GMAT

GMAT™ 官方指南
2020版

来自GMAT™考试官方出题机构的权威指南

线下学习 + 在线学习 + 移动应用

GMAT™ Official Prep

GMAT™考试历年真题的唯一来源

此版本包含

新增！移动应用方便随时随地练习

更多试题！试题比2019版多出100余道

更新！GMAT™考试题型重点划分——哪些题型会考，哪些不会

 mba.com

GMAT™ OFFICIAL GUIDE 2020

Copyright © 2019 by the Graduate Management Admission Council (GMAC). All rights reserved.

Published by John Wiley & Sons, Inc., Hoboken, New Jersey.

No part of this publication may be reproduced, stored in a retrieval system or transmitted in any form or by any means, electronic, mechanical, photocopying, recording, scanning or otherwise, except as permitted under Sections 107 or 108 of the 1976 United States Copyright Act, without either the prior written permission of the Publisher, or authorization through payment of the appropriate per-copy fee to the Copyright Clearance Center, 222 Rosewood Drive, Danvers, MA 01923, (978) 750-8400, fax (978) 646-8600, or on the web at www.copyright.com. Requests to the Publisher for permission should be addressed to the Permissions Department, John Wiley & Sons, Inc., 111 River Street, Hoboken, NJ 07030, (201) 748-6011, fax (201) 748-6008, or online at http://www.wiley.com/go/permissions.

The publisher and the author make no representations or warranties with respect to the accuracy or completeness of the contents of this work and specifically disclaim all warranties, including without limitation warranties of fitness for a particular purpose. No warranty may be created or extended by sales or promotional materials. The advice and strategies contained herein may not be suitable for every situation. This work is sold with the understanding that the publisher is not engaged in rendering legal, accounting, or other professional services. If professional assistance is required, the services of a competent professional person should be sought. Neither the publisher nor the author shall be liable for damages arising here from. The fact that an organization or Website is referred to in this work as a citation and/or a potential source of further information does not mean that the author or the publisher endorses the information the organization or Website may provide or recommendations it may make. Further, readers should be aware that Internet Websites listed in this work may have changed or disappeared between when this work was written and when it is read.

Trademarks: Wiley, the Wiley logo, and related trademarks are trademarks or registered trademarks of John Wiley & Sons, Inc. and/or its affiliates. The GMAT logo, GMAC™, GMASS™, GMAT™, Graduate Management Admission Council™, and Graduate Management Admission Test™ are trademarks of GMAC in the United States and other countries. All other trademarks are the property of their respective owners. John Wiley & Sons, Inc., is not associated with any product or vendor mentioned in this book.

For general information on our other products and services or to obtain technical support please contact our Customer Care Department within the U.S. at (877) 762-2974, outside the U.S. at (317) 572-3993 or fax (317) 572-4002.

John Wiley & Sons, Inc., also publishes its books in a variety of electronic formats and by print-on-demand. Not all content that is available in standard print versions of this book may appear or be packaged in all book formats. If you have purchased a version of this book that did not include media that is referenced by or accompanies a standard print version, you may request this media by visiting http://booksupport.wiley.com. For more information about Wiley products, visit us at www.wiley.com.

ISBN 978-1-119-57612-9 (pbk)

Printed and bound in Singapore by Markono Print Media Pte Ltd

10 9 8 7 6 5 4 3 2 1

Table of Contents

Letter from the President and CEO, GMAC™ — v

1.0	**What Is the GMAT™ Exam?**	**2**
1.0	What Is the GMAT™ Exam?	3
1.1	Why Take the GMAT™ Exam?	3
1.2	GMAT™ Exam Format	4
1.3	What Is the Content of the Exam Like?	6
1.4	Analytical Writing Assessment	6
1.5	Integrated Reasoning Section	6
1.6	Quantitative Reasoning Section	7
1.7	Verbal Reasoning Section	7
1.8	What Are the Test Centers Like?	7
1.9	How Are Scores Calculated?	8
2.0	**How to Prepare**	**10**
2.0	How to Prepare	11
2.1	How Should I Prepare to Take the Test?	11
2.2	Using GMAT Official Prep Products	11
2.3	Where Can I Get Additional Practice?	12
2.4	General Test-Taking Suggestions	12
3.0	**Diagnostic Test**	**14**
3.0	Diagnostic Test	15
3.1	Quantitative Questions	16
3.2	Verbal Questions	23
3.3	Quantitative and Verbal Answer Keys	40
3.4	Interpretive Guide	40
3.5	Quantitative Answer Explanations	41
3.6	Verbal Answer Explanations	60
4.0	**Math Review**	**100**
4.0	Math Review	101
4.1	Arithmetic	102
4.2	Algebra	114
4.3	Geometry	122
4.4	Word Problems	134
5.0	**Problem Solving**	**142**
5.0	Problem Solving	143
5.1	Test-Taking Strategies	144
5.2	Section Instructions	144
5.3	Practice Questions	146
5.4	Answer Key	182
5.5	Answer Explanations	184
6.0	**Data Sufficiency**	**266**
6.0	Data Sufficiency	267
6.1	Test-Taking Strategies	268
6.2	Section Instructions	270
6.3	Practice Questions	272
6.4	Answer Key	295
6.5	Answer Explanations	297

7.0	**Reading Comprehension**	**386**
7.0	Reading Comprehension	387
7.1	What Is Measured	388
7.2	Test-Taking Strategies	396
7.3	Section Instructions	397
7.4	Practice Questions	398
7.5	Answer Key	461
7.6	Answer Explanations	462
8.0	**Critical Reasoning**	**550**
8.0	Critical Reasoning	551
8.1	What Is Measured	551
8.2	Test-Taking Strategies	553
8.3	Reasoning Concepts to Know for the GMAT Exam	555
8.4	Section Instructions	561
8.5	Practice Questions	562
8.6	Answer Key	609
8.7	Answer Explanations	610
9.0	**Sentence Correction**	**760**
9.0	Sentence Correction	761
9.1	Some Comments About How It Works	761
9.2	The Eight Sentence Correction Categories	762
9.3	Study Suggestions	783
9.4	What Is Measured	783
9.5	Test-Taking Strategies	783
9.6	Section Instructions	784
9.7	Practice Questions	785
9.8	Answer Key	815
9.9	Answer Explanations	816
10.0	**Integrated Reasoning**	**902**
10.0	Integrated Reasoning	903
10.1	What Is Measured	904
10.2	Question Types and Test-Taking Strategies	905
10.3	Section Instructions	911
11.0	**Analytical Writing Assessment**	**912**
11.0	Analytical Writing Assessment	913
11.1	What Is Measured	913
11.2	Test-Taking Strategies	914
11.3	The Directions	914
11.4	GMAT™ Scoring Guide: Analysis of an Argument	915
11.5	Sample: Analysis of an Argument	917
11.6	Analysis of an Argument Sample Topics	921
12.0	**Official Guide Question Index**	**954**
13.0	**GMAT™ Official Guide Online Index**	**968**
Appendix A	**Answer Sheets**	**977**
	Diagnostic Answer Sheet—Quantitative	977
	Diagnostic Answer Sheet—Verbal	977
	Problem Solving Answer Sheet	978
	Data Sufficiency Answer Sheet	979
	Reading Comprehension Answer Sheet	980
	Critical Reasoning Answer Sheet	981
	Sentence Correction Answer Sheet	982

Dear GMAT Test-Taker,

Thank you for your interest in graduate management education. Today more than 7,000 graduate programs around the world use the GMAT™ exam to establish their MBA, business master's, and other graduate-level management degree programs as hallmarks of excellence. Nine of out 10 new MBA enrollments globally are made using a GMAT score.*

By using the *GMAT™ Official Guide* to prepare for the GMAT exam, you're taking a very important step toward achieving your goals and pursuing admission to the MBA or business master's program that is the best fit for you.

This book, *GMAT™ Official Guide 2020*, is designed to help you prepare for and build confidence to do your best on the GMAT exam. It's the only guide that features real questions from past exams published by the Graduate Management Admission Council (GMAC), the makers of the GMAT™ exam

For more than 60 years, the GMAT exam has helped candidates like you demonstrate their command of the skills needed for success in the classroom and showcase to schools their commitment to pursuing a graduate business degree. Schools use and trust the GMAT exam as part of their admissions process because it's a proven predictor of classroom success and your ability to excel in your chosen program.

The mission of GMAC is to ensure no talent goes undiscovered. We are driven to continue improving the GMAT exam as well as helping you find and connect with the best-fit schools and programs for you. I applaud your commitment to educational success. This guide and the other GMAT™ Official Prep products available at mba.com will give you the confidence to achieve your personal best on the GMAT exam and launch or reinvigorate a rewarding career.

I wish you the best success on all your future educational and professional endeavors.

Sincerely,

Sangeet Chowfla
President & CEO of the Graduate Management Admission Council

*Refers to the FT-100 Global MBA Programs, 2017

GMAC 首席心理测评专家对于"机经"的看法：

使用"机经"不仅是得不偿失的复习方法，考生更可能因此被取消 GMAT 成绩，甚至构成刑事犯罪。GMAC 鼓励考生端正心态，正确备考。

虽然许多人可能认为使用"机经"是备考 GMAT 的捷径，但实际上这是对"机经"和 GMAT 考试的认识误区，而且这是直接违反《中华人民共和国著作权法》和其他知识产权法律法规，以及国际知识产权法规的行为，严重违反者将受到刑事处罚。在 GMAT 考试中，使用"机经"属于舞弊行为，GMAC 严禁考生使用"机经"帮助他们备考 GMAT。

如果考生一旦被发现使用"机经"，他们将会承担严重后果。虽然考生可能认为这类作弊行为不容易被发现，但是 GMAC 有能力识别这些违反考试规章的行为。GMAC 打击"机经"的法律行动从未停止。例如，GMAC 曾经将一家把"机经"公布于自己网站上的网络公司告上法庭。公司的所有者被法院起诉并被判违反当地法律以及国际知识产权法规。GMAC 没收了这家公司的数据库，进行了数据取证，识别曾经使用"机经"的每个考生并取消了他们的分数，他们的考试资格也被永久剥夺，GMAC 还通知了那些已经收到这些作弊考生分数的学校。

实际上"机经"在 GMAT 这种自适应考试机制下，几乎很难发挥作用。在 2009 年的一份研究报告《CAT 泄露考题对成绩的量化影响》(Quantifying the Impact of Compromised Items in CAT) 中，我们发现即使考生事先知道五道考题，对他们的定量推理或者文本逻辑推理部分成绩也几乎没有影响。以下图表列出了事先知道五道 GMAT 定量推理或者文本逻辑推理题目对于考生分数变化的平均影响。

定量推理

考生 %	分数变化
0.5%	≤ -1 point
94.7%	**= 0 points**
2.2%	= +1 point
1.3%	= +2 points
1.2%	≥ +3 points

文本逻辑推理

考生 %	分数变化
0.4%	≤ -1 point
94.8%	**= 0 points**
2.5%	= +1 point
1.4%	= +2 points
0.9%	≥ +3 points

为什么使用"机经"得不偿失？

像 GMAT 这样的计算机自适应式考试 (CAT)，通常会从一个巨大的题库中根据考生具体的考试表现来选择适合其答题能力的考题。碰见已知题目的几率非常小。

CAT 考试具备自我校正的能力。如果一位考生碰巧答对了一道难度大于他／她真实能力的题目，那下一道题目会更难，这样这位考生就会倾向于答错，考试也会在两至三道这样的错题之后恢复到适应考生真实水平的难度。

在 CAT 的分数计算中，并不是每道答对的题目都会有相同的得分。

GMAC 承诺将维持 GMAT 考试的公正性和有效性。我们邀请您和我们一起加入到抵制"机经"的努力当中，并且鼓励其他考生也一起加入。如果您发现任何组织或个人使用或者鼓励他人使用机经，请通过电子邮箱 testsecurity@gmac.com 向 GMAC 举报。

韩景泽 博士
GMAC 测评研究部资深总监

GMAT™ 官方指南 2020 版

1.0 什么是 GMAT™ 考试?

1.0 什么是 GMAT™ 考试？

GMAT™考试 (Graduate Management Admission Test™) 是一项标准化考试，全球大约有 2300 所研究生商学院的 7000 余个管理专业研究生项目采用该考试做出招生决策。GMAT 考试可帮助考生进行自我评估，并向所申请的院校展示您具备能够顺利完成管理专业研究生项目的学术潜力。

考试分为四个部分，分别考查分析性写作、综合推理、文本逻辑推理和定量推理技能。世界各地的管理学院、招生人员和雇主均认为这些高阶推理技能对于入学新生来说至关重要。"高阶"推理技能涉及复杂的判断，包括批判性思维、分析和问题求解。本科成绩和课程在不同地区及院校的标准会有所不同，GMAT 则并非如此。对考生在管理专业研究生项目核心课程中可能具有的学术表现，GMAT 成绩可进行标准化、统计学上有效且可靠的衡量。经过大量的学术研究，GMAT 考试的有效性、公正性以及在招生方面的价值已得到广泛认可。

GMAT 考试是一项全程用计算机完成的全英文考试。该考试并不测试商学知识、学科掌握程度、英语词汇或高级计算技能。它也不评估与顺利完成管理专业研究生阶段学习相关的其他因素，比如工作经验、领导能力、自我激励和人际交往技能等。您的 GMAT 成绩将与申请文书和面试表现等其他更主观的项目一起，作为学校作出录取决策的标准。

1.1 为什么要参加 GMAT™ 考试？

GMAT 考试由九所商学院于 1954 年共同设立，旨在提供一个统一的考查标准，考查顺利完成其学业项目所需的学术技能。如今，全球大约有 2300 所院校的超过 7000 个管理专业研究生项目采用该考试。

参加 GMAT 考试可帮助您从申请者中脱颖而出，展现您对管理专业研究生教育的热情以及准备的情况。院校使用 GMAT 成绩来帮助选择最符合资格的申请者，因为他们知道，参加 GMAT 考试的考生是真心希望获得商学硕士学位。该成绩也是一项经过验证的预测指标，可用于预测学生是否能够顺利完成所选项目。当您考虑要申请哪些项目时，您可将院校对 GMAT 考试的使用情况作为一项教学质量参考指标。使用 GMAT 考试的院校通常会在其班级介绍中列出分数范围或平均分数。您会发现这些介绍有助于您衡量所考虑项目的学术竞争力，还可与该项目录取学生的分数进行比较，了解自己的分数处于哪一水平。

> **误区 -与- 真相**
>
> **误区** – 如果我在 GMAT 中没有取得高分，我将不能被首选院校录取。
>
> **真相** – 取得任何 GMAT 成绩的考生，都有很棒的院校可供选择。
>
> 每年参加 GMAT 考试的 250,000 多名考生中，取得满分 800 分的不到 50 人；但每年都有许多人被全球顶级的商学院项目录取。招生官在做出招生决策时，GMAT 成绩只是其考虑的一个方面，他们在决定录取哪些申请者加入项目时，还会结合本科成绩、申请文书、面试表现、推荐信及其他信息。访问 mba.com 上的 "School Finder"（院校查找器）工具，了解最适合您的院校。

无论您在 GMAT 考试中表现如何，您都应当主动联系您感兴趣的院校来了解更多信息，询问他们在招生流程中如何使用 GMAT 成绩和其他标准（比如您的本科成绩、申请文书和推荐信）。当您研究想就读哪所商学院时，您可从院校的招生办公室、网站和院校发布的资料中搜索相关信息，这些都是重要的信息来源。

如需关于 GMAT、备考资料、注册报名、如何使用 GMAT 成绩并将其发送给院校，以及申请商学院的更多信息，请访问 mba.com。

1.2 GMAT™ 考试形式

GMAT 考试由四个独立计时的考核部分组成（见下一页中的表格）。分析性写作 (AWA) 部分包含一篇作文。综合推理 (Integrated Reasoning) 部分包含图解和数据分析问题，并有多种作答形式。定量推理 (Quantitative Reasoning) 和文本逻辑推理 (Verbal Reasoning) 部分包含选择题。

GMAT 考试的定量推理和文本逻辑推理部分采用计算机自适应性考试形式，这意味着计算机会根据您的能力水平，从包含大量试题的题库中选择与您能力相当的试题。因此，您不会遇到太多对您而言难度过高或过低的试题。第一道试题难度适中。当您解答每道试题时，计算机将对您的答案进行计分，使用该答案并结合您之前试题的作答情况，为您选择下一题。

根据计算机自适应性机制，您正确回答的试题数量越多，接下来的试题就会越难。但是如果您遇到的试题似乎比上一题简单，也不一定意味着上一题您答错了。考试会涵盖一定范围的题型和学科知识。

> **误区 -与- 真相**
>
> **误区** – 遇到更简单的试题意味着我上一题答错了。
>
> **真相** – 您不应该因试题的难度水平而分心。
>
> 试题难度由很多不同因素造成，所以参加考试时不要担心，也不要将宝贵的时间浪费在判断试题难度上面。
>
> 为确保每位考生被考查的范围一致，考试针对每种题型选择特定数量的试题。例如，考试系统需要调取一道相对较难的涉及算术运算的数据充分性分析试题，但题库中已经没有此类试题，那么可能会为您提供一道更简单的试题。

由于计算机使用您的回答来为您选择下一题，您不能跳过某道试题，也不能返回之前的试题修改答案。如果您不知道某个试题的答案，请尽量多排除几个选项，然后选择您认为最佳的答案。

虽然单个的试题不尽相同，但每次 GMAT 考试所包含的题型是相同的。您的成绩取决于您所解答试题的难度和统计特征，以及您答对的试题数量。GMAT 考试通过适应每位考生的能力，能准确有效地考查其在各种能力上所具备的技能水平，从极高到极低。

考试包含本书所述题型和在线题型 gmat.wiley.com，但计算机屏幕上的试题形式和呈现方式会有所不同。当您参加考试时：

- 计算机屏幕上一次仅会显示一道试题或题干。
- 多项选择题的答案选项前为单选按钮而不是字母。
- 在选择题和综合推理部分，将随机出现不同的题型。

- 您必须使用计算机选择您的答案。
- 您必须选择一个答案并进行确认，然后才能继续解答下一题。
- 您不能返回之前的屏幕更改前面试题的答案。

GMAT™ 考试形式

	题量	考试时间
分析性写作部分	1	30 分钟
综合推理 　多源推理 　表格分析 　图表解读 　二段式分析	12	30 分钟
定量推理 　问题求解 　数据充分性分析	31	62 分钟
文本逻辑推理 　阅读理解 　批判性推理 　句子改错	36	65 分钟
考试时长：		187 分钟

在开始作答前，您可当即从以下三个选项中灵活选择 GMAT 各部分考题的答题次序。

次序 1	次序 2	次序 3
分析性写作部分	文本逻辑推理	定量推理
综合推理		
可选择休息 8 分钟		
定量推理	定量推理	文本逻辑推理
可选择休息 8 分钟		
文本逻辑推理	综合推理	综合推理
	分析性写作部分	分析性写作部分

所选答题次序会于考试当天 GMAT 开考之前，在考试中心生效。

1.3 考试内容介绍

GMAT 考试会考查包含几种推理能力在内的高阶分析能力。分析性写作部分要求您进行论证推理分析，并以写作的形式作答；综合推理部分要求您阐述并整合以不同形式出现的多源信息，得出合理的结论；定量推理部分要求您运用基本算术、代数和几何知识来进行定量推理；文本逻辑推理部分要求您阅读并理解书面材料，进行推理并评估论点。

考试试题可能涉及多类学科知识，但解答试题所需的全部信息都涵盖在考试范围内，您无需具备学科知识以外的信息。GMAT 考试并不考查商学知识、英语词汇或高级计算技能。要在考试中良好发挥，您需要具备英语阅读和写作能力以及基本的数学和英语技能。然而，真正的考试难点在于分析和批判性思维能力。

本书中的试题按照题型由易到难进行编排，但请记住，当您参加考试时，每个部分中的各类题型会以任意顺序出现。

1.4 分析性写作部分

分析性写作部分 (AWA) 的考试时间为 30 分钟，您需要完成一篇论证分析作文。该部分考查您进行批判性思考、表达自己的想法以及提出恰当且具建设性的批判观点的能力。您需要通过计算机键盘输入您的作文。

如需获取论证分析写作应试技巧、范文、答案解析和示例，请参阅第 11 章。

1.5 综合推理部分

在如今数据驱动的世界中，企业管理者需要分析复杂的数据和解决复杂的问题。综合推理部分重点考查与此相关的技能。综合推理部分会考查您理解和评估彼此相关的不同来源和不同形式信息的能力，比如图表、数字和文本。该部分要求您使用定量推理和文本逻辑推理来解决复杂的问题和彼此相关的多个问题。

综合推理部分包含四种题型：

- 多源推理
- 表格分析
- 图表解读
- 二段式分析

综合推理部分的试题可能考查定量推理或文本逻辑推理技能，或是两者的结合。您需要解读图表并对表格进行排序，从数据中提取有价值的信息，但您无需具备高级统计学知识和电子表格操作技能。在综合推理部分，您将可以使用具有基本功能的屏显计算器，但请注意，定量推理部分不提供计算器。

如需查看综合推理题型和应试技巧,请参阅第 10 章。如需获取各题型的练习题及其完整答案解析,请使用本书封面内页中唯一的访问代码,访问 gmat.wiley.com。

1.6 定量推理部分

GMAT 定量推理部分考查您进行定量推理、解决定量问题和解读图表数据的能力。

定量推理部分包含两类选择题:

- 问题求解
- 数据充分性分析

这两种题型将在定量推理部分混合出现,需要的基础知识包括:算术、初等代数和一般的几何概念。

如需查看解答定量推理试题所需的基本数学概念,请参阅第 4 章的"数学复习"部分。如需针对定量推理部分特定题型的应试技巧、练习题和答案解析,请参阅第 5 章和第 6 章。

1.7 文本逻辑推理部分

GMAT 文本逻辑推理部分考查您阅读和理解书面材料以及推理和评估论点的能力。该部分涵盖几个不同内容领域的阅读材料。尽管您可能会对某些材料有一定了解,但是在阅读篇章或试题中,均不会涉及有关该主题的任何详细知识点。

以下三类选择题在文本逻辑推理部分混合出现:

- 阅读理解
- 批判性推理
- 句子改错

这三种题型均需您掌握基本的英语知识,但文本逻辑推理部分并非考查高级词汇。

如需针对文本逻辑推理部分特定题型的应试技巧、练习题和答案解析,请参阅第 7 章到第 9 章。

1.8 考试中心环境

GMAT 考试是在全球逾 700 个考试中心标准化的环境下进行的。每个考试中心的考场均有监考,并为每位考生配备个人机位,让您能在安静和拥有一定隐私的环境中完成整场考试。考试期间,您有两次可选择的休息时间,每次时长为 8 分钟。您不能将笔记或草稿纸带入考场,但考试中心会为您提供一个可擦性记事本和一支记号笔,供您在考试过程中使用。如需有关考试当天的更多详情,请访问 mba.com。

1.9 成绩计算方式

文本逻辑推理部分和定量推理部分的分数范围在 6 分到 51 分之间，分数递增单位为 1 分。GMAT 总成绩根据您在上述两部分的表现得出，分数区间为 200 分到 800 分。您的分数由以下几方面决定：

- 您所解答的试题总数
- 您正确或错误回答的试题数量
- 每道试题的难度和其他统计特征

您的文本逻辑推理部分分数、定量推理部分分数和 GMAT 总成绩根据特定算法得出，该算法会综合考虑呈现给您的试题的难度和您的答题表现。如果您正确解答了难度较低的试题，便有机会解答更高难度的试题，从而可能得到一个更高的分数。当您完成整场考试的所有试题后，或者当考试时间结束时，计算机便会计算您的分数。

您会获得三个分数：总分数（取决于您的定量推理和文本逻辑推理分数）、综合推理分数和分析性写作分数。下表汇总了不同的分数类型、分数区间和分数递增单位。

分数类型	分数区间	分数递增单位
总分数（取决于您的定量推理和文本逻辑推理分数）	200–800	10
定量推理	6–51	1
文本逻辑推理	6–51	1
综合推理	1–8	1
分析性写作部分	0–6	.5

您指定的成绩单接收院校可能会收到一份成绩单外加您的分析性写作作文副本。您自己的成绩单将不会随附您实际的作文。

您的 GMAT 成绩单包含一项成绩百分位排名，该排名根据您的技能水平与过去三年所有其他考生的技能水平比较得出。成绩百分位排名显示了成绩在您之下的考生百分比数。每年 7 月，百分位排名表都会更新。如需查看最新的百分位排名表，请访问 mba.com。

欲报名 GMAT 考试，请前往 www.mba.com

2.0 如何备考

2.0 如何备考

2.1 如何准备考试？

GMAT 考试专门用于考查管理学教育所需的推理能力。参加考试前，您至少应该熟悉考试形式和各类题型。由于 GMAT 考试有时间限制，您应练习模拟题。这不仅能帮助您更好地了解题型及相应的应试技能，还有助于您在参加考试时调整答题节奏，顺利完成各个部分。

由于考试考查的是推理能力，而不是对学科知识的掌握，所以您很可能会发现牢记知识点并没有什么帮助。您不需要学习高等数学概念，但您需要确保对基本算术、代数和几何有很好的掌握，和足以使用这些技能来解答定量问题。同样，您无需学习高阶词汇，但您应该牢固掌握基本英语词汇和语法，以应对阅读、写作和推理部分。

本书及 Graduate Management Admission Council (GMAC) 发布的其他学习资料是 GMAT 考试历年真题的唯一来源。GMAT 考试中出现或出现过的所有试题的版权及所有权归 GMAC 所有，严禁在其他地方转载和重印这些内容。提前获取综合推理、定量推理或文本逻辑推理部分的试题，或在考试期间或之后分享考试内容（机经），均属于严重违规行为。这可能导致您的考试成绩被取消，我们还将会通知您所申请的院校。如果情节恶劣，可能会禁止您参加今后的考试，并追究相关法律责任。

> **误区 -与- 真相**
>
> **误区** – 需要具备非常高级的数学技能才能在 GMAT 考试中取得高分。
>
> **真相** – GMAT 主要考查推理和批判性思维能力，而非高等数学技能。
>
> GMAT 考试只需要运用基本的定量分析技能。您需要查看本指南（第 4 章）及《GMAT™ 定量推理复习官方指南 2020 版》中列出的数学技能（代数、几何、基本算术）。GMAT 定量推理试题的难度来自于解决问题所需要运用的逻辑与分析能力，而非基本的数学技能。

2.2 使用GMAT官方备考产品

由于 GMAT 考试采用机考，建议您访问 gmat.wiley.com，在线练习 GMAT™ 官方指南中的测试题。本书中的所有测试题均可在该网站上查看，您还可创建练习题集，轻松跟踪学习进度。此外，GMAT™ 官方指南在线版还包含74道本书中没有的综合推理测试题。

除官方指南外，建议您在备考期间从我们的六套 GMAT 官方模考练习中选几套来做，或六套全做。由于 GMAT 考试是机考，也就是说，在考试作答时会根据您的能力进行调整，所以做 GMAT 官方模考练习是最佳模考。如同真实考试场景，官方模考练习可根据您的能力进行调整，并使用与 GMAT 实际考试相同的评分算法进行评分。

要实现最佳学习成效，建议您先了解 GMAT 考试以及 GMAT™ 官方指南和 GMAT™ 官方入门工具包中的考试题型。之后，您可以先做一次 GMAT 官方模考练习，熟悉考试流程，了解自己能取得的大致成绩。无需担心首次模考中的分数！第一次模考练习的目标是熟悉考试，设一个大致成绩目标，以便评估您的进步。之后，前往 gmat.wiley.com，练习官方指南中的测试题，将重点放在需要您注意的地方。您可以边练习边做更多官方模考练习，评估自己的进步。在参加真正的 GMAT 考试前,做最后一次官方模考练习,以便了解自己的水平,这也是一次考试演练。

注意:免费的 GMAT™ 官方入门工具包 + 模考练习 1 和模考练习 2 (GMAT™ Official Starter Kit + Practice Exams 1 and 2) 包含两次免费的 GMAT 官方模考练习和 90 道免费的练习题,有 mba.com 帐号的用户均可查看。

2.3 从哪里可以获得更多的练习?

如果您想进行更多的练习,《GMAT™ 定量推理复习官方指南 2020 版》和《GMAT™ 文本逻辑推理复习官方指南 2020 版》分别额外提供了逾 300 道本指南中未出现的试题。您还可在 mba.com 上找到更多的定量推理、文本逻辑推理和综合推理练习题、完整的计算机自适应性模考练习、分析性写作练习提示以及其他有用的学习资料。

2.4 一般性备考建议

针对不同题型的具体应试策略将在本书后面部分进行介绍。以下是帮助您在考试中发挥最佳水平的一般性建议:

1. **合理运用您的时间。**
   尽管 GMAT 考试更强调准确性而非速度,但是,合理运用您的时间仍然相当重要。平均来说,您有大约 1 分 48 秒的时间解答一道文本逻辑推理试题,大约 2 分钟的时间解答一道定量推理试题,大约 2 分 30 秒的时间解答一道综合推理试题(部分试题包含多个问题)。一旦您开始考试,屏幕上的时钟会显示您还剩下的时间。您可以选择隐藏时间显示,但非常建议您定期查看时钟,密切关注进程。在离您正回答的每个部分结束前剩 5 分钟时,时钟会自动提醒。

2. **您可在参加真正的考试前确定好自己喜欢的答题顺序。**
   GMAT 考试允许考生自主选择答题顺序。您可使用 GMAT 官方模考练习来进行练习并确定答题顺序。注意:没有"正确"的考试答题顺序。您可多练习几种答题顺序,找到最适合自己的一种。

3. **提前完成练习题。**
   在您熟悉所有的题型之后,可以使用本书和在线练习题 gmat.wiley.com 来准备实战考试(请注意,综合推理试题只可在线获取)。您可以在解答练习题时自行计时,大概估算一下实战考试时每道试题所需的时间,判断您是否能够在规定时间内完成相应试题。

4. **仔细阅读各部分的考试说明。**
   考试说明准确阐述了解答每种题型的注意事项。如果您读得很匆忙,可能会忽略重要提示并影响正确作答。如需在考试过程中重温考试说明,请点击"Help"(帮助)图标。但请注意,您查看考试说明所花费的时间将计入该部分考试的规定时间。

5. 认真仔细地阅读每一道试题。

在您解答每一道试题前，请明确试题问的到底是什么，然后选出或给出最佳答案。请不要只是粗略地浏览试题或任何可能的答案，这么做可能会让您遗漏重要信息或细微差别。

6. 不要在任何一道试题上花费过多时间。

如果您不知道某道试题的正确答案，或者在某道试题上已耗时太长，请尽可能多地排除您认为错误的选项，在余下选项中选出相对最佳的答案，然后继续解答下一题。

未完成某些部分，以及在各部分即将结束时随机猜测试题答案，可能会显著降低您的成绩。只要您参加了一个部分的测试，就会获得一个分数，即使您未能在规定时间内完成一个或多个部分。如果您连试题都没看到，自然无法得分。

7. 只有在您准备好继续进行下一题时才确认答案。

在定量推理和文本逻辑推理部分，一旦您选择了某道选择题的答案，您会被要求进行确认。一旦确认答案，您将不能返回和更改。您不能够跳过任何试题。在综合推理部分，同一试题提示信息下可能会有多个问题。当一个屏幕上有多个回答时，您可以在进入下一个屏幕前，更改当前屏幕上的任一试题答案。但是，您不能返回之前的屏幕更改任何答案。

8. 在开始写作前构思您的作文。

应对论证分析写作的最佳方法是仔细阅读试题说明，花几分钟时间审清题目，在作答之前构思清楚。花些时间组织好想法并充分展开，但记得留些时间重读一遍文章，并进行任何您认为可提升行文质量的修改。

误区 -与- 真相

误区 – 正确回答试题比完成考试更为重要。

真相 – 未答完的GMAT考题将严重影响考生分数。

考试节奏非常重要。如果您被某一道试题难住了，尽量猜测最有可能的答案并继续进行下一题。如果您猜错了，计算机程序接下来很可能会给出一道相对容易的试题，并且您也容易正确作答。计算机也会迅速调整，根据您的实际能力匹配出题。如果未能完成考试，将会扣分。例如，如果您未能回答5道文本逻辑推理试题，您的成绩百分位数就会从91降到77。

误区 -与- 真相

误区 – 前10道试题尤其重要，应该在这些试题上投入更多时间。

真相 – 所有试题都同样重要。

计算机自适应性考试算法使用所有已解答的试题来对您的能力做出初步评估。但是，随着您继续解答接下来的试题，该算法会根据您已解答的所有试题，实时评估并自行调整，进而给出最符合您当时能力水平的试题。您的最终成绩取决于您作答的准确性及所解答试题的难度水平。在前10道试题上花费额外的时间并不能影响计分系统，却可能导致您没有足够的时间完成考试，得不偿失。

3.0 Diagnostic Test

3.0 Diagnostic Test

Like the practice sections later in the book, the Diagnostic Test uses questions from real GMAT™ exams. The purpose of the Diagnostic Test is to help you determine how skilled you are in answering each of the five types of questions on the GMAT exam: problem solving, data sufficiency, reading comprehension, critical reasoning, and sentence correction.

Scores on the Diagnostic Test are designed to help you answer the question, "If all the questions on the GMAT exam were like the questions in this section, how well would I do?" Your scores are classified as being *excellent, above average, average,* or *below average,* relative to the scores of other test-takers. You can use this information to focus your test-preparation activities.

Instructions

1. Take your time answering these questions. The Diagnostic Test is not timed.
2. If you are stumped by a question, you should guess and move on, just like you should do on the real GMAT exam.
3. You can take one segment at a time, if you want. It is better to finish an entire section (Quantitative or Verbal Reasoning) in one sitting, but this is not a requirement.
4. You can go back and change your answers in the Diagnostic Test.
5. After you take the test, check your answers using the answer key that follows the test. The number of correct answers is your raw score.
6. Convert your raw score, using the table provided.

Note: The Diagnostic Test is designed to give you guidance on how to prepare for the GMAT exam; however, a strong score on one type of question does not guarantee that you will perform as well on the real GMAT exam. The statistical reliability of scores on the Diagnostic Test ranges from 0.75 to 0.89, and the subscale classification is about 85%–90% accurate, meaning that your scores on the Diagnostic Test are a good, but not perfect, measure of how you are likely to perform on the real test. Use the tests on the free online software to obtain a good estimate of your expected GMAT Verbal, Quantitative, and Total scores.

You should not compare the number of questions you got right in each section. Instead, you should compare how your responses are rated in each section.

3.1 Quantitative Questions

Problem Solving

Solve the problem and indicate the best of the answer choices given.
Numbers: All numbers used are real numbers.
Figures: All figures accompanying problem solving questions are intended to provide information useful in solving the problems. Figures are drawn as accurately as possible. Exceptions will be clearly noted. Lines shown as straight are straight, and lines that appear jagged are also straight. The positions of points, angles, regions, etc., exist in the order shown, and angle measures are greater than zero. All figures lie in a plane unless otherwise indicated.

1. Last month a certain music club offered a discount to preferred customers. After the first compact disc purchased, preferred customers paid $3.99 for each additional compact disc purchased. If a preferred customer purchased a total of 6 compact discs and paid $15.95 for the first compact disc, then the dollar amount that the customer paid for the 6 compact discs is equivalent to which of the following?

   (A) 5(4.00) + 15.90
   (B) 5(4.00) + 15.95
   (C) 5(4.00) + 16.00
   (D) 5(4.00 − 0.01) + 15.90
   (E) 5(4.00 − 0.05) + 15.95

2. The average (arithmetic mean) of the integers from 200 to 400, inclusive, is how much greater than the average of the integers from 50 to 100, inclusive?

   (A) 150
   (B) 175
   (C) 200
   (D) 225
   (E) 300

3. The sequence $a_1, a_2, a_3, \ldots, a_n, \ldots$ is such that $a_n = \dfrac{a_{n-1} + a_{n-2}}{2}$ for all $n \geq 3$. If $a_3 = 4$ and $a_5 = 20$ what is the value of a_6?

   (A) 12
   (B) 16
   (C) 20
   (D) 24
   (E) 28

4. Among a group of 2,500 people, 35 percent invest in municipal bonds, 18 percent invest in oil stocks, and 7 percent invest in both municipal bonds and oil stocks. If 1 person is to be randomly selected from the 2,500 people, what is the probability that the person selected will be one who invests in municipal bonds but NOT in oil stocks?

   (A) $\dfrac{9}{50}$
   (B) $\dfrac{7}{25}$
   (C) $\dfrac{7}{20}$
   (D) $\dfrac{21}{50}$
   (E) $\dfrac{27}{50}$

5. A closed cylindrical tank contains 36π cubic feet of water and is filled to half its capacity. When the tank is placed upright on its circular base on level ground, the height of the water in the tank is 4 feet. When the tank is placed on its side on level ground, what is the height, in feet, of the surface of the water above the ground?

   (A) 2
   (B) 3
   (C) 4
   (D) 6
   (E) 9

6. A marketing firm determined that, of 200 households surveyed, 80 used neither Brand A nor Brand B soap, 60 used only Brand A soap, and for every household that used both brands of soap, 3 used only Brand B soap. How many of the 200 households surveyed used both brands of soap?

   (A) 15
   (B) 20
   (C) 30
   (D) 40
   (E) 45

7. A certain club has 10 members, including Harry. One of the 10 members is to be chosen at random to be the president, one of the remaining 9 members is to be chosen at random to be the secretary, and one of the remaining 8 members is to be chosen at random to be the treasurer. What is the probability that Harry will be either the member chosen to be the secretary or the member chosen to be the treasurer?

   (A) $\frac{1}{720}$
   (B) $\frac{1}{80}$
   (C) $\frac{1}{10}$
   (D) $\frac{1}{9}$
   (E) $\frac{1}{5}$

8. If a certain toy store's revenue in November was $\frac{2}{5}$ of its revenue in December and its revenue in January was $\frac{1}{4}$ of its revenue in November, then the store's revenue in December was how many times the average (arithmetic mean) of its revenues in November and January?

   (A) $\frac{1}{4}$
   (B) $\frac{1}{2}$
   (C) $\frac{2}{3}$
   (D) 2
   (E) 4

9. A researcher computed the mean, the median, and the standard deviation for a set of performance scores. If 5 were to be added to each score, which of these three statistics would change?

   (A) The mean only
   (B) The median only
   (C) The standard deviation only
   (D) The mean and the median
   (E) The mean and the standard deviation

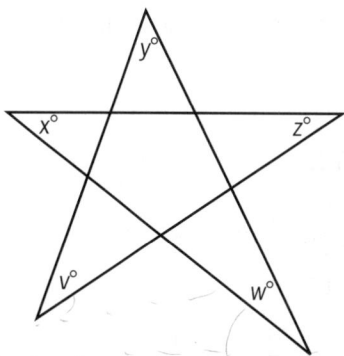

10. In the figure shown, what is the value of $v + x + y + z + w$?

    (A) 45
    (B) 90
    (C) 180
    (D) 270
    (E) 360

17

11. Of the three-digit integers greater than 700, how many have two digits that are equal to each other and the remaining digit different from the other two?

    (A) 90
    (B) 82
    (C) 80
    (D) 45
    (E) 36

12. Positive integer y is 50 percent of 50 percent of positive integer x, and y percent of x equals 100. What is the value of x ?

    (A) 50
    (B) 100
    (C) 200
    (D) 1,000
    (E) 2,000

13. If s and t are positive integers such that $\frac{s}{t} = 64.12$, which of the following could be the remainder when s is divided by t ?

    (A) 2
    (B) 4
    (C) 8
    (D) 20
    (E) 45

14. Of the 84 parents who attended a meeting at a school, 35 volunteered to supervise children during the school picnic and 11 volunteered both to supervise children during the picnic and to bring refreshments to the picnic. If the number of parents who volunteered to bring refreshments was 1.5 times the number of parents who neither volunteered to supervise children during the picnic nor volunteered to bring refreshments, how many of the parents volunteered to bring refreshments?

    (A) 25
    (B) 36
    (C) 38
    (D) 42
    (E) 45

15. The product of all the prime numbers less than 20 is closest to which of the following powers of 10 ?

    (A) 10^9
    (B) 10^8
    (C) 10^7
    (D) 10^6
    (E) 10^5

16. If $\sqrt{3-2x} = \sqrt{2x} + 1$, then $4x^2 =$

    (A) 1
    (B) 4
    (C) 2 – 2x
    (D) 4x – 2
    (E) 6x – 1

17. If $n = \sqrt{\frac{16}{81}}$, what is the value of $\sqrt{n}$?

    (A) $\frac{1}{9}$
    (B) $\frac{1}{4}$
    (C) $\frac{4}{9}$
    (D) $\frac{2}{3}$
    (E) $\frac{9}{2}$

18. If n is the product of the integers from 1 to 8, inclusive, how many different prime factors greater than 1 does n have?

    (A) Four
    (B) Five
    (C) Six
    (D) Seven
    (E) Eight

19. If k is an integer and 2 < k < 7, for how many different values of k is there a triangle with sides of lengths 2, 7, and k ?

    (A) One
    (B) Two
    (C) Three
    (D) Four
    (E) Five

18

20. A right circular cone is inscribed in a hemisphere so that the base of the cone coincides with the base of the hemisphere. What is the ratio of the height of the cone to the radius of the hemisphere?

   (A) $\sqrt{3}:1$
   (B) $1:1$
   (C) $\frac{1}{2}:1$
   (D) $\sqrt{2}:1$
   (E) $2:1$

21. John deposited $10,000 to open a new savings account that earned 4 percent annual interest, compounded quarterly. If there were no other transactions in the account, what was the amount of money in John's account 6 months after the account was opened?

   (A) $10,100
   (B) $10,101
   (C) $10,200
   (D) $10,201
   (E) $10,400

22. A container in the shape of a right circular cylinder is $\frac{1}{2}$ full of water. If the volume of water in the container is 36 cubic inches and the height of the container is 9 inches, what is the diameter of the base of the cylinder, in inches?

   (A) $\frac{16}{9\pi}$
   (B) $\frac{4}{\sqrt{\pi}}$
   (C) $\frac{12}{\sqrt{\pi}}$
   (D) $\sqrt{\frac{2}{\pi}}$
   (E) $4\sqrt{\frac{2}{\pi}}$

23. If the positive integer x is a multiple of 4 and the positive integer y is a multiple of 6, then xy must be a multiple of which of the following?

   I. 8
   II. 12
   III. 18

   (A) II only
   (B) I and II only
   (C) I and III only
   (D) II and III only
   (E) I, II, and III

24. Aaron will jog from home at x miles per hour and then walk back home by the same route at y miles per hour. How many miles from home can Aaron jog so that he spends a total of t hours jogging and walking?

   (A) $\dfrac{xt}{y}$
   (B) $\dfrac{x+t}{xy}$
   (C) $\dfrac{xyt}{x+y}$
   (D) $\dfrac{x+y+t}{xy}$
   (E) $\dfrac{y+t}{x}-\dfrac{t}{y}$

Data Sufficiency

Each data sufficiency problem consists of a question and two statements, labeled (1) and (2), which contain certain data. Using these data and your knowledge of mathematics and everyday facts (such as the number of days in July or the meaning of the word *counterclockwise*), decide whether the data given are sufficient for answering the question and then indicate one of the following answer choices:

A   Statement (1) ALONE is sufficient, but statement (2) alone is not sufficient.
B   Statement (2) ALONE is sufficient, but statement (1) alone is not sufficient.
C   BOTH statements TOGETHER are sufficient, but NEITHER statement ALONE is sufficient.
D   EACH statement ALONE is sufficient.
E   Statements (1) and (2) TOGETHER are NOT sufficient.

Note: In data sufficiency problems that ask for the value of a quantity, the data given in the statements are sufficient only when it is possible to determine exactly one numerical value for the quantity.

Example:

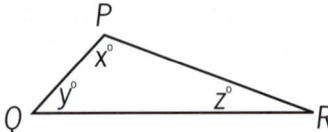

In $\triangle PQR$, what is the value of x?

(1) $PQ = PR$

(2) $y = 40$

Explanation: According to statement (1) $PQ = PR$; therefore, $\triangle PQR$ is isosceles and $y = z$. Since $x + y + z = 180$, it follows that $x + 2y = 180$. Since statement (1) does not give a value for y, you cannot answer the question using statement (1) alone. According to statement (2), $y = 40$; therefore, $x + z = 140$. Since statement (2) does not give a value for z, you cannot answer the question using statement (2) alone. Using both statements together, since $x + 2y = 180$ and the value of y is given, you can find the value of x. Therefore, BOTH statements (1) and (2) TOGETHER are sufficient to answer the question, but NEITHER statement ALONE is sufficient.

Numbers: All numbers used are real numbers.

Figures:
- Figures conform to the information given in the question, but will not necessarily conform to the additional information given in statements (1) and (2).
- Lines shown as straight are straight, and lines that appear jagged are also straight.
- The positions of points, angles, regions, etc., exist in the order shown, and angle measures are greater than zero.
- All figures lie in a plane unless otherwise indicated.

25. If the units digit of integer *n* is greater than 2, what is the units digit of *n*?

    (1) The units digit of *n* is the same as the units digit of n^2.
    (2) The units digit of *n* is the same as the units digit of n^3.

26. What is the value of the integer *p*?

    (1) Each of the integers 2, 3, and 5 is a factor of *p*.
    (2) Each of the integers 2, 5, and 7 is a factor of *p*.

27. If the length of Wanda's telephone call was rounded up to the nearest whole minute by her telephone company, then Wanda was charged for how many minutes for her telephone call?

    (1) The total charge for Wanda's telephone call was $6.50.
    (2) Wanda was charged $0.50 more for the first minute of the telephone call than for each minute after the first.

28. What is the perimeter of isosceles triangle *MNP*?

    (1) *MN* = 16
    (2) *NP* = 20

29. In a survey of retailers, what percent had purchased computers for business purposes?

    (1) 85 percent of the retailers surveyed who owned their own store had purchased computers for business purposes.
    (2) 40 percent of the retailers surveyed owned their own store.

30. The only gift certificates that a certain store sold yesterday were worth either $100 each or $10 each. If the store sold a total of 20 gift certificates yesterday, how many gift certificates worth $10 each did the store sell yesterday?

    (1) The gift certificates sold by the store yesterday were worth a total of between $1,650 and $1,800.
    (2) Yesterday the store sold more than 15 gift certificates worth $100 each.

31. Is the standard deviation of the set of measurements $x_1, x_2, x_3, x_4, \ldots, x_{20}$ less than 3?

    (1) The variance for the set of measurements is 4.
    (2) For each measurement, the difference between the mean and that measurement is 2.

32. Is the range of the integers 6, 3, *y*, 4, 5, and *x* greater than 9?

    (1) *y* > 3*x*
    (2) *y* > *x* > 3

33. Is $\dfrac{5^{x+2}}{25} < 1$?

    (1) $5^x < 1$
    (2) $x < 0$

34. Of the companies surveyed about the skills they required in prospective employees, 20 percent required both computer skills and writing skills. What percent of the companies surveyed required neither computer skills nor writing skills?

    (1) Of those companies surveyed that required computer skills, half required writing skills.
    (2) 45 percent of the companies surveyed required writing skills but not computer skills.

35. What is the value of *w* + *q*?

    (1) 3*w* = 3 − 3*q*
    (2) 5*w* + 5*q* = 5

36. If *X* and *Y* are points in a plane and *X* lies inside the circle *C* with center *O* and radius 2, does *Y* lie inside circle *C*?

    (1) The length of line segment *XY* is 3.
    (2) The length of line segment *OY* is 1.5.

37. Is *x* > *y*?

    (1) *x* = *y* + 2
    (2) $\dfrac{x}{2} = y - 1$

38. If Paula drove the distance from her home to her college at an average speed that was greater than 70 kilometers per hour, did it take her less than 3 hours to drive this distance?

    (1) The distance that Paula drove from her home to her college was greater than 200 kilometers.
    (2) The distance that Paula drove from her home to her college was less than 205 kilometers.

39. In the xy-plane, if line k has negative slope and passes through the point (–5,r), is the x-intercept of line k positive?

    (1) The slope of line k is –5.
    (2) r > 0

40. If $5,000 invested for one year at p percent simple annual interest yields $500, what amount must be invested at k percent simple annual interest for one year to yield the same number of dollars?

    (1) k = 0.8p
    (2) k = 8

41. If $\frac{x+y}{z} > 0$, is x < 0 ?

    (1) x < y
    (2) z < 0

42. Does the integer k have at least three different positive prime factors?

    (1) $\frac{k}{15}$ is an integer.
    (2) $\frac{k}{10}$ is an integer.

43. In City X last April, was the average (arithmetic mean) daily high temperature greater than the median daily high temperature?

    (1) In City X last April, the sum of the 30 daily high temperatures was 2,160°.
    (2) In City X last April, 60 percent of the daily high temperatures were less than the average daily high temperature.

44. If m and n are positive integers, is $\left(\sqrt{m}\right)^n$ an integer?

    (1) $\left(\sqrt{m}\right)$ is an integer.
    (2) $\left(\sqrt{n}\right)$ is an integer.

45. Of the 66 people in a certain auditorium, at most 6 people have their birthdays in any one given month. Does at least one person in the auditorium have a birthday in January?

    (1) More of the people in the auditorium have their birthday in February than in March.
    (2) Five of the people in the auditorium have their birthday in March.

46. Last year the average (arithmetic mean) salary of the 10 employees of Company X was $42,800. What is the average salary of the same 10 employees this year?

    (1) For 8 of the 10 employees, this year's salary is 15 percent greater than last year's salary.
    (2) For 2 of the 10 employees, this year's salary is the same as last year's salary.

47. In a certain classroom, there are 80 books, of which 24 are fiction and 23 are written in Spanish. How many of the fiction books are written in Spanish?

    (1) Of the fiction books, there are 6 more that are not written in Spanish than are written in Spanish.
    (2) Of the books written in Spanish, there are 5 more nonfiction books than fiction books.

48. If p is the perimeter of rectangle Q, what is the value of p ?

    (1) Each diagonal of rectangle Q has length 10.
    (2) The area of rectangle Q is 48.

3.2 Verbal Questions

Reading Comprehension

Each of the reading comprehension questions is based on the content of a passage. After reading the passage, answer all questions pertaining to it on the basis of what is stated or implied in the passage. For each question, select the best answer of the choices given.

Line According to economic signaling theory, consumers may perceive the frequency with which an unfamiliar brand is advertised as a cue that the brand is of high quality. The notion that
(5)   highly advertised brands are associated with high-quality products does have some empirical support. Marquardt and McGann found that heavily advertised products did indeed rank high on certain measures of product quality. **Because**
(10) **large advertising expenditures represent a significant investment on the part of a manufacturer, only companies that expect to recoup these costs in the long run, through consumers' repeat purchases of the product,**
(15) **can afford to spend such amounts.**
      However, two studies by Kirmani have found that although consumers initially perceive expensive advertising as a signal of high brand quality, at some level of spending the manufacturer's
(20) advertising effort may be perceived as unreasonably high, implying low manufacturer confidence in product quality. If consumers perceive excessive advertising effort as a sign of a manufacturer's desperation, the result may be less favorable
(25) brand perceptions. In addition, a third study by Kirmani, of print advertisements, found that the use of color affected consumer perception of brand quality. Because consumers recognize that color advertisements are more expensive than
(30) black and white, the point at which repetition of an advertisement is perceived as excessive comes sooner for a color advertisement than for a black-and-white advertisement.

49. Which of the following best describes the purpose of the sentence in lines 10–15 ?

    (A) To show that economic signaling theory fails to explain a finding
    (B) To introduce a distinction not accounted for by economic signaling theory
    (C) To account for an exception to a generalization suggested by Marquardt and McGann
    (D) To explain why Marquardt and McGann's research was conducted
    (E) To offer an explanation for an observation reported by Marquardt and McGann

50. The primary purpose of the passage is to

    (A) present findings that contradict one explanation for the effects of a particular advertising practice
    (B) argue that theoretical explanations about the effects of a particular advertising practice are of limited value without empirical evidence
    (C) discuss how and why particular advertising practices may affect consumers' perceptions
    (D) contrast the research methods used in two different studies of a particular advertising practice
    (E) explain why a finding about consumer responses to a particular advertising practice was unexpected

51. Kirmani's research, as described in the passage, suggests which of the following regarding consumers' expectations about the quality of advertised products?

    (A) Those expectations are likely to be highest if a manufacturer runs both black-and-white and color advertisements for the same product.
    (B) Those expectations can be shaped by the presence of color in an advertisement as well as by the frequency with which an advertisement appears.
    (C) Those expectations are usually high for frequently advertised new brands but not for frequently advertised familiar brands.
    (D) Those expectations are likely to be higher for products whose black-and-white advertisements are often repeated than for those whose color advertisements are less often repeated.
    (E) Those expectations are less definitively shaped by the manufacturer's advertisements than by information that consumers gather from other sources.

52. Kirmani's third study, as described in the passage, suggests which of the following conclusions about a black-and-white advertisement?

    (A) It can be repeated more frequently than a comparable color advertisement could before consumers begin to suspect low manufacturer confidence in the quality of the advertised product.
    (B) It will have the greatest impact on consumers' perceptions of the quality of the advertised product if it appears during periods when a color version of the same advertisement is also being used.
    (C) It will attract more attention from readers of the print publication in which it appears if it is used only a few times.
    (D) It may be perceived by some consumers as more expensive than a comparable color advertisement.
    (E) It is likely to be perceived by consumers as a sign of higher manufacturer confidence in the quality of the advertised product than a comparable color advertisement would be.

53. The passage suggests that Kirmani would be most likely to agree with which of the following statements about consumers' perceptions of the relationship between the frequency with which a product is advertised and the product's quality?

    (A) Consumers' perceptions about the frequency with which an advertisement appears are their primary consideration when evaluating an advertisement's claims about product quality.
    (B) Because most consumers do not notice the frequency of advertisement, it has little impact on most consumers' expectations regarding product quality.
    (C) Consumers perceive frequency of advertisement as a signal about product quality only when the advertisement is for a product that is newly on the market.
    (D) The frequency of advertisement is not always perceived by consumers to indicate that manufacturers are highly confident about their products' quality.
    (E) Consumers who try a new product that has been frequently advertised are likely to perceive the advertisement's frequency as having been an accurate indicator of the product's quality.

Line The idea of the brain as an information
      processor—a machine manipulating blips of energy
      according to fathomable rules—has come to
      dominate neuroscience. However, one enemy of
(5)   the brain-as-computer metaphor is John R. Searle,
      a philosopher who argues that since computers
      simply follow algorithms, they cannot deal with
      important aspects of human thought such as
      meaning and content. Computers are syntactic,
(10) rather than semantic, creatures. People, on the
      other hand, understand meaning because they have
      something Searle obscurely calls the causal powers
      of the brain.
        Yet how would a brain work if not by reducing
(15) what it learns about the world to information—some
      kind of code that can be transmitted from neuron
      to neuron? What else could meaning and content
      be? If the code can be cracked, a computer should
      be able to simulate it, at least in principle. But
(20) even if a computer could simulate the workings
      of the mind, Searle would claim that the machine
      would not really be thinking; it would just be acting
      as if it were. His argument proceeds thus: if a
      computer were used to simulate a stomach, with
(25) the stomach's churnings faithfully reproduced on a
      video screen, the machine would not be digesting
      real food. It would just be blindly manipulating the
      symbols that generate the visual display.
        Suppose, though, that a stomach were simulated
(30) using plastic tubes, a motor to do the churning, a
      supply of digestive juices, and a timing mechanism.
      If food went in one end of the device, what came out
      the other end would surely be digested food. Brains,
      unlike stomachs, are information processors, and if
(35) one information processor were made to simulate
      another information processor, it is hard to see
      how one and not the other could be said to think.
      Simulated thoughts and real thoughts are made of
      the same element: information. The representations
(40) of the world that humans carry around in their heads
      are already simulations. To accept Searle's argument,
      one would have to deny the most fundamental notion
      in psychology and neuroscience: that brains work
      by processing information.

54. The main purpose of the passage is to

    (A) propose an experiment
    (B) analyze a function
    (C) refute an argument
    (D) explain a contradiction
    (E) simulate a process

55. Which of the following is most consistent with Searle's reasoning as presented in the passage?

    (A) Meaning and content cannot be reduced to algorithms.
    (B) The process of digestion can be simulated mechanically, but not on a computer.
    (C) Simulated thoughts and real thoughts are essentially similar because they are composed primarily of information.
    (D) A computer can use "causal powers" similar to those of the human brain when processing information.
    (E) Computer simulations of the world can achieve the complexity of the brain's representations of the world.

56. The author of the passage would be most likely to agree with which of the following statements about the simulation of organ functions?

    (A) An artificial device that achieves the functions of the stomach could be considered a valid model of the stomach.
    (B) Computer simulations of the brain are best used to crack the brain's codes of meaning and content.
    (C) Computer simulations of the brain challenge ideas that are fundamental to psychology and neuroscience.
    (D) Because the brain and the stomach both act as processors, they can best be simulated by mechanical devices.
    (E) The computer's limitations in simulating digestion suggest equal limitations in computer-simulated thinking.

57. It can be inferred that the author of the passage believes that Searle's argument is flawed by its failure to

    (A) distinguish between syntactic and semantic operations
    (B) explain adequately how people, unlike computers, are able to understand meaning
    (C) provide concrete examples illustrating its claims about thinking
    (D) understand how computers use algorithms to process information
    (E) decipher the code that is transmitted from neuron to neuron in the brain

58. From the passage, it can be inferred that the author would agree with Searle on which of the following points?

    (A) Computers operate by following algorithms.
    (B) The human brain can never fully understand its own functions.
    (C) The comparison of the brain to a machine is overly simplistic.
    (D) The most accurate models of physical processes are computer simulations.
    (E) Human thought and computer-simulated thought involve similar processes of representation.

59. Which of the following most accurately represents Searle's criticism of the brain-as-computer metaphor, as that criticism is described in the passage?

    (A) The metaphor is not experimentally verifiable.
    (B) The metaphor does not take into account the unique powers of the brain.
    (C) The metaphor suggests that a brain's functions can be simulated as easily as those of a stomach.
    (D) The metaphor suggests that a computer can simulate the workings of the mind by using the codes of neural transmission.
    (E) The metaphor is unhelpful because both the brain and the computer process information.

Line Women's grassroots activism and their vision of a new civic consciousness lay at the heart of social reform in the United States throughout the Progressive Era, the period between the depression
(5) of 1893 and America's entry into the Second World War. Though largely disenfranchised except for school elections, white middle-class women reformers won a variety of victories, notably in the improvement of working conditions, especially
(10) for women and children. Ironically, though, child labor legislation pitted women of different classes against one another. To the reformers, child labor and industrial home work were equally inhumane practices that should be outlawed, but,
(15) as a number of women historians have recently observed, working-class mothers did not always share this view. Given the precarious finances of working-class families and the necessity of pooling the wages of as many family members as possible,
(20) working-class families viewed the passage and enforcement of stringent child labor statutes as a personal economic disaster and made strenuous efforts to circumvent child labor laws. Yet reformers rarely understood this resistance in terms
(25) of the desperate economic situation of working-class families, interpreting it instead as evidence of poor parenting. This is not to dispute women reformers' perception of child labor as a terribly exploitative practice, but their understanding of
(30) child labor and their legislative solutions for ending it failed to take account of the economic needs of working-class families.

60. The primary purpose of the passage is to

(A) explain why women reformers of the Progressive Era failed to achieve their goals

(B) discuss the origins of child labor laws in the late nineteenth and early twentieth centuries

(C) compare the living conditions of working-class and middle-class women in the Progressive Era

(D) discuss an oversight on the part of women reformers of the Progressive Era

(E) revise a traditional view of the role played by women reformers in enacting Progressive Era reforms

61. The view mentioned in line 17 of the passage refers to which of the following?

(A) Some working-class mothers' resistance to the enforcement of child labor laws

(B) Reformers' belief that child labor and industrial home work should be abolished

(C) Reformers' opinions about how working-class families raised their children

(D) Certain women historians' observation that there was a lack of consensus between women of different classes on the issue of child labor and industrial home work

(E) Working-class families' fears about the adverse consequences that child labor laws would have on their ability to earn an adequate living

62. The author of the passage mentions the observations of women historians (lines 15–17) most probably in order to

(A) provide support for an assertion made in the preceding sentence (lines 10–12)

(B) raise a question that is answered in the last sentence of the passage (lines 27–32)

(C) introduce an opinion that challenges a statement made in the first sentence of the passage

(D) offer an alternative view to the one attributed in the passage to working-class mothers

(E) point out a contradiction inherent in the traditional view of child labor reform as it is presented in the passage

63. The passage suggests that which of the following was a reason for the difference of opinion between working-class mothers and women reformers on the issue of child labor?

    (A) Reformers' belief that industrial home work was preferable to child labor outside the home
    (B) Reformers' belief that child labor laws should pertain to working conditions but not to pay
    (C) Working-class mothers' resentment at reformers' attempts to interfere with their parenting
    (D) Working-class mothers' belief that child labor was an inhumane practice
    (E) Working-class families' need for every employable member of their families to earn money

64. The author of the passage asserts which of the following about women reformers who tried to abolish child labor?

    (A) They alienated working-class mothers by attempting to enlist them in agitating for progressive causes.
    (B) They underestimated the prevalence of child labor among the working classes.
    (C) They were correct in their conviction that child labor was deplorable but shortsighted about the impact of child labor legislation on working-class families.
    (D) They were aggressive in their attempts to enforce child labor legislation, but were unable to prevent working-class families from circumventing them.
    (E) They were prevented by their nearly total disenfranchisement from making significant progress in child labor reform.

65. According to the passage, one of the most striking achievements of white middle-class women reformers during the Progressive Era was

    (A) gaining the right to vote in school elections
    (B) mobilizing working-class women in the fight against child labor
    (C) uniting women of different classes in grassroots activism
    (D) improving the economic conditions of working-class families
    (E) improving women's and children's working conditions

Critical Reasoning

Each of the critical reasoning questions is based on a short argument, a set of statements, or a plan of action. For each question, select the best answer of the choices given.

66. Vasquez-Morrell Assurance specializes in insuring manufacturers. Whenever a policyholder makes a claim, a claims adjuster determines the amount that Vasquez-Morrell is obligated to pay. Vasquez-Morrell is cutting its staff of claims adjusters by 15 percent. To ensure that the company's ability to handle claims promptly is affected as little as possible by the staff cuts, consultants recommend that Vasquez-Morrell lay off those adjusters who now take longest, on average, to complete work on claims assigned to them.

    Which of the following, if true, most seriously calls into question the consultants' criterion for selecting the staff to be laid off?

    (A) If the time that Vasquez-Morrell takes to settle claims increases significantly, it could lose business to other insurers.
    (B) Supervisors at Vasquez-Morrell tend to assign the most complex claims to the most capable adjusters.
    (C) At Vasquez-Morrell, no insurance payments are made until a claims adjuster has reached a final determination on the claim.
    (D) There are no positions at Vasquez-Morrell to which staff currently employed as claims adjusters could be reassigned.
    (E) The premiums that Vasquez-Morrell currently charges are no higher than those charged for similar coverage by competitors.

67. Prolonged spells of hot, dry weather at the end of the grape-growing season typically reduce a vineyard's yield, because the grapes stay relatively small. In years with such weather, wine producers can make only a relatively small quantity of wine from a given area of vineyards. Nonetheless, in regions where wine producers generally grow their own grapes, analysts typically expect a long, hot, dry spell late in the growing season to result in increased revenues for local wine producers.

    Which of the following, if true, does most to justify the analysts' expectation?

    (A) The lower a vineyard's yield, the less labor is required to harvest the grapes.
    (B) Long, hot, dry spells at the beginning of the grape-growing season are rare, but they can have a devastating effect on a vineyard's yield.
    (C) Grapes grown for wine production are typically made into wine at or near the vineyard in which they were grown.
    (D) When hot, dry spells are followed by heavy rains, the rains frequently destroy grape crops.
    (E) Grapes that have matured in hot, dry weather make significantly better wine than ordinary grapes.

68. In the past, most children who went sledding in the winter snow in Verland used wooden sleds with runners and steering bars. Ten years ago, smooth plastic sleds became popular; they go faster than wooden sleds but are harder to steer and slow. The concern that plastic sleds are more dangerous is clearly borne out by the fact that the number of children injured while sledding was much higher last winter than it was 10 years ago.

Which of the following, if true in Verland, most seriously undermines the force of the evidence cited?

(A) A few children still use traditional wooden sleds.
(B) Very few children wear any kind of protective gear, such as helmets, while sledding.
(C) Plastic sleds can be used in a much wider variety of snow conditions than wooden sleds can.
(D) Most sledding injuries occur when a sled collides with a tree, a rock, or another sled.
(E) Because the traditional wooden sleds can carry more than one rider, an accident involving a wooden sled can result in several children being injured.

69. Metal rings recently excavated from seventh-century settlements in the western part of Mexico were made using the same metallurgical techniques as those used by Ecuadorian artisans before and during that period. These techniques are sufficiently complex to make their independent development in both areas unlikely. Since the people of these two areas were in cultural contact, archaeologists hypothesize that the metallurgical techniques used to make the rings found in Mexico were learned by Mexican artisans from Ecuadorian counterparts.

Which of the following would it be most useful to establish in order to evaluate the archaeologists' hypothesis?

(A) Whether metal objects were traded from Ecuador to western Mexico during the seventh century
(B) Whether travel between western Mexico and Ecuador in the seventh century would have been primarily by land or by sea
(C) Whether artisans from western Mexico could have learned complex metallurgical techniques from their Ecuadorian counterparts without actually leaving western Mexico
(D) Whether metal tools were used in the seventh-century settlements in western Mexico
(E) Whether any of the techniques used in the manufacture of the metal rings found in western Mexico are still practiced among artisans in Ecuador today

70. Following several years of declining advertising sales, the Greenville Times reorganized its advertising sales force. Before reorganization, the sales force was organized geographically, with some sales representatives concentrating on city-center businesses and others concentrating on different outlying regions. The reorganization attempted to increase the sales representatives' knowledge of clients' businesses by having each sales representative deal with only one type of industry or of retailing. After the reorganization, revenue from advertising sales increased.

In assessing whether the improvement in advertising sales can properly be attributed to the reorganization, it would be most helpful to find out which of the following?

(A) What proportion of the total revenue of the Greenville Times is generated by advertising sales?
(B) Has the circulation of the Greenville Times increased substantially in the last two years?
(C) Among all the types of industry and retailing that use the Greenville Times as an advertising vehicle, which type accounts for the largest proportion of the newspaper's advertising sales?
(D) Do any clients of the sales representatives of the Greenville Times have a standing order with the Times for a fixed amount of advertising per month?
(E) Among the advertisers in the Greenville Times, are there more types of retail business or more types of industrial business?

71. Motorists in a certain country frequently complain that traffic congestion is much worse now than it was 20 years ago. No real measure of how much traffic congestion there was 20 years ago exists, but the motorists' complaints are almost certainly unwarranted. The country's highway capacity has tripled in the last twenty years, thanks to a vigorous highway construction program, whereas the number of automobiles registered in the country has increased by only 75 percent.

    Which of the following, if true, most seriously weakens the argument?

    (A) Most automobile travel is local, and the networks of roads and streets in the country's settled areas have changed little over the last 20 years.
    (B) Gasoline prices are high, and miles traveled per car per year have not changed much over the last 20 years.
    (C) The country's urban centers have well-developed public transit systems that carry most of the people who commute into those centers.
    (D) The average age of automobiles registered in the country is lower now than it was 20 years ago.
    (E) Radio stations have long been broadcasting regular traffic reports that inform motorists about traffic congestion.

72. The percentage of households with an annual income of more than $40,000 is higher in Merton County than in any other county. However, the percentage of households with an annual income of $60,000 or more is higher in Sommer County.

    If the statements above are true, which of the following must also be true?

    (A) The percentage of households with an annual income of $80,000 is higher in Sommer County than in Merton County.
    (B) Merton County has the second highest percentage of households with an annual income of $60,000 or more.
    (C) Some households in Merton County have an annual income between $40,000 and $60,000.
    (D) The number of households with an annual income of more than $40,000 is greater in Merton County than in Sommer County.
    (E) Average annual household income is higher in Sommer County than in Merton County.

73. Tiger beetles are such fast runners that they can capture virtually any nonflying insect. However, when running toward an insect, a tiger beetle will intermittently stop and then, a moment later, resume its attack. Perhaps the beetles cannot maintain their pace and must pause for a moment's rest; but an alternative hypothesis is that while running, tiger beetles are unable to adequately process the resulting rapidly changing visual information and so quickly go blind and stop.

    Which of the following, if discovered in experiments using artificially moved prey insects, would support one of the two hypotheses and undermine the other?

    (A) When a prey insect is moved directly toward a beetle that has been chasing it, the beetle immediately stops and runs away without its usual intermittent stopping.
    (B) In pursuing a swerving insect, a beetle alters its course while running and its pauses become more frequent as the chase progresses.
    (C) In pursuing a moving insect, a beetle usually responds immediately to changes in the insect's direction, and it pauses equally frequently whether the chase is up or down an incline.
    (D) If, when a beetle pauses, it has not gained on the insect it is pursuing, the beetle generally ends its pursuit.
    (E) The faster a beetle pursues an insect fleeing directly away from it, the more frequently the beetle stops.

74. Guillemots are birds of Arctic regions. They feed on fish that gather beneath thin sheets of floating ice, and they nest on nearby land. Guillemots need 80 consecutive snow-free days in a year to raise their chicks, so until average temperatures in the Arctic began to rise recently, the guillemots' range was limited to the southernmost Arctic coast. Therefore, if the warming continues, the guillemots' range will probably be enlarged by being extended northward along the coast.

    Which of the following, if true, most seriously weakens the argument?

    (A) Even if the warming trend continues, there will still be years in which guillemot chicks are killed by an unusually early snow.
    (B) If the Arctic warming continues, guillemots' current predators are likely to succeed in extending their own range farther north.
    (C) Guillemots nest in coastal areas, where temperatures are generally higher than in inland areas.
    (D) If the Arctic warming continues, much of the thin ice in the southern Arctic will disappear.
    (E) The fish that guillemots eat are currently preyed on by a wider variety of predators in the southernmost Arctic regions than they are farther north.

75. Some batches of polio vaccine used around 1960 were contaminated with SV40, a virus that in monkeys causes various cancers. Some researchers now claim that this contamination caused some cases of a certain cancer in humans, mesothelioma. This claim is not undercut by the fact that a very careful survey made in the 1960s of people who had received the contaminated vaccine found no elevated incidence of any cancer, since _____.

    (A) most cases of mesothelioma are caused by exposure to asbestos
    (B) in some countries, there was no contamination of the vaccine
    (C) SV40 is widely used in laboratories to produce cancers in animals
    (D) mesotheliomas take several decades to develop
    (E) mesothelioma was somewhat less common in 1960 than it is now

76. Gortland has long been narrowly self-sufficient in both grain and meat. However, as per capita income in Gortland has risen toward the world average, per capita consumption of meat has also risen toward the world average, and it takes several pounds of grain to produce one pound of meat. Therefore, since per capita income continues to rise, whereas domestic grain production will not increase, Gortland will soon have to import either grain or meat or both.

    Which of the following is an assumption on which the argument depends?

    (A) The total acreage devoted to grain production in Gortland will soon decrease.
    (B) Importing either grain or meat will not result in a significantly higher percentage of Gortlanders' incomes being spent on food than is currently the case.
    (C) The per capita consumption of meat in Gortland is increasing at roughly the same rate across all income levels.
    (D) The per capita income of meat producers in Gortland is rising faster than the per capita income of grain producers.
    (E) People in Gortland who increase their consumption of meat will not radically decrease their consumption of grain.

77. The Hazelton coal-processing plant is a major employer in the Hazelton area, but national environmental regulations will force it to close if it continues to use old, polluting processing methods. However, to update the plant to use newer, cleaner methods would be so expensive that the plant will close unless it receives the tax break it has requested. In order to prevent a major increase in local unemployment, the Hazelton government is considering granting the plant's request.

    Which of the following would be most important for the Hazelton government to determine before deciding whether to grant the plant's request?

    (A) Whether the company that owns the plant would open a new plant in another area if the present plant were closed
    (B) Whether the plant would employ far fewer workers when updated than it does now
    (C) Whether the level of pollutants presently being emitted by the plant is high enough to constitute a health hazard for local residents
    (D) Whether the majority of the coal processed by the plant is sold outside the Hazelton area
    (E) Whether the plant would be able to process more coal when updated than it does now

78. A physically active lifestyle has been shown to help increase longevity. In the Wistar region of Bellaria, the average age at death is considerably higher than in any other part of the country. Wistar is the only mountainous part of Bellaria. A mountainous terrain makes even such basic activities as walking relatively strenuous; it essentially imposes a physically active lifestyle on people. Clearly, this circumstance explains the long lives of people in Wistar.

    Which of the following, if true, most seriously weakens the argument?

    (A) In Bellaria all medical expenses are paid by the government, so that personal income does not affect the quality of health care a person receives.
    (B) The Wistar region is one of Bellaria's least populated regions.
    (C) Many people who live in the Wistar region have moved there in middle age or upon retirement.
    (D) The many opportunities for hiking, skiing, and other outdoor activities that Wistar's mountains offer make it a favorite destination for vacationing Bellarians.
    (E) Per capita spending on recreational activities is no higher in Wistar than it is in other regions of Bellaria.

79. Cheever College offers several online courses via remote computer connection, in addition to traditional classroom-based courses. A study of student performance at Cheever found that, overall, the average student grade for online courses matched that for classroom-based courses. In this calculation of the average grade, course withdrawals were weighted as equivalent to a course failure, and the rate of withdrawal was much lower for students enrolled in classroom-based courses than for students enrolled in online courses.

    If the statements above are true, which of the following must also be true of Cheever College?

    (A) Among students who did not withdraw, students enrolled in online courses got higher grades, on average, than students enrolled in classroom-based courses.
    (B) The number of students enrolled per course at the start of the school term is much higher, on average, for the online courses than for the classroom-based courses.
    (C) There are no students who take both an online and a classroom-based course in the same school term.
    (D) Among Cheever College students with the best grades, a significant majority take online, rather than classroom-based, courses.
    (E) Courses offered online tend to deal with subject matter that is less challenging than that of classroom-based courses.

80. For years the beautiful Renaissance buildings in Palitito have been damaged by exhaust from the many tour buses that come to the city. There has been little parking space, so most buses have idled at the curb during each stop on their tour, and idling produces as much exhaust as driving. The city has now provided parking that accommodates a third of the tour buses, so damage to Palitito's buildings from the buses' exhaust will diminish significantly.

    Which of the following, if true, most strongly supports the argument?

    (A) The exhaust from Palitito's few automobiles is not a significant threat to Palitito's buildings.

    (B) Palitito's Renaissance buildings are not threatened by pollution other than engine exhaust.

    (C) Tour buses typically spend less than one-quarter of the time they are in Palitito transporting passengers from one site to another.

    (D) More tourists come to Palitito by tour bus than by any other single means of transportation.

    (E) Some of the tour buses that are unable to find parking drive around Palitito while their passengers are visiting a site.

81. During the 1980s and 1990s, the annual number of people who visited the Sordellian Mountains increased continually, and many new ski resorts were built. Over the same period, however, the number of visitors to ski resorts who were caught in avalanches decreased, even though there was no reduction in the annual number of avalanches in the Sordellian Mountains.

    Which of the following, if true in the Sordellian Mountains during the 1980s and 1990s, most helps to explain the decrease?

    (A) Avalanches were most likely to happen when a large new snowfall covered an older layer of snow.

    (B) Avalanches destroyed at least some buildings in the Sordellian Mountains in every year.

    (C) People planning new ski slopes and other resort facilities used increasingly accurate information about which locations are likely to be in the path of avalanches.

    (D) The average length of stay for people visiting the Sordellian Mountains increased slightly.

    (E) Construction of new ski resorts often led to the clearing of wooded areas that had helped to prevent avalanches.

82. A year ago, Dietz Foods launched a yearlong advertising campaign for its canned tuna. Last year Dietz sold 12 million cans of tuna compared to the 10 million sold during the previous year, an increase directly attributable to new customers brought in by the campaign. Profits from the additional sales, however, were substantially less than the cost of the advertising campaign. Clearly, therefore, the campaign did nothing to further Dietz's economic interests.

    Which of the following, if true, most seriously weakens the argument?

    (A) Sales of canned tuna account for a relatively small percentage of Dietz Foods' profits.

    (B) Most of the people who bought Dietz's canned tuna for the first time as a result of the campaign were already loyal customers of other Dietz products.

    (C) A less expensive advertising campaign would have brought in significantly fewer new customers for Dietz's canned tuna than did the campaign Dietz Foods launched last year.

    (D) Dietz made money on sales of canned tuna last year.

    (E) In each of the past five years, there was a steep, industry-wide decline in sales of canned tuna.

Sentence Correction

Each of the sentence correction questions presents a sentence, part or all of which is underlined. Beneath the sentence you will find five ways of phrasing the underlined part. The first of these repeats the original; the other four are different. Follow the requirements of standard written English to choose your answer, paying attention to grammar, word choice, and sentence construction. Select the answer that produces the most effective sentence; your answer should make the sentence clear, exact, and free of grammatical error. It should also minimize awkwardness, ambiguity, and redundancy.

83. Unlike the buildings in Mesopotamian cities, which were arranged haphazardly, the same basic plan was followed for all cities of the Indus Valley: with houses laid out on a north-south, east-west grid, and houses and walls were built of standard-size bricks.

    (A) the buildings in Mesopotamian cities, which were arranged haphazardly, the same basic plan was followed for all cities of the Indus Valley: with houses
    (B) the buildings in Mesopotamian cities, which were haphazard in arrangement, the same basic plan was used in all cities of the Indus Valley: houses were
    (C) the arrangement of buildings in Mesopotamian cities, which were haphazard, the cities of the Indus Valley all followed the same basic plan: houses
    (D) Mesopotamian cities, in which buildings were arranged haphazardly, the cities of the Indus Valley all followed the same basic plan: houses were
    (E) Mesopotamian cities, which had buildings that were arranged haphazardly, the same basic plan was used for all cities in the Indus Valley: houses that were

84. New data from United States Forest Service ecologists show that for every dollar spent on controlled small-scale burning, forest thinning, and the training of fire-management personnel, it saves seven dollars that would not be spent on having to extinguish big fires.

    (A) that for every dollar spent on controlled small-scale burning, forest thinning, and the training of fire-management personnel, it saves seven dollars that would not be spent on having to extinguish
    (B) that for every dollar spent on controlled small-scale burning, forest thinning, and the training of fire-management personnel, seven dollars are saved that would have been spent on extinguishing
    (C) that for every dollar spent on controlled small-scale burning, forest thinning, and the training of fire-management personnel saves seven dollars on not having to extinguish
    (D) for every dollar spent on controlled small-scale burning, forest thinning, and the training of fire-management personnel, that it saves seven dollars on not having to extinguish
    (E) for every dollar spent on controlled small-scale burning, forest thinning, and the training of fire-management personnel, that seven dollars are saved that would not have been spent on extinguishing

85. Like the grassy fields and old pastures that the upland sandpiper needs for feeding and nesting when it returns in May after wintering in the Argentine Pampas, the sandpipers vanishing in the northeastern United States is a result of residential and industrial development and of changes in farming practices.

   (A) the sandpipers vanishing in the northeastern United States is a result of residential and industrial development and of changes in
   (B) the bird itself is vanishing in the northeastern United States as a result of residential and industrial development and of changes in
   (C) that the birds themselves are vanishing in the northeastern United States is due to residential and industrial development and changes to
   (D) in the northeastern United States, sandpipers' vanishing due to residential and industrial development and to changes in
   (E) in the northeastern United States, the sandpipers' vanishing, a result of residential and industrial development and changing

86. The results of two recent unrelated studies support the idea that dolphins may share certain cognitive abilities with humans and great apes; the studies indicate dolphins as capable of recognizing themselves in mirrors—an ability that is often considered a sign of self-awareness—and to grasp spontaneously the mood or intention of humans.

   (A) dolphins as capable of recognizing themselves in mirrors—an ability that is often considered a sign of self-awareness—and to grasp spontaneously
   (B) dolphins' ability to recognize themselves in mirrors—an ability that is often considered as a sign of self-awareness—and of spontaneously grasping
   (C) dolphins to be capable of recognizing themselves in mirrors—an ability that is often considered a sign of self-awareness—and to grasp spontaneously
   (D) that dolphins have the ability of recognizing themselves in mirrors—an ability that is often considered as a sign of self-awareness—and spontaneously grasping
   (E) that dolphins are capable of recognizing themselves in mirrors—an ability that is often considered a sign of self-awareness—and of spontaneously grasping

87. According to scholars, the earliest writing was probably not a direct rendering of speech, but was more likely to begin as a separate and distinct symbolic system of communication, and only later merged with spoken language.

   (A) was more likely to begin as
   (B) more than likely began as
   (C) more than likely beginning from
   (D) it was more than likely begun from
   (E) it was more likely that it began

88. In 1995 Richard Stallman, a well-known critic of the patent system, testified in Patent Office hearings that, to test the system, a colleague of his had managed to win a patent for one of Kirchhoff's laws, an observation about electric current first made in 1845 and now included in virtually every textbook of elementary physics.

   (A) laws, an observation about electric current first made in 1845 and
   (B) laws, which was an observation about electric current first made in 1845 and it is
   (C) laws, namely, it was an observation about electric current first made in 1845 and
   (D) laws, an observation about electric current first made in 1845, it is
   (E) laws that was an observation about electric current, first made in 1845, and is

89. Excavators at the Indus Valley site of Harappa in eastern Pakistan say the discovery of inscribed shards dating to circa 2800–2600 B.C. indicate their development of a Harappan writing system, the use of inscribed seals impressed into clay for marking ownership, and the standardization of weights for trade or taxation occurred many decades, if not centuries, earlier than was previously believed.

   (A) indicate their development of a Harappan writing system, the use of
   (B) indicate that the development of a Harappan writing system, using
   (C) indicates that their development of a Harappan writing system, using
   (D) indicates the development of a Harappan writing system, their use of
   (E) indicates that the development of a Harappan writing system, the use of

90. The Supreme Court has ruled that public universities can collect student activity fees even with students' objections to particular activities, so long as the groups they give money to will be chosen without regard to their views.

    (A) with students' objections to particular activities, so long as the groups they give money to will be
    (B) if they have objections to particular activities and the groups that are given the money are
    (C) if they object to particular activities, but the groups that the money is given to have to be
    (D) from students who object to particular activities, so long as the groups given money are
    (E) though students have an objection to particular activities, but the groups that are given the money be

91. Despite the increasing number of women graduating from law school and passing bar examinations, the proportion of judges and partners at major law firms who are women have not risen to a comparable extent.

    (A) the proportion of judges and partners at major law firms who are women have not risen to a comparable extent
    (B) the proportion of women judges and partners at major law firms have not risen comparably
    (C) the proportion of judges and partners at major law firms who are women has not risen comparably
    (D) yet the proportion of women judges and partners at major law firms has not risen to a comparable extent
    (E) yet the proportion of judges and partners at major law firms who are women has not risen comparably

92. Seldom more than 40 feet wide and 12 feet deep, but it ran 363 miles across the rugged wilderness of upstate New York, the Erie Canal connected the Hudson River at Albany to the Great Lakes at Buffalo, providing the port of New York City with a direct water link to the heartland of the North American continent.

    (A) Seldom more than 40 feet wide and 12 feet deep, but it ran 363 miles across the rugged wilderness of upstate New York, the Erie Canal connected
    (B) Seldom more than 40 feet wide or 12 feet deep but running 363 miles across the rugged wilderness of upstate New York, the Erie Canal connected
    (C) It was seldom more than 40 feet wide and 12 feet deep, and ran 363 miles across the rugged wilderness of upstate New York, but the Erie Canal, connecting
    (D) The Erie Canal was seldom more than 40 feet wide or 12 feet deep and it ran 363 miles across the rugged wilderness of upstate New York, which connected
    (E) The Erie Canal, seldom more than 40 feet wide and 12 feet deep, but running 363 miles across the rugged wilderness of upstate New York, connecting

93. In 1923, the Supreme Court declared a minimum wage for women and children in the District of Columbia as unconstitutional, and ruling that it was a form of price-fixing and, as such, an abridgment of the right of contract.

    (A) the Supreme Court declared a minimum wage for women and children in the District of Columbia as unconstitutional, and
    (B) the Supreme Court declared as unconstitutional a minimum wage for women and children in the District of Columbia, and
    (C) the Supreme Court declared unconstitutional a minimum wage for women and children in the District of Columbia,
    (D) a minimum wage for women and children in the District of Columbia was declared unconstitutional by the Supreme Court,
    (E) when the Supreme Court declared a minimum wage for women and children in the District of Columbia as unconstitutional,

94. Researchers have found that individuals who have been blind from birth, and who thus have never seen anyone gesture, nevertheless make hand motions when speaking just as frequently and in virtually the same way as sighted people do, and that they will gesture even when conversing with another blind person.

    (A) who thus have never seen anyone gesture, nevertheless make hand motions when speaking just as frequently and in virtually the same way as sighted people do, and that they will gesture

    (B) who thus never saw anyone gesturing, nevertheless make hand motions when speaking just as frequent and in virtually the same way as sighted people did, and that they will gesture

    (C) who thus have never seen anyone gesture, nevertheless made hand motions when speaking just as frequently and in virtually the same way as sighted people do, as well as gesturing

    (D) thus never having seen anyone gesture, nevertheless made hand motions when speaking just as frequent and in virtually the same way as sighted people did, as well as gesturing

    (E) thus never having seen anyone gesture, nevertheless to make hand motions when speaking just as frequently and in virtually the same way as sighted people do, and to gesture

95. Like embryonic germ cells, which are cells that develop early in the formation of the fetus and that later generate eggs or sperm, embryonic stem cells have the ability of developing themselves into different kinds of body tissue.

    (A) embryonic stem cells have the ability of developing themselves into different kinds of body tissue

    (B) embryonic stem cells have the ability to develop into different kinds of body tissue

    (C) in embryonic stem cells there is the ability to develop into different kinds of body tissue

    (D) the ability to develop themselves into different kinds of body tissue characterizes embryonic stem cells

    (E) the ability of developing into different kinds of body tissue characterizes embryonic stem cells

96. Critics contend that the new missile is a weapon whose importance is largely symbolic, more a tool for manipulating people's perceptions than to fulfill a real military need.

    (A) for manipulating people's perceptions than to fulfill

    (B) for manipulating people's perceptions than for fulfilling

    (C) to manipulate people's perceptions rather than that it fulfills

    (D) to manipulate people's perceptions rather than fulfilling

    (E) to manipulate people's perceptions than for fulfilling

97. As an actress and, more importantly, as a teacher of acting, Stella Adler was one of the most influential artists in the American theater, who trained several generations of actors including Marlon Brando and Robert De Niro.

    (A) Stella Adler was one of the most influential artists in the American theater, who trained several generations of actors including

    (B) Stella Adler, one of the most influential artists in the American theater, trained several generations of actors who include

    (C) Stella Adler was one of the most influential artists in the American theater, training several generations of actors whose ranks included

    (D) one of the most influential artists in the American theater was Stella Adler, who trained several generations of actors including

    (E) one of the most influential artists in the American theater, Stella Adler, trained several generations of actors whose ranks included

98. By developing the Secure Digital Music Initiative, the recording industry associations of North America, Japan, and Europe hope to create a standardized way of distributing songs and full-length recordings on the Internet that will protect copyright holders and foil the many audio pirates who copy and distribute digital music illegally.

    (A) of distributing songs and full-length recordings on the Internet that will protect copyright holders and foil the many audio pirates who copy and distribute

    (B) of distributing songs and full-length recordings on the Internet and to protect copyright holders and foiling the many audio pirates copying and distributing

    (C) for distributing songs and full-length recordings on the Internet while it protects copyright holders and foils the many audio pirates who copy and distribute

    (D) to distribute songs and full-length recordings on the Internet while they will protect copyright holders and foil the many audio pirates copying and distributing

    (E) to distribute songs and full-length recordings on the Internet and it will protect copyright holders and foiling the many audio pirates who copy and distribute

99. Whereas a ramjet generally cannot achieve high speeds without the initial assistance of a rocket, high speeds can be attained by scramjets, or supersonic combustion ramjets, in that they reduce airflow compression at the entrance of the engine and letting air pass through at supersonic speeds.

    (A) high speeds can be attained by scramjets, or supersonic combustion ramjets, in that they reduce

    (B) that high speeds can be attained by scramjets, or supersonic combustion ramjets, is a result of their reducing

    (C) the ability of scramjets, or supersonic combustion ramjets, to achieve high speeds is because they reduce

    (D) scramjets, or supersonic combustion ramjets, have the ability of attaining high speeds when reducing

    (E) scramjets, or supersonic combustion ramjets, can attain high speeds by reducing

100. It will not be possible to implicate melting sea ice in the coastal flooding that many global warming models have projected: just like a glass of water that will not overflow due to melting ice cubes, so melting sea ice does not increase oceanic volume.

    (A) like a glass of water that will not overflow due to melting ice cubes,

    (B) like melting ice cubes that do not cause a glass of water to overflow,

    (C) a glass of water will not overflow because of melting ice cubes,

    (D) as melting ice cubes that do not cause a glass of water to overflow,

    (E) as melting ice cubes do not cause a glass of water to overflow,

3.3 Quantitative and Verbal Answer Keys

Quantitative

1. A	17. D	33. D
2. D	18. A	34. C
3. E	19. A	35. D
4. B	20. B	36. B
5. B	21. D	37. A
6. A	22. E	38. B
7. E	23. B	39. E
8. E	24. C	40. D
9. D	25. E	41. C
10. C	26. E	42. C
11. C	27. E	43. B
12. C	28. E	44. A
13. E	29. E	45. D
14. B	30. A	46. E
15. C	31. D	47. D
16. E	32. C	48. C

Verbal

49. E	67. E	85. B
50. C	68. C	86. E
51. B	69. A	87. B
52. A	70. B	88. A
53. D	71. A	89. E
54. C	72. C	90. D
55. A	73. B	91. C
56. A	74. D	92. B
57. B	75. D	93. C
58. A	76. E	94. A
59. B	77. B	95. B
60. D	78. C	96. B
61. B	79. A	97. C
62. A	80. C	98. A
63. E	81. C	99. E
64. C	82. E	100. E
65. E	83. D	
66. B	84. B	

3.4 Interpretive Guide

The following table provides a guide for interpreting your score, on the basis of the number of questions you got right.

Interpretive Guide	Excellent	Above Average	Average	Below Average
Problem Solving	19–24	16–18	10–15	0–9
Data Sufficiency	19–24	16–18	10–15	0–9
Reading Comprehension	16–17	14–15	9–13	0–8
Critical Reasoning	14–17	9–13	6–8	0–5
Sentence Correction	16–18	11–15	8–10	0–7

Remember, you should not compare the number of questions you got right in each section. Instead, you should compare how your response rated in each section.

3.5 Quantitative Answer Explanations

Problem Solving

The following discussion is intended to familiarize you with the most efficient and effective approaches to the kinds of problems common to problem solving questions. The particular questions in this chapter are generally representative of the kinds of quantitative questions you will encounter on the GMAT exam. Remember that it is the problem solving strategy that is important, not the specific details of a particular question.

1. Last month a certain music club offered a discount to preferred customers. After the first compact disc purchased, preferred customers paid $3.99 for each additional compact disc purchased. If a preferred customer purchased a total of 6 compact discs and paid $15.95 for the first compact disc, then the dollar amount that the customer paid for the 6 compact discs is equivalent to which of the following?

   (A) 5(4.00) + 15.90
   (B) 5(4.00) + 15.95
   (C) 5(4.00) + 16.00
   (D) 5(4.00 − 0.01) + 15.90
   (E) 5(4.00 − 0.05) + 15.95

   Arithmetic Operations on rational numbers

   The cost of the 6 compact discs, with $15.95 for the first one and $3.99 for the other 5 discs, can be expressed as 5(3.99) + 15.95. It is clear from looking at the answer choices that some regrouping of the values is needed because none of the answer choices uses $3.99 in the calculation.

   If $4.00 is used instead of $3.99, each one of the 5 additional compact discs is calculated at $0.01 too much, and the total cost is 5(0.01) = $0.05 too high. There is an overage of $0.05 that must be subtracted from the $15.95, or thus $15.95 − $0.05 = $15.90. Therefore, the cost can be expressed as 5(4.00) + 15.90.

   The correct answer is A.

2. The average (arithmetic mean) of the integers from 200 to 400, inclusive, is how much greater than the average of the integers from 50 to 100, inclusive?

   (A) 150
   (B) 175
   (C) 200
   (D) 225
   (E) 300

   Arithmetic Statistics

   In the list of integers from 200 to 400 inclusive, the middle value is 300. For every integer above 300, there exists an integer below 300 that is the same distance away from 300; thus the average of the integers from 200 to 400, inclusive, will be kept at 300. In the same manner, the average of the integers from 50 to 100, inclusive, is 75.

   The difference is 300 − 75 = 225.

   The correct answer is D.

3. The sequence $a_1, a_2, a_3, \ldots, a_n, \ldots$ is such that $a_n = \frac{a_{n-1} + a_{n-2}}{2}$ for all $n \geq 3$. If $a_3 = 4$ and $a_5 = 20$, what is the value of a_6?

   (A) 12
   (B) 16
   (C) 20
   (D) 24
   (E) 28

Algebra Applied problems

According to this formula, it is necessary to know the two prior terms in the sequence to determine the value of a term; that is, it is necessary to know both a_{n-1} and a_{n-2} to find a_n. Therefore, to find a_6, the values of a_5 and a_4 must be determined. To find a_4, let $a_n = a_5$, which makes $a_{n-1} = a_4$ and $a_{n-2} = a_3$. Then, by substituting the given values into the formula

$$a_n = \frac{a_{n-1} + a_{n-2}}{2}$$

$$a_5 = \frac{a_4 + a_3}{2}$$

$20 = \dfrac{a_4 + 4}{2}$ substitute known values

$40 = a_4 + 4$ multiply both sides

$36 = a_4$ subtract 4 from both sides

Then, letting $a_n = a_6$, substitute the known values:

$$a_6 = \frac{a_5 + a_4}{2}$$

$a_6 = \dfrac{20 + 36}{2}$ substitute known values

$a_6 = \dfrac{56}{2}$ simplify

$a_6 = 28$

The correct answer is E.

4. Among a group of 2,500 people, 35 percent invest in municipal bonds, 18 percent invest in oil stocks, and 7 percent invest in both municipal bonds and oil stocks. If 1 person is to be randomly selected from the 2,500 people, what is the probability that the person selected will be one who invests in municipal bonds but NOT in oil stocks?

(A) $\dfrac{9}{50}$

(B) $\dfrac{7}{25}$

(C) $\dfrac{7}{20}$

(D) $\dfrac{21}{50}$

(E) $\dfrac{27}{50}$

Arithmetic Probability

Since there are 2,500 people, 2,500(0.35) = 875 people invest in municipal bonds, and 2,500(0.07) = 175 of those people invest in both municipal bonds and oil stocks. Therefore, there are 875 – 175 = 700 people who invest in municipal bonds but not in oil stocks. Probability of an event =

$$\frac{\text{Number of desired outcomes}}{\text{Total number of outcomes that can occur}}.$$

Probability of investing in municipal bonds but not in oil stocks = $\dfrac{700}{2,500} = \dfrac{7}{25}$

The correct answer is B.

5. A closed cylindrical tank contains 36π cubic feet of water and is filled to half its capacity. When the tank is placed upright on its circular base on level ground, the height of the water in the tank is 4 feet. When the tank is placed on its side on level ground, what is the height, in feet, of the surface of the water above the ground?

(A) 2
(B) 3
(C) 4
(D) 6
(E) 9

Geometry Volume

Since the cylinder is half full, it will be filled to half its height, whether it is upright or on its side. When the cylinder is on its side, half its height is equal to its radius.

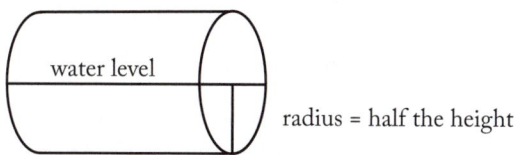

Using the information about the volume of water in the upright cylinder, solve for this radius to determine the height of the water when the cylinder is on its side.

$V = \pi r^2 h$	volume = $(\pi)(\text{radius}^2)(\text{height})$
$36\pi = \pi r^2 h$	known volume of water is 36π
$36 = r^2(4)$	substitute 4 for h; divide both sides by π
$9 = r^2$	solve for r
$3 = r$	radius = height of the water in the cylinder on its side

The correct answer is B.

6. A marketing firm determined that, of 200 households surveyed, 80 used neither Brand A nor Brand B soap, 60 used only Brand A soap, and for every household that used both brands of soap, 3 used only Brand B soap. How many of the 200 households surveyed used both brands of soap?

   (A) 15
   (B) 20
   (C) 30
   (D) 40
   (E) 45

   Arithmetic Operations on rational numbers

   Since it is given that 80 households use neither Brand A nor Brand B, then $200 - 80 = 120$ must use Brand A, Brand B, or both. It is also given that 60 households use only Brand A and that three times as many households use Brand B exclusively as use both brands. If x is the number of households that use both Brand A and Brand B, then $3x$ use Brand B alone. A Venn diagram can be helpful for visualizing the logic of the given information for this item:

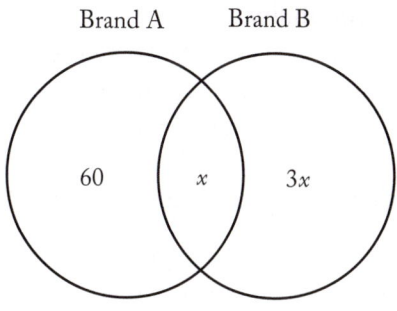

All the sections in the circles can be added up and set equal to 120, and then the equation can be solved for x:

$60 + x + 3x = 120$	
$60 + 4x = 120$	combine like terms
$4x = 60$	subtract 60 from both sides
$x = 15$	divide both sides by 4

The correct answer is A.

7. A certain club has 10 members, including Harry. One of the 10 members is to be chosen at random to be the president, one of the remaining 9 members is to be chosen at random to be the secretary, and one of the remaining 8 members is to be chosen at random to be the treasurer. What is the probability that Harry will be either the member chosen to be the secretary or the member chosen to be the treasurer?

   (A) $\dfrac{1}{720}$
   (B) $\dfrac{1}{80}$
   (C) $\dfrac{1}{10}$
   (D) $\dfrac{1}{9}$
   (E) $\dfrac{1}{5}$

Arithmetic Probability

Two probabilities must be calculated here: (1) the probability of Harry's being chosen for secretary and (2) the probability of Harry's being chosen for treasurer. For any probability, the probability of an event's occurring

$$\frac{\text{number of desired outcomes}}{\text{total number of outcomes that can occur}}.$$

(1) If Harry is to be secretary, he first CANNOT have been chosen for president, and then he must be chosen for secretary. The probability that he will be chosen for president is $\frac{1}{10}$, so the probability of his NOT being chosen for president is $1-\frac{1}{10}=\frac{9}{10}$. Then, the probability of his being chosen for secretary is $\frac{1}{9}$.

Once he is chosen, the probability that he will be selected for treasurer is 0, so the probability that he will NOT be selected for treasurer is $1-0=1$. Thus, the probability that Harry will be chosen for secretary is $\left(\frac{9}{10}\right)\left(\frac{1}{9}\right)(1)=\frac{1}{10}$.

(2) If Harry is to be treasurer, he needs to be NOT chosen for president, then NOT chosen for secretary, and then finally chosen for treasurer.

The probability that he will NOT be chosen for president is again $1-\frac{1}{10}=\frac{9}{10}$. The probability of his NOT being chosen for secretary is $1-\frac{1}{9}=\frac{8}{9}$. The probability of his being chosen for treasurer is $\frac{1}{8}$, so the probability that Harry will be chosen for treasurer is $\left(\frac{9}{10}\right)\left(\frac{8}{9}\right)\left(\frac{1}{8}\right)=\frac{1}{10}$.

(3) So, finally, the probability of Harry's being chosen as either secretary or treasurer is thus $\frac{1}{10}+\frac{1}{10}=\frac{2}{10}=\frac{1}{5}$.

The correct answer is E.

8. If a certain toy store's revenue in November was $\frac{2}{5}$ of its revenue in December and its revenue in January was $\frac{1}{4}$ of its revenue in November, then the store's revenue in December was how many times the average (arithmetic mean) of its revenues in November and January?

(A) $\frac{1}{4}$

(B) $\frac{1}{2}$

(C) $\frac{2}{3}$

(D) 2

(E) 4

Arithmetic Statistics

Let n be the store's revenue in November, d be the store's revenue in December, and j be the store's revenue in January. The information from the problem can be expressed as $n=\frac{2}{5}d$ and $j=\frac{1}{4}n$. Substituting $\frac{2}{5}d$ for n in the second equation gives $j=\frac{1}{4}\left(\frac{2}{5}d\right)=\frac{1}{10}d$. Then, the average of the revenues in November and January can be found by using these values in the formula

$$\text{average} = \frac{\text{sum of values}}{\text{number of values}}, \text{ as follows:}$$

$$\text{average} = \frac{\frac{2}{5}d+\frac{1}{10}d}{2} = \frac{\frac{4}{10}d+\frac{1}{10}d}{2} = \frac{\frac{5}{10}d}{2} = \frac{1}{2}d\left(\frac{1}{2}\right)=\frac{1}{4}d$$

Solve for the store's revenue in December by multiplying both sides of this equation by 4:

$$\text{average} = \frac{1}{4}d$$
$$4(\text{average}) = d$$

Thus, the store's revenue in December was 4 times its average revenue in November and January.

The correct answer is E.

9. A researcher computed the mean, the median, and the standard deviation for a set of performance scores. If 5 were to be added to each score, which of these three statistics would change?

   (A) The mean only
   (B) The median only
   (C) The standard deviation only
   (D) The mean and the median
   (E) The mean and the standard deviation

   Arithmetic Statistics

   If 5 were added to each score, the mean would go up by 5, as would the median. However, the spread of the values would remain the same, simply centered around a new value. So, the standard deviation would **NOT** change.

   The correct answer is D.

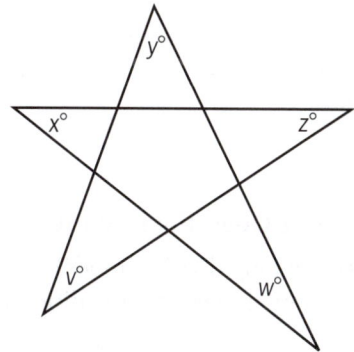

10. In the figure shown, what is the value of $v + x + y + z + w$?

    (A) 45
    (B) 90
    (C) 180
    (D) 270
    (E) 360

    Geometry Angles and their measure

    In the following figure, the center section of the star is a pentagon.

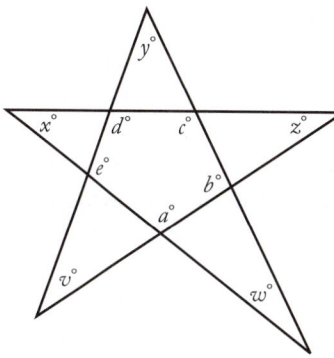

    The sum of the interior angles of any polygon is $180(n - 2)$, where n is the number of sides. Thus, $a + b + c + d + e = 180(5 - 2) = 180(3) = 540$.

    Each of the interior angles of the pentagon defines a triangle with two of the angles at the points of the star. This gives the following five equations:

    $a + x + z = 180$
    $b + v + y = 180$
    $c + x + w = 180$
    $d + v + z = 180$
    $e + y + w = 180$

    Summing these 5 equations gives:

    $a + b + c + d + e + 2v + 2x + 2y + 2z + 2w = 900$.

    Substituting 540 for $a + b + c + d + e$ gives:

    $540 + 2v + 2x + 2y + 2w = 900$.

    From this:

    $2v + 2x + 2y + 2z + 2w = 360$ subtract 540 from both sides

    $2(v + x + y + z + w) = 360$ factor out 2 on the left side

    $v + x + y + z + w = 180$ divide both sides by 2

    The correct answer is C.

11. Of the three-digit integers greater than 700, how many have two digits that are equal to each other and the remaining digit different from the other two?

    (A) 90
    (B) 82
    (C) 80
    (D) 45
    (E) 36

Arithmetic Properties of numbers

In three-digit integers, there are three pairs of digits that can be the same while the other digit is different: tens and ones, hundreds and tens, and hundreds and ones. In each of these pairs, there are 9 options for having the third digit be different from the other two. The single exception to this is in the 700–799 set, where the number 700 cannot be included because the problem calls for integers "greater than 700." So, in the 700–799 set, there are only 8 options for when the tens and ones are the same. This is shown in the table below.

Number of digits available for the third digit when two given digits are the same			
Same	701–799	800–899	900–999
tens and ones	8	9	9
hundreds and tens	9	9	9
hundreds and ones	9	9	9

Thus, of the three-digit integers greater than 700, there are $9(9) - 1 = 80$ numbers that have two digits that are equal to each other when the remaining digit is different from these two.

The correct answer is C.

12. Positive integer y is 50 percent of 50 percent of positive integer x, and y percent of x equals 100. What is the value of x?

    (A) 50
    (B) 100
    (C) 200
    (D) 1,000
    (E) 2,000

**Arithmetic; Algebra Percents
Simultaneous equations**

Because y is a positive integer, y percent is notated as $\frac{y}{100}$. According to the problem, $y = 0.50(0.50x)$ and $\left(\frac{y}{100}\right)x = 100$.

The first equation simplifies to $y = 0.25x$, and multiplying the second equation by 100 gives $xy = 10,000$.

Substituting the simplified first equation into this second equation gives:

$x(0.25x) = 10,000$

$0.25x^2 = 10,000$ simplify left side

$x^2 = 40,000$ divide both sides by 0.25

$x = 200$ solve for the value of x

The correct answer is C.

13. If s and t are positive integers such that $\frac{s}{t} = 64.12$, which of the following could be the remainder when s is divided by t?

    (A) 2
    (B) 4
    (C) 8
    (D) 20
    (E) 45

Arithmetic Operations on rational numbers

By using a long division model, it can be seen that the remainder after dividing s by t is $s - 64t$:

$$\begin{array}{r} 64 \\ t\overline{)s} \\ \underline{-64t} \\ s - 64t \end{array}$$

Then, the given equation can be written as $64.12t = s$. By splitting portions of t into its integer multiple and its decimal multiple, this becomes $64t + 0.12t = s$, or $0.12t = s - 64t$, which is the remainder. So, $0.12t =$ remainder. Test the answer choices to find the situation in which t is an integer.

A $0.12t = 2$ or $t = 16.67$ NOT an integer
B $0.12t = 4$ or $t = 33.33$ NOT an integer
C $0.12t = 8$ or $t = 66.67$ NOT an integer
D $0.12t = 20$ or $t = 166.67$ NOT an integer
E $0.12t = 45$ or $t = 375$ INTEGER

The correct answer is E.

14. Of the 84 parents who attended a meeting at a school, 35 volunteered to supervise children during the school picnic and 11 volunteered both to supervise children during the picnic and to bring refreshments to the picnic. If the number of parents who volunteered to bring refreshments was 1.5 times the number of parents who neither volunteered to supervise children during the picnic nor volunteered to bring refreshments, how many of the parents volunteered to bring refreshments?

    (A) 25
    (B) 36
    (C) 38
    (D) 42
    (E) 45

    Arithmetic Operations on rational numbers

    Out of the 35 parents who agreed to supervise children during the school picnic, 11 parents are also bringing refreshments, so 35 − 11 = 24 parents are only supervising children. Let x be the number of parents who volunteered to bring refreshments, and let y be the number of parents who declined to supervise or to bring refreshments. The fact that the number of parents who volunteered to bring refreshments is 1.5 times the number who did not volunteer at all can then be expressed as $x = 1.5y$. A Venn diagram, such as the one below, can be helpful in answering problems of this kind.

    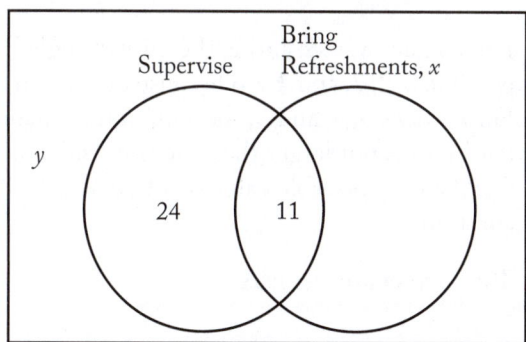

    Then, the sum of the sections can be set equal to the total number of parents at the picnic, and the equation can be solved for y:

$y + 24 + x = 84$	sum of sections = total parents at picnic
$y + x = 60$	subtract 24 from each side
$y = 60 - x$	subtract x from each side

Then, substituting the value $60 - x$ for y in the equation $x = 1.5y$ gives the following:

$x = 1.5(60 - x)$	
$x = 90 - 1.5x$	distribute the 1.5
$2.5x = 90$	add $1.5x$ to both sides
$x = 36$	divide both sides by 2.5

The correct answer is B.

15. The product of all the prime numbers less than 20 is closest to which of the following powers of 10 ?

    (A) 10^9
    (B) 10^8
    (C) 10^7
    (D) 10^6
    (E) 10^5

    Arithmetic Properties of numbers

    The prime numbers less than 20 are 2, 3, 5, 7, 11, 13, 17, and 19. Their product is 9,699,690 (arrived at as follows: $2 \times 3 \times 5 \times 7 \times 11 \times 13 \times 17 \times 19 = 9,699,690$). This is closest to $10,000,000 = 10^7$ ($10 \times 10 \times 10 \times 10 \times 10 \times 10 \times 10 = 10,000,000$).

    The correct answer is C.

16. If $\sqrt{3-2x} = \sqrt{2x}+1$ then, $4x^2 =$

    (A) 1
    (B) 4
    (C) $2 - 2x$
    (D) $4x - 2$
    (E) $6x - 1$

Algebra Second-degree equations

Work with the equation to create $4x^2$ on one side.

$\sqrt{3-2x} = \sqrt{2x}+1$

$(\sqrt{3-2x})^2 = (\sqrt{2x}+1)^2$ square both sides

$3-2x = 2x + 2\sqrt{2x}+1$

$2-4x = 2\sqrt{2x}$ move all non-square-root terms to one side (i.e., subtract $2x$ and 1)

$1-2x = \sqrt{2x}$ divide both sides by 2

$(1-2x)^2 = (\sqrt{2x})^2$ square both sides

$1-4x+4x^2 = 2x$

$4x^2 = 6x-1$ isolate the $4x^2$ (add $4x$ and subtract 1 from both sides)

The correct answer is E.

17. If $n = \sqrt{\frac{16}{81}}$, what is the value of $\sqrt{n}$?

    (A) $\frac{1}{9}$
    (B) $\frac{1}{4}$
    (C) $\frac{4}{9}$
    (D) $\frac{2}{3}$
    (E) $\frac{9}{2}$

Arithmetic Operations on radical expressions

Work the problem.

Since $n = \sqrt{\frac{16}{81}} = \frac{4}{9}$, then $\sqrt{n} = \sqrt{\frac{4}{9}} = \frac{2}{3}$.

The correct answer is D.

18. If n is the product of the integers from 1 to 8, inclusive, how many different prime factors greater than 1 does n have?

    (A) Four
    (B) Five
    (C) Six
    (D) Seven
    (E) Eight

Arithmetic Properties of numbers

If n is the product of the integers from 1 to 8, then its prime factors will be the prime numbers from 1 to 8. There are four prime numbers between 1 and 8: 2, 3, 5, and 7.

The correct answer is A.

19. If k is an integer and $2 < k < 7$, for how many different values of k is there a triangle with sides of lengths 2, 7, and k?

    (A) One
    (B) Two
    (C) Three
    (D) Four
    (E) Five

Geometry Triangles

In a triangle, the sum of the smaller two sides must be larger than the largest side.

For k values 3, 4, 5, and 6, the only triangle possible is 2, 7, and $k = 6$ because only $2 + 6 > 7$. For k values 3, 4, and 5, the sum of the smaller two sides is not larger than the third side; thus, 6 is the only possible value of k that satisfies the conditions.

The correct answer is A.

20. A right circular cone is inscribed in a hemisphere so that the base of the cone coincides with the base of the hemisphere. What is the ratio of the height of the cone to the radius of the hemisphere?

   (A) $\sqrt{3}:1$
   (B) $1:1$
   (C) $\frac{1}{2}:1$
   (D) $\sqrt{2}:1$
   (E) $2:1$

Geometry Volume

As the diagram below shows, the height of the cone will be the radius of the hemisphere, so the ratio is 1:1.

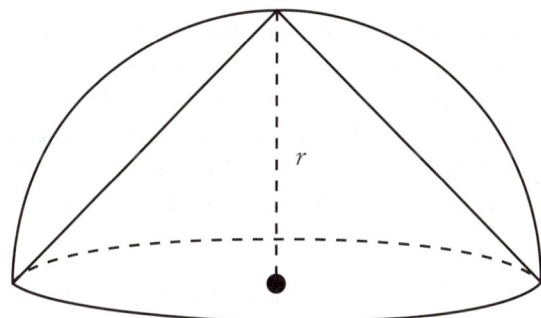

The correct answer is B.

21. John deposited $10,000 to open a new savings account that earned 4 percent annual interest, compounded quarterly. If there were no other transactions in the account, what was the amount of money in John's account 6 months after the account was opened?

   (A) $10,100
   (B) $10,101
   (C) $10,200
   (D) $10,201
   (E) $10,400

Arithmetic Operations on rational numbers

Since John's account is compounded quarterly, he receives $\frac{1}{4}$ of his annual interest, or 1%, every 3 months. This is added to the amount already in the account to accrue interest for the next quarter. After 6 months, this process will have occurred twice, so the amount in John's account will then be ($10,000)(1.01)(1.01) = $10,000(1.01)^2 = $10,201.

The correct answer is D.

22. A container in the shape of a right circular cylinder is $\frac{1}{2}$ full of water. If the volume of water in the container is 36 cubic inches and the height of the container is 9 inches, what is the diameter of the base of the cylinder, in inches?

   (A) $\frac{16}{9\pi}$
   (B) $\frac{4}{\sqrt{\pi}}$
   (C) $\frac{12}{\sqrt{\pi}}$
   (D) $\sqrt{\frac{2}{\pi}}$
   (E) $4\sqrt{\frac{2}{\pi}}$

Geometry Volume

For a right cylinder, volume = $\pi(\text{radius})^2(\text{height})$. Since the volume of water is 36 cubic inches and since this represents $\frac{1}{2}$ the container, the water is occupying $\frac{1}{2}$ the container's height, or $9\left(\frac{1}{2}\right) = 4.5$ inches. Let r be the radius of the cylinder.

$36 = \pi r^2 (4.5)$

$8 = \pi r^2$ divide both sides by 4.5

$\frac{8}{\pi} = r^2$ divide both sides by π

$\sqrt{\frac{8}{\pi}} = r$ take the square root of both sides

$\frac{2\sqrt{2}}{\sqrt{\pi}} = r$ simplify the $\sqrt{8}$ to get the radius

Then, since the diameter is twice the length of the radius, the diameter equals

$$2\left(\frac{2\sqrt{2}}{\sqrt{\pi}}\right) = 4\frac{\sqrt{2}}{\sqrt{\pi}} = 4\sqrt{\frac{2}{\pi}}.$$

The correct answer is E.

23. If the positive integer x is a multiple of 4 and the positive integer y is a multiple of 6, then xy must be a multiple of which of the following?

    I.   8
    II. 12
    III. 18

    (A) II only
    (B) I and II only
    (C) I and III only
    (D) II and III only
    (E) I, II, and III

Arithmetic Properties of numbers

The product xy must be a multiple of $4(6) = 24$ and any of its factors. Test each alternative.

I. $\frac{24}{8} = 3$ 8 is a factor of 24
MUST be a multiple of 8

II. $\frac{24}{12} = 2$ 12 is a factor of 24
MUST be a multiple of 12

III. $\frac{24}{18} = 1\frac{1}{3}$ 18 is NOT a factor of 24
NEED NOT be a multiple of 18

The correct answer is B.

24. Aaron will jog from home at x miles per hour and then walk back home by the same route at y miles per hour. How many miles from home can Aaron jog so that he spends a total of t hours jogging and walking?

    (A) $\frac{xt}{y}$

    (B) $\frac{x+t}{xy}$

    (C) $\frac{xyt}{x+y}$

    (D) $\frac{x+y+t}{xy}$

    (E) $\frac{y+t}{x} - \frac{t}{y}$

Algebra Simplifying algebraic expressions

Let j be the number of hours Aaron spends jogging; then let $t - j$ be the total number of hours he spends walking. It can be stated that Aaron jogs a distance of xj miles and walks a distance of $y(t - j)$ miles. Because Aaron travels the same route, the miles jogged must equal the miles walked, and they can be set equal.

$xj = y(t - j)$ set number of miles equal to each other

$xj = yt - jy$ distribute the y

$xj + jy = yt$ add jy to both sides to get all terms with j to one side

$j(x + y) = yt$ factor out the j

$j = \frac{yt}{x+y}$.   divide both sides by $x + y$

So, the number of hours Aaron spends jogging is $j = \frac{yt}{x+y}$.

The number of miles he can jog is xj or, by substitution of this value of j, $x\left(\frac{yt}{x+y}\right) = \frac{xyt}{x+y}$.

The correct answer is C.

3.5 Diagnostic Test Quantitative Answer Explanations

Data Sufficiency

The following section on data sufficiency is intended to familiarize you with the most efficient and effective approaches to the kinds of problems common to data sufficiency. The particular questions in this chapter are generally representative of the kinds of data sufficiency questions you will encounter on the GMAT exam. Remember that it is the problem solving strategy that is important, not the specific details of a particular question.

25. If the units digit of integer n is greater than 2, what is the units digit of n?

    (1) The units digit of n is the same as the units digit of n^2.
    (2) The units digit of n is the same as the units digit of n^3.

    Arithmetic Arithmetic operations

    If the units digit of n is greater than 2, then it can only be the digits 3, 4, 5, 6, 7, 8, or 9.

    (1) To solve this problem, it is necessary to find a digit that is the same as the units digit of its square. For example, both 43 squared (1,849) and 303 squared (91,809) have a units digit of 9, which is different from the units digit of 43 and 303. However, 25 squared (625) and 385 squared (148,225) both have a units digit of 5, and 16 and 226 both have a units digit of 6 and their squares (256 and 51,076, respectively) do, too. However, there is no further information to choose between 5 or 6; NOT sufficient.

    (2) Once again, 5 and 6 are the only numbers which, when cubed, will both have a 5 or 6 respectively in their units digits. However, the information given does not distinguish between them; NOT sufficient.

    Since (1) and (2) together yield the same information but with no direction as to which to choose, there is not enough information to determine the answer.

    The correct answer is E; both statements together are still not sufficient.

26. What is the value of the integer p?

    (1) Each of the integers 2, 3, and 5 is a factor of p.
    (2) Each of the integers 2, 5, and 7 is a factor of p.

    Arithmetic Properties of numbers

    (1) These are factors of p, but it is not clear that they are the only factors of p; NOT sufficient.

    (2) These are factors of p, but it is not clear that they are the only factors of p; NOT sufficient.

    Taken together, (1) and (2) overlap, but again there is no clear indication that these are the only factors of p.

    The correct answer is E; both statements together are still not sufficient.

27. If the length of Wanda's telephone call was rounded up to the nearest whole minute by her telephone company, then Wanda was charged for how many minutes for her telephone call?

    (1) The total charge for Wanda's telephone call was $6.50.
    (2) Wanda was charged $0.50 more for the first minute of the telephone call than for each minute after the first.

    Arithmetic Arithmetic operations

    (1) This does not give any information as to the call's cost per minute; NOT sufficient.

    (2) From this, it can be determined only that the call was longer than one minute and that the charge for the first minute was $0.50 more than the charge for each succeeding minute; NOT sufficient.

51

Taking (1) and (2) together, the number of minutes cannot be determined as long as the cost of each minute after the first is unknown. For example, if the cost of each minute after the first minute were $0.40, then the cost of the first minute would be $0.90. Then the total cost of the other minutes would be $6.50 − $0.90 = $5.60, and $5.60 ÷ $0.40 would yield 14. In this case, the time of the call would be 1 + 14 = 15 minutes. If, however, the cost of each minute after the first minute were $0.15, then the cost of the first minute would be $0.65. Then $6.50 − $0.65 would be $5.85, and this in turn, when divided by $0.15, would yield 39 minutes, for a total call length of 40 minutes. More information on the cost of each minute after the first minute is still needed.

**The correct answer is E;
both statements together are still not sufficient.**

28. What is the perimeter of isosceles triangle *MNP* ?

    (1) *MN* = 16
    (2) *NP* = 20

    Geometry Triangles

    The perimeter of a triangle is the sum of all three sides. In the case of an isosceles triangle, two of the sides are equal. To determine the perimeter of this triangle, it is necessary to know both the length of an equal side and the length of the base of the triangle.

    (1) Only gives the length of one side; NOT sufficient.

    (2) Only gives the length of one side; NOT sufficient.

    Since it is unclear whether *MN* or *NP* is one of the equal sides, it is not possible to determine the length of the third side or the perimeter of the triangle. The perimeter could be either ((2)(16)) + 20 = 52 or ((2)(20)) + 16 = 56.

    **The correct answer is E;
    both statements together are still not sufficient.**

29. In a survey of retailers, what percent had purchased computers for business purposes?

    (1) 85 percent of the retailers surveyed who owned their own store had purchased computers for business purposes.
    (2) 40 percent of the retailers surveyed owned their own store.

    Arithmetic Percents

    (1) With only this, it cannot be known what percent of the retailers not owning their own store had purchased computers, and so it cannot be known how many retailers purchased computers overall; NOT sufficient.

    (2) While this permits the percent of owners and nonowners in the survey to be deduced, the overall percent of retailers who had purchased computers cannot be determined; NOT sufficient.

    Using the information from both (1) and (2), the percent of surveyed owner-retailers who had purchased computers can be deduced, and the percent of nonowner-retailers can also be deduced. However, the information that would permit a determination of either the percent of nonowner-retailers who had purchased computers or the overall percent of all retailers (both owners and nonowners) who had purchased computers is still not provided.

    **The correct answer is E;
    both statements together are still not sufficient.**

30. The only gift certificates that a certain store sold yesterday were worth either $100 each or $10 each. If the store sold a total of 20 gift certificates yesterday, how many gift certificates worth $10 each did the store sell yesterday?

    (1) The gift certificates sold by the store yesterday were worth a total of between $1,650 and $1,800.
    (2) Yesterday the store sold more than 15 gift certificates worth $100 each.

    Algebra Applied problems; Simultaneous equations; Inequalities

    Let x represent the number of $100 certificates sold, and let y represent the number of $10 certificates sold. Then the given information can be expressed as $x + y = 20$ or thus $y = 20 − x$. The value of the $100 certificates sold is $100x$, and the value of the $10 certificates sold is $10y$.

(1) From this, it is known that $100x + 10y > 1,650$. Since $y = 20 - x$, this value can be substituted for y, and the inequality can be solved for x:

$100x + 10y > 1,650$
$100x + 10(20 - x) > 1,650$ substitute for y
$100x + 200 - 10x > 1,650$ distribute
$90x + 200 > 1,650$ simplify
$90x > 1,450$ subtract 200 from both sides
$x > 16.1$

Thus, more than 16 of the $100 certificates were sold. If 17 $100 certificates were sold, then it must be that 3 $10 certificates were also sold for a total of $1,730, which satisfies the condition of being between $1,650 and $1,800. If, however, 18 $100 certificates were sold, then it must be that 2 $10 certificates were sold, and this totals $1,820, which is more than $1,800 and fails to satisfy the condition. Therefore, 3 of the $10 certificates were sold; SUFFICIENT.

(2) From this it can be known only that the number of $10 certificates sold was 4 or fewer; NOT sufficient.

The correct answer is A; statement 1 alone is sufficient.

31. Is the standard deviation of the set of measurements $x_1, x_2, x_3, x_4, ..., x_{20}$ less than 3 ?

 (1) The variance for the set of measurements is 4.
 (2) For each measurement, the difference between the mean and that measurement is 2.

Arithmetic Statistics

In determining the standard deviation, the difference between each measurement and the mean is squared, and then the squared differences are added and divided by the number of measurements. The quotient is the variance and the positive square root of the variance is the standard deviation.

(1) If the variance is 4, then the standard deviation = $\sqrt{4} = 2$, which is less than 3; SUFFICIENT.

(2) For each measurement, the difference between the mean and that measurement is 2. Therefore, the square of each difference is 4, and the sum of all the squares is $4 \times 20 = 80$. The standard deviation is $\sqrt{\frac{80}{20}} = \sqrt{4} = 2$, which is less than 3; SUFFICIENT.

The correct answer is D; each statement alone is sufficient.

32. Is the range of the integers 6, 3, y, 4, 5, and x greater than 9 ?

 (1) $y > 3x$
 (2) $y > x > 3$

Arithmetic Statistics

The range of a set of integers is equal to the difference between the largest integer and the smallest integer. The range of the set of integers 3, 4, 5, and 6 is 3, which is derived from $6 - 3$.

(1) Although it is known that $y > 3x$, the value of x is unknown. If, for example, $x = 1$, then the value of y would be greater than 3. However, if $x = 2$, then the value of y would be greater than 6, and, since 6 would no longer be the largest integer, the range would be affected. Because the actual values of x and y are unknown, the value of the range is also unknown; NOT sufficient.

(2) If $x > 3$ and $y > x$, then x could be 4 and y could be 5. Then the range of the 6 integers would still be $6 - 3$ or 3. However, if x were 4 and y were 15, then the range of the 6 integers would be $15 - 3$, or 12. There is no means to establish the values of x and y, beyond the fact that they both are greater than 3; NOT sufficient.

Taking (1) and (2) together, it is known that $x > 3$ and that $y > 3x$. Since the smallest integer that x could be is thus 4, then $y > 3(4)$ or $y > 12$. Therefore, the integer y must be 13 or larger. When y is equal to 13, the range of the 6 integers is $13 - 3 = 10$, which is larger than 9. As y increases in value, the value of the range will also increase.

The correct answer is C; both statements together are sufficient.

53

33. Is $\dfrac{5^{x+2}}{25} < 1$?

    (1) $5^x < 1$
    (2) $x < 0$

    Algebra Inequalities

    Note that $x^{r+s} = (x^r)(x^s)$.

    (1) If $5^x < 1$, then $\dfrac{5^{x+2}}{25} < 1$ since
    $\dfrac{5^{x+2}}{25} = \dfrac{5^x \cdot 5^2}{25} = 5^x$; SUFFICIENT.

    (2) If $x < 0$, then
    $x + 2 < 2$ add 2 to both sides
    $5^{x+2} < 5^2$ because $a < b$ implies $5^a < 5^b$
    $\dfrac{5^{x+2}}{25} < 1$ divide both sides by $5^2 = 25$;
    SUFFICIENT.

    **The correct answer is D;
    each statement alone is sufficient.**

34. Of the companies surveyed about the skills they required in prospective employees, 20 percent required both computer skills and writing skills. What percent of the companies surveyed required neither computer skills nor writing skills?

    (1) Of those companies surveyed that required computer skills, half required writing skills.
    (2) 45 percent of the companies surveyed required writing skills but not computer skills.

    Arithmetic Percents

    The surveyed companies could be placed into one of the following four categories:

    1. Requiring computer skills and requiring writing skills
    2. Requiring computer skills but not requiring writing skills
    3. Not requiring computer skills but requiring writing skills
    4. Not requiring either computer skills or writing skills

    It is given that 20 percent of the surveyed companies fell into category 1. It is necessary to determine what percent of the surveyed companies fell into category 4.

    (1) This helps identify the percentage in category 2. Since $\dfrac{1}{2}$ the companies that required computer skills also required writing skills (i.e., those in category 1), then the other $\dfrac{1}{2}$ of the companies that required computer skills did not require writing skills (thus category 2 = category 1). However, this information only establishes that 20 percent required computer skills, but not writing skills; NOT sufficient.

    (2) While this establishes category 3, that is, that 45 percent required writing skills but not computer skills, no further information is available; NOT sufficient.

    Taking (1) and (2) together, the first three categories add up to 85 percent (20 + 20 + 45). Therefore, category 4 would be equal to 100 − 85 = 15 percent of the surveyed companies required neither computer skills nor writing skills.

    **The correct answer is C;
    both statements together are sufficient.**

35. What is the value of $w + q$?

    (1) $3w = 3 - 3q$
    (2) $5w + 5q = 5$

    Algebra First- and second-degree equations

    (1) If $3q$ is added to both sides of this equation, it can be rewritten as $3w + 3q = 3$. When each term is then divided by 3, it yields $w + q = 1$; SUFFICIENT.

    (2) When each term in this equation is divided by 5, it becomes $w + q = 1$; SUFFICIENT.

    **The correct answer is D;
    each statement alone is sufficient.**

36. If X and Y are points in a plane and X lies inside the circle C with center O and radius 2, does Y lie inside circle C?

   (1) The length of line segment XY is 3.
   (2) The length of line segment OY is 1.5.

   Geometry Circles

   (1) The maximum distance between two points that lie on a circle is equal to the diameter, or 2 times the radius. Since the radius of circle C is 2, the diameter in this case is 4. It cannot be assumed, however, that X and Y are points on the diameter; X can lie anywhere within the circle. When the distance between X and Y is 3, it is still possible either that Y is within the circle or that Y is outside the circle; NOT sufficient.

   (2) If the length of the line segment OY is 1.5 and the circle has a radius of 2, then the distance from the center O to point Y is less than the radius, and point Y must therefore lie within the circle; SUFFICIENT.

   The correct answer is B; statement 2 alone is sufficient.

37. Is $x > y$?

   (1) $x = y + 2$
   (2) $\frac{x}{2} = y - 1$

   Algebra First- and second-degree equations

   (1) Since 2 has to be added to y in order to make it equal to x, it can be reasoned that $x > y$; SUFFICIENT.

   (2) Multiplying both sides of this equation by 2 results in $x = 2(y - 1)$ or $x = 2y - 2$. If y were 0, then x would be -2, and y would be greater than x. If y were a negative number like -2, then $x = 2(-2) - 2 - 6$, and again y would be greater than x. However, if y were a positive number such as 4, then $x = 2(4) - 2 = 6$, and $x > y$. Since there is no other information concerning the value of y, it cannot be determined if $x > y$; NOT sufficient.

   The correct answer is A; statement 1 alone is sufficient.

38. If Paula drove the distance from her home to her college at an average speed that was greater than 70 kilometers per hour, did it take her less than 3 hours to drive this distance?

   (1) The distance that Paula drove from her home to her college was greater than 200 kilometers.
   (2) The distance that Paula drove from her home to her college was less than 205 kilometers.

   Arithmetic Distance problem

   A distance problem uses the formula distance = rate × time. To find the time, the formula would be rearranged as time = $\frac{\text{distance}}{\text{rate}}$. To solve this problem, it is necessary to know the rate (given here as 70 kilometers per hour) and the distance.

   (1) If D is the distance Paula drove then $D > 200$ and $\frac{D}{70} > \frac{200}{70} = 2\frac{6}{7}$ so $t > 2\frac{6}{7}$ and t may or may not be less than 3; NOT sufficient.

   (2) If D is the distance Paula drove then $D < 205$ and $\frac{D}{70} < \frac{205}{70} = 2\frac{13}{14}$ so $t < 2\frac{13}{14} < 3$; SUFFICIENT.

   The correct answer is B; statement 2 alone is sufficient.

39. In the xy-plane, if line k has negative slope and passes through the point (–5,r), is the x-intercept of line k positive?

   (1) The slope of line k is –5.
   (2) $r > 0$

55

Geometry Coordinate geometry

The x-intercept is the x-coordinate of the point in which the line k crosses the x-axis and would have the coordinates $(x,0)$.

(1) Knowing the slope of the line does not help in determining the x-intercept, since from point $(-5,r)$ the line k extends in both directions. Without knowing the value of r, the x-intercept could be -5 if r were 0, or it could be other numbers, both positive and negative, depending on the value of r; NOT sufficient.

(2) Knowing that $r > 0$ suggests that the x-intercept is not -5; the point $(-5,r)$, where r is a positive number, does lie in quadrant II. It could, however, be any point with an x-coordinate of -5 in that quadrant and line k could have any negative slope, and so the line k would vary with the value of r. Therefore, the x-intercept of line k cannot be determined; NOT sufficient.

Using (1) and (2) together does not help in the determination of the x-intercept, since the point $(-5,r)$ could have any positive y-coordinate and thus line k could cross the x-axis at many different places.

**The correct answer is E;
both statements together are still not sufficient.**

40. If $5,000 invested for one year at p percent simple annual interest yields $500, what amount must be invested at k percent simple annual interest for one year to yield the same number of dollars?

    (1) $k = 0.8p$
    (2) $k = 8$

Arithmetic Interest problem

With simple annual interest, the formula to use is interest = principal × rate × time. It is given that $500 = \$5,000 \times \frac{p}{100} \times 1$ (year), so $p = 10$ percent interest.

(1) If p is 10 percent, then $k = 0.8\,p$ is 0.08. Using the same formula, the time is again 1 year; the interest is the same amount; and the rate is 0.08, or 8 percent. Thus, $500 = $ principal $\times 0.08 \times 1$, or principal $6,250; SUFFICIENT.

(2) If $k = 8$, then the rate is 8 percent, and the same formula and procedure as above are employed again; SUFFICIENT.

**The correct answer is D;
each statement alone is sufficient.**

41. If $\dfrac{x+y}{z} > 0$, is $x < 0$?

    (1) $x < y$
    (2) $z < 0$

Algebra Inequalities

If $\dfrac{x+y}{z} > 0$, then either one of two cases holds true. Either $(x+y) > 0$ **and** $z > 0$, or $(x+y) < 0$ **and** $z < 0$. In other words, in order for the term to be greater than zero, it must be true that either 1) both the numerator and denominator are greater than 0 or 2) both the numerator and denominator are less than 0.

(1) Regardless of whether $(x+y)$ is positive or negative, the positive or negative value of z must be in agreement with the sign of $(x+y)$ in order for $\dfrac{x+y}{z} > 0$. However, there is no information about z here; NOT sufficient.

(2) If $z < 0$, then $(x+y)$ must be less than 0. However, this statement gives no information about $(x+y)$; NOT sufficient.

This can be solved using (1) and (2) together. From (2), it is known that $z < 0$, and, going back to the original analysis, for the term to be greater than zero, $(x+y)$ must also be less than 0. If $x + y < 0$ then $x < -y$. But $x < y$ from (1) so

$x + x < -y + y$

$2x < 0$

$x < 0$.

**The correct answer is C;
both statements together are sufficient.**

42. Does the integer k have at least three different positive prime factors?

    (1) $\frac{k}{15}$ is an integer.
    (2) $\frac{k}{10}$ is an integer.

Arithmetic Properties of numbers

(1) The prime factors of 15 are 3 and 5. So in this case, k has at least 2 different positive prime factors, but it is unknown if there are more positive prime factors; NOT sufficient.

(2) The prime factors of 10 are 2 and 5, showing that k has at least these 2 different positive prime factors, but k might or might not have more; NOT sufficient.

Taking (1) and (2) together, since k is divisible by both 10 and 15, it must be divisible by their different positive prime factors of 2, 3, and 5. Thus k has at least 3 different positive prime factors.

The correct answer is C; both statements together are sufficient.

43. In City X last April, was the average (arithmetic mean) daily high temperature greater than the median daily high temperature?

    (1) In City X last April, the sum of the 30 daily high temperatures was 2,160°.
    (2) In City X last April, 60 percent of the daily high temperatures were less than the average daily high temperature.

Arithmetic Statistics

The formula for calculating the arithmetic mean, or the average, is as follows:

$$\text{Average} = \frac{\text{sum of } v \text{ values}}{v}$$

(1) These data will produce an average of $\frac{2160}{30} = 72°$ for last April in City X. However, there is no information regarding the median for comparison; NOT sufficient.

(2) The median is the middle temperature of the data. As such, 50 percent of the daily high temperatures will be at or above the median, and 50 percent will be at or below the median. If 60 percent of the daily high temperatures were less than the average daily high temperature, then the average of the daily highs must be greater than the median; SUFFICIENT.

The correct answer is B; statement 2 alone is sufficient.

44. If m and n are positive integers, is $(\sqrt{m})^n$ an integer?

    (1) $(\sqrt{m})$ is an integer.
    (2) $(\sqrt{n})$ is an integer.

Arithmetic Properties of numbers

(1) If $(\sqrt{m})$ is an integer and n is a positive integer, then $(\sqrt{m})^n$ is an integer because an integer raised to a positive integer is an integer; SUFFICIENT.

(2) The information that $(\sqrt{n})$ is an integer is not helpful in answering the question. For example, if $m = 2$ and $n = 9$, $\sqrt{9} = 3$, which is an integer, but $(\sqrt{2})^9 = (16\sqrt{2})$, which is not an integer. But if $m = 4$ and $n = 9$, then $\sqrt{9} = 3$, which is an integer, and $(\sqrt{4})^9 = 2^9 = 512$ is an integer; NOT sufficient.

The correct answer is A; statement 1 alone is sufficient.

45. Of the 66 people in a certain auditorium, at most 6 people have birthdays in any one given month. Does at least one person in the auditorium have a birthday in January?

    (1) More of the people in the auditorium have birthdays in February than in March.
    (2) Five of the people in the auditorium have birthdays in March.

    Algebra Sets and functions

    Because it is given that 6 is the greatest number of individuals who can have birthdays in any particular month, these 66 people could be evenly distributed across 11 of the 12 months of the year. That is to say, it could be possible for the distribution to be $11 \times 6 = 66$, and thus any given month, such as January, would not have a person with a birthday. Assume that January has no people with birthdays, and see if this assumption is disproved.

    (1) The information that more people have February birthdays than March birthdays indicates that the distribution is not even. Therefore, March is underrepresented and must thus have fewer than 6 birthdays. Since no month can have more than 6 people with birthdays, and every month but January already has as many people with birthdays as it can have, January has to have at least 1 person with a birthday; SUFFICIENT.

    (2) Again, March is underrepresented with only 5 birthdays, and none of the other months can have more than 6 birthdays. Therefore, the extra birthday (from March) must occur in January; SUFFICIENT.

    The correct answer is D;
    each statement alone is sufficient.

46. Last year the average (arithmetic mean) salary of the 10 employees of Company X was $42,800. What is the average salary of the same 10 employees this year?

    (1) For 8 of the 10 employees, this year's salary is 15 percent greater than last year's salary.
    (2) For 2 of the 10 employees, this year's salary is the same as last year's salary.

    Arithmetic Statistics

    (1) Since all 10 employees did not receive the same 15 percent increase, it cannot be assumed that the mean this year is 15 percent higher than last year. It remains unknown whether these 8 salaries were the top 8 salaries, the bottom 8 salaries, or somewhere in-between. Without this type of information from last year, the mean for this year cannot be determined; NOT sufficient.

    (2) If 2 salaries remained the same as last year, then 8 salaries changed. Without further information about the changes, the mean for this year cannot be determined; NOT sufficient.

    Even taking (1) and (2) together, it remains impossible to tell the mean salary for this year without additional data.

    The correct answer is E;
    both statements together are still not sufficient.

47. In a certain classroom, there are 80 books, of which 24 are fiction and 23 are written in Spanish. How many of the fiction books are written in Spanish?

    (1) Of the fiction books, there are 6 more that are not written in Spanish than are written in Spanish.
    (2) Of the books written in Spanish, there are 5 more nonfiction books than fiction books.

    Algebra Sets and functions

    Let x represent the fiction books that are written in Spanish. A table could be set up like the one below, filling in the information that is known or able to be known:

	Spanish	Non-Spanish	Total
Fiction	x		24
Nonfiction			56
Total	23	57	80

    (1) If x represents the fiction books written in Spanish, then $x + 6$ can now be used to represent the fiction books that are not written in Spanish. From the table above, it can be seen then that $x + x + 6 = 24$, or $2x = 18$. Therefore, x, or the number of fiction books written in Spanish, is 9; SUFFICIENT.

(2) If x represents the fiction books written in Spanish, then $x + 5$ can now be used to represent the nonfiction books written in Spanish. From the table, it can be said that $x + x + 5 = 23$, or $2x = 18$. Therefore, x, or the number of fiction books written in Spanish, is 9; SUFFICIENT.

**The correct answer is D;
each statement alone is sufficient.**

48. If p is the perimeter of rectangle Q, what is the value of p?

    (1) Each diagonal of rectangle Q has length 10.
    (2) The area of rectangle Q is 48.

Geometry Rectangles; Perimeter; Area

The perimeter of a rectangle is equal to 2 times the rectangle's length plus 2 times the rectangle's width, or $p = 2l + 2w$. The diagonals of a rectangle are equal. In a rectangle, because a diagonal forms a right triangle, the length of a diagonal is equal to the square root of the length squared plus the width squared, or $d = \sqrt{l^2 + w^2}$.

(1) If a diagonal = 10, then $10 = \sqrt{l^2 + w^2}$, or, by squaring both sides, $100 = l^2 + w^2$. Without knowing the value or the relationship between the other two sides of the right triangle, it is impossible to solve for l or w, and thus for the perimeter of the rectangle; NOT sufficient.

(2) If the area of the rectangle is 48, then it can be stated that $lw = 48$. However, without further information, the perimeter cannot be determined. For example, l could be 6 and w could be 8, and the perimeter would then be $12 + 16 = 28$. However, it could also be that l is 4 and w is 12, and in that case the perimeter would be $8 + 24 = 32$; NOT sufficient.

Using (1) and (2) together, it is possible to solve this problem. Since from (2) $lw = 48$, then $w = \dfrac{48}{l}$. Substituting this into $100 = l^2 + w^2$ from (1) the equation can be solved as follows:

$100 = l^2 + \left(\dfrac{48}{l}\right)^2$ substitution

$100l^2 = l^4 + 2,304$ multiply both sides by l^2

$l^4 - 100l^2 + 2,304 = 0$ move all terms to one side

$(l^2 - 64)(l^2 - 36) = 0$ factor like a quadratic

$l^2 = 64,\ l^2 = 36$ solve for l^2

Since l is a length, it must be positive, so l is either 8 or 6. When $l = 8, w = \dfrac{48}{8} = 6$, and when $l = 6, w = \dfrac{48}{6} = 8$, both of which give the same perimeter.

**The correct answer is C;
both statements together are sufficient.**

3.6 Verbal Answer Explanations

Reading Comprehension

The following discussion is intended to familiarize you with the most efficient and effective approaches to the kinds of problems common to reading comprehension. The particular questions in this chapter are generally representative of the kinds of reading comprehension questions you will encounter on the GMAT exam. Remember that it is the problem solving strategy that is important, not the specific details of a particular question.

Questions 1–5 refer to the passage on page 23.

49. Which of the following best describes the purpose of the sentence in lines 10–15 ?

    (A) To show that economic signaling theory fails to explain a finding
    (B) To introduce a distinction not accounted for by economic signaling theory
    (C) To account for an exception to a generalization suggested by Marquardt and McGann
    (D) To explain why Marquardt and McGann's research was conducted
    (E) To offer an explanation for an observation reported by Marquardt and McGann

    Logical structure

    Marquardt and McGann found a correlation between highly advertised products and high-quality products. The connection can be explained by understanding that companies may invest heavily in such advertising, anticipating that recurring purchases of high-quality products will eventually recover these advertising costs. The consumers will continue to buy these products over time because of loyalty to their high quality. The statement in bold provides this explanation for the correlation noted by Marquardt and McGann.

    A   The sentence does not explain a failure of the economic signaling theory.
    B   Economic signaling theory is about perceptions of quality, but this explanation is about actual quality and its correlation with advertising.
    C   No exception is mentioned in Marquardt and McGann's work.
    D   The sentence does not examine why or how the research was undertaken.
    E   **Correct.** This statement provides an explanation of why highly advertised products *did indeed rank high on certain measures of product quality*.

    The correct answer is E.

50. The primary purpose of the passage is to

    (A) present findings that contradict one explanation for the effects of a particular advertising practice
    (B) argue that theoretical explanations about the effects of a particular advertising practice are of limited value without empirical evidence
    (C) discuss how and why particular advertising practices may affect consumers' perceptions
    (D) contrast the research methods used in two different studies of a particular advertising practice
    (E) explain why a finding about consumer responses to a particular advertising practice was unexpected

Main idea

The primary purpose can be determined only by evaluating the whole passage. The first paragraph discusses consumers' perceptions of quality based on frequency of advertising. The second paragraph discusses three studies that show how consumers base their evaluations of products on the kinds of advertising they see. Therefore, the purpose of the whole passage is to show how consumers' perceptions of products are shaped by certain advertising practices.

A   The passage shows that expensive advertising works to a certain point, but not after it; this method examines a continuum, not a contradiction.

B   Most of the passage is devoted to empirical evidence.

C   **Correct.** The passage shows how the frequency and the kind of advertising influence consumers' perceptions about the quality of the products advertised.

D   The passage reports the findings of four studies but does not mention research methods.

E   The passage does not indicate that any of the findings were unexpected.

The correct answer is C.

51. Kirmani's research, as described in the passage, suggests which of the following regarding consumers' expectations about the quality of advertised products?

(A) Those expectations are likely to be highest if a manufacturer runs both black-and-white and color advertisements for the same product.

(B) Those expectations can be shaped by the presence of color in an advertisement as well as by the frequency with which an advertisement appears.

(C) Those expectations are usually high for frequently advertised new brands but not for frequently advertised familiar brands.

(D) Those expectations are likely to be higher for products whose black-and-white advertisements are often repeated than for those whose color advertisements are less often repeated.

(E) Those expectations are less definitively shaped by the manufacturer's advertisements than by information that consumers gather from other sources.

Inference

The question's use of the word *suggests* means that the answer depends on making an inference. This research is discussed in the second paragraph. Kirmani found that too much advertising tended to make the consumers believe that manufacturers were desperate. The use of color was also found to affect consumers' perceptions of brand quality. Realizing that color advertising is more expensive than black-and-white, consumers react more quickly to what they perceive to be its overuse than they do to a repetition of black-and-white advertisements.

61

A   This situation is not discussed in the research, at least as it is reported in this passage.

B   **Correct.** It can be inferred that consumers' perceptions of product quality are influenced by the use of color in an advertisement and by the frequency of the advertisement's appearance.

C   The research does not make a distinction between new and familiar brands.

D   The research indicates only that consumers can tolerate black-and-white advertisements for a longer time than color advertisements before dismissing them as excessive.

E   There is no discussion of what consumers learn from other sources.

The correct answer is B.

52. Kirmani's third study, as described in the passage, suggests which of the following conclusions about a black-and-white advertisement?

    (A) It can be repeated more frequently than a comparable color advertisement could before consumers begin to suspect low manufacturer confidence in the quality of the advertised product.

    (B) It will have the greatest impact on consumers' perceptions of the quality of the advertised product if it appears during periods when a color version of the same advertisement is also being used.

    (C) It will attract more attention from readers of the print publication in which it appears if it is used only a few times.

    (D) It may be perceived by some consumers as more expensive than a comparable color advertisement.

    (E) It is likely to be perceived by consumers as a sign of higher manufacturer confidence in the quality of the advertised product than a comparable color advertisement would be.

Inference

Kirmani's third study is discussed in the final two sentences. Consumers suspect expensive advertising results from a manufacturer's lack of confidence in the quality of the product. Consumers reach the point at which they find advertising *excessive* more quickly with color advertising than with black-and-white advertising because they understand that the addition of color increases advertising expenses. It is reasonable to infer that the reverse is also true and thus that consumers will tolerate lengthier repetitions of black-and-white advertising without becoming suspicious of product quality.

A   **Correct.** Consumers find color advertising excessive more quickly and thus can be expected to find black-and-white advertising excessive less quickly.

B   The study does not discuss concurrent appearances of color and black-and-white advertisements for the same product.

C   The sole conclusion about frequency is that consumers can tolerate a greater frequency of black-and-white advertisements than color advertisements.

D   It is stated that consumers understand that color advertisements are more expensive.

E   The research certainly does not report this finding.

The correct answer is A.

3.6 Diagnostic Test Verbal Answer Explanations

53. The passage suggests that Kirmani would be most likely to agree with which of the following statements about consumers' perceptions of the relationship between the frequency with which a product is advertised and the product's quality?

    (A) Consumers' perceptions about the frequency with which an advertisement appears are their primary consideration when evaluating an advertisement's claims about product quality.

    (B) Because most consumers do not notice the frequency of advertisement, it has little impact on most consumers' expectations regarding product quality.

    (C) Consumers perceive frequency of advertisement as a signal about product quality only when the advertisement is for a product that is newly on the market.

    (D) The frequency of advertisement is not always perceived by consumers to indicate that manufacturers are highly confident about their products' quality.

    (E) Consumers who try a new product that has been frequently advertised are likely to perceive the advertisement's frequency as having been an accurate indicator of the product's quality.

Inference

The first sentence of the second paragraph provides the answer to this question: *at some level of spending the manufacturer's advertising effort may be perceived as unreasonably high, implying low manufacturer confidence in product quality.* Thus, it is logical to assume that if a product is advertised too frequently, consumers may believe that the manufacturer is spending excessive amounts on advertising because that manufacturer is not confident of the product's quality.

A   Kirmani's research, as reported here, does not support this claim.

B   Kirmani's research examines how consumers respond to the frequency of advertising; the research does not indicate that consumers do not notice frequency.

C   The research does not distinguish between new and familiar products.

D   **Correct.** Excessive advertising may lead consumers to believe that the manufacturer lacks confidence in the quality of the product.

E   Kirmani's research does not specifically address new products.

The correct answer is D.

Questions 6–11 refer to the passage on page 25.

54. The main purpose of the passage is to

    (A) propose an experiment
    (B) analyze a function
    (C) refute an argument
    (D) explain a contradiction
    (E) simulate a process

Main idea

Determining the main purpose comes from considering the passage as a whole. The first paragraph begins by noting that *the idea of the brain as an information processor* is generally accepted by neuroscientists. The author then presents Searle as an *enemy* of this position and explains Searle's belief that human thought is more than information processing. The second paragraph questions Searle's position, and the third asserts that the brain is an information processor, refuting Searle's argument.

63

A   The author uses the idea of a mechanical simulation of a stomach as a metaphor for a computer's simulation of thought; this is not a proposal for an experiment.

B   The author analyzes Searle's position, but no function is analyzed.

C   **Correct.** The author explains Searle's argument in order to refute it.

D   The author points out a weakness in Searle's thinking, but not a contradiction.

E   The simulation of a process is included as a metaphor, but it is not essential to the passage.

The correct answer is C.

55. Which of the following is most consistent with Searle's reasoning as presented in the passage?

    (A) Meaning and content cannot be reduced to algorithms.
    (B) The process of digestion can be simulated mechanically, but not on a computer.
    (C) Simulated thoughts and real thoughts are essentially similar because they are composed primarily of information.
    (D) A computer can use "causal powers" similar to those of the human brain when processing information.
    (E) Computer simulations of the world can achieve the complexity of the brain's representations of the world.

Evaluation

Searle's position is stated in the first paragraph: because computers merely follow algorithms, *they cannot deal with important aspects of human thought such as meaning and content.* Thus, Searle believes that meaning and content cannot be reduced to algorithms.

A   **Correct.** Searle believes that meaning and content cannot be reduced to algorithms.

B   The author argues for the mechanical simulation, but offers no evidence that Searle would agree.

C   This statement reflects the author's position, but it is the opposite of Searle's.

D   Searle asserts that only people, not computers, have *the causal powers of the brain.*

E   The passage does not discuss computer simulations of the world.

The correct answer is A.

56. The author of the passage would be most likely to agree with which of the following statements about the simulation of organ functions?

    (A) An artificial device that achieves the functions of the stomach could be considered a valid model of the stomach.
    (B) Computer simulations of the brain are best used to crack the brain's codes of meaning and content.
    (C) Computer simulations of the brain challenge ideas that are fundamental to psychology and neuroscience.
    (D) Because the brain and the stomach both act as processors, they can best be simulated by mechanical devices.
    (E) The computer's limitations in simulating digestion suggest equal limitations in computer-simulated thinking.

Application

To answer this question, think about how the author would respond to each statement. Anticipating the author's response depends on understanding the author's point of view. In this passage, the author is arguing against Searle's view of the brain and in favor of the brain as information processor. The author believes that the computer can be a model of the brain and uses the example of the mechanical stomach to support his position on simulations.

A	**Correct.** The first two sentences of the third paragraph imply that a mechanical device is a valid model.	
B	The author believes a computer can simulate the brain but does not comment on how these simulations should be used. There is no way to predict the author's reaction to this statement.	
C	The author would reject this statement since neuroscience and psychology do in fact see the brain as an information processor.	
D	The author agrees that both the brain and the stomach act as processors; believes that the computer, a nonmechanical device, can simulate the brain; and offers a way that a mechanical device could simulate the stomach. The author does not suggest that mechanical devices are the best way to simulate both their processes.	
E	This statement reflects Searle's viewpoint, which the author rejects.	

The correct answer is A.

57. It can be inferred that the author of the passage believes that Searle's argument is flawed by its failure to

(A) distinguish between syntactic and semantic operations
(B) explain adequately how people, unlike computers, are able to understand meaning
(C) provide concrete examples illustrating its claims about thinking
(D) understand how computers use algorithms to process information
(E) decipher the code that is transmitted from neuron to neuron in the brain

Inference

The author's attitude toward Searle's argument is apparent in the first paragraph, which ends with the author's summary of what Searle is saying. Computers understand structures, Searle argues, but only people understand meaning. How do people understand meaning? The author notes that Searle is not able to answer this question and is able only to assert that people have *causal powers of the brain*.

A	The author makes it clear in the first paragraph that Searle does distinguish between the two. In Searle's view computers are syntactic, interpreting structure or arrangement, rather than semantic, understanding meaning.
B	**Correct.** The first paragraph ends with the contrast between people and computers: *People, on the other hand, understand meaning because they have something Searle obscurely calls the causal powers of the brain.* By calling Searle's explanation obscure, the author implies that Searle has not adequately clarified how people understand meaning.
C	Nothing in the passage criticizes Searle for not providing concrete examples. Indeed, in the second paragraph, the author anticipates how Searle would react to one concrete example, the computer simulation of the stomach.
D	In the first paragraph, the author says that Searle argues that *computers simply follow algorithms*; whether or not Searle understands how they use algorithms is irrelevant.
E	Since, as the author suggests in the first paragraph, Searle does not believe information could be a code transmitted from neuron to neuron, he cannot be expected to decipher that code.

The correct answer is B.

58. From the passage, it can be inferred that the author would agree with Searle on which of the following points?

   (A) Computers operate by following algorithms.
   (B) The human brain can never fully understand its own functions.
   (C) The comparison of the brain to a machine is overly simplistic.
   (D) The most accurate models of physical processes are computer simulations.
   (E) Human thought and computer-simulated thought involve similar processes of representation.

Inference

An inference requires going beyond the material explicitly stated in the passage to the author's ideas that underlie that material. The author and Searle take opposite points of view on the brain as information processor. Their area of agreement is narrow. However, they do both agree that computers work by following algorithms.

A **Correct.** The first paragraph explains that Searle dismisses computers because they *simply follow algorithms*; while the author disagrees with Searle on virtually every other point, no disagreement is voiced here.

B The first paragraph shows this to be Searle's position, but not the author's.

C The first paragraph shows this to be Searle's position, but not the author's.

D The second paragraph explains Searle's rejection of this position.

E The final paragraph establishes this as the author's position, but not Searle's.

The correct answer is A.

59. Which of the following most accurately represents Searle's criticism of the brain-as-computer metaphor, as that criticism is described in the passage?

   (A) The metaphor is not experimentally verifiable.
   (B) The metaphor does not take into account the unique powers of the brain.
   (C) The metaphor suggests that a brain's functions can be simulated as easily as those of a stomach.
   (D) The metaphor suggests that a computer can simulate the workings of the mind by using the codes of neural transmission.
   (E) The metaphor is unhelpful because both the brain and the computer process information.

Inference

Searle's criticism of the brain-as-computer metaphor is discussed in the first paragraph. Computers are merely machines; only people are endowed with *causal powers of the brain* that allow them to understand meaning and content.

A Searle does not believe in the value of the metaphor, so its verification is beside the point.

B **Correct.** Searle believes that people have something computers do not, *causal powers of the brain* for understanding *important aspects of human thought*.

C Comparing the brain to a computer, the metaphor does not make this suggestion.

D In the second paragraph, the author says, *but even if a computer could simulate the workings of the mind*, making it clear that presently it cannot; this statement does not reflect why Searle rejects the metaphor.

E This is not the basis of Searle's objection since he does not accept the premise that the brain is an information processor.

The correct answer is B.

Questions 12–17 refer to the passage on page 27.

60. The primary purpose of the passage is to

    (A) explain why women reformers of the Progressive Era failed to achieve their goals
    (B) discuss the origins of child labor laws in the late nineteenth and early twentieth centuries
    (C) compare the living conditions of working-class and middle-class women in the Progressive Era
    (D) discuss an oversight on the part of women reformers of the Progressive Era
    (E) revise a traditional view of the role played by women reformers in enacting Progressive Era reforms

Main idea

Understanding the author's purpose comes only from reflecting on the passage as a whole. The beginning of the passage notes the success of middle-class women reformers in improving working conditions for women and children. The middle discusses the position of working-class mothers, who were more concerned with the economic survival of their families than with labor reform and consequently tried to circumvent the laws. The close of the passage observes that, although middle-class reformers were right to point out exploitation of children, they failed to understand the economic plight of working-class families, who needed the income earned by every possible member. The purpose of this passage is to show the failure of middle-class reformers to understand the economic position of working-class families.

A   Lines 6–10 emphasize the victories of the reformers.
B   The passage discusses the effects, rather than the origins, of child labor laws.
C   Living conditions of middle-class and working-class women are not compared.
D   **Correct.** As is made clear, especially in the final sentence of the passage, women reformers failed to understand the economic needs of working-class families.
E   A traditional view is not compared with a newer, revised view of the reformers.

The correct answer is D.

61. The *view* mentioned in line 17 of the passage refers to which of the following?

    (A) Some working-class mothers' resistance to the enforcement of child labor laws
    (B) Reformers' belief that child labor and industrial home work should be abolished
    (C) Reformers' opinions about how working-class families raised their children
    (D) Certain women historians' observation that there was a lack of consensus between women of different classes on the issue of child labor and industrial home work
    (E) Working-class families' fears about the adverse consequences that child labor laws would have on their ability to earn an adequate living

Inference

To find what this appearance of *view* refers to, it is necessary to look back to the beginning of the sentence. *This view*, not shared by working-class mothers, refers to the reformers' conviction that *child labor and industrial home work were equally inhumane practices that should be outlawed.*

A *This view* must refer back to a point already stated; resistance to child labor laws is not discussed until the following sentence.

B **Correct.** *This view* refers to the position of reformers stated earlier in the same sentence: that *child labor and industrial home work…should be outlawed.*

C *This view* must refer back to a point already stated; the reformers' belief that resistance to child labor laws was due to poor parenting is discussed later in the passage.

D A number of women historians have said that working-class mothers did not always share the *view* of middle-class women reformers about child labor.

E *This view* must refer back to a point already stated; the fears of working-class families are examined in the following sentence.

The correct answer is B.

62. The author of the passage mentions the observations of women historians (lines 15–17) most probably in order to

   (A) provide support for an assertion made in the preceding sentence (lines 10–12)
   (B) raise a question that is answered in the last sentence of the passage (lines 27–32)
   (C) introduce an opinion that challenges a statement made in the first sentence of the passage
   (D) offer an alternative view to the one attributed in the passage to working-class mothers
   (E) point out a contradiction inherent in the traditional view of child labor reform as it is presented in the passage

Evaluation

In lines 10–12, the author asserts that child labor laws *pitted women of different classes against one another.* The view of the middle-class women reformers is stated, and then, to show that working-class mothers did not hold the same opinion, the author turns to the recent work of women historians to support this statement.

A **Correct.** The author uses the recent work of women historians to support the statement that women of different social classes were pitted against one another.

B The women historians *have recently observed*; the verb *observed* introduces a statement rather than a question.

C The reference to women historians has to do with working-class mothers; it does not challenge women's activism and role in social reform.

D The passage supports what the women historians say about working-class mothers.

E The author does not define or present the *traditional* view of child labor reform, nor is any inherent contradiction pointed out.

The correct answer is A.

63. The passage suggests that which of the following was a reason for the difference of opinion between working-class mothers and women reformers on the issue of child labor?

   (A) Reformers' belief that industrial home work was preferable to child labor outside the home
   (B) Reformers' belief that child labor laws should pertain to working conditions but not to pay
   (C) Working-class mothers' resentment at reformers' attempts to interfere with their parenting
   (D) Working-class mothers' belief that child labor was an inhumane practice
   (E) Working-class families' need for every employable member of their families to earn money

3.6 Diagnostic Test Verbal Answer Explanations

Inference

The question's use of the word *suggests* means that the answer depends on making an inference. Lines 12–23 examine the different views of middle-class reformers and working-class mothers on child labor laws. While the reformers saw child labor as an *inhumane* practice that should be *outlawed*, working class mothers understood *the necessity of pooling the wages of as many family members as possible* and viewed child labor legislation as *a personal economic disaster*.

A   Lines 12–14 show that reformers regarded both kinds of work as *equally inhumane practices that should be outlawed*.

B   Pay is not specifically discussed in the passage.

C   Lines 24–27 indicate that the reformers believed working-class resistance to child labor laws was a sign of poor parenting, but nothing is said about the working-class response to this view.

D   Lines 12–17 say that the reformers held this position, but *working class mothers did not always share this view*.

E   **Correct.** Lines 17–23 explain that working-class families needed *the wages of as many family members as possible*.

The correct answer is E.

64. The author of the passage asserts which of the following about women reformers who tried to abolish child labor?

(A) They alienated working-class mothers by attempting to enlist them in agitating for progressive causes.

(B) They underestimated the prevalence of child labor among the working classes.

(C) They were correct in their conviction that child labor was deplorable but shortsighted about the impact of child labor legislation on working-class families.

(D) They were aggressive in their attempts to enforce child labor legislation, but were unable to prevent working-class families from circumventing them.

(E) They were prevented by their nearly total disenfranchisement from making significant progress in child labor reform.

Supporting ideas

This question is based on information explicitly stated in the final sentence of the passage. Women reformers viewed *child labor as a terribly exploitative practice* but they *failed to take account of the economic needs of working-class families*.

A   The passage does not say that reformers tried to enlist working-class mothers in progressive causes.

B   No evidence is offered to support such a statement.

C   **Correct.** The final sentence makes clear that the reformers recognized child labor as *exploitative* but did not understand *the economic needs of working-class families*.

D   The reformers' activities involved promoting legislation; there is no evidence in the passage that the reformers themselves attempted to enforce these laws.

E   Lines 6–10 show that the reformers improved working conditions for women and children, despite their disenfranchisement.

The correct answer is C.

65. According to the passage, one of the most striking achievements of white middle-class women reformers during the Progressive Era was

    (A) gaining the right to vote in school elections
    (B) mobilizing working-class women in the fight against child labor
    (C) uniting women of different classes in grassroots activism
    (D) improving the economic conditions of working-class families
    (E) improving women's and children's working conditions

Supporting ideas

The question's use of the phrase *according to the passage* indicates that the answer can be found through careful reading of the passage. This question is based on information explicitly stated in lines 7–10, which state that *white middle-class women reformers won a variety of victories, notably in the improvement of working conditions, especially for women and children*.

A   Lines 6–7 show that women already had the right to vote in school elections.

B   Lines 20–24 show that working-class families tried to *circumvent child labor laws*.

C   Lines 11–12 say that one product of grassroots activism, child labor legislation, *pitted women of different classes against one another*.

D   Lines 31–32 say that the reformers *failed to take account of the economic needs of working-class families*.

E   **Correct**. The passage states that reformers improved the working conditions of women and children.

The correct answer is E.

Critical Reasoning

The following discussion is intended to familiarize you with the most efficient and effective approaches to critical reasoning questions. The particular questions in this chapter are generally representative of the kinds of critical reasoning questions you will encounter on the GMAT exam. Remember that it is the problem solving strategy that is important, not the specific details of a particular question.

66. Vasquez-Morrell Assurance specializes in insuring manufacturers. Whenever a policyholder makes a claim, a claims adjuster determines the amount that Vasquez-Morrell is obligated to pay. Vasquez-Morrell is cutting its staff of claims adjusters by 15 percent. To ensure that the company's ability to handle claims promptly is affected as little as possible by the staff cuts, consultants recommend that Vasquez-Morrell lay off those adjusters who now take longest, on average, to complete work on claims assigned to them.

    Which of the following, if true, most seriously calls into question the consultants' criterion for selecting the staff to be laid off?

    (A) If the time that Vasquez-Morrell takes to settle claims increases significantly, it could lose business to other insurers.
    (B) Supervisors at Vasquez-Morrell tend to assign the most complex claims to the most capable adjusters.
    (C) At Vasquez-Morrell, no insurance payments are made until a claims adjuster has reached a final determination on the claim.
    (D) There are no positions at Vasquez-Morrell to which staff currently employed as claims adjusters could be reassigned.
    (E) The premiums that Vasquez-Morrell currently charges are no higher than those charged for similar coverage by competitors.

    Evaluation of a Plan

    Situation   An insurance company must reduce its staff of claims adjusters. To ensure continuing promptness in handling claims, consultants advise the company to lay off those adjusters who take the longest to complete claims.

    Reasoning   *What problem could there be with the criterion?* The consultants' criterion is the time an adjuster takes to settle a claim. However, some claims are naturally more complicated and require more time. If it is true that the company now assigns these time-consuming cases to its most capable adjusters, then these adjusters would be likely to be the ones who take longest to complete their cases. Laying off the adjusters who take the longest would thus mean laying off the company's most capable staff, which could very well decrease its ability to handle claims promptly.

    A   The consultants' advice makes sense if increased time to handle claims causes the company to lose business.
    B   **Correct.** This statement properly identifies the problem with the consultants' criterion.
    C   This statement merely describes the process of handling a claim; it does not provide any information about the criterion for layoffs.
    D   The consultants make no recommendations for reassigning staff, so indicating that there are no positions available does not call their advice into question.
    E   The consultants do not recommend a change in premiums; noting that they are similar to competitors' premiums does not undermine the plan that the consultants recommend.

    The correct answer is B.

67. Prolonged spells of hot, dry weather at the end of the grape-growing season typically reduce a vineyard's yield, because the grapes stay relatively small. In years with such weather, wine producers can make only a relatively small quantity of wine from a given area of vineyards. Nonetheless, in regions where wine producers generally grow their own grapes, analysts typically expect a long, hot, dry spell late in the growing season to result in increased revenues for local wine producers.

    Which of the following, if true, does most to justify the analysts' expectation?

    (A) The lower a vineyard's yield, the less labor is required to harvest the grapes.
    (B) Long, hot, dry spells at the beginning of the grape-growing season are rare, but they can have a devastating effect on a vineyard's yield.
    (C) Grapes grown for wine production are typically made into wine at or near the vineyard in which they were grown.
    (D) When hot, dry spells are followed by heavy rains, the rains frequently destroy grape crops.
    (E) Grapes that have matured in hot, dry weather make significantly better wine than ordinary grapes.

    Argument Construction

    Situation   Hot, dry weather at the end of the grape-growing season reduces yield, so winemakers can only produce a small quantity of wine. However, analysts expect that this weather will increase winemakers' revenues.

    Reasoning   *What additional piece of information explains the analysts' expectations?* The same conditions that lead to low quantity also lead to something that increases revenues. What could this be? If these weather conditions lead to higher-quality wine that will sell for higher prices, the analysts' expectations for increased revenues are justified.

    A   Lower labor costs mean less expenditure for the winemakers; this does not explain how revenues would increase.

    B   This statement about low yields does not explain an increase in revenues.

    C   The proximity of production to the vineyard is irrelevant to the question of how hot, dry weather can be responsible for decreased yield and increased revenues.

    D   This statement gives another example of weather's effect on grape crops, but it does not explain how revenues are increased.

    E   **Correct.** This statement properly provides the explanation that the weather conditions will lead to better wines. With better wines typically commanding higher prices, the winemakers will gain the increased revenues that the analysts anticipate.

    The correct answer is E.

68. In the past, most children who went sledding in the winter snow in Verland used wooden sleds with runners and steering bars. Ten years ago, smooth plastic sleds became popular; they go faster than wooden sleds but are harder to steer and slow. The concern that plastic sleds are more dangerous is clearly borne out by the fact that the number of children injured while sledding was much higher last winter than it was 10 years ago.

Which of the following, if true in Verland, most seriously undermines the force of the evidence cited?

(A) A few children still use traditional wooden sleds.
(B) Very few children wear any kind of protective gear, such as helmets, while sledding.
(C) Plastic sleds can be used in a much wider variety of snow conditions than wooden sleds can.
(D) Most sledding injuries occur when a sled collides with a tree, a rock, or another sled.
(E) Because the traditional wooden sleds can carry more than one rider, an accident involving a wooden sled can result in several children being injured.

Argument Evaluation

Situation   Ten years ago, wooden sleds began to be replaced by plastic sleds that go faster but are harder to control. Plastic sleds are more dangerous than wooden sleds because more children suffered injuries last year than they did 10 years ago.

Reasoning   *What weakens this argument?* This argument depends on a comparison of two kinds of sleds. Any evidence that would either strengthen or weaken the argument must indicate a comparison. Evidence that applies only to one kind of sled or to both kinds of sleds equally cannot weaken this argument. Consider the implications of the evidence presented in the answer choices. If plastic sleds can be used in a wider variety of conditions than wooden sleds can, then plastic sleds can be used more frequently. It is possible that more frequent use, rather than the sleds themselves, has led to more accidents.

A   The limited use of some wooden sleds does not weaken the argument.
B   The absence of protective gear would affect accidents with both kinds of sleds.
C   **Correct.** This statement weakens the argument by providing an alternate explanation for the increased accidents.
D   This statement is true of accidents with both kinds of sleds.
E   This explains why wooden sleds may be dangerous but does not weaken the argument that plastic sleds are even more dangerous.

The correct answer is C.

69. Metal rings recently excavated from seventh-century settlements in the western part of Mexico were made using the same metallurgical techniques as those used by Ecuadorian artisans before and during that period. These techniques are sufficiently complex to make their independent development in both areas unlikely. Since the people of these two areas were in cultural contact, archaeologists hypothesize that the metallurgical techniques used to make the rings found in Mexico were learned by Mexican artisans from Ecuadorian counterparts.

    Which of the following would it be most useful to establish in order to evaluate the archaeologists' hypothesis?

    (A) Whether metal objects were traded from Ecuador to western Mexico during the seventh century
    (B) Whether travel between western Mexico and Ecuador in the seventh century would have been primarily by land or by sea
    (C) Whether artisans from western Mexico could have learned complex metallurgical techniques from their Ecuadorian counterparts without actually leaving western Mexico
    (D) Whether metal tools were used in the seventh-century settlements in western Mexico
    (E) Whether any of the techniques used in the manufacture of the metal rings found in western Mexico are still practiced among artisans in Ecuador today

    Argument Evaluation

    Situation	Metal rings excavated from seventh-century settlements in western Mexico were made with the same complex techniques used in Ecuador before and during a period when the two cultures were known to be in contact. Mexican artisans are thought to have learned the techniques from Ecuadorian artisans.

    Reasoning	*What point could best be applied in evaluating this hypothesis?* Consider what specific information would help to assess the archaeologists' theory. It is given that the two areas had some cultural contact. If it were determined that metal objects were traded from one culture to the other, it could be possible that the metalworking techniques were passed along as well. Such evidence would be relevant to the hypothesis that Mexican artisans saw the work of their Ecuadorian counterparts and, from this exchange, learned the techniques to make the metal rings.

    A	**Correct.** This statement properly identifies information that would be useful in the evaluation of the archaeologists' hypothesis.
    B	The means of travel is irrelevant to the hypothesis about the source of the techniques.
    C	The hypothesis is not about where Mexican artisans learned the techniques, but whether they learned them from the Ecuadorians.
    D	The existence of metal tools provides no helpful information in establishing whether the Ecuadorians were the source of the metallurgical techniques.
    E	The comparison to the present day is irrelevant to the hypothesis.

    The correct answer is A.

70. Following several years of declining advertising sales, the *Greenville Times* reorganized its advertising sales force. Before reorganization, the sales force was organized geographically, with some sales representatives concentrating on city-center businesses and others concentrating on different outlying regions. The reorganization attempted to increase the sales representatives' knowledge of clients' businesses by having each sales representative deal with only one type of industry or of retailing. After the reorganization, revenue from advertising sales increased.

In assessing whether the improvement in advertising sales can properly be attributed to the reorganization, it would be most helpful to find out which of the following?

(A) What proportion of the total revenue of the *Greenville Times* is generated by advertising sales?
(B) Has the circulation of the *Greenville Times* increased substantially in the last two years?
(C) Among all the types of industry and retailing that use the *Greenville Times* as an advertising vehicle, which type accounts for the largest proportion of the newspaper's advertising sales?
(D) Do any clients of the sales representatives of the *Greenville Times* have a standing order with the *Times* for a fixed amount of advertising per month?
(E) Among the advertisers in the *Greenville Times*, are there more types of retail business or more types of industrial business?

Evaluation of a Plan

Situation   In the face of declining advertising sales, a newspaper reorganizes its sales force so that sales representatives have a better understanding of businesses. Revenue from advertising sales increased after the reorganization.

Reasoning   *What additional evidence would help determine the source of the increased revenue?* In order to attribute the increased revenue to the reorganization of the sales force, other possible causes must be eliminated. Newspaper advertising rates are linked to circulation; when circulation increases, higher rates can be charged and revenues will increase. An alternate explanation might be a significant rise in circulation, so it would be particularly helpful to know if circulation had increased.

A   The question concerns only increased revenue from advertising sales; the proportion of advertising revenue to total revenue is outside the scope of the question.

B   **Correct.** This statement provides another possible explanation for increased revenue of advertising sales, and so the answer to this question would help to clarify the reason for the increased revenue.

C   Knowing how the advertising sales break down by type of business might be useful for other purposes, but it does not help to show the cause of the increase.

D   A fixed amount of advertising would not explain increased revenue, so the answer to this question would be irrelevant.

E   Distinguishing between the types of businesses will not contribute to determining whether the reorganization was responsible for the increased revenue.

The correct answer is B.

71. Motorists in a certain country frequently complain that traffic congestion is much worse now than it was 20 years ago. No real measure of how much traffic congestion there was 20 years ago exists, but the motorists' complaints are almost certainly unwarranted. The country's highway capacity has tripled in the last twenty years, thanks to a vigorous highway construction program, whereas the number of automobiles registered in the country has increased by only 75 percent.

    Which of the following, if true, most seriously weakens the argument?

    (A) Most automobile travel is local, and the networks of roads and streets in the country's settled areas have changed little over the last twenty years.
    (B) Gasoline prices are high, and miles traveled per car per year have not changed much over the last 20 years.
    (C) The country's urban centers have well-developed public transit systems that carry most of the people who commute into those centers.
    (D) The average age of automobiles registered in the country is lower now than it was 20 years ago.
    (E) Radio stations have long been broadcasting regular traffic reports that inform motorists about traffic congestion.

    Argument Evaluation

    Situation   Motorists complain that traffic congestion in their country is much worse than it was twenty years ago. But these complaints have no basis since the highway capacity in this country has tripled in the same period, whereas the number of cars registered has risen by only 75 percent.

    Reasoning   *Which point most undermines the argument that the complaints are unwarranted?* Consider that the response to the generalized complaints about congestion discusses only the topic of highway capacity. What if the congestion that motorists are complaining about is not on highways but on local roads? Discovering that travel tends to be local in this country and that the local roads have not been improved in the last twenty years would seriously weaken the argument.

    A   **Correct.** This statement properly identifies a weakness in the argument: the response to the broad complaint addresses a different subject, highway capacity, not the issue of traffic congestion encountered by most motorists.
    B   If high gas prices actually prevented motorists from driving, and if motorists' driving habits were the same as they were twenty years ago, then these points should strengthen the argument that there is no basis for their complaints.
    C   The number of commuters who use public transit does not affect the argument that the motorists' complaints have no basis.
    D   The age of registered cars is irrelevant to the argument.
    E   The radio broadcasts attest to the existence of traffic, but not to its increase, so they do not affect the argument.

    The correct answer is A.

72. The percentage of households with an annual income of more than $40,000 is higher in Merton County than in any other county. However, the percentage of households with an annual income of $60,000 or more is higher in Sommer County.

    If the statements above are true, which of the following must also be true?

    (A) The percentage of households with an annual income of $80,000 is higher in Sommer County than in Merton County.
    (B) Merton County has the second highest percentage of households with an annual income of $60,000 or more.
    (C) Some households in Merton County have an annual income between $40,000 and $60,000.
    (D) The number of households with an annual income of more than $40,000 is greater in Merton County than in Sommer County.
    (E) Average annual household income is higher in Sommer County than in Merton County.

    Argument Construction

    Situation   The percentage of households with annual incomes of more than $40,000 is higher in Merton County than in any other county; the percentage of households with annual incomes of $60,000 or more is higher in Sommer County.

    Reasoning   *On the basis of this information, what point must be true?* The given information makes clear that Merton County has some households that exceed $40,000 in annual income. Sommer County has a higher percentage of households with annual incomes at or above $60,000. A higher percentage of the Merton County households must in turn have annual incomes of $60,000 or less. Thus, the annual income of some households in Merton County is between $40,000 and $60,000.

    A   Since it is possible that there are no households with an annual income of $80,000 in Sommer County, this statement does not follow from the situation.

    B   It is not possible to make this determination on the basis of the available evidence; Merton County may have no households at all with an income of more than $60,000.

    C   **Correct.** This statement properly identifies a conclusion that can be drawn from the given information: in order for the percentage of $40,000-plus incomes to be higher in Merton county than any other county while Sommer has the highest percentage of $60,000-plus incomes, there must be some households in Merton County that bring in between $40,000 and $60,000 annually.

    D   On the basis of information about the *percentages* of households, it is not possible to arrive at this conclusion about the *number* of households.

    E   From the given information, it is not possible to determine where the average income is greater. It is entirely possible that the number of $60,000-plus incomes in Sommer County is quite small and that the number of $40,000-plus incomes in Merton County is substantial.

    The correct answer is C.

73. Tiger beetles are such fast runners that they can capture virtually any nonflying insect. However, when running toward an insect, a tiger beetle will intermittently stop and then, a moment later, resume its attack. Perhaps the beetles cannot maintain their pace and must pause for a moment's rest; but an alternative hypothesis is that while running, tiger beetles are unable to adequately process the resulting rapidly changing visual information and so quickly go blind and stop.

Which of the following, if discovered in experiments using artificially moved prey insects, would support one of the two hypotheses and undermine the other?

(A) When a prey insect is moved directly toward a beetle that has been chasing it, the beetle immediately stops and runs away without its usual intermittent stopping.

(B) In pursuing a swerving insect, a beetle alters its course while running and its pauses become more frequent as the chase progresses.

(C) In pursuing a moving insect, a beetle usually responds immediately to changes in the insect's direction, and it pauses equally frequently whether the chase is up or down an incline.

(D) If, when a beetle pauses, it has not gained on the insect it is pursuing, the beetle generally ends its pursuit.

(E) The faster a beetle pursues an insect fleeing directly away from it, the more frequently the beetle stops.

Argument Evaluation

Situation   Two hypotheses are offered to explain the sudden stop that tiger beetles make while pursuing their prey: (1) they cannot maintain the rapid pace and must rest, and (2) they run too quickly to process visual information and so temporarily go blind.

Reasoning   *What point would strengthen one of the two hypotheses and weaken the other?* Consider the information provided in each answer choice, remembering that information that supports one hypothesis must necessarily detract from the other. Any information that is not about pursuit or that affects the two hypotheses equally may be dismissed from consideration. If the frequency of stopping increases when the beetle follows a swerving insect and must constantly change its course, then the second hypothesis is strengthened; the beetle's pauses increase as the variety of visual information that it needs to deal with increases.

A   The hypotheses concern ongoing pursuit; since this information is not about the beetle's continuing pursuit of prey, it neither strengthens nor weakens either hypothesis.

B   **Correct.** This statement provides information that strengthens the second hypothesis: the swerving pursuit and the resulting continual course adjustments appear to be forcing the beetle to stop with increasing frequency to sort out the erratic visual information.

C   In this experiment, since neither vision nor tiredness appears to be problematic, the beetle could be stopping for either reason; this information neither strengthens nor weakens either hypothesis.

D   This information is irrelevant since both the hypotheses are about mid-pursuit behaviors.

E   The correlation of frequency of stops with speed affects both hypotheses equally; the pauses could be equally due to an inability to maintain the pace or due to a need to process the visual information.

The correct answer is B.

74. Guillemots are birds of Arctic regions. They feed on fish that gather beneath thin sheets of floating ice, and they nest on nearby land. Guillemots need 80 consecutive snow-free days in a year to raise their chicks, so until average temperatures in the Arctic began to rise recently, the guillemots' range was limited to the southernmost Arctic coast. Therefore, if the warming continues, the guillemots' range will probably be enlarged by being extended northward along the coast.

    Which of the following, if true, most seriously weakens the argument?

    (A) Even if the warming trend continues, there will still be years in which guillemot chicks are killed by an unusually early snow.
    (B) If the Arctic warming continues, guillemots' current predators are likely to succeed in extending their own range farther north.
    (C) Guillemots nest in coastal areas, where temperatures are generally higher than in inland areas.
    (D) If the Arctic warming continues, much of the thin ice in the southern Arctic will disappear.
    (E) The fish that guillemots eat are currently preyed on by a wider variety of predators in the southernmost Arctic regions than they are farther north.

    Argument Evaluation

    Situation   In the southern Arctic, guillemots find their prey beneath thin sheets of ice, nest nearby, and require 80 snow-free days to raise their young. A warming trend means that their range may be enlarged by extending northward along the coast.

    Reasoning   *Which point weakens the argument about the enlargement of the guillemots' range?* How could the birds move northward and simultaneously not enlarge their range? Consider the assumption implied by the idea of *enlargement*. If the guillemots lost their southern habitat, then their northward move would be a displacement rather than an enlargement. If their source of food was no longer available to them in the southern Arctic, then they would abandon that area as part of their range.

    A   An exceptional year is not an argument against an enlarged range because *an unusually early snow* could happen in the southern Arctic as well.
    B   If their current predators also migrate northward, then the guillemots' situation has not changed, so this is not an argument against their enlarged range.
    C   The argument suggests that they will move not inland, but *northward along the coast*.
    D   **Correct.** This statement properly identifies a factor that weakens the argument: the guillemots' move northward would not enlarge their range if they lost their food source, fish found under thin ice, in the southern Arctic.
    E   The possibility that they may find prey more easily in the north does not mean that they would abandon the southern Arctic, and so this point does not weaken the argument.

    The correct answer is D.

75. Some batches of polio vaccine used around 1960 were contaminated with SV40, a virus that in monkeys causes various cancers. Some researchers now claim that this contamination caused some cases of a certain cancer in humans, mesothelioma. This claim is not undercut by the fact that a very careful survey made in the 1960s of people who had received the contaminated vaccine found no elevated incidence of any cancer, since _____.

   (A) most cases of mesothelioma are caused by exposure to asbestos
   (B) in some countries, there was no contamination of the vaccine
   (C) SV40 is widely used in laboratories to produce cancers in animals
   (D) mesotheliomas take several decades to develop
   (E) mesothelioma was somewhat less common in 1960 than it is now

   Argument Construction

   Situation Researchers claim that contaminated polio vaccine administered in 1960 caused some cases of mesothelioma, a type of cancer. Their claim is not undermined by the results of a 1960s survey showing that those who received the contaminated vaccine had no elevated incidence of cancer.

   Reasoning *Why did the survey results not challenge the researchers' claim?* The survey did not reveal a higher incidence of mesothelioma. This question then requires completing a sentence that establishes cause. What could be the reason that the people surveyed in the 1960s showed no signs of the disease? If the disease takes decades to develop, then those people surveyed would not yet have shown any signs of it; less than a decade had passed between their exposure to the vaccine and the survey.

   A The contaminated vaccine is said to have caused *some* cases, not *most*; the question remains why the survey results pose no obstacle to the researchers' claim.

   B The claim is only about contaminated vaccine, not uncontaminated vaccine.

   C That the virus can cause cancers in laboratory animals had already been provided as a given; this additional information is irrelevant to the survey of people who received contaminated vaccine.

   D **Correct.** This statement properly identifies the reason that the survey does not call into question the researchers' claim: the people surveyed in the 1960s showed no signs of disease because the cancer takes decades to develop.

   E The frequency of mesothelioma in the general population is not related to the claim that contaminated vaccine caused the disease in a specific population.

   The correct answer is D.

76. Gortland has long been narrowly self-sufficient in both grain and meat. However, as per capita income in Gortland has risen toward the world average, per capita consumption of meat has also risen toward the world average, and it takes several pounds of grain to produce one pound of meat. Therefore, since per capita income continues to rise, whereas domestic grain production will not increase, Gortland will soon have to import either grain or meat or both.

    Which of the following is an assumption on which the argument depends?

    (A) The total acreage devoted to grain production in Gortland will soon decrease.
    (B) Importing either grain or meat will not result in a significantly higher percentage of Gortlanders' incomes being spent on food than is currently the case.
    (C) The per capita consumption of meat in Gortland is increasing at roughly the same rate across all income levels.
    (D) The per capita income of meat producers in Gortland is rising faster than the per capita income of grain producers.
    (E) People in Gortland who increase their consumption of meat will not radically decrease their consumption of grain.

    Argument Construction

    Situation A country previously self-sufficient in grain and meat will soon have to import one or the other or both. Consumption of meat has risen as per capita income has risen, and it takes several pounds of grain to produce one pound of meat.

    Reasoning *What conditions must be true for the conclusion to be true?* Meat consumption is rising. What about grain consumption? A sharp reduction in the amount of grain consumed could compensate for increased meat consumption, making the conclusion false. If people did radically decrease their grain consumption, it might not be necessary to import grain or meat or both. Since the argument concludes that the imports are necessary, it assumes grain consumption will not plunge.

    A The argument makes no assumptions about the acreage devoted to grain; it assumes only that the demand for grain will rise.
    B The argument does not discuss the percentage of their income that Gortlanders spend on food, so an assumption about this topic is not needed.
    C The argument involves only meat consumption in general, not its distribution by income level.
    D Since the argument does not refer to the incomes of meat producers and grain producers, it cannot depend on an assumption about them.
    E **Correct.** This statement properly identifies the assumption that there will be no great decrease in grain consumption.

    The correct answer is E.

77. The Hazelton coal-processing plant is a major employer in the Hazelton area, but national environmental regulations will force it to close if it continues to use old, polluting processing methods. However, to update the plant to use newer, cleaner methods would be so expensive that the plant will close unless it receives the tax break it has requested. In order to prevent a major increase in local unemployment, the Hazelton government is considering granting the plant's request.

    Which of the following would be most important for the Hazelton government to determine before deciding whether to grant the plant's request?

    (A) Whether the company that owns the plant would open a new plant in another area if the present plant were closed
    (B) Whether the plant would employ far fewer workers when updated than it does now
    (C) Whether the level of pollutants presently being emitted by the plant is high enough to constitute a health hazard for local residents
    (D) Whether the majority of the coal processed by the plant is sold outside the Hazelton area
    (E) Whether the plant would be able to process more coal when updated than it does now

    Evaluation of a Plan

    Situation Because of the expenses of mandatory updating, a plant that is a major employer in the local area will close unless it receives the tax break it has requested from the local government.

    Reasoning *What point is most critical to the evaluation of the request?* Consider the information provided in the answer choices. The plant is important to the local government primarily because it is a major employer of local residents. What if updating the plant significantly reduced the number of employees needed? It is crucial for the local government to determine whether the plant will continue to employ the same number of people once it has updated.

    A The local government is concerned only with the local area, so a new site outside that area is irrelevant.
    B **Correct**. This statement properly identifies a factor that is critical to the plant's argument and the local government's decision.
    C Updating is mandatory under national environmental regulations, whether the local residents are affected by the plant's pollutants or not.
    D At issue is the plant's role as a major employer; where its product is sold is irrelevant.
    E The amount of coal processed by the updated plant is irrelevant to the critical issue of the number of people employed to process that coal.

    The correct answer is B.

78. A physically active lifestyle has been shown to help increase longevity. In the Wistar region of Bellaria, the average age at death is considerably higher than in any other part of the country. Wistar is the only mountainous part of Bellaria. A mountainous terrain makes even such basic activities as walking relatively strenuous; it essentially imposes a physically active lifestyle on people. Clearly, this circumstance explains the long lives of people in Wistar.

Which of the following, if true, most seriously weakens the argument?

(A) In Bellaria all medical expenses are paid by the government, so that personal income does not affect the quality of health care a person receives.
(B) The Wistar region is one of Bellaria's least populated regions.
(C) Many people who live in the Wistar region have moved there in middle age or upon retirement.
(D) The many opportunities for hiking, skiing, and other outdoor activities that Wistar's mountains offer make it a favorite destination for vacationing Bellarians.
(E) Per capita spending on recreational activities is no higher in Wistar than it is in other regions of Bellaria.

Argument Evaluation

Situation   People in one region of a country live longer than people in other areas. The higher average age at time of death is attributed to the healthy lifestyle of the people in this region, where the mountainous terrain demands a physically active life.

Reasoning   *What point weakens the argument?* Consider what assumption underlies the argument that the physically active lifestyle required of living in Wistar is responsible for its residents' relative longevity. The mountainous environment necessitates lifelong levels of rigorous physical activity that build a more robust population. What if a significant portion of the population has not been conditioned since childhood to the demands of the terrain? It is assumed here that the healthy lifestyle imposed by the terrain has shaped residents from birth and accounts for their longer life span. If many residents only moved there later in life, the argument is weakened.

A   The argument is not about the quality of health care throughout the country, but the length of the residents' lives in a particular region.
B   The rate of population density does not affect the argument.
C   **Correct.** This statement properly identifies a point that weakens the argument.
D   The area's popularity as a vacation destination does not affect the longevity of the local residents.
E   The argument establishes that merely living in the region is strenuous; the spending on recreational activities is irrelevant.

The correct answer is C.

79. Cheever College offers several online courses via remote computer connection, in addition to traditional classroom-based courses. A study of student performance at Cheever found that, overall, the average student grade for online courses matched that for classroom-based courses. In this calculation of the average grade, course withdrawals were weighted as equivalent to a course failure, and the rate of withdrawal was much lower for students enrolled in classroom-based courses than for students enrolled in online courses.

If the statements above are true, which of the following must also be true of Cheever College?

(A) Among students who did not withdraw, students enrolled in online courses got higher grades, on average, than students enrolled in classroom-based courses.

(B) The number of students enrolled per course at the start of the school term is much higher, on average, for the online courses than for the classroom-based courses.

(C) There are no students who take both an online and a classroom-based course in the same school term.

(D) Among Cheever College students with the best grades, a significant majority take online, rather than classroom-based, courses.

(E) Courses offered online tend to deal with subject matter that is less challenging than that of classroom-based courses.

Argument Construction

Situation   A comparison of online and classroom courses showed similar average grades. In determining average grades, a course withdrawal was weighted as a course failure. The rate of withdrawal was higher from online than from classroom courses.

Reasoning   *What conclusion about the courses can be derived from this comparison?* Consider the ramifications of the methodology used to calculate the grade averages for the two types of courses. Because of course withdrawals, the online courses experienced a higher rate of failure, but the average grade for these courses still matched the average grade for classroom courses. From this it is logical to conclude that, for the two averages to match, the students who remained in the online courses must have had higher initial average grades than those in classroom courses.

A   **Correct.** This statement properly identifies the logical conclusion that the higher percentage of withdrawals from online classes requires higher grades, on average, to compensate for the higher rate of failure.

B   A number of students cannot be derived from a discussion of average grades and rates of withdrawal.

C   This conclusion cannot be determined on the basis of the information provided.

D   The information is about average grades; the argument does not provide any basis for a conclusion about best grades.

E   It is impossible to determine the difficulty of subject matter from this information.

The correct answer is A.

80. For years the beautiful Renaissance buildings in Palitito have been damaged by exhaust from the many tour buses that come to the city. There has been little parking space, so most buses have idled at the curb during each stop on their tour, and idling produces as much exhaust as driving. The city has now provided parking that accommodates a third of the tour buses, so damage to Palitito's buildings from the buses' exhaust will diminish significantly.

    Which of the following, if true, most strongly supports the argument?

    (A) The exhaust from Palitito's few automobiles is not a significant threat to Palitito's buildings.
    (B) Palitito's Renaissance buildings are not threatened by pollution other than engine exhaust.
    (C) Tour buses typically spend less than one-quarter of the time they are in Palitito transporting passengers from one site to another.
    (D) More tourists come to Palitito by tour bus than by any other single means of transportation.
    (E) Some of the tour buses that are unable to find parking drive around Palitito while their passengers are visiting a site.

    Argument Evaluation

    Situation   Tour buses have damaged Renaissance buildings with their exhaust fumes because lack of parking has kept the buses idling at curbs. Providing new parking for a third of the buses should significantly reduce the damage caused by the exhaust.

    Reasoning   *What point strengthens the argument?* The argument for reduced damage relies on the reduction of the vehicles' exhaust fumes. Any additional evidence regarding the extent to which the vehicular emissions are likely to be reduced also supports the argument for the benefits of the new parking spaces. Learning that tour buses spend not just a few minutes but most of their time idling at the curb strengthens the argument. The new parking spaces will allow a third of the tour buses to spend 75 percent of their time with their engines off, causing no damage at all.

    A   If automobile exhaust is not a threat, the argument is not affected.
    B   This statement does not address the question of whether the new parking will reduce the damage caused by engine exhaust from the buses.
    C   **Correct.** This statement properly cites a factor that supports the argument: since most of the buses' time has been spent producing damaging exhaust, the new parking should reduce the damage significantly.
    D   This statement about tourists' chosen means of transportation is irrelevant to the issue of what the buses do while in the city.
    E   It is given that the new parking will only provide space for a third of the buses, and thus some buses will continue to idle and some to drive around, continuing to contribute equally to the building damage. This statement does not strengthen the argument.

    The correct answer is C.

81. During the 1980s and 1990s, the annual number of people who visited the Sordellian Mountains increased continually, and many new ski resorts were built. Over the same period, however, the number of visitors to ski resorts who were caught in avalanches decreased, even though there was no reduction in the annual number of avalanches in the Sordellian Mountains.

    Which of the following, if true in the Sordellian Mountains during the 1980s and 1990s, most helps to explain the decrease?

    (A) Avalanches were most likely to happen when a large new snowfall covered an older layer of snow.
    (B) Avalanches destroyed at least some buildings in the Sordellian Mountains in every year.
    (C) People planning new ski slopes and other resort facilities used increasingly accurate information about which locations are likely to be in the path of avalanches.
    (D) The average length of stay for people visiting the Sordellian Mountains increased slightly.
    (E) Construction of new ski resorts often led to the clearing of wooded areas that had helped prevent avalanches.

    Argument Construction

    Situation   Over a certain period, new ski resorts accommodated an increasing number of visitors at the same time that fewer visitors were caught in avalanches. Yet there were no fewer avalanches than usual during this period.

    Reasoning   *What explains the apparent contradiction of increased visitors but fewer visitors caught in avalanches?* More resort visitors would imply more avalanche-related accidents, but the average has shifted so that fewer visitors are being caught in the avalanches. It must be that fewer visitors are exposed to this danger; consider the answer choices to identify a logical reason for this improvement in their exposure. If the likely paths of avalanches had become better understood, that information would have been applied to identify safer locations for new ski slopes and ski resorts. The facilities would thus have been built well out of the way of avalanches, resulting in fewer visitors trapped in avalanches.

    A   This likelihood would remain true from year to year; it does not explain the decrease.
    B   This point does not explain why fewer visitors were caught in these avalanches.
    C   **Correct.** This statement properly identifies a factor that explains the decreased number of accidents.
    D   The greater length of stay would seem to expose visitors to greater danger.
    E   This information points to an expected increase, rather than decrease, in visitors who might be caught by avalanches.

    The correct answer is C.

82. A year ago, Dietz Foods launched a yearlong advertising campaign for its canned tuna. Last year Dietz sold 12 million cans of tuna compared to the 10 million sold during the previous year, an increase directly attributable to new customers brought in by the campaign. Profits from the additional sales, however, were substantially less than the cost of the advertising campaign. Clearly, therefore, the campaign did nothing to further Dietz's economic interests.

Which of the following, if true, most seriously weakens the argument?

(A) Sales of canned tuna account for a relatively small percentage of Dietz Foods' profits.
(B) Most of the people who bought Dietz's canned tuna for the first time as a result of the campaign were already loyal customers of other Dietz products.
(C) A less expensive advertising campaign would have brought in significantly fewer new customers for Dietz's canned tuna than did the campaign Dietz Foods launched last year.
(D) Dietz made money on sales of canned tuna last year.
(E) In each of the past five years, there was a steep, industry-wide decline in sales of canned tuna.

Argument Evaluation

Situation   An advertising campaign was responsible for increased sales of canned tuna. Since the profits from the increased sales were less than the costs of the campaign, the campaign did not contribute to the company's economic interests.

Reasoning   *Which point weakens the argument?* Consider the basis of the argument: if profits are lower than costs, the campaign made no contribution to the company's financial well-being. In what case might this be untrue? What if the advertising campaign reversed an industry-wide trend of declining sales? If Dietz experienced increasing sales, while other companies experienced decreased sales, then the campaign did contribute to the economic interests of the company, and the argument is considerably weakened.

A   The issue is not the percentage of profits that canned tuna contributes, but the success of the advertising campaign.
B   If the customers bought the tuna because of the campaign, it is irrelevant to the argument that they also bought other Dietz products.
C   This information neither strengthens nor weakens the argument.
D   The argument is not about profits only, but about whether the advertising campaign contributed to the economic interests of the company.
E   **Correct.** This statement properly identifies a factor that weakens the argument: the campaign secured the benefits of increased sales at a time when the entire industry was experiencing a decline in sales.

The correct answer is E.

Sentence Correction

The following discussion is intended to familiarize you with the most efficient and effective approaches to sentence correction questions. The particular questions in this chapter are generally representative of the kinds of sentence correction questions you will encounter on the GMAT exam. Remember that it is the problem solving strategy that is important, not the specific details of a particular question.

83. Unlike the buildings in Mesopotamian cities, which were arranged haphazardly, the same basic plan was followed for all cities of the Indus Valley: with houses laid out on a north-south, east-west grid, and houses and walls were built of standard-size bricks.

    (A) the buildings in Mesopotamian cities, which were arranged haphazardly, the same basic plan was followed for all cities of the Indus Valley: with houses

    (B) the buildings in Mesopotamian cities, which were haphazard in arrangement, the same basic plan was used in all cities of the Indus Valley: houses were

    (C) the arrangement of buildings in Mesopotamian cities, which were haphazard, the cities of the Indus Valley all followed the same basic plan: houses

    (D) Mesopotamian cities, in which buildings were arranged haphazardly, the cities of the Indus Valley all followed the same basic plan: houses were

    (E) Mesopotamian cities, which had buildings that were arranged haphazardly, the same basic plan was used for all cities in the Indus Valley: houses that were

    Comparison-contrast; Modifying clause

    The contrast introduced by *unlike* must be logical and clear. Contrasting *the buildings in Mesopotamian cities* with *the same basic plan* does not make sense; *Mesopotamian cities* should be contrasted with *the cities of the Indus Valley*. Also, it needs to be clear that it was the *buildings* in the cities that were *arranged haphazardly* rather than the *cities*. The second half of the sentence needs *houses were laid out* to be parallel in structure to *and houses and walls were built*.

    A   Illogically contrasts *the buildings in Mesopotamian cities* with *the same basic plan*; not clear whether *which were arranged haphazardly* modifies *cities or buildings*; *with houses* lacks parallelism and is confusing.

    B   Illogically contrasts *the buildings in Mesopotamian cities* with *the same basic plan*; does not clarify what *which were haphazard in arrangement* modifies.

    C   Illogically contrasts *the arrangement of buildings* with *the cities of the Indus Valley*; not clear whether *which were haphazard* modifies *buildings* or *cities*; *houses* not followed by a verb.

    D   **Correct.** In this sentence, *Mesopotamian cities* are properly contrasted with *the cities of the Indus Valley; in which buildings were arranged haphazardly* expresses the idea clearly; and *houses* is followed by *were* as required.

    E   Illogically contrasts *Mesopotamian cities* with *the same basic plan; houses that were* lacks parallelism and is confusing.

    The correct answer is D.

84. New data from United States Forest Service ecologists show that for every dollar spent on controlled small-scale burning, forest thinning, and the training of fire-management personnel, it saves seven dollars that would not be spent on having to extinguish big fires.

(A) that for every dollar spent on controlled small-scale burning, forest thinning, and the training of fire-management personnel, it saves seven dollars that would not be spent on having to extinguish

(B) that for every dollar spent on controlled small-scale burning, forest thinning, and the training of fire-management personnel, seven dollars are saved that would have been spent on extinguishing

(C) that for every dollar spent on controlled small-scale burning, forest thinning, and the training of fire-management personnel saves seven dollars on not having to extinguish

(D) for every dollar spent on controlled small-scale burning, forest thinning, and the training of fire-management personnel, that it saves seven dollars on not having to extinguish

(E) for every dollar spent on controlled small-scale burning, forest thinning, and the training of fire-management personnel, that seven dollars are saved that would not have been spent on extinguishing

Logical predication; Rhetorical construction

The pronoun *it* (*it saves seven dollars*) has no referent. Making *seven dollars* the subject of the clause eliminates this problem, and it also fulfills a reader's expectation that after the phrase beginning *for every dollar* another specific amount will be given to balance it. This change in structure also allows the awkward and wordy clause *that would not be spent on having to extinguish* to be rewritten so that *spent* balances *saved: seven dollars are saved that would have been spent on extinguishing*, and the unnecessary *having to* is omitted.

A *It* has no referent; *not be spent* is awkward; *on having to extinguish* is wordy.

B **Correct.** This sentence properly uses *seven dollars* as the subject of the clause to balance *every dollar* in the introductory phrase; the phrasing is concise and parallel.

C *Saves* does not have a subject; construction is not a complete sentence; *not having to extinguish* is wordy and awkward.

D *That* introduces a subordinate rather than main clause, making a sentence fragment; *it* has no referent; *not having to extinguish* is wordy and awkward.

E Introductory *that* makes a sentence fragment; *that would not have been spent on extinguishing* is awkward and illogical.

The correct answer is B.

85. Like the grassy fields and old pastures that the upland sandpiper needs for feeding and nesting when it returns in May after wintering in the Argentine Pampas, the sandpipers vanishing in the northeastern United States is a result of residential and industrial development and of changes in farming practices.

(A) the sandpipers vanishing in the northeastern United States is a result of residential and industrial development and of changes in

(B) the bird itself is vanishing in the northeastern United States as a result of residential and industrial development and of changes in

(C) that the birds themselves are vanishing in the northeastern United States is due to residential and industrial development and changes to

(D) in the northeastern United States, sandpipers' vanishing due to residential and industrial development and to changes in

(E) in the northeastern United States, the sandpipers' vanishing, a result of residential and industrial development and changing

Comparison; Sentence structure

The comparison introduced by *like* must be logical and clear; the point of this comparison is that both the habitat and the bird are disappearing for similar reasons. The comparison must use comparable grammatical components; *the bird itself* is a noun phrase and matches the noun phrases *grassy fields* and *old pastures*.

A   Illogically compares *the sandpipers vanishing* to *grassy fields and old pastures*; omits apostrophe in *sandpipers' vanishing*; wordy.

B   **Correct.** This sentence properly compares *the bird itself* to *grassy fields and old pastures*; *is vanishing* as the verb strengthens the sentence by making the comparison clearer.

C   Does not finish the comparison begun with *like* but instead substitutes a clause (*that the birds themselves are vanishing*).

D   Illogically compares *the sandpipers' vanishing* to *grassy fields and old pastures*; creates a sentence fragment.

E   Illogically compares *the sandpipers' vanishing* to *grassy fields and old pastures*; creates a sentence fragment.

The correct answer is B.

86. The results of two recent unrelated studies support the idea that dolphins may share certain cognitive abilities with humans and great apes; the studies indicate <u>dolphins as capable of recognizing themselves in mirrors—an ability that is often considered a sign of self-awareness—and to grasp spontaneously</u> the mood or intention of humans.

(A) dolphins as capable of recognizing themselves in mirrors—an ability that is often considered a sign of self-awareness—and to grasp spontaneously

(B) dolphins' ability to recognize themselves in mirrors—an ability that is often considered as a sign of self-awareness—and of spontaneously grasping

(C) dolphins to be capable of recognizing themselves in mirrors—an ability that is often considered a sign of self-awareness—and to grasp spontaneously

(D) that dolphins have the ability of recognizing themselves in mirrors—an ability that is often considered as a sign of self-awareness—and spontaneously grasping

(E) that dolphins are capable of recognizing themselves in mirrors—an ability that is often considered a sign of self-awareness—and of spontaneously grasping

Grammatical construction; Parallelism

In the context of this sentence, *the studies indicate* must introduce a clause; the clause must begin with *that* and have a subject, *dolphins*, and a verb, *are* (the complete verb phrase would be *are capable of*). The two capabilities should be parallel: *capable of recognizing…and of spontaneously grasping*.

A   Context requires a clause, but this construction is not a clause; *capable of recognizing* is not parallel to *to grasp spontaneously*.

B   Construction is not a clause, and a clause is required; *dolphins' ability to recognize* is not parallel to *of spontaneously grasping*.

C   A clause is required following *the studies indicate*; *to be capable of recognizing* is not parallel to *to grasp spontaneously*.

D   *Have the ability of* is wordy and unidiomatic; *of recognizing* and *spontaneously grasping* are not parallel.

E   **Correct.** *That* introduces the subordinate clause necessary to complete this sentence properly; *of recognizing* and *of spontaneously grasping* are parallel.

The correct answer is E.

87. According to scholars, the earliest writing was probably not a direct rendering of speech, but was more likely to begin as a separate and distinct symbolic system of communication, and only later merged with spoken language.

    (A) was more likely to begin as
    (B) more than likely began as
    (C) more than likely beginning from
    (D) it was more than likely begun from
    (E) it was more likely that it began

Idiom; Verb form

This sentence is a comparison in which *probably not x* is balanced by *but more than likely y*. When *more* is used in the comparative form of an adjective (*more difficult*) or adverb (*more likely*), it is followed by *than*. The words used to show the comparison between *x* and *y*, *but more than likely*, must also introduce the correct verb form, allowing *y* to fit grammatically into the rest of the sentence. The subject of the sentence has three verbs, all of which should be parallel: *the earliest writing was…began…merged*. *Was…to begin* is not parallel and results in a construction that is not grammatically correct.

A   In this context, *more likely* is not a complete idiomatic expression; *was…to begin* is not parallel to *was* and *merged*.

B   **Correct.** In this sentence, *more than likely* is the correct comparative construction; the simple past tense *began*, parallel to *was* and *merged*, fits grammatically into the sentence.

C   Subject should be followed by three verbs; *beginning from* is not a verb.

D   Use of the pronoun *it* makes this construction a main clause, in which case the comma after *communication* must be omitted and *began* must be used to be parallel to *merged*; *was…begun* is not the correct tense.

E   In this awkward, unclear, and wordy construction, the first *it* must be followed by *is*, not *was*, because the theory is current; the second *it* acts as the subject of the subordinate clause, and this usage requires the omission of the comma after *communication*.

The correct answer is B.

88. In 1995 Richard Stallman, a well-known critic of the patent system, testified in Patent Office hearings that, to test the system, a colleague of his had managed to win a patent for one of Kirchhoff's laws, an observation about electric current first made in 1845 and now included in virtually every textbook of elementary physics.

    (A) laws, an observation about electric current first made in 1845 and
    (B) laws, which was an observation about electric current first made in 1845 and it is
    (C) laws, namely, it was an observation about electric current first made in 1845 and
    (D) laws, an observation about electric current first made in 1845, it is
    (E) laws that was an observation about electric current, first made in 1845, and is

Logical predication; Parallelism

The function of the entire long phrase (*observation…physics*) that follows *one of Kirchhoff's laws* is to describe that law. It is a noun phrase in apposition, which means that it has the same syntactic relation to all the other parts of the sentence that the noun phrase *one of Kirchhoff's laws* does. Within the long modifying phrase, parallelism is maintained by balancing *an observation…first made* with *and now included*.

- **A** **Correct.** In this sentence, the noun phrase in apposition properly identifies and explains the law, using parallel structure and concise expression.
- **B** *Which* is ambiguous because it could refer to *one* or to *laws*; *it is* violates the parallelism of *first made* and *now included*.
- **C** *It* is ambiguous; the introduction of *it was* does not allow this construction to fit grammatically into the sentence.
- **D** The referent of *it* is unclear; *it is* creates a run-on sentence and violates the parallelism of *first made* and *now included*.
- **E** *That* appears to refer to *laws* rather than *one*, but the verb is singular; setting off the phrase *first made in 1845* in commas distorts meaning; *is* violates parallelism.

The correct answer is A.

89. Excavators at the Indus Valley site of Harappa in eastern Pakistan say the discovery of inscribed shards dating to circa 2800–2600 B.C. <u>indicate their development of a Harappan writing system, the use of</u> inscribed seals impressed into clay for marking ownership, and the standardization of weights for trade or taxation occurred many decades, if not centuries, earlier than was previously believed.

(A) indicate their development of a Harappan writing system, the use of
(B) indicate that the development of a Harappan writing system, using
(C) indicates that their development of a Harappan writing system, using
(D) indicates the development of a Harappan writing system, their use of
(E) indicates that the development of a Harappan writing system, the use of

Agreement; Idiom; Parallelism

In long sentences such as this one, the relationship between parts of the sentence may be difficult to see. Here, the main clause of the sentence is *excavators…say* and the logical sequence that follows is *the discovery…indicates that*. The subject of this first subordinate clause is the singular noun *discovery*, which should be followed by the singular verb *indicates* rather than by the plural *indicate*, as is done in the original sentence. *Their*, used with either *development* or *use*, has no clear or logical referent in any of the alternatives. The subject of the following subordinate (*that*) clause, which has *occurred* as its verb, is a series of three phrases, which must be parallel, especially in a sentence of this length and complexity: *the development of…, the use of…, and the standardization of…*.

- **A** *Indicate* does not agree with *discovery*; the pronoun *their* has no logical referent, and *their development* is not parallel to *the use* and *the standardization*.
- **B** *Indicate* does not agree with *discovery*; *using* is not parallel to *the development* and *the standardization*.
- **C** *Their* has no logical referent; the series of three elements should be parallel, but here all are different.
- **D** The pronoun *their* has no logical referent, and *their use* is not parallel to *the development* and *the standardization*; the preferred sentence structure would have *indicates* followed by *that* when introducing a clause.
- **E** **Correct.** In this sentence, *indicates* agrees with *discovery* and is followed by *that* to introduce a clause; the three parallel phrases begin with an article (*the*), a noun, and the preposition *of*.

The correct answer is E.

90. The Supreme Court has ruled that public universities can collect student activity fees even <u>with students' objections to particular activities, so long as the groups they give money to will be</u> chosen without regard to their views.

    (A) with students' objections to particular activities, so long as the groups they give money to will be
    (B) if they have objections to particular activities and the groups that are given the money are
    (C) if they object to particular activities, but the groups that the money is given to have to be
    (D) from students who object to particular activities, so long as the groups given money are
    (E) though students have an objection to particular activities, but the groups that are given the money be

Logical predication; Rhetorical construction

The underlined portion of the sentence fails to establish a clear relationship among *universities*, *students*, and *groups*. To which of these three does *they* refer? It would appear that the *universities* must give the money, but *they* does not have a referent. Furthermore, *they* is followed by *their views*, and in this case *their* must refer to *groups*. Wordy and awkward phrasing as well as an unnecessary shift in verb tense (*will be chosen*) compound the difficulty of understanding this sentence in its original form.

A   *With students' objections…* is awkward and dense; *they* does not have a referent; the future *will be* is incorrect since the Supreme Court *has* already *ruled*.

B   Referent for *they* is *student activity fees*, which cannot possibly *have objections…*; the use of *and* is illogical.

C   *They* refers to student *activity fees* rather than *students*; *but* does not have the requisite sense of *with the provision that*; *have to be* is wordy.

D   **Correct.** In this sentence, *from students who object* is clear and idiomatic; *so long as* is used appropriately; *groups given money* eliminates the problem of a pronoun without a referent; *are* is the proper tense.

E   *Have an objection* is an unnecessarily wordy way to say *object*; the verb *be* does not complete the latter part of the sentence.

The correct answer is D.

91. Despite the increasing number of women graduating from law school and passing bar examinations, <u>the proportion of judges and partners at major law firms who are women have not risen to a comparable extent.</u>

    (A) the proportion of judges and partners at major law firms who are women have not risen to a comparable extent
    (B) the proportion of women judges and partners at major law firms have not risen comparably
    (C) the proportion of judges and partners at major law firms who are women has not risen comparably
    (D) yet the proportion of women judges and partners at major law firms has not risen to a comparable extent
    (E) yet the proportion of judges and partners at major law firms who are women has not risen comparably

Agreement; Rhetorical construction

When a number of plural nouns appear in phrases between a singular subject and the verb, it can be easy to overlook the true subject of the verb. Here, *judges, partners, firms,* and *women* all occur between the singular subject, *proportion*, and the verb, which should also be singular, *has risen*. Concise expression is particularly important in a long construction; *to a comparable extent* may be more concisely expressed as *comparably*.

A   Plural verb, *have risen*, does not agree with the singular subject, *proportion*.

B   *Have risen* does not agree with *proportion*; here, *women* applies only to *judges*, not to *partners at major law firms*.

C   **Correct.** In this sentence, *has risen* agrees with *proportion*, and *comparably* is more concise than *to a comparable extent*. The modifying clause *who are women* follows (1) *judges* and (2) *partners at major law firms* as closely as is possible given the content of the sentence; this positioning has the virtue of being clear in its meaning.

D   The contrast has already been introduced by *despite*, so the addition of *yet* is illogical and ungrammatical; *to a comparable extent* is wordy.

E   *Despite* introduces the contrast; adding *yet* is illogical and results in an ungrammatical construction.

The correct answer is C.

92. Seldom more than 40 feet wide and 12 feet deep, but it ran 363 miles across the rugged wilderness of upstate New York, the Erie Canal connected the Hudson River at Albany to the Great Lakes at Buffalo, providing the port of New York City with a direct water link to the heartland of the North American continent.

(A) Seldom more than 40 feet wide and 12 feet deep, but it ran 363 miles across the rugged wilderness of upstate New York, the Erie Canal connected

(B) Seldom more than 40 feet wide or 12 feet deep but running 363 miles across the rugged wilderness of upstate New York, the Erie Canal connected

(C) It was seldom more than 40 feet wide and 12 feet deep, and ran 363 miles across the rugged wilderness of upstate New York, but the Erie Canal, connecting

(D) The Erie Canal was seldom more than 40 feet wide or 12 feet deep and it ran 363 miles across the rugged wilderness of upstate New York, which connected

(E) The Erie Canal, seldom more than 40 feet wide and 12 feet deep, but running 363 miles across the rugged wilderness of upstate New York, connecting

Logical predication; Grammatical construction

The phrase *seldom…deep* is the first half of a modifier that describes *the Erie Canal*. However, because a comma incorrectly follows *deep*, this phrase appears to be the entire modifier, which must agree with the noun or pronoun that immediately follows it. This phrase cannot modify the conjunction *but*, and *it* has no referent; *but it ran* is not a logical or grammatical construction following the modifying phrase. Substituting *running* for *it ran* creates an adjective phrase parallel to the first adjective phrase (*seldom…deep*). To contrast the small size reported in the first phrase with the great distance reported in the second, the two phrases may be joined with *but*; together they create a single modifier correctly modifying *the Erie Canal*. *The Erie Canal* is then the subject of the sentence and requires the verb *connected* to provide a logical statement.

A *But it ran* cannot logically or grammatically follow the modifying phrase.

B **Correct.** This sentence properly has the single modifier consisting of two contrasting parts.

C Neither *and* nor *but* acts as a logical connector; the use of *connecting* results in a sentence fragment.

D The paired concepts of width and depth should be joined by *and*, not *or*; this construction calls for two main clauses to be separated by a comma after *deep*; *which* is ambiguous.

E The two halves of the modifier should not be separated by a comma after *deep*; the subject is awkwardly and confusingly placed at a great distance from the predicate; the use of *connecting* rather than *connected* creates a sentence fragment.

The correct answer is B.

93. In 1923, the Supreme Court declared a minimum wage for women and children in the District of Columbia as unconstitutional, and ruling that it was a form of price-fixing and, as such, an abridgment of the right of contract.

(A) the Supreme Court declared a minimum wage for women and children in the District of Columbia as unconstitutional, and

(B) the Supreme Court declared as unconstitutional a minimum wage for women and children in the District of Columbia, and

(C) the Supreme Court declared unconstitutional a minimum wage for women and children in the District of Columbia,

(D) a minimum wage for women and children in the District of Columbia was declared unconstitutional by the Supreme Court,

(E) when the Supreme Court declared a minimum wage for women and children in the District of Columbia as unconstitutional,

Idiom; Grammatical construction

This sentence depends on the correct use of an idiom: *the court declares x unconstitutional*. The inverted form should be used here because of the long phrases involved: *the court declares unconstitutional x*. *The Supreme Court* is the subject of the sentence; *declared* is the verb. *Ruling... contract* acts as a modifier describing the action of the main clause; because the modifier is subordinate to the main clause, the conjunction *and* must be omitted. *And* is used to join two independent clauses, not a clause and its modifier.

A   *Declared...as unconstitutional* is not the correct idiom; the use of *and* creates an ungrammatical construction.

B   *Declared as unconstitutional* is not the correct idiom; the use of *and* creates an ungrammatical construction.

C   **Correct**. In this sentence, the correct idiom is used, and the modifier is grammatically and logically attached to the main clause.

D   Passive voice construction is weak and wordy; its use causes the modifier to be misplaced and ambiguous.

E   *Declared...as unconstitutional* is not the correct idiom; *when* transforms the main clause into a subordinate clause, resulting in a sentence fragment.

The correct answer is C.

94. Researchers have found that individuals who have been blind from birth, and <u>who thus have never seen anyone gesture, nevertheless make hand motions when speaking just as frequently and in virtually the same way as sighted people do, and that they will gesture</u> even when conversing with another blind person.

(A)   who thus have never seen anyone gesture, nevertheless make hand motions when speaking just as frequently and in virtually the same way as sighted people do, and that they will gesture

(B)   who thus never saw anyone gesturing, nevertheless make hand motions when speaking just as frequent and in virtually the same way as sighted people did, and that they will gesture

(C)   who thus have never seen anyone gesture, nevertheless made hand motions when speaking just as frequently and in virtually the same way as sighted people do, as well as gesturing

(D)   thus never having seen anyone gesture, nevertheless made hand motions when speaking just as frequent and in virtually the same way as sighted people did, as well as gesturing

(E)   thus never having seen anyone gesture, nevertheless to make hand motions when speaking just as frequently and in virtually the same way as sighted people do, and to gesture

Parallelism; Verb form; Diction

The researchers have found (1) *that individuals... make hand motions...as sighted people do* and (2) *that they will gesture...with another blind person*. In the original sentence, the two findings are reported in two parallel subordinate clauses introduced by *that*. The verb tenses are logical and parallel: *who have been blind* and *who have never seen* indicate a condition that began in the past and continues in the present; *make* and *do* refer to present actions. The verb *make (hand motions)* is correctly modified by the adverb *frequently* to show how the action of the verb is carried out. The emphatic future *will gesture* is properly used here with *even* to emphasize the extreme or the unexpected.

A **Correct.** Although the original sentence is complicated, the parallelism of its structure and phrasing allows its meaning to be clear and its expression effective.

B Verbs *saw* and *did* indicate action completed in the past; the simple past tense is not appropriate in either case; the adjective *frequent* cannot modify the verb; awkward and muddy.

C *Made* indicates past action, but the present tense is logically required; *as well as gesturing* violates the parallelism of the two subordinate (*that*) clauses; choppy and unclear.

D *Having seen* is not parallel to *have been*; *made* and *did* do not show ongoing action; *frequent* incorrectly modifies the verb; *as well as gesturing* destroys the parallelism of the two subordinate (*that*) clauses; awkward and unclear.

E Replacing the verb *make* with the infinitive *to make* results in an ungrammatical construction that fails to complete the sentence.

The correct answer is A.

95. Like embryonic germ cells, which are cells that develop early in the formation of the fetus and that later generate eggs or sperm, embryonic stem cells have the ability of developing themselves into different kinds of body tissue.

    (A) embryonic stem cells have the ability of developing themselves into different kinds of body tissue
    (B) embryonic stem cells have the ability to develop into different kinds of body tissue
    (C) in embryonic stem cells there is the ability to develop into different kinds of body tissue
    (D) the ability to develop themselves into different kinds of body tissue characterizes embryonic stem cells
    (E) the ability of developing into different kinds of body tissue characterizes embryonic stem cells

Idiom; Grammatical construction

Two constructions create problems in the original sentence. The first is the unidiomatic construction *have the ability of developing*; *ability* must be followed by an infinitive, *to develop*, not a phrase. The second problematic construction is *to develop themselves into*. In this biological context, the verb *develop* means to progress from an earlier to a later stage; it is used intransitively, which means that it cannot take an object. The pronoun *themselves* acts as an object, creating a construction that is not grammatical or logical. Omitting the pronoun removes the problem.

A *Ability* is incorrectly followed by *of developing*; a pronoun cannot follow *develop*, when it is used, as it is here, in its intransitive sense.

B **Correct.** *Ability* is properly followed by the infinitive in this sentence, and the pronoun *themselves* is omitted.

C This awkward and wordy construction violates the parallelism of *like embryonic germ cells…embryonic stem cells….*

D The two parts of the comparison must be parallel; *like embryonic germ cells* must be followed by *embryonic stem cells*, not *the ability to develop*.

E *Ability* is followed by the unidiomatic *of developing* rather than *to develop*; the main clause must begin with *embryonic stem cells* to balance and complete *like embryonic germ cells*.

The correct answer is B.

96. Critics contend that the new missile is a weapon whose importance is largely symbolic, more a tool for manipulating people's perceptions than to fulfill a real military need.

    (A) for manipulating people's perceptions than to fulfill
    (B) for manipulating people's perceptions than for fulfilling
    (C) to manipulate people's perceptions rather than that it fulfills
    (D) to manipulate people's perceptions rather than fulfilling
    (E) to manipulate people's perceptions than for fulfilling

Parallelism

This sentence uses the comparative construction *more x than y* where *x* and *y* must be parallel. Here, *x* is *a tool for manipulating people's perceptions*, and *y* is *to fulfill a real military need*. A *tool* does not need to be repeated in the second half of the comparison because it is understood, but the wording of the two phrases does need to match. There are two acceptable solutions: (1) *for manipulating* can be followed by *for fulfilling* or (2) *to manipulate* can be followed by *to fulfill*.

A   *For manipulating* is not parallel to *to fulfill*.

B   **Correct**. *For manipulating* and *for fulfilling* are parallel in this sentence.

C   *To manipulate* is not parallel to *that it fulfills*.

D   *To manipulate* is not parallel to *fulfilling*.

E   *To manipulate* is not parallel to *for fulfilling*.

The correct answer is B.

97. As an actress and, more importantly, as a teacher of acting, <u>Stella Adler was one of the most influential artists in the American theater, who trained several generations of actors including</u> Marlon Brando and Robert De Niro.

   (A) Stella Adler was one of the most influential artists in the American theater, who trained several generations of actors including

   (B) Stella Adler, one of the most influential artists in the American theater, trained several generations of actors who include

   (C) Stella Adler was one of the most influential artists in the American theater, training several generations of actors whose ranks included

   (D) one of the most influential artists in the American theater was Stella Adler, who trained several generations of actors including

   (E) one of the most influential artists in the American theater, Stella Adler, trained several generations of actors whose ranks included

Logical predication

The original sentence contains a number of modifiers, but not all of them are correctly expressed. The clause *who trained...* describes *Stella Adler*, yet a relative clause such as this one must be placed immediately after the noun or pronoun it modifies, and this clause follows *theater* rather than *Adler*. Replacing *who trained* with *training* corrects the error because the phrase *training...* modifies the whole preceding clause rather than the single preceding noun. *Several generations of actors including* shows the same error in reverse; *including* modifies the whole phrase, but the two actors named are not *generations of actors*. The more limiting clause *whose ranks included* (referring to *actors*) is appropriate here.

A   Relative (*who*) clause follows *theater* rather than *Adler*; *including* refers to *generations of actors*, when the reference should be to *actors* only.

B   This construction, in which the subject is both preceded and followed by modifiers, is awkward; the verbs should be consistently in the past tense, but *include* is present tense.

C   **Correct**. In this sentence, substituting *training* for *who trained* and *whose ranks included* for *including* eliminates the modification errors.

D   Introductory modifier must be immediately followed by *Stella Adler*, not *one...*; *including* refers to *generations of actors* rather than to *actors* only.

E   Introductory modifier must be immediately followed by *Stella Adler*, not one.

The correct answer is C.

98. By developing the Secure Digital Music Initiative, the recording industry associations of North America, Japan, and Europe hope to create a standardized way <u>of distributing songs and full-length recordings on the Internet that will protect copyright holders and foil the many audio pirates who copy and distribute</u> digital music illegally.

    (A) of distributing songs and full-length recordings on the Internet that will protect copyright holders and foil the many audio pirates who copy and distribute

    (B) of distributing songs and full-length recordings on the Internet and to protect copyright holders and foiling the many audio pirates copying and distributing

    (C) for distributing songs and full-length recordings on the Internet while it protects copyright holders and foils the many audio pirates who copy and distribute

    (D) to distribute songs and full-length recordings on the Internet while they will protect copyright holders and foil the many audio pirates copying and distributing

    (E) to distribute songs and full-length recordings on the Internet and it will protect copyright holders and foiling the many audio pirates who copy and distribute

    Parallelism

    The original sentence depends on the parallelism of its verbs to make its point clearly and effectively. *A standardized way…will protect* and (*will* understood) *foil*; *pirates…copy and distribute*. In the first pair of parallel verbs, *will* does not need to be repeated because it is understood.

    A **Correct.** The verbs *will protect* and (*will*) *foil* are parallel in this sentence, as are the verbs *copy* and *distribute*.

    B *And to protect* distorts meaning, suggesting that protection comes in addition to *the standardized way*; *foiling* is not parallel to *to protect*.

    C *Way for* should instead be *way of*; the pronoun reference in *while it protects* is ambiguous; construction suggests that protection comes from something other than the *standardized way*.

    D Pronoun *they* has no referent; use of *while* suggests that protection comes from something other than the *standardized way* of distribution.

    E *And it will protect* distorts meaning, suggesting that protection comes in addition to *the standardized way*; *will protect* and *foiling* are not parallel.

    The correct answer is A.

99. Whereas a ramjet generally cannot achieve high speeds without the initial assistance of a rocket, <u>high speeds can be attained by scramjets, or supersonic combustion ramjets, in that they reduce</u> airflow compression at the entrance of the engine and letting air pass through at supersonic speeds.

    (A) high speeds can be attained by scramjets, or supersonic combustion ramjets, in that they reduce

    (B) that high speeds can be attained by scramjets, or supersonic combustion ramjets, is a result of their reducing

    (C) the ability of scramjets, or supersonic combustion ramjets, to achieve high speeds is because they reduce

    (D) scramjets, or supersonic combustion ramjets, have the ability of attaining high speeds when reducing

    (E) scramjets, or supersonic combustion ramjets, can attain high speeds by reducing

Rhetorical construction

The underlined portion of the original sentence is wordy and ineffective. Transforming it from passive (*high speeds can be attained by scramjets*) to active voice (*scramjets can attain high speeds*) eliminates much of the problem. As the subject of the main clause, *scramjets* correctly parallels *a ramjet*, the subject of the subordinate clause; the contrast is thus clearly and effectively drawn. *In that they reduce* is wordy and awkward; it can be replaced by the more concise phrase *by reducing*.

A Passive voice contributes to a wordy, awkward, and ineffective construction; *in that they reduce* is also wordy and awkward.

B Passive voice and subordinate (*that*) clause constructions are wordy, awkward, and ineffective.

C *The ability…is because* is not a grammatical construction; *scramjets*, not *the ability*, should be parallel to *a ramjet*.

D *Have the ability of attaining* is wordy; *when* does not indicate the cause-and-effect relationship.

E **Correct**. *Scramjets* parallels *a ramjet* for an effective contrast in this sentence; the active voice is clear and concise; *by reducing* shows how scramjets attain high speeds.

The correct answer is E.

100. It will not be possible to implicate melting sea ice in the coastal flooding that many global warming models have projected: just <u>like a glass of water that will not overflow due to melting ice cubes,</u> so melting sea ice does not increase oceanic volume.

  (A) like a glass of water that will not overflow due to melting ice cubes,

  (B) like melting ice cubes that do not cause a glass of water to overflow,

  (C) a glass of water will not overflow because of melting ice cubes,

  (D) as melting ice cubes that do not cause a glass of water to overflow,

  (E) as melting ice cubes do not cause a glass of water to overflow,

Diction; Parallelism

The preposition *like* introduces nouns and noun phrases; the conjunction *as* introduces verbs or clauses, so *as* is required here. The comparative construction used here is *just as x so y; x* and *y* must be parallel. The *y* clause is written in effective subject-verb-object order: *melting sea ice does not increase oceanic volume*. The original wordy, awkward *x* clause is not parallel. To make it parallel, *melting ice cubes* should be the subject of the clause, *do not cause…to overflow* the verb phrase, and *a glass of water* the object.

A *Like* is used in place of *as*; the two elements of comparison are not parallel.

B *Like* is used in place of *as*; *that* violates parallelism.

C *As* or *just as* is needed to introduce the clause; the two clauses are not parallel.

D *That* violates the parallelism of the two clauses and creates an ungrammatical construction.

E **Correct**. This sentence has *just as* properly introducing the first clause, and the two clauses are parallel.

The correct answer is E.

4.0 Math Review

4.0 Math Review

To answer Quantitative Reasoning questions on the GMAT exam, you will need to be familiar with basic mathematical concepts and formulas. This chapter contains a list of the basic mathematical concepts, terms, and formulas that may appear or can be useful for answering Quantitative Reasoning questions on the GMAT exam. This chapter offers only a high-level overview, so if you find unfamiliar terms or concepts, you should consult other resources for a more detailed discussion and explanation.

Keep in mind that this knowledge of basic math, while necessary, is seldom sufficient in answering GMAT questions. Unlike traditional math problems that you may have encountered in school, GMAT Quantitative Reasoning questions require you to *apply* your knowledge of math. For example, rather than asking you to demonstrate your knowledge of prime factorization by listing the prime factors of a number, a GMAT question may require you to apply your knowledge of prime factorization and properties of exponents to simplify an algebraic expression with a radical.

To prepare for the GMAT Quantitative Reasoning section, we recommend starting with a review of the basic mathematical concepts and formulas to ensure that you have the foundational knowledge necessary for answering the questions, before moving on to practicing the application of this knowledge on real GMAT questions from past exams.

Section 4.1, "Arithmetic," includes the following topics:

1. Properties of Integers
2. Fractions
3. Decimals
4. Real Numbers
5. Ratio and Proportion
6. Percents
7. Powers and Roots of Numbers
8. Descriptive Statistics
9. Sets
10. Counting Methods
11. Discrete Probability

Section 4.2, "Algebra," does not extend beyond what is usually covered in a first-year high school algebra course. The topics included are as follows:

1. Simplifying Algebraic Expressions
2. Equations
3. Solving Linear Equations with One Unknown
4. Solving Two Linear Equations with Two Unknowns
5. Solving Equations by Factoring
6. Solving Quadratic Equations
7. Exponents
8. Inequalities
9. Absolute Value
10. Functions

Section 4.3, "Geometry," is limited primarily to measurement and intuitive geometry or spatial visualization. Extensive knowledge of theorems and the ability to construct proofs, skills that are usually developed in a formal geometry course, are not tested. The topics included in this section are the following:

1. Lines
2. Intersecting Lines and Angles
3. Perpendicular Lines
4. Parallel Lines
5. Polygons (Convex)
6. Triangles
7. Quadrilaterals
8. Circles
9. Rectangular Solids and Cylinders
10. Coordinate Geometry

Section 4.4, "Word Problems," presents examples of and solutions to the following types of word problems:

1. Rate Problems
2. Work Problems
3. Mixture Problems
4. Interest Problems
5. Discount
6. Profit
7. Sets
8. Geometry Problems
9. Measurement Problems
10. Data Interpretation

4.1 Arithmetic

1. Properties of Integers

An *integer* is any number in the set $\{\ldots -3, -2, -1, 0, 1, 2, 3, \ldots\}$. If x and y are integers and $x \neq 0$, then x is a *divisor* (*factor*) of y provided that $y = xn$ for some integer n. In this case, y is also said to be *divisible* by x or to be a *multiple* of x. For example, 7 is a divisor or factor of 28 since $28 = (7)(4)$, but 8 is not a divisor of 28 since there is no integer n such that $28 = 8n$.

If x and y are positive integers, there exist unique integers q and r, called the *quotient* and *remainder*, respectively, such that $y = xq + r$ and $0 \leq r < x$. For example, when 28 is divided by 8, the quotient is 3 and the remainder is 4 since $28 = (8)(3) + 4$. Note that y is divisible by x if and only if the remainder r is 0; for example, 32 has a remainder of 0 when divided by 8 because 32 is divisible by 8. Also, note that when a smaller integer is divided by a larger integer, the quotient is 0 and the remainder is the smaller integer. For example, 5 divided by 7 has the quotient 0 and the remainder 5 since $5 = (7)(0) + 5$.

Any integer that is divisible by 2 is an *even integer*; the set of even integers is $\{\ldots -4, -2, 0, 2, 4, 6, 8, \ldots\}$. Integers that are not divisible by 2 are *odd integers*; $\{\ldots -3, -1, 1, 3, 5, \ldots\}$ is the set of odd integers.

If at least one factor of a product of integers is even, then the product is even; otherwise the product is odd. If two integers are both even or both odd, then their sum and their difference are even. Otherwise, their sum and their difference are odd.

A *prime* number is a positive integer that has exactly two different positive divisors, 1 and itself. For example, 2, 3, 5, 7, 11, and 13 are prime numbers, but 15 is not, since 15 has four different positive divisors, 1, 3, 5, and 15. The number 1 is not a prime number since it has only one positive divisor. Every integer greater than 1 either is prime or can be uniquely expressed as a product of prime factors. For example, $14 = (2)(7)$, $81 = (3)(3)(3)(3)$, and $484 = (2)(2)(11)(11)$.

The numbers $-2, -1, 0, 1, 2, 3, 4, 5$ are *consecutive integers*. Consecutive integers can be represented by $n, n + 1, n + 2, n + 3, \ldots$, where n is an integer. The numbers $0, 2, 4, 6, 8$ are *consecutive even integers*, and $1, 3, 5, 7, 9$ are *consecutive odd integers*. Consecutive even integers can be represented by $2n, 2n + 2, 2n + 4, \ldots$, and consecutive odd integers can be represented by $2n + 1, 2n + 3, 2n + 5, \ldots$, where n is an integer.

Properties of the integer 1. If n is any number, then $1 \cdot n = n$, and for any number $n \neq 0$, $n \cdot \frac{1}{n} = 1$.

The number 1 can be expressed in many ways; for example, $\frac{n}{n} = 1$ for any number $n \neq 0$.

Multiplying or dividing an expression by 1, in any form, does not change the value of that expression.

Properties of the integer 0. The integer 0 is neither positive nor negative. If n is any number, then $n + 0 = n$ and $n \cdot 0 = 0$. Division by 0 is not defined.

2. Fractions

In a fraction $\frac{n}{d}$, n is the *numerator* and d is the *denominator*. The denominator of a fraction can never be 0, because division by 0 is not defined.

Two fractions are said to be *equivalent* if they represent the same number. For example, $\frac{8}{36}$ and $\frac{14}{63}$ are equivalent since they both represent the number $\frac{2}{9}$. In each case, the fraction is reduced to lowest terms by dividing both numerator and denominator by their *greatest common divisor* (gcd). The gcd of 8 and 36 is 4 and the gcd of 14 and 63 is 7.

Addition and subtraction of fractions.

Two fractions with the same denominator can be added or subtracted by performing the required operation with the numerators, leaving the denominators the same. For example, $\frac{3}{5} + \frac{4}{5} = \frac{3+4}{5} = \frac{7}{5}$ and $\frac{5}{7} - \frac{2}{7} = \frac{5-2}{7} = \frac{3}{7}$. If two fractions do not have the same denominator, express them as equivalent fractions with the same denominator. For example, to add $\frac{3}{5}$ and $\frac{4}{7}$, multiply the numerator and denominator of the first fraction by 7 and the numerator and denominator of the second fraction by 5, obtaining $\frac{21}{35}$ and $\frac{20}{35}$, respectively; $\frac{21}{35} + \frac{20}{35} = \frac{41}{35}$.

For the new denominator, choosing the *least common multiple* (lcm) of the denominators usually lessens the work. For $\frac{2}{3} + \frac{1}{6}$, the lcm of 3 and 6 is 6 (not $3 \times 6 = 18$), so $\frac{2}{3} + \frac{1}{6} = \frac{2}{3} \times \frac{2}{2} + \frac{1}{6} = \frac{4}{6} + \frac{1}{6} = \frac{5}{6}$.

Multiplication and division of fractions.

To multiply two fractions, simply multiply the two numerators and multiply the two denominators. For example, $\frac{2}{3} \times \frac{4}{7} = \frac{2 \times 4}{3 \times 7} = \frac{8}{21}$.

To divide by a fraction, invert the divisor (that is, find its *reciprocal*) and multiply. For example, $\frac{2}{3} \div \frac{4}{7} = \frac{2}{3} \times \frac{7}{4} = \frac{14}{12} = \frac{7}{6}$.

In the problem above, the reciprocal of $\frac{4}{7}$ is $\frac{7}{4}$. In general, the reciprocal of a fraction $\frac{n}{d}$ is $\frac{d}{n}$, where n and d are not zero.

Mixed numbers.

A number that consists of a whole number and a fraction, for example, $7\frac{2}{3}$, is a mixed number: $7\frac{2}{3}$ means $7 + \frac{2}{3}$.

To change a mixed number into a fraction, multiply the whole number by the denominator of the fraction and add this number to the numerator of the fraction; then put the result over the denominator of the fraction. For example, $7\frac{2}{3} = \frac{(3 \times 7) + 2}{3} = \frac{23}{3}$.

3. Decimals

In the decimal system, the position of the period or *decimal point* determines the place value of the digits. For example, the digits in the number 7,654.321 have the following place values:

Thousands		Hundreds	Tens	Ones or units		Tenths	Hundredths	Thousandths
7	,	6	5	4	.	3	2	1

Some examples of decimals follow.

$$0.321 = \frac{3}{10} + \frac{2}{100} + \frac{1}{1,000} = \frac{321}{1,000}$$

$$0.0321 = \frac{0}{10} + \frac{3}{100} + \frac{2}{1,000} + \frac{1}{10,000} = \frac{321}{10,000}$$

$$1.56 = 1 + \frac{5}{10} + \frac{6}{100} = \frac{156}{100}$$

Sometimes decimals are expressed as the product of a number with only one digit to the left of the decimal point and a power of 10. This is called *scientific notation*. For example, 231 can be written as 2.31×10^2 and 0.0231 can be written as 2.31×10^{-2}. When a number is expressed in scientific notation, the exponent of the 10 indicates the number of places that the decimal point is to be moved in the number that is to be multiplied by a power of 10 in order to obtain the product. The decimal point is moved to the right if the exponent is positive and to the left if the exponent is negative. For example, 2.013×10^4 is equal to 20,130 and 1.91×10^{-4} is equal to 0.000191.

Addition and subtraction of decimals.

To add or subtract two decimals, the decimal points of both numbers should be lined up. If one of the numbers has fewer digits to the right of the decimal point than the other, zeros may be inserted to the right of the last digit. For example, to add 17.6512 and 653.27, set up the numbers in a column and add:

$$\begin{array}{r} 17.6512 \\ + 653.2700 \\ \hline 670.9212 \end{array}$$

Likewise for 653.27 minus 17.6512:

$$\begin{array}{r} 653.2700 \\ -17.6512 \\ \hline 635.6188 \end{array}$$

Multiplication of decimals.

To multiply decimals, multiply the numbers as if they were whole numbers and then insert the decimal point in the product so that the number of digits to the right of the decimal point is equal to the sum of the numbers of digits to the right of the decimal points in the numbers being multiplied. For example:

$$
\begin{array}{r}
2.09 \quad \text{(2 digits to the right)} \\
\times 1.3 \quad \text{(1 digit to the right)} \\
\hline
627 \\
2090 \\
\hline
2.717 \quad \text{(2+1=3 digits to the right)}
\end{array}
$$

Division of decimals.

To divide a number (the dividend) by a decimal (the divisor), move the decimal point of the divisor to the right until the divisor is a whole number. Then move the decimal point of the dividend the same number of places to the right, and divide as you would by a whole number. The decimal point in the quotient will be directly above the decimal point in the new dividend. For example, to divide 698.12 by 12.4:

$$12.4\overline{)698.12}$$

will be replaced by:

$$124\overline{)6981.2}$$

and the division would proceed as follows:

$$
\begin{array}{r}
56.3 \\
124\overline{)6981.2} \\
\underline{620} \\
781 \\
\underline{744} \\
372 \\
\underline{372} \\
0
\end{array}
$$

4. Real Numbers

All *real* numbers correspond to points on the number line and all points on the number line correspond to real numbers. All real numbers except zero are either positive or negative.

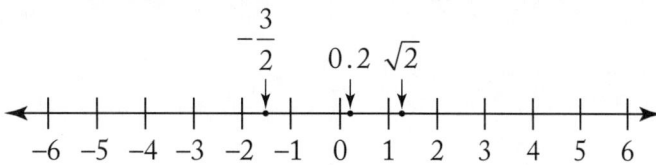

On a number line, numbers corresponding to points to the left of zero are negative and numbers corresponding to points to the right of zero are positive. For any two numbers on the number line, the number to the left is less than the number to the right; for example, $-4 < -3 < -\frac{3}{2} < -1$, and $1 < \sqrt{2} < 2$.

To say that the number n is between 1 and 4 on the number line means that $n > 1$ and $n < 4$, that is, $1 < n < 4$. If n is "between 1 and 4, inclusive," then $1 \leq n \leq 4$.

The distance between a number and zero on the number line is called the *absolute value* of the number. Thus 3 and −3 have the same absolute value, 3, since they are both three units from zero. The absolute value of 3 is denoted $|3|$. Examples of absolute values of numbers are

$$|-5| = |5| = 5, \left|-\frac{7}{2}\right| = \frac{7}{2}, \text{ and } |0| = 0.$$

Note that the absolute value of any nonzero number is positive.

Here are some properties of real numbers that are used frequently. If x, y, and z are real numbers, then

(1) $x + y = y + x$ and $xy = yx$.
For example, $8 + 3 = 3 + 8 = 11$, and $(17)(5) = (5)(17) = 85$.

(2) $(x + y) + z = x + (y + z)$ and $(xy)z = x(yz)$.
For example, $(7 + 5) + 2 = 7 + (5 + 2) = 7 + (7) = 14$, and $\left(5\sqrt{3}\right)\left(\sqrt{3}\right) = (5)\left(\sqrt{3}\sqrt{3}\right) = (5)(3) = 15$.

(3) $xy + xz = x(y + z)$.
For example, $718(36) + 718(64) = 718(36 + 64) = 718(100) = 71{,}800$.

(4) If x and y are both positive, then $x + y$ and xy are positive.

(5) If x and y are both negative, then $x + y$ is negative and xy is positive.

(6) If x is positive and y is negative, then xy is negative.

(7) If $xy = 0$, then $x = 0$ or $y = 0$. For example, $3y = 0$ implies $y = 0$.

(8) $|x + y| \leq |x| + |y|$. For example, if $x = 10$ and $y = 2$, then $|x + y| = |12| = 12 = |x| + |y|$; and if $x = 10$ and $y = -2$, then $|x + y| = |8| = 8 < 12 = |x| + |y|$.

5. Ratio and Proportion

The *ratio* of the number a to the number b ($b \neq 0$) is $\frac{a}{b}$.

A ratio may be expressed or represented in several ways. For example, the ratio of 2 to 3 can be written as 2 to 3, 2:3, or $\frac{2}{3}$. The order of the terms of a ratio is important. For example, the ratio of the number of months with exactly 30 days to the number with exactly 31 days is $\frac{4}{7}$, not $\frac{7}{4}$.

A *proportion* is a statement that two ratios are equal; for example, $\frac{2}{3} = \frac{8}{12}$ is a proportion. One way to solve a proportion involving an unknown is to cross multiply, obtaining a new equality. For example, to solve for n in the proportion $\frac{2}{3} = \frac{n}{12}$, cross multiply, obtaining $24 = 3n$; then divide both sides by 3, to get $n = 8$.

6. Percents

Percent means *per hundred* or *number out of 100*. A percent can be represented as a fraction with a denominator of 100, or as a decimal. For example:

$$37\% = \frac{37}{100} = 0.37.$$

To find a certain percent of a number, multiply the number by the percent expressed as a decimal or fraction. For example:

$$20\% \text{ of } 90 = 0.2 \times 90 = 18$$

or

$$20\% \text{ of } 90 = \frac{20}{100} \times 90 = \frac{1}{5} \times 90 = 18.$$

Percents greater than 100%.

Percents greater than 100% are represented by numbers greater than 1. For example:

$$300\% = \frac{300}{100} = 3$$

$$250\% \text{ of } 80 = 2.5 \times 80 = 200.$$

Percents less than 1%.

The percent 0.5% means $\frac{1}{2}$ of 1 percent. For example, 0.5% of 12 is equal to $0.005 \times 12 = 0.06$.

Percent change.

Often a problem will ask for the percent increase or decrease from one quantity to another quantity. For example, "If the price of an item increases from $24 to $30, what is the percent increase in price?" To find the percent increase, first find the amount of the increase; then divide this increase by the original amount, and express this quotient as a percent. In the example above, the percent increase would be found in the following way: the amount of the increase is $(30 - 24) = 6$. Therefore, the percent increase is $\frac{6}{24} = 0.25 = 25\%$.

Likewise, to find the percent decrease (for example, the price of an item is reduced from $30 to $24), first find the amount of the decrease; then divide this decrease by the original amount, and express this quotient as a percent. In the example above, the amount of decrease is $(30 - 24) = 6$. Therefore, the percent decrease is $\frac{6}{30} = 0.20 = 20\%$.

Note that the percent increase from 24 to 30 is not the same as the percent decrease from 30 to 24.

In the following example, the increase is greater than 100 percent: If the cost of a certain house in 1983 was 300 percent of its cost in 1970, by what percent did the cost increase?

If n is the cost in 1970, then the percent increase is equal to $\frac{3n-n}{n} = \frac{2n}{n} = 2$, or 200%.

7. Powers and Roots of Numbers

When a number k is to be used n times as a factor in a product, it can be expressed as k^n, which means the nth power of k. For example, $2^2 = 2 \times 2 = 4$ and $2^3 = 2 \times 2 \times 2 = 8$ are powers of 2.

Squaring a number that is greater than 1, or raising it to a higher power, results in a larger number; squaring a number between 0 and 1 results in a smaller number. For example:

$$3^2 = 9 \qquad (9 > 3)$$
$$\left(\frac{1}{3}\right)^2 = \frac{1}{9} \qquad \left(\frac{1}{9} < \frac{1}{3}\right)$$
$$(0.1)^2 = 0.01 \quad (0.01 < 0.1)$$

A *square root* of a number n is a number that, when squared, is equal to n. The square root of a negative number is not a real number. Every positive number n has two square roots, one positive and the other negative, but $\sqrt{n}$ denotes the positive number whose square is n. For example, $\sqrt{9}$ denotes 3. The two square roots of 9 are $\sqrt{9} = 3$ and $-\sqrt{9} = -3$.

Every real number r has exactly one real *cube root*, which is the number s such that $s^3 = r$. The real cube root of r is denoted by $\sqrt[3]{r}$. Since $2^3 = 8$, $\sqrt[3]{8} = 2$. Similarly, $\sqrt[3]{-8} = -2$, because $(-2)^3 = -8$.

8. Descriptive Statistics

A list of numbers, or numerical data, can be described by various statistical measures. One of the most common of these measures is the *average*, or *(arithmetic) mean,* which locates a type of "center" for the data. The average of n numbers is defined as the sum of the n numbers divided by n. For example, the average of 6, 4, 7, 10, and 4 is $\frac{6+4+7+10+4}{5} = \frac{31}{5} = 6.2$.

The *median* is another type of center for a list of numbers. To calculate the median of n numbers, first order the numbers from least to greatest; if n is odd, the median is defined as the middle number, whereas if n is even, the median is defined as the average of the two middle numbers. In the example above, the numbers, in order, are 4, 4, 6, 7, 10, and the median is 6, the middle number.

For the numbers 4, 6, 6, 8, 9, 12, the median is $\frac{6+8}{2} = 7$. Note that the mean of these numbers is 7.5.

The median of a set of data can be less than, equal to, or greater than the mean. Note that for a large set of data (for example, the salaries of 800 company employees), it is often true that about half of the data is less than the median and about half of the data is greater than the median; but this is not always the case, as the following data show.

3, 5, 7, 7, 7, 7, 7, 7, 8, 9, 9, 9, 9, 10, 10

Here the median is 7, but only $\frac{2}{15}$ of the data is less than the median.

The *mode* of a list of numbers is the number that occurs most frequently in the list. For example, the mode of 1, 3, 6, 4, 3, 5 is 3. A list of numbers may have more than one mode. For example, the list 1, 2, 3, 3, 3, 5, 7, 10, 10, 10, 20 has two modes, 3 and 10.

The degree to which numerical data are spread out or dispersed can be measured in many ways. The simplest measure of dispersion is the *range*, which is defined as the greatest value in the numerical data minus the least value. For example, the range of 11, 10, 5, 13, 21 is $21 - 5 = 16$. Note how the range depends on only two values in the data.

One of the most common measures of dispersion is the *standard deviation*. Generally speaking, the more the data are spread away from the mean, the greater the standard deviation. The standard deviation of n numbers can be calculated as follows: (1) find the arithmetic mean, (2) find the differences between the mean and each of the n numbers, (3) square each of the differences, (4) find the average of the squared differences, and (5) take the nonnegative square root of this average. Shown below is this calculation for the data 0, 7, 8, 10, 10, which have arithmetic mean 7.

x	$x - 7$	$(x - 7)^2$
0	-7	49
7	0	0
8	1	1
10	3	9
10	3	9
Total		68

Standard deviation $\sqrt{\dfrac{68}{5}} \approx 3.7$

Notice that the standard deviation depends on every data value, although it depends most on values that are farthest from the mean. This is why a distribution with data grouped closely around the mean will have a smaller standard deviation than will data spread far from the mean. To illustrate this, compare the data 6, 6, 6.5, 7.5, 9, which also have mean 7. Note that the numbers in the second set of data seem to be grouped more closely around the mean of 7 than the numbers in the first set. This is reflected in the standard deviation, which is less for the second set (approximately 1.1) than for the first set (approximately 3.7).

There are many ways to display numerical data that show how the data are distributed. One simple way is with a *frequency distribution*, which is useful for data that have values occurring with varying frequencies. For example, the 20 numbers

$$-4 \quad 0 \quad 0 \quad -3 \quad -2 \quad -1 \quad -1 \quad 0 \quad -1 \quad -4$$
$$-1 \quad -5 \quad 0 \quad -2 \quad 0 \quad -5 \quad -2 \quad 0 \quad 0 \quad -1$$

are displayed on the next page in a frequency distribution by listing each different value x and the frequency f with which x occurs.

Data Value x	Frequency f
−5	2
−4	2
−3	1
−2	3
−1	5
0	7
Total	20

From the frequency distribution, one can readily compute descriptive statistics:

Mean: $=\dfrac{(-5)(2)+(-4)(2)+(-3)(1)+(-2)(3)+(-1)(5)+(0)(7)}{20}=-1.6$

Median: −1 (the average of the 10th and 11th numbers)

Mode: 0 (the number that occurs most frequently)

Range: $0-(-5)=5$

Standard deviation: $\sqrt{\dfrac{(-5+1.6)^2(2)+(-4+1.6)^2(2)+\ldots+(0+1.6)^2(7)}{20}}\approx 1.7$

9. Sets

In mathematics a *set* is a collection of numbers or other objects. The objects are called the *elements* of the set. If S is a set having a finite number of elements, then the number of elements is denoted by $|S|$. Such a set is often defined by listing its elements; for example, $S = \{-5, 0, 1\}$ is a set with $|S| = 3$. The order in which the elements are listed in a set does not matter; thus $\{-5, 0, 1\} = \{0, 1, -5\}$. If all the elements of a set S are also elements of a set T, then S is a *subset* of T; for example, $S = \{-5, 0, 1\}$ is a subset of $T = \{-5, 0, 1, 4, 10\}$.

For any two sets A and B, the *union* of A and B is the set of all elements that are in A or in B or in both. The *intersection* of A and B is the set of all elements that are both in A and in B. The union is denoted by $A \cup B$ and the intersection is denoted by $A \cap B$. As an example, if $A = \{3, 4\}$ and $B = \{4, 5, 6\}$, then $A \cup B = \{3, 4, 5, 6\}$ and $A \cap B = \{4\}$. Two sets that have no elements in common are said to be *disjoint* or *mutually exclusive*.

The relationship between sets is often illustrated with a *Venn diagram* in which sets are represented by regions in a plane. For two sets S and T that are not disjoint and neither is a subset of the other, the intersection $S \cap T$ is represented by the shaded region of the diagram below.

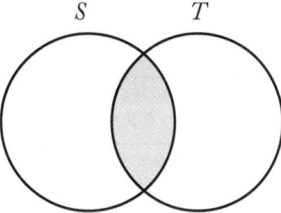

This diagram illustrates a fact about any two finite sets S and T: the number of elements in their union equals the sum of their individual numbers of elements minus the number of elements in their intersection (because the latter are counted twice in the sum); more concisely,

$$|S \cup T| = |S| + |T| - |S \cap T|.$$

This counting method is called the general addition rule for two sets. As a special case, if S and T are disjoint, then

$$|S \cup T| = |S| + |T|$$

since $|S \cap T| = 0$.

10. Counting Methods

There are some useful methods for counting objects and sets of objects without actually listing the elements to be counted. The following principle of multiplication is fundamental to these methods.

If an object is to be chosen from a set of m objects and a second object is to be chosen from a different set of n objects, then there are mn ways of choosing both objects simultaneously.

As an example, suppose the objects are items on a menu. If a meal consists of one entree and one dessert and there are 5 entrees and 3 desserts on the menu, then there are $5 \times 3 = 15$ different meals that can be ordered from the menu. As another example, each time a coin is flipped, there are two possible outcomes, heads and tails. If an experiment consists of 8 consecutive coin flips, then the experiment has 2^8 possible outcomes, where each of these outcomes is a list of heads and tails in some order.

A symbol that is often used with the multiplication principle is the *factorial*. If n is an integer greater than 1, then n factorial, denoted by the symbol $n!$, is defined as the product of all the integers from 1 to n. Therefore,

$$2! = (1)(2) = 2,$$
$$3! = (1)(2)(3) = 6,$$
$$4! = (1)(2)(3)(4) = 24, \text{ etc.}$$

Also, by definition, $0! = 1! = 1$.

The factorial is useful for counting the number of ways that a set of objects can be ordered. If a set of n objects is to be ordered from 1st to nth, then there are n choices for the 1st object, $n - 1$ choices for the 2nd object, $n - 2$ choices for the 3rd object, and so on, until there is only 1 choice for the nth object.

Thus, by the multiplication principle, the number of ways of ordering the n objects is

$n(n-1)(n-2)\cdots(3)(2)(1) = n!.$

For example, the number of ways of ordering the letters A, B, and C is 3!, or 6:

ABC, ACB, BAC, BCA, CAB, and CBA.

These orderings are called the *permutations* of the letters A, B, and C.

A permutation can be thought of as a selection process in which objects are selected one by one in a certain order. If the order of selection is not relevant and only k objects are to be selected from a larger set of n objects, a different counting method is employed.

Specifically, consider a set of n objects from which a complete selection of k objects is to be made without regard to order, where $0 \leq k \leq n$. Then the number of possible complete selections of k objects is called the number of *combinations* of n objects taken k at a time and is denoted by $\binom{n}{k}$.

The value of $\binom{n}{k}$ is given by $\binom{n}{k} = \dfrac{n!}{k!(n-k)!}$.

Note that $\binom{n}{k}$ is the number of k-element subsets of a set with n elements. For example, if $S = \{A, B, C, D, E\}$, then the number of 2-element subsets of S, or the number of combinations of 5 letters taken 2 at a time, is $\binom{5}{2} = \dfrac{5!}{2!3!} = \dfrac{120}{(2)(6)} = 10.$

The subsets are {A, B}, {A, C}, {A, D}, {A, E}, {B, C}, {B, D}, {B, E}, {C, D}, {C, E}, and {D, E}. Note that $\binom{5}{2} = 10 = \binom{5}{3}$ because every 2-element subset chosen from a set of 5 elements corresponds to a unique 3-element subset consisting of the elements *not* chosen.

In general, $\binom{n}{k} = \binom{n}{n-k}$.

11. Discrete Probability

Many of the ideas discussed in the preceding three topics are important to the study of discrete probability. Discrete probability is concerned with *experiments* that have a finite number of *outcomes*. Given such an experiment, an *event* is a particular set of outcomes. For example, rolling a number cube with faces numbered 1 to 6 (similar to a 6-sided die) is an experiment with 6 possible outcomes: 1, 2, 3, 4, 5, or 6. One event in this experiment is that the outcome is 4, denoted {4}; another event is that the outcome is an odd number: {1, 3, 5}.

The probability that an event E occurs, denoted by $P(E)$, is a number between 0 and 1, inclusive. If E has no outcomes, then E is *impossible* and $P(E) = 0$; if E is the set of all possible outcomes of the experiment, then E is *certain* to occur and $P(E) = 1$. Otherwise, E is possible but uncertain, and $0 < P(E) < 1$. If F is a subset of E, then $P(F) \leq P(E)$. In the example above, if the probability of each of the 6 outcomes is the same, then the probability of each outcome is $\dfrac{1}{6}$, and the outcomes are said to be *equally likely*. For experiments in which all the individual outcomes are equally likely, the probability of an event E is

$$P(E) = \frac{\text{The number of outcomes in } E}{\text{The total number of possible outcomes}}.$$

In the example, the probability that the outcome is an odd number is

$$P(\{1,3,5\}) = \frac{|\{1,3,5\}|}{6} = \frac{3}{6} = \frac{1}{2}.$$

Given an experiment with events E and F, the following events are defined:
"*not E*" is the set of outcomes that are not outcomes in E;
"*E or F*" is the set of outcomes in E or F or both, that is, $E \cup F$;
"*E and F*" is the set of outcomes in both E and F, that is, $E \cap F$.

The probability that E does not occur is $P(\text{not } E) = 1 - P(E)$. The probability that "$E$ or F" occurs is $P(E \text{ or } F) = P(E) + P(F) - P(E \text{ and } F)$, using the general addition rule at the end of section 4.1.9 ("Sets"). For the number cube, if E is the event that the outcome is an odd number, $\{1, 3, 5\}$, and F is the event that the outcome is a prime number, $\{2, 3, 5\}$, then $P(E \text{ and } F) = P(\{3,5\}) = \frac{2}{6} = \frac{1}{3}$ and so

$$P(E \text{ or } F) = P(E) + P(F) - P(E \text{ and } F) = \frac{3}{6} + \frac{3}{6} - \frac{2}{6} = \frac{4}{6} = \frac{2}{3}.$$

Note that the event "E or F" is $E \cup F = \{1, 2, 3, 5\}$, and hence $P(E \text{ or } F) = \frac{|\{1,2,3,5\}|}{6} = \frac{4}{6} = \frac{2}{3}$.

If the event "E and F" is impossible (that is, $E \cap F$ has no outcomes), then E and F are said to be *mutually exclusive* events, and $P(E \text{ and } F) = 0$. Then the general addition rule is reduced to $P(E \text{ or } F) = P(E) + P(F)$.

This is the special addition rule for the probability of two mutually exclusive events.

Two events A and B are said to be *independent* if the occurrence of either event does not alter the probability that the other event occurs. For one roll of the number cube, let $A = \{2, 4, 6\}$ and let $B = \{5, 6\}$. Then the probability that A occurs is $P(A) = \frac{|A|}{6} = \frac{3}{6} = \frac{1}{2}$, while, *presuming B occurs*, the probability that A occurs is

$$\frac{|A \cap B|}{|B|} = \frac{|\{6\}|}{|\{5,6\}|} = \frac{1}{2}.$$

Similarly, the probability that B occurs is $P(B) = \frac{|B|}{6} = \frac{2}{6} = \frac{1}{3}$, while, *presuming A occurs*, the probability that B occurs is

$$\frac{|B \cap A|}{|A|} = \frac{|\{6\}|}{|\{2,4,6\}|} = \frac{1}{3}.$$

Thus, the occurrence of either event does not affect the probability that the other event occurs. Therefore, A and B are independent.

The following multiplication rule holds for any independent events E and F: $P(E \text{ and } F) = P(E)P(F)$. For the independent events A and B above, $P(A \text{ and } B) = P(A)P(B) = \left(\frac{1}{2}\right)\left(\frac{1}{3}\right) = \left(\frac{1}{6}\right)$.

Note that the event "A and B" is $A \cap B = \{6\}$, and hence $P(A \text{ and } B) = P(\{6\}) = \frac{1}{6}$. It follows from the general addition rule and the multiplication rule above that if E and F are independent, then

$$P(E \text{ or } F) = P(E) + P(F) - P(E)P(F).$$

For a final example of some of these rules, consider an experiment with events A, B, and C for which $P(A) = 0.23$, $P(B) = 0.40$, and $P(C) = 0.85$. Also, suppose that events A and B are mutually exclusive and events B and C are independent. Then

$$P(A \text{ or } B) = P(A) + P(B) \text{ (since } A \text{ or } B \text{ are mutually exclusive)}$$
$$= 0.23 + 0.40$$
$$= 0.63$$
$$P(B \text{ or } C) = P(B) + P(C) - P(B)P(C) \text{ (by independence)}$$
$$= 0.40 + 0.85 - (0.40)(0.85)$$
$$= 0.91$$

Note that $P(A \text{ or } C)$ and $P(A \text{ and } C)$ cannot be determined using the information given. But it can be determined that A and C are *not* mutually exclusive since $P(A) + P(C) = 1.08$, which is greater than 1, and therefore cannot equal $P(A \text{ or } C)$; from this it follows that $P(A \text{ and } C) \geq 0.08$. One can also deduce that $P(A \text{ and } C) \leq P(A) = 0.23$, since $A \cap C$ is a subset of A, and that $P(A \text{ or } C) \geq P(C) = 0.85$ since C is a subset of $A \cup C$. Thus, one can conclude that $0.85 \leq P(A \text{ or } C) \leq 1$ and $0.08 \leq P(A \text{ and } C) \leq 0.23$.

4.2 Algebra

Algebra is based on the operations of arithmetic and on the concept of an *unknown quantity*, or *variable*. Letters such as x or n are used to represent unknown quantities. For example, suppose Pam has 5 more pencils than Fred. If F represents the number of pencils that Fred has, then the number of pencils that Pam has is $F + 5$. As another example, if Jim's present salary S is increased by 7%, then his new salary is $1.07S$. A combination of letters and arithmetic operations, such as

$F + 5, \dfrac{3x^2}{2x-5}$, and $19x^2 - 6x + 3$, is called an *algebraic expression*.

The expression $19x^2 - 6x + 3$ consists of the *terms* $19x^2$, $-6x$, and 3, where 19 is the *coefficient* of x^2, -6 is the coefficient of x^1, and 3 is a *constant term* (or coefficient of $x^0 = 1$). Such an expression is called a *second degree* (or *quadratic*) *polynomial in x* since the highest power of x is 2. The expression $F + 5$ is a *first degree* (or *linear*) *polynomial in F* since the highest power of F is 1. The expression $\dfrac{3x^2}{2x-5}$ is not a polynomial because it is not a sum of terms that are each powers of x multiplied by coefficients.

1. Simplifying Algebraic Expressions

Often when working with algebraic expressions, it is necessary to simplify them by factoring or combining *like* terms. For example, the expression $6x + 5x$ is equivalent to $(6 + 5)x$, or $11x$. In the expression $9x - 3y$, 3 is a factor common to both terms: $9x - 3y = 3(3x - y)$. In the expression $5x^2 + 6y$, there are no like terms and no common factors.

If there are common factors in the numerator and denominator of an expression, they can be divided out, provided that they are not equal to zero.

For example, if $x \neq 3$, then $\frac{x-3}{x-3}$ is equal to 1; therefore,

$$\frac{3xy - 9y}{x - 3} = \frac{3y(x-3)}{x-3}$$
$$= (3y)(1)$$
$$= 3y$$

To multiply two algebraic expressions, each term of one expression is multiplied by each term of the other expression. For example:

$$(3x - 4)(9y + x) = 3x(9y + x) - 4(9y + x)$$
$$= (3x)(9y) + (3x)(x) + (-4)(9y) + (-4)(x)$$
$$= 27xy + 3x^2 - 36y - 4x$$

An algebraic expression can be evaluated by substituting values of the unknowns in the expression. For example, if $x = 3$ and $y = -2$, then $3xy - x^2 + y$ can be evaluated as

$$3(3)(-2) - (3)^2 + (-2) = -18 - 9 - 2 = -29$$

2. Equations

A major focus of algebra is to solve equations involving algebraic expressions. Some examples of such equations are

$5x - 2 = 9 - x$ (a linear equation with one unknown)

$3x + 1 = y - 2$ (a linear equation with two unknowns)

$5x^2 + 3x - 2 = 7x$ (a quadratic equation with one unknown)

$\frac{x(x-3)(x^2+5)}{x-4} = 0$ (an equation that is factored on one side with 0 on the other)

The *solutions* of an equation with one or more unknowns are those values that make the equation true, or "satisfy the equation," when they are substituted for the unknowns of the equation. An equation may have no solution or one or more solutions. If two or more equations are to be solved together, the solutions must satisfy all the equations simultaneously.

Two equations having the same solution(s) are *equivalent equations*. For example, the equations

$$2 + x = 3$$
$$4 + 2x = 6$$

each have the unique solution $x = 1$. Note that the second equation is the first equation multiplied by 2. Similarly, the equations

$$3x - y = 6$$
$$6x - 2y = 12$$

have the same solutions, although in this case each equation has infinitely many solutions. If any value is assigned to x, then $3x - 6$ is a corresponding value for y that will satisfy both equations; for example, $x = 2$ and $y = 0$ is a solution to both equations, as is $x = 5$ and $y = 9$.

3. Solving Linear Equations with One Unknown

To solve a linear equation with one unknown (that is, to find the value of the unknown that satisfies the equation), the unknown should be isolated on one side of the equation. This can be done by performing the same mathematical operations on both sides of the equation. Remember that if the same number is added to or subtracted from both sides of the equation, this does not change the equality; likewise, multiplying or dividing both sides by the same nonzero number does not change the equality. For example, to solve the equation $\frac{5x - 6}{3} = 4$ for x, the variable x can be isolated using the following steps:

$$5x - 6 = 12 \quad \text{(multiplying by 3)}$$
$$5x = 18 \quad \text{(adding 6)}$$
$$x = \frac{18}{5} \quad \text{(dividing by 5)}$$

The solution, $\frac{18}{5}$, can be checked by substituting it for x in the original equation to determine whether it satisfies that equation:

$$\frac{5\left(\frac{18}{5}\right) - 6}{3} = \frac{18 - 6}{3} = \frac{12}{3} = 4$$

Therefore, $x = \frac{18}{5}$ is the solution.

4. Solving Two Linear Equations with Two Unknowns

For two linear equations with two unknowns, if the equations are equivalent, then there are infinitely many solutions to the equations, as illustrated at the end of section 4.2.2 ("Equations"). If the equations are not equivalent, then they have either one unique solution or no solution. The latter case is illustrated by the two equations:

$$3x + 4y = 17$$
$$6x + 8y = 35$$

Note that $3x + 4y = 17$ implies $6x + 8y = 34$, which contradicts the second equation. Thus, no values of x and y can simultaneously satisfy both equations.

There are several methods of solving two linear equations with two unknowns. With any method, if a contradiction is reached, then the equations have no solution; if a trivial equation such as $0 = 0$ is reached, then the equations are equivalent and have infinitely many solutions. Otherwise, a unique solution can be found.

One way to solve for the two unknowns is to express one of the unknowns in terms of the other using one of the equations, and then substitute the expression into the remaining equation to obtain an equation with one unknown. This equation can be solved and the value of the unknown substituted into either of the original equations to find the value of the other unknown. For example, the following two equations can be solved for x and y.

$$(1) \quad 3x + 2y = 11$$
$$(2) \quad x - y = 2$$

In equation (2), $x = 2 + y$. Substitute $2 + y$ in equation (1) for x:

$$3(2 + y) + 2y = 11$$
$$6 + 3y + 2y = 11$$
$$6 + 5y = 11$$
$$5y = 5$$
$$y = 1$$

If $y = 1$, then $x - 1 = 2$ and $x = 2 + 1 = 3$.

There is another way to solve for x and y by eliminating one of the unknowns. This can be done by making the coefficients of one of the unknowns the same (disregarding the sign) in both equations and either adding the equations or subtracting one equation from the other. For example, to solve the equations

$$(1) \quad 6x + 5y = 29$$
$$(2) \quad 4x - 3y = -6$$

by this method, multiply equation (1) by 3 and equation (2) by 5 to get

$$18x + 15y = 87$$
$$20x - 15y = -30$$

Adding the two equations eliminates y, yielding $38x = 57$, or $x = \frac{3}{2}$. Finally, substituting $\frac{3}{2}$ for x in one of the equations gives $y = 4$. These answers can be checked by substituting both values into both of the original equations.

5. Solving Equations by Factoring

Some equations can be solved by factoring. To do this, first add or subtract expressions to bring all the expressions to one side of the equation, with 0 on the other side. Then try to factor the nonzero side into a product of expressions. If this is possible, then using property (7) in section 4.1.4 ("Real Numbers") each of the factors can be set equal to 0, yielding several simpler equations that possibly can be solved. The solutions of the simpler equations will be solutions of the factored equation. As an example, consider the equation $x^3 - 2x^2 + x = -5(x-1)^2$:

$$x^3 - 2x^2 + x + 5(x-1)^2 = 0$$
$$x(x^2 - 2x + 1) + 5(x-1)^2 = 0$$
$$x(x-1)^2 + 5(x-1)^2 = 0$$
$$(x+5)(x-1)^2 = 0$$
$$x+5 = 0 \text{ or } (x-1)^2 = 0$$
$$x = -5 \text{ or } x = 1.$$

For another example, consider $\dfrac{x(x-3)(x^2+5)}{x-4} = 0$. A fraction equals 0 if and only if its numerator equals 0. Thus, $x(x-3)(x^2+5) = 0$:

$$x = 0 \text{ or } x - 3 = 0 \text{ or } x^2 + 5 = 0$$
$$x = 0 \text{ or } x = 3 \text{ or } x^2 + 5 = 0.$$

But $x^2 + 5 = 0$ has no real solution because $x^2 + 5 > 0$ for every real number. Thus, the solutions are 0 and 3.

The solutions of an equation are also called the *roots* of the equation. These roots can be checked by substituting them into the original equation to determine whether they satisfy the equation.

6. Solving Quadratic Equations

The standard form for a *quadratic equation* is

$$ax^2 + bx + c = 0,$$

where a, b, and c are real numbers and $a \neq 0$; for example:

$$x^2 + 6x + 5 = 0$$
$$3x^2 - 2x = 0, \text{ and}$$
$$x^2 + 4 = 0$$

Some quadratic equations can easily be solved by factoring. For example:

(1) $$x^2 + 6x + 5 = 0$$
$$(x+5)(x+1) = 0$$
$$x+5 = 0 \text{ or } x+1 = 0$$
$$x = -5 \text{ or } x = -1$$

(2)
$$3x^2 - 3 = 8x$$
$$3x^2 - 8x - 3 = 0$$
$$(3x+1)(x-3) = 0$$
$$3x+1 = 0 \text{ or } x-3 = 0$$
$$x = -\frac{1}{3} \text{ or } x = 3$$

A quadratic equation has at most two real roots and may have just one or even no real root. For example, the equation $x^2 - 6x + 9 = 0$ can be expressed as $(x-3)^2 = 0$, or $(x-3)(x-3) = 0$; thus the only root is 3. The equation $x^2 + 4 = 0$ has no real root; since the square of any real number is greater than or equal to zero, $x^2 + 4$ must be greater than zero.

An expression of the form $a^2 - b^2$ can be factored as $(a-b)(a+b)$.

For example, the quadratic equation $9x^2 - 25 = 0$ can be solved as follows.

$$(3x-5)(3x+5) = 0$$
$$3x-5 = 0 \text{ or } 3x+5 = 0$$
$$x = \frac{5}{3} \text{ or } x = -\frac{5}{3}$$

If a quadratic expression is not easily factored, then its roots can always be found using the *quadratic formula:* If $ax^2 + bx + c = 0$ $(a \neq 0)$, then the roots are

$$x = \frac{-b + \sqrt{b^2 - 4ac}}{2a} \text{ and } x = \frac{-b - \sqrt{b^2 - 4ac}}{2a}$$

These are two distinct real numbers unless $b^2 - 4ac \leq 0$. If $b^2 - 4ac = 0$, then these two expressions for x are equal to $-\frac{b}{2a}$, and the equation has only one root. If $b^2 - 4ac < 0$, then $\sqrt{b^2 - 4ac}$ is not a real number and the equation has no real roots.

7. Exponents

A positive integer exponent of a number or a variable indicates a product, and the positive integer is the number of times that the number or variable is a factor in the product. For example, x^5 means $(x)(x)(x)(x)(x)$; that is, x is a factor in the product 5 times.

Some rules about exponents follow.

Let x and y be any positive numbers, and let r and s be any positive integers.

(1) $(x^r)(x^s) = x^{(r+s)}$; for example, $(2^2)(2^3) = 2^{(2+3)} = 2^5 = 32$.

(2) $\dfrac{x^r}{x^s} = x^{(r-s)}$; for example, $\dfrac{4^5}{4^2} = 4^{5-2} = 4^3 = 64$.

(3) $(x^r)(y^r) = (xy)^r$; for example, $(3^3)(4^3) = 12^3 = 1{,}728$.

(4) $\left(\dfrac{x}{y}\right)^r = \dfrac{x^r}{y^r}$; for example, $\left(\dfrac{2}{3}\right)^3 = \dfrac{2^3}{3^3} = \dfrac{8}{27}$.

(5) $(x^r)^s = x^{rs} = (x^s)^r$; for example, $(x^3)^4 = x^{12} = (x^4)^3$.

(6) $x^{-r} = \dfrac{1}{x^r}$; for example, $3^{-2} = \dfrac{1}{3^2} = \dfrac{1}{9}$.

(7) $x^0 = 1$; for example, $6^0 = 1$.

(8) $x^{\frac{r}{s}} = \left(x^{\frac{1}{s}}\right)^r = (x^r)^{\frac{1}{s}} = \sqrt[s]{x^r}$; for example, $8^{\frac{2}{3}} = \left(8^{\frac{1}{3}}\right)^2 = (8^2)^{\frac{1}{3}} = \sqrt[3]{8^2} = \sqrt[3]{64} = 4$ and $9^{\frac{1}{2}} = \sqrt{9} = 3$.

It can be shown that rules 1 – 6 also apply when r and s are not integers and are not positive, that is, when r and s are any real numbers.

8. Inequalities

An *inequality* is a statement that uses one of the following symbols:

$\neq$ not equal to

$>$ greater than

$\geq$ greater than or equal to

$<$ less than

$\leq$ less than or equal to

Some examples of inequalities are $5x - 3 < 9$, $6x \geq y$, and $\dfrac{1}{2} < \dfrac{3}{4}$. Solving a linear inequality with one unknown is similar to solving an equation; the unknown is isolated on one side of the inequality. As in solving an equation, the same number can be added to or subtracted from both sides of the inequality, or both sides of an inequality can be multiplied or divided by a positive number without changing the truth of the inequality. However, multiplying or dividing an inequality by a negative number reverses the order of the inequality. For example, $6 > 2$, but $(-1)(6) < (-1)(2)$.

To solve the inequality $3x - 2 > 5$ for x, isolate x by using the following steps:

$$3x - 2 > 5$$
$$3x > 7 \quad \text{(adding 2 to both sides)}$$
$$x > \dfrac{7}{3} \quad \text{(dividing both sides by 3)}$$

To solve the inequality $\dfrac{5x - 1}{-2} < 3$ for x, isolate x by using the following steps:

$$\dfrac{5x - 1}{-2} < 3$$
$$5x - 1 > -6 \quad \text{(multiplying both sides by } -2\text{)}$$
$$5x > -5 \quad \text{(adding 1 to both sides)}$$
$$x > -1 \quad \text{(dividing both sides by 5)}$$

9. **Absolute Value**

    The absolute value of x, denoted $|x|$, is defined to be x if $x \geq 0$ and $-x$ if $x < 0$. Note that $\sqrt{x^2}$ denotes the nonnegative square root of x^2, and so $\sqrt{x^2} = |x|$.

10. **Functions**

    An algebraic expression in one variable can be used to define a *function* of that variable. A function is denoted by a letter such as f or g along with the variable in the expression. For example, the expression $x^3 - 5x^2 + 2$ defines a function f that can be denoted by

    $$f(x) = x^3 - 5x^2 + 2.$$

    The expression $\dfrac{2z+7}{\sqrt{z+1}}$ defines a function g that can be denoted by

    $$g(z) = \dfrac{2z+7}{\sqrt{z+1}}.$$

    The symbols "$f(x)$" or "$g(z)$" do not represent products; each is merely the symbol for an expression, and is read "f of x" or "g of z."

    Function notation provides a short way of writing the result of substituting a value for a variable. If $x = 1$ is substituted in the first expression, the result can be written $f(1) = -2$, and $f(1)$ is called the "value of f at $x = 1$." Similarly, if $z = 0$ is substituted in the second expression, then the value of g at $z = 0$ is $g(0) = 7$.

    Once a function $f(x)$ is defined, it is useful to think of the variable x as an input and $f(x)$ as the corresponding output. In any function there can be no more than one output for any given input. However, more than one input can give the same output; for example, if $h(x) = |x + 3|$, then $h(-4) = 1 = h(-2)$.

    The set of all allowable inputs for a function is called the *domain* of the function. For f and g defined above, the domain of f is the set of all real numbers and the domain of g is the set of all numbers greater than -1. The domain of any function can be arbitrarily specified, as in the function defined by "$h(x) = 9x - 5$ for $0 \leq x \leq 10$." Without such a restriction, the domain is assumed to be all values of x that result in a real number when substituted into the function.

    The domain of a function can consist of only the positive integers and possibly 0. For example, $a(n) = n^2 + \dfrac{n}{5}$ for $n = 0, 1, 2, 3, \ldots$.

    Such a function is called a *sequence* and $a(n)$ is denoted by a_n. The value of the sequence a_n at $n = 3$ is $a_3 = 3^2 + \dfrac{3}{5} = 9.60$. As another example, consider the sequence defined by $b_n = (-1)^n (n!)$ for $n = 1, 2, 3, \ldots$ A sequence like this is often indicated by listing its values in the order $b_1, b_2, b_3, \ldots, b_n, \ldots$ as follows:

    $-1, 2, -6, \ldots, (-1)^n (n!), \ldots,$ and $(-1)^n (n!)$ is called the nth term of the sequence.

4.3 Geometry

1. Lines

In geometry, the word "line" refers to a straight line that extends without end in both directions.

The line above can be referred to as line *PQ* or line ℓ. The part of the line from *P* to *Q* is called a *line segment*. *P* and *Q* are the *endpoints* of the segment. The notation $\overline{PQ}$ is used to denote line segment *PQ* and *PQ* is used to denote the length of the segment.

2. Intersecting Lines and Angles

If two lines intersect, the opposite angles are called *vertical angles* and have the same measure. In the figure

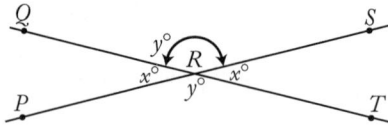

∠*PRQ* and ∠*SRT* are vertical angles and ∠*QRS* and ∠*PRT* are vertical angles. Also, $x + y = 180°$ since *PRS* is a straight line.

3. Perpendicular Lines

An angle that has a measure of 90° is a *right angle*. If two lines intersect at right angles, the lines are *perpendicular*. For example:

ℓ_1 and ℓ_2 above are perpendicular, denoted by $\ell_1 \perp \ell_2$. A right angle symbol in an angle of intersection indicates that the lines are perpendicular.

4. Parallel Lines

If two lines that are in the same plane do not intersect, the two lines are *parallel*. In the figure

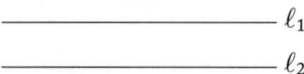

lines ℓ_1 and ℓ_2 are parallel, denoted by $\ell_1 \parallel \ell_2$. If two parallel lines are intersected by a third line, as shown below, then the angle measures are related as indicated, where $x + y = 180°$.

5. Polygons (Convex)

A *polygon* is a closed plane figure formed by three or more line segments, called the *sides* of the polygon. Each side intersects exactly two other sides at their endpoints. The points of intersection of the sides are *vertices*. The term "polygon" will be used to mean a convex polygon, that is, a polygon in which each interior angle has a measure of less than 180°.

The following figures are polygons:

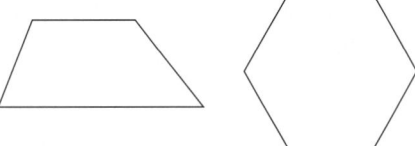

The following figures are not polygons:

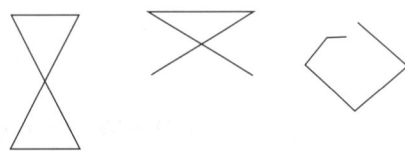

A polygon with three sides is a *triangle*; with four sides, a *quadrilateral*; with five sides, a *pentagon*; and with six sides, a *hexagon*.

The sum of the interior angle measures of a triangle is 180°. In general, the sum of the interior angle measures of a polygon with n sides is equal to $(n - 2)180°$. For example, this sum for a pentagon is $(5 - 2)180° = (3)180° = 540°$.

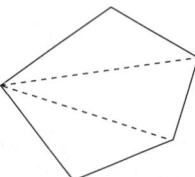

Note that a pentagon can be partitioned into three triangles and therefore the sum of the angle measures can be found by adding the sum of the angle measures of three triangles.

The *perimeter* of a polygon is the sum of the lengths of its sides.

The commonly used phrase "area of a triangle" (or any other plane figure) is used to mean the area of the region enclosed by that figure.

6. Triangles

There are several special types of triangles with important properties. But one property that all triangles share is that the sum of the lengths of any two of the sides is greater than the length of the third side, as illustrated below.

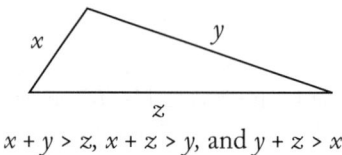

$x + y > z$, $x + z > y$, and $y + z > x$

An *equilateral* triangle has all sides of equal length. All angles of an equilateral triangle have equal measure. An *isosceles* triangle has at least two sides of the same length. If two sides of a triangle have the same length, then the two angles opposite those sides have the same measure. Conversely, if two angles of a triangle have the same measure, then the sides opposite those angles have the same length. In isosceles triangle *PQR* below, $x = y$ since $PQ = QR$.

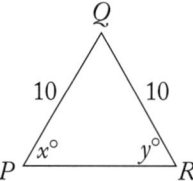

A triangle that has a right angle is a *right* triangle. In a right triangle, the side opposite the right angle is the *hypotenuse,* and the other two sides are the *legs*. An important theorem concerning right triangles is the *Pythagorean theorem,* which states: In a right triangle, the square of the length of the hypotenuse is equal to the sum of the squares of the lengths of the legs.

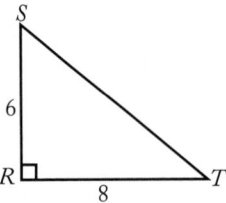

In the figure above, $\triangle RST$ is a right triangle, so $(RS)^2 + (RT)^2 = (ST)^2$. Here, $RS = 6$ and $RT = 8$, so $ST = 10$, since $6^2 + 8^2 = 36 + 64 = 100 = (ST)^2$ and $ST = \sqrt{100}$. Any triangle in which the lengths of the sides are in the ratio 3:4:5 is a right triangle. In general, if *a*, *b*, and *c* are the lengths of the sides of a triangle and $a^2 + b^2 = c^2$, then the triangle is a right triangle.

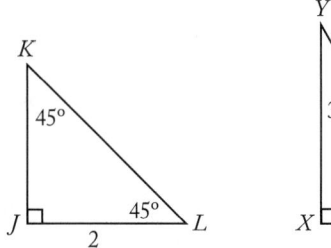

In 45°–45°–90° triangles, the lengths of the sides are in the ratio $1:1:\sqrt{2}$. For example, in $\triangle JKL$, if $JL = 2$, then $JK = 2$ and $KL = 2\sqrt{2}$. In 30°–60°–90° triangles, the lengths of the sides are in the ratio $1:\sqrt{3}:2$. For example, in $\triangle XYZ$, if $XZ = 3$, then $XY = 3\sqrt{3}$ and $YZ = 6$.

The *altitude* of a triangle is the segment drawn from a vertex perpendicular to the side opposite that vertex. Relative to that vertex and altitude, the opposite side is called the *base*.

The area of a triangle is equal to:

$$\frac{(\text{the length of the altitude}) \times (\text{the length of the base})}{2}$$

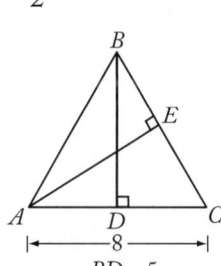

In $\triangle ABC$, $\overline{BD}$ is the altitude to base $\overline{AC}$ and $\overline{AE}$ is the altitude to base $\overline{BC}$. The area of $\triangle ABC$ is equal to

$$\frac{BD \times AC}{2} = \frac{5 \times 8}{2} = 20.$$

The area is also equal to $\dfrac{AE \times BC}{2}$. If $\triangle ABC$ above is isosceles and $AB = BC$, then altitude $\overline{BD}$ bisects the base; that is, $AD = DC = 4$. Similarly, any altitude of an equilateral triangle bisects the side to which it is drawn.

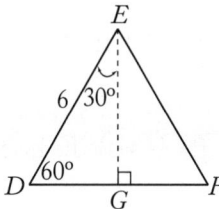

In equilateral triangle DEF, if $DE = 6$, then $DG = 3$ and $EG = 3\sqrt{3}$. The area of $\triangle DEF$ is equal to $\dfrac{3\sqrt{3} \times 6}{2} = 9\sqrt{3}.$

125

7. Quadrilaterals

A polygon with four sides is a *quadrilateral*. A quadrilateral in which both pairs of opposite sides are parallel is a *parallelogram*. The opposite sides of a parallelogram also have equal length.

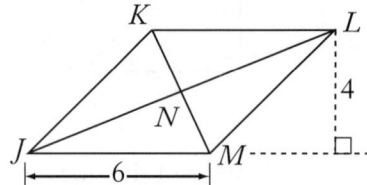

In parallelogram *JKLM*, $\overline{JK} \parallel \overline{LM}$ and *JK* = *LM*; $\overline{KL} \parallel \overline{JM}$ and *KL* = *JM*.

The diagonals of a parallelogram bisect each other (that is, *KN* = *NM* and *JN* = *NL*).

The area of a parallelogram is equal to

(the length of the altitude) × (the length of the base).

The area of *JKLM* is equal to 4 × 6 = 24.

A parallelogram with right angles is a *rectangle*, and a rectangle with all sides of equal length is a *square*.

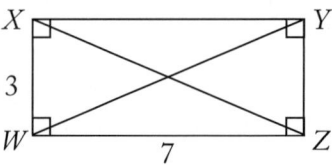

The perimeter of *WXYZ* = 2(3) + 2(7) = 20 and the area of *WXYZ* is equal to 3 × 7 = 21. The diagonals of a rectangle are equal; therefore $WY = XZ = \sqrt{9+49} = \sqrt{58}$.

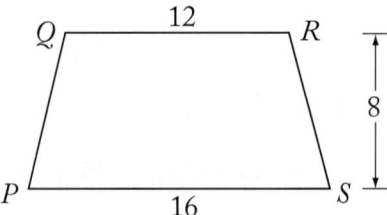

A quadrilateral with two sides that are parallel, as shown above, is a *trapezoid*. The area of trapezoid *PQRS* may be calculated as follows:

$\frac{1}{2}$(the sum of the lengths of the bases)(the height) = $\frac{1}{2}(QR + PS)(8) = \frac{1}{2}(28 \times 8) = 112$.

8. Circles

A *circle* is a set of points in a plane that are all located the same distance from a fixed point (the *center* of the circle).

A *chord* of a circle is a line segment that has its endpoints on the circle. A chord that passes through the center of the circle is a *diameter* of the circle. A *radius* of a circle is a segment from the center of the circle to a point on the circle. The words "diameter" and "radius" are also used to refer to the lengths of these segments.

The *circumference* of a circle is the distance around the circle. If r is the radius of the circle, then the circumference is equal to $2\pi r$, where π is approximately $\frac{22}{7}$ or 3.14. The *area* of a circle of radius r is equal to πr^2.

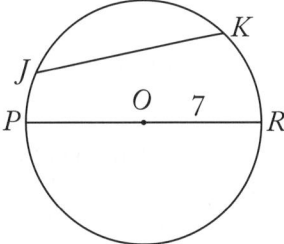

In the circle above, O is the center of the circle and $\overline{JK}$ and $\overline{PR}$ are chords. $\overline{PR}$ is a diameter and $\overline{OR}$ is a radius. If $OR = 7$, then the circumference of the circle is $2\pi(7) = 14\pi$ and the area of the circle is $\pi(7)^2 = 49\pi$.

The number of degrees of arc in a circle (or the number of degrees in a complete revolution) is 360.

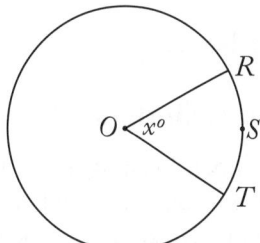

In the circle with center O above, the length of arc RST is $\frac{x}{360}$ of the circumference of the circle; for example, if $x = 60$, then arc RST has length $\frac{1}{6}$ of the circumference of the circle.

A line that has exactly one point in common with a circle is said to be *tangent* to the circle, and that common point is called the *point of tangency*. A radius or diameter with an endpoint at the point of tangency is perpendicular to the tangent line, and, conversely, a line that is perpendicular to a radius or diameter at one of its endpoints is tangent to the circle at that endpoint.

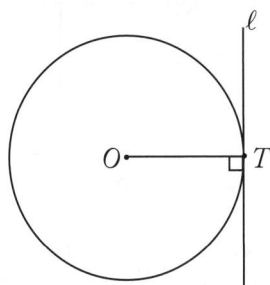

The line ℓ above is tangent to the circle and radius $\overline{OT}$ is perpendicular to ℓ.

If each vertex of a polygon lies on a circle, then the polygon is *inscribed* in the circle and the circle is *circumscribed* about the polygon. If each side of a polygon is tangent to a circle, then the polygon is *circumscribed* about the circle and the circle is *inscribed* in the polygon.

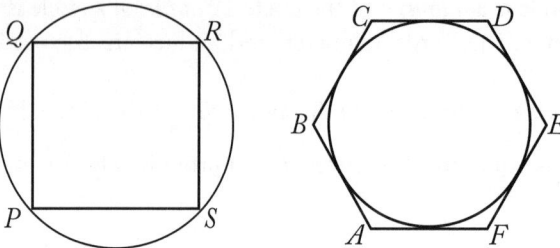

In the figure above, quadrilateral *PQRS* is inscribed in a circle and hexagon *ABCDEF* is circumscribed about a circle.

If a triangle is inscribed in a circle so that one of its sides is a diameter of the circle, then the triangle is a right triangle.

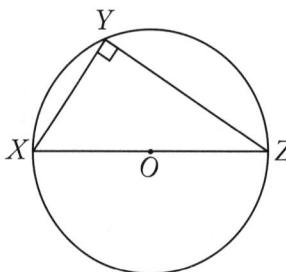

In the circle above, $\overline{XZ}$ is a diameter and the measure of $\angle XYZ$ is 90°.

9. Rectangular Solids and Cylinders

A *rectangular solid* is a three-dimensional figure formed by 6 rectangular surfaces, as shown below. Each rectangular surface is a *face*. Each solid or dotted line segment is an *edge*, and each point at which the edges meet is a *vertex*. A rectangular solid has 6 faces, 12 edges, and 8 vertices. Opposite faces are parallel rectangles that have the same dimensions. A rectangular solid in which all edges are of equal length is a *cube*.

The *surface area* of a rectangular solid is equal to the sum of the areas of all the faces. The *volume* is equal to

(length) × (width) × (height);

in other words, (area of base) × (height).

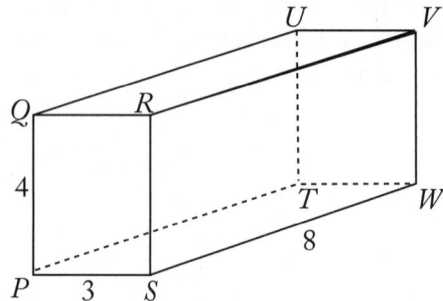

In the rectangular solid above, the dimensions are 3, 4, and 8. The surface area is equal to $2(3 \times 4) + 2(3 \times 8) + 2(4 \times 8) = 136$. The volume is equal to $3 \times 4 \times 8 = 96$.

The figure above is a right circular *cylinder*. The two bases are circles of the same size with centers O and P, respectively, and altitude (height) $\overline{OP}$ is perpendicular to the bases. The surface area of a right circular cylinder with a base of radius r and height h is equal to $2(\pi r^2) + 2\pi rh$ (the sum of the areas of the two bases plus the area of the curved surface).

The volume of a cylinder is equal to $\pi r^2 h$, that is,

$$(\text{area of base}) \times (\text{height}).$$

In the cylinder above, the surface area is equal to

$$2(25\pi) + 2\pi(5)(8) = 130\pi,$$

and the volume is equal to

$$25\pi(8) = 200\pi.$$

10. Coordinate Geometry

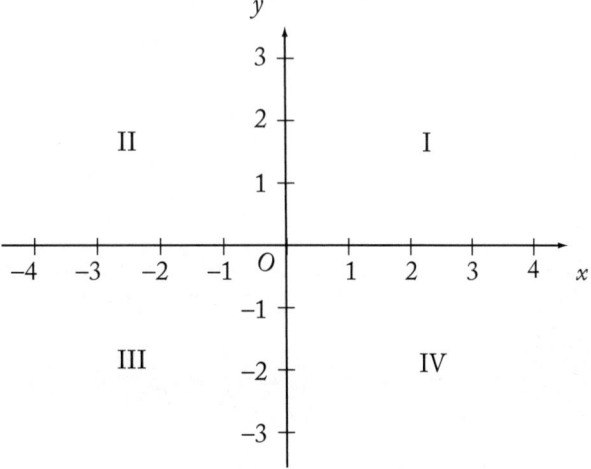

The figure above shows the (rectangular) *coordinate plane*. The horizontal line is called the *x-axis* and the perpendicular vertical line is called the *y-axis*. The point at which these two axes intersect, designated O, is called the *origin*. The axes divide the plane into four quadrants, I, II, III, and IV, as shown.

Each point in the plane has an *x-coordinate* and a *y-coordinate*. A point is identified by an ordered pair (x,y) of numbers in which the x-coordinate is the first number and the y-coordinate is the second number.

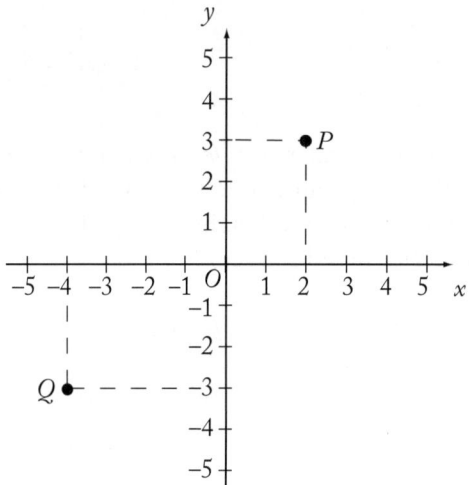

In the graph above, the (x,y) coordinates of point P are (2,3) since P is 2 units to the right of the y-axis (that is, x = 2) and 3 units above the x-axis (that is, y = 3). Similarly, the (x,y) coordinates of point Q are (−4,−3). The origin O has coordinates (0,0).

One way to find the distance between two points in the coordinate plane is to use the Pythagorean theorem.

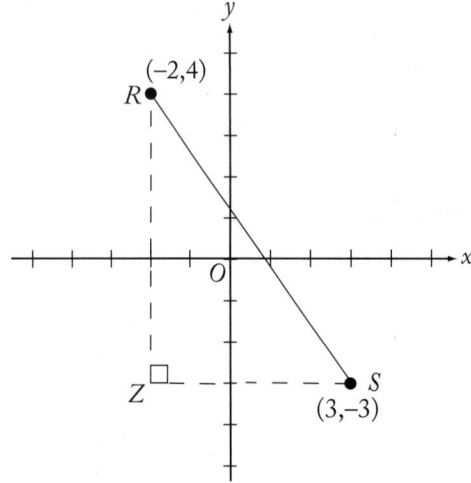

To find the distance between points R and S using the Pythagorean theorem, draw the triangle as shown. Note that Z has (x,y) coordinates (−2,−3), RZ = 7, and ZS = 5. Therefore, the distance between R and S is equal to

$$\sqrt{7^2 + 5^2} = \sqrt{74}.$$

For a line in the coordinate plane, the coordinates of each point on the line satisfy a linear equation of the form y = mx + b (or the form x = a if the line is vertical). For example, each point on the line on the next page satisfies the equation $y = -\frac{1}{2}x + 1$. One can verify this for the points (−2,2), (2,0), and (0,1) by substituting the respective coordinates for x and y in the equation.

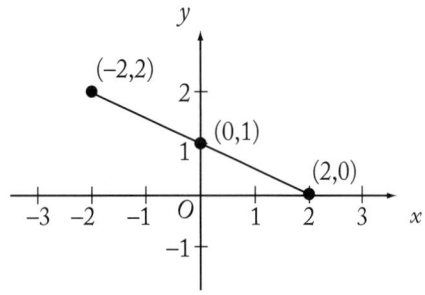

In the equation $y = mx + b$ of a line, the coefficient m is the *slope* of the line and the constant term b is the *y-intercept* of the line. For any two points on the line, the slope is defined to be the ratio of the difference in the y-coordinates to the difference in the x-coordinates. Using $(-2, 2)$ and $(2, 0)$ above, the slope is

$$\frac{\text{The difference in the } y\text{-coordinates}}{\text{The difference in the } x\text{-coordinates}} = \frac{0-2}{2-(-2)} = \frac{-2}{4} = -\frac{1}{2}.$$

The y-intercept is the y-coordinate of the point at which the line intersects the y-axis. For the line above, the y-intercept is 1, and this is the resulting value of y when x is set equal to 0 in the equation $y = -\frac{1}{2}x + 1$. The *x-intercept* is the x-coordinate of the point at which the line intersects the x-axis. The x-intercept can be found by setting $y = 0$ and solving for x. For the line $y = -\frac{1}{2}x + 1$, this gives

$$-\frac{1}{2}x + 1 = 0$$

$$-\frac{1}{2}x = -1$$

$$x = 2.$$

Thus, the x-intercept is 2.

Given any two points (x_1, y_1) and (x_2, y_2) with $x_1 \neq x_2$, the equation of the line passing through these points can be found by applying the definition of slope. Since the slope is $m = \frac{y_2 - y_1}{x_2 - x_1}$, then using a point known to be on the line, say (x_1, y_1), any point (x, y) on the line must satisfy $\frac{y - y_1}{x - x_1} = m$, or $y - y_1 = m(x - x_1)$. (Using (x_2, y_2) as the known point would yield an equivalent equation.) For example, consider the points $(-2, 4)$ and $(3, -3)$ on the line below.

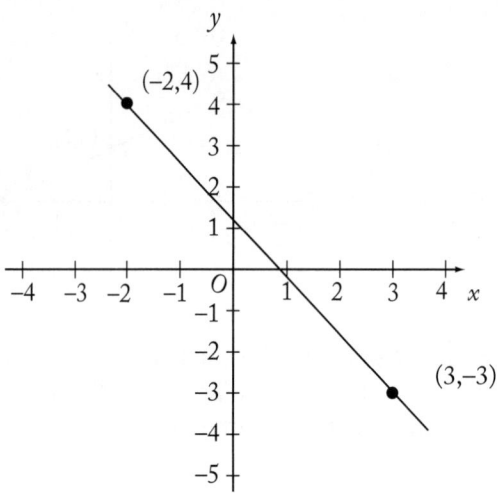

The slope of this line is $\frac{-3-4}{3-(-2)} = \frac{-7}{5}$, so an equation of this line can be found using the point $(3,-3)$ as follows:

$$y - (-3) = -\frac{7}{5}(x - 3)$$

$$y + 3 = -\frac{7}{5}x + \frac{21}{5}$$

$$y = -\frac{7}{5}x + \frac{6}{5}$$

The y-intercept is $\frac{6}{5}$. The *x-intercept* can be found as follows:

$$0 = -\frac{7}{5}x + \frac{6}{5}$$

$$\frac{7}{5}x = \frac{6}{5}$$

$$x = \frac{6}{7}$$

Both of these intercepts can be seen on the graph.

If the slope of a line is negative, the line slants downward from left to right; if the slope is positive, the line slants upward. If the slope is 0, the line is horizontal; the equation of such a line is of the form $y = b$ since $m = 0$. For a vertical line, slope is not defined, and the equation is of the form $x = a$, where a is the x-intercept.

There is a connection between graphs of lines in the coordinate plane and solutions of two linear equations with two unknowns. If two linear equations with unknowns x and y have a unique solution, then the graphs of the equations are two lines that intersect in one point, which is the solution. If the equations are equivalent, then they represent the same line with infinitely many points or solutions. If the equations have no solution, then they represent parallel lines, which do not intersect.

There is also a connection between functions (see section 4.2.10) and the coordinate plane. If a function is graphed in the coordinate plane, the function can be understood in different and useful ways. Consider the function defined by

$$f(x) = -\frac{7}{5}x + \frac{6}{5}.$$

If the value of the function, $f(x)$, is equated with the variable y, then the graph of the function in the xy-coordinate plane is simply the graph of the equation

$$y = -\frac{7}{5}x + \frac{6}{5}$$

shown above. Similarly, any function $f(x)$ can be graphed by equating y with the value of the function:

$$y = f(x).$$

So for any x in the domain of the function f, the point with coordinates $(x, f(x))$ is on the graph of f, and the graph consists entirely of these points.

As another example, consider a quadratic polynomial function defined by $f(x) = x^2 - 1$. One can plot several points $(x, f(x))$ on the graph to understand the connection between a function and its graph:

x	$f(x)$
−2	3
−1	0
0	−1
1	0
2	3

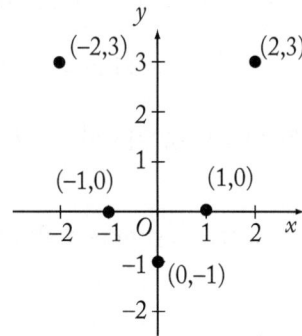

If all the points were graphed for $-2 \leq x \leq 2$, then the graph would appear as follows.

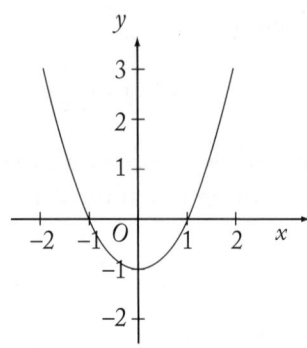

The graph of a quadratic function is called a *parabola* and always has the shape of the curve above, although it may be upside down or have a greater or lesser width. Note that the roots of the equation $f(x) = x^2 - 1 = 0$ are $x = 1$ and $x = -1$; these coincide with the x-intercepts since x-intercepts are found by setting $y = 0$ and solving for x. Also, the y-intercept is $f(0) = -1$ because this is the value of y corresponding to $x = 0$. For any function f, the x-intercepts are the solutions of the equation $f(x) = 0$ and the y-intercept is the value $f(0)$.

4.4 Word Problems

Many of the principles discussed in this chapter are used to solve word problems. The following discussion of word problems illustrates some of the techniques and concepts used in solving such problems.

1. Rate Problems

The distance that an object travels is equal to the product of the average speed at which it travels and the amount of time it takes to travel that distance, that is,

$$\text{Rate} \times \text{Time} = \text{Distance}.$$

Example 1: If a car travels at an average speed of 70 kilometers per hour for 4 hours, how many kilometers does it travel?

Solution: Since rate × time = distance, simply multiply 70 km/hour × 4 hours. Thus, the car travels 280 kilometers in 4 hours.

To determine the average rate at which an object travels, divide the total distance traveled by the total amount of traveling time.

Example 2: On a 400-mile trip, Car X traveled half the distance at 40 miles per hour (mph) and the other half at 50 mph. What was the average speed of Car X ?

Solution: First it is necessary to determine the amount of traveling time. During the first 200 miles, the car traveled at 40 mph; therefore, it took $\dfrac{200}{40} = 5$ hours to travel the first 200 miles.

During the second 200 miles, the car traveled at 50 mph; therefore, it took $\frac{200}{50} = 4$ hours to travel the second 200 miles. Thus, the average speed of Car X was $\frac{400}{9} = 44\frac{4}{9}$ mph. Note that the average speed is not $\frac{40+50}{2} = 45$.

Some rate problems can be solved by using ratios.

Example 3: If 5 shirts cost $44, then, at this rate, what is the cost of 8 shirts?

Solution: If c is the cost of the 8 shirts, then $\frac{5}{44} = \frac{8}{c}$. Cross multiplication results in the equation

$$5c = 8 \times 44 = 352$$

$$c = \frac{352}{5} = 70.40$$

The 8 shirts cost $70.40.

2. Work Problems

In a work problem, the rates at which certain persons or machines work alone are usually given, and it is necessary to compute the rate at which they work together (or vice versa).

The basic formula for solving work problems is $\frac{1}{r} + \frac{1}{s} = \frac{1}{h}$, where r and s are, for example, the number of hours it takes Rae and Sam, respectively, to complete a job when working alone, and h is the number of hours it takes Rae and Sam to do the job when working together. The reasoning is that in 1 hour Rae does $\frac{1}{r}$ of the job, Sam does $\frac{1}{s}$ of the job, and Rae and Sam together do $\frac{1}{h}$ of the job.

Example 1: If Machine X can produce 1,000 bolts in 4 hours and Machine Y can produce 1,000 bolts in 5 hours, in how many hours can Machines X and Y, working together at these constant rates, produce 1,000 bolts?

Solution:

$$\frac{1}{4} + \frac{1}{5} = \frac{1}{h}$$

$$\frac{5}{20} + \frac{4}{20} = \frac{1}{h}$$

$$\frac{9}{20} = \frac{1}{h}$$

$$9h = 20$$

$$h = \frac{20}{9} = 2\frac{2}{9}$$

Working together, Machines X and Y can produce 1,000 bolts in $2\frac{2}{9}$ hours.

Example 2: If Art and Rita can do a job in 4 hours when working together at their respective constant rates and Art can do the job alone in 6 hours, in how many hours can Rita do the job alone?

Solution:

$$\frac{1}{6} + \frac{1}{R} = \frac{1}{4}$$

$$\frac{R+6}{6R} = \frac{1}{4}$$

$$4R + 24 = 6R$$

$$24 = 2R$$

$$12 = R$$

Working alone, Rita can do the job in 12 hours.

3. Mixture Problems

In mixture problems, substances with different characteristics are combined, and it is necessary to determine the characteristics of the resulting mixture.

Example 1: If 6 pounds of nuts that cost $1.20 per pound are mixed with 2 pounds of nuts that cost $1.60 per pound, what is the cost per pound of the mixture?

Solution: The total cost of the 8 pounds of nuts is

$$6(\$1.20) + 2(\$1.60) = \$10.40.$$

The cost per pound is

$$\frac{\$10.40}{8} = \$1.30.$$

Example 2: How many liters of a solution that is 15 percent salt must be added to 5 liters of a solution that is 8 percent salt so that the resulting solution is 10 percent salt?

Solution: Let n represent the number of liters of the 15% solution. The amount of salt in the 15% solution $[0.15n]$ plus the amount of salt in the 8% solution $[(0.08)(5)]$ must be equal to the amount of salt in the 10% mixture $[0.10(n + 5)]$. Therefore,

$$0.15n + 0.08(5) = 0.10(n + 5)$$

$$15n + 40 = 10n + 50$$

$$5n = 10$$

$$n = 2 \text{ liters}$$

Two liters of the 15% salt solution must be added to the 8% solution to obtain the 10% solution.

4. Interest Problems

Interest can be computed in two basic ways. With simple annual interest, the interest is computed on the principal only and is equal to (principal) × (interest rate) × (time). If interest is compounded, then interest is computed on the principal as well as on any interest already earned.

Example 1: If $8,000 is invested at 6 percent simple annual interest, how much interest is earned after 3 months?

Solution: Since the annual interest rate is 6%, the interest for 1 year is

$$(0.06)(\$8,000) = \$480.$$

The interest earned in 3 months is $\frac{3}{12}(\$480) = \$120.$

Example 2: If $10,000 is invested at 10 percent annual interest, compounded semiannually, what is the balance after 1 year?

Solution: The balance after the first 6 months would be

$$10,000 + (10,000)(0.05) = \$10,500.$$

The balance after one year would be $10,500 + (10,500)(0.05) = \$11,025.$

Note that the interest rate for each 6-month period is 5%, which is half of the 10% annual rate. The balance after one year can also be expressed as

$$10,000\left(1 + \frac{0.10}{2}\right)^2 \text{ dollars.}$$

5. Discount

If a price is discounted by n percent, then the price becomes $(100 - n)$ percent of the original price.

Example 1: A certain customer paid $24 for a dress. If that price represented a 25 percent discount on the original price of the dress, what was the original price of the dress?

Solution: If p is the original price of the dress, then $0.75p$ is the discounted price and $0.75p = \$24$, or $p = \$32.$ The original price of the dress was $32.

Example 2: The price of an item is discounted by 20 percent and then this reduced price is discounted by an additional 30 percent. These two discounts are equal to an overall discount of what percent?

Solution: If p is the original price of the item, then $0.8p$ is the price after the first discount. The price after the second discount is $(0.7)(0.8)p = 0.56p.$ This represents an overall discount of 44 percent (100% − 56%).

6. Profit

Gross profit is equal to revenues minus expenses, or selling price minus cost.

Example: A certain appliance costs a merchant $30. At what price should the merchant sell the appliance in order to make a gross profit of 50 percent of the cost of the appliance?

Solution: If s is the selling price of the appliance, then $s - 30 = (0.5)(30)$, or $s = \$45.$ The merchant should sell the appliance for $45.

7. Sets

If S is the set of numbers 1, 2, 3, and 4, you can write $S = \{1, 2, 3, 4\}$. Sets can also be represented by Venn diagrams. That is, the relationship among the members of sets can be represented by circles.

Example 1: Each of 25 people is enrolled in history, mathematics, or both. If 20 are enrolled in history and 18 are enrolled in mathematics, how many are enrolled in both history and mathematics?

Solution: The 25 people can be divided into three sets: those who study history only, those who study mathematics only, and those who study history and mathematics. Thus a Venn diagram may be drawn as follows, where n is the number of people enrolled in both courses, $20 - n$ is the number enrolled in history only, and $18 - n$ is the number enrolled in mathematics only.

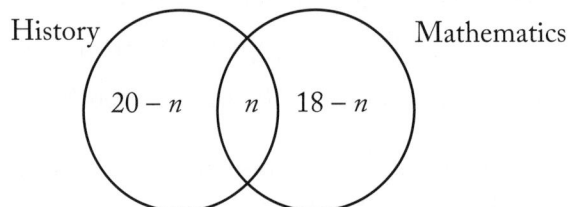

Since there is a total of 25 people, $(20 - n) + n + (18 - n) = 25$, or $n = 13$. Thirteen people are enrolled in both history and mathematics. Note that $20 + 18 - 13 = 25$, which is the general addition rule for two sets (see section 4.1.9).

Example 2: In a certain production lot, 40 percent of the toys are red and the remaining toys are green. Half of the toys are small and half are large. If 10 percent of the toys are red and small, and 40 toys are green and large, how many of the toys are red and large?

Solution: For this kind of problem, it is helpful to organize the information in a table:

	Red	Green	Total
Small	10%		50%
Large			50%
Total	40%	60%	100%

The numbers in the table are the percentages given. The following percentages can be computed on the basis of what is given:

	Red	Green	Total
Small	10%	40%	50%
Large	30%	20%	50%
Total	40%	60%	100%

Since 20% of the number of toys (n) are green and large, $0.20n = 40$ (40 toys are green and large), or $n = 200$. Therefore, 30% of the 200 toys, or $(0.3)(200) = 60$, are red and large.

8. Geometry Problems

The following is an example of a word problem involving geometry.

Example:

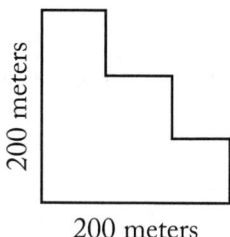

The figure above shows an aerial view of a piece of land. If all angles shown are right angles, what is the perimeter of the piece of land?

Solution: For reference, label the figure as

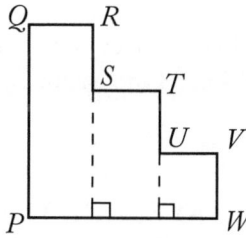

If all the angles are right angles, then $QR + ST + UV = PW$, and $RS + TU + VW = PQ$. Hence, the perimeter of the land is $2PW + 2PQ = 2 \times 200 + 2 \times 200 = 800$ meters.

9. Measurement Problems

Some questions on the GMAT involve metric units of measure, whereas others involve English units of measure. However, except for units of time, if a question requires conversion from one unit of measure to another, the relationship between those units will be given.

Example: A train travels at a constant rate of 25 meters per second. How many kilometers does it travel in 5 minutes? (1 kilometer = 1,000 meters)

Solution: In 1 minute the train travels $(25)(60) = 1,500$ meters, so in 5 minutes it travels 7,500 meters. Since 1 kilometer = 1,000 meters, it follows that 7,500 meters equals $\frac{7,500}{1,000}$, or 7.5 kilometers.

10. Data Interpretation

Occasionally a question or set of questions will be based on data provided in a table or graph. Some examples of tables and graphs are given below.

Example 1:

Population by Age Group
(in thousands)

Age	Population
17 years and under	63,376
18–44 years	86,738
45–64 years	43,845
65 years and over	24,054

How many people are 44 years old or younger?

Solution: The figures in the table are given in thousands. The answer in thousands can be obtained by adding 63,376 thousand and 86,738 thousand. The result is 150,114 thousand, which is 150,114,000.

Example 2:

AVERAGE TEMPERATURE AND PRECIPITATION IN CITY X

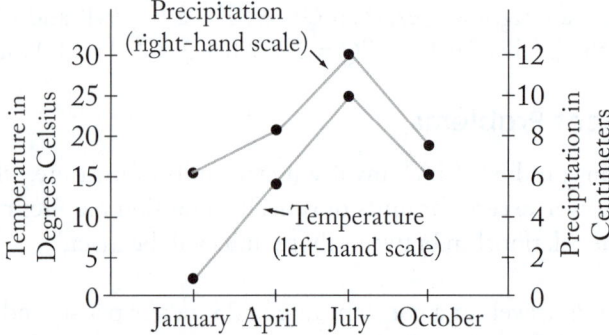

What are the average temperature and precipitation in City X during April?

Solution: Note that the scale on the left applies to the temperature line graph and the one on the right applies to the precipitation line graph. According to the graph, during April the average temperature is approximately 14° Celsius and the average precipitation is approximately 8 centimeters.

Example 3:

DISTRIBUTION OF AL'S WEEKLY NET SALARY

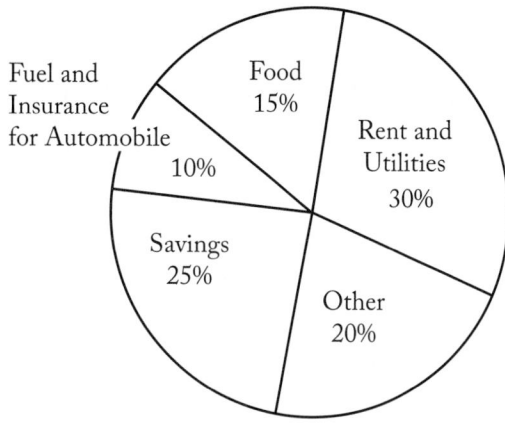

Al's weekly net salary is $350. To how many of the categories listed was at least $80 of Al's weekly net salary allocated?

Solution: In the circle graph, the relative sizes of the sectors are proportional to their corresponding values and the sum of the percents given is 100%. Note that $\frac{80}{350}$ is approximately 23%, so at least $80 was allocated to each of 2 categories—Rent and Utilities, and Savings—since their allocations are each greater than 23%.

5.0 Problem Solving

5.0 Problem Solving

The Quantitative Reasoning section of the GMAT™ exam uses problem solving and data sufficiency questions to gauge your skill level. This chapter focuses on problem solving questions. Remember that quantitative questions require knowledge of the following:

- Arithmetic
- Elementary algebra
- Commonly known concepts of geometry

Problem solving questions are designed to test your basic mathematical skills and understanding of elementary mathematical concepts, as well as your ability to reason quantitatively, solve quantitative problems, and interpret graphic data. The mathematics knowledge required to answer the questions is no more advanced than what is generally taught in secondary school (or high school) mathematics classes.

In these questions, you are asked to solve each problem and select the best of the five answer choices given. Begin by reading the question thoroughly to determine exactly what information is given and to make sure you understand what is being asked. Scan the answer choices to understand your options. If the problem seems simple, take a few moments to see whether you can determine the answer. Then, check your answer against the choices provided.

If you do not see your answer among the choices, or if the problem is complicated, take a closer look at the answer choices and think again about what the problem is asking. See whether you can eliminate some of the answer choices and narrow down your options. If you are still unable to narrow the answer down to a single choice, reread the question. Keep in mind that the answer will be based solely on the information provided in the question—don't allow your own experience and assumptions to interfere with your ability to find the correct answer to the question.

If you find yourself stuck on a question or unable to select the single correct answer, keep in mind that you have about two minutes to answer each quantitative question. You may run out of time if you take too long to answer any one question; you may simply need to pick the answer that seems to make the most sense. Although guessing is generally not the best way to achieve a high GMAT score, making an educated guess is a good strategy for answering questions you are unsure of. Even if your answer to a particular question is incorrect, your answers to other questions will allow the test to accurately gauge your ability level.

The following pages include test-taking strategies, directions that will apply to questions of this type, sample questions, an answer key, and explanations for all the problems. These explanations present problem solving strategies that could be helpful in answering the questions.

5.1 Test-Taking Strategies

1. **Pace yourself.**

   Consult the on-screen timer periodically. Work as carefully as possible, but do not spend valuable time checking answers or pondering problems that you find difficult.

2. **Use the erasable notepad provided at the test center.**

   Working a problem out may help you avoid errors in solving the problem. If diagrams or figures are not presented, it may help to draw your own.

3. **Read each question carefully to determine what is being asked.**

   For word problems, take one step at a time, reading each sentence carefully and translating the information into equations or other useful mathematical representations.

4. **Scan the answer choices before attempting to answer a question.**

   Scanning the answers can prevent you from putting answers in a form that is not given (e.g., finding the answer in decimal form, such as 0.25, when the choices are given in fractional form, such as $\frac{1}{4}$). Also, if the question requires approximations, a shortcut could serve well (e.g., you may be able to approximate 48 percent of a number by using half).

5. **Don't waste time trying to solve a problem that is too difficult for you.**

   Make your best guess and then move on to the next question.

5.2 Section Instructions

Go to www.mba.com/tutorial to view instructions for the section and get a feel for what the test center screens will look at on the actual GMAT exam.

5.3 Practice Questions

Solve the problem and indicate the best of the answer choices given.
Numbers: All numbers used are real numbers.
Figures: A figure accompanying a problem solving question is intended to provide information useful in solving the problem. Figures are drawn as accurately as possible. Exceptions will be clearly noted. Lines shown as straight are straight, and lines that appear jagged are also straight. The positions of points, angles, regions, etc., exist in the order shown, and angle measures are greater than zero. All figures lie in a plane unless otherwise indicated.

1. In the figure, the 6 small squares are identical, each with sides of length 1. What is the outer perimeter (shown in bold) of the entire figure?

   (A) 8
   (B) 12
   (C) 16
   (D) 20
   (E) 24

Performance Time	Ticket Price	Number of Tickets Sold
Thursday night	$40	200
Friday night	$50	240
Saturday afternoon	$40	220
Saturday night	$50	300

2. The table shows a summary of the ticket sales from four performances of a certain play. What is the difference between the maximum and the minimum ticket-sale revenue from a single performance?

   (A) $4,000
   (B) $5,100
   (C) $6,200
   (D) $7,000
   (E) $9,600

3. During a trip that they took together, Carmen, Juan, Maria, and Rafael drove an average (arithmetic mean) of 80 miles each. Carmen drove 72 miles, Juan drove 78 miles, and Maria drove 83 miles. How many miles did Rafael drive?

   (A) 80
   (B) 82
   (C) 85
   (D) 87
   (E) 89

4. Each week, a clothing salesperson receives a commission equal to 15 percent of the first $500 in sales and 20 percent of all additional sales that week. What commission would the salesperson receive on total sales for the week of $1,300 ?

   (A) $195
   (B) $227
   (C) $235
   (D) $260
   (E) $335

5. A certain restaurant that regularly advertises through the mail has 1,040 cover letters and 3,000 coupons in stock. In its next mailing, each envelope will contain 1 cover letter and 2 coupons. If all of the cover letters in stock are used, how many coupons will remain in stock after this mailing?

   (A) 920
   (B) 1,040
   (C) 1,500
   (D) 1,960
   (E) 2,080

5.3 Problem Solving Practice Questions

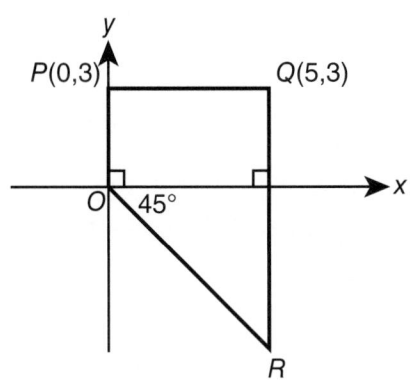

PS02599
6. In the figure above, what are the coordinates of point R?

(A) (3,–5)
(B) (3,–3)
(C) (5,5)
(D) (5,–3)
(E) (5,–5)

PS08877
7. The price of a coat in a certain store is $500. If the price of the coat is to be reduced by $150, by what percent is the price to be reduced?

(A) 10%
(B) 15%
(C) 20%
(D) 25%
(E) 30%

PS05410
8. $\left(\dfrac{1}{2}-\dfrac{1}{3}\right)+\left(\dfrac{1}{3}-\dfrac{1}{4}\right)+\left(\dfrac{1}{4}-\dfrac{1}{5}\right)+\left(\dfrac{1}{5}-\dfrac{1}{6}\right) =$

(A) $-\dfrac{1}{6}$
(B) 0
(C) $\dfrac{1}{3}$
(D) $\dfrac{1}{2}$
(E) $\dfrac{2}{3}$

PS05001
9. While a family was away on vacation, they paid a neighborhood boy $11 per week to mow their lawn and $4 per day to feed and walk their dog. If the family was away for exactly 3 weeks, how much did they pay the boy for his services?

(A) $45
(B) $54
(C) $71
(D) $95
(E) $117

PS17812
10. Last year $48,000 of a certain store's profit was shared by its 2 owners and their 10 employees. Each of the 2 owners received 3 times as much as each of their 10 employees. How much did each owner receive from the $48,000 ?

(A) $12,000
(B) $9,000
(C) $6,000
(D) $4,000
(E) $3,000

PS02295
11. On a vacation, Rose exchanged $500.00 for euros at an exchange rate of 0.80 euro per dollar and spent $\dfrac{3}{4}$ of the euros she received. If she exchanged the remaining euros for dollars at an exchange rate of $1.20 per euro, what was the dollar amount she received?

(A) $60.00
(B) $80.00
(C) $100.00
(D) $120.00
(E) $140.00

147

x	x	x	y	y	v
v	x	x	y	w	w

12. Each of the 12 squares shown is labeled x, y, v, or w. What is the ratio of the number of these squares labeled x or y to the number of these squares labeled v or w?

    (A) 1:2
    (B) 2:3
    (C) 4:3
    (D) 3:2
    (E) 2:1

13. In the xy-coordinate plane, if the point (0,2) lies on the graph of the line $2x + ky = 4$, what is the value of the constant k?

    (A) 2
    (B) 1
    (C) 0
    (D) −1
    (E) −2

14. Bouquets are to be made using white tulips and red tulips, and the ratio of the number of white tulips to the number of red tulips is to be the same in each bouquet. If there are 15 white tulips and 85 red tulips available for the bouquets, what is the greatest number of bouquets that can be made using all the tulips available?

    (A) 3
    (B) 5
    (C) 8
    (D) 10
    (E) 13

15. Over the past 7 weeks, the Smith family had weekly grocery bills of $74, $69, $64, $79, $64, $84, and $77. What was the Smiths' average (arithmetic mean) weekly grocery bill over the 7-week period?

    (A) $64
    (B) $70
    (C) $73
    (D) $74
    (E) $85

16. 125% of 5 =

    (A) 5.125
    (B) 5.25
    (C) 6
    (D) 6.125
    (E) 6.25

17. During a recent storm, 9 neighborhoods experienced power failures of durations 34, 29, 27, 46, 18, 25, 12, 35, and 16 minutes, respectively. For these 9 neighborhoods, what was the median duration, in minutes, of the power failures?

    (A) 34
    (B) 29
    (C) 27
    (D) 25
    (E) 18

18. When traveling at a constant speed of 32 miles per hour, a certain motorboat consumes 24 gallons of fuel per hour. What is the fuel consumption of this boat at this speed measured in miles traveled per gallon of fuel?

    (A) $\frac{2}{3}$
    (B) $\frac{3}{4}$
    (C) $\frac{4}{5}$
    (D) $\frac{4}{3}$
    (E) $\frac{3}{2}$

19. A technician makes a round-trip to and from a certain service center by the same route. If the technician completes the drive to the center and then completes 10 percent of the drive from the center, what percent of the round-trip has the technician completed?

    (A) 5%
    (B) 10%
    (C) 25%
    (D) 40%
    (E) 55%

20. From 2000 to 2003, the number of employees at a certain company increased by a factor of $\frac{1}{4}$. From 2003 to 2006, the number of employees at this company decreased by a factor of $\frac{1}{3}$. If there were 100 employees at the company in 2006, how many employees were there at the company in 2000 ?

   (A) 200
   (B) 120
   (C) 100
   (D) 75
   (E) 60

21. Which of the following statements must be true about the average (arithmetic mean) and the median of 5 consecutive integers?

   I. The average is one of the integers.
   II. The median is one of the integers.
   III. The median equals the average.

   (A) I only
   (B) II only
   (C) III only
   (D) I and II only
   (E) I, II, and III

22. A collection of 16 coins, each with a face value of either 10 cents or 25 cents, has a total face value of $2.35. How many of the coins have a face value of 25 cents?

   (A) 3
   (B) 5
   (C) 7
   (D) 9
   (E) 11

23. A retailer purchased eggs at $2.80 per dozen and sold the eggs at 3 eggs for $0.90. What was the retailer's gross profit from purchasing and selling 5 dozen eggs? (1 dozen eggs = 12 eggs)

   (A) $0.90
   (B) $2.40
   (C) $4.00
   (D) $11.30
   (E) $12.00

24. In a set of 24 cards, each card is numbered with a different positive integer from 1 to 24. One card will be drawn at random from the set. What is the probability that the card drawn will have either a number that is divisible by both 2 and 3 or a number that is divisible by 7 ?

   (A) $\frac{3}{24}$
   (B) $\frac{4}{24}$
   (C) $\frac{7}{24}$
   (D) $\frac{8}{24}$
   (E) $\frac{17}{24}$

25. If the circumference of a circle inscribed in a square is 25π, what is the perimeter of the square?

   (A) 20
   (B) 25
   (C) 40
   (D) 50
   (E) 100

26. If $1 < x < y < z$, which of the following has the greatest value?

   (A) $z(x + 1)$
   (B) $z(y + 1)$
   (C) $x(y + z)$
   (D) $y(x + z)$
   (E) $z(x + y)$

27. Set X consists of eight consecutive integers. Set Y consists of all the integers that result from adding 4 to each of the integers in set X and all the integers that result from subtracting 4 from each of the integers in set X. How many more integers are there in set Y than in set X?

   (A) 0
   (B) 4
   (C) 8
   (D) 12
   (E) 16

28. Of the following, which is the closest to $\frac{60.2}{1.03 \times 4.86}$?

   (A) 10
   (B) 12
   (C) 13
   (D) 14
   (E) 15

29. Thabo owns exactly 140 books, and each book is either paperback fiction, paperback nonfiction, or hardcover nonfiction. If he owns 20 more paperback nonfiction books than hardcover nonfiction books, and twice as many paperback fiction books as paperback nonfiction books, how many hardcover nonfiction books does Thabo own?

   (A) 10
   (B) 20
   (C) 30
   (D) 40
   (E) 50

30. If the average (arithmetic mean) of the four numbers 3, 15, 32, and (N + 1) is 18, then N =

   (A) 19
   (B) 20
   (C) 21
   (D) 22
   (E) 29

31. Abdul, Barb, and Carlos all live on the same straight road, on which their school is also located. The school is halfway between Abdul's house and Barb's house. Barb's house is halfway between the school and Carlos's house. If the school is 4 miles from Carlos's house, how many miles is Abdul's house from Carlos's house?

   (A) $1\frac{1}{3}$
   (B) 2
   (C) 4
   (D) 6
   (E) 8

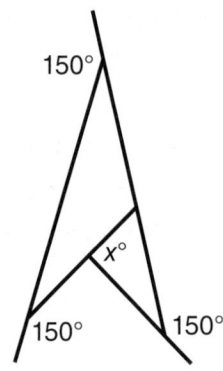

32. In the figure shown, what is the value of x?

   (A) 60
   (B) 80
   (C) 85
   (D) 90
   (E) 95

33. During a certain time period, Car X traveled north along a straight road at a constant rate of 1 mile per minute and used fuel at a constant rate of 5 gallons every 2 hours. During this time period, if Car X used exactly 3.75 gallons of fuel, how many miles did Car X travel?

   (A) 36
   (B) 37.5
   (C) 40
   (D) 80
   (E) 90

34. Cheryl purchased 5 identical hollow pine doors and 6 identical solid oak doors for the house she is building. The regular price of each solid oak door was twice the regular price of each hollow pine door. However, Cheryl was given a discount of 25% off the regular price of each solid oak door. If the regular price of each hollow pine door was $40, what was the total price of all 11 doors?

    (A) $320
    (B) $540
    (C) $560
    (D) $620
    (E) $680

35. A certain store will order 25 crates of apples. The apples will be of three different varieties—McIntosh, Rome, and Winesap—and each crate will contain apples of only one variety. If the store is to order more crates of Winesap than crates of McIntosh and more crates of Winesap than crates of Rome, what is the least possible number of crates of Winesap that the store will order?

    (A) 7
    (B) 8
    (C) 9
    (D) 10
    (E) 11

36. A bicycle store purchased two bicycles, one for $250 and the other for $375, and sold both bicycles at a total gross profit of $250. If the store sold one of the bicycles for $450, which of the following could be the store's gross profit from the sale of the other bicycle?

    (A) $75
    (B) $100
    (C) $125
    (D) $150
    (E) $175

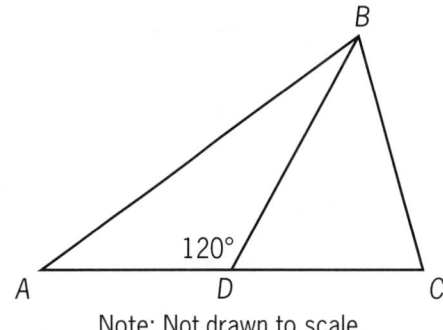

Note: Not drawn to scale.

37. In the figure shown, $AC = 2$ and $BD = DC = 1$. What is the measure of angle ABD?

    (A) 15°
    (B) 20°
    (C) 30°
    (D) 40°
    (E) 45°

38. If $k^2 = m^2$, which of the following must be true?

    (A) $k = m$
    (B) $k = -m$
    (C) $k = |m|$
    (D) $k = -|m|$
    (E) $|k| = |m|$

39. Makoto, Nishi, and Ozuro were paid a total of $780 for waxing the floors at their school. Each was paid in proportion to the number of hours he or she worked. If Makoto worked 15 hours, Nishi worked 20 hours, and Ozuro worked 30 hours, how much was Makoto paid?

    (A) $52
    (B) $117
    (C) $130
    (D) $180
    (E) $234

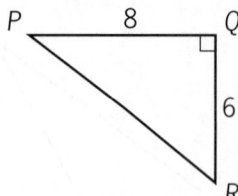

40. The figure above shows a path around a triangular piece of land. Mary walked the distance of 8 miles from P to Q and then walked the distance of 6 miles from Q to R. If Ted walked directly from P to R, by what percent did the distance that Mary walked exceed the distance that Ted walked?

(A) 30%
(B) 40%
(C) 50%
(D) 60%
(E) 80%

41. If x is a positive integer and $4^x - 3 = y$, which of the following CANNOT be a value of y?

(A) 1
(B) 7
(C) 13
(D) 61
(E) 253

42. If $(1 - 1.25)N = 1$, then N =

(A) −400
(B) −140
(C) −4
(D) 4
(E) 400

43. The quotient when a certain number is divided by $\frac{2}{3}$ is $\frac{9}{2}$. What is the number?

(A) $\frac{4}{27}$
(B) $\frac{1}{3}$
(C) 3
(D) 6
(E) $\frac{27}{4}$

44. If a sphere with radius r is inscribed in a cube with edges of length e, which of the following expresses the relationship between r and e?

(A) $r = \frac{1}{2}e$
(B) $r = e$
(C) $r = 2e$
(D) $r = \sqrt{e}$
(E) $r = \frac{1}{4}e^2$

45. The price of gasoline at a service station increased from $1.65 per gallon last week to $1.82 per gallon this week. Sally paid $26.40 for gasoline last week at the station. How much more will Sally pay this week at the station for the same amount of gasoline?

(A) $1.70
(B) $2.55
(C) $2.64
(D) $2.72
(E) $2.90

Monthly Charge for Low-Use Telephone Contract Offered by Company X

Monthly rate (up to 75 message units)	20% less than standard rate of $10.00
Per unit in excess of 75 message units	$0.065

46. Based on the rates above, how much would Company X charge a customer with a low-use contract for using 95 message units in a month?

(A) $9.30
(B) $11.30
(C) $12.88
(D) $14.88
(E) $16.18

5.3 Problem Solving Practice Questions

47. If $2x + y = 7$ and $x + 2y = 5$, then $\frac{x+y}{3} =$

(A) 1
(B) $\frac{4}{3}$
(C) $\frac{17}{5}$
(D) $\frac{18}{5}$
(E) 4

48. City X has a population 4 times as great as the population of City Y, which has a population twice as great as the population of City Z. What is the ratio of the population of City X to the population of City Z?

(A) 1:8
(B) 1:4
(C) 2:1
(D) 4:1
(E) 8:1

Tides at Bay Cove on July 13

49. The graph above shows the height of the tide, in feet, above or below a baseline. Which of the following is closest to the difference, in feet, between the heights of the highest and lowest tides on July 13 at Bay Cove?

(A) 1.7
(B) 1.9
(C) 2.2
(D) 2.5
(E) 2.7

50. If $S = 1 + \frac{1}{2^2} + \frac{1}{3^2} + \frac{1}{4^2} + \frac{1}{5^2} + \frac{1}{6^2} + \frac{1}{7^2} + \frac{1}{8^2} + \frac{1}{9^2} + \frac{1}{10^2}$, which of the following is true?

(A) $S > 3$
(B) $S = 3$
(C) $2 < S < 3$
(D) $S = 2$
(E) $S < 2$

51. A manufacturer of a certain product can expect that between 0.3 percent and 0.5 percent of the units manufactured will be defective. If the retail price is $2,500 per unit and the manufacturer offers a full refund for defective units, how much money can the manufacturer expect to need to cover the refunds on 20,000 units?

(A) Between $15,000 and $25,000
(B) Between $30,000 and $50,000
(C) Between $60,000 and $100,000
(D) Between $150,000 and $250,000
(E) Between $300,000 and $500,000

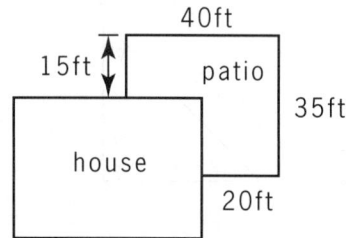

52. A flat patio was built alongside a house as shown in the figure above. If all angles are right angles, what is the area of the patio in square feet?

(A) 800
(B) 875
(C) 1,000
(D) 1,100
(E) 1,125

53. Which of the following is closest to $\sqrt{\frac{4.2(1,590)}{15.7}}$?

(A) 20
(B) 40
(C) 60
(D) 80
(E) 100

54. The sum of the weekly salaries of 5 employees is $3,250. If each of the 5 salaries is to increase by 10 percent, then the average (arithmetic mean) weekly salary per employee will increase by

(A) $52.50
(B) $55.00
(C) $57.50
(D) $62.50
(E) $65.00

55. Last week Chris earned x dollars per hour for the first 40 hours worked plus 22 dollars per hour for each hour worked beyond 40 hours. If last week Chris earned a total of 816 dollars by working 48 hours, what is the value of x ?

(A) 13
(B) 14
(C) 15
(D) 16
(E) 17

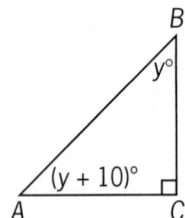

56. In the figure above, what is the ratio of the measure of angle B to the measure of angle A ?

(A) 2 to 3
(B) 3 to 4
(C) 3 to 5
(D) 4 to 5
(E) 5 to 6

57. The value of $\dfrac{\tfrac{7}{8}+\tfrac{1}{9}}{\tfrac{1}{2}}$ is closest to which of the following?

(A) 2
(B) $\dfrac{3}{2}$
(C) 1
(D) $\dfrac{1}{2}$
(E) 0

58. The positive two-digit integers x and y have the same digits, but in reverse order. Which of the following must be a factor of x + y ?

(A) 6
(B) 9
(C) 10
(D) 11
(E) 14

59. In a certain sequence of 8 numbers, each number after the first is 1 more than the previous number. If the first number is –5, how many of the numbers in the sequence are positive?

(A) None
(B) One
(C) Two
(D) Three
(E) Four

60. A total of s oranges are to be packaged in boxes that will hold r oranges each, with no oranges left over. When n of these boxes have been completely filled, what is the number of boxes that remain to be filled?

(A) $s - nr$
(B) $s - \dfrac{n}{r}$
(C) $rs - n$
(D) $\dfrac{s}{n} - r$
(E) $\dfrac{s}{r} - n$

PS03371
61. If $0 < a < b < c$, which of the following statements must be true?

  I. $2a > b + c$
  II. $c - a > b - a$
  III. $\frac{c}{a} < \frac{b}{a}$

  (A) I only
  (B) II only
  (C) III only
  (D) I and II
  (E) II and III

PS00096
62. In the xy-plane, the origin O is the midpoint of line segment PQ. If the coordinates of P are (r,s), what are the coordinates of Q ?

  (A) (r,s)
  (B) (s,–r)
  (C) (–s,–r)
  (D) (–r,s)
  (E) (–r,–s)

	Monday	Tuesday	Wednesday	Thursday
Company A	45	55	50	50
Company B	10	30	30	10
Company C	34	28	28	30
Company D	39	42	41	38
Company E	50	60	60	70

PS10568
63. The table shows the numbers of packages shipped daily by each of five companies during a 4-day period. The standard deviation of the numbers of packages shipped daily during the period was greatest for which of the five companies?

  (A) A
  (B) B
  (C) C
  (D) D
  (E) E

PS15523
64. Company Q plans to make a new product next year and sell each unit of this new product at a selling price of $2. The variable costs per unit in each production run are estimated to be 40% of the selling price, and the fixed costs for each production run are estimated to be $5,040. Based on these estimated costs, how many units of the new product will Company Q need to make and sell in order for their revenue to equal their total costs for each production run?

  (A) 4,200
  (B) 3,150
  (C) 2,520
  (D) 2,100
  (E) 1,800

PS07197
65. A small business invests $9,900 in equipment to produce a product. Each unit of the product costs $0.65 to produce and is sold for $1.20. How many units of the product must be sold before the revenue received equals the total expense of production, including the initial investment in equipment?

  (A) 12,000
  (B) 14,500
  (C) 15,230
  (D) 18,000
  (E) 20,000

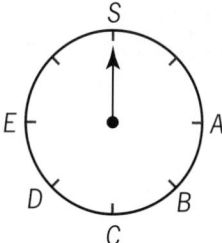

PS05682
66. The dial shown above is divided into equal-sized intervals. At which of the following letters will the pointer stop if it is rotated clockwise from S through 1,174 intervals?

  (A) A
  (B) B
  (C) C
  (D) D
  (E) E

Estimated Number of Home-Schooled
Students by State, January 2001

State	Number (in thousands)
A	181
B	125
C	103
D	79
E	72

PS12287
67. According to the table shown, the estimated number of home-schooled students in State A is approximately what percent greater than the number in State D ?

(A) 25%
(B) 55%
(C) 100%
(D) 125%
(E) 155%

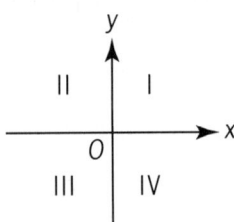

PS02695
68. The graph of the equation $xy = k$, where $k < 0$, lies in which two of the quadrants shown above?

(A) I and II
(B) I and III
(C) II and III
(D) II and IV
(E) III and IV

PS00526
69. When n liters of fuel were added to a tank that was already $\frac{1}{3}$ full, the tank was filled to $\frac{7}{9}$ of its capacity. In terms of n, what is the capacity of the tank, in liters?

(A) $\frac{10}{9}n$
(B) $\frac{4}{3}n$
(C) $\frac{3}{2}n$
(D) $\frac{9}{4}n$
(E) $\frac{7}{3}n$

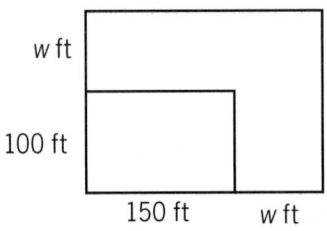
Note: Not drawn to scale.

PS06601
70. The smaller rectangle in the figure above represents the original size of a parking lot before its length and width were each extended by w feet to make the larger rectangular lot shown. If the area of the enlarged lot is twice the area of the original lot, what is the value of w ?

(A) 25
(B) 50
(C) 75
(D) 100
(E) 200

PS02209
71. Kevin invested $8,000 for one year at a simple annual interest rate of 6 percent and invested $10,000 for one year at an annual interest rate of 8 percent compounded semiannually. What is the total amount of interest that Kevin earned on the two investments?

(A) $880
(B) $1,088
(C) $1,253
(D) $1,280
(E) $1,296

5.3 Problem Solving Practice Questions

2 feet

72. The figure above represents a semicircular archway over a flat street. The semicircle has a center at O and a radius of 6 feet. What is the height h, in feet, of the archway 2 feet from its center?

(A) $\sqrt{2}$
(B) 2
(C) 3
(D) $4\sqrt{2}$
(E) 6

73. The harvest yield from a certain apple orchard was 350 bushels of apples. If x of the trees in the orchard each yielded 10 bushels of apples, what fraction of the harvest yield was from these x trees?

(A) $\dfrac{x}{35}$
(B) $1 - \dfrac{x}{35}$
(C) $10x$
(D) $35 - x$
(E) $350 - 10x$

74. In a certain fraction, the denominator is 16 greater than the numerator. If the fraction is equivalent to 80 percent, what is the denominator of the fraction?

(A) 32
(B) 64
(C) 72
(D) 80
(E) 120

75. Greg assembles units of a certain product at a factory. Each day he is paid $2.00 per unit for the first 40 units that he assembles and $2.50 for each additional unit that he assembles that day. If Greg assembled at least 30 units on each of two days and was paid a total of $180.00 for assembling units on the two days, what is the greatest possible number of units that he could have assembled on one of the two days?

(A) 48
(B) 52
(C) 56
(D) 60
(E) 64

76. Which of the following is greatest?

(A) $10\sqrt{3}$
(B) $9\sqrt{4}$
(C) $8\sqrt{5}$
(D) $7\sqrt{6}$
(E) $6\sqrt{7}$

77. Al and Ben are drivers for SD Trucking Company. One snowy day, Ben left SD at 8:00 a.m. heading east and Al left SD at 11:00 a.m. heading west. At a particular time later that day, the dispatcher retrieved data from SD's vehicle tracking system. The data showed that, up to that time, Al had averaged 40 miles per hour and Ben had averaged 20 miles per hour. It also showed that Al and Ben had driven a combined total of 240 miles. At what time did the dispatcher retrieve data from the vehicle tracking system?

(A) 1:00 p.m.
(B) 2:00 p.m.
(C) 3:00 p.m.
(D) 5:00 p.m.
(E) 6:00 p.m.

78. Of the land owned by a farmer, 90 percent was cleared for planting. Of the cleared land, 40 percent was planted with soybeans and 50 percent of the cleared land was planted with wheat. If the remaining 720 acres of cleared land was planted with corn, how many acres did the farmer own?

   (A) 5,832
   (B) 6,480
   (C) 7,200
   (D) 8,000
   (E) 8,889

79. At the start of an experiment, a certain population consisted of 3 animals. At the end of each month after the start of the experiment, the population size was double its size at the beginning of that month. Which of the following represents the population size at the end of 10 months?

   (A) 2^3
   (B) 3^2
   (C) $2(3^{10})$
   (D) $3(2^{10})$
   (E) $3(10^2)$

80. If $\left(\frac{1}{3}+\frac{1}{4}+\frac{1}{5}+\frac{1}{6}\right)=r\left(\frac{1}{9}+\frac{1}{12}+\frac{1}{15}+\frac{1}{18}\right)$, then $r =$

   (A) $\frac{1}{3}$
   (B) $\frac{4}{3}$
   (C) 3
   (D) 4
   (E) 12

81. If x and y are positive integers such that y is a multiple of 5 and $3x + 4y = 200$, then x must be a multiple of which of the following?

   (A) 3
   (B) 6
   (C) 7
   (D) 8
   (E) 10

82. Which of the following expressions can be written as an integer?

   I. $\left(\sqrt{82}+\sqrt{82}\right)^2$
   II. $(82)(\sqrt{82})$
   III. $\dfrac{(\sqrt{82})(\sqrt{82})}{82}$

   (A) None
   (B) I only
   (C) III only
   (D) I and II
   (E) I and III

83. Pumping alone at their respective constant rates, one inlet pipe fills an empty tank to $\frac{1}{2}$ of capacity in 3 hours and a second inlet pipe fills the same empty tank to $\frac{2}{3}$ of capacity in 6 hours. How many hours will it take both pipes, pumping simultaneously at their respective constant rates, to fill the empty tank to capacity?

   (A) 3.25
   (B) 3.6
   (C) 4.2
   (D) 4.4
   (E) 5.5

84. In the xy-coordinate plane, which of the following points must lie on the line $kx + 3y = 6$ for every possible value of k?

   (A) (1,1)
   (B) (0,2)
   (C) (2,0)
   (D) (3,6)
   (E) (6,3)

PS11091
85. If $x^2 - 2 < 0$, which of the following specifies all the possible values of x?

(A) $0 < x < 2$
(B) $0 < x < \sqrt{2}$
(C) $-\sqrt{2} < x < \sqrt{2}$
(D) $-2 < x < 0$
(E) $-2 < x < 2$

Book number	Pages in book	Total pages read
1	253	253
2	110	363
3	117	480
4	170	650
5	155	805
6	50	855
7	205	1,060
8	70	1,130
9	165	1,295
10	105	1,400
11	143	1,543
12	207	1,750

PS14467
86. Shawana made a schedule for reading books during 4 weeks (28 days) of her summer vacation. She has checked out 12 books from the library. The number of pages in each book and the order in which she plans to read the books are shown in the table above. She will read exactly 50 pages each day. The only exception will be that she will never begin the next book on the same day that she finishes the previous one, and therefore on some days she may read fewer than 50 pages. At the end of the 28th day, how many books will Shawana have finished?

(A) 7
(B) 8
(C) 9
(D) 10
(E) 11

PS07465
87. In Western Europe, x bicycles were sold in each of the years 1990 and 1993. The bicycle producers of Western Europe had a 42 percent share of this market in 1990 and a 33 percent share in 1993. Which of the following represents the decrease in the annual number of bicycles produced and sold in Western Europe from 1990 to 1993?

(A) 9% of $\frac{x}{100}$
(B) 14% of $\frac{x}{100}$
(C) 75% of $\frac{x}{100}$
(D) 9% of x
(E) 14% of x

PS06946
88. If k is a positive integer, what is the remainder when $(k + 2)(k^3 - k)$ is divided by 6?

(A) 0
(B) 1
(C) 2
(D) 3
(E) 4

PS14989
89. Which of the following fractions is closest to $\frac{1}{2}$?

(A) $\frac{4}{7}$
(B) $\frac{5}{9}$
(C) $\frac{6}{11}$
(D) $\frac{7}{13}$
(E) $\frac{9}{16}$

90. If $p \neq 0$ and $p - \dfrac{1-p^2}{p} = \dfrac{r}{p}$, then $r =$

    (A) $p + 1$
    (B) $2p - 1$
    (C) $p^2 + 1$
    (D) $2p^2 - 1$
    (E) $p^2 + p - 1$

91. If the range of the six numbers 4, 3, 14, 7, 10, and x is 12, what is the difference between the greatest possible value of x and the least possible value of x?

    (A) 0
    (B) 2
    (C) 12
    (D) 13
    (E) 15

92. What number is 108 more than two-thirds of itself?

    (A) 72
    (B) 144
    (C) 162
    (D) 216
    (E) 324

93. Company P had 15 percent more employees in December than it had in January. If Company P had 460 employees in December, how many employees did it have in January?

    (A) 391
    (B) 400
    (C) 410
    (D) 423
    (E) 445

94. A doctor prescribed 18 cubic centimeters of a certain drug to a patient whose body weight was 120 pounds. If the typical dosage is 2 cubic centimeters per 15 pounds of body weight, by what percent was the prescribed dosage greater than the typical dosage?

    (A) 8%
    (B) 9%
    (C) 11%
    (D) 12.5%
    (E) 14.8%

95. The function f is defined by $f(x) = \sqrt{x} - 10$ for all positive numbers x. If $u = f(t)$ for some positive numbers t and u, what is t in terms of u?

    (A) $\sqrt{\sqrt{u}+10}$
    (B) $\left(\sqrt{u}+10\right)^2$
    (C) $\sqrt{u^2+10}$
    (D) $(u+10)^2$
    (E) $(u^2+10)^2$

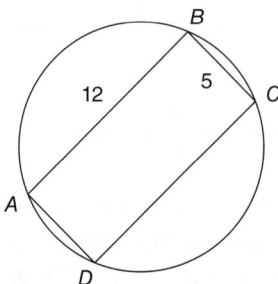

96. If rectangle ABCD is inscribed in the circle above, what is the area of the circular region?

    (A) 36.00π
    (B) 42.25π
    (C) 64.00π
    (D) 84.50π
    (E) 169.00π

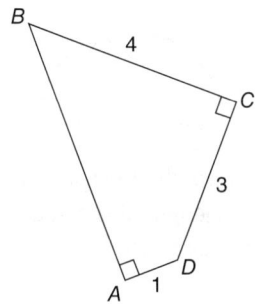

97. In quadrilateral ABCD above, what is the length of AB ?

   (A) $\sqrt{26}$
   (B) $2\sqrt{5}$
   (C) $2\sqrt{6}$
   (D) $3\sqrt{2}$
   (E) $3\sqrt{3}$

98. Three-fourths of the area of a rectangular lawn 30 feet wide by 40 feet long is to be enclosed by a rectangular fence. If the enclosure has full width and reduced length rather than full length and reduced width, how much less fence will be needed?

   (A) $2\frac{1}{2}$
   (B) 5
   (C) 10
   (D) 15
   (E) 20

99. In the floor plan of an executive's beach house above, the north and south walls of the living room are parallel. What is the floor area, in square feet, of the bedroom?

   (A) $450\sqrt{3}$
   (B) 450
   (C) $225\sqrt{3}$
   (D) 225
   (E) It cannot be determined from the information given.

100. On a scale drawing, a rectangle 1 inch by $1\frac{1}{3}$ inches represents the floor of a room and the indicated scale is 1 inch equals 15 feet. How many square tiles 6 inches on a side will be needed to cover this floor? (1 foot = 12 inches)

   (A) 40
   (B) 70
   (C) 120
   (D) 700
   (E) 1,200

101. If m and p are positive integers and $m^2 + p^2 < 100$, what is the greatest possible value of mp ?

   (A) 36
   (B) 42
   (C) 48
   (D) 49
   (E) 51

102. If $\dfrac{x}{y} = \dfrac{c}{d}$ and $\dfrac{d}{c} = \dfrac{b}{a}$, which of the following must be true?

   I. $\dfrac{y}{x} = \dfrac{b}{a}$

   II. $\dfrac{x}{a} = \dfrac{y}{b}$

   III. $\dfrac{y}{a} = \dfrac{x}{b}$

   (A) I only
   (B) II only
   (C) I and II only
   (D) I and III only
   (E) I, II, and III

103. If k is an integer and $(0.0025)(0.025)(0.00025) \times 10^k$ is an integer, what is the least possible value of k?

   (A) −12
   (B) −6
   (C) 0
   (D) 6
   (E) 12

104. If $a(a + 2) = 24$ and $b(b + 2) = 24$, where $a \ne b$, then $a + b =$

   (A) −48
   (B) −2
   (C) 2
   (D) 46
   (E) 48

105. In a recent election, Ms. Robbins received 8,000 votes cast by independent voters, that is, voters not registered with a specific political party. She also received 10 percent of the votes cast by those voters registered with a political party. If N is the total number of votes cast in the election and 40 percent of the votes cast were cast by independent voters, which of the following represents the number of votes that Ms. Robbins received?

   (A) $0.06N + 3{,}200$
   (B) $0.1N + 7{,}200$
   (C) $0.4N + 7{,}200$
   (D) $0.1N + 8{,}000$
   (E) $0.06N + 8{,}000$

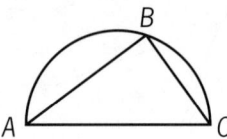

106. In the figure shown, the triangle is inscribed in the semicircle. If the length of line segment AB is 8 and the length of line segment BC is 6, what is the length of arc ABC?

   (A) 15π
   (B) 12π
   (C) 10π
   (D) 7π
   (E) 5π

107. A manufacturer makes and sells 2 products, P and Q. The revenue from the sale of each unit of P is $20.00 and the revenue from the sale of each unit of Q is $17.00. Last year the manufacturer sold twice as many units of Q as P. What was the manufacturer's average (arithmetic mean) revenue per unit sold of these 2 products last year?

   (A) $28.50
   (B) $27.00
   (C) $19.00
   (D) $18.50
   (E) $18.00

108. A worker carries jugs of liquid soap from a production line to a packing area, carrying 4 jugs per trip. If the jugs are packed into cartons that hold 7 jugs each, how many jugs are needed to fill the last partially filled carton after the worker has made 17 trips?

   (A) 1
   (B) 2
   (C) 4
   (D) 5
   (E) 6

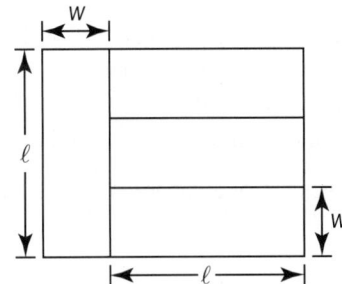

109. The figure shown above represents a modern painting that consists of four differently colored rectangles, each of which has length ℓ and width w. If the area of the painting is 4,800 square inches, what is the width, in inches, of each of the four rectangles?

(A) 15
(B) 20
(C) 25
(D) 30
(E) 40

110. Working simultaneously and independently at an identical constant rate, four machines of a certain type can produce a total of x units of product P in 6 days. How many of these machines, working simultaneously and independently at this constant rate, can produce a total of $3x$ units of product P in 4 days?

(A) 24
(B) 18
(C) 16
(D) 12
(E) 8

111. The symbol Δ denotes one of the four arithmetic operations: addition, subtraction, multiplication, or division. If $6 \Delta 3 \leq 3$, which of the following must be true?

I. $2 \Delta 2 = 0$
II. $2 \Delta 2 = 1$
III. $4 \Delta 2 = 2$

(A) I only
(B) II only
(C) III only
(D) I and II only
(E) I, II, and III

112. If $mn \neq 0$ and 25 percent of n equals $37\frac{1}{2}$ percent of m, what is the value of $\frac{12n}{m}$?

(A) 18
(B) $\frac{32}{3}$
(C) 8
(D) 3
(E) $\frac{9}{8}$

113. Last year Joe grew 1 inch and Sally grew 200 percent more than Joe grew. How many inches did Sally grow last year?

(A) 0
(B) 1
(C) 2
(D) 3
(E) 4

Technique	Percent of Consumers
Television ads	35%
Coupons	22%
Store displays	18%
Samples	15%

114. The table shows partial results of a survey in which consumers were asked to indicate which one of six promotional techniques most influenced their decision to buy a new food product. Of those consumers who indicated one of the four techniques listed, what fraction indicated either coupons or store displays?

(A) $\frac{2}{7}$
(B) $\frac{1}{3}$
(C) $\frac{2}{5}$
(D) $\frac{4}{9}$
(E) $\frac{1}{2}$

115. The cost C, in dollars, to remove p percent of a certain pollutant from a pond is estimated by using the formula $C = \dfrac{100{,}000P}{100-P}$. According to this estimate, how much more would it cost to remove 90 percent of the pollutant from the pond than it would cost to remove 80 percent of the pollutant?

    (A) $500,000
    (B) $100,000
    (C) $50,000
    (D) $10,000
    (E) $5,000

116. If $xy \ne 0$ and $x^2y^2 - xy = 6$, which of the following could be y in terms of x?

    I. $\dfrac{1}{2x}$
    II. $-\dfrac{2}{x}$
    III. $\dfrac{3}{x}$

    (A) I only
    (B) II only
    (C) I and II
    (D) I and III
    (E) II and III

117. $\sqrt{4.8 \times 10^9}$ is closest in value to

    (A) 2,200
    (B) 70,000
    (C) 220,000
    (D) 7,000,000
    (E) 22,000,000

118. Three printing presses, R, S, and T, working together at their respective constant rates, can do a certain printing job in 4 hours. S and T, working together at their respective constant rates, can do the same job in 5 hours. How many hours would it take R, working alone at its constant rate, to do the same job?

    (A) 8
    (B) 10
    (C) 12
    (D) 15
    (E) 20

119. For a party, three solid cheese balls with diameters of 2 inches, 4 inches, and 6 inches, respectively, were combined to form a single cheese ball. What was the approximate diameter, in inches, of the new cheese ball? (The volume of a sphere is $\dfrac{4}{3}\pi r^3$, where r is the radius.)

    (A) 12
    (B) 16
    (C) $\sqrt[3]{16}$
    (D) $3\sqrt[3]{8}$
    (E) $2\sqrt[3]{36}$

120. The sum of all the integers k such that $-26 < k < 24$ is

    (A) 0
    (B) -2
    (C) -25
    (D) -49
    (E) -51

121. The number line shown contains three points R, S, and T, whose coordinates have absolute values r, s, and t, respectively. Which of the following equals the average (arithmetic mean) of the coordinates of the points R, S, and T?

    (A) s
    (B) $s+t-r$
    (C) $\dfrac{r-s-t}{3}$
    (D) $\dfrac{r+s+t}{3}$
    (E) $\dfrac{s+t-r}{3}$

122. Mark and Ann together were allocated n boxes of cookies to sell for a club project. Mark sold 10 boxes less than n and Ann sold 2 boxes less than n. If Mark and Ann have each sold at least one box of cookies, but together they have sold less than n boxes, what is the value of n?

(A) 11
(B) 12
(C) 13
(D) 14
(E) 15

123. A certain high school has 5,000 students. Of these students, x are taking music, y are taking art, and z are taking both music and art. How many students are taking neither music nor art?

(A) $5{,}000 - z$
(B) $5{,}000 - x - y$
(C) $5{,}000 - x + z$
(D) $5{,}000 - x - y - z$
(E) $5{,}000 - x - y + z$

124. Each person who attended a company meeting was either a stockholder in the company, an employee of the company, or both. If 62 percent of those who attended the meeting were stockholders and 47 percent were employees, what percent were stockholders who were not employees?

(A) 34%
(B) 38%
(C) 45%
(D) 53%
(E) 62%

Accounts	Amount Budgeted	Amount Spent
Payroll	$110,000	$117,000
Taxes	40,000	42,000
Insurance	2,500	2,340

125. The table shows the amount budgeted and the amount spent for each of three accounts in a certain company. For which of these accounts did the amount spent differ from the amount budgeted by more than 6 percent of the amount budgeted?

(A) Payroll only
(B) Taxes only
(C) Insurance only
(D) Payroll and Insurance
(E) Taxes and Insurance

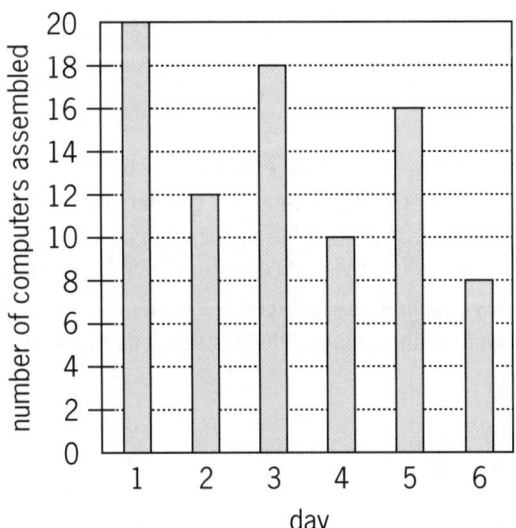

126. The graph shows the number of computers assembled during each of 6 consecutive days. From what day to the next day was the percent change in the number of computers assembled the greatest in magnitude?

(A) From Day 1 to Day 2
(B) From Day 2 to Day 3
(C) From Day 3 to Day 4
(D) From Day 4 to Day 5
(E) From Day 5 to Day 6

127. If $n = 20! + 17$, then n is divisible by which of the following?

   I. 15
   II. 17
   III. 19

   (A) None
   (B) I only
   (C) II only
   (D) I and II
   (E) II and III

128. The product of two negative numbers is 160. If the lesser of the two numbers is 4 less than twice the greater, what is the greater number?

   (A) −20
   (B) −16
   (C) −10
   (D) −8
   (E) −4

129. According to a certain estimate, the depth $N(t)$, in centimeters, of the water in a certain tank at t hours past 2:00 in the morning is given by $N(t) = -20(t - 5)^2 + 500$ for $0 \leq t \leq 10$. According to this estimate, at what time in the morning does the depth of the water in the tank reach its maximum?

   (A) 5:30
   (B) 7:00
   (C) 7:30
   (D) 8:00
   (E) 9:00

130. After driving to a riverfront parking lot, Bob plans to run south along the river, turn around, and return to the parking lot, running north along the same path. After running 3.25 miles south, he decides to run for only 50 minutes more. If Bob runs at a constant rate of 8 minutes per mile, how many miles farther south can he run and still be able to return to the parking lot in 50 minutes?

   (A) 1.5
   (B) 2.25
   (C) 3.0
   (D) 3.25
   (E) 4.75

131. Alex deposited x dollars into a new account that earned 8 percent annual interest, compounded annually. One year later Alex deposited an additional x dollars into the account. If there were no other transactions and if the account contained w dollars at the end of two years, which of the following expresses x in terms of w?

   (A) $\dfrac{w}{1+1.08}$
   (B) $\dfrac{w}{1.08+1.16}$
   (C) $\dfrac{w}{1.16+1.24}$
   (D) $\dfrac{w}{1.08+(1.08)^2}$
   (E) $\dfrac{w}{(1.08)^2+(1.08)^3}$

132. M is the sum of the reciprocals of the consecutive integers from 201 to 300, inclusive. Which of the following is true?

   (A) $\dfrac{1}{3} < M < \dfrac{1}{2}$
   (B) $\dfrac{1}{5} < M < \dfrac{1}{3}$
   (C) $\dfrac{1}{7} < M < \dfrac{1}{5}$
   (D) $\dfrac{1}{9} < M < \dfrac{1}{7}$
   (E) $\dfrac{1}{12} < M < \dfrac{1}{9}$

PS00428
133. Working simultaneously at their respective constant rates, Machines A and B produce 800 nails in x hours. Working alone at its constant rate, Machine A produces 800 nails in y hours. In terms of x and y, how many hours does it take Machine B, working alone at its constant rate, to produce 800 nails?

(A) $\dfrac{x}{x+y}$

(B) $\dfrac{y}{x+y}$

(C) $\dfrac{xy}{x+y}$

(D) $\dfrac{xy}{x-y}$

(E) $\dfrac{xy}{y-x}$

10, 4, 26, 16

PS08966
134. What is the median of the numbers shown?

(A) 10
(B) 13
(C) 14
(D) 15
(E) 16

	Number of Marbles in Each of Three Bags	Percent of Marbles in Each Bag That Are Blue (to the nearest tenth)
Bag P	37	10.8%
Bag Q	x	66.7%
Bag R	32	50.0%

PS03823
135. If $\dfrac{1}{3}$ of the total number of marbles in the three bags listed in the table above are blue, how many marbles are there in bag Q?

(A) 5
(B) 9
(C) 12
(D) 23
(E) 46

Age Category (in years)	Number of Employees
Less than 20	29
20–29	58
30–39	36
40–49	21
50–59	10
60–69	5
70 and over	2

PS11600
136. The table above gives the age categories of the 161 employees at Company X and the number of employees in each category. According to the table, if m is the median age, in years, of the employees at Company X, then m must satisfy which of the following?

(A) $20 \leq m \leq 29$
(B) $25 \leq m \leq 34$
(C) $30 \leq m \leq 39$
(D) $35 \leq m \leq 44$
(E) $40 \leq m \leq 49$

PS02749
137. Ron is 4 inches taller than Amy, and Barbara is 1 inch taller than Ron. If Barbara's height is 65 inches, what is the median height, in inches, of these three people?

(A) 60
(B) 61
(C) 62
(D) 63
(E) 64

PS02777
138. If x and y are positive numbers such that $x + y = 1$, which of the following could be the value of $100x + 200y$?

I. 80
II. 140
III. 199

(A) II only
(B) III only
(C) I and II
(D) I and III
(E) II and III

PS02017
139. If X is the hundredths digit in the decimal 0.1X and if Y is the thousandths digit in the decimal 0.02Y, where X and Y are nonzero digits, which of the following is closest to the greatest possible value of $\dfrac{0.1X}{0.02Y}$?

(A) 4
(B) 5
(C) 6
(D) 9
(E) 10

PS13724
140. Clarissa will create her summer reading list by randomly choosing 4 books from the 10 books approved for summer reading. She will list the books in the order in which they are chosen. How many different lists are possible?

(A) 6
(B) 40
(C) 210
(D) 5,040
(E) 151,200

PS10982
141. If n is a positive integer and the product of all the integers from 1 to n, inclusive, is divisible by 990, what is the least possible value of n?

(A) 8
(B) 9
(C) 10
(D) 11
(E) 12

PS02111
142. The probability that event M will not occur is 0.8 and the probability that event R will not occur is 0.6. If events M and R cannot both occur, which of the following is the probability that either event M or event R will occur?

(A) $\dfrac{1}{5}$
(B) $\dfrac{2}{5}$
(C) $\dfrac{3}{5}$
(D) $\dfrac{4}{5}$
(E) $\dfrac{12}{25}$

PS16410
143. The total cost for Company X to produce a batch of tools is $10,000 plus $3 per tool. Each tool sells for $8. The gross profit earned from producing and selling these tools is the total income from sales minus the total production cost. If a batch of 20,000 tools is produced and sold, then Company X's gross profit per tool is

(A) $3.00
(B) $3.75
(C) $4.50
(D) $5.00
(E) $5.50

PS07357
144. If Q is an odd number and the median of Q consecutive integers is 120, what is the largest of these integers?

(A) $\dfrac{Q-1}{2}+120$
(B) $\dfrac{Q}{2}+119$
(C) $\dfrac{Q}{2}+120$
(D) $\dfrac{Q+119}{2}$
(E) $\dfrac{Q+120}{2}$

PS02649
145. A ladder of a fire truck is elevated to an angle of 60° and extended to a length of 70 feet. If the base of the ladder is 7 feet above the ground, how many feet above the ground does the ladder reach?

(A) 35
(B) 42
(C) $35\sqrt{3}$
(D) $7+35\sqrt{3}$
(E) $7+42\sqrt{3}$

5.3 Problem Solving Practice Questions

PS13827
146. The window in the figure above consists of a rectangle and a semicircle with dimensions as shown. What is the area, in square feet, of the window?

(A) $40 + 8\pi$
(B) $40 + 2\pi$
(C) $32 + 8\pi$
(D) $32 + 4\pi$
(E) $32 + 2\pi$

PS00562
147. If there are fewer than 8 zeros between the decimal point and the first nonzero digit in the decimal expansion of $\left(\dfrac{t}{1{,}000}\right)^4$, which of the following numbers could be the value of t?

I. 3
II. 5
III. 9

(A) None
(B) I only
(C) II only
(D) III only
(E) II and III

PS08280
148. A three-digit code for certain locks uses the digits 0, 1, 2, 3, 4, 5, 6, 7, 8, 9 according to the following constraints. The first digit cannot be 0 or 1, the second digit must be 0 or 1, and the second and third digits cannot both be 0 in the same code. How many different codes are possible?

(A) 144
(B) 152
(C) 160
(D) 168
(E) 176

PS02903
149. Jackie has two solutions that are 2 percent sulfuric acid and 12 percent sulfuric acid by volume, respectively. If these solutions are mixed in appropriate quantities to produce 60 liters of a solution that is 5 percent sulfuric acid, approximately how many liters of the 2 percent solution will be required?

(A) 18
(B) 20
(C) 24
(D) 36
(E) 42

PS16259
150. If Jake loses 8 pounds, he will weigh twice as much as his sister. Together they now weigh 278 pounds. What is Jake's present weight, in pounds?

(A) 131
(B) 135
(C) 139
(D) 147
(E) 188

PS03768
151. For each student in a certain class, a teacher adjusted the student's test score using the formula $y = 0.8x + 20$, where x is the student's original test score and y is the student's adjusted test score. If the standard deviation of the original test scores of the students in the class was 20, what was the standard deviation of the adjusted test scores of the students in the class?

(A) 12
(B) 16
(C) 28
(D) 36
(E) 40

PS01987
152. Last year 26 members of a certain club traveled to England, 26 members traveled to France, and 32 members traveled to Italy. Last year no members of the club traveled to both England and France, 6 members traveled to both England and Italy, and 11 members traveled to both France and Italy. How many members of the club traveled to at least one of these three countries last year?

(A) 52
(B) 67
(C) 71
(D) 73
(E) 79

153. A store reported total sales of $385 million for February of this year. If the total sales for the same month last year was $320 million, approximately what was the percent increase in sales?

(A) 2%
(B) 17%
(C) 20%
(D) 65%
(E) 83%

154. When positive integer x is divided by positive integer y, the remainder is 9. If $\frac{x}{y} = 96.12$, what is the value of y?

(A) 96
(B) 75
(C) 48
(D) 25
(E) 12

155. If $x(2x+1) = 0$ and $\left(x + \frac{1}{2}\right)(2x - 3) = 0$, then $x =$

(A) -3
(B) $-\frac{1}{2}$
(C) 0
(D) $\frac{1}{2}$
(E) $\frac{3}{2}$

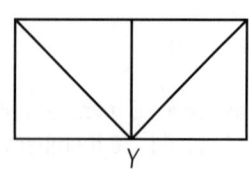

X   Y

156. Figures X and Y above show how eight identical triangular pieces of cardboard were used to form a square and a rectangle, respectively. What is the ratio of the perimeter of X to the perimeter of Y?

(A) $2:3$
(B) $\sqrt{2}:2$
(C) $2\sqrt{2}:3$
(D) $1:1$
(E) $\sqrt{2}:1$

157. A certain experimental mathematics program was tried out in 2 classes in each of 32 elementary schools and involved 37 teachers. Each of the classes had 1 teacher and each of the teachers taught at least 1, but not more than 3, of the classes. If the number of teachers who taught 3 classes is n, then the least and greatest possible values of n, respectively, are

(A) 0 and 13
(B) 0 and 14
(C) 1 and 10
(D) 1 and 9
(E) 2 and 8

158. For the positive numbers, n, $n+1$, $n+2$, $n+4$, and $n+8$, the mean is how much greater than the median?

(A) 0
(B) 1
(C) $n+1$
(D) $n+2$
(E) $n+3$

159. The interior of a rectangular carton is designed by a certain manufacturer to have a volume of x cubic feet and a ratio of length to width to height of 3:2:2. In terms of x, which of the following equals the height of the carton, in feet?

(A) $\sqrt[3]{x}$
(B) $\sqrt[3]{\frac{2x}{3}}$
(C) $\sqrt[3]{\frac{3x}{2}}$
(D) $\frac{2}{3}\sqrt[3]{x}$
(E) $\frac{3}{2}\sqrt[3]{x}$

160. The present ratio of students to teachers at a certain school is 30 to 1. If the student enrollment were to increase by 50 students and the number of teachers were to increase by 5, the ratio of students to teachers would then be 25 to 1. What is the present number of teachers?

    (A) 5
    (B) 8
    (C) 10
    (D) 12
    (E) 15

161. What is the smallest integer n for which $25^n > 5^{12}$?

    (A) 6
    (B) 7
    (C) 8
    (D) 9
    (E) 10

162. Sixty percent of the members of a study group are women, and 45 percent of those women are lawyers. If one member of the study group is to be selected at random, what is the probability that the member selected is a woman lawyer?

    (A) 0.10
    (B) 0.15
    (C) 0.27
    (D) 0.33
    (E) 0.45

163. Each year for 4 years, a farmer increased the number of trees in a certain orchard by $\frac{1}{4}$ of the number of trees in the orchard the preceding year. If all of the trees thrived and there were 6,250 trees in the orchard at the end of the 4-year period, how many trees were in the orchard at the beginning of the 4-year period?

    (A) 1,250
    (B) 1,563
    (C) 2,250
    (D) 2,560
    (E) 2,752

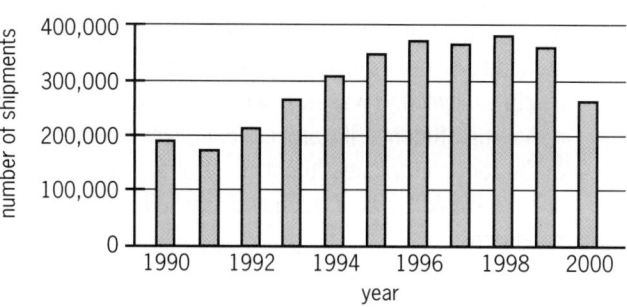

Number of Shipments of Manufactured Homes in the United States, 1990–2000

164. According to the chart shown, which of the following is closest to the median annual number of shipments of manufactured homes in the United States for the years from 1990 to 2000, inclusive?

    (A) 250,000
    (B) 280,000
    (C) 310,000
    (D) 325,000
    (E) 340,000

165. For the positive integers a, b, and k, $a^k \| b$ means that a^k is a divisor of b, but a^{k+1} is not a divisor of b. If k is a positive integer and $2^k \| 72$, then k is equal to

    (A) 2
    (B) 3
    (C) 4
    (D) 8
    (E) 18

166. A certain characteristic in a large population has a distribution that is symmetric about the mean m. If 68 percent of the distribution lies within one standard deviation d of the mean, what percent of the distribution is less than $m + d$?

    (A) 16%
    (B) 32%
    (C) 48%
    (D) 84%
    (E) 92%

167. Four extra-large sandwiches of exactly the same size were ordered for m students, where m > 4. Three of the sandwiches were evenly divided among the students. Since 4 students did not want any of the fourth sandwich, it was evenly divided among the remaining students. If Carol ate one piece from each of the four sandwiches, the amount of sandwich that she ate would be what fraction of a whole extra-large sandwich?

(A) $\dfrac{m+4}{m(m-4)}$

(B) $\dfrac{2m-4}{m(m-4)}$

(C) $\dfrac{4m-4}{m(m-4)}$

(D) $\dfrac{4m-8}{m(m-4)}$

(E) $\dfrac{4m-12}{m(m-4)}$

168. Which of the following equations has $1 + \sqrt{2}$ as one of its roots?

(A) $x^2 + 2x - 1 = 0$
(B) $x^2 - 2x + 1 = 0$
(C) $x^2 + 2x + 1 = 0$
(D) $x^2 - 2x - 1 = 0$
(E) $x^2 - x - 1 = 0$

169. In Country C, the unemployment rate among construction workers dropped from 16 percent on September 1, 1992, to 9 percent on September 1, 1996. If the number of construction workers was 20 percent greater on September 1, 1996, than on September 1, 1992, what was the approximate percent change in the number of unemployed construction workers over this period?

(A) 50% decrease
(B) 30% decrease
(C) 15% decrease
(D) 30% increase
(E) 55% increase

170. In a box of 12 pens, a total of 3 are defective. If a customer buys 2 pens selected at random from the box, what is the probability that neither pen will be defective?

(A) $\dfrac{1}{6}$
(B) $\dfrac{2}{9}$
(C) $\dfrac{6}{11}$
(D) $\dfrac{9}{16}$
(E) $\dfrac{3}{4}$

171. At a certain fruit stand, the price of each apple is 40 cents and the price of each orange is 60 cents. Mary selects a total of 10 apples and oranges from the fruit stand, and the average (arithmetic mean) price of the 10 pieces of fruit is 56 cents. How many oranges must Mary put back so that the average price of the pieces of fruit that she keeps is 52 cents?

(A) 1
(B) 2
(C) 3
(D) 4
(E) 5

172. A pharmaceutical company received $3 million in royalties on the first $20 million in sales of the generic equivalent of one of its products and then $9 million in royalties on the next $108 million in sales. By approximately what percent did the ratio of royalties to sales decrease from the first $20 million in sales to the next $108 million in sales?

(A) 8%
(B) 15%
(C) 45%
(D) 52%
(E) 56%

Times at Which the Door
Opened from 8:00 to 10:00

8:00	8:06	8:30	9:05
8:03	8:10	8:31	9:11
8:04	8:18	8:54	9:29
8:04	8:19	8:57	9:31

173. The light in a restroom operates with a 15-minute timer that is reset every time the door opens as a person goes in or out of the room. Thus, after someone enters or exits the room, the light remains on for only 15 minutes unless the door opens again and resets the timer for another 15 minutes. If the times listed above are the times at which the door opened from 8:00 to 10:00, approximately how many minutes during this two-hour period was the light off?

(A) 10
(B) 25
(C) 35
(D) 40
(E) 70

174. The parallelogram shown has four sides of equal length. What is the ratio of the length of the shorter diagonal to the length of the longer diagonal?

(A) $\frac{1}{2}$
(B) $\frac{1}{\sqrt{2}}$
(C) $\frac{1}{2\sqrt{2}}$
(D) $\frac{1}{\sqrt{3}}$
(E) $\frac{1}{2\sqrt{3}}$

175. If p is the product of the integers from 1 to 30, inclusive, what is the greatest integer k for which 3^k is a factor of p?

(A) 10
(B) 12
(C) 14
(D) 16
(E) 18

176. If $n = 3^8 - 2^8$, which of the following is NOT a factor of n?

(A) 97
(B) 65
(C) 35
(D) 13
(E) 5

177. In the figure shown, if the area of the shaded region is 3 times the area of the smaller circular region, then the circumference of the larger circle is how many times the circumference of the smaller circle?

(A) 4
(B) 3
(C) 2
(D) $\sqrt{3}$
(E) $\sqrt{2}$

178. Club X has more than 10 but fewer than 40 members. Sometimes the members sit at tables with 3 members at one table and 4 members at each of the other tables, and sometimes they sit at tables with 3 members at one table and 5 members at each of the other tables. If they sit at tables with 6 members at each table except one and fewer than 6 members at that one table, how many members will be at the table that has fewer than 6 members?

    (A) 1
    (B) 2
    (C) 3
    (D) 4
    (E) 5

179. In order to complete a reading assignment on time, Terry planned to read 90 pages per day. However, she read only 75 pages per day at first, leaving 690 pages to be read during the last 6 days before the assignment was to be completed. How many days in all did Terry have to complete the assignment on time?

    (A) 15
    (B) 16
    (C) 25
    (D) 40
    (E) 46

180. If $s > 0$ and $\sqrt{\frac{r}{s}} = s$, what is r in terms of s?

    (A) $\frac{1}{s}$
    (B) $\sqrt{s}$
    (C) $s\sqrt{s}$
    (D) s^3
    (E) $s^2 - s$

181. If $3 < x < 100$, for how many values of x is $\frac{x}{3}$ the square of a prime number?

    (A) Two
    (B) Three
    (C) Four
    (D) Five
    (E) Nine

182. A researcher plans to identify each participant in a certain medical experiment with a code consisting of either a single letter or a pair of distinct letters written in alphabetical order. What is the least number of letters that can be used if there are 12 participants, and each participant is to receive a different code?

    (A) 4
    (B) 5
    (C) 6
    (D) 7
    (E) 8

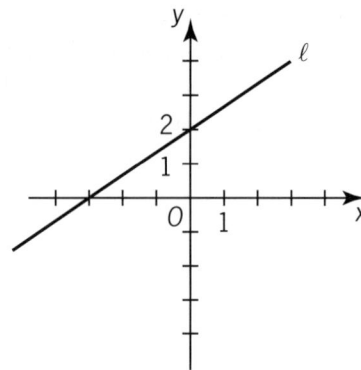

183. The graph of which of the following equations is a straight line that is parallel to line ℓ in the figure above?

    (A) $3y - 2x = 0$
    (B) $3y + 2x = 0$
    (C) $3y + 2x = 6$
    (D) $2y - 3x = 6$
    (E) $2y + 3x = -6$

184. An object thrown directly upward is at a height of h feet after t seconds, where $h = -16(t - 3)^2 + 150$. At what height, in feet, is the object 2 seconds after it reaches its maximum height?

    (A) 6
    (B) 86
    (C) 134
    (D) 150
    (E) 166

185. Which of the following is equivalent to the pair of inequalities x + 6 > 10 and x − 3 ≤ 5 ?

(A)   2 ≤ x < 16
(B)   2 ≤ x < 4
(C)   2 < x ≤ 8
(D)   4 < x ≤ 8
(E)   4 ≤ x < 16

186. David has d books, which is 3 times as many as Jeff and $\frac{1}{2}$ as many as Paula. How many books do the three of them have altogether, in terms of d?

(A) $\frac{5}{6}d$
(B) $\frac{7}{3}d$
(C) $\frac{10}{3}d$
(D) $\frac{7}{2}d$
(E) $\frac{9}{2}d$

187. There are 8 teams in a certain league and each team plays each of the other teams exactly once. If each game is played by 2 teams, what is the total number of games played?

(A)   15
(B)   16
(C)   28
(D)   56
(E)   64

188. At his regular hourly rate, Don had estimated the labor cost of a repair job as $336 and he was paid that amount. However, the job took 4 hours longer than he had estimated and, consequently, he earned $2 per hour less than his regular hourly rate. What was the time Don had estimated for the job, in hours?

(A)   28
(B)   24
(C)   16
(D)   14
(E)   12

189. If $\frac{p}{q} < 1$, and p and q are positive integers, which of the following must be greater than 1 ?

(A) $\sqrt{\frac{p}{q}}$
(B) $\frac{p}{q^2}$
(C) $\frac{p}{2q}$
(D) $\frac{q}{p^2}$
(E) $\frac{q}{p}$

190. To mail a package, the rate is x cents for the first pound and y cents for each additional pound, where x > y. Two packages weighing 3 pounds and 5 pounds, respectively, can be mailed separately or combined as one package. Which method is cheaper, and how much money is saved?

(A)   Combined, with a savings of x − y cents
(B)   Combined, with a savings of y − x cents
(C)   Combined, with a savings of x cents
(D)   Separately, with a savings of x − y cents
(E)   Separately, with a savings of y cents

191. If money is invested at r percent interest, compounded annually, the amount of the investment will double in approximately $\frac{70}{r}$ years. If Pat's parents invested $5,000 in a long-term bond that pays 8 percent interest, compounded annually, what will be the approximate total amount of the investment 18 years later, when Pat is ready for college?

(A) $20,000
(B) $15,000
(C) $12,000
(D) $10,000
(E) $9,000

192. On a recent trip, Cindy drove her car 290 miles, rounded to the nearest 10 miles, and used 12 gallons of gasoline, rounded to the nearest gallon. The actual number of miles per gallon that Cindy's car got on this trip must have been between

   (A) $\frac{290}{12.5}$ and $\frac{290}{11.5}$
   (B) $\frac{295}{12}$ and $\frac{285}{11.5}$
   (C) $\frac{285}{12}$ and $\frac{295}{12}$
   (D) $\frac{285}{12.5}$ and $\frac{295}{11.5}$
   (E) $\frac{295}{12.5}$ and $\frac{285}{11.5}$

193. Which of the following inequalities is an algebraic expression for the shaded part of the number line above?

   (A) $|x| \leq 3$
   (B) $|x| \leq 5$
   (C) $|x - 2| \leq 3$
   (D) $|x - 1| \leq 4$
   (E) $|x + 1| \leq 4$

194. In a small snack shop, the average (arithmetic mean) revenue was $400 per day over a 10-day period. During this period, if the average daily revenue was $360 for the first 6 days, what was the average daily revenue for the last 4 days?

   (A) $420
   (B) $440
   (C) $450
   (D) $460
   (E) $480

195. If y is the smallest positive integer such that 3,150 multiplied by y is the square of an integer, then y must be

   (A) 2
   (B) 5
   (C) 6
   (D) 7
   (E) 14

196. If [x] is the greatest integer less than or equal to x, what is the value of [–1.6] + [3.4] + [2.7] ?

   (A) 3
   (B) 4
   (C) 5
   (D) 6
   (E) 7

197. In the first week of the year, Nancy saved $1. In each of the next 51 weeks, she saved $1 more than she had saved in the previous week. What was the total amount that Nancy saved during the 52 weeks?

   (A) $1,326
   (B) $1,352
   (C) $1,378
   (D) $2,652
   (E) $2,756

198. In a certain sequence, the term x_n is given by the formula $x_n = 2x_{n-1} - \frac{1}{2}(x_{n-2})$ for all $n \geq 2$. If $x_0 = 3$ and $x_1 = 2$, what is the value of x_3 ?

   (A) 2.5
   (B) 3.125
   (C) 4
   (D) 5
   (E) 6.75

199. During a trip, Francine traveled x percent of the total distance at an average speed of 40 miles per hour and the rest of the distance at an average speed of 60 miles per hour. In terms of x, what was Francine's average speed for the entire trip?

(A) $\dfrac{180-x}{2}$

(B) $\dfrac{x+60}{4}$

(C) $\dfrac{300-x}{5}$

(D) $\dfrac{600}{115-x}$

(E) $\dfrac{12{,}000}{x+200}$

200. If $n = (33)^{43} + (43)^{33}$, what is the units digit of n?

(A) 0
(B) 2
(C) 4
(D) 6
(E) 8

201. Team A and Team B are competing against each other in a game of tug-of-war. Team A, consisting of 3 males and 3 females, decides to line up male, female, male, female, male, female. The lineup that Team A chooses will be one of how many different possible lineups?

(A) 9
(B) 12
(C) 15
(D) 36
(E) 720

202. A border of uniform width is placed around a rectangular photograph that measures 8 inches by 10 inches. If the area of the border is 144 square inches, what is the width of the border, in inches?

(A) 3
(B) 4
(C) 6
(D) 8
(E) 9

203. If $d = \dfrac{1}{2^3 \times 5^7}$ is expressed as a terminating decimal, how many nonzero digits will d have?

(A) One
(B) Two
(C) Three
(D) Seven
(E) Ten

204. For any positive integer n, the sum of the first n positive integers equals $\dfrac{n(n+1)}{2}$. What is the sum of all the even integers between 99 and 301?

(A) 10,100
(B) 20,200
(C) 22,650
(D) 40,200
(E) 45,150

205. How many prime numbers between 1 and 100 are factors of 7,150?

(A) One
(B) Two
(C) Three
(D) Four
(E) Five

206. A sequence of numbers a_1, a_2, a_3, ... is defined as follows: $a_1 = 3$, $a_2 = 5$, and every term in the sequence after a_2 is the product of all terms in the sequence preceding it, e.g., $a_3 = (a_1)(a_2)$ and $a_4 = (a_1)(a_2)(a_3)$. If $a_n = t$ and $n > 2$, what is the value of a_{n+2} in terms of t?

(A) $4t$
(B) t^2
(C) t^3
(D) t^4
(E) t^8

207. Last year the price per share of Stock X increased by k percent and the earnings per share of Stock X increased by m percent, where k is greater than m. By what percent did the ratio of price per share to earnings per share increase, in terms of k and m?

(A) $\dfrac{k}{m}\%$

(B) $(k-m)\%$

(C) $\dfrac{100(k-m)}{100+k}\%$

(D) $\dfrac{100(k-m)}{100+m}\%$

(E) $\dfrac{100(k-m)}{100+k+m}\%$

208. Of the 300 subjects who participated in an experiment using virtual-reality therapy to reduce their fear of heights, 40 percent experienced sweaty palms, 30 percent experienced vomiting, and 75 percent experienced dizziness. If all of the subjects experienced at least one of these effects and 35 percent of the subjects experienced exactly two of these effects, how many of the subjects experienced only one of these effects?

(A) 105
(B) 125
(C) 130
(D) 180
(E) 195

209. If $m^{-1} = -\dfrac{1}{3}$, then m^{-2} is equal to

(A) -9
(B) -3
(C) $-\dfrac{1}{9}$
(D) $\dfrac{1}{9}$
(E) 9

210. A photography dealer ordered 60 Model X cameras to be sold for $250 each, which represents a 20 percent markup over the dealer's initial cost for each camera. Of the cameras ordered, 6 were never sold and were returned to the manufacturer for a refund of 50 percent of the dealer's initial cost. What was the dealer's approximate profit or loss as a percent of the dealer's initial cost for the 60 cameras?

(A) 7% loss
(B) 13% loss
(C) 7% profit
(D) 13% profit
(E) 15% profit

211. Seven pieces of rope have an average (arithmetic mean) length of 68 centimeters and a median length of 84 centimeters. If the length of the longest piece of rope is 14 centimeters more than 4 times the length of the shortest piece of rope, what is the maximum possible length, in centimeters, of the longest piece of rope?

(A) 82
(B) 118
(C) 120
(D) 134
(E) 152

212. What is the difference between the sixth and the fifth terms of the sequence 2, 4, 7, … whose nth term is $n + 2^{n-1}$?

(A) 2
(B) 3
(C) 6
(D) 16
(E) 17

213. From the consecutive integers −10 to 10, inclusive, 20 integers are randomly chosen with repetitions allowed. What is the least possible value of the product of the 20 integers?

(A) $(-10)^{20}$
(B) $(-10)^{10}$
(C) 0
(D) $-(10)^{19}$
(E) $-(10)^{20}$

178

5.3 Problem Solving Practice Questions

PS05140
214. The letters D, G, I, I, and T can be used to form 5-letter strings such as DIGIT or DGIIT. Using these letters, how many 5-letter strings can be formed in which the two occurrences of the letter I are separated by at least one other letter?

  (A) 12
  (B) 18
  (C) 24
  (D) 36
  (E) 48

PS00574
215. $\dfrac{0.99999999}{1.0001} - \dfrac{0.99999991}{1.0003} =$

  (A) 10^{-8}
  (B) $3(10^{-8})$
  (C) $3(10^{-4})$
  (D) $2(10^{-4})$
  (E) 10^{-4}

PS03144
216. Last Sunday a certain store sold copies of Newspaper A for $1.00 each and copies of Newspaper B for $1.25 each, and the store sold no other newspapers that day. If r percent of the store's revenue from newspaper sales was from Newspaper A and if p percent of the newspapers that the store sold were copies of Newspaper A, which of the following expresses r in terms of p?

  (A) $\dfrac{100p}{125-p}$
  (B) $\dfrac{150p}{250-p}$
  (C) $\dfrac{300p}{375-p}$
  (D) $\dfrac{400p}{500-p}$
  (E) $\dfrac{500p}{625-p}$

PS16890
217. For the past n days, the average (arithmetic mean) daily production at a company was 50 units. If today's production of 90 units raises the average to 55 units per day, what is the value of n?

  (A) 30
  (B) 18
  (C) 10
  (D) 9
  (E) 7

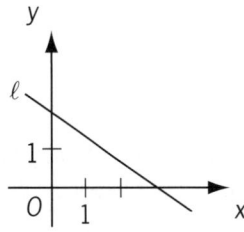

PS16893
218. In the coordinate system above, which of the following is the equation of line ℓ?

  (A) $2x - 3y = 6$
  (B) $2x + 3y = 6$
  (C) $3x + 2y = 6$
  (D) $2x - 3y = -6$
  (E) $3x - 2y = -6$

PS16894
219. If a two-digit positive integer has its digits reversed, the resulting integer differs from the original by 27. By how much do the two digits differ?

  (A) 3
  (B) 4
  (C) 5
  (D) 6
  (E) 7

179

220. In an electric circuit, two resistors with resistances x and y are connected in parallel. In this case, if r is the combined resistance of these two resistors, then the reciprocal of r is equal to the sum of the reciprocals of x and y. What is r in terms of x and y?

(A) xy
(B) $x+y$
(C) $\dfrac{1}{x+y}$
(D) $\dfrac{xy}{x+y}$
(E) $\dfrac{x+y}{xy}$

221. Xavier, Yvonne, and Zelda each try independently to solve a problem. If their individual probabilities for success are $\dfrac{1}{4}$, $\dfrac{1}{2}$, and $\dfrac{5}{8}$, respectively, what is the probability that Xavier and Yvonne, but not Zelda, will solve the problem?

(A) $\dfrac{11}{8}$
(B) $\dfrac{7}{8}$
(C) $\dfrac{9}{64}$
(D) $\dfrac{5}{64}$
(E) $\dfrac{3}{64}$

222. If $\dfrac{1}{x} - \dfrac{1}{x+1} = \dfrac{1}{x+4}$, then x could be

(A) 0
(B) −1
(C) −2
(D) −3
(E) −4

223. $\left(\dfrac{1}{2}\right)^{-3}\left(\dfrac{1}{4}\right)^{-2}\left(\dfrac{1}{16}\right)^{-1}$

(A) $\left(\dfrac{1}{2}\right)^{-48}$
(B) $\left(\dfrac{1}{2}\right)^{-11}$
(C) $\left(\dfrac{1}{2}\right)^{-6}$
(D) $\left(\dfrac{1}{8}\right)^{-11}$
(E) $\left(\dfrac{1}{8}\right)^{-6}$

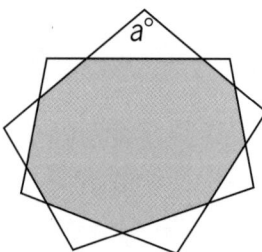

224. The figure shown above consists of a shaded 9-sided polygon and 9 unshaded isosceles triangles. For each isosceles triangle, the longest side is a side of the shaded polygon and the two sides of equal length are extensions of the two adjacent sides of the shaded polygon. What is the value of a?

(A) 100
(B) 105
(C) 110
(D) 115
(E) 120

225. List T consists of 30 positive decimals, none of which is an integer, and the sum of the 30 decimals is S. The estimated sum of the 30 decimals, E, is defined as follows. Each decimal in T whose tenths digit is even is rounded up to the nearest integer, and each decimal in T whose tenths digit is odd is rounded down to the nearest integer; E is the sum of the resulting integers. If $\frac{1}{3}$ of the decimals in T have a tenths digit that is even, which of the following is a possible value of E − S ?

   I.   −16
   II. 6
   III. 10

   (A) I only
   (B) I and II only
   (C) I and III only
   (D) II and III only
   (E) I, II, and III

226. If $5 - \frac{6}{x} = x$, then x has how many possible values?

   (A) None
   (B) One
   (C) Two
   (D) A finite number greater than two
   (E) An infinite number

227. Seed mixture X is 40 percent ryegrass and 60 percent bluegrass by weight; seed mixture Y is 25 percent ryegrass and 75 percent fescue. If a mixture of X and Y contains 30 percent ryegrass, what percent of the weight of the mixture is X ?

   (A) 10%
   (B) $33\frac{1}{3}$%
   (C) 40%
   (D) 50%
   (E) $66\frac{2}{3}$%

228. How many of the integers that satisfy the inequality $\frac{(x+2)(x+3)}{x-2} \geq 0$ are less than 5 ?

   (A) 1
   (B) 2
   (C) 3
   (D) 4
   (E) 5

229. Of the 150 houses in a certain development, 60 percent have air-conditioning, 50 percent have a sunporch, and 30 percent have a swimming pool. If 5 of the houses have all three of these amenities and 5 have none of them, how many of the houses have exactly two of these amenities?

   (A) 10
   (B) 45
   (C) 50
   (D) 55
   (E) 65

230. The value of $\frac{2^{-14} + 2^{-15} + 2^{-16} + 2^{-17}}{5}$ is how many times the value of $2^{(-17)}$?

   (A) $\frac{3}{2}$
   (B) $\frac{5}{2}$
   (C) 3
   (D) 4
   (E) 5

5.4 Answer Key

1.	B	31.	D	61.	B	91.	D
2.	D	32.	D	62.	E	92.	E
3.	D	33.	E	63.	B	93.	B
4.	C	34.	C	64.	A	94.	D
5.	A	35.	C	65.	D	95.	D
6.	E	36.	E	66.	E	96.	B
7.	E	37.	C	67.	D	97.	C
8.	C	38.	E	68.	D	98.	B
9.	E	39.	D	69.	D	99.	C
10.	B	40.	B	70.	B	100.	E
11.	D	41.	B	71.	E	101.	D
12.	E	42.	C	72.	D	102.	C
13.	A	43.	C	73.	A	103.	E
14.	B	44.	A	74.	D	104.	B
15.	C	45.	D	75.	C	105.	E
16.	E	46.	A	76.	B	106.	E
17.	C	47.	B	77.	B	107.	E
18.	D	48.	E	78.	D	108.	B
19.	E	49.	E	79.	D	109.	B
20.	B	50.	E	80.	C	110.	B
21.	E	51.	D	81.	E	111.	C
22.	B	52.	C	82.	E	112.	A
23.	C	53.	A	83.	B	113.	D
24.	C	54.	E	84.	B	114.	D
25.	E	55.	D	85.	C	115.	A
26.	E	56.	D	86.	B	116.	E
27.	C	57.	A	87.	D	117.	B
28.	B	58.	D	88.	A	118.	E
29.	B	59.	C	89.	D	119.	E
30.	C	60.	E	90.	D	120.	D

5.4 Problem Solving Answer Key

121.	E	151.	B	181.	B	211.	D
122.	A	152.	B	182.	B	212.	E
123.	E	153.	C	183.	A	213.	E
124.	E	154.	B	184.	B	214.	D
125.	D	155.	B	185.	D	215.	D
126.	D	156.	C	186.	C	216.	D
127.	C	157.	A	187.	C	217.	E
128.	D	158.	B	188.	B	218.	B
129.	B	159.	B	189.	E	219.	A
130.	A	160.	E	190.	A	220.	D
131.	D	161.	B	191.	A	221.	E
132.	A	162.	C	192.	D	222.	C
133.	E	163.	D	193.	E	223.	B
134.	B	164.	C	194.	D	224.	A
135.	B	165.	B	195.	E	225.	B
136.	A	166.	D	196.	A	226.	C
137.	E	167.	E	197.	C	227.	B
138.	E	168.	D	198.	C	228.	D
139.	D	169.	B	199.	E	229.	D
140.	D	170.	C	200.	A	230.	C
141.	D	171.	E	201.	D		
142.	C	172.	C	202.	A		
143.	C	173.	B	203.	B		
144.	A	174.	D	204.	B		
145.	D	175.	C	205.	D		
146.	E	176.	C	206.	D		
147.	A	177.	C	207.	D		
148.	B	178.	E	208.	D		
149.	E	179.	B	209.	D		
150.	E	180.	D	210.	D		

5.5 Answer Explanations

The following discussion is intended to familiarize you with the most efficient and effective approaches to the kinds of problems common to problem solving questions. The particular questions in this chapter are generally representative of the kinds of problem solving questions you will encounter on the GMAT exam. Remember that it is the problem solving strategy that is important, not the specific details of a particular question.

*PS02991
1. In the figure, the 6 small squares are identical, each with sides of length 1. What is the outer perimeter (shown in bold) of the entire figure?

(A) 8
(B) 12
(C) 16
(D) 20
(E) 24

Geometry Perimeter

The labeled figure shows the 6 horizontal sides of the boundary, 4 sides of length 1 and 2 sides of length 2, and the 6 vertical sides of the boundary, 2 sides of length 1 and 1 side each of lengths a, b, c, and d. The perimeter is the sum of the lengths of these 12 sides, or $4(1) + 2(2) + 2(1) + a + b + c + d$, or $10 + a + b + c + d$. To determine the value of $a + b + c + d$, note that the vertical width of the squares is 2. On the left side, this vertical width is the sum of the lengths of 3 vertical sides of the boundary, 1 side of length 1 and 1 side each of lengths a and b, and thus $2 = 1 + a + b$, or $a + b = 1$. On the right side, this vertical width is the sum of the lengths of 3 vertical sides of the boundary, 1 side of length 1 and 1 side each of lengths c and d, and thus $2 = 1 + c + d$, or $c + d = 1$. Therefore, the perimeter is $10 + (a + b) + (c + d) = 10 + 1 + 1 = 12$.

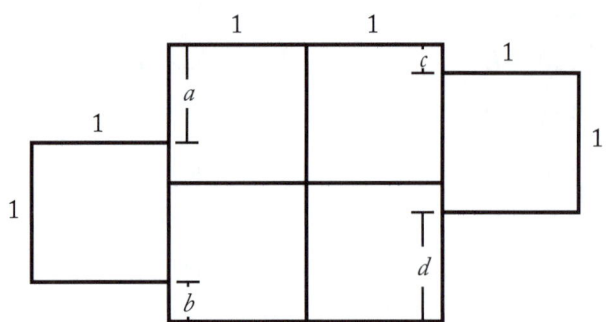

The correct answer is B.

Performance Time	Ticket Price	Number of Tickets Sold
Thursday night	$40	200
Friday night	$50	240
Saturday afternoon	$40	220
Saturday night	$50	300

PS09868
2. The table shows a summary of the ticket sales from four performances of a certain play. What is the difference between the maximum and the minimum ticket-sale revenue from a single performance?

(A) $4,000
(B) $5,100
(C) $6,200
(D) $7,000
(E) $9,600

Arithmetic Interpretation of tables

For each performance, the product of the ticket price and the number of tickets sold is the ticket-sale revenue. The following table shows these values.

*These numbers correlate with the online test bank question number. See the GMAT Official Guide Online Index in the back of this book.

Performance Time	Ticket-sale Revenue
Thursday night	200($40) = $8,000
Friday night	240($50) = $12,000
Saturday afternoon	220($40) = $8,800
Saturday night	300($50) = $15,000

From these values it follows that for a single performance, the maximum ticket-sale revenue is $15,000 and the minimum ticket-sale revenue is $8,000, and therefore the difference between these two revenues is $15,000 − $8,000 = $7,000.

The correct answer is D.

PS10002

3. During a trip that they took together, Carmen, Juan, Maria, and Rafael drove an average (arithmetic mean) of 80 miles each. Carmen drove 72 miles, Juan drove 78 miles, and Maria drove 83 miles. How many miles did Rafael drive?

   (A) 80
   (B) 82
   (C) 85
   (D) 87
   (E) 89

Arithmetic Statistics

Let $C, J, M,$ and R be the numbers of miles, respectively, that Carmen, Juan, Maria, and Rafael drove. Since the average of the numbers of miles they drove is 80, it follows that $\frac{C+J+M+R}{4} = 80$, or $C+J+M+R = 4(80) = 320$. It is given that $C = 72, J = 78,$ and $M = 83$. Therefore, $72 + 78 + 83 + R = 320$, or $R = 87$.

The correct answer is D.

PS07308

4. Each week, a clothing salesperson receives a commission equal to 15 percent of the first $500 in sales and 20 percent of all additional sales that week. What commission would the salesperson receive on total sales for the week of $1,300 ?

   (A) $195
   (B) $227
   (C) $235
   (D) $260
   (E) $335

Arithmetic Applied problems

The commission on the total sales can be calculated as follows:

$$\text{commission on first \$500} + \text{commission on amount over \$500}$$
$$= (0.15)(\$500) + (0.20)(\$1{,}300 - \$500)$$
$$= \$75 + \$160$$

Therefore, the commission on the total sales is $75 + $160 = $235.

The correct answer is C.

PS07799

5. A certain restaurant that regularly advertises through the mail has 1,040 cover letters and 3,000 coupons in stock. In its next mailing, each envelope will contain 1 cover letter and 2 coupons. If all of the cover letters in stock are used, how many coupons will remain in stock after this mailing?

   (A) 920
   (B) 1,040
   (C) 1,500
   (D) 1,960
   (E) 2,080

Arithmetic Applied problems

In the next mailing there will be 1,040 cover letters and 2(1,040) = 2,080 coupons. Therefore, after the next mailing the number of coupons remaining in stock will be 3,000 − 2,080 = 920.

The correct answer is A.

PS02599

6. In the figure above, what are the coordinates of point R?

(A) (3,–5)
(B) (3,–3)
(C) (5,5)
(D) (5,–3)
(E) (5,–5)

Geometry Simple coordinate geometry; Triangles

In the figure, each of the points M and R has x-coordinate 5 because these two points lie on a vertical line that contains Q and it is given that the x-coordinate of Q is 5. Also, the measure of $\angle MRO$ is 45°, and hence $OM = MR$, because $\triangle OMR$ is a right triangle and it is given that the measure of $\angle ROM$ is 45°. Since it is given that $OM = 5$, it follows that $MR = 5$ and the coordinates of R are $(5,y) = (5,-5)$.

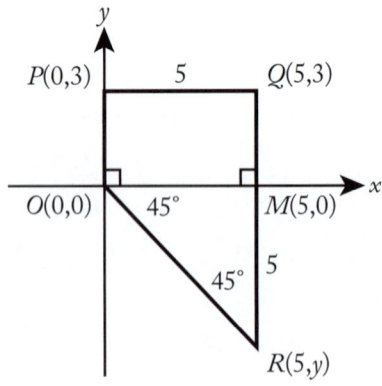

The correct answer is E.

PS08877

7. The price of a coat in a certain store is $500. If the price of the coat is to be reduced by $150, by what percent is the price to be reduced?

(A) 10%
(B) 15%
(C) 20%
(D) 25%
(E) 30%

Arithmetic Percents

A reduction of $150 from $500 represents a percent decrease of $\left(\dfrac{150}{500} \times 100\right)\% = 30\%$. Therefore, the price of the coat was reduced by 30%.

The correct answer is E.

PS05410

8. $\left(\dfrac{1}{2}-\dfrac{1}{3}\right)+\left(\dfrac{1}{3}-\dfrac{1}{4}\right)+\left(\dfrac{1}{4}-\dfrac{1}{5}\right)+\left(\dfrac{1}{5}-\dfrac{1}{6}\right)=$

(A) $-\dfrac{1}{6}$
(B) 0
(C) $\dfrac{1}{3}$
(D) $\dfrac{1}{2}$
(E) $\dfrac{2}{3}$

Arithmetic Operations on rational numbers

The parentheses can be removed without any change of signs, and after doing this most of the terms can be additively cancelled as shown below.

$$\dfrac{1}{2}-\cancel{\dfrac{1}{3}}+\cancel{\dfrac{1}{3}}-\cancel{\dfrac{1}{4}}+\cancel{\dfrac{1}{4}}-\cancel{\dfrac{1}{5}}+\cancel{\dfrac{1}{5}}-\dfrac{1}{6}=\dfrac{1}{2}-\dfrac{1}{6}$$
$$=\dfrac{1}{3}$$

The correct answer is C.

5.5 Problem Solving Answer Explanations

PS05001

9. While a family was away on vacation, they paid a neighborhood boy $11 per week to mow their lawn and $4 per day to feed and walk their dog. If the family was away for exactly 3 weeks, how much did they pay the boy for his services?

   (A) $45
   (B) $54
   (C) $71
   (D) $95
   (E) $117

Arithmetic Applied problems

A period of exactly 3 weeks consists of exactly $3(7) = 21$ days. Therefore, the boy was paid for 3 weeks of mowing the lawn and for 21 days of feeding and walking the dog, for a total pay of $3(\$11) + 21(\$4) = \$33 + \$84 = \$117$.

The correct answer is E.

PS17812

10. Last year $48,000 of a certain store's profit was shared by its 2 owners and their 10 employees. Each of the 2 owners received 3 times as much as each of their 10 employees. How much did each owner receive from the $48,000 ?

    (A) $12,000
    (B) $9,000
    (C) $6,000
    (D) $4,000
    (E) $3,000

Algebra First-degree equations

Let A be the amount received by each owner and let B be the amount received by each employee. From the given information it follows that $A = 3B$ and $2A + 10B = 48,000$. Thus, $2(3B) + 10B = 48,000$, or $16B = 48,000$, or $B = 3,000$. Therefore, the amount received by each owner was $A = 3B = 3(\$3,000) = \$9,000$.

The correct answer is B.

PS02295

11. On a vacation, Rose exchanged $500.00 for euros at an exchange rate of 0.80 euro per dollar and spent $\frac{3}{4}$ of the euros she received. If she exchanged the remaining euros for dollars at an exchange rate of $1.20 per euro, what was the dollar amount she received?

    (A) $60.00
    (B) $80.00
    (C) $100.00
    (D) $120.00
    (E) $140.00

Arithmetic Operations with rational numbers

At the exchange rate of 0.80 euro per dollar, Rose exchanged $500.00 for $(0.80)(500) = 400$ euros. She spent $\frac{3}{4}(400) = 300$ euros, had $400 - 300 = 100$ euros left, and exchanged them for dollars at the exchange rate of $1.20 per euro. Therefore, the dollar amount she received was $(1.20)(100) = \$120.00$.

The correct answer is D.

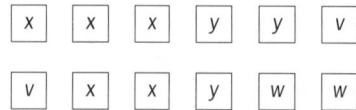

PS08461

12. Each of the 12 squares shown is labeled x, y, v, or w. What is the ratio of the number of these squares labeled x or y to the number of these squares labeled v or w?

    (A) 1:2
    (B) 2:3
    (C) 4:3
    (D) 3:2
    (E) 2:1

Arithmetic Ratio and proportion

By a direct count, there are 8 squares labeled x or y (5 labeled x, 3 labeled y) and there are 4 squares labeled v or w (2 labeled v, 2 labeled w). Therefore, the ratio of the number of squares labeled x or y to the number of squares labeled v or w is 8:4, which reduces to 2:1.

The correct answer is E.

13. In the xy-coordinate plane, if the point (0,2) lies on the graph of the line 2x + ky = 4, what is the value of the constant k ?

    (A) 2
    (B) 1
    (C) 0
    (D) −1
    (E) −2

    Algebra First-degree equations

    It is given that the point (0,2) lies on the graph of 2x + ky = 4. Therefore, 2(0) + k(2) = 4, or 0 + 2k = 4, or k = 2.

    The correct answer is A.

14. Bouquets are to be made using white tulips and red tulips, and the ratio of the number of white tulips to the number of red tulips is to be the same in each bouquet. If there are 15 white tulips and 85 red tulips available for the bouquets, what is the greatest number of bouquets that can be made using all the tulips available?

    (A) 3
    (B) 5
    (C) 8
    (D) 10
    (E) 13

    Arithmetic Applied problems; Properties of numbers

    Because all the tulips are to be used and the same number of white tulips will be in each bouquet, the number of white tulips in each bouquet times the number of bouquets must equal the total number of white tulips, or 15. Thus, the number of bouquets must be a factor of 15, and so the number must be 1, 3, 5, or 15. Also, the number of red tulips in each bouquet times the number of bouquets must equal the total number of red tulips, or 85. Thus, the number of bouquets must be a factor of 85, and so the number must be 1, 5, 17, or 85. Since the number of bouquets must be 1, 3, 5, or 15, and the number of bouquets must be 1, 5, 17, or 85, it follows that the number of bouquets must be 1 or 5, and thus the greatest number of bouquets that can be made is 5. Note that each of the 5 bouquets will have 3 white tulips, because (5)(3) = 15, and each of the 5 bouquets will have 17 red tulips, because (5)(17) = 85.

    The correct answer is B.

15. Over the past 7 weeks, the Smith family had weekly grocery bills of $74, $69, $64, $79, $64, $84, and $77. What was the Smiths' average (arithmetic mean) weekly grocery bill over the 7-week period?

    (A) $64
    (B) $70
    (C) $73
    (D) $74
    (E) $85

    Arithmetic Statistics

    The average weekly grocery bill over the 7-week period can be calculated by dividing the total of the 7 weekly grocery bills by 7.

    $$\frac{\$74+\$69+\$64+\$79+\$64+\$84+\$77}{7} = \frac{\$511}{7} = \$73$$

    An alternate method that involves less computation by hand is to calculate the average by dividing the total of the differences of the weekly bills from a fixed value (chosen so that these differences can be calculated easily), dividing this total by 7, and then adding the result to the fixed value chosen. The computations below illustrate and justify this method when the fixed value is 70. In using this method when the fixed value is 70 (and not also justifying the method, as is done below), the numbers 4, −1, −6, 9, −6, 14, and 7 would be obtained by inspection and added together, then divided by 7 with the result added to 70.

    $$\frac{(70+4)+(70-1)+(70-6)+(70+9)+(70-6)+(70+14)+(70+7)}{7}$$
    $$= \frac{7(70)}{7} + \frac{4-1-6+9-6+14+7}{7}$$
    $$= 70 + \frac{21}{7}$$
    $$= 70 + 3$$
    $$= 73$$

    The correct answer is C.

5.5 Problem Solving Answer Explanations

16. 125% of 5 =

    (A) 5.125
    (B) 5.25
    (C) 6
    (D) 6.125
    (E) 6.25

    Arithmetic Percents

    125% of 5 represents $\frac{125}{100} \times 5$, or $1.25 \times 5 = 6.25$.

    The correct answer is E.

17. During a recent storm, 9 neighborhoods experienced power failures of durations 34, 29, 27, 46, 18, 25, 12, 35, and 16 minutes, respectively. For these 9 neighborhoods, what was the median duration, in minutes, of the power failures?

    (A) 34
    (B) 29
    (C) 27
    (D) 25
    (E) 18

    Arithmetic Statistics

    To determine the median of these 9 numbers, put the numbers in numerical order in a list and determine the middle value in the list:

    12, 16, 18, 25, **27**, 29, 34, 35, 46

    From this list it follows that the median is 27.

    The correct answer is C.

18. When traveling at a constant speed of 32 miles per hour, a certain motorboat consumes 24 gallons of fuel per hour. What is the fuel consumption of this boat at this speed measured in miles traveled per gallon of fuel?

    (A) $\frac{2}{3}$
    (B) $\frac{3}{4}$
    (C) $\frac{4}{5}$
    (D) $\frac{4}{3}$
    (E) $\frac{3}{2}$

    Arithmetic Operations with rational numbers

    If the motorboat consumes 24 gallons of fuel in 1 hour, then it consumes 1 gallon of fuel in $\frac{1}{24}$ hour. If the motorboat travels 32 miles in 1 hour, then it travels $\frac{32}{24} = \frac{4}{3}$ miles in $\frac{1}{24}$ hour, which is the length of time it takes to consume 1 gallon of fuel. Thus, the motorboat travels $\frac{4}{3}$ miles per gallon of fuel.

    The correct answer is D.

19. A technician makes a round-trip to and from a certain service center by the same route. If the technician completes the drive to the center and then completes 10 percent of the drive from the center, what percent of the round-trip has the technician completed?

    (A) 5%
    (B) 10%
    (C) 25%
    (D) 40%
    (E) 55%

    Arithmetic Percents

    In completing the drive to the service center, the technician has completed 50% of the round-trip. The drive from the center is the other 50% of the round-trip. In completing 10% of the drive from the center, the technician has completed an additional 10% of 50%, or 5% of the round-trip. Thus, the technician has completed 50% + 5% = 55% of the round-trip.

The correct answer is E.

PS15957
20. From 2000 to 2003, the number of employees at a certain company increased by a factor of $\frac{1}{4}$. From 2003 to 2006, the number of employees at this company decreased by a factor of $\frac{1}{3}$. If there were 100 employees at the company in 2006, how many employees were there at the company in 2000?

(A) 200
(B) 120
(C) 100
(D) 75
(E) 60

Algebra First-degree equations

Let N be the number of employees in 2000. In 2003 there were $\frac{1}{4}$(number in 2000) $= \frac{1}{4}N$ more employees than in 2000, for a total of $N + \frac{1}{4}N = \frac{5}{4}N$ employees. In 2006 there were $\frac{1}{3}$(number in 2003) $= \frac{1}{3}\left(\frac{5}{4}\right)N$ fewer employees than in 2003, for a total of $\frac{5}{4}N - \frac{1}{3}\left(\frac{5}{4}N\right) = \frac{5}{6}N$ employees. It is given that there were 100 employees in 2006, so $\frac{5}{6}N = 100$, or $N = \frac{6}{5}(100) = 120$.

The correct answer is B.

PS00984
21. Which of the following statements must be true about the average (arithmetic mean) and the median of 5 consecutive integers?

I. The average is one of the integers.
II. The median is one of the integers.
III. The median equals the average.

(A) I only
(B) II only
(C) III only
(D) I and II only
(E) I, II, and III

Algebra Statistics

If n is the least of the 5 consecutive integers then, in increasing order, the integers are

$n, n+1, n+2, n+3, n+4$.

Statement I must be true because the average of the integers is $\frac{n+(n+1)+(n+2)+(n+3)+(n+4)}{5}$, or $\frac{5n+10}{5} = n+2$, and $n+2$ is one of the integers.

Statement II must be true because the median is the middle number in the list, which is $n+2$, and $n+2$ is one of the integers.

Statement III must be true because $n+2$ is both the average and the median.

The correct answer is E.

PS15358
22. A collection of 16 coins, each with a face value of either 10 cents or 25 cents, has a total face value of $2.35. How many of the coins have a face value of 25 cents?

(A) 3
(B) 5
(C) 7
(D) 9
(E) 11

Algebra First-degree equations

Let x represent the number of coins each with a face value of 25 cents. Then, since there are 16 coins in all, $16 - x$ represents the number of coins each with a face value of 10 cents. The total face value of the coins is $2.35 or 235 cents so,

$25x + 10(16 - x) = 235$ given
$25x + 160 - 10x = 235$ distributive property
$15x + 160 = 235$ combine like terms
$15x = 75$ subtract 160 from both sides
$x = 5$ divide both sides by 15

Therefore, 5 of the coins have a face value of 25 cents.

The correct answer is B.

5.5 Problem Solving Answer Explanations

PS09707
23. A retailer purchased eggs at $2.80 per dozen and sold the eggs at 3 eggs for $0.90. What was the retailer's gross profit from purchasing and selling 5 dozen eggs? (1 dozen eggs = 12 eggs)

   (A) $0.90
   (B) $2.40
   (C) $4.00
   (D) $11.30
   (E) $12.00

Arithmetic Applied problems

The retailer's cost was $2.80 per dozen eggs and the retailer's revenue was $0.90 per 3 eggs, or 4($0.90) = $3.60 per dozen eggs. Therefore, the retailer's profit for 5 dozen eggs—revenue minus cost for 5 dozen eggs—was 5($3.60 − $2.80) = 5($0.80) = $4.00.

The correct answer is C.

PS02127
24. In a set of 24 cards, each card is numbered with a different positive integer from 1 to 24. One card will be drawn at random from the set. What is the probability that the card drawn will have either a number that is divisible by both 2 and 3 or a number that is divisible by 7?

   (A) $\frac{3}{24}$
   (B) $\frac{4}{24}$
   (C) $\frac{7}{24}$
   (D) $\frac{8}{24}$
   (E) $\frac{17}{24}$

Arithmetic Probability

The desired probability is N divided by 24, where N is the number of positive integers from 1 through 24 that are either divisible by both 2 and 3, or divisible by 7. Since an integer is divisible by both 2 and 3 if and only if the integer is divisible by 6, it follows that N is the number of positive integers from 1 through 24 that are either divisible by 6 or divisible by 7. There are 4 numbers from 1 through 24 that are divisible by 6, namely 6, 12, 18, and 24. There are 3 numbers from 1 through 24 that are divisible by 7, namely 7, 14, and 21. Since these numbers are all different from each other, it follows that $N = 4 + 3 = 7$ and the desired probability is $\frac{N}{24} = \frac{7}{24}$.

The correct answer is C.

PS12542
25. If the circumference of a circle inscribed in a square is 25π, what is the perimeter of the square?

   (A) 20
   (B) 25
   (C) 40
   (D) 50
   (E) 100

Geometry Circles; Circumference; Perimeter

For any circle inscribed in a square, the length of the diameter of the circle is equal to the length of a side of the square. Let d be the length of the diameter of the circle. Then πd is the circumference of the circle. Also, d is the length of each of the 4 sides of the square, and so $4d$ is the perimeter of the square. From the information given, $\pi d = 25\pi$, or $d = 25$, and therefore the perimeter of the square is $4d = 4(25) = 100$.

The correct answer is E.

PS03972
26. If $1 < x < y < z$, which of the following has the greatest value?

   (A) $z(x + 1)$
   (B) $z(y + 1)$
   (C) $x(y + z)$
   (D) $y(x + z)$
   (E) $z(x + y)$

Algebra Inequalities

This problem can be solved by calculating each of the options for a fixed and appropriate choice of values for each of the variables. For example, if

191

$x = 2$, $y = 3$, and $z = 4$, then $1 < x < y < z$ and the values of the options are as follows:

A $z(x + 1) = 4(2 + 1) = 12$
B $z(y + 1) = 4(3 + 1) = 16$
C $x(y + z) = 2(3 + 4) = 14$
D $y(x + z) = 3(2 + 4) = 18$
E $z(x + y) = 4(2 + 3) = 20$

This problem can also be solved by the use of algebraic ordering principles in a way that does not assume the same answer option is true for each choice of values of x, y, and z such that $1 < x < y < z$. First, note that neither the value of the expression in A nor the value of the expression in B can ever have the greatest value, since the value of the expression in E is greater than the value of the expression in A (because $y > 1$) and the value of the expression in E is greater than the value of the expression in B (because $x > 1$). Also, the value of the expression in D is greater than the value of the expression in C, since $y > x$ implies $yz > xz$, which implies $xy + yz > xy + xz$, which implies $y(x + z) > x(y + z)$, and so the value of the expression in C cannot be the greatest. Finally, the value of the expression in E is greater than the value of the expression in D, since $z > y$ implies $xz > xy$, which implies $xz + yz > xy + yz$, which implies $z(x + y) > y(x + z)$, and so the value of the expression in D cannot be the greatest. Since none of the values of the expressions in A, B, C, or D can be the greatest, it follows that the value of the expression in E is the greatest.

The correct answer is E.

PS00087

27. Set X consists of eight consecutive integers. Set Y consists of all the integers that result from adding 4 to each of the integers in set X and all the integers that result from subtracting 4 from each of the integers in set X. How many more integers are there in set Y than in set X?

   (A) 0
   (B) 4
   (C) 8
   (D) 12
   (E) 16

Arithmetic Operations with integers

Let n be the least integer in Set X. Then the 8 integers in Set X are

| n, | $n + 1$, | ..., | $n + 6$, | $n + 7$. |

Adding 4 to each of the integers in Set X gives

| $n + 4$, | $n + 5$, | ..., | $n + 10$, | $n + 11$. |

Subtracting 4 from each of the integers in Set X gives

| $n - 4$, | $n - 3$, | ..., | $n + 2$, | $n + 3$. |

Combining the last two lists gives the integers in Set Y:

| $n - 4$, | $n - 3$, | ..., | $n + 10$, | $n + 11$. |

Therefore, the integers in Set Y consist of the 4 integers $n - 4$, $n - 3$, $n - 2$, $n - 1$ along with the integers in Set X along with the 4 integers $n + 8$, $n + 9$, $n + 10$, $n + 11$. It follows that Set Y contains a total of $4 + 4 = 8$ more integers than Set X.

The correct answer is C.

PS05239

28. Of the following, which is the closest to $\dfrac{60.2}{1.03 \times 4.86}$?

   (A) 10
   (B) 12
   (C) 13
   (D) 14
   (E) 15

Arithmetic Estimation

Replace the three numbers appearing in the expression with three nearby integers that allow the arithmetic operations to be carried out easily to get an approximation.

$$\dfrac{60.2}{1.03 \times 4.86} \approx \dfrac{\cancel{60}^{12}}{1 \times \cancel{5}^{1}} = \dfrac{12}{1 \times 1} = 12$$

The correct answer is B.

PS15402

29. Thabo owns exactly 140 books, and each book is either paperback fiction, paperback nonfiction, or hardcover nonfiction. If he owns 20 more paperback nonfiction books than hardcover nonfiction books, and twice as many paperback fiction books as paperback nonfiction books, how many hardcover nonfiction books does Thabo own?

(A) 10
(B) 20
(C) 30
(D) 40
(E) 50

Algebra Simultaneous first-degree equations

Let F represent the number of paperback fiction books that Thabo owns; N_p, the number of paperback nonfiction books; and N_h, the number of hardcover nonfiction books. It is given that $F + N_p + N_h = 140$, $N_p = N_h + 20$, and $F = 2N_p = 2(N_h + 20)$. It follows that

$$\begin{aligned} F + N_p + N_h &= 140 \text{ given} \\ 2(N_h + 20) + (N_h + 20) + N_h &= 140 \text{ by substitution} \\ 4N_h + 60 &= 140 \text{ combine like terms} \\ 4N_h &= 80 \text{ subtract 60 from both sides} \\ N_h &= 20 \text{ divide both sides by 4} \end{aligned}$$

The correct answer is B.

PS04571

30. If the average (arithmetic mean) of the four numbers 3, 15, 32, and $(N + 1)$ is 18, then $N =$

(A) 19
(B) 20
(C) 21
(D) 22
(E) 29

Arithmetic Statistics

From the given information and the definition of average, it follows that
$$\frac{3 + 15 + 32 + (N + 1)}{4} = 18, \text{ or } \frac{51 + N}{4} = 18.$$
Multiplying both sides of the last equation by 4 gives $51 + N = 72$. Therefore, $N = 72 - 51 = 21$.

The correct answer is C.

PS13801

31. Abdul, Barb, and Carlos all live on the same straight road, on which their school is also located. The school is halfway between Abdul's house and Barb's house. Barb's house is halfway between the school and Carlos's house. If the school is 4 miles from Carlos's house, how many miles is Abdul's house from Carlos's house?

(A) $1\frac{1}{3}$
(B) 2
(C) 4
(D) 6
(E) 8

Geometry Applied problems

In the diagram, A represents the location of Abdul's house, S represents the location of the school, B represents the location of Barb's house, and C represents the location of Carlos's house. Because the school is halfway between Abdul's house and Barb's house, S is the midpoint of $\overline{AB}$, and because Barb's house is halfway between the school and Carlos's house, B is the midpoint of $\overline{SC}$. Therefore, $AS = SB = BC$. Finally, since $SC = 4$, it follows that $AS = SB = BC = 2$ and hence $AC = 2 + 2 + 2 = 6$.

The correct answer is D.

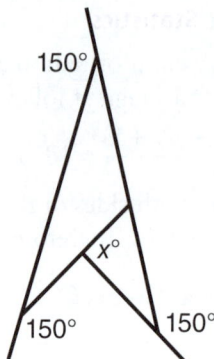

PS00534
32. In the figure shown, what is the value of x?

(A) 60
(B) 80
(C) 85
(D) 90
(E) 95

Geometry Angles and their measure

The revised figure shows three angles, each with measure 150°, and their three corresponding supplementary angles, each with measure 30°. Since the sum of the measures of the angles in $\triangle PQR$ is 180°, it follows that the measure of $\angle PRQ$ is $180° - (30° + 30°) = 120°$, and hence the measure of $\angle SRT$ is $180° - 120° = 60°$. Finally, since the sum of the measures of the angles in $\triangle RST$ is 180°, it follows that $x° = 180° - (30° + 60°) = 90°$.

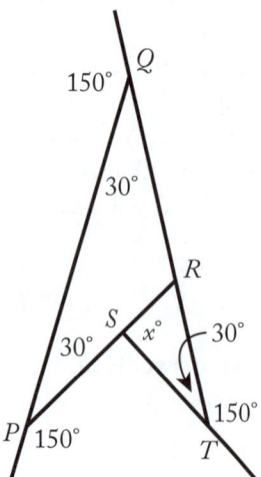

The correct answer is D.

PS17479
33. During a certain time period, Car X traveled north along a straight road at a constant rate of 1 mile per minute and used fuel at a constant rate of 5 gallons every 2 hours. During this time period, if Car X used exactly 3.75 gallons of fuel, how many miles did Car X travel?

(A) 36
(B) 37.5
(C) 40
(D) 80
(E) 90

Arithmetic Applied problems

The car traveled at a rate of
$$1\frac{\text{mi}}{\text{min}} = \left(1\frac{\text{mi}}{\text{min}}\right)\left(60\frac{\text{min}}{\text{hr}}\right) = 60\frac{\text{mi}}{\text{hr}}$$ using fuel at a rate of 5 gallons every 2 hours, or $\frac{5\text{ gal}}{2\text{ hr}}$. If the usage rate in miles per gallon was known, then that usage rate times 3.75 gallons would give the number of miles.

One approach to finding this usage rate is to consider whether multiplying or dividing the known rates $60\frac{\text{mi}}{\text{hr}}$ and $\frac{5\text{ gal}}{2\text{ hr}}$ will lead to unit cancellations that result in miles per gallon. The following calculation shows that dividing these two known rates leads to the appropriate unit cancellations:
$$60\frac{\text{mi}}{\text{hr}} \div \frac{5\text{ gal}}{2\text{ hr}} = 60\frac{\text{mi}}{\text{hr}} \times \frac{2\text{ hr}}{5\text{ gal}} = 24\frac{\text{mi}}{\text{gal}}.$$
Therefore, after using 3.75 gal of fuel, the car has traveled $24\frac{\text{mi}}{\text{gal}} \times 3.75\text{ gal} = 90$ miles.

The correct answer is E.

PS13707
34. Cheryl purchased 5 identical hollow pine doors and 6 identical solid oak doors for the house she is building. The regular price of each solid oak door was twice the regular price of each hollow pine door. However, Cheryl was given a discount of 25% off the regular price of each solid oak door. If the regular price of each hollow pine door was $40, what was the total price of all 11 doors?

(A) $320
(B) $540
(C) $560
(D) $620
(E) $680

Algebra Applied problems; Percents

The price of each pine door is $40, so the price of 5 pine doors is 5($40) = $200. The price of each oak door is twice that of a pine door, and thus $80, which becomes (0.75)($80) = $60 when the 25% discount is applied. Therefore, the price of 6 oak doors at the 25% discount is 6($60) = $360, and hence the total price of all 11 doors is $200 + $360 = $560.

The correct answer is C.

PS01233
35. A certain store will order 25 crates of apples. The apples will be of three different varieties—McIntosh, Rome, and Winesap—and each crate will contain apples of only one variety. If the store is to order more crates of Winesap than crates of McIntosh and more crates of Winesap than crates of Rome, what is the least possible number of crates of Winesap that the store will order?

(A) 7
(B) 8
(C) 9
(D) 10
(E) 11

Arithmetic Applied problems

Let M, R, and W be the numbers of crates, respectively, of McIntosh, Rome, and Winesap apples. From the given information it follows that $M + R + W = 25$ and $M \leq R < W$. Find the least possible value of W such that positive integer values of M, R, and W satisfy these two conditions.

Since the values 8, 8, and 9 for M, R, and W satisfy these two conditions, $W = 9$ is possible. Thus, the least possible value of W is less than or equal to 9. It is not possible for the value of W to be less than 9, since if the value of W were less than 9, then $M + R + W < 25$. This is because in this case, the greatest possible values of M, R, and W would be 7, 7, and 8, which have a sum less than 25. Therefore, the least possible value of W is 9.

The correct answer is C.

PS02007
36. A bicycle store purchased two bicycles, one for $250 and the other for $375, and sold both bicycles at a total gross profit of $250. If the store sold one of the bicycles for $450, which of the following could be the store's gross profit from the sale of the other bicycle?

(A) $75
(B) $100
(C) $125
(D) $150
(E) $175

Arithmetic Profit and loss

Let $450 and $R be the individual revenues from selling the two bicycles. Then the unknown profit from selling one of the bicycles is either $R − $250 or $R − $375.

total profit = (total revenue) − (total cost)
$250 = ($450 + $R) − ($250 + $375)
$250 = $R − $175
$425 = $R

From this it follows that the unknown profit is either $425 − $250 = $175 or $425 − $375 = $50.

The correct answer is E.

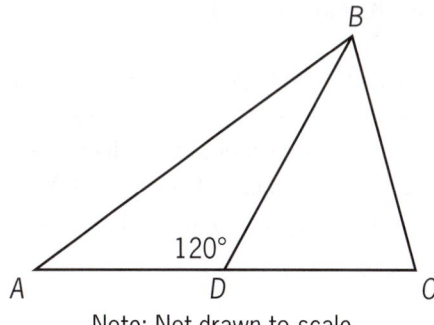

Note: Not drawn to scale.

PS10628
37. In the figure shown, $AC = 2$ and $BD = DC = 1$. What is the measure of angle ABD?

(A) 15°
(B) 20°
(C) 30°
(D) 40°
(E) 45°

195

Geometry Triangles

Since $AC = AD + DC$, and it is given that $AC = 2$ and $DC = 1$, it follows that $AD = 1$. Therefore, $AD = BD = 1$ and $\triangle ABD$ is an isosceles triangle where the measure of $\angle ABD$ is equal to the measure of $\angle BAD$. Letting $x°$ be the common degree measure of these two angles, it follows that $x° + x° + 120° = 180°$, or $2x° = 60°$, or $x° = 30°$.

The correct answer is C.

PS12786
38. If $k^2 = m^2$, which of the following must be true?

(A) $k = m$
(B) $k = -m$
(C) $k = |m|$
(D) $k = -|m|$
(E) $|k| = |m|$

Algebra Simplifying algebraic expressions

One method of solving this is to first take the nonnegative square root of both sides of the equation $k^2 = m^2$ and then make use of the fact that $\sqrt{u^2} = |u|$. Doing this gives $|k| = |m|$. Alternatively, if (k, m) is equal to either of the pairs $(1,1)$ or $(-1,1)$, then $k^2 = m^2$ is true. However, each of the answer choices except $|k| = |m|$ is false for at least one of these two pairs.

The correct answer is E.

PS13831
39. Makoto, Nishi, and Ozuro were paid a total of $780 for waxing the floors at their school. Each was paid in proportion to the number of hours he or she worked. If Makoto worked 15 hours, Nishi worked 20 hours, and Ozuro worked 30 hours, how much was Makoto paid?

(A) $52
(B) $117
(C) $130
(D) $180
(E) $234

Arithmetic Ratio and proportion

Makoto, Nishi, and Ozuro worked a total of $15 + 20 + 30 = 65$ hours and were paid a total of $780. Each was paid in proportion to the number of hours he or she worked. Therefore, Makoto was paid $\frac{15}{65}(\$780) = \$180$.

The correct answer is D.

PS05680
40. The figure above shows a path around a triangular piece of land. Mary walked the distance of 8 miles from P to Q and then walked the distance of 6 miles from Q to R. If Ted walked directly from P to R, by what percent did the distance that Mary walked exceed the distance that Ted walked?

(A) 30%
(B) 40%
(C) 50%
(D) 60%
(E) 80%

Geometry Pythagorean theorem

Mary walked a distance of $6 + 8 = 14$ miles. The distance that Ted walked, PR, can be found by using the Pythagorean theorem $6^2 + 8^2 = (PR)^2$, or $(PR)^2 = 100$. Taking square roots, it follows that Ted walked 10 miles. Therefore, the distance Mary walked exceeded the distance Ted walked by $14 - 10 = 4$ miles and 4 is 40% of 10.

The correct answer is B.

PS04797
41. If x is a positive integer and $4^x - 3 = y$, which of the following CANNOT be a value of y?

(A) 1
(B) 7
(C) 13
(D) 61
(E) 253

Arithmetic Exponents

This can be solved by calculating the value of $4^x - 3$ for the first few positive integer values of x.

x	4^x	$4^x - 3$	answer choice
1	4	1	A
2	16	13	C
3	64	61	D
4	256	253	E

Alternatively, this can be solved by observing that 4^x always has units digit 4 or 6—the product of two integers with units digit 4 has units digit 6, the product of two integers with units digit 6 has units digit 4, etc.—and therefore any integer that does not have units digit $4 - 3 = 1$ or $6 - 3 = 3$ cannot be the value of $4^x - 3$ for some positive integer value of x.

The correct answer is B.

PS05747

42. If $(1 - 1.25)N = 1$, then $N =$

   (A) −400
   (B) −140
   (C) −4
   (D) 4
   (E) 400

Algebra Operations with rational numbers

Since $(1 - 1.25)N = -0.25N = -\frac{1}{4}N$, the equation becomes $-\frac{1}{4}N = 1$, which has solution $N = -4$.

The correct answer is C.

PS14972

43. The quotient when a certain number is divided by $\frac{2}{3}$ is $\frac{9}{2}$. What is the number?

   (A) $\frac{4}{27}$
   (B) $\frac{1}{3}$
   (C) 3
   (D) 6
   (E) $\frac{27}{4}$

Arithmetic Operations with rational numbers

Recall the definition of division: $a \div b = c$ means $a = bc$. For example, if a certain number divided by 2 equals 3, then the number is $2 \times 3 = 6$. For this problem, a certain number divided by $\frac{2}{3}$ equals $\frac{9}{2}$, so the number is $\frac{2}{3} \times \frac{9}{2} = 3$. This problem can also be solved by algebra. Let N be the number. Then $\frac{N}{\frac{2}{3}} = \frac{9}{2}$, or $N = \frac{2}{3} \times \frac{9}{2} = 3$.

The correct answer is C.

PS06592

44. If a sphere with radius r is inscribed in a cube with edges of length e, which of the following expresses the relationship between r and e?

   (A) $r = \frac{1}{2}e$
   (B) $r = e$
   (C) $r = 2e$
   (D) $r = \sqrt{e}$
   (E) $r = \frac{1}{4}e^2$

Geometry Volume

A sphere inscribed in a cube touches, but does not extend beyond, each of the 6 sides of the cube, and thus the diameter of the sphere is equal to the distance between a pair of opposite sides of the cube, which is equal to the edge length of the cube. Therefore, the radius of the sphere is equal to half the edge length of the cube, or $r = \frac{1}{2}e$.

The correct answer is A.

PS13159

45. The price of gasoline at a service station increased from $1.65 per gallon last week to $1.82 per gallon this week. Sally paid $26.40 for gasoline last week at the station. How much more will Sally pay this week at the station for the same amount of gasoline?

   (A) $1.70
   (B) $2.55
   (C) $2.64
   (D) $2.72
   (E) $2.90

Arithmetic Applied problems

The amount that Sally purchased last week is equal to the total price that Sally paid last week divided by the price per gallon last week, or $\frac{26.4}{1.65}$ gallons. Since $\frac{26.4}{1.65}$ gallons is the amount that Sally purchased this week at a price of $1.82 per gallon, the amount that Sally paid this week is $\$1.82\left(\frac{26.4}{1.65}\right)$, which is $(\$1.82 - \$1.65)\left(\frac{26.4}{1.65}\right) = \$0.17\left(\frac{26.4}{1.65}\right)$ more than Sally paid last week.

One way to lessen the arithmetic computations is to work with integers and factor:

$$0.17\left(\frac{26.4}{1.65}\right) = \frac{(17)(264)}{1,650} = \frac{(17)(\cancel{3} \times 8 \times \cancel{11})}{\cancel{3} \times 5 \times \cancel{11} \times 10}$$

$$= \frac{17 \times 8}{50} = \frac{136}{50} = \frac{13.6}{5}.$$

Now divide 5 into 13.6 to get 2.72.

Another way to lessen the arithmetic computations is to estimate and keep track of the error:

$$0.17\left(\frac{26.4}{1.65}\right) = 26.4\left(\frac{17}{165}\right) = 26.4\left(\frac{16.5}{165} + \frac{0.5}{165}\right)$$

$$= 26.4\left(\frac{1}{10} + \frac{1}{330}\right) = 2.64 + \frac{26.4}{330}.$$

It follows that the desired value is greater than 2.64, and hence none of the first three answer choices is correct. Moreover, since $\frac{26.4}{330} < \frac{27}{330} = \frac{9}{110} < 0.09$, it follows that the desired value is less than $2.64 + 0.09 = 2.73$ and hence the last answer choice is not correct.

The correct answer is D.

Monthly Charge for Low-Use Telephone
Contract Offered by Company X

Monthly rate (up to 75 message units)	20% less than standard rate of $10.00
Per unit in excess of 75 message units	$0.065

PS02534

46. Based on the rates above, how much would Company X charge a customer with a low-use contract for using 95 message units in a month?

(A) $9.30
(B) $11.30
(C) $12.88
(D) $14.88
(E) $16.18

Arithmetic Interpretation of tables

The low-use contract charge for using 95 message units in a month can be calculated by $(100\% - 20\%)(\$10.00) + (95 - 75)(\$0.065)$, which equals $\$8.00 + \$1.30 = \$9.30$.

The correct answer is A.

PS02338

47. If $2x + y = 7$ and $x + 2y = 5$, then $\frac{x+y}{3} =$

(A) 1
(B) $\frac{4}{3}$
(C) $\frac{17}{5}$
(D) $\frac{18}{5}$
(E) 4

Algebra Simultaneous equations

Adding the equations $2x + y = 7$ and $x + 2y = 5$ gives $3x + 3y = 12$, or $x + y = 4$. Dividing both sides of the last equation by 3 gives $\frac{x+y}{3} = \frac{4}{3}$.

The correct answer is B.

PS14250

48. City X has a population 4 times as great as the population of City Y, which has a population twice as great as the population of City Z. What is the ratio of the population of City X to the population of City Z?

(A) 1:8
(B) 1:4
(C) 2:1
(D) 4:1
(E) 8:1

Arithmetic Ratio and Proportion

Let X, Y, and Z be the populations of Cities X, Y, and Z, respectively. It is given that $X = 4Y$, and $Y = 2Z$ or $Z = \frac{Y}{2}$. Then, $\frac{X}{Z} = \frac{4Y}{\frac{Y}{2}} = (4Y)\left(\frac{2}{Y}\right) = \frac{8}{1}$.

The correct answer is E.

5.5 Problem Solving Answer Explanations

Tides at Bay Cove on July 13

PS05100

49. The graph above shows the height of the tide, in feet, above or below a baseline. Which of the following is closest to the difference, in feet, between the heights of the highest and lowest tides on July 13 at Bay Cove?

   (A) 1.7
   (B) 1.9
   (C) 2.2
   (D) 2.5
   (E) 2.7

Arithmetic Interpretation of graphs and tables

From the graph, the highest tide is 2.2 ft above the baseline and the lowest tide is 0.5 ft below the baseline. Therefore, the difference between the heights of the highest tide and the lowest tide is [2.2 − (−0.5)] ft = (2.2 + 0.5) ft = 2.7 ft.

The correct answer is E.

PS06243

50. If $S = 1 + \frac{1}{2^2} + \frac{1}{3^2} + \frac{1}{4^2} + \frac{1}{5^2} + \frac{1}{6^2} + \frac{1}{7^2} + \frac{1}{8^2} + \frac{1}{9^2} + \frac{1}{10^2}$, which of the following is true?

   (A) $S > 3$
   (B) $S = 3$
   (C) $2 < S < 3$
   (D) $S = 2$
   (E) $S < 2$

Arithmetic Estimation

By appropriately grouping the fractions being added and then replacing each fraction within a group by the greatest fraction in that group, the value of S can be shown to be less than 2 without extensive calculation.

$$S = 1 + \left(\frac{1}{2^2} + \frac{1}{3^2}\right) + \left(\frac{1}{4^2} + \frac{1}{5^2} + \frac{1}{6^2} + \frac{1}{7^2}\right) + \left(\frac{1}{8^2} + \frac{1}{9^2} + \frac{1}{10^2}\right)$$

$$< 1 + \left(\frac{1}{2^2} + \frac{1}{2^2}\right) + \left(\frac{1}{4^2} + \frac{1}{4^2} + \frac{1}{4^2} + \frac{1}{4^2}\right) + \left(\frac{1}{8^2} + \frac{1}{8^2} + \frac{1}{8^2}\right)$$

$$= 1 + \left(\frac{2}{4}\right) + \left(\frac{4}{16}\right) + \left(\frac{3}{64}\right)$$

$$= 1 + \frac{1}{2} + \frac{1}{4} + \frac{3}{64}$$

$$< 2$$

The correct answer is E.

PS05308

51. A manufacturer of a certain product can expect that between 0.3 percent and 0.5 percent of the units manufactured will be defective. If the retail price is $2,500 per unit and the manufacturer offers a full refund for defective units, how much money can the manufacturer expect to need to cover the refunds on 20,000 units?

   (A) Between $15,000 and $25,000
   (B) Between $30,000 and $50,000
   (C) Between $60,000 and $100,000
   (D) Between $150,000 and $250,000
   (E) Between $300,000 and $500,000

Arithmetic Applied problems

The expected number of defective units is between 0.3% and 0.5% of 20,000, or between (0.003)(20,000) = 60 and (0.005)(20,000) = 100. Since each unit has a retail price of $2,500, the amount of money needed to cover the refunds for the expected number of defective units is between 60($2,500) and 100($2,500), or between $150,000 and $250,000.

The correct answer is D.

199

52. A flat patio was built alongside a house as shown in the figure above. If all angles shown are right angles, what is the area of the patio in square feet?

   (A) 800
   (B) 875
   (C) 1,000
   (D) 1,100
   (E) 1,125

Geometry Area

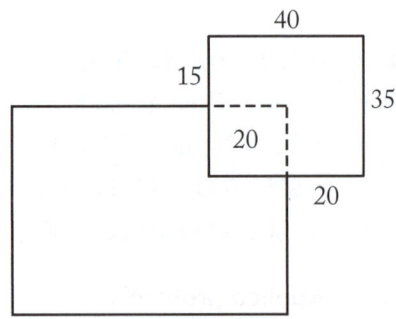

The area of the patio can be calculated by imagining the patio to be a rectangle of dimensions 40 ft by 35 ft that has a lower-left square corner of dimensions 20 ft by 20 ft covered up, as shown in the figure above. The area of the patio will be the area of the uncovered part of the rectangle, and therefore the area of the patio, in square feet, is $(40)(35) - (20)(20) = 1,400 - 400 = 1,000$.

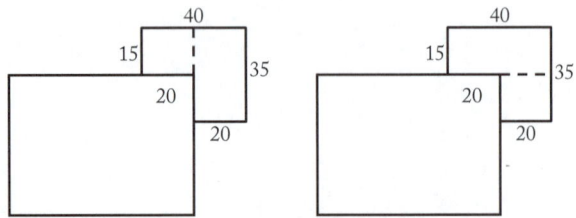

Alternatively, the area of the patio can be calculated by dividing the patio into two rectangles and adding the areas of the two rectangles. This can be done in two ways:

by using rectangles of dimensions 20 ft by 35 ft and 20 ft by 15 ft, as shown in the figure above on the left (for a total area of $700 \text{ ft}^2 + 300 \text{ ft}^2 = 1,000 \text{ ft}^2$), or by using rectangles of dimensions 40 ft by 15 ft and 20 ft by 20 ft, as shown in the figure above on the right (for a total area of $600 \text{ ft}^2 + 400 \text{ ft}^2 = 1,000 \text{ ft}^2$).

The correct answer is C.

53. Which of the following is closest to $\sqrt{\dfrac{4.2(1,590)}{15.7}}$?

   (A) 20
   (B) 40
   (C) 60
   (D) 80
   (E) 100

Arithmetic Estimation

Replace the numbers that appear with nearly equal values that are perfect squares and then evaluate the resulting expression:

$$\sqrt{\dfrac{4(1,600)}{16}} = \sqrt{\dfrac{4 \times 16 \times 100}{16}} = \sqrt{4 \times 100}$$
$$= \sqrt{4} \times \sqrt{100} = 2 \times 10 = 20.$$

The correct answer is A.

54. The sum of the weekly salaries of 5 employees is $3,250. If each of the 5 salaries is to increase by 10 percent, then the average (arithmetic mean) weekly salary per employee will increase by

   (A) $52.50
   (B) $55.00
   (C) $57.50
   (D) $62.50
   (E) $65.00

Arithmetic Applied problems; Percents

Let S_1, S_2, S_3, S_4, and S_5 be the salaries, in dollars, of the 5 employees. Since the sum of the 5 salaries is 3,250, then $S_1 + S_2 + S_3 + S_4 + S_5 = 3,250$ and the average salary is $\dfrac{S_1 + S_2 + S_3 + S_4 + S_5}{5} = \dfrac{3,250}{5} = 650$.

After each salary is increased by 10%, the salaries will be $(1.1)S_1, (1.1)S_2, (1.1)S_3, (1.1)S_4,$ and

$(1.1)S_5$ and the average salary, in dollars, will be
$$\frac{(1.1)S_1 + (1.1)S_2 + (1.1)S_3 + (1.1)S_4 + (1.1)S_5}{5} =$$
$$1.1 \times \left(\frac{S_1 + S_2 + S_3 + S_4 + S_5}{5}\right) = 1.1 \times 650 = 715.$$
Therefore, the increase in the average salary is $715 − $650 = $65.

The correct answer is E.

PS08173

55. Last week Chris earned x dollars per hour for the first 40 hours worked plus 22 dollars per hour for each hour worked beyond 40 hours. If last week Chris earned a total of 816 dollars by working 48 hours, what is the value of x ?

(A) 13
(B) 14
(C) 15
(D) 16
(E) 17

Algebra Applied problems

Chris worked 40 hours at a rate of $x per hour, 48 − 40 = 8 hours at a rate of $22 per hour, and earned a total of $816.

$40x + 8(22) = 816$	given information
$40x + 176 = 816$	multiply 8 and 22
$40x = 640$	subtract 176 from both sides
$x = 16$	divide both sides by 40

The correct answer is D.

PS07408

56. In the figure above, what is the ratio of the measure of angle B to the measure of angle A ?

(A) 2 to 3
(B) 3 to 4
(C) 3 to 5
(D) 4 to 5
(E) 5 to 6

Geometry Angles

Because the sum of the degree measures of the three interior angles of a triangle is 180, it follows that $y + (y + 10) + 90 = 180$. Therefore, $2y = 80$, and hence $y = 40$. The ratio of the measure of angle B to the measure of angle A can now be determined: $\frac{y}{y+10} = \frac{40}{50} = \frac{4}{5}$.

The correct answer is D.

PS08768

57. The value of $\dfrac{\frac{7}{8} + \frac{1}{9}}{\frac{1}{2}}$ is closest to which of the following?

(A) 2
(B) $\frac{3}{2}$
(C) 1
(D) $\frac{1}{2}$
(E) 0

Arithmetic Estimation

First, note that $\left(\frac{7}{8} + \frac{1}{9}\right) \div \frac{1}{2} = \left(\frac{7}{8} + \frac{1}{9}\right) \times 2.$

One approach is to calculate and then estimate:

$$2\left(\frac{7}{8} + \frac{1}{9}\right) = 2\left(\frac{63+8}{72}\right) = 2\left(\frac{71}{72}\right) \approx 2\left(\frac{72}{72}\right) = 2(1) = 2.$$

Another approach is to estimate and then calculate:

$$2\left(\frac{7}{8} + \frac{1}{9}\right) \approx 2\left(\frac{7}{8} + \frac{1}{8}\right) = 2\left(\frac{8}{8}\right) = 2(1) = 2.$$

The correct answer is A.

58. The positive two-digit integers x and y have the same digits, but in reverse order. Which of the following must be a factor of $x + y$?

(A) 6
(B) 9
(C) 10
(D) 11
(E) 14

Arithmetic Properties of numbers

Let m and n be digits. If $x = 10m + n$, then $y = 10n + m$. Adding x and y gives $x + y = (10m + n) + (10n + m) = 11m + 11n = 11(m + n)$, and therefore 11 is a factor of $x + y$.

The correct answer is D.

59. In a certain sequence of 8 numbers, each number after the first is 1 more than the previous number. If the first number is –5, how many of the numbers in the sequence are positive?

(A) None
(B) One
(C) Two
(D) Three
(E) Four

Arithmetic Sequences

The sequence consists of eight consecutive integers beginning with –5:

$-5, -4, -3, -2, -1, 0, 1, 2$

In this sequence exactly two of the numbers are positive.

The correct answer is C.

60. A total of s oranges are to be packaged in boxes that will hold r oranges each, with no oranges left over. When n of these boxes have been completely filled, what is the number of boxes that remain to be filled?

(A) $s - nr$
(B) $s - \dfrac{n}{r}$
(C) $rs - n$
(D) $\dfrac{s}{n} - r$
(E) $\dfrac{s}{r} - n$

Algebra Algebraic expressions

If s oranges are packed r oranges to a box with no oranges left over, then the number of boxes that will be filled is $\dfrac{s}{r}$. If n of these boxes are already filled, then $\dfrac{s}{r} - n$ boxes remain to be filled.

The correct answer is E.

61. If $0 < a < b < c$, which of the following statements must be true?

I. $2a > b + c$
II. $c - a > b - a$
III. $\dfrac{c}{a} < \dfrac{b}{a}$

(A) I only
(B) II only
(C) III only
(D) I and II
(E) II and III

Algebra Inequalities

Given $0 < a < b < c$, Statement I is not necessarily true. If, for example, $a = 1$, $b = 2$, and $c = 3$, then $0 < a < b < c$, but $2a = 2(1) < 2 + 3 = b + c$.

Given $0 < a < b < c$, then $c > b$, and subtracting a from both sides gives $c - a > b - a$. Therefore, Statement II is true.

Given $0 < a < b < c$, Statement III is not necessarily true. If, for example, $a = 1$, $b = 2$, and $c = 3$, then $0 < a < b < c$, but $\dfrac{c}{a} = \dfrac{3}{1} > \dfrac{2}{1} = \dfrac{b}{a}$.

The correct answer is B.

62. In the xy-plane, the origin O is the midpoint of line segment PQ. If the coordinates of P are (r,s), what are the coordinates of Q?

(A) (r,s)
(B) $(s,-r)$
(C) $(-s,-r)$
(D) $(-r,s)$
(E) $(-r,-s)$

Algebra Coordinate geometry

Let (x,y) be the coordinates of Q. The midpoint of (r,s) and (x,y) is $\left(\frac{r+x}{2}, \frac{s+y}{2}\right)$. Since the midpoint is $(0,0)$, it follows that $\frac{r+x}{2} = 0$ and $\frac{s+y}{2} = 0$. Therefore, $r + x = 0$ and $s + y = 0$, or $x = -r$ and $y = -s$, or $(x,y) = (-r,-s)$.

This problem can also be solved by observing that Q is the reflection of P about the origin, and so $Q = (-r,-s)$ (i.e., change the sign of each of the coordinates of P to obtain the coordinates of Q).

The correct answer is E.

	Monday	Tuesday	Wednesday	Thursday
Company A	45	55	50	50
Company B	10	30	30	10
Company C	34	28	28	30
Company D	39	42	41	38
Company E	50	60	60	70

PS10568

63. The table shows the numbers of packages shipped daily by each of five companies during a 4-day period. The standard deviation of the numbers of packages shipped daily during the period was greatest for which of the five companies?

    (A) A
    (B) B
    (C) C
    (D) D
    (E) E

Arithmetic Statistics

Since the standard deviation of a data set is a measure of how widely the data are scattered about their mean, find the mean number of packages shipped by each company and then determine the company for which the data is most widely scattered about its mean.

For Company A, the mean number of packages shipped is $\frac{45 + 55 + 2(50)}{4} = 50$. Two of the data points are each 50 and the other two each differ from 50 by 5.

For Company B, the mean number of packages shipped is $\frac{2(10) + 2(30)}{4} = 20$. Each of the data points differs from 20 by 10. Thus, the data for Company B is more widely scattered about its mean of 20 than the data for Company A is about its mean of 50.

For Company C, the mean number of packages shipped is $\frac{34 + 2(28) + 30}{4} = 30$. One data point is 30, two others each differ from 30 by only 2, and the fourth data point differs from 30 by only 4. Therefore, the data for Company C is not as widely scattered about its mean of 30 as the data for Company B is about its mean of 20.

For Company D, the mean number of packages shipped is $\frac{39 + 42 + 41 + 38}{4} = 40$. Two of the data points each differ from 40 by only 1 and the other two each differ from 40 by only 2. Therefore, the data for Company D is not as widely scattered about its mean of 40 as the data for Company B is about its mean of 20.

For Company E, the mean number of packages shipped is $\frac{50 + 2(60) + 70}{4} = 60$. Two of the data points are each 60 and the other two each differ from 60 by 10. Therefore, the data for Company E is not as widely scattered about its mean of 60 as the data for Company B is about its mean of 20.

Thus, the data for Company B is most widely scattered about its mean and, therefore, the standard deviation of the number of packages shipped daily by the five companies is greatest for Company B.

For those interested, the standard deviations for the five companies can be calculated as follows:

For A: $\sqrt{\frac{(45-50)^2 + (55-50)^2 + 2(50-50)^2}{4}}$

$= \sqrt{\frac{2(25)}{4}} = \sqrt{\frac{25}{2}} = \sqrt{12.5}$.

For B: $\sqrt{\dfrac{2(10-20)^2 + 2(30-20)^2}{4}} = \sqrt{\dfrac{4(100)}{4}}$

$= \sqrt{100}$.

For C: $\sqrt{\dfrac{(34-30)^2 + 2(28-30)^2 + (30-30)^2}{4}}$

$= \sqrt{\dfrac{24}{4}} = \sqrt{6}$.

For D:

$\sqrt{\dfrac{(39-40)^2 + (42-40)^2 + (41-40)^2 + (38-40)^2}{4}}$

$= \sqrt{\dfrac{10}{4}} = \sqrt{2.5}$.

For E: $\sqrt{\dfrac{(50-60)^2 + 2(60-60)^2 + (70-60)^2}{4}}$

$= \sqrt{\dfrac{200}{4}} = \sqrt{50}$.

The correct answer is B.

PS15523

64. Company Q plans to make a new product next year and sell each unit of this new product at a selling price of $2. The variable costs per unit in each production run are estimated to be 40% of the selling price, and the fixed costs for each production run are estimated to be $5,040. Based on these estimated costs, how many units of the new product will Company Q need to make and sell in order for their revenue to equal their total costs for each production run?

(A) 4,200
(B) 3,150
(C) 2,520
(D) 2,100
(E) 1,800

Algebra Applied problems

Let x be the desired number of units to be sold at a price of $2 each. Then the revenue for selling these units is $2x$, and the total cost for selling these units is $(40\%)(\$2.00)x = \$0.80x$ plus a fixed cost of $5,040.

revenue = total cost	given requirement
$2x = 0.8x + 5{,}040$	given information
$1.2x = 5{,}040$	subtract $0.8x$ from both sides
$x = 4{,}200$	divide both sides by 1.2

The correct answer is A.

PS07197

65. A small business invests $9,900 in equipment to produce a product. Each unit of the product costs $0.65 to produce and is sold for $1.20. How many units of the product must be sold before the revenue received equals the total expense of production, including the initial investment in equipment?

(A) 12,000
(B) 14,500
(C) 15,230
(D) 18,000
(E) 20,000

Arithmetic Rate

Let n be the number of units desired. Then, in dollars, the revenue received is $1.2n$ and the total expense is $9{,}900 + 0.65n$. These two amounts are equal when $1.2n = 9{,}900 + 0.65n$, or $0.55n = 9{,}900$. Therefore,

$n = \dfrac{9{,}900}{0.55} = \dfrac{990{,}000}{55} = \dfrac{90{,}000}{5} = 18{,}000$.

The correct answer is D.

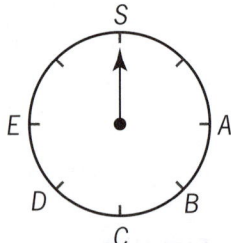

PS05682

66. The dial shown above is divided into equal-sized intervals. At which of the following letters will the pointer stop if it is rotated clockwise from S through 1,174 intervals?

(A) A
(B) B
(C) C
(D) D
(E) E

204

Arithmetic Properties of numbers

There are 8 intervals in each complete revolution. Dividing 8 into 1,174 gives 146 with remainder 6. Therefore, 1,174 intervals is equivalent to 146 complete revolutions followed by an additional 6 intervals measured clockwise from S, which places the pointer at E.

The correct answer is E.

Estimated Number of Home-Schooled Students by State, January 2001

State	Number (in thousands)
A	181
B	125
C	103
D	79
E	72

67. According to the table shown, the estimated number of home-schooled students in State A is approximately what percent greater than the number in State D ?

(A) 25%
(B) 55%
(C) 100%
(D) 125%
(E) 155%

Arithmetic Percents

The percent increase from the number in State D to the number in State A is

$= \left(\dfrac{181{,}000 - 79{,}000}{79{,}000} \times 100 \right)\%$ expression for percent increase

$= \left(\dfrac{181 - 79}{79} \times 100 \right)\%$ reduce fraction

$= \left(\dfrac{102}{79} \times 100 \right)\%$ subtract

$\approx \left(\dfrac{100}{80} \times 100 \right)\%$ approximate

$= (1.25 \times 100)\%$ divide

$= 125\%$ multiply

The correct answer is D.

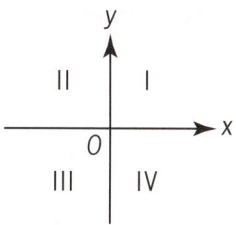

68. The graph of the equation $xy = k$, where $k < 0$, lies in which two of the quadrants shown above?

(A) I and II
(B) I and III
(C) II and III
(D) II and IV
(E) III and IV

Algebra Coordinate geometry

If a point lies on the graph of $xy = k$, then the product of the point's x- and y-coordinates is k. Since k is negative, it follows that for any such point, the product of the point's x- and y-coordinates is negative. Therefore, for any such point, the point's x- and y-coordinates have opposite signs, and hence the point must be in quadrant II or in quadrant IV.

The correct answer is D.

69. When n liters of fuel were added to a tank that was already $\dfrac{1}{3}$ full, the tank was filled to $\dfrac{7}{9}$ of its capacity. In terms of n, what is the capacity of the tank, in liters?

(A) $\dfrac{10}{9}n$
(B) $\dfrac{4}{3}n$
(C) $\dfrac{3}{2}n$
(D) $\dfrac{9}{4}n$
(E) $\dfrac{7}{3}n$

205

Algebra Applied problems

Let C represent the capacity of the tank, in liters. It follows that

$\frac{1}{3}C + n = \frac{7}{9}C$ given

$n = \frac{7}{9}C - \frac{1}{3}C$ subtract $\frac{1}{3}C$ from both sides

$n = \frac{4}{9}C$ combine like terms

$\frac{9}{4}n = C$ divide both sides by $\frac{4}{9}$

The correct answer is D.

Note: Not drawn to scale.

PS06601
70. The smaller rectangle in the figure above represents the original size of a parking lot before its length and width were each extended by w feet to make the larger rectangular lot shown. If the area of the enlarged lot is twice the area of the original lot, what is the value of w?

(A) 25
(B) 50
(C) 75
(D) 100
(E) 200

Geometry Area

From the given information it follows that $(100 + w)(150 + w) = 2(100)(150)$, or $(100 + w)(150 + w) = (200)(150)$. This is a quadratic equation that can be solved by several methods. One method is by inspection. The left side is clearly equal to the right side when $w = 50$. Another method is by factoring. Expanding the left side gives $(100)(150) + 250w + w^2 = (200)(150)$, or $w^2 + 250w - (100)(150) = 0$. Factoring the left side gives $(w - 50)(w + 300) = 0$, which has $w = 50$ as its only positive solution.

The correct answer is B.

PS02209
71. Kevin invested $8,000 for one year at a simple annual interest rate of 6 percent and invested $10,000 for one year at an annual interest rate of 8 percent compounded semiannually. What is the total amount of interest that Kevin earned on the two investments?

(A) $880
(B) $1,088
(C) $1,253
(D) $1,280
(E) $1,296

Arithmetic Applied problems

The amount of interest after one year is the total value of the investment after one year minus the total initial value of the investment. The total value of the investment after one year is $\$8,000(1.06) + \$10,000(1.04)^2 = \$8,480 + \$10,816$, so the amount of interest is $(\$8,480 + \$10,816) - (\$8,000 + \$10,000) = \$480 + \$816 = \$1,296$.

The correct answer is E.

PS05957
72. The figure above represents a semicircular archway over a flat street. The semicircle has a center at O and a radius of 6 feet. What is the height h, in feet, of the archway 2 feet from its center?

(A) $\sqrt{2}$
(B) 2
(C) 3
(D) $4\sqrt{2}$
(E) 6

Geometry Circles; Pythagorean theorem

In the figure, $\triangle ABO$ is a right triangle with legs of lengths 2 and h. From the Pythagorean theorem, it follows that $(AO)^2 = 2^2 + h^2 = 4 + h^2$. Also, $AO = 6$ since the radius of the semicircle is 6. Thus, $6^2 = 4 + h^2$, or $36 = 4 + h^2$, or $h^2 = 32$. Therefore, $h = \sqrt{32} = \sqrt{16 \cdot 2} = 4\sqrt{2}$.

5.5 Problem Solving Answer Explanations

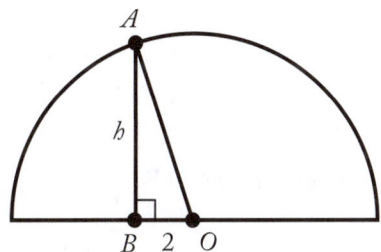

The correct answer is D.

PS01315

73. The harvest yield from a certain apple orchard was 350 bushels of apples. If x of the trees in the orchard each yielded 10 bushels of apples, what fraction of the harvest yield was from these x trees?

(A) $\dfrac{x}{35}$

(B) $1 - \dfrac{x}{35}$

(C) $10x$

(D) $35 - x$

(E) $350 - 10x$

Algebra Algebraic expressions

Since each of the x trees yielded 10 bushels, the total number of bushels yielded by these trees was 10x. Since the yield of the entire orchard was 350 bushels, $\dfrac{10x}{350} = \dfrac{x}{35}$ was the fraction of the total yield from these x trees.

The correct answer is A.

PS00907

74. In a certain fraction, the denominator is 16 greater than the numerator. If the fraction is equivalent to 80 percent, what is the denominator of the fraction?

(A) 32
(B) 64
(C) 72
(D) 80
(E) 120

Algebra First-degree equations

Let n be the numerator of the fraction. Then $n + 16$ is the denominator of the fraction. From the given information it follows that $\dfrac{n}{n+16} = 80\%$, which is solved below.

$\dfrac{n}{n+16} = \dfrac{4}{5}$ convert 80% to a fraction

$5n = 4(n + 16)$ clear fractions

$5n = 4n + 64$ simplify

$n = 64$ subtract $4n$ from both sides

Therefore, the denominator of the fraction is $n + 16 = 64 + 16 = 80$.

The correct answer is D.

PS02102

75. Greg assembles units of a certain product at a factory. Each day he is paid $2.00 per unit for the first 40 units that he assembles and $2.50 for each additional unit that he assembles that day. If Greg assembled at least 30 units on each of two days and was paid a total of $180.00 for assembling units on the two days, what is the greatest possible number of units that he could have assembled on one of the two days?

(A) 48
(B) 52
(C) 56
(D) 60
(E) 64

Arithmetic Applied problems

The day that Greg assembled the greatest possible number of units, Day D, is the day for which the other day, Day E, is the day that Greg assembled the least possible number of units. Determine the number of units that Greg assembled on Day D.

From the given information, on Day E Greg assembled 30 units, for which he was paid ($2)(30) = $60. Thus, Greg was paid $180 − $60 = $120 for work done on Day D. Of this $120, Greg was paid ($2)(40) = $80 for assembling 40 units at the rate of $2 per unit. From this it follows that on Day D Greg was paid $120 − $80 = $40 for assembling units at the rate of $2.5 per unit. Hence, on Day D Greg assembled $\dfrac{40}{2.5} = 16$ units at the rate of $2.5 per unit. Therefore, on Day D Greg assembled a total of $40 + 16 = 56$ units.

The correct answer is C.

207

PS00419
76. Which of the following is greatest?

   (A) $10\sqrt{3}$
   (B) $9\sqrt{4}$
   (C) $8\sqrt{5}$
   (D) $7\sqrt{6}$
   (E) $6\sqrt{7}$

Arithmetic Operations on radical expressions

Since all the expressions represent positive numbers, the expression that has the greatest squared value will be the expression that has the greatest value.

$\left(10\sqrt{3}\right)^2 = 100 \times 3 = 300$ (not greatest)

$\left(9\sqrt{4}\right)^2 = 81 \times 4 = 324$ (greatest)

$\left(8\sqrt{5}\right)^2 = 64 \times 5 = 320$ (not greatest)

$\left(7\sqrt{6}\right)^2 = 49 \times 6 = 294$ (not greatest)

$\left(6\sqrt{7}\right)^2 = 36 \times 7 = 252$ (not greatest)

The correct answer is B.

PS14236
77. Al and Ben are drivers for SD Trucking Company. One snowy day, Ben left SD at 8:00 a.m. heading east and Al left SD at 11:00 a.m. heading west. At a particular time later that day, the dispatcher retrieved data from SD's vehicle tracking system. The data showed that, up to that time, Al had averaged 40 miles per hour and Ben had averaged 20 miles per hour. It also showed that Al and Ben had driven a combined total of 240 miles. At what time did the dispatcher retrieve data from the vehicle tracking system?

   (A) 1:00 p.m.
   (B) 2:00 p.m.
   (C) 3:00 p.m.
   (D) 5:00 p.m.
   (E) 6:00 p.m.

Algebra Applied problems

Let t be the number of hours after 8:00 a.m. that Ben drove. Then, in t hours, Ben drove $20t$ miles and Al, who began driving 3 hours after Ben began driving, drove $40(t-3)$ miles. Therefore, their combined total distance at that time can be expressed as

$(20t + 40t - 120)$ miles = $(60t - 120)$ miles. It follows that $60t - 120 = 240$, or $60t = 360$, or $t = 6$, which corresponds to 6 hours after 8:00 a.m. or 2:00 p.m.

The correct answer is B.

PS02996
78. Of the land owned by a farmer, 90 percent was cleared for planting. Of the cleared land, 40 percent was planted with soybeans and 50 percent of the cleared land was planted with wheat. If the remaining 720 acres of cleared land was planted with corn, how many acres did the farmer own?

   (A) 5,832
   (B) 6,480
   (C) 7,200
   (D) 8,000
   (E) 8,889

Arithmetic Applied problems; Percents

Corn was planted on 100% − (40% + 50%) = 10% of the cleared land, and the cleared land represents 90% of the farmer's land. Therefore, corn was planted on 10% of 90%, or $(0.10)(0.90) = 0.09 = 9\%$, of the farmer's land. It is given that corn was planted on 720 acres, so if x is the number of acres the farmer owns, then $0.09x = 720$ and $x = \dfrac{720}{0.09} = 8,000$.

The correct answer is D.

PS00307
79. At the start of an experiment, a certain population consisted of 3 animals. At the end of each month after the start of the experiment, the population size was double its size at the beginning of that month. Which of the following represents the population size at the end of 10 months?

   (A) 2^3
   (B) 3^2
   (C) $2(3^{10})$
   (D) $3(2^{10})$
   (E) $3(10^2)$

Arithmetic Applied problems; Sequences

The population doubles each month, so multiply the previous month's population by 2 to get the next month's population. Thus, at the end of the 1st month the population will be (3)(2), at the end of the 2nd month the population will be (3)(2)(2), at the end of the 3rd month the population will be (3)(2)(2)(2), and so on. Therefore, at the end of the 10th month the population will be the product of 3 and ten factors of 2, which equals $3(2^{10})$.

The correct answer is D.

PS03635

80. If $\left(\dfrac{1}{3}+\dfrac{1}{4}+\dfrac{1}{5}+\dfrac{1}{6}\right)=r\left(\dfrac{1}{9}+\dfrac{1}{12}+\dfrac{1}{15}+\dfrac{1}{18}\right)$, then $r=$

(A) $\dfrac{1}{3}$

(B) $\dfrac{4}{3}$

(C) 3

(D) 4

(E) 12

Arithmetic Operations with rational numbers

$\left(\dfrac{1}{3}+\dfrac{1}{4}+\dfrac{1}{5}+\dfrac{1}{6}\right)=r\left(\dfrac{1}{9}+\dfrac{1}{12}+\dfrac{1}{15}+\dfrac{1}{18}\right)$

$\left(\dfrac{1}{3}+\dfrac{1}{4}+\dfrac{1}{5}+\dfrac{1}{6}\right)=r\left(\dfrac{1}{3}\right)\left(\dfrac{1}{3}+\dfrac{1}{4}+\dfrac{1}{5}+\dfrac{1}{6}\right)$

$1=r\left(\dfrac{1}{3}\right)$

$3=r$

Alternatively,

$\left(\dfrac{1}{3}+\dfrac{1}{4}+\dfrac{1}{5}+\dfrac{1}{6}\right)=r\left(\dfrac{1}{9}+\dfrac{1}{12}+\dfrac{1}{15}+\dfrac{1}{18}\right)$

$\left(\dfrac{20}{60}+\dfrac{15}{60}+\dfrac{12}{60}+\dfrac{10}{60}\right)=r\left(\dfrac{20}{180}+\dfrac{15}{180}+\dfrac{12}{180}+\dfrac{10}{180}\right)$

$\left(\dfrac{20+15+12+10}{60}\right)=r\left(\dfrac{20+15+12+10}{180}\right)$

$\left(\dfrac{20+15+12+10}{60}\right)\left(\dfrac{180}{20+15+12+10}\right)=r$

$\dfrac{180}{60}=r$

$3=r$

The correct answer is C.

PS03214

81. If x and y are positive integers such that y is a multiple of 5 and $3x + 4y = 200$, then x must be a multiple of which of the following?

(A) 3
(B) 6
(C) 7
(D) 8
(E) 10

Arithmetic Properties of numbers

Since it is given that y is a multiple of 5, let $y = 5q$, where q is a positive integer. It is given that $3x + 4y = 200$, so $3x + 4(5q) = 200$ or $3x + 20q = 200$. It follows that $3x = 200 - 20q = 20(10 - q)$. Since 3 is prime and is not a factor of 20, then 3 must be a factor of $10 - q$, which means the only possible values of q are 1, 4, and 7. This is summarized in the following table.

q	10 − q	20(10 − q)	3x	x
1	9	180	180	60
4	6	120	120	40
7	3	60	60	20

In each case, the value of x is a multiple of 10.

Alternatively, since $3x = 20(10 - q)$, the factors of the product of 3 and x must correspond to the factors of the product of 20 and $(10 - q)$. Since the factors of 20 include 10, then x must have a factor of 10, which means that x is a multiple of 10.

The correct answer is E.

PS12764

82. Which of the following expressions can be written as an integer?

I. $\left(\sqrt{82}+\sqrt{82}\right)^2$

II. $(82)\left(\sqrt{82}\right)$

III. $\dfrac{\left(\sqrt{82}\right)\left(\sqrt{82}\right)}{82}$

(A) None
(B) I only
(C) III only
(D) I and II
(E) I and III

Arithmetic Operations with radical expressions

Expression I represents an integer because
$\left(\sqrt{82}+\sqrt{82}\right)^2 = \left(2\sqrt{82}\right)^2 = (4)(82)$.

Expression II does not represent an integer because $(82)\sqrt{82} = \sqrt{82^3}$ and $82^3 = 2^3 \times 41^3$ is not a perfect square. Regarding this last assertion, note that the square of any integer has the property that each of its distinct prime factors is repeated an even number of times. For example, $24^2 = (2^3 \times 3)^2 = 2^6 \times 3^2$ has the prime factor 2 repeated 6 times and the prime factor 3 repeated twice. Expression III represents an integer, because $\dfrac{\left(\sqrt{82}\right)\left(\sqrt{82}\right)}{82} = \dfrac{82}{82} = 1$.

The correct answer is E.

83. Pumping alone at their respective constant rates, one inlet pipe fills an empty tank to $\dfrac{1}{2}$ of capacity in 3 hours and a second inlet pipe fills the same empty tank to $\dfrac{2}{3}$ of capacity in 6 hours. How many hours will it take both pipes, pumping simultaneously at their respective constant rates, to fill the empty tank to capacity?

(A) 3.25
(B) 3.6
(C) 4.2
(D) 4.4
(E) 5.5

Arithmetic Applied problems

The first pipe can fill $\dfrac{1}{2}$ of the tank in 3 hours, which is equivalent to the rate of filling $\dfrac{1}{2} \div 3 = \dfrac{1}{6}$ of the tank per hour. The second pipe can fill $\dfrac{2}{3}$ of the tank in 6 hours, which is equivalent to the rate of filling $\dfrac{2}{3} \div 6 = \dfrac{1}{9}$ of the tank per hour. Together, they can fill the tank at a rate of $\dfrac{1}{6} + \dfrac{1}{9} = \dfrac{5}{18}$ of the tank per hour. Thus, when both pipes are used at the same time, they will fill the tank in $\dfrac{18}{5} = 3.6$ hours.

The correct answer is B.

84. In the xy-coordinate plane, which of the following points must lie on the line $kx + 3y = 6$ for every possible value of k?

(A) (1,1)
(B) (0,2)
(C) (2,0)
(D) (3,6)
(E) (6,3)

Algebra Coordinate geometry

Substituting the various answer choices for (x,y) into $kx + 3y = 6$ gives the following equations:

A $\quad k + 3 = 6$
B $\quad 0 + 3(2) = 6$
C $\quad 2k + 3(0) = 6$
D $\quad 3k + 3(6) = 6$
E $\quad 6k + 3(3) = 6$

Each of these, except for the equation in B, holds for only one value of k. The equation in B does not include k and therefore holds for every value of k.

The correct answer is B.

85. If $x^2 - 2 < 0$, which of the following specifies all the possible values of x?

(A) $0 < x < 2$
(B) $0 < x < \sqrt{2}$
(C) $-\sqrt{2} < x < \sqrt{2}$
(D) $-2 < x < 0$
(E) $-2 < x < 2$

Algebra Inequalities

The corresponding equality $x^2 - 2 = 0$ has two solutions, $x = \sqrt{2}$ and $x = -\sqrt{2}$, and thus there are three intervals to test for inclusion in the solution of the inequality: $x < -\sqrt{2}$, $-\sqrt{2} < x < \sqrt{2}$, and $x > \sqrt{2}$. Choose $x = -2$, $x = 0$, and $x = 2$ from these intervals, respectively, to test whether the inequality holds. Then for these choices, the inequality becomes $(-2)^2 - 2 < 0$ (False), $(0)^2 - 2 < 0$ (True), and $(2)^2 - 2 < 0$ (False). Therefore, the solution consists of only the interval $-\sqrt{2} < x < \sqrt{2}$. Alternatively, the graph of $y = x^2 - 2$ is easily seen to be a parabola that opens upward with vertex at $(0, -2)$ and x-intercepts at $x = \sqrt{2}$ and $x = -\sqrt{2}$. The solution to the inequality is the set of the x-coordinates of the portion of this parabola that lies below the x-axis, which is $-\sqrt{2} < x < \sqrt{2}$.

The correct answer is C.

Book number	Pages in book	Total pages read
1	253	253
2	110	363
3	117	480
4	170	650
5	155	805
6	50	855
7	205	1,060
8	70	1,130
9	165	1,295
10	105	1,400
11	143	1,543
12	207	1,750

PS14467

86. Shawana made a schedule for reading books during 4 weeks (28 days) of her summer vacation. She has checked out 12 books from the library. The number of pages in each book and the order in which she plans to read the books are shown in the table above. She will read exactly 50 pages each day. The only exception will be that she will never begin the next book on the same day that she finishes the previous one, and therefore on some days she may read fewer than 50 pages. At the end of the 28th day, how many books will Shawana have finished?

(A) 7
(B) 8
(C) 9
(D) 10
(E) 11

Arithmetic Operations with integers

Book 1: 6 days—50 pages on each of Days 1–5, 3 pages on Day 6 [5(50) + 3 = 253]

Book 2: 3 days—50 pages on each of Days 7 and 8, 10 pages on Day 9 [2(50) + 10 = 110]

Book 3: 3 days—50 pages on each of Days 10 and 11, 17 pages on Day 12 [2(50) + 17 = 117]

Book 4: 4 days—50 pages on each of Days 13–15, 20 pages on Day 16 [3(50) + 20 = 170]

Book 5: 4 days—50 pages on each of Days 17–19, 5 pages on Day 20 [3(50) + 5 = 155]

Book 6: 1 day—50 pages on Day 21 [1(50) = 50]

Book 7: 5 days—50 pages on each of Days 22–25, 5 pages on Day 26 [4(50) + 5 = 205]

Book 8: 2 days—50 pages on Day 27, 20 pages on Day 28 [50 + 20 = 70]

At this point, Shawana has read on a total of 28 days and has finished 8 books.

The correct answer is B.

PS07465

87. In Western Europe, x bicycles were sold in each of the years 1990 and 1993. The bicycle producers of Western Europe had a 42 percent share of this market in 1990 and a 33 percent share in 1993. Which of the following represents the decrease in the annual number of bicycles produced and sold in Western Europe from 1990 to 1993?

(A) 9% of $\dfrac{x}{100}$

(B) 14% of $\dfrac{x}{100}$

(C) 75% of $\dfrac{x}{100}$

(D) 9% of x

(E) 14% of x

Arithmetic Percents

Of the x bicycles sold in Western Europe in 1990, 42% of them were produced in Western Europe. It follows that the number of bicycles produced and sold in Western Europe in 1990 was $0.42x$. Similarly, of the x bicycles sold in Western Europe in 1993, 33% were produced in

Western Europe. It follows that the number of bicycles produced and sold in Western Europe in 1993 was $0.33x$. Therefore, the decrease in the annual number of bicycles produced and sold in Western Europe from 1990 to 1993 was $0.42x - 0.33x = 0.09x$, which is 9% of x.

The correct answer is D.

PS06946

88. If k is a positive integer, what is the remainder when $(k + 2)(k^3 - k)$ is divided by 6 ?

    (A) 0
    (B) 1
    (C) 2
    (D) 3
    (E) 4

Algebra Properties of numbers

Since k can be any positive integer, the remainder must be the same regardless of the value of k. If $k = 2$, for example, then $(k + 2)(k^3 - k) = (2 + 2)(2^3 - 2) = (4)(6)$, which is a multiple of 6, and therefore, the remainder when divided by 6 is 0.

Alternatively, factor the given expression:

$(k + 2)(k^3 - k) = (k + 2)(k)(k^2 - 1)$
$= (k + 2)(k)(k + 1)(k - 1)$

Now, rearrange the factors in ascending order $(k - 1)(k)(k + 1)(k + 2)$, and observe that for any positive integer k, the factors are 4 consecutive integers, two of which are even and one of which is divisible by 3. Therefore, $(k + 2)(k^3 - k)$ is divisible by both 2 and 3. Thus, $(k + 2)(k^3 - k)$ is divisible by 6 with 0 remainder.

The correct answer is A.

PS14989

89. Which of the following fractions is closest to $\frac{1}{2}$?

    (A) $\frac{4}{7}$
    (B) $\frac{5}{9}$
    (C) $\frac{6}{11}$
    (D) $\frac{7}{13}$
    (E) $\frac{9}{16}$

Arithmetic Fractions

Find the distance between each fraction and $\frac{1}{2}$:

$\left|\frac{4}{7} - \frac{1}{2}\right| = \left|\frac{8}{14} - \frac{7}{14}\right| = \frac{1}{14}$

$\left|\frac{5}{9} - \frac{1}{2}\right| = \left|\frac{10}{18} - \frac{9}{18}\right| = \frac{1}{18}$

$\left|\frac{6}{11} - \frac{1}{2}\right| = \left|\frac{12}{22} - \frac{11}{22}\right| = \frac{1}{22}$

$\left|\frac{7}{13} - \frac{1}{2}\right| = \left|\frac{14}{26} - \frac{13}{26}\right| = \frac{1}{26}$

$\left|\frac{9}{16} - \frac{1}{2}\right| = \left|\frac{9}{16} - \frac{8}{16}\right| = \frac{1}{16}$

Each distance is the reciprocal of a positive integer, the greatest of which is 26. Therefore, $\frac{1}{26}$ is the least of the distances and $\frac{7}{13}$ is the fraction closest to $\frac{1}{2}$.

Alternatively, asking which fraction is closest to $\frac{1}{2}$ is equivalent to asking which of the fractions, when doubled, is closest to 1. The fractions after doubling are $\frac{8}{7}, \frac{10}{9}, \frac{12}{11}, \frac{14}{13}$, and $\frac{18}{16} = \frac{9}{8}$. Each of these fractions can be expressed as $\frac{n + 1}{n} = 1 + \frac{1}{n}$ for some integer n. Of these fractions, the one closest to 1 is the one for which $\frac{1}{n}$ is least, or in other words, the one for which n is greatest. That fraction is $\frac{14}{13}$, and therefore the closest of the original fractions to $\frac{1}{2}$ is $\left(\frac{1}{2}\right)\left(\frac{14}{13}\right) = \frac{7}{13}$.

The correct answer is D.

PS12949

90. If $p \neq 0$ and $p - \frac{1 - p^2}{p} = \frac{r}{p}$, then $r =$

    (A) $p + 1$
    (B) $2p - 1$
    (C) $p^2 + 1$
    (D) $2p^2 - 1$
    (E) $p^2 + p - 1$

Algebra Simplifying algebraic expressions

$$p - \frac{1-p^2}{p} = \frac{r}{p} \quad \text{given}$$
$$p^2 - (1-p^2) = r \quad \text{multiply both sides by } p$$
$$2p^2 - 1 = r \quad \text{combine like terms}$$

The correct answer is D.

PS12760

91. If the range of the six numbers 4, 3, 14, 7, 10, and x is 12, what is the difference between the greatest possible value of x and the least possible value of x ?

(A) 0
(B) 2
(C) 12
(D) 13
(E) 15

Arithmetic Statistics

The range of the six numbers 3, 4, 7, 10, 14, and x is 12. If x were neither the greatest nor the least of the six numbers, then the greatest and least of the six numbers would be 14 and 3. But, this cannot be possible because the range of the six numbers would be $14 - 3 = 11$ and not 12 as stated. Therefore, x must be either the greatest or the least of the six numbers. If x is the greatest of the six numbers, then 3 is the least, and $x - 3 = 12$. It follows that $x = 15$. On the other hand, if x is the least of the six numbers, then 14 is the greatest, and $14 - x = 12$. It follows that $x = 2$. Thus, there are only two possible values of x, namely 15 and 2, and so the difference between the greatest and least possible values of x is $15 - 2 = 13$.

The correct answer is D.

PS04734

92. What number is 108 more than two-thirds of itself?

(A) 72
(B) 144
(C) 162
(D) 216
(E) 324

Algebra First-degree equations

Let x be the number that is 108 more than two-thirds of itself. Then, $108 + \frac{2}{3}x = x$. Solve for x as follows:

$$108 + \frac{2}{3}x = x$$
$$108 = \frac{1}{3}x$$
$$324 = x$$

The correct answer is E.

PS11396

93. Company P had 15 percent more employees in December than it had in January. If Company P had 460 employees in December, how many employees did it have in January?

(A) 391
(B) 400
(C) 410
(D) 423
(E) 445

Arithmetic Percents

It is given that 460 is 115% of the number of employees in January. Therefore, the number of employees in January was

$$\frac{460}{1.15} = \frac{460}{1.15}\left(\frac{100}{100}\right) = \left(\frac{460}{115}\right)(100) = (4)(100) = 400.$$

The correct answer is B.

PS07672

94. A doctor prescribed 18 cubic centimeters of a certain drug to a patient whose body weight was 120 pounds. If the typical dosage is 2 cubic centimeters per 15 pounds of body weight, by what percent was the prescribed dosage greater than the typical dosage?

(A) 8%
(B) 9%
(C) 11%
(D) 12.5%
(E) 14.8%

Arithmetic Percents

If the typical dosage is 2 cubic centimeters per 15 pounds of body weight, then the typical dosage for a person who weighs 120 pounds is $2\left(\frac{120}{15}\right) = 2(8) = 16$ cubic centimeters. The prescribed dosage of 18 cubic centimeters is, therefore, $\left(\left(\frac{18-16}{16}\right) \times 100\right)\%$ or 12.5% greater than the typical dosage.

The correct answer is D.

PS09899

95. The function f is defined by $f(x) = \sqrt{x} - 10$ for all positive numbers x. If $u = f(t)$ for some positive numbers t and u, what is t in terms of u?

(A) $\sqrt{\sqrt{u}+10}$
(B) $\left(\sqrt{u}+10\right)^2$
(C) $\sqrt{u^2+10}$
(D) $(u+10)^2$
(E) $(u^2+10)^2$

Algebra Functions

The question can be answered by solving $u = \sqrt{t} - 10$ for t in terms of u. Adding 10 to both sides of this equation gives $u+10 = \sqrt{t}$. Squaring both sides of the last equation gives $(u+10)^2 = t$, which gives t in terms of u.

The correct answer is D.

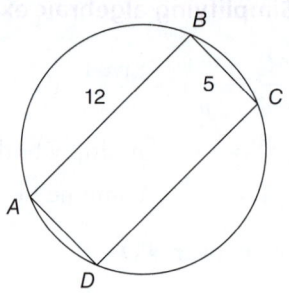

PS77502.01

96. If rectangle ABCD is inscribed in the circle above, what is the area of the circular region?

(A) 36.00π
(B) 42.25π
(C) 64.00π
(D) 84.50π
(E) 169.00π

Geometry Circles; Rectangles

The diagonal $\overline{AC}$ is the hypotenuse of a right triangle, $\triangle ABC$, that is inscribed in the circle, and thus $\overline{AC}$ is a diameter of the circle. Applying the Pythagorean theorem gives $(AC)^2 = 12^2 + 5^2 = 144 + 25 = 169$, or $AC = 13$. Therefore, the radius of the circle is $\frac{13}{2}$ and the area of the circle is $\pi\left(\frac{13}{2}\right)^2 = 42.25\pi$.

The correct answer is B.

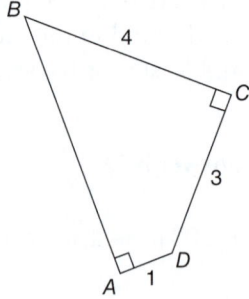

PS58502.01

97. In quadrilateral ABCD above, what is the length of AB?

(A) $\sqrt{26}$
(B) $2\sqrt{5}$
(C) $2\sqrt{6}$
(D) $3\sqrt{2}$
(E) $3\sqrt{3}$

5.5 Problem Solving Answer Explanations

Geometry Quadrilaterals; Pythagorean theorem

First, apply the Pythagorean theorem to $\triangle BCD$ to get $(BD)^2 = 3^2 + 4^2 = 25$, or $BD = 5$. Next, apply the Pythagorean theorem to $\triangle DAB$ to get $1^2 + (AB)^2 = 5^2$, or $(AB)^2 = 24$. Therefore, $AB = \sqrt{24} = 2\sqrt{6}$.

The correct answer is C.

PS98502.01

98. Three-fourths of the area of a rectangular lawn 30 feet wide by 40 feet long is to be enclosed by a rectangular fence. If the enclosure has full width and reduced length rather than full length and reduced width, how much less fence will be needed?

(A) $2\frac{1}{2}$
(B) 5
(C) 10
(D) 15
(E) 20

Geometry Rectangles

Let L ft be the reduced length. Then from $(30\text{ ft})(L\text{ ft}) = \frac{3}{4}(30\text{ ft})(40\text{ ft})$ it follows that $L = 30$, and hence in this case the amount of fence needed is $2(30\text{ ft} + 30\text{ ft}) = 120$ ft. Let W ft be the reduced width. Then from $(W\text{ ft})(40\text{ ft}) = \frac{3}{4}(30\text{ ft})(40\text{ ft})$ it follows that $W = 22.5$, and hence in this case the amount of fence needed is $2(22.5\text{ ft} + 40\text{ ft}) = 125$ ft. Therefore, the former case requires 5 ft less fence than the latter case.

The correct answer is B.

PS19502.01

99. In the floor plan of an executive's beach house above, the north and south walls of the living room are parallel. What is the floor area, in square feet, of the bedroom?

(A) $450\sqrt{3}$
(B) 450
(C) $225\sqrt{3}$
(D) 225
(E) It cannot be determined from the information given.

Geometry Triangles; Area

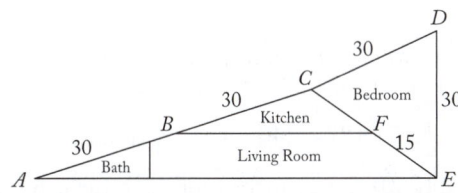

Using the labels in the figure above, it is given that $\overline{BF}$ is parallel to $\overline{AE}$ and so $\frac{BC}{AC} = \frac{CF}{CE}$ because, if a line parallel to one side of a triangle intersects the other two sides, it cuts off segments that are proportional to these sides. Therefore, $\frac{30}{30+30} = \frac{CF}{CF+15}$ or $\frac{1}{2} = \frac{CF}{CF+15}$. Solving for CF gives $CF + 15 = 2CF$ and so $CF = 15$. It follows that $CE = 15 + 15 = 30$, $\triangle CDE$ is equilateral, and each of its angles measures 60°. Then, $\triangle CDF$ is a 30°–60°–90° triangle with its sides in the ratio $1:\sqrt{3}:2$, from which it follows that $DF = 15\sqrt{3}$. Thus, the area, in square feet, of $\triangle CDE$, which is the bedroom, is $\frac{1}{2}(30)(15\sqrt{3}) = 225\sqrt{3}$.

The correct answer is C.

100. On a scale drawing, a rectangle 1 inch by $1\frac{1}{3}$ inches represents the floor of a room and the indicated scale is 1 inch equals 15 feet. How many square tiles 6 inches on a side will be needed to cover this floor? (1 foot = 12 inches)

(A) 40
(B) 70
(C) 120
(D) 700
(E) 1,200

Geometry Quadrilaterals; Area

In feet, the floor is $(1)(15)$ feet = 15 feet by $\left(1\frac{1}{3}\right)(15) = 20$ feet with an area of $(15)(20) = 300$ square feet and each tile is $\frac{1}{2}$ foot by $\frac{1}{2}$ foot with an area of $\left(\frac{1}{2}\right)\left(\frac{1}{2}\right) = \frac{1}{4}$ square feet. The number of tiles needed to cover the floor is then $\frac{300}{\frac{1}{4}} = 1,200$.

Alternatively, in inches, the floor is $(1)(15)(12)$ inches = 180 inches by $\left(1\frac{1}{3}\right)(15)(12) = 240$ inches with an area of $(180)(240)$ square inches and each tile is 6 inches by 6 inches with an area of $(6)(6)$ square inches. The number of tiles needed to cover the floor is then $\frac{(180)(240)}{(6)(6)} = \left(\frac{180}{6}\right)\left(\frac{240}{6}\right) = (30)(40) = 1,200$.

The correct answer is E.

101. If m and p are positive integers and $m^2 + p^2 < 100$, what is the greatest possible value of mp?

(A) 36
(B) 42
(C) 48
(D) 49
(E) 51

Arithmetic Operations with integers

Trying various integer values for m and corresponding values of p that satisfy $m^2 + p^2 < 100$ might be the quickest way to solve this problem. First, $m < 10$ and $p < 10$; otherwise, $m^2 + p^2 < 100$ is not true.

If $m = 9$, then for $m^2 + p^2 < 100$ to be true, $p < \sqrt{100 - 81} = \sqrt{19}$, so $p \leq 4$, and the greatest possible value for mp is $(9)(4) = 36$.

Similarly, if $m = 8$, then $p < \sqrt{100 - 64} = \sqrt{36}$, so $p \leq 5$, and the greatest possible value for mp is $(8)(5) = 40$.

If $m = 7$, then $p < \sqrt{100 - 49} = \sqrt{51}$, so $p \leq 7$, and the greatest possible value for mp is $(7)(7) = 49$.

If $m = 6$, then $p < \sqrt{100 - 36} = \sqrt{64}$, so $p \leq 7$, and the greatest possible value for mp is $(6)(7) = 42$.

If $m \leq 5$ and $p \leq 9$, it follows that $mp \leq 45$.

Thus, the greatest possible value for mp is 49.

The correct answer is D.

102. If $\frac{x}{y} = \frac{c}{d}$ and $\frac{d}{c} = \frac{b}{a}$, which of the following must be true?

I. $\frac{y}{x} = \frac{b}{a}$

II. $\frac{x}{a} = \frac{y}{b}$

III. $\frac{y}{a} = \frac{x}{b}$

(A) I only
(B) II only
(C) I and II only
(D) I and III only
(E) I, II, and III

Algebra Ratio and proportion

Equation I is true:

$\frac{x}{y} = \frac{c}{d}$ given

$\frac{y}{x} = \frac{d}{c}$ take reciprocals

$\frac{d}{c} = \frac{b}{a}$ given

$\frac{y}{x} = \frac{b}{a}$ use last two equations

216

Equation II is true:

$\frac{y}{x} = \frac{b}{a}$ Equation I (shown true)

$y = \frac{bx}{a}$ multiply both sides by x

$\frac{y}{b} = \frac{x}{a}$ divide both sides by b

Equation III is false, since otherwise it would follow that:

$y = \frac{bx}{a}$ from above

$\frac{y}{a} = \frac{bx}{a^2}$ divide both sides by a

$\frac{x}{b} = \frac{bx}{a^2}$ use Equation III (assumed true)

$x = \frac{b^2 x}{a^2}$ multiply both sides by b

From this it follows that Equation III will hold only if $\frac{b^2}{a^2} = 1$, which can be false. For example, if $x = a = c = 1$ and $y = b = d = 2$ (a choice of values for which $\frac{x}{y} = \frac{c}{d}$ and $\frac{d}{c} = \frac{b}{a}$ are true), then $\frac{b^2}{a^2} \neq 1$ and Equation III is $\frac{2}{1} = \frac{1}{2}$, which is false.

The correct answer is C.

PS10391
103. If k is an integer and $(0.0025)(0.025)(0.00025) \times 10^k$ is an integer, what is the least possible value of k?

(A) −12
(B) −6
(C) 0
(D) 6
(E) 12

Arithmetic Properties of numbers

Let $N = (0.0025)(0.025)(0.00025) \times 10^k$. Rewriting each of the decimals as an integer times a power of 10 gives $N = (25 \times 10^{-4})(25 \times 10^{-3})(25 \times 10^{-5}) \times 10^k = (25)^3 \times 10^{k-12}$. Since the units digit of $(25)^3$ is 5, it follows that if $k = 11$, then the tenths digit of N would be 5, and thus N would not be an

integer; and if $k = 12$, then N would be $(25)^3 \times 10^0 = (25)^3$, which is an integer. Therefore, the least value of k such that N is an integer is 12.

The correct answer is E.

PS07325
104. If $a(a + 2) = 24$ and $b(b + 2) = 24$, where $a \neq b$, then $a + b =$

(A) −48
(B) −2
(C) 2
(D) 46
(E) 48

Algebra Second-degree equations

$a(a + 2) = 24$ given

$a^2 + 2a = 24$ use distributive property

$a^2 + 2a - 24 = 0$ subtract 24 from both sides

$(a + 6)(a - 4) = 0$ factor

So, $a + 6 = 0$, which means that $a = -6$, or $a - 4 = 0$, which means $a = 4$. The equation with the variable b has the same solutions, and so $b = -6$ or $b = 4$.

Since $a \neq b$, then $a = -6$ and $b = 4$, which means $a + b = -6 + 4 = -2$, or $a = 4$ and $b = -6$, which means that $a + b = 4 + (-6) = -2$

The correct answer is B.

PS05560
105. In a recent election, Ms. Robbins received 8,000 votes cast by independent voters, that is, voters not registered with a specific political party. She also received 10 percent of the votes cast by those voters registered with a political party. If N is the total number of votes cast in the election and 40 percent of the votes cast were cast by independent voters, which of the following represents the number of votes that Ms. Robbins received?

(A) $0.06N + 3,200$
(B) $0.1N + 7,200$
(C) $0.4N + 7,200$
(D) $0.1N + 8,000$
(E) $0.06N + 8,000$

217

Algebra Percents

If N represents the total number of votes cast and 40% of the votes cast were cast by independent voters, then 60% of the votes cast, or $0.6N$ votes, were cast by voters registered with a political party. Ms. Robbins received 10% of these, and so Ms. Robbins received $(0.10)(0.6N) = 0.06N$ votes cast by voters registered with a political party. Thus, Ms. Robbins received $0.06N$ votes cast by voters registered with a political party and 8,000 votes cast by independent voters, so she received $0.06N + 8,000$ votes in all.

The correct answer is E.

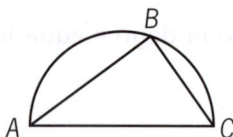

PS11308
106. In the figure shown, the triangle is inscribed in the semicircle. If the length of line segment AB is 8 and the length of line segment BC is 6, what is the length of arc ABC ?

(A) 15π
(B) 12π
(C) 10π
(D) 7π
(E) 5π

Geometry Circles, triangles

Because $\triangle ABC$ is inscribed in a semicircle, $\angle ABC$ is a right angle. Applying the Pythagorean theorem gives $(AB)^2 + (BC)^2 = (AC)^2$. Then substituting the given lengths, $8^2 + 6^2 = (AC)^2$, and so $(AC)^2 = 100$ and $AC = 10$. Thus, the diameter of the circle is 10, the circumference of the entire circle is 10π, and the length of arc ABC is half the circumference of the circle, or 5π.

The correct answer is E.

PS15517
107. A manufacturer makes and sells 2 products, P and Q. The revenue from the sale of each unit of P is $20.00 and the revenue from the sale of each unit of Q is $17.00. Last year the manufacturer sold twice as many units of Q as P. What was the manufacturer's average (arithmetic mean) revenue per unit sold of these 2 products last year?

(A) $28.50
(B) $27.00
(C) $19.00
(D) $18.50
(E) $18.00

Arithmetic Statistics

Let x represent the number of units of Product P the manufacturer sold last year. Then $2x$ represents the number of units of Product Q the manufacturer sold last year, and $x + 2x = 3x$ represents the total number of units of Products P and Q the manufacturer sold last year. The total revenue from the sale of Products P and Q was $\$(20x) + \$(17(2x)) = \$(54x)$, so the average revenue per unit sold was $\dfrac{\$(54x)}{3x} = \$18$.

The correct answer is E.

PS11756
108. A worker carries jugs of liquid soap from a production line to a packing area, carrying 4 jugs per trip. If the jugs are packed into cartons that hold 7 jugs each, how many jugs are needed to fill the last partially filled carton after the worker has made 17 trips?

(A) 1
(B) 2
(C) 4
(D) 5
(E) 6

Arithmetic Remainders

Carrying 4 jugs per trip, the worker carries a total of $4(17) = 68$ jugs in 17 trips. At 7 jugs per carton, these jugs will completely fill 9 cartons with 5 jugs left over since $(9)(7) + 5 = 68$. To fill the 10th carton, $7 - 5 = 2$ jugs are needed.

The correct answer is B.

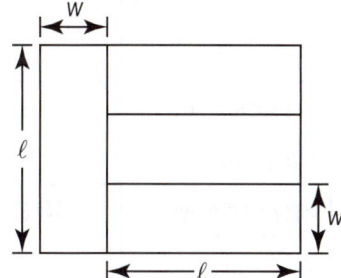

PS02820

109. The figure shown above represents a modern painting that consists of four differently colored rectangles, each of which has length ℓ and width w. If the area of the painting is 4,800 square inches, what is the width, in inches, of each of the four rectangles?

(A) 15
(B) 20
(C) 25
(D) 30
(E) 40

Geometry Area

From the figure, $\ell = 3w$, and the area of the painting is $\ell(w + \ell)$. Substituting $3w$ for ℓ gives $3w(w + 3w) = 3w(4w) = 12w^2$. It is given that the area is 4,800 square inches, so $12w^2 = 4,800$, $w^2 = 400$, and $w = 20$.

The correct answer is B.

PS09737

110. Working simultaneously and independently at an identical constant rate, 4 machines of a certain type can produce a total of x units of product P in 6 days. How many of these machines, working simultaneously and independently at this constant rate, can produce a total of 3x units of product P in 4 days?

(A) 24
(B) 18
(C) 16
(D) 12
(E) 8

Algebra Applied problems

Define a *machine day* as 1 machine working for 1 day. Then, 4 machines each working 6 days is equivalent to $(4)(6) = 24$ machine days. Thus, x units of product P were produced in 24 machine days, and 3x units of product P will require $(3)(24) = 72$ machine days, which is equivalent to $\frac{72}{4} = 18$ machines working independently and simultaneously for 4 days.

The correct answer is B.

PS01622

111. The symbol Δ denotes one of the four arithmetic operations: addition, subtraction, multiplication, or division. If 6 Δ 3 ≤ 3, which of the following must be true?

I.   2 Δ 2 = 0
II. 2 Δ 2 = 1
III. 4 Δ 2 = 2

(A) I only
(B) II only
(C) III only
(D) I and II only
(E) I, II, and III

Arithmetic Operations with integers

If Δ represents addition, subtraction, multiplication, or division, then 6 Δ 3 is equal to either $6 + 3 = 9$, or $6 - 3 = 3$, or $6 \times 3 = 18$, or $6 \div 3 = 2$. Since it is given that 6 Δ 3 ≤ 3, Δ represents either subtraction or division.

Statement I is true for subtraction since $2 - 2 = 0$ but not true for division since $2 \div 2 = 1$.

Statement II is not true for subtraction since $2 - 2 = 0$ but is true for division since $2 \div 2 = 1$.

Statement III is true for subtraction since $4 - 2 = 2$ and is true for division since $4 \div 2 = 2$. Therefore, only Statement III must be true.

The correct answer is C.

PS04448

112. If $mn \neq 0$ and 25 percent of n equals $37\frac{1}{2}$ percent of m, what is the value of $\frac{12n}{m}$?

(A) 18
(B) $\frac{32}{3}$
(C) 8
(D) 3
(E) $\frac{9}{8}$

Algebra Percents; First-degree equations

It is given that $(25\%)n = (37.5\%)m$, or $0.25n = 0.375m$. The value of $\dfrac{12n}{m}$ can be found by first finding the value of $\dfrac{n}{m}$ and then multiplying the result by 12. Doing this gives $\dfrac{12n}{m} = \left(\dfrac{0.375}{0.25}\right)(12) = 18$. Alternatively, the numbers involved allow for a series of simple equation transformations to be carried out, such as the following:

$0.25n = 0.375m$	given
$25n = 37.5m$	multiply both sides by 100
$50n = 75m$	multiply both sides by 2
$2n = 3m$	divide both sides by 25
$12n = 18m$	multiply both sides by 6
$\dfrac{12n}{m} = 18$	divide both sides by m

The correct answer is A.

PS02555

113. Last year Joe grew 1 inch and Sally grew 200 percent more than Joe grew. How many inches did Sally grow last year?

(A) 0
(B) 1
(C) 2
(D) 3
(E) 4

Arithmetic Percents

Joe grew 1 inch last year and Sally grew 200 percent more than Joe grew, so Sally grew 1 inch plus 200 percent of 1 inch or $1 + 2(1) = 3$ inches.

The correct answer is D.

Technique	Percent of Consumers
Television ads	35%
Coupons	22%
Store displays	18%
Samples	15%

PS10307

114. The table shows <u>partial</u> results of a survey in which consumers were asked to indicate which one of six promotional techniques most influenced their decision to buy a new food product. Of those consumers who indicated one of the four techniques listed, what fraction indicated either coupons or store displays?

(A) $\dfrac{2}{7}$
(B) $\dfrac{1}{3}$
(C) $\dfrac{2}{5}$
(D) $\dfrac{4}{9}$
(E) $\dfrac{1}{2}$

Arithmetic Percents; Ratio and proportion

Let T be the total number of consumers who were asked. Then the table shows $35\% + 22\% + 18\% + 15\% = 90\%$ of this total, or $0.9T$ consumers. Also, the number of consumers who indicated either coupons or store displays was $0.22T + 0.18T = 0.4T$. Therefore, the number of consumers who indicated either coupons or store displays divided by the number of consumers shown in the table is $\dfrac{0.4T}{0.9T} = \dfrac{4}{9}$.

The correct answer is D.

5.5 Problem Solving Answer Explanations

PS09708

115. The cost C, in dollars, to remove p percent of a certain pollutant from a pond is estimated by using the formula $C = \dfrac{100,000p}{100 - p}$. According to this estimate, how much more would it cost to remove 90 percent of the pollutant from the pond than it would cost to remove 80 percent of the pollutant?

(A) $500,000
(B) $100,000
(C) $50,000
(D) $10,000
(E) $5,000

Algebra; Arithmetic Simplifying algebraic expressions; Operations on rational numbers

Removing 90% of the pollutant from the pond would cost $\dfrac{(100,000)(90)}{100-90} = \dfrac{9,000,000}{10} = 900,000$ dollars, and removing 80% of the pollutant would cost $\dfrac{(100,000)(80)}{100-80} = \dfrac{8,000,000}{20} = 400,000$ dollars. The difference is, then, $900,000 - $400,000 = $500,000.

The correct answer is A.

PS11121

116. If $xy \neq 0$ and $x^2y^2 - xy = 6$, which of the following could be y in terms of x?

I. $\dfrac{1}{2x}$

II. $-\dfrac{2}{x}$

III. $\dfrac{3}{x}$

(A) I only
(B) II only
(C) I and II
(D) I and III
(E) II and III

Algebra Second-degree equations

$\begin{array}{ll} x^2y^2 - xy = 6 & \text{given} \\ x^2y^2 - xy - 6 = 0 & \text{subtract 6 from both sides} \\ (xy + 2)(xy - 3) = 0 & \text{factor} \end{array}$

So, $xy + 2 = 0$, which means $xy = -2$ and $y = -\dfrac{2}{x}$, or $xy - 3 = 0$, which means that $xy = 3$ and $y = \dfrac{3}{x}$. Thus, y in terms of x could be given by the expressions in II or III.

The correct answer is E.

PS00633

117. $\sqrt{4.8 \times 10^9}$ is closest in value to

(A) 2,200
(B) 70,000
(C) 220,000
(D) 7,000,000
(E) 22,000,000

Arithmetic Operations on radical expressions

$\sqrt{4.8} \times \sqrt{10^9} = \sqrt{48 \times 10^8}$ substitute 48×10^8 for 4.8×10^9

$= \sqrt{48} \times \sqrt{10^8}$ $\sqrt{ab} = \sqrt{a} \times \sqrt{b}$

$\approx \sqrt{49} \times \sqrt{10^8}$ $49 \approx 48$

and then

$\sqrt{49} \times \sqrt{10^8} = 7 \times 10^4$ $\sqrt{49} = 7, \sqrt{10^8} = \sqrt{(10^4)^2} = 10^4$

$= 70,000$

The correct answer is B.

PS08865

118. Three printing presses, R, S, and T, working together at their respective constant rates, can do a certain printing job in 4 hours. S and T, working together at their respective constant rates, can do the same job in 5 hours. How many hours would it take R, working alone at its constant rate, to do the same job?

(A) 8
(B) 10
(C) 12
(D) 15
(E) 20

221

Algebra Applied problems

Let r be the portion of the job that printing press R, working alone, completes in 1 hour; and let s and t be the corresponding portions, respectively, for printing press S and printing press T. From the given information, it follows that $r + s + t = \frac{1}{4}$ and $s + t = \frac{1}{5}$. Subtracting these two equations gives $r = \frac{1}{4} - \frac{1}{5} = \frac{1}{20}$. It follows that printing press R, working alone, will complete $\frac{1}{20}$ of the job in 1 hour, and therefore printing press R, working alone, will complete the job in 20 hours.

The correct answer is E.

PS07112

119. For a party, three solid cheese balls with diameters of 2 inches, 4 inches, and 6 inches, respectively, were combined to form a single cheese ball. What was the approximate diameter, in inches, of the new cheese ball? (The volume of a sphere is $\frac{4}{3}\pi r^3$, where r is the radius.)

(A) 12
(B) 16
(C) $\sqrt[3]{16}$
(D) $3\sqrt[3]{8}$
(E) $2\sqrt[3]{36}$

Geometry Volume

Since the diameters of the cheese balls are given as 2 inches, 4 inches, and 6 inches, the radii of the cheese balls are 1 inch, 2 inches, and 3 inches, respectively. Using $V = \frac{4}{3}\pi r^3$, the combined volume of the 3 cheese balls is $\frac{4}{3}\pi(1^3 + 2^3 + 3^3)$ or $\frac{4}{3}\pi(36)$ cubic inches.

Thus, if R represents the radius of the new cheese ball, then the volume of the new cheese ball is $\frac{4}{3}\pi R^3 = \frac{4}{3}\pi(36)$ and $R^3 = 36$, from which it follows that $R = \sqrt[3]{36}$ inches. Therefore, the diameter of the new cheese ball is $2R = 2\sqrt[3]{36}$ inches.

The correct answer is E.

PS02325

120. The sum of all the integers k such that $-26 < k < 24$ is

(A) 0
(B) −2
(C) −25
(D) −49
(E) −51

Arithmetic Operations on integers

In the sum of all integers k such that $-26 < k < 24$, the positive integers from 1 through 23 can be paired with the negative integers from -1 through -23. The sum of these pairs is 0 because $a + (-a) = 0$ for all integers a. Therefore, the sum of all integers k such that $-26 < k < 24$ is $-25 + (-24) + (23)(0) = -49$.

The correct answer is D.

PS08399

121. The number line shown contains three points R, S, and T, whose coordinates have absolute values r, s, and t, respectively. Which of the following equals the average (arithmetic mean) of the coordinates of the points R, S, and T?

(A) s
(B) $s + t - r$
(C) $\frac{r - s - t}{3}$
(D) $\frac{r + s + t}{3}$
(E) $\frac{s + t - r}{3}$

Arithmetic Absolute value; Number line

Because point R is to the left of 0 on the number line, the coordinate of R is negative. It is given that r is the absolute value of the coordinate of R and so the coordinate of R is $-r$. Because points S and T are to the right of 0 on the number line, their coordinates are positive. It is given that s and t are the absolute values of the coordinates of S and T, and so the coordinates of S and T are s and t. The arithmetic mean of the coordinates of R, S, and T is $\frac{s + t - r}{3}$.

The correct answer is E.

5.5 Problem Solving Answer Explanations

PS05962

122. Mark and Ann together were allocated n boxes of cookies to sell for a club project. Mark sold 10 boxes less than n and Ann sold 2 boxes less than n. If Mark and Ann have each sold at least one box of cookies, but together they have sold less than n boxes, what is the value of n?

(A) 11
(B) 12
(C) 13
(D) 14
(E) 15

Algebra Inequalities

Mark sold $n - 10$ boxes and Ann sold $n - 2$ boxes. Because each person sold at least one box, it follows that $n - 10 \geq 1$ and $n - 2 \geq 1$, which implies that $n \geq 11$. On the other hand, together they sold less than n boxes, so $(n - 10) + (n - 2) < n$, which implies that $n < 12$. Therefore, n is an integer such that $n \geq 11$ and $n < 12$, which implies that $n = 11$.

The correct answer is A.

PS04089

123. A certain high school has 5,000 students. Of these students, x are taking music, y are taking art, and z are taking both music and art. How many students are taking neither music nor art?

(A) $5,000 - z$
(B) $5,000 - x - y$
(C) $5,000 - x + z$
(D) $5,000 - x - y - z$
(E) $5,000 - x - y + z$

Algebra Sets

Since x students are taking music, y students are taking art, and z students are taking both music and art, the number of students taking only music is $x - z$, and the number of students taking only art is $y - z$, as illustrated by the following Venn diagram.

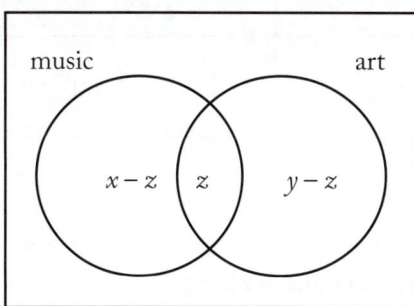

Therefore, the number of students taking neither music nor art is
$5,000 - [(x - z) + z + (y - z)] = 5,000 - x - y + z$.

The correct answer is E.

PS06133

124. Each person who attended a company meeting was either a stockholder in the company, an employee of the company, or both. If 62 percent of those who attended the meeting were stockholders and 47 percent were employees, what percent were stockholders who were *not* employees?

(A) 34%
(B) 38%
(C) 45%
(D) 53%
(E) 62%

Arithmetic Sets

Let M represent the number of meeting attendees. Then, since 62% of M or $0.62M$ were stockholders and 47% of M or $0.47M$ were employees, it follows that $0.62M + 0.47M = 1.09M$ were either stockholders, employees, or both. Since $1.09M$ exceeds M, the excess $1.09M - M = 0.09M$ must be the number of attendees who were both stockholders and employees, leaving the rest $0.62M - 0.09M = 0.53M$, or 53%, of the meeting attendees to be stockholders but not employees.

The correct answer is D.

Accounts	Amount Budgeted	Amount Spent
Payroll	$110,000	$117,000
Taxes	40,000	42,000
Insurance	2,500	2,340

PS08441

125. The table shows the amount budgeted and the amount spent for each of three accounts in a certain company. For which of these accounts did the amount spent differ from the amount budgeted by more than 6 percent of the amount budgeted?

(A) Payroll only
(B) Taxes only
(C) Insurance only
(D) Payroll and Insurance
(E) Taxes and Insurance

223

Arithmetic Percents

For Payroll, 6% of the budgeted amount is (0.06)($110,000) = $6,600. Since $117,000 − $110,000 = $7,000 > $6,600, the amount spent differed from the amount budgeted by more than 6%.

For Taxes, 6% of the budgeted amount is (0.06)($40,000) = $2,400. Since $42,000 − $40,000 = $2,000 < $2,400, the amount spent did not differ from the amount budgeted by more than 6%.

For Insurance, 6% of the budgeted amount is (0.06)($2,500) = $150. Since $2,500 − $2,340 = $160 > $150, the amount spent differed from the amount budgeted by more than 6%.

Thus, the amount spent differed from the amount budgeted by more than 6% for Payroll and Insurance.

The correct answer is D.

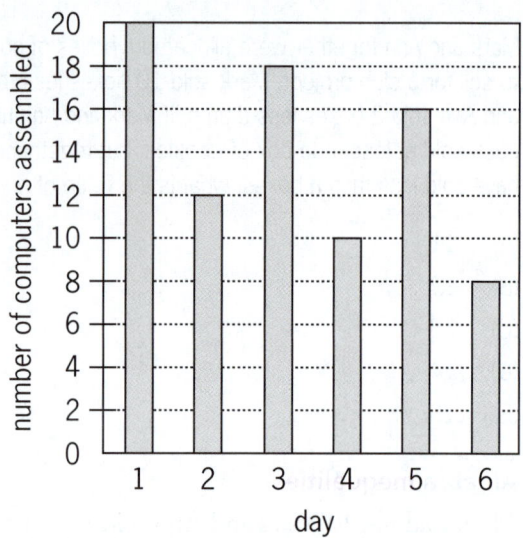

PS15111
126. The graph shows the number of computers assembled during each of 6 consecutive days. From what day to the next day was the percent change in the number of computers assembled the greatest in magnitude?

(A) From Day 1 to Day 2
(B) From Day 2 to Day 3
(C) From Day 3 to Day 4
(D) From Day 4 to Day 5
(E) From Day 5 to Day 6

Arithmetic Percents

The following table shows the percent change from each day to the next and the magnitude of the percent change.

Time period	Percent change	Magnitude of percent change
From Day 1 to Day 2	$\left(\frac{12-20}{20} \times 100\right)\% = \left(-\frac{8}{20} \times 100\right)\% = -40\%$	40
From Day 2 to Day 3	$\left(\frac{18-12}{12} \times 100\right)\% = \left(\frac{6}{12} \times 100\right)\% = 50\%$	50
From Day 3 to Day 4	$\left(\frac{10-18}{18} \times 100\right)\% = \left(-\frac{8}{18} \times 100\right)\% \approx -44\%$	44
From Day 4 to Day 5	$\left(\frac{16-10}{10} \times 100\right)\% = \left(\frac{6}{10} \times 100\right)\% = 60\%$	60
From Day 5 to Day 6	$\left(\frac{8-16}{16} \times 100\right)\% = \left(-\frac{8}{16} \times 100\right)\% = -50\%$	50

The correct answer is D.

5.5 Problem Solving Answer Explanations

PS02704
127. If $n = 20! + 17$, then n is divisible by which of the following?

   I.   15
   II. 17
   III. 19

   (A) None
   (B) I only
   (C) II only
   (D) I and II
   (E) II and III

Arithmetic Properties of numbers

Because 20! is the product of all integers from 1 through 20, it follows that 20! is divisible by each integer from 1 through 20. In particular, 20! is divisible by each of the integers 15, 17, and 19. Since 20! and 17 are both divisible by 17, their sum is divisible by 17, and hence the correct answer will include II. If n were divisible by 15, then $n - 20!$ would be divisible by 15. But, $n - 20! = 17$ and 17 is not divisible by 15. Therefore, the correct answer does not include I. If n were divisible by 19, then $n - 20!$ would be divisible by 19. But, $n - 20! = 17$ and 17 is not divisible by 19. Therefore, the correct answer does not include III.

The correct answer is C.

PS02600
128. The product of two negative numbers is 160. If the lesser of the two numbers is 4 less than twice the greater, what is the greater number?

   (A) −20
   (B) −16
   (C) −10
   (D) −8
   (E) −4

Algebra Second-degree equations

Let x and y be the two numbers, where x is the lesser of the two numbers and y is the number desired. From the given information it follows that $xy = 160$ and $x = 2y - 4$, from which it follows that $(2y - 4)y = 160$. Dividing both sides of the last equation by 2 gives $(y - 2)y = 80$. Thus, 80 is to be written as a product of two negative numbers, one that is 2 less than the other. Trying simple factorizations of 80 quickly leads to the value of y: $(-40)(-2) = 80$, $(-20)(-4) = 80$, $(-10)(-8) = 80$. Therefore, $y = -8$. Note that because −8 is one of the answer choices, it is not necessary to ensure there are no other negative solutions to the equation $(y - 2)y = 80$.

Alternatively, $(y - 2)y = 80$ can be written as $y^2 - 2y - 80 = 0$. Factoring the left side gives $(y + 8)(y - 10) = 0$, and $y = -8$ is the only negative solution.

The correct answer is D.

PS10546
129. According to a certain estimate, the depth $N(t)$, in centimeters, of the water in a certain tank at t hours past 2:00 in the morning is given by $N(t) = -20(t - 5)^2 + 500$ for $0 \le t \le 10$. According to this estimate, at what time in the morning does the depth of the water in the tank reach its maximum?

   (A) 5:30
   (B) 7:00
   (C) 7:30
   (D) 8:00
   (E) 9:00

Algebra Functions

When $t = 5$, the value of $-20(t - 5)^2 + 500$ is 500. For all values of t between 0 and 10, inclusive, except $t = 5$, the value of $-20(t - 5)^2$ is negative and $-20(t - 5)^2 + 500 < 500$. Therefore, the tank reaches its maximum depth 5 hours after 2:00 in the morning, which is 7:00 in the morning.

The correct answer is B.

PS04617
130. After driving to a riverfront parking lot, Bob plans to run south along the river, turn around, and return to the parking lot, running north along the same path. After running 3.25 miles south, he decides to run for only 50 minutes more. If Bob runs at a constant rate of 8 minutes per mile, how many miles farther south can he run and still be able to return to the parking lot in 50 minutes?

   (A) 1.5
   (B) 2.25
   (C) 3.0
   (D) 3.25
   (E) 4.75

225

Algebra Applied problems

After running 3.25 miles south, Bob has been running for $(3.25 \text{ miles})\left(8 \dfrac{\text{minutes}}{\text{mile}}\right) = 26$ minutes. Thus, if t is the number of additional minutes that Bob can run south before turning around, then the number of minutes that Bob will run north, after turning around, will be $t + 26$. Since Bob will be running a total of 50 minutes after the initial 26 minutes of running, it follows that $t + (t + 26) = 50$, or $t = 12$. Therefore, Bob can run south an additional $\dfrac{12 \text{ minutes}}{8 \dfrac{\text{minutes}}{\text{mile}}} = 1.5$ miles before turning around.

The correct answer is A.

PS12577
131. Alex deposited x dollars into a new account that earned 8 percent annual interest, compounded annually. One year later Alex deposited an additional x dollars into the account. If there were no other transactions and if the account contained w dollars at the end of two years, which of the following expresses x in terms of w?

(A) $\dfrac{w}{1 + 1.08}$

(B) $\dfrac{w}{1.08 + 1.16}$

(C) $\dfrac{w}{1.16 + 1.24}$

(D) $\dfrac{w}{1.08 + (1.08)^2}$

(E) $\dfrac{w}{(1.08)^2 + (1.08)^3}$

Algebra Applied problems

At the end of the first year, the value of Alex's initial investment was $x(1.08)$ dollars, and after he deposited an additional x dollars into the account, its value was $[x(1.08) + x]$ dollars. At the end of the second year, the value was w dollars, where $w = [x(1.08) + x](1.08) = x(1.08)^2 + x(1.08) = x[(1.08)^2 + 1.08]$. Thus, $x = \dfrac{w}{1.08 + (1.08)^2}$.

The correct answer is D.

PS05973
132. M is the sum of the reciprocals of the consecutive integers from 201 to 300, inclusive. Which of the following is true?

(A) $\dfrac{1}{3} < M < \dfrac{1}{2}$

(B) $\dfrac{1}{5} < M < \dfrac{1}{3}$

(C) $\dfrac{1}{7} < M < \dfrac{1}{5}$

(D) $\dfrac{1}{9} < M < \dfrac{1}{7}$

(E) $\dfrac{1}{12} < M < \dfrac{1}{9}$

Arithmetic Estimation

Because $\dfrac{1}{300}$ is less than each of the 99 numbers $\dfrac{1}{201}, \dfrac{1}{202}, \ldots, \dfrac{1}{299}$, it follows that $\dfrac{1}{300} + \dfrac{1}{300} + \cdots + \dfrac{1}{300}$ (the sum of 99 identical values) is less than $\dfrac{1}{201} + \dfrac{1}{202} + \cdots + \dfrac{1}{299}$. Therefore, adding $\dfrac{1}{300}$ to both sides of this last inequality, it follows that $\dfrac{1}{300} + \dfrac{1}{300} + \cdots + \dfrac{1}{300}$ (the sum of 100 identical values) is less than $\dfrac{1}{201} + \dfrac{1}{202} + \cdots + \dfrac{1}{299} + \dfrac{1}{300} = M$. Hence, $(100)\left(\dfrac{1}{300}\right) < M$ or $\dfrac{1}{3} < M$. Also, because $\dfrac{1}{200}$ is greater than each of the 100 numbers $\dfrac{1}{201}, \dfrac{1}{202}, \ldots, \dfrac{1}{300}$, it follows that $\dfrac{1}{200} + \dfrac{1}{200} + \cdots + \dfrac{1}{200}$ (the sum of 100 identical values) is greater than $\dfrac{1}{201} + \dfrac{1}{202} + \cdots + \dfrac{1}{300}$. Hence, $(100)\left(\dfrac{1}{200}\right) > M$ or $\dfrac{1}{2} > M$. From $\dfrac{1}{3} < M$ and $\dfrac{1}{2} > M$, it follows that $\dfrac{1}{3} < M < \dfrac{1}{2}$.

The correct answer is A.

5.5 Problem Solving Answer Explanations

PS00428

133. Working simultaneously at their respective constant rates, Machines A and B produce 800 nails in x hours. Working alone at its constant rate, Machine A produces 800 nails in y hours. In terms of x and y, how many hours does it take Machine B, working alone at its constant rate, to produce 800 nails?

(A) $\dfrac{x}{x+y}$

(B) $\dfrac{y}{x+y}$

(C) $\dfrac{xy}{x+y}$

(D) $\dfrac{xy}{x-y}$

(E) $\dfrac{xy}{y-x}$

Algebra Applied problems

Let R_A and R_B be the constant rates, in nails per hour, at which Machines A and B work, respectively. Then it follows from the given information that $R_A + R_B = \dfrac{800}{x}$ and $R_A = \dfrac{800}{y}$. Hence, $\dfrac{800}{y} + R_B = \dfrac{800}{x}$, or

$R_B = \dfrac{800}{x} - \dfrac{800}{y} = 800\left(\dfrac{1}{x} - \dfrac{1}{y}\right) = 800\left(\dfrac{y-x}{xy}\right)$.

Therefore, the time, in hours, it would take Machine B to produce 800 nails is given by

$\dfrac{800}{800\left(\dfrac{y-x}{xy}\right)} = \dfrac{xy}{y-x}$.

The correct answer is E.

PS08966

134. What is the median of the numbers shown?

10, 4, 26, 16

(A) 10
(B) 13
(C) 14
(D) 15
(E) 16

Arithmetic Statistics

To determine the median of these 4 numbers, put the numbers in numerical order in a list and determine the average of the two middle values in the list:

4, **10**, **16**, 26

From this list it follows that the median is the average of 10 and 16, which is $\dfrac{10+16}{2} = 13$.

The correct answer is B.

	Number of Marbles in Each of Three Bags	Percent of Marbles in Each Bag That Are Blue (to the nearest tenth)
Bag P	37	10.8%
Bag Q	x	66.7%
Bag R	32	50.0%

PS03823

135. If $\dfrac{1}{3}$ of the total number of marbles in the three bags listed in the table above are blue, how many marbles are there in bag Q?

(A) 5
(B) 9
(C) 12
(D) 23
(E) 46

Algebra Percents

What is the value of x, the number of marbles in bag Q? From the given information and rounded to the nearest integer, bag P has $(37)(0.108) = 4$ blue marbles, bag Q has $(x)(0.667) = \dfrac{2}{3}x$ blue marbles, and bag R has $(32)(0.5) = 16$ blue marbles. Therefore, the total number of blue marbles is equal to $4 + \dfrac{2}{3}x + 16 = 20 + \dfrac{2}{3}x$. It is given that $\dfrac{1}{3}$ of the total number of marbles are blue, so the total number of blue marbles is also equal to $\dfrac{1}{3}(37 + x + 32) = \dfrac{1}{3}x + 23$. It follows that $20 + \dfrac{2}{3}x = \dfrac{1}{3}x + 23$, or $\dfrac{1}{3}x = 3$, or $x = 9$.

The correct answer is B.

227

Age Category (in years)	Number of Employees
Less than 20	29
20–29	58
30–39	36
40–49	21
50–59	10
60–69	5
70 and over	2

PS11600

136. The table above gives the age categories of the 161 employees at Company X and the number of employees in each category. According to the table, if m is the median age, in years, of the employees at Company X, then m must satisfy which of the following?

(A) $20 \leq m \leq 29$
(B) $25 \leq m \leq 34$
(C) $30 \leq m \leq 39$
(D) $35 \leq m \leq 44$
(E) $40 \leq m \leq 49$

Arithmetic Statistics

The median of 161 ages is the 81st age when the ages are listed in order. Since 29 of the ages are less than 20, the median age must be greater than or equal to 20. Since 58 of the ages are between 20 and 29, a total of $29 + 58 = 87$ of the ages are less than or equal to 29, and thus the median age is less than or equal to 29. Therefore, the median age is greater than or equal to 20 and less than or equal to 29.

The correct answer is A.

PS02749

137. Ron is 4 inches taller than Amy, and Barbara is 1 inch taller than Ron. If Barbara's height is 65 inches, what is the median height, in inches, of these three people?

(A) 60
(B) 61
(C) 62
(D) 63
(E) 64

Arithmetic Operations with integers

Let R, A, and B be the heights, respectively and in inches, of Ron, Amy, and Barbara. It is given that $R = 4 + A$, $B = 1 + R$, and $B = 65$. Therefore, $R = B - 1 = 65 - 1 = 64$ and $A = R - 4 = 64 - 4 = 60$. From this it follows that the three heights, in inches, are 60, 64, and 65. The median of these three heights is 64.

The correct answer is E.

PS02777

138. If x and y are positive numbers such that $x + y = 1$, which of the following could be the value of $100x + 200y$?

I. 80
II. 140
III. 199

(A) II only
(B) III only
(C) I and II
(D) I and III
(E) II and III

Algebra Simultaneous equations; Inequalities

Since $x + y = 1$, then $y = 1 - x$ and $100x + 200y$ can be expressed as $100x + 200(1 - x) = 200 - 100x$. Test each value.

I. If $200 - 100x = 80$, then $x = \dfrac{200 - 80}{100} = 1.2$ and $y = 1 - 1.2 = -0.2$. Since y must be positive, 80 cannot be a value of $100x + 200y$.

II. If $200 - 100x = 140$, then $x = \dfrac{200 - 140}{100} = 0.6$ and $y = 1 - 0.6 = 0.4$, so 140 can be a value of $100x + 200y$.

III. If $200 - 100x = 199$, then $x = \dfrac{200 - 199}{100} = 0.01$ and $y = 1 - 0.01 = 0.99$, so 199 can be a value of $100x + 200y$.

The correct answer is E.

PS02017

139. If X is the hundredths digit in the decimal $0.1X$ and if Y is the thousandths digit in the decimal $0.02Y$, where X and Y are nonzero digits, which of the following is closest to the greatest possible value of $\dfrac{0.1X}{0.02Y}$?

(A) 4
(B) 5
(C) 6
(D) 9
(E) 10

Arithmetic Operations with decimals; Place value

The greatest possible value of $\frac{0.1X}{0.02Y}$ will occur when $0.1X$ has the greatest possible value and $0.02Y$ has the least possible value. Since X and Y are nonzero digits, this means than X must be 9 and Y must be 1. The greatest possible value of $\frac{0.1X}{0.02Y}$ is then $\frac{0.19}{0.021} \approx 9.05$, which is closest to 9.

The correct answer is D.

PS13724
140. Clarissa will create her summer reading list by randomly choosing 4 books from the 10 books approved for summer reading. She will list the books in the order in which they are chosen. How many different lists are possible?

(A) 6
(B) 40
(C) 210
(D) 5,040
(E) 151,200

Arithmetic Elementary combinatorics

Any of the 10 books can be listed first. Any of the 9 books remaining after the first book is listed can be listed second. Any of the 8 books remaining after the first and second books are listed can be listed third. Any of the 7 books remaining after the first, second, and third books are listed can be listed fourth. By the multiplication principle, there are $(10)(9)(8)(7) = 5{,}040$ different lists possible.

The correct answer is D.

PS10982
141. If n is a positive integer and the product of all the integers from 1 to n, inclusive, is divisible by 990, what is the least possible value of n?

(A) 8
(B) 9
(C) 10
(D) 11
(E) 12

Arithmetic Properties of numbers

For convenience, let N represent the product of all integers from 1 through n. Then, since N is divisible by 990, every prime factor of 990 must also be a factor of N. The prime factorization of 990 is $2 \times 3^2 \times 5 \times 11$, and therefore, 11 must be a factor of N. Then, the least possible value of N with factors of 2, 5, 3^2, and 11 is $1 \times 2 \times 3 \times \cdots \times 11$, and the least possible value of n is 11.

The correct answer is D.

PS02111
142. The probability that event M will not occur is 0.8 and the probability that event R will not occur is 0.6. If events M and R cannot both occur, which of the following is the probability that either event M or event R will occur?

(A) $\frac{1}{5}$
(B) $\frac{2}{5}$
(C) $\frac{3}{5}$
(D) $\frac{4}{5}$
(E) $\frac{12}{25}$

Arithmetic Probability

Let $P(M)$ be the probability that event M will occur, let $P(R)$ be the probability that event R will occur, and let $P(M \text{ and } R)$ be the probability that events M and R both occur. Then the probability that either event M or event R will occur is $P(M) + P(R) - P(M \text{ and } R)$. From the given information, it follows that $P(M) = 1.0 - 0.8 = 0.2$, $P(R) = 1.0 - 0.6 = 0.4$, and $P(M \text{ and } R) = 0$. Therefore, the probability that either event M or event R will occur is $0.2 + 0.4 - 0 = 0.6 = \frac{3}{5}$.

The correct answer is C.

143. The total cost for Company X to produce a batch of tools is $10,000 plus $3 per tool. Each tool sells for $8. The gross profit earned from producing and selling these tools is the total income from sales minus the total production cost. If a batch of 20,000 tools is produced and sold, then Company X's gross profit per tool is

(A) $3.00
(B) $3.75
(C) $4.50
(D) $5.00
(E) $5.50

Arithmetic Applied problems

The total cost to produce 20,000 tools is $10,000 + $3(20,000) = $70,000. The revenue resulting from the sale of 20,000 tools is $8(20,000) = $160,000. The gross profit is $160,000 − $70,000 = $90,000, and the gross profit per tool is $\frac{\$90,000}{20,000} = \$4.50$.

The correct answer is C.

144. If Q is an odd number and the median of Q consecutive integers is 120, what is the largest of these integers?

(A) $\frac{Q-1}{2} + 120$

(B) $\frac{Q}{2} + 119$

(C) $\frac{Q}{2} + 120$

(D) $\frac{Q+119}{2}$

(E) $\frac{Q+120}{2}$

Arithmetic Statistics

For an odd number of data values, the median is the middle number. Thus, 120 is the middle number, and so half of the $Q - 1$ remaining values are at most 120 and the other half of the $Q - 1$ remaining values are at least 120. In particular, $\frac{Q-1}{2}$ data values lie to the right of 120 when the data values are listed in increasing order from left to right, and so the largest data value is $120 + \frac{Q-1}{2}$. Alternatively, it is evident that (B), (C), or (E) cannot be correct since these

expressions do not have an integer value when Q is odd. For the list consisting of the single number 120 (i.e., if $Q = 1$), (D) fails because $\frac{Q+119}{2} = \frac{1+119}{2} = 60 \neq 120$ and (A) does not fail because $\frac{Q-1}{2} + 120 = \frac{1-1}{2} + 120 = 120$.

The correct answer is A.

145. A ladder of a fire truck is elevated to an angle of 60° and extended to a length of 70 feet. If the base of the ladder is 7 feet above the ground, how many feet above the ground does the ladder reach?

(A) 35
(B) 42
(C) $35\sqrt{3}$
(D) $7 + 35\sqrt{3}$
(E) $7 + 42\sqrt{3}$

Geometry Triangles

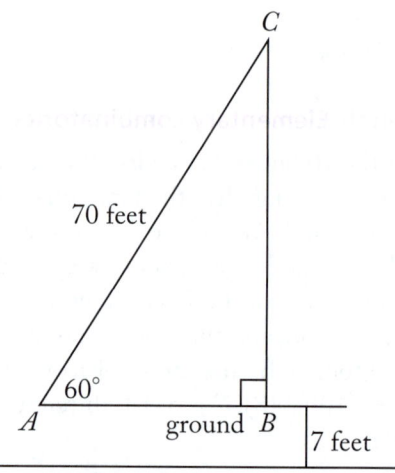

Given the figure above, determine BC. Then add 7 to determine how far above the ground the ladder reaches.

Triangle $\triangle ABC$ is a 30°–60°–90° triangle with hypotenuse AC of length 70 feet. Since the lengths of the sides of a 30°–60°–90° triangle are in the ratio $1:2:\sqrt{3}$, $\frac{AB}{AC} = \frac{1}{2}$ and so $AB = \frac{1}{2}AC = 35$, and $\frac{AB}{BC} = \frac{1}{\sqrt{3}}$ and so $BC = AB\sqrt{3} = 35\sqrt{3}$. Therefore, the ladder reaches $7 + 35\sqrt{3}$ feet above the ground.

The correct answer is D.

5.5 Problem Solving Answer Explanations

PS13827
146. The window in the figure above consists of a rectangle and a semicircle with dimensions as shown. What is the area, in square feet, of the window?

(A) $40 + 8\pi$
(B) $40 + 2\pi$
(C) $32 + 8\pi$
(D) $32 + 4\pi$
(E) $32 + 2\pi$

Geometry Area

The semicircle has a radius of 2 ft, and thus its area is $\frac{1}{2}\pi(2^2) = 2\pi$ ft². The rectangle has dimensions 4 ft by 8 ft, where $8 = 10 - 2$ is the full height of the window minus the radius of the semicircle, and thus has area $(4)(8) = 32$ ft². Therefore, in square feet, the area of the window is $32 + 2\pi$.

The correct answer is E.

PS00562
147. If there are fewer than 8 zeros between the decimal point and the first nonzero digit in the decimal expansion of $\left(\dfrac{t}{1,000}\right)^4$, which of the following numbers could be the value of t?

  I. 3
  II. 5
  III. 9

(A) None
(B) I only
(C) II only
(D) III only
(E) II and III

Arithmetic Properties of numbers; Decimals

The decimal expansion of $\left(\dfrac{1}{1,000}\right)^4 = 10^{-12}$ has 11 zeros to the right of the decimal point followed by a single digit that is 1. Therefore, in the decimal expansion of $\left(\dfrac{t}{1,000}\right)^4 = t^4 \times 10^{-12}$, the number of zeros between the decimal point and the first nonzero digit is equal to 12 minus the number of digits in the integer t^4. Since this number of zeros is fewer than 8, it follows that the number of digits in the integer t^4 is greater than 4. The integer t cannot be 3, because the number of digits in $3^4 = 81$ is not greater than 4. The integer t cannot be 5, because the number of digits in $5^4 = 625$ is not greater than 4. The integer t cannot be 9, because the number of digits in $9^4 = 6,561$ is not greater than 4. Therefore, none of 3, 5, or 9 could be the value of t.

The correct answer is A.

PS08280
148. A three-digit code for certain locks uses the digits 0, 1, 2, 3, 4, 5, 6, 7, 8, 9 according to the following constraints. The first digit cannot be 0 or 1, the second digit must be 0 or 1, and the second and third digits cannot both be 0 in the same code. How many different codes are possible?

(A) 144
(B) 152
(C) 160
(D) 168
(E) 176

Arithmetic Elementary combinatorics

Since the first digit cannot be 0 or 1, there are 8 digits possible for the first digit. Since the second digit must be 0 or 1, there are 2 digits possible for the second digit. If there were no other restrictions, all 10 digits would be possible for the third digit, making the total number of possible codes $8 \times 2 \times 10 = 160$. But, the additional restriction that the second and third digits cannot both be 0 in the same code eliminates the 8 codes 2-0-0, 3-0-0, 4-0-0, 5-0-0, 6-0-0, 7-0-0, 8-0-0, and 9-0-0. Therefore, there are $160 - 8 = 152$ possible codes.

The correct answer is B.

231

149. Jackie has two solutions that are 2 percent sulfuric acid and 12 percent sulfuric acid by volume, respectively. If these solutions are mixed in appropriate quantities to produce 60 liters of a solution that is 5 percent sulfuric acid, approximately how many liters of the 2 percent solution will be required?

(A) 18
(B) 20
(C) 24
(D) 36
(E) 42

Algebra Simultaneous equations

Let x represent the quantity of the 2% sulfuric acid solution in the mixture, from which it follows that the 2% sulfuric acid solution contributes $0.02x$ liters of sulfuric acid to the mixture. Let y represent the quantity of the 12% sulfuric acid solution in the mixture, from which it follows that the 12% sulfuric acid solution contributes $0.12y$ liters of sulfuric acid to the mixture. Since there are 60 liters of the mixture, $x + y = 60$. The quantity of sulfuric acid in the mixture, which is 5% sulfuric acid, is then $(0.05)(60) = 3$ liters. Therefore, $0.02x + 0.12y = 3$. Substituting $60 - x$ for y gives $0.02x + 0.12(60 - x) = 3$. Then,

$0.02x + 0.12(60 - x) = 3$	given
$0.02x + 7.2 - 0.12x = 3$	use distributive property
$7.2 - 0.1x = 3$	combine like terms
$-0.1x = -4.2$	subtract 7.2 from both sides
$x = 42$	divide both sides by -0.1

The correct answer is E.

150. If Jake loses 8 pounds, he will weigh twice as much as his sister. Together they now weigh 278 pounds. What is Jake's present weight, in pounds?

(A) 131
(B) 135
(C) 139
(D) 147
(E) 188

Algebra Systems of equations

Let J represent Jake's weight and S represent his sister's weight. Then $J - 8 = 2S$ and $J + S = 278$. Solve the second equation for S and get $S = 278 - J$. Substituting the expression for S into the first equation gives

$$J - 8 = 2(278 - J)$$
$$J - 8 = 556 - 2J$$
$$J + 2J = 556 + 8$$
$$3J = 564$$
$$J = 188$$

The correct answer is E.

151. For each student in a certain class, a teacher adjusted the student's test score using the formula $y = 0.8x + 20$, where x is the student's original test score and y is the student's adjusted test score. If the standard deviation of the original test scores of the students in the class was 20, what was the standard deviation of the adjusted test scores of the students in the class?

(A) 12
(B) 16
(C) 28
(D) 36
(E) 40

Arithmetic Statistics

Let n be the number of students in the class, let $\mu = \dfrac{\Sigma x}{n}$ be the mean of the students' unadjusted scores. It follows that the standard deviation of the unadjusted scores is $20 = \sqrt{\dfrac{\Sigma(x-\mu)^2}{n}}$.

To find the standard deviation of the adjusted scores, first find their mean: $\dfrac{\Sigma(0.8x + 20)}{n} = \dfrac{0.8\Sigma x}{n} + \dfrac{20n}{n} = 0.8\mu + 20$. Then, subtract the adjusted mean from each adjusted score: $(0.8x + 20) - (0.8\mu + 20) = 0.8(x - \mu)$. Next, square each difference: $(0.8(x - \mu))^2 = 0.64(x - \mu)^2$. Next, find the average of the squared differences: $\dfrac{\Sigma 0.64(x-\mu)^2}{n} = \dfrac{0.64\Sigma(x-\mu)^2}{n}$.

Finally, take the nonnegative square root:

$$\sqrt{\frac{0.64\Sigma(x-\mu)^2}{n}} = 0.8\sqrt{\frac{\Sigma(x-\mu)^2}{n}} = 0.8(20) = 16.$$

The correct answer is B.

PS01987

152. Last year 26 members of a certain club traveled to England, 26 members traveled to France, and 32 members traveled to Italy. Last year no members of the club traveled to both England and France, 6 members traveled to both England and Italy, and 11 members traveled to both France and Italy. How many members of the club traveled to at least one of these three countries last year?

   (A) 52
   (B) 67
   (C) 71
   (D) 73
   (E) 79

Arithmetic Applied problems

The numbers in the following diagram represent the numbers of members of the club who traveled to the indicated countries, and these numbers can be determined as follows. Since no members traveled to both England and France, both regions that form the overlap of England and France are labeled with 0. It follows that none of the 6 members who traveled to both England and Italy traveled to France, and so the region corresponding to England and Italy only is labeled with 6. It also follows that none of the 11 members who traveled to both France and Italy traveled to England, and so the region corresponding to France and Italy only is labeled with 11. At this point it can be determined that 26 – 6 = 20 members traveled to England only, 26 – 11 = 15 members traveled to France only, and 32 – (6 + 11) = 15 members traveled to Italy only.

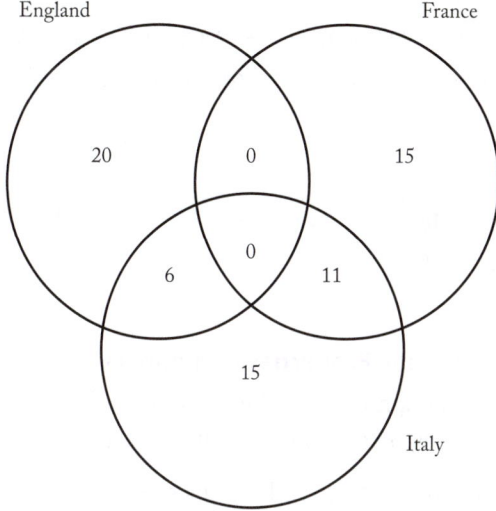

From the diagram it follows that 20 + 15 + 6 + 11 + 15 = 67 members traveled to at least one of these three countries.

The correct answer is B.

PS16088

153. A store reported total sales of $385 million for February of this year. If the total sales for the same month last year was $320 million, approximately what was the percent increase in sales?

   (A)   2%
   (B) 17%
   (C) 20%
   (D) 65%
   (E) 83%

Arithmetic Percents

The percent increase in sales from last year to this year is 100 times the quotient of the difference in sales for the two years divided by the sales last year. Thus, the percent increase is

$$\frac{385-320}{320} \times 100 = \frac{65}{320} \times 100$$

$$= \frac{13}{64} \times 100$$

$$\approx \frac{13}{65} \times 100$$

$$= \frac{1}{5} \times 100$$

$$= 20\%$$

The correct answer is C.

233

154. When positive integer x is divided by positive integer y, the remainder is 9. If $\frac{x}{y} = 96.12$, what is the value of y?

   (A) 96
   (B) 75
   (C) 48
   (D) 25
   (E) 12

Arithmetic Properties of numbers

The remainder is 9 when x is divided by y, so $x = yq + 9$ for some positive integer q. Dividing both sides by y gives $\frac{x}{y} = q + \frac{9}{y}$.
But, $\frac{x}{y} = 96.12 = 96 + 0.12$. Equating the two expressions for $\frac{x}{y}$ gives $q + \frac{9}{y} = 96 + 0.12$.
Thus, $q = 96$ and $\frac{9}{y} = 0.12$.

$9 = 0.12 y$

$y = \frac{9}{0.12}$

$y = 75$

The correct answer is B.

155. If $x(2x + 1) = 0$ and $\left(x + \frac{1}{2}\right)(2x - 3) = 0$, then x =

   (A) -3
   (B) $-\frac{1}{2}$
   (C) 0
   (D) $\frac{1}{2}$
   (E) $\frac{3}{2}$

Algebra Second-degree equations; Simultaneous equations

Setting each factor equal to 0, it can be seen that the solution set to the first equation is $\left\{0, -\frac{1}{2}\right\}$ and the solution set to the second equation is $\left\{-\frac{1}{2}, \frac{3}{2}\right\}$. Therefore, $-\frac{1}{2}$ is the solution to both equations.

The correct answer is B.

X   Y

156. Figures X and Y above show how eight identical triangular pieces of cardboard were used to form a square and a rectangle, respectively. What is the ratio of the perimeter of X to the perimeter of Y?

   (A) $2:3$
   (B) $\sqrt{2}:2$
   (C) $2\sqrt{2}:3$
   (D) $1:1$
   (E) $\sqrt{2}:1$

Geometry Perimeter

Because Figure X is a square and the diagonals of a square are the same length, are perpendicular, and bisect each other, it follows that each triangular piece is a 45°–45°–90° triangle. Thus, the length of each side of the square is $a\sqrt{2}$, and the perimeter is $4a\sqrt{2}$. The perimeter of the rectangle is $2(a + 2a) = 6a$. It follows that the ratio of the perimeter of the square to the perimeter of the rectangle is $\frac{4a\sqrt{2}}{6a} = \frac{2\sqrt{2}}{3}$, or $2\sqrt{2}:3$.

The correct answer is C.

157. A certain experimental mathematics program was tried out in 2 classes in each of 32 elementary schools and involved 37 teachers. Each of the classes had 1 teacher and each of the teachers taught at least 1, but not more than 3, of the classes. If the number of teachers who taught 3 classes is n, then the least and greatest possible values of n, respectively, are

   (A) 0 and 13
   (B) 0 and 14
   (C) 1 and 10
   (D) 1 and 9
   (E) 2 and 8

5.5 Problem Solving Answer Explanations

Algebra Simultaneous equations; Inequalities

It is given that $2(32) = 64$ classes are taught by 37 teachers. Let k, m, and n be the number of teachers who taught, respectively, 1, 2, and 3 of the classes. Then $k + m + n = 37$ and $k + 2m + 3n = 64$. Subtracting these two equations gives $m + 2n = 64 - 37 = 27$, or $2n = 27 - m$, and therefore $2n \leq 27$. Because n is an integer, it follows that $n \leq 13$ and B cannot be the answer. Since $n = 0$ is possible, which can be seen by using $m = 27$ and $k = 10$ (obtained by solving $2n = 27 - m$ with $n = 0$, then by solving $k + m + n = 37$ with $n = 0$ and $m = 27$), the answer must be A.

It is not necessary to ensure that $n = 13$ is possible to answer the question. However, it is not difficult to see that $k = 23$, $m = 1$, and $n = 13$ satisfy the given conditions.

The correct answer is A.

PS16214
158. For the positive numbers, n, $n + 1$, $n + 2$, $n + 4$, and $n + 8$, the mean is how much greater than the median?

(A) 0
(B) 1
(C) $n + 1$
(D) $n + 2$
(E) $n + 3$

Algebra Statistics

Since the five positive numbers n, $n + 1$, $n + 2$, $n + 4$, and $n + 8$ are in ascending order, the median is the third number, which is $n + 2$. The mean of the five numbers is

$$\frac{n + (n+1) + (n+2) + (n+4) + (n+8)}{5}$$
$$= \frac{5n + 15}{5}$$
$$= n + 3$$

Since $(n + 3) - (n + 2) = 1$, the mean is 1 greater than the median.

The correct answer is B.

PS08313
159. The interior of a rectangular carton is designed by a certain manufacturer to have a volume of x cubic feet and a ratio of length to width to height of 3:2:2. In terms of x, which of the following equals the height of the carton, in feet?

(A) $\sqrt[3]{x}$
(B) $\sqrt[3]{\frac{2x}{3}}$
(C) $\sqrt[3]{\frac{3x}{2}}$
(D) $\frac{2}{3}\sqrt[3]{x}$
(E) $\frac{3}{2}\sqrt[3]{x}$

Geometry; Arithmetic Volume; Ratio and proportion

Letting c represent the constant of proportionality, the length, width, and height, in feet, of the carton can be expressed as $3c$, $2c$, and $2c$, respectively. The volume of the carton is then $(3c)(2c)(2c) = 12c^3$ cubic feet. But, the volume is x cubic feet, and so $12c^3 = x$. Then, $c^3 = \frac{x}{12}$ and $c = \sqrt[3]{\frac{x}{12}}$. The height of the carton is $2c$ and in terms of x, $2c = 2\sqrt[3]{\frac{x}{12}}$. Since $2 = \sqrt[3]{8}$ and $\left(\sqrt[3]{a}\right)\left(\sqrt[3]{b}\right) = \sqrt[3]{ab}$, the height of the carton can be expressed as $2\sqrt[3]{\frac{x}{12}} = \sqrt[3]{8\left(\frac{x}{12}\right)} = \sqrt[3]{\frac{2x}{3}}$.

The correct answer is B.

PS16810
160. The present ratio of students to teachers at a certain school is 30 to 1. If the student enrollment were to increase by 50 students and the number of teachers were to increase by 5, the ratio of students to teachers would then be 25 to 1. What is the present number of teachers?

(A) 5
(B) 8
(C) 10
(D) 12
(E) 15

235

Algebra Applied problems

Let s be the present number of students, and let t be the present number of teachers. According to the problem, the following two equations apply:

$\frac{30}{1} = \frac{s}{t}$ Current student to teacher ratio

$\frac{s+50}{t+5} = \frac{25}{1}$ Future student to teacher ratio

Solving the first equation for s gives $s = 30t$. Substitute this value of s into the second equation, and solve for t.

$\frac{30t + 50}{t+5} = \frac{25}{1}$

$30t + 50 = 25t + 125$ multiply both sides by $t + 5$

$5t = 75$ simplify by subtraction

$t = 15$

The correct answer is E.

PS16811

161. What is the smallest integer n for which $25^n > 5^{12}$?

(A) 6
(B) 7
(C) 8
(D) 9
(E) 10

Arithmetic Operations with rational numbers

Because $5^2 = 25$, a common base is 5. Rewrite the left side with 5 as a base: $25^n = (5^2)^n = 5^{2n}$. It follows that the desired integer is the least integer n for which $5^{2n} > 5^{12}$. This will be the least integer n for which $2n > 12$, or the least integer n for which $n > 6$, which is 7.

The correct answer is B.

PS16122

162. Sixty percent of the members of a study group are women, and 45 percent of those women are lawyers. If one member of the study group is to be selected at random, what is the probability that the member selected is a woman lawyer?

(A) 0.10
(B) 0.15
(C) 0.27
(D) 0.33
(E) 0.45

Arithmetic Probability

For simplicity, suppose there are 100 members in the study group. Since 60 percent of the members are women, there are 60 women in the group. Also, 45 percent of the women are lawyers so there are $0.45(60) = 27$ women lawyers in the study group. Therefore the probability of selecting a woman lawyer is $\frac{27}{100} = 0.27$.

The correct answer is C.

PS06570

163. Each year for 4 years, a farmer increased the number of trees in a certain orchard by $\frac{1}{4}$ of the number of trees in the orchard the preceding year. If all of the trees thrived and there were 6,250 trees in the orchard at the end of the 4-year period, how many trees were in the orchard at the beginning of the 4-year period?

(A) 1,250
(B) 1,563
(C) 2,250
(D) 2,560
(E) 2,752

Arithmetic Operations on rational numbers

Increasing the number of trees each year by $\frac{1}{4}$ of the number of trees in the orchard the preceding year is equivalent to making the number of trees increase 25% per year, compounded yearly. If there were n trees at the beginning of the 4-year period, then there will be $1.25n$ trees at the end of the first year, $1.25(1.25n) = (1.25)^2 n$ trees at the end of the second year, $1.25[(1.25)^2 n] = (1.25)^3 n$ trees at the end of the third year, and $1.25[(1.25)^3 n] = (1.25)^4 n$ trees at the end of the fourth year. Hence, $6,250 = (1.25)^4 n$ and $n = \frac{6,250}{(1.25)^4}$. The arithmetic can be greatly simplified by rewriting $(1.25)^4$ as $\left(\frac{5}{4}\right)^4 = \frac{5^4}{4^4}$ and 6,250 as $(625)(10) = (5^4)(10)$. Then

$\frac{6,250}{(1.25)^4} = (5^4)(10)\left(\frac{4^4}{5^4}\right) = (10)(4^4) = 2,560.$

The correct answer is D.

Number of Shipments of Manufactured Homes
in the United States, 1990–2000

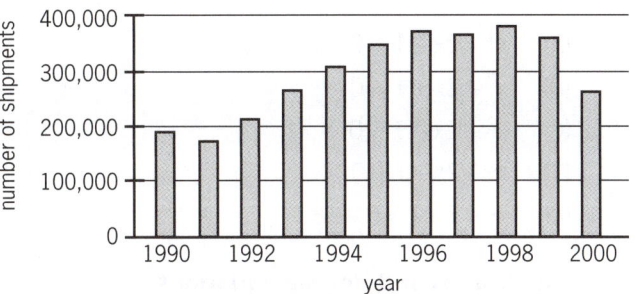

PS00422

164. According to the chart shown, which of the following is closest to the median annual number of shipments of manufactured homes in the United States for the years from 1990 to 2000, inclusive?

(A) 250,000
(B) 280,000
(C) 310,000
(D) 325,000
(E) 340,000

Arithmetic Interpretation of graphs and tables; Statistics

From the chart, the approximate numbers of shipments are as follows:

Year	Number of shipments
1990	190,000
1991	180,000
1992	210,000
1993	270,000
1994	310,000
1995	350,000
1996	380,000
1997	370,000
1998	390,000
1999	360,000
2000	270,000

Since there are 11 entries in the table and 11 is an odd number, the median of the numbers of shipments is the 6th entry when the numbers of shipments are arranged in order from least to greatest. In order, from least to greatest, the first 6 entries are:

Number of shipments
180,000
190,000
210,000
270,000
270,000
310,000

The 6th entry is 310,000.

The correct answer is C.

PS08209

165. For the positive integers a, b, and k, $a^k \| b$ means that a^k is a divisor of b, but a^{k+1} is not a divisor of b. If k is a positive integer and $2^k \| 72$, then k is equal to

(A) 2
(B) 3
(C) 4
(D) 8
(E) 18

Arithmetic Property of numbers

Since $72 = (2^3)(3^2)$, it follows that 2^3 is a divisor of 72 and 2^4 is not a divisor of 72. Therefore, $2^3 \| 72$, and hence $k = 3$.

The correct answer is B.

PS06674

166. A certain characteristic in a large population has a distribution that is symmetric about the mean m. If 68 percent of the distribution lies within one standard deviation d of the mean, what percent of the distribution is less than $m + d$?

(A) 16%
(B) 32%
(C) 48%
(D) 84%
(E) 92%

Arithmetic Statistics

Since 68% lies between $m - d$ and $m + d$, a total of $(100 - 68)\% = 32\%$ lies to the left of $m - d$ and to the right of $m + d$. Because the distribution is symmetric about m, half of the 32% lies to the right of $m + d$. Therefore, 16% lies to the right of $m + d$, and hence $(100 - 16)\% = 84\%$ lies to the left of $m + d$.

The correct answer is D.

PS07459

167. Four extra-large sandwiches of exactly the same size were ordered for m students, where $m > 4$. Three of the sandwiches were evenly divided among the students. Since 4 students did not want any of the fourth sandwich, it was evenly divided among the remaining students. If Carol ate one piece from each of the four sandwiches, the amount of sandwich that she ate would be what fraction of a whole extra-large sandwich?

(A) $\dfrac{m+4}{m(m-4)}$

(B) $\dfrac{2m-4}{m(m-4)}$

(C) $\dfrac{4m-4}{m(m-4)}$

(D) $\dfrac{4m-8}{m(m-4)}$

(E) $\dfrac{4m-12}{m(m-4)}$

Algebra Applied problems

Since each of 3 of the sandwiches was evenly divided among m students, each piece was $\dfrac{1}{m}$ of a sandwich. Since the fourth sandwich was evenly divided among $m - 4$ students, each piece was $\dfrac{1}{m-4}$ of the fourth sandwich. Carol ate 1 piece from each of the four sandwiches, so she ate a total of

$$(3)\dfrac{1}{m} + \dfrac{1}{m-4} = \dfrac{3(m-4)+m}{m(m-4)} = \dfrac{4m-12}{m(m-4)}$$

The correct answer is E.

PS05888

168. Which of the following equations has $1 + \sqrt{2}$ as one of its roots?

(A) $x^2 + 2x - 1 = 0$
(B) $x^2 - 2x + 1 = 0$
(C) $x^2 + 2x + 1 = 0$
(D) $x^2 - 2x - 1 = 0$
(E) $x^2 - x - 1 = 0$

Algebra Second-degree equations

This problem can be solved by working backwards to construct a quadratic equation with $1 + \sqrt{2}$ as a root that does not involve radicals.

$x = 1 + \sqrt{2}$	set x to the desired value
$x - 1 = \sqrt{2}$	subtract 1 from both sides
$(x - 1)^2 = 2$	square both sides
$x^2 - 2x + 1 = 2$	expand the left side
$x^2 - 2x - 1 = 0$	subtract 2 from both sides

The correct answer is D.

PS07730

169. In Country C, the unemployment rate among construction workers dropped from 16 percent on September 1, 1992, to 9 percent on September 1, 1996. If the number of construction workers was 20 percent greater on September 1, 1996, than on September 1, 1992, what was the approximate percent change in the number of unemployed construction workers over this period?

(A) 50% decrease
(B) 30% decrease
(C) 15% decrease
(D) 30% increase
(E) 55% increase

Arithmetic Percents

Let U_1 and U_2 be the numbers of unemployed construction workers on September 1, 1992, and September 1, 1996, respectively, and let N be the number of construction workers on September 1, 1992. Then, from the given information, $1.2N$ is the number of construction workers on September 1, 1996, $U_1 = 0.16N$, and $U_2 = 0.09(1.2N)$. Therefore, the percent change from September 1, 1992, to September 1, 1996, of unemployed construction workers is given by

$$\left(\frac{U_2 - U_1}{U_1} \times 100\right)\%$$
$$= \left(\frac{0.09(1.2N) - 0.16N}{0.16N} \times 100\right)\%$$
$$= \left(\frac{0.108 - 0.16}{0.16} \times 100\right)\%$$
$$= \left(\frac{108 - 160}{160} \times 100\right)\%$$
$$= \left(-\frac{13}{40} \times 100\right)\%$$
$$\approx \left(-\frac{13}{39} \times 100\right)\%$$
$$\approx \left(-\frac{1}{3} \times 100\right)\%$$
$$\approx -30\%$$

The correct answer is B.

PS06215

170. In a box of 12 pens, a total of 3 are defective. If a customer buys 2 pens selected at random from the box, what is the probability that neither pen will be defective?

    (A) $\frac{1}{6}$
    (B) $\frac{2}{9}$
    (C) $\frac{6}{11}$
    (D) $\frac{9}{16}$
    (E) $\frac{3}{4}$

Arithmetic Probability

Let A represent the event that the first pen purchased is not defective and let B represent the event that the second pen purchased is not defective, where A and B are dependent events. Since there are 3 defective pens in the box of 12 pens, there are 9 pens in the box that are not defective. Using standard probability notation, $P(A) = \frac{9}{12}$ and $P(B$, given that A has occurred$) = \frac{8}{11}$. (Event A has occurred so there are 11 pens left in the box and 8 of them are not defective.) Then, using the multiplication rule for dependent events, P(neither pen is defective) $= P(A$ and $B) = P(A) \times P(B$, given that A has occurred$) = \frac{9}{12} \times \frac{8}{11} = \frac{6}{11}$.

Alternately, the probability of selecting 2 pens, neither of which is defective, from a box containing 12 pens, 3 of which are defective, and therefore, 9 of which are non-defective is the number of ways to select 2 non-defective pens from 9 non-defective pens over the number of ways to select 2 pens from 12 pens

$$= \frac{\binom{9}{2}}{\binom{12}{2}} = \frac{\frac{9 \times 8}{2}}{\frac{12 \times 11}{2}} = \frac{6}{11}.$$

The correct answer is C.

PS13244

171. At a certain fruit stand, the price of each apple is 40 cents and the price of each orange is 60 cents. Mary selects a total of 10 apples and oranges from the fruit stand, and the average (arithmetic mean) price of the 10 pieces of fruit is 56 cents. How many oranges must Mary put back so that the average price of the pieces of fruit that she keeps is 52 cents?

    (A) 1
    (B) 2
    (C) 3
    (D) 4
    (E) 5

Algebra Statistics

If Mary selected x apples, then she selected $(10 - x)$ oranges. The average price of the 10 pieces of fruit is $\frac{40x + 60(10 - x)}{10} = 56$. From this,

$$\frac{40x + 60(10 - x)}{10} = 56 \quad \text{given}$$
$$40x + 60(10 - x) = 560 \quad \text{multiply both sides by 10}$$
$$40x + 600 - 60x = 560 \quad \text{distribution property}$$
$$600 - 20x = 560 \quad \text{combine like terms}$$
$$-20x = -40 \quad \text{subtract 600 from both sides}$$
$$x = 2 \quad \text{divide both sides by } -20$$

Thus, Mary selected 2 apples and 8 oranges. Next, let y be the number of oranges Mary needs to put back, so that the average price of the $[2 + (8 - y)]$ pieces of fruit Mary keeps is 52 cents. Then,

$$\frac{(40)(2) + (60)(8 - y)}{2 + (8 - y)} = 52 \quad \text{given}$$
$$\frac{80 + 480 - 60y}{10 - y} = 52 \quad \text{distributive property}$$
$$80 + 480 - 60y = 52(10 - y) \quad \text{multiply both sides by } 10 - y$$
$$560 - 60y = 520 - 52y \quad \text{distributive property}$$
$$8y = 40 \quad \text{subtract } 520 - 60y \text{ from both sides}$$
$$y = 5 \quad \text{divide both sides by 8}$$

Therefore, Mary must put back 5 oranges, so that the average price of the fruit she keeps (that is, the average price of 2 apples and 3 oranges) is 52 cents.

The correct answer is E.

PS04688
172. A pharmaceutical company received $3 million in royalties on the first $20 million in sales of the generic equivalent of one of its products and then $9 million in royalties on the next $108 million in sales. By approximately what percent did the ratio of royalties to sales decrease from the first $20 million in sales to the next $108 million in sales?

(A) 8%
(B) 15%
(C) 45%
(D) 52%
(E) 56%

Arithmetic Percents

The ratio of royalties to sales for the first $20 million in sales is $\frac{3}{20}$, and the ratio of royalties to sales for the next $108 million in sales is $\frac{9}{108} = \frac{1}{12}$. The percent decrease in the royalties to sales ratios is 100 times the quotient of the difference in the ratios divided by the ratio of royalties to sales for the first $20 million in sales or

$$\frac{\frac{1}{12} - \frac{3}{20}}{\frac{3}{20}} \times 100 = \left(\frac{1}{12} - \frac{3}{20}\right) \times \frac{20}{3} \times 100$$

$$= \left(\frac{1}{12} \times \frac{20}{3} - 1\right) \times 100$$

$$= \left(\frac{5}{9} - 1\right) \times 100$$

$$= -\frac{4}{9} \times 100$$

$$\approx -0.44 \times 100$$

$$\approx 45\% \text{ decrease}$$

The correct answer is C.

5.5 Problem Solving Answer Explanations

Times at Which the Door Opened from 8:00 to 10:00

8:00	8:06	8:30	9:05
8:03	8:10	8:31	9:11
8:04	8:18	8:54	9:29
8:04	8:19	8:57	9:31

PS06497

173. The light in a restroom operates with a 15-minute timer that is reset every time the door opens as a person goes in or out of the room. Thus, after someone enters or exits the room, the light remains on for only 15 minutes unless the door opens again and resets the timer for another 15 minutes. If the times listed above are the times at which the door opened from 8:00 to 10:00, approximately how many minutes during this two-hour period was the light off?

(A) 10
(B) 25
(C) 35
(D) 40
(E) 70

Arithmetic Operations with integers

Look for two consecutive times that are more than 15 minutes apart

8:03 − 8:00 = 3 minutes

8:04 − 8:03 = 1 minute

8:04 − 8:04 = 0 minutes

8:06 − 8:04 = 2 minutes

8:10 − 8:06 = 4 minutes

8:18 − 8:10 = 8 minutes

8:19 − 8:18 = 1 minute

8:30 − 8:19 = 11 minutes

8:31 − 8:30 = 1 minute

8:54 − 8:31 = 23 minutes, so the light is off for 23 − 15 = 8 minutes

8:57 − 8:54 = 3 minutes

9:05 − 8:57 = 8 minutes

9:11 − 9:05 = 6 minutes

9:29 − 9:11 = 18 minutes, so the light is off for 18 − 15 = 3 minutes

9:31 − 9:29 = 2 minutes

10:00 − 9:31 = 29 minutes, so the light is off for 29 − 15 = 14 minutes

Thus, the light is off for a total of 8 + 3 + 14 = 25 minutes during the two-hour period.

Alternatively, the light comes on at 8:00 when the door is opened and is scheduled to go off at 8:15. So, when the door is opened at 8:03, twice at 8:04, at 8:06, and 8:10, the light is still on, but by the door being opened at these times, the timer has been reset to turn the light off at 8:18, 8:19, 8:21, and 8:25, respectively. Therefore, the light is still on when the door is opened at 8:18, 8:19, 8:30, and 8:31, but the timer has been reset to turn the light off at 8:33, 8:34, 8:45, and 8:46, respectively. The light is therefore off from 8:46 until the door is opened again at 8:54, which is an interval of 8 minutes. The light is still on when the door is opened at 8:57, 9:05, and 9:11, but the timer has been reset to turn the light off at 9:12, 9:20, and 9:26, respectively. The light is off from 9:26 until the door is opened again at 9:29, which is an interval of 3 minutes. The light is still on when the door is opened again at 9:31, and the timer has been reset to turn the light off at 9:46. Since, according to the chart, the door is not opened again before 10:00, the light remains off from 9:46 until 10:00, which is an interval of 14 minutes. Thus, the light is off a total of 8 + 3 + 14 = 25 minutes during the two-hour period.

The correct answer is B.

PS07536
174. The parallelogram shown has four sides of equal length. What is the ratio of the length of the shorter diagonal to the length of the longer diagonal?

(A) $\dfrac{1}{2}$

(B) $\dfrac{1}{\sqrt{2}}$

(C) $\dfrac{1}{2\sqrt{2}}$

(D) $\dfrac{1}{\sqrt{3}}$

(E) $\dfrac{1}{2\sqrt{3}}$

Geometry Quadrilaterals; Triangles

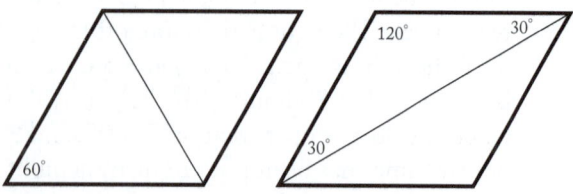

First, opposite angles of a parallelogram have equal measure, and the sum of the measures of adjacent angles is 180°. This means that each of the angles adjacent to the angle labeled 60° has measure 120°.

Since all four sides of the parallelogram have equal length, say x units, the shorter diagonal divides the parallelogram into two isosceles triangles. An isosceles triangle with one angle measuring 60° is equilateral, and so the shorter diagonal has length x units.

The longer diagonal divides the parallelogram into two isosceles triangles with one angle measuring 120° and each of the other angles measuring $\dfrac{180-120}{2} = 30°$, as shown in the figure above on the right.

Then, because the diagonals of a parallelogram are perpendicular and bisect each other, the two diagonals divide the parallelogram into four 30°-60°-90° triangles, each with hypotenuse x units long. The sides of a 30°-60°-90° triangle are in the ratio of $1 : \sqrt{3} : 2$ and so, if y represents the length of the side opposite the 60° angle, then $\dfrac{x}{2} = \dfrac{y}{\sqrt{3}}$ and $y = \dfrac{x\sqrt{3}}{2}$. But, y is half the length of the longer diagonal, so the longer diagonal has length $x\sqrt{3}$ units. Therefore, the ratio of the length of the shorter diagonal to the length of the longer diagonal is $\dfrac{x}{x\sqrt{3}} = \dfrac{1}{\sqrt{3}}$.

The correct answer is D.

PS00041
175. If p is the product of the integers from 1 to 30, inclusive, what is the greatest integer k for which 3^k is a factor of p?

(A) 10
(B) 12
(C) 14
(D) 16
(E) 18

Arithmetic Properties of numbers

The table below shows the numbers from 1 to 30, inclusive, that have at least one factor of 3 and how many factors of 3 each has.

Multiples of 3 between 1 and 30	Number of factors of 3
3	1
$6 = 2 \times 3$	1
$9 = 3 \times 3$	2
$12 = 2 \times 2 \times 3$	1
$15 = 3 \times 5$	1
$18 = 2 \times 3 \times 3$	2
$21 = 3 \times 7$	1
$24 = 2 \times 2 \times 2 \times 3$	1
$27 = 3 \times 3 \times 3$	3
$30 = 2 \times 3 \times 5$	1

The sum of the numbers in the right column is 14. Therefore, 3^{14} is the greatest power of 3 that is a factor of the product of the first 30 positive integers.

The correct answer is C.

PS04651
176. If $n = 3^8 - 2^8$, which of the following is NOT a factor of n?

(A) 97
(B) 65
(C) 35
(D) 13
(E) 5

Arithmetic Properties of numbers

Since $3^8 - 2^8$ is the difference of the perfect squares $(3^4)^2$ and $(2^4)^2$, then $3^8 - 2^8 = (3^4 + 2^4)(3^4 - 2^4)$. But $3^4 - 2^4$ is also the difference of the perfect squares $(3^2)^2$ and $(2^2)^2$ so $3^4 - 2^4 = (3^2 + 2^2)(3^2 - 2^2)$ and therefore $3^8 - 2^8 = (3^4 + 2^4)(3^2 + 2^2)(3^2 - 2^2)$. It follows that $3^8 - 2^8$ can be factored as $(81 + 16)(9 + 4)(9 - 4) = (97)(13)(5)$. Therefore, 7 is not a factor of $3^8 - 2^8$, and hence $35 = 5 \times 7$ is not a factor of $3^8 - 2^8$. It is easy to see that each of 97, 13, and 5 is a factor of $3^8 - 2^8$, and so is 65, since $65 = 5 \times 13$, although this additional analysis is not needed to arrive at the correct answer.

The correct answer is C.

PS12078
177. In the figure shown, if the area of the shaded region is 3 times the area of the smaller circular region, then the circumference of the larger circle is how many times the circumference of the smaller circle?

(A) 4
(B) 3
(C) 2
(D) $\sqrt{3}$
(E) $\sqrt{2}$

Geometry Circles

Let R represent the radius of the larger circle and r represent the radius of the smaller circle. Then the area of the shaded region is the area of the larger circular region minus the area of the smaller circular region, or $\pi R^2 - \pi r^2$. It is given that the area of the shaded region is three times the area of the smaller circular region, and so $\pi R^2 - \pi r^2 = 3\pi r^2$. Then $R^2 - r^2 = 3r^2$, and so $R^2 = 4r^2$ and $R = 2r$. The circumference of the larger circle is $2\pi R = 2\pi(2r) = 2(2\pi r)$, which is 2 times the circumference of the smaller circle.

The correct answer is C.

PS12177
178. Club X has more than 10 but fewer than 40 members. Sometimes the members sit at tables with 3 members at one table and 4 members at each of the other tables, and sometimes they sit at tables with 3 members at one table and 5 members at each of the other tables. If they sit at tables with 6 members at each table except one and fewer than 6 members at that one table, how many members will be at the table that has fewer than 6 members?

(A) 1
(B) 2
(C) 3
(D) 4
(E) 5

243

Arithmetic Properties of numbers

Let n be the number of members that Club X has. Since the members can be equally divided into groups of 4 each with 3 left over, and the members can be equally divided into groups of 5 each with 3 left over, it follows that $n - 3$ is divisible by both 4 and 5. Therefore, $n - 3$ must be a multiple of $(4)(5) = 20$. Also, because the only multiple of 20 that is greater than 10 and less than 40 is 20, it follows that $n - 3 = 20$, or $n = 23$. Finally, when these 23 members are divided into the greatest number of groups of 6 each, there will be 5 members left over, since $23 = (3)(6) + 5$.

The correct answer is E.

PS07081

179. In order to complete a reading assignment on time, Terry planned to read 90 pages per day. However, she read only 75 pages per day at first, leaving 690 pages to be read during the last 6 days before the assignment was to be completed. How many days in all did Terry have to complete the assignment on time?

    (A) 15
    (B) 16
    (C) 25
    (D) 40
    (E) 46

Algebra Applied problems

Let n be the number of days that Terry read at the slower rate of 75 pages per day. Then $75n$ is the number of pages Terry read at this slower rate, and $75n + 690$ is the total number of pages Terry needs to read. Also, $n + 6$ is the total number of days that Terry will spend on the reading assignment. The requirement that Terry average 90 pages per day is equivalent to $\frac{75n + 690}{n + 6} = 90$.

Then

$$\frac{75n + 690}{n + 6} = 90$$
$$75n + 690 = 90n + 540$$
$$150 = 15n$$
$$10 = n$$

Therefore, the total number of days that Terry has to complete the assignment on time is $n + 6 = 10 + 6 = 16$.

The correct answer is B.

PS13996

180. If $s > 0$ and $\sqrt{\frac{r}{s}} = s$, what is r in terms of s?

    (A) $\frac{1}{s}$
    (B) $\sqrt{s}$
    (C) $s\sqrt{s}$
    (D) s^3
    (E) $s^3 - s$

Algebra Equations

Solve the equation for r as follows:

$$\sqrt{\frac{r}{s}} = s$$

$\frac{r}{s} = s^2$ square both sides of the equation

$r = s^3$ multiply both sides by s

The correct answer is D.

PS12536

181. If $3 < x < 100$, for how many values of x is $\frac{x}{3}$ the square of a prime number?

    (A) Two
    (B) Three
    (C) Four
    (D) Five
    (E) Nine

Arithmetic Properties of numbers

If $\frac{x}{3}$ is the square of a prime number, then possible values of $\frac{x}{3}$ are $2^2, 3^2, 5^2, 7^2, \ldots$. Therefore, possible values of x are $3 \times 2^2 = 12$, $3 \times 3^2 = 27$, $3 \times 5^2 = 75$, $3 \times 7^2 = 147, \ldots$. Since only three of these values, namely 12, 27, and 75, are between 3 and 100, there are three values of x such that $\frac{x}{3}$ is the square of a prime number.

The correct answer is B.

PS07547

182. A researcher plans to identify each participant in a certain medical experiment with a code consisting of either a single letter or a pair of distinct letters written in alphabetical order. What is the least number of letters that can be used if there are 12 participants, and each participant is to receive a different code?

(A) 4
(B) 5
(C) 6
(D) 7
(E) 8

Arithmetic Elementary combinatorics

None of the essential aspects of the problem is affected if the letters are restricted to be the first n letters of the alphabet, for various positive integers n. With the 3 letters a, b, and c, there are 6 codes: a, b, c, ab, ac, and bc. With the 4 letters a, b, c, and d, there are 10 codes: a, b, c, d, ab, ac, ad, bc, bd, and cd. Clearly, more than 12 codes are possible with 5 or more letters, so the least number of letters that can be used is 5.

The correct answer is B.

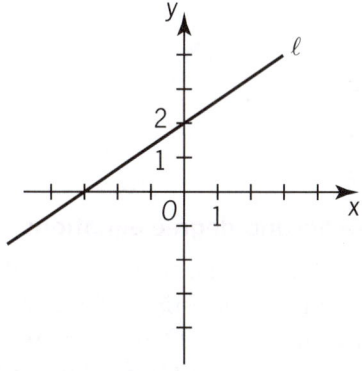

PS06948

183. The graph of which of the following equations is a straight line that is parallel to line ℓ in the figure above?

(A) $3y - 2x = 0$
(B) $3y + 2x = 0$
(C) $3y + 2x = 6$
(D) $2y - 3x = 6$
(E) $2y + 3x = -6$

Algebra Coordinate geometry

From the graph, line ℓ contains points $(-3,0)$ and $(0,2)$, so the slope of line ℓ is $\frac{0-2}{-3-0} = \frac{2}{3}$. Any line parallel to line ℓ has slope $\frac{2}{3}$. Rewrite each of the equations given in the answer choices in slope-intercept form $y = mx + b$, where m is the slope and b is the y-intercept, to find the equation whose graph is a line with slope $\frac{2}{3}$. For answer choice A, $3y - 2x = 0$ so $3y = 2x$ and $y = \frac{2}{3}x$. The graph of this equation is a line with slope $\frac{2}{3}$.

The correct answer is A.

PS06562

184. An object thrown directly upward is at a height of h feet after t seconds, where $h = -16(t-3)^2 + 150$. At what height, in feet, is the object 2 seconds after it reaches its maximum height?

(A) 6
(B) 86
(C) 134
(D) 150
(E) 166

Algebra Applied problems

Since $(t-3)^2$ is positive when $t \neq 3$ and zero when $t = 3$, it follows that the *minimum* value of $(t-3)^2$ occurs when $t = 3$. Therefore, the *maximum* value of $-16(t-3)^2$, and also the maximum value of $-16(t-3)^2 + 150$, occurs when $t = 3$. Hence, the height 2 seconds after the maximum height is the value of h when $t = 5$, or $-16(5-3)^2 + 150 = 86$.

The correct answer is B.

PS16107

185. Which of the following is equivalent to the pair of inequalities $x + 6 > 10$ and $x - 3 \leq 5$?

(A) $2 \leq x < 16$
(B) $2 \leq x < 4$
(C) $2 < x \leq 8$
(D) $4 < x \leq 8$
(E) $4 \leq x < 16$

245

Algebra Inequalities

Solve the inequalities separately and combine the results.

$x + 6 > 10$

$\quad x > 4$

$x - 3 \leq 5$

$\quad x \leq 8$

Since $x > 4$, then $4 < x$. Combining $4 < x$ and $x \leq 8$ gives $4 < x \leq 8$.

The correct answer is D.

PS16823

186. David has d books, which is 3 times as many as Jeff and $\frac{1}{2}$ as many as Paula. How many books do the three of them have altogether, in terms of d?

(A) $\frac{5}{6}d$

(B) $\frac{7}{3}d$

(C) $\frac{10}{3}d$

(D) $\frac{7}{2}d$

(E) $\frac{9}{2}d$

Algebra Applied problems; Simultaneous equations

Let J be the number of books that Jeff has, and let P be the number of books Paula has. Then, the given information about David's books can be expressed as $d = 3J$ and $d = \frac{1}{2}P$. Solving these two equations for J and P gives $\frac{d}{3} = J$ and $2d = P$. Thus, $d + J + P = d + \frac{d}{3} + 2d = 3\frac{1}{3}d = \frac{10}{3}d$.

The correct answer is C.

PS16824

187. There are 8 teams in a certain league and each team plays each of the other teams exactly once. If each game is played by 2 teams, what is the total number of games played?

(A) 15
(B) 16
(C) 28
(D) 56
(E) 64

Arithmetic Operations on rational numbers

Since no team needs to play itself, each team needs to play 7 other teams. In addition, each game needs to be counted only once, rather than once for each team that plays that game. Since two teams play each game, $\frac{8 \times 7}{2} = 28$ games are needed.

The correct answer is C.

PS07491

188. At his regular hourly rate, Don had estimated the labor cost of a repair job as $336 and he was paid that amount. However, the job took 4 hours longer than he had estimated and, consequently, he earned $2 per hour less than his regular hourly rate. What was the time Don had estimated for the job, in hours?

(A) 28
(B) 24
(C) 16
(D) 14
(E) 12

Algebra Second-degree equations

Let r be Don's regular hourly rate and t be the number of hours he estimated the repair job to take. Then $rt = 336$ is Don's estimated labor cost. Since Don was paid $336 for doing $t + 4$ hours of work at an hourly rate of $r - 2$, it also follows that $(r - 2)(t + 4) = 336$. Then

$(r - 2)(t + 4) = 336$

$rt - 2t + 4r - 8 = 336$

$-2t + 4r - 8 = 0$ since $rt = 336$ from above

$-2t^2 + 4rt - 8t = 0$ multiply both sides by t

$-2t^2 + 4(336) - 8t = 0$ since $rt = 336$

$t^2 + 4t - 672 = 0$ divide both sides by -2

$(t - 24)(t + 28) = 0$ factor

Alternatively, from the third line above,

$$-2t + 4r - 8 = 0$$

$-2t + 4\left(\dfrac{336}{t}\right) - 8 = 0$ since $rt = 336$ from above

gives $r = \dfrac{336}{t}$

$-2t^2 + 4(336) - 8t = 0$ multiply both sides by t

$t^2 + 4t - 672 = 0$ divide both sides by -2

$(t - 24)(t + 28) = 0$ factor

So, $t - 24 = 0$, which means $t = 24$, or $t + 28 = 0$, which means $t = -28$. Since an estimated time cannot be negative, $t = 24$.

The correct answer is B.

PS16828

189. If $\dfrac{p}{q} < 1$, and p and q are positive integers, which of the following must be greater than 1 ?

(A) $\sqrt{\dfrac{p}{q}}$

(B) $\dfrac{p}{q^2}$

(C) $\dfrac{p}{2q}$

(D) $\dfrac{q}{p^2}$

(E) $\dfrac{q}{p}$

Arithmetic Properties of numbers

Since p and q are positive integers, $0 < \dfrac{p}{q} < 1$.

A   Since $\dfrac{p}{q} < 1$, then $q > p$. Taking the square root of both sides of the inequality gives $\sqrt{q} > \sqrt{p}$. Then, $\sqrt{\dfrac{p}{q}} = \dfrac{\sqrt{p}}{\sqrt{q}}$, so here the denominator will still be larger than the numerator. CANNOT be greater than 1.

B   Squaring the denominator increases the denominator, which decreases the value of the fraction. CANNOT be greater than 1.

C   Multiplying the denominator by 2 increases the denominator, which decreases the value of the fraction. CANNOT be greater than 1.

D   Since $\dfrac{p}{q} < 1$, then $q > p$. When $p^2 < q$, this expression will be greater than 1, but p^2 need not be less than q. For example, if $p = 2$ and $q = 100$, $\dfrac{p}{q} = \dfrac{2}{100}$ and $\dfrac{q}{p^2} = \dfrac{100}{2^2} = \dfrac{100}{4} = 25 > 1$.

However, if $p = 3$ and $q = 4$, then $\dfrac{p}{q} = \dfrac{3}{4}$ and $\dfrac{q}{p^2} = \dfrac{4}{3^2} = \dfrac{4}{9} < 1$. NEED NOT be greater than 1.

E   Again, since $\dfrac{p}{q} < 1$, then $q > p$. Thus, the reciprocal, $\dfrac{q}{p}$, always has a value greater than 1 because the numerator will always be a larger positive integer than the denominator. MUST be greater than 1.

The correct answer is E.

PS16830

190. To mail a package, the rate is x cents for the first pound and y cents for each additional pound, where $x > y$. Two packages weighing 3 pounds and 5 pounds, respectively, can be mailed separately or combined as one package. Which method is cheaper, and how much money is saved?

(A)   Combined, with a savings of $x - y$ cents
(B)   Combined, with a savings of $y - x$ cents
(C)   Combined, with a savings of x cents
(D)   Separately, with a savings of $x - y$ cents
(E)   Separately, with a savings of y cents

Algebra Applied problems

Shipping the two packages separately would cost $1x + 2y$ for the 3-pound package and $1x + 4y$ for the 5-pound package. Shipping them together (as a single 8-pound package) would cost $1x + 7y$. By calculating the sum of the costs for shipping the two packages separately minus the cost for

247

shipping the one combined package, it is possible to determine the difference in cost, as shown.

$((1x+2y)+(1x+4y))-(1x+7y)$ (cost for 3 lb. + cost for 5 lb.) − cost for 8 lb.

$=(2x+6y)-(1x+7y)$ combine like terms

$=2x+6y-1x-7y$ distribute the negative

$=x-y$ combine like terms

Since $x > y$, this value is positive, which means it costs more to ship two packages separately. Thus it is cheaper to mail one combined package at a cost savings of $x - y$ cents.

The correct answer is A.

PS16831
191. If money is invested at r percent interest, compounded annually, the amount of the investment will double in approximately $\frac{70}{r}$ years. If Pat's parents invested $5,000 in a long-term bond that pays 8 percent interest, compounded annually, what will be the approximate total amount of the investment 18 years later, when Pat is ready for college?

(A) $20,000
(B) $15,000
(C) $12,000
(D) $10,000
(E) $9,000

Algebra Applied problems

Since the investment will double in $\frac{70}{r} = \frac{70}{8} = 8.75 \approx 9$ years, the value of the investment over 18 years can be approximated by doubling its initial value twice. Therefore, the approximate value will be $(\$5,000)(2)(2) = \$20,000$.

The correct answer is A.

PS16832
192. On a recent trip, Cindy drove her car 290 miles, rounded to the nearest 10 miles, and used 12 gallons of gasoline, rounded to the nearest gallon. The actual number of miles per gallon that Cindy's car got on this trip must have been between

(A) $\frac{290}{12.5}$ and $\frac{290}{11.5}$
(B) $\frac{295}{12}$ and $\frac{285}{11.5}$
(C) $\frac{285}{12}$ and $\frac{295}{12}$
(D) $\frac{285}{12.5}$ and $\frac{295}{11.5}$
(E) $\frac{295}{12.5}$ and $\frac{285}{11.5}$

Arithmetic Estimation

The lowest number of miles per gallon can be calculated using the lowest possible miles and the highest amount of gasoline. Also, the highest number of miles per gallon can be calculated using the highest possible miles and the lowest amount of gasoline.

Since the miles are rounded to the nearest 10 miles, the number of miles is between 285 and 295. Since the gallons are rounded to the nearest gallon, the number of gallons is between 11.5 and 12.5. Therefore, the lowest number of miles per gallon is $\frac{\text{lowest miles}}{\text{highest gallons}} = \frac{285}{12.5}$ and the highest number of miles per gallon is $\frac{\text{highest miles}}{\text{lowest gallons}} = \frac{295}{11.5}$

The correct answer is D.

PS16833
193. Which of the following inequalities is an algebraic expression for the shaded part of the number line above?

(A) $|x| \leq 3$
(B) $|x| \leq 5$
(C) $|x-2| \leq 3$
(D) $|x-1| \leq 4$
(E) $|x+1| \leq 4$

Algebra Inequalities

The number line above shows $-5 \leq x \leq 3$. To turn this into absolute value notation, as all the choices are written, the numbers need to be opposite signs of the same value.

Since the distance between -5 and 3 is 8 ($3 - (-5) = 8$), that distance needs to be split in half with -4 to one side and 4 to the other. Each of these two values is 1 more than the values in the inequality above, so adding 1 to all terms in the inequality gives $-4 \leq x + 1 \leq 4$, which is the same as $|x + 1| \leq 4$.

The correct answer is E.

PS16835

194. In a small snack shop, the average (arithmetic mean) revenue was $400 per day over a 10-day period. During this period, if the average daily revenue was $360 for the first 6 days, what was the average daily revenue for the last 4 days?

(A) $420
(B) $440
(C) $450
(D) $460
(E) $480

Arithmetic; Algebra Statistics; Applied problems

Let x be the average daily revenue for the last 4 days. Using the formula $\text{average} = \dfrac{\text{sum of values}}{\text{number of values}}$, the information regarding the average revenues for the 10-day and 6-day periods can be expressed as follows and solved for x:

$\$400 = \dfrac{6(\$360) + 4x}{10}$

$\$4,000 = \$2,160 + 4x$ multiply both sides by 10

$\$1,840 = 4x$ subtract $2,160 from both sides

$\$460 = x$ divide both sides by 4

The correct answer is D.

PS05882

195. If y is the smallest positive integer such that 3,150 multiplied by y is the square of an integer, then y must be

(A) 2
(B) 5
(C) 6
(D) 7
(E) 14

Arithmetic Properties of numbers

To find the smallest positive integer y such that $3,150y$ is the square of an integer, first find the prime factorization of 3,150 by a method similar to the following:

$3,150 = 10 \times 315$
$= (2 \times 5) \times (3 \times 105)$
$= 2 \times 5 \times 3 \times (5 \times 21)$
$= 2 \times 5 \times 3 \times 5 \times (3 \times 7)$
$= 2 \times 3^2 \times 5^2 \times 7$

To be a perfect square, $3,150y$ must have an even number of each of its prime factors. At a minimum, y must have one factor of 2 and one factor of 7 so that $3,150y$ has two factors of each of the primes 2, 3, 5, and 7. The smallest positive integer value of y is then $(2)(7) = 14$.

The correct answer is E.

PS16116

196. If [x] is the greatest integer less than or equal to x, what is the value of $[-1.6] + [3.4] + [2.7]$?

(A) 3
(B) 4
(C) 5
(D) 6
(E) 7

Arithmetic Profit and loss

The greatest integer that is less than or equal to -1.6 is -2. It cannot be -1 because -1 is greater than -1.6. The greatest integer that is less than or equal to 3.4 is 3. It cannot be 4 because 4 is greater than 3.4. The greatest integer that is less than or equal to 2.7 is 2. It cannot be 3 because 3 is greater than 2.7. Therefore, $[-1.6] + [3.4] + [2.7] = -2 + 3 + 2 = 3$.

The correct answer is A.

249

PS06558

197. In the first week of the year, Nancy saved $1. In each of the next 51 weeks, she saved $1 more than she had saved in the previous week. What was the total amount that Nancy saved during the 52 weeks?

(A) $1,326
(B) $1,352
(C) $1,378
(D) $2,652
(E) $2,756

Arithmetic Operations on rational numbers

In dollars, the total amount saved is the sum of 1, (1 + 1), (1 + 1 + 1), and so on, up to and including the amount saved in the 52nd week, which was $52. Therefore, the total amount saved in dollars was $1 + 2 + 3 + \ldots + 50 + 51 + 52$. This sum can be easily evaluated by grouping the terms as $(1 + 52) + (2 + 51) + (3 + 50) + \ldots + (26 + 27)$, which results in the number 53 added to itself 26 times. Therefore, the sum is $(26)(53) = 1,378$.

Alternatively, the formula for the sum of the first n positive integers is $\frac{n(n+1)}{2}$. Therefore, the sum of the first 52 positive integers is $\frac{52(53)}{2} = 26(53) = 1,378$.

The correct answer is C.

PS16100

198. In a certain sequence, the term x_n is given by the formula $x_n = 2x_{n-1} - \frac{1}{2}(x_{n-2})$ for all $n \geq 2$. If $x_0 = 3$ and $x_1 = 2$, what is the value of x_3?

(A) 2.5
(B) 3.125
(C) 4
(D) 5
(E) 6.75

Algebra Simplifying algebraic expressions

Given the formula $x_n = 2x_{n-1} - \frac{1}{2}(x_{n-2})$ with $x_0 = 3$ and $x_1 = 2$, then

$$x_2 = 2x_1 - \frac{1}{2}x_0$$
$$= 2(2) - \frac{1}{2}(3)$$
$$= \frac{5}{2}$$

$$x_3 = 2x_2 - \frac{1}{2}x_1$$
$$= 2\left(\frac{5}{2}\right) - \frac{1}{2}(2)$$
$$= 5 - 1$$
$$= 4$$

The correct answer is C.

PS08570

199. During a trip, Francine traveled x percent of the total distance at an average speed of 40 miles per hour and the rest of the distance at an average speed of 60 miles per hour. In terms of x, what was Francine's average speed for the entire trip?

(A) $\frac{180 - x}{2}$
(B) $\frac{x + 60}{4}$
(C) $\frac{300 - x}{5}$
(D) $\frac{600}{115 - x}$
(E) $\frac{12,000}{x + 200}$

Algebra Applied problems

Assume for simplicity that the total distance of Francine's trip is 100 miles. Then the table below gives all of the pertinent information.

Distance	Rate	Time = $\frac{\text{Distance}}{\text{Rate}}$
x	40	$\frac{x}{40}$
$100 - x$	60	$\frac{100 - x}{60}$

The total time for Francine's trip is

$$\frac{x}{40} + \frac{100-x}{60} = \frac{3x}{120} + \frac{2(100-x)}{120}$$
$$= \frac{3x + 2(100-x)}{120}$$
$$= \frac{3x + 200 - 2x}{120}$$
$$= \frac{x + 200}{120}$$

Francine's average speed over the entire trip is

$$\frac{\text{total distance}}{\text{total time}} = \frac{100}{\frac{x+200}{120}} = \frac{12{,}000}{x+200}.$$

The correct answer is E.

PS00564

200. If $n = (33)^{43} + (43)^{33}$, what is the units digit of n?

(A) 0
(B) 2
(C) 4
(D) 6
(E) 8

Arithmetic Properties of numbers

If the units digit of an integer n is 3, then the units digits of $n^1, n^2, n^3, n^4, n^5, n^6, n^7$, and n^8 are, respectively, 3, 9, 7, 1, 3, 9, 7, and 1. Thus, the units digit of the powers of n form the sequence in which the digits 3, 9, 7, and 1 repeat indefinitely in that order. Since $43 = (10)(4) + 3$, the 43rd number in the sequence is 7, and therefore the units digit of $(33)^{43}$ is 7. Since $33 = (8)(4) + 1$, the 33rd number of this sequence is 3, and therefore, the units digit of $(43)^{33}$ is 3. Thus, the units digit of $(33)^{43} + (43)^{33}$ is the units digit of $7 + 3$, which is 0.

The correct answer is A.

PS13691

201. Team A and Team B are competing against each other in a game of tug-of-war. Team A, consisting of 3 males and 3 females, decides to line up male, female, male, female, male, female. The lineup that Team A chooses will be one of how many different possible lineups?

(A) 9
(B) 12
(C) 15
(D) 36
(E) 720

Arithmetic Elementary combinatorics

Any of the 3 males can be first in the line, and any of the 3 females can be second. Either of the 2 remaining males can be next, followed by either of the 2 remaining females. The last 2 places in the line are filled with the only male left followed by the only female left. By the multiplication principle, there are $3 \times 3 \times 2 \times 2 \times 1 \times 1 = 36$ different lineups possible.

The correct answer is D.

PS08480

202. A border of uniform width is placed around a rectangular photograph that measures 8 inches by 10 inches. If the area of the border is 144 square inches, what is the width of the border, in inches?

(A) 3
(B) 4
(C) 6
(D) 8
(E) 9

Algebra Second-degree equations

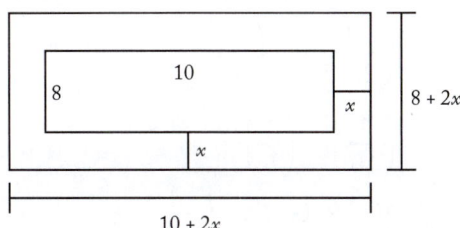

Note: Figure not drawn to scale.

Let x be the width, in inches, of the border. The photograph with the border has dimensions $(10 + 2x)$ inches and $(8 + 2x)$ inches with an area of $(10 + 2x)(8 + 2x) = (80 + 36x + 4x^2)$ square inches. The photograph without the border has dimensions 10 inches and 8 inches with an area of $(10)(8) = 80$ square inches. The area of the border is then the difference between the areas of the photograph with and without the border or $(80 + 36x + 4x^2) - 80 = 36x + 4x^2$ square inches. It is given that the area of the border is 144 square inches so,

$$36x + 4x^2 = 144$$
$$4x^2 + 36x - 144 = 0$$
$$x^2 + 9x - 36 = 0$$
$$(x - 3)(x + 12) = 0$$

So, $x - 3 = 0$, which means $x = 3$, or $x + 12 = 0$, which means $x = -12$.

Thus, after discarding $x = -12$ since the width of the border must be positive, $x = 3$.

The correct answer is A.

PS09403
203. If $d = \dfrac{1}{2^3 \times 5^7}$ is expressed as a terminating decimal, how many nonzero digits will d have?

(A) One
(B) Two
(C) Three
(D) Seven
(E) Ten

Arithmetic Operations on rational numbers

It will be helpful to use the fact that a factor that is an integer power of 10 has no effect on the number of nonzero digits a terminating decimal has.

$$\dfrac{1}{2^3 \times 5^7} = \dfrac{1}{2^3 \times 5^3} \times \dfrac{1}{5^4}$$
$$= \left(\dfrac{1}{2 \times 5}\right)^3 \times \left(\dfrac{1}{5}\right)^4$$
$$= \left(\dfrac{1}{10}\right)^3 \times \left(\dfrac{1}{5}\right)^4$$
$$= 10^{-3} \times (0.2)^4$$
$$= 10^{-3} \times (0.0016)$$
$$= 0.0000016$$

The correct answer is B.

PS03513
204. For any positive integer n, the sum of the first n positive integers equals $\dfrac{n(n+1)}{2}$. What is the sum of all the even integers between 99 and 301 ?

(A) 10,100
(B) 20,200
(C) 22,650
(D) 40,200
(E) 45,150

Algebra Simplifying expressions; Arithmetic Computation with integers

The given formula translates into
$1 + 2 + \ldots + n = \sum\limits_{k=1}^{n} k = \dfrac{n(n+1)}{2}$. The sum of the even integers between 99 and 301 is the sum of the even integers from 100 through 300, or the sum of the 50th even integer through the 150th even integer. To get this sum, find the sum of the first 150 even integers and subtract the sum of the first 49 even integers. In symbols,

$$\sum_{k=1}^{150} 2k - \sum_{k=1}^{49} 2k = 2\sum_{k=1}^{150} k - 2\sum_{k=1}^{49} k$$
$$= 2\left(\dfrac{150(150+1)}{2}\right) - 2\left(\dfrac{49(49+1)}{2}\right)$$
$$= 150(151) - 49(50)$$
$$= 50(3(151) - 49)$$
$$= 50(453 - 49)$$
$$= 50(404)$$
$$= 20,200$$

The correct answer is B.

PS06498
205. How many prime numbers between 1 and 100 are factors of 7,150 ?

(A) One
(B) Two
(C) Three
(D) Four
(E) Five

Arithmetic Rate

To find the number of prime numbers between 1 and 100 that are factors of 7,150, find the prime factorization of 7,150 using a method similar to the following:

$$7{,}150 = 10 \times 715$$
$$= (2 \times 5) \times (5 \times 143)$$
$$= 2 \times 5 \times 5 \times (11 \times 13)$$

Thus, 7,150 has four prime factors: 2, 5, 11, and 13.

The correct answer is D.

PS08732

206. A sequence of numbers $a_1, a_2, a_3, \ldots$ is defined as follows: $a_1 = 3$, $a_2 = 5$, and every term in the sequence after a_2 is the product of all terms in the sequence preceding it, e.g., $a_3 = (a_1)(a_2)$ and $a_4 = (a_1)(a_2)(a_3)$. If $a_n = t$ and $n > 2$, what is the value of a_{n+2} in terms of t?

(A) $4t$
(B) t^2
(C) t^3
(D) t^4
(E) t^8

Algebra Sequences

It is given that $a_n = (a_1)(a_2) \ldots (a_{n-1})$ and $a_n = t$. Therefore, $a_{n+1} = (a_1)(a_2) \ldots (a_{n-1})(a_n) = (a_n)(a_n) = t^2$ and $a_{n+2} = (a_1)(a_2) \ldots (a_n)(a_{n+1}) = (a_{n+1})(a_{n+1}) = (t^2)(t^2) = t^4$.

The correct answer is D.

PS08552

207. Last year the price per share of Stock X increased by k percent and the earnings per share of Stock X increased by m percent, where k is greater than m. By what percent did the ratio of price per share to earnings per share increase, in terms of k and m?

(A) $\dfrac{k}{m}\%$
(B) $(k - m)\%$
(C) $\dfrac{100(k-m)}{100+k}\%$
(D) $\dfrac{100(k-m)}{100+m}\%$
(E) $\dfrac{100(k-m)}{100+k+m}\%$

Algebra Percents

If P and E are the price and earnings per share before the increase, then $\left(1 + \dfrac{k}{100}\right)P$ and $\left(1 + \dfrac{m}{100}\right)E$ are the price and earnings per share after the increase. Therefore, the percent increase in the ratio of price per share to earnings per share can be expressed as follows:

$$\left(\frac{(\text{ratio after increases}) - (\text{ratio before increases})}{(\text{ratio before increases})} \times 100\right)\%$$

$$= \left(\left(\frac{(\text{ratio after increases})}{(\text{ratio before increases})} - 1\right) \times 100\right)\%$$

$$= \left(\left(\frac{\frac{\left(1 + \frac{k}{100}\right)P}{\left(1 + \frac{m}{100}\right)E}}{\frac{P}{E}} - 1\right) \times 100\right)\%$$

$$= \left(\left(\frac{\frac{1 + \frac{k}{100}}{1 + \frac{m}{100}} \times \frac{P}{E}}{\frac{P}{E}} - 1\right) \times 100\right)\%$$

$$= \left(\left(\frac{\frac{1 + \frac{k}{100}}{1 + \frac{m}{100}}}{1} - 1\right) \times 100\right)\%$$

$$= \left(\left(\frac{1 + \frac{k}{100}}{1 + \frac{m}{100}} - 1\right) \times 100\right)\%$$

$$= \left(\left(\frac{1+\frac{k}{100}}{1+\frac{m}{100}} \times \frac{100}{100} - 1\right) \times 100\right)\%$$

$$= \left(\left(\frac{100+k}{100+m} - 1\right) \times 100\right)\%$$

$$= \left(\frac{(100+k)-(100+m)}{100+m} \times 100\right)\%$$

$$= \left(\frac{k-m}{100+m} \times 100\right)\%$$

$$= \frac{100(k-m)}{100+m}\%$$

The correct answer is D.

PS04677

208. Of the 300 subjects who participated in an experiment using virtual-reality therapy to reduce their fear of heights, 40 percent experienced sweaty palms, 30 percent experienced vomiting, and 75 percent experienced dizziness. If all of the subjects experienced at least one of these effects and 35 percent of the subjects experienced exactly two of these effects, how many of the subjects experienced only one of these effects?

(A) 105
(B) 125
(C) 130
(D) 180
(E) 195

Arithmetic Applied problems

Let a be the number who experienced only one of the effects, b be the number who experienced exactly two of the effects, and c be the number who experienced all three of the effects. Then $a + b + c = 300$, since each of the 300 participants experienced at least one of the effects. From the given information, $b = 105$ (35% of 300), which gives $a + 105 + c = 300$, or $a + c = 195$ (Eq. 1). Also, if the number who experienced sweaty palms (40% of 300, or 120) is added to the number who experienced vomiting (30% of 300, or 90), and this sum is added to the number who experienced dizziness (75% of 300, or 225), then each participant who experienced only one of the effects is counted exactly once, each participant who experienced exactly two of the effects is counted exactly twice, and each participant who experienced all three of the effects is counted exactly 3 times. Therefore, $a + 2b + 3c = 120 + 90 + 225 = 435$. Using $b = 105$, it follows that $a + 2(105) + 3c = 435$, or $a + 3c = 225$ (Eq. 2). Then solving the system defined by Eq. 1 and Eq. 2,

$$\begin{cases} a+c = 195 \\ a+3c = 225 \end{cases} \quad \text{multiply 1st equation by } -3$$

$$\begin{cases} -3a-3c = -585 \\ a+3c = 225 \end{cases} \quad \text{add equations}$$

$-2a = -360$, or $a = 180$

The correct answer is D.

PS03686

209. If $m^{-1} = \frac{1}{3}$, then m^{-2} is equal to

(A) -9
(B) -3
(C) $-\frac{1}{9}$
(D) $\frac{1}{9}$
(E) 9

Arithmetic Negative exponents

Using rules of exponents, $m^{-2} = m^{-1 \times 2} = (m^{-1})^2$, and since $m^{-1} = -\frac{1}{3}$, $m^{-2} = \left(-\frac{1}{3}\right)^2 = \frac{1}{9}$.

The correct answer is D.

PS07555

210. A photography dealer ordered 60 Model X cameras to be sold for $250 each, which represents a 20 percent markup over the dealer's initial cost for each camera. Of the cameras ordered, 6 were never sold and were returned to the manufacturer for a refund of 50 percent of the dealer's initial cost. What was the dealer's approximate profit or loss as a percent of the dealer's initial cost for the 60 cameras?

(A) 7% loss
(B) 13% loss
(C) 7% profit
(D) 13% profit
(E) 15% profit

Arithmetic Percents

Given that $250 is 20% greater than a camera's initial cost, it follows that the initial cost for each camera was $\left(\$\dfrac{250}{1.2}\right)$. Therefore, the initial cost for the 60 cameras was $60\left(\$\dfrac{250}{1.2}\right)$. The total revenue is the sum of the amount obtained from selling $60 - 6 = 54$ cameras for $250 each and the $\left(\dfrac{1}{2}\right)\left(\$\dfrac{250}{1.2}\right)$ refund for each of 6 cameras, or $(54)(\$250)+(6)\left(\dfrac{1}{2}\right)\left(\$\dfrac{250}{1.2}\right)$. The total profit, as a percent of the total initial cost, is

$\left(\dfrac{(\text{total revenue})-(\text{total initial cost})}{(\text{total initial cost})}\times 100\right)\% =$

$\left(\left(\dfrac{(\text{total revenue})}{(\text{total initial cost})}-1\right)\times 100\right)\%$. Using the numerical expressions obtained above,

$\dfrac{(\text{total revenue})}{(\text{total initial cost})}-1$

$= \dfrac{(54)(250)+6\left(\dfrac{1}{2}\right)\left(\dfrac{250}{1.2}\right)}{(60)\left(\dfrac{250}{1.2}\right)}-1$ by substitution

$= \dfrac{54+3\left(\dfrac{1}{1.2}\right)}{(60)\left(\dfrac{1}{1.2}\right)}-1$ by canceling 250s

$= \dfrac{54(1.2)+3}{60}-1$ by multiplying top and bottom by 1.2 and then canceling 1.2

$= \dfrac{67.8}{60}-1$

$= 1.13 - 1$

$= 0.13$

Finally, $(0.13 \times 100)\% = 13\%$, which represents a profit since it is positive.

The correct answer is D.

PS04305
211. Seven pieces of rope have an average (arithmetic mean) length of 68 centimeters and a median length of 84 centimeters. If the length of the longest piece of rope is 14 centimeters more than 4 times the length of the shortest piece of rope, what is the maximum possible length, in centimeters, of the longest piece of rope?

(A)   82
(B)   118
(C)   120
(D)   134
(E)   152

Algebra Statistics

Let $a, b, c, d, e, f,$ and g be the lengths, in centimeters, of the pieces of rope, listed from least to greatest. From the given information it follows that $d = 84$ and $g = 4a + 14$. Therefore, listed from least to greatest, the lengths are $a, b, c, 84, e, f,$ and $4a + 14$. The maximum value of $4a + 14$ will occur when the maximum value of a is used, and this will be the case only if the shortest 3 pieces all have the same length. Therefore, listed from least to greatest, the lengths are $a, a, a, 84, e, f,$ and $4a + 14$. The maximum value for $4a + 14$ will occur when e and f are as small as possible. Since e and f are to the right of the median, they must be at least 84 and so 84 is the least possible value for each of e and f. Therefore, listed from least to greatest, the lengths are $a, a, a, 84, 84, 84,$ and $4a + 14$. Since the average length is 68, it follows that $\dfrac{a+a+a+84+84+84+(4a+14)}{7} = 68$, or $a = 30$.

Hence, the maximum length of the longest piece is $(4a + 14) = [4(30) + 14] = 134$ centimeters.

The correct answer is D.

PS16146
212. What is the difference between the sixth and the fifth terms of the sequence 2, 4, 7, ... whose nth term is $n + 2^{n-1}$?

(A)   2
(B)   3
(C)   6
(D)   16
(E)   17

Algebra Simplifying algebraic expressions

According to the given formula, the sixth term of the sequence is $6 + 2^{6-1} = 6 + 2^5$ and the fifth term is $5 + 2^{5-1} = 5 + 2^4$. Then,

$$(6 + 2^5) - (5 + 2^4) = (6 - 5) + (2^5 - 2^4)$$
$$= 1 + 2^4(2 - 1)$$
$$= 1 + 2^4$$
$$= 1 + 16$$
$$= 17$$

The correct answer is E.

PS02405

213. From the consecutive integers −10 to 10, inclusive, 20 integers are randomly chosen with repetitions allowed. What is the least possible value of the product of the 20 integers?

(A) $(-10)^{20}$
(B) $(-10)^{10}$
(C) 0
(D) $-(10)^{19}$
(E) $-(10)^{20}$

Arithmetic Properties of numbers

If −10 is chosen an odd number of times and 10 is chosen the remaining number of times (for example, choose −10 once and choose 10 nineteen times, or choose −10 three times and choose 10 seventeen times), then the product of the 20 chosen numbers will be $-(10)^{20}$. Note that $-(10)^{20}$ is less than $-(10)^{19}$, the only other negative value among the answer choices.

The correct answer is E.

PS05140

214. The letters D, G, I, I, and T can be used to form 5-letter strings such as DIGIT or DGIIT. Using these letters, how many 5-letter strings can be formed in which the two occurrences of the letter I are separated by at least one other letter?

(A) 12
(B) 18
(C) 24
(D) 36
(E) 48

Arithmetic Elementary combinatorics

There are 6 ways to select the locations of the 2 occurrences of the letter I, and this number can be determined by listing all such ways as shown below, where the symbol * is used in place of the letters D, G, and T:

I*I**, I**I*, I***I, *I*I*, *I**I, **I*I

Alternatively, the number of ways to select the locations of the 2 occurrences of the letter I can be determined by using $\binom{5}{2} - 4 = \frac{5!}{(2!)(3!)} - 4 = 10 - 4 = 6$, which is the number of ways to select 2 of the 5 locations minus the 4 ways in which the 2 selected locations are adjacent.

For each of these 6 ways to select the locations of the 2 occurrences of the letter I, there are 6 ways to select the locations of the letters D, G, and T, which can be determined by using 3! = 6 or by listing all such ways:

DGT, DTG, GDT, GTD, TDG, TGD

It follows that the number of ways to select the locations of the 5 letters to form 5-letter strings is (6)(6) = 36.

The correct answer is D.

PS00574

215. $\dfrac{0.99999999}{1.0001} - \dfrac{0.99999991}{1.0003} =$

(A) 10^{-8}
(B) $3(10^{-8})$
(C) $3(10^{-4})$
(D) $2(10^{-4})$
(E) 10^{-4}

Arithmetic Operations on rational numbers

Calculations with lengthy decimals can be avoided by writing 0.99999999 as $1 - 10^{-8}$, 0.99999991 as $1 - 9(10^{-8})$, 1.0001 as $1 + 10^{-4}$, and 1.0003 as $1 + 3(10^{-4})$. Doing this gives

$$\frac{1-10^{-8}}{1+10^{-4}} - \frac{1-9(10^{-8})}{1+3(10^{-4})}$$

$$= \frac{[1+10^{-4}][1-10^{-4}]}{1+10^{-4}} - \frac{1-9(10^{-8})}{1+3(10^{-4})}$$

$$= \frac{1-10^{-4}}{1} - \frac{1-9(10^{-8})}{1+3(10^{-4})}$$

$$= \frac{[1-10^{-4}][1+3(10^{-4})]-[1-9(10^{-8})]}{1+3(10^{-4})}$$

$$= \frac{1+3(10^{-4})-10^{-4}-3(10^{-8})-1+9(10^{-8})}{1+3(10^{-4})}$$

$$= \frac{2(10^{-4})+6(10^{-8})}{1+3(10^{-4})}$$

$$= \frac{[2(10^{-4})][1+3(10^{-4})]}{1+3(10^{-4})}$$

$$= 2(10^{-4})$$

The correct answer is D.

PS03144

216. Last Sunday a certain store sold copies of Newspaper A for $1.00 each and copies of Newspaper B for $1.25 each, and the store sold no other newspapers that day. If r percent of the store's revenue from newspaper sales was from Newspaper A and if p percent of the newspapers that the store sold were copies of Newspaper A, which of the following expresses r in terms of p?

(A) $\dfrac{100p}{125-p}$

(B) $\dfrac{150p}{250-p}$

(C) $\dfrac{300p}{375-p}$

(D) $\dfrac{400p}{500-p}$

(E) $\dfrac{500p}{625-p}$

Algebra Simultaneous equations

Let N be the total number of newspapers that the store sold. Then, the number of copies of Newspaper A the store sold was $p\%$ of $N = \left(\dfrac{p}{100}\right)N$ and the revenue from those copies of Newspaper A, in dollars, was $(1.00)\left(\dfrac{p}{100}\right)N = \left(\dfrac{p}{100}\right)N$. The number of copies of Newspaper B the store sold was $(100-p)\%$ of $N = \left(\dfrac{100-p}{100}\right)N$ and the revenue from those copies of Newspaper B, in dollars, was $(1.25)\left(\dfrac{100-p}{100}\right)N = \left(\dfrac{5}{4}\right)\left(\dfrac{100-p}{100}\right)N$. The store's total revenue from newspaper sales, in dollars, was $\left(\dfrac{p}{100}\right)N + \left(\dfrac{5}{4}\right)\left(\dfrac{100-p}{100}\right)N$, and the fraction of that revenue from the sale of Newspaper A was

$$\frac{\dfrac{p}{100}N}{\dfrac{p}{100}N + \left(\dfrac{5}{4}\right)\left(\dfrac{100-p}{100}\right)N} = \frac{\dfrac{p}{100}}{\dfrac{4p}{400} + \left(\dfrac{500-5p}{400}\right)}$$

$$= \frac{\dfrac{p}{100}}{\dfrac{4p+500-5p}{400}}$$

$$= \frac{\dfrac{p}{100}}{\dfrac{500-p}{400}}$$

$$= \left(\dfrac{p}{100}\right)\left(\dfrac{400}{500-p}\right)$$

$$= \frac{4p}{500-p}$$

Since r percent of the store's newspaper sales revenue was from Newspaper A, $\dfrac{r}{100} = \dfrac{4p}{500-p}$, and so $r = \dfrac{400p}{500-p}$.

The correct answer is D.

PS16890
217. For the past n days, the average (arithmetic mean) daily production at a company was 50 units. If today's production of 90 units raises the average to 55 units per day, what is the value of n?

(A) 30
(B) 18
(C) 10
(D) 9
(E) 7

Arithmetic; Algebra Statistics; Applied problems; Simultaneous equations

Let x be the total production of the past n days. Using the formula average = $\frac{\text{sum of values}}{\text{number of values}}$, the information in the problem can be expressed in the following two equations

$50 = \frac{x}{n}$ daily average of 50 units over the past n days

$55 = \frac{x + 90}{n + 1}$ increased daily average when including today's 90 units

Solving the first equation for x gives $x = 50n$. Then substituting $50n$ for x in the second equation gives the following that can be solved for n:

$55 = \frac{50n + 90}{n + 1}$

$55(n + 1) = 50n + 90$ multiply both sides by $(n + 1)$

$55n + 55 = 50n + 90$ distribute the 55

$5n = 35$ subtract $50n$ and 55 from both sides

$n = 7$ divide both sides by 5

The correct answer is E.

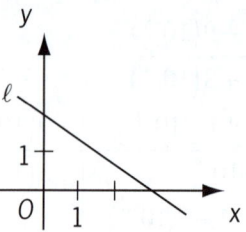

PS16893
218. In the coordinate system above, which of the following is the equation of line ℓ?

(A) $2x - 3y = 6$
(B) $2x + 3y = 6$
(C) $3x + 2y = 6$
(D) $2x - 3y = -6$
(E) $3x - 2y = -6$

Geometry Simple coordinate geometry

The line is shown going through the points $(0,2)$ and $(3,0)$. The slope of the line can be found with the formula slope = $\frac{\text{change in } y}{\text{change in } x} = \frac{y_2 - y_1}{x_2 - x_1}$ for two points (x_1, y_1) and (x_2, y_2). Thus, the slope of this line equals $\frac{0 - 2}{3 - 0} = -\frac{2}{3}$. Using the formula for a line of $y = mx + b$, where m is the slope and b is the y-intercept (in this case, 2), an equation for this line is $y = -\frac{2}{3}x + 2$. Since this equation must be compared to the available answer choices, the following further steps should be taken:

$y = -\frac{2}{3}x + 2$

$3y = -2x + 6$ multiply both sides by 3

$2x + 3y = 6$ add $2x$ to both sides

This problem can also be solved as follows. From the graph, when $x = 0$, y is positive; when $y = 0$, x is positive. This eliminates all but B and C. Of these, B is the only line containing $(0,2)$. Still another way is to use $(0,2)$ to eliminate A, C, and E, and then use $(3,0)$ to eliminate D.

The correct answer is B.

5.5 Problem Solving Answer Explanations

PS16894

219. If a two-digit positive integer has its digits reversed, the resulting integer differs from the original by 27. By how much do the two digits differ?

(A) 3
(B) 4
(C) 5
(D) 6
(E) 7

Algebra Applied problems

Let the one two-digit integer be represented by $10t + s$, where s and t are digits, and let the other integer with the reversed digits be represented by $10s + t$. The information that the difference between the integers is 27 can be expressed in the following equation, which can be solved for the answer.

$(10s + t) - (10t + s) = 27$
$10s + t - 10t - s = 27$ distribute the negative
$9s - 9t = 27$ combine like terms
$s - t = 3$ divide both sides by 9

Thus, it is seen that the two digits s and t differ by 3.

The correct answer is A.

PS16896

220. In an electric circuit, two resistors with resistances x and y are connected in parallel. In this case, if r is the combined resistance of these two resistors, then the reciprocal of r is equal to the sum of the reciprocals of x and y. What is r in terms of x and y?

(A) xy
(B) $x + y$
(C) $\dfrac{1}{x+y}$
(D) $\dfrac{xy}{x+y}$
(E) $\dfrac{x+y}{xy}$

Algebra Applied problems

Note that two numbers are reciprocals of each other if and only if their product is 1. Thus the reciprocals of r, x, and y are $\dfrac{1}{r}$, $\dfrac{1}{x}$, and $\dfrac{1}{y}$, respectively. So, according to the problem,

$\dfrac{1}{r} = \dfrac{1}{x} + \dfrac{1}{y}$. To solve this equation for r, begin by creating a common denominator on the right side by multiplying the first fraction by $\dfrac{y}{y}$ and the second fraction by $\dfrac{x}{x}$:

$\dfrac{1}{r} = \dfrac{1}{x} + \dfrac{1}{y}$

$\dfrac{1}{r} = \dfrac{y}{xy} + \dfrac{x}{xy}$

$\dfrac{1}{r} = \dfrac{x+y}{xy}$ combine the fractions on the right side

$r = \dfrac{xy}{x+y}$ invert the fractions on both sides

The correct answer is D.

PS16897

221. Xavier, Yvonne, and Zelda each try independently to solve a problem. If their individual probabilities for success are $\dfrac{1}{4}$, $\dfrac{1}{2}$, and $\dfrac{5}{8}$, respectively, what is the probability that Xavier and Yvonne, but not Zelda, will solve the problem?

(A) $\dfrac{11}{8}$
(B) $\dfrac{7}{8}$
(C) $\dfrac{9}{64}$
(D) $\dfrac{5}{64}$
(E) $\dfrac{3}{64}$

Arithmetic Probability

Since the individuals' probabilities are independent, they can be multiplied to figure out the combined probability. The probability of Xavier's success is given as $\dfrac{1}{4}$, and the probability of Yvonne's success is given as $\dfrac{1}{2}$. Since the probability of Zelda's success is given as $\dfrac{5}{8}$, then the probability of her NOT solving the problem is $1 - \dfrac{5}{8} = \dfrac{3}{8}$.

Thus, the combined probability is

$\left(\dfrac{1}{4}\right)\left(\dfrac{1}{2}\right)\left(\dfrac{3}{8}\right) = \dfrac{3}{64}$.

The correct answer is E.

PS16898

222. If $\dfrac{1}{x} - \dfrac{1}{x+1} = \dfrac{1}{x+4}$, then x could be

(A) 0
(B) −1
(C) −2
(D) −3
(E) −4

Algebra Second-degree equations

Solve the equation for x. Begin by multiplying all the terms by $x(x+1)(x+4)$ to eliminate the denominators.

$$\dfrac{1}{x} - \dfrac{1}{x+1} = \dfrac{1}{x+4}$$

$(x+1)(x+4) - x(x+4) = x(x+1)$

$(x+4)(x+1-x) = x(x+1)$ factor the $(x+4)$ out front on the left side

$(x+4)(1) = x(x+1)$ simplify

$(x+4) = x^2 + x$ distribute the x on the right side

$4 = x^2$ subtract x from both sides

$\pm 2 = x$ take the square root of both sides

Both − 2 and 2 are square roots of 4 since $(-2^2) = 4$ and $(2^2) = 4$. Thus, x could be − 2.

This problem can also be solved as follows. Rewrite the left side as, $\dfrac{(x+1)-x}{x(x+1)} = \dfrac{1}{x(x+1)}$, then set equal to the right side to get $\dfrac{1}{x(x+1)} = \dfrac{1}{x+4}$. Next, cross multiply: $(1)(x+4) = x(x+1)(1)$. Therefore, $x+4 = x^2 + x$, or $x^2 = 4$, so $x = \pm 2$.

The correct answer is C.

PS16899

223. $\left(\dfrac{1}{2}\right)^{-3} \left(\dfrac{1}{4}\right)^{-2} \left(\dfrac{1}{16}\right)^{-1} =$

(A) $\left(\dfrac{1}{2}\right)^{-48}$

(B) $\left(\dfrac{1}{2}\right)^{-11}$

(C) $\left(\dfrac{1}{2}\right)^{-6}$

(D) $\left(\dfrac{1}{8}\right)^{-11}$

(E) $\left(\dfrac{1}{8}\right)^{-6}$

Arithmetic Operations on rational numbers

It is clear from the answer choices that all three factors need to be written with a common denominator, and they thus become

$\left(\dfrac{1}{2}\right)^{-3} = \left(\dfrac{1}{2}\right)^{-3}$

$\left(\dfrac{1}{4}\right)^{-2} = \left(\left(\dfrac{1}{2}\right)^2\right)^{-2} = \left(\dfrac{1}{2}\right)^{-4}$

$\left(\dfrac{1}{16}\right)^{-1} = \left(\left(\dfrac{1}{2}\right)^4\right)^{-1} = \left(\dfrac{1}{2}\right)^{-4}$

So, $\left(\dfrac{1}{2}\right)^{-3} \left(\dfrac{1}{4}\right)^{-2} \left(\dfrac{1}{16}\right)^{-1} =$

$\left(\dfrac{1}{2}\right)^{-3} \left(\dfrac{1}{2}\right)^{-4} \left(\dfrac{1}{2}\right)^{-4} = \left(\dfrac{1}{2}\right)^{-3-4-4} = \left(\dfrac{1}{2}\right)^{-11}$.

The correct answer is B.

5.5 Problem Solving Answer Explanations

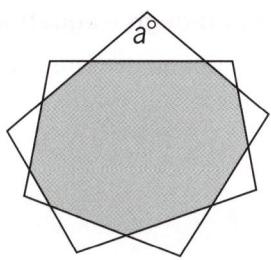

PS00947
224. The figure shown above consists of a shaded 9-sided polygon and 9 unshaded isosceles triangles. For each isosceles triangle, the longest side is a side of the shaded polygon and the two sides of equal length are extensions of the two adjacent sides of the shaded polygon. What is the value of a?

(A) 100
(B) 105
(C) 110
(D) 115
(E) 120

Geometry Polygons

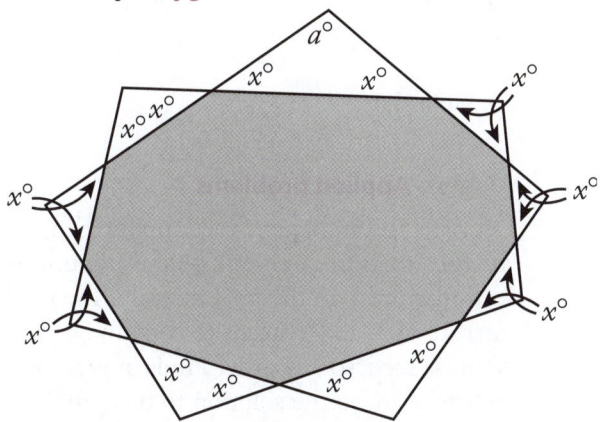

Let $x°$ represent the measure of each base angle of the triangle with vertex angle labeled $a°$. Each base angle of this triangle and one base angle of a triangle with which it shares a vertex are vertical angles and have the same measure. Thus, the base angles of these triangles also have measure $x°$. This pattern continues for the base angles of each pair of triangles that share a vertex, so each base angle of each of the 9 triangles has measure $x°$, as shown above. Also, the vertex angle of each of the 9 triangles has measure $a° = 180° − 2x°$.

Each interior angle of the shaded polygon has measure $(180 − x)°$ since each forms a straight angle with an angle that has measure $x°$, and the sum of the measures is $(9)(180 − x)°$. But

the sum of the interior angles of a polygon with n sides is $(n − 2)(180°)$, so the sum of the interior angles of a 9-sided polygon is $(7)(180°) = 1{,}260°$. Therefore, $(9)(180 − x)° = 1{,}260°$ and $x = 40$. Finally, $a = 180 − 2x = 180 − 2(40) = 100$.

The correct answer is A.

PS01648
225. List T consists of 30 positive decimals, none of which is an integer, and the sum of the 30 decimals is S. The underlined sum of the 30 decimals, E, is defined as follows. Each decimal in T whose tenths digit is even is rounded up to the nearest integer, and each decimal in T whose tenths digit is odd is rounded down to the nearest integer; E is the sum of the resulting integers. If $\frac{1}{3}$ of the decimals in T have a tenths digit that is even, which of the following is a possible value of $E − S$?

I.   −16
II.   6
III. 10

(A) I only
(B) I and II only
(C) I and III only
(D) II and III only
(E) I, II, and III

Arithmetic Operations on rational numbers

Since $\frac{1}{3}$ of the 30 decimals in T have an even tenths digit, it follows that $\frac{1}{3}(30) = 10$ decimals in T have an even tenths digit. Let T_E represent the list of these 10 decimals, let S_E represent the sum of all 10 decimals in T_E, and let E_E represent the estimated sum of all 10 decimals in T_E after rounding. The remaining 20 decimals in T have an odd tenths digit. Let T_O represent the list of these 20 remaining decimals, let S_O represent the sum of all 20 decimals in T_O, and let E_O represent the estimated sum of all 20 decimals in T_O after rounding. Note that $E = E_E + E_O$ and $S = S_E + S_O$ and hence $E − S = (E_E + E_O) − (S_E + S_O) = (E_E − S_E) + (E_O − S_O)$.

The least values of $E_E − S_E$ occur at the extreme where each decimal in T_E has tenths digit 8. Here, the difference between the rounded integer and the original decimal is greater than 0.1. (For example, the difference between the integer 15

261

and 14.899 that has been rounded to 15 is 0.101.) Hence, $E_E - S_E > 10(0.1) = 1$. The greatest values of $E_E - S_E$ occur at the other extreme, where each decimal in T_E has tenths digit 0. Here, the difference between the rounded integer and the original decimal is less than 1. (For example, the difference between the integer 15 and 14.001 that has been rounded to 15 is 0.999.) Hence, $E_E - S_E < 10(1) = 10$. Thus, $1 < E_E - S_E < 10$.

Similarly, the least values of $E_O - S_O$ occur at the extreme where each decimal in T_O has tenths digit 9. Here, the difference between the rounded integer and the original decimal is greater than -1. (For example, the difference between the integer 14 and 14.999 that has been rounded to 14 is -0.999.) Hence $E_O - S_O > 20(-1) = -20$. The greatest values of $E_O - S_O$ occur at the other extreme where each decimal in T_O has tenths digit 1. Here, the difference between the rounded integer and the original decimal is less than or equal to -0.1. (For example, the difference between the integer 14 and 14.1 that has been rounded to 14 is -0.1.) Hence, $E_O - S_O \leq 20(-0.1) = -2$. Thus, $-20 < E_O - S_O \leq -2$.

Adding the inequalities $1 < E_E - S_E < 10$ and $-20 < E_O - S_O \leq -2$ gives $-19 < (E_E - S_E) + (E_O - S_O) < 8$. Therefore, $-19 < (E_E + E_O) - (S_E + S_O) < 8$ and $-19 < E - S < 8$. Thus, of the values -16, 6, and 10 for $E - S$, only -16 and 6 are possible.

Note that if T contains 10 repetitions of the decimal 1.8 and 20 repetitions of the decimal 1.9, $S = 10(1.8) + 20(1.9) = 18 + 38 = 56$, $E = 10(2) + 20(1) = 40$, and $E - S = 40 - 56 = -16$. Also, if T contains 10 repetitions of the decimal 1.2 and 20 repetitions of the decimal 1.1, $S = 10(1.2) + 20(1.1) = 12 + 22 = 34$, $E = 10(2) + 20(1) = 40$, and $E - S = 40 - 34 = 6$.

The correct answer is B.

PS16115

226. If $5 - \dfrac{6}{x} = x$, then x has how many possible values?

(A) None
(B) One
(C) Two
(D) A finite number greater than two
(E) An infinite number

Algebra Second-degree equations

Solve the equation to determine how many values are possible for x.

$$5 - \dfrac{6}{x} = x$$
$$5x - 6 = x^2$$
$$0 = x^2 - 5x + 6$$
$$0 = (x-3)(x-2)$$
$$x = 3 \text{ or } 2$$

The correct answer is C.

PS16904

227. Seed mixture X is 40 percent ryegrass and 60 percent bluegrass by weight; seed mixture Y is 25 percent ryegrass and 75 percent fescue. If a mixture of X and Y contains 30 percent ryegrass, what percent of the weight of the mixture is X ?

(A) 10%
(B) $33\dfrac{1}{3}$%
(C) 40%
(D) 50%
(E) $66\dfrac{2}{3}$%

Algebra Applied problems

Let X be the amount of seed mixture X in the final mixture, and let Y be the amount of seed mixture Y in the final mixture. The final mixture of X and Y needs to contain 30 percent ryegrass seed, so any other kinds of grass seed are irrelevant to the solution to this problem. The information about the ryegrass percentages for X, Y, and the final mixture can be expressed in the following equation and solved for X.

$0.40X + 0.25Y = 0.30(X+Y)$
$0.40X + 0.25Y = 0.30X + 0.30Y$ distribute the 0.30 on the right side

$0.10X = 0.05Y$ subtract $0.30X$ and $0.25Y$ from both sides

$X = 0.5Y$ divide both sides by 0.10

Using this, the percent of the weight of the combined mixture $(X+Y)$ that is X is

$$\frac{X}{X+Y} = \frac{0.5Y}{0.5Y+Y} = \frac{0.5Y}{1.5Y} = \frac{0.5}{1.5} = 0.33\overline{3} = 33\frac{1}{3}\%$$

The correct answer is B.

PS14203

228. How many of the integers that satisfy the inequality $\frac{(x+2)(x+3)}{x-2} \geq 0$ are less than 5 ?

(A) 1
(B) 2
(C) 3
(D) 4
(E) 5

Algebra Inequalities

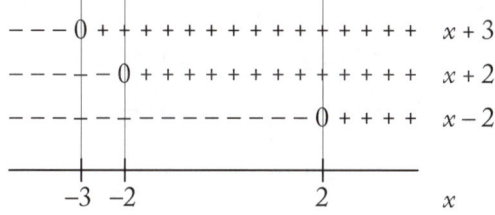

Pictorially, the number line above shows the algebraic signs of the expressions $(x+3)$, $(x+2)$, and $(x-2)$. For example, $x+3$ is 0 when $x = -3$, $x + 3$ is negative when $x < -3$, and $x + 3$ is positive when $x > -3$. The expression $\frac{(x+2)(x+3)}{x-2}$ will be positive in the intervals of the number line where the number of minus signs is even. Therefore $\frac{(x+2)(x+3)}{x-2}$ is positive for values of x such that $-3 < x < -2$ and for values of x such that $x > 2$. The only integer values of x in these intervals that are also less than 5 are 3 and 4. Also, $\frac{(x+2)(x+3)}{x-2}$ will be zero if and only if $(x+2)(x+3) = 0$, which has two integer solutions less than 5, namely, $x = -2$ and $x = -3$.

Therefore, there are four integers less than 5 that satisfy $\frac{(x+2)(x+3)}{x-2} \geq 0$ and those integers are $-3, -2, 3,$ and 4.

Alternatively, $\frac{(x+2)(x+3)}{x-2}$ will be zero if and only if $(x+2)(x+3) = 0$, which has two integer solutions less than 5, namely, $x = -2$ and $x = -3$.

Also, $\frac{(x+2)(x+3)}{x-2}$ will be positive if $(x+2)(x+3)$ and $x - 2$ are both positive or both negative, and for no other values of x. On the one hand, $(x+2)(x+3)$ will be positive when $x + 2$ and $x + 3$ are both positive, which will be the case when $x > -2$ and $x > -3$ and thus when $x > -2$. On the other hand, $(x+2)(x+3)$ will be positive when $x + 2$ and $x + 3$ are both negative, which will be the case when $x < -2$ and $x < -3$ and thus when $x < -3$. So, $(x+2)(x+3)$ will be positive when $x < -3$ or $x > -2$. (This result can also be deduced from the fact that the graph of $y = (x+2)(x+3)$ is a parabola with x-intercepts $(-2,0)$ and $(-3,0)$ that opens upward.) Since $x - 2$ will be positive when $x > 2$, it follows that $(x+2)(x+3)$ and $x - 2$ are both positive when $x > 2$, which includes exactly two integer values less than 5, namely, $x = 3$ and $x = 4$. There are no integer values of x such that $(x+2)(x+3)$ and $x - 2$ are both negative, since $(x+2)(x+3)$ is negative if and only if x lies between -3 and -2 and there are no integers between -3 and -2. Therefore, there are exactly 4 integer values of x less than 5 such that $\frac{(x+2)(x+3)}{x-2} \geq 0$.

Two of the values, $x = -2$ and $x = -3$, arise from solutions to $\frac{(x+2)(x+3)}{x-2} = 0$, and two of the values, $x = 3$ and $x = 4$, arise from solutions to $\frac{(x+2)(x+3)}{x-2} > 0$.

The correct answer is D.

PS07712
229. Of the 150 houses in a certain development, 60 percent have air-conditioning, 50 percent have a sunporch, and 30 percent have a swimming pool. If 5 of the houses have all three of these amenities and 5 have none of them, how many of the houses have exactly two of these amenities?

(A) 10
(B) 45
(C) 50
(D) 55
(E) 65

Arithmetic Sets

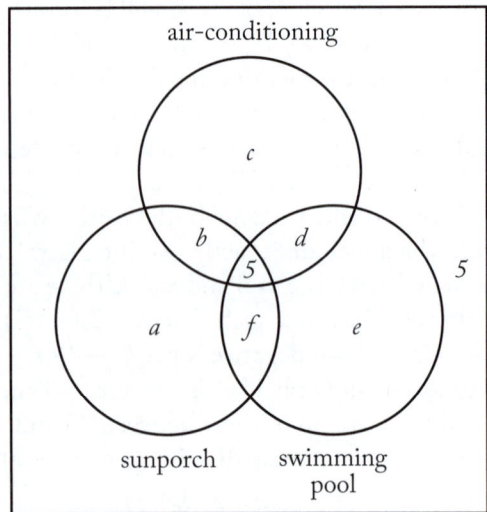

Since 60% of the 150 houses have air-conditioning, $b + c + d + 5 = 0.6(150) = 90$, so $b + c + d = 85$ (i). Similarly, since 50% have a sunporch, $a + b + f + 5 = 0.5(150) = 75$, so $a + b + f = 70$ (ii). Likewise, since 30% have a swimming pool, $d + e + f + 5 = 0.3(150) = 45$, so $d + e + f = 40$ (iii). Adding equations (i), (ii), and (iii) gives $(b + c + d) + (a + b + f) + (d + e + f) = 195$, or $a + 2b + c + 2d + e + 2f = 195$ (iv). But $a + b + c + d + e + f + 5 + 5 = 150$, or $a + b + c + d + e + f = 140$ (v). Subtracting equation (v) from equation (iv) gives $b + d + f = 55$, so 55 houses have exactly two of the amenities.

The correct answer is D.

PS08886
230. The value of $\dfrac{2^{-14} + 2^{-15} + 2^{-16} + 2^{-17}}{5}$ is how many times the value of $2^{(-17)}$?

(A) $\dfrac{3}{2}$
(B) $\dfrac{5}{2}$
(C) 3
(D) 4
(E) 5

Arithmetic Negative exponents

If the value of $\dfrac{2^{-14} + 2^{-15} + 2^{-16} + 2^{-17}}{5}$ is x times the value of 2^{-17}, then

$x(2^{-17}) = \dfrac{2^{-14} + 2^{-15} + 2^{-16} + 2^{-17}}{5}$

$x = \dfrac{\dfrac{2^{-14} + 2^{-15} + 2^{-16} + 2^{-17}}{5}}{2^{-17}}$

$= \dfrac{2^{-14} + 2^{-15} + 2^{-16} + 2^{-17}}{5} \times 2^{17}$

$= \dfrac{(2^{-14} + 2^{-15} + 2^{-16} + 2^{-17}) \times 2^{17}}{5}$

$= \dfrac{2^{-14+17} + 2^{-15+17} + 2^{-16+17} + 2^{-17+17}}{5}$

$= \dfrac{2^3 + 2^2 + 2^1 + 2^0}{5}$

$= \dfrac{8 + 4 + 2 + 1}{5}$

$= 3$

The correct answer is C.

To register for the GMAT exam go to www.mba.com

6.0 Data Sufficiency

6.0 Data Sufficiency

Data sufficiency questions appear in the Quantitative Reasoning section of the GMAT® exam. Multiple-choice data sufficiency questions are intermingled with problem solving questions throughout the section. You will have 62 minutes to complete the Quantitative Reasoning section of the GMAT exam, or about 2 minutes to answer each question. These questions require knowledge of the following topics:

- Arithmetic
- Elementary algebra
- Commonly known concepts of geometry

Data sufficiency questions are designed to measure your ability to analyze a quantitative problem, recognize which given information is relevant, and determine at what point there is sufficient information to solve a problem. In these questions, you are to classify each problem according to the five fixed answer choices, rather than find a solution to the problem.

Each data sufficiency question consists of a question, often accompanied by some initial information, and two statements, labeled (1) and (2), which contain additional information. You must decide whether the information in each statement is sufficient to answer the question or—if neither statement provides enough information—whether the information in the two statements together is sufficient. It is also possible that the statements, in combination, do not give enough information to answer the question.

Begin by reading the initial information and the question carefully. Next, consider the first statement. Does the information provided by the first statement enable you to answer the question? Go on to the second statement. Try to ignore the information given in the first statement when you consider whether the second statement provides information that, by itself, allows you to answer the question. Now you should be able to say, for each statement, whether it is sufficient to determine the answer.

Next, consider the two statements in tandem. Do they, together, enable you to answer the question?

Look again at your answer choices. Select the one that most accurately reflects whether the statements provide the information required to answer the question.

6.1 Test-Taking Strategies

1. **Do not waste valuable time solving a problem.**

   You only need to determine whether sufficient information is given to solve it.

2. **Consider each statement separately.**

   First, decide whether each statement alone gives sufficient information to solve the problem. Be sure to disregard the information given in statement (1) when you evaluate the information given in statement (2). If either, or both, of the statements give(s) sufficient information to solve the problem, select the answer corresponding to the description of which statement(s) give(s) sufficient information to solve the problem.

3. **Judge the statements in tandem if neither statement is sufficient by itself.**

   It is possible that the two statements together do not provide sufficient information. Once you decide, select the answer corresponding to the description of whether the statements together give sufficient information to solve the problem.

4. **Answer the question asked.**

   For example, if the question asks, "What is the value of y?" for an answer statement to be sufficient, you must be able to find one and only one value for y. Being able to determine minimum or maximum values for an answer (e.g., $y = x + 2$) is not sufficient, because such answers constitute a range of values rather than the specific value of y.

5. **Be very careful not to make unwarranted assumptions based on the images represented.**

   Figures are not necessarily drawn to scale; they are generalized figures showing little more than intersecting line segments and the relationships of points, angles, and regions. For example, if a figure described as a rectangle looks like a square, do *not* conclude that it is actually a square just by looking at the figure.

If statement 1 is sufficient, then the answer must be **A or D.**

If statement 2 is not sufficient, then the answer must be **A.**

If statement 2 is sufficient, then the answer must be **D.**

If statement 1 is not sufficient, then the answer must be **B, C, or E.**

If statement 2 is sufficient, then the answer must be **B.**

If statement 2 is not sufficient, then the answer must be **C or E.**

If both statements together are sufficient, then the answer must be **C.**

If both statements together are still not sufficient, then the answer must be **E.**

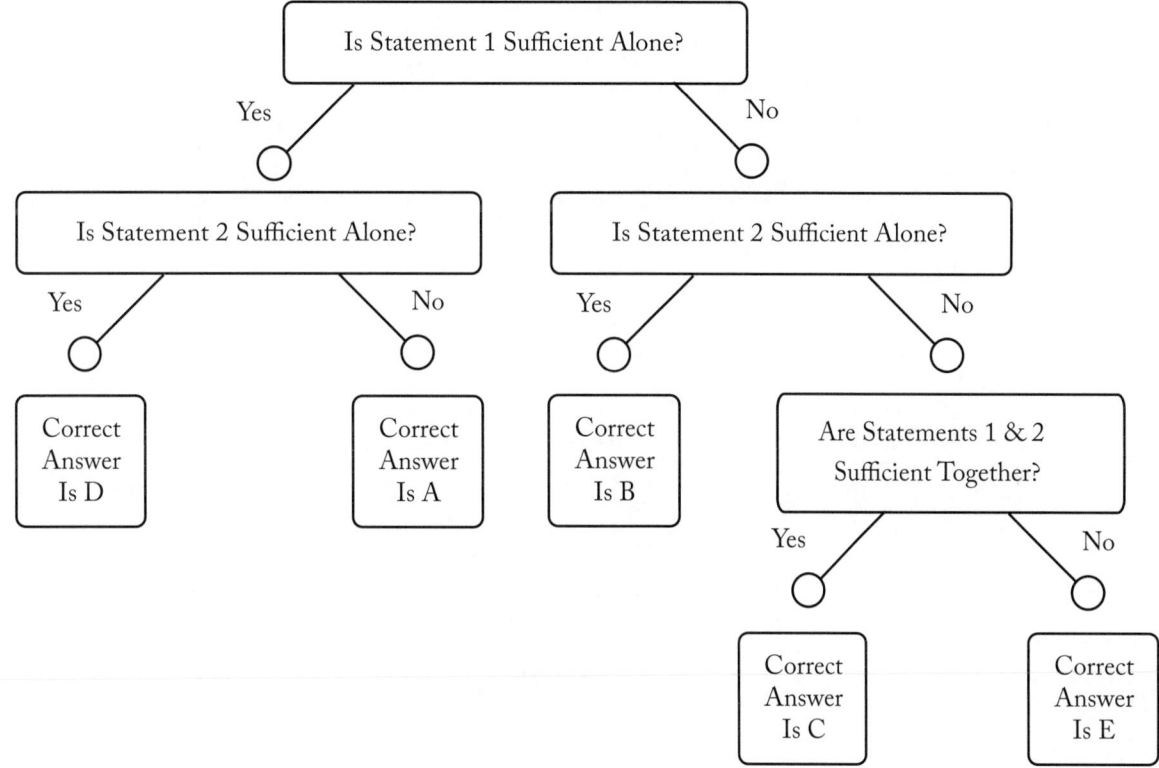

6.2 Section Instructions

Go to www.mba.com/tutorial to view instructions for the section and get a feel for what the test center screens will look at on the actual GMAT exam.

6.3 Practice Questions

Each <u>data sufficiency</u> problem consists of a question and two statements, labeled (1) and (2), which contain certain data. Using these data and your knowledge of mathematics and everyday facts (such as the number of days in July or the meaning of the word *counterclockwise*), decide whether the data given are sufficient for answering the question and then indicate one of the following answer choices:

A   Statement (1) ALONE is sufficient, but statement (2) alone is not sufficient.
B   Statement (2) ALONE is sufficient, but statement (1) alone is not sufficient.
C   BOTH statements TOGETHER are sufficient, but NEITHER statement ALONE is sufficient.
D   EACH statement ALONE is sufficient.
E   Statements (1) and (2) TOGETHER are NOT sufficient.

<u>Note:</u> In data sufficiency problems that ask for the value of a quantity, the data given in the statements are sufficient only when it is possible to determine exactly one numerical value for the quantity.

<u>Example:</u>

In, $\triangle PQR$ what is the value of x?

(1) $PQ = PR$

(2) $y = 40$

<u>Explanation:</u> According to statement (1) $PQ = PR$; therefore, $\triangle PQR$ is isosceles and $y = z$. Since $x + y + z = 180$, it follows that $x + 2y = 180$. Since statement (1) does not give a value for y, you cannot answer the question using statement (1) alone. According to statement (2), $y = 40$; therefore, $x + z = 140$. Since statement (2) does not give a value for z, you cannot answer the question using statement (2) alone. Using both statements together, since $x + 2y = 180$ and the value of y is given, you can find the value of x. Therefore, BOTH statements (1) and (2) TOGETHER are sufficient to answer the questions, but NEITHER statement ALONE is sufficient.

<u>Numbers:</u> All numbers used are real numbers.

<u>Figures:</u>
- Figures conform to the information given in the question, but will not necessarily conform to the additional information given in statements (1) and (2).
- Lines shown as straight are straight, and lines that appear jagged are also straight.
- The positions of points, angles, regions, etc., exist in the order shown, and angle measures are greater than zero.
- All figures lie in a plane unless otherwise indicated.

*DS02562
231. What is the number of pages of a certain journal article?

   (1) The size of each page is $5\frac{1}{2}$ inches by 8 inches.
   (2) The average (arithmetic mean) number of words per page is 250.

DS10471
232. If a certain vase contains only roses and tulips, how many tulips are there in the vase?

   (1) The number of roses in the vase is 4 times the number of tulips in the vase.
   (2) There is a total of 20 flowers in the vase.

DS03802
233. The cost of 10 pounds of apples and 2 pounds of grapes was $12. What was the cost per pound of apples?

   (1) The cost per pound of grapes was $2.
   (2) The cost of 2 pounds of apples was less than the cost of 1 pound of grapes.

DS05863
234. What was the median annual salary for the employees at Company X last year?

   (1) Last year there were 29 employees at Company X.
   (2) Last year 12 employees at Company X had an annual salary of $24,000.

DS03422
235. How many basic units of currency X are equivalent to 250 basic units of currency Y ?

   (1) 100 basic units of currency X are equivalent to 625 basic units of currency Y.
   (2) 2,000 basic units of currency X are equivalent to 12,500 basic units of currency Y.

DS12265
236. A company bought 3 printers and 1 scanner. What was the price of the scanner?

   (1) The total price of the printers and the scanner was $1,300.
   (2) The price of each printer was 4 times the price of the scanner.

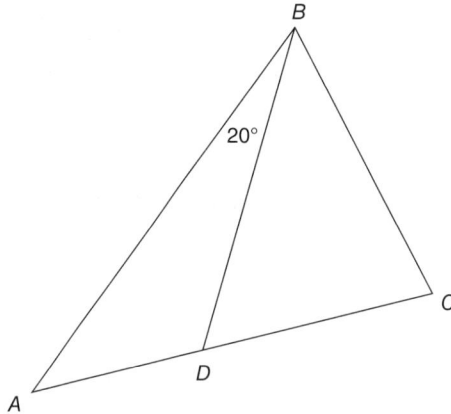

DS17639
237. In the figure above, point D is on $\overline{AC}$. What is the degree measure of ∠BAC ?

   (1) The measure of ∠BDC is 60°.
   (2) The degree measure of ∠BAC is less than the degree measure of ∠BCD.

DS07822
238. Each of the 256 solid-colored marbles in a box is either blue, green, or purple. What is the ratio of the number of blue marbles to the number of purple marbles in the box?

   (1) The number of green marbles in the box is 4 times the number of blue marbles in the box.
   (2) There are 192 green marbles in the box.

DS15940
239. A certain mixture of paint requires blue, yellow, and red paints in ratios of 2:3:1, respectively, and no other ingredients. If there are ample quantities of the blue and red paints available, is there enough of the yellow paint available to make the desired amount of the mixture?

   (1) Exactly 20 quarts of the mixture are needed.
   (2) Exactly 10 quarts of the yellow paint are available.

DS05338
240. The research funds of a certain company were divided among three departments, X, Y, and Z. Which one of the three departments received the greatest proportion of the research funds?

   (1) The research funds received by departments X and Y were in the ratio 3 to 5, respectively.
   (2) The research funds received by departments X and Z were in the ratio 2 to 1, respectively.

*These numbers correlate with the online test bank question number. See the GMAT Official Online Index in the back of this book.

241. In a certain class, some students donated cans of food to a local food bank. What was the average (arithmetic mean) number of cans donated per student in the class?

    (1) The students donated a total of 56 cans of food.
    (2) The total number of cans donated was 40 greater than the total number of students in the class.

242. Each of the n employees at a certain company has a different annual salary. What is the median of the annual salaries of the n employees?

    (1) When the annual salaries of the n employees are listed in increasing order, the median is the 15th salary.
    (2) The sum of the annual salaries of the n employees is $913,500.

243. In a recent town election, what was the ratio of the number of votes in favor of a certain proposal to the number of votes against the proposal?

    (1) There were 60 more votes in favor of the proposal than against the proposal.
    (2) There were 240 votes in favor of the proposal.

244. How many men are in a certain company's vanpool program?

    (1) The ratio of men to women in the program is 3 to 2.
    (2) The men and women in the program fill 6 vans.

245. Each of the marbles in a jar is either red or white or blue. If one marble is to be selected at random from the jar, what is the probability that the marble will be blue?

    (1) There are a total of 24 marbles in the jar, 8 of which are red.
    (2) The probability that the marble selected will be white is $\frac{1}{2}$.

246. In the figure above, what is the value of z?

    (1) $x = y = 1$
    (2) $w = 2$

247. What is the value of 10 percent of y?

    (1) 5 percent of y is 60.
    (2) y is 80 percent of 1,500.

248. Last semester, Professor K taught two classes, A and B. Each student in class A handed in 7 assignments, and each student in class B handed in 5 assignments. How many students were in class A?

    (1) The students in both classes combined handed in a total of 85 assignments.
    (2) There were 10 students in class B.

249. Was the amount of John's heating bill for February greater than it was for January?

    (1) The ratio of the amount of John's heating bill for February to that for January was $\frac{26}{25}$.
    (2) The sum of the amounts of John's heating bills for January and February was $183.60.

250. If sequence S has 120 terms, what is the 105th term of S?

    (1) The first term of S is –8.
    (2) Each term of S after the first term is 10 more than the preceding term.

251. Machine R and machine S work at their respective constant rates. How much time does it take machine R, working alone, to complete a certain job?

    (1) The amount of time that it takes machine S, working alone, to complete the job is $\frac{3}{4}$ the amount of time that it takes machine R, working alone, to complete the job.
    (2) Machine R and machine S, working together, take 12 minutes to complete the job.

252. If $u > 0$ and $v > 0$, which is greater, u^v or v^u?

 (1) $u = 1$
 (2) $v > 2$

253. What was the range of the selling prices of the 30 wallets sold by a certain store yesterday?

 (1) $\frac{1}{3}$ of the wallets had a selling price of $24 each.
 (2) The lowest selling price of the wallets was $\frac{1}{3}$ the highest selling price of the wallets.

254. Three houses are being sold through a real estate agent. What is the asking price for the house with the second-largest asking price?

 (1) The difference between the greatest and the least asking price is $130,000.
 (2) The difference between the two greater asking prices is $85,000.

255. If $a + b + c = 12$, what is the value of b?

 (1) $a + b = 8$
 (2) $b + c = 6$

256. Is $rw = 0$?

 (1) $-6 < r < 5$
 (2) $6 < w < 10$

257. Is $x = \frac{1}{y}$?

 (1) $xy = 1$
 (2) $\frac{1}{xy} = 1$

258. How many people in a group of 50 own neither a fax machine nor a laser printer?

 (1) The total number of people in the group who own a fax machine or a laser printer or both is less than 50.
 (2) The total number of people in the group who own both a fax machine and a laser printer is 15.

259. What is the value of w^{-2}?

 (1) $w^{-1} = \frac{1}{2}$
 (2) $w^3 = 8$

260. A certain investment earned a fixed rate of 4 percent interest per year, compounded annually, for five years. The interest earned for the third year of the investment was how many dollars greater than that for the first year?

 (1) The amount of the investment at the beginning of the second year was $4,160.00.
 (2) The amount of the investment at the beginning of the third year was $4,326.40.

261. What is the circumference of circle C?

 (1) The radius of circle C is 2π.
 (2) The center of circle C is located at point (7,8) in the xy-plane.

262. What is the value of t?

 (1) $s + t = 6 + s$
 (2) $t^3 = 216$

263. For a certain car repair, the total charge consisted of a charge for parts, a charge for labor, and a 6 percent sales tax on both the charge for parts and the charge for labor. If the charge for parts, excluding sales tax, was $50.00, what was the total charge for the repair?

 (1) The sales tax on the charge for labor was $9.60.
 (2) The total sales tax was $12.60.

264. George has a total of B books in his library, 25 of which are hardcover fiction books. What is the value of B?

 (1) 40 of the B books are fiction and the rest are nonfiction.
 (2) 60 of the B books are hardcovers and the rest are paperbacks.

265. Is $w + h^4$ positive?

 (1) h is positive.
 (2) w is positive.

266. If *a* is a 3-digit integer and *b* is a 3-digit integer, is the units digit of the product of *a* and *b* greater than 5 ?

    (1) The units digit of *a* is 4.
    (2) The units digit of *b* is 7.

267. In each of the last five years, Company K donated *p* percent of its annual profits to a certain scholarship fund. Did Company K donate more than $10,000 to the scholarship fund last year?

    (1) Two years ago, Company K had annual profits of $3 million and donated $15,000 to the scholarship fund.
    (2) Last year, Company K had annual profits of $2.5 million.

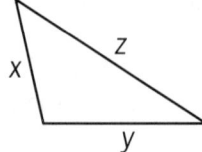

268. Is the area of the triangular region above less than 20 ?

    (1) $x^2 + y^2 \neq z^2$
    (2) $x + y < 13$

269. *A*, *B*, *C*, and *D* are points on a line. If *C* is the midpoint of line segment *AB* and if *D* is the midpoint of line segment *CB*, is the length of line segment *DB* greater than 5 ?

    (1) The length of line segment *AC* is greater than 8.
    (2) The length of line segment *CD* is greater than 6.

270. The people in a line waiting to buy tickets to a show are standing one behind the other. Adam and Beth are among the people in the line, and Beth is standing behind Adam with a number of people between them. If the number of people in front of Adam plus the number of people behind Beth is 18, how many people in the line are behind Beth?

    (1) There are a total of 32 people in the line.
    (2) 23 people in the line are behind Adam.

271. Square *ABCD* is inscribed in circle *O*. What is the area of square region *ABCD* ?

    (1) The area of circular region *O* is 64π.
    (2) The circumference of circle *O* is 16π.

272. Lines *k* and *m* are parallel to each other. Is the slope of line *k* positive?

    (1) Line *k* passes through the point (3,2).
    (2) Line *m* passes through the point (–3,2).

273. In cross section, a tunnel that carries one lane of one-way traffic is a semicircle with radius 4.2 m. Is the tunnel large enough to accommodate the truck that is approaching the entrance to the tunnel?

    (1) The maximum width of the truck is 2.4 m.
    (2) The maximum height of the truck is 4 m.

274. In a certain group of 50 people, how many are doctors who have a law degree?

    (1) In the group, 36 people are doctors.
    (2) In the group, 18 people have a law degree.

275. Of a group of 50 households, how many have at least one cat or at least one dog, but not both?

    (1) The number of households that have at least one cat and at least one dog is 4.
    (2) The number of households that have no cats and no dogs is 14.

276. Robin invested a total of $12,000 in two investments, X and Y, so that the investments earned the same amount of simple annual interest. How many dollars did Robin invest in investment Y ?

    (1) Investment X paid 3 percent simple annual interest, and investment Y paid 6 percent simple annual interest.
    (2) Robin invested more than $1,000 in investment X.

277. In a real estate office that employs *n* salespeople, *f* of them are females and *x* of the females are new employees. What is the value of *n*?

    (1) If an employee were randomly selected from the *n* employees, the probability of selecting a female would be $\frac{2}{3}$.

    (2) If an employee were randomly selected from the *f* female employees, the probability of selecting a new employee would be $\frac{1}{2}$.

278. Is $\frac{x+1}{y+1} > \frac{x}{y}$?

    (1) $0 < x < y$
    (2) $xy > 0$

279. Do at least 60 percent of the students in Pat's class walk to school?

    (1) At least 60 percent of the female students in Pat's class walk to school.
    (2) The number of students in Pat's class who walk to school is twice the number of students who do not walk to school.

280. A certain plumber charges $92 for each job completed in 4 hours or less and $23 per hour for each job completed in more than 4 hours. If it took the plumber a total of 7 hours to complete two separate jobs, what was the total amount charged by the plumber for the two jobs?

    (1) The plumber charged $92 for one of the two jobs.
    (2) The plumber charged $138 for one of the two jobs.

281. If *x* and *y* are positive numbers, is $\frac{x+1}{y+1} > \frac{x}{y}$?

    (1) $x > 1$
    (2) $x < y$

282. If *a* and *b* are positive integers, is $\frac{a}{b} < \frac{9}{11}$?

    (1) $\frac{a}{b} < 0.818$
    (2) $\frac{b}{a} > 1.223$

283. Every object in a box is either a sphere or a cube, and every object in the box is either red or green. How many objects are in the box?

    (1) There are six cubes and five green objects in the box.
    (2) There are two red spheres in the box.

284. If *x* and *y* are positive integers, is *xy* even?

    (1) $x^2 + y^2 - 1$ is divisible by 4.
    (2) $x + y$ is odd.

285. If *a* and *b* are integers, is $a + b + 3$ an odd integer?

    (1) *ab* is an odd integer.
    (2) $a - b$ is an even integer.

286. If *x* and *y* are positive integers, what is the value of $\sqrt{x} + \sqrt{y}$?

    (1) $x + y = 15$
    (2) $\sqrt{xy} = 6$

287. A certain truck uses $\frac{1}{12} + kv^2$ gallons of fuel per mile when its speed is *v* miles per hour, where *k* is a constant. At what speed should the truck travel so that it uses $\frac{5}{12}$ gallon of fuel per mile?

    (1) The value of *k* is $\frac{1}{10,800}$.
    (2) When the truck travels at 30 miles per hour, it uses $\frac{1}{6}$ gallon of fuel per mile.

288. If *r* and *s* are positive integers, is $r + s$ even?

    (1) *r* is even.
    (2) *s* is even.

289. In the figure above, △PQR has angle measures as shown. Is x < y ?

    (1) PQ = QR
    (2) PR > QR

290. If S is a set of odd integers and 3 and −1 are in S, is −15 in S ?

    (1) 5 is in S.
    (2) Whenever two numbers are in S, their product is in S.

291. Is the integer x a 3-digit integer?

    (1) x is the square of an integer.
    (2) 90 < x < 150

292. If the 1st term of a sequence is 0 and the 2nd term is 1, is the 5th term 2 ?

    (1) Each odd-numbered term is either 0 or 2.
    (2) The 3rd term is 2.

293. Is the sum of four particular integers even?

    (1) Two of the integers are odd and two are even.
    (2) The average (arithmetic mean) of the four integers is an integer.

294. If a school district paid a total of $35 per desk for x desks and a total of $30 per table for y tables, what was the total amount that the district paid for these desks and tables?

    (1) The total amount the district paid for the y tables was $900.
    (2) x = 90, and the total amount the district paid for the x desks was 3.5 times the total amount the district paid for the y tables.

295. Three children inherited a total of X dollars. If the oldest child inherited $7,000 more than the youngest child, and the youngest child inherited $9,000 less than the middle child, what is the value of X ?

    (1) The middle child inherited $27,000.
    (2) The youngest child and the middle child together inherited a total of $45,000.

296. If xyz ≠ 0, what is the value of $\dfrac{x^4 z^2}{z^2 y^2}$?

    (1) $y^2 = x^4$
    (2) x = 2 and y = 4

297. If a and b are integers, and b > 0, does $\dfrac{a-1}{b+1} = \dfrac{a}{b}$?

    (1) a = b − 4
    (2) a = −b

298. In a sequence of numbers in which each term is 2 more than the preceding term, what is the fourth term?

    (1) The last term is 90.
    (2) The first term is 2.

299. Is the integer p divisible by 5 ?

    (1) p is divisible by 10.
    (2) p is not divisible by 15.

300. The 9 squares above are to be filled with x's and o's, with only one symbol in each square. How many of the squares will contain an x ?

    (1) More than $\dfrac{1}{2}$ of the number of squares will contain an o.
    (2) Each of the 4 corner squares will contain an x.

301. Is the sum of two integers divisible by 10 ?

   (1) One of the integers is even.
   (2) One of the integers is a multiple of 5.

302. Is x an integer?

   (1) $x^3 = 8$
   (2) $x = \sqrt{4}$

303. If a building has 6,000 square meters of floor space, how many offices are in the building?

   (1) Exactly $\frac{1}{4}$ of the floor space is not used for offices.
   (2) There are exactly 20 executive offices and each of these occupies 3 times as much floor space as the average for all of the remaining offices.

304. If p, r, and s are consecutive integers in ascending order and x is the average (arithmetic mean) of the three integers, what is the value of x ?

   (1) Twice x is equal to the sum of p, r, and s.
   (2) The sum of p, r, and s is zero.

305. If m and n are integers, what is the value of $m + n$?

   (1) $(x + m)(x + n) = x^2 + 5x + mn$ and $x \neq 0$.
   (2) $mn = 4$

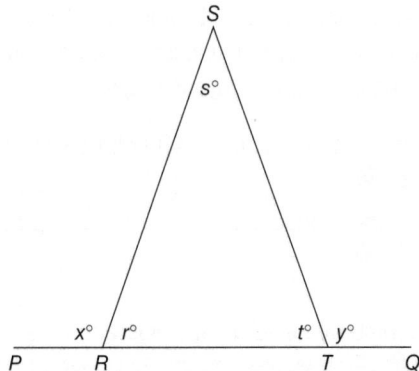

306. In the figure above, RST is a triangle with angle measures as shown and $PRTQ$ is a line segment. What is the value of $x + y$?

   (1) $s = 40$
   (2) $r = 70$

307. If R, S, and T are points on a line, and if R is 5 meters from T and 2 meters from S, how far is S from T ?

   (1) R is between S and T.
   (2) S is to the left of R, and T is to the right of R.

308. Is n equal to zero?

   (1) The product of n and some nonzero number is 0.
   (2) The sum of n and 0 is 0.

309. On a map, $\frac{1}{2}$ inch represents 100 miles. According to this map, how many miles is City X from City Y ?

   (1) City X is 3 inches from City Y on the map.
   (2) Cities X and Y are each 300 miles from City Z.

310. What is the remainder when the positive integer n is divided by 5 ?

   (1) When n is divided by 3, the quotient is 4 and the remainder is 1.
   (2) When n is divided by 4, the remainder is 1.

311. If r and s are positive numbers and θ is one of the operations, $+$, $-$, $\times$, or $\div$, which operation is θ ?

   (1) If $r = s$, then $r \, \theta \, s = 0$.
   (2) If $r \neq s$, then $r \, \theta \, s \neq s \, \theta \, r$.

312. In any sequence of n nonzero numbers, a pair of consecutive terms with opposite signs represents a sign change. For example, the sequence –2, 3, –4, 5 has three sign changes. Does the sequence of nonzero numbers s_1, s_2, s_3, . . . , s_n have an even number of sign changes?

   (1) $s_k = (-1)^k$ for all positive integers k from 1 to n.
   (2) n is odd.

313. Jack picked 76 apples. Of these, he sold $4y$ apples to Juanita and $3t$ apples to Sylvia. If he kept the remaining apples, how many apples did he keep? (t and y are positive integers.)

   (1) $y \geq 15$ and $t = 2$
   (2) $y = 17$

314. What number is 6 more than $x + y$?

    (1) y is 3 less than x.
    (2) y is twice x.

315. The total price of 5 pounds of regular coffee and 3 pounds of decaffeinated coffee was $21.50. What was the price of the 5 pounds of regular coffee?

    (1) If the price of the 5 pounds of regular coffee had been reduced 10 percent and the price of the 3 pounds of decaffeinated coffee had been reduced 20 percent, the total price would have been $18.45.
    (2) The price of the 5 pounds of regular coffee was $3.50 more than the price of the 3 pounds of decaffeinated coffee.

316. If a and b are integers, is $a^5 < 4^b$?

    (1) $a^3 = -27$
    (2) $b^2 = 16$

317. If each side of parallelogram P has length 1, what is the area of P?

    (1) One angle of P measures 45 degrees.
    (2) The altitude of P is $\frac{\sqrt{2}}{2}$.

318. If x is an integer greater than 0, what is the remainder when x is divided by 4?

    (1) The remainder is 3 when $x + 1$ is divided by 4.
    (2) The remainder is 0 when $2x$ is divided by 4.

319. A certain painting job requires a mixture of yellow, green, and white paint. If 12 quarts of paint are needed for the job, how many quarts of green paint are needed?

    (1) The ratio of the amount of green paint to the amount of yellow and white paint combined needs to be 1 to 3.
    (2) The ratio of the amount of yellow paint to the amount of green paint needs to be 3 to 2.

320. Is the average (arithmetic mean) of the numbers x, y, and z greater than z?

    (1) $z - x < y - z$
    (2) $x < z < y$

321. Is the point Q on the circle with center C?

    (1) R is a point on the circle and the distance from Q to R is equal to the distance from Q to C.
    (2) S is a point on the circle and the distance from Q to S is equal to the distance from S to C.

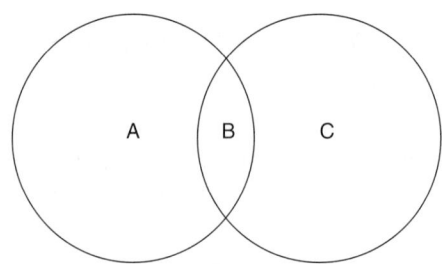

322. In the figure above, if A, B, and C are the areas, respectively, of the three nonoverlapping regions formed by the intersection of two circles of equal area, what is the value of $B + C$?

    (1) $A + 2B + C = 24$
    (2) $A + C = 18$ and $B = 3$

323. A company produces a certain toy in only 2 sizes, small or large, and in only 2 colors, red or green. If, for each size, there are equal numbers of red and green toys in a certain production lot, what fraction of the total number of green toys is large?

    (1) In the production lot, 400 of the small toys are green.
    (2) In the production lot, $\frac{2}{3}$ of the toys produced are small.

324. Is quadrilateral $PQRS$ a parallelogram?

    (1) Adjacent sides PQ and QR have the same length.
    (2) Adjacent sides RS and SP have the same length.

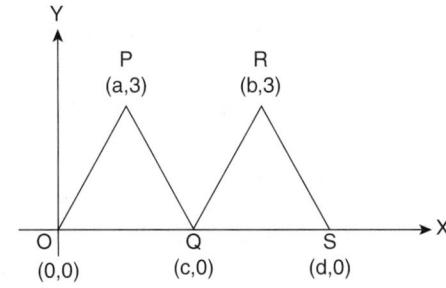

325. In the figure above, the vertices of △OPQ and △QRS have coordinates as indicated. Do △OPQ and △QRS have equal areas?

   (1) $b = 2a$
   (2) $d = 2c$

326. After the first two terms in a sequence of numbers, each term in the sequence is formed by adding all of the preceding terms. Is 12 the fifth term in the sequence?

   (1) The sum of the first 3 terms in the sequence is 6.
   (2) The fourth term in the sequence is 6.

327. Jones has worked at Firm X twice as many years as Green, and Green has worked at Firm X four years longer than Smith. How many years has Green worked at Firm X ?

   (1) Jones has worked at Firm X 9 years longer than Smith.
   (2) Green has worked at Firm X 5 years less than Jones.

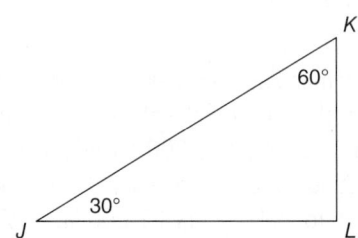

328. In △JKL shown above, what is the length of segment JL ?

   (1) $JK = 10$
   (2) $KL = 5$

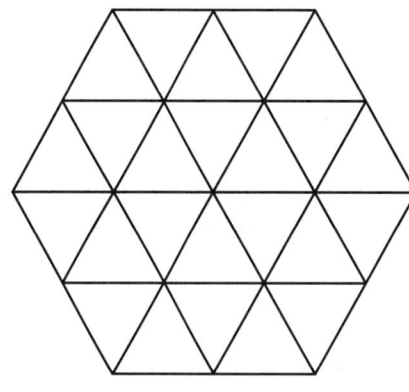

329. A six-sided mosaic contains 24 triangular pieces of tile of the same size and shape, as shown in the figure above. If the sections of tile fit together perfectly, how many square centimeters of tile are in the mosaic?

   (1) Each side of each triangular piece of tile is 9 centimeters long.
   (2) The mosaic can be put inside a rectangular frame that is 40 centimeters wide.

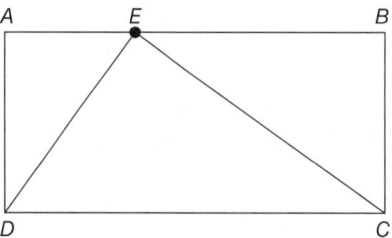

330. If, in the figure above, ABCD is a rectangular region, what is the value of the ratio $\frac{\text{area of } \triangle EDA}{\text{area of } \triangle EBC}$?

   (1) $AD = 4$
   (2) $AE = 2$ and $EB = 4$

331. A noncompressible ball in the shape of a sphere is to be passed through a square opening in a board. What is the perimeter of the opening?

   (1) The radius of the ball is equal to 2 inches.
   (2) The square opening is the smallest square opening through which the ball will fit.

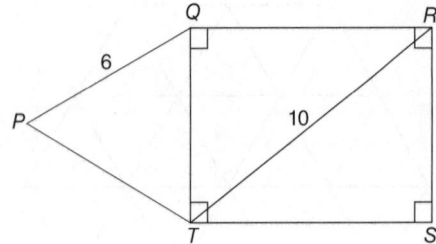

332. In the figure above, what is the area of region PQRST?

    (1) PQ = RS
    (2) PT = QT

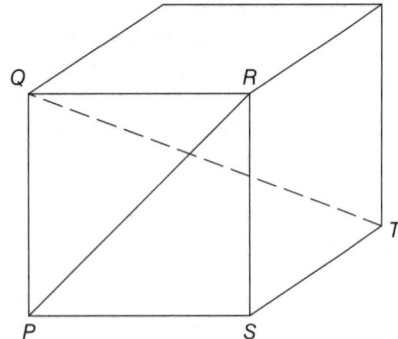

333. The figure above represents a box that has the shape of a cube. What is the volume of the box?

    (1) PR = 10 cm
    (2) QT = $5\sqrt{6}$ cm

334. If x and y are the lengths of the legs of a right triangle, what is the value of xy?

    (1) The hypotenuse of the triangle is $10\sqrt{2}$.
    (2) The area of the triangular region is 50.

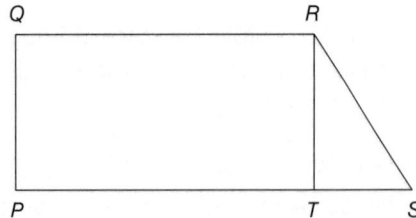

335. In the figure above, PQRT is a rectangle. What is the length of segment PQ?

    (1) The area of region PQRS is 39 and TS = 6.
    (2) The area of region PQRT is 30 and QR = 10.

336. On June 1, Mary paid Omar $360 for rent and utilities for the month of June. Mary moved out early, and Omar refunded the money she paid for utilities, but not for rent, for the days in June after she moved out. How many dollars did Omar refund to Mary?

    (1) Mary moved out on June 24.
    (2) The amount Mary paid for utilities was less than $\frac{1}{5}$ the amount Mary paid for rent.

337. If $x = 2t$ and $y = \frac{t}{3}$, what is the value of $x^2 - y^2$?

    (1) $t^2 - 3 = 6$
    (2) $t^3 = -27$

338. The 10 students in a history class recently took an examination. What was the maximum score on the examination?

    (1) The mean of the scores was 75.
    (2) The standard deviation of the scores was 5.

339. Last school year, each of the 200 students at a certain high school attended the school for the entire year. If there were 8 cultural performances at the school during the last school year, what was the average (arithmetic mean) number of students attending each cultural performance?

    (1) Last school year, each student attended at least one cultural performance.
    (2) Last school year, the average number of cultural performances attended per student was 4.

340. A clothing manufacturer makes jackets that are wool or cotton or a combination of wool and cotton. The manufacturer has 3,000 pounds of wool and 2,000 pounds of cotton on hand. Is this enough wool and cotton to make at least 1,000 jackets?

    (1) Each wool jacket requires 4 pounds of wool, and no cotton.
    (2) Each cotton jacket requires 6 pounds of cotton, and no wool.

341. If *n* is an integer, what is the greatest common divisor of 12 and *n* ?

    (1) The product of 12 and *n* is 432.
    (2) The greatest common divisor of 24 and *n* is 12.

342. Each month, Jim receives a base salary plus a 10 percent commission on the price of each car he sells that month. If Jim sold 15 cars last month, what was the total amount of base salary and commissions that Jim received that month?

    (1) Last month, Jim's base salary was $3,000.
    (2) Last month, Jim sold 3 cars whose prices totaled $60,000 and 5 cars whose prices totaled $120,000.

343. If *x* is a positive integer greater than 1, what is the value of *x* ?

    (1) 2*x* is a common factor of 18 and 24.
    (2) *x* is a factor of 6.

344. By what percentage was the price of a certain television set discounted for a sale?

    (1) The price of the television set before it was discounted for the sale was 25 percent greater than the discounted price.
    (2) The price of the television set was discounted by $60 for the sale.

345. Jack wants to use a circular rug on his rectangular office floor to cover two small circular stains, each less than $\frac{\pi}{100}$ square feet in area and each more than 3 feet from the nearest wall. Can the rug be placed to cover both stains?

    (1) Jack's rug covers an area of 9π square feet.
    (2) The centers of the stains are less than 4 feet apart.

346. A paint mixture was formed by mixing exactly 3 colors of paint. By volume, the mixture was *x*% blue paint, *y*% green paint, and *z*% red paint. If exactly 1 gallon of blue paint and 3 gallons of red paint were used, how many gallons of green paint were used?

    (1) *x* = *y*
    (2) *z* = 60

×	a	b	c
a	d	e	f
b	e	g	h
c	f	h	j

347. In the multiplication table above, each letter represents an integer. What is the value of *c* ?

    (1) *c* = *f*
    (2) *h* ≠ 0

348. If *n* is an integer, is $(0.1)^n$ greater than $(10)^n$?

    (1) *n* > −10
    (2) *n* < 10

349. For a basic monthly fee of *F* yen (¥*F*), Naoko's first cell phone plan allowed him to use a maximum of 420 minutes on calls during the month. Then, for each of *x* additional minutes he used on calls, he was charged ¥*M*, making his total charge for the month ¥*T*, where *T* = *F* + *xM*. What is the value of *F* ?

    (1) Naoko used 450 minutes on calls the first month and the total charge for the month was ¥13,755.
    (2) Naoko used 400 minutes on calls the second month and the total charge for the month was ¥13,125.

350. Is the sum of the prices of the 3 books that Shana bought less than $48 ?

    (1) The price of the most expensive of the 3 books that Shana bought is less than $17.
    (2) The price of the least expensive of the 3 books that Shana bought is exactly $3 less than the price of the second most expensive book.

351. If *r* and *t* are three-digit positive integers, is *r* greater than *t* ?

    (1) The tens digit of *r* is greater than each of the three digits of *t*.
    (2) The tens digit of *r* is less than either of the other two digits of *r*.

352. Is the product of two positive integers x and y divisible by the sum of x and y?

    (1) $x = y$
    (2) $x = 2$

353. If a and b are constants, is the expression $\dfrac{x+b}{\sqrt{x+a}}$ defined for $x = -2$?

    (1) $a = 5$
    (2) $b = 6$

354. A company makes and sells two products, P and Q. The costs per unit of making and selling P and Q are $8.00 and $9.50, respectively, and the selling prices per unit of P and Q are $10.00 and $13.00, respectively. In one month the company sold a total of 834 units of these products. Was the total profit on these items more than $2,000.00?

    (1) During the month, more units of P than units of Q were sold.
    (2) During the month, at least 100 units of Q were sold.

355. Jill has applied for a job with each of two different companies. What is the probability that she will get job offers from both companies?

    (1) The probability that she will get a job offer from neither company is 0.3.
    (2) The probability that she will get a job offer from exactly one of the two companies is 0.5.

356. A conveyor belt moves bottles at a constant speed of 120 centimeters per second. If the conveyor belt moves a bottle from a loading dock to an unloading dock, is the distance that the conveyor belt moves the bottle less than 90 meters? (1 meter = 100 centimeters)

    (1) It takes the conveyor belt less than 1.2 minutes to move the bottle from the loading dock to the unloading dock.
    (2) It takes the conveyor belt more than 1.1 minutes to move the bottle from the loading dock to the unloading dock.

357. If x, y, and z are positive numbers, what is the value of the average (arithmetic mean) of x and z?

    (1) $x - y = y - z$
    (2) $x^2 - y^2 = z$

358. The rectangular rug shown in the figure above has an accent border. What is the area of the portion of the rug that excludes the border?

    (1) The perimeter of the rug is 44 feet.
    (2) The width of the border on all sides is 1 foot.

359. If $y \neq 2xz$, what is the value of $\dfrac{2xz + yz}{2xz - y}$?

    (1) $2x + y = 3$
    (2) $z = 2$

360. In the parallelogram shown, what is the value of x?

    (1) $y = 2x$
    (2) $x + z = 120$

361. In a product test of a common cold remedy, x percent of the patients tested experienced side effects from the use of the drug and y percent experienced relief of cold symptoms. What percent of the patients tested experienced both side effects and relief of cold symptoms?

    (1) Of the 1,000 patients tested, 15 percent experienced neither side effects nor relief of cold symptoms.
    (2) Of the patients tested, 30 percent experienced relief of cold symptoms without side effects.

362. Is $x < 5$?

    (1) $x^2 > 5$
    (2) $x^2 + x < 5$

363. Three roommates—Bela, Gyorgy, and Janos—together saved money for a trip. The amount that Bela saved was equal to 8% of his monthly income. The amount that Gyorgy saved was exactly $\frac{1}{3}$ of the total amount saved by all 3 roommates. What was the total amount saved for the trip by all 3 roommates?

    (1) Bela had a monthly income of $2,000.
    (2) Janos saved 1.5 times as much for the trip as Bela.

364. Is zp negative?

    (1) $pz^4 < 0$
    (2) $p + z^4 = 14$

365. In each game of a certain tournament, a contestant either loses 3 points or gains 2 points. If Pat had 100 points at the beginning of the tournament, how many games did Pat play in the tournament?

    (1) At the end of the tournament, Pat had 104 points.
    (2) Pat played fewer than 10 games.

366. At the beginning of the year, the Finance Committee and the Planning Committee of a certain company each had n members, and no one was a member of both committees. At the end of the year, 5 members left the Finance Committee and 3 members left the Planning Committee. How many members did the Finance Committee have at the beginning of the year?

    (1) The ratio of the total number of members who left at the end of the year to the total number of members at the beginning of the year was 1:6.
    (2) At the end of the year, 21 members remained on the Planning Committee.

367. If $xy \neq 0$, is $x^3 + y^3 > 0$?

    (1) $x + y > 0$
    (2) $xy > 0$

368. Max purchased a guitar for a total of $624, which consisted of the price of the guitar and the sales tax. Was the sales tax rate greater than 3 percent?

    (1) The price of the guitar that Max purchased was less than $602.
    (2) The sales tax for the guitar that Max purchased was less than $30.

369. A pentagon with 5 sides of equal length and 5 interior angles of equal measure is inscribed in a circle. Is the perimeter of the pentagon greater than 26 centimeters?

    (1) The area of the circle is 16π square centimeters.
    (2) The length of each diagonal of the pentagon is less than 8 centimeters.

370. If $2.00X$ and $3.00Y$ are 2 numbers in decimal form with thousandths digits X and Y, is $3(2.00X) > 2(3.00Y)$?

    (1) $3X < 2Y$
    (2) $X < Y - 3$

371. The length, width, and height of a rectangular box, in centimeters, are L, W, and H. If the volume of this box is V cubic centimeters and the total area of the 6 sides of this box is A square centimeters, what is the value of $\frac{V}{A}$?

    (1) At least 2 of L, W, and H are equal to 5.
    (2) L, W, and H all have the same value.

372. What is the sum of a certain pair of consecutive odd integers?

    (1) At least one of the integers is negative.
    (2) At least one of the integers is positive.

373. Is $x = y$?

    (1) $\frac{2x}{3} - \frac{y}{3} = \frac{1}{3}$
    (2) $\frac{x}{4} - \frac{y}{4} = 0$

374. The sum of 4 different odd integers is 64. What is the value of the greatest of these integers?

    (1) The integers are consecutive odd numbers.
    (2) Of these integers, the greatest is 6 more than the least.

375. Was the number of books sold at Bookstore X last week greater than the number of books sold at Bookstore Y last week?

    (1) Last week, more than 1,000 books were sold at Bookstore X on Saturday and fewer than 1,000 books were sold at Bookstore Y on Saturday.
    (2) Last week, less than 20 percent of the books sold at Bookstore X were sold on Saturday and more than 20 percent of the books sold at Bookstore Y were sold on Saturday.

376. A rectangular solid has length, width, and height of L cm, W cm, and H cm, respectively. If these dimensions are increased by $x\%$, $y\%$, and $z\%$, respectively, what is the percentage increase in the total surface area of the solid?

    (1) L, W, and H are in the ratios of 5:3:4.
    (2) $x = 5$, $y = 10$, $z = 20$

377. A certain list, L, contains a total of n numbers, not necessarily distinct, that are arranged in increasing order. If L_1 is the list consisting of the first n_1 numbers in L and L_2 is the list consisting of the last n_2 numbers in L, is 17 a mode for L?

    (1) 17 is a mode for L_1 and 17 is a mode for L_2.
    (2) $n_1 + n_2 = n$

378. From May 1 to May 30 in the same year, the balance in a checking account increased. What was the balance in the checking account on May 30?

    (1) If, during this period of time, the increase in the balance in the checking account had been 12 percent, then the balance in the account on May 30 would have been $504.
    (2) During this period of time, the increase in the balance in the checking account was 8 percent.

379. A merchant discounted the sale price of a coat and the sale price of a sweater. Which of the two articles of clothing was discounted by the greater dollar amount?

    (1) The percent discount on the coat was 2 percentage points greater than the percent discount on the sweater.
    (2) Before the discounts, the sale price of the coat was $10 less than the sale price of the sweater.

380. If the positive integer n is added to each of the integers 69, 94, and 121, what is the value of n?

    (1) $69 + n$ and $94 + n$ are the squares of two consecutive integers.
    (2) $94 + n$ and $121 + n$ are the squares of two consecutive integers.

381. If a merchant purchased a sofa from a manufacturer for $400 and then sold it, what was the selling price of the sofa?

    (1) The selling price of the sofa was greater than 140 percent of the purchase price.
    (2) The merchant's gross profit from the purchase and sale of the sofa was $\frac{1}{3}$ of the selling price.

382. Last year, in a certain housing development, the average (arithmetic mean) price of 20 new houses was $160,000. Did more than 9 of the 20 houses have prices that were less than the average price last year?

    (1) Last year the greatest price of one of the 20 houses was $219,000.
    (2) Last year the median of the prices of the 20 houses was $150,000.

383. For a certain city's library, the average cost of purchasing each new book is $28. The library receives $15,000 from the city each year; the library also receives a bonus of $2,000 if the total number of items checked out over the course of the year exceeds 5,000. Did the library receive the bonus last year?

    (1) The library purchased an average of 50 new books each month last year and received enough money from the city to cover this cost.
    (2) The lowest number of items checked out in one month was 459.

286

7, 9, 6, 4, 5, x

384. If x is a number in the list above, what is the median of the list?

   (1) x > 7
   (2) The median of the list equals the arithmetic mean of the list.

385. Three dice, each of which has its 6 sides numbered 1 through 6, are tossed. The sum of the 3 numbers that are facing up is 12. Is at least 1 of these numbers 5 ?

   (1) None of the 3 numbers that are facing up is divisible by 3.
   (2) Of the numbers that are facing up, 2, but not all 3, are equal.

386. On the number line, point R has coordinate r and point T has coordinate t. Is t < 0 ?

   (1) −1 < r < 0
   (2) The distance between R and T is equal to r^2.

387. S is a set of points in the plane. How many distinct triangles can be drawn that have three of the points in S as vertices?

   (1) The number of distinct points in S is 5.
   (2) No three of the points in S are collinear.

388. Stores L and M each sell a certain product at a different regular price. If both stores discount their regular price of the product, is the discount price at Store M less than the discount price at Store L ?

   (1) At Store L the discount price is 10 percent less than the regular price; at Store M the discount price is 15 percent less than the regular price.
   (2) At Store L the discount price is $5 less than the regular store price; at Store M the discount price is $6 less than the regular price.

389. If d denotes a decimal, is d ≥ 0.5 ?

   (1) When d is rounded to the nearest tenth, the result is 0.5.
   (2) When d is rounded to the nearest integer, the result is 1.

390. In the two-digit integers 3■ and 2▲, the symbols ■ and ▲ represent different digits, and the product (3■)(2▲) is equal to 864. What digit does ■ represent?

   (1) The sum of ■ and ▲ is 10.
   (2) The product of ■ and ▲ is 24.

```
•————————————————————ℓ
M
```

391. Two points, N and Q (not shown), lie to the right of point M on line ℓ. What is the ratio of the length of QN to the length of MQ ?

   (1) Twice the length of MN is 3 times the length of MQ.
   (2) Point Q is between points M and N.

392. Did the sum of the prices of three shirts exceed $60 ?

   (1) The price of the most expensive of the shirts exceeded $30.
   (2) The price of the least expensive of the shirts exceeded $20.

393. What is the total number of coins that Bert and Claire have?

   (1) Bert has 50 percent more coins than Claire.
   (2) The total number of coins that Bert and Claire have is between 21 and 28.

394. A telephone station has x processors, each of which can process a maximum of y calls at any particular time, where x and y are positive integers. If 500 calls are sent to the station at a particular time, can the station process all of the calls?

   (1) x = 600
   (2) 100 < y < 200

	Price per Flower
Roses	$1.00
Daisies	$0.50

395. Kim and Sue each bought some roses and some daisies at the prices shown above. If Kim bought the same total number of roses and daisies as Sue, was the price of Kim's purchase of roses and daisies higher than the price of Sue's purchase of roses and daisies?

   (1) Kim bought twice as many daisies as roses.
   (2) Kim bought 4 more roses than Sue bought.

396. Jazz and blues recordings accounted for 6 percent of the $840 million revenue from the sales of recordings in Country Y in 2000. What was the revenue from the sales of jazz and blues recordings in Country Y in 1998?

   (1) Jazz and blues recordings accounted for 5 percent of the revenue from the sales of recordings in Country Y in 1998.
   (2) The revenue from the sales of jazz and blues recordings in Country Y increased by 40 percent from 1998 to 2000.

397. On a certain nonstop trip, Marta averaged x miles per hour for 2 hours and y miles per hour for the remaining 3 hours. What was her average speed, in miles per hour, for the entire trip?

   (1) $2x + 3y = 280$
   (2) $y = x + 10$

398. If x is a positive integer, what is the value of $\sqrt{x + 24} - \sqrt{x}$?

   (1) $\sqrt{x}$ is an integer.
   (2) $\sqrt{x + 24}$ is an integer.

399. A tank is filled with gasoline to a depth of exactly 2 feet. The tank is a cylinder resting horizontally on its side, with its circular ends oriented vertically. The inside of the tank is exactly 6 feet long. What is the volume of the gasoline in the tank?

   (1) The inside of the tank is exactly 4 feet in diameter.
   (2) The top surface of the gasoline forms a rectangle that has an area of 24 square feet.

400. Of the four numbers represented on the number line above, is r closest to zero?

   (1) $q = -s$
   (2) $-t < q$

401. A group consisting of several families visited an amusement park where the regular admission fees were ¥5,500 for each adult and ¥4,800 for each child. Because there were at least 10 people in the group, each paid an admission fee that was 10% less than the regular admission fee. How many children were in the group?

   (1) The total of the admission fees paid for the adults in the group was ¥29,700.
   (2) The total of the admission fees paid for the children in the group was ¥4,860 more than the total of the admission fees paid for the adults in the group.

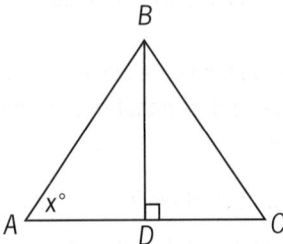

402. What is the area of triangular region ABC above?

   (1) The product of BD and AC is 20.
   (2) $x = 45$

403. In the xy-coordinate plane, is point R equidistant from points $(-3, -3)$ and $(1, -3)$?

   (1) The x-coordinate of point R is -1.
   (2) Point R lies on the line $y = -3$.

404. What is the ratio of the average (arithmetic mean) height of students in class X to the average height of students in class Y?

   (1) The average height of the students in class X is 120 centimeters.
   (2) The average height of the students in class X and class Y combined is 126 centimeters.

DS04631
405. Is the positive two-digit integer N less than 40 ?

   (1) The units digit of N is 6 more than the tens digit.
   (2) N is 4 less than 4 times the units digit.

DS06318
406. If $2^{x+y} = 4^8$, what is the value of y ?

   (1) $x^2 = 81$
   (2) $x - y = 2$

DS03680
407. Each week a certain salesman is paid a fixed amount equal to $300, plus a commission equal to 5 percent of the amount of his sales that week over $1,000. What is the total amount the salesman was paid last week?

   (1) The total amount the salesman was paid last week is equal to 10 percent of the amount of his sales last week.
   (2) The salesman's sales last week totaled $5,000.

DS01383
408. At a bakery, all donuts are priced equally and all bagels are priced equally. What is the total price of 5 donuts and 3 bagels at the bakery?

   (1) At the bakery, the total price of 10 donuts and 6 bagels is $12.90.
   (2) At the bakery, the price of a donut is $0.15 less than the price of a bagel.

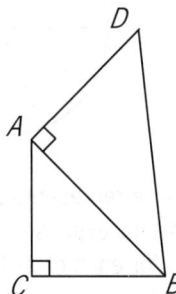

DS06869
409. In the figure above, is the area of triangular region ABC equal to the area of triangular region DBA ?

   (1) $(AC)^2 = 2(AD)^2$
   (2) $\triangle ABC$ is isosceles.

DS08105
410. If r and s are positive integers, can the fraction $\frac{r}{s}$ be expressed as a decimal with only a finite number of nonzero digits?

   (1) s is a factor of 100.
   (2) r is a factor of 100.

DS16384
411. If $r > 0$ and $s > 0$, is $\frac{r}{s} < \frac{s}{r}$?

   (1) $\frac{r}{3s} = \frac{1}{4}$
   (2) $s = r + 4$

DS06789
412. If k is an integer such that $56 < k < 66$, what is the value of k ?

   (1) If k were divided by 2, the remainder would be 1.
   (2) If $k + 1$ were divided by 3, the remainder would be 0.

DS13965
413. If x is a positive integer, then is x prime?

   (1) $3x + 1$ is prime.
   (2) $5x + 1$ is prime.

DS00172
              k, n, 12, 6, 17
414. What is the value of n in the list above?

   (1) $k < n$
   (2) The median of the numbers in the list is 10.

DS07508
415. If x and y are integers, what is the value of $x + y$?

   (1) $3 < \frac{x+y}{2} < 4$
   (2) $2 < x < y < 5$

DS00764
416. Last year, if Arturo spent a total of $12,000 on his mortgage payments, real estate taxes, and home insurance, how much did he spend on his real estate taxes?

   (1) Last year, the total amount that Arturo spent on his real estate taxes and home insurance was $33\frac{1}{3}$ percent of the amount that he spent on his mortgage payments.
   (2) Last year, the amount that Arturo spent on his real estate taxes was 20 percent of the total amount he spent on his mortgage payments and home insurance.

417. If a, b, c, and d are positive numbers, is $\dfrac{a}{b} < \dfrac{c}{d}$?

   (1) $0 < \dfrac{c-a}{d-b}$

   (2) $\left(\dfrac{ad}{bc}\right)^2 < \dfrac{ad}{bc}$

418. Is the number of members of Club X greater than the number of members of Club Y ?

   (1) Of the members of Club X, 20 percent are also members of Club Y.
   (2) Of the members of Club Y, 30 percent are also members of Club X.

419. On the number line above, p, q, r, s, and t are five consecutive even integers in increasing order. What is the average (arithmetic mean) of these five integers?

   (1) $q + s = 24$
   (2) The average (arithmetic mean) of q and r is 11.

420. If $\lceil x \rceil$ denotes the least integer greater than or equal to x, is $\lceil x \rceil = 0$?

   (1) $-1 < x < 1$
   (2) $x < 0$

421. If x and y are integers, is $x > y$?

   (1) $x + y > 0$
   (2) $y^x < 0$

422. If r and s are the roots of the equation $x^2 + bx + c = 0$, where b and c are constants, is $rs < 0$?

   (1) $b < 0$
   (2) $c < 0$

423. The figure above represents an L-shaped garden. What is the value of k ?

   (1) The area of the garden is 189 square feet.
   (2) The perimeter of the garden is 60 feet.

424. The only articles of clothing in a certain closet are shirts, dresses, and jackets. The ratio of the number of shirts to the number of dresses to the number of jackets in the closet is 9:4:5, respectively. If there are more than 7 dresses in the closet, what is the total number of articles of clothing in the closet?

   (1) The total number of shirts and jackets in the closet is less than 30.
   (2) The total number of shirts and dresses in the closet is 26.

TOTAL EXPENSES FOR THE
FIVE DIVISIONS OF COMPANY H

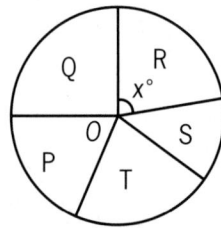

425. The figure above represents a circle graph of Company H's total expenses broken down by the expenses for each of its five divisions. If O is the center of the circle and if Company H's total expenses are $5,400,000, what are the expenses for Division R ?

   (1) $x = 94$
   (2) The total expenses for Divisions S and T are twice as much as the expenses for Division R.

426. If x is negative, is $x < -3$?

   (1) $x^2 > 9$
   (2) $x^3 < -9$

6.3 Data Sufficiency Practice Questions

DS04897
427. What is the number of cans that can be packed in a certain carton?

(1) The interior volume of this carton is 2,304 cubic inches.
(2) The exterior of each can is 6 inches high and has a diameter of 4 inches.

r	s	t
u	v	w
x	y	z

DS08301
428. Each of the letters in the table above represents one of the numbers 1, 2, or 3, and each of these numbers occurs exactly once in each row and exactly once in each column. What is the value of r?

(1) v + z = 6
(2) s + t + u + x = 6

DS00328
429. Material A costs $3 per kilogram, and Material B costs $5 per kilogram. If 10 kilograms of Material K consists of x kilograms of Material A and y kilograms of Material B, is x > y?

(1) y > 4
(2) The cost of the 10 kilograms of Material K is less than $40.

DS16164
430. At what speed was a train traveling on a trip when it had completed half of the total distance of the trip?

(1) The trip was 460 miles long and took 4 hours to complete.
(2) The train traveled at an average rate of 115 miles per hour on the trip.

DS12047
431. Tom, Jane, and Sue each purchased a new house. The average (arithmetic mean) price of the three houses was $120,000. What was the median price of the three houses?

(1) The price of Tom's house was $110,000.
(2) The price of Jane's house was $120,000.

DS13958
432. What is the value of x if $x^3 < x^2$?

(1) −2 < x < 2
(2) x is an integer greater than −2.

DS08451
433. For any integers x and y, min(x, y) and max(x, y) denote the minimum and the maximum of x and y, respectively. For example, min(5, 2) = 2 and max(5, 2) = 5. For the integer w, what is the value of min(10, w)?

(1) w = max(20, z) for some integer z
(2) w = max(10, w)

DS01473
434. A certain bookcase has 2 shelves of books. On the upper shelf, the book with the greatest number of pages has 400 pages. On the lower shelf, the book with the least number of pages has 475 pages. What is the median number of pages for all of the books on the 2 shelves?

(1) There are 25 books on the upper shelf.
(2) There are 24 books on the lower shelf.

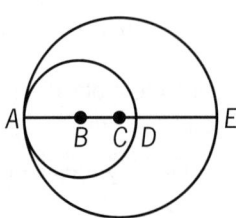

DS12070
435. In the figure above, points A, B, C, D, and E lie on a line. A is on both circles, B is the center of the smaller circle, C is the center of the larger circle, D is on the smaller circle, and E is on the larger circle. What is the area of the region inside the larger circle and outside the smaller circle?

(1) AB = 3 and BC = 2
(2) CD = 1 and DE = 4

291

DS08995
436. In planning for a car trip, Joan estimated both the distance of the trip, in miles, and her average speed, in miles per hour. She accurately divided her estimated distance by her estimated average speed to obtain an estimate for the time, in hours, that the trip would take. Was her estimate within 0.5 hour of the actual time that the trip took?

(1) Joan's estimate for the distance was within 5 miles of the actual distance.
(2) Joan's estimate for her average speed was within 10 miles per hour of her actual average speed.

DS12239
437. A certain list consists of 3 different numbers. Does the median of the 3 numbers equal the average (arithmetic mean) of the 3 numbers?

(1) The range of the 3 numbers is equal to twice the difference between the greatest number and the median.
(2) The sum of the 3 numbers is equal to 3 times one of the numbers.

DS12806
438. Line ℓ lies in the xy-plane and does not pass through the origin. What is the slope of line ℓ?

(1) The x-intercept of line ℓ is twice the y-intercept of line ℓ.
(2) The x- and y-intercepts of line ℓ are both positive.

$$y = ax - 5$$
$$y = x + 6$$
$$y = 3x + b$$

DS07713
439. In the xy-plane, the straight-line graphs of the three equations above each contain the point (p,r). If a and b are constants, what is the value of b?

(1) $a = 2$
(2) $r = 17$

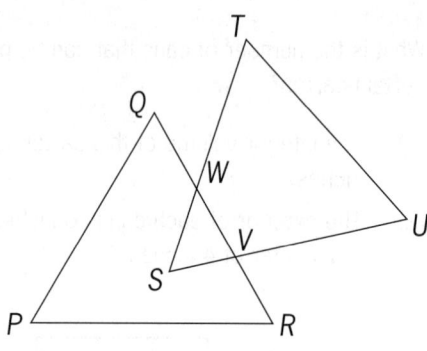

DS06861
440. In the figure above, PQR and STU are identical equilateral triangles, and PQ = 6. What is the perimeter of polygon PQWTUVR?

(1) Triangle SWV has perimeter 9.
(2) VW has length 3.5.

DS09973
441. The range of the numbers in set S is x, and the range of the numbers in set T is y. If all of the numbers in set T are also in set S, is x greater than y?

(1) Set S consists of 7 numbers.
(2) Set T consists of 6 numbers.

DS13857
442. The hypotenuse of a right triangle is 10 cm. What is the perimeter, in centimeters, of the triangle?

(1) The area of the triangle is 25 square centimeters.
(2) The 2 legs of the triangle are of equal length.

Shipment	S1	S2	S3	S4	S5	S6
Fraction of the Total Value of the Six Shipments	$\frac{1}{4}$	$\frac{1}{5}$	$\frac{1}{6}$	$\frac{3}{20}$	$\frac{2}{15}$	$\frac{1}{10}$

DS01427
443. Six shipments of machine parts were shipped from a factory on two trucks, with each shipment entirely on one of the trucks. Each shipment was labeled either S1, S2, S3, S4, S5, or S6. The table shows the value of each shipment as a fraction of the total value of the six shipments. If the shipments on the first truck had a value greater than $\frac{1}{2}$ of the total value of the six shipments, was S3 shipped on the first truck?

(1) S2 and S4 were shipped on the first truck.
(2) S1 and S6 were shipped on the second truck.

444. If x, y, and z are three-digit positive integers and if x = y + z, is the hundreds digit of x equal to the sum of the hundreds digits of y and z?

    (1) The tens digit of x is equal to the sum of the tens digits of y and z.
    (2) The units digit of x is equal to the sum of the units digits of y and z.

	Favorable	Unfavorable	Not Sure
Candidate M	40	20	40
Candidate N	30	35	35

445. The table above shows the results of a survey of 100 voters who each responded "Favorable" or "Unfavorable" or "Not Sure" when asked about their impressions of Candidate M and of Candidate N. What was the number of voters who responded "Favorable" for both candidates?

    (1) The number of voters who did not respond "Favorable" for either candidate was 40.
    (2) The number of voters who responded "Unfavorable" for both candidates was 10.

446. A school administrator will assign each student in a group of n students to one of m classrooms. If 3 < m < 13 < n, is it possible to assign each of the n students to one of the m classrooms so that each classroom has the same number of students assigned to it?

    (1) It is possible to assign each of 3n students to one of m classrooms so that each classroom has the same number of students assigned to it.
    (2) It is possible to assign each of 13n students to one of m classrooms so that each classroom has the same number of students assigned to it.

447. If q, s, and t are all different numbers, is q < s < t?

    (1) $t - q = |t - s| + |s - q|$
    (2) $t > q$

448. What is the median number of employees assigned per project for the projects at Company Z?

    (1) 25 percent of the projects at Company Z have 4 or more employees assigned to each project.
    (2) 35 percent of the projects at Company Z have 2 or fewer employees assigned to each project.

449. Last year, a certain company began manufacturing product X and sold every unit of product X that it produced. Last year the company's total expenses for manufacturing product X were equal to $100,000 plus 5 percent of the company's total revenue from all units of product X sold. If the company made a profit on product X last year, did the company sell more than 21,000 units of product X last year?

    (1) The company's total revenue from the sale of product X last year was greater than $110,000.
    (2) For each unit of product X sold last year, the company's revenue was $5.

450. Beginning in January of last year, Carl made deposits of $120 into his account on the 15th of each month for several consecutive months and then made withdrawals of $50 from the account on the 15th of each of the remaining months of last year. There were no other transactions in the account last year. If the closing balance of Carl's account for May of last year was $2,600, what was the range of the monthly closing balances of Carl's account last year?

    (1) Last year the closing balance of Carl's account for April was less than $2,625.
    (2) Last year the closing balance of Carl's account for June was less than $2,675.

451. Are all of the numbers in a certain list of 15 numbers equal?

    (1) The sum of all the numbers in the list is 60.
    (2) The sum of any 3 numbers in the list is 12.

452. If the average (arithmetic mean) of six numbers is 75, how many of the numbers are equal to 75?

    (1) None of the six numbers is less than 75.
    (2) None of the six numbers is greater than 75.

DS16188
453. What amount did Jean earn from the commission on her sales in the first half of 1988 ?

(1) In 1988 Jean's commission was 5 percent of the total amount of her sales.
(2) The amount of Jean's sales in the second half of 1988 averaged $10,000 per month more than in the first half.

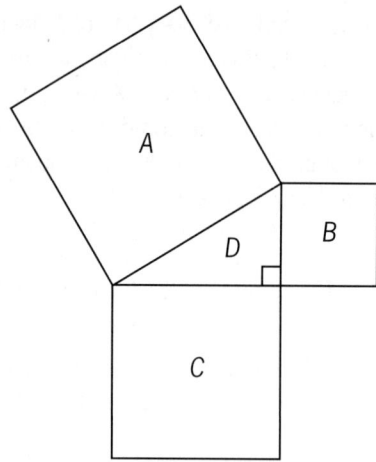

DS16572
454. In the figure above, if the area of triangular region D is 4, what is the length of a side of square region A ?

(1) The area of square region B is 9.
(2) The area of square region C is $\frac{64}{9}$.

DS16168
455. If n is a positive integer and $k = 5.1 \times 10^n$, what is the value of k ?

(1) $6{,}000 < k < 500{,}000$
(2) $k^2 = 2.601 \times 10^9$

DS06875
456. What is the value of $x + y$ in the figure above?

(1) $w = 95$
(2) $z = 125$

DS16370
457. If n and k are positive integers, is $\sqrt{n+k} > 2\sqrt{n}$?

(1) $k > 3n$
(2) $n + k > 3n$

DS16589
458. In a certain business, production index p is directly proportional to efficiency index e, which is in turn directly proportional to investment index i. What is p if $i = 70$?

(1) $e = 0.5$ whenever $i = 60$.
(2) $p = 2.0$ whenever $i = 50$.

DS16085
459. If n is a positive integer, what is the tens digit of n ?

(1) The hundreds digit of 10n is 6.
(2) The tens digit of $n + 1$ is 7.

DS16204
460. What is the value of $\frac{2t + t - x}{t - x}$?

(1) $\frac{2t}{t - x} = 3$
(2) $t - x = 5$

6.4 Answer Key

231.	E	266.	C	301.	E	336.	E	371.	C
232.	C	267.	C	302.	D	337.	D	372.	C
233.	A	268.	E	303.	E	338.	E	373.	B
234.	E	269.	B	304.	D	339.	B	374.	D
235.	D	270.	C	305.	A	340.	C	375.	C
236.	C	271.	D	306.	A	341.	D	376.	C
237.	A	272.	E	307.	D	342.	E	377.	A
238.	C	273.	C	308.	D	343.	A	378.	C
239.	C	274.	E	309.	A	344.	A	379.	E
240.	C	275.	C	310.	A	345.	C	380.	D
241.	C	276.	A	311.	A	346.	D	381.	B
242.	E	277.	E	312.	C	347.	E	382.	B
243.	C	278.	A	313.	C	348.	E	383.	D
244.	E	279.	B	314.	C	349.	B	384.	A
245.	C	280.	B	315.	D	350.	C	385.	C
246.	C	281.	B	316.	A	351.	C	386.	C
247.	D	282.	D	317.	D	352.	C	387.	C
248.	C	283.	E	318.	A	353.	A	388.	C
249.	A	284.	D	319.	A	354.	E	389.	B
250.	C	285.	D	320.	A	355.	C	390.	D
251.	C	286.	C	321.	E	356.	A	391.	A
252.	C	287.	D	322.	D	357.	E	392.	B
253.	E	288.	C	323.	B	358.	E	393.	C
254.	E	289.	D	324.	E	359.	E	394.	A
255.	C	290.	C	325.	B	360.	D	395.	B
256.	E	291.	C	326.	D	361.	E	396.	B
257.	D	292.	E	327.	D	362.	B	397.	A
258.	E	293.	D	328.	D	363.	C	398.	E
259.	D	294.	B	329.	A	364.	E	399.	D
260.	D	295.	D	330.	B	365.	E	400.	A
261.	A	296.	D	331.	C	366.	D	401.	C
262.	D	297.	B	332.	C	367.	A	402.	A
263.	D	298.	B	333.	D	368.	A	403.	A
264.	E	299.	A	334.	B	369.	D	404.	E
265.	B	300.	C	335.	B	370.	D	405.	D

406.	B	417.	B	428.	D	439.	D	450.	C
407.	D	418.	C	429.	B	440.	A	451.	B
408.	A	419.	D	430.	E	441.	E	452.	D
409.	C	420.	C	431.	B	442.	D	453.	E
410.	A	421.	C	432.	B	443.	B	454.	D
411.	D	422.	B	433.	D	444.	A	455.	D
412.	E	423.	A	434.	C	445.	A	456.	C
413.	E	424.	D	435.	D	446.	B	457.	A
414.	C	425.	A	436.	E	447.	A	458.	B
415.	D	426.	A	437.	D	448.	C	459.	A
416.	B	427.	E	438.	A	449.	B	460.	A

6.5 Answer Explanations

The following discussion of data sufficiency is intended to familiarize you with the most efficient and effective approaches to the kinds of problems common to data sufficiency. The particular questions in this chapter are generally representative of the kinds of data sufficiency questions you will encounter on the GMAT exam. Remember that it is the problem solving strategy that is important, not the specific details of a particular question.

*DS02562

231. What is the number of pages of a certain journal article?

    (1) The size of each page is $5\frac{1}{2}$ inches by 8 inches.
    (2) The average (arithmetic mean) number of words per page is 250.

Arithmetic Applied problems

(1) Given that the size of each page is $5\frac{1}{2}$ inches by 8 inches, it is clearly not possible to determine the number of pages; NOT sufficient.

(2) Given that the average number of words per page is 250, it is not possible to determine the number of pages because nothing is known about the number of words other than the number of words is a positive integer multiple of 250; NOT sufficient.

Taking (1) and (2) together, it is still not possible to determine the number of pages, because the total number of words is not known.

The correct answer is E;
both statements together are still not sufficient.

DS10471

232. If a certain vase contains only roses and tulips, how many tulips are there in the vase?

    (1) The number of roses in the vase is 4 times the number of tulips in the vase.
    (2) There is a total of 20 flowers in the vase.

Algebra Simultaneous equations

Let R and T, respectively, be the number of roses and tulips in the vase. What is the value of T?

(1) Given that $R = 4T$, it is not possible to determine the value of T. For example, $R = 4$ and $T = 1$ is possible. However, $R = 8$ and $T = 2$ is also possible; NOT sufficient.

(2) Given that $R + T = 20$, it is not possible to determine the value of T. For example, $R = 10$ and $T = 10$ is possible. However, $R = 15$ and $T = 5$ is also possible; NOT sufficient.

Taking (1) and (2) together, substituting $R = 4T$ into $R + T = 20$ gives $4T + T = 20$, or $5T = 20$, or $T = 4$.

The correct answer is C;
both statements together are sufficient.

DS03802

233. The cost of 10 pounds of apples and 2 pounds of grapes was $12. What was the cost per pound of apples?

    (1) The cost per pound of grapes was $2.
    (2) The cost of 2 pounds of apples was less than the cost of 1 pound of grapes.

Algebra Simultaneous equations

Let A be the cost, in dollars per pound, of the apples and let G be the cost, in dollars per pound, of the grapes. It is given that $10A + 2G = 12$. What is the value of A?

(1) Given that $G = 2$, it follows that $10A + 2(2) = 12$, or $10A = 8$, or $A = 0.8$; SUFFICIENT.

(2) Given that $2A < G$, different possible values of A can be found by using $10A + 2G = 12$, or $2G = 12 - 10A$, or $G = 6 - 5A$, and picking values for A, determining the corresponding values for G, and then determining whether the inequality $2A < G$ is true. Thus, the values of A and B could be, respectively, 0.8 and 2, since both

---

*These numbers correlate with the online test bank question number. See the GMAT Official Guide Online Index in the back of this book.

$10(0.8) + 2(2) = 8 + 4 = 12$ and $2(0.8) < 2$ are true. On the other hand, the values of A and B could be, respectively, 0.6 and 3, since both $10(0.6) + 2(3) = 6 + 6 = 12$ and $2(0.6) < 3$ are true; NOT sufficient.

**The correct answer is A;
statement 1 alone is sufficient.**

DS05863

234. What was the median annual salary for the employees at Company X last year?

    (1) Last year there were 29 employees at Company X.
    (2) Last year 12 employees at Company X had an annual salary of $24,000.

Arithmetic Statistics

(1) Given that there were 29 employees, the median salary cannot be determined because no information about the salaries is given; NOT sufficient.

(2) Given that there were 12 salaries of $24,000, the median salary cannot be determined. For example, if there were 12 salaries of $24,000 and 17 salaries of $20,000, then the median salary would be $20,000. On the other hand, if there were 12 salaries of $24,000 and 17 salaries of $30,000, then the median salary would be $30,000; NOT sufficient.

Taking (1) and (2) together is still not sufficient because the same examples used in (2) also satisfy (1).

**The correct answer is E;
both statements together are still not sufficient.**

DS03422

235. How many basic units of currency X are equivalent to 250 basic units of currency Y?

    (1) 100 basic units of currency X are equivalent to 625 basic units of currency Y.
    (2) 2,000 basic units of currency X are equivalent to 12,500 basic units of currency Y.

Arithmetic Ratio and proportion

Let x be the number of basic units of currency X that are equivalent to 1 basic unit of currency Y. What is the value of $250x$?

(1) Given that 100 basic units of currency X are equivalent to 625 basic units of currency Y, it follows that $\frac{100}{625}$ basic units of currency X are equivalent to 1 basic unit of currency Y. Therefore, $x = \frac{100}{625}$ and $250x = 250\left(\frac{100}{625}\right)$; SUFFICIENT.

(2) Given that 2,000 basic units of currency X are equivalent to 12,500 basic units of currency Y, it follows that $\frac{2,000}{12,500}$ basic units of currency X are equivalent to 1 basic unit of currency Y. Therefore, $x = \frac{2,000}{12,500}$ and $250x = 250\left(\frac{2,000}{12,500}\right)$; SUFFICIENT.

**The correct answer is D;
each statement alone is sufficient.**

DS12265

236. A company bought 3 printers and 1 scanner. What was the price of the scanner?

    (1) The total price of the printers and the scanner was $1,300.
    (2) The price of each printer was 4 times the price of the scanner.

Algebra Simultaneous equations

Let P_1, P_2, and P_3 be the prices, in dollars, of the 3 printers and let S be the price, in dollars, of the scanner. What is the value of S?

(1) Given that $P_1 + P_2 + P_3 + S = 1,300$, it is clear that the value of S cannot be determined; NOT sufficient.

(2) Given that $P_1 = P_2 = P_3 = 4S$, it is possible that $P_1 = P_2 = P_3 = 400$ and $S = 100$. On the other hand, it is also possible that $P_1 = P_2 = P_3 = 800$ and $S = 200$; NOT sufficient.

Taking (1) and (2) together, substituting $P_1 = 4S$, $P_2 = 4S$, and $P_3 = 4S$ into $P_1 + P_2 + P_3 + S = 1,300$ gives $4S + 4S + 4S + S = 1,300$, or $13S = 1,300$, and therefore $S = 100$.

**The correct answer is C;
both statements together are sufficient.**

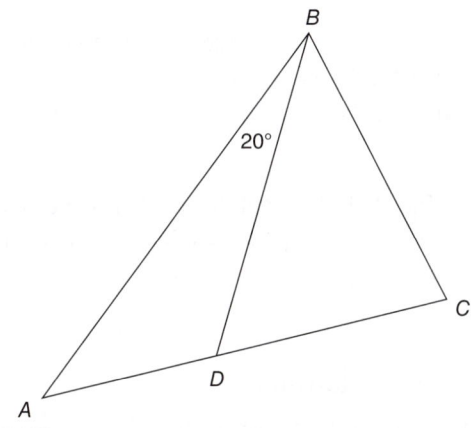

237. In the figure above, point D is on $\overline{AC}$. What is the degree measure of $\angle BAC$?

    (1) The measure of $\angle BDC$ is 60°.
    (2) The degree measure of $\angle BAC$ is less than the degree measure of $\angle BCD$.

Geometry Angles

(1) Given that the measure of $\angle BDC$ is 60°, it follows that the measure of $\angle BDA$ is 180° − 60° = 120°. Therefore, since the measures of the angles in a triangle add to 180°, the measure of $\angle BAC$ is $180 - (20° + 120°) = 40°$; SUFFICIENT.

(2) Given that the degree measure of $\angle BAC$ is less than the degree measure of $\angle BCD$, when the line segment $\overline{AC}$ rotates a few degrees counterclockwise about point A and point D stays on $\overline{AC}$, then the degree measure of $\angle BAC$ decreases (and the degree measure of $\angle BCD$ increases, and the degree measure of $\angle ABD$ remains 20°). Therefore, the degree measure of $\angle BAC$ can vary; NOT sufficient.

The correct answer is A; statement 1 alone is sufficient.

DS07822

238. Each of the 256 solid-colored marbles in a box is either blue, green, or purple. What is the ratio of the number of blue marbles to the number of purple marbles in the box?

    (1) The number of green marbles in the box is 4 times the number of blue marbles in the box.
    (2) There are 192 green marbles in the box.

Arithmetic Ratio and Proportion

Let B, G, and P be the numbers of marbles, respectively, that are blue, green, and purple.

From the given information it follows that $B + G + P = 256$. What is the value of $\frac{B}{P}$?

(1) Given that $G = 4B$, it is possible that $\frac{B}{P} = \frac{1}{251}$ (choose $B = 1$, $G = 4$, and $P = 251$) and it is possible that $\frac{B}{P} = \frac{1}{123}$ (choose $B = 2$, $G = 8$, and $P = 246$); NOT sufficient.

(2) Given that $G = 192$, it is possible that $\frac{B}{P} = \frac{1}{63}$ (choose $B = 1$, $G = 192$, and $P = 63$) and it is possible that $\frac{B}{P} = \frac{1}{31}$ (choose $B = 2$, $G = 192$, and $P = 62$); NOT sufficient.

Taking (1) and (2) together, it follows from $G = 4B$ and $G = 192$ that $192 = 4B$, or $B = 48$. Thus, $B + G + P = 256$ becomes $48 + 192 + P = 256$, and so $P = 256 − 48 − 192 = 16$. Therefore, $\frac{B}{P} = \frac{48}{16}$.

The correct answer is C; both statements together are sufficient.

DS15940

239. A certain mixture of paint requires blue, yellow, and red paints in ratios of 2:3:1, respectively, and no other ingredients. If there are ample quantities of the blue and red paints available, is there enough of the yellow paint available to make the desired amount of the mixture?

    (1) Exactly 20 quarts of the mixture are needed.
    (2) Exactly 10 quarts of the yellow paint are available.

Arithmetic Ratios

Given that the mixture requires blue paint, yellow paint, and red paint in the ratios 2:3:1, it follows that $\frac{3}{2 + 3 + 1} = \frac{1}{2}$ of the mixture will be yellow paint. Determining whether there is enough yellow paint available depends on how much of the mixture is needed and how much yellow paint is available.

(1) This indicates that exactly 20 quarts of the paint mixture are needed, so $\frac{1}{2}(20) = 10$ quarts of yellow paint are needed. However, there is no information about how much yellow paint is available; NOT sufficient.

299

(2) This indicates that exactly 10 quarts of yellow paint are available, but there is no information about how much of the mixture or how much yellow paint is needed; NOT sufficient.

Taking (1) and (2) together, 10 quarts of yellow paint are needed and 10 quarts are available.

The correct answer is C; both statements together are sufficient.

DS05338
240. The research funds of a certain company were divided among three departments, X, Y, and Z. Which one of the three departments received the greatest proportion of the research funds?

(1) The research funds received by departments X and Y were in the ratio 3 to 5, respectively.

(2) The research funds received by departments X and Z were in the ratio 2 to 1, respectively.

Algebra Order; Ratio

Let x, y, and z be the research funds, respectively, of departments X, Y, and Z. Which of $\frac{x}{x+y+z}$, $\frac{y}{x+y+z}$, or $\frac{z}{x+y+z}$ is the greatest, or respectively, which of x, y, or z is the greatest?

(1) Given that $\frac{x}{y} = \frac{3}{5}$ where x and y are positive, it follows that $x < y$. However, nothing is known about z other than z is positive, so it cannot be determined which of x, y, or z is the greatest; NOT sufficient.

(2) Given that $\frac{x}{z} = \frac{2}{1}$ where x and z are positive, it follows that $z < x$. However, nothing is known about y other than y is positive, so it cannot be determined which of x, y, or z is the greatest; NOT sufficient.

Taking (1) and (2) together, it follows from (1) that $x < y$ and it follows from (2) that $z < x$. Therefore, $z < x < y$ and y is the greatest.

The correct answer is C; both statements together are sufficient.

DS03138
241. In a certain class, some students donated cans of food to a local food bank. What was the average (arithmetic mean) number of cans donated per student in the class?

(1) The students donated a total of 56 cans of food.

(2) The total number of cans donated was 40 greater than the total number of students in the class.

Arithmetic Statistics

Let s be the number of students and let c be the number of cans. What is the value of $\frac{c}{s}$?

(1) Given that $c = 56$, it is not possible to determine the value of $\frac{c}{s}$ because nothing is known about the value of s other than s is a positive integer; NOT sufficient.

(2) Given that $c = 40 + s$, it is not possible to determine the value of $\frac{c}{s}$. For example, if $c = 40$ and $s = 40$, then $\frac{c}{s} = 1$. However, if $c = 80$ and $s = 40$, then $\frac{c}{s} = 2$; NOT sufficient.

Taking (1) and (2) together, it follows that $40 + s = c = 56$, or $s = 56 - 40 = 16$. Therefore, $c = 56$, $s = 16$, and $\frac{c}{s} = \frac{56}{16}$.

The correct answer is C; both statements together are sufficient.

DS00254
242. Each of the n employees at a certain company has a different annual salary. What is the median of the annual salaries of the n employees?

(1) When the annual salaries of the n employees are listed in increasing order, the median is the 15th salary.

(2) The sum of the annual salaries of the n employees is $913,500.

Arithmetic Statistics

(1) Given that the median is the 15th salary when the n salaries, which are all different from each other, are listed in increasing order, it follows that n is an odd number. This is because if there were an even number of salaries, where S_k and S_{k+1} are the two

middle salaries, then the median salary would be midway between the different numbers S_k and S_{k+1}, and thus the median salary could not be any of the salaries. Also, since the 15th salary is the middle salary, there must be a total of 29 salaries, as indicated below.

first 14 salaries	15th salary	last 14 salaries
$S_1, S_2, \ldots, S_{14}$	S_{15}	$S_{16}, S_{17}, \ldots, S_{29}$

However, no explicit values are given for any of the salaries, and therefore the median of the 29 salaries cannot be determined; NOT sufficient.

(2) Given that the sum of the annual salaries is $913,500, the median salary cannot be determined. For example, since $913,500 = 21 × $43,500, there could be 21 different salaries each greater than $40,000, and so the median could be greater than $40,000. However, since $913,500 = 29 × $31,500, there could be 29 different salaries each less than $35,000, and so the median could be less than $35,000; NOT sufficient.

Taking (1) and (2) together, it follows from (1) that there are 29 salaries and it follows from (2) that the sum of the salaries is $913,500. However, the median salary still cannot be determined. For example, let the first 13 salaries be $31,500 − $1,400, $31,500 − $1,300, ..., and $31,500 − $200; and let the last 13 salaries be $31,500 + $200, $31,500 + $300, ..., and $31,500 + $1,400. Then the 3 middle salaries (the 14th, 15th, and 16th salaries) could be $31,500 − $100, $31,500, and $31,500 + $100, and thus the median salary could be $31,500. However, the 3 middle salaries (the 14th, 15th, and 16th salaries) could be $31,500 − $100, $31,500 + $40, and $31,500 + $60, and thus the median salary could be $31,540.

**The correct answer is E;
both statements together are still not sufficient.**

DS10687

243. In a recent town election, what was the ratio of the number of votes in favor of a certain proposal to the number of votes against the proposal?

(1) There were 60 more votes in favor of the proposal than against the proposal.
(2) There were 240 votes in favor of the proposal.

Arithmetic Ratio and Proportion

Let F be the number of votes in favor and let A be the number of votes against. What is the value of $\frac{F}{A}$?

(1) Given that $F = 60 + A$, it is possible that $\frac{F}{A} = 2$ (choose $F = 120$ and $A = 60$) and it is possible that $\frac{F}{A} = 3$ (choose $F = 90$ and $A = 30$); NOT sufficient.

(2) Given that $F = 240$, it is possible that $\frac{F}{A} = 1$ (choose $F = 240$ and $A = 240$) and it is possible that $\frac{F}{A} = 2$ (choose $F = 240$ and $A = 120$); NOT sufficient.

Taking (1) and (2) together, substitute $F = 240$ into $F = 60 + A$ to get $240 = 60 + A$, or $A = 180$. Therefore, $\frac{F}{A} = \frac{240}{180}$.

**The correct answer is C;
both statements together are sufficient.**

DS02541

244. How many men are in a certain company's vanpool program?

(1) The ratio of men to women in the program is 3 to 2.
(2) The men and women in the program fill 6 vans.

Arithmetic Applied problems

Let m be the number of men in the program and let w be the number of women in the program. What is the value of m?

(1) Given that $\frac{m}{w} = \frac{3}{2}$, it is not possible to determine the value of m. For example, if $m = 3$ and $w = 2$, then $\frac{m}{w} = \frac{3}{2}$ is true; and if $m = 6$ and $w = 4$, then $\frac{m}{w} = \frac{3}{2}$ is true; NOT sufficient.

(2) Given that the men and women fill 6 vans, it is clearly not possible to determine the value of *m*; NOT sufficient.

Taking (1) and (2) together, it is still not possible to determine the value of *m*. Even if it is assumed that each van has the same maximum capacity, it is possible that *m* = 18 and *w* = 12 (a total of 30 people, which would fill 6 vans each having a capacity of 5 people) and it is possible that *m* = 36 and *w* = 24 (a total of 60 people, which would fill 6 vans each having a capacity of 10 people).

**The correct answer is E;
both statements together are still not sufficient.**

DS08054
245. Each of the marbles in a jar is either red or white or blue. If one marble is to be selected at random from the jar, what is the probability that the marble will be blue?

(1) There are a total of 24 marbles in the jar, 8 of which are red.
(2) The probability that the marble selected will be white is $\frac{1}{2}$.

Arithmetic Probability

This problem can be solved by determining the number of marbles in the jar and the number that are blue.

(1) This indicates that there are 24 marbles in the jar and 8 of them are red. The number of marbles that are blue is not known; NOT sufficient.

(2) This indicates neither the number of marbles in the jar nor the number that are blue; NOT sufficient.

Taking (1) and (2) together, there are 24 marbles in the jar, 8 of which are red and $\frac{1}{2}$(24) = 12 of which are white. Then, the number of blue marbles is 24 − 8 − 12 = 4, and the probability that one marble selected at random will be blue is $\frac{4}{24} = \frac{1}{6}$.

**The correct answer is C;
both statements together are sufficient.**

DS04594
246. In the figure above, what is the value of *z* ?

(1) $x = y = 1$
(2) $w = 2$

Geometry Triangles; Pythagorean theorem

(1) Given that $x = y = 1$, the length of the base of the triangle to the right, which equals $z - y = z - 1$, can vary, and thus the value of *z* can vary; NOT sufficient.

(2) Given that $w = 2$, all dimensions of the rectangle to the left can vary, and thus the value of *z* can vary; NOT sufficient.

Taking (1) and (2) together, then $z = y + (z - y) = 1 + (z - 1)$, and the value of $z - 1$ can be determined by applying the Pythagorean theorem to the triangle that has hypotenuse of length $w = 2$ and sides of lengths $x = 1$ and $z - 1$. Specifically, the Pythagorean theorem gives $1^2 + (z - 1)^2 = 2^2$, or $1 + (z - 1)^2 = 4$, and solving this equation gives $(z - 1)^2 = 3$, or $z - 1 = \sqrt{3}$, or $z = 1 + \sqrt{3}$.

**The correct answer is C;
both statements together are sufficient.**

DS04630
247. What is the value of 10 percent of *y* ?

(1) 5 percent of *y* is 60.
(2) *y* is 80 percent of 1,500.

Arithmetic Percents

This problem can be solved by determining the value of *y*.

(1) If 5 percent of *y* is 60, then $0.05y = 60$ and $y = \frac{60}{0.05} = 1,200$; SUFFICIENT.

(2) If *y* is 80 percent of 1,500, then $y = (0.80)(1,500) = 1,200$; SUFFICIENT.

**The correct answer is D;
each statement alone is sufficient.**

6.5 Data Sufficiency Answer Explanations

DS12062

248. Last semester, Professor K taught two classes, A and B. Each student in class A handed in 7 assignments, and each student in class B handed in 5 assignments. How many students were in class A?

    (1) The students in both classes combined handed in a total of 85 assignments.
    (2) There were 10 students in class B.

Algebra Simultaneous equations

Let a be the number of students in class A and let b be the number of students in class B. Then the students in class A handed in a total of $7a$ assignments and the students in class B handed in a total of $5b$ assignments. What is the value of a?

(1) Given that $7a + 5b = 85$, it is not possible to determine the value of a. For example, it is possible that $a = 5$ and $b = 10$, since $7(5) + 5(10) = 85$. On the other hand, it is also possible that $a = 10$ and $b = 3$, since $7(10) + 5(3) = 85$; NOT sufficient.

(2) Given that $b = 10$, it is not possible to determine the value of a. For example, it is possible that $a = b = 10$; and it is also possible that $a = 5$ and $b = 10$; NOT sufficient.

Taking (1) and (2) together, substituting $b = 10$ into $7a + 5b = 85$ gives $7a + 5(10) = 85$, or $7a = 35$, or $a = 5$.

The correct answer is C; both statements together are sufficient.

DS06802

249. Was the amount of John's heating bill for February greater than it was for January?

    (1) The ratio of the amount of John's heating bill for February to that for January was $\frac{26}{25}$.
    (2) The sum of the amounts of John's heating bills for January and February was $183.60.

Arithmetic Applied problems

Let J and F be the amounts, respectively and in dollars, of the heating bills for January and February. Is $F > J$?

(1) Given that $\frac{F}{J} = \frac{26}{25}$, it follows that $\frac{F}{J} > 1$. Multiplying both sides of the inequality $\frac{F}{J} > 1$ by the positive quantity J gives $F > J$; SUFFICIENT.

(2) Given that $J + F = 183.60$, it is not possible to determine whether $F > J$. For example, if $J = 83.60$ and $F = 100.00$, then $J + F = 183.60$ and $F > J$. On the other hand, if $J = 100.00$ and $F = 83.60$, then $J + F = 183.60$ and $F < J$; NOT sufficient.

The correct answer is A; statement 1 alone is sufficient.

DS06662

250. If sequence S has 120 terms, what is the 105th term of S?

    (1) The first term of S is -8.
    (2) Each term of S after the first term is 10 more than the preceding term.

Arithmetic Sequences

This problem can be solved by determining at least one term of the sequence and how each term is derived from the preceding term(s).

(1) This indicates that the first term of the sequence is -8, but does not indicate how subsequent terms are derived; NOT sufficient.

(2) This indicates how each term is derived from the preceding term, but does not indicate at least one term of the sequence; NOT sufficient.

Taking (1) and (2) together, the first term is -8 and each subsequent term is 10 more than the preceding term from which the 105th term can be determined.

The correct answer is C; both statements together are sufficient.

DS00858

251. Machine R and machine S work at their respective constant rates. How much time does it take machine R, working alone, to complete a certain job?

    (1) The amount of time that it takes machine S, working alone, to complete the job is $\frac{3}{4}$ the amount of time that it takes machine R, working alone, to complete the job.

(2) Machine R and machine S, working together, take 12 minutes to complete the job.

Algebra Applied problems

For machines R and S, let r_R and r_S be their respective rates, in jobs per minute; and let t_R and t_S be their respective times, in minutes, to complete 1 job. Then $1 = r_R t_R$ (i.e. 1 job is completed by machine R working at rate r_R for t_R minutes) and $1 = r_S t_S$ (i.e. 1 job is completed by machine S working at rate r_S for t_S minutes). What is the value of t_R?

(1) Given that $t_S = \frac{3}{4} t_R$, the value of t_R cannot be determined because nothing else is known about t_R and t_S other than they are positive real numbers; NOT sufficient.

(2) Given that 1 job is completed by machines R and S working together at a combined rate $r_R + r_S$ for 12 minutes, or $1 = (r_R + r_S)(12)$, the value of t_R cannot be determined. For example, if $r_R = \frac{1}{24}$ and $r_S = \frac{1}{24}$, then $1 = (r_R + r_S)(12)$ is true and from $1 = r_R t_R$, or $1 = \left(\frac{1}{24}\right) t_R$, it follows that $t_R = 24$. However, if $r_R = \frac{1}{48}$ and $r_S = \frac{3}{48}$, then $1 = (r_R + r_S)(12)$ is true and from $1 = r_R t_R$, or $1 = \left(\frac{1}{48}\right) t_R$, it follows that $t_R = 48$; NOT sufficient.

Taking (1) and (2) together, from (1) it follows that $t_S = \frac{3}{4} t_R$ and from (2) it follows that $(r_R + r_S)(12) = 1$, or $r_R + r_S = \frac{1}{12}$. Using $r_R = \frac{1}{t_R}$ and $r_S = \frac{1}{t_S}$ (obtained from $1 = r_R t_R$ and $1 = r_S t_S$), the last equality in the previous sentence becomes $\frac{1}{t_R} + \frac{1}{t_S} = \frac{1}{12}$. Substituting $t_S = \frac{3}{4} t_R$ into $\frac{1}{t_R} + \frac{1}{t_S} = \frac{1}{12}$ gives $\frac{1}{t_R} + \frac{1}{(3/4)t_R} = \frac{1}{12}$, or $\frac{1}{t_R} + \frac{4}{3} \times \frac{1}{t_R} = \frac{1}{12}$, or $\frac{7}{3} \times \frac{1}{t_R} = \frac{1}{12}$. Therefore, $\frac{1}{t_R} = \frac{3}{7} \times \frac{1}{12} = \frac{1}{28}$, or $t_R = 28$.

The correct answer is C; both statements together are sufficient.

DS06065
252. If $u > 0$ and $v > 0$, which is greater, u^v or v^u?

(1) $u = 1$
(2) $v > 2$

Arithmetic Exponents

(1) Given that $u = 1$, then $u^v = 1^v = 1$ and $v^u = v^1 = v$. If $v = 2$, then $u^v = 1$ is less than $v^u = 2$. However, if $v = 0.5$, then $u^v = 1$ is greater than $v^u = 0.5$; NOT sufficient.

(2) Given that $v > 2$, it is possible that u^v is less than v^u (for example, if $u = 1$ and $v = 4$, then $u^v = 1^4 = 1$ and $v^u = 4^1 = 4$), and it is possible that u^v is greater than v^u (for example, if $u = 3$ and $v = 4$, then $u^v = 3^4 = 81$ and $v^u = 4^3 = 64$); NOT sufficient.

Taking (1) and (2) together, it follows from (1) that $u^v = 1$ and $v^u = v$, and it follows from (2) that $v > 2$. Therefore, $u^v = 1 < 2 < v = v^u$, and so v^u is greater than u^v.

The correct answer is C; both statements together are sufficient.

DS00660
253. What was the range of the selling prices of the 30 wallets sold by a certain store yesterday?

(1) $\frac{1}{3}$ of the wallets had a selling price of $24 each.
(2) The lowest selling price of the wallets was $\frac{1}{3}$ the highest selling price of the wallets.

Arithmetic Statistics

Since the range of a data set is the greatest value in the data set minus the least value in the data set, this problem can be solved if the least selling price and the greatest selling price of the wallets sold by the store yesterday can be determined.

(1) This indicates that 10 of the wallets had a selling price of $24 each, but does not indicate the least selling price or the greatest selling price of the wallets sold by the store yesterday; NOT sufficient.

(2) This indicates that $L = \frac{1}{3} G$, where L represents the least selling price and G represents the greatest selling price, but does

not give enough information to determine $G - L$; NOT sufficient.

Taking (1) and (2) together, the least and greatest selling prices of the wallets sold by the store yesterday could be $10 and $30 for a range of $30 − $10 = $20, or the least and greatest selling prices of the wallets sold by the store yesterday could be $20 and $60 for a range of $60 − $20 = $40.

**The correct answer is E;
both statements together are still not sufficient.**

DS08723

254. Three houses are being sold through a real estate agent. What is the asking price for the house with the second-largest asking price?

(1) The difference between the greatest and the least asking price is $130,000.
(2) The difference between the two greater asking prices is $85,000.

Algebra Simultaneous equations

Let x, y, and z, where $x \leq y \leq z$, be the asking prices of the three houses. This problem can be solved by determining the value of y.

(1) This indicates that $z − x = \$130,000$, but does not give the value of y; NOT sufficient.

(2) This indicates that $z − y = \$85,000$, but does not give the value of y; NOT sufficient.

Taking (1) and (2) together, x, y, and z could be $100,000, $145,000, and $230,000, respectively, in which case the second highest selling price is $145,000, or they could be $200,000, $245,000, and $330,000, respectively, in which case the second highest selling price is $245,000.

**The correct answer is E;
both statements together are still not sufficient.**

DS04605

255. If $a + b + c = 12$, what is the value of b?

(1) $a + b = 8$
(2) $b + c = 6$

Algebra Simultaneous equations

(1) Given that $a + b = 8$, it follows from $(a + b) + c = 12$ that $8 + c = 12$, or $c = 4$. However, the value of b still cannot be determined. For example, if $a = 6$, $b = 2$, and $c = 4$, then $a + b + c = 12$ and $a + b = 8$. On the other hand, if $a = 4$, $b = 4$, and $c = 4$, then $a + b + c = 12$ and $a + b = 8$; NOT sufficient.

(2) Given that $b + c = 6$, it follows from $a + (b + c) = 12$ that $a + 6 = 12$, or $a = 6$. However, the value of b still cannot be determined. For example, if $a = 6$, $b = 3$, and $c = 3$, then $a + b + c = 12$ and $b + c = 6$. On the other hand, if $a = 6$, $b = 2$, and $c = 4$, then $a + b + c = 12$ and $b + c = 6$; NOT sufficient.

Taking (1) and (2) together, it follows from (1) that $c = 4$ and it follows from (2) that $a = 6$. Substituting these values in $a + b + c = 12$ gives $6 + b + 4 = 12$, or $b = 2$.

**The correct answer is C;
both statements together are sufficient.**

DS11254

256. Is $rw = 0$?

(1) $-6 < r < 5$
(2) $6 < w < 10$

Algebra Inequalities

This problem can be solved if it can be determined that either or both of r and w is zero or that neither r nor w is zero.

(1) This indicates that r can be, but does not have to be, zero and gives no indication of the value of w; NOT sufficient.

(2) This indicates that w cannot be zero, but gives no indication of the value of r; NOT sufficient.

Taking (1) and (2) together, r could be zero, in which case $rw = 0$ **or** r could be nonzero, in which case $rw \neq 0$.

**The correct answer is E;
both statements together are still not sufficient.**

257. Is $x = \frac{1}{y}$?

   (1) $xy = 1$
   (2) $\frac{1}{xy} = 1$

   Algebra Equations

   (1) This indicates that neither x nor y can be zero because if $x = 0$ or $y = 0$, then $xy = 0$. Since $xy = 1$ and $y \neq 0$, then dividing both sides by y gives $x = \frac{1}{y}$; SUFFICIENT.

   (2) This indicates that neither x nor y can be zero because if $x = 0$ or $y = 0$, then $xy = 0$, and division by zero is undefined. Multiplying both sides of the equation $\frac{1}{xy} = 1$ by x gives $\frac{1}{y} = x$; SUFFICIENT.

   **The correct answer is D;
   each statement alone is sufficient.**

258. How many people in a group of 50 own neither a fax machine nor a laser printer?

   (1) The total number of people in the group who own a fax machine or a laser printer or both is less than 50.
   (2) The total number of people in the group who own both a fax machine and a laser printer is 15.

   Algebra Sets

   (1) This indicates that the total number who own either a fax machine or a laser printer or both is less than 50, but does not indicate how much less than 50 the total number is. Thus, the number of people in the group who own neither a fax machine nor a laser printer cannot be determined; NOT sufficient.

   (2) This indicates that, of the 50 people, 15 own both a fax machine and a laser printer, but does not indicate how many own one or the other. Thus, the number of people in the group who own neither a fax machine nor a laser printer cannot be determined; NOT sufficient.

   Taking (1) and (2) together, it is known that 15 people own both a fax machine and a laser printer and that the total number who own either a fax machine or a laser printer or both is less than 50, but the exact number who own neither still cannot be determined. For example, if 20 people own only a fax machine and 10 people own only a laser printer, then both (1) and (2) are true and the number of people who own neither a fax machine nor a laser printer is $50 - 20 - 10 - 15 = 5$. However, if 10 people own only a fax machine and 10 people own only a laser printer, then both (1) and (2) are true and the number of people who own neither a fax machine nor a laser printer is $50 - 10 - 10 - 15 = 15$.

   **The correct answer is E;
   both statements together are still not sufficient.**

259. What is the value of w^{-2}?

   (1) $w^{-1} = \frac{1}{2}$
   (2) $w^3 = 8$

   Algebra Exponents

   (1) Since $w^{-1} = \frac{1}{2}$, then $(w^{-1})^2 = \left(\frac{1}{2}\right)^2 = \frac{1}{4}$ or $w^{-2} = \frac{1}{4}$; SUFFICIENT.

   (2) Since $w^3 = 8$, then $w = \sqrt[3]{8} = 2$ and $w^{-2} = 2^{-2} = \frac{1}{4}$; SUFFICIENT.

   **The correct answer is D;
   each statement alone is sufficient.**

260. A certain investment earned a fixed rate of 4 percent interest per year, compounded annually, for five years. The interest earned for the third year of the investment was how many dollars greater than that for the first year?

   (1) The amount of the investment at the beginning of the second year was $4,160.00.
   (2) The amount of the investment at the beginning of the third year was $4,326.40.

   Arithmetic Applied problems; Percents

   This problem can be solved by determining the dollar amount of the interest earned for the third year minus the dollar amount of interest earned in the first year, or, in symbols, $[A(1.04)^3 - A(1.04)^2] - [A(1.04)^1 - A]$, where A represents the dollar amount of the investment.

This can be determined if the value of A can be determined.

(1) This indicates that $A(1.04)^1 = \$4,160.00$, since the amount of the investment at the beginning of the second year is the same as the amount of the investment at the end of the first year. Thus, the value of A can be determined by dividing 4,160.00 by 1.04; SUFFICIENT.

(2) This indicates that $A(1.04)^2 = \$4,326.40$, since the amount of the investment at the beginning of the third year is the same as the amount of the investment at the end of the second year. Thus, the value of A can be determined by dividing 4,326.40 by $(1.04)^2$; SUFFICIENT.

The correct answer is D; each statement alone is sufficient.

DS06397

261. What is the circumference of circle C?

(1) The radius of circle C is 2π.
(2) The center of circle C is located at point (7,8) in the xy-plane.

Geometry Circles

What is the value of $2\pi r$, where r is the radius of circle C?

(1) Given that $r = 2\pi$, the value of $2\pi r$ is $2\pi \cdot 2\pi$; SUFFICIENT.
(2) Given that the center of circle C is located at $(7,8)$, the radius of circle C can be any positive real number, and therefore the value of $2\pi r$ cannot be determined; NOT sufficient.

The correct answer is A; statement 1 alone is sufficient.

DS07813

262. What is the value of t?

(1) $s + t = 6 + s$
(2) $t^3 = 216$

Algebra Equations

(1) Given that $s + t = 6 + s$, subtracting s from both sides gives $t = 6$; SUFFICIENT.
(2) Given that $t^3 = 216$, taking the cube root of both sides gives $t = 6$; SUFFICIENT.

The correct answer is D; each statement alone is sufficient.

DS11109

263. For a certain car repair, the total charge consisted of a charge for parts, a charge for labor, and a 6 percent sales tax on both the charge for parts and the charge for labor. If the charge for parts, excluding sales tax, was $50.00, what was the total charge for the repair?

(1) The sales tax on the charge for labor was $9.60.
(2) The total sales tax was $12.60.

Arithmetic Applied problems; Percents

To find the total charge, T, for the repair, requires determining the value, in dollars, of $T = (1.06)(50 + L) = 53 + 1.06L$, where L represents the charge, in dollars, for labor. This value can be determined if the value of L can be determined.

(1) This indicates that $0.06L = 9.60$, from which L can be determined by dividing 9.60 by 0.06; SUFFICIENT.
(2) This indicates that $(0.06)(50 + L) = 12.60$. So, $3.00 + 0.06L = 12.60$ or $0.06L = 9.60$, which is the same as the equation in (1); SUFFICIENT.

The correct answer is D; each statement alone is sufficient.

DS06905

264. George has a total of B books in his library, 25 of which are hardcover fiction books. What is the value of B?

(1) 40 of the B books are fiction and the rest are nonfiction.
(2) 60 of the B books are hardcovers and the rest are paperbacks.

Arithmetic Applied problems

The diagram below incorporates the given information that George has a total of B books, of which 25 are both fiction and hardcover. In the diagram, x represents the number of books that are fiction and not hardcover, and y represents the number of books that are hardcover and not fiction.

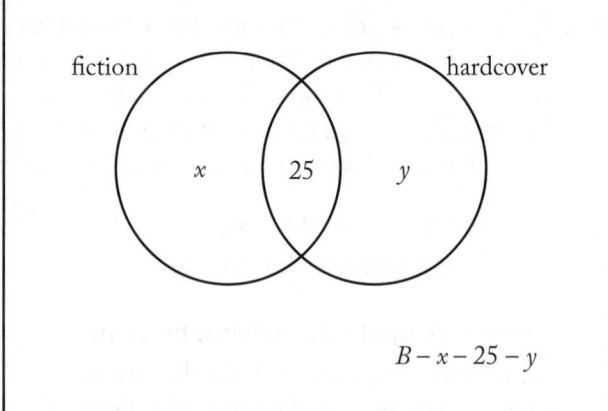

(1) Given that 40 of the books are fiction, it follows that $x + 25 = 40$, or $x = 15$. Using this additional information, the diagram (shown below) clearly shows that the value of B cannot be determined. For example, $y = 35$ and $B = 80$ is possible (note that $B - 40 - y = 5$), and $y = 35$ and $B = 100$ is possible (note that $B - 40 - y = 25$); NOT sufficient.

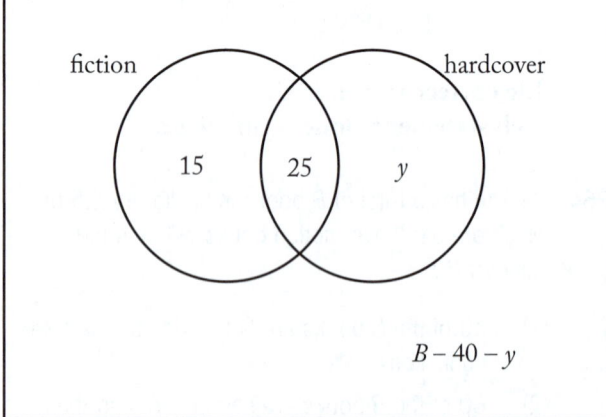

(2) Given that 60 of the books are hardcover, it follows that $25 + y = 60$, or $y = 35$. Using this additional information, the diagram (shown below) clearly shows that the value of B cannot be determined. For example, $x = 15$ and $B = 80$ is possible (note that $B - x - 60 = 5$), and $x = 15$ and $B = 100$ is possible (note that $B - x - 60 = 25$); NOT sufficient.

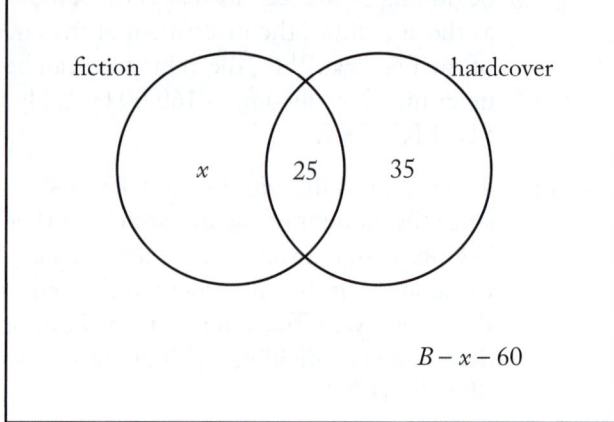

Taking (1) and (2) together, there is still not enough information to determine the value of B, since in the diagram below $B = 80$ is possible and $B = 100$ is possible.

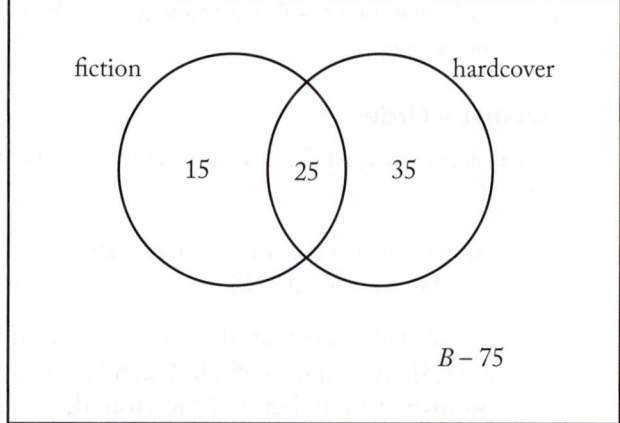

The correct answer is E; both statements together are still not sufficient.

DS12031
265. Is $w + h^4$ positive?

(1) h is positive.
(2) w is positive.

Arithmetic Properties of numbers

(1) Given that h is positive, then $w + h^4$ can be positive (for example, when $w = 1$ and $h = 1$) and $w + h^4$ can be negative (for example, when $w = -2$ and $h = 1$); NOT sufficient.

(2) Given that w is positive, then because $h^4 \geq 0$, it follows that $w + h^4 \geq w + 0 = w$ and thus $w + h^4 > 0$ since $w > 0$; SUFFICIENT.

The correct answer is B; statement 2 alone is sufficient.

DS15377
266. If a is a 3-digit integer and b is a 3-digit integer, is the units digit of the product of a and b greater than 5 ?

(1) The units digit of a is 4.
(2) The units digit of b is 7.

Arithmetic Operations with integers

Determine whether the units digit of the product of the two 3-digit integers a and b is greater than 5.

(1) It is given that the units digit of a is 4. If the units digit of b is 0 or 1, then the units digit of ab is not greater than 5. However, if the units digit of b is 2, then the units digit of ab is greater than 5; NOT sufficient.

(2) It is given that the units digit of b is 7. If the units digit of a is 0, then the units digit of ab is not greater than 5. However, if the units digit of a is 1, then the units digit of ab is greater than 5; NOT sufficient.

Taking (1) and (2) together, the units digit of a is 4 and the units digit of b is 7. Therefore, the units digit of ab is 8, which is greater than 5.

The correct answer is C; both statements together are sufficient.

DS02450
267. In each of the last five years, Company K donated p percent of its annual profits to a certain scholarship fund. Did Company K donate more than \$10,000 to the scholarship fund last year?

(1) Two years ago, Company K had annual profits of \$3 million and donated \$15,000 to the scholarship fund.
(2) Last year, Company K had annual profits of \$2.5 million.

Arithmetic Applied problems; Percents

Let \$$k$ be Company K's profit last year. Is $\left(\dfrac{p}{100}\right)k > 10{,}000$?

(1) Given that $\left(\dfrac{p}{100}\right)(3 \text{ million}) = 15{,}000$, it follows that $p = \dfrac{(15{,}000)(100)}{3 \text{ million}} = \dfrac{1}{2}$. However, the question cannot be answered since no information is available about the value of k. For example, if $k = 3$ million, then $\left(\dfrac{p}{100}\right)k = 15{,}000$, and the answer to the question is yes. However, if $k = 1$ million, then $\left(\dfrac{p}{100}\right)k = 5{,}000$, and the answer to the question is no; NOT sufficient.

(2) Given that $k = 2.5$ million, it follows that $\left(\dfrac{p}{100}\right)k = \left(\dfrac{p}{100}\right)(2.5 \text{ million})$. However, the question cannot be answered since no information is available about the value of p. For example, if $p = 1$, then $\left(\dfrac{p}{100}\right)k = 25{,}000$, and the answer to the question is yes. However, if $p = 0.1$, then $\left(\dfrac{p}{100}\right)k = 2{,}500$, and the answer to the question is no; NOT sufficient.

Taking (1) and (2) together, the values of both p and k can be determined. Therefore, the value of $\left(\dfrac{p}{100}\right)k$ can be determined, and thus the answer to the question can be determined.

The correct answer is C; both statements together are sufficient.

268. Is the area of the triangular region above less than 20 ?

    (1) $x^2 + y^2 \ne z^2$
    (2) $x + y < 13$

Geometry Triangles; Area

Determine whether the area of the given triangle is less than 20.

(1) This indicates the triangle is not a right triangle but gives no information about the base and height or how to determine them in order to find the area; NOT sufficient.

(2) This indicates that two sides of the triangle have lengths x and y such that $x + y < 13$. If, for example, the triangle is a right triangle with $x = 3$ and $y = 4$, then $x + y = 3 + 4 = 7 < 13$ and the area of the triangle is $\frac{1}{2}(3)(4) = 6$, which is less than 20. But if the triangle is a right triangle with $x = y = \sqrt{42}$, then $x + y = \sqrt{42} + \sqrt{42} = 2\sqrt{42} = \sqrt{168} < \sqrt{169} = 13$ and the area is $\frac{1}{2}(\sqrt{42})(\sqrt{42}) = 21$, which is greater than 20; NOT sufficient.

Taking (1) and (2) together, since the triangle is not a right triangle from (1), the diagrams show two other possibilities: an obtuse triangle and an acute triangle.

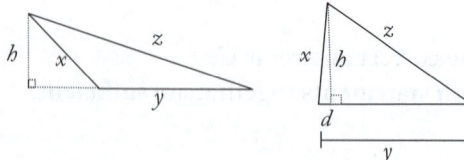

For the obtuse triangle, $h < x$ since because h is a leg of a right triangle with hypotenuse x. The area A is given by $A = \frac{1}{2}yh < \frac{1}{2}xy$. If $x = y = 6$, then $x + y = 6 + 6 = 12 < 13$ and $A < \frac{1}{2}(6^2) = 18$.

The area of the triangular region is less than 20 for the obtuse triangle. For the acute triangle,

if $x = y = \sqrt{42}$, then $x + y = \sqrt{42} + \sqrt{42} = 2\sqrt{42} = \sqrt{168} < \sqrt{169} = 13$. Let $d = 1$. Then, $h^2 = (\sqrt{42})^2 - 1 = 42 - 1 = 41$ and $h = \sqrt{41}$. Thus, for the acute triangle, the area of the triangular region is $\frac{1}{2}yh = \frac{1}{2}(\sqrt{42})(\sqrt{41})$ and $\frac{1}{2}(\sqrt{42})(\sqrt{41}) > \frac{1}{2}(\sqrt{40})(\sqrt{40})$ or $\frac{1}{2}(\sqrt{42})(\sqrt{41}) > 20$. Therefore, it is possible that the area of the triangular region can be less than 20 (in the case of the obtuse triangle) and it is possible that the area of the triangular region can be greater than 20 (in the case of the acute triangle).

The correct answer is E; both statements together are still not sufficient.

269. A, B, C, and D are points on a line. If C is the midpoint of line segment AB and if D is the midpoint of line segment CB, is the length of line segment DB greater than 5 ?

    (1) The length of line segment AC is greater than 8.
    (2) The length of line segment CD is greater than 6.

Geometry Lines and segments

It is given that C is the midpoint of $\overline{AB}$, so $AC = CB = \frac{1}{2}(AB)$. It is given that D is the midpoint of $\overline{CB}$, so $CD = DB = \frac{1}{2}(CB)$. Determine if $DB > 5$.

(1) Given that $AC > 8$, it follows that $CB > 8$ since $AC = CB$, and so $DB = \frac{1}{2}(CB) > \frac{1}{2}(8)$ or $DB > 4$. However, this means that DB could be 6 and $6 > 5$ or DB could be 4.1 and $4.1 < 5$; NOT sufficient.

(2) Given that $CD > 6$, it follows that $DB > 6$ since $CD = DB$; SUFFICIENT.

The correct answer is B; statement 2 alone is sufficient.

DS11805

270. The people in a line waiting to buy tickets to a show are standing one behind the other. Adam and Beth are among the people in the line, and Beth is standing behind Adam with a number of people between them. If the number of people in front of Adam plus the number of people behind Beth is 18, how many people in the line are behind Beth?

(1) There are a total of 32 people in the line.
(2) 23 people in the line are behind Adam.

Arithmetic Order

Beth is standing in line behind Adam with a number of people between them. Let x be the number of people ahead of Adam, let y be the number of people between Adam and Beth, and let z be the number of people behind Beth. It is given that $x + z = 18$. Determine z.

(1) This indicates that there are 32 people in the line. Two of these people are Adam and Beth, so there are 30 other people in line besides Adam and Beth. Therefore, $x + y + z = 30$ and $x + z = 18$. From this, $y = 12$, but z cannot be determined uniquely. For example, if $x = 5$, then $z = 13$, but if $x = 10$, then $z = 8$; NOT sufficient.

(2) This indicates that $y + 1 + z = 23$ because the people behind Adam consist of the people between Adam and Beth, Beth herself, and the people behind Beth. If, for example, $y = 4$, then $z = 18$, but if $y = 9$, then $z = 13$; NOT sufficient.

Taking (1) and (2) together, $y = 12$ from (1) and $y + z = 22$ from (2). Therefore, $z = 10$, and there are 10 people in line behind Beth.

**The correct answer is C;
both statements together are sufficient.**

DS08730

271. Square ABCD is inscribed in circle O. What is the area of square region ABCD ?

(1) The area of circular region O is 64π.
(2) The circumference of circle O is 16π.

Geometry Circles; Area

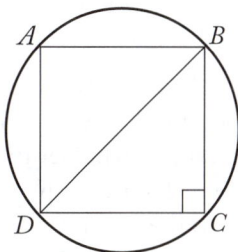

Since the area of square ABCD is the square of its side length, to solve this problem it is necessary to determine the side length of ABCD. From the figure, a diameter of the circle coincides with a diagonal of the square. If the length of a diameter of the circle can be determined, then the length of a diagonal of the square can be determined, from which the side length of the square can be determined using the Pythagorean theorem.

(1) This indicates that the area of the circle is 64π, so letting r represent the radius of the circle, $\pi r^2 = 64\pi$. Thus, $r^2 = 64$, $r = 8$, and $d = 2(8) = 16$, where d represents the length of the diameter of the circle and also the diagonal of the square; SUFFICIENT.

(2) This indicates that the circumference of the circle is 16π, so letting d represent the length of the diameter of the circle as well as the diagonal of the square, $\pi d = 16\pi$. Thus, $d = 16$; SUFFICIENT.

**The correct answer is D;
each statement alone is sufficient.**

DS12533

272. Lines k and m are parallel to each other. Is the slope of line k positive?

(1) Line k passes through the point (3,2).
(2) Line m passes through the point (–3,2).

Geometry Coordinate geometry

(1) This indicates that line k passes through the point (3,2). One point is not enough to determine whether the slope of line k is positive. If, for example, line k also passes through the point (0,0), then the slope of line k is $\frac{2-0}{3-0} = \frac{2}{3}$, which is positive. But if line k also passes through the point (5,0),

311

then the slope of line k is $\frac{2-0}{3-5} = \frac{2}{-2}$, which is negative; NOT sufficient.

(2) This indicates that line m passes through the point $(-3,2)$. One point is not enough to determine whether the slope of line m is positive. If, for example, line m also passes through the point $(0,0)$, then the slope of line m is $\frac{2-0}{-3-0} = \frac{2}{-3}$, which is negative. In this case, the slope of line k is also negative since parallel lines k and m have the same slope. But if line m also passes through the point $(0,5)$, then the slope of line m is $\frac{2-5}{-3-0} = \frac{-3}{-3}$, which is positive. In this case, the slope of line k is also positive since parallel lines k and m have the same slope; NOT sufficient.

Taking (1) and (2) together gives no more information than (1) or (2) alone and so whether the slope of line k is positive cannot be determined.

The correct answer is E; both statements together are still not sufficient.

DS19520

273. In cross section, a tunnel that carries one lane of one-way traffic is a semicircle with radius 4.2 m. Is the tunnel large enough to accommodate the truck that is approaching the entrance to the tunnel?

    (1) The maximum width of the truck is 2.4 m.
    (2) The maximum height of the truck is 4 m.

Geometry Circles; Pythagorean theorem

(1) Given that the maximum width of the truck is 2.4 m, it is possible that the tunnel is large enough (for example, if the maximum height of the truck is sufficiently small) and it is possible that the tunnel is not large enough (for example, if the maximum height of the truck is sufficiently large); NOT sufficient.

(2) Given that the maximum height of the truck is 4 m, it is possible that the tunnel is large enough (for example, if the maximum width is sufficiently small) and it is possible that the tunnel is not large enough (for example, if the maximum width of the truck is sufficiently large); NOT sufficient.

Taking (1) and (2) together, it is possible for the truck to pass through the tunnel, because even if the truck were rectangular with width 2.4 m and height 4 m, the truck could pass through the tunnel if it were centered in the tunnel as shown in the diagram. In this position, it follows from the Pythagorean theorem that every point on the truck is located at most a distance of $\sqrt{(1.2)^2 + 4^2}$ meters from the center axis of the tunnel, and this distance is less than 4.2 meters, the radius of the tunnel, since $(1.2)^2 + 4^2 = 17.44$ is less than $(4.2)^2 = 17.64$.

The correct answer is C; both statements together are sufficient.

DS13122

274. In a certain group of 50 people, how many are doctors who have a law degree?

    (1) In the group, 36 people are doctors.
    (2) In the group, 18 people have a law degree.

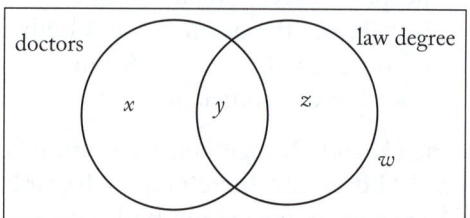

Arithmetic Sets

Using the labels in the Venn diagram, $w + x + y + z = 50$. Determine the value of y.

(1) This indicates that $x + y = 36$ but does not give a unique value for y. For example, if $x = 18$, then $y = 18$; but if $x = 10$, then $y = 26$; NOT sufficient.

(2) This indicates that $y + z = 18$ but does not give a unique value for y. For example, if $z = 8$, then $y = 10$; but if $z = 10$, then $y = 8$; NOT sufficient.

Taking (1) and (2) together, if $w = 6$, $x = 26$, $y = 10$, and $z = 8$, then $w + x + y + z = 50$, $x + y = 36$, and $y + z = 18$. In this case, $y = 10$. However, if $w = 2$, $x = 30$, $y = 6$, and $z = 12$, then $w + x + y + z = 50$, $x + y = 36$, and $y + z = 18$. In this case, $y = 6$.

Alternatively, this problem can be solved by means of a contingency table. Letting n represent the number of doctors with a law degree, the table with the given information is shown below.

	doctor	not a doctor	total
law degree	n		
no law degree			
total			50

(1) This indicates that there are 36 doctors, so the number of people who are not doctors is $50 - 36 = 14$. The table with this information is shown below.

	doctor	not a doctor	total
law degree	n		
no law degree			
total	36	14	50

It is obvious from the table that there is not enough information to determine the value of n, the number of doctors with a law degree; NOT sufficient.

(2) This indicates that there are 18 people with a law degree, so the number of people without a law degree is $50 - 18 = 32$. The table with this information is shown below.

	doctor	not a doctor	total
law degree	n		18
no law degree			32
total			50

It is obvious from the table that there is not enough information to determine the value of n, the number of doctors with a law degree; NOT sufficient.

The table with the information from both (1) and (2) is shown below.

	doctor	not a doctor	total
law degree	n		18
no law degree			32
total	36	14	50

It is obvious from the table that there is still not enough information to determine the value of n, the number of doctors with a law degree.

The correct answer is E; both statements together are still not sufficient.

DS01544

275. Of a group of 50 households, how many have at least one cat or at least one dog, but not both?

    (1) The number of households that have at least one cat and at least one dog is 4.
    (2) The number of households that have no cats and no dogs is 14.

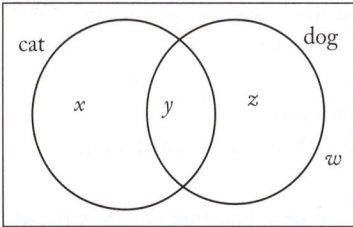

Arithmetic Sets

Using the labels on the Venn diagram, $w + x + y + z = 50$. Determine the value of $x + z$.

(1) This indicates that $y = 4$, so $w + x + z = 46$, but the value of $x + z$ cannot be uniquely determined; NOT sufficient.

(2) This indicates that $w = 14$, so $x + y + z = 36$, but the value of $x + z$ cannot be uniquely determined; NOT sufficient.

Taking (1) and (2) together, $14 + x + 4 + z = 50$, so $x + z = 50 - 14 - 4 = 32$.

The correct answer is C; both statements together are sufficient.

DS02441

276. Robin invested a total of $12,000 in two investments, X and Y, so that the investments earned the same amount of simple annual interest. How many dollars did Robin invest in investment Y?

(1) Investment X paid 3 percent simple annual interest, and investment Y paid 6 percent simple annual interest.

(2) Robin invested more than $1,000 in investment X.

Algebra Applied problems

For investments X and Y, let r_X and r_Y be the annual percentage interest rates, respectively, and let x and y be the investment amounts, respectively and in dollars. Then $x + y = 12{,}000$ and $r_X \cdot x = r_Y \cdot y$. What is the value of y?

(1) Given that $r_X = 3$ and $r_Y = 6$, then from $r_X \cdot x = r_Y \cdot y$ it follows that $3x = 6y$, or $x = 2y$. Therefore, $x + y = 12{,}000$ becomes $2y + y = 12{,}000$, or $3y = 12{,}000$, or $y = 4{,}000$; SUFFICIENT.

(2) Given that $x > 1{,}000$, it is not possible to determine the value of y. For example, $y = 4{,}000$ is possible (choose $r_X = 3$, $r_Y = 6$, and $x = 8{,}000$) and $y = 6{,}000$ is possible (choose $r_X = 3$, $r_Y = 3$, and $x = 6{,}000$); NOT sufficient.

The correct answer is A; statement 1 alone is sufficient.

DS03999

277. In a real estate office that employs n salespeople, f of them are females and x of the females are new employees. What is the value of n?

(1) If an employee were randomly selected from the n employees, the probability of selecting a female would be $\frac{2}{3}$.

(2) If an employee were randomly selected from the f female employees, the probability of selecting a new employee would be $\frac{1}{2}$.

Arithmetic Probability

(1) Given that $\frac{f}{n} = \frac{2}{3}$, it is possible that $n = 3$ (choose $f = 2$ and $x = 1$) and it is possible that $n = 6$ (choose $f = 4$ and $x = 2$); NOT sufficient.

(2) Given that $\frac{x}{f} = \frac{1}{2}$, the value of n cannot be determined because $\frac{x}{f} = \frac{1}{2}$ is true for each

of the two choices of values of $n, f,$ and x that were used in (1); NOT sufficient.

Taking (1) and (2) together is still not sufficient because both (1) and (2) hold for each of the two choices of values of $n, f,$ and x that were used in (1).

The correct answer is E; both statements together are still not sufficient.

DS09315

278. Is $\frac{x+1}{y+1} > \frac{x}{y}$?

(1) $0 < x < y$

(2) $xy > 0$

Algebra Inequalities

(1) Given that $0 < x < y$, the following steps show how to obtain $\frac{x+1}{y+1} > \frac{x}{y}$.

y	>	x	given
$xy + y$	>	$xy + x$	add xy to both sides
$y(x + 1)$	>	$x(y + 1)$	factor
$\frac{x+1}{y+1}$	>	$\frac{x}{y}$	divide both sides by $y(y + 1)$

In the last step, the direction of the inequality is not changed because both y and $y + 1$ are positive, and hence the product $y(y + 1)$ is positive. These steps can be discovered by performing standard algebraic manipulations that transform $\frac{x+1}{y+1} > \frac{x}{y}$ into $y > x$, and then verifying that it is mathematically valid to reverse the steps; SUFFICIENT.

(2) Given that $xy > 0$, it is possible that $\frac{x+1}{y+1} > \frac{x}{y}$ can be true (choosing $x = 1$ and $y = 2$, the inequality becomes $\frac{2}{3} > \frac{1}{2}$) and it is possible that $\frac{x+1}{y+1} > \frac{x}{y}$ can be false (choosing $x = -1$ and $y = -2$, the inequality becomes $\frac{0}{-1} > \frac{-1}{-2}$ or $0 > \frac{1}{2}$); NOT sufficient.

The correct answer is A; statement 1 alone is sufficient.

DS01216
279. Do at least 60 percent of the students in Pat's class walk to school?

(1) At least 60 percent of the female students in Pat's class walk to school.
(2) The number of students in Pat's class who walk to school is twice the number of students who do not walk to school.

Arithmetic Percents

This problem can be solved by determining the total number of students in Pat's class and the number who walk to school.

(1) This indicates that at least 60% of the female students in Pat's class walk to school. However, it does not give any information about the other students in Pat's class; NOT sufficient.

(2) Letting x represent the number of students in Pat's class who do not walk to school, this indicates that $2x$ students in Pat's class walk to school and that the total number of students in Pat's class is $x + 2x = 3x$. From this, the percent of students in Pat's class who walk to school is $\left[\frac{2x}{3x}100\right]\% = \left[\frac{2}{3}(100)\right]\%$; SUFFICIENT.

**The correct answer is B;
statement 2 alone is sufficient.**

DS03628
280. A certain plumber charges $92 for each job completed in 4 hours or less and $23 per hour for each job completed in more than 4 hours. If it took the plumber a total of 7 hours to complete two separate jobs, what was the total amount charged by the plumber for the two jobs?

(1) The plumber charged $92 for one of the two jobs.
(2) The plumber charged $138 for one of the two jobs.

Arithmetic Applied problems

Find the total amount charged for two jobs lasting a total of 7 hours if the plumber charges $92 for a job lasting 4 hours or less and $23 per hour for a job lasting more than 4 hours.

(1) This indicates that one of the two jobs lasted 4 hours or less. If that job lasted 2 hours, then the other job lasted 5 hours, and the charge for that job would be ($23)(5) = $115, making the total for the two jobs $92 + $115 = $207. However, if the jobs lasted 1 hour and 6 hours, respectively, then the total charge for the two jobs would be $92 + (6)($23) = $92 + $138 = $230; NOT sufficient.

(2) This indicates that one job lasted $\frac{\$138}{\$23} = 6$ hours. Therefore, the other job lasted for 1 hour and the charge for that job was $92, making the total charge for the two jobs $92 + $138 = $230; SUFFICIENT.

**The correct answer is B;
statement 2 alone is sufficient.**

DS02585
281. If x and y are positive numbers, is $\frac{x+1}{y+1} > \frac{x}{y}$?

(1) $x > 1$
(2) $x < y$

Algebra Inequalities

Since y is positive, multiplying both sides of the inequality $\frac{x+1}{y+1} > \frac{x}{y}$ by $y(y+1)$ gives $y(x+1) > x(y+1)$ or $xy + y > xy + x$, which is equivalent to $y > x$. So, determining whether the inequality $\frac{x+1}{y+1} > \frac{x}{y}$ is true is equivalent to determining whether the inequality $y > x$ is true.

(1) This indicates that $x > 1$. If, for example, $x = 3$ and $y = 4$, then $y > x$ is true. However, if $x = 4$ and $y = 3$, then $y > x$ is not true; NOT sufficient.

(2) This indicates that $x < y$, so $y > x$ is true; SUFFICIENT.

**The correct answer is B;
statement 2 alone is sufficient.**

DS01619
282. If a and b are positive integers, is $\frac{a}{b} < \frac{9}{11}$?

(1) $\frac{a}{b} < 0.818$
(2) $\frac{b}{a} > 1.223$

Arithmetic Inequalities

If $11a < 9b$ and b is positive, then $\frac{11a}{b} < 9$ and $\frac{a}{b} < \frac{9}{11}$. Therefore, this problem can be solved by determining if $11a < 9b$.

(1) From this,

$\frac{a}{b} <$ 0.818   given

$a <$ 0.818b multiply both sides by b, which is positive

$11a <$ 8.998b multiply both sides by 11

Then, since $8.998b < 9b$, it follows that $11a < 9b$; SUFFICIENT.

(2) From this,

$\frac{b}{a} >$ 1.223   given

$b >$ 1.223a multiply both sides by a, which is positive

$9b >$ 11.007a multiply both sides by 9

Then, since $11.007a > 11a$, it follows that $9b > 11a$; SUFFICIENT.

The correct answer is D; each statement alone is sufficient.

DS04536

283. Every object in a box is either a sphere or a cube, and every object in the box is either red or green. How many objects are in the box?

    (1) There are six cubes and five green objects in the box.
    (2) There are two red spheres in the box.

Arithmetic Sets

This problem can be solved using a contingency table set up as shown below, where T represents the number to be determined.

	cube	sphere	total
red			
green			
total			T

(1) The following table displays the information that there are 6 cubes and 5 green objects:

	cube	sphere	total
red			
green			5
total	6		T

It is obvious that there is not enough information to determine a unique value for T; NOT sufficient.

(2) The following table displays the information that there are 2 red spheres:

	cube	sphere	total
red		2	
green			
total			T

It is obvious that there is not enough information to determine a unique value for T; NOT sufficient.

The following table displays the information from (1) and (2) taken together:

	cube	sphere	total
red		2	
green			5
total	6		T

It is obvious that there is still not enough information to determine a unique value for T.

The correct answer is E; both statements together are still not sufficient.

DS01425

284. If x and y are positive integers, is xy even?

    (1) $x^2 + y^2 - 1$ is divisible by 4.
    (2) $x + y$ is odd.

Arithmetic Properties of numbers

Determine whether the product of two positive integers, x and y, is even.

(1) This indicates that $x^2 + y^2 - 1$ is divisible by 4, so $x^2 + y^2 - 1 = 4q$ for some integer q. Then $x^2 + y^2 = 4q + 1$, which means $x^2 + y^2$ is odd. Both x^2 and y^2 cannot be even because, in that case, their sum would be even, and both cannot be odd because, in that case, their sum would also be even. Therefore, one of x^2 and y^2 is even, and the

other is odd. It follows that one of x or y is even and the other is odd, so xy is even; SUFFICIENT.

(2) If $x + y$ is odd, then one of x and y is even and the other is odd because if both were even or both were odd, the sum would be even. It follows that xy is even; SUFFICIENT.

The correct answer is D; each statement alone is sufficient.

DS14502

285. If a and b are integers, is $a + b + 3$ an odd integer?

(1) ab is an odd integer.
(2) $a - b$ is an even integer.

Arithmetic Properties of numbers

Determine whether $a + b + 3$ is odd for integers a and b.

(1) This indicates that, since ab is odd, both a and b are odd because if one of a or b is even or both a and b are even, then ab is even. Therefore, $a + b$ is even and $a + b + 3$ is odd; SUFFICIENT.

(2) This indicates that, since $a - b$ is even, both a and b are even or both are odd because if one of them is even and the other is odd, then $a - b$ is odd. Therefore, $a + b$ is even, and $a + b + 3$ is odd; SUFFICIENT.

The correct answer is D; each statement alone is sufficient.

DS08308

286. If x and y are positive integers, what is the value of $\sqrt{x} + \sqrt{y}$?

(1) $x + y = 15$
(2) $\sqrt{xy} = 6$

Algebra Operations with radicals

(1) From this, if $x = 1$ and $y = 14$, then $x + y = 15$ and $\sqrt{x} + \sqrt{y} = \sqrt{1} + \sqrt{14} = 1 + \sqrt{14}$. But $\sqrt{14} < \sqrt{16} = 4$, so $1 + \sqrt{14} < 1 + 4 = 5$. However, if $x = 9$ and $y = 6$, then $x + y = 15$ and $\sqrt{x} + \sqrt{y} = \sqrt{9} + \sqrt{6} = 3 + \sqrt{6}$. But $\sqrt{6} > \sqrt{4} = 2$ so, $3 + \sqrt{6} > 3 + 2 = 5$; NOT sufficient.

(2) From this, if $x = 1$ and $y = 36$, then $\sqrt{xy} = 6$ and $\sqrt{x} + \sqrt{y} = \sqrt{1} + \sqrt{36} = 1 + 6 = 7$. However, if $x = 4$ and $y = 9$, then $\sqrt{xy} = 6$ and $\sqrt{x} + \sqrt{y} = \sqrt{4} + \sqrt{9} = 2 + 3 = 5$; NOT sufficient.

Taking (1) and (2) together, $x + y = 15$ and $\sqrt{xy} = 6$, so

$$\sqrt{x(15-x)} = 6 \quad \text{substitute } 15 - x \text{ for } y$$
$$x(15-x) = 36 \quad \text{square both sides}$$
$$15x - x^2 = 36 \quad \text{use distributive property}$$
$$x^2 - 15x + 36 = 0 \quad \text{collect like terms}$$
$$(x - 12)(x - 3) = 0 \quad \text{factor}$$

Thus, $x = 12$ or $x = 3$. If $x = 12$, then $y = 3$ and $\sqrt{x} + \sqrt{y} = \sqrt{12} + \sqrt{3}$. If $x = 3$, then $y = 12$ and $\sqrt{x} + \sqrt{y} = \sqrt{3} + \sqrt{12}$.

Algebraically, if the value of $\left(\sqrt{x} + \sqrt{y}\right)^2 = \left(\sqrt{x}\right)^2 + 2\sqrt{xy} + \left(\sqrt{y}\right)^2 = x + y + 2\sqrt{xy}$ can be determined, then the value of $\sqrt{x} + \sqrt{y}$ can be determined, and conversely.

(1) From this, $\left(\sqrt{x} + \sqrt{y}\right)^2 = x + y + 2\sqrt{xy} = 15 + 2\sqrt{x(15-x)}$, but the value of x is unknown, and the value of $\left(\sqrt{x} + \sqrt{y}\right)^2$ cannot be determined; NOT sufficient.

(2) From this, $\left(\sqrt{x} + \sqrt{y}\right)^2 = x + y + 2\sqrt{xy} = x + \frac{36}{x} + 2(6)$, but the value of x is unknown, and the value of $\left(\sqrt{x} + \sqrt{y}\right)^2$ cannot be determined; NOT sufficient.

Taking (1) and (2) together, $\left(\sqrt{x} + \sqrt{y}\right)^2 = x + y + 2\sqrt{xy} = 15 + (2)(6) = 27$ and so $\sqrt{x} + \sqrt{y} = \sqrt{27} = 3\sqrt{3}$. Note that in the nonalgebraic solution $\sqrt{x} + \sqrt{y} = \sqrt{3} + \sqrt{12}$ and $\sqrt{3} + \sqrt{12} = \sqrt{3} + 2\sqrt{3} = 3\sqrt{3}$.

The correct answer is C; both statements together are sufficient.

287. A certain truck uses $\frac{1}{12} + kv^2$ gallons of fuel per mile when its speed is v miles per hour, where k is a constant. At what speed should the truck travel so that it uses $\frac{5}{12}$ gallon of fuel per mile?

(1) The value of k is $\frac{1}{10,800}$.

(2) When the truck travels at 30 miles per hour, it uses $\frac{1}{6}$ gallon of fuel per mile.

Algebra Applied problems

This problem can be solved by determining the positive value of v so that $\frac{1}{12} + kv^2 = \frac{5}{12}$.

(1) This indicates the value of k and so the value of v can be determined by solving $\frac{1}{12} + \frac{1}{10,800}v^2 = \frac{5}{12}$ for v; SUFFICIENT.

(2) This indicates that $\frac{1}{12} + k(30)^2 = \frac{1}{6}$. The value of k can be determined by solving this equation for k. Then that value of k can be substituted into $\frac{1}{12} + kv^2 = \frac{5}{12}$, which can then be solved for the value of v; SUFFICIENT.

The correct answer is D; each statement alone is sufficient.

288. If r and s are positive integers, is $r + s$ even?

(1) r is even.
(2) s is even.

Arithmetic Properties of integers

An integer m is even if and only if m is divisible by 2, or equivalently, if and only if $m = 2M$ for some integer M. Is $r + s$ even?

(1) Given that r is even, $r + s$ could be even (choose $r = 2$ and $s = 2$) and $r + s$ could be odd (choose $r = 2$ and $s = 1$); NOT sufficient.

(2) Given that s is even, $r + s$ could be even (choose $r = 2$ and $s = 2$) and $r + s$ could be odd (choose $r = 1$ and $s = 2$); NOT sufficient.

Taking (1) and (2) together, let R and S be integers such that $r = 2R$ and $s = 2S$. Then $r + s = 2R + 2S = 2(R + S)$, where $R + S$ is an integer. Therefore, $r + s$ is even.

The correct answer is C; both statements together are sufficient.

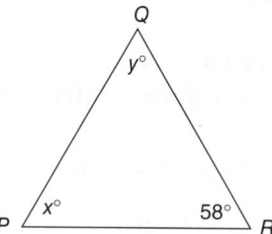

289. In the figure above, $\triangle PQR$ has angle measures as shown. Is $x < y$?

(1) $PQ = QR$
(2) $PR > QR$

Geometry Triangles

(1) Given that $PQ = QR$, it follows that the angle at vertex R has the same measure as the angle at vertex P, or $58 = x$. Therefore, using $x + y + 58 = 180$ gives $58 + y + 58 = 180$, or $y = 64$. Since the values of both x and y are now known, it can be determined whether $x < y$; SUFFICIENT.

(2) Given that $PR > QR$, it follows that the measure of the angle at vertex Q is greater than the measure of the angle at vertex P, or $y > x$; SUFFICIENT.

The correct answer is D; each statement alone is sufficient.

290. If S is a set of odd integers and 3 and −1 are in S, is −15 in S?

(1) 5 is in S.
(2) Whenever two numbers are in S, their product is in S.

Arithmetic Operations with integers

(1) Given that 5 is in S, it is not possible to determine whether −15 is in S. For example, if $S = \{-15, -1, 3, 5\}$, then S is a set of odd

integers, 3 and −1 are in S, and −15 is in S. However, if $S = \{−1, 3, 5\}$, then S is a set of odd integers, 3 and −1 are in S, and −15 is not in S; NOT sufficient.

(2) Given that xy is in S whenever x is in S and y is in S, it is possible that −15 is in S, since S could be the set of all odd integers, and in this case S contains 3 and −1, along with −15, and S is such that the product of any two of its members is a member (because an odd integer times an odd integer is an odd integer). However, it is also possible that −15 is not in S, since S could be the set of all nonnegative integer powers of 3, along with their negatives, namely $S = \{…, −27, −9, −3, −1, 1, 3, 9, 27, …\}$. In this case, S is a set of odd integers that contains 3 and −1, but not −15, and S is such that the product of any two of its members is a member (if m and n are integers, then 3^m times 3^n is 3^{m+n}); NOT sufficient.

Taking (1) and (2) together, apply (2) for $x = 3$ and $y = 5$ to get $(3)(5) = 15$ in S. Now apply (2) for $x = −1$ and $y = 15$ to get −15 in S.

The correct answer is C; both statements together are sufficient.

DS01602.01
291. Is the integer x a 3-digit integer?

(1) x is the square of an integer.
(2) $90 < x < 150$

Arithmetic Properties of integers

(1) Given that x is the square of an integer, both $x = 16$ (not a 3-digit integer) and $x = 100$ (a 3-digit integer) are possible; NOT sufficient.

(2) Given that $90 < x < 150$, both $x = 95$ (not a 3-digit integer) and $x = 100$ (a 3-digit integer) are possible; NOT sufficient.

From (1) and (2) taken together, it follows that x is among the numbers …, 81, 100, 121, 144, 169, … and $90 < x < 150$. Therefore, x must be one of the three numbers 100, 121, 144, and hence x must be a 3-digit integer.

The correct answer is C; both statements together are sufficient.

DS11602.01
292. If the 1st term of a sequence is 0 and the 2nd term is 1, is the 5th term 2?

(1) Each odd-numbered term is either 0 or 2.
(2) The 3rd term is 2.

Arithmetic Series and sequences

Let the sequence be 0, 1, a, b, c. Is $c = 2$?

(1) Given that $a = 0$ or $a = 2$, and $c = 0$ or $c = 2$, it is possible that $c = 2$ (consider the sequence 0, 1, 2, 2, 2) and it is possible that $c \neq 2$ (consider the sequence 0, 1, 2, 0, 0); NOT sufficient.

(2) Given that $a = 2$, the same examples given in (1) show that it is not possible to determine whether $c = 2$; NOT sufficient.

Taking (1) and (2) together, it is still not possible to determine whether $c = 2$ because the same examples were used for both (1) and (2).

The correct answer is E; both statements together are still not sufficient.

DS21602.01
293. Is the sum of four particular integers even?

(1) Two of the integers are odd and two are even.
(2) The average (arithmetic mean) of the four integers is an integer.

Arithmetic Properties of integers

(1) Given that two of the integers are odd and two of the integers are even, the sum of the four integers must be the sum of an even integer (this being the sum of the two odd integers) and an even integer (this being the sum of the two even integers). Since the sum of two even integers is even, it follows that the sum of the four integers is even; SUFFICIENT.

(2) Given that the average of the four integers is an integer, it follows that the sum of the four integers divided by four is an integer, and hence the sum of the integers is four times an integer. Since four times an integer is even, it follows that the sum of the four integers is even; SUFFICIENT.

The correct answer is D; each statement alone is sufficient.

DS70602.01
294. If a school district paid a total of $35 per desk for x desks and a total of $30 per table for y tables, what was the total amount that the district paid for these desks and tables?

(1) The total amount the district paid for the y tables was $900.
(2) x = 90, and the total amount the district paid for the x desks was 3.5 times the total amount the district paid for the y tables.

Algebra Simultaneous equations

Determine the value of $35x + 30y$.

(1) Given that $30y = 900$, it follows that $y = 30$. However, it is not possible to determine the value of $35x + 30y = 35x + 900$ because more than one possible value of x is possible; NOT sufficient.

(2) Given that $x = 90$ and $35x = 3.5(30y)$, it follows that $(35)(90) = (3.5)(30)y$, or $y = \frac{35}{3.5} \times \frac{90}{30} = 10 \times 3 = 30$, and therefore $35x + 30y = 35(90) + 30(30)$; SUFFICIENT.

**The correct answer is B;
statement 2 alone is sufficient.**

DS90602.01
295. Three children inherited a total of X dollars. If the oldest child inherited $7,000 more than the youngest child, and the youngest child inherited $9,000 less than the middle child, what is the value of X?

(1) The middle child inherited $27,000.
(2) The youngest child and the middle child together inherited a total of $45,000.

Algebra Simultaneous equations

Let A, B, and C be the amounts inherited, respectively and in dollars, of the oldest, middle, and youngest child. It is given that $A = 7{,}000 + C$ and $C = B - 9{,}000$. Then $A = 7{,}000 + (B - 9{,}000) = B - 2{,}000$. Determine the value of $A + B + C$, or equivalently, determine the value of $(B - 2{,}000) + B + (B - 9{,}000) = 3B - 11{,}000$.

(1) Given that $B = 27{,}000$, it follows that $3B - 11{,}000 = 70{,}000$; SUFFICIENT.

(2) Given that $B + C = 45{,}000$, then using $C = B - 9{,}000$ it follows that $B + (B - 9{,}000) = 45{,}000$, which can be solved to obtain $B = 27{,}000$. Therefore, $3B - 11{,}000 = 70{,}000$; SUFFICIENT.

**The correct answer is D;
each statement alone is sufficient.**

DS41602.01
296. If xyz ≠ 0, what is the value of $\frac{x^4 z^2}{z^2 y^2}$?

(1) $y^2 = x^4$
(2) $x = 2$ and $y = 4$

Algebra Simplifying algebraic expressions

What is the value of $\frac{x^4 z^2}{z^2 y^2}$? Equivalently (since $z \neq 0$), what is the value of $\frac{x^4}{y^2}$?

(1) Given that $y^2 = x^4$, then dividing both sides of this equation by y^2 gives $1 = \frac{x^4}{y^2}$; SUFFICIENT.

(2) Given that $x = 2$ and $y = 4$, then $\frac{x^4}{y^2} = \frac{2^4}{4^2} = \frac{16}{16} = 1$; SUFFICIENT.

**The correct answer is D;
each statement alone is sufficient.**

DS81602.01
297. If a and b are integers, and b > 0, does $\frac{a-1}{b+1} = \frac{a}{b}$?

(1) $a = b - 4$
(2) $a = -b$

Algebra Ratios

(1) Given that $a = b - 4$, then $\frac{a-1}{b+1} = \frac{a}{b}$ can be true (use $a = -2$ and $b = 2$) and $\frac{a-1}{b+1} = \frac{a}{b}$ can be false (use $a = -3$ and $b = 1$); NOT sufficient.

(2) Given that $a = -b$, then $\frac{a-1}{b+1} = \frac{-b-1}{b+1} = \frac{-(b+1)}{b+1} = -1$ and $\frac{a}{b} = \frac{-b}{b} = -1$; SUFFICIENT.

**The correct answer is B;
statement 2 alone is sufficient.**

298. In a sequence of numbers in which each term is 2 more than the preceding term, what is the fourth term?

   (1) The last term is 90.
   (2) The first term is 2.

   Arithmetic Series and sequences

   (1) Given that the last term is 90, then the sequence could be 2, 4, 6, 8, …, 90 with the fourth term equal to 8, and the sequence could be 84, 86, 88, 90 with the fourth term equal to 90; NOT sufficient.

   (2) Given that the first term is 2, then the second term must be $2 + 2 = 4$, the third term must be $4 + 2 = 6$, and the fourth term must be $6 + 2 = 8$; SUFFICIENT.

   The correct answer is B; statement 2 alone is sufficient.

299. Is the integer p divisible by 5?

   (1) p is divisible by 10.
   (2) p is not divisible by 15.

   Arithmetic Properties of integers

   (1) If p is divisible by 10, then $p = 10q$ for some integer q. So, $p = (5)(2q)$ and p is divisible by 5; SUFFICIENT.

   (2) If p is not divisible by 15, then p could be 20, for example, and 20 is divisible by 5. But, p could also be 21, for example, and 21 is not divisible by 5; NOT sufficient.

   The correct answer is A; statement 1 alone is sufficient.

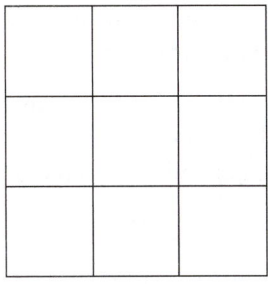

300. The 9 squares above are to be filled with x's and o's, with only one symbol in each square. How many of the squares will contain an x?

   (1) More than $\frac{1}{2}$ of the number of squares will contain an o.
   (2) Each of the 4 corner squares will contain an x.

   Arithmetic Properties of numbers

   (1) If more than $\frac{1}{2}$ of the squares will contain an o, then 5, 6, 7, 8, or 9 of the squares will contain an o. The rest will contain x's, and so 4, 3, 2, 1, or 0 of the squares will contain an x; NOT sufficient.

   (2) Since each of the 4 corner squares will contain an x, the number of squares that will contain an x could be 4, 5, 6, 7, 8, or 9; NOT sufficient.

   Taking (1) and (2) together, from (1), the number of squares containing x's will be 4, 3, 2, 1, or 0, while from (2), the number of squares containing x's will be 4, 5, 6, 7, 8, or 9. Therefore, the number of squares containing x's will be 4.

   The correct answer is C; both statements together are sufficient.

301. Is the sum of two integers divisible by 10?

   (1) One of the integers is even.
   (2) One of the integers is a multiple of 5.

   Arithmetic Properties of integers

   (1) If one of the integers is 10, which is even, and the other is 2, then $10 + 2 = 12$, which is not divisible by 10. However, if the other integer is 20, then $10 + 20 = 30$, which is divisible by 10; NOT sufficient.

321

(2) Note that the examples in (1) also satisfy (2); NOT sufficient.

Since the examples used to show that (1) is not sufficient also show that (2) is not sufficient, it follows that (1) and (2) taken together are not sufficient.

The correct answer is E; both statements together are still not sufficient.

DS22602.01

302. Is x an integer?

   (1) $x^3 = 8$
   (2) $x = \sqrt{4}$

Algebra Exponents and radicals

(1) If $x^3 = 8$, then $x = \sqrt[3]{8} = 2$, which is an integer; SUFFICIENT.

(2) If $x = \sqrt{4}$, then $x = 2$, which is an integer; SUFFICIENT.

The correct answer is D; each statement alone is sufficient.

DS42602.01

303. If a building has 6,000 square meters of floor space, how many offices are in the building?

   (1) Exactly $\frac{1}{4}$ of the floor space is not used for offices.
   (2) There are exactly 20 executive offices and each of these occupies 3 times as much floor space as the average for all of the remaining offices.

Algebra Simultaneous equations

(1) If exactly $\frac{1}{4}$ of the floor space is not used for offices, then a total of $\frac{3}{4}(6,000) = 4,500$ square meters of floor space is used for offices. However, there is no information on how this floor space is divided up among the offices. There could be 10 offices each occupying 450 square meters of floor space, or there could be 100 offices each occupying 45 square meters of floor space; NOT sufficient.

(2) Since there is no information on how much of the 6,000 square meters of floor space is occupied by offices, it is not possible to determine how many offices are in the building. For example, if all 6,000 square feet of floor space is used for offices, there could be 40 non-executive offices each occupying 60 square meters and 20 executive offices each occupying $(3)(60) = 180$ square meters since $(40)(60) + (20)(180) = 2,400 + 3,600 = 6,000$. Or, if offices occupy only 4,500 square meters of floor space, there could be 30 non-executive offices each occupying 50 square meters and 20 executive offices each occupying $(3)(50) = 150$ square meters since $(30)(50) + (20)(150) = 1,500 + 3,000 = 4,500$; NOT sufficient.

With (1) and (2) taken together, (1) implies that 4,500 square meters of floor space is used for offices. If n represents the number of non-executive offices and f represents the average amount, in square meters, occupied by these offices then nf represents the total square meters of floor space occupied by the non-executive offices. By (2), there are 20 executive offices, each occupying $3f$ square meters of floor space. Thus, the total square meters of floor space occupied by all of the offices combined is $nf + (20)(3f) = 4,500$, or $f(n + 60) = 4,500$. Multiple values for n and f satisfy this equation. For example, if $n = 30$ and $f = 50$, then $(50)(30 + 60) = (50)(90) = 4,500$. Also, if $n = 15$ and $f = 60$, then $(60)(15 + 60) = (60)(75) = 4,500$.

The correct answer is E; both statements together are still not sufficient.

DS43602.01

304. If p, r, and s are consecutive integers in ascending order and x is the average (arithmetic mean) of the three integers, what is the value of x?

   (1) Twice x is equal to the sum of p, r, and s.
   (2) The sum of p, r, and s is zero.

Algebra Statistics

(1) It is given that twice x is equal to the sum of p, r, and s, or $2x = p + r + s$. Because x is the average of p, r, and s, it follows that $3x = p + r + s$ and so $2x = 3x$. Therefore, $x = 0$; SUFFICIENT

(2) It is given that $p + r + s = 0$. Since $x = \frac{p+r+s}{3}$, it follows that $x = \frac{0}{3} = 0$; SUFFICIENT.

The correct answer is D; each statement alone is sufficient.

DS53602.01

305. If m and n are integers, what is the value of $m + n$?

   (1) $(x + m)(x + n) = x^2 + 5x + mn$ and $x \neq 0$.
   (2) $mn = 4$

Algebra Simplifying algebraic expressions

(1) Since it is given that $(x + m)(x + n) = x^2 + 5x + mn$ and it is also true that $(x + m)(x + n) = x^2 + (m + n)x + mn$, it follows that $m + n = 5$; SUFFICIENT.

(2) Given that $mn = 4$, it is possible that $m = 1$ and $n = 4$, which means that $m + n = 5$. But it is also possible that $m = 2$ and $n = 2$, which means that $m + n = 4$; NOT sufficient.

The correct answer is A; statement 1 alone is sufficient.

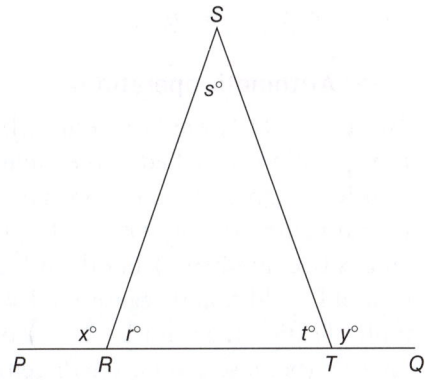

DS63602.01

306. In the figure above, RST is a triangle with angle measures as shown and $PRTQ$ is a line segment. What is the value of $x + y$?

   (1) $s = 40$
   (2) $r = 70$

Geometry Triangles

(1) Given that $s = 40$, then $180 = 40 + r + t$ and $140 = r + t$. Also, $x + r = 180$ and $t + y = 180$, so $(x + y) + (r + t) = 360$, which means that $(x + y) + 140 = 360$. Therefore, $(x + y) = 360 - 140 = 220$; SUFFICIENT.

(2) If $r = 70$, then $x = 180 - 70 = 110$. Since $r + s + t = 180$, then $s + t = 180 - r = 180 - 70 = 110$, from which it follows that $x = s + t$. By similar reasoning, $y = r + s = 70 + s$. Therefore, the value of $x + y$ depends on the values of s and t, which can be any two positive integers whose sum is 110. For example, if $s = 70$ and $t = 40$, then $x + y = 110 + 140 = 250$, but if $s = 50$ and $t = 60$, then $x + y = 110 + 120 = 230$; NOT sufficient.

The correct answer is A; statement 1 alone is sufficient.

DS04602.01

307. If R, S, and T are points on a line, and if R is 5 meters from T and 2 meters from S, how far is S from T?

   (1) R is between S and T.
   (2) S is to the left of R, and T is to the right of R.

Geometry Lines and segments

(1) It is given that R is between S and T, so the placement of R, S, and T is shown by either

or

In either case, the distance from S to T is 7 meters; SUFFICIENT.

(2) It is given that S is to the left of R, and T is to the right of R, so the placement of R, S, and T is shown by

The distance from S to T is 7 meters; SUFFICIENT.

The correct answer is D; each statement alone is sufficient.

308. Is n equal to zero?

   (1) The product of n and some nonzero number is 0.
   (2) The sum of n and 0 is 0.

   Arithmetic Properties of numbers

   (1) If x represents a nonzero number, then from (1), $nx = 0$. If the product of two numbers is 0, one or both of the numbers must be 0. Since x is nonzero, it follows that $n = 0$; SUFFICIENT.

   (2) Given $n + 0 = 0$, then by a property of the integer 0, namely that $n + 0 = n$ for any number n, it follows that $n = 0$; SUFFICIENT.

   The correct answer is D; each statement alone is sufficient.

309. On a map, $\frac{1}{2}$ inch represents 100 miles. According to this map, how many miles is City X from City Y?

   (1) City X is 3 inches from City Y on the map.
   (2) Cities X and Y are each 300 miles from City Z.

   Algebra Measurement conversion

   (1) Letting d represent the distance, in miles, from City X to City Y, given that City X is 3 inches from City Y on a map where $\frac{1}{2}$ inch represents 100 miles, the following proportion can be solved for d.
   $$\frac{\frac{1}{2}}{3} = \frac{100}{d}; \text{SUFFICIENT.}$$

   (2) Given that each of Cities X and Y is 300 miles from City Z, if points X, Y, and Z representing these cities on the map are on a straight line, then the distance between Cities X and Y is $300 + 300 = 600$ miles. However, if points X, Y, and Z are the vertices of a triangle on the map, the distance is less than 600 miles because the length of the third side of a triangle is less than the sum of the lengths of the other two sides; NOT sufficient.

   The correct answer is A; statement 1 alone is sufficient.

310. What is the remainder when the positive integer n is divided by 5?

   (1) When n is divided by 3, the quotient is 4 and the remainder is 1.
   (2) When n is divided by 4, the remainder is 1.

   Arithmetic Properties of integers

   (1) Given that the quotient is 4 and the remainder is 1 when n is divided by 3, it follows that $n = (3)(4) + 1 = 13$. Since 13 is 3 more than a multiple of 5, the remainder when n is divided by 5 is 3; SUFFICIENT.

   (2) Given that the remainder is 1 when n is divided by 4, $n = 5$ is possible (has remainder 0 when divided by 5) and $n = 9$ is possible (has remainder 4 when divided by 5); NOT sufficient.

   The correct answer is A; statement 1 alone is sufficient.

311. If r and s are positive numbers and θ is one of the operations, $+$, $-$, $\times$, or $\div$, which operation is θ?

   (1) If $r = s$, then $r \theta s = 0$.
   (2) If $r \neq s$, then $r \theta s \neq s \theta r$.

   Arithmetic Arithmetic operations

   (1) Given that 0 is always the result when the operation is applied to the same two positive numbers, then the operation can be subtraction (because $r - r = 0$ is true for all positive numbers r), but the operation cannot be addition (because $1 + 1 \neq 0$), multiplication (because $1 \times 1 \neq 0$), or division (because $1 \div 1 \neq 0$). Therefore, the operation must be subtraction; SUFFICIENT.

   (2) Given that if $r \neq s$, then $r \theta s \neq s \theta r$, or equivalently (by forming the logical contrapositive), if $r \theta s = s \theta r$, then $r = s$, it is not possible to determine the operation θ. Subtraction satisfies this condition, because from $r - s = s - r$ it follows that $2r = 2s$ and $r = s$. Division satisfies this condition, because from $r \div s = s \div r$, or $\frac{r}{s} = \frac{s}{r}$, it follows that $r^2 = s^2$ and $r = s$ (the possibility $r = -s$ is excluded because r and

s are nonzero positive numbers). Therefore, both subtraction and division satisfy this condition; NOT sufficient.

The correct answer is A; statement 1 alone is sufficient.

DS57502.01

312. In any sequence of n nonzero numbers, a pair of consecutive terms with opposite signs represents a sign change. For example, the sequence –2, 3, –4, 5 has three sign changes. Does the sequence of nonzero numbers $s_1, s_2, s_3, \ldots, s_n$ have an even number of sign changes?

    (1) $s_k = (-1)^k$ for all positive integers k from 1 to n.
    (2) n is odd.

Arithmetic Series and sequences

(1) Given that the sequence is a certain number of initial terms of $(-1)^1 = -1, (-1)^2 = 1, (-1)^3 = -1, (-1)^4 = 1, \ldots$, then it is possible to have an even number of sign changes (–1, 1, –1 has 2 sign changes) and it is possible to have an odd number of sign changes (–1, 1 has 1 sign change); NOT sufficient.

(2) Given that n is odd, then it is possible to have an even number of sign changes (–1, 1, –1 has 2 sign changes and $n = 3$) and it is possible to have an odd number of sign changes (1, 1, –1 has 1 sign change and $n = 3$); NOT sufficient.

Taking (1) and (2) together, then the sequence begins with –1 followed by a certain number of repetitions (possibly zero repetitions) of 1, –1. For example, if $n = 1$, then the sequence consists of the single term –1 (has 0 sign changes). If $n = 3$, then the sequence consists of the 3 terms –1, 1, –1 (has 2 sign changes). If $n = 5$, then the sequence consists of the 5 terms –1, 1, –1, 1, –1 (has 4 sign changes). Since each of these has an even number of sign changes, and each additional inclusion of the two terms 1, –1 adds 2 additional sign changes, the number of sign changes will always be even.

The correct answer is C; both statements together are sufficient.

DS86502.01

313. Jack picked 76 apples. Of these, he sold 4y apples to Juanita and 3t apples to Sylvia. If he kept the remaining apples, how many apples did he keep? (t and y are positive integers.)

    (1) $y \geq 15$ and $t = 2$
    (2) $y = 17$

Algebra Simultaneous equations

Determine the value of the nonnegative integer $76 - 4y - 3t$.

(1) Given that $y \geq 15$ and $t = 2$, it follows that $76 - 4y - 3t = 76 - 4y - 6 = 70 - 4y$ could have the value $70 - 4(15) = 10$, $70 - 4(16) = 6$, or $70 - 4(17) = 2$; NOT sufficient.

(2) Given that $y = 17$, it follows that $76 - 4y - 3t = 76 - 68 - 3t = 8 - 3t$ could have the value $8 - 3(1) = 5$ or $8 - 3(2) = 2$; NOT sufficient.

Taking (1) and (2) together, it follows that $76 - 4y - 3t = 76 - 4(17) - 3(2) = 2$.

The correct answer is C; both statements together are sufficient.

DS47502.01

314. What number is 6 more than $x + y$?

    (1) y is 3 less than x.
    (2) y is twice x.

Algebra Simultaneous equations

Determine the value of $x + y + 6$.

(1) Given that $y = x - 3$, $x + y + 6$ could be 15 (use $x = 6$ and $y = 3$) and $x + y + 6$ could be 21 (use $x = 9$ and $y = 6$); NOT sufficient.

(2) Given that $y = 2x$, $x + y + 6$ could be 9 (use $x = 1$ and $y = 2$) and $x + y + 6$ could be 12 (use $x = 2$ and $y = 4$); NOT sufficient.

Taking (1) and (2) together, then $y = x - 3$ and $y = 2x$ both hold. Therefore, $x - 3 = 2x$, or $x = -3$, and hence $y = 2(-3) = -6$. It follows that $x + y + 6 = (-3) + (-6) + 6 = -3$.

The correct answer is C; both statements together are sufficient.

315. The total price of 5 pounds of regular coffee and 3 pounds of decaffeinated coffee was $21.50. What was the price of the 5 pounds of regular coffee?

(1) If the price of the 5 pounds of regular coffee had been reduced 10 percent and the price of the 3 pounds of decaffeinated coffee had been reduced 20 percent, the total price would have been $18.45.
(2) The price of the 5 pounds of regular coffee was $3.50 more than the price of the 3 pounds of decaffeinated coffee.

Algebra Simultaneous equations

Let x be the price of 5 pounds of regular coffee and let y be the price of 3 pounds of decaffeinated coffee. Then $x + y = 21.5$. Determine the value of x.

(1) Given that $0.9x + 0.8y = 18.45$, then the values of both x and y can be determined, because $x + y = 21.5$ and $0.9x + 0.8y = 18.45$ can be interpreted as equations of nonparallel lines in the coordinate plane that have a single point of intersection. One way to determine that the lines are not parallel is to show that their slopes are different. In the case of $x + y = 21.5$, the equation can be rewritten as $y = -x + 21.5$, and hence the slope is -1. In the case of $0.9x + 0.8y = 18.45$, the equation can be rewritten as $0.8y = -0.9x + 18.45$, or $y = -\frac{0.9}{0.8}x + \frac{18.45}{0.8}$, and hence the slope is $-\frac{0.9}{0.8}$. Since $-1 \neq -\frac{0.9}{0.8}$, the slopes are different, and therefore the lines are not parallel. Although showing that the lines are not parallel is enough to show that (1) is sufficient, one may instead solve the equations simultaneously. This gives the solution $x = 12.5$ and $y = 9$; SUFFICIENT.

(2) Given that $x = 3.5 + y$, then the values of both x and y can be determined in the same way as in (1) above. The slope of $x + y = 21.5$ was shown above to be -1 and the slope of $x = 3.5 + y$ is easily seen to be 1. Since $-1 \neq 1$, the slopes are different, and therefore the lines are not parallel. Solving the equations simultaneously will give the solution $x = 12.5$ and $y = 9$; SUFFICIENT.

The correct answer is D; each statement alone is sufficient.

316. If a and b are integers, is $a^5 < 4^b$?

(1) $a^3 = -27$
(2) $b^2 = 16$

Arithmetic Exponents

(1) Given that $a^3 = -27$, it follows that $a = -3$, and hence $a < 0$. Therefore, $a^5 < 0$ (the 5th power of a negative number is negative), from which it follows that $a^5 < 4^b$ because a^5 is less than zero and 4 raised to an integer power is greater than zero; SUFFICIENT.

(2) Given that $b^2 = 16$, it follows that $b = 4$ or $b = -4$, but there is no restriction on the value of a. If $a = 1$ and $b = 4$, then $a^5 = 1$ is less than $4^b = 4^4$. However, if $a = 5$ and $b = 4$, then $a^5 = 5^5$ is greater than $4^b = 4^4$; NOT sufficient.

The correct answer is A; statement 1 alone is sufficient.

317. If each side of parallelogram P has length 1, what is the area of P?

(1) One angle of P measures 45 degrees.
(2) The altitude of P is $\frac{\sqrt{2}}{2}$.

Geometry Quadrilaterals; Area

The figure below shows parallelogram P, its altitude h, and an interior angle with degree measure θ. The area of a parallelogram is its base times its altitude. Therefore, the area of parallelogram P is $(h)(1) = h$. Determine the value of h.

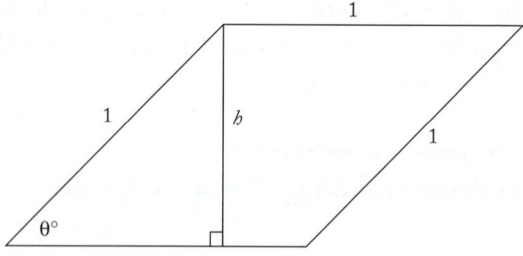

(1) Given that $\theta = 45$, it follows that the right triangle in the figure with hypotenuse 1 and side length h is a 45°-45°-90° triangle. Therefore, the length of each of its legs is $\frac{\sqrt{2}}{2}$ times the length of its hypotenuse, and hence $h = \frac{\sqrt{2}}{2}$; SUFFICIENT.

(2) Given that $h = \frac{\sqrt{2}}{2}$, it follows from the comments above that the area of P is $h = \frac{\sqrt{2}}{2}$; SUFFICIENT.

The correct answer is D; each statement alone is sufficient.

DS49502.01
318. If x is an integer greater than 0, what is the remainder when x is divided by 4 ?

(1) The remainder is 3 when x + 1 is divided by 4.
(2) The remainder is 0 when 2x is divided by 4.

Arithmetic Properties of integers

(1) Given that the remainder is 3 when $x + 1$ is divided by 4, or equivalently, that $x + 1$ is 3 more than a multiple of 4, then it follows that x is 2 more than a multiple of 4, or equivalently, that the remainder is 2 when $x + 1$ is divided by 4; SUFFICIENT.

(2) Given that the remainder is 0 when $2x$ is divided by 4, it is possible that the remainder when x is divided by 4 is 0 (choose $x = 4$; then $2x = 8$ has remainder 0 and $x = 4$ has remainder 0) and it is possible that the remainder when x is divided by 4 is 2 (choose $x = 6$; then $2x = 12$ has remainder 0 and $x = 6$ has remainder 2); NOT sufficient.

The correct answer is A; statement 1 alone is sufficient.

DS00602.01
319. A certain painting job requires a mixture of yellow, green, and white paint. If 12 quarts of paint are needed for the job, how many quarts of green paint are needed?

(1) The ratio of the amount of green paint to the amount of yellow and white paint combined needs to be 1 to 3.
(2) The ratio of the amount of yellow paint to the amount of green paint needs to be 3 to 2.

Algebra Ratios; Simultaneous equations

Let Y, G, and W be the number of quarts, respectively, of yellow, green, and white paint. It is given that $Y + G + W = 12$. Determine the value of G.

(1) Given that $\frac{G}{Y+W} = \frac{1}{3}$, it follows that $Y + W = 3G$. Therefore, $Y + G + W = 12$, which can be written as $(Y + W) + G = 12$, which becomes $3G + G = 12$, or $G = 3$; SUFFICIENT.

(2) Given that $\frac{Y}{G} = \frac{3}{2}$, it is not possible to determine the value of G. For example, it is possible that $G = 2$ (using $Y = 3$, $G = 2$, and $W = 7$, then $\frac{Y}{G} = \frac{3}{2}$ and $Y + G + W = 12$) and it is possible that $G = 4$ (using $Y = 6$, $G = 4$, and $W = 2$, then $\frac{Y}{G} = \frac{3}{2}$ and $Y + G + W = 12$); NOT sufficient.

The correct answer is A; statement 1 alone is sufficient.

DS69502.01
320. Is the average (arithmetic mean) of the numbers x, y, and z greater than z ?

(1) $z - x < y - z$
(2) $x < z < y$

Algebra Inequalities

Determine whether $\frac{x+y+z}{3} > z$, or $x + y + z > 3z$. Equivalently, determine whether $x + y > 2z$.

327

(1) Given that $z - x < y - z$, it follows by adding $x + z$ to each side that $2z < x + y$; SUFFICIENT.

(2) Given that $x < z < y$, it is not possible to determine whether $x + y > 2z$. For example, if $x = 1$, $y = 4$, and $z = 2$, then $x < z < y$ and $x + y = 5$ is greater than $2z = 4$. However, if $x = 1$, $y = 4$, and $z = 3$, then $x < z < y$ and $x + y = 5$ is less than $2z = 6$; NOT sufficient.

The correct answer is A; statement 1 alone is sufficient.

DS30602.01

321. Is the point Q on the circle with center C?

   (1) R is a point on the circle and the distance from Q to R is equal to the distance from Q to C.
   (2) S is a point on the circle and the distance from Q to S is equal to the distance from S to C.

Geometry Circles

(1) Given that R is on the circle with center C and $QR = QC$, it is possible that Q is on the circle with center C and it is possible that Q is not on the circle with center C. In the figure below, several possible locations for Q are shown on the perpendicular bisector of $\overline{CR}$, and for each of these $QR = QC$; NOT sufficient.

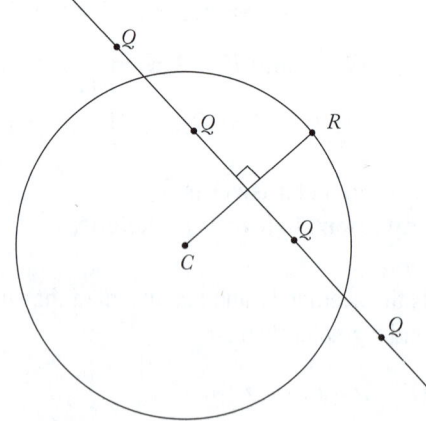

(2) Given that S is on the circle with center C and $QS = SC$, it is possible that Q is on the circle with center C and it is possible that Q is not on the circle with center C. In the figure below, several possible locations for Q are shown on the circle with center S and radius SC, and for each of these $QS = SC$; NOT sufficient.

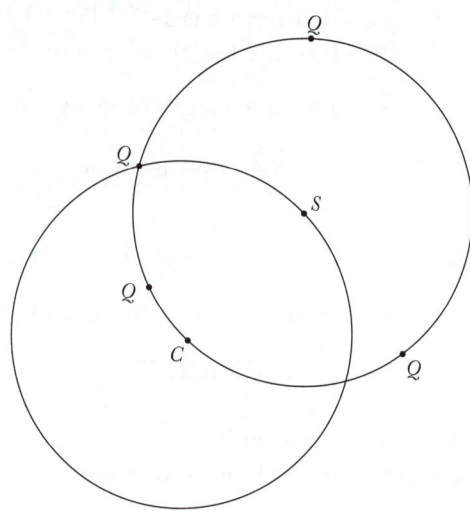

Taking (1) and (2) together, the figures below show that it is possible for Q to be on the circle with center C (when $R = S$) and it is possible for Q to not be on the circle with center C (when $R \neq S$). In the case $R = S$, when Q is on the perpendicular bisector of $\overline{CR}$, then $QR = QC$, and when Q is on the circle with center S, then $QS = SC$, or $QR = RC$ using $R = S$. Therefore, $QR = QC$ and $QR = RC$, hence $QC = RC$, and it follows that Q is on the circle with center C since the distance between Q and C is equal to the radius of the circle with center C (that radius being RC, since R is on the circle with center C).

In the case $R \neq S$, it is clear that it is possible for Q to not be on the circle with center C, especially when $\overline{CR}$ and $\overline{CS}$ are perpendicular.

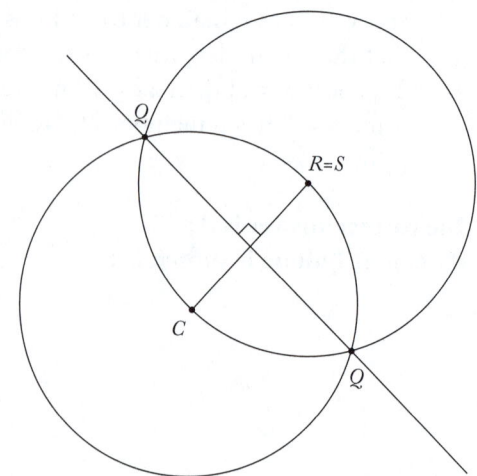

6.5 Data Sufficiency Answer Explanations

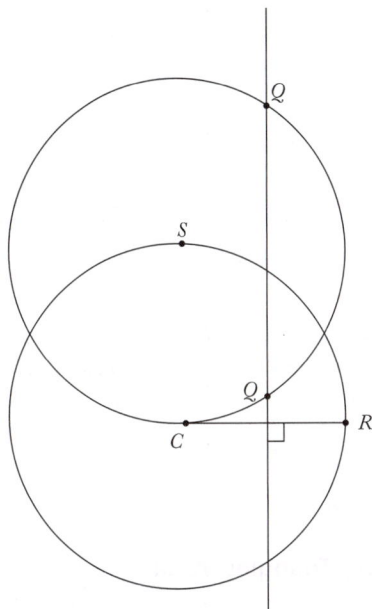

Therefore, $B = 3$ and $C = 9$, and hence $B + C = 12$; SUFFICIENT.

The correct answer is D; each statement alone is sufficient.

DS61602.01

323. A company produces a certain toy in only 2 sizes, small or large, and in only 2 colors, red or green. If, for each size, there are equal numbers of red and green toys in a certain production lot, what fraction of the total number of green toys is large?

    (1) In the production lot, 400 of the small toys are green.
    (2) In the production lot, $\frac{2}{3}$ of the toys produced are small.

Algebra Ratios

Let x be the number of small toys of each color, and let y be the number of large toys of each color. The contingency table below gives a summary of the information given. Determine the value of $\frac{y}{x+y}$.

	small	large	total
red	x	y	$x + y$
green	x	y	$x + y$
total	$2x$	$2y$	$2x + 2y$

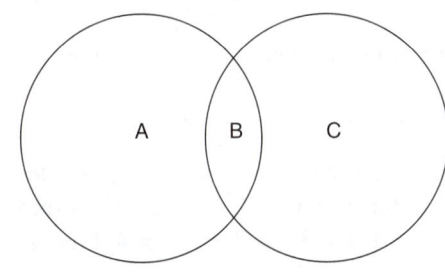

DS59502.01

322. In the figure above, if A, B, and C are the areas, respectively, of the three nonoverlapping regions formed by the intersection of two circles of equal area, what is the value of $B + C$?

    (1) $A + 2B + C = 24$
    (2) $A + C = 18$ and $B = 3$

Geometry Circles; Area

It is given that the area of the left circle is equal to the area of the right circle, or $A + B = B + C$. Subtracting B from each side of this equation gives $A = C$. Determine the value of $B + C$.

(1) Given that $A + 2B + C = 24$, it follows from $A = C$ that $C + 2B + C = 24$, or $2B + 2C = 24$, or $B + C = 12$; SUFFICIENT.

(2) Given that $A + C = 18$ and $B = 3$, it follows from $A = C$ that the first equation is equivalent to $C + C = 18$, or $C = 9$.

(1) Given that $x = 400$, it is clearly not possible to determine the value of $\frac{y}{x+y} = \frac{y}{400+y}$; NOT sufficient.

(2) Given that $\frac{2}{3}$ of the toys are small, then because there are $(2x + 2y)$ toys altogether and $2x$ small toys, it follows that $\frac{2x}{2x+2y} = \frac{2}{3}$. Therefore, $3(2x) = 2(2x + 2y)$, or $x = 2y$, and hence $\frac{y}{x+y} = \frac{y}{2y+y} = \frac{y}{3y} = \frac{1}{3}$; SUFFICIENT.

The correct answer is B; statement 2 alone is sufficient.

329

DS51602.01
324. Is quadrilateral PQRS a parallelogram?

    (1) Adjacent sides PQ and QR have the same length.
    (2) Adjacent sides RS and SP have the same length.

Geometry Quadrilaterals

(1) Given that $PQ = QR$, it is not possible to determine whether quadrilateral PQRS is a parallelogram. For example, if quadrilateral PQRS is a square, then $PQ = QR$ and quadrilateral PQRS is a parallelogram. However, if quadrilateral PQRS is as shown in the figure below, then $PQ = QR$ and quadrilateral PQRS is not a parallelogram; NOT sufficient.

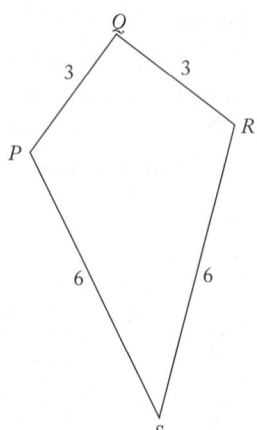

(2) Given that $RS = SP$, it is not possible to determine whether quadrilateral PQRS is a parallelogram. For example, if quadrilateral PQRS is a square, then $RS = SP$ and quadrilateral PQRS is a parallelogram. However, if quadrilateral PQRS is as shown in the figure above, then $RS = SP$ and quadrilateral PQRS is not a parallelogram; NOT sufficient.

Taking (1) and (2) together, it is not possible to determine whether quadrilateral PQRS is a parallelogram because the same examples used in (1) also satisfy (2).

The correct answer is E; both statements together are still not sufficient.

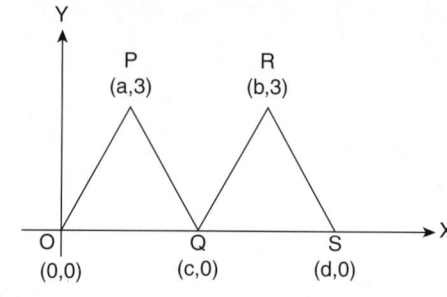

DS71602.01
325. In the figure above, the vertices of $\triangle OPQ$ and $\triangle QRS$ have coordinates as indicated. Do $\triangle OPQ$ and $\triangle QRS$ have equal areas?

    (1) $b = 2a$
    (2) $d = 2c$

Geometry Triangles; Area

The area of $\triangle OPQ$ is $\frac{1}{2}(c-0)(3-0) = \frac{3}{2}c$ and the area of $\triangle QRS$ is $\frac{1}{2}(d-c)(3-0) = \frac{3}{2}(d-c)$. Determine whether $\frac{3}{2}c = \frac{3}{2}(d-c)$, or equivalently, whether $d = 2c$.

(1) Given that $b = 2a$, it is not possible to determine whether $d = 2c$. For example, if $a = 1$, $b = 3$, $c = 2$, and $d = 4$, then $d = 2c$. However, if $a = 1$, $b = 3$, $c = 2$, and $d = 10$, then $d \neq 2c$; NOT sufficient.

(2) Given that $d = 2c$, then as explained in the preliminary comments above, it follows that $\triangle OPQ$ and $\triangle QRS$ have equal areas; SUFFICIENT.

The correct answer is B; statement 2 alone is sufficient.

DS92602.01
326. After the first two terms in a sequence of numbers, each term in the sequence is formed by adding all of the preceding terms. Is 12 the fifth term in the sequence?

    (1) The sum of the first 3 terms in the sequence is 6.
    (2) The fourth term in the sequence is 6.

Algebra Series and sequences

If the first term is a and the second term is b, then the third term is $a + b$, the fourth term is $a + b + (a + b) = 2a + 2b$, and the fifth term is $a + b + (a + b) + (2a + 2b) = 4a + 4b$. Is $4a + 4b = 12$?

(1) It is given that the sum of the first 3 terms is 6, and since the sum of the first 3 terms is the fourth term, it follows that $2a + 2b = 6$. Therefore $a + b = 3$ and $4(a + b) = 4a + 4b = 12$; SUFFICIENT.

(2) It is given that the fourth term is 6. Since the fourth term is $2a + 2b$, the same reasoning used in (1) applies, and $4a + 4b = 12$; SUFFICIENT.

The correct answer is D; each statement alone is sufficient.

DS13602.01

327. Jones has worked at Firm X twice as many years as Green, and Green has worked at Firm X four years longer than Smith. How many years has Green worked at Firm X ?

(1) Jones has worked at Firm X 9 years longer than Smith.
(2) Green has worked at Firm X 5 years less than Jones.

Algebra Simultaneous equations

Let J, G, and S be the number of years Jones, Green, and Smith, respectively, have worked at Firm X. Then $J = 2G$ and $G = 4 + S$. What is the value of G ?

(1) Given that $J = 9 + S$, then from $J = 2G$ it follows that $2G = 9 + S$. From $G = 4 + S$ it follows that $S = G - 4$, and therefore $G - 4$ can be substituted for S in the equation $2G = 9 + S$ to obtain $2G = 9 + (G - 4)$, or $G = 5$; SUFFICIENT.

(2) Given that $G = J - 5$, it follows from $J = 2G$ that $G = 2G - 5$, or $G = 5$; SUFFICIENT.

The correct answer is D; each statement alone is sufficient.

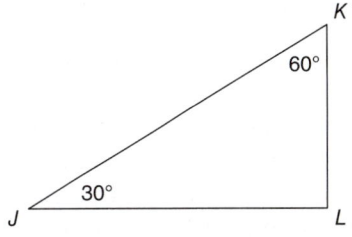

DS83602.01

328. In $\triangle JKL$ shown above, what is the length of segment JL ?

(1) $JK = 10$
(2) $KL = 5$

Geometry Triangles

Since $\triangle JKL$ is a 30°-60°-90° triangle, its side lengths are in the ratio $1:\sqrt{3}:2$. Therefore, if the length of $\overline{KL}$ is represented by x, then the length of $\overline{JL}$ is represented by $x\sqrt{3}$, and the length of $\overline{JK}$ is represented by $2x$.

(1) $JK = 10$, so $2x = 10$ and $x = 5$. Therefore, from above, $JL = 5\sqrt{3}$; SUFFICIENT.

(2) $KL = 5$, so $x = 5$ and $JL = 5\sqrt{3}$; SUFFICIENT.

The correct answer is D; each statement alone is sufficient.

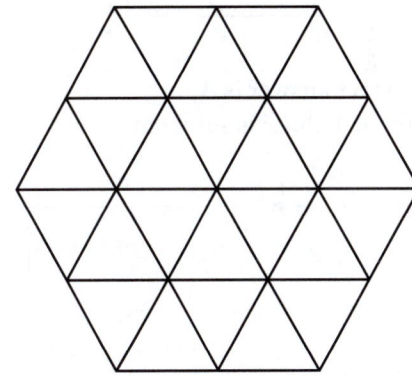

DS24602.01

329. A six-sided mosaic contains 24 triangular pieces of tile of the same size and shape, as shown in the figure above. If the sections of tile fit together perfectly, how many square centimeters of tile are in the mosaic?

(1) Each side of each triangular piece of tile is 9 centimeters long.
(2) The mosaic can be put inside a rectangular frame that is 40 centimeters wide.

Geometry Triangles; Area

(1) It is given that each side of each triangle is 9 centimeters long. The height of each triangle can be determined using the ratios for 30°-60°-90° triangles, and thus the area of each of the 24 triangular tiles can be determined. Then, multiplying by 24 will give the area of the tile in the mosaic; SUFFICIENT.

(2) It is given that the mosaic can be put inside a rectangular frame that is 40 centimeters wide. This means that the distance from A to E on the figure below is a maximum of 40 centimeters, but no information is given on the exact width of the mosaic. There is also no information on the distance from C to G; NOT sufficient.

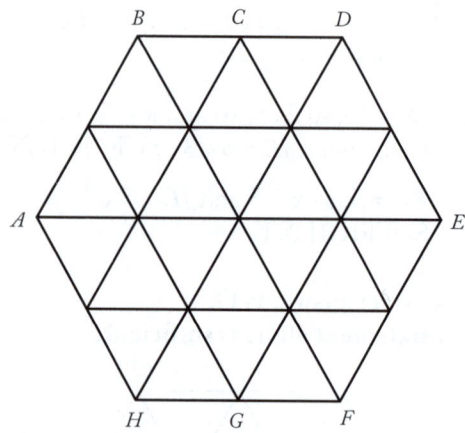

The correct answer is A; statement 1 alone is sufficient.

DS34602.01
330. If, in the figure above, $ABCD$ is a rectangular region, what is the value of the ratio $\frac{\text{area of } \triangle EDA}{\text{area of } \triangle EBC}$?

(1) $AD = 4$
(2) $AE = 2$ and $EB = 4$

Geometry Triangles

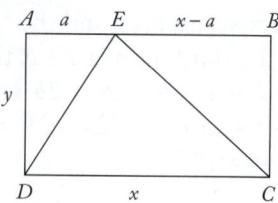

Using the figure above,

$$\frac{\text{area of } \triangle EDA}{\text{area of } \triangle EBC} = \frac{\frac{1}{2}ay}{\frac{1}{2}(x-a)y} = \frac{a}{x-a}.$$

(1) In the notation introduced in the figure above, this gives $y = 4$. However, the desired ratio depends only on the value of a and x and no information is given for these values; NOT sufficient.

(2) In the notation introduced in the figure above, this gives $a = 2$ and $x - a = 4$. With these values for a and $x - a$, the value of the desired ratio can be determined; SUFFICIENT.

The correct answer is B; statement 2 alone is sufficient.

DS64602.01
331. A noncompressible ball in the shape of a sphere is to be passed through a square opening in a board. What is the perimeter of the opening?

(1) The radius of the ball is equal to 2 inches.
(2) The square opening is the smallest square opening through which the ball will fit.

Geometry Quadrilaterals; Perimeter

(1) The radius of the ball is 2 inches, so the diameter of the ball is 4 inches. The square opening must be at least 4 inches on a side, so the perimeter of the opening must be at least 16 inches. However, there is not enough information to determine the exact perimeter of the opening; NOT sufficient.

(2) Knowing that the square opening is the smallest through which the ball will fit is not enough information to determine the perimeter of the opening because there is no information on the diameter of the ball; NOT sufficient.

Given (1) and (2), the perimeter of the square opening must be at least 16 inches and as small as possible. Therefore, the perimeter of the square opening is 16 inches.

**The correct answer is C;
both statements together are sufficient.**

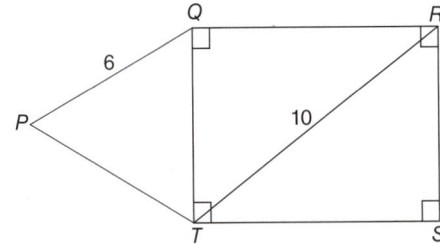

DS74602.01
332. In the figure above, what is the area of region PQRST ?

(1) PQ = RS
(2) PT = QT

Geometry Triangles; Area

From the figure, PQRST is composed of △PQT and quadrilateral QRST, which is a rectangle because each of its angles is a right angle. The area of PQRST is the sum of the areas of △PQT and rectangle QRST.

(1) It is given that PQ = RS, where PQ is given as 6. The length of the rectangle is $\sqrt{10^2 - 6^2} = 8$, so the area of the rectangle is then (6)(8) = 48. Because QRST is a rectangle, QT = RS. It follows that △PQT is isosceles, but no other information about △PQT can be obtained from (1) or what is given in the figure. If PT = 6, then △PQT is equilateral and its area is $\frac{1}{2}(6)(3\sqrt{3}) = 9\sqrt{3}$. Therefore, the area of PQRST is $48 + 9\sqrt{3}$. However, If PT = 8, then △PQT is isosceles (PQ = QT) with base 8 and area $\frac{1}{2}(8)(2\sqrt{5}) = 8\sqrt{5}$. The area of PQRST is $48 + 8\sqrt{5}$; NOT sufficient.

(2) It is given that PT = QT. It follows that △PQT is isosceles with base PQ = 6. If PT = QT = 6, then △PQT is equilateral and its area is $\frac{1}{2}(6)(3\sqrt{3}) = 9\sqrt{3}$. Since RT = 10, the length of the rectangle is $\sqrt{100 - 36} = 8$ and the area of the rectangle is (6)(8) = 48. The area of PQRST is $48 + 9\sqrt{3}$. However, if PT = QT = 8, the area of △PQT is $\frac{1}{2}(6)(\sqrt{64 - 9}) = 3\sqrt{55}$. Since RT = 10, and QT = 8, the length of the rectangle is $\sqrt{100 - 64} = 6$ and the area of the rectangle is (6)(8) = 48. The area of PQRST is $48 + 3\sqrt{55}$; NOT sufficient.

Taking (1) and (2) together, PQ = RS = 6 from (1) and QT = RS = 6 because QRST is a rectangle. From (2), PT = QT, so PT = 6. All three sides of △PQT are known and therefore the area of △PQT can be determined. Also, from the figure, TR = 10. Using this and the Pythagorean theorem applied to △TQR (or △TSR), which gives QR (or TS), the area of QRST can be determined. With both the area of △PQT and QRST known, the area of PQRST can be determined.

**The correct answer is C;
both statements together are sufficient.**

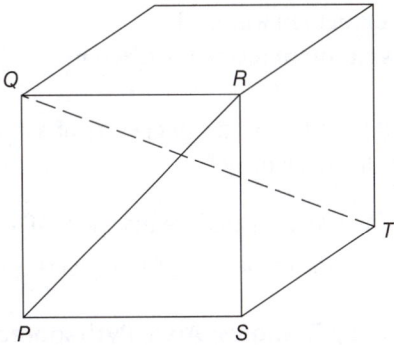

DS84602.01
333. The figure above represents a box that has the shape of a cube. What is the volume of the box?

(1) PR = 10 cm
(2) QT = $5\sqrt{6}$ cm

Geometry Volume

Letting s represent the side length of the cube, if the value of s can be determined, then the volume of the cube, s^3, can be determined.

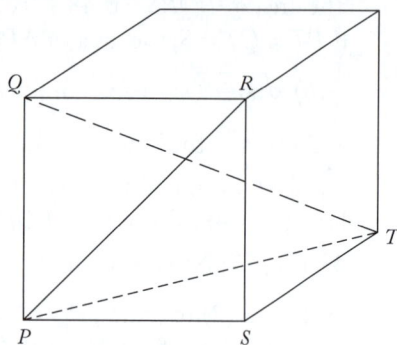

(1) It is given that $PR = 10$. Applying the Pythagorean theorem to $\triangle PSR$, it follows that $10^2 = 2s^2$, from which the value of s can be determined; SUFFICIENT.

(2) It is given that $QT = 5\sqrt{6}$. Applying the Pythagorean theorem to $\triangle PST$, it follows that $PT^2 = 2s^2$. Then applying the Pythagorean theorem to $\triangle QPT$, it follows that $QT^2 = QP^2 + PT^2$ or $(5\sqrt{6})^2 = s^2 + 2s^2 = 3s^2$, from which the value of s can be determined; SUFFICIENT.

The correct answer is D; each statement alone is sufficient.

DS94602.01

334. If x and y are the lengths of the legs of a right triangle, what is the value of xy?

(1) The hypotenuse of the triangle is $10\sqrt{2}$.
(2) The area of the triangular region is 50.

Geometry Triangles; Area; Pythagorean theorem

(1) Given that the hypotenuse of the triangle is $10\sqrt{2}$, it follows that $x^2 + y^2 = (10\sqrt{2})^2 = 200$. It is possible that $x = y = 10$ ($x^2 + y^2 = 200$), in which case $xy = 100$. However, it is also possible that $x = 5\sqrt{6}$ and $y = 5\sqrt{2}$ (($5\sqrt{6})^2 + (5\sqrt{2})^2 = 150 + 50 = 200$), in which case $xy = 50\sqrt{3}$; NOT sufficient.

(2) Given that the area of the triangle is 50, it follows that $\frac{xy}{2} = 50$, so $xy = 100$; SUFFICIENT.

The correct answer is B; statement 2 alone is sufficient.

DS75602.01

335. In the figure above, PQRT is a rectangle. What is the length of segment PQ?

(1) The area of region PQRS is 39 and $TS = 6$.
(2) The area of region PQRT is 30 and $QR = 10$.

Geometry Quadrilaterals

Since $PQRT$ is a rectangle, $\overline{QR}$ is parallel to $\overline{PT}$, and since $\overline{PT}$ is part of the same line as $\overline{PS}$, it follows that $\overline{QR}$ is parallel to $\overline{PS}$. Therefore, quadrilateral PQRS is a trapezoid with area given by $\frac{1}{2}(QR + PS)(PQ)$.

(1) Given that the area of PQRS is 39, it follows that $\frac{1}{2}(QR + PS)(PQ) = 39$. But, $PS = PT + TS$, where $TS = 6$, and $QR = PT$ since PQRT is a rectangle. Therefore, $39 = \frac{1}{2}(2PT + 6)(PQ)$ or $78 = (2PT + 6)(PQ)$. This equation has two unknowns, namely PT and PQ, and many values for PT and PQ satisfy the equation; NOT sufficient.

(2) Since PQRT is a rectangle with area given by $(QR)(QP)$, from (2), $30 = (10)(QP)$, so $QP = 3$; SUFFICIENT.

The correct answer is B; statement 2 alone is sufficient.

6.5 Data Sufficiency Answer Explanations

DS08420

336. On June 1, Mary paid Omar $360 for rent and utilities for the month of June. Mary moved out early, and Omar refunded the money she paid for utilities, but not for rent, for the days in June after she moved out. How many dollars did Omar refund to Mary?

(1) Mary moved out on June 24.
(2) The amount Mary paid for utilities was less than $\frac{1}{5}$ the amount Mary paid for rent.

Algebra Applied problems; Proportions

Let R and U be the amounts, respectively and in dollars, that Mary paid for rent and utilities for the month of June. Given that $R + U = 360$, find the value of $\left(\frac{n}{30}\right)U$, where n is the number of days in June—which has 30 days—after Mary moved out.

(1) Given that $n = 6$, it follows that $\left(\frac{n}{30}\right)U = \frac{1}{5}U$. However, it is clear that more than one value of U is possible, and thus the value of $\left(\frac{n}{30}\right)U$ cannot be determined; NOT sufficient.

(2) Given that $U < \frac{1}{5}R$, it is clear that more than one value of U is possible, and thus the value of $\left(\frac{n}{30}\right)U$ cannot be determined; NOT sufficient.

Taking (1) and (2) together, the problem reduces to whether the value of $\frac{1}{5}U$, or equivalently the value of U, can be determined when $R + U = 360$ and $U < \frac{1}{5}R$. However, it is still the case that the value of U cannot be determined. For example, if $U = \frac{1}{10}(360) = 36$ and $R = \frac{9}{10}(360) = 324$, then both $R + U = 360$ and $U < \frac{1}{5}R$ are true. On the other hand, if $U = \frac{1}{36}(360) = 10$ and $R = \frac{35}{36}(360) = 350$, then both $R + U = 360$ and $U < \frac{1}{5}R$ are true.

**The correct answer is E;
both statements together are still not sufficient.**

DS04057

337. If $x = 2t$ and $y = \frac{t}{3}$, what is the value of $x^2 - y^2$?

(1) $t^2 - 3 = 6$
(2) $t^3 = -27$

Algebra Simplifying algebraic expressions

This problem can be solved by determining the value of $x^2 - y^2 = (2t)^2 - \left(\frac{t}{3}\right)^2 = 4t^2 - \frac{t^2}{9}$, and this can be determined if the value of t^2 or the value of t can be determined.

(1) This indicates that $t^2 - 3 = 6$ and so $t^2 = 6 + 3 = 9$; SUFFICIENT.

(2) This indicates that $t^3 = -27$ and so $t = -3$; SUFFICIENT.

**The correct answer is D;
each statement alone is sufficient.**

DS02939

338. The 10 students in a history class recently took an examination. What was the maximum score on the examination?

(1) The mean of the scores was 75.
(2) The standard deviation of the scores was 5.

Arithmetic Statistics

(1) Given that the mean of the scores was 75, then all 10 scores could have been 75 and the maximum score would be 75. However, it is also possible that the scores were 74, 76, and 8 scores of 75, and the maximum would be 76; NOT sufficient.

(2) Given that the standard deviation was 5, it will be helpful to use a specific value for the mean, such as 75. From the definition of standard deviation, it follows that $\sqrt{\frac{\sum(S-75)^2}{10}} = 5$, where $\sum(S-75)^2$ denotes the sum of the squares of the differences of the scores from 75. It will be useful to solve for $\sum(S-75)^2$. Doing this gives $\frac{\sum(S-75)^2}{10} = 25$, and so the condition $\sum(S-75)^2 = 250$ will ensure that the standard deviation of the scores is 5. One list of 10 scores with standard deviation 5 and mean 75 is five occurrences of 70

335

and five occurrences of 80, since for these scores we have $\sum (S-75)^2 = 5(70-75)^2 + 5(80-75)^2$, which equals $5(25) + 5(25) = 250$; and the mean is 75 because the sum of the differences of the scores from 75 is equal to 0. Another list of 10 scores with standard deviation 5 and mean 75 is 70, 70, 70, 70, 75, 75, 75, 80, 80, and 85, since for these scores we have $\sum (S-75)^2 = 4(70-75)^2 + 3(75-75)^2 + 2(80-75)^2 + (85-75)^2$, which equals $4(25) + 2(25) + 100 = 250$; and the mean is 75 because the sum of the differences of the scores from 75 is equal to 0. The maximum for the first list is 80, and the maximum for the second list is 85; NOT sufficient.

Taking (1) and (2) together is still not sufficient because both (1) and (2) hold for the lists used in (2).

The correct answer is E;
both statements together are still not sufficient.

DS01341

339. Last school year, each of the 200 students at a certain high school attended the school for the entire year. If there were 8 cultural performances at the school during the last school year, what was the average (arithmetic mean) number of students attending each cultural performance?

    (1) Last school year, each student attended at least one cultural performance.
    (2) Last school year, the average number of cultural performances attended per student was 4.

Arithmetic Statistics

Determine the average number of students attending each of 8 cultural performances at a school that has 200 students.

(1) This indicates that each student attended at least one cultural performance, but the average number of students attending each performance cannot be uniquely determined. It could be as low as $\frac{200}{8} = 25$ students if each student attended exactly one performance, or it could be as high as $\frac{200}{1} = 200$ if each student attended every performance; NOT sufficient.

(2) This indicates that, since the average number of performances attended per student was 4, $\frac{\text{total attendance at performances}}{\text{total number of students}} = 4$, so the total attendance at the performances is $(4)(200) = 800$ students. It follows that the average number of students attending each performance is $\frac{800}{8} = 100$; SUFFICIENT.

The correct answer is B;
statement 2 alone is sufficient.

DS14569

340. A clothing manufacturer makes jackets that are wool or cotton or a combination of wool and cotton. The manufacturer has 3,000 pounds of wool and 2,000 pounds of cotton on hand. Is this enough wool and cotton to make at least 1,000 jackets?

    (1) Each wool jacket requires 4 pounds of wool, and no cotton.
    (2) Each cotton jacket requires 6 pounds of cotton, and no wool.

Arithmetic Applied problems

(1) Given that each wool jacket requires 4 pounds of wool and no cotton, then at most a total of 750 wool jackets can be made (because $\frac{3,000}{4} = 750$), and possibly no other jackets. Therefore, it is possible that there is enough wool and cotton to make at least 1,000 jackets (for example, if there is enough cotton to make 250 cotton jackets) and it is possible that there is not enough wool and cotton to make at least 1,000 jackets (for example, if there is less than the amount of cotton needed to make 250 cotton jackets); NOT sufficient.

(2) Given that each cotton jacket requires 6 pounds of cotton and no wool, then at most a total of 333 cotton jackets can be made (because rounding $\frac{2,000}{6}$ down to the nearest integer gives 333), and possibly no other jackets. Therefore, it is possible that there is enough wool and cotton to make at least 1,000 jackets (for example, if there is enough wool to make 667 wool jackets), and it is possible that there is not enough wool

and cotton to make at least 1,000 jackets (for example, if there is less than the amount of wool needed to make 667 wool jackets); NOT sufficient.

Taking (1) and (2) together, there is enough wool and cotton to make 750 wool jackets and 333 cotton jackets for a total of 1,083 jackets.

The correct answer is C; both statements together are sufficient.

DS05377

341. If n is an integer, what is the greatest common divisor of 12 and n ?

    (1) The product of 12 and n is 432.
    (2) The greatest common divisor of 24 and n is 12.

Arithmetic Properties of integers

(1) Given that $12n = 432$, it follows that $n = 36$ and the greatest common divisor of 12 and 36 is 12. However, it is not necessary to **solve** this equation and then **calculate** the greatest common divisor of two numbers to determine whether it is possible to answer the question asked. It is sufficient to observe that the value of n can be determined by solving this equation and then observe that the greatest common divisor of 12 and the value of n can be determined; SUFFICIENT.

(2) Given that 12 is the greatest common divisor of 24 and n, it follows that 12 is a common divisor of 24 and n, and hence 12 is a divisor of n. Thus, 12 is a common divisor of 12 and n because 12 is a divisor of 12 and 12 is a divisor of n. Also, no number greater than 12 can be a common divisor of 12 and n because no number greater than 12 can be a divisor of 12. Therefore, 12 is the greatest common divisor of 12 and n; SUFFICIENT.

The correct answer is D; each statement alone is sufficient.

DS11287

342. Each month, Jim receives a base salary plus a 10 percent commission on the price of each car he sells that month. If Jim sold 15 cars last month, what was the total amount of base salary and commissions that Jim received that month?

    (1) Last month, Jim's base salary was $3,000.
    (2) Last month, Jim sold 3 cars whose prices totaled $60,000 and 5 cars whose prices totaled $120,000.

Arithmetic Applied problems

Determine the total of Jim's base salary plus a 10% commission on the price of each of the 15 cars he sold last month.

(1) This indicates that Jim's base salary was $3,000 but gives no information about the prices of the 15 cars he sold last month; NOT sufficient.

(2) This indicates that Jim's commission on 8 cars that he sold last month can be determined but gives no information about his base salary or about the prices of the other 7 cars he sold last month; NOT sufficient.

Taking (1) and (2) together gives Jim's base salary and information about the prices of 8 of the 15 cars he sold last month, but does not provide information about the selling prices of the other 7 cars he sold.

The correct answer is E; both statements together are still not sufficient.

DS17615

343. If x is a positive integer greater than 1, what is the value of x ?

    (1) $2x$ is a common factor of 18 and 24.
    (2) x is a factor of 6.

Arithmetic Properties of numbers

(1) Given that $2x$, where x is an integer greater than 1, is a common factor of 18 and 24, then $2x$ is an even integer greater than or equal to 4 that is a factor of 18 and 24. The factors of 18 are 1, 2, 3, 6, 9, and 18. The factors of 24 are 1, 2, 3, 4, 6, 8, 12, and 24. Since the only even integer greater than or equal to 4 that belongs to both lists is 6, it follows that $2x = 6$, or $x = 3$; SUFFICIENT.

337

(2) Given that x, an integer greater than 1, is a factor of 6, then x could be 2, 3, or 6; NOT sufficient.

The correct answer is A; statement 1 alone is sufficient.

DS13408

344. By what percent was the price of a certain television set discounted for a sale?

    (1) The price of the television set before it was discounted for the sale was 25 percent greater than the discounted price.
    (2) The price of the television set was discounted by $60 for the sale.

Arithmetic Percents

Let B represent the price, in dollars, for the television before the sale and let D represent the discounted price, in dollars. The percent by which B was discounted to obtain D can be determined if the value of $\frac{B-D}{B}$ can be determined.

(1) This indicates that B is 25% greater than D or that $B = 1.25D$. Then, $\frac{B-D}{B} = \frac{1.25D - D}{1.25D} = \frac{0.25}{1.25} = 0.2$ or 20%; SUFFICIENT.

(2) This indicates that $D = B - 60$, but B is unknown. For example, B could be 100 and the value of $\frac{B-D}{B}$ would be $\frac{60}{100}$, or B could be 500 and the value of $\frac{B-D}{B}$ would be $\frac{60}{500}$; NOT sufficient.

The correct answer is A; statement 1 alone is sufficient.

DS05049

345. Jack wants to use a circular rug on his rectangular office floor to cover two small circular stains, each less than $\frac{\pi}{100}$ square feet in area and each more than 3 feet from the nearest wall. Can the rug be placed to cover both stains?

    (1) Jack's rug covers an area of 9π square feet.
    (2) The centers of the stains are less than 4 feet apart.

Geometry Applied problems; Circles

If a circle with radius r has area less than $\frac{\pi}{100}$, then $\pi r^2 < \frac{\pi}{100}$, or $r^2 < \frac{1}{100}$. Hence, $r < \frac{1}{10}$, so the circle's radius is less than $\frac{1}{10}$ ft.

(1) Given that the circular rug has area 9π ft^2, the radius of the rug, R ft, satisfies the equation $\pi R^2 = 9\pi$, and so $R^2 = 9$, or $R = 3$. If the centers of the circular stains are 4 ft apart, then the midpoint of the centers will be a distance of at most $\left(\frac{1}{10} + 2 + \frac{1}{10}\right)$ ft = 2.2 ft from any point on the stains. Thus, if the circular rug (which has radius 3 ft) were placed so that its center lies on that midpoint, then the rug would cover both stains. However, if the centers of the circular stains are 7 ft apart, then the circular rug (which has diameter 6 ft) cannot be placed to cover both stains; NOT sufficient.

(2) Given that the centers of the circular stains are less than 4 ft apart, it is not possible to determine whether the circular rug can be placed to cover both stains since nothing is given about the size of the circular rug; NOT sufficient.

Taking (1) and (2) together, the centers of the circular stains are less than 4 ft apart and it follows from the discussion in (1) that the circular rug can be placed to cover both stains.

The correct answer is C; both statements together are sufficient.

DS24751.01

346. A paint mixture was formed by mixing exactly 3 colors of paint. By volume, the mixture was x% blue paint, y% green paint, and z% red paint. If exactly 1 gallon of blue paint and 3 gallons of red paint were used, how many gallons of green paint were used?

    (1) $x = y$
    (2) $z = 60$

Algebra First-degree equations

Letting T represent the total number of gallons of the paint in the mixture, and B, G, and R the amounts of blue paint, green paint, and red paint, respectively, in the mixture, then $B = \frac{x}{100}T$, $G = \frac{y}{100}T$, and $R = \frac{z}{100}T$. It is given that $\frac{x}{100}T = 1$ and $\frac{z}{100}T = 3$, from which it follows that $z = 3x$. Also, since there are exactly three colors of paint, $x + y + z = 100$ and $B + G + R = T$. Determine the value of G, or equivalently, the value $\frac{y}{100}T$.

(1) Given that $x = y$ and $\frac{x}{100}T = 1$, it follows that $\frac{y}{100}T = 1$; SUFFICIENT.

(2) Given that $z = 60$ and $\frac{z}{100}T = 3$, it follows that $T = 5$. Knowing that the total amount of paint in the mixture is 5 gallons of which 1 gallon is blue paint and 3 gallons are red paint, the amount of green paint can be determined; SUFFICIENT.

The correct answer is D; each statement alone is sufficient.

×	a	b	c
a	d	e	f
b	e	g	h
c	f	h	j

DS05772

347. In the multiplication table above, each letter represents an integer. What is the value of c?

(1) $c = f$
(2) $h \neq 0$

Arithmetic Properties of numbers

(1) Given that $c = f$, the examples below, in which $a = b = 1$, show that the value of c could be 1 and the value of c could be 2; NOT sufficient.

×	1	1	1
1	1	1	1
1	1	1	1
1	1	1	1

×	1	1	2
1	1	1	2
1	1	1	2
2	2	2	4

(2) Given that $h \neq 0$, the examples in (1) show that the value of c could be 1 and the value of c could be 2; NOT sufficient.

Taking (1) and (2) together is of no more help than either (1) or (2) taken separately because the same examples used to show that (1) is not sufficient also show that (2) is not sufficient.

The correct answer is E; both statements together are still not sufficient.

DS09379

348. If n is an integer, is $(0.1)^n$ greater than $(10)^n$?

(1) $n > -10$
(2) $n < 10$

Arithmetic Exponents

$(0.1)^n = \frac{1}{10^n}$ will be greater than 10^n if 1 is greater than 10^{2n}, and this will be the case if and only if $n < 0$. Determine if $n < 0$.

(1) This indicates that n is greater than -10. This includes nonnegative values of n as well as negative values of n; NOT sufficient.

(2) This indicates that n is less than 10, but this includes negative values of n as well as nonnegative values of n; NOT sufficient.

Taking (1) and (2) together, n can have any value between -10 and 10 and can therefore be negative or nonnegative.

The correct answer is E; both statements together are still not sufficient.

DS19199

349. For a basic monthly fee of F yen (¥F), Naoko's first cell phone plan allowed him to use a maximum of 420 minutes on calls during the month. Then, for each of x additional minutes he used on calls, he was charged ¥M, making his total charge for the month ¥T, where $T = F + xM$. What is the value of F?

    (1) Naoko used 450 minutes on calls the first month and the total charge for the month was ¥13,755.
    (2) Naoko used 400 minutes on calls the second month and the total charge for the month was ¥13,125.

Algebra Simultaneous equations

(1) Given that Naoko used 450 minutes and was charged ¥13,125, it follows that $F + (450 - 420)M = 13,755$, or $F + 30M = 13,755$. However, the value of F cannot be determined. For example, $F = 13,005$ and $M = 25$ is possible, and $F = 13,035$ and $M = 24$ is possible; NOT sufficient.

(2) Given that Naoko used 400 minutes and was charged ¥13,125, it follows that $F = 13,125$, since Naoko did not use more than 420 minutes; SUFFICIENT.

**The correct answer is B;
statement 2 alone is sufficient.**

DS13949

350. Is the sum of the prices of the 3 books that Shana bought less than $48?

    (1) The price of the most expensive of the 3 books that Shana bought is less than $17.
    (2) The price of the least expensive of the 3 books that Shana bought is exactly $3 less than the price of the second most expensive book.

Arithmetic Operations with integers; Order

Let B_1, B_2, and B_3 be the prices, in dollars and in numerical order, of the 3 books. Thus, $B_1 \leq B_2 \leq B_3$. Determine whether $B_1 + B_2 + B_3 < 48$.

(1) Given that $B_3 < 17$, it is possible that $B_1 + B_2 + B_3 < 48$ (choose $B_1 = B_2 = 15$ and $B_3 = 16$) and it is possible that $B_1 + B_2 + B_3 > 48$ (choose $B_1 = B_2 = 16$ and $B_3 = 16.5$); NOT sufficient.

(2) Given that $B_1 = B_2 - 3$, it is possible that $B_1 + B_2 + B_3 < 48$ (choose $B_1 = 3$, $B_2 = 6$, and $B_3 = 10$) and it is possible that $B_1 + B_2 + B_3 > 48$ (choose $B_1 = 3$, $B_2 = 6$, and $B_3 = 48$); NOT sufficient.

Taking (1) and (2) together, from (1) and the information given it follows that $B_3 < 17$ and $B_2 \leq B_3 < 17$, or $B_2 < 17$. Also, from $B_2 < 17$ and (2), it follows that $B_1 < 17 - 3$, or $B_1 < 14$. Therefore, $B_1 + B_2 + B_3$ is the sum of 3 numbers—a number less than 14, a number less than 17, and a number less than 17—and thus $B_1 + B_2 + B_3 < 14 + 17 + 17 = 48$.

**The correct answer is C;
both statements together are sufficient.**

DS12943

351. If r and t are three-digit positive integers, is r greater than t?

    (1) The tens digit of r is greater than each of the three digits of t.
    (2) The tens digit of r is less than either of the other two digits of r.

Arithmetic Properties of numbers

Let r_3, r_2, and r_1 be the hundreds, tens, and units digits, respectively, of the 3-digit integer r, and let t_3, t_2, and t_1 be the hundreds, tens, and units digits, respectively, of the 3-digit integer t.

(1) Given that r_2 is greater than each of t_3, t_2, and t_1, then r could be greater than t (for example, if $r = 242$ and $t = 222$) and r could be less than t (for example, if $r = 242$ and $t = 333$); NOT sufficient.

(2) Given that r_2 is less than either of r_1 or r_3, then r could be greater than t (for example, if $r = 212$ and $t = 111$) and r could be less than t (for example, if $r = 212$ and $t = 222$); NOT sufficient.

Taking (1) and (2) together, $r_3 > r_2$ follows from (2) and $r_2 > t_3$ follows from (1). Therefore, $r_3 > t_3$ and hence r is greater than t.

**The correct answer is C;
both statements together are sufficient.**

352. Is the product of two positive integers x and y divisible by the sum of x and y?

    (1) $x = y$
    (2) $x = 2$

Arithmetic Properties of numbers

(1) Given that $x = y$, then xy could be divisible by $x + y$ (for example, if $x = y = 2$, then $xy = 4$ is divisible by $x + y = 4$) and xy could fail to be divisible by $x + y$ (for example, if $x = y = 3$, then $xy = 9$ is not divisible by $x + y = 6$); NOT sufficient.

(2) Given that $x = 2$, then xy could be divisible by $x + y$ (for example, if $x = y = 2$, then $xy = 4$ is divisible by $x + y = 4$) and xy could fail to be divisible by $x + y$ (for example, if $x = 2$ and $y = 3$, then $xy = 6$ is not divisible by $x + y = 5$); NOT sufficient.

Taking (1) and (2) together, it follows that $x = y = 2$, and so $xy = 4$ is divisible by $x + y = 4$.

The correct answer is C; both statements together are sufficient.

353. If a and b are constants, is the expression $\dfrac{x+b}{\sqrt{x+a}}$ defined for $x = -2$?

    (1) $a = 5$
    (2) $b = 6$

Algebra Functions

In the set of real numbers, the radical expression $\dfrac{x+b}{\sqrt{x+a}}$ is defined for all values of x for which $\sqrt{x+a}$ is a nonzero real number, from which it follows that $\dfrac{x+b}{\sqrt{x+a}}$ is defined for all values of x such that $x > -a$. If $-2 > -a$ or equivalently if $a > 2$, then $\dfrac{x+b}{\sqrt{x+a}}$ is defined for $x = -2$. Determine if $a > 2$.

(1) If $a = 5$, then $a > 2$; SUFFICIENT.

(2) Given information only about the value of b, if $a = 5$, for example, then a is greater than 2. On the other hand, if $a = -5$, then a is not greater than 2; NOT sufficient.

The correct answer is A; statement 1 alone is sufficient.

354. A company makes and sells two products, P and Q. The costs per unit of making and selling P and Q are $8.00 and $9.50, respectively, and the selling prices per unit of P and Q are $10.00 and $13.00, respectively. In one month the company sold a total of 834 units of these products. Was the total profit on these items more than $2,000.00?

    (1) During the month, more units of P than units of Q were sold.
    (2) During the month, at least 100 units of Q were sold.

Arithmetic Applied problems

It is given that the profit on each unit of P is $10.00 - $8.00 = $2.00, and the profit on each unit of Q is $13.00 - $9.50 = $3.50. Also if p and q represent the number of units of Products P and Q made and sold, then it is given that $p + q = 834$. Determining if the total profit on these items was more than $2,000 requires determining how many units of at least one of the products were sold.

(1) This indicates that $p > q$, but does not give a specific value for p or q; NOT sufficient.

(2) This indicates that $q \geq 100$, but does not give a specific value for q; NOT sufficient.

Taking (1) and (2) together, $p > q$ and $q \geq 100$, so $p > 100$, but a specific value for p or q cannot be determined.

The correct answer is E; both statements together are still not sufficient.

355. Jill has applied for a job with each of two different companies. What is the probability that she will get job offers from both companies?

    (1) The probability that she will get a job offer from neither company is 0.3.
    (2) The probability that she will get a job offer from exactly one of the two companies is 0.5.

Arithmetic Probability

Let $P(2)$ be the probability that she will get a job offer from both companies, $P(1)$ be the probability that she will get a job offer from exactly one of the companies, and $P(0)$ be the probability that she will get a job offer from neither company. Then $P(2) + P(1) + P(0) = 1$. What is the value of $P(2)$?

(1) Given that $P(0) = 0.3$, it follows that $P(2) + P(1) + 0.3 = 1$, or $P(2) + P(1) = 0.7$. However, the value of $P(2)$ cannot be determined, since nothing is known about the value of $P(1)$ other than $0 \leq P(1) \leq 0.7$; NOT sufficient.

(2) (2) Given that $P(1) = 0.5$, it follows that $P(2) + 0.5 + P(0) = 1$, or $P(2) + P(0) = 0.5$. However, the value of $P(2)$ cannot be determined, since nothing is known about the value of $P(0)$ other than $0 \leq P(1) \leq 0.5$; NOT sufficient.

Taking (1) and (2) together, it follows that $P(2) + 0.5 + 0.3 = 1$, or $P(2) = 0.2$.

**The correct answer is C;
both statements together are sufficient.**

DS01257

356. A conveyor belt moves bottles at a constant speed of 120 centimeters per second. If the conveyor belt moves a bottle from a loading dock to an unloading dock, is the distance that the conveyor belt moves the bottle less than 90 meters? (1 meter = 100 centimeters)

    (1) It takes the conveyor belt less than 1.2 minutes to move the bottle from the loading dock to the unloading dock.
    (2) It takes the conveyor belt more than 1.1 minutes to move the bottle from the loading dock to the unloading dock.

Arithmetic Applied problems

Since the rate at which the conveyor belt moves is given as 120 centimeters per second, which is equivalent to $\frac{120}{100} = 1.2$ meters per second, the conveyor will move less than 90 meters if it moves for less than $\frac{90}{1.2} = 75$ seconds.

(1) This indicates that the length of time the conveyor belt moves is less than 1.2 minutes, which is equivalent to $(1.2)(60) = 72$ seconds and $72 < 75$; SUFFICIENT.

(2) This indicates that the length of time the conveyor belt moves is more than 1.1 minutes, which is equivalent to $(1.1)(60) = 66$ seconds, but does not indicate how much more than 66 seconds the conveyor moves. If the conveyor moves for 70 seconds ($70 > 66$), for example, it moves less than 90 meters since $70 < 75$. However, if the conveyor belt moves for 80 seconds ($80 > 66$), then it moves more than 90 meters since $80 > 75$; NOT sufficient.

**The correct answer is A;
statement 1 alone is sufficient.**

DS02706

357. If x, y, and z are positive numbers, what is the value of the average (arithmetic mean) of x and z?

    (1) $x - y = y - z$
    (2) $x^2 - y^2 = z$

Algebra Statistics; Simplifying algebraic expressions

(1) Given that $x - y = y - z$, it follows that $x + z = 2y$, or $y = \frac{x+z}{2}$. Therefore, y is the average of x and z. However, it is not possible to determine the value of y. For example, $x = y = z = 3$ gives three positive numbers that satisfy $x - y = y - z$, and $x = y = z = 4$ gives three positive numbers that satisfy $x - y = y - z$; NOT sufficient.

(2) Given that $x^2 - y^2 = z$, it is not possible to determine the value of $\frac{x+z}{2}$, the average of the x and z. For example, if $x = 3$, $y = 2$, and $z = 5$, then $x^2 - y^2 = z$ is true (because $3^2 - 2^2 = 9 - 4 = 5$) and $\frac{x+z}{2} = \frac{3+5}{2} = 4$. However, if $x = 5$, $y = 4$, and $z = 9$, then $x^2 - y^2 = z$ is true (because $5^2 - 4^2 = 25 - 16 = 9$) and $\frac{x+z}{2} = \frac{5+9}{2} = 7$; NOT sufficient.

Taking (1) and (2) together, it follows that $x + z = 2y$ and $x^2 - y^2 = z$, so $x + (x^2 - y^2) = 2y$, or $x + x^2 = y^2 + 2y$. Adding 1 to both sides of this last equation gives $x + x^2 + 1 = y^2 + 2y + 1 = (y+1)^2$, which simplifies the task of finding positive numbers $x, y,$ and z that satisfy both (1) and (2) and for which the values of $\frac{x+z}{2} = y$ can be different. For one example, letting $x = 1$ gives $x + x^2 + 1 = 3$, and thus $(y + 1)^2 = 3$. Solving for a positive value of y gives $y + 1 = \sqrt{3}$, or $y = \sqrt{3} - 1$, and by using $x + z = 2y$, the corresponding value of z is $2y - x = 2(\sqrt{3} - 1) - 1 = 2\sqrt{3} - 3$. Note that $2\sqrt{3} - 3$ is positive because $(2\sqrt{3})^2 = 4(3) = 12$ is greater than $3^2 = 9$. The values $x = 1$, $y = \sqrt{3} - 1$, and $z = 2\sqrt{3} - 3$ satisfy both (1) and (2), and for this choice of values of $x, y,$ and z, the value of $\frac{x+z}{2} = y$ is $\sqrt{3} - 1$. For another example, letting $x = 2$ gives $x + x^2 + 1 = 7$, and thus $(y + 1)^2 = 7$. Solving for a positive value of y gives $y + 1 = \sqrt{7}$, or $y = \sqrt{7} - 1$, and by using $x + z = 2y$, the corresponding value of z is $2y - x = 2(\sqrt{7} - 1) - 2 = 2\sqrt{7} - 4$. Note that $2\sqrt{7} - 4$ is positive because $(2\sqrt{7})^2 = 4(7) = 28$ is greater than $4^2 = 16$. The values $x = 2, y = \sqrt{7} - 1,$ and $z = 2\sqrt{7} - 4$ satisfy both (1) and (2), and for this choice of values of $x, y,$ and z, the value of $\frac{x+z}{2} = y$ is $\sqrt{7} - 1$; NOT sufficient.

**The correct answer is E;
both statements together are still not sufficient.**

DS04428

358. The rectangular rug shown in the figure above has an accent border. What is the area of the portion of the rug that excludes the border?

    (1) The perimeter of the rug is 44 feet.
    (2) The width of the border on all sides is 1 foot.

Geometry Rectangles; Perimeter

(1) Given that the perimeter of the rug is 44 ft, then the rectangular rug could have area 121 ft² (length = 11 ft and width = 11 ft) and the rectangular rug could have area 96 ft² (length = 16 ft and width = 6 ft). Moreover, no information is given about the width of the accent border, so even if the area of the rectangular rug could be determined, it would still not be possible to determine the area of the portion of the rug that excludes the border; NOT sufficient.

(2) Given that the width of the border is 1 ft, the area of the portion of the rug that excludes the border is $(L-2)(W-2)$ ft², where L ft and W ft are the length and width, respectively, of the rug. If $L = W = 11$, then $(L-2)(W-2) = 81$. However, if $L = 16$ and $W = 6$, then $(L-2)(W-2) = 56$; NOT sufficient.

Taking (1) and (2) together, the area could be 81 ft² or 56 ft² as shown by the examples in (1) and (2).

**The correct answer is E;
both statements together are still not sufficient.**

DS06537

359. If $y \neq 2xz$, what is the value of $\frac{2xz + yz}{2xz - y}$?

    (1) $2x + y = 3$
    (2) $z = 2$

Algebra Simplifying algebraic expressions

The task is to determine the value of
$$\frac{2xz + yz}{2xz - y} = \frac{z(2x + y)}{2xz - y}.$$

(1) This indicates $2x + y = 3$, and so $\frac{2xz + yz}{2xz - y} = \frac{3z}{2xz - y}$. However, this is not enough to determine the value of $\frac{2xz + yz}{2xz - y}$. For example, if $x = 1, y = 1,$ and $z = 2$, then $2x + y = 3$ and $\frac{2xz + yz}{2xz - y} = 2$, but if $x = 0, y = 3,$ and $z = 2$, then $2x + y = 3$ and $\frac{2xz + yz}{2xz - y} = -2$; NOT sufficient.

(2) This indicates that $z = 2$, and so $\frac{2xz + yz}{2xz - y} = \frac{4x + 2y}{4x - y}$. However, this is not enough to determine the value of $\frac{2xz + yz}{2xz - y}$. For example, if $x = 1, y = 1,$ and $z = 2$, then $\frac{2xz + yz}{2xz - y} = 2$, but if $x = 0, y = 3,$ and $z = 2$, then $\frac{2xz + yz}{2xz - y} = -2$; NOT sufficient.

Taking (1) and (2) together is not enough to determine the value of $\frac{2xz + yz}{2xz - y}$ because the same examples used to show that (1) is not sufficient were also used to show that (2) is not sufficient.

The correct answer is E; both statements together are still not sufficient.

DS04852
360. In the parallelogram shown, what is the value of x?

(1) $y = 2x$
(2) $x + z = 120$

Geometry Angles

(1) Given that $y = 2x$ and the fact that adjacent angles of a parallelogram are supplementary, it follows that $180 = x + y = x + 2x = 3x$, or $180 = 3x$. Solving this equation gives $x = 60$; SUFFICIENT.

(2) Given that $x + z = 120$ and the fact that opposite angles of a parallelogram have the same measure, it follows that $120 = x + z = x + x$, or $120 = 2x$. Solving this equation gives $x = 60$; SUFFICIENT.

The correct answer is D; each statement alone is sufficient.

DS06096
361. In a product test of a common cold remedy, x percent of the patients tested experienced side effects from the use of the drug and y percent experienced relief of cold symptoms. What percent of the patients tested experienced both side effects and relief of cold symptoms?

(1) Of the 1,000 patients tested, 15 percent experienced neither side effects nor relief of cold symptoms.
(2) Of the patients tested, 30 percent experienced relief of cold symptoms without side effects.

Algebra Sets

One way to solve problems about sets is by using a contingency table. For the information given in this problem with T representing the total number of people tested, the table might be as follows:

	side effects	no side effects	totals
relief of symptoms			$\left(\frac{y}{100}\right)T$
no relief of symptoms			
totals	$\left(\frac{x}{100}\right)T$		T

(1) Using the information in (1) gives the following table, where 15% of 1,000 is 150.

	side effects	no side effects	totals
relief of symptoms			$\left(\frac{y}{100}\right)(1{,}000)$
no relief of symptoms		150	
totals	$\left(\frac{x}{100}\right)(1{,}000)$		1,000

If $x = 55$ and $y = 55$, then the table becomes

	side effects	no side effects	totals
relief of symptoms	250	300	550
no relief of symptoms	300	150	450
totals	550	450	1,000

and this gives $\frac{250}{1{,}000} = 25\%$ as the percent of patients tested who experienced both side effects and relief of cold symptoms.

However, if $x = 55$ and $y = 50$, then the table becomes

	side effects	no side effects	totals
relief of symptoms	200	300	500
no relief of symptoms	350	150	500
totals	550	450	1,000

and this gives $\frac{200}{1,000} = 20\%$ as the percent of patients tested who experienced both side effects and relief of cold symptoms; NOT sufficient.

(2) This indicates that 30% of the patients tested experienced relief of cold symptoms without side effects. The same examples that were used for (1) can be used here, also, to show that different values can be obtained for the percent of patients tested who experienced both side effects and relief of cold symptoms; NOT sufficient.

Since the examples satisfy both (1) and (2), these statements taken together are not sufficient to determine the percent of patients tested who experienced both side effects and relief of cold symptoms.

The correct answer is E; both statements together are still not sufficient.

DS13588

362. Is $x < 5$?

(1) $x^2 > 5$
(2) $x^2 + x < 5$

Algebra Inequalities

(1) Given that $x^2 > 5$, then $x < 5$ can be true (for example, if $x = -3$) and $x < 5$ can be false (for example, if $x = 6$); NOT sufficient.

(2) Given that $x^2 + x < 5$, then $x < 5 - x^2$. Also, since $x^2 \geq 0$ is true for any real number x, it follows that $-x^2 \leq 0$, or after adding 5 to both sides, $5 - x^2 \leq 5$. From $x < 5 - x^2$ and $5 - x^2 \leq 5$, it follows that $x < 5$; SUFFICIENT.

The correct answer is B; statement 2 alone is sufficient.

DS72951.01

363. Three roommates—Bela, Gyorgy, and Janos—together saved money for a trip. The amount that Bela saved was equal to 8% of his monthly income. The amount that Gyorgy saved was exactly $\frac{1}{3}$ of the total amount saved by all 3 roommates. What was the total amount saved for the trip by all 3 roommates?

(1) Bela had a monthly income of $2,000.
(2) Janos saved 1.5 times as much for the trip as Bela.

Algebra First-degree equations

Letting B, G, and J represent the amounts saved by Bela, Gyorgy, and Janos, respectively, then $B = 0.08I$, where I represents Bela's monthly income, $G = \frac{1}{3}(B + G + J)$, and $G = \frac{1}{2}(B + J)$. Determine the value of $B + G + J$.

(1) This allows the value of B to be determined, but gives no information about the values of G or J; NOT sufficient.

(2) This gives the relationship between the values of J and B, but no information to determine the value of either B or J; NOT sufficient.

Taking (1) and (2) together, the values of both B and J can be determined as can the value of G since $G = \frac{1}{2}(B + J)$. Thus, the value of $B + G + J$ can be determined.

The correct answer is C; both statements together are sufficient.

DS11257

364. Is zp negative?

(1) $pz^4 < 0$
(2) $p + z^4 = 14$

Arithmetic Properties of numbers

(1) Given that $pz^4 < 0$, zp can be negative (choose $p = -2$ and $z = 2$) and zp can be nonnegative (choose $p = -2$ and $z = -2$); NOT sufficient.

(2) Given that $p + z^4 = 14$, the same examples used to show that (1) is not sufficient can be used for (2); NOT sufficient.

Taking (1) and (2) together is of no more help than either (1) or (2) taken separately because the same examples used to show that (1) is not sufficient also show that (2) is not sufficient.

**The correct answer is E;
both statements together are still not sufficient.**

DS04157

365. In each game of a certain tournament, a contestant either loses 3 points or gains 2 points. If Pat had 100 points at the beginning of the tournament, how many games did Pat play in the tournament?

(1) At the end of the tournament, Pat had 104 points.
(2) Pat played fewer than 10 games.

Arithmetic Computation with integers

Pat either lost 3 points or gained 2 points in each game she played. Therefore, since she had 100 points at the beginning of the tournament, her score at the end of the tournament was $100 - 3x + 2y$, where x and y represent, respectively, the number of games in which she lost 3 points and the number of games in which she gained 2 points. Determine the value of $x + y$.

(1) This indicates that $100 - 3x + 2y = 104$, but no information is given about the values of x or y. For example, the values of x and y could be 0 and 2, respectively, so that $x + y = 2$ or the values of x and y could be 2 and 5, respectively, so that $x + y = 7$; NOT sufficient.

(2) This indicates that Pat played fewer than 10 games, but in each of the examples above, Pat played fewer than 10 games; NOT sufficient.

Since the examples given satisfy both (1) and (2), taking (1) and (2) together does not give enough information to determine the value of $x + y$.

**The correct answer is E;
both statements together are still not sufficient.**

DS05631

366. At the beginning of the year, the Finance Committee and the Planning Committee of a certain company each had n members, and no one was a member of both committees. At the end of the year, 5 members left the Finance Committee and 3 members left the Planning Committee. How many members did the Finance Committee have at the beginning of the year?

(1) The ratio of the total number of members who left at the end of the year to the total number of members at the beginning of the year was 1:6.
(2) At the end of the year, 21 members remained on the Planning Committee.

Algebra Applied problems

(1) It is given that $\frac{8}{2n} = \frac{1}{6}$, since a total of $3 + 5 = 8$ members left at the end of the year and there were a total of $n + n = 2n$ members at the beginning of the year. It follows that $(8)(6) = (2n)(1)$, or $n = 24$; SUFFICIENT.

(2) It is given that $n - 3 = 21$, since 3 members from the original n members left the Planning Committee at the end of the year. It follows that $n = 21 + 3 = 24$; SUFFICIENT.

**The correct answer is D;
each statement alone is sufficient.**

DS15561

367. If $xy \neq 0$, is $x^3 + y^3 > 0$?

(1) $x + y > 0$
(2) $xy > 0$

Algebra Inequalities

(1) Given that $x + y > 0$, factor $x^3 + y^3$ as $(x + y)(x^2 - xy + y^2)$ and consider $x^2 - xy + y^2$. If $xy < 0$, then $x^2 - xy + y^2$ is the sum of $x^2 + y^2$ (which is greater than or equal to 0) and $-xy$ (which is greater than 0), and so $x^2 - xy + y^2 > 0$. (In fact, $x^2 + y^2 > 0$, since from $xy \neq 0$ it follows that $x \neq 0$ and $y \neq 0$.) If $xy > 0$, then $xy < 2xy$ and $2xy \leq x^2 + y^2$ (this follows from $0 \leq x^2 - 2xy + y^2$, which in turn follows from $0 \leq (x - y)^2$), and therefore $xy < x^2 + y^2$, or $x^2 - xy + y^2 > 0$. Finally, $xy = 0$ is not possible from the information given. Thus, from the information given, it is always the case that

$x^2 - xy + y^2$ is positive, and hence $x^3 + y^3$ is the product of two positive quantities, $x + y$ and $x^2 - xy + y^2$, and therefore $x^3 + y^3 > 0$.

By using ideas involving functions and their graphs, a shorter argument can be given. The function $f(x) = x^3$ is a strictly increasing function, which is evident from its graph. Thus, if $a < b$, then $f(a) < f(b)$, or $a^3 < b^3$. From (1) it follows that $x > -y$. Therefore, $x^3 < (-y)^3$, or $x^3 < -y^3$, or $x^3 + y^3 < 0$; SUFFICIENT.

(2) Given that $xy > 0$, it is possible that $x^3 + y^3 > 0$ (choose $x = y = 1$) and it is possible that $x^3 + y^3 < 0$ (choose $x = y = -1$); NOT sufficient.

The correct answer is A; statement 1 alone is sufficient.

DS13541
368. Max purchased a guitar for a total of $624, which consisted of the price of the guitar and the sales tax. Was the sales tax rate greater than 3 percent?

(1) The price of the guitar that Max purchased was less than $602.
(2) The sales tax for the guitar that Max purchased was less than $30.

Arithmetic Applied problems; Percents

Letting P be the price, in dollars, of the guitar and $r\%$ be the sales tax rate, it is given that $P\left(1 + \dfrac{r}{100}\right) = 624$. Determine if $r > 3$.

(1) Given that $P < 602$, then $624 = P\left(1 + \dfrac{r}{100}\right) < 602\left(1 + \dfrac{r}{100}\right)$, and so

$1 + \dfrac{r}{100} > \dfrac{624}{602}$. Therefore, $\dfrac{r}{100} >$

$\dfrac{624}{602} - 1 = \dfrac{22}{602} = \dfrac{11}{301} > \dfrac{3}{100}$, because

$(11)(100) > (3)(301)$, and so $r >$

$100\left(\dfrac{3}{100}\right) = 3$; SUFFICIENT.

(2) Given that the sales tax was less than $30, it is not possible to determine whether the sales tax rate was greater than 3%. Since $(0.03)(\$624) = \$18.72$, a 3% sales tax rate on the price corresponds to a sales tax that is less than $18.72, since the price is less than $624. Therefore, it is possible that the sales tax is less than $30 and the sales tax rate is less than 3%, since any sales tax rate less than 3% would give a sales tax that is less than $18.72 (and hence less than $30). However, it is also possible that the sales tax is less than $30 and the sales tax rate is 4% (which is greater than 3%), since a 4% sales tax rate implies $P\left(1 + \dfrac{4}{100}\right) = 624$, or $P = \dfrac{62,400}{104} = 600$, and thus the sales tax would be $0.04(\$600) = \$24 < \$30$; NOT sufficient.

The correct answer is A; statement 1 alone is sufficient.

DS75271.01
369. A pentagon with 5 sides of equal length and 5 interior angles of equal measure is inscribed in a circle. Is the perimeter of the pentagon greater than 26 centimeters?

(1) The area of the circle is 16π square centimeters.
(2) The length of each diagonal of the pentagon is less than 8 centimeters.

Geometry Polygons

A regular pentagon can be partitioned into 5 isosceles triangles, one of which is shown in the figure below. The vertex angle of each of these triangles has measure $72°$. If $s = r$, then each of the 5 triangles would be equilateral with vertex angle measuring $60°$, not $72°$. If $s < r$, then the vertex of each of the 5 triangles would measure less than $60°$. Therefore, $s > r$. If P represents the perimeter, determine if $P > 26$.

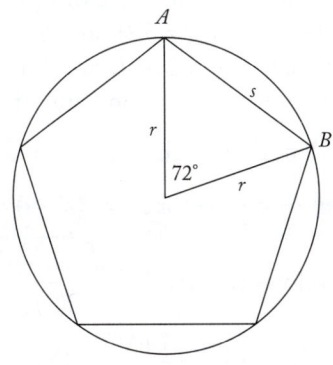

(1) This gives $r = 4$, so the circumference of the circle is 8π. The length of arc $\overset{\frown}{AB}$ is

347

$\left(\frac{72}{360}\right)(8\pi) = \frac{8\pi}{5}$. Also, $s < \frac{8\pi}{5}$ because a straight line is the shortest distance between two points, so $P < 8\pi$, or equivalently, $\frac{P}{8} < \pi$. If $P > 26$ were true, then $\frac{P}{8} > 3.25$ would be true. But $3.25 > \pi$ so $\frac{P}{8} > \pi$, which contradicts $\frac{P}{8} < \pi$ and so contradicts $P > 26$. It follows that the answer to "Is P greater than 26?" is definitively "no"; SUFFICIENT.

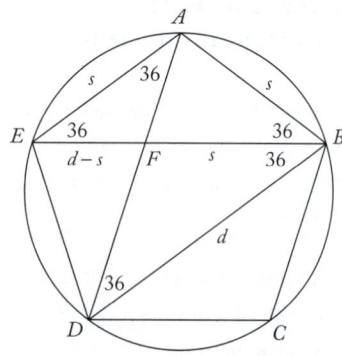

(2) Diagonals $\overline{AD}$, $\overline{BD}$, and $\overline{BE}$ are shown in the figure above. Using these diagonals, each with length d, plus the facts that all the sides of the pentagon are the same length, the degree measure of each of the pentagon's interior angles is 108, and the base angles of an isosceles triangle have equal degree measures, the angle measures, in degrees, shown in the figure can be verified. Also it can be shown that $\triangle ABF$ is isosceles (the degree measure of $\angle FAB$ is $108 - 36 = 72$ and the degree measure of $\angle AFB$ is $180 - (36 + 72) = 72$), so $FB = s$. It follows that $\triangle AFE$ and $\triangle BFD$ are similar and their sides are in proportion. Thus, if d represents the length of each diagonal of the pentagon, then $\frac{s}{d} = \frac{d-s}{s}$ or $s^2 = d(d-s) = d^2 - ds$.

It follows that $d = \frac{s \pm \sqrt{s^2 + 4(1)s^2}}{2(1)}$, which simplifies to $d = \frac{1+\sqrt{5}}{2}s$. (Note that $d = \frac{s - \sqrt{s^2 + 4(1)s^2}}{2(1)} = \frac{1-\sqrt{5}}{2}s$ has been

discarded because $\frac{1-\sqrt{5}}{2}$ is negative and $\frac{1-\sqrt{5}}{2}s$ cannot be a length.) It is given that $d < 8$ from which it follows that $\frac{1+\sqrt{5}}{2}s < 8$ and thus $s < \frac{16}{1+\sqrt{5}}$. Since $P = 5s$, it follows that $P < \frac{80}{1+\sqrt{5}} = \left(\frac{80}{1+\sqrt{5}}\right)\left(\frac{1-\sqrt{5}}{1-\sqrt{5}}\right) = \frac{80(1-\sqrt{5})}{-4} = 20(\sqrt{5}-1)$. It is true that $20(\sqrt{5}-1) < 26$ because if $20(\sqrt{5}-1) \geq 26$, then $(\sqrt{5}-1) \geq \frac{13}{10}$, and $\sqrt{5} \geq \frac{23}{10}$, from which it follows that $5 \geq \frac{529}{100}$ or $5 \geq 5.29$. But, this is not true and so $20(\sqrt{5}-1) < 26$ and $P < 26$. Therefore, the answer to the question "Is P greater than 26?" is definitively "no"; SUFFICIENT.

The correct answer is D; each statement alone is sufficient.

DS13841.01
370. If 2.00X and 3.00Y are 2 numbers in decimal form with thousandths digits X and Y, is 3(2.00X) > 2(3.00Y)?

(1) $3X < 2Y$
(2) $X < Y - 3$

Arithmetic Operations with integers

The decimals $3(2.00X)$ and $2(3.00Y)$ can also be expressed as $3\left(2 + \frac{X}{1,000}\right) = 6 + \frac{3X}{1,000}$ and $2\left(3 + \frac{Y}{1,000}\right) = 6 + \frac{2Y}{1,000}$. Then, $3(2.00X) > 2(3.00Y)$ only if $3X > 2Y$. Determine if $3X > 2Y$ is true.

(1) Given that $3X < 2Y$, it follows that $3X > 2Y$ is not true and so $3(2.00X) > 2(3.00Y)$ is not true for all integer values of X and Y from 0 through 9; SUFFICIENT.

(2) Given that $X < Y - 3$, if $X = 0$, then the possible values for Y are 4, 5, 6, 7, 8, and 9. For each of these values, $3X > 2Y$ is not true. If $X = 1$, then the possible values for

Y are 5, 6, 7, 8, and 9 and for each of these values, $3X > 2Y$ is not true. If $X = 2$, then the possible values for *Y* are 6, 7, 8, and 9 and for each of these values, $3X > 2Y$ is not true. If $X = 3$, then the possible values for *Y* are 7, 8, and 9 and for each of these values, $3X > 2Y$ is not true. If $X = 4$, then the possible values for *Y* are 8 and 9 and for each of these values, $3X > 2Y$ is not true. If $X = 5$, then the only possible value for *Y* is 9 and for this value, $3X > 2Y$ is not true. If $X \geq 6$, there are no integer values from 0 through 9 for which $X < Y - 3$. In all possible cases, $3X > 2Y$ is not true, so $3(2.00X) > 2(3.00Y)$ is not true; SUFFICIENT.

Alternatively, if $X < Y - 3$, then $X + 3 < Y$. If $3X > 2Y$ were true, or equivalently, if $Y < \frac{3}{2}X$ were true, then $X + 3 < Y < \frac{3}{2}X$ would be true, from which it follows that $X + 3 < \frac{3}{2}X$ would be true. But, this would imply $X > 6$ is true, which cannot be true because if $X + 3 < Y$, then $Y > 9$, and *Y* cannot be greater than 9 because *Y* is a digit.

**The correct answer is D;
each statement alone is sufficient.**

DS50351.01
371. The length, width, and height of a rectangular box, in centimeters, are *L*, *W*, and *H*. If the volume of this box is *V* cubic centimeters and the total area of the 6 sides of this box is *A* square centimeters, what is the value of $\frac{V}{A}$?

(1) At least 2 of *L*, *W*, and *H* are equal to 5.
(2) *L*, *W*, and *H* all have the same value.

Geometry Volume; Surface area

For a rectangular box with dimensions *L*, *W*, and *H*, $V = LWH$ and $A = 2(LW + LH + WH)$. Determine the value of $\frac{V}{A}$.

(1) Given that at least 2 of the dimensions are 5, if $L = W = 5$ and $H = 1$, then $\frac{V}{A} = \frac{(5)(5)(1)}{2[(5)(5)+(2)(5)(1)]} = \frac{25}{70} = \frac{5}{14}$. However, if $L = W = 5$ and $H = 2$, then $\frac{V}{A} = \frac{(5)(5)(2)}{2[(5)(5)+(2)(5)(2)]} = \frac{50}{90} = \frac{5}{9}$; NOT sufficient.

(2) Given that *L*, *W*, and *H* all have the same value, then letting *s* represent that value, $\frac{V}{A} = \frac{s^3}{2(3s^2)}$ and this value differs as *s* differs; NOT sufficient.

Taking (1) and (2) together, $L = W = H = 5$ and a unique value for $\frac{V}{A}$ can be determined.

**The correct answer is C;
both statements together are sufficient.**

DS06027
372. What is the sum of a certain pair of consecutive odd integers?

(1) At least one of the integers is negative.
(2) At least one of the integers is positive.

Arithmetic Properties of numbers

(1) Given that at least one of the integers is negative, the sum could be –4 (if the integers were –3 and –1) and the sum could be 0 (if the integers were –1 and 1); NOT sufficient.

(2) Given that at least one of the integers is positive, the sum could be 0 (if the integers were –1 and 1) and the sum could be 4 (if the integers were 1 and 3); NOT sufficient.

Taking (1) and (2) together, the smaller of the two numbers cannot be less than –1 (otherwise (2) would not be true) and the larger of the two numbers cannot be greater than 1 (otherwise (1) would not be true). Therefore, the integers must be –1 and 1, and the sum must be 0.

**The correct answer is C;
both statements together are sufficient.**

DS45530.01
373. Is $x = y$?

(1) $\frac{2x}{3} - \frac{y}{3} = \frac{1}{3}$
(2) $\frac{x}{4} - \frac{y}{4} = 0$

349

Algebra First-degree equations

(1) Given that $\frac{2x}{3} - \frac{y}{3} = \frac{1}{3}$, or equivalently $2x - y = 1$, it is not possible to determine whether $x = y$ is true. For example, if $x = 1$ and $y = 1$, then $2(1) - 1 = 1$ and $x = y$. However, if $x = 2$ and $y = 3$, then $2(2) - 3 = 1$ and $x \neq y$; NOT sufficient.

(2) Given that $\frac{x}{4} - \frac{y}{4} = 0$, then multiplying both sides by 4 gives $x - y = 0$, which means $x = y$; SUFFICIENT.

The correct answer is B; statement 2 alone is sufficient.

DS08197
374. The sum of 4 different odd integers is 64. What is the value of the greatest of these integers?

(1) The integers are consecutive odd numbers.
(2) Of these integers, the greatest is 6 more than the least.

Arithmetic Properties of numbers

Determine the greatest of four odd integers whose sum is 64.

(1) This indicates that the integers are consecutive odd integers. Letting z represent the greatest of the four integers, it follows that $(z - 6) + (z - 4) + (z - 2) + z = 64$, from which a unique value of z can be determined; SUFFICIENT.

(2) Letting w, x, y, and z represent four different odd integers, where $w < x < y < z$, this indicates that $z - w = 6$ or $w = z - 6$. This means that $x = z - 4$ and $y = z - 2$ since $w, x, y,$ and z must be different odd integers and it must be true that $w < x < y < z$. From $w + x + y + z = 64$, it follows that $(z - 6) + (z - 4) + (z - 2) + z = 64$ from which a unique value of z can be determined; SUFFICIENT.

The correct answer is D; each statement alone is sufficient.

DS13130
375. Was the number of books sold at Bookstore X last week greater than the number of books sold at Bookstore Y last week?

(1) Last week, more than 1,000 books were sold at Bookstore X on Saturday and fewer than 1,000 books were sold at Bookstore Y on Saturday.
(2) Last week, less than 20 percent of the books sold at Bookstore X were sold on Saturday and more than 20 percent of the books sold at Bookstore Y were sold on Saturday.

Arithmetic Inequalities

Determine if Bookstore X sold more books last week than Bookstore Y.

(1) This indicates that Bookstore X sold more books on Saturday than Bookstore Y, but it gives no information about the numbers of books sold by the two bookstores on the other days of last week; NOT sufficient.

(2) This gives information about the percents of the books sold last week that were sold on Saturday, but it gives no information about the actual numbers of books sold at the two bookstores last week. Therefore, a comparison of the numbers of books sold last week by Bookstore X and Bookstore Y is not possible; NOT sufficient.

Taking (1) and (2) together, if x represents the number of books that Bookstore X sold on Saturday and T_X represents the total number of books that Bookstore X sold last week, then $x > 1,000$ and $x < 0.2T_X$. It follows that $1,000 < 0.2T_X$ and so $T_X > 5,000$. Similarly, if y represents the number of books that Bookstore Y sold on Saturday and T_Y represents the total number of books that Bookstore Y sold last week, then $y < 1,000$ and $y > 0.2T_Y$. It follows that $0.2T_Y < 1,000$, and so $T_Y < 5,000$. Combining the inequalities gives $T_Y < 5,000 < T_X$, and so $T_Y < T_X$, which means that Bookstore X sold more books last week than Bookstore Y.

The correct answer is C; both statements together are sufficient.

DS47651.01
376. A rectangular solid has length, width, and height of L cm, W cm, and H cm, respectively. If these dimensions are increased by x%, y%, and z%, respectively, what is the percentage increase in the total surface area of the solid?

  (1) L, W, and H are in the ratios of 5:3:4.
  (2) x = 5, y = 10, z = 20

Geometry Surface area

The total surface area of a rectangular solid with dimensions l, w, and h is given by $2(lw + lh + wh)$.

  (1) This gives the relationships among the dimensions of the solid, but gives no information about the percentages by which the dimensions are increased; NOT sufficient.

  (2) This gives the percentages by which the dimensions are increased, but gives no information about the dimensions themselves; NOT sufficient.

Taking (1) and (2) together gives both the relationships among the dimensions and the percentages by which the dimensions are increased. From the ratios given in (1) and letting the constant of proportionality be 1, which causes no loss of generality, $L = 5$, $W = 3$, and $H = 4$. The dimensions of the enlarged solid can be determined by multiplying L by 1.05, W by 1.1, and H by 1.2. The percent increase in the surface area of the solid is given by
$$\frac{\text{SA of enlarged solid} - \text{SA of original solid}}{\text{SA of original solid}} \times 100,$$
where SA is short for surface area. The total surface area of the original solid and the enlarged solid can be determined by substituting their dimensions into the formula for total surface area. Thus, the percent increase can be determined. Note that it is not necessary to do the actual calculations.

The correct answer is C; both statements together are sufficient.

DS08091.01
377. A certain list, L, contains a total of n numbers, not necessarily distinct, that are arranged in increasing order. If L_1 is the list consisting of the first n_1 numbers in L and L_2 is the list consisting of the last n_2 numbers in L, is 17 a mode for L?

  (1) 17 is a mode for L_1 and 17 is a mode for L_2.
  (2) $n_1 + n_2 = n$

Arithmetic Statistics

  (1) By (1), 17 is a mode of both L_1 and L_2. Therefore, 17 must occur in L_1 and either more times or the same number of times as any other number in L_1. Similarly, 17 must occur in L_2 and either more times or the same number of times as any other number in L_2. Since the numbers in L are in ascending order, every number between the last occurrence of 17 in L_1 and the first occurrence of 17 in L_2 must be 17; otherwise the least number in L_2 would be greater than 17 and 17 would not occur in L_2. Thus, 17 occurs either more times or the same number of times as any other number in L and 17 is a mode of L; SUFFICIENT.

  (2) If, for example, $n = 7$, $n_1 = 3$ and $n_2 = 4$, then L could be 1, 2, 3, 17, 17, 18, 19 where L_1 is 1, 2, 3 and L_2 is 17, 17, 18, 19, and 17 is the only mode of L. But, L could also be 5, 5, 5, 16, 17, 18, 19 where L_1 is 5, 5, 5 and L_2 is 16, 17, 18, 19, and 5 is the only mode of L; NOT sufficient.

The correct answer is A; statement 1 alone is sufficient.

DS04540
378. From May 1 to May 30 in the same year, the balance in a checking account increased. What was the balance in the checking account on May 30?

  (1) If, during this period of time, the increase in the balance in the checking account had been 12 percent, then the balance in the account on May 30 would have been $504.
  (2) During this period of time, the increase in the balance in the checking account was 8 percent.

Arithmetic Applied problems; Percents

  (1) Given that the amount on May 30 would have been $504 if the increase had been

12%, it follows that the amount on May 1 was $\frac{504}{1.12}$ = $450. However, the balance on May 30 cannot be determined because the (actual) percent increase is not given. For example, if the increase had been 10%, then the balance on May 30 would have been (1.1)($450) = $495, which is different from $504; NOT sufficient.

(2) Given that the increase was 8%, the amount on May 30 could be $108 (if the amount on May 1 was $100) and the amount on May 30 could be $216 (if the amount on May 1 was $200); NOT sufficient.

Taking (1) and (2) together, it follows that the amount on May 30 was ($450)(1.08) = $486.

The correct answer is C;
both statements together are sufficient.

DS08365

379. A merchant discounted the sale price of a coat and the sale price of a sweater. Which of the two articles of clothing was discounted by the greater dollar amount?

(1) The percent discount on the coat was 2 percentage points greater than the percent discount on the sweater.

(2) Before the discounts, the sale price of the coat was $10 less than the sale price of the sweater.

Arithmetic Applied problems; Percents

(1) Given that the discount on the coat was 2 percentage points greater than the discount on the sweater, the sweater could have been discounted by the greater dollar amount ($30 sweater with 10% discount is a discount of $3; $20 coat with 12% discount is a discount of $2.40) and the coat could have been discounted by the greater dollar amount ($110 sweater with 10% discount is a discount of $11; $100 coat with 12% discount is a discount of $12); NOT sufficient.

(2) Given that the coat's sale price was $10 less than the sweater's sale price, the same examples used to show that (1) is not sufficient can be used for (2); NOT sufficient.

Taking (1) and (2) together is of no more help than either (1) or (2) taken separately because the same examples used to show that (1) is not sufficient also show that (2) is not sufficient.

The correct answer is E;
both statements together are still not sufficient.

DS01168

380. If the positive integer n is added to each of the integers 69, 94, and 121, what is the value of n?

(1) $69 + n$ and $94 + n$ are the squares of two consecutive integers.

(2) $94 + n$ and $121 + n$ are the squares of two consecutive integers.

Algebra Computation with integers

Determine the value of the positive integer n.

(1) This indicates that $69 + n$ and $94 + n$ are the squares of two consecutive integers. Letting x and $(x + 1)$ represent the consecutive integers, it follows that $(x + 1)^2 - x^2 = x^2 + 2x + 1 - x^2 = 2x + 1$. Therefore, $(94 + n) - (69 + n) = 2x + 1$ or $25 = 2x + 1$, from which $x = 12$. Then $12^2 = 69 + n$ and $n = 144 - 69 = 75$ or $(12 + 1)^2 = 94 + n$ and $n = 169 - 94 = 75$; SUFFICIENT.

(2) This indicates that $94 + n$ and $121 + n$ are the squares of two consecutive integers. Letting x and $(x + 1)$ represent the consecutive integers, it follows that $(x + 1)^2 - x^2 = x^2 + 2x + 1 - x^2 = 2x + 1$. Therefore, $(121 + n) - (94 + n) = 2x + 1$ or $27 = 2x + 1$, from which $x = 13$. Then $13^2 = 94 + n$ and $n = 169 - 94 = 75$ or $(13 + 1)^2 = 121 + n$ and $n = 196 - 121 = 75$; SUFFICIENT.

The correct answer is D;
each statement alone is sufficient.

DS71521.01

381. If a merchant purchased a sofa from a manufacturer for $400 and then sold it, what was the selling price of the sofa?

(1) The selling price of the sofa was greater than 140 percent of the purchase price.

(2) The merchant's gross profit from the purchase and sale of the sofa was $\frac{1}{3}$ of the selling price.

Algebra Applied problems

Letting s represent the selling price of the sofa, in dollars, determine the value of s.

(1) The condition that the selling price of the sofa was greater than 140 percent of the purchase price is equivalent to $s > 1.4(400)$, from which it is not possible to determine the selling price; NOT sufficient.

(2) Given that the gross profit from the purchase and sale of the sofa was $\frac{1}{3}$ of the selling price, it follows that $s - 400 = \frac{1}{3}s$ since gross profit is defined to be the selling price minus the purchase price. From this, a unique value of s can be determined; SUFFICIENT.

The correct answer is B; statement 2 alone is sufficient.

DS05269

382. Last year, in a certain housing development, the average (arithmetic mean) price of 20 new houses was $160,000. Did more than 9 of the 20 houses have prices that were less than the average price last year?

    (1) Last year the greatest price of one of the 20 houses was $219,000.

    (2) Last year the median of the prices of the 20 houses was $150,000.

Arithmetic Statistics

(1) Given that the greatest price was $219,000, it is possible that only one of the houses had a price less than $160,000. For example, the 20 houses that have an average price of $160,000 could have been 18 houses each at $160,000, one house at $219,000 = $160,000 + $59,000 and one house at $101,000 = $160,000 − $59,000. On the other hand, it is possible that 19 of the houses had a price less than $160,000. For example, the 20 houses that have an average price of $160,000 could have been 18 houses each at $159,000 = $160,000 − $1,000, one house at $219,000 = $160,000 + $59,000 and one house at $119,000 = $160,000 − $59,000 + $18,000. Therefore, it is not possible to determine whether more than 9 of the houses had prices less than $160,000; NOT sufficient.

(2) Given that the median of the 20 prices was $150,000, then when the prices are listed in numerical order from least to greatest, it follows that at least 10 of the prices are less than or equal to $150,000, and hence more than 9 of the prices are less than $160,000. For one of these 10 prices this is true because the median is the average of the 10th and 11th prices, and so the 10th price cannot be greater than $150,000, otherwise both the 10th and 11th prices would be greater than $150,000 and their average would be greater than $150,000. The other 9 of these 10 prices are the 1st through 9th prices, since each of these is less than or equal to the 10th price; SUFFICIENT.

The correct answer is B; statement 2 alone is sufficient.

DS14527

383. For a certain city's library, the average cost of purchasing each new book is $28. The library receives $15,000 from the city each year; the library also receives a bonus of $2,000 if the total number of items checked out over the course of the year exceeds 5,000. Did the library receive the bonus last year?

    (1) The library purchased an average of 50 new books each month last year and received enough money from the city to cover this cost.

    (2) The lowest number of items checked out in one month was 459.

Arithmetic Applied problems

(1) Given that the library purchased an average of 50 new books each month, for the entire year the library purchased a total of $(50)(12) = 600$ books for a total cost of $(600)(\$28) = \$16,800$. Excluding any possible bonus, the library received $15,000 from the city. Since this amount received from the city is not enough to cover the cost of the books, and the information provided in (1) says that the total amount received from the city was enough to cover the cost of the books, it follows that the library received a bonus; SUFFICIENT.

(2) Given that the least number of books checked out in one month was 459, it follows that the total number of books checked out for the year was at least (12)(459) = 5,508. Since this is greater than 5,000, it follows that the total number of books checked out for the year was greater than 5,000 and the library received a bonus; SUFFICIENT.

**The correct answer is D;
each statement alone is sufficient.**

DS89950.01

7, 9, 6, 4, 5, x

384. If x is a number in the list above, what is the median of the list?

(1) $x > 7$

(2) The median of the list equals the arithmetic mean of the list.

Arithmetic Statistics

(1) The given numbers in the list, in order, are 4, 5, 6, 7, 9. From (1), $x > 7$, so the list could be 4, 5, 6, 7, x, 9 or the list could be 4, 5, 6, 7, 9, x. In either case, the two middle numbers are 6 and 7 and the median is $\frac{6+7}{2} = \frac{13}{2}$; SUFFICIENT.

(2) The mean of the list is $\frac{7+9+6+4+5+x}{6} = \frac{31+x}{6}$, which depends on the value of x. Likewise, the median depends on the value of x. If $x = 2$, then the list is 2, 4, 5, 6, 7, 9, which has median $\frac{5+6}{2} = \frac{11}{2}$ and arithmetic mean $\frac{31+2}{6} = \frac{33}{6} = \frac{11}{2}$, thereby satisfying (2). However, if $x = 8$, then the list is 4, 5, 6, 7, 8, 9, which has median $\frac{6+7}{2} = \frac{13}{2}$ and arithmetic mean $\frac{31+8}{6} = \frac{39}{6} = \frac{13}{2}$, thereby satisfying (2); NOT sufficient.

**The correct answer is A;
statement 1 alone is sufficient.**

DS15045

385. Three dice, each of which has its 6 sides numbered 1 through 6, are tossed. The sum of the 3 numbers that are facing up is 12. Is at least 1 of these numbers 5 ?

(1) None of the 3 numbers that are facing up is divisible by 3.

(2) Of the numbers that are facing up, 2, but not all 3, are equal.

Arithmetic Properties of integers

When three dice, each with its 6 faces numbered 1 through 6, are tossed and the sum of the three integers facing up is 12, the possible outcomes are {1, 5, 6}, {2, 4, 6}, {2, 5, 5}, {3, 3, 6}, {3, 4, 5}, and {4, 4, 4}. Determine if, in the outcome described, at least one of the numbers is 5.

(1) This indicates that none of the numbers is divisible by three. The outcome could be {4, 4, 4}. In this case, none of the three numbers is 5. On the other hand, the outcome could be {2, 5, 5}. In this case, at least one of the numbers is 5; NOT sufficient.

(2) This indicates that two of the numbers, but not all three, are equal. The outcome could be {3, 3, 6}. In this case, none of the three numbers is 5. On the other hand, the outcome could be {2, 5, 5}. In this case, at least one of the numbers is 5; NOT sufficient.

Taking (1) and (2) together, of the possible outcomes {1, 5, 6}, {2, 4, 6}, {3, 3, 6}, and {3, 4, 5} are eliminated because they do not satisfy (1), and {4, 4, 4} is eliminated because it does not satisfy (2). This leaves only {2, 5, 5}, and at least one number is 5.

**The correct answer is C;
both statements together are sufficient.**

DS01324

386. On the number line, point R has coordinate r and point T has coordinate t. Is $t < 0$?

(1) $-1 < r < 0$

(2) The distance between R and T is equal to r^2.

Arithmetic Number line

Determine if t, the coordinate of point T on the number line, is negative.

(1) This indicates that r, the coordinate of point R on the number line, lies between −1 and 0, but gives no information about the location of T in relation to either point R or 0; NOT sufficient.

(2) This indicates that the distance between R and T, which can be expressed as $|r - t|$, is r^2. If $r = 2$, for example, then $|2 - t| = 4$ so $2 - t = 4$ or $2 - t = -4$. If $2 - t = 4$, then $t = -2$, which is negative. If $2 - t = -4$, then $t = 6$, which is not negative; NOT sufficient.

Taking (1) and (2) together, if $r - t \geq 0$, then $r - t = r^2$ and $t = r - r^2 = r(1 - r)$. Since $-1 < r < 0$, it follows that $1 < 1 - r < 2$, and so t is the product of a negative number (r) and a positive number ($1 - r$) and is therefore negative. Similarly, if $r - t < 0$, then $|r - t| = -(r - t) = t - r = r^2$ and $t = r^2 + r = r(r + 1)$. Since $-1 < r < 0$, it follows that $0 < r + 1 < 1$, and so t is the product of a negative number (r) and the positive number ($r + 1$) and is therefore negative.

The correct answer is C; both statements together are sufficient.

DS06659

387. S is a set of points in the plane. How many distinct triangles can be drawn that have three of the points in S as vertices?

(1) The number of distinct points in S is 5.
(2) No three of the points in S are collinear.

Arithmetic Elementary combinatorics

(1) Given that the number of points in S is 5, the number of triangles can be 0 (if the points are collinear) and the number of triangles can be greater than 0 (if the points are not all collinear); NOT sufficient.

(2) Given that no three points of S are collinear, the number of triangles can be 1 (if S consists of 3 points) and the number of triangles can be 4 (if S consists of 4 points); NOT sufficient.

Taking (1) and (2) together, the number of distinct triangles must be $\binom{5}{3} = \frac{5!}{3!(5-3)!} = 10$, which is the number of combinations of 5 points taken 3 at a time.

The correct answer is C; both statements together are sufficient.

DS16078

388. Stores L and M each sell a certain product at a different regular price. If both stores discount their regular price of the product, is the discount price at Store M less than the discount price at Store L?

(1) At Store L the discount price is 10 percent less than the regular price; at Store M the discount price is 15 percent less than the regular price.
(2) At Store L the discount price is $5 less than the regular store price; at Store M the discount price is $6 less than the regular price.

Arithmetic Percents

Let L_r and L_d be the regular and discounted prices, respectively, at Store L, and let M_r and M_d be the regular and discounted prices, respectively, at Store M. Determine if $M_d < L_d$.

(1) Knowing that $L_d = (1 - 0.10)L_r = 0.90L_r$ and that $M_d = (1 - 0.15)M_r = 0.85M_r$ gives no information for comparing M_d and L_d; NOT sufficient.

(2) Knowing that $L_d = L_r - 5$ and that $M_d = M_r - 6$ gives no information for comparing M_d and L_d; NOT sufficient.

Taking (1) and (2) together gives $0.90L_r = L_r - 5$ and $0.85 M_r = M_r - 6$, from which it follows that $0.10L_r = 5$ or $L_r = 50$ and $0.15M_r = 6$ or $M_r = 40$. Then $L_d = 50 - 5 = 45$ and $M_d = 40 - 6 = 34$. Therefore, $M_d < L_d$.

The correct answer is C; both statements together are sufficient.

DS16529

389. If d denotes a decimal, is $d \geq 0.5$?

(1) When d is rounded to the nearest tenth, the result is 0.5.
(2) When d is rounded to the nearest integer, the result is 1.

355

Arithmetic Rounding; Estimating

(1) In this case, for example, the value of d could range from the decimal 0.45 to 0.54. Some of these, such as 0.51 or 0.52, are greater than or equal to 0.5, and others, such as 0.47 or 0.48, are less than 0.5; NOT sufficient.

(2) When the result of rounding d to the nearest integer is 1, d could range in value from the decimal 0.50 to 1.49, which are greater than or equal to 0.5; SUFFICIENT.

The correct answer is B; statement 2 alone is sufficient.

DS08231

390. In the two-digit integers 3■ and 2▲, the symbols ■ and ▲ represent different digits, and the product (3■)(2▲) is equal to 864. What digit does ■ represent?

(1) The sum of ■ and ▲ is 10.
(2) The product of ■ and ▲ is 24.

Arithmetic Properties of numbers

(1) Given that ■ + ▲ = 10, then the possible products ■▲ are (1)(9) = (9)(1) = 9, (2)(8) = (8)(2) = 16, (3)(7) = (7)(3) = 21, (4)(6) = (6)(4) = 24, and (5)(5) = 25. Since (3■)(2▲) = 864 has units digit 4, it follows that ■▲ must also have units digit 4. Since only two of the possible products of ■▲ has units digit 4, it follows that ■ = 4 and ▲ = 6, or ■ = 6 and ▲ = 4. If ■ = 4 and ▲ = 6, then (3■)(2▲) = (34)(26) = 884 ≠ 864, and if ■ = 6 and ▲ = 4, then (3■)(2▲) = (36)(24) = 864. Therefore, ■ = 6; SUFFICIENT.

(2) Given that ■▲ = 24, and that both ■ and ▲ are digits, there are four possibilities for the values of ■ and ▲.
  (a) ■ = 3 and ▲ = 8, which gives (3■)(2▲) = (33)(28) = 924 ≠ 864;
  (b) ■ = 4 and ▲ = 6, which gives (3■)(2▲) = (34)(26) = 884 ≠ 864;
  (c) ■ = 6 and ▲ = 4, which gives (3■)(2▲) = (36)(24) = 864;
  (d) ■ = 8 and ▲ = 3, which gives (3■)(2▲) = (38)(23) = 874 ≠ 864.
  Therefore, ■ = 6; SUFFICIENT.

The correct answer is D; each statement alone is sufficient.

———•———————ℓ
   M

DS07262

391. Two points, N and Q (not shown), lie to the right of point M on line ℓ. What is the ratio of the length of QN to the length of MQ?

(1) Twice the length of MN is 3 times the length of MQ.
(2) Point Q is between points M and N.

Algebra Order

(1) Given that twice the length of MN is 3 times the length of MQ, it follows that the points are ordered from left to right as M, Q, and N. Thus, letting $MQ = x$ and $QN = y$, it is given that $2(x + y) = 3x$ and the value of $\frac{y}{x}$ is to be determined. The given equation can be rewritten as $2x + 2y = 3x$, or $2y = x$, or $\frac{y}{x} = \frac{1}{2}$; SUFFICIENT.

(2) Given that Q is between M and N, the ratio of QN to MQ can be close to zero (if Q and N are close together and both far from M) and the ratio of QN to MQ can be large (if M and Q are close together and both far from N); NOT sufficient.

The correct answer is A; statement 1 alone is sufficient.

DS05639

392. Did the sum of the prices of three shirts exceed $60?

(1) The price of the most expensive of the shirts exceeded $30.
(2) The price of the least expensive of the shirts exceeded $20.

Arithmetic Applied problems

(1) Given that the price of the most expensive shirt exceeded $30, the sum of the prices of the shirts can be under $60 (if the prices were $10, $10, and $35) and the sum of the prices of the shirts can be over $60 (if the prices were $10, $10, and $50); NOT sufficient.

(2) Given that the price of the least expensive shirt exceeded $20, it follows that the sum of the prices of the shirts exceeds 3($20) = $60; SUFFICIENT.

The correct answer is B; statement 2 alone is sufficient.

393. What is the total number of coins that Bert and Claire have?

    (1) Bert has 50 percent more coins than Claire.
    (2) The total number of coins that Bert and Claire have is between 21 and 28.

Arithmetic Computation with integers

Determine the total number of coins Bert and Claire have. If B represents the number of coins that Bert has and C represents the number of coins that Claire has, determine $B + C$.

(1) Bert has 50% more coins than Claire, so $B = 1.5C$, and $B + C = 1.5C + C = 2.5C$, but the value of C can vary; NOT sufficient.

(2) The total number of coins Bert and Claire have is between 21 and 28, so $21 < B + C < 28$ and, therefore, $B + C$ could be 22, 23, 24, 25, 26, or 27; NOT sufficient.

Taking (1) and (2) together, $21 < 2.5C < 28$ and then $\frac{21}{2.5} < C < \frac{28}{2.5}$ or $8.4 < C < 11.2$.

If $C = 9$, then $B = (1.5)(9) = 13.5$; if $C = 10$, then $B = (1.5)(10) = 15$; and if $C = 11$, then $B = (1.5)(11) = 16.5$. Since B represents a number of coins, B is an integer. Therefore, $B = 15$, $C = 10$, and $B + C = 25$.

The correct answer is C; both statements together are sufficient.

394. A telephone station has x processors, each of which can process a maximum of y calls at any particular time, where x and y are positive integers. If 500 calls are sent to the station at a particular time, can the station process all of the calls?

    (1) $x = 600$
    (2) $100 < y < 200$

Algebra Applied problems

At a particular time, the telephone station can process a maximum of xy calls, where x and y are positive integers. Determine whether $xy \geq 500$.

(1) Given that $x = 600$, it follows that $xy \geq 600$ since $y \geq 1$ (y is a positive integer); SUFFICIENT.

(2) Given that $100 < y < 200$, $xy < 500$ is possible (if $x = 3$ and $y = 150$) and $xy \geq 500$ is possible (if $x = 10$ and $y = 150$); NOT sufficient.

The correct answer is A; statement 1 alone is sufficient.

	Price per Flower
Roses	$1.00
Daisies	$0.50

395. Kim and Sue each bought some roses and some daisies at the prices shown above. If Kim bought the same total number of roses and daisies as Sue, was the price of Kim's purchase of roses and daisies higher than the price of Sue's purchase of roses and daisies?

    (1) Kim bought twice as many daisies as roses.
    (2) Kim bought 4 more roses than Sue bought.

Algebra Applied problems

Let R_K be the number of roses that Kim bought, let R_S be the number of roses that Sue bought, and let T be the total number of roses and daisies each bought. Then Kim bought $(T - R_K)$ daisies and Sue bought $(T - R_S)$ daisies. For the roses and daisies, Kim paid a total of $[R_K + \frac{1}{2}(T - R_K)] = \$\frac{1}{2}(R_K + T)$ and Sue paid a total of $[R_S + \frac{1}{2}(T - R_S)] = \$\frac{1}{2}(R_S + T)$. Determine whether $\frac{1}{2}(R_K + T) > \frac{1}{2}(R_S + T)$, or equivalently, determine whether $R_K > R_S$.

(1) Given that $T - R_K = 2R_K$, or $T = 3R_K$, it is not possible to determine whether $R_K > R_S$ because no information is provided about the value of R_S; NOT sufficient.

(2) Given that $R_K = R_S + 4$, it follows that $R_K > R_S$; SUFFICIENT.

The correct answer is B; statement 2 alone is sufficient.

357

396. Jazz and blues recordings accounted for 6 percent of the $840 million revenue from the sales of recordings in Country Y in 2000. What was the revenue from the sales of jazz and blues recordings in Country Y in 1998?

(1) Jazz and blues recordings accounted for 5 percent of the revenue from the sales of recordings in Country Y in 1998.

(2) The revenue from the sales of jazz and blues recordings in Country Y increased by 40 percent from 1998 to 2000.

Arithmetic Percents

It is given that jazz and blues recordings accounted for 6% of the $840 million revenue of recordings in Country Y in 2000. Determine the revenue from the sales of jazz and blues recordings in 1998.

(1) This indicates that jazz and blues recordings accounted for 5% of the revenue from the sales of recordings in Country Y in 1998. However, no information is given to indicate what the revenue from the sales of recordings was in 1998. Therefore, the revenue from sales of jazz and blues recordings in 1998 cannot be determined; NOT sufficient.

(2) This indicates that the revenue from the sales of jazz and blues recordings in Country Y increased by 40% from 1998 to 2000. Letting R_{1998} and R_{2000} represent the revenue from the sales of jazz and blues recordings in 1998 and 2000, respectively, then $R_{2000} = 1.4 R_{1998}$, and so $(0.06)(\$840 \text{ million}) = 1.4 R_{1998}$, from which R_{1998} can be determined; SUFFICIENT.

The correct answer is B; statement 2 alone is sufficient.

397. On a certain nonstop trip, Marta averaged x miles per hour for 2 hours and y miles per hour for the remaining 3 hours. What was her average speed, in miles per hour, for the entire trip?

(1) $2x + 3y = 280$
(2) $y = x + 10$

Algebra Rate problems

Marta traveled a total of $(2x + 3y)$ miles in $2 + 3 = 5$ hours for an average speed of $\left(\dfrac{2x+3y}{5}\right)$ miles per hour. Determine the value of $\dfrac{2x+3y}{5}$.

(1) Given that $2x + 3y = 280$, it follows that $\dfrac{2x+3y}{5} = \dfrac{280}{5}$; SUFFICIENT.

(2) Given that $y = x + 10$, it follows that $\dfrac{2x+3y}{5} = \dfrac{2x+3(x+10)}{5} = x + 6$. Therefore, the value of $\dfrac{2x+3y}{5}$ can be 56 (if $x = 50$ and $y = 60$) and the value of $\dfrac{2x+3y}{5}$ can be 61 (if $x = 55$ and $y = 65$); NOT sufficient.

The correct answer is A; statement 1 alone is sufficient.

398. If x is a positive integer, what is the value of $\sqrt{x+24} - \sqrt{x}$?

(1) $\sqrt{x}$ is an integer.
(2) $\sqrt{x+24}$ is an integer.

Arithmetic Operations with radicals

Determine the value of $\sqrt{x+24} - \sqrt{x}$.

(1) This indicates that x is a perfect square. If $x = 1$, then $\sqrt{x+24} - \sqrt{x} = \sqrt{1+24} - \sqrt{1} = 5 - 1 = 4$. However, if $x = 25$, then $\sqrt{x+24} - \sqrt{x} = \sqrt{25+24} - \sqrt{25} = 7 - 5 = 2$; NOT sufficient.

(2) This indicates that $\sqrt{x+24}$ is an integer. In each of the examples above, $\sqrt{x+24}$ is an integer; NOT sufficient.

Because the same examples were used to establish that neither (1) nor (2) is sufficient, it is not possible to determine the value of $\sqrt{x+24} - \sqrt{x}$ from the given information.

The correct answer is E; both statements together are still not sufficient.

DS13982
399. A tank is filled with gasoline to a depth of exactly 2 feet. The tank is a cylinder resting horizontally on its side, with its circular ends oriented vertically. The inside of the tank is exactly 6 feet long. What is the volume of the gasoline in the tank?

(1) The inside of the tank is exactly 4 feet in diameter.
(2) The top surface of the gasoline forms a rectangle that has an area of 24 square feet.

Geometry Cylinders; Volume

(1) Given that the diameter of the cylindrical tank is 4 ft, it follows that its radius is 2 ft. Therefore, the radius and height of the cylindrical tank are known, and hence the volume of the gasoline is half the volume of the cylinder, or $\frac{1}{2}\pi r^2 h = \frac{1}{2}\pi (2 \text{ ft})^2 (6 \text{ ft}) = 12\pi \text{ ft}^3$; SUFFICIENT.

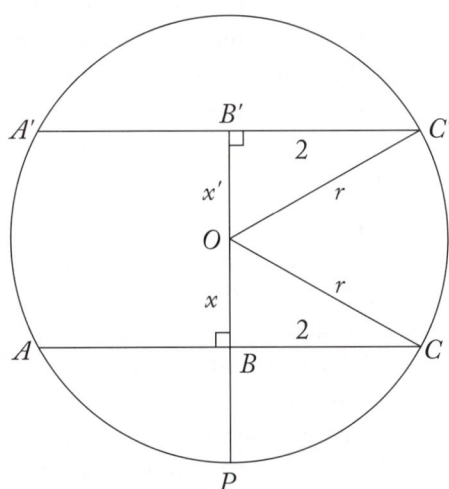

(2) Given that the rectangular surface of the gasoline forms a rectangle with area 24 ft² and length 6 ft, the width of the rectangular surface is 4 ft. Let r ft be the radius of the cylinder. The figure shows a vertical cross-section of the cylindrical tank—a circle with center O—with the two possibilities for the location of the top surface of the gasoline: the depth of the gasoline is less than or equal to r ft ($\overline{AC}$ marks the location of the top surface of the gasoline and $BP = 2$ ft is the depth of the gasoline) or the depth of the gasoline is greater than or equal to r ft ($\overline{A'C'}$ marks the location of the top surface of the gasoline and $B'P = 2$ ft

is the depth of the gasoline). For the first possibility, $\triangle OBC$ is a right triangle with hypotenuse $\overline{OC}$ of length r ft, so letting $OB = x$ ft, it follows from the Pythagorean theorem that $r^2 = x^2 + 2^2 = x^2 + 4$. However, because $r = OB + BP = x + 2$, it follows that $r^2 = (x+2)^2 = x^2 + 4x + 4$. Therefore, $x^2 + 4 = x^2 + 4x + 4$, so $4x = 0$, $x = 0$, and $\overline{AC}$ is a diameter of the circle. Thus, the diameter of the cylindrical tank is 4 ft, and by the same reasoning used in (1), the volume of the gasoline can be determined. For the second possibility, $\triangle OB'C'$ is a right triangle with hypotenuse $\overline{OC'}$ of length r ft, so letting $B'O = x'$ ft, it follows from the Pythagorean theorem that $r^2 = (x')^2 + 2^2 = (x')^2 + 4$. However, because $r = B'P - B'O = 2 - x'$, it follows that $r^2 = (2 - x')^2 = 4 - 4x' + (x')^2$. Therefore, $(x')^2 + 4 = 4 - 4x' + (x')^2$, so $0 = -4x'$, $x' = 0$, and $\overline{A'C'}$ is a diameter of the circle. Thus, the diameter of the cylindrical tank is 4 ft, and by the same reasoning used in (1), the volume of the gasoline can be determined; SUFFICIENT.

The correct answer is D; each statement alone is sufficient.

DS16197
400. Of the four numbers represented on the number line above, is r closest to zero?

(1) $q = -s$
(2) $-t < q$

Algebra Order

Referring to the figure above, in which it may be assumed that q, r, s, and t are different numbers, determine if r is closest to 0.

359

(1) Since $q = -s$, one of q and s is positive and the other is negative. Since s is to the right of q, then s is positive and q is negative. Also, 0 is halfway between q and s, so q and s are the same distance from 0. If $r = 0$, then, of $q, r, s,$ and t, r is closest to 0 because it IS 0. If $r \ne 0$ then either (i) $q < 0 < r < s < t$ or (ii) $q < r < 0 < s < t$.

(i) If $q < 0 < r < s < t$, as shown above, r is closer to 0 than s is because r is between 0 and s, and r is clearly closer to 0 than t is because t is farther away from 0 than s is. Also, since q and s are the same distance from 0 and r is closer to 0 than s is, then r is closer to 0 than q is. Therefore, r is closest to 0.

(ii) If $q < r < 0 < s < t$, as shown above, r is closer to 0 than q is because r is between 0 and q. Also, r is closer to 0 than s is because r is closer to 0 than q is and q and s are the same distance from 0. Moreover, r is closer to 0 than t is because t is farther away from 0 than s is. Therefore, r is closest to 0.

In each case, r is closest to 0; SUFFICIENT.

(2) If $-t < q$, then $-t$ is to the left of q. If $t = 5, s = 4, r = 3,$ and $q = -2$, then $-5 < -2$, so (2) is satisfied. In this case, q is closest to 0. On the other hand, if $t = 5, s = 4, r = -1,$ and $q = -2$, then $-5 < -2$, so (2) is satisfied, but r is closest to 0; NOT sufficient.

The correct answer is A; statement 1 alone is sufficient.

DS18414
401. A group consisting of several families visited an amusement park where the regular admission fees were ¥5,500 for each adult and ¥4,800 for each child. Because there were at least 10 people in the group, each paid an admission fee that was 10% less than the regular admission fee. How many children were in the group?

(1) The total of the admission fees paid for the adults in the group was ¥29,700.
(2) The total of the admission fees paid for the children in the group was ¥4,860 more than the total of the admission fees paid for the adults in the group.

Arithmetic Simultaneous equations

Determine the number of children in a group of at least 10 people who visited an amusement park.

(1) This indicates that $(0.9)(5,500)A = 29,700$, where A represents the number of adults in the group. From this, the number of adults can be determined. However, the number of children in the group cannot be determined without additional information about the exact number of people in the group; NOT sufficient.

(2) If C and A represent the numbers of children and adults, respectively, in the group, this indicates that $(0.9)(4,800)C = (0.9)(5,500)A + 4,860$, or $48C = 55A + 54$, or $48C - 55A = 54$, which is a single equation with two variables from which unique values of C and A cannot be determined, even under the assumptions that C and A are integers such that $C + A \ge 10$. For example, the values of C and A could be 8 and 6, respectively, since $(48)(8) - (55)(6) = 54$, or the values of C and A could be 63 and 54, respectively, since $(48)(63) - (55)(54) = 54$; NOT sufficient.

Taking (1) and (2) together, it follows that
$$A = \frac{29,700}{(0.9)(5,500)} = 6 \text{ and}$$
$$C = \frac{(0.9)(5,500)(6) + 4,860}{(0.9)(4,800)} = 8.$$

The correct answer is C; both statements together are sufficient.

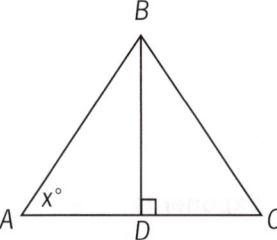

402. What is the area of triangular region ABC above?

   (1) The product of BD and AC is 20.
   (2) x = 45

Geometry Triangles; Area

The area of $\triangle ABC = \dfrac{BD \times AC}{2}$.

(1) The product of BD and AC is given as 20, so the area of $\triangle ABC$ is $\dfrac{20}{2}$ or 10; SUFFICIENT.

(2) With the measurement of x being 45, it is concluded that $\triangle ABD$ is a 45–45–90 right triangle, where the length of side BD is equal to the length of side AD. However, with no lengths of any side known, there is not enough information to calculate the area; NOT sufficient.

**The correct answer is A;
statement 1 alone is sufficient.**

403. In the xy-coordinate plane, is point R equidistant from points (–3,–3) and (1,–3)?

   (1) The x-coordinate of point R is –1.
   (2) Point R lies on the line y = –3.

Algebra Coordinate geometry

Determine if point R is equidistant from (–3,–3) and (1,–3). Letting $R = (x,y)$, then R will be equidistant from (–3,–3) and (1,–3) if and only if R lies on the perpendicular bisector of the line segment with endpoints (–3,–3) and (1,–3), or equivalently, if and only if R lies on the vertical line that consists of all points with x-coordinate equal to $\dfrac{-3+1}{2} = -1$. Therefore, determine if $x = -1$.

(1) Given that $x = -1$, then R will be equidistant from (–3,–3) and (1,–3); SUFFICIENT.

(2) Given that $y = -3$, then both $x = -1$ and $x \neq -1$ are possible; NOT sufficient.

Alternatively, letting $R = (x,y)$, then R will be equidistant from (–3,–3) and (1,–3) if and only if the distance between (x,y) and (–3,–3) is the same as the distance between (x,y) and (1,–3), or if and only if $\sqrt{(x+3)^2 + (y+3)^2} = \sqrt{(x-1)^2 + (y+3)^2}$ or if and only if $(x+3)^2 + (y+3)^2 = (x-1)^2 + (y+3)^2$, or if and only if $(x+3)^2 = (x-1)^2$.

(1) Given that $x = -1$, then $(-1+3)^2 = 4$ and $(-1-1)^2 = 4$; SUFFICIENT.

(2) Given that $y = -3$, then it is impossible to determine if $(x+3)^2 = (x-1)^2$; NOT sufficient.

**The correct answer is A;
statement 1 alone is sufficient.**

404. What is the ratio of the average (arithmetic mean) height of students in class X to the average height of students in class Y?

   (1) The average height of the students in class X is 120 centimeters.
   (2) The average height of the students in class X and class Y combined is 126 centimeters.

Arithmetic Statistics

(1) Given that the average height of the students in class X is 120 cm, but given no information about the average height of the students in class Y, the desired ratio cannot be determined; NOT sufficient.

(2) Given that the average height of the students in class X and class Y combined is 126 cm, the ratio of the averages of the individual classes cannot be determined. For example, if class X consists of 10 students, each of whom has height 120 cm, and class Y consists of 10 students, each of whom has height 132 cm, then the average height of the students in class X and class Y combined is $\dfrac{10(120) + 10(132)}{20} = 126$ cm

and the ratio of the averages of the individual classes is $\frac{120}{132}$. However, if class X consists of 10 students, each of whom has height 120 cm and class Y consists of 20 students, each of whom has height 129 cm, then the average height of the students in class X and class Y combined is $\frac{10(120) + 20(129)}{30} = 126$ cm and the ratio of the averages of the individual classes is $\frac{120}{129}$; NOT sufficient.

Taking (1) and (2) together is of no more help than either (1) or (2) taken separately because the same examples used to show that (2) is not sufficient include the information from (1).

The correct answer is E; both statements together are still not sufficient.

DS04631
405. Is the positive two-digit integer N less than 40?

(1) The units digit of N is 6 more than the tens digit.
(2) N is 4 less than 4 times the units digit.

Arithmetic Place value

Determine if the two-digit integer N is less than 40. Letting the tens digit be t and the units digit be u, then $N = 10t + u$. Determine if $10t + u < 40$.

(1) Given that $u = t + 6$, then $N = 10t + (t + 6) = 11t + 6$. Since u is a digit, $u = t + 6 \leq 9$, so $t \leq 3$. Therefore, $N = 11t + 6 \leq 11(3) + 6 = 39$; SUFFICIENT.

(2) Given that $N = 4u - 4$, then since u is a digit and $u \leq 9$, it follows that $N = 4u - 4 \leq 4(9) - 4 = 32$; SUFFICIENT.

The correct answer is D; each statement alone is sufficient.

DS06318
406. If $2^{x+y} = 4^8$, what is the value of y?

(1) $x^2 = 81$
(2) $x - y = 2$

Algebra Exponents

Since $4^8 = (2^2)^8 = 2^{16}$, the equation $2^{x+y} = 4^8$ becomes $2^{x+y} = 2^{16}$, which is equivalent to $x + y = 16$.

(1) Given that $x^2 = 81$, then both $x = 9$ and $x = -9$ are possible. Therefore, $y = 7$ is possible (choose $x = 9$) and $y = 25$ is possible (choose $x = -9$); NOT sufficient.

(2) Given that $x - y = 2$, it follows that $-x + y = -2$. Adding the last equation to $x + y = 16$ gives $2y = 14$, or $y = 7$; SUFFICIENT.

The correct answer is B; statement 2 alone is sufficient.

DS03680
407. Each week a certain salesman is paid a fixed amount equal to $300, plus a commission equal to 5 percent of the amount of his sales that week over $1,000. What is the total amount the salesman was paid last week?

(1) The total amount the salesman was paid last week is equal to 10 percent of the amount of his sales last week.
(2) The salesman's sales last week totaled $5,000.

Algebra Applied problems

Let P be the salesman's pay for last week and let S be the amount of his sales last week. Then $P = 300 + 0.05(S - 1,000)$. Determine the value of P.

(1) Given $P = 0.10S$, then $0.10S = 300 + 0.05(S - 1,000)$. This equation can be solved for a unique value of S, from which the value of P can be determined; SUFFICIENT.

(2) Given $S = 5,000$, then $P = 300 + 0.05(5,000 - 1,000)$; SUFFICIENT.

The correct answer is D; each statement alone is sufficient.

6.5 Data Sufficiency Answer Explanations

DS01383

408. At a bakery, all donuts are priced equally and all bagels are priced equally. What is the total price of 5 donuts and 3 bagels at the bakery?

   (1) At the bakery, the total price of 10 donuts and 6 bagels is $12.90.
   (2) At the bakery, the price of a donut is $0.15 less than the price of a bagel.

Algebra Simultaneous equations

Let x be the price, in dollars, of each donut and let y be the price, in dollars, of each bagel. Find the value of $5x + 3y$.

   (1) Given that $10x + 6y = 12.90$, since $5x + 3y = \frac{1}{2}(10x + 6y)$, it follows that $5x + 3y = \frac{1}{2}(12.90)$; SUFFICIENT.

   (2) Given that $x = y - 0.15$, then $5x + 3y = 5(y - 0.15) + 3y = 8y - 0.75$, which varies as y varies; NOT sufficient.

The correct answer is A; statement 1 alone is sufficient.

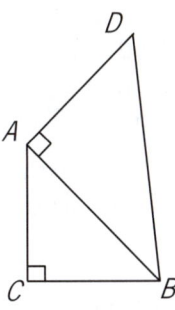

DS06869

409. In the figure above, is the area of triangular region ABC equal to the area of triangular region DBA?

   (1) $(AC)^2 = 2(AD)^2$
   (2) $\triangle ABC$ is isosceles.

Geometry Triangles; Area

Determine whether $\frac{1}{2}(AC)(CB) = \frac{1}{2}(AD)(AB)$ or, equivalently, whether $(AC)(CB) = (AD)(AB)$.

   (1) Given that $(AC)^2 = 2(AD)^2$, then $\sqrt{2}$ and 1 could be the values of AC and AD, respectively. If, for example, $CB = \sqrt{2}$, then $AB = \sqrt{\left(\sqrt{2}\right)^2 + \left(\sqrt{2}\right)^2} = 2$ by the Pythagorean theorem applied to $\triangle ABC$. Hence, $(AC)(CB) = (\sqrt{2})(\sqrt{2})$ and $(AD)(AB) = (1)(2)$, from which it follows that $(AC)(CB) = (AD)(AB)$. On the other hand, if $CB = 1$, then $AB = \sqrt{\left(\sqrt{2}\right)^2 + 1^2} = \sqrt{3}$ by the Pythagorean theorem applied to $\triangle ABC$. Hence, $(AC)(CB) = (\sqrt{2})(1)$ and $(AD)(AB) = (1)(\sqrt{3})$, from which it follows that $(AC)(CB) \neq (AD)(AB)$; NOT sufficient.

   (2) Given that $\triangle ABC$ is isosceles then, by varying the value of AD, the area of $\triangle ABC$ may or may not be equal to the area of $\triangle DBA$. For example, if $AC = CB = 1$, then $(AC)(CB) = (1)(1) = 1$ and $AB = \sqrt{2}$ by the Pythagorean theorem applied to $\triangle ABC$. If $AD = \frac{1}{\sqrt{2}}$, then $(AD)(AB) = \left(\frac{1}{\sqrt{2}}\right)(\sqrt{2}) = 1$, and $(AC)(CB) = (AD)(AB)$. On the other hand, if $AD = 1$, $(AD)(AB) = (1)(\sqrt{2}) = \sqrt{2}$ and $(AC)(CB) \neq (AD)(AB)$; NOT sufficient.

Given (1) and (2) together, let $AC = CB = x$ be the length of the legs of the isosceles triangle ABC. Then, from $(AC)^2 = 2(AD)^2$, it follows that $x^2 = 2(AD)^2$, and hence $AD = \frac{x}{\sqrt{2}}$. Also, by the Pythagorean theorem applied to $\triangle ABC$, it follows that $AB = \sqrt{x^2 + x^2} = x\sqrt{2}$. Therefore, it follows that $(AC)(CB) = (x)(x) = x^2$ and $(AD)(AB) = \left(\frac{x}{\sqrt{2}}\right)(x\sqrt{2}) = x^2$, and so $(AC)(CB) = (AD)(AB)$.

The correct answer is C; both statements together are sufficient.

DS08105

410. If r and s are positive integers, can the fraction $\frac{r}{s}$ be expressed as a decimal with only a finite number of nonzero digits?

   (1) s is a factor of 100.
   (2) r is a factor of 100.

Arithmetic Properties of numbers

Determine if $\frac{r}{s}$, where r and s are positive integers, can be expressed as a decimal with a finite number of nonzero decimal digits.

(1) It is given that s is a factor of 100 and so $s = 1, 2, 4, 5, 10, 20, 25, 50,$ or 100. This means that $\frac{r}{s}$ must be one of the quotients $\frac{r}{1}, \frac{r}{2}, \frac{r}{4}, \frac{r}{5}, \frac{r}{10}, \frac{r}{20}, \frac{r}{25}, \frac{r}{50},$ or $\frac{r}{100}$. Thus, $\frac{r}{s}$ must be one of the products $r(1)$, $r(0.5), r(0.25), r(0.20), r(0.1), r(0.05), r(0.04), r(0.02),$ or $r(0.01)$. In each case, $\frac{r}{s}$ is the product of an integer and a decimal with a finite number of nonzero digits, and hence, $\frac{r}{s}$ can be expressed as a decimal with a finite number of nonzero digits. In fact, it suffices to note this is true for $\frac{r}{100}$, since each of the other possibilities is a positive integer times $\frac{r}{100}$ (for example, $\frac{r}{20}$ is 5 times $\frac{r}{100}$); SUFFICIENT.

(2) It is given that r is a factor of 100. If $r = 4$ and $s = 5$, then $\frac{r}{s} = 0.8$, which is a decimal with a finite number of nonzero digits. On the other hand, if $r = 4$ and $s = 7$, then $\frac{r}{s} = 0.\overline{571428}$, which is not a decimal with a finite number of nonzero digits; NOT sufficient.

**The correct answer is A;
statement 1 alone is sufficient.**

DS16384

411. If $r > 0$ and $s > 0$, is $\frac{r}{s} < \frac{s}{r}$?

(1) $\frac{r}{3s} = \frac{1}{4}$

(2) $s = r + 4$

Algebra Ratios

Given positive numbers r and s, determine if $\frac{r}{s} < \frac{s}{r}$.

(1) If $\frac{r}{3s} = \frac{1}{4}$, then $\frac{r}{s} = \frac{3}{4}, \frac{s}{r} = \frac{4}{3}$, and so $\frac{r}{s} < \frac{s}{r}$, since $\frac{3}{4} < \frac{4}{3}$; SUFFICIENT.

(2) If $s = r + 4$, then $\frac{r}{s} = \frac{r}{r+4}$ and $\frac{s}{r} = \frac{r+4}{r}$. Since $r + 4 > r$, $\frac{r}{r+4} < 1$ and $\frac{r+4}{r} > 1$, so $\frac{r}{s} < \frac{s}{r}$; SUFFICIENT.

**The correct answer is D;
each statement alone is sufficient.**

DS06789

412. If k is an integer such that $56 < k < 66$, what is the value of k?

(1) If k were divided by 2, the remainder would be 1.
(2) If $k + 1$ were divided by 3, the remainder would be 0.

Arithmetic Properties of integers

Determine the value of the integer k, where $56 < k < 66$.

(1) It is given that the remainder is 1 when k is divided by 2, which implies that k is odd. Therefore, the value of k can be 57, 59, 61, 63, or 65; NOT sufficient.

(2) It is given that the remainder is 0 when $k + 1$ is divided by 3, which implies that $k + 1$ is divisible by 3. Since $56 < k < 66$ (equivalently, $57 < k + 1 < 67$), the value of $k + 1$ can be 60, 63, or 66 so the value of k can be 59, 62, or 65; NOT sufficient.

Taking (1) and (2) together, 59 and 65 appear in both lists of possible values for k; NOT sufficient.

**The correct answer is E;
both statements together are still not sufficient.**

DS13965

413. If x is a positive integer, then is x prime?

(1) $3x + 1$ is prime.
(2) $5x + 1$ is prime.

Arithmetic Properties of numbers

Determine if the positive integer x is prime.

(1) This indicates that $3x + 1$ is prime. If $x = 2$, then $3x + 1 = 7$ is prime and so is x. However, if $x = 6$, then $3x + 1 = 19$ is prime, but 6 is not prime; NOT sufficient.

(2) This indicates that $5x + 1$ is prime. If $x = 2$, then $5x + 1 = 11$ is prime and so is x. However, if $x = 6$, then $5x + 1 = 31$ is prime, but 6 is not prime; NOT sufficient.

Because the same examples were used to establish that neither (1) nor (2) is sufficient, it is not possible to determine whether x is prime from the given information.

**The correct answer is E;
both statements together are still not sufficient.**

$$k, n, 12, 6, 17$$

DS00172
414. What is the value of n in the list above?

(1) $k < n$
(2) The median of the numbers in the list is 10.

Arithmetic Statistics

Given the list $k, n, 12, 6, 17$, determine the value of n.

(1) Although $k < n$, no information is given about the value of k or n; NOT sufficient.

(2) Since the median of the numbers in the list is 10 and there are 5 numbers in the list, 10 is one of those 5 numbers. Therefore, $n = 10$ or $k = 10$. If $n = 10$, then the value of n has been determined. However, if $k = 10$, then n can be any number that is 10 or less, so the value of n cannot be determined; NOT sufficient.

Taking (1) and (2) together, if $k < n$ and the median of the list is 10, then 12 and 17 are to the right of the median and the list in ascending order is either $6, k, n, 12, 17$ or $k, 6, n, 12, 17$. In either case, n is the middle number, and since the median is 10, $n = 10$.

**The correct answer is C;
both statements together are sufficient.**

DS07508
415. If x and y are integers, what is the value of $x + y$?

(1) $3 < \dfrac{x+y}{2} < 4$
(2) $2 < x < y < 5$

Arithmetic Computation with integers

Determine the value of $x + y$ for integers x and y.

(1) Given that $3 < \dfrac{x+y}{2} < 4$, then $6 < x + y < 8$. Since $x + y$ is an integer and 7 is the only integer greater than 6 and less than 8, it follows that the value of $x + y$ is 7; SUFFICIENT.

(2) Given that $2 < x < y < 5$, then $2 < x < 5$, and hence $x = 3$ or $x = 4$. Likewise, $2 < y < 5$, and hence $y = 3$ or $y = 4$. With the additional restriction that $x < y$, it follows that $x = 3$ and $y = 4$, and thus $x + y = 7$; SUFFICIENT.

**The correct answer is D;
each statement alone is sufficient.**

DS00764
416. Last year, if Arturo spent a total of $12,000 on his mortgage payments, real estate taxes, and home insurance, how much did he spend on his real estate taxes?

(1) Last year, the total amount that Arturo spent on his real estate taxes and home insurance was $33\dfrac{1}{3}$ percent of the amount that he spent on his mortgage payments.

(2) Last year, the amount that Arturo spent on his real estate taxes was 20 percent of the total amount he spent on his mortgage payments and home insurance.

Arithmetic Applied problems

Let M, R, and H be the amounts that Arturo spent last year on mortgage payments, real estate taxes, and home insurance, respectively. Given that $M + R + H = 12,000$, determine the value of R.

(1) Given that $R + H = \dfrac{1}{3}M$ and $M + R + H = 12,000$, then $M + \dfrac{1}{3}M = 12,000$, or $M = 9,000$. However, the value of R cannot be determined, since it is possible that $R = 2,000$ (use $M = 9,000$ and $H = 1,000$) and it is possible that $R = 1,000$ (use $M = 9,000$ and $H = 2,000$); NOT sufficient.

(2) Given that $R = \frac{1}{5}(M+H)$, or $5R = M+H$ and $M+R+H = 12{,}000$, which can be rewritten as $(M+H) + R = 12{,}000$, then $5R + R = 12{,}000$, or $R = 2{,}000$; SUFFICIENT.

The correct answer is B; statement 2 alone is sufficient.

DS06038
417. If a, b, c, and d are positive numbers, is $\frac{a}{b} < \frac{c}{d}$?

(1) $0 < \frac{c-a}{d-b}$

(2) $\left(\frac{ad}{bc}\right)^2 < \frac{ad}{bc}$

Algebra Inequalities

Determine whether $\frac{a}{b} < \frac{c}{d}$, where a, b, c, and d are positive numbers.

(1) Given that $0 < \frac{c-a}{d-b}$, then $a = 2$, $b = 3$, $c = 6$, and $d = 8$ are possible values for a, b, c, and d because $\frac{c-a}{d-b} = \frac{6-2}{8-3} = \frac{4}{5}$ and $\frac{4}{5} > 0$. For these values, $\frac{a}{b} < \frac{c}{d}$ is true because $\frac{2}{3} < \frac{6}{8}$. On the other hand, $a = 4$, $b = 6$, $c = 2$, and $d = 3$ are also possible values of a, b, c, and d because $\frac{c-a}{d-b} = \frac{2-4}{3-6} = \frac{2}{3}$ and $\frac{2}{3} > 0$. For these values, $\frac{a}{b} < \frac{c}{d}$ is false because $\frac{4}{6} = \frac{2}{3}$; NOT sufficient.

(2) Given that $\left(\frac{ad}{bc}\right)^2 < \frac{ad}{bc}$, then

$\frac{ad}{bc} < 1$ dividing both sides by the positive number $\frac{ad}{bc}$

$\frac{ad}{b} < c$ multiplying both sides by the positive number c

$\frac{a}{b} < \frac{c}{d}$ dividing both sides by the positive number d; SUFFICIENT

The correct answer is B; statement 2 alone is sufficient.

DS12008
418. Is the number of members of Club X greater than the number of members of Club Y ?

(1) Of the members of Club X, 20 percent are also members of Club Y.

(2) Of the members of Club Y, 30 percent are also members of Club X.

Arithmetic Sets

Let a be the number of members in Club X that do not belong to Club Y, let b be the number of members in Club Y that do not belong to Club X, and let c be the number of members that belong to both Club X and to Club Y. Determine whether $a + c > b + c$, or equivalently, whether $a > b$.

(1) If $a = 80$, $b = 79$, and $c = 20$, then 20 percent of the members of Club X are also members of Club Y (because $c = 20$ is 20 percent of $a + c = 100$) and $a > b$ is true. However, if $a = 80$, $b = 80$, and $c = 20$, then 20 percent of the members of Club X are also members of Club Y (because $c = 20$ is 20 percent of $a + c = 100$) and $a > b$ is false. Therefore, it cannot be determined whether $a > b$; NOT sufficient.

(2) If $a = 71$, $b = 70$, and $c = 30$, then 30 percent of the members of Club Y are also members of Club X (because $c = 30$ is 30 percent of $b + c = 100$) and $a > b$ is true. However, if $a = 70$, $b = 70$, and $c = 30$, then 30 percent of the members of Club Y are also members of Club X (because $c = 30$ is 30 percent of $b + c = 100$) and $a > b$ is false. Therefore, it cannot be determined whether $a > b$; NOT sufficient.

Now assume both (1) and (2). From (1) it follows that $\frac{c}{a+c} = 0.20 = \frac{1}{5}$, or $5c = a + c$, and so $a = 4c$. From (2) it follows that $\frac{c}{b+c} = 0.30 = \frac{3}{10}$, or $10c = 3b + 3c$, and so $7c = 3b$ and $b = \frac{7}{3}c$. Since $4c > \frac{7}{3}c$ (from the statements it can be deduced that $c > 0$), it follows that $a > b$. Therefore, (1) and (2) together are sufficient.

The correct answer is C; both statements together are sufficient.

419. On the number line above, p, q, r, s, and t are five consecutive even integers in increasing order. What is the average (arithmetic mean) of these five integers?

    (1) $q + s = 24$
    (2) The average (arithmetic mean) of q and r is 11.

Arithmetic Properties of numbers

Since $p, q, r, s,$ and t are consecutive even integers listed in numerical order, the 5 integers can also be given as $p, p + 2, p + 4, p + 6,$ and $p + 8$. Determine the average of these 5 integers, which is the value of $\frac{p + (p + 2) + (p + 4) + (p + 6) + (p + 8)}{5} = \frac{5p + 20}{5} = p + 4$

(1) Given that $q + s = 24$, then $(p + 2) + (p + 6) = 24$. Therefore, $2p + 8 = 24$, or $p = 8$, and hence $p + 4 = 12$; SUFFICIENT.

(2) Given that $\frac{q + r}{2} = 11$, then $q + r = (2)(11) = 22$, or $(p + 2) + (p + 4) = 22$. Therefore, $2p + 6 = 22$, or $p = 8$, and hence $p + 4 = 12$; SUFFICIENT.

The correct answer is D; each statement alone is sufficient.

DS06657

420. If $\lceil x \rceil$ denotes the least integer greater than or equal to x, is $\lceil x \rceil = 0$?

    (1) $-1 < x < 1$
    (2) $x < 0$

Algebra Functions

Determine if $\lceil x \rceil$, the least integer greater than or equal to x, is equal to 0, which is the same as determining if x satisfies $-1 < x \leq 0$.

(1) Given that $-1 < x < 1$, then it is possible that $\lceil x \rceil = 0$ (for example, if $x = 0$, then $\lceil x \rceil = 0$) and it is possible that $\lceil x \rceil \neq 0$ (for example, if $x = \frac{1}{2}$, then $\lceil x \rceil = 1 \neq 0$); NOT sufficient.

(2) Given that $x < 0$, then it is possible that $\lceil x \rceil = 0$ (for example, if $x = -\frac{1}{2}$, then $\lceil x \rceil = 0$) and it is possible that $\lceil x \rceil \neq 0$ (for example, if $x = -5$, then $\lceil x \rceil = -5 \neq 0$); NOT sufficient.

Taking (1) and (2) together gives $-1 < x < 0$, which implies that $\lceil x \rceil = 0$.

The correct answer is C; both statements together are sufficient.

DS12718

421. If x and y are integers, is $x > y$?

    (1) $x + y > 0$
    (2) $y^x < 0$

Arithmetic Properties of integers

Determine if the integer x is greater than the integer y.

(1) It is given that $x + y > 0$, and so $-x < y$. If, for example, $x = -3$ and $y = 4$, then $x + y = -3 + 4 = 1 > 0$ and $x < y$. On the other hand, if $x = 4$ and $y = -3$, then $x + y = 4 - 3 = 1 > 0$ and $x > y$; NOT sufficient.

(2) It is given that $y^x < 0$, so $y < 0$. If, for example, $x = 3$ and $y = -2$, then $(-2)^3 = -8 < 0$ and $x > y$. On the other hand, if $x = -3$ and $y = -2$, then $(-2)^{-3} = -\frac{1}{8} < 0$ and $x < y$; NOT sufficient.

Taking (1) and (2) together, from (2) y is negative and from (1) $-x$ is less than y. Therefore, $-x$ is negative, and hence x is positive. Since x is positive and y is negative, it follows that $x > y$.

The correct answer is C; both statements together are sufficient.

422. If r and s are the roots of the equation $x^2 + bx + c = 0$, where b and c are constants, is $rs < 0$?

(1) $b < 0$
(2) $c < 0$

Algebra Second-degree equations

Determine whether the product of the roots to $x^2 + bx + c = 0$, where b and c are constants, is negative.

If r and s are the roots of the given equation, then $(x - r)(x - s) = x^2 + bx + c$. This implies that $x^2 - (r + s)x + rs = x^2 + bx + c$, and so $rs = c$. Therefore, rs is negative if and only if c is negative.

(1) Given that $b < 0$, then c could be negative or positive. For example, if $b = -1$ and $c = -6$, then the given equation would be $x^2 - x - 6 = (x - 3)(x + 2) = 0$, and the product of its roots would be $(3)(-2)$, which is negative. On the other hand, if $b = -6$ and $c = 5$, then the given equation would be $x^2 - 6x + 5 = (x - 5)(x - 1) = 0$, and the product of its roots would be $(5)(1)$, which is positive; NOT sufficient.

(2) Given that $c < 0$, it follows from the explanation above that $rs < 0$; SUFFICIENT.

**The correct answer is B;
statement 2 alone is sufficient.**

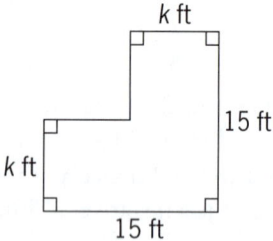

423. The figure above represents an L-shaped garden. What is the value of k?

(1) The area of the garden is 189 square feet.
(2) The perimeter of the garden is 60 feet.

Geometry Polygons

(1) Given that the area of the garden is 189 ft², and observing that area of the garden can be calculated by imagining the garden as a square with dimensions 15 ft by 15 ft from which its upper-right square corner with dimensions $(15 - k)$ ft by $(15 - k)$ ft is removed, it follows that $189 = (15)^2 - (15 - k)^2$. Therefore, $(15 - k)^2 = 225 - 189 = 36$, so $15 - k = 6$ or $15 - k = -6$. The figure implies $15 - k > 0$, so it follows that $15 - k = 6$, or $k = 9$; SUFFICIENT.

(2) Given that the perimeter of the garden is 60 ft, and because $15 + 15 + k + (15 - k) + (15 - k) + k = 60$, any value of k between 0 and 15 is possible, since for any such value of k the sum of the lengths of all the sides would be 60 ft; NOT sufficient.

**The correct answer is A;
statement 1 alone is sufficient.**

424. The only articles of clothing in a certain closet are shirts, dresses, and jackets. The ratio of the number of shirts to the number of dresses to the number of jackets in the closet is 9:4:5, respectively. If there are more than 7 dresses in the closet, what is the total number of articles of clothing in the closet?

(1) The total number of shirts and jackets in the closet is less than 30.
(2) The total number of shirts and dresses in the closet is 26.

Arithmetic Ratio and proportion

Letting s, d, and j represent, respectively, the numbers of shirts, dresses, and jackets in the closet, then $s = 9x$, $d = 4x$, and $j = 5x$, where x is a positive integer. It is given that $4x > 7$, and so $4x \geq 8$ or $x \geq 2$ since x is an integer. Determine the value of $9x + 4x + 5x = 18x$.

(1) This indicates that $9x + 5x < 30$, and so $14x \leq 28$ or $x \leq 2$ since x is an integer. It follows from $x \geq 2$ and $x \leq 2$ that $x = 2$ and $18x = 36$; SUFFICIENT.

(2) This indicates that $9x + 4x = 26$ or $13x = 26$, or $x = 2$. It follows that $18x = 36$; SUFFICIENT.

**The correct answer is D;
each statement alone is sufficient.**

6.5 Data Sufficiency Answer Explanations

TOTAL EXPENSES FOR THE
FIVE DIVISIONS OF COMPANY H

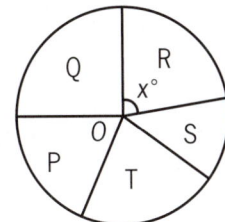

DS16542

425. The figure above represents a circle graph of Company H's total expenses broken down by the expenses for each of its five divisions. If O is the center of the circle and if Company H's total expenses are $5,400,000, what are the expenses for Division R ?

(1) $x = 94$

(2) The total expenses for Divisions S and T are twice as much as the expenses for Division R.

Geometry Circles

In this circle graph, the expenses of Division R are equal to the value of $\frac{x}{360}$ multiplied by $5,400,000, or $15,000x$. Therefore, it is necessary to know the value of x in order to determine the expenses for Division R.

(1) The value of x is given as 94, so the expenses of Division R can be determined; SUFFICIENT.

(2) This gives a comparison among the expenses of some of the divisions of Company H, but no information is given about the value of x; NOT sufficient.

**The correct answer is A;
statement 1 alone is sufficient.**

DS13641

426. If x is negative, is $x < -3$?

(1) $x^2 > 9$
(2) $x^3 < -9$

Algebra Properties of numbers

(1) Given that $x^2 > 9$, it follows that $x < -3$ or $x > 3$, a result that can be obtained in a variety of ways. For example, consider the equivalent inequality $\left(|x|\right)^2 > 9$ that reduces to $|x| > 3$, or consider when the two factors of $x^2 - 9$ are both positive and when the two factors of $x^2 - 9$ are both negative, or consider where the graph of the parabola $y = x^2 - 9$ is above the x-axis, etc. Since it is also given that x is negative, it follows that $x < -3$; SUFFICIENT.

(2) Given that $x^3 < -9$, if $x = -4$, then $x^3 = -64$, and so $x^3 < -9$ and it is true that $x < -3$. However, if $x = -3$, then $x^3 = -27$, and so $x^3 < -9$, but it is not true that $x < -3$; NOT sufficient.

**The correct answer is A;
statement 1 alone is sufficient.**

DS04897

427. What is the number of cans that can be packed in a certain carton?

(1) The interior volume of this carton is 2,304 cubic inches.

(2) The exterior of each can is 6 inches high and has a diameter of 4 inches.

Geometry Rectangular solids and cylinders

(1) No information about the size of the cans is given; NOT sufficient.

(2) No information about the size of the carton is given; NOT sufficient.

Taking (1) and (2) together, there is still not enough information to answer the question. If the carton is a rectangular solid that is 1 inch by 1 inch by 2,304 inches and the cans are cylindrical with the given dimensions, then 0 cans can be packed into the carton. However, if the carton is a rectangular solid that is 16 inches by 12 inches by 12 inches and the cans are cylindrical with the given dimensions, then 1 or more cans can be packed into the carton.

**The correct answer is E;
both statements together are still not sufficient.**

369

r	s	t
u	v	w
x	y	z

428. Each of the letters in the table above represents one of the numbers 1, 2, or 3, and each of these numbers occurs exactly once in each row and exactly once in each column. What is the value of r?

    (1) $v + z = 6$
    (2) $s + t + u + x = 6$

Arithmetic Properties of numbers

In the following discussion, "row/column convention" means that each of the numbers 1, 2, and 3 appears exactly once in any given row and exactly once in any given column.

(1) Given that $v + z = 6$, then both v and z are equal to 3, since no other sum of the possible values is equal to 6. Applying the row/column convention to row 2, and then to row 3, it follows that neither u nor x can be 3. Since neither u nor x can be 3, the row/column convention applied to column 1 forces r to be 3; SUFFICIENT.

(2) If $u = 3$, then $s + t + x = 3$. Hence, $s = t = x = 1$, since the values these variables can have does not permit another possibility. However, this assignment of values would violate the row/column convention for row 1, and thus u cannot be 3. If $x = 3$, then $s + t + u = 3$. Hence, $s = t = u = 1$, since the values these variables can have does not permit another possibility. However, this assignment of values would violate the row/column convention for row 1, and thus x cannot be 3. Since neither u nor x can be 3, the row/column convention applied to column 1 forces r to be 3; SUFFICIENT.

The correct answer is D; each statement alone is sufficient.

429. Material A costs $3 per kilogram, and Material B costs $5 per kilogram. If 10 kilograms of Material K consists of x kilograms of Material A and y kilograms of Material B, is $x > y$?

    (1) $y > 4$
    (2) The cost of the 10 kilograms of Material K is less than $40.

Algebra Inequalities

Since $x + y = 10$, the relation $x > y$ is equivalent to $x > 10 - x$, or $x > 5$.

(1) The given information is consistent with $x = 5.5$ and $y = 4.5$, and the given information is also consistent with $x = y = 5$. Therefore, it is possible for $x > y$ to be true and it is possible for $x > y$ to be false; NOT sufficient.

(2) Given that $3x + 5y < 40$, or $3x + 5(10 - x) < 40$, then $3x - 5x < 40 - 50$. It follows that $-2x < -10$, or $x > 5$; SUFFICIENT.

The correct answer is B; statement 2 alone is sufficient.

430. At what speed was a train traveling on a trip when it had completed half of the total distance of the trip?

    (1) The trip was 460 miles long and took 4 hours to complete.
    (2) The train traveled at an average rate of 115 miles per hour on the trip.

Arithmetic Applied problems

Determine the speed of the train when it had completed half the total distance of the trip.

(1) Given that the train traveled 460 miles in 4 hours, the train could have traveled at the constant rate of 115 miles per hour for 4 hours, and thus it could have been traveling 115 miles per hour when it had completed half the total distance of the trip. However, the train could have traveled 150 miles per hour for the first 2 hours (a distance of 300 miles) and 80 miles per hour for the last 2 hours (a distance of 160 miles), and thus it could have been traveling 150 miles per hour when it had completed half the total distance of the trip; NOT sufficient.

(2) Given that the train traveled at an average rate of 115 miles per hour, each of the possibilities given in the explanation for (1) could occur, since 460 miles in 4 hours gives an average speed of $\frac{460}{4} = 115$ miles per hour; NOT sufficient.

Assuming (1) and (2), each of the possibilities given in the explanation for (1) could occur. Therefore, (1) and (2) together are not sufficient.

**The correct answer is E;
both statements together are still not sufficient.**

DS12047
431. Tom, Jane, and Sue each purchased a new house. The average (arithmetic mean) price of the three houses was $120,000. What was the median price of the three houses?

(1) The price of Tom's house was $110,000.
(2) The price of Jane's house was $120,000.

Arithmetic Statistics

Let $T, J,$ and S be the purchase prices for Tom's, Jane's, and Sue's new houses. Given that the average purchase price is 120,000, or $T + J + S = 3(120,000)$, determine the median purchase price.

(1) Given $T = 110,000$, the median could be 120,000 (if $J = 120,000$ and $S = 130,000$) or 125,000 (if $J = 125,000$ and $S = 125,000$); NOT sufficient.

(2) Given $J = 120,000$, the following two cases include every possibility consistent with $T + J + S = (3)(120,000)$, or $T + S = (2)(120,000)$.

  (i) $T = S = 120,000$
  (ii) One of T or S is less than 120,000 and the other is greater than 120,000.

In each case, the median is clearly 120,000; SUFFICIENT.

**The correct answer is B;
statement 2 alone is sufficient.**

DS13958
432. What is the value of x if $x^3 < x^2$?

(1) $-2 < x < 2$
(2) x is an integer greater than –2.

Algebra Inequalities

The inequality $x^3 < x^2$ is equivalent to $x^3 - x^2 < 0$, or $x^2(x - 1) < 0$. Since this inequality is false for $x = 0$, it follows that $x \neq 0$, and hence $x^2 > 0$. Therefore, $x^2(x - 1) < 0$ can only hold if $x - 1 < 0$, or if $x < 1$. Thus, the problem is equivalent to determining the value of x given that $x \neq 0$ and $x < 1$.

(1) Given that $-2 < x < 2$, it is not possible to determine the value of x. For example, the value of x could be -1 (note that $-1 < 1$) and the value of x could be 0.5 (note that $0.125 < 0.25$); NOT sufficient.

(2) Given that the value of x is an integer greater than -2, then the value of x must be among the integers $-1, 0, 1, 2, 3, \ldots$. However, from the discussion above, $x \neq 0$ and $x < 1$, so the value of x can only be -1; SUFFICIENT.

**The correct answer is B;
statement 2 alone is sufficient.**

DS08451
433. For any integers x and y, min(x, y) and max(x, y) denote the minimum and the maximum of x and y, respectively. For example, min(5, 2) = 2 and max(5, 2) = 5. For the integer w, what is the value of min(10, w) ?

(1) w = max(20, z) for some integer z.
(2) w = max(10, w)

Arithmetic Properties of numbers

If $w \geq 10$, then $(10, w) = 10$, and if $w < 10$, then $(10, w) = w$. Therefore, the value of min(10, w) can be determined if the value of w can be determined.

(1) Given that $w = \max(20, z)$ then $w \geq 20$. Hence, $w \geq 10$, and so min(10, w) = 10; SUFFICIENT.

(2) Given that $w = \max(10, w)$, then $w \geq 10$, and so min(10, w) = 10; SUFFICIENT.

**The correct answer is D;
each statement alone is sufficient.**

DS01473
434. A certain bookcase has 2 shelves of books. On the upper shelf, the book with the greatest number of pages has 400 pages. On the lower shelf, the book with the least number of pages has 475 pages. What is the median number of pages for all of the books on the 2 shelves?

(1) There are 25 books on the upper shelf.
(2) There are 24 books on the lower shelf.

Arithmetic Statistics

(1) The information given says nothing about the number of books on the lower shelf. If there are fewer than 25 books on the lower shelf, then the median number of pages will be the number of pages in one of the books on the upper shelf or the average number of pages in two books on the upper shelf. Hence, the median will be at most 400. If there are more than 25 books on the lower shelf, then the median number of pages will be the number of pages in one of the books on the lower shelf or the average number of pages in two books on the lower shelf. Hence, the median will be at least 475; NOT sufficient.

(2) An analysis very similar to that used in (1) shows the information given is not sufficient to determine the median; NOT sufficient.

Given both (1) and (2), it follows that there is a total of 49 books. Therefore, the median will be the 25th book when the books are ordered by number of pages. Since the 25th book in this ordering is the book on the upper shelf with the greatest number of pages, the median is 400. Therefore, (1) and (2) together are sufficient.

**The correct answer is C;
both statements together are sufficient.**

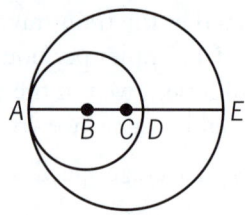

DS12070
435. In the figure above, points A, B, C, D, and E lie on a line. A is on both circles, B is the center of the smaller circle, C is the center of the larger circle, D is on the smaller circle, and E is on the larger circle. What is the area of the region inside the larger circle and outside the smaller circle?

(1) $AB = 3$ and $BC = 2$
(2) $CD = 1$ and $DE = 4$

Geometry Circles

If R is the radius of the larger circle and r is the radius of the smaller circle, then the desired area is $\pi R^2 - \pi r^2$. Thus, if both the values of R and r can be determined, then the desired area can be determined.

(1) Given that $AB = r = 3$ and $BC = 2$, then $AB + BC = R = 3 + 2 = 5$; SUFFICIENT.

(2) Given that $CD = 1$ and $DE = 4$, then $CD + DE = R = 1 + 4 = 5$. Since $\overline{AE}$ is a diameter of the larger circle, then $AD + DE = 2R$. Also, since $\overline{AD}$ is a diameter of the smaller circle, then $AD = 2r$. Thus, $2r + DE = 2R$ or $2r + 4 = 10$, and so $r = 3$; SUFFICIENT.

**The correct answer is D;
each statement alone is sufficient.**

DS08995
436. In planning for a trip, Joan estimated both the distance of the trip, in miles, and her average speed, in miles per hour. She accurately divided her estimated distance by her estimated average speed to obtain an estimate for the time, in hours, that the trip would take. Was her estimate within 0.5 hour of the actual time that the trip took?

(1) Joan's estimate for the distance was within 5 miles of the actual distance.
(2) Joan's estimate for her average speed was within 10 miles per hour of her actual average speed.

Arithmetic Applied problems; Estimating

(1) Given that Joan's estimate for the distance was within 5 miles of the actual distance, it is not possible to determine whether her estimate for the time was within 0.5 hour without information about her estimated average speed. For example, if her estimated distance was 20 miles and was within 5 miles of the actual distance, then the actual distance would be between 15 and 25 miles. If her estimated speed was 20 miles per hour (mph) and was within, say, 10 mph of her actual speed, then her actual speed would be between 10 and 30 mph. Her estimated time would then be $\frac{20}{20} = 1.0$ hour and the actual time would be between $\frac{15}{30} = 0.5$ hour (least distance over greatest speed) and $\frac{25}{10} = 2.5$ hours (greatest distance over least speed). Since 1.0 hour is between 0.5 hour and 2.5 hours, her estimate for the time could equal the actual time, and thus it is possible that her estimate of the time is within 0.5 hour of the actual time. However, her estimate for the time could be as much as $2.5 - 1.0 = 1.5$ hours over the actual time, and thus it is possible that her estimate of the time is not within 0.5 hour; NOT sufficient.

(2) Given that Joan's estimate for her average speed was within 10 miles per hour of her actual average speed, the same examples used in (1) can be used to show that it cannot be determined whether her estimate for the time would be within 0.5 hour of the actual time; NOT sufficient.

Taking (1) and (2) together is of no more help than either (1) or (2) taken separately because the same examples used to show that (1) is not sufficient also show that (2) is not sufficient.

**The correct answer is E;
both statements together are still not sufficient.**

DS12239
437. A certain list consists of 3 different numbers. Does the median of the 3 numbers equal the average (arithmetic mean) of the 3 numbers?

(1) The range of the 3 numbers is equal to twice the difference between the greatest number and the median.

(2) The sum of the 3 numbers is equal to 3 times one of the numbers.

Arithmetic Statistics

Let the numbers be x, y, and z so that $x < y < z$. Determine whether $y = \frac{x + y + z}{3}$, or equivalently, whether $3y = x + y + z$, or equivalently, whether $2y = x + z$.

(1) Given that the range is equal to twice the difference between the greatest number and the median, it follows that $z - x = 2(z - y)$, or $z - x = 2z - 2y$, or $2y = x + z$; SUFFICIENT.

(2) Given that the sum of the 3 numbers equals 3 times one of the numbers, it follows that $x + y + z = 3x$ or $x + y + z = 3y$ or $x + y + z = 3z$. If $x + y + z = 3x$, then $y + z = 2x$, or $(y - x) + (z - x) = 0$. Also, if $x + y + z = 3z$, then $x + y = 2z$, or $0 = (z - x) + (z - y)$. In each of these cases, the sum of two positive numbers is zero, which is impossible. Therefore, it must be true that $x + y + z = 3y$, from which it follows that $x + z = 2y$, and hence by the initial comments, the median of the 3 numbers equals the average of the 3 numbers; SUFFICIENT.

**The correct answer is D;
each statement alone is sufficient.**

DS12806
438. Line ℓ lies in the xy-plane and does not pass through the origin. What is the slope of line ℓ?

(1) The x-intercept of line ℓ is twice the y-intercept of line ℓ.

(2) The x- and y-intercepts of line ℓ are both positive.

373

Geometry Coordinate geometry

Since the line does not pass through the origin, the line is either vertical and given by the equation $x = c$ for some constant c such that $c \neq 0$, or the line is not vertical and given by the equation $y = mx + b$ for some constants m and b such that $b \neq 0$. Determine whether the line is not vertical, and if so, determine the slope of the line, which is the value of m.

(1) Given that the x-intercept of the line is twice the y-intercept of the line, it follows that the line is not vertical, since a vertical line that does not pass through the origin will not have a y-intercept. Thus, the line is given by the equation $y = mx + b$. The x-intercept of the line is the solution to $0 = mx + b$, or $mx = -b$, which has solution $x = -\frac{b}{m}$, and the y-intercept of the line is b. Therefore, $-\frac{b}{m} = 2b$. Since $b \neq 0$, both sides of the last equation can be divided by b to get $-\frac{1}{m} = 2$, or $m = -\frac{1}{2}$; SUFFICIENT.

(2) Given that the x- and y-intercepts of the line are both positive, it is not possible to determine the slope of the line. For example, if the line is given by $y = -x + 1$, then the x-intercept is 1 (solve $-x + 1 = 0$), the y-intercept is 1 ($b = 1$), and the slope is -1. However, if the line is given by $y = -2x + 2$, then the x-intercept is 1 (solve $-2x + 2 = 0$), the y-intercept is 2 ($b = 2$), and the slope is -2; NOT sufficient.

The correct answer is A; statement 1 alone is sufficient.

$$y = ax - 5$$
$$y = x + 6$$
$$y = 3x + b$$

DS07713

439. In the xy-plane, the straight-line graphs of the three equations above each contain the point (p,r). If a and b are constants, what is the value of b?

(1) $a = 2$
(2) $r = 17$

Algebra Coordinate geometry

Since (p,r) is on each of the lines, each of the following three equations is true:

(i) $r = ap - 5$
(ii) $r = p + 6$
(iii) $r = 3p + b$

Determine the value of b.

(1) Given that $a = 2$, Equations (i) and (ii) become $r = 2p - 5$ and $r = p + 6$. Subtracting equations gives $0 = p - 11$, or $p = 11$. Now using $r = p + 6$, it follows that $r = 11 + 6 = 17$. Finally, using $p = 11$ and $r = 17$ in Equation (iii) gives $17 = 3(11) + b$, or $b = 17 - 33 = -16$; SUFFICIENT.

(2) Given that $r = 17$, Equation (ii) becomes $17 = p + 6$, and so $p = 17 - 6 = 11$. Using $r = 17$ and $p = 11$, Equation (iii) becomes $17 = 3(11) + b$, or $b = 17 - 33 = -16$; SUFFICIENT.

The correct answer is D; each statement alone is sufficient.

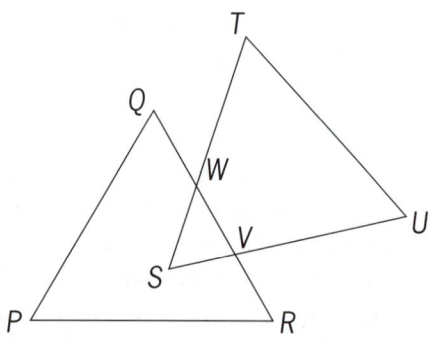

DS06861

440. In the figure above, PQR and STU are identical equilateral triangles, and PQ = 6. What is the perimeter of polygon PQWTUVR?

(1) Triangle SWV has perimeter 9.
(2) VW has length 3.5.

Geometry Triangles; Perimeter

(1) Given that triangle SWV has perimeter 9, the perimeter of polygon PQWTUVR can be determined, since the perimeter of polygon PQWTUVR equals the sum of the perimeters of the two equilateral triangles,

which is 3(6) + 3(6) = 36, minus the perimeter of triangle *SWV*; SUFFICIENT.

Figure 1

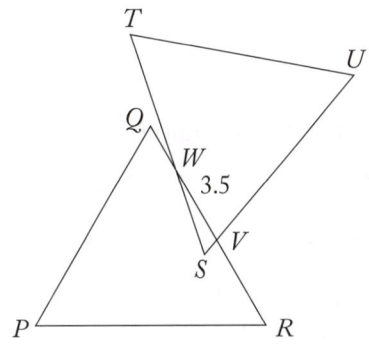

Figure 2

(2) Given that *VW* = 3.5, and using the fact that the perimeter of polygon *PQWTUVR* equals the sum of the perimeters of the two equilateral triangles, which is 3(6) + 3(6) = 36, minus the perimeter of triangle *SWV*, it is not possible to determine the perimeter of polygon *PQWTUVR*. For example, the perimeter of polygon *PQWTUVR* could be 36 − 3(3.5) = 25.5 (arrange triangles *PQR* and *STU* so that *VW* = *WS* = *SV* = 3.5, as shown in Figure 1), and the perimeter of polygon *PQWTUVR* could be greater than 25.5 (arrange triangles *PQR* and *STU* so that *VW* = 3.5, *WS* is slightly greater than 3.5, and *SV* is close to 0, as shown in Figure 2); NOT sufficient.

The correct answer is A; statement 1 alone is sufficient.

DS09973
441. The range of the numbers in set *S* is *x*, and the range of the numbers in set *T* is *y*. If all of the numbers in set *T* are also in set *S*, is *x* greater than *y*?

(1) Set *S* consists of 7 numbers.
(2) Set *T* consists of 6 numbers.

Arithmetic Statistics

Set *S* has a range of *x*, set *T* has a range of *y*, and *T* is a subset of *S*. Determine if *x* is greater than *y*.

(1) It is given that *S* contains exactly 7 numbers, but nothing additional is known about *T*. Thus, if *S* = {1, 2, 3, 4, 5, 6, 7} and *T* = {1, 2, 3, 4, 5, 6}, then $x = 7 − 1 = 6$, $y = 6 − 1 = 5$, and *x* is greater than *y*. On the other hand, if *S* = {1, 2, 3, 4, 5, 6, 7} and *T* = {1, 3, 4, 5, 6, 7}, then $x = 7 − 1 = 6$, $y = 7 − 1 = 6$, and *x* is not greater than *y*; NOT sufficient.

(2) It is given that *T* contains exactly 6 numbers, but nothing additional is known about *T*. Since the same examples given in (1) can also be used in (2), it cannot be determined if *x* is greater than *y*; NOT sufficient.

Taking (1) and (2) together, the examples used in (1) can be used to show that it cannot be determined if *x* is greater than *y*.

The correct answer is E; both statements together are still not sufficient.

DS13857
442. The hypotenuse of a right triangle is 10 cm. What is the perimeter, in centimeters, of the triangle?

(1) The area of the triangle is 25 square centimeters.
(2) The 2 legs of the triangle are of equal length.

Geometry Triangles

If *x* and *y* are the lengths of the legs of the triangle, then it is given that $x^2 + y^2 = 100$. Determining the value of $x + y + 10$, the perimeter of the triangle, is equivalent to determining the value of $x + y$.

(1) Given that the area is 25, then $\frac{1}{2}xy = 25$, or $xy = 50$. Since $(x + y)^2 = x^2 + y^2 + 2xy$, it follows that $(x + y)^2 = 100 + 2(50)$, or $x + y = \sqrt{200}$; SUFFICIENT.

(2) Given that $x = y$, since $x^2 + y^2 = 100$, it follows that $2x^2 = 100$, or $x = \sqrt{50}$. Hence, $x + y = x + x = 2x = 2\sqrt{50}$; SUFFICIENT.

The correct answer is D; each statement alone is sufficient.

Shipment	S1	S2	S3	S4	S5	S6
Fraction of the Total Value of the Six Shipments	$\frac{1}{4}$	$\frac{1}{5}$	$\frac{1}{6}$	$\frac{3}{20}$	$\frac{2}{15}$	$\frac{1}{10}$

DS01427

443. Six shipments of machine parts were shipped from a factory on two trucks, with each shipment entirely on one of the trucks. Each shipment was labeled either S1, S2, S3, S4, S5, or S6. The table shows the value of each shipment as a fraction of the total value of the six shipments. If the shipments on the first truck had a value greater than $\frac{1}{2}$ of the total value of the six shipments, was S3 shipped on the first truck?

(1) S2 and S4 were shipped on the first truck.
(2) S1 and S6 were shipped on the second truck.

Arithmetic Operations on rational numbers

Given that the shipments on the first truck had a value greater than $\frac{1}{2}$ of the total value of the 6 shipments, determine if S3 was shipped on the first truck.

To avoid dealing with fractions, it will be convenient to create scaled values of the shipments by multiplying each fractional value by 60, which is the least common denominator of the fractions. Thus, the scaled values associated with S1, S2, S3, S4, S5, and S6 are 15, 12, 10, 9, 8, and 6, respectively. The given information is that the scaled value of the shipments on the first truck is greater than $\left(\frac{1}{2}\right)(60) = 30$.

(1) Given that the first truck includes shipments with scaled values 12 and 9, it may or may not be the case that S3 (the shipment with scaled value 10) is on the first truck. For example, the first truck could contain only S2, S3, and S4, for a total scaled value $12 + 10 + 9 = 31 > 30$. Or, the first truck could contain only S1, S2, and S4, for a total scaled value $15 + 12 + 9 = 36 > 30$; NOT sufficient.

(2) Given that the second truck includes shipments with scaled values 15 and 6, the second truck cannot contain S3. Otherwise, the second truck would contain shipments with scaled values 15, 6, and 10, for a total scaled value $15 + 6 + 10 = 31$, leaving at most a total scaled value 29 (which is not greater than 30) for the first truck; SUFFICIENT.

The correct answer is B; statement 2 alone is sufficient.

DS11723

444. If x, y, and z are three-digit positive integers and if $x = y + z$, is the hundreds digit of x equal to the sum of the hundreds digits of y and z?

(1) The tens digit of x is equal to the sum of the tens digits of y and z.
(2) The units digit of x is equal to the sum of the units digits of y and z.

Arithmetic Place value

Letting $x = 100a + 10b + c$, $y = 100p + 10q + r$, and $z = 100t + 10u + v$, where a, b, c, p, q, r, t, u, and v are digits, determine if $a = p + t$.

(1) It is given that $b = q + u$ (which implies that $c + v \leq 9$ because if $c + v > 9$, then in the addition process a ten would need to be carried over to the tens column and b would be $q + u + 1$). Since b is a digit, $0 \leq b \leq 9$. Hence, $0 \leq q + u \leq 9$, and so $0 \leq 10(q + u) \leq 90$. Therefore, in the addition process, there are no hundreds to carry over from the tens column to the hundreds column, so $a = p + t$; SUFFICIENT.

(2) It is given that $c = r + v$. If $x = 687$, $y = 231$, and $z = 456$, then, $y + z = 231 + 456 = 687 = x$, $r + v = 1 + 6 = 7 = c$, and $p + t = 2 + 4 = 6 = a$. On the other hand, if $x = 637$, $y = 392$, and $z = 245$, then $y + z = 392 + 245 = 637 = x$, $r + v = 2 + 5 = 7 = c$, and $p + t = 3 + 2 = 5 \neq 6 = a$; NOT sufficient.

The correct answer is A; statement 1 alone is sufficient.

	Favorable	Unfavorable	Not Sure
Candidate M	40	20	40
Candidate N	30	35	35

DS05162

445. The table above shows the results of a survey of 100 voters who each responded "Favorable" or "Unfavorable" or "Not Sure" when asked about their impressions of Candidate M and of Candidate N. What was the number of voters who responded "Favorable" for both candidates?

   (1) The number of voters who did not respond "Favorable" for either candidate was 40.
   (2) The number of voters who responded "Unfavorable" for both candidates was 10.

Arithmetic Sets

If x is the number of voters who responded "Favorable" for both candidates, then it follows from the table that the number of voters who responded "Favorable" to at least one candidate is $40 + 30 - x = 70 - x$. This is because $40 + 30$ represents the number of voters who responded "Favorable" for Candidate M added to the number of voters who responded "Favorable" for Candidate N, a calculation that counts twice each of the x voters who responded "Favorable" for both candidates.

   (1) Given that there were 40 voters who did not respond "Favorable" for either candidate and there were 100 voters surveyed, the number of voters who responded "Favorable" to at least one candidate is $100 - 40 = 60$. Therefore, from the comments above, it follows that $70 - x = 60$, and hence $x = 10$; SUFFICIENT.

   (2) The information given affects only the numbers of voters in the categories "Unfavorable" for Candidate M only, "Unfavorable" for Candidate N only, and "Unfavorable" for both candidates. Thus, the numbers of voters in the categories "Favorable" for Candidate M only, "Favorable" for Candidate N only, and "Favorable" for both candidates are not affected. Since these latter categories are only constrained to have certain integer values that have a total sum of $70 - x$, more than one possibility exists for the value of x. For example, the numbers of voters in the categories "Favorable" for Candidate M only, "Favorable" for Candidate N only, and "Favorable" for both candidates could be 25, 15, and 15, respectively, which gives $70 - x = 25 + 15 + 15$, or $x = 15$. However, the numbers of voters in the categories "Favorable" for Candidate M only, "Favorable" for Candidate N only, and "Favorable" for both candidates could be 30, 20, and 10, respectively, which gives $70 - x = 30 + 20 + 10$, or $x = 10$; NOT sufficient.

The correct answer is A; statement 1 alone is sufficient.

DS00340

446. A school administrator will assign each student in a group of n students to one of m classrooms. If $3 < m < 13 < n$, is it possible to assign each of the n students to one of the m classrooms so that each classroom has the same number of students assigned to it?

   (1) It is possible to assign each of $3n$ students to one of m classrooms so that each classroom has the same number of students assigned to it.
   (2) It is possible to assign each of $13n$ students to one of m classrooms so that each classroom has the same number of students assigned to it.

Arithmetic Properties of numbers

Determine if n is divisible by m.

   (1) Given that $3n$ is divisible by m, then n is divisible by m if $m = 9$ and $n = 27$ (note that $3 < m < 13 < n$, $3n = 81$, and $m = 9$, so $3n$ is divisible by m) and n is not divisible by m if $m = 9$ and $n = 30$ (note that $3 < m < 13 < n$, $3n = 90$, and $m = 9$, so $3n$ is divisible by m); NOT sufficient.

   (2) Given that $13n$ is divisible by m, then $13n = qm$, or $\frac{n}{m} = \frac{q}{13}$, for some integer q.

Since 13 is a prime number that divides qm (because $13n = qm$) and 13 does not divide m (because $m < 13$), it follows that 13 divides q.

Therefore, $\frac{q}{13}$ is an integer, and since $\frac{n}{m} = \frac{q}{13}$, then $\frac{n}{m}$ is an integer. Thus, n is divisible by m; SUFFICIENT.

The correct answer is B; statement 2 alone is sufficient.

DS07441

447. If q, s, and t are all different numbers, is $q < s < t$?

    (1) $t - q = |t - s| + |s - q|$
    (2) $t > q$

    Algebra Absolute value

    (1) It is given that $t - q = |t - s| + |s - q|$, which can be rewritten without absolute values in four mutually exclusive and collectively exhaustive cases by making use of the algebraic definition of absolute value. Recall that $|x| = x$ if $x > 0$, and $|x| = -x$ if $x < 0$. Thus, for example, if $t - s < 0$, then $|t - s| = -(t - s)$.
    Case 1: $t > s$ and $s > q$. In this case, $t - s > 0$ and $s - q > 0$, and so $t - q = |t - s| + |s - q|$ is equivalent to $t - q = (t - s) + (s - q)$, which is an identity. Therefore, the case for which $t > s$ and $s > q$ is consistent with the given information and the assumption $t - q = |t - s| + |s - q|$.
    Case 2: $t > s$ and $s < q$. In this case, $t - s > 0$ and $s - q < 0$, and so $t - q = |t - s| + |s - q|$ is equivalent to $t - q = (t - s) - (s - q)$, or $s = q$, which is not consistent with the assumption that q, s, and t are all different numbers. Therefore, the case for which $t > s$ and $s < q$ is not consistent with the given information and the assumption $t - q = |t - s| + |s - q|$.
    Case 3: $t < s$ and $s > q$. In this case, $t - s < 0$ and $s - q > 0$, and so $t - q = |t - s| + |s - q|$ is equivalent to $t - q = -(t - s) + (s - q)$, or $t = s$, which is not consistent with the assumption that q, s, and t are all different numbers. Therefore, the case for which $t < s$ and $s > q$ is not consistent with the given information and the assumption $t - q = |t - s| + |s - q|$.
    Case 4: $t < s$ and $s < q$. In this case, $t - s < 0$ and $s - q < 0$, and so $t - q = |t - s| + |s - q|$ is equivalent to $t - q = -(t - s) - (s - q)$, or $t = q$, which is not consistent with the assumption that q, s, and t are all different numbers. Therefore, the case for which $t < s$ and $s < q$ is not consistent with the given information and the assumption $t - q = |t - s| + |s - q|$. The only case that is consistent with the given information and the assumption $t - q = |t - s| + |s - q|$ is Case 1. Therefore, it follows that $t > s$ and $s > q$, and this implies $q < s < t$; SUFFICIENT.

    (2) Given that $t > q$, it is possible that $q < s < t$ is true (for example, when s is between t and q) and it is possible that $q < s < t$ is false (for example, when s is greater than t); NOT sufficient.

    The correct answer is A; statement 1 alone is sufficient.

DS11538

448. What is the median number of employees assigned per project for the projects at Company Z?

    (1) 25 percent of the projects at Company Z have 4 or more employees assigned to each project.
    (2) 35 percent of the projects at Company Z have 2 or fewer employees assigned to each project.

    Arithmetic Statistics

    (1) Although 25 percent of the projects have 4 or more employees, there is essentially no information about the middle values of the numbers of employees per project. For example, if there were a total of 100 projects, then the median could be 2 (75 projects that have exactly 2 employees each and 25 projects that have exactly 4 employees each) or the median could be 3 (75 projects that have exactly 3 employees each and 25 projects that have exactly 4 employees each); NOT sufficient.

    (2) Although 35 percent of the projects have 2 or fewer employees, there is essentially no information about the middle values of the numbers of employees per project. For example, if there were a total of 100 projects, then the median could be 3 (35 projects

that have exactly 2 employees each and 65 projects that have exactly 3 employees each) or the median could be 4 (35 projects that have exactly 2 employees each and 65 projects that have exactly 4 employees each); NOT sufficient.

Given both (1) and (2), 100 − (25 + 35) percent = 40 percent of the projects have exactly 3 employees. Therefore, when the numbers of employees per project are listed from least to greatest, 35 percent of the numbers are 2 or less and (35 + 40) percent = 75 percent are 3 or less, and hence the median is 3.

The correct answer is C; both statements together are sufficient.

DS04409

449. Last year, a certain company began manufacturing product X and sold every unit of product X that it produced. Last year the company's total expenses for manufacturing product X were equal to $100,000 plus 5 percent of the company's total revenue from all units of product X sold. If the company made a profit on product X last year, did the company sell more than 21,000 units of product X last year?

  (1) The company's total revenue from the sale of product X last year was greater than $110,000.
  (2) For each unit of product X sold last year, the company's revenue was $5.

Algebra Applied problems

For a company that made a profit last year from selling product X and had total expenses for product X of $100,000 + 0.05R$, where R is the total revenue for selling product X, determine whether the company sold more than 21,000 units of product X last year.

Note that since the company made a profit, revenue − cost, which is given by $R − (\$100,000 + 0.05R) = 0.95R − \$100,000$, must be positive.

  (1) It is given that $R > \$110,000$. It is possible to vary the unit price and the number of units sold so that $R > \$110,000$ and *more than* 21,000 units were sold, and also so that $R > \$110,000$ and *less than* 21,000 units were sold. For example, if 25,000 units were sold for $10 per unit, then

$R = 25,000(\$10) = \$250,000 > \$110,000$ and $25,000 > 21,000$. On the other hand, if 20,000 units were sold for $10 per unit, then $R = 20,000(\$10) = \$200,000 > \$110,000$ and $20,000 < 21,000$; NOT sufficient.

  (2) It is given that the company's revenue for each unit of product X was $5. If the company manufactured and sold x units of product X, then its revenue was $\$5x$. Because the company made a profit, $0.95(\$5x) − \$100,000 > 0$, and so

$$0.95(\$5x) − \$100,000 > 0$$
$$\$4.75x − \$100,000 > 0$$
$$\$4.75x > \$100,000$$
$$x > 21,052; \text{SUFFICIENT.}$$

To avoid long division in the last step, note that $4.75(21,000) = 99,750$, and thus from $4.75x > 100,000$, it follows that $x > 21,000$.

The correct answer is B; statement 2 alone is sufficient.

DS01641

450. Beginning in January of last year, Carl made deposits of $120 into his account on the 15th of each month for several consecutive months and then made withdrawals of $50 from the account on the 15th of each of the remaining months of last year. There were no other transactions in the account last year. If the closing balance of Carl's account for May of last year was $2,600, what was the range of the monthly closing balances of Carl's account last year?

  (1) Last year the closing balance of Carl's account for April was less than $2,625.
  (2) Last year the closing balance of Carl's account for June was less than $2,675.

Arithmetic Statistics

  (1) If Carl began making $50 withdrawals on or before May 15, his account balance on April 16 would be at least $50 greater than it was on the last day of May. Thus, his account balance on April 16 would be at least $2,600 + $50 = $2,650, which is contrary to the information given in (1). Therefore, Carl did not begin making $50 withdrawals until June 15 or later. These observations can be used to give at least two possible ranges. Carl could have had an account balance of

$2,000 on January 1, made $120 deposits in each of the first 11 months of the year, and then made a $50 withdrawal on December 15, which gives a range of monthly closing balances of (120)(10). Also, Carl could have had an account balance of $2,000 on January 1, made $120 deposits in each of the first 10 months of the year, and then made $50 withdrawals on November 15 and on December 15, which gives a range of monthly closing balances of (120)(9); NOT sufficient.

(2) On June 1, Carl's account balance was the same as its closing balance was for May, namely $2,600. Depending on whether Carl made a $120 deposit or a $50 withdrawal on June 15, Carl's account balance on June 16 was either $2,720 or $2,550. It follows from the information given in (2) that Carl's balance on June 16 was $2,550. Therefore, Carl began making $50 withdrawals on or before June 15. These observations can be used to give at least two possible ranges. Carl could have had an account balance of $2,680 on January 1, made one $120 deposit on January 15, and then made a $50 withdrawal in each of the remaining 11 months of the year (this gives a closing balance of $2,600 for May), which gives a range of monthly closing balances of (50)(11). Also, Carl could have had an account balance of $2,510 on January 1, made $120 deposits on January 15 and on February 15, and then made a $50 withdrawal in each of the remaining 10 months of the year (this gives a closing balance of $2,600 for May), which gives a range of monthly closing balances of (50)(10); NOT sufficient.

Given both (1) and (2), it follows from the remarks above that Carl began making $50 withdrawals on June 15. Therefore, the changes to Carl's account balance for each month of last year are known. Since the closing balance for May is given, it follows that the closing balances for each month of last year are known, and hence the range of these 12 known values can be determined.

**The correct answer is C;
both statements together are sufficient.**

DS16368
451. Are all of the numbers in a certain list of 15 numbers equal?

(1) The sum of all the numbers in the list is 60.
(2) The sum of any 3 numbers in the list is 12.

Arithmetic Properties of numbers

(1) If there are 15 occurrences of the number 4 in the list, then the sum of the numbers in the list is 60 and all the numbers in the list are equal. If there are 13 occurrences of the number 4 in the list, 1 occurrence of the number 3 in the list, and 1 occurrence of the number 5 in the list, then the sum of the numbers in the list is 60 and not all the numbers in the list are equal; NOT sufficient.

(2) Given that the sum of any 3 numbers in the list is 12, arrange the numbers in the list in numerical order, from least to greatest: $a_1 \leq a_2 \leq a_3 \leq \ldots \leq a_{15}$.

If $a_1 < 4$, then $a_1 + a_2 + a_3 < 4 + a_2 + a_3$. Therefore, from (2), $12 < 4 + a_2 + a_3$, or $8 < a_2 + a_3$, and so at least one of the values a_2 and a_3 must be greater than 4. Because $a_2 \leq a_3$, it follows that $a_3 > 4$. Since the numbers are arranged from least to greatest, it follows that $a_4 > 4$ and $a_5 > 4$. But then, $a_3 + a_4 + a_5 > 4 + 4 + 4 = 12$, contrary to (2), and so $a_1 < 4$ is not true. Therefore, $a_1 \geq 4$. Since a_1 is the least of the 15 numbers, $a_n \geq 4$ for $n = 1, 2, 3, \ldots, 15$.

If $a_{15} > 4$, then $a_{13} + a_{14} + a_{15} > a_{13} + a_{14} + 4$. Therefore, from (2), $12 > a_{13} + a_{14} + 4$, or $8 > a_{13} + a_{14}$, and so at least one of the values a_{13} and a_{14} must be less than 4. Because $a_{13} \leq a_{14}$, it follows that $a_{13} < 4$. Since the numbers are arranged from least to greatest, it follows that $a_{11} < 4$ and $a_{12} < 4$. But then $a_{11} + a_{12} + a_{13} < 4 + 4 + 4 = 12$, contrary to (2). Therefore, $a_{15} \leq 4$. Since a_{15} is the greatest of the 15 numbers, $a_n \leq 4$ for $n = 1, 2, 3, \ldots, 15$.

It has been shown that, for $n = 1, 2, 3, \ldots, 15$, each of $a_n \geq 4$ and $a_n \leq 4$ is true. Therefore, $a_n = 4$ for $n = 1, 2, 3, \ldots, 15$; SUFFICIENT.

**The correct answer is B;
statement 2 alone is sufficient.**

6.5 Data Sufficiency Answer Explanations

DS16565

452. If the average (arithmetic mean) of six numbers is 75, how many of the numbers are equal to 75?

    (1) None of the six numbers is less than 75.
    (2) None of the six numbers is greater than 75.

Arithmetic Statistics

If the average of six numbers is 75, then $\frac{1}{6}$ of the sum of the numbers is 75. Therefore, the sum of the numbers is (6)(75).

(1) If one of the numbers is greater than 75, then we can write that number as $75 + x$ for some positive number x. Consequently, the sum of the 6 numbers must be at least $(5)(75) + (75 + x) = (6)(75) + x$, which is greater than (6)(75), contrary to the fact that the sum is equal to (6)(75). Hence, none of the numbers can be greater than 75. Since none of the numbers can be less than 75 (given information) and none of the numbers can be greater than 75, it follows that each of the numbers is equal to 75; SUFFICIENT.

(2) If one of the numbers is less than 75, then we can write that number as $75 - x$ for some positive number x. Consequently, the sum of the 6 numbers must be at most $(5)(75) + (75 - x) = (6)(75) - x$, which is less than (6)(75), contrary to the fact that the sum is equal to (6)(75). Hence, none of the numbers can be less than 75. Since none of the numbers can be less than 75 and none of the numbers can be greater than 75 (given information), it follows that each of the numbers is equal to 75; SUFFICIENT.

**The correct answer is D;
each statement alone is sufficient.**

DS16188

453. What amount did Jean earn from the commission on her sales in the first half of 1988?

    (1) In 1988 Jean's commission was 5 percent of the total amount of her sales.
    (2) The amount of Jean's sales in the second half of 1988 averaged $10,000 per month more than in the first half.

Arithmetic Applied problems

Let A be the amount of Jean's sales in the first half of 1988. Determine the value of A.

(1) If the amount of Jean's sales in the first half of 1988 was $10,000, then her commission in the first half of 1988 would have been (5%)($10,000) = $500. On the other hand, if the amount of Jean's sales in the first half of 1988 was $100,000, then her commission in the first half of 1988 would have been (5%)($100,000) = $5,000; NOT sufficient.

(2) No information is given that relates the amount of Jean's sales to the amount of Jean's commission; NOT sufficient.

Given (1) and (2), from (1) the amount of Jean's commission in the first half of 1988 is (5%)A. From (2) the amount of Jean's sales in the second half of 1988 is $A + $60,000. Both statements together do not give information to determine the value of A.

**The correct answer is E;
both statements together are still not sufficient.**

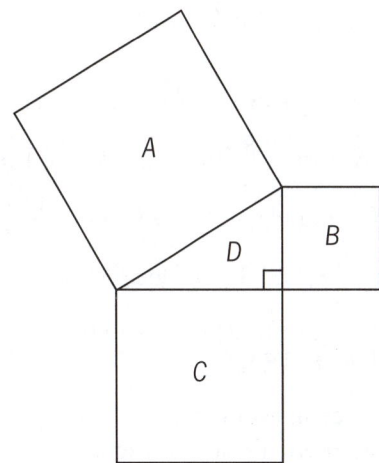

DS16572

454. In the figure above, if the area of triangular region D is 4, what is the length of a side of square region A?

    (1) The area of square region B is 9.
    (2) The area of square region C is $\frac{64}{9}$.

Geometry Area

The area of the triangular region D can be represented by $\frac{1}{2}bh$, where b is the base of the triangle (and is equal to the length of a side of

381

the square region C) and h is the height of the triangle (and is equal to the length of a side of the square region B). The area of any square is equal to the length of a side squared. The Pythagorean theorem is used to find the length of a side of a right triangle, when the length of the other 2 sides of the triangle are known and is represented by $a^2 + b^2 = c^2$, where a and b are the lengths of the 2 perpendicular sides of the triangle and c is the length of the hypotenuse.

Although completed calculations are provided in what follows, keep in mind that completed calculations are not needed to solve this problem.

(1) If the area of B is 9, then the length of each side is 3. Therefore, $h = 3$. Then, b can be determined, since the area of the triangle is, by substitution, $4 = \frac{1}{2}(3b)$ or $8 = 3b$ or $\frac{8}{3} = b$. Once b is known, the Pythagorean theorem can be used: $\left(\frac{8}{3}\right)^2 + 3^2 = c^2$ or $\frac{64}{9} + 9 = c^2$ or $\frac{145}{9} = c^2$. The length of a side of A is thus $\sqrt{\frac{145}{9}}$; SUFFICIENT.

(2) If the area of C is $\frac{64}{9}$, then the length of each side is $\frac{8}{3}$. Therefore, $b = \frac{8}{3}$. The area of a triangle is $A = \frac{1}{2}bh$ so $4 = \frac{1}{2}\left(\frac{8}{3}h\right)$, $8 = \frac{8}{3}h$, and $3 = h$. Once h is known, the Pythagorean theorem can be used as above; SUFFICIENT.

The correct answer is D; each statement alone is sufficient.

DS16168
455. If n is a positive integer and $k = 5.1 \times 10^n$, what is the value of k?

(1) $6{,}000 < k < 500{,}000$
(2) $k^2 = 2.601 \times 10^9$

Arithmetic Properties of numbers

Given that $k = 5.1 \times 10^n$, where n is a positive integer, then the value of k must follow the pattern shown in the following table:

n	k
1	51
2	510
3	5,100
4	51,000
5	510,000
6	5,100,000
.	.
.	.
.	.

(1) Given that $6{,}000 < k < 500{,}000$, then k must have the value 51,000, and so $n = 4$; SUFFICIENT.

(2) Given that $k^2 = 2.601 \times 10^9$, then $k = \sqrt{2.601 \times 10^9} = \sqrt{2{,}601 \times 10^6} = \sqrt{2{,}601} \times \sqrt{10^6}$ $= 51 \times 10^3 = 51{,}000$, and so $n = 4$; SUFFICIENT.

The correct answer is D; each statement alone is sufficient.

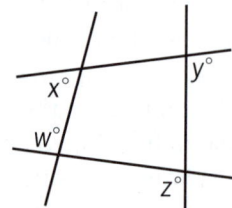

DS06875
456. What is the value of $x + y$ in the figure above?

(1) $w = 95$
(2) $z = 125$

Geometry Angles

In the figure above, a, b, c, and d are the degree measures of the interior angles of the quadrilateral formed by the four lines and $a + b + c + d = 360$. Then

$w + x + y + z$
$= (180 − a) + (180 − d) + (180 − c) + (180 − b)$
$= 720 − (a + b + c + d)$
$= 720 − 360$
$= 360$.

Determine the value of $x + y$.

(1) Given that $w = 95$, then $95 + x + y + z = 360$ and $x + y + z = 265$. If $z = 65$, for example, then $x + y = 200$. On the other hand, if $z = 100$, then $x + y = 165$; NOT sufficient.

(2) Given that $z = 125$, then $w + x + y + 125 = 360$ and $w + x + y = 235$. If $w = 35$, for example, then $x + y = 200$. On the other hand, if $w = 100$, then $x + y = 135$; NOT sufficient.

Taking (1) and (2) together, $95 + x + y + 125 = 360$, and so $x + y = 140$.

The correct answer is C; both statements together are sufficient.

DS16370

457. If n and k are positive integers, is $\sqrt{n+k} > 2\sqrt{n}$?

(1) $k > 3n$
(2) $n + k > 3n$

Algebra Inequalities

Determine if $\sqrt{n+k} > 2\sqrt{n}$. Since each side is positive, squaring each side preserves the inequality, so $\sqrt{n+k} > 2\sqrt{n}$ is equivalent to $(\sqrt{n+k})(\sqrt{n+k}) > (2\sqrt{n})(2\sqrt{n})$, which in turn is equivalent to $n + k > 4n$, or to $k > 3n$.

(1) Given that $k > 3n$, then $\sqrt{n+k} > 2\sqrt{n}$; SUFFICIENT.

(2) Given that $n + k > 3n$, then $k > 2n$. However, it is possible for $k > 2n$ to be true and $k > 3n$ to be false (for example, $k = 3$ and $n = 1$) and it is possible for $k > 2n$ to be true and $k > 3n$ to be true (for example, $k = 4$ and $n = 1$); NOT sufficient.

The correct answer is A; statement 1 alone is sufficient.

DS16589

458. In a certain business, production index p is directly proportional to efficiency index e, which is in turn directly proportional to investment index i. What is p if $i = 70$?

(1) $e = 0.5$ whenever $i = 60$.
(2) $p = 2.0$ whenever $i = 50$.

Arithmetic Proportions

(1) This gives only values for e and i, and, while p is directly proportional to e, the nature of this proportion is unknown. Therefore, p cannot be determined; NOT sufficient.

(2) Since p is directly proportional to e, which is directly proportional to i, then p is directly proportional to i. Therefore, the following proportion can be set up: $\frac{p}{i} = \frac{2.0}{50}$. If $i = 70$, then $\frac{p}{70} = \frac{2.0}{50}$. Through cross multiplying, this equation yields $50p = 140$, or $p = 2.8$; SUFFICIENT.

The preceding approach is one method that can be used. Another approach is as follows: It is given that $p = Ke = K(Li) = (KL)i$, where K and L are the proportionality constants, and the value of $70KL$ is to be determined. Statement (1) allows us to determine the value of L, but gives nothing about K, and thus (1) is not sufficient. Statement (2) allows us to determine the value of KL, and thus (2) is sufficient.

The correct answer is B; statement 2 alone is sufficient.

DS16085

459. If n is a positive integer, what is the tens digit of n ?

(1) The hundreds digit of $10n$ is 6.
(2) The tens digit of $n + 1$ is 7.

Arithmetic Properties of numbers

(1) Given that the hundreds digit of $10n$ is 6, the tens digit of n is 6, since the hundreds digit of $10n$ is always equal to the tens digit of n; SUFFICIENT.

(2) Given that the tens digit of $n + 1$ is 7, it is possible that the tens digit of n is 7 (for example, $n = 70$) and it is possible that the tens digit of n is 6 (for example, $n = 69$); NOT sufficient.

The correct answer is A; statement 1 alone is sufficient.

DS16204
460. What is the value of $\frac{2t + t - x}{t - x}$?

(1) $\frac{2t}{t - x} = 3$

(2) $t - x = 5$

Algebra Simplifying algebraic expressions

Determine the value of $\frac{2t + t - x}{t - x}$.

(1) Since $\frac{2t}{t - x} = 3$ and
$\frac{2t + t - x}{t - x} = \frac{2t}{t - x} + \frac{t - x}{t - x} = \frac{2t}{t - x} + 1$,
it follows that $\frac{2t + t - x}{t - x} = 3 + 1$; SUFFICIENT.

(2) Given that $t - x = 5$, it follows that $\frac{2t + t - x}{t - x} = \frac{2t + 5}{5} = \frac{2}{5}t + 1$, which can vary when the value of t varies. For example, $\frac{2}{5}t + 1 = 3$ if $t = 5$ (choose $x = 0$ to have $t - x = 5$) and $\frac{2}{5}t + 1 = 5$ if $t = 10$ (choose $x = 5$ to have $t - x = 5$); NOT sufficient.

The correct answer is A; statement 1 alone is sufficient.

7.0 Reading Comprehension

7.0 Reading Comprehension

Reading comprehension questions appear in the Verbal Reasoning section of the GMAT™ exam. The Verbal Reasoning section uses multiple-choice questions to measure your ability to read and comprehend written material, to reason and evaluate arguments, and to correct written material to conform to standard written English. Because the Verbal Reasoning section includes content from a variety of topics, you may be generally familiar with some of the material; however, neither the passages nor the questions assume knowledge of the topics discussed. Reading comprehension questions are intermingled with critical reasoning and sentence correction questions throughout the Verbal Reasoning section of the test.

You will have 65 minutes to complete the Verbal Reasoning section, or an average of about 1¾ minutes to answer each question. Keep in mind you will need time to read the passages, so the average time you spend on the reading comprehension questions will probably be slightly longer than the overall Verbal Reasoning section average. However, the difference will typically be offset by shorter times spent on some of the less time-consuming sentence correction questions if you work efficiently and manage your time wisely throughout the section.

Reading comprehension questions refer to written passages consisting of around 200 words or around 350 words. The passages discuss topics in the social sciences, humanities, and physical or biological sciences and such business-related fields as marketing, economics, and human resource management. Each passage is accompanied by a short series of questions that will ask you to interpret the text, apply the information you gather from the reading, and make inferences (or informed assumptions) based on the reading. For these questions, you will see a split computer screen. The written passage will remain visible on the left side as each question associated with that passage appears, in turn, on the right side. You will see only one question at a time. However, the number of questions associated with each passage may vary.

As you move through the reading comprehension sample questions, try to determine a process that works best for you. You might begin by reading a passage carefully and thoroughly. Some test-takers prefer to skim the passages the first time through, or even to read the first question before reading the passage. You may want to reread any sentences that present complicated ideas or introduce terms that are new to you. Read each question and series of answers carefully. Make sure you understand exactly what the question is asking and what the answer choices are.

If you need to, you may reread any parts of the passage that are relevant to answering the question that you are currently viewing, but you will not be able to return to other questions after you have answered them and moved on. Some questions ask explicitly about particular portions of the passages to which they refer. In some cases, the portion referred to is highlighted while the relevant question is displayed. In such cases, the question will explicitly refer to the highlighted part.

The following pages describe what reading comprehension questions are designed to measure, present the directions that will precede questions of this type, and describe the various question types. This chapter also provides test-taking strategies, sample questions, and detailed explanations of all the questions. The explanations further illustrate the ways in which reading comprehension questions evaluate basic reading skills.

7.1 What Is Measured

Reading comprehension questions measure your ability to understand, analyze, apply, and evaluate information and concepts presented in written form. All questions are to be answered on the basis of what is stated or implied in the reading material, and no specific prior knowledge of the material is required. Success in all types of GMAT questions—except those that are purely mathematical—requires strong reading skills. People without the necessary level of reading skill will be less likely than proficient readers to do well on those questions. Thus, for some examinees, critical reasoning, sentence correction, and word-based quantitative questions inevitably test reading comprehension in addition to the skills that they primarily target. But they do so only indirectly and only at the level of proficiency needed to demonstrate the skills that are directly targeted. By contrast, the reading comprehension questions are designed to focus directly on various components of reading comprehension and to measure different levels of skill in those components.

The GMAT reading comprehension questions evaluate your ability to do the following:

- **Understand complex, sophisticated nontechnical writing.**
  Effective reading involves both understanding words and phrases in context and accurately interpreting the overall messages conveyed by the writer. Although the questions do not directly measure your vocabulary knowledge (they will not ask you to show that you know the standard meanings of terms), some of them may test your ability to interpret special meanings of terms as they are used in the reading passages.

- **Understand the purposes and functions of passage components and the logical and rhetorical relationships among concepts and among pieces of information.**
  Questions that focus on this type of skill may ask you, for example, to determine how a part of a passage relates to other parts, to determine the strong and weak points of an argument, or to evaluate the relative importance of arguments and ideas in a passage.

- **Draw inferences from facts and statements.**
  Anyone who thoroughly comprehends a text should be able, with a little reflection, to determine what further information can be inferred from it. The inference questions will ask you to consider factual statements, authors' claims and opinions, or other components of a reading passage and reach conclusions on the basis of those components.

- **Understand and follow the development of quantitative concepts as they are presented in written material.**
  Reading comprehension questions do not measure mathematical knowledge. However, the passages sometimes contain quantitative information or opinions about such matters as percentages, proportions, trends, probabilities, or statistics, expressed in ways that should be understandable without technical mathematical training. You may be asked to interpret, evaluate, or apply such quantitative information or to draw inferences from it. In some cases, you might need to use some very simple arithmetic.

There are six kinds of reading comprehension questions, each of which focuses directly on a different skill. However, there is inevitably some peripheral overlap between the skills tested by one kind of question and those tested by others. For example, identifying the main point of a passage often depends on recognizing the logical or rhetorical structure of the text, and drawing inferences or applying information depends on an accurate understanding of the passage's main idea and supporting ideas.

During the test, there will be no label telling which kind of reading comprehension question you are looking at, but the wording of each question will clearly indicate what you need to do. Most of the reading comprehension question types will be represented among the several reading comprehension sets in your test, but you may not see all of the types.

The reading comprehension questions ask about the following areas:

Main idea

Each passage is a unified whole—that is, the individual sentences and paragraphs support and develop one main idea or central point and have a single unified purpose. Sometimes you will be told the central point in the passage itself, and sometimes it will be necessary for you to determine the central point from the overall organization or development of the passage. You may be asked in this kind of question to

- recognize an accurate summary, restatement, or paraphrase of the main idea of a passage
- identify the author's primary purpose or objective in writing the passage
- assign a title that summarizes, briefly and pointedly, the main idea developed in the passage.

Main idea questions are usually easy to identify as such. They generally ask explicitly about the main idea or main purpose, using phrases such as "Which of the following most accurately expresses the main idea of the passage?" "The primary purpose of the passage as a whole is to …" or "In the passage, the author seeks primarily to …"

Incorrect answer choices for these questions often take the form of ideas in the passage that are subsidiary or tangential to the main point rather than the main point of the passage as a whole, statements that are superficially similar to the main idea but are demonstrably inaccurate, or statements that are simply outside the scope of the passage discussion even though they may be conceptually related to it.

You may find it helpful, as you read through a passage, to consider the type of rhetorical strategy the author is using. For example, is the author primarily reporting facts, events, or other writers' views; arguing for a point of view; or commenting on others' views or on events or states of affairs? This is essential in answering main idea questions that ask for the passage's purpose but can also help focus your thoughts for those that ask for a main idea as such. Here are some major rhetorical types that you may encounter in the reading passages:

Argumentation (primarily presenting reasons or evidence in support of a position). In passages of this type, the correct answer to a main-idea question will typically be a paraphrase or description of the conclusion of the argument—that is, the position that the author wants readers to accept. That position is sometimes, but not always, stated explicitly in the passage. When it is not, the nature of the argumentation will make it clear to careful, perceptive readers what the author is arguing for. The correct answer choice may also include a brief reference to the reasons given in support of the position. For example, "An analysis of recent findings supports the hypothesis that …" Argumentative passages have many different purposes and follow many different reasoning strategies. Some of the major types are:

- prescriptive (primarily advocating the adoption or rejection of policies, procedures, or laws or arguing for the acceptance of ethical viewpoints)

- evaluative (primarily arguing that something is good or bad, desirable or undesirable, without advocating any particular policy or course of action)
- causal (primarily arguing for or against an account of the causes, reasons, or motivations underlying an event, condition, decision, or outcome or an account of the influences underlying a literary or artistic style or movement). In some passages of this type, the author offers reasons for or against another author's scientific, historical, or social hypothesis
- interpretive (primarily arguing for or against an account of the meaning, importance, or implications of a set of observations, a theory, an artistic or literary work, or a historical event).

Exposition (primarily presenting established facts, conveying other information, or reporting someone else's views, actions, or research findings). Like argumentative passages, expository passages follow many different strategies. Some of the major types are:

- narrative (primarily reporting or describing sequences of events). The answer to a main idea question about a narrative passage can take various forms, depending on the author's purpose and focus. For example, it may be expressed as a concise one-sentence summary of the events described or a statement of the overall outcome of the events, depending on the author's focus.
- reporting (primarily telling the views or findings of another author, researcher, theorist, or critic or reporting research findings, artistic accomplishments, innovations, etc.)
- descriptive (primarily describing the appearance, nature, or characteristics of something—for example, a place, society, artistic work, device, invention, etc.)
- informative with no further function (primarily informing readers of established scientific, historical, or other facts without arguing for any particular viewpoint regarding them).

Supporting idea

These questions measure your ability to comprehend ideas that are directly expressed in a passage and differentiate them from ideas that are neither expressed nor implied in the passage. They also measure your ability to differentiate supporting ideas from the main idea and from ideas that are implied by the author but are not explicitly stated.

Like main idea questions, supporting idea questions simply assess whether you understand the messages conveyed in the writing, without asking you to do anything further with the information. *Supporting* does not refer only to ideas that are expressed as premises supporting a main conclusion. Since each GMAT reading comprehension passage has an overall main point or purpose, every part of the writing can be thought of as supporting that main point or purpose in some way, either directly or tangentially. Therefore, supporting idea questions may ask you to understand and identify anything (other than the main point) that is said in the passage.

Correct answers to supporting idea questions almost never consist of verbatim quotations from the passage, so you will need to be able to recognize paraphrases or more abstract expressions of the passage material. Among the passage components you may be asked to understand and recognize are:

- a premise of an argument
- a tangential point such as an acknowledgment of a potential objection to the author's position or a mention of an exception to a principle or generalization
- an example given to illustrate a principle or generalization

- a counterexample intended to provide evidence against a principle or generalization
- a fact cited as background information relevant to the main idea or to a subsidiary idea
- a component of a complex explanation, description, or narration
- a brief statement of a position against which the author's reasoning is directed
- a descriptive detail used to support or elaborate on the main idea.

Whereas questions about the main idea ask you to determine the meaning of a passage as a whole, questions about supporting ideas ask you to determine the meanings of individual phrases, sentences, and paragraphs that contribute to the meaning of the passage as a whole. In many cases, these questions can be thought of as asking for the main point of one small part of the passage. Supporting idea questions often contain key phrases such as: "According to the passage …" "Which of the following does the author cite as …" "The passage mentions which of the following …" or "Which of the following does the author propose …?"

Success in answering supporting idea questions depends on remembering or quickly locating the relevant information in the passage. Occasionally, it may be possible to answer a question by quickly glancing to find the needed information without first reading through the passage, but as a general approach, that could be risky and even time-consuming. Supporting idea questions typically require a good understanding of the relationships among parts of the passage. In many cases, they will ask you to identify a piece of information that plays a specified role or is presented in a specified context. Thus, they may contain phrases such as: "Which of the following does the author offer as an objection to the theory discussed in the second paragraph?" "According to the passage, new businesses are more likely to fail if they …" "The passage compares the sea turtle's thermoregulation to …".

Inference

These questions ask about ideas that are not explicitly stated in a passage but are implied by the author or otherwise follow logically from the information in the passage. Unlike questions about supporting ideas, which ask about information that is directly expressed in a passage, inference questions ask about ideas or meanings that must be inferred from information that is directly stated.

Authors can make their points in indirect ways, suggesting ideas without actually stating them. Inference questions measure your ability to understand an author's intended meaning in parts of a passage where the meaning is only suggested. They sometimes also measure your ability to understand further implications that clearly follow from the information in the passage, even if the author does not directly intend them to be inferred. Therefore, when you read a passage, you should concentrate not only on the explicit meaning of the author's words, but also on the subtler meanings and unstated implications of those words. These questions do not ask about obscure or tenuous implications that are very remote from the passage; rather, they ask about things that any astute, observant reader should be able to infer from the passage after a little reflection.

Among the types of inferences that you may be asked to draw are:

- a likely cause of a phenomenon or situation described in the passage
- a likely effect of a phenomenon or situation described in the passage
- a specific instance or subset based on a generalization given in the passage. For example, if the passage indicates that all reptiles have a certain property and also mentions that crocodiles are reptiles, you could infer that crocodiles have the property in question

- a statement that the author (or someone referred to in the passage) likely considers true or false
- an evaluative position that the author (or someone referred to in the passage) likely holds. For example, it may be possible to infer from the author's words that she or he disapproves of something that is discussed in the passage
- the intended meaning of a word or phrase based on how it is used in the passage. However, GMAT reading comprehension questions will not ask you to define a word that is used in the passage with a standard meaning that could be accurately guessed from background vocabulary knowledge.

In some cases, the inference you are asked to draw will follow from a single statement or series of statements in the passage. In other cases, it will require consideration of two or more separate parts of the passage, and none of those parts will be sufficient when considered alone. The relevant parts may be close together or far apart, but in either case, they will be significant aspects of the passage, not irrelevant or highly obscure details. The question may refer explicitly to one or more portions of the passage or it may leave it up to you to locate or remember the relevant information.

Inference questions often contain phrases such as: "Which of the following statements about … is most strongly supported by the passage?" "It can be inferred from the passage that …" "If the claims made by the author about … are true, which of the following is most likely also true?" "The passage implies that …" "The information in the passage suggests that …".

Some of the inferences might depend on commonly known and obviously true facts in addition to the information supplied by the passage. For example, if the passage says that an event happened during a snowstorm, you could reasonably infer that the weather was not hot at that location at that time.

Incorrect answer choices for inference questions are often statements that appear superficially related to the passage but are not supported by the information in question. When the question asks what can be inferred from a specific aspect of the passage, you should be careful not to select an answer that follows from some other part of the passage but not from the part in question.

You should not expect to be able to tell which answer choice is correct on the basis of whether it is true or false. Incorrect answers are often true even though they are not supported by the information in the passage. In other cases, the correct answer could be a false statement that is implied by false information in the passage. For example, when the author explains why a theory is mistaken, you might be asked to infer that if the theory were true, such incorrect information would also have to be true.

Occasionally, it may not be possible to tell, merely from the wording of a question, whether it is asking for an inference or for recognition of something that is directly expressed. For example, "In the passage, the author suggests …" could be asking you to note that the author explicitly makes a certain suggestion in the passage. More typically, a phrase like "The passage suggests …" will be asking you about something the text implies even though the author does not directly claim that it does so. However, if you understand the passage and the relationships and implications of its parts, you will be able to find the correct answer without having to worry about how the test writers may have classified the question.

Application

Application questions measure your ability to discern relationships between situations or ideas presented in the passage and other situations or ideas beyond the direct scope of the passage. The most crucial skill involved in answering these questions is that of abstracting key features or principles from one context and applying them effectively to other contexts. This is a skill that people often need when working with scholarly, legal, professional, or business writings. The relevant features can be of various types, especially logical, practical, functional, or structural.

Application questions take many forms. They are often hypothetical or speculative, and therefore may contain words such as *would*, *could*, *might*, or *should*, or phrases such as *most clearly exemplifies*, *is most similar to*, or *is most likely ruled out by*. Some of these questions pose analogies between passage topics and other topics.

Because application questions can be about the relationships of the passage to topics outside its scope, you should not expect to be able to eliminate any answer choice based on the fact that its topic does not appear in the passage. For instance, all the answer choices for an analogy question relating to a passage's explanation of a water-treatment process might refer to book-publishing processes.

Here are some major application types that you may encounter in the test:

Analogies. These could include:

- a function or purpose that is similar to the function or purpose of something described in the passage. A question might ask, for instance, "In which of the following is the role played by a computer program most analogous to the role of the protein molecule in the pesticide discussed in the passage?"

- a method or procedure that is similar to one described in the passage even though it is used in a different context

- a goal or purpose that is similar to the goal or purpose of something discussed in the passage. For example, a protest demonstration's goal of bringing about a change in one country's environmental policies would be more analogous to a political speaker's goal of changing another country's food-safety regulations than it would to an employee's goal of finding a new job

- a part–whole relationship that is similar to a part–whole relationship described in the passage. This could be, for example, the way in which a machine or organism relates to the rest of the system or the way in which a book chapter relates to the book as a whole

- a logical relationship that is similar to the relationship between parts of the passage or between elements of someone's reasoning described in the passage.

Principles, policies, and procedures. You may be asked to identify, for example,

- a rule or policy that if enforced could help bring about a goal presented in the passage

- a principle that is not explicitly formulated in the passage but can be understood as underlying the author's reasoning

- a generalization that is likely to be true based on a range of specific instances referred to in the passage

- an action or situation that would violate or conform to a rule or policy mentioned in the passage
- a potential solution to a problem discussed in the passage
- an alternative approach that could have the same effect as one discussed in the passage.

Extensions of the author's rhetorical strategies. These include such things as:

- an example that would effectively illustrate a point made by the author
- a statement representing how the author would most likely respond to an objection to her or his position
- an additional topic that could be relevantly added to the discussion in the passage
- an idea that is not expressed in the passage but that the author would probably agree or disagree with on the basis of statements made in the passage.

What-if scenarios. You might need to identify, for example,

- a hypothetical extension of a trend or series of developments described in the passage: What would be a likely consequence if the trend continued?
- how a researcher's conclusions would have been logically affected if some observed data had been different from the data reported in the passage
- how circumstances would likely have been different if a set of developments described in the passage had not occurred
- how someone whose views are described in the passage would likely respond if that person read the passage.

Evaluation

These questions require you to analyze and evaluate the organization and logic of a passage. They fall broadly into two subcategories, analysis and critique.

Analysis-type evaluation questions require you to determine how parts of the passage work and how they relate to other parts. These are often expressed in terms of the author's purpose. Thus, they have something in common with main idea questions that ask about authors' purposes, but for main idea questions you will identify a holistic purpose of the entire passage. In those cases, you probably will not need to explicitly analyze relationships among parts. In contrast, evaluation questions target the purposes of specific elements within the passage, and those purposes usually involve relationships to other parts. Some evaluation questions may ask you to identify the logical structure of the passage or of a portion of the passage.

Critique-type evaluation questions require you to judge the strengths, weaknesses, relevance, or effectiveness of parts of the passage and their relationships to potential objections or justifications. These often involve some of the same types of reasoning that you would encounter in critical reasoning questions but with a slightly different approach and in a different context. Neither critical reasoning questions nor reading comprehension evaluation questions rely on technical knowledge of formal logic—nor do they require you to be familiar with specific terms of logic or argumentation. You can answer these using the information in the passage and careful reasoning.

Evaluation questions often contain phrases such as "The purpose of …", "Most accurately describes the structure of …", "Most strengthens …", "Would most justify …", "Is most vulnerable to the objection that …", "Which … additional information would most help …". Answer choices are often abstract and might not contain any words or concepts that appear in the passage. For example, a question that asks about the function of a paragraph might have answer choices of the form: "It rejects a theory that is presented in the preceding paragraph and offers some criteria that an alternative theory would need to meet."

Here are some major application types that you may encounter in the test:

Analysis. Answers to these questions might be, for example, statements or descriptions of:

- how the passage as a whole is constructed. In such a case, the answer will sometimes be expressed as an abstract summary of the elements that make up the passage
- how a portion of the passage is constructed
- the purpose or function of a specified part of the passage—for instance, does it define, compare or contrast, present a new idea, or refute an idea?
- how a specified portion of the passage relates logically or rhetorically to surrounding parts
- how the author tries to persuade readers to accept his or her assertions
- a likely reason or motivation for a view that the author expresses or attributes to someone

Critique. In these questions, you may be asked to identify, for example,

- an assumption that is involved in the author's reasoning or in someone else's reasoning discussed in the passage
- crucial gaps in the information provided in the passage
- a potential discovery that would help resolve an issue discussed in the passage
- a statement that, if true, would strengthen or weaken the author's reasoning or someone else's reasoning presented in the passage
- a potential counterexample to a general claim made in the passage.

Style and tone

Effective reading often depends on recognizing and evaluating the author's attitude toward a topic and the effect that the author intends the writing to have on readers. These things are often implicit in the passage's style and tone rather than stated explicitly.

Some questions focus directly and exclusively on the style or tone of the passage as a whole. They often involve phrases such as "The overall tone of the passage can be most accurately described as …", "The passage, as a whole, functions primarily as a …" or "The author's approach to … can be most accurately described as …". In the answer choices, you may be asked to select an adjective or adjective phrase that accurately describes the tone of a passage—for instance, *critical, questioning, objective, dismissive,* or *enthusiastic*. Answers may also take the form of nouns or noun phrases such as *advocacy for a political position, a sarcastic portrayal of a historical trend,* or *a journalistic exploration of some attempts to solve a problem*. They may also be more complex descriptions of the author's approach.

To answer this type of question, you will typically have to consider the language of the passage as a whole. It takes more than one pointed, critical word to make the tone of an entire passage or section critical. Sometimes, style and tone questions ask what audience the passage was probably intended for or what type of publication it would most appropriately appear in. To answer any question involving style and tone, you must ask yourself what attitudes or objectives are conveyed by the words of a passage beyond the literal meanings.

You may sometimes need to consider style and tone in answering any type of reading comprehension question, even one that does not explicitly ask about that aspect of the passage. Some question types are more likely than others to involve this type of consideration. An inference question, for example, may ask you to infer the author's attitude toward a topic, you may need to consider the passage's tone in order to confidently identify its purpose, and some evaluation questions require you to recognize the rhetorical approach the author takes in a portion of the passage.

7.2 Test-Taking Strategies

1. **Do not expect to be completely familiar with any of the material presented in reading comprehension passages.**
   You may find some passages easier to understand than others, but all passages are designed to present a challenge. If you have some familiarity with the material presented in a passage, do not let this knowledge influence your choice of answers to the questions. Answer all questions on the basis of what is *stated or implied* in the passage itself.

2. **Analyze each passage carefully, because the questions require you to have a specific and detailed understanding of the material.**
   You may find it easier to do the analysis first before moving to the questions. You may find that you prefer to skim the passage the first time and read more carefully once you understand what a question asks. You may even want to read the question before reading the passage. You should choose the method most suitable for you.

3. **Focus on key words and phrases, and make every effort to avoid losing the sense of what is discussed in the passage.**
   Keep the following in mind:
   - Note how each fact relates to an idea or an argument
   - Note where the passage moves from one idea to the next
   - Separate main ideas from supporting ideas
   - Determine what conclusions are reached and why.

4. **Read the questions carefully, making certain that you understand what is asked.**
   An answer choice that accurately restates information in the passage may be incorrect if it does not answer the question. If you need to, refer back to the passage for clarification.

5. **Read all the choices carefully.**
   Never assume that you have selected the best answer without first reading all the choices.

6. **Select the choice that answers the question best in terms of the information given in the passage.**
   Do not rely on outside knowledge of the material to help you answer the questions.

7. **Remember that comprehension—not speed—is the critical success factor when it comes to reading comprehension questions.**

7.3 Section Instructions

Go to www.mba.com/tutorial to view instructions for the section and get a feel for what the test center screens will look at on the actual GMAT exam.

7.4 Practice Questions

Each of the reading comprehension questions is based on the content of a passage. After reading the passage answer all questions pertaining to it on the basis of what is stated or implied in the passage. For each question, select the best answer of the choices given.

Line   Scientists long believed that two nerve clusters in the human hypothalamus, called suprachiasmatic nuclei (SCNs), were what controlled our circadian rhythms. Those rhythms are the biological cycles
(5)   that recur approximately every 24 hours in synchronization with the cycle of sunlight and darkness caused by Earth's rotation. Studies have demonstrated that in some animals, the SCNs control daily fluctuations in blood pressure, body
(10)   temperature, activity level, and alertness, as well as the nighttime release of the sleep-promoting agent melatonin. Furthermore, cells in the human retina dedicated to transmitting information about light levels to the SCNs have recently been discovered.
(15)   Four critical genes governing circadian cycles have been found to be active in every tissue, however, not just the SCNs, of flies, mice, and humans. In addition, when laboratory rats that usually ate at will were fed only once a day, peak
(20)   activity of a clock gene in their livers shifted by 12 hours, whereas the same clock gene in the SCNs remained synchronized with light cycles. While scientists do not dispute the role of the SCNs in controlling core functions such as the regulation of
(25)   body temperature and blood pressure, scientists now believe that circadian clocks in other organs and tissues may respond to external cues other than light—including temperature changes—that recur regularly every 24 hours.

Questions 461–463 refer to the passage.

461. The primary purpose of the passage is to

    (A) challenge recent findings that appear to contradict earlier findings
    (B) present two sides of an ongoing scientific debate
    (C) report answers to several questions that have long puzzled researchers
    (D) discuss evidence that has caused a long-standing belief to be revised
    (E) attempt to explain a commonly misunderstood biological phenomenon

462. The passage mentions each of the following as a function regulated by the SCNs in some animals EXCEPT

    (A) activity level
    (B) blood pressure
    (C) alertness
    (D) vision
    (E) temperature

463. The author of the passage would probably agree with which of the following statements about the SCNs?

   (A) The SCNs are found in other organs and tissues of the body besides the hypothalamus.
   (B) The SCNs play a critical but not exclusive role in regulating circadian rhythms.
   (C) The SCNs control clock genes in a number of tissues and organs throughout the body.
   (D) The SCNs are a less significant factor in regulating blood pressure than scientists once believed.
   (E) The SCNs are less strongly affected by changes in light levels than they are by other external cues.

In their study of whether offering a guarantee of service quality will encourage customers to visit a particular restaurant, Tucci and Talaga have found that the effect of such guarantees is mixed. For higher-priced restaurants, there is some evidence that offering a guarantee increases the likelihood of customer selection, probably reflecting the greater financial commitment involved in choosing an expensive restaurant. For lower-priced restaurants, where one expects less assiduous service, Tucci and Talaga found that a guarantee could actually have a negative effect: a potential customer might think that a restaurant offering a guarantee is worried about its service. Moreover, since customers understand a restaurant's product and know what to anticipate in terms of service, they are empowered to question its quality. This is not generally true in the case of skilled activities such as electrical work, where, consequently, a guarantee might have greater customer appeal.

For restaurants generally, the main benefit of a service guarantee probably lies not so much in customer appeal as in managing and motivating staff. Staff members would know what service standards are expected of them and also know that the success of the business relies on their adhering to those standards. Additionally, guarantees provide some basis for defining the skills needed for successful service in areas traditionally regarded as unskilled, such as waiting tables.

Questions 464–466 refer to the passage.

464. The primary purpose of the passage is to

  (A) question the results of a study that examined the effect of service-quality guarantees in the restaurant industry
  (B) discuss potential advantages and disadvantages of service-quality guarantees in the restaurant industry
  (C) examine the conventional wisdom regarding the effect of service-quality guarantees in the restaurant industry
  (D) argue that only certain restaurants would benefit from the implementation of service-quality guarantees
  (E) consider the impact that service-quality guarantees can have on the service provided by a restaurant

465. It can be inferred that the author of the passage would agree with which of the following statements about the appeal of service guarantees to customers?

  (A) Such guarantees are likely to be somewhat more appealing to customers of restaurants than to customers of other businesses.
  (B) Such guarantees are likely to be more appealing to customers who know what to anticipate in terms of service.
  (C) Such guarantees are likely to have less appeal in situations where customers are knowledgeable about a business's product or service.
  (D) In situations where a high level of financial commitment is involved, a service guarantee is not likely to be very appealing.
  (E) In situations where customers expect a high level of customer service, a service guarantee is likely to make customers think that a business is worried about its service.

466. According to the passage, Tucci and Talaga found that service guarantees, when offered by lower-priced restaurants, can have which of the following effects?

(A) Customers' developing unreasonably high expectations regarding service

(B) Customers' avoiding such restaurants because they fear that the service guarantee may not be fully honored

(C) Customers' interpreting the service guarantee as a sign that management is not confident about the quality of its service

(D) A restaurant's becoming concerned that its service will not be assiduous enough to satisfy customers

(E) A restaurant's becoming concerned that customers will be more emboldened to question the quality of the service they receive

One proposal for preserving rain forests is to promote the adoption of new agricultural technologies, such as improved plant varieties and use of chemical herbicides, which would increase
(5) productivity and slow deforestation by reducing demand for new cropland. Studies have shown that farmers in developing countries who have achieved certain levels of education, wealth, and security of land tenure are more likely to adopt such
(10) technologies. But these studies have focused on villages with limited land that are tied to a market economy rather than on the relatively isolated, self-sufficient communities with ample land characteristic of rain-forest regions. A recent study of the Tawahka
(15) people of the Honduran rain forest found that farmers with some formal education were more likely to adopt improved plant varieties but less likely to use chemical herbicides and that those who spoke Spanish (the language of the market economy) were
(20) more likely to adopt both technologies. Nonland wealth was also associated with more adoption of both technologies, but availability of uncultivated land reduced the incentive to employ the productivity-enhancing technologies. Researchers also measured
(25) land-tenure security: in Tawahka society, kinship ties are a more important indicator of this than are legal property rights, so researchers measured it by a household's duration of residence in its village. They found that longer residence correlated with more
(30) adoption of improved plant varieties but less adoption of chemical herbicides.

Questions 467–468 refer to the passage.

467. The passage suggests that in the study mentioned in line 14 the method for gathering information about security of land tenure reflects which of the following pairs of assumptions about Tawahka society?

   (A) The security of a household's land tenure depends on the strength of that household's kinship ties, and the duration of a household's residence in its village is an indication of the strength of that household's kinship ties.

   (B) The ample availability of land makes security of land tenure unimportant, and the lack of a need for secure land tenure has made the concept of legal property rights unnecessary.

   (C) The strength of a household's kinship ties is a more reliable indicator of that household's receptivity to new agricultural technologies than is its quantity of nonland wealth, and the duration of a household's residence in its village is a more reliable indicator of that household's security of land tenure than is the strength of its kinship ties.

   (D) Security of land tenure based on kinship ties tends to make farmers more receptive to the use of improved plant varieties, and security of land tenure based on long duration of residence in a village tends to make farmers more receptive to the use of chemical herbicides.

   (E) A household is more likely to be receptive to the concept of land tenure based on legal property rights if it has easy access to uncultivated land, and a household is more likely to uphold the tradition of land tenure based on kinship ties if it possesses a significant degree of nonland wealth.

468. According to the passage, the proposal mentioned in line 1 is aimed at preserving rain forests by encouraging farmers in rain-forest regions to do each of the following EXCEPT

　(A)　adopt new agricultural technologies

　(B)　grow improved plant varieties

　(C)　decrease their use of chemical herbicides

　(D)　increase their productivity

　(E)　reduce their need to clear new land for cultivation

Line   The argument for "monetizing"—or putting a monetary value on—ecosystem functions may be stated thus: Concern about the depletion of natural resources is widespread, but this concern, in the
(5)   absence of an economic argument for conservation, has not translated into significant conservational progress. Some critics blame this impasse on environmentalists, whom they believe fail to address the economic issues of environmental degradation.
(10)   Conservation can appear unprofitable when compared with the economic returns derived from converting natural assets (pristine coastlines, for example) into explicitly commercial ones (such as resort hotels). But according to David Pearce, that illusion stems
(15)   from the fact that "services" provided by ecological systems are not traded on the commodities market, and thus have no readily *quantifiable* value. To remedy this, says Pearce, one has to show that all ecosystems have economic value—indeed, that all
(20)   ecological services are economic services. Tourists visiting wildlife preserves, for example, create jobs and generate income for national economies; undisturbed forests and wetlands regulate water runoff and act as water-purifying systems, saving
(25)   millions of dollars worth of damage to property and to marine ecosystems. In Gretchen Daily's view, monetization, while unpopular with many environmentalists, reflects the dominant role that economic considerations play in human behavior,
(30)   and the expression of economic value in a common currency helps inform environmental decision-making processes.

Questions 469–472 refer to the passage.

469. Information in the passage suggests that David Pearce would most readily endorse which of the following statements concerning monetization?

   (A) Monetization represents a strategy that is attractive to both environmentalists and their critics.
   (B) Monetization is an untested strategy, but it is increasingly being embraced by environmentalists.
   (C) Monetization should at present be restricted to ecological services and should only gradually be extended to such commercial endeavors as tourism and recreation.
   (D) Monetization can serve as a means of representing persuasively the value of environmental conservation.
   (E) Monetization should inform environmental decision-making processes only if it is accepted by environmentalist groups.

470. Which of the following most clearly represents an example of an "ecological service" as that term is used in line 20 ?

   (A) A resort hotel located in an area noted for its natural beauty
   (B) A water-purifying plant that supplements natural processes with nontoxic chemicals
   (C) A wildlife preserve that draws many international travelers
   (D) A nonprofit firm that specializes in restoring previously damaged ecosystems
   (E) A newsletter that keeps readers informed of ecological victories and setbacks

471. According to the passage, Daily sees monetization as an indication of which of the following?

   (A) The centrality of economic interests to people's actions
   (B) The reluctance of the critics of environmentalism to acknowledge the importance of conservation
   (C) The inability of financial interests and ecological interests to reach a common ideological ground
   (D) The inevitability of environmental degradation
   (E) The inevitability of the growth of ecological services in the future

472. Which of the following can be inferred from the passage concerning the environmentalists mentioned in line 8 ?

   (A) They are organized in opposition to the generation of income produced by the sale of ecological services.
   (B) They are fewer in number but better organized and better connected to the media than their opponents.
   (C) They have sometimes been charged with failing to use a particular strategy in their pursuit of conservational goals.
   (D) They have been in the forefront of publicizing the extent of worldwide environmental degradation.
   (E) They define environmental progress differently and more conservatively than do other organized groups of environmentalists.

Line	Much research has been devoted to investigating what motivates consumers to try new products. Previous consumer research suggests that both the price of a new product and the way it is advertised
(5)	affect consumers' perceptions of the product's performance risk (the possibility that the product will not function as consumers expect and/or will not provide the desired benefits). Some of this research has concluded that a relatively high price will reduce
(10)	a consumer's perception of the performance risk associated with purchasing a particular product, while other studies have reported that price has little or no effect on perceived performance risk. These conflicting findings may simply be due to the nature
(15)	of product advertisements: a recent study indicates that the presentation of an advertised message has a marked effect on the relationship between price and perceived performance risk.
      Researchers have identified consumers' perception
(20)	of the credibility of the source of an advertised message—i.e., the manufacturer—as another factor affecting perceived performance risk: one study found that the greater the source credibility, the lower the consumer's perception of the risk of purchasing
(25)	an advertised new product. However, past research suggests that the relationship between source credibility and perceived performance risk may be more complex: source credibility may interact with price in a subtle way to affect consumers' judgments
(30)	of the performance risk associated with an advertised product.

Questions 473–476 refer to the passage.

473. According to the passage, the studies referred to in line 12 reported which of the following about the effect of price on consumers' perception of the performance risk associated with a new product?

(A) Although most consumers regard price as an important factor, their perception of the performance risk associated with a new product is ultimately determined by the manufacturer's reputation.

(B) Price interacts with the presentation of an advertised message to affect perceived performance risk.

(C) Price does not significantly affect consumers' perception of the performance risk associated with a new product.

(D) Consumers tend to regard price as more important than the manufacturer's credibility when they are buying from that manufacturer for the first time.

(E) Consumers are generally less concerned about a new product's performance risk when that product is relatively expensive.

474. The "past research" mentioned in line 25 suggests which of the following about perceived performance risk?

(A) The more expensive a new product is, the more likely consumers may be to credit advertised claims about that product.

(B) The more familiar consumers are with a particular manufacturer, the more willing they may be to assume some risk in the purchase of a new product being advertised by that manufacturer.

(C) Consumers' perception of the performance risk associated with a new product being advertised may be influenced by an interplay between the product's price and the manufacturer's credibility.

(D) Consumers may be more likely to believe that a product will function as it is advertised to do when they have bought products from a particular manufacturer before.

(E) The price of a particular advertised product may have less impact than the manufacturer's credibility on consumers' assessment of the performance risk associated with that product.

475. The passage is primarily concerned with

(A) challenging the implications of previous research into why consumers try new products
(B) suggesting new marketing strategies for attracting consumers to new products
(C) reconciling two different views about the effect of price on consumers' willingness to try new products
(D) describing a new approach to researching why consumers try new products
(E) discussing certain findings regarding why consumers try new products

476. Which of the following, if true, would most tend to weaken the conclusions drawn from "some of this research" (line 8)?

(A) In a subsequent study, consumers who were asked to evaluate new products with relatively low prices had the same perception of the products' performance risk as did consumers who were shown the same products priced more expensively.
(B) In a subsequent study, the quality of the advertising for the products that consumers perceived as having a lower performance risk was relatively high, while the quality of the advertising for the products that consumers perceived as having a higher performance risk was relatively poor.
(C) In a subsequent study, the products that consumers perceived as having a lower performance risk were priced higher than the highest priced products in the previous research.
(D) None of the consumers involved in this research had ever before bought products from the manufacturers involved in the research.
(E) Researchers found that the higher the source credibility for a product, the more consumers were willing to pay for it.

Line   Historians remain divided over the role of
        banks in facilitating economic growth in the
        United States in the late eighteenth and early
        nineteenth centuries. Some scholars contend
(5)   that banks played a minor role in the nation's
        growing economy. Financial institutions, they
        argue, appeared only after the economy had
        begun to develop, and once organized, followed
        conservative lending practices, providing aid to
(10)   established commercial enterprises but
        shunning those, such as manufacturing and
        transportation projects, that were more
        uncertain and capital-intensive (i.e., requiring
        greater expenditures in the form of capital than in
(15)   labor).
           A growing number of historians argue, in
        contrast, that banks were crucial in transforming
        the early national economy. When state
        legislatures began granting more bank charters
(20)   in the 1790s and early 1800s, the supply of
        credit rose accordingly. Unlike the earliest banks,
        which had primarily provided short-term loans to
        well-connected merchants, the banks of the early
        nineteenth century issued credit widely. As Paul
(25)   Gilje asserts, the expansion and democratization
        of credit in the early nineteenth century became
        the driving force of the American economy, as
        banks began furnishing large amounts of capital
        to transportation and industrial enterprises. The
(30)   exception, such historians argue, was in the
        South; here, the overwhelmingly agrarian nature
        of the economy generated outright opposition
        to banks, which were seen as monopolistic
        institutions controlled by an elite group of
(35)   planters.

Questions 477–481 refer to the passage.

477. The primary purpose of the passage is to

   (A) compare the economic role played by southern banks with the economic role played by banks in the rest of the United States during the late eighteenth and early nineteenth centuries

   (B) reevaluate a conventional interpretation of the role played by banks in the American economy during the late eighteenth and early nineteenth centuries

   (C) present different interpretations of the role played by banks in the American economy during the late eighteenth and early nineteenth centuries

   (D) analyze how the increasing number of banks in the late eighteenth and early nineteenth centuries affected the American economy

   (E) examine how scholarly opinion regarding the role played by banks in the American economy during the late eighteenth and early nineteenth centuries has changed over time

478. The passage suggests that the scholars mentioned in line 4 would argue that the reason banks tended not to fund manufacturing and transportation projects in the late eighteenth and early nineteenth centuries was that

   (A) these projects, being well established and well capitalized, did not need substantial long-term financing from banks

   (B) these projects entailed a level of risk that was too great for banks' conservative lending practices

   (C) banks preferred to invest in other, more speculative projects that offered the potential for higher returns

   (D) bank managers believed that these projects would be unlikely to contribute significantly to economic growth in the new country

   (E) bank managers believed funding these projects would result in credit being extended to too many borrowers

479. The passage suggests that Paul Gilje would be most likely to agree with which of the following claims about the lending practices of the "earliest banks" (see line 21)?

(A) These lending practices were unlikely to generate substantial profits for banks.
(B) These lending practices only benefited a narrow sector of the economy.
(C) The restrictive nature of these lending practices generated significant opposition outside of the South.
(D) The restrictive nature of these lending practices forced state legislatures to begin granting more bank charters by the early nineteenth century.
(E) These lending practices were likely to be criticized by economic elites as being overly restrictive.

480. The passage suggests that the opposition to banks in the South in the early nineteenth century stemmed in part from the perception that banks

(A) did not benefit more than a small minority of the people
(B) did not support the interests of elite planters
(C) were too closely tied to transportation and industrial interests
(D) were unwilling to issue the long-term loans required by agrarian interests
(E) were too willing to lend credit widely

481. Which of the following statements best describes the function of the last sentence of the passage?

(A) It provides evidence tending to undermine the viewpoint of the scholars mentioned in line 5.
(B) It resolves a conflict over the role of banks summarized in the first paragraph.
(C) It clarifies some of the reasons state legislatures began granting more bank charters.
(D) It qualifies a claim made earlier in the passage about the impact of banks on the American economy in the early nineteenth century.
(E) It supports a claim made earlier in the passage about how the expansion of credit affected the economy.

Line   In recent years, Western business managers have been heeding the exhortations of business journalists and academics to move their companies toward long-term, collaborative "strategic partnerships" with
(5)   their external business partners (e.g., suppliers). The experts' advice comes as a natural reaction to numerous studies conducted during the past decade that compared Japanese production and supply practices with those of the rest of the world. The
(10)   link between the success of a certain well-known Japanese automaker and its effective management of its suppliers, for example, has led to an unquestioning belief within Western management circles in the value of strategic partnerships. Indeed, in the automobile
(15)   sector all three United States manufacturers and most of their European competitors have launched programs to reduce their total number of suppliers and move toward having strategic partnerships with a few.
(20)   However, new research concerning supplier relationships in various industries demonstrates that the widespread assumption of Western managers and business consultants that Japanese firms manage their suppliers primarily through strategic
(25)   partnerships is unjustified. Not only do Japanese firms appear to conduct a far smaller proportion of their business through strategic partnerships than is commonly believed, but they also make extensive use of "market-exchange" relationships, in which
(30)   either party can turn to the marketplace and shift to different business partners at will, a practice usually associated with Western manufacturers.

Questions 482–485 refer to the passage.

482. The passage is primarily concerned with

   (A)   examining economic factors that may have contributed to the success of certain Japanese companies
   (B)   discussing the relative merits of strategic partnerships as compared with those of market-exchange relationships
   (C)   challenging the validity of a widely held assumption about how Japanese firms operate
   (D)   explaining why Western companies have been slow to adopt a particular practice favored by Japanese companies
   (E)   pointing out certain differences between Japanese and Western supplier relationships

483. According to the passage, the advice referred to in line 6 was a response to which of the following?

   (A)   A recent decrease in the number of available suppliers within the United States automobile industry
   (B)   A debate within Western management circles during the past decade regarding the value of strategic partnerships
   (C)   The success of certain European automobile manufacturers that have adopted strategic partnerships
   (D)   An increase in demand over the past decade for automobiles made by Western manufacturers
   (E)   Research comparing Japanese business practices with those of other nations

RC00458-03
484. The author mentions "the success of a certain well-known Japanese automaker" in lines 10–11, most probably in order to

   (A) demonstrate some of the possible reasons for the success of a certain business practice
   (B) cite a specific case that has convinced Western business experts of the value of a certain business practice
   (C) describe specific steps taken by Western automakers that have enabled them to compete more successfully in a global market
   (D) introduce a paradox about the effect of a certain business practice in Japan
   (E) indicate the need for Western managers to change their relationships with their external business partners

RC00458-05
485. Which of the following is cited in the passage as evidence supporting the author's claim about what the new research referred to in line 20 demonstrates?

   (A) The belief within Western management circles regarding the extent to which Japanese firms rely on strategic partnerships
   (B) The surprising number of European and United States businesses that have strategic partnerships with their suppliers
   (C) The response of Western automobile manufacturers to the advice that they adopt strategic partnerships with their suppliers
   (D) The prevalence of "market-exchange" relationships between Japanese firms and their suppliers
   (E) The success of a particular Japanese automobile manufacturer that favors strategic partnerships with its suppliers

In an effort to explain why business acquisitions often fail, scholars have begun to focus on the role of top executives of acquired companies. Acquired companies that retain their top executives tend to
(5) have more successful outcomes than those that do not. Furthermore, existing research suggests that retaining the highest-level top executives, such as the CEO (chief executive officer) and COO (chief operating officer), is related more positively to postacquisition
(10) success than retaining lower-ranked top executives. However, this explanation, while insightful, suffers from two limitations. First, the focus on positional rank does not recognize the variation in length of service that may exist in top executive posts across companies,
(15) nor does it address which particular top executives (with respect to length of service) should be retained to achieve a successful acquisition outcome. Second, the relationship between retained top executives and acquisition outcomes offered by existing research
(20) is subject to opposing theoretical explanations related to length of service. The resource-based view (RBV) suggests that keeping acquired company top executives with longer organizational tenure would lead to more successful outcomes, as those executives
(25) have idiosyncratic and nontransferable knowledge of the acquired company that would be valuable for the effective implementation of the acquisition. The opposing position, offered by the upper echelons perspective (UEP), suggests that retaining top
(30) executives having short organizational tenure would lead to more successful outcomes, as they would have the adaptability to manage most effectively during the uncertainty of the acquisition process.

Responding to these limitations, Bergh conducted
(35) a study of executive retention and acquisition outcome that focused on the organizational tenure of retained company top executives in 104 acquisitions, followed over 5 years. Bergh considered the acquisition successful if the acquired company was
(40) retained and unsuccessful if it was divested. Bergh's findings support the RBV position. Apparently, the benefits of long organizational tenure lead to more successful outcomes than the benefits of short organizational tenure. While longer tenured top
(45) executives may have trouble adapting to change, it appears that their perspectives and knowledge bases offer unique value after the acquisition. Although from the UEP position it seems sensible to retain less tenured executives and allow more tenured
(50) ones to leave, such a strategy appears to lower the probability of acquisition success.

Questions 486–489 refer to the passage.

486. According to the passage, the research mentioned in line 6 suggests which of the following about lower-ranked top executives and postacquisition success?

(A) Given that these executives are unlikely to contribute to postacquisition success, little effort should be spent trying to retain them.
(B) The shorter their length of service, the less likely it is that these executives will play a significant role in postacquisition success.
(C) These executives are less important to postacquisition success than are more highly ranked top executives.
(D) If they have long tenures, these executives may prove to be as important to postacquisition success as are more highly ranked top executives.
(E) Postacquisition success is unlikely if these executives are retained.

487. The resource-based view, as described in the passage, is based on which of the following ideas?

(A) The managerial skills of top executives become strongest after the first five years of their tenure.
(B) Company-specific knowledge is an important factor in the success of an acquisition process.
(C) The amount of nontransferable knowledge possessed by long-tenured top executives tends to be underestimated.
(D) Effective implementation of an acquisition depends primarily on the ability of executives to adapt to change.
(E) Short-tenured executives are likely to impede the implementation of a successful acquisition strategy.

488. The passage suggests that Bergh and a proponent of the upper echelons perspective would be most likely to disagree over which of the following?

- (A) Whether there is a positive correlation between short organizational tenure and managerial adaptability
- (B) Whether there is a positive correlation between long organizational tenure and the acquisition of idiosyncratic and nontransferable knowledge
- (C) Whether adaptability is a useful trait for an executive who is managing an acquisition process
- (D) Whether retaining less-tenured top executives of an acquired company is an optimal strategy for achieving postacquisition success
- (E) Whether retaining highest-level top executives of acquired companies is more important than retaining lower-ranked top executives

489. According to the passage, prior to Bergh's study, research on the role of top executives of acquired companies in business acquisition success was limited in which of the following ways?

- (A) It did not address how the organizational tenure of top executives affects postacquisition success.
- (B) It did not address why some companies have longer-tenured CEOs than others.
- (C) It did not consider strategies for retaining long-tenured top executives of acquired companies.
- (D) It failed to differentiate between the contribution of highest-level top executives to postacquisition success and that of lower-ranked top executives.
- (E) It underestimated the potential contribution that lower-level top executives can make to postacquisition success.

Line   When Jamaican-born social activist Marcus
        Garvey came to the United States in 1916, he
        arrived at precisely the right historical moment.
        What made the moment right was the return of
(5)   African American soldiers from the First World War
        in 1918, which created an ideal constituency for
        someone with Garvey's message of unity, pride,
        and improved conditions for African American
        communities.
(10)   Hoping to participate in the traditional American
        ethos of individual success, many African American
        people entered the armed forces with enthusiasm,
        only to find themselves segregated from white
        troops and subjected to numerous indignities. They
(15)   returned to a United States that was as segregated
        as it had been before the war. Considering similar
        experiences, anthropologist Anthony F. C. Wallace
        has argued that when a perceptible gap arises
        between a culture's expectations and the reality of
(20)   that culture, the resulting tension can inspire a
        revitalization movement: an organized, conscious
        effort to construct a culture that fulfills long-
        standing expectations.
            Some scholars have argued that Garvey created
(25)   the consciousness from which he built, in the 1920s,
        the largest revitalization movement in
        African American history. But such an argument only
        tends to obscure the consciousness of
        identity, strength, and sense of history that already
(30)   existed in the African American community. Garvey
        did not create this consciousness; rather, he gave
        this consciousness its political expression.

Questions 490–493 refer to the passage.

490. According to the passage, which of the following contributed to Marcus Garvey's success?

    (A) He introduced cultural and historical consciousness to the African American community.
    (B) He believed enthusiastically in the traditional American success ethos.
    (C) His audience had already formed a consciousness that made it receptive to his message.
    (D) His message appealed to critics of African American support for United States military involvement in the First World War.
    (E) He supported the movement to protest segregation that had emerged prior to his arrival in the United States.

491. The passage suggests that many African American people responded to their experiences in the armed forces in which of the following ways?

    (A) They maintained as civilians their enthusiastic allegiance to the armed forces.
    (B) They questioned United States involvement in the First World War.
    (C) They joined political organizations to protest the segregation of African American troops and the indignities they suffered in the military.
    (D) They became aware of the gap between their expectations and the realities of American culture.
    (E) They repudiated Garvey's message of pride and unity.

492. It can be inferred from the passage that the "scholars" mentioned in line 24 believe which of the following to be true?

(A) Revitalization resulted from the political activism of returning African American soldiers following the First World War.
(B) Marcus Garvey had to change a number of prevailing attitudes in order for his mass movement to find a foothold in the United States.
(C) The prevailing sensibility of the African American community provided the foundation of Marcus Garvey's political appeal.
(D) Marcus Garvey hoped to revitalize consciousness of cultural and historical identity in the African American community.
(E) The goal of the mass movement that Marcus Garvey helped bring into being was to build on the pride and unity among African Americans.

493. According to the passage, many African American people joined the armed forces during the First World War for which of the following reasons?

(A) They wished to escape worsening economic conditions in African American communities.
(B) They expected to fulfill ideals of personal attainment.
(C) They sought to express their loyalty to the United States.
(D) They hoped that joining the military would help advance the cause of desegregation.
(E) They saw military service as an opportunity to fulfill Marcus Garvey's political vision.

Arboria is floundering in the global marketplace, incurring devastating losses in market position and profits. The problem is not Arboria's products, but Arboria's trade policy. Arboria faces the prospect
(5) of continuing economic loss until Arborian business and political leaders recognize the fundamental differences between Arborian and foreign economic systems. Today the key trade issue is not free trade versus protectionism but diminishing trade versus
(10) expanding trade.

Arboria is operating with an obsolete trade policy, an artifact of the mid-1940s when Arboria and Whorfland dominated the global economy, tariffs were the principal obstacle to trade, and Arborian
(15) supremacy was uncontested in virtually all industries. In the intervening decades, economic circumstances have shifted radically. Arborian trade policy has not.

Today, Arboria's trade policy seems paralyzed by the relentless conflict between proponents of
(20) "free" and "fair" trade. The free traders argue that Arborian markets should be open, and the movement of goods and services across national borders unrestrained. The fair traders assert that access to Arborian markets should be restricted until Arborian
(25) businesses are granted equal access to foreign markets. They contend that free trade is impossible while other nations erect barriers to Arborian exports.

Both are correct: fair trade requires equal access and equal access leads to free trade. But both sides
(30) base their positions on the same two outdated premises:

1. Global commerce is conducted under the terms of the General Agreement on Tariffs and Trade (GATT) and dominated by Arboria and similar economic
(35) systems abroad.
2. Multilateral negotiations are the most effective way to resolve pressing trade issues.

Both assumptions are wrong. The 40-year-old GATT
(40) now covers less than 7 percent of global commerce. World trade is no longer dominated by the free-trade economies; nearly 75 percent is conducted by economic systems operating with principles at odds with those of Arboria. Forging a multilateral
(45) trade policy consensus among so many diverse economic systems has become virtually impossible. And while multilateral talks drag on, Arboria misses opportunities for trade expansion.

Questions 494–501 refer to the passage.

494. Which of the following best states the difference between free trade and fair trade, as explained in the passage?

(A) Free trade requires no trade tariffs whatsoever, whereas fair trade assumes multilateral agreement on tariffs for goods of equal worth.

(B) Free trade is based on the unrestricted movement of goods across all national boundaries, whereas fair trade is based on a nation's restriction of commerce with each nation that erects trade barriers to the first nation's exports.

(C) The trade policies of countries like Arboria are based on the principles of free trade, whereas the trade policies of other types of world economies are based on fair trade.

(D) Free-trade nations negotiate individual trade agreements with each of their trading partners, whereas fair-trade nations conduct multilateral trade negotiations.

(E) Free trade assumes a constant level of global commerce, whereas fair trade promotes a steady expansion of international trade.

495. It can be inferred that the author of the passage would most likely agree with which of the following statements about multilateral trade negotiations?

(A) They are the most effective way to resolve trade problems.

(B) They are most effective in dealing with fair-trade issues between nations.

(C) They have only recently begun to make an impact on world trade.

(D) Arborian reliance on multilateral trade negotiations, while appropriate in the past, is inadequate for today's global marketplace.

(E) The principles of multilateral trade negotiations are incompatible with current Arborian foreign trade policy.

496. Which of the following statements best summarizes the author's opinion of "free traders" and "fair traders"?

(A) The free and the fair traders' continuing debate provides a healthy and effective forum for examining Arborian trade policy.
(B) The proponents of fair trade are essentially correct, while those who advocate free trade are not.
(C) The proponents of free trade are better able to deal with current economic problems than are the fair traders.
(D) Neither the free nor the fair traders can come up with a workable trade policy because neither takes multilateral negotiations into account.
(E) The proponents of both free and fair trade have based their positions on out-of-date premises that do not reflect current economic conditions.

497. The author mentions all of the following as characteristic of world trade in the mid-1940s EXCEPT:

(A) Arboria played a major role in the global marketplace.
(B) Whorfland played a major role in the global marketplace.
(C) Tariffs were the main obstacle to trade.
(D) Fair-trade economies dominated international trade.
(E) Arborian manufacturers were unsurpassed in most industries.

498. In presenting the argument in the passage, the author uses all of the following EXCEPT:

(A) statistical information about global commerce
(B) definitions of terms concerning world trade
(C) generalizations about Arboria's economic system
(D) historical background of Arborian trade policy
(E) an example of an economic system whose principles differ from those of Arboria

499. The author asserts which of the following about Arboria's trade policy?

(A) A dramatic revision of Arboria's trade policy will be necessary unless Arborian manufacturers improve the quality of their goods.
(B) The most crucial issue facing Arborian trade policymakers is that of free trade versus protectionism.
(C) Arboria's current trade policy was essentially developed during the 1940s and has changed little since that time.
(D) Arboria's trade policy is widely emulated throughout the world, to the extent that most international commerce is modeled on Arboria's principles.
(E) Arboria's trade policy has evolved gradually over the last eighty years, constantly readjusting itself in response to shifts in global commerce.

500. The passage is primarily concerned with

(A) illustrating the erosion of Arboria's position in the world marketplace
(B) examining the differences between "free" and "fair" traders
(C) advocating a reassessment of Arboria's trade policy
(D) criticizing the terms of the General Agreement on Tariffs and Trade (GATT)
(E) comparing the different economic circumstances of Arboria's trade partners

501. The author implies that the main obstacle to a truly effective Arborian trade policy is the

(A) weak position that Arboria currently holds in the global marketplace
(B) inability of Arborian leaders to recognize that foreign economic systems are based on principles fundamentally different from their own
(C) dominance of the supporters of free trade in the conflict between free-trade and fair-trade advocates
(D) apparent inability of Arborian industries to produce goods that are competitive in the world market
(E) protectionism that characterizes the foreign trade policies of so many of Arboria's trade partners

Line   In *Winters v. United States* (1908), the Supreme
Court held that the right to use waters flowing through
or adjacent to the Fort Berthold Indian Reservation
was reserved to American Indians by the treaty
(5) establishing the reservation. Although this treaty did
not mention water rights, the Court ruled that the
federal government, when it created the reservation,
intended to deal fairly with American Indians by
reserving for them the waters without which their
(10) lands would have been useless. Later decisions,
citing Winters, established that courts can find federal
rights to reserve water for particular purposes if
(1) the land in question lies within an enclave under
exclusive federal jurisdiction; (2) the land has been
(15) formally withdrawn from federal public lands—i.e.,
withdrawn from the stock of federal lands available
for private use under federal land use laws—and set
aside or reserved; and (3) the circumstances reveal
the government intended to reserve water as well as
(20) land when establishing the reservation.
    Some American Indian tribes have also established
water rights through the courts based on their
traditional diversion and use of certain waters prior
to the United States' acquisition of sovereignty. For
(25) example, the Rio Grande pueblos already existed
when the United States acquired sovereignty over
New Mexico in 1848. Although they at that time
became part of the United States, the pueblo lands
never formally constituted a part of federal public
(30) lands; in any event, no treaty, statute, or executive
order has ever designated or withdrawn the pueblos
from public lands as American Indian reservations.
This fact, however, has not barred application of the
Winters doctrine. What constitutes an American Indian
(35) reservation is a question of practice, not of legal
definition, and the pueblos have always been treated
as reservations by the United States. This pragmatic
approach is buttressed by *Arizona v. California*
(1963), wherein the Supreme Court indicated that
(40) the manner in which any type of federal reservation
is created does not affect the application to it of the
Winters doctrine. Therefore, the reserved water rights
of Pueblo Indians have priority over other citizens'
water rights as of 1848, the year in which pueblos
(45) must be considered to have become reservations.

Questions 502–509 refer to the passage.

RC74000-01.01
502. According to the passage, which of the following was true of the treaty establishing the Fort Berthold Indian Reservation?

(A) It was challenged in the Supreme Court a number of times.
(B) It was rescinded by the federal government, an action that gave rise to the Winters case.
(C) It cited American Indians' traditional use of the land's resources.
(D) It failed to mention water rights to be enjoyed by the reservation's inhabitants.
(E) It was modified by the Supreme Court in *Arizona v. California*.

RC74000-02.01
503. The passage suggests that, if the criteria discussed in lines 10–20 of the text were the only criteria for establishing a reservation's water rights, which of the following would be true?

(A) The water rights of the inhabitants of the Fort Berthold Indian Reservation would not take precedence over those of other citizens.
(B) Reservations established before 1848 would be judged to have no water rights.
(C) There would be no legal basis for the water rights of the Rio Grande pueblos.
(D) Reservations other than American Indian reservations could not be created with reserved water rights.
(E) Treaties establishing reservations would have to mention water rights explicitly in order to reserve water for a particular purpose.

RC74000-03.01
504. Which of the following most accurately summarizes the relationship between *Arizona v. California*, as that decision is described in the passage, and the criteria discussed in lines 10–20?

(A) *Arizona v. California* abolishes these criteria and establishes a competing set of criteria for applying the Winters doctrine.
(B) *Arizona v. California* establishes that the Winters doctrine applies to a broader range of situations than those defined by these criteria.

(C) *Arizona v. California* represents the sole example of an exception to the criteria as they were set forth in the Winters doctrine.

(D) *Arizona v. California* does not refer to the Winters doctrine to justify water rights, whereas these criteria do rely on the Winters doctrine.

(E) *Arizona v. California* applies the criteria derived from the Winters doctrine only to federal lands other than American Indian reservations.

505. The "pragmatic approach" mentioned in lines 37–38 of the passage is best defined as one that

(A) grants recognition to reservations that were never formally established but that have traditionally been treated as such

(B) determines the water rights of all citizens in a particular region by examining the actual history of water usage in that region

(C) gives federal courts the right to reserve water along with land even when it is clear that the government originally intended to reserve only the land

(D) bases the decision to recognize the legal rights of a group on the practical effect such a recognition is likely to have on other citizens

(E) dictates that courts ignore precedents set by such cases as *Winters v. United States* in deciding what water rights belong to reserved land

506. It can be inferred from the passage that the Winters doctrine has been used to establish which of the following?

(A) A rule that the government may reserve water only by explicit treaty or agreement

(B) A legal distinction between federal lands reserved for American Indians and federal lands reserved for other purposes

(C) Criteria governing when the federal government may set land aside for a particular purpose

(D) The special status of American Indian tribes' rights to reserved land

(E) The federal right to reserve water implicitly as well as explicitly under certain conditions

507. The author cites the fact that the Rio Grande pueblos were never formally withdrawn from public lands primarily in order to do which of the following?

(A) Suggest why it might have been argued that the Winters doctrine ought not to apply to pueblo lands

(B) Imply that the United States never really acquired sovereignty over pueblo lands

(C) Argue that the pueblo lands ought still to be considered part of federal public lands

(D) Support the argument that the water rights of citizens other than American Indians are limited by the Winters doctrine

(E) Suggest that federal courts cannot claim jurisdiction over cases disputing the traditional diversion and use of water by Pueblo Indians

508. The primary purpose of the passage is to

(A) trace the development of laws establishing American Indian reservations

(B) explain the legal bases for the water rights of American Indian tribes

(C) question the legal criteria often used to determine the water rights of American Indian tribes

(D) discuss evidence establishing the earliest date at which the federal government recognized the water rights of American Indians

(E) point out a legal distinction between different types of American Indian reservations

509. The passage suggests that the legal rights of citizens other than American Indians to the use of water flowing into the Rio Grande pueblos are

(A) guaranteed by the precedent set in *Arizona v. California*

(B) abolished by the Winters doctrine

(C) deferred to the Pueblo Indians whenever treaties explicitly require this

(D) guaranteed by federal land-use laws

(E) limited by the prior claims of the Pueblo Indians

Line   In corporate purchasing, competitive scrutiny is typically limited to suppliers of items that are directly related to end products. With "indirect" purchases (such as computers, advertising, and legal services),
(5) which are not directly related to production, corporations often favor "supplier partnerships" (arrangements in which the purchaser forgoes the right to pursue alternative suppliers), which can inappropriately shelter suppliers from rigorous
(10) competitive scrutiny that might afford the purchaser economic leverage. There are two independent variables—availability of alternatives and ease of changing suppliers—that companies should use to evaluate the feasibility of subjecting suppliers of
(15) indirect purchases to competitive scrutiny. This can create four possible situations.

In Type 1 situations, there are many alternatives and change is relatively easy. Open pursuit of alternatives—by frequent competitive bidding, if
(20) possible—will likely yield the best results. In Type 2 situations, where there are many alternatives but change is difficult—as for providers of employee health-care benefits—it is important to continuously test the market and use the results to secure
(25) concessions from existing suppliers. Alternatives provide a credible threat to suppliers, even if the ability to switch is constrained. In Type 3 situations, there are few alternatives, but the ability to switch without difficulty creates a threat that companies
(30) can use to negotiate concessions from existing suppliers. In Type 4 situations, where there are few alternatives and change is difficult, partnerships may be unavoidable.

Questions 510–514 refer to the passage.

510. Which of the following can be inferred about supplier partnerships, as they are described in the passage?

(A) They cannot be sustained unless the goods or services provided are available from a large number of suppliers.

(B) They can result in purchasers paying more for goods and services than they would in a competitive-bidding situation.

(C) They typically are instituted at the urging of the supplier rather than the purchaser.

(D) They are not feasible when the goods or services provided are directly related to the purchasers' end products.

(E) They are least appropriate when the purchasers' ability to change suppliers is limited.

511. Which of the following best describes the relation of the second paragraph to the first?

(A) The second paragraph offers proof of an assertion made in the first paragraph.

(B) The second paragraph provides an explanation for the occurrence of a situation described in the first paragraph.

(C) The second paragraph discusses the application of a strategy proposed in the first paragraph.

(D) The second paragraph examines the scope of a problem presented in the first paragraph.

(E) The second paragraph discusses the contradictions inherent in a relationship described in the first paragraph.

512. It can be inferred that the author of the passage would be most likely to make which of the following recommendations to a company purchasing health care benefits for its employees?

   (A) Devise strategies for circumventing the obstacles to replacing the current provider of health care benefits.
   (B) Obtain health care benefits from a provider that also provides other indirect products and services.
   (C) Obtain bids from other providers of health care benefits in order to be in a position to negotiate a better deal with the current provider.
   (D) Switch providers of health care benefits whenever a different provider offers a more competitive price.
   (E) Acknowledge the difficulties involved in replacing the current provider of health care benefits and offer to form a partnership with the provider.

513. Which of the following is one difference between Type 2 situations and Type 4 situations, as they are described in the passage?

   (A) The number of alternative suppliers available to the purchaser
   (B) The most effective approach for the purchaser to use in obtaining competitive bids from potential suppliers
   (C) The degree of difficulty the purchaser encounters when changing suppliers
   (D) The frequency with which each type of situation occurs in a typical business environment
   (E) The likelihood that any given purchase will be an indirect purchase

514. According to the passage, which of the following factors distinguishes an indirect purchase from other purchases?

   (A) The ability of the purchasing company to subject potential suppliers of the purchased item to competitive scrutiny
   (B) The number of suppliers of the purchased item available to the purchasing company
   (C) The methods of negotiation that are available to the purchasing company
   (D) The relationship of the purchased item to the purchasing company's end product
   (E) The degree of importance of the purchased item in the purchasing company's business operations

Line Carotenoids, a family of natural pigments, form
an important part of the colorful signals used by
many animals. Animals acquire carotenoids either
directly (from the plants and algae that produce
(5)   them) or indirectly (by eating insects) and store them
in a variety of tissues. Studies of several animal
species have shown that when choosing mates,
females prefer males with brighter carotenoid-based
coloration. Owens and Olson hypothesize that the
(10) presence of carotenoids, as signaled by coloration,
would be meaningful in the context of mate selection
if carotenoids were either rare or required for
health. The conventional view is that carotenoids
are meaningful because they are rare: healthier
(15) males can forage for more of the pigments than
can their inferior counterparts. Although this may be
true, there is growing evidence that carotenoids are
meaningful also because they are required: they are
used by the immune system and for detoxification
(20) processes that are important for maintaining health.
It may be that males can use scarce carotenoids
either for immune defense and detoxification or for
attracting females. Males that are more susceptible
to disease and parasites will have to use their
(25) carotenoids to boost their immune systems, whereas
males that are genetically resistant will use fewer
carotenoids for fighting disease and will advertise
this by using the pigments for flashy display instead.

Questions 515–519 refer to the passage.

RC00423-01

515. According to the "conventional view" referred to in line 13 of the passage, brighter carotenoid-based coloration in certain species suggests that an individual

(A) lives in a habitat rich in carotenoid-bearing plants and insects
(B) has efficient detoxification processes
(C) has a superior immune system
(D) possesses superior foraging capacity
(E) is currently capable of reproducing

RC00423-02

516. The idea that carotenoid-based coloration is significant partly because carotenoids are required for health suggests that a lack of bright coloration in a male is most likely to indicate which of the following?

(A) Inefficient detoxification processes
(B) Immunity to parasite infestation
(C) Low genetic resistance to disease
(D) Lack of interest in mating
(E) Lack of carotenoid-storing tissues

RC00423-03

517. The passage suggests that relatively bright carotenoid-based coloration is a signal of which of the following characteristics in males of certain animal species?

(A) Readiness for mating behavior
(B) Ability to fight
(C) Particular feeding preferences
(D) Recovery from parasite infestation
(E) Fitness as a mate

RC00423-04

518. The passage implies which of the following about the insects from which animals acquire carotenoids?

(A) They do not produce carotenoids themselves.
(B) They use carotenoids primarily for coloration.
(C) They maintain constant levels of carotenoids in their tissues.
(D) They are unable to use carotenoids to boost their immune system.
(E) They are available in greater abundance than are carotenoid-bearing plants.

519. Information in the passage suggests that which of the following is true of carotenoids that a male animal uses for detoxification processes?

  (A) They were not acquired directly from plants and algae.
  (B) They cannot be replenished through foraging.
  (C) They cannot be used simultaneously to brighten coloration.
  (D) They do not affect the animal's susceptibility to parasites.
  (E) They increase the chances that the animal will be selected as a mate.

Linda Kerber argued in the mid-1980s that after the American Revolution (1775–1783), an ideology of "republican motherhood" resulted in a surge of educational opportunities for women in the United States. Kerber maintained that the leaders of the new nation wanted women to be educated in order to raise politically virtuous sons. A virtuous citizenry was considered essential to the success of the country's republican form of government; virtue was to be instilled not only by churches and schools, but by families, where the mother's role was crucial. Thus, according to Kerber, motherhood became pivotal to the fate of the republic, providing justification for an unprecedented attention to female education.

Introduction of the "republican motherhood" thesis dramatically changed historiography. Prior to Kerber's work, educational historians barely mentioned women and girls; Thomas Woody's 1929 work is the notable exception. Examining newspaper advertisements for academies, Woody found that educational opportunities increased for both girls and boys around 1750. Pointing to "An Essay on Woman" (1753) as reflecting a shift in view, Woody also claimed that practical education for females had many advocates before the Revolution. Woody's evidence challenges the notion that the Revolution changed attitudes regarding female education, although it may have accelerated earlier trends. Historians' reliance on Kerber's "republican motherhood" thesis may have obscured the presence of these trends, making it difficult to determine to what extent the Revolution really changed women's lives.

Questions 520–524 refer to the passage.

520. According to the passage, Kerber maintained that which of the following led to an increase in educational opportunities for women in the United States after the American Revolution?

(A) An unprecedented demand by women for greater educational opportunities in the decades following the Revolution

(B) A new political ideology calling for equality of opportunity between women and men in all aspects of life

(C) A belief that the American educational system could be reformed only if women participated more fully in that system

(D) A belief that women needed to be educated if they were to contribute to the success of the nation's new form of government

(E) A recognition that women needed to be educated if they were to take an active role in the nation's schools and churches

521. According to the passage, within the field of educational history, Thomas Woody's 1929 work was

(A) innovative because it relied on newspaper advertisements as evidence

(B) exceptional in that it concentrated on the period before the American Revolution

(C) unusual in that it focused on educational attitudes rather than on educational practices

(D) controversial in its claims regarding educational opportunities for boys

(E) atypical in that it examined the education of girls

522. The passage suggests that Woody would have agreed with which of the following claims regarding "An Essay on Woman"?

    (A) It expressed attitudes concerning women's education that were reflected in new educational opportunities for women after 1750.
    (B) It persuaded educators to offer greater educational opportunities to women in the 1750s.
    (C) It articulated ideas about women's education that would not be realized until after the American Revolution.
    (D) It offered one of the most original arguments in favor of women's education in the United States in the eighteenth century.
    (E) It presented views about women's education that were still controversial in Woody's own time.

523. The passage suggests that, with regard to the history of women's education in the United States, Kerber's work differs from Woody's primarily concerning which of the following?

    (A) The extent to which women were interested in pursuing educational opportunities in the eighteenth century
    (B) The extent of the support for educational opportunities for girls prior to the American Revolution
    (C) The extent of public resistance to educational opportunities for women after the American Revolution
    (D) Whether attitudes toward women's educational opportunities changed during the eighteenth century
    (E) Whether women needed to be educated in order to contribute to the success of a republican form of government

524. According to the passage, Kerber argued that political leaders thought that the form of government adopted by the United States after the American Revolution depended on which of the following for its success?

    (A) Women assuming the sole responsibility for instilling political virtue in children
    (B) Girls becoming the primary focus of a reformed educational system that emphasized political virtue
    (C) The family serving as one of the primary means by which children were imbued with political virtue
    (D) The family assuming many of the functions previously performed by schools and churches
    (E) Men and women assuming equal responsibility for the management of schools, churches, and the family

In the Sonoran Desert of northwestern Mexico and southern Arizona, the flowers of several species of columnar cacti—cardon, saguaro, and organ pipe—were once exclusively pollinated at night by
(5) nectar-feeding bats, as their close relatives in arid tropical regions of southern Mexico still are. In these tropical regions, diurnal (daytime) visitors to columnar cactus flowers are ineffective pollinators because, by sunrise, the flowers' stigmas become unreceptive
(10) or the flowers close. Yet the flowers of the Sonoran Desert cacti have evolved to remain open after sunrise, allowing pollination by such diurnal visitors as bees and birds. Why have these cacti expanded their range of pollinators by remaining open and receptive in daylight?
(15) This development at the northernmost range of columnar cacti may be due to a yearly variation in the abundance—and hence the reliability—of migratory nectar-feeding bats. Pollinators can be unreliable for several reasons. They can be dietary generalists
(20) whose fidelity to a particular species depends on the availability of alternative food sources. Or, they can be dietary specialists, but their abundance may vary widely from year to year, resulting in variable pollination of their preferred food species. Finally, they
(25) may be dietary specialists, but their abundance may be chronically low relative to the availability of flowers.
Recent data reveals that during spring in the Sonoran Desert, the nectar-feeding bats are specialists feeding on cardon, saguaro, and
(30) organpipe flowers. However, whereas cactus-flower abundance tends to be high during spring, bat population densities tend to be low except near maternity roosts. Moreover, in spring, diurnal cactus-pollinating birds are significantly more abundant in
(35) this region than are the nocturnal bats. Thus, with bats being unreliable cactus-flower pollinators, and daytime pollinators more abundant and therefore more reliable, selection favors the cactus flowers with traits that increase their range of pollinators. While data suggest
(40) that population densities of nectar-feeding bats are also low in tropical areas of southern Mexico, where bats are the exclusive pollinators of many species of columnar cacti, cactus-flower density and bat population density appear to be much more evenly
(45) balanced there: compared with the Sonoran Desert's cardon and saguaro, columnar cacti in southern Mexico produce far fewer flowers per night. Accordingly, despite their low population density, bats are able to pollinate nearly 100 percent of the available flowers.

Questions 525–527 refer to the passage.

525. The primary purpose of the passage is to

   (A) compare the adaptive responses of several species of columnar cacti in the Sonoran Desert with those in the arid tropical regions of southern Mexico

   (B) discuss some of the possible causes of the relatively low abundance of migratory nectar-feeding bats in the Sonoran Desert

   (C) provide a possible explanation for a particular evolutionary change in certain species of columnar cacti in the Sonoran Desert

   (D) present recent findings that challenge a particular theory as to why several species of columnar cacti in the Sonoran Desert have expanded their range of pollinators

   (E) compare the effectiveness of nocturnal and diurnal pollination for several different species of columnar cacti in the Sonoran Desert

526. According to the passage, which of the following types of nectar-feeding pollinators is likely to be an unreliable pollinator of a particular cactus flower?

   (A) A dietary specialist whose abundance is typically high in relation to that of the flower

   (B) A dietary specialist whose abundance is at times significantly lower than that of the flower

   (C) A dietary generalist for whom that flower's nectar is not a preferred food but is the most consistently available food

   (D) A dietary generalist for whom that flower's nectar is slightly preferred to other available foods

   (E) A dietary generalist that evolved from a species of dietary specialists

527. According to the passage, present-day columnar cacti in the Sonoran Desert differ from their close relatives in southern Mexico in that the Sonoran cacti

(A) have flowers that remain open after sunset
(B) are pollinated primarily by dietary specialists
(C) can be pollinated by nectar-feeding bats
(D) have stigmas that are unreceptive to pollination at night
(E) are sometimes pollinated by diurnal pollinators

Manufacturers have to do more than build large manufacturing plants to realize economies of scale. It is true that as the capacity of a manufacturing operation rises, costs per unit of output fall as plant
(5) size approaches "minimum efficient scale," where the cost per unit of output reaches a minimum, determined roughly by the state of existing technology and size of the potential market. However, minimum efficient scale cannot be fully realized unless a steady
(10) "throughput" (the flow of materials through a plant) is attained. The throughput needed to maintain the optimal scale of production requires careful coordination not only of the flow of goods through the production process, but also of the flow of input from
(15) suppliers and the flow of output to wholesalers and final consumers. If throughput falls below a critical point, unit costs rise sharply and profits disappear. A manufacturer's fixed costs and "sunk costs" (original capital investment in the physical plant) do not
(20) decrease when production declines due to inadequate supplies of raw materials, problems on the factory floor, or inefficient sales networks. Consequently, potential economies of scale are based on the physical and engineering characteristics of the
(25) production facilities—that is, on tangible capital—but realized economies of scale are operational and organizational, and depend on knowledge, skills, experience, and teamwork—that is, on organized human capabilities, or intangible capital.
(30) The importance of investing in intangible capital becomes obvious when one looks at what happens in new capital-intensive manufacturing industries. Such industries are quickly dominated, not by the first firms to acquire technologically sophisticated plants of
(35) theoretically optimal size, but rather by the first to exploit the full potential of such plants. Once some firms achieve this, a market becomes extremely hard to enter. Challengers must construct comparable plants and do so after the first movers have already
(40) worked out problems with suppliers or with new production processes. Challengers must create distribution networks and marketing systems in markets where first movers have all the contacts and know-how. And challengers must recruit management
(45) teams to compete with those that have already mastered these functional and strategic activities.

Questions 528–532 refer to the passage.

528. The passage suggests that in order for a manufacturer in a capital-intensive industry to have a decisive advantage over competitors making similar products, the manufacturer must

   (A) be the first in the industry to build production facilities of theoretically optimal size
   (B) make every effort to keep fixed and sunk costs as low as possible
   (C) be one of the first to operate its manufacturing plants at minimum efficient scale
   (D) produce goods of higher quality than those produced by direct competitors
   (E) stockpile raw materials at production sites in order to ensure a steady flow of such materials

529. The passage suggests that which of the following is true of a manufacturer's fixed and sunk costs?

   (A) The extent to which they are determined by market conditions for the goods being manufactured is frequently underestimated.
   (B) If they are kept as low as possible, the manufacturer is very likely to realize significant profits.
   (C) They are the primary factor that determines whether a manufacturer will realize economies of scale.
   (D) They should be on a par with the fixed and sunk costs of the manufacturer's competitors.
   (E) They are not affected by fluctuations in a manufacturing plant's throughput.

530. In the context of the passage as a whole, the second paragraph serves primarily to

   (A) provide an example to support the argument presented in the first paragraph
   (B) evaluate various strategies discussed in the first paragraph
   (C) introduce evidence that undermines the argument presented in the first paragraph
   (D) anticipate possible objections to the argument presented in the first paragraph
   (E) demonstrate the potential dangers of a commonly used strategy

RC00121-05
531. The passage LEAST supports the inference that a manufacturer's throughput could be adversely affected by

(A) a mistake in judgment regarding the selection of a wholesaler
(B) a breakdown in the factory's machinery
(C) a labor dispute on the factory floor
(D) an increase in the cost per unit of output
(E) a drop in the efficiency of the sales network

RC00121-07
532. The primary purpose of the passage is to

(A) point out the importance of intangible capital for realizing economies of scale in manufacturing
(B) show that manufacturers frequently gain a competitive advantage from investment in large manufacturing facilities
(C) argue that large manufacturing facilities often fail because of inadequate investment in both tangible and intangible capital
(D) suggest that most new industries are likely to be dominated by firms that build large manufacturing plants early
(E) explain why large manufacturing plants usually do not help manufacturers achieve economies of scale

A small number of the forest species of lepidoptera (moths and butterflies, which exist as caterpillars during most of their life cycle) exhibit regularly recurring patterns of population growth and decline—such fluctuations in population are known as population cycles. Although many different variables influence population levels, a regular pattern such as a population cycle seems to imply a dominant, driving force. Identification of that driving force, however, has proved surprisingly elusive despite considerable research. The common approach of studying causes of population cycles by measuring the mortality caused by different agents, such as predatory birds or parasites, has been unproductive in the case of lepidoptera. Moreover, population ecologists' attempts to alter cycles by changing the caterpillars' habitat and by reducing caterpillar populations have not succeeded. In short, the evidence implies that these insect populations, if not self-regulating, may at least be regulated by an agent more intimately connected with the insect than are predatory birds or parasites.

Recent work suggests that this agent may be a virus. For many years, viral disease had been reported in declining populations of caterpillars, but population ecologists had usually considered viral disease to have contributed to the decline once it was underway rather than to have initiated it. The recent work has been made possible by new techniques of molecular biology that allow viral DNA to be detected at low concentrations in the environment. Nuclear polyhedrosis viruses are hypothesized to be the driving force behind population cycles in lepidoptera in part because the viruses themselves follow an infectious cycle in which, if protected from direct sunlight, they may remain virulent for many years in the environment, embedded in durable crystals of polyhedrin protein. Once ingested by a caterpillar, the crystals dissolve, releasing the virus to infect the insect's cells. Late in the course of the infection, millions of new virus particles are formed and enclosed in polyhedrin crystals. These crystals reenter the environment after the insect dies and decomposes, thus becoming available to infect other caterpillars.

One of the attractions of this hypothesis is its broad applicability. Remarkably, despite significant differences in habitat and behavior, many species of lepidoptera have population cycles of similar length, between eight and eleven years. Nuclear polyhedrosis viral infection is one factor these disparate species share.

Questions 533–538 refer to the passage.

533. The primary purpose of the passage is to

(A) describe the development of new techniques that may help to determine the driving force behind population cycles in lepidoptera

(B) present evidence that refutes a particular theory about the driving force behind population cycles in lepidoptera

(C) present a hypothesis about the driving force behind population cycles in lepidoptera

(D) describe the fluctuating patterns of population cycles in lepidoptera

(E) question the idea that a single driving force is behind population cycles in lepidoptera

534. It can be inferred from the passage that the mortality caused by agents such as predatory birds or parasites was measured in an attempt to

(A) develop an explanation for the existence of lepidoptera population cycles

(B) identify behavioral factors in lepidoptera that affect survival rates

(C) identify possible methods for controlling lepidoptera population growth

(D) provide evidence that lepidoptera populations are self-regulating

(E) determine the life stages of lepidoptera at which mortality rates are highest

7.4 Reading Comprehension Practice Questions

RC00120-01
535. Which of the following, if true, would most weaken the author's conclusion in lines 18–22 ?

(A) New research reveals that the number of species of birds and parasites that prey on lepidoptera has dropped significantly in recent years.

(B) New experiments in which the habitats of lepidoptera are altered in previously untried ways result in the shortening of lepidoptera population cycles.

(C) Recent experiments have revealed that the nuclear polyhedrosis virus is present in a number of predators and parasites of lepidoptera.

(D) Differences among the habitats of lepidoptera species make it difficult to assess the effects of weather on lepidoptera population cycles.

(E) Viral disease is typically observed in a large proportion of the lepidoptera population.

RC00120-02
536. According to the passage, before the discovery of new techniques for detecting viral DNA, population ecologists believed that viral diseases

(A) were not widely prevalent among insect populations generally

(B) affected only the caterpillar life stage of lepidoptera

(C) were the driving force behind lepidoptera population cycles

(D) attacked already declining caterpillar populations

(E) infected birds and parasites that prey on various species of lepidoptera

RC00120-03
537. According to the passage, nuclear polyhedrosis viruses can remain virulent in the environment only when

(A) the polyhedrin protein crystals dissolve

(B) caterpillar populations are in decline

(C) they are present in large numbers

(D) their concentration in a particular area remains low

(E) they are sheltered from direct sunlight

RC00120-04
538. It can be inferred from the passage that while inside its polyhedrin protein crystals, the nuclear polyhedrosis virus

(A) is exposed to direct sunlight

(B) is attractive to predators

(C) cannot infect caterpillars' cells

(D) cannot be ingested by caterpillars

(E) cannot be detected by new techniques of molecular biology

Line   Resin is a plant secretion that hardens when
exposed to air; fossilized resin is called amber.
Although Pliny in the first century recognized that
amber was produced from "marrow discharged by
(5)   trees," amber has been widely misunderstood to be
a semiprecious gem and has even been described
in mineralogy textbooks. Confusion also persists
surrounding the term "resin," which was defined
before rigorous chemical analyses were available.
(10)   Resin is often confused with gum, a substance
produced in plants in response to bacterial infections,
and with sap, an aqueous solution transported
through certain plant tissues. Resin differs from both
gum and sap in that scientists have not determined a
(15)   physiological function for resin.
    In the 1950s, entomologists posited that resin
may function to repel or attract insects. Fraenkel
conjectured that plants initially produced resin in
nonspecific chemical responses to insect attack
(20)   and that, over time, plants evolved that produced
resin with specific repellent effects. But some insect
species, he noted, might overcome the repellent
effects, actually becoming attracted to the resin.
This might induce the insects to feed on those
(25)   plants or aid them in securing a breeding site.
Later researchers suggested that resin mediates
the complex interdependence, or "coevolution," of
plants and insects over time. Such ideas led to the
development of the specialized discipline of chemical
(30)   ecology, which is concerned with the role of plant
chemicals in interactions with other organisms and
with the evolution and ecology of plant antiherbivore
chemistry (plants' chemical defenses against attack
by herbivores such as insects).

Questions 539–542 refer to the passage.

RC00223-03

539. According to the passage, which of the following is true of plant antiherbivore chemistry?

(A) Changes in a plant's antiherbivore chemistry may affect insect feeding behavior.
(B) A plant's repellent effects often involve interactions between gum and resin.
(C) A plant's antiherbivore responses assist in combating bacterial infections.
(D) Plant antiherbivore chemistry plays only a minor role in the coevolution of plants and insects.
(E) Researchers first studied repellent effects in plants beginning in the 1950s.

RC00223-04

540. Of the following topics, which would be most likely to be studied within the discipline of chemical ecology as it is described in the passage?

(A) Seeds that become attached to certain insects, which in turn carry away the seeds and aid in the reproductive cycle of the plant species in question
(B) An insect species that feeds on weeds detrimental to crop health and yield, and how these insects might aid in agricultural production
(C) The effects of deforestation on the life cycles of subtropical carnivorous plants and the insect species on which the plants feed
(D) The growth patterns of a particular species of plant that has proved remarkably resistant to herbicides
(E) Insects that develop a tolerance for feeding on a plant that had previously been toxic to them, and the resultant changes within that plant species

541. The author refers to "bacterial infections" (see line 11) most likely in order to

- (A) describe the physiological function that gum performs in plants
- (B) demonstrate that sap is not the only substance that is transported through a plant's tissues
- (C) explain how modern chemical analysis has been used to clarify the function of resin
- (D) show that gum cannot serve as an effective defense against herbivores
- (E) give an example of how confusion has arisen with regard to the nature of resin

542. The author of the passage refers to Pliny most probably in order to

- (A) give an example of how the nature of amber has been misunderstood in the past
- (B) show that confusion about amber has long been more pervasive than confusion about resin
- (C) make note of the first known reference to amber as a semiprecious gem
- (D) point out an exception to a generalization about the history of people's understanding of amber
- (E) demonstrate that Pliny believed amber to be a mineral

Line   During the 1980s, many economic historians
studying Latin America focused on the impact of
the Great Depression of the 1930s. Most of these
historians argued that although the Depression
(5) began earlier in Latin America than in the United
States, it was less severe in Latin America and did
not significantly impede industrial growth there.
The historians' argument was grounded in national
government records concerning tax revenues and
(10) exports and in government-sponsored industrial
censuses, from which historians have drawn
conclusions about total manufacturing output
and profit levels across Latin America. However,
economic statistics published by Latin American
(15) governments in the early twentieth century are
neither reliable nor consistent; this is especially
true of manufacturing data, which were gathered
from factory owners for taxation purposes and
which therefore may well be distorted. Moreover,
(20) one cannot assume a direct correlation between
the output level and the profit level of a given
industry as these variables often move in opposite
directions. Finally, national and regional economies
are composed of individual firms and industries,
(25) and relying on general, sweeping economic
indicators may mask substantial variations among
these different enterprises. For example, recent
analyses of previously unexamined data on textile
manufacturing in Brazil and Mexico suggest that the
(30) Great Depression had a more severe impact on this
Latin American industry than scholars
had recognized.

Questions 543–545 refer to the passage.

RC00333-01
543. The primary purpose of the passage is to

(A) compare the impact of the Great Depression on Latin America with its impact on the United States

(B) criticize a school of economic historians for failing to analyze the Great Depression in Latin America within a global context

(C) illustrate the risks inherent in comparing different types of economic enterprises to explain economic phenomena

(D) call into question certain scholars' views concerning the severity of the Great Depression in Latin America

(E) demonstrate that the Great Depression had a more severe impact on industry in Latin America than in certain other regions

RC00333-02
544. Which of the following conclusions about the Great Depression is best supported by the passage?

(A) It did not impede Latin American industrial growth as much as historians had previously thought.

(B) It had a more severe impact on the Brazilian and the Mexican textile industries than it had on Latin America as a region.

(C) It affected the Latin American textile industry more severely than it did any other industry in Latin America.

(D) The overall impact on Latin American industrial growth should be reevaluated by economic historians.

(E) Its impact on Latin America should not be compared with its impact on the United States.

545. Which of the following, if true, would most strengthen the author's assertion regarding economic indicators in lines 25–27 ?

   (A) During an economic depression, European textile manufacturers' profits rise while their industrial output remains steady.

   (B) During a national economic recession, United States microchips manufacturers' profits rise sharply while United States steel manufacturers' profits plunge.

   (C) During the years following a severe economic depression, textile manufacturers' output levels and profit levels increase in Brazil and Mexico but not in the rest of Latin America.

   (D) Although Japanese industry as a whole recovers after an economic recession, it does not regain its previously high levels of production.

   (E) While European industrial output increases in the years following an economic depression, total output remains below that of Japan or the United States.

Among the myths taken as fact by the environmental managers of most corporations is the belief that environmental regulations affect all competitors in a given industry uniformly. In reality, regulatory costs—and therefore compliance—fall unevenly, economically disadvantaging some companies and benefiting others. For example, a plant situated near a number of larger noncompliant competitors is less likely to attract the attention of local regulators than is an isolated plant, and less attention means lower costs.

Additionally, large plants can spread compliance costs such as waste treatment across a larger revenue base; on the other hand, some smaller plants may not even be subject to certain provisions such as permit or reporting requirements by virtue of their size. Finally, older production technologies often continue to generate toxic wastes that were not regulated when the technology was first adopted. New regulations have imposed extensive compliance costs on companies still using older industrial coal-fired burners that generate high sulfur dioxide and nitrogen oxide outputs, for example, whereas new facilities generally avoid processes that would create such waste products. By realizing that they have discretion and that not all industries are affected equally by environmental regulation, environmental managers can help their companies to achieve a competitive edge by anticipating regulatory pressure and exploring all possibilities for addressing how changing regulations will affect their companies specifically.

Questions 546–549 refer to the passage.

546. It can be inferred from the passage that a large plant might have to spend more than a similar but smaller plant on environmental compliance because the larger plant is

(A) more likely to attract attention from local regulators
(B) less likely to be exempt from permit and reporting requirements
(C) less likely to have regulatory costs passed on to it by companies that supply its raw materials
(D) more likely to employ older production technologies
(E) more likely to generate wastes that are more environmentally damaging than those generated by smaller plants

547. According to the passage, which of the following statements about sulfur dioxide and nitrogen oxide outputs is true?

(A) Older production technologies cannot be adapted so as to reduce production of these outputs as waste products.
(B) Under the most recent environmental regulations, industrial plants are no longer permitted to produce these outputs.
(C) Although these outputs are environmentally hazardous, some plants still generate them as waste products despite the high compliance costs they impose.
(D) Many older plants have developed innovative technological processes that reduce the amounts of these outputs generated as waste products.
(E) Since the production processes that generate these outputs are less costly than alternative processes, these less expensive processes are sometimes adopted despite their acknowledged environmental hazards.

548. Which of the following best describes the relationship of the statement about large plants (lines 12–17) to the passage as a whole?

(A) It presents a hypothesis that is disproved later in the passage.
(B) It highlights an opposition between two ideas mentioned in the passage.
(C) It provides examples to support a claim made earlier in the passage.
(D) It exemplifies a misconception mentioned earlier in the passage.
(E) It draws an analogy between two situations described in the passage.

549. The primary purpose of the passage is to

(A) address a widespread environmental management problem and suggest possible solutions
(B) illustrate varying levels of compliance with environmental regulation among different corporations
(C) describe the various alternatives to traditional methods of environmental management
(D) advocate increased corporate compliance with environmental regulation
(E) correct a common misconception about the impact of environmental regulations

Two works published in 1984 demonstrate contrasting approaches to writing the history of United States women. Buel and Buel's biography of Mary Fish (1736–1818) makes little effort to
(5) place her story in the context of recent historiography on women. Lebsock, meanwhile, attempts not only to write the history of women in one southern community, but also to redirect two decades of historiographical debate as to
(10) whether women gained or lost status in the nineteenth century as compared with the eighteenth century. Although both books offer the reader the opportunity to assess this controversy regarding women's status, only Lebsock's deals with
(15) it directly. She examines several different aspects of women's status, helping to refine and resolve the issues. She concludes that while women gained autonomy in some areas, especially in the private sphere, they lost it in
(20) many aspects of the economic sphere. More importantly, she shows that the debate itself depends on frame of reference: in many respects, women lost power in relation to men, for example, as certain jobs (delivering babies, supervising
(25) schools) were taken over by men. Yet women also gained power in comparison with their previous status, owning a higher proportion of real estate, for example. In contrast, Buel and Buel's biography provides ample raw material for
(30) questioning the myth, fostered by some historians, of a colonial golden age in the eighteenth century but does not give the reader much guidance in analyzing the controversy over women's status.

Questions 550–555 refer to the passage.

550. The primary purpose of the passage is to

(A) examine two sides of a historiographical debate
(B) call into question an author's approach to a historiographical debate
(C) examine one author's approach to a historiographical debate
(D) discuss two authors' works in relationship to a historiographical debate
(E) explain the prevalent perspective on a historiographical debate

551. The author of the passage mentions the supervision of schools primarily in order to

(A) remind readers of the role education played in the cultural changes of the nineteenth century in the United States
(B) suggest an area in which nineteenth-century American women were relatively free to exercise power
(C) provide an example of an occupation for which accurate data about women's participation are difficult to obtain
(D) speculate about which occupations were considered suitable for United States women of the nineteenth century
(E) illustrate how the answers to questions about women's status depend on particular contexts

552. With which of the following characterizations of Lebsock's contribution to the controversy concerning women's status in the nineteenth-century United States would the author of the passage be most likely to agree?

(A) Lebsock has studied women from a formerly neglected region and time period.
(B) Lebsock has demonstrated the importance of frame of reference in answering questions about women's status.
(C) Lebsock has addressed the controversy by using women's current status as a frame of reference.
(D) Lebsock has analyzed statistics about occupations and property that were previously ignored.
(E) Lebsock has applied recent historiographical methods to the biography of a nineteenth-century woman.

553. According to the passage, Lebsock's work differs from Buel and Buel's work in that Lebsock's work

(A) uses a large number of primary sources
(B) ignores issues of women's legal status
(C) refuses to take a position on women's status in the eighteenth century
(D) addresses larger historiographical issues
(E) fails to provide sufficient material to support its claims

554. The passage suggests that Lebsock believes that compared to nineteenth-century American women, eighteenth-century American women were

(A) in many respects less powerful in relation to men
(B) more likely to own real estate
(C) generally more economically independent
(D) more independent in conducting their private lives
(E) less likely to work as school superintendents

555. The passage suggests that Buel and Buel's biography of Mary Fish provides evidence for which of the following views of women's history?

(A) Women have lost power in relation to men since the colonial era.
(B) Women of the colonial era were not as likely to be concerned with their status as were women in the nineteenth century.
(C) The colonial era was not as favorable for women as some historians have believed.
(D) Women had more economic autonomy in the colonial era than in the nineteenth century.
(E) Women's occupations were generally more respected in the colonial era than in the nineteenth century.

Line   Acting on the recommendation of a British government committee investigating the high incidence in white lead factories of illness among employees, most of whom were women, the Home
(5)   Secretary proposed in 1895 that Parliament enact legislation that would prohibit women from holding most jobs in white lead factories. Although the Women's Industrial Defence Committee (WIDC), formed in 1892 in response to earlier legislative
(10)   attempts to restrict women's labor, did not discount the white lead trade's potential health dangers, it opposed the proposal, viewing it as yet another instance of limiting women's work opportunities.

Also opposing the proposal was the Society for
(15)   Promoting the Employment of Women (SPEW), which attempted to challenge it by investigating the causes of illness in white lead factories. SPEW contended, and WIDC concurred, that controllable conditions in such factories were responsible for
(20)   the development of lead poisoning. SPEW provided convincing evidence that lead poisoning could be avoided if workers were careful and clean and if already extant workplace safety regulations were stringently enforced. However, the Women's Trade
(25)   Union League (WTUL), which had ceased in the late 1880s to oppose restrictions on women's labor, supported the eventually enacted proposal, in part because safety regulations were generally not being enforced in white lead factories, where there were
(30)   no unions (and little prospect of any) to pressure employers to comply with safety regulations.

Questions 556–558 refer to the passage.

RC00558-01

556. The passage suggests that WIDC differed from WTUL in which of the following ways?

(A) WIDC believed that the existing safety regulations were adequate to protect women's health, whereas WTUL believed that such regulations needed to be strengthened.

(B) WIDC believed that unions could not succeed in pressuring employers to comply with such regulations, whereas WTUL believed that unions could succeed in doing so.

(C) WIDC believed that lead poisoning in white lead factories could be avoided by controlling conditions there, whereas WTUL believed that lead poisoning in such factories could not be avoided no matter how stringently safety regulations were enforced.

(D) At the time that the legislation concerning white lead factories was proposed, WIDC was primarily concerned with addressing health conditions in white lead factories, whereas WTUL was concerned with improving working conditions in all types of factories.

(E) At the time that WIDC was opposing legislative attempts to restrict women's labor, WTUL had already ceased to do so.

557. Which of the following, if true, would most clearly support the contention attributed to SPEW in lines 17–20?

(A) Those white lead factories that most strongly enforced regulations concerning worker safety and hygiene had the lowest incidences of lead poisoning among employees.

(B) The incidence of lead poisoning was much higher among women who worked in white lead factories than among women who worked in other types of factories.

(C) There were many household sources of lead that could have contributed to the incidence of lead poisoning among women who also worked outside the home in the late nineteenth century.

(D) White lead factories were more stringent than were certain other types of factories in their enforcement of workplace safety regulations.

(E) Even brief exposure to the conditions typically found in white lead factories could cause lead poisoning among factory workers.

558. The passage is primarily concerned with

(A) presenting various groups' views of the motives of those proposing certain legislation

(B) contrasting the reasoning of various groups concerning their positions on certain proposed legislation

(C) tracing the process whereby certain proposed legislation was eventually enacted

(D) assessing the success of tactics adopted by various groups with respect to certain proposed legislation

(E) evaluating the arguments of various groups concerning certain proposed legislation

It is an odd but indisputable fact that the seventeenth-century English women who are generally regarded as among the forerunners of modern feminism are almost all identified with the
(5) Royalist side in the conflict between Royalists and Parliamentarians known as the English Civil Wars. Since Royalist ideology is often associated with the radical patriarchalism of seventeenth-century political theorist Robert Filmer—a patriarchalism
(10) that equates family and kingdom and asserts the divinely ordained absolute power of the king and, by analogy, of the male head of the household—historians have been understandably puzzled by the fact that Royalist women wrote the earliest
(15) extended criticisms of the absolute subordination of women in marriage and the earliest systematic assertions of women's rational and moral equality with men. Some historians have questioned the facile equation of Royalist ideology with Filmerian
(20) patriarchalism; and indeed, there may have been no consistent differences between Royalists and Parliamentarians on issues of family organization and women's political rights, but in that case one would expect early feminists to be equally divided
(25) between the two sides.

Catherine Gallagher argues that Royalism engendered feminism because the ideology of absolute monarchy provided a transition to an ideology of the absolute self. She cites the example
(30) of the notoriously eccentric author Margaret Cavendish (1626–1673), duchess of Newcastle. Cavendish claimed to be as ambitious as any woman could be, but knowing that as a woman she was excluded from the pursuit of power in the real
(35) world, she resolved to be mistress of her own world, the "immaterial world" that any person can create within her own mind—and, as a writer, on paper. In proclaiming what she called her "singularity," Cavendish insisted that she was a
(40) self-sufficient being within her mental empire, the center of her own subjective universe rather than a satellite orbiting a dominant male planet. In justifying this absolute singularity, Cavendish repeatedly invoked the model of the absolute
(45) monarch, a figure that became a metaphor for the self-enclosed, autonomous nature of the individual person. Cavendish's successors among early feminists retained her notion of woman's sovereign self, but they also sought to break free from the
(50) complete political and social isolation that her absolute singularity entailed.

Questions 559–564 refer to the passage.

559. The author of the passage refers to Robert Filmer (see line 9) primarily in order to

    (A) show that Royalist ideology was somewhat more radical than most historians appear to realize
    (B) qualify the claim that patriarchalism formed the basis of Royalist ideology
    (C) question the view that most early feminists were associated with the Royalist faction
    (D) highlight an apparent tension between Royalist ideology and the ideas of early feminists
    (E) argue that Royalists held conflicting opinions on issues of family organization and women's political rights

560. The passage suggests which of the following about the seventeenth-century English women mentioned in line 2 ?

   (A) Their status as forerunners of modern feminism is not entirely justified.
   (B) They did not openly challenge the radical patriarchalism of Royalist Filmerian ideology.
   (C) Cavendish was the first among these women to criticize women's subordination in marriage and assert women's equality with men.
   (D) Their views on family organization and women's political rights were diametrically opposed to those of both Royalist and Parliamentarian ideology.
   (E) Historians would be less puzzled if more of them were identified with the Parliamentarian side in the English Civil Wars.

561. The passage suggests that Margaret Cavendish's decision to become an author was motivated, at least in part, by a desire to

   (A) justify her support for the Royalist cause
   (B) encourage her readers to work toward eradicating Filmerian patriarchalism
   (C) persuade other women to break free from their political and social isolation
   (D) analyze the causes for women's exclusion from the pursuit of power
   (E) create a world over which she could exercise total control

562. The phrase "a satellite orbiting a dominant male planet" (lines 41–42) refers most directly to

   (A) Cavendish's concept that each woman is a sovereign self
   (B) the complete political and social isolation of absolute singularity
   (C) the immaterial world that a writer can create on paper
   (D) the absolute subordination of women in a patriarchal society
   (E) the metaphorical figure of the absolute monarch

563. The primary purpose of the passage is to

   (A) trace the historical roots of a modern sociopolitical movement
   (B) present one scholar's explanation for a puzzling historical phenomenon
   (C) contrast two interpretations of the ideological origins of a political conflict
   (D) establish a link between the ideology of an influential political theorist and that of a notoriously eccentric writer
   (E) call attention to some points of agreement between opposing sides in an ideological debate

564. Which of the following, if true, would most clearly undermine Gallagher's explanation of the link between Royalism and feminism?

   (A) Because of their privileged backgrounds, Royalist women were generally better educated than were their Parliamentarian counterparts.
   (B) Filmer himself had read some of Cavendish's early writings and was highly critical of her ideas.
   (C) Cavendish's views were highly individual and were not shared by the other Royalist women who wrote early feminist works.
   (D) The Royalist and Parliamentarian ideologies were largely in agreement on issues of family organization and women's political rights.
   (E) The Royalist side included a sizable minority faction that was opposed to the more radical tendencies of Filmerian patriarchalism.

Line   Frazier and Mosteller assert that medical research could be improved by a move toward larger, simpler clinical trials of medical treatments. Currently, researchers collect far more background information
(5) on patients than is strictly required for their trials—substantially more than hospitals collect—thereby escalating costs of data collection, storage, and analysis. Although limiting information collection could increase the risk that researchers will overlook
(10) facts relevant to a study, Frazier and Mosteller contend that such risk, never entirely eliminable from research, would still be small in most studies. Only in research on entirely new treatments are new and unexpected variables likely to arise.
(15)   Frazier and Mosteller propose not only that researchers limit data collection on individual patients but also that researchers enroll more patients in clinical trials, thereby obtaining a more representative sample of the total population with
(20) the disease under study. Often researchers restrict study participation to patients who have no ailments besides those being studied. A treatment judged successful under these ideal conditions can then be evaluated under normal conditions. Broadening the
(25) range of trial participants, Frazier and Mosteller suggest, would enable researchers to evaluate a treatment's efficacy for diverse patients under various conditions and to evaluate its effectiveness for different patient subgroups. For example, the value
(30) of a treatment for a progressive disease may vary according to a patient's stage of disease. Patients' ages may also affect a treatment's efficacy.

Questions 565–569 refer to the passage.

565. The passage is primarily concerned with

    (A) identifying two practices in medical research that may affect the accuracy of clinical trials
    (B) describing aspects of medical research that tend to drive up costs
    (C) evaluating an analysis of certain shortcomings of current medical research practices
    (D) describing proposed changes to the ways in which clinical trials are conducted
    (E) explaining how medical researchers have traditionally conducted clinical trials and how such trials are likely to change

566. Which of the following can be inferred from the passage about a study of the category of patients referred to in lines 20–22 ?

    (A) Its findings might have limited applicability.
    (B) It would be prohibitively expensive in its attempt to create ideal conditions.
    (C) It would be the best way to sample the total population of potential patients.
    (D) It would allow researchers to limit information collection without increasing the risk that important variables could be overlooked.
    (E) Its findings would be more accurate if it concerned treatments for a progressive disease than if it concerned treatments for a nonprogressive disease.

567. It can be inferred from the passage that a study limited to patients like those mentioned in lines 20–22 would have which of the following advantages over the kind of study proposed by Frazier and Mosteller?

   (A) It would yield more data and its findings would be more accurate.
   (B) It would cost less in the long term, though it would be more expensive in its initial stages.
   (C) It would limit the number of variables researchers would need to consider when evaluating the treatment under study.
   (D) It would help researchers to identify subgroups of patients with secondary conditions that might also be treatable.
   (E) It would enable researchers to assess the value of an experimental treatment for the average patient.

568. The author mentions patients' ages (line 32) primarily in order to

   (A) identify the most critical variable differentiating subgroups of patients
   (B) cast doubt on the advisability of implementing Frazier and Mosteller's proposals about medical research
   (C) indicate why progressive diseases may require different treatments at different stages
   (D) illustrate a point about the value of enrolling a wide range of patients in clinical trials
   (E) substantiate an argument about the problems inherent in enrolling large numbers of patients in clinical trials

569. According to the passage, which of the following describes a result of the way in which researchers generally conduct clinical trials?

   (A) They expend resources on the storage of information likely to be irrelevant to the study they are conducting.
   (B) They sometimes compromise the accuracy of their findings by collecting and analyzing more information than is strictly required for their trials.
   (C) They avoid the risk of overlooking variables that might affect their findings, even though doing so raises their research costs.
   (D) Because they attempt to analyze too much information, they overlook facts that could emerge as relevant to their studies.
   (E) In order to approximate the conditions typical of medical treatment, they base their methods of information collection on those used by hospitals.

There are recent reports of apparently drastic declines in amphibian populations and of extinctions of a number of the world's endangered amphibian species. These declines, if real, may be signs of a
(5) general trend toward extinction, and many environmentalists have claimed that immediate environmental action is necessary to remedy this "amphibian crisis," which, in their view, is an indicator of general and catastrophic environmental
(10) degradation due to human activity.

To evaluate these claims, it is useful to make a preliminary distinction that is far too often ignored. A declining population should not be confused with an endangered one. An endangered population is
(15) always rare, almost always small, and, by definition, under constant threat of extinction even without a proximate cause in human activities. Its disappearance, however unfortunate, should come as no great surprise. Moreover, chance events—which may
(20) indicate nothing about the direction of trends in population size—may lead to its extinction. The probability of extinction due to such random factors depends on the population size and is independent of the prevailing direction of change in that size.

(25) For biologists, population declines are potentially more worrisome than extinctions. Persistent declines, especially in large populations, indicate a changed ecological context. Even here, distinctions must again be made among declines that are only
(30) apparent (in the sense that they are part of habitual cycles or of normal fluctuations), declines that take a population to some lower but still acceptable level, and those that threaten extinction (e.g., by taking the number of individuals below the minimum
(35) viable population). Anecdotal reports of population decreases cannot distinguish among these possibilities, and some amphibian populations have shown strong fluctuations in the past.

It is indisputably true that there is simply not
(40) enough long-term scientific data on amphibian populations to enable researchers to identify real declines in amphibian populations. Many fairly common amphibian species declared all but extinct after severe declines in the 1950s and 1960s
(45) have subsequently recovered, and so might the apparently declining populations that have generated the current appearance of an amphibian crisis. Unfortunately, long-term data will not soon be forthcoming, and postponing environmental
(50) action while we wait for it may doom species and whole ecosystems to extinction.

Questions 570–575 refer to the passage.

570. The primary purpose of the passage is to

   (A) assess the validity of a certain view
   (B) distinguish between two phenomena
   (C) identify the causes of a problem
   (D) describe a disturbing trend
   (E) allay concern about a particular phenomenon

571. It can be inferred from the passage that the author believes which of the following to be true of the environmentalists mentioned in lines 5–6 ?

   (A) They have wrongly chosen to focus on anecdotal reports rather than on the long-term data that are currently available concerning amphibians.
   (B) Their recommendations are flawed because their research focuses too narrowly on a single category of animal species.
   (C) Their certainty that population declines in general are caused by environmental degradation is not warranted.
   (D) They have drawn premature conclusions concerning a crisis in amphibian populations from recent reports of declines.
   (E) They have overestimated the effects of chance events on trends in amphibian populations.

572. It can be inferred from the passage that the author believes which of the following to be true of the amphibian extinctions that have recently been reported?

   (A) They have resulted primarily from human activities causing environmental degradation.
   (B) They could probably have been prevented if timely action had been taken to protect the habitats of amphibian species.
   (C) They should not come as a surprise, because amphibian populations generally have been declining for a number of years.
   (D) They have probably been caused by a combination of chance events.
   (E) They do not clearly constitute evidence of general environmental degradation.

573. According to the passage, each of the following is true of endangered amphibian species EXCEPT:

(A) They are among the rarest kinds of amphibians.
(B) They generally have populations that are small in size.
(C) They are in constant danger of extinction.
(D) Those with decreasing populations are the most likely candidates for immediate extinction.
(E) They are in danger of extinction due to events that sometimes have nothing to do with human activities.

574. Which of the following most accurately describes the organization of the passage?

(A) A question is raised, a distinction regarding it is made, and the question is answered.
(B) An interpretation is presented, its soundness is examined, and a warning is given.
(C) A situation is described, its consequences are analyzed, and a prediction is made.
(D) Two interpretations of a phenomenon are described, and one of them is rejected as invalid.
(E) Two methods for analyzing a phenomenon are compared, and further study of the phenomenon is recommended.

575. Which of the following best describes the function of the sentence in lines 35–38 ?

(A) To give an example of a particular kind of study
(B) To cast doubt on an assertion made in the previous sentence
(C) To raise an objection to a view presented in the first paragraph
(D) To provide support for a view presented in the first paragraph
(E) To introduce an idea that will be countered in the following paragraph

Line   While the most abundant and dominant species within a particular ecosystem is often crucial in perpetuating the ecosystem, a "keystone" species, here defined as one whose effects are much larger
(5)   than would be predicted from its abundance, can also play a vital role. But because complex species interactions may be involved, identifying a keystone species by removing the species and observing changes in the ecosystem is problematic. It might
(10)   seem that certain traits would clearly define a species as a keystone species; for example, *Pisaster ochraceus* is often a keystone predator because it consumes and suppresses mussel populations, which in the absence of this starfish
(15)   can be a dominant species. But such predation on a dominant or potentially dominant species occurs in systems that do as well as in systems that do not have species that play keystone roles. Moreover, whereas *P. ochraceus* occupies an unambiguous
(20)   keystone role on wave-exposed rocky headlands, in more wave-sheltered habitats the impact of *P. ochraceus* predation is weak or nonexistent, and at certain sites sand burial is responsible for eliminating mussels. Keystone status appears to
(25)   depend on context, whether of particular geography or of such factors as community diversity (for example, a reduction in species diversity may thrust more of the remaining species into keystone roles) and length of species
(30)   interaction (since newly arrived species in particular may dramatically affect ecosystems).

Questions 576–579 refer to the passage.

RC00556-03

576. The passage mentions which of the following as a factor that affects the role of *P. ochraceus* as a keystone species within different habitats?

(A) The degree to which the habitat is sheltered from waves

(B) The degree to which other animals within a habitat prey on mussels

(C) The fact that mussel populations are often not dominant within some habitats occupied by *P. ochraceus*

(D) The size of the *P. ochraceus* population within the habitat

(E) The fact that there is great species diversity within some habitats occupied by *P. ochraceus*

RC00556-04

577. Which of the following hypothetical experiments most clearly exemplifies the method of identifying species' roles that the author considers problematic?

(A) A population of seals in an Arctic habitat is counted in order to determine whether it is the dominant species in that ecosystem.

(B) A species of fish that is a keystone species in one marine ecosystem is introduced into another marine ecosystem to see whether the species will come to occupy a keystone role.

(C) In order to determine whether a species of monkey is a keystone species within a particular ecosystem, the monkeys are removed from that ecosystem and the ecosystem is then studied.

(D) Different mountain ecosystems are compared to determine how geography affects a particular species' ability to dominate its ecosystem.

(E) In a grassland experiencing a changing climate, patterns of species extinction are traced in order to evaluate the effect of climate changes on keystone species in that grassland.

578. Which of the following, if true, would most clearly support the argument about keystone status advanced in the last sentence of the passage (lines 24–31) ?

   (A) A species of bat is primarily responsible for keeping insect populations within an ecosystem low, and the size of the insect population in turn affects bird species within that ecosystem.

   (B) A species of iguana occupies a keystone role on certain tropical islands, but does not play that role on adjacent tropical islands that are inhabited by a greater number of animal species.

   (C) Close observation of a savannah ecosystem reveals that more species occupy keystone roles within that ecosystem than biologists had previously believed.

   (D) As a keystone species of bee becomes more abundant, it has a larger effect on the ecosystem it inhabits.

   (E) A species of moth that occupies a keystone role in a prairie habitat develops coloration patterns that camouflage it from potential predators.

579. The passage suggests which of the following about the identification of a species as a keystone species?

   (A) Such an identification depends primarily on the species' relationship to the dominant species.

   (B) Such an identification can best be made by removing the species from a particular ecosystem and observing changes that occur in the ecosystem.

   (C) Such an identification is likely to be less reliable as an ecosystem becomes less diverse.

   (D) Such an identification seems to depend on various factors within the ecosystem.

   (E) Such an identification can best be made by observing predation behavior.

Line Conodonts, the spiky phosphatic remains (bones and teeth composed of calcium phosphate) of tiny marine animals that probably appeared about 520 million years ago, were once among the most
(5) controversial of fossils. Both the nature of the organism to which the remains belonged and the function of the remains were unknown. However, since the 1981 discovery of fossils preserving not just the phosphatic elements but also other remains
(10) of the tiny soft-bodied animals (also called conodonts) that bore them, scientists' reconstructions of the animals' anatomy have had important implications for hypotheses concerning the development of the vertebrate skeleton.
(15) The vertebrate skeleton had traditionally been regarded as a defensive development, champions of this view postulating that it was only with the much later evolution of jaws that vertebrates became predators. The first vertebrates, which were soft-
(20) bodied, would have been easy prey for numerous invertebrate carnivores, especially if these early vertebrates were sedentary suspension feeders. Thus, traditionalists argued, these animals developed coverings of bony scales or plates, and teeth were
(25) secondary features, adapted from the protective bony scales. Indeed, external skeletons of this type are common among the well-known fossils of ostracoderms, jawless vertebrates that existed from approximately 500 to 400 million years ago.
(30) However, other paleontologists argued that many of the definitive characteristics of vertebrates, such as paired eyes and muscular and skeletal adaptations for active life, would not have evolved unless the first vertebrates were predatory. Teeth were more
(35) primitive than external armor according to this view, and the earliest vertebrates were predators.
 The stiffening notochord along the back of the body, V-shaped muscle blocks along the sides, and posterior tail fins help to identify conodonts as
(40) among the most primitive of vertebrates. The lack of any mineralized structures apart from the elements in the mouth indicates that conodonts were more primitive than the armored jawless fishes such as the ostracoderms. It now appears that the hard parts that
(45) first evolved in the mouth of an animal improved its efficiency as a predator, and that aggression rather than protection was the driving force behind the origin of the vertebrate skeleton.

Questions 580–582 refer to the passage.

580. According to the passage, the anatomical evidence provided by the preserved soft bodies of conodonts led scientists to conclude that

(A) conodonts had actually been invertebrate carnivores
(B) conodonts' teeth were adapted from protective bony scales
(C) conodonts were primitive vertebrate suspension feeders
(D) primitive vertebrates with teeth appeared earlier than armored vertebrates
(E) scientists' original observations concerning the phosphatic remains of conodonts were essentially correct

581. The second paragraph in the passage serves primarily to

(A) outline the significance of the 1981 discovery of conodont remains to the debate concerning the development of the vertebrate skeleton
(B) contrast the traditional view of the development of the vertebrate skeleton with a view derived from the 1981 discovery of conodont remains
(C) contrast the characteristics of the ostracoderms with the characteristics of earlier soft-bodied vertebrates
(D) explain the importance of the development of teeth among the earliest vertebrate predators
(E) present the two sides of the debate concerning the development of the vertebrate skeleton

582. It can be inferred that on the basis of the 1981 discovery of conodont remains, paleontologists could draw which of the following conclusions?

   (A) The earliest vertebrates were sedentary suspension feeders.
   (B) Ostracoderms were not the earliest vertebrates.
   (C) Defensive armor preceded jaws among vertebrates.
   (D) Paired eyes and adaptations for activity are definitive characteristics of vertebrates.
   (E) Conodonts were unlikely to have been predators.

Line   Jon Clark's study of the effect of the modernization
of a telephone exchange on exchange maintenance
work and workers is a solid contribution to a debate
that encompasses two lively issues in the history and
(5) sociology of technology: technological determinism
and social constructivism.
    Clark makes the point that the characteristics of a
technology have a decisive influence on job skills and
work organization. Put more strongly, technology can
(10) be a primary determinant of social and managerial
organization. Clark believes this possibility has
been obscured by the recent sociological fashion,
exemplified by Braverman's analysis, that emphasizes
the way machinery reflects social choices. For
(15) Braverman, the shape of a technological system is
subordinate to the manager's desire to wrest control
of the labor process from the workers. Technological
change is construed as the outcome of negotiations
among interested parties who seek to incorporate
(20) their own interests into the design and configuration
of the machinery. This position represents the new
mainstream called social constructivism.
    The constructivists gain acceptance by
misrepresenting technological determinism:
(25) technological determinists are supposed to believe,
for example, that machinery imposes appropriate
forms of order on society. The alternative to
constructivism, in other words, is to view technology
as existing outside society, capable of directly
(30) influencing skills and work organization.
    Clark refutes the extremes of the constructivists
by both theoretical and empirical arguments.
Theoretically he defines "technology" in terms of
relationships between social and technical variables.
(35) Attempts to reduce the meaning of technology to
cold, hard metal are bound to fail, for machinery is
just scrap unless it is organized functionally and
supported by appropriate systems of operation and
maintenance. At the empirical level Clark shows how
(40) a change at the telephone exchange from
maintenance-intensive electromechanical switches
to semielectronic switching systems altered work
tasks, skills, training opportunities, administration,
and organization of workers. Some changes Clark
(45) attributes to the particular way management and
labor unions negotiated the introduction of the
technology, whereas others are seen as arising from
the capabilities and nature of the technology itself.
Thus Clark helps answer the question: "When is
(50) social choice decisive and when are the concrete
characteristics of technology more important?"

Questions 583–590 refer to the passage.

RC00013-01
583. The primary purpose of the passage is to

(A) advocate a more positive attitude toward technological change
(B) discuss the implications for employees of the modernization of a telephone exchange
(C) consider a successful challenge to the constructivist view of technological change
(D) challenge the position of advocates of technological determinism
(E) suggest that the social causes of technological change should be studied in real situations

RC00013-02
584. Which of the following statements about the modernization of the telephone exchange is supported by information in the passage?

(A) The new technology reduced the role of managers in labor negotiations.
(B) The modernization was implemented without the consent of the employees directly affected by it.
(C) The modernization had an impact that went significantly beyond maintenance routines.
(D) Some of the maintenance workers felt victimized by the new technology.
(E) The modernization gave credence to the view of advocates of social constructivism.

RC00013-03
585. Which of the following most accurately describes Clark's opinion of Braverman's position?

(A) He respects its wide-ranging popularity.
(B) He disapproves of its misplaced emphasis on the influence of managers.
(C) He admires the consideration it gives to the attitudes of the workers affected.
(D) He is concerned about its potential to impede the implementation of new technologies.
(E) He is sympathetic to its concern about the impact of modern technology on workers.

586. The information in the passage suggests that which of the following statements from hypothetical sociological studies of change in industry most clearly exemplifies the social constructivists' version of technological determinism?

(A) It is the available technology that determines workers' skills, rather than workers' skills influencing the application of technology.

(B) All progress in industrial technology grows out of a continuing negotiation between technological possibility and human need.

(C) Some organizational change is caused by people; some is caused by computer chips.

(D) Most major technological advances in industry have been generated through research and development.

(E) Some industrial technology eliminates jobs, but educated workers can create whole new skills areas by the adaptation of the technology.

587. The information in the passage suggests that Clark believes that which of the following would be true if social constructivism had not gained widespread acceptance?

(A) Businesses would be more likely to modernize without considering the social consequences of their actions.

(B) There would be greater understanding of the role played by technology in producing social change.

(C) Businesses would be less likely to understand the attitudes of employees affected by modernization.

(D) Modernization would have occurred at a slower rate.

(E) Technology would have played a greater part in determining the role of business in society.

588. According to the passage, constructivists employed which of the following to promote their argument?

(A) Empirical studies of business situations involving technological change

(B) Citation of managers supportive of their position

(C) Construction of hypothetical situations that support their view

(D) Contrasts of their view with a misstatement of an opposing view

(E) Descriptions of the breadth of impact of technological change

589. The author of the passage uses the expression "are supposed to" in line 25 primarily in order to

(A) suggest that a contention made by constructivists regarding determinists is inaccurate

(B) define the generally accepted position of determinists regarding the implementation of technology

(C) engage in speculation about the motivation of determinists

(D) lend support to a comment critical of the position of determinists

(E) contrast the historical position of determinists with their position regarding the exchange modernization

590. Which of the following statements about Clark's study of the telephone exchange can be inferred from information in the passage?

(A) Clark's reason for undertaking the study was to undermine Braverman's analysis of the function of technology.

(B) Clark's study suggests that the implementation of technology should be discussed in the context of conflict between labor and management.

(C) Clark examined the impact of changes in the technology of switching at the exchange in terms of overall operations and organization.

(D) Clark concluded that the implementation of new switching technology was equally beneficial to management and labor.

(E) Clark's analysis of the change in switching systems applies only narrowly to the situation at the particular exchange that he studied.

Because the framers of the United States Constitution (written in 1787) believed that protecting property rights relating to inventions would encourage the new nation's economic growth, they gave
(5) Congress—the national legislature—a constitutional mandate to grant patents for inventions. The resulting patent system has served as a model for those in other nations. Recently, however, scholars have questioned whether the American system helped
(10) achieve the framers' goals. These scholars have contended that from 1794 to roughly 1830, American inventors were unable to enforce property rights because judges were "antipatent" and routinely invalidated patents for arbitrary reasons. This
(15) argument is based partly on examination of court decisions in cases where patent holders ("patentees") brought suit alleging infringement of their patent rights. In the 1820s, for instance, 75 percent of verdicts were decided against the patentee.
(20) The proportion of verdicts for the patentee began to increase in the 1830s, suggesting to these scholars that judicial attitudes toward patent rights began shifting then.

Not all patent disputes in the early nineteenth
(25) century were litigated, however, and litigated cases were not drawn randomly from the population of disputes. Therefore the rate of verdicts in favor of patentees cannot be used by itself to gauge changes in judicial attitudes
(30) or enforceability of patent rights. If early judicial decisions were prejudiced against patentees, one might expect that subsequent courts—allegedly more supportive of patent rights—would reject the former legal precedents. But pre-1830
(35) cases have been cited as frequently as later decisions, and they continue to be cited today, suggesting that the early decisions, many of which clearly declared that patent rights were a just recompense for inventive ingenuity,
(40) provided a lasting foundation for patent law. The proportion of judicial decisions in favor of patentees began to increase during the 1830s because of a change in the underlying population of cases brought to trial. This change was partly
(45) due to an 1836 revision to the patent system: an examination procedure, still in use today, was instituted in which each application is scrutinized for its adherence to patent law. Previously, patents were automatically granted upon payment
(50) of a $30 fee.

Questions 591–595 refer to the passage.

591. The passage implies that which of the following was a reason that the proportion of verdicts in favor of patentees began to increase in the 1830s?

(A) Patent applications approved after 1836 were more likely to adhere closely to patent law.
(B) Patent laws enacted during the 1830s better defined patent rights.
(C) Judges became less prejudiced against patentees during the 1830s.
(D) After 1836, litigated cases became less representative of the population of patent disputes.
(E) The proportion of patent disputes brought to trial began to increase after 1836.

592. The passage implies that the scholars mentioned in line 8 would agree with which of the following criticisms of the American patent system before 1830?

(A) Its definition of property rights relating to inventions was too vague to be useful.
(B) Its criteria for the granting of patents were not clear.
(C) It made it excessively difficult for inventors to receive patents.
(D) It led to excessive numbers of patent-infringement suits.
(E) It failed to encourage national economic growth.

593. It can be inferred from the passage that the frequency with which pre-1830 cases have been cited in court decisions is an indication that

(A) judicial support for patent rights was strongest in the period before 1830
(B) judicial support for patent rights did not increase after 1830
(C) courts have returned to judicial standards that prevailed before 1830
(D) verdicts favoring patentees in patent-infringement suits did not increase after 1830
(E) judicial bias against patentees persisted after 1830

594. It can be inferred from the passage that the author and the scholars referred to in line 21 disagree about which of the following aspects of the patents defended in patent-infringement suits before 1830 ?

   (A) Whether the patents were granted for inventions that were genuinely useful
   (B) Whether the patents were actually relevant to the growth of the United States economy
   (C) Whether the patents were particularly likely to be annulled by judges
   (D) Whether the patents were routinely invalidated for reasons that were arbitrary
   (E) Whether the patents were vindicated at a significantly lower rate than patents in later suits

595. The author of the passage cites which of the following as evidence challenging the argument referred to in lines 14–15 ?

   (A) The proportion of cases that were decided against patentees in the 1820s
   (B) The total number of patent disputes that were litigated from 1794 to 1830
   (C) The fact that later courts drew upon the legal precedents set in pre-1830 patent cases
   (D) The fact that the proportion of judicial decisions in favor of patentees began to increase during the 1830s
   (E) The constitutional rationale for the 1836 revision of the patent system

Jacob Burckhardt's view that Renaissance European women "stood on a footing of perfect equality" with Renaissance men has been repeatedly cited by feminist scholars as a prelude to their
(5) presentation of rich historical evidence of women's inequality. In striking contrast to Burckhardt, Joan Kelly in her famous 1977 essay, "Did Women Have a Renaissance?" argued that the Renaissance was a period of economic and social decline for women
(10) relative both to Renaissance men and to medieval women. Recently, however, a significant trend among feminist scholars has entailed a rejection of both Kelly's dark vision of the Renaissance and Burckhardt's rosy one. Many recent works by these
(15) scholars stress the ways in which differences among Renaissance women—especially in terms of social status and religion—work to complicate the kinds of generalizations both Burckhardt and Kelly made on the basis of their observations about
(20) upper-class Italian women.

The trend is also evident, however, in works focusing on those middle- and upper-class European women whose ability to write gives them disproportionate representation in the historical
(25) record. Such women were, simply by virtue of their literacy, members of a tiny minority of the population, so it is risky to take their descriptions of their experiences as typical of "female experience" in any general sense. Tina Krontiris, for example, in
(30) her fascinating study of six Renaissance women writers, does tend at times to conflate "women" and "women writers," assuming that women's gender, irrespective of other social differences, including literacy, allows us to view women as a homogeneous
(35) social group and make that group an object of analysis. Nonetheless, Krontiris makes a significant contribution to the field and is representative of those authors who offer what might be called a cautiously optimistic assessment of Renaissance
(40) women's achievements, although she also stresses the social obstacles Renaissance women faced when they sought to raise their "oppositional voices." Krontiris is concerned to show women intentionally negotiating some power for themselves
(45) (at least in the realm of public discourse) against potentially constraining ideologies, but in her sober and thoughtful concluding remarks, she suggests that such verbal opposition to cultural stereotypes was highly circumscribed; women seldom attacked
(50) the basic assumptions in the ideologies that oppressed them.

Questions 596–602 refer to the passage.

596. The author of the passage discusses Krontiris primarily to provide an example of a writer who

(A) is highly critical of the writings of certain Renaissance women
(B) supports Kelly's view of women's status during the Renaissance
(C) has misinterpreted the works of certain Renaissance women
(D) has rejected the views of both Burckhardt and Kelly
(E) has studied Renaissance women in a wide variety of social and religious contexts

597. According to the passage, Krontiris's work differs from that of the scholars mentioned in line 12 in which of the following ways?

(A) Krontiris's work stresses the achievements of Renaissance women rather than the obstacles to their success.
(B) Krontiris's work is based on a reinterpretation of the work of earlier scholars.
(C) Krontiris's views are at odds with those of both Kelly and Burkhardt.
(D) Krontiris's work focuses on the place of women in Renaissance society.
(E) Krontiris's views are based exclusively on the study of a privileged group of women.

RC00313-03
598. According to the passage, feminist scholars cite Burckhardt's view of Renaissance women primarily for which of the following reasons?

(A) Burckhardt's view forms the basis for most arguments refuting Kelly's point of view.
(B) Burckhardt's view has been discredited by Kelly.
(C) Burckhardt's view is one that many feminist scholars wish to refute.
(D) Burckhardt's work provides rich historical evidence of inequality between Renaissance women and men.
(E) Burckhardt's work includes historical research supporting the arguments of the feminist scholars.

RC00313-04
599. It can be inferred that both Burckhardt and Kelly have been criticized by the scholars mentioned in line 12 for which of the following?

(A) Assuming that women writers of the Renaissance are representative of Renaissance women in general
(B) Drawing conclusions that are based on the study of an atypical group of women
(C) Failing to describe clearly the relationship between social status and literacy among Renaissance women
(D) Failing to acknowledge the role played by Renaissance women in opposing cultural stereotypes
(E) Failing to acknowledge the ways in which social status affected the creative activities of Renaissance women

RC00313-05
600. The author of the passage suggests that Krontiris incorrectly assumes that

(A) social differences among Renaissance women are less important than the fact that they were women
(B) literacy among Renaissance women was more prevalent than most scholars today acknowledge
(C) during the Renaissance, women were able to successfully oppose cultural stereotypes relating to gender
(D) Renaissance women did not face many difficult social obstacles relating to their gender
(E) in order to attain power, Renaissance women attacked basic assumptions in the ideologies that oppressed them

RC00313-06
601. The last sentence in the passage serves primarily to

(A) suggest that Krontiris's work is not representative of recent trends among feminist scholars
(B) undermine the argument that literate women of the Renaissance sought to oppose social constraints imposed on them
(C) show a way in which Krontiris's work illustrates a "cautiously optimistic" assessment of Renaissance women's achievements
(D) summarize Krontiris's view of the effect of literacy on the lives of upper- and middle-class Renaissance women
(E) illustrate the way in which Krontiris's study differs from the studies done by Burckhardt and Kelly

RC00313-08
602. The author of the passage implies that the women studied by Krontiris are unusual in which of the following ways?

(A) They faced obstacles less formidable than those faced by other Renaissance women.
(B) They have been seen by historians as more interesting than other Renaissance women.
(C) They were more concerned about recording history accurately than were other Renaissance women.
(D) Their perceptions are more likely to be accessible to historians than are those of most other Renaissance women.
(E) Their concerns are likely to be of greater interest to feminist scholars than are the ideas of most other Renaissance women.

Line When asteroids collide, some collisions cause
an asteroid to spin faster; others slow it down. If
asteroids are all monoliths—single rocks—undergoing
random collisions, a graph of their rotation rates
(5) should show a bell-shaped distribution with statistical
"tails" of very fast and very slow rotators. If asteroids
are rubble piles, however, the tail representing the
very fast rotators would be missing, because any
loose aggregate spinning faster than once every few
(10) hours (depending on the asteroid's bulk density)
would fly apart. Researchers have discovered that
all but five observed asteroids obey a strict limit on
rate of rotation. The exceptions are all smaller than
200 meters in diameter, with an abrupt cutoff for
(15) asteroids larger than that.
  The evident conclusion—that asteroids larger than
200 meters across are multicomponent structures or
rubble piles—agrees with recent computer modeling
of collisions, which also finds a transition at that
(20) diameter. A collision can blast a large asteroid to bits,
but after the collision those bits will usually move
slower than their mutual escape velocity. Over several
hours, gravity will reassemble all but the fastest
pieces into a rubble pile. Because collisions among
(25) asteroids are relatively frequent, most large bodies
have already suffered this fate. Conversely, most
small asteroids should be monolithic, because impact
fragments easily escape their feeble gravity.

Questions 603–606 refer to the passage.

603. The passage implies which of the following about the five asteroids mentioned in line 12 ?

(A) Their rotation rates are approximately the same.
(B) They have undergone approximately the same number of collisions.
(C) They are monoliths.
(D) They are composed of fragments that have escaped the gravity of larger asteroids.
(E) They were detected only recently.

604. The discovery of which of the following would call into question the conclusion mentioned in line 16 ?

(A) An asteroid 100 meters in diameter rotating at a rate of once per week
(B) An asteroid 150 meters in diameter rotating at a rate of 20 times per hour
(C) An asteroid 250 meters in diameter rotating at a rate of once per week
(D) An asteroid 500 meters in diameter rotating at a rate of once per hour
(E) An asteroid 1,000 meters in diameter rotating at a rate of once every 24 hours

RC00524-06
605. According to the passage, which of the following is a prediction that is based on the strength of the gravitational attraction of small asteroids?

   (A) Small asteroids will be few in number.
   (B) Small asteroids will be monoliths.
   (C) Small asteroids will collide with other asteroids very rarely.
   (D) Most small asteroids will have very fast rotation rates.
   (E) Almost no small asteroids will have very slow rotation rates.

RC00524-07
606. The author of the passage mentions "escape velocity" (see line 22) in order to help explain which of the following?

   (A) The tendency for asteroids to become smaller rather than larger over time
   (B) The speed with which impact fragments reassemble when they do not escape an asteroid's gravitational attraction after a collision
   (C) The frequency with which collisions among asteroids occur
   (D) The rotation rates of asteroids smaller than 200 meters in diameter
   (E) The tendency for large asteroids to persist after collisions

Line   Most attempts by physicists to send particles faster than the speed of light involve a remarkable phenomenon called quantum tunneling, in which particles travel through solid barriers that appear
(5)   to be impenetrable. If you throw a ball at a wall, you expect it to bounce back, not to pass straight through it. Yet subatomic particles perform the equivalent feat. Quantum theory says that there is a distinct, albeit small, probability that such a particle
(10)   will tunnel its way through a barrier; the probability declines exponentially as the thickness of the barrier increases. Though the extreme rapidity of quantum tunneling was noted as early as 1932, not until 1955 was it hypothesized—by Wigner and
(15)   Eisenbud—that tunneling particles sometimes travel faster than light. Their grounds were calculations that suggested that the time it takes a particle to tunnel through a barrier increases with the thickness of the barrier until tunneling time
(20)   reaches a maximum; beyond that maximum, tunneling time stays the same regardless of barrier thickness. This would imply that once maximum tunneling time is reached, tunneling speed will increase without limit as barrier thickness increases. Several recent
(25)   experiments have supported this hypothesis that tunneling particles sometimes reach superluminal speed. According to measurements performed by Raymond Chiao and colleagues, for example, photons can pass through an optical filter at 1.7 times the
(30)   speed of light.

Questions 607–609 refer to the passage.

607. The author of the passage mentions calculations about tunneling time and barrier thickness in order to

    (A) suggest that tunneling time is unrelated to barrier thickness
    (B) explain the evidence by which Wigner and Eisenbud discovered the phenomenon of tunneling
    (C) describe data recently challenged by Raymond Chiao and colleagues
    (D) question why particles engaged in quantum tunneling rarely achieve extremely high speeds
    (E) explain the basis for Wigner and Eisenbud's hypothesis

608. The passage implies that if tunneling time reached no maximum in increasing with barrier thickness, then

    (A) tunneling speed would increase with barrier thickness
    (B) tunneling speed would decline with barrier thickness
    (C) tunneling speed would vary with barrier thickness
    (D) tunneling speed would not be expected to increase without limit
    (E) successful tunneling would occur even less frequently than it does

609. Which of the following statements about the earliest scientific investigators of quantum tunneling can be inferred from the passage?

    (A) They found it difficult to increase barrier thickness continually.
    (B) They anticipated the later results of Chiao and his colleagues.
    (C) They did not suppose that tunneling particles could travel faster than light.
    (D) They were unable to observe instances of successful tunneling.
    (E) They made use of photons to study the phenomenon of tunneling.

7.5 Answer Key

461. D	491. D	521. E	551. E	581. E
462. D	492. B	522. A	552. B	582. B
463. B	493. B	523. B	553. D	583. C
464. B	494. B	524. C	554. C	584. C
465. C	495. D	525. C	555. C	585. B
466. C	496. E	526. B	556. E	586. A
467. A	497. D	527. E	557. A	587. B
468. C	498. E	528. C	558. B	588. D
469. D	499. C	529. E	559. D	589. A
470. C	500. C	530. A	560. E	590. C
471. A	501. B	531. D	561. E	591. A
472. C	502. D	532. A	562. D	592. E
473. C	503. C	533. C	563. B	593. B
474. C	504. B	534. A	564. C	594. D
475. E	505. A	535. B	565. D	595. C
476. A	506. E	536. D	566. A	596. D
477. C	507. A	537. E	567. C	597. E
478. B	508. B	538. C	568. D	598. C
479. B	509. E	539. A	569. A	599. B
480. A	510. B	540. E	570. A	600. A
481. D	511. C	541. A	571. D	601. C
482. C	512. C	542. D	572. E	602. D
483. E	513. A	543. D	573. D	603. C
484. B	514. D	544. D	574. B	604. D
485. D	515. D	545. B	575. C	605. B
486. C	516. C	546. B	576. A	606. E
487. B	517. E	547. C	577. C	607. E
488. D	518. A	548. C	578. B	608. D
489. A	519. C	549. E	579. D	609. C
490. C	520. D	550. D	580. D	

7.6 Answer Explanations

The following discussion of reading comprehension is intended to familiarize you with the most efficient and effective approaches to the kinds of problems common to reading comprehension. The particular questions in this chapter are generally representative of the kinds of reading comprehension questions you will encounter on the GMAT exam. Remember that it is the problem solving strategy that is important, not the specific details of a particular question.

Questions 461–463 refer to the passage on page 398.

461. The primary purpose of the passage is to

   (A) challenge recent findings that appear to contradict earlier findings
   (B) present two sides of an ongoing scientific debate
   (C) report answers to several questions that have long puzzled researchers
   (D) discuss evidence that has caused a long-standing belief to be revised
   (E) attempt to explain a commonly misunderstood biological phenomenon

Main idea

This question depends on understanding the passage as a whole. The passage begins by describing a long-held belief regarding humans' circadian rhythms: that the SCNs control them. It then goes on to explain that new findings have led scientists to believe that other organs and tissues may be involved in regulating the body's circadian rhythms as well.

A The passage does not challenge the more-recent findings. Furthermore, the recent findings that the passage recounts do not contradict earlier findings; rather, when placed alongside those earlier findings, they have led scientists to reach additional conclusions.

B The passage does not discuss a two-sided debate; no findings or conclusions are disputed by any figures in the passages.

C There is only one question at issue in the passage: whether the SCN alone control human circadian rhythms. Furthermore, nothing in the passage suggests that researchers have been puzzled for a long time about this.

D **Correct.** The new evidence regarding circadian rhythm–related gene activity in all the body's tissue has led scientists to revise their long-standing belief that the SCN alone control circadian rhythms.

E The biological phenomenon of circadian rhythms is not, at least as far as the passage is concerned, misunderstood. Its causes are being investigated and refined.

The correct answer is D.

462. The passage mentions each of the following as a function regulated by the SCNs in some animals EXCEPT

   (A) activity level
   (B) blood pressure
   (C) alertness
   (D) vision
   (E) temperature

---
*These numbers correlate with the online test bank question number. See the GMAT Official Guide Online Index in the back of this book.

Supporting idea

This question asks about what is NOT specifically mentioned in the passage with regard to functions regulated by the SCN. Those functions, as identified in the passage, are blood pressure, body temperature, activity level, alertness, and the release of melatonin.

A   The passage includes activity level in its list of functions regulated by the SCN.
B   The passage includes blood pressure in its list of functions regulated by the SCN.
C   The passage includes alertness in its list of functions regulated by the SCN.
D   **Correct.** While the passage does say that cells in the human retina transmit information to the SCN, there is no suggestion that the SCN reciprocally control vision.
E   The passage includes temperature in its list of functions regulated by the SCN.

The correct answer is D.

RC00504-04
463. The author of the passage would probably agree with which of the following statements about the SCNs?

(A) The SCNs are found in other organs and tissues of the body besides the hypothalamus.
(B) The SCNs play a critical but not exclusive role in regulating circadian rhythms.
(C) The SCNs control clock genes in a number of tissues and organs throughout the body.
(D) The SCNs are a less significant factor in regulating blood pressure than scientists once believed.
(E) The SCNs are less strongly affected by changes in light levels than they are by other external cues.

Main idea

The author of the passage discusses the SCN in the passage in order to explain that they are most likely not, as long believed, solely responsible for the control of our circadian rhythms.

A   The author states that the SCN are nerve clusters in the hypothalamus, and nothing in the passage contradicts or undermines the supposition that they are only in the hypothalamus.
B   **Correct.** The author points out in the second paragraph that the SCN control core circadian function, but that circadian clocks found elsewhere in the body have an effect as well.
C   The evidence offered in the second paragraph about the activity of the clock gene in rat livers suggests that these clock genes are not under the SCN's control. The passage does not suggest that the SCN control any of the non-SCN controllers of circadian rhythms.
D   The author states in the second paragraph that scientists do not dispute the idea that the SCN regulate blood pressure.
E   The first paragraph indicates that the SCN respond to light levels; clock genes in other tissues are the ones that may respond to other external cues.

The correct answer is B.

Questions 464–466 refer to the passage on page 400.

464. The primary purpose of the passage is to

(A) question the results of a study that examined the effect of service-quality guarantees in the restaurant industry
(B) discuss potential advantages and disadvantages of service-quality guarantees in the restaurant industry
(C) examine the conventional wisdom regarding the effect of service-quality guarantees in the restaurant industry
(D) argue that only certain restaurants would benefit from the implementation of service-quality guarantees
(E) consider the impact that service-quality guarantees can have on the service provided by a restaurant

Main idea

This question depends on understanding the passage as a whole. The first paragraph describes Tucci and Talaga's findings regarding the effect of service-quality guarantees: that they have different, more positive results for higher-priced restaurants than for lower-priced ones, which could be affected negatively. The second paragraph explains that a particular benefit from service guarantees could accrue to restaurants generally.

A The passage does not question the results of Tucci and Talaga's study; rather, the passage appears to accept the results of the study as accurate.

B **Correct.** The potential advantages involve the management and motivation of service staff, as well as, for higher-priced restaurants, a greater likelihood of being selected by customers over other restaurants. Potential disadvantages for lower-priced restaurants include the possibility that potential customers may believe that such restaurants are concerned about the quality of their service.

C The passage does not indicate whether there is any conventional wisdom regarding service-quality guarantees in the restaurant industry.

D The second paragraph of the passage suggests that restaurants in general could potentially enjoy some benefits from the implementation of service-quality guarantees. For lower-priced restaurants, these benefits could offset the possible negative effects of service-quality guarantees described in the first paragraph.

E The second paragraph of the passage indicates an effect that service-quality guarantees could have on a restaurant's staff and the service that the staff provides, but this is only one of the subsidiary points contributing to the focus of the passage as a whole. The first is more concerned with the question of what effect these guarantees would have on whether customers choose to patronize that restaurant.

The correct answer is B.

465. It can be inferred that the author of the passage would agree with which of the following statements about the appeal of service guarantees to customers?

(A) Such guarantees are likely to be somewhat more appealing to customers of restaurants than to customers of other businesses.
(B) Such guarantees are likely to be more appealing to customers who know what to anticipate in terms of service.
(C) Such guarantees are likely to have less appeal in situations where customers are knowledgeable about a business's product or service.
(D) In situations where a high level of financial commitment is involved, a service guarantee is not likely to be very appealing.
(E) In situations where customers expect a high level of customer service, a service guarantee is likely to make customers think that a business is worried about its service.

Inference

This question asks for an inference from the passage about the author's view of why and how service guarantees would appeal to customers. The question does not ask specifically about service guarantees in the context of restaurants, but rather service guarantees in general. The end of the first paragraph addresses this general question: a service guarantee may appeal most to customers in the case of activities whose quality they are less likely to know how to question.

A   The author states that a service guarantee might have greater appeal in the case of skilled activities than it would for restaurant customers.

B   According to the author, customers who know what to expect in terms of service—a group that includes restaurant customers—would likely find service guarantees less appealing.

C   **Correct.** The author makes clear that service guarantees would be less appealing to restaurant customers when they know what to expect in terms of the quality of service.

D   The passage provides some evidence that where a high level of financial commitment is involved, a service guarantee may be more rather than less appealing than in other situations. In discussing higher-priced restaurants, which require a relatively high level of financial commitment, the author states that Tucci and Talaga found evidence that a service guarantee would likely appeal to customers.

E   The author implies that customers of higher-priced restaurants expect a high level of service, certainly a level higher than that expected by customers of lower-priced restaurants. But it is at lower-priced restaurants that Tucci and Talaga found that a service guarantee makes customers think a given restaurant is concerned about its service.

The correct answer is C.

RC00525-07
466. According to the passage, Tucci and Talaga found that service guarantees, when offered by lower-priced restaurants, can have which of the following effects?

(A) Customers' developing unreasonably high expectations regarding service

(B) Customers' avoiding such restaurants because they fear that the service guarantee may not be fully honored

(C) Customers' interpreting the service guarantee as a sign that management is not confident about the quality of its service

(D) A restaurant's becoming concerned that its service will not be assiduous enough to satisfy customers

(E) A restaurant's becoming concerned that customers will be more emboldened to question the quality of the service they receive

Supporting ideas

This question requires identifying Tucci and Talaga's findings regarding service guarantees offered by lower-priced restaurants. The passage states directly that these researchers found in these situations that a guarantee could lead potential customers to think that the restaurant has concerns about its service.

A   The passage does not report that Tucci and Talaga found that service guarantees create unreasonably high expectations regarding service.

B   The passage does not report that Tucci and Talaga found that customers doubted that service guarantees would be honored.

C   **Correct.** The passage explicitly indicates that Tucci and Talaga found that potential customers of lower-priced restaurants could interpret service guarantees as indicating worries about the quality of service.

D   The passage indicates that Tucci and Talaga found that customers might think that lower-priced restaurants are offering service guarantees because they are concerned that the quality of their service is too low, but the passage does not indicate that service guarantees lead such restaurants to have concerns about the quality of their service, and in fact it may be that such guarantees could lead to improvements in service.

E The passage indicates that service guarantees offered at lower-priced restaurants may empower customers to question the quality of service, but it does not indicate that service guarantees lead restaurants to have concerns about this.

The correct answer is C.

Questions 467–468 refer to the passage on page 402.

RC00455-03

467. The passage suggests that in the study mentioned in line 14 the method for gathering information about security of land tenure reflects which of the following pairs of assumptions about Tawahka society?

(A) The security of a household's land tenure depends on the strength of that household's kinship ties, and the duration of a household's residence in its village is an indication of the strength of that household's kinship ties.

(B) The ample availability of land makes security of land tenure unimportant, and the lack of a need for secure land tenure has made the concept of legal property rights unnecessary.

(C) The strength of a household's kinship ties is a more reliable indicator of that household's receptivity to new agricultural technologies than is its quantity of nonland wealth, and the duration of a household's residence in its village is a more reliable indicator of that household's security of land tenure than is the strength of its kinship ties.

(D) Security of land tenure based on kinship ties tends to make farmers more receptive to the use of improved plant varieties, and security of land tenure based on long duration of residence in a village tends to make farmers more receptive to the use of chemical herbicides.

(E) A household is more likely to be receptive to the concept of land tenure based on legal property rights if it has easy access to uncultivated land, and a household is more likely to uphold the tradition of land tenure based on kinship ties if it possesses a significant degree of nonland wealth.

Evaluation

In discussing the study, the passage notes that the strength of kinship ties is a more important indicator of land-tenure security than are legal property rights. The researchers, knowing this, measured land-tenure security by indirectly measuring the strength of kinship ties. How long a household had resided in its village was taken as an indicator of the strength of kinship ties, and indirectly, of the household's degree of land-tenure security.

A **Correct.** This summarizes two assumptions that the passage suggests were made by the researchers.

B The passage notes that ample availability of land is characteristic of rain-forest communities, which presumably includes the Tawahka people on whom the study focused. However, based on the information in the passage, the study did not assume that land-tenure security was unimportant in that community.

C The passage reports that the study took a household's duration of residence in its village as a reliable indicator of the strength of the household's kinship ties. Thus, the researchers did not assume that duration of residence was a more reliable measure of land-tenure security than kinship ties.

D The passage does not indicate that the researchers assumed this. As already stated, the researchers in effect equated a household's strength of kinship ties with its length of residence in its village. Though only the latter was directly measured, both were regarded as guarantors and indicators of land-tenure security. According to the passage, the researchers found that "longer residence correlated with more adoption of improved plant varieties but with less adoption of chemical herbicides." This was a finding based on research data, not an assumption.

E The passage does not attribute to the researchers an assumption that "a household is more likely to be receptive to the concept of land tenure based on legal property rights if it has easy access to uncultivated land."

The correct answer is A.

468. According to the passage, the proposal mentioned in line 1 is aimed at preserving rain forests by encouraging farmers in rain-forest regions to do each of the following EXCEPT

(A) adopt new agricultural technologies
(B) grow improved plant varieties
(C) decrease their use of chemical herbicides
(D) increase their productivity
(E) reduce their need to clear new land for cultivation

Supporting ideas

The goal of the proposal is to help preserve rain forests by encouraging the adoption of new agricultural technologies, including use of chemical herbicides. The latter would presumably help improve crop yields on existing land, reducing the need to clear portions of rain forest to expand agricultural production.

A The proposal aims to encourage farmers to adopt new agricultural technologies.

B The proposal aims to encourage farmers to grow improved plant varieties.

C **Correct.** The proposal aims to encourage farmers to adopt new agricultural technologies, such as increased use of chemical herbicides. So persuading farmers to reduce their use of chemical herbicides is not part of the proposal.

D The proposal aims to encourage farmers to increase their productivity.

E The proposal aims to encourage farmers to reduce their need to clear rain-forest land for cultivation.

The correct answer is C.

Questions 469–472 refer to the passage on page 404.

469. Information in the passage suggests that David Pearce would most readily endorse which of the following statements concerning monetization?

(A) Monetization represents a strategy that is attractive to both environmentalists and their critics.

(B) Monetization is an untested strategy, but it is increasingly being embraced by environmentalists.

(C) Monetization should at present be restricted to ecological services and should only gradually be extended to such commercial endeavors as tourism and recreation.

(D) Monetization can serve as a means of representing persuasively the value of environmental conservation.

(E) Monetization should inform environmental decision-making processes only if it is accepted by environmentalist groups.

Inference

This question requires an understanding of David Pearce's view of monetization. According to the passage, Pearce finds the idea that conservation is unprofitable to be an illusion. He argues for showing the economic value of ecosystems in order to make progress in conserving those ecosystems.

A The passage attributes to Gretchen Daily the view that monetization is unpopular with environmentalists. The passage gives no reason to believe that Pearce would endorse the idea that environmentalists currently find monetization attractive.

B The passage gives no indication that monetization is increasingly being embraced by environmentalists, even if Pearce thinks it should be.

C The passage indicates Pearce's belief that some types of tourism are also types of ecological services that have economic value and that they should be monetized.

D **Correct.** Pearce believes that monetization quantifies the value of the services provided by ecological systems—and if that value is quantified, people are more likely to be persuaded to conserve those systems.

E Pearce is arguing, against some environmentalists, that monetization should inform the decision-making process with regard to preserving ecosystems.

The correct answer is D.

470. Which of the following most clearly represents an example of an "ecological service" as that term is used in line 20 ?

(A) A resort hotel located in an area noted for its natural beauty
(B) A water-purifying plant that supplements natural processes with nontoxic chemicals
(C) A wildlife preserve that draws many international travelers
(D) A nonprofit firm that specializes in restoring previously damaged ecosystems
(E) A newsletter that keeps readers informed of ecological victories and setbacks

Application

Based on the passage, *ecological services* are services provided by natural assets that have not been converted into commercial assets. Thus any example of such an ecological service requires that the area providing it is natural.

A The passage mentions resort hotels as an example of explicitly commercial assets. Although some hotels might be situated in ecologically valuable natural environments, any ecological services in such cases would be contributed by the natural environments, not by the hotels themselves.
B Water purifying is *an ecological* service if it is supplied by *undisturbed forests and wetlands*. The word *plant* here must mean a technological installation, not a botanical organism, because it is said to supplement—not to be part of—the natural processes. Thus it is not a natural asset and therefore does not provide an ecological service as described in the passage.
C **Correct.** The passage states that a wildlife preserve that creates jobs and generates income would be providing an ecological service.
D A nonprofit firm that restores damaged ecosystems would be performing a valuable ecology-related service, but it would not itself be an example of a natural asset providing an ecological service.

E Environmentalists and others would most likely find such a newsletter informative, but it would not be an ecological service, because it is not a service provided by a natural asset.

The correct answer is C.

471. According to the passage, Daily sees monetization as an indication of which of the following?

(A) The centrality of economic interests to people's actions
(B) The reluctance of the critics of environmentalism to acknowledge the importance of conservation
(C) The inability of financial interests and ecological interests to reach a common ideological ground
(D) The inevitability of environmental degradation
(E) The inevitability of the growth of ecological services in the future

Supporting ideas

This question asks about Daily's view of monetization, and according to the passage, she sees monetization as a practice that *reflects the dominant role that economic decisions play in human behavior.*

A **Correct.** According to the passage, Daily believes that economic interests are central to people's actions, and monetization of ecological services would take that central role realistically into account.
B Monetization, as Daily sees it, is a way of assigning value to conservation and thus acknowledging its importance. Many environmentalists, rather than their critics, are reluctant to embrace monetization, according to Daily.
C For Daily, monetization represents a way for financial interests and ecological interests to reach a common ground; by using this *common currency*, both sides can make good decisions about the environment.
D Monetization, on Daily's view, would help to prevent environmental degradation; the passage does not suggest that she regards such degradation as at all inevitable.

E   Daily does not see monetization as inevitably spurring the growth of ecological services but as more likely preventing their decline by leaving those *services* undisturbed.

The correct answer is A.

RC00344-06

472. Which of the following can be inferred from the passage concerning the environmentalists mentioned in line 8 ?

(A) They are organized in opposition to the generation of income produced by the sale of ecological services.

(B) They are fewer in number but better organized and better connected to the media than their opponents.

(C) They have sometimes been charged with failing to use a particular strategy in their pursuit of conservational goals.

(D) They have been in the forefront of publicizing the extent of worldwide environmental degradation.

(E) They define environmental progress differently and more conservatively than do other organized groups of environmentalists.

Inference

The sentence in question states that critics blame environmentalists for their failure *to address the economic issues of environmental degradation.*

A   The passage states that in the absence of monetization, conservation can appear unprofitable. But this does not mean that the environmentalists in question are opposed to conservation generating income.

B   The passage does not address the issue of the number of environmentalists in question, the number of those opposed to them, or whether either group is better connected to the media.

C   **Correct.** The passage indicates that critics of the environmentalists in question believe environmentalists are to blame for not using an effective economics-based strategy to promote conservation.

D   Although it may be the case that the environmentalists in question have been prominent in publicizing worldwide environmental degradation, the passage does not provide grounds for inferring that they have been.

E   The passage suggests that certain critics consider environmentalists in general to be at fault for failing to address economic issues. In this respect, the passage makes no distinctions among different environmentalist groups, organized or otherwise.

The correct answer is C.

Questions 473–476 refer to the passage on page 406.

RC00359-01

473. According to the passage, the studies referred to in line 12 reported which of the following about the effect of price on consumers' perception of the performance risk associated with a new product?

(A) Although most consumers regard price as an important factor, their perception of the performance risk associated with a new product is ultimately determined by the manufacturer's reputation.

(B) Price interacts with the presentation of an advertised message to affect perceived performance risk.

(C) Price does not significantly affect consumers' perception of the performance risk associated with a new product.

(D) Consumers tend to regard price as more important than the manufacturer's credibility when they are buying from that manufacturer for the first time.

(E) Consumers are generally less concerned about a new product's performance risk when that product is relatively expensive.

Supporting ideas

The question asks about information explicitly provided in the passage. The first paragraph explains that there are *conflicting findings* in the research about how the price of a product affects a consumer's perception of the performance risk of that product. Some studies have found that higher priced products reduce the perception of performance risk. The *other studies* referred to in line 12, however, have found little or no connection between price and perceived performance risk.

A   The passage does not mention that these studies consider the manufacturer's reputation.
B   The passage does not mention that these studies consider advertising messages.
C   **Correct.** The passage indicates that these studies have found little or no connection between relative price and consumers' perception of performance risk.
D   The passage does not mention that these studies consider the manufacturer's credibility.
E   Although some studies have found that a relatively high price reduces the perception of performance risk, the passage explains that the studies referred to in line 12 have not confirmed that finding.

The correct answer is C.

RC00359-03

474. The "past research" mentioned in line 25 suggests which of the following about perceived performance risk?

    (A) The more expensive a new product is, the more likely consumers may be to credit advertised claims about that product.
    (B) The more familiar consumers are with a particular manufacturer, the more willing they may be to assume some risk in the purchase of a new product being advertised by that manufacturer.
    (C) Consumers' perception of the performance risk associated with a new product being advertised may be influenced by an interplay between the product's price and the manufacturer's credibility.
    (D) Consumers may be more likely to believe that a product will function as it is advertised to do when they have bought products from a particular manufacturer before.
    (E) The price of a particular advertised product may have less impact than the manufacturer's credibility on consumers' assessment of the performance risk associated with that product.

Supporting ideas

The question asks about information explicitly provided in the passage. The second paragraph explains that, according to some research, consumers perceive a product as having less performance risk when they trust the source of advertising about that product. *Past research*, however, suggests that performance risk is affected not merely by the credibility of the source, but by an interaction between source credibility and the price of the product.

A   The passage does not indicate that the past research addressed the question of how the price of a product affects consumers' perception of advertised claims. It only says that the research suggests that the two factors *interact*.
B   Although the passage discusses consumers' perception of how risky a purchase might be, it does not address the relationship between familiarity and willingness to assume risk.
C   **Correct.** The *past research* suggests that performance risk is affected by an interaction between the price of the product and the credibility of the source of the advertising about the product—in other words, the manufacturer.
D   The *past research* suggests that consumers' beliefs about a product's performance are affected not merely by their perception of the manufacturer, but by an interplay between source credibility and product price. The passage does not mention any possible role of prior experience in this interplay.
E   The passage does not discuss whether price or the manufacturer's credibility has more of an effect on perceived performance risk.

The correct answer is C.

RC00359-05

475. The passage is primarily concerned with

    (A) challenging the implications of previous research into why consumers try new products
    (B) suggesting new marketing strategies for attracting consumers to new products
    (C) reconciling two different views about the effect of price on consumers' willingness to try new products
    (D) describing a new approach to researching why consumers try new products
    (E) discussing certain findings regarding why consumers try new products

Main idea

The question depends on understanding the passage as a whole. The passage begins with a statement explaining that much research has investigated *what motivates consumers to try new products*. It then defines one such motivating factor—perception of performance risk. The remainder of the passage summarizes research into how price and a manufacturer's advertising affect consumers' perception of performance risk.

- A The passage summarizes research findings that conflict with one another but does not support some findings over others.
- B The passage does not suggest any new marketing strategies.
- C The first paragraph mentions a study that could reconcile two conflicting findings, but this is only a supporting point in the passage's larger purpose of summarizing research.
- D The passage does not describe new research approaches.
- E **Correct.** The passage discusses studies about performance risk, which is a factor that motivates consumers to try new products.

The correct answer is E.

RC00359-06

476. Which of the following, if true, would most tend to weaken the conclusions drawn from "some of this research" (see line 8)?

(A) In a subsequent study, consumers who were asked to evaluate new products with relatively low prices had the same perception of the products' performance risk as did consumers who were shown the same products priced more expensively.

(B) In a subsequent study, the quality of the advertising for the products that consumers perceived as having a lower performance risk was relatively high, while the quality of the advertising for the products that consumers perceived as having a higher performance risk was relatively poor.

(C) In a subsequent study, the products that consumers perceived as having a lower performance risk were priced higher than the highest priced products in the previous research.

(D) None of the consumers involved in this research had ever before bought products from the manufacturers involved in the research.

(E) Researchers found that the higher the source credibility for a product, the more consumers were willing to pay for it.

Evaluation

The question depends on evaluating the reasoning behind the conclusions of some research and deciding which evidence would weaken them. The research concludes that higher prices reduce consumers' perception of performance risk associated with a particular product. This conclusion involves a claim of cause and effect, so evidence showing that higher prices do not cause that effect would weaken the argument.

- A **Correct.** If lowering prices has no effect on consumers' perception of performance risk, the conclusions of the research are called into question.
- B A correlation between quality of advertising and perceived performance risk is not clearly relevant to the research conclusions about the effects of price.
- C This answer choice provides no basis for comparison among prices within the subsequent study. For all we can tell, the prices that correlated with higher perceived performance risk in the subsequent study may have been lower than those that correlated with lower perceived risk. In that case, the subsequent study would tend to strengthen, not weaken, the conclusions drawn from the earlier research.
- D Consumers' lack of familiarity with other products from the manufacturers is not clearly relevant to the studies' conclusions about the effects of price.
- E Credibility of the source of advertisements is discussed as a separate issue in the second paragraph and is not clearly relevant to these studies' conclusions about the effects of price. To the extent that it may be obliquely relevant, it tends to strengthen, rather than to weaken, the conclusions.

The correct answer is A.

Questions 477–481 refer to the passage on page 408.

RC00419-01

477. The primary purpose of the passage is to

(A) compare the economic role played by southern banks with the economic role played by banks in the rest of the United States during the late eighteenth and early nineteenth centuries
(B) reevaluate a conventional interpretation of the role played by banks in the American economy during the late eighteenth and early nineteenth centuries
(C) present different interpretations of the role played by banks in the American economy during the late eighteenth and early nineteenth centuries
(D) analyze how the increasing number of banks in the late eighteenth and early nineteenth centuries affected the American economy
(E) examine how scholarly opinion regarding the role played by banks in the American economy during the late eighteenth and early nineteenth centuries has changed over time

Main idea

The question depends on understanding the passage as a whole. The passage describes two contrasting views about the role banks played in the economic growth of the United States around the turn of the nineteenth century. The first paragraph describes the view that banks played only a small role. The second paragraph describes the contrasting view that banks played a critical role.

A   The mention of banks in the South is a small part of a larger discussion about the role of banks in the country as a whole.
B   The passage describes two major views held by historians; it does not reevaluate either of those views.
C   **Correct.** The passage describes two different views about the role that banks played in America's growing economy.
D   The passage does not analyze any aspect of the relationship between the increasing number of banks and the economy. It alludes to the increase in numbers only within a broader description of two contrasting views about how banks affected the economy.
E   The passage suggests that at the time when it was written, the two views it describes were both still held among historians.

The correct answer is C.

RC00419-02

478. The passage suggests that the scholars mentioned in line 4 would argue that the reason banks tended not to fund manufacturing and transportation projects in the late eighteenth and early nineteenth centuries was that

(A) these projects, being well established and well capitalized, did not need substantial long-term financing from banks
(B) these projects entailed a level of risk that was too great for banks' conservative lending practices
(C) banks preferred to invest in other, more speculative projects that offered the potential for higher returns
(D) bank managers believed that these projects would be unlikely to contribute significantly to economic growth in the new country
(E) bank managers believed funding these projects would result in credit being extended to too many borrowers

Inference

The question asks about information implied by the passage. According to the scholars' view described in the first paragraph, banks followed conservative lending practices: they shunned projects that were uncertain and that required substantial investments in capital. It follows that, according to those scholars, the reason banks chose not to fund certain projects was that they entailed too great a risk.

A   The passage indicates that manufacturing and transportation projects were less well established than those the banks preferred to fund, not more so.
B   **Correct.** Because the projects were *uncertain* and required a great deal of capital, banks considered them too risky.
C   The passage indicates that banks followed conservative lending practices and avoided investments that were uncertain.
D   The passage does not mention banks' beliefs about economic growth, and it does not provide any basis for inferring that the scholars in question held any particular views regarding such beliefs.
E   The passage does not mention, or provide a basis for inferences about, bank managers' concerns about numbers of borrowers.

The correct answer is B.

7.6 Reading Comprehension Answer Explanations

479. The passage suggests that Paul Gilje would be most likely to agree with which of the following claims about the lending practices of the "earliest banks" (see line 21)?

(A) These lending practices were unlikely to generate substantial profits for banks.
(B) These lending practices only benefited a narrow sector of the economy.
(C) The restrictive nature of these lending practices generated significant opposition outside of the South.
(D) The restrictive nature of these lending practices forced state legislatures to begin granting more bank charters by the early nineteenth century.
(E) These lending practices were likely to be criticized by economic elites as being overly restrictive.

Inference

This question asks about conclusions that can be logically inferred from information provided in the passage. According to the second paragraph, Paul Gilje believes that a driving force in American economic growth in the early nineteenth century was banks' lending to a larger and more diverse group of borrowers. The question asks what this would imply about Gilje's view toward earlier banks—which, the passage explains, offered credit only to *well-connected merchants*.

A   The profitability of banks' lending practices is not at issue in the discussion.
B   **Correct.** The passage says that the earliest banks had primarily made loans only to a narrow sector—well-connected merchants—and that they began lending more broadly in the early nineteenth century. It then cites Gilje's view to corroborate and explicate this claim. This strongly suggests that Gilje agrees with the claim.
C   Opposition to the earliest banks is not mentioned or alluded to in the discussion.
D   The passage provides no basis for inferring that Gilje held any particular view as to why legislatures began granting more bank charters.
E   The passage does not mention or provide a basis for inference about the views of economic elites regarding the lending practices of the earliest banks in the United States. It thus provides no basis for inferring that Gilje would have any particular opinion on this topic.

The correct answer is B.

480. The passage suggests that the opposition to banks in the South in the early nineteenth century stemmed in part from the perception that banks

(A) did not benefit more than a small minority of the people
(B) did not support the interests of elite planters
(C) were too closely tied to transportation and industrial interests
(D) were unwilling to issue the long-term loans required by agrarian interests
(E) were too willing to lend credit widely

Inference

The question asks about statements that can be inferred from information provided in the passage. The second paragraph explains that people who opposed banks in the South saw them as monopolies controlled by elite planters. This would imply that those who opposed banks believed that most people in the South did not benefit from them.

A   **Correct.** Since people opposed the banks on the grounds that they were monopolies controlled by an elite group of planters, they likely thought banks did not benefit most of the population.
B   The passage implies that people believed the banks did serve the interests of elite planters.
C   The passage indicates that people believed banks in the South were tied to planters, not to transportation and industrial interests.
D   Southern banks' willingness to provide long-term loans is not discussed or alluded to in the passage.
E   The passage does not imply that anyone believed banks in the South were willing to lend credit widely. Since people believed the banks were controlled by the elite, they more likely thought banks were unwilling to lend credit widely.

The correct answer is A.

RC00419-06
481. Which of the following statements best describes the function of the last sentence of the passage?

(A) It provides evidence tending to undermine the viewpoint of the scholars mentioned in line 5.
(B) It resolves a conflict over the role of banks summarized in the first paragraph.
(C) It clarifies some of the reasons state legislatures began granting more bank charters.
(D) It qualifies a claim made earlier in the passage about the impact of banks on the American economy in the early nineteenth century.
(E) It supports a claim made earlier in the passage about how the expansion of credit affected the economy.

Evaluation

This question asks about the function of the last sentence in relation to the rest of the passage. The first paragraph describes the view of one set of historians. The second paragraph describes the contrasting view of a second set of historians. The last sentence of the passage points out an exception mentioned by the second set of historians.

A The last sentence pertains to the view of historians described in the second paragraph, not those described in the first paragraph.
B The conflict between the two differing views is not resolved by the passage.
C The passage does not explain why legislatures began granting more bank charters.
D **Correct.** The second set of historians claim banks spurred American economic growth at the turn of the nineteenth century, but the last sentence adds an exception to that claim.
E The last sentence does not support the claim made by the second set of historians, but rather serves as an exception to that claim.

The correct answer is D.

Questions 482–485 refer to the passage on page 410.

RC00458-01
482. The passage is primarily concerned with

(A) examining economic factors that may have contributed to the success of certain Japanese companies
(B) discussing the relative merits of strategic partnerships as compared with those of market-exchange relationships
(C) challenging the validity of a widely held assumption about how Japanese firms operate
(D) explaining why Western companies have been slow to adopt a particular practice favored by Japanese companies
(E) pointing out certain differences between Japanese and Western supplier relationships

Main idea

This question asks for an assessment of what the passage as a whole is doing. The passage discusses how Western business managers have been following the advice of academics and journalists to pursue strategic partnerships with their suppliers. The advice is based on studies comparing Japanese production and supply practices with those of the rest of the world. Newer research, however, indicates that Japanese practices actually differ from those indicated in the earlier studies and are not significantly different from practices associated with Western manufacturers.

A The passage is not primarily concerned with economic factors contributing to the success of Japanese companies, but rather with whether Japanese relationships with suppliers conform to the practices recently adopted by Western business manufacturers.
B Although the passage discusses strategic partnerships and market-exchange relationships, it does not discuss their relative merits.
C **Correct.** The passage does question the view promoted by several studies regarding the relationship Japanese firms have with their suppliers.

D   The passage does not indicate that Western companies have been slow to adopt any particular practice favored by Japanese companies.

E   Rather than pointing out differences between Japanese and Western supplier relationships, it actually suggests that they are more similar than generally realized.

The correct answer is C.

RC00458-02

483. According to the passage, the advice referred to in line 6 was a response to which of the following?

(A)   A recent decrease in the number of available suppliers within the United States automobile industry

(B)   A debate within Western management circles during the past decade regarding the value of strategic partnerships

(C)   The success of certain European automobile manufacturers that have adopted strategic partnerships

(D)   An increase in demand over the past decade for automobiles made by Western manufacturers

(E)   Research comparing Japanese business practices with those of other nations

Supporting idea

This question is concerned with identifying what the passage says about certain experts' advice. The passage indicates that the experts' advice is based on numerous studies carried out over the previous decade that compared Japanese manufacturing and supply practices with those of the rest of the world.

A   The passage indicates that the major automobile manufacturers in the United States have decreased the number of suppliers they deal with, but the experts' advice was not in response to such a decrease; rather, the decrease was in response to the manufacturers' adoption of the experts' advice.

B   The passage does not say anything about a debate within Western management circles regarding management partnerships.

C   The passage mentions that European manufacturers have adopted strategic partnerships, but it does not indicate how successful those manufacturers have been.

D   The passage does not indicate whether demand for automobiles has increased over the past decade.

E   **Correct.** The passage indicates that the experts' advice was made in reaction to studies that compared Japanese business practices regarding production and suppliers with those of other companies.

The correct answer is E.

RC00458-03

484. The author mentions "the success of a certain well-known Japanese automaker" in lines 10–11, most probably in order to

(A)   demonstrate some of the possible reasons for the success of a certain business practice

(B)   cite a specific case that has convinced Western business experts of the value of a certain business practice

(C)   describe specific steps taken by Western automakers that have enabled them to compete more successfully in a global market

(D)   introduce a paradox about the effect of a certain business practice in Japan

(E)   indicate the need for Western managers to change their relationships with their external business partners

Evaluation

The question requires the test-taker to determine the author's reason for mentioning *the success of a certain well-known Japanese automaker*. Most likely, the author wishes to present a specific case that was crucial in leading Western management circles to value strategic partnerships.

A   The passage does not discuss reasons for the success of the business practice.

B   **Correct.** The well-known success of a certain Japanese automaker is offered as a reason for Western management circles to believe in the value of the business practice of forming strategic partnerships.

C   Although the passage does indicate that Western automakers have adopted strategic partnerships with suppliers, it does not indicate whether this has enabled them to become more successful globally.

D   The passage does not specifically discuss any paradox related to the effects of Japanese business practices.

E   Although the passage does give reason to think that the changes adopted by Western managers may have made their relationships with external business partners less, rather than more, like the relationships Japanese managers have, the passage does not indicate whether the Western managers need to make any further changes.

The correct answer is B.

485. Which of the following is cited in the passage as evidence supporting the author's claim about what the new research referred to in line 20 demonstrates?

(A) The belief within Western management circles regarding the extent to which Japanese firms rely on strategic partnerships

(B) The surprising number of European and United States businesses that have strategic partnerships with their suppliers

(C) The response of Western automobile manufacturers to the advice that they adopt strategic partnerships with their suppliers

(D) The prevalence of "market-exchange" relationships between Japanese firms and their suppliers

(E) The success of a particular Japanese automobile manufacturer that favors strategic partnerships with its suppliers

Supporting idea

To answer this question, you must identify what evidence is cited in the passage regarding the author's claim that new research casts doubt on the widespread view that Japanese firms primarily manage their supplier relationships through strategic partnerships. To support this claim regarding the new research, the author points out that Japanese firms make extensive use of "market-exchange relationships," which are alternatives to the strategic relationships discussed in the preceding paragraph.

A   This is the belief that the author claims that the new research casts doubt on, so it would not make sense for the author to cite this as evidence for the author's claim.

B   This is cited as a result of the belief that the author claims the new research casts doubt on, not as evidence for the author's claim.

C   The new research undermines the basis of the advice referred to here—advice that the Western automobile manufacturers heed—so it would make little sense for the author to cite this as evidence in support of the author's claim about the new research.

D   **Correct.** The passage does cite this prevalence as evidence for the author's claim that the new research casts doubt on the widely held view about Japanese firms.

E   Citing this firm's success would tend to support the widespread view about Japanese firms, not undermine that view.

The correct answer is D.

Questions 486–489 refer to the passage on page 412.

486. According to the passage, the research mentioned in line 6 suggests which of the following about lower-ranked top executives and postacquisition success?

(A) Given that these executives are unlikely to contribute to postacquisition success, little effort should be spent trying to retain them.

(B) The shorter their length of service, the less likely it is that these executives will play a significant role in postacquisition success.

(C) These executives are less important to postacquisition success than are more highly ranked top executives.

(D) If they have long tenures, these executives may prove to be as important to postacquisition success as are more highly ranked top executives.

(E) Postacquisition success is unlikely if these executives are retained.

Supporting idea

The question asks about information provided by the passage. According to the third sentence, research suggests that retaining the highest-level top executives in an acquisition is more strongly associated with success than retaining lower-ranked top executives—which suggests, in turn, that lower-ranked top executives are less important than top-level executives to postacquisition success, though it does not suggest that they are unimportant to such success.

A   The research indicates that lower-ranked top executives are less strongly associated with success than are higher-ranked executives but does not provide advice about retention efforts.
B   The research mentioned in the third sentence does not consider length of service.
C   **Correct.** The research indicates that lower-ranked top executives are less strongly associated with postacquisition success than are the highest-ranked executives.
D   The research mentioned in the third sentence does not consider length of service.
E   The research suggests that lower-ranked top executives are less strongly associated with postacquisition success but does not suggest that they decrease the likelihood of success.

The correct answer is C.

RC00497-03
487. The resource-based view, as described in the passage, is based on which of the following ideas?

(A) The managerial skills of top executives become strongest after the first five years of their tenure.
(B) Company-specific knowledge is an important factor in the success of an acquisition process.
(C) The amount of nontransferable knowledge possessed by long-tenured top executives tends to be underestimated.
(D) Effective implementation of an acquisition depends primarily on the ability of executives to adapt to change.
(E) Short-tenured executives are likely to impede the implementation of a successful acquisition strategy.

Evaluation

This question requires analysis of the reasoning underlying one of the two explanations described in the passage. The resource-based view (RBV) holds that retaining high-level executives with long tenure will contribute to success because those people have important company-specific knowledge. This view rests on the assumption that company-specific knowledge is valuable to postacquisition success.

A   In RBV, executives with long tenure are valuable not specifically for their managerial skills but for their knowledge about the acquired company. The passage does not restrict to five years the period in which this knowledge is gained.
B   **Correct.** RBV values executives' knowledge of the acquired company and is based on the belief that company-specific knowledge is valuable for postacquisition success.
C   The passage does not indicate that RBV claims that executives' company-specific knowledge is generally undervalued. But the passage does indicate that RBV regards such knowledge as valuable to postacquisition success.
D   In RBV, executives with long tenure are valuable not for their ability to adapt to change, but for their knowledge about the acquired company.
E   RBV does not suggest that short-tenured executives impede postacquisition success, only that they are less important to success than the highest-ranked executives.

The correct answer is B.

488. The passage suggests that Bergh and a proponent of the upper echelons perspective would be most likely to disagree over which of the following?

(A) Whether there is a positive correlation between short organizational tenure and managerial adaptability

(B) Whether there is a positive correlation between long organizational tenure and the acquisition of idiosyncratic and nontransferable knowledge

(C) Whether adaptability is a useful trait for an executive who is managing an acquisition process

(D) Whether retaining less-tenured top executives of an acquired company is an optimal strategy for achieving postacquisition success

(E) Whether retaining highest-level top executives of acquired companies is more important than retaining lower-ranked top executives

Inference

The question asks about conclusions that can reasonably be drawn from the information provided in the passage. Bergh's study supports the resource-based view (RBV), which suggests that top executives with long tenure are more valuable to postacquisition success than other executives. The upper echelons perspective (UEP), in contrast, suggests that top executives with shorter tenure are more valuable to postacquisition success. Thus, Bergh and a proponent of UEP would likely disagree about whether long or short tenure top executives are more valuable to a positive outcome in a postacquisition situation.

A   The passage does not provide sufficiently specific information about statistical relationships to determine whether Bergh and proponents of UEP would agree or disagree about whether there is such a positive correlation.

B   There is a weak suggestion in the passage that Bergh believes such a positive correlation exists, but there is no indication that a proponent of UEP would question such a correlation.

C   The passage does not indicate that Bergh would disagree with proponents of UEP that adaptability is a valuable trait in an executive who is managing an acquisition.

D   **Correct.** The passage suggests that proponents of UEP believe that retaining less-tenured top executives during and after an acquisition is a better strategy, while Bergh believes that retaining longer-tenured top executives is better.

E   The passage suggests that Bergh and proponents of UEP agree that retaining the highest-level top executives is more important to postacquisition success than is retaining lower-ranked top executives.

The correct answer is D.

489. According to the passage, prior to Bergh's study, research on the role of top executives of acquired companies in business acquisition success was limited in which of the following ways?

(A) It did not address how the organizational tenure of top executives affects postacquisition success.

(B) It did not address why some companies have longer-tenured CEOs than others.

(C) It did not consider strategies for retaining long-tenured top executives of acquired companies.

(D) It failed to differentiate between the contribution of highest-level top executives to postacquisition success and that of lower-ranked top executives.

(E) It underestimated the potential contribution that lower-level top executives can make to postacquisition success.

Supporting idea

This question asks about information explicitly provided in the passage. The first paragraph summarizes research indicating that retaining highest-level top executives during and after an acquisition is more strongly associated with successful outcomes than retaining lower-ranking top executives. The paragraph then states that this research has limitations, including failing to take into account how long the highest-ranking executives have worked for the company. The second paragraph explains that Bergh's study responds to those limitations by analyzing the role of tenure (length of service in the organization).

A   **Correct.** The passage indicates that the research about the role of highest-level executives in acquisitions is limited by its failure to consider tenure.
B   The passage does not portray the failure of the research to address this as a limitation of the research in question.
C   The passage does not portray the failure of the research to consider this as a limitation of the research in question.
D   The passage indicates that the research does, in fact, differentiate between the respective contributions of these two groups of top executives.
E   Undervaluing the contributions of lower-level top executives is not one of the limitations mentioned in the passage.

The correct answer is A.

Questions 490–493 refer to the passage on page 414.

RC00017-02

490. According to the passage, which of the following contributed to Marcus Garvey's success?

(A) He introduced cultural and historical consciousness to the African American community.
(B) He believed enthusiastically in the traditional American success ethos.
(C) His audience had already formed a consciousness that made it receptive to his message.
(D) His message appealed to critics of African American support for United States military involvement in the First World War.
(E) He supported the movement to protest segregation that had emerged prior to his arrival in the United States.

Supporting idea

To answer this question, find what the passage states explicitly about how Marcus Garvey achieved his success. The passage begins by stating that Garvey arrived at the right time: that returning African American soldiers were primed to receive what he had to say about the African American community. These soldiers already held strong beliefs about their rights to opportunities for success; the passage concludes that the divide between the soldiers' expectations and their experiences led to Garvey's success.

A   The passage states that African American people were in possession of a strong cultural and historical consciousness prior to Garvey's arrival in the United States.
B   The passage attributes belief in the traditional American success ethos to African American people who joined the armed forces; it does not mention Garvey's beliefs on this subject.
C   **Correct.** African American soldiers who had experienced segregation during the First World War were ready to hear what Garvey had to say.
D   Critics of African American support for United States involvement in the First World War are not mentioned in the passage.
E   While Garvey most likely would have supported a movement to protest segregation, such a movement is not discussed in the passage.

The correct answer is C.

RC00017-03

491. The passage suggests that many African American people responded to their experiences in the armed forces in which of the following ways?

(A) They maintained as civilians their enthusiastic allegiance to the armed forces.
(B) They questioned United States involvement in the First World War.
(C) They joined political organizations to protest the segregation of African American troops and the indignities they suffered in the military.
(D) They became aware of the gap between their expectations and the realities of American culture.
(E) They repudiated Garvey's message of pride and unity.

Inference

According to the passage, African Americans enthusiastically joined the armed services but were confronted with continued segregation, both in the military and when they returned home. The passage does not explicitly state their response to these experiences, but a response can be inferred. The second paragraph refers to anthropologist Anthony F. C. Wallace, who argued that a revitalization movement may be brought about by the perception of a gap between expectations and reality, and such a revitalization did occur in African American communities following the First World War; thus, many African American people may have become aware of a gap such as Wallace described.

- A   The passage states that African American troops experienced segregation and other indignities while in the military; these experiences could reasonably be inferred to have dampened their enthusiasm for the armed forces. Regardless, the passage does not suggest an enthusiastic allegiance.
- B   The passage describes African American people's enthusiasm about joining the military. Although they experienced segregation and other indignities while in the military, the passage does not suggest that their opinion about involvement in the war changed.
- C   While African American troops may have joined political organizations, the passage does not provide any actual evidence of this having occurred.
- D   **Correct.** The fact that, as the passage states, a revitalization movement occurred in the African American community following the First World War suggests that the returning soldiers did become aware of the gap between their expectations of an improved situation with regard to segregation and the reality of continued segregation in the United States.
- E   The passage does not suggest that African American troops repudiated Garvey's message. On the contrary, it states that Garvey built *the largest revitalization movement in African American history*. This suggests that the members of the African American community, including the returning soldiers, were extremely receptive to Garvey's message.

The correct answer is D.

RC00017-04

492. It can be inferred from the passage that the "scholars" mentioned in line 24 believe which of the following to be true?

- (A) Revitalization resulted from the political activism of returning African American soldiers following the First World War.
- (B) Marcus Garvey had to change a number of prevailing attitudes in order for his mass movement to find a foothold in the United States.
- (C) The prevailing sensibility of the African American community provided the foundation of Marcus Garvey's political appeal.
- (D) Marcus Garvey hoped to revitalize consciousness of cultural and historical identity in the African American community.
- (E) The goal of the mass movement that Marcus Garvey helped bring into being was to build on the pride and unity among African Americans.

Inference

To determine what it is logical to infer regarding the scholars discussed in the third paragraph, look at the context in which they are mentioned. According to the passage, these scholars argue that Garvey was responsible for creating a particular consciousness within the African American community, a consciousness that the passage identifies as *identity, strength, and* [a] *sense of history*. Unlike the passage author, these scholars believe strongly in Garvey's responsibility for this consciousness, so they would most likely reject any suggestion that it existed prior to his arrival and activism.

- A   According to the passage, the scholars believe that Garvey was responsible for the creation of the consciousness that led to revitalization, which suggests that revitalization resulted from Garvey's activism, not soldiers' activism.
- B   **Correct.** According to the passage, the scholars believe that Garvey created the consciousness that led to his revitalization

movement. This suggests that he had to change prevailing attitudes in order to foster this new consciousness.

C According to the passage, the scholars believe that Garvey created a new consciousness in the African American community; thus, the prevailing sensibility could not have provided a foundation for his appeal.

D According to the passage, the scholars believe that Garvey built his revitalization movement on a new consciousness of cultural and historical identity, not a previously existing one.

E According to the passage, the scholars' position is that Garvey's movement was built on a new sense of pride and unity that he provided, and that that sense did not precede Garvey's work.

The correct answer is B.

RC00017-05

493. According to the passage, many African American people joined the armed forces during the First World War for which of the following reasons?

(A) They wished to escape worsening economic conditions in African American communities.

(B) They expected to fulfill ideals of personal attainment.

(C) They sought to express their loyalty to the United States.

(D) They hoped that joining the military would help advance the cause of desegregation.

(E) They saw military service as an opportunity to fulfill Marcus Garvey's political vision.

Supporting idea

This question depends on identifying what the passage states directly about African American people's reasons for joining the armed forces. The reason offered by the passage is that the African American people who entered the armed forces did so because they were *hoping to participate in the traditional American ethos of individual success.*

A Although this is a plausible reason for entering the armed forces, the passage does not discuss economic conditions.

B **Correct.** The passage states that African American people who joined the armed forces during the First World War wanted to achieve individual success.

C The passage does not discuss African American people's loyalty to the United States.

D The passage states that African American troops experienced segregation, but it does not suggest that they had hoped their joining the military would promote desegregation.

E The passage suggests that African American troops did not become aware of Marcus Garvey's political vision until after they returned from the First World War.

The correct answer is B.

Questions 494–501 refer to the passage on page 416.

RC38200-01.01

494. Which of the following best states the difference between free trade and fair trade, as explained in the passage?

(A) Free trade requires no trade tariffs whatsoever, whereas fair trade assumes multilateral agreement on tariffs for goods of equal worth.

(B) Free trade is based on the unrestricted movement of goods across all national boundaries, whereas fair trade is based on a nation's restriction of commerce with each nation that erects trade barriers to the first nation's exports.

(C) The trade policies of countries like Arboria are based on the principles of free trade, whereas the trade policies of other types of world economies are based on fair trade.

(D) Free-trade nations negotiate individual trade agreements with each of their trading partners, whereas fair-trade nations conduct multilateral trade negotiations.

(E) Free trade assumes a constant level of global commerce, whereas fair trade promotes a steady expansion of international trade.

Evaluation

This question requires you to understand how the passage explains the difference between free trade and fair trade. The passage discusses international trade as viewed from the perspective of the nation of Arboria. The distinction between free trade and fair trade is discussed in the third paragraph. Free trade between two countries is understood as free movement of goods in each direction across countries' borders. From the Arborian perspective, fair trade is understood as mutually beneficial trading arrangements, where access to the Arborian market is granted only to nations that allow Arborian exports equal access to their own markets.

- A The distinction between free trade and fair trade in the passage does not hinge on the absence or presence of tariffs in a trading regime, even though the passage implies that asymmetric application of tariffs would render a trading regime unfair.
- B **Correct.** As explained above, free trade implies open access to markets; fair trade implies that each of any two trading partner nations should allow the same level of access for imports from the other nation.
- C Whether true or false, this is a claim of a factual kind, and does not provide anything resembling a definition of the two terms, *free trade* and *fair trade*. The passage suggests that Arboria has a free-trade economy and many other nations do not.
- D The passage tells us that both the free-trade advocates and the fair-trade advocates base their positions, in part, on the idea that multilateral negotiations are the most effective way of resolving pressing trade issues.
- E The passage suggests that free trade without fair trade would hinder the expansion of trade (especially Arborian trade) and that fair trade would eventually lead to free trade. But the passage also suggests that international trade between two countries can be simultaneously free and fair. As presented in the passage, the distinction between the two aspects of trade does not hinge on whether the regime promotes a steady expansion of international trade.

The correct answer is B.

495. It can be inferred that the author of the passage would most likely agree with which of the following statements about multilateral trade negotiations?

- (A) They are the most effective way to resolve trade problems.
- (B) They are most effective in dealing with fair-trade issues between nations.
- (C) They have only recently begun to make an impact on world trade.
- (D) Arborian reliance on multilateral trade negotiations, while appropriate in the past, is inadequate for today's global marketplace.
- (E) The principles of multilateral trade negotiations are incompatible with current Arborian foreign trade policy.

Inference

Answering this question requires you to infer from the given information what claim about multilateral trade negotiations the author would most likely agree with. According to the passage, the advocates of free trade and the advocates of fair trade both assume that multilateral negotiations are the most effective way to resolve trading issues. But the passage claims that this assumption is wrong and outdated for current trading conditions. The passage argues that nearly 75 percent of trade is conducted by widely divergent economic systems in countries not subscribing to the same trading principles as Arboria and that this makes negotiation of multilateral trade agreements virtually impossible.

- A As explained above, the author of the passage takes a position opposed to this.
- B According to the passage, it is virtually impossible to negotiate multilateral agreements with countries that do not accept the same trading principles as Arboria and that therefore may have differing notions of what makes trade fair.
- C The passage suggests that the assumption concerning multilateral trade negotiations had for 40 years been accepted by the free-trade countries that dominated world trade—as well as possibly by other trading countries.

D **Correct.** As explained above, this is a part of the argument in the passage.

E The passage does not argue that a principle concerning multilateral approaches in negotiating trade policy, long accepted by Arborian trading authorities, was incompatible with "current" foreign-trade policy. Rather, the passage suggests that that principle and the associated policy should be questioned and rejected, with a view to formulating a policy more relevant to current conditions.

The correct answer is D.

RC38200-03.01

496. Which of the following statements best summarizes the author's opinion of "free traders" and "fair traders"?

(A) The free and the fair traders' continuing debate provides a healthy and effective forum for examining Arborian trade policy.

(B) The proponents of fair trade are essentially correct, while those who advocate free trade are not.

(C) The proponents of free trade are better able to deal with current economic problems than are the fair traders.

(D) Neither the free nor the fair traders can come up with a workable trade policy because neither takes multilateral negotiations into account.

(E) The proponents of both free and fair trade have based their positions on out-of-date premises that do not reflect current economic conditions.

Supporting Ideas

This question requires an understanding of what the author has to say about "free traders" and "fair traders." The final paragraph of the passage states that "both sides," i.e. the proponents of free trade and the proponents of fair trade, base their positions on two assumptions that, according to the passage, are outdated. The passage attributes this outdatedness to changes that have occurred in the composition of international trade.

A The passage implies that the debate between the free traders and the fair traders is unlikely to make progress because of two outdated assumptions that both sides make.

B The passage implies that fair trade ultimately leads to free trade. The passage implies that trade can be both free and fair.

C The passage indicates that assumptions on which the free traders and the fair traders rely are incompatible with the current realities of international trade.

D The passage argues that both free traders and fair traders wrongly assume that the best way to resolve trade issues is through the use of multilateral negotiations.

E **Correct.** This is a claim that is central to the argument in the passage, as explained above.

The correct answer is E.

RC38200-04.01

497. The author mentions all of the following as characteristic of world trade in the mid-1940s EXCEPT:

(A) Arboria played a major role in the global marketplace.

(B) Whorfland played a major role in the global marketplace.

(C) Tariffs were the main obstacle to trade.

(D) Fair-trade economies dominated international trade.

(E) Arborian manufacturers were unsurpassed in most industries.

Supporting Ideas

The word "mentions" in the question is to be taken as meaning "explicitly states" (as opposed to implies or suggests), so this question requires that you recognize what is and is NOT explicitly stated in the passage regarding world trade in the mid-1940s. The passage states that Arboria and Whorfland dominated the global economy for a long period, but no longer do so. It also states that tariffs were the main obstacle to trade during the time of Arboria's trade supremacy and that in most industries, Arboria had no close competitors. The passage neither states nor implies that at that time fair-trade economies dominated world trade.

A The passage states that this was so in the mid-1940s.

B This is stated in the passage.

C The passage states: "tariffs were the principal obstacle to trade."

D **Correct.** The passage does NOT mention this; it neither states nor implies that in the mid-1940s, fair-trade economies dominated world trade.

E The passage states: "Arborian supremacy was uncontested in virtually all industries."

The correct answer is D.

RC38200-05.01

498. In presenting the argument in the passage, the author uses all of the following EXCEPT:

(A) statistical information about global commerce
(B) definitions of terms concerning world trade
(C) generalizations about Arboria's economic system
(D) historical background of Arborian trade policy
(E) an example of an economic system whose principles differ from those of Arboria

Evaluation

This question concerns rhetorical techniques used in the passage, and we are asked to identify a technique that is NOT used.

A The passage gives some statistical information about global commerce: e.g., 75% of world trade involves countries with divergent economic systems that differ from those of Arboria.

B The passage defines free trade and fair trade.

C The passage states that the supremacy of Arboria in most industries was for a long time uncontested.

D The passage indicates how the trade regime in which Arboria participates was established 40 years previously.

E **Correct.** No individual economic system besides that of Whorfland—which has adopted the same trading principles as Arboria—is cited in the passage.

The correct answer is E.

RC38200-06.01

499. The author asserts which of the following about Arboria's trade policy?

(A) A dramatic revision of Arboria's trade policy will be necessary unless Arborian manufacturers improve the quality of their goods.
(B) The most crucial issue facing Arborian trade policymakers is that of free trade versus protectionism.
(C) Arboria's current trade policy was essentially developed during the 1940s and has changed little since that time.
(D) Arboria's trade policy is widely emulated throughout the world, to the extent that most international commerce is modeled on Arboria's principles.
(E) Arboria's trade policy has evolved gradually over the last eighty years, constantly readjusting itself in response to shifts in global commerce.

Supporting Ideas

This question asks us to identify something stated in the passage—though not necessarily in the exact words given. We should look for the statement that is the most precise paraphrase of a statement made in the passage.

A Although the passage indicates that some revision of Arborian trade policy is needed, the passage does not indicate that such a revision would be unnecessary if the quality of Arborian manufactures improved.

B The passage states: "Today the key trade issue is not free trade versus protectionism."

C **Correct.** The passage states that the current trade policy is obsolete and "an artifact of the mid-1940s," and adds that although economic circumstances have changed, Arborian trade policy has not.

D The passage states: "nearly 75 percent [of world trade] is conducted by economic systems operating with principles at odds with those of Arboria."

E The passage does not state that this is so; in fact, it emphasizes the lack of change over the previous 40 years in Arborian trade policy and the absence of readjustment in response to significant changes in conditions affecting global trade.

The correct answer is C.

7.6 Reading Comprehension Answer Explanations

RC38200-07.01
500. The passage is primarily concerned with

(A) illustrating the erosion of Arboria's position in the world marketplace
(B) examining the differences between "free" and "fair" traders
(C) advocating a reassessment of Arboria's trade policy
(D) criticizing the terms of the General Agreement on Tariffs and Trade (GATT)
(E) comparing the different economic circumstances of Arboria's trade partners

Main Point

We are asked here to select the phrase that most accurately identifies the topic that is the central theme of the passage. The discussion revolves around trade policy—specifically the way in which it has affected the interests of the nation of Arboria. In the course of exploring this central topic, several issues are touched on: the loss of Arborian dominance in global trade; the distinction between free trade and fair trade; the impact of GATT on the governance of global trade; and the percentage of total trade conducted by countries other than Arboria and Whorfland.

A   Illustrating something generally involves providing a specific example. But the passage gives no example to show how the Arborian trade position has declined relative to that of other countries.

B   The distinction between free trade and fair trade, as understood by the advocates of each of these, is explained in the broader context of considering Arborian trade policy. But the passage emphasizes the common assumptions relied on by both free traders and fair traders.

C   **Correct.** This is the theme of the passage, which advocates a reconsideration of Arborian trade policy and the longstanding assumptions on which it has been based. This central concern prompts the discussion of other relevant, but subsidiary, topics.

D   The individual terms of GATT are not examined or criticized in any detail, but the relevance of GATT to current global trade is minimized.

E   No such comparison is made, even though the divergence of economic systems involved in world trade is emphasized with a view to demonstrating the difficulty in negotiating multilateral trade deals and the obsolescence of the multilateral approach.

The correct answer is C.

RC38200-08.01
501. The author implies that the main obstacle to a truly effective Arborian trade policy is the

(A) weak position that Arboria currently holds in the global marketplace
(B) inability of Arborian leaders to recognize that foreign economic systems are based on principles fundamentally different from their own
(C) dominance of the supporters of free trade in the conflict between free-trade and fair-trade advocates
(D) apparent inability of Arborian industries to produce goods that are competitive in the world market
(E) protectionism that characterizes the foreign trade policies of so many of Arboria's trade partners

Inference

Correctly answering this question requires you to infer from the given information what the main obstacle to an effective Arborian trade policy is. The correct response is to be found in the first paragraph of the passage, which contains the following sentence: "Arboria faces the prospect of continuing economic loss until Arborian business and political leaders recognize the fundamental differences between Arborian and foreign economic systems." The phrase *continuing economic loss* indicates, from the author's perspective, an ineffective trade policy. The *until*-clause signifies that a necessary condition of improving the situation is a recognition by leaders that Arborian and foreign economic systems are fundamentally different. The final paragraph emphasizes that such differences exist: "75 percent [of world trade] is conducted by economic systems operating with principles at odds with those of Arboria."

A The passage does not state or imply that Arboria has a "weak position" in global trade; rather, it emphasizes that Arboria can gain a much stronger position and "misses opportunities for trade expansion."

B **Correct.** See the detailed analysis given above.

C The passage nowhere states or implies that the free-trade advocates are dominant in the dispute with fair-trade advocates, even though the passage suggests that developed economies such as Arboria and Whorfland have long practiced free trade and been dominant in global trade.

D The passage neither states nor implies that the goods produced by Arborian industries are deficient in quality or are overpriced, but it does suggest that some countries that export to Arboria have trade barriers, such as tariffs, that impede importation of Arborian products.

E The passage suggests that some trading partners of Arboria have trade barriers impeding imports from Arboria, but the passage asserts the following: "Today the key trade issue is not free trade versus protectionism but diminishing trade versus expanding trade."

The correct answer is B.

Questions 502–509 refer to the passage on page 418.

RC74000-01.01

502. According to the passage, which of the following was true of the treaty establishing the Fort Berthold Indian Reservation?

(A) It was challenged in the Supreme Court a number of times.

(B) It was rescinded by the federal government, an action that gave rise to the Winters case.

(C) It cited American Indians' traditional use of the land's resources.

(D) It failed to mention water rights to be enjoyed by the reservation's inhabitants.

(E) It was modified by the Supreme Court in *Arizona v. California*.

Supporting Idea

This question depends on recognizing what the passage says about the treaty that established the Fort Berthold Indian Reservation. The passage indicates that the treaty does not mention water rights, but the federal government had intended, according to the Supreme Court, to reserve for the inhabitants of the reservation the waters that were essential to the usefulness of the land.

A The passage does discuss Supreme Court cases, but it does not explicitly mention any challenges in the Supreme Court to the treaty.

B The passage does not state that the federal government rescinded the treaty.

C The passage does not indicate that the treaty made any reference to the traditional use of the land's resources.

D **Correct.** The passage indicates that the treaty does not mention water rights.

E The passage's reference to *Arizona v. California* relates to the treaty that established the Fort Berthold Indian Reservation only in that *Arizona v. California* refers to the Winters doctrine, which was established in a case regarding that treaty; *Arizona v. California* does not modify that treaty in any way.

The correct answer is D.

RC74000-02.01

503. The passage suggests that, if the criteria discussed in lines 10–20 of the text were the only criteria for establishing a reservation's water rights, which of the following would be true?

(A) The water rights of the inhabitants of the Fort Berthold Indian Reservation would not take precedence over those of other citizens.

(B) Reservations established before 1848 would be judged to have no water rights.

(C) There would be no legal basis for the water rights of the Rio Grande pueblos.

(D) Reservations other than American Indian reservations could not be created with reserved water rights.

(E) Treaties establishing reservations would have to mention water rights explicitly in order to reserve water for a particular purpose.

Inference

The question requires you to make an inference based on a hypothetical situation in which the criteria discussed in lines 10–20 are the only criteria relevant to establishing a reservation's water rights. These criteria relate to any reservation that has been formally withdrawn from federal public lands, in which the circumstances of that withdrawal make clear that the government had intended to reserve both water and land when the reservation was established. Because the Rio Grande pueblos never formally constituted a part of federal public lands, they were never formally withdrawn from these lands, and so this set of criteria does not apply to these pueblos. Thus, if these were the only legal criteria for establishing water rights, then there would be no legal basis for water rights for the Rio Grande pueblos.

A   The criteria, which were established on the precedent set in the *Winters v. United States* ruling, all apply to the Fort Berthold Indian Reservation.

B   Although in actual fact there were no Indian reservations formally established before 1848, nothing in the passage suggests that there were not any, or that none would have met the criteria.

C   **Correct.** If the criteria were the only criteria relevant for establishing water rights, then the passage suggests that, because the Rio Grande pueblos were never formally withdrawn from federal public lands, there would be no legal basis for water rights for these pueblos.

D   The criteria as expressed in the passage do not restrict the type of reservation covered to American Indian reservations.

E   The criteria are meant to cover any circumstances in which the government intended to reserve water rights, whether water rights are explicitly mentioned or not.

The correct answer is C.

RC74000-03.01
504. Which of the following most accurately summarizes the relationship between *Arizona v. California*, as that decision is described in the passage, and the criteria discussed in lines 10–20?

(A)   *Arizona v. California* abolishes these criteria and establishes a competing set of criteria for applying the Winters doctrine.

(B)   *Arizona v. California* establishes that the Winters doctrine applies to a broader range of situations than those defined by these criteria.

(C)   *Arizona v. California* represents the sole example of an exception to the criteria as they were set forth in the Winters doctrine.

(D)   *Arizona v. California* does not refer to the Winters doctrine to justify water rights, whereas these criteria do rely on the Winters doctrine.

(E)   *Arizona v. California* applies the criteria derived from the Winters doctrine only to federal lands other than American Indian reservations.

Evaluation

This question requires you to determine how *Arizona v. California*, as it is described in the passage, relates to the criteria discussed in lines 10–20. Those criteria, which were established in various decisions based on the precedent of *Winters v. United States*, lay down conditions under which courts can uphold federal rights to reserve water. One of the criteria is related to land formally withdrawn from federal public lands. *Arizona v. California* establishes that the Winters doctrine—which stipulates that water rights need not have been granted explicitly—applies to a broader range of situations than those defined by the criteria. For instance, the doctrine can apply in cases in which the land in question was never formally withdrawn from public lands.

A   The passage does not indicate that *Arizona v. California* abolishes these criteria. It merely indicates that *Arizona v. California* recognizes further situations to which the Winters doctrine can apply.

B   **Correct.** The passage indicates that *Arizona v. California* applies the Winters doctrine to a situation that falls outside these criteria.

C   The passage does not indicate that there are no other exceptions besides *Arizona v. California* to these criteria.

D   The passage indicates that *Arizona v. California* does refer to the Winters doctrine to justify water rights.

E   The passage does not indicate that *Arizona v. California* applies these criteria at all; instead, *Arizona v. California* broadens the range of situations to which the Winters doctrine applies.

The correct answer is B.

RC74000-04.01

505. The "pragmatic approach" mentioned in lines 37–38 of the passage is best defined as one that

(A) grants recognition to reservations that were never formally established but that have traditionally been treated as such

(B) determines the water rights of all citizens in a particular region by examining the actual history of water usage in that region

(C) gives federal courts the right to reserve water along with land even when it is clear that the government originally intended to reserve only the land

(D) bases the decision to recognize the legal rights of a group on the practical effect such a recognition is likely to have on other citizens

(E) dictates that courts ignore precedents set by such cases as *Winters v. United States* in deciding what water rights belong to reserved land

Evaluation

This question depends on determining how the term *pragmatic approach* is used in lines 37–38. The passage states that what constitutes an American Indian reservation is a matter not of legal definition, but of practice. The Rio Grande pueblos, though they were never formally established by a withdrawal from federal public lands, have always been treated in practice as reservations. This is what is described in the passage as a *pragmatic approach*.

A   **Correct.** The passage refers to the idea that *[w]hat constitutes an American Indian reservation is a question of practice, not of legal definition* as a *pragmatic approach*. Thus, the pragmatic approach does not require that a reservation has been formally established, but only that it has been traditionally treated as such.

B   The passage does not concern itself with the water rights of all citizens.

C   The passage clearly indicates that determining whether the government intended to reserve water along with the land is crucial for courts.

D   The passage does not specifically consider the likely practical effect of recognizing a particular group's legal rights on other citizens.

E   The passage indicates that the pragmatic approach is supported by *Arizona v. California*, which used, and expanded on, the precedent set by *Winters v. United States*.

The correct answer is A.

RC74000-05.01

506. It can be inferred from the passage that the Winters doctrine has been used to establish which of the following?

(A) A rule that the government may reserve water only by explicit treaty or agreement

(B) A legal distinction between federal lands reserved for American Indians and federal lands reserved for other purposes

(C) Criteria governing when the federal government may set land aside for a particular purpose

(D) The special status of American Indian tribes' rights to reserved land

(E) The federal right to reserve water implicitly as well as explicitly under certain conditions

Inference

This question requires you to make an inference based on facts the passage cites regarding the Winters doctrine. The passage indicates that the Supreme Court ruled in *Winters v. United States* that, despite the fact that the treaty establishing the Berthold Indian Reservation made no explicit mention of water rights, the federal government had intended to reserve such rights to the American Indians living on that reservation. Later court rulings that cited the Winters ruling as precedent further refined this doctrine such that water rights can be reserved implicitly if *circumstances reveal [that] the government intended to reserve water as well as land when establishing the reservation*.

A   The passage states that the Winters doctrine ruled that even if a treaty has not explicitly reserved water, water may be reserved if conditions reveal that the reservation of water had been intended.

B The passage indicates that the Winters doctrine presupposes such a legal distinction; it does not establish it.

C The passage does not give any information that suggests that the Winters doctrine has been used to establish any criteria governing when the federal government may set land aside for a particular purpose.

D The passage indicates that the Winters doctrine gives special status to the water flowing through reserved lands, but it does not suggest that the doctrine has been used to establish any special status of American Indian tribes' rights to those lands.

E **Correct.** The passage provides information suggesting that the Winters doctrine has been used to establish a federal right to implicitly reserve water under certain conditions.

The correct answer is E.

RC74000-06.01

507. The author cites the fact that the Rio Grande pueblos were never formally withdrawn from public lands primarily in order to do which of the following?

(A) Suggest why it might have been argued that the Winters doctrine ought not to apply to pueblo lands

(B) Imply that the United States never really acquired sovereignty over pueblo lands

(C) Argue that the pueblo lands ought still to be considered part of federal public lands

(D) Support the argument that the water rights of citizens other than American Indians are limited by the Winters doctrine

(E) Suggest that federal courts cannot claim jurisdiction over cases disputing the traditional diversion and use of water by Pueblo Indians

Evaluation

The passage in the first paragraph outlines a set of criteria that, through various court decisions using the Winters decision as precedent, refined what came to be known as the Winters doctrine. These decisions established that courts can uphold federal rights to reserve water (specifically, for use by American Indians) if, among other conditions, *the land has been formally withdrawn from federal public lands.* Because the Rio Grande pueblos never formally constituted a part of federal public lands, it might appear that the Winters doctrine would not apply to them. The passage indicates, however, that *Arizona v. California* established that this doctrine did apply to them.

A **Correct.** Because the Rio Grande pueblo lands were never formally withdrawn from federal public lands—because they never were a part of federal public lands—it might have appeared that the Winters doctrine did not apply to them, because that doctrine had traditionally been taken to apply only to land that had been formally withdrawn from federal public lands.

B The passage does suggest that the federal government never acquired sovereignty over the Rio Grande pueblos. But the passage indicates this not by citing the fact that the pueblos were never formally withdrawn from public lands, but by pointing out that these pueblos were never part of federal public lands in the first place.

C The passage states that the pueblo lands were never considered to be part of federal public lands.

D It is not the fact that these lands were never withdrawn from federal public lands that is cited in support of this argument; it is, rather, the fact that these lands were never part of federal public lands that is cited for this purpose.

E The passage actually suggests the opposite of what this says, namely, that federal courts can claim jurisdiction over such cases.

The correct answer is A.

RC74000-07.01

508. The primary purpose of the passage is to

(A) trace the development of laws establishing American Indian reservations

(B) explain the legal bases for the water rights of American Indian tribes

(C) question the legal criteria often used to determine the water rights of American Indian tribes

489

(D) discuss evidence establishing the earliest date at which the federal government recognized the water rights of American Indians

(E) point out a legal distinction between different types of American Indian reservations

Main idea

Answering this question requires identifying the primary purpose of the passage. The passage is mainly concerned with describing the legal bases of American Indian tribal water rights.

A The passage does not discuss the development of laws establishing reservations. It is concerned with American Indian water rights.

B **Correct.** The passage's primary concern is to discuss certain principles relating to American Indian water rights established in various court cases.

C The passage does not question the legal criteria it discusses.

D The passage indicates that a groundbreaking Supreme Court ruling regarding the water rights of American Indians was handed down in 1908, but that ruling suggested that the federal government had intended at an earlier stage, in the treaty establishing the Fort Berthold Indian Reservation, to recognize water rights; the passage gives no indication, though, of the date of that treaty, nor whether that treaty would have been the first recognition in law of such rights. The passage is concerned with the legal bases of American Indian water rights, not with when the federal government first recognized them.

E The passage does discuss both lands that have been explicitly created as reservations by treaty and lands that have been treated as reservations although they had never been legally constituted as such; however, (1) the passage indicates that in crucial ways there are no legal distinctions between these two different types of American reservation, and (2) this is not the primary focus of the passage, which, instead, concerns the legal bases of American Indian water rights.

The correct answer is B.

509. The passage suggests that the legal rights of citizens other than American Indians to the use of water flowing into the Rio Grande pueblos are

(A) guaranteed by the precedent set in *Arizona v. California*

(B) abolished by the Winters doctrine

(C) deferred to the Pueblo Indians whenever treaties explicitly require this

(D) guaranteed by federal land-use laws

(E) limited by the prior claims of the Pueblo Indians

Inference

The question requires you to make an inference regarding the legal rights of citizens other than American Indians to the use of water flowing into the Rio Grande pueblos. The second paragraph of the passage discusses the Rio Grande pueblos, the rights to the water flowing into them, and the legal bases regarding those rights. Most relevantly to this question, the final sentence of the passage indicates that *the reserved water rights of Pueblo Indians have priority over other citizens' water rights*.

A The passage indicates that the precedent set in *Arizona v. California* declares that the Winters doctrine applies to the pueblos, despite their never having been explicitly set aside as a reservation. This gave the inhabitants of the pueblos priority rights to water. Thus, the legal rights of citizens other than American Indians are not guaranteed by the precedent set in that ruling.

B The passage does not rule out the possibility that citizens other than American Indians may have some rights to the water; their rights are merely limited by the prior claims of the Pueblo Indians.

C The passage does not explicitly discuss treaties to which Pueblo Indians are a party.

D The passage gives no indication that federal land-use laws guarantee the legal rights of citizens other than American Indians to water flowing into the Rio Grande pueblos.

E. **Correct.** The passage explicitly states that the reserved water rights of Pueblo Indians have priority over other citizens' water rights.

The correct answer is E.

Questions 510–514 refer to the passage on page 420.

RC00394-02

510. Which of the following can be inferred about supplier partnerships, as they are described in the passage?

(A) They cannot be sustained unless the goods or services provided are available from a large number of suppliers.

(B) They can result in purchasers paying more for goods and services than they would in a competitive-bidding situation.

(C) They typically are instituted at the urging of the supplier rather than the purchaser.

(D) They are not feasible when the goods or services provided are directly related to the purchasers' end products.

(E) They are least appropriate when the purchasers' ability to change suppliers is limited.

Inference

According to the passage, in supplier partnerships a corporate purchaser forgoes the right to pursue alternative suppliers for certain goods or services. This tends to reduce or eliminate the threat of competition for the supplier in the partnership. It can be inferred that the corporate purchaser in a supplier partnership risks paying more for goods or services than it would if the supplier had to compete for the business.

A   The passage suggests something incompatible with this, i.e., that availability of the relevant goods or services from many suppliers would undermine rather than strengthen a supplier partnership.

B   **Correct.** The passage indicates that supplier partnerships, by definition, reduce the supplier's exposure to competition, and it can be inferred from this that a purchaser in such a partnership could sometimes pay more for the supplied goods or services than if not in the partnership.

C   The passage is silent on how supplier partnerships are initiated, and the passage gives no reason to believe that these would usually be initiated by suppliers.

D   The passage indicates that supplier partnerships are usually instituted for the supply of goods or services that do not contribute directly to the company's end products, though the passage gives no reason to believe that such partnerships would never make sense for supply of items directly related to end products.

E   The passage states that where alternative suppliers for certain goods or services are few and change from an existing supplier is difficult, partnerships may be "unavoidable." This seems to imply that in such cases, supplier partnerships are the most appropriate.

The correct answer is B.

RC00394-03

511. Which of the following best describes the relation of the second paragraph to the first?

(A) The second paragraph offers proof of an assertion made in the first paragraph.

(B) The second paragraph provides an explanation for the occurrence of a situation described in the first paragraph.

(C) The second paragraph discusses the application of a strategy proposed in the first paragraph.

(D) The second paragraph examines the scope of a problem presented in the first paragraph.

(E) The second paragraph discusses the contradictions inherent in a relationship described in the first paragraph.

Evaluation

The first paragraph recommends that a corporate purchaser of certain categories of goods and services should consider two variables to evaluate how, if at all, it might exert pressure on a supplier to gain economic advantage. Applying the two variables, the second paragraph identifies four different scenarios and, for each scenario, explains how the purchaser can gain some economic advantage.

A   The second paragraph is not focused on proving anything; rather it conducts an analysis of the ways in which, under various conditions, a corporate purchaser can gain economic advantage from a supplier.

B   The second paragraph conducts an analysis of various situations affecting the feasibility of a purchaser's exerting pressure to gain economic advantage from a supplier; it is not focused on explaining what causes the occurrence of any situation mentioned in the first paragraph.

C   **Correct.** The first paragraph recommends that corporate purchasers consider two variables in analyzing the feasibility of exerting pressure on suppliers with a view to economic advantage; the second paragraph shows how purchasers can apply those variables to identify four different types of situations affecting the degree to which economic advantage can be gained by exerting competitive pressure.

D   The first paragraph is not focused on presenting a problem, but rather on indicating an approach that purchasers might use in evaluating the feasibility of exerting economic pressure on suppliers with a view to economic advantage. The second paragraph elaborates on the suggested approach.

E   The second paragraph does not characterize as contradictory any relationship involved in the four types of situations it discusses. The first paragraph discusses supplier partnerships and identifies a disadvantage that they sometimes involve for purchasers; but the discussion in the second paragraph does not focus exclusively on situations that involve a supplier partnership.

The correct answer is C.

RC00394-04

512. It can be inferred that the author of the passage would be most likely to make which of the following recommendations to a company purchasing health care benefits for its employees?

(A)   Devise strategies for circumventing the obstacles to replacing the current provider of health care benefits.

(B)   Obtain health care benefits from a provider that also provides other indirect products and services.

(C)   Obtain bids from other providers of health care benefits in order to be in a position to negotiate a better deal with the current provider.

(D)   Switch providers of health care benefits whenever a different provider offers a more competitive price.

(E)   Acknowledge the difficulties involved in replacing the current provider of health care benefits and offer to form a partnership with the provider.

Inference

In the passage, health care benefits are used as an example of a Type 2 situation, where there are many competing providers, but where changing from one provider to another is difficult. In Type 2 situations, the author of the passage recommends that the corporate purchaser examine the alternative providers to provide leverage in bargaining with the existing provider.

A   Presumably handling any obstacles to replacement would be necessary if a corporate purchaser had decided to change providers. The author of the passage does not preclude the possibility that this may sometimes be a reasonable decision but does not recommend it.

B   The author of the passage does not consider such a possibility, and does not even recommend switching from the existing provider in a Type 2 situation.

C   **Correct.** The recommendation offered in the passage is to review competitive alternatives to the existing provider, with a view to bargaining effectively for better terms with the existing provider.

D   As already noted, the author of the passage does not recommend switching from the existing provider, but recommends reviewing competitive alternatives to exert pressure on the existing provider to grant more favorable terms.

E   The author of the passage does not recommend this course of action in a Type 2 situation, which the corporate purchase of health care benefits exemplifies. The only situation in which the author views a supplier partnership as possibly the best of a set of bad options is a Type 4 situation, where there are few competitive alternatives available and change is difficult.

The correct answer is C.

513. Which of the following is one difference between Type 2 situations and Type 4 situations, as they are described in the passage?

(A) The number of alternative suppliers available to the purchaser

(B) The most effective approach for the purchaser to use in obtaining competitive bids from potential suppliers

(C) The degree of difficulty the purchaser encounters when changing suppliers

(D) The frequency with which each type of situation occurs in a typical business environment

(E) The likelihood that any given purchase will be an indirect purchase

Evaluation

According to the passage, Type 2 situations are those where there are several competitive alternative suppliers available but where changing from the existing supplier would be difficult. Type 4 situations are those where there are few competitive alternative suppliers and changing from the existing supplier would be difficult.

A **Correct.** The two types of situations differ in the number of competitive alternatives to the existing supplier that are available: in Type 2 situations there are several; in Type 4 situations there are few.

B How should the prospective purchaser ensure that potential suppliers submit truly competitive bids, or can a prospective purchaser even ensure it? The passage gives no answer to such questions that helps to identify a difference between the two types of situations.

C In both types of situations as described in the passage, changing to a new supplier is difficult, and no difference in the degree of difficulty is mentioned.

D How frequently each of the two types of situations typically occur is not addressed in the passage.

E Indirect purchases, as described in the passage, are goods or services that are not embodied in the corporation's end products. Many corporate producers currently make indirect purchases such as computers or business consultancy services. The passage does not compare the proportion of a corporation's total purchases that are indirect (the proportion would presumably vary widely depending on the nature of a corporation's production); so the passage provides no rational basis for estimating a universally applicable likelihood that a given purchase would be indirect.

The correct answer is A.

514. According to the passage, which of the following factors distinguishes an indirect purchase from other purchases?

(A) The ability of the purchasing company to subject potential suppliers of the purchased item to competitive scrutiny

(B) The number of suppliers of the purchased item available to the purchasing company

(C) The methods of negotiation that are available to the purchasing company

(D) The relationship of the purchased item to the purchasing company's end product

(E) The degree of importance of the purchased item in the purchasing company's business operations

Supporting ideas

The passage characterizes a purchase of goods or services as indirect when the goods or services are not directly related to the end products of the purchasing corporation. Examples given are computers, advertising, and legal services. By implication, direct purchases by an automobile manufacturer could include steel, batteries, and tires: these would obviously be inputs embodied in the final products.

A   The passage suggests that "competitive scrutiny" is typically applied only to suppliers of direct purchases, but makes the case that it could be applied also to suppliers of indirect purchases. The exposure to competitive scrutiny is not the characteristic that the passage uses to distinguish direct from indirect purchases.

B   The number of available suppliers clearly can vary for both direct purchases and indirect purchases, and the passage provides no reason to think otherwise.

C   The passage provides no information about the methods of negotiation that are available for direct purchases. The passage does not base the distinction between direct and indirect purchases on differences in methods of negotiation.

D   **Correct.** The passage defines direct purchases as those directly related to the purchasing firm's end products; indirect purchases are purchases that are not related to the end products.

E   The type of purchase—direct or indirect—is not, according to the passage, determined by the degree of importance of the purchase in facilitating the purchasing firm's business operations. For example, purchase of advertising by an accounting firm could be critically important for success of the firm's business operations, but such a purchase would likely count as indirect, given the way the passage defines indirect purchases.

The correct answer is D.

Questions 515–519 refer to the passage on page 422.

RC00423-01

515. According to the "conventional view" referred to in line 13 of the passage, brighter carotenoid-based coloration in certain species suggests that an individual

(A) lives in a habitat rich in carotenoid-bearing plants and insects

(B) has efficient detoxification processes

(C) has a superior immune system

(D) possesses superior foraging capacity

(E) is currently capable of reproducing

Supporting ideas

According to the passage, the conventional view is that carotenoids in a male animal—recognizable by brighter coloration—are meaningful in the context of mate selection because they are rare and not easily acquired. A male that displays brighter coloration than other males would appear to a female of the species to have foraged more effectively and would therefore seem healthier, and more eligible as a mate, than some less brightly colored males.

A   Male animals in a carotenoid-rich environment might, on average, have brighter coloration, but the passage does not imply that this is part of the conventional view. The passage represents the conventional view as emphasizing the rarity of carotenoids, and the consequent difficulty of finding them.

B   The conventional view holds that a brightly colored male might appear healthier than less brightly colored males to a female of the species. If the male were healthier, this would presumably require having efficient detoxification processes. But the passage does not treat this as part of the conventional view.

C   If a male animal is healthier than other males of the species, presumably that male has a superior immune system, but the passage does not represent this as part of the conventional view.

D   **Correct.** The passage represents the conventional view as holding that more brightly colored males seem to females to be more effective foragers, and therefore healthier.

E   The passage does not represent the conventional view as holding that brighter coloration in a male animal would be taken by a female of the species as indicating a current ability to reproduce.

The correct answer is D.

516. The idea that carotenoid-based coloration is significant partly because carotenoids are required for health suggests that a lack of bright coloration in a male is most likely to indicate which of the following?

(A) Inefficient detoxification processes
(B) Immunity to parasite infestation
(C) Low genetic resistance to disease
(D) Lack of interest in mating
(E) Lack of carotenoid-storing tissues

Inference

The passage states that carotenoids are used by the immune system and for detoxification processes that help maintain health. Males that are more susceptible to disease and parasites, i.e., males that lack high genetic resistance to such things, must use up the carotenoids they accumulate to boost their immune systems. The passage suggests that consequently male animals perceived by females of the species as having used up their carotenoids would be perceived as having relatively low genetic resistance to disease and parasites.

A   Even if an animal has efficient detoxification processes, the passage suggests that carotenoids would be used up in such processes. Thus, having relatively less bright coloration (and therefore less carotenoids) would not necessarily indicate inefficient detoxification processes.

B   The information in the passage suggests that having low genetic resistance to parasite infections is consistent with having immunity to at least some parasite infections, because carotenoids can be used to boost immunity. But this comes at the cost of lacking bright coloration.

C   **Correct.** The passage indicates that a male's having relatively bright coloration could indicate relatively high genetic resistance to disease, and having relatively less bright coloration could indicate relatively low genetic resistance, because the carotenoids that create bright coloration would have been used to boost immunity or aid detoxification processes.

D   The passage does not suggest that male animals lacking bright coloration would be perceived by a female of the species as lacking interest in mating.

E   The passage does not address the issue of whether carotenoid-storing tissues may be lacking in a male of a species that would normally have such tissues. The passage only states that "many" animal species use colorful signals made possible by carotenoids.

The correct answer is C.

517. The passage suggests that relatively bright carotenoid-based coloration is a signal of which of the following characteristics in males of certain animal species?

(A) Readiness for mating behavior
(B) Ability to fight
(C) Particular feeding preferences
(D) Recovery from parasite infestation
(E) Fitness as a mate

Application

According to the passage, "studies of several animal species have shown that when choosing mates, females prefer males with brighter, carotenoid-based coloration." The passage examines two mechanisms by which carotenoid-based coloration might affect mate selection: either signaling good health or signaling high genetic resistance to infection. It is implicit in the discussion that whichever mechanism is in question, bright coloration would function to signal fitness as a mate.

A   The passage discusses how bright carotenoid-based coloration may affect mate selection but does not cite perceived bright coloration as signaling readiness for mating behavior.

B   The passage suggests that bright carotenoid-based coloration tends to signal good health or genetic resistance to factors that cause illness. The passage does not refer to ability to fight.

C   The passage does not refer to feeding preferences, but only indicates that animals with bright carotenoid-based coloration would have consumed organisms that are rich in carotenoids.

D The passage explores the possibility that bright carotenoid-based coloration could signal high genetic resistance to infection, but implies that recovery from infection could arise from strong immune resistance rather than from high genetic resistance, and could be signaled by lack of carotenoid-based brightness.

E **Correct.** The passage discussion indicates that, whatever the precise mechanism, bright carotenoid-based coloration in males of certain species functions to signal fitness as a mate.

The correct answer is E.

RC00423-04

518. The passage implies which of the following about the insects from which animals acquire carotenoids?

(A) They do not produce carotenoids themselves.
(B) They use carotenoids primarily for coloration.
(C) They maintain constant levels of carotenoids in their tissues.
(D) They are unable to use carotenoids to boost their immune system.
(E) They are available in greater abundance than are carotenoid-bearing plants.

Inference

The passage says that animals "acquire carotenoids either directly (from the plants and algae that produce them) or indirectly (by eating insects)."

A **Correct.** The passage indicates that the phrase *acquire .... directly* signifies in this context acquisition from the ultimate source of carotenoids, so the phrase *acquire ... indirectly* signifies an acquisition that is not from the ultimate source. This implies that insects do not produce their own carotenoids, but derive them by consuming plants, algae, or other insects.

B This may well be true of some insects, but no information in the passage implies it.

C No information in the passage implies that carotenoid levels in insect tissue remain constant over time.

D The passage contains no information that relates to the immune system of any insect species.

E Even if this is true, the passage contains no information that implies it.

The correct answer is A.

RC00423-05

519. Information in the passage suggests that which of the following is true of carotenoids that a male animal uses for detoxification processes?

(A) They were not acquired directly from plants and algae.
(B) They cannot be replenished through foraging.
(C) They cannot be used simultaneously to brighten coloration.
(D) They do not affect the animal's susceptibility to parasites.
(E) They increase the chances that the animal will be selected as a mate.

Inference

The passage states that carotenoids are used by the immune system and for detoxification processes. To the extent that any carotenoids are used for these purposes, the passage suggests, they would not also be available for bright-colored display to potential mates.

A The passage states that animals can acquire carotenoids from insects, as well as from plants and algae. Nothing indicates that a male animal's use of the carotenoids would determine which of these sources they are acquired from.

B No information in the passage suggests this. The passage tells us that males acquire carotenoids by foraging.

C **Correct.** The passage implies that the quantity of carotenoids used for detoxification is no longer available for any other purpose, such as display of bright coloration.

D The passage suggests that carotenoids could benefit immune response; this implies the possibility of better resistance to parasitic infections.

E The passage conjectures that a male animal's use of carotenoids for detoxification processes could reduce the chances of being selected as a mate.

The correct answer is C.

7.6 Reading Comprehension Answer Explanations

Questions 520–524 refer to the passage on page 424.

RC00349-02

520. According to the passage, Kerber maintained that which of the following led to an increase in educational opportunities for women in the United States after the American Revolution?

(A) An unprecedented demand by women for greater educational opportunities in the decades following the Revolution

(B) A new political ideology calling for equality of opportunity between women and men in all aspects of life

(C) A belief that the American educational system could be reformed only if women participated more fully in that system

(D) A belief that women needed to be educated if they were to contribute to the success of the nation's new form of government

(E) A recognition that women needed to be educated if they were to take an active role in the nation's schools and churches

Supporting ideas

The passage ascribes to Linda Kerber the claim that there was "a surge of educational opportunities for women in the United States" after the American Revolution, and that this surge resulted from a new ideology of "republic motherhood." According to the passage, Kerber argued that the nation's leaders advocated education for women to equip them, in their family role, to raise politically virtuous sons.

A The passage attributes no claim to Kerber concerning a demand by women for education.

B The passage attributes no claim to Kerber concerning a new ideology calling for equality between women and men.

C Kerber's argument as represented in the passage did not claim that an increase in education opportunities for women resulted from a belief that such an increase was required for successful reform of the American educational system.

D **Correct.** According to the passage, Kerber argued that educational opportunities for women increased because the nation's leaders believed that successful democratic government would require that women raise politically virtuous sons within their families, and that women could do so only if they had access to education themselves.

E According to the passage, Kerber's thesis primarily concerns the roles that it was believed educated women could play in raising politically virtuous sons in the context of the family, not in the nation's schools or churches.

The correct answer is D.

RC00349-03

521. According to the passage, within the field of educational history, Thomas Woody's 1929 work was

(A) innovative because it relied on newspaper advertisements as evidence

(B) exceptional in that it concentrated on the period before the American Revolution

(C) unusual in that it focused on educational attitudes rather than on educational practices

(D) controversial in its claims regarding educational opportunities for boys

(E) atypical in that it examined the education of girls

Supporting ideas

According to the passage, Woody's work was a "notable exception" as contrast to the work of other educational historians, who "barely mentioned women and girls."

A Other historians prior to Woody's 1929 work may have used newspaper advertisements as evidence, but the passage provides no information as to whether this was so.

B The passage is silent as to whether educational historians besides Woody concentrated on the period before the American Revolution.

C The passage does not provide information as to the extent to which either Woody or other historians focused on educational attitudes as opposed to educational practices.

497

D   According to the passage, Woody noted that educational opportunities increased for both girls and boys around 1750. But the passage does not indicate that this claim, or any other claim Woody may have made about educational opportunities for boys, was controversial.

E   **Correct.** As stated above, the passage describes Woody's work as a "notable exception," i.e., atypical, with respect to his discussion of education for girls.

The correct answer is E.

RC00349-04

522. The passage suggests that Woody would have agreed with which of the following claims regarding "An Essay on Woman"?

(A) It expressed attitudes concerning women's education that were reflected in new educational opportunities for women after 1750.

(B) It persuaded educators to offer greater educational opportunities to women in the 1750s.

(C) It articulated ideas about women's education that would not be realized until after the American Revolution.

(D) It offered one of the most original arguments in favor of women's education in the United States in the eighteenth century.

(E) It presented views about women's education that were still controversial in Woody's own time.

Application

According to the passage, Woody characterized "An Essay on Woman" (1753) as reflecting a shift in view, and the context indicates that this shift concerned new attitudes that accompanied increased opportunities after 1750 for girls to become educated women.

A   **Correct.** Based on the passage, this is a claim with which Woody would likely have agreed.

B   The passage represents Woody as claiming that "An Essay on Woman" reflected changes that had already occurred around 1750. The passage does not indicate whether Woody would have agreed with this claim about a persuasive effect on educators.

C   Nothing in the passage represents Woody as thinking that "An Essay on Woman" had ideas about women's education that did not come to fruition until after the American Revolution. The tenor of Woody's thinking, as the passage represents it, is that the essay reflected changes already occurring.

D   The passage indicates that Woody characterizes "An Essay on Woman" as "reflecting" a view that had already gained some currency; so it is unlikely that Woody saw the essay as offering any highly original arguments in favor of women's education.

E   It may be true that "An Essay on Woman" presented some views that were at least somewhat controversial even around 1929, but the passage provides no information that addresses this point.

The correct answer is A.

RC00349-05

523. The passage suggests that, with regard to the history of women's education in the United States, Kerber's work differs from Woody's primarily concerning which of the following?

(A) The extent to which women were interested in pursuing educational opportunities in the eighteenth century

(B) The extent of the support for educational opportunities for girls prior to the American Revolution

(C) The extent of public resistance to educational opportunities for women after the American Revolution

(D) Whether attitudes toward women's educational opportunities changed during the eighteenth century

(E) Whether women needed to be educated in order to contribute to the success of a republican form of government

Evaluation

The passage represents Kerber as claiming that the American Revolution led to a surge in educational opportunities for women because the nation's leaders believed women needed to be educated if they were to raise politically virtuous sons. Woody, however, is represented as claiming that there was a significant increase in such opportunities and significant advocacy for women's education well before the Revolution.

7.6 Reading Comprehension Answer Explanations

A The passage does not represent either Kerber or Woody as addressing the extent to which women were interested in pursuing educational opportunities in the eighteenth century.

B **Correct.** The passage attributes to Woody the view that "practical education for females had many advocates before the Revolution," notably in the 1750s, and that the Revolution at most accelerated an earlier trend of changing attitudes. This is contrary to the views attributed to Kerber.

C The passage gives no information as to whether Kerber or Woody addresses this issue, nor does it discuss to what extent, if any, such resistance may have occurred.

D The passage indicates that Kerber and Woody hold that there was a change in attitudes toward women's educational opportunities during the eighteenth century, disagreeing, however, as to whether the most significant change occurred before or after the Revolution.

E Neither Kerber nor Woody is represented by the passage as holding divergent views on this point, and it would be reasonable to think that they may have agreed.

The correct answer is B.

RC00349-06

524. According to the passage, Kerber argued that political leaders thought that the form of government adopted by the United States after the American Revolution depended on which of the following for its success?

(A) Women assuming the sole responsibility for instilling political virtue in children
(B) Girls becoming the primary focus of a reformed educational system that emphasized political virtue
(C) The family serving as one of the primary means by which children were imbued with political virtue
(D) The family assuming many of the functions previously performed by schools and churches
(E) Men and women assuming equal responsibility for the management of schools, churches, and the family

Supporting ideas

The passage attributes to Kerber the claim that the nation's leaders believed a virtuous citizenry was essential to the success of the nation's republican form of government, and that women would play a primary role in raising future citizens who would be politically virtuous.

A According to the passage, Kerber indicates that the nation's leaders believed churches and schools, as well as families, would work to imbue political virtue, though they emphasized the crucial role of families.

B Kerber argues that the educational system underwent reform in the sense that educational opportunities for women increased; but does not claim that schools or families would change focus to imbue girls with political virtue.

C **Correct.** Kerber argues that political leaders emphasized the family as the primary means by which future citizens would be imbued with political virtue.

D Kerber does not claim the nation's leaders proposed that the family would take over functions previously fulfilled by schools and churches.

E Kerber does not attribute to the nation's leaders the view that men and women would exercise equal roles in managing schools, churches, and the family.

The correct answer is C.

Questions 525–527 refer to the passage on page 426.

RC00633-01

525. The primary purpose of the passage is to

(A) compare the adaptive responses of several species of columnar cacti in the Sonoran Desert with those in the arid tropical regions of southern Mexico
(B) discuss some of the possible causes of the relatively low abundance of migratory nectar-feeding bats in the Sonoran Desert
(C) provide a possible explanation for a particular evolutionary change in certain species of columnar cacti in the Sonoran Desert
(D) present recent findings that challenge a particular theory as to why several species of columnar cacti in the Sonoran Desert have expanded their range of pollinators

499

(E) compare the effectiveness of nocturnal and diurnal pollination for several different species of columnar cacti in the Sonoran Desert

Main idea

This question depends on understanding the passage as a whole. The first paragraph discusses an evolutionary change undergone by columnar cacti in the Sonoran Desert with regard to pollination. The second paragraph offers a possible reason for this change—migratory nectar-feeding bats are unreliable pollinators—and the third paragraph goes on to provide evidence that supports the reason given in the second paragraph.

A The passage does compare the adaptations of cacti in the Sonoran Desert with those of cacti in southern Mexico, but it does so in support of a larger point about the Sonoran Desert cacti.

B The relatively low abundance of migratory nectar-feeding bats in the Sonoran Desert is important to the passage in that it provides a reason why the columnar cacti in that region have made certain adaptations. But the passage does not explain why the bats are not particularly abundant.

C **Correct.** The flowers of the columnar cacti in the Sonoran Desert have evolved to remain open after sunrise, and the passage is primarily concerned with explaining why this change may have taken place.

D The passage presents recent findings that support, rather than challenge, a theory as to why the columnar cacti of the Sonoran Desert have expanded their range of pollinators. The passage does not allude to any competing theory that may be challenged by the findings.

E Any comparison of the effectiveness of nocturnal and diurnal pollination for columnar cacti in the Sonoran Desert is made in support of the passage's primary concern: explaining why these cacti have come to remain open and receptive to pollination in daylight.

The correct answer is C.

526. According to the passage, which of the following types of nectar-feeding pollinators is likely to be an unreliable pollinator of a particular cactus flower?

(A) A dietary specialist whose abundance is typically high in relation to that of the flower
(B) A dietary specialist whose abundance is at times significantly lower than that of the flower
(C) A dietary generalist for whom that flower's nectar is not a preferred food but is the most consistently available food
(D) A dietary generalist for whom that flower's nectar is slightly preferred to other available foods
(E) A dietary generalist that evolved from a species of dietary specialists

Supporting idea

This question depends on recognizing the qualities of an unreliable pollinator, as described in the passage. The second paragraph addresses this issue: it explains that the unreliability of pollinators can arise in any of three ways: they may be dietary generalists with alternative sources of food; they may be dietary specialists whose own abundance varies; or they may be dietary specialists whose abundance is chronically low in relation to the flowers.

A A dietary specialist whose abundance is high in relation to the flowers on which it feeds would likely be a reliable pollinator.

B **Correct.** A dietary specialist whose abundance is at times significantly lower than that of the flower it pollinates would be, according to the passage, unreliable.

C A dietary generalist who finds the flower of a particular species more consistently available than other suitable food sources would most likely be a reliable pollinator of that flower.

D A dietary generalist who prefers the flower's nectar would likely be a reliable pollinator of that flower compared to other flowers.

E The passage provides no reason to believe that the evolution of a pollinator's dietary preference has any bearing on its reliability as a pollinator.

The correct answer is B.

527. According to the passage, present-day columnar cacti in the Sonoran Desert differ from their close relatives in southern Mexico in that the Sonoran cacti

(A) have flowers that remain open after sunset
(B) are pollinated primarily by dietary specialists
(C) can be pollinated by nectar-feeding bats
(D) have stigmas that are unreceptive to pollination at night
(E) are sometimes pollinated by diurnal pollinators

Supporting idea

This question depends on identifying a difference noted in the passage between columnar cacti in the Sonoran Desert and their relatives in southern Mexico. The first paragraph states that in southern Mexico, columnar cactus flowers are not receptive to pollination by diurnal pollinators, whereas in the Sonoran Desert, the flowers have evolved to allow diurnal pollination.

A The cacti in both the Sonoran Desert and southern Mexico have flowers that remain open after sunset, because cacti in both locations can be pollinated nocturnally.
B Sonoran Desert cacti are pollinated, at least partially, by nectar-feeding bats, which are dietary specialists. But the cacti in southern Mexico are pollinated by these specialists, too.
C Sonoran Desert cacti can be pollinated by nectar-feeding bats—but so can cacti in southern Mexico.
D Cacti in the Sonoran Desert have stigmas that have evolved to be receptive to pollination both at night and during the day.
E **Correct.** The distinction between cacti in the Sonoran Desert and those in southern Mexico is that Sonoran Desert cacti have evolved to allow pollination during the day—that is, pollination by diurnal pollinators.

The correct answer is E.

Questions 528–532 refer to the passage on page 428.
RC00121-01

528. The passage suggests that in order for a manufacturer in a capital-intensive industry to have a decisive advantage over competitors making similar products, the manufacturer must

(A) be the first in the industry to build production facilities of theoretically optimal size
(B) make every effort to keep fixed and sunk costs as low as possible
(C) be one of the first to operate its manufacturing plants at minimum efficient scale
(D) produce goods of higher quality than those produced by direct competitors
(E) stockpile raw materials at production sites in order to ensure a steady flow of such materials

Inference

This question asks for an inference about what a manufacturer in a capital-intensive industry must do to have an advantage over competitors making similar products. The passage addresses this question by stating that advantage accrues to those firms that are the first to exploit the full potential of optimally sized, technologically sophisticated plants. In this context, exploiting the full potential of such plants means operating them at *minimum efficient scale*. Based on the definition in the first paragraph, this means that the plant must have an output of such a size that the cost per unit of output is at a minimum.

A The passage says that for new capital-intensive firms to dominate the market, it is not enough for them to have optimally sized plants; the plants must also be operated in a way that fully exploits their potential.
B While keeping fixed and sunk costs low would obviously help keep overall costs low, the passage does not suggest that this is decisive in enabling a firm to have an advantage over competitors.
C **Correct.** Being among the first manufacturers to operate plants at minimum efficient scale means that those plants are being exploited to their full potential. This strategy would most likely give such manufacturers a decisive advantage over new firms hoping to compete effectively.
D The passage does not discuss the quality of goods made by manufacturers.
E The passage does not suggest that stockpiling raw materials is the most efficient way to ensure a steady flow of raw materials into the manufacturing process, though the passage states that such a steady flow is a factor in achieving minimum efficient scale.

The correct answer is C.

RC00121-02
529. The passage suggests that which of the following is true of a manufacturer's fixed and sunk costs?

(A) The extent to which they are determined by market conditions for the goods being manufactured is frequently underestimated.
(B) If they are kept as low as possible, the manufacturer is very likely to realize significant profits.
(C) They are the primary factor that determines whether a manufacturer will realize economies of scale.
(D) They should be on a par with the fixed and sunk costs of the manufacturer's competitors.
(E) They are not affected by fluctuations in a manufacturing plant's throughput.

Inference

This question asks about what the passage implies about fixed and sunk costs. The passage states that when production declines due to certain factors, such costs remain at the same level (which may be high), and the cost per unit produced (*unit costs*) rises sharply.

A The passage discusses the impact of market conditions on determining what the optimal size of a manufacturing plant is (which affects fixed and sunk costs). But it makes no claim about the frequency with which such an impact is "underestimated."

B The passage emphasizes that failing to keep throughput at an efficiently high level reduces profitability because that failure results in increased cost per unit (to which, of course, the plant's fixed and sunk costs contribute). But the passage does not claim that keeping aggregate fixed and sunk costs very low is necessary in order to have the most competitive production operation.

C The passage emphasizes that the crucial factor in achieving economies of scale is efficient operation of the production facilities, not the size of the firm's fixed and sunk costs (even though such costs are clearly in part determined by the size and design of the production facilities).

D While a manufacturer's fixed and sunk costs may be on a par with those of the manufacturer's competitors, the passage provides no grounds for inferring that there is any need for them to be (for example,

physical plants that employ different technologies may have different price tags).

E **Correct.** According to the passage, "throughput" refers to the flow of materials through a plant. This flow can vary as a result of various factors, but fixed and sunk costs—financial resources already committed—remain the same regardless of such variation.

The correct answer is E.

RC00121-03
530. In the context of the passage as a whole, the second paragraph serves primarily to

(A) provide an example to support the argument presented in the first paragraph
(B) evaluate various strategies discussed in the first paragraph
(C) introduce evidence that undermines the argument presented in the first paragraph
(D) anticipate possible objections to the argument presented in the first paragraph
(E) demonstrate the potential dangers of a commonly used strategy

Evaluation

This question asks about the rhetorical function of the second paragraph. While the first paragraph argues that a crucial factor in achieving economies of scale is intangible capital, or organized human capabilities, the second paragraph uses the example of new capital-intensive manufacturing industries to help show that this is indeed the case.

A **Correct.** The second paragraph provides an example that illustrates the claims made in the first paragraph. It discusses the way in which intangible capital—e.g., distribution networks, marketing systems, smooth production processes, and qualified management teams—enables manufacturers in new capital-intensive manufacturing industries to realize economies of scale and achieve market dominance.

B The second paragraph does, in a sense, "evaluate" investment in intangible capital: it suggests that such investment is necessary. However, investment in intangible capital is the only strategy it discusses.

C   The second paragraph supports rather than undermines the first paragraph's argument.
D   Nothing in the second paragraph suggests that there are, or could be, any objections to the first paragraph's argument.
E   The second paragraph discusses the potential positive outcomes of investing in intangible capital. It suggests that there might be negative consequences to not making such investments, but it does not indicate that avoiding such investments is a commonly used strategy.

The correct answer is A.

RC00121-05
531. The passage LEAST supports the inference that a manufacturer's throughput could be adversely affected by

(A)   a mistake in judgment regarding the selection of a wholesaler
(B)   a breakdown in the factory's machinery
(C)   a labor dispute on the factory floor
(D)   an increase in the cost per unit of output
(E)   a drop in the efficiency of the sales network

Application

This question may be best approached by using an elimination strategy—first finding the four choices that can reasonably be inferred from the passage, and then checking to make sure that the remaining choice cannot reasonably be inferred. This requires understanding the information the passage gives about throughput, then making inferences about what can cause throughput to drop. The passage defines throughput generally as *the flow of materials through a plant* and goes on to explain that it involves coordination of the production process itself, as well as obtaining materials from suppliers and marketing and distributing the manufactured products. Anything that damages this flow of materials and products would be said to have an adverse effect on throughput.

A   Making a poor judgment about a wholesaler would most likely have an adverse effect on throughput, in that it could affect *the flow of output to wholesalers and final consumers*.

B   A breakdown in machinery would likely fall into the category of *problems on the factory floor* mentioned in the passage and would likely prove damaging to throughput because of its effect on the production process itself.
C   A labor dispute would also likely fall into the category of *problems on the factory floor* mentioned in the passage and would probably cause a decline in production and thus adversely affect throughput.
D   **Correct.** The passage emphasizes that changes in throughput can cause increases or decreases in costs per unit. But the passage is not committed to any claims about how changes in costs per unit might affect throughput.
E   The passage suggests that inefficient sales networks could cause a decline in production. Thus a decrease in sales efficiency would most likely adversely affect a manufacturer's ability to provide goods to consumers, and thus would create problems with throughput.

The correct answer is D.

RC00121-07
532. The primary purpose of the passage is to

(A)   point out the importance of intangible capital for realizing economies of scale in manufacturing
(B)   show that manufacturers frequently gain a competitive advantage from investment in large manufacturing facilities
(C)   argue that large manufacturing facilities often fail because of inadequate investment in both tangible and intangible capital
(D)   suggest that most new industries are likely to be dominated by firms that build large manufacturing plants early
(E)   explain why large manufacturing plants usually do not help manufacturers achieve economies of scale

Main idea

This question depends on understanding the passage as a whole. In general, it makes an argument for investing in intangible capital as a way for manufacturers to realize economies of scale, and it supports its argument with an example.

A **Correct.** The passage focuses on intangible capital as a crucial factor in realizing economies of scale.
B According to the passage, manufacturers gain competitive advantage by building plants of optimal size that they then fully exploit; nothing in the passage suggests that large plants are frequently optimal.
C The passage assumes that manufacturers invest appropriately in tangible capital and argues that it is important for them to invest in intangible capital as well.
D The passage states that new capital-intensive manufacturing industries are dominated not by firms that are the first to build large plants, but by firms that exploit the full potential of their plants.
E The passage indicates that economies of scale can be achieved in plants of optimal size. The passage does not suggest that large plants cannot be optimal.

The correct answer is A.

Questions 533–538 refer to the passage on page 430.

RC00120-05
533. The primary purpose of the passage is to

(A) describe the development of new techniques that may help to determine the driving force behind population cycles in lepidoptera
(B) present evidence that refutes a particular theory about the driving force behind population cycles in lepidoptera
(C) present a hypothesis about the driving force behind population cycles in lepidoptera
(D) describe the fluctuating patterns of population cycles in lepidoptera
(E) question the idea that a single driving force is behind population cycles in lepidoptera

Main idea

This question depends on understanding the passage as a whole in order to identify its purpose. The first paragraph defines population cycles of lepidoptera and discusses some ways those cycles have been studied. It suggests that a particular agent may regulate these cycles. The second paragraph describes a candidate for this agent: nuclear polyhedrosis viruses. The third paragraph explains why this hypothesis is compelling.

A The passage mentions new techniques in molecular biology, but it does so in order to explain why a particular candidate for the agent behind population cycles has come to light.
B The theory the passage presents is that there is a driving force behind lepidoptera population cycles. It does not refute this theory; rather, it offers a convincing case for nuclear polyhedrosis viruses as that force. It also discusses some previous approaches to seeking plausible hypotheses but does not focus on refuting any particular hypothesis.
C **Correct.** The passage is primarily concerned with presenting the hypothesis that nuclear polyhedrosis viruses are the driving force behind lepidoptera population cycles.
D The first paragraph describes the fluctuating patterns of lepidoptera population cycles, but it does so to explain what population cycles are, so that it can then go on to attempt to account for those cycles.
E The passage is concerned with making a case for nuclear polyhedrosis viruses as the driving force behind at least some lepidoptera population cycles, not with questioning the idea that there is a driving force.

The correct answer is C.

RC00120-06
534. It can be inferred from the passage that the mortality caused by agents such as predatory birds or parasites was measured in an attempt to

(A) develop an explanation for the existence of lepidoptera population cycles
(B) identify behavioral factors in lepidoptera that affect survival rates
(C) identify possible methods for controlling lepidoptera population growth
(D) provide evidence that lepidoptera populations are self-regulating
(E) determine the life stages of lepidoptera at which mortality rates are highest

Inference

The passage states that mortality caused by various agents, birds and parasites among them, was measured because this was the common approach to studying causes of population cycles. This in turn suggests that those scientists engaged in such measuring in the case of lepidoptera were attempting to come up with a definitive explanation for why those lepidoptera population cycles occurred.

- A **Correct.** Measuring mortality caused by various agents was part of the attempt to determine the driving force behind lepidoptera population cycles.
- B The passage does not indicate that behavioral factors in lepidoptera are related to their mortality as caused by agents such as predatory birds or parasites.
- C The passage is concerned not with controlling lepidoptera population growth, but rather with determining why population cycles occur.
- D According to the information in the passage, scientists sought to measure mortality caused by particular agents in order to determine the driving force behind lepidoptera population cycles. In suggesting that mortality caused by these agents is not that force, the measurements may have indicated that the cycles could be self-regulating, but they were not undertaken in order to provide such evidence.
- E The passage discusses mortality primarily in the caterpillar stage and does not suggest that any research was directed toward comparing caterpillar mortality rates with mortality rates in other life stages of the insects.

The correct answer is A.

RC00120-01

535. Which of the following, if true, would most weaken the author's conclusion in lines 18–22 ?

  (A) New research reveals that the number of species of birds and parasites that prey on lepidoptera has dropped significantly in recent years.
  (B) New experiments in which the habitats of lepidoptera are altered in previously untried ways result in the shortening of lepidoptera population cycles.
  (C) Recent experiments have revealed that the nuclear polyhedrosis virus is present in a number of predators and parasites of lepidoptera.
  (D) Differences among the habitats of lepidoptera species make it difficult to assess the effects of weather on lepidoptera population cycles.
  (E) Viral disease is typically observed in a large proportion of the lepidoptera population.

Evaluation

The sentence in question presents the author's conclusion that lepidoptera populations may be self-regulating or regulated by something more closely connected to the insects than predatory birds or parasites are. To weaken that conclusion requires weakening its support, namely, that mortality caused by predators and parasites seems not to affect population cycles, and that changing habitats and reducing populations has not altered population cycles either.

- A A drop in birds and parasites preying on lepidoptera would not weaken the author's conclusion; mortality caused by these predators has not affected population cycles.
- B **Correct.** New experiments involving changes in habitat that did succeed in altering population cycles would suggest that the populations are not in fact self-regulating, and that the search for another cycle-altering agent may be unnecessary.
- C This finding would support the idea that the nuclear polyhedrosis virus is responsible for population cycles—that is, that the virus is the closely connected agent the author concludes is responsible.
- D The suggestion that the effects of weather may not have been adequately assessed is remotely relevant to the author's conclusion, but the mere difficulty of assessing the effects provides no positive reason to suppose that weather may be the cause of the cycles. On the other hand, answer choice B does offer evidence for an alternative explanation.
- E Viral disease is what the author ultimately suggests is the agent that drives the lepidoptera population cycles in question. The wide presence of viruses in lepidoptera could help support the author's conclusion.

The correct answer is B.

536. According to the passage, before the discovery of new techniques for detecting viral DNA, population ecologists believed that viral diseases

(A) were not widely prevalent among insect populations generally
(B) affected only the caterpillar life stage of lepidoptera
(C) were the driving force behind lepidoptera population cycles
(D) attacked already declining caterpillar populations
(E) infected birds and parasites that prey on various species of lepidoptera

Supporting idea

This question addresses what the passage states directly about population ecologists' beliefs regarding viral diseases prior to the discovery of new viral DNA–detection techniques. The second paragraph of the passage states that these ecologists believed viral disease contributed to population decline that was already underway rather than initiating it.

A The second paragraph states that viral disease had been reported; thus, population ecologists were aware of its existence in insect populations. The passage is consistent with ecologists having believed that it was prevalent.
B The passage focuses mainly on the caterpillar life stage of lepidoptera, but there is nothing to suggest that scientists held particular beliefs regarding viral diseases' restriction to that life stage.
C It is after, not before, the discovery of new techniques for detecting viral DNA when populations ecologists came to believe that such diseases were the driving force behind the population cycles.
D **Correct.** As stated in the passage, population ecologists believed that viral diseases contributed to already occurring population decline.
E The passage does not discuss whether viral diseases may infect any lepidoptera predators.

The correct answer is D.

537. According to the passage, nuclear polyhedrosis viruses can remain virulent in the environment only when

(A) the polyhedrin protein crystals dissolve
(B) caterpillar populations are in decline
(C) they are present in large numbers
(D) their concentration in a particular area remains low
(E) they are sheltered from direct sunlight

Supporting idea

The passage states in the second paragraph that these viruses remain virulent for many years if they are protected from direct sunlight. They are embedded in crystals of polyhedrin protein.

A The viruses remain virulent partially because of their being contained in polyhedrin protein crystals. They would most likely not remain virulent if those crystals dissolved.
B The viruses remain virulent even when caterpillar populations are not in decline; that is how the viruses initiate new population declines.
C According to the passage, viral DNA has been detected in the environment at low concentrations, yet the viruses are still virulent. Thus, they need not be present in large numbers.
D Nothing in the passage indicates that the concentration of these viruses must be low for them to be virulent.
E **Correct.** The passage says that if the viruses are protected from direct sunlight, they remain virulent for many years. The context strongly suggests that if they are not so protected, they do not remain virulent.

The correct answer is E.

538. It can be inferred from the passage that while inside its polyhedrin protein crystals, the nuclear polyhedrosis virus

(A) is exposed to direct sunlight
(B) is attractive to predators
(C) cannot infect caterpillars' cells
(D) cannot be ingested by caterpillars
(E)

Inference

The passage indicates that the polyhedrin protein crystals protect the nuclear polyhedrosis virus when it is in the environment. When a caterpillar ingests those crystals, they dissolve. That releases the virus, whereupon it infects the caterpillar's cells. Thus it is reasonable to infer that the virus must be released from the crystals before it can infect the caterpillar.

A

540. Of the following topics, which would be most likely to be studied within the discipline of chemical ecology as it is described in the passage?

- (A) Seeds that become attached to certain insects, which in turn carry away the seeds and aid in the reproductive cycle of the plant species in question
- (B) An insect species that feeds on weeds detrimental to crop health and yield, and how these insects might aid in agricultural production
- (C) The effects of deforestation on the life cycles of subtropical carnivorous plants and the insect species on which the plants feed
- (D) The growth patterns of a particular species of plant that has proved remarkably resistant to herbicides
- (E) Insects that develop a tolerance for feeding on a plant that had previously been toxic to them, and the resultant changes within that plant species

Application

The discipline of chemical ecology, as it is described in the passage, deals with how plants use chemicals to interact with other organisms—in particular, how they defend against attack—and how those interactions have evolved. To be studied within that discipline, a specific topic would need to address some aspect of that chemical interaction.

- A The passage provides no reason to suppose that the topic of seeds and how they travel would be studied within chemical ecology, given that it does not discuss how chemicals might be involved in the reproductive cycle.
- B The passage provides no indication that chemical ecology would be concerned with how weed-destroying insects would aid agricultural production.
- C The passage provides no indication that deforestation would involve plant chemicals or that its effects would be studied in chemical ecology.
- D The passage provides no indication that a plant's resistance to herbicides would be studied in chemical ecology, but the passage does suggest that the focus of chemical ecology is on how plants chemically interact with other organisms.
- E **Correct.** Chemical ecology developed to deal with the interdependence between plants and insects. Insects' developing a tolerance for feeding on a once-toxic plant, and the plants' resultant changes, is a situation of just such interdependence: plants and insects coevolving.

The correct answer is E.

541. The author refers to "bacterial infections" (see line 11) most likely in order to

- (A) describe the physiological function that gum performs in plants
- (B) demonstrate that sap is not the only substance that is transported through a plant's tissues
- (C) explain how modern chemical analysis has been used to clarify the function of resin
- (D) show that gum cannot serve as an effective defense against herbivores
- (E) give an example of how confusion has arisen with regard to the nature of resin

Evaluation

The author mentions *bacterial infections* in the first paragraph as the reason why plants produce the substance known as gum.

- A **Correct.** The author states directly that plants produce gum in response to bacterial infections.
- B The author states directly that sap is transported through plant tissues. The passage does not address the question of whether bacterial infections or anything related to them are similarly transported.
- C The passage indicates that rigorous chemical analysis is now available, but scientists still do not know resin's function. The reference to bacterial infections is related to gum, not resin.
- D The reference to bacterial infections indicates the actual purpose served by gum; it does not function to show ways in which gum is inadequate.
- E Gum itself serves as an example of the confusion surrounding the nature of resin; bacterial infections, to which gum production is a response, do not serve as that example.

The correct answer is A.

542. The author of the passage refers to Pliny most probably in order to

(A) give an example of how the nature of amber has been misunderstood in the past
(B) show that confusion about amber has long been more pervasive than confusion about resin
(C) make note of the first known reference to amber as a semiprecious gem
(D) point out an exception to a generalization about the history of people's understanding of amber
(E) demonstrate that Pliny believed amber to be a mineral

Evaluation

The passage states generally that *amber has been widely misunderstood* but cites Pliny as noting correctly, in the first century, that amber resulted from a substance discharged by trees.

A   Pliny's observation was, according to the author, accurate and not a misunderstanding.
B   The author equates confusion about amber with confusion about resin; the reference to Pliny does not indicate which of the two, amber or resin, has been more widely misunderstood.
C   The author indicates that others, not Pliny, mischaracterized amber as a semiprecious gem—and when that mischaracterization first occurred is not identified.
D   **Correct.** Pliny's recognition that amber came from a substance discharged by trees stands, in the author's account, as an exception to the widespread incorrect identifications of the substance.
E   Others held the belief that amber was a mineral. The passage indicates that Pliny recognized that amber came from trees but provides no evidence that he also considered it a mineral.

The correct answer is D.

Questions 543–545 refer to the passage on page 434.

543. The primary purpose of the passage is to

(A) compare the impact of the Great Depression on Latin America with its impact on the United States
(B) criticize a school of economic historians for failing to analyze the Great Depression in Latin America within a global context
(C) illustrate the risks inherent in comparing different types of economic enterprises to explain economic phenomena
(D) call into question certain scholars' views concerning the severity of the Great Depression in Latin America
(E) demonstrate that the Great Depression had a more severe impact on industry in Latin American than in certain other regions

Main idea

This question depends on understanding the passage as a whole. The passage first describes the view of many economic historians of the 1980s. It next describes the evidence on which that view is based. The remainder of the passage raises issues about the rationale for that view.

A   The comparison between Latin America and the United States is only a small part of a larger argument analyzing studies of the Great Depression in Latin America.
B   The passage does not discuss a global context for the Great Depression.
C   The passage does not primarily aim to illustrate risks that may be generally inherent in explaining economic phenomena.
D   **Correct.** The passage claims that certain scholars underestimate the severity of the Great Depression in Latin America.
E   The passage does not claim that the impact of the Great Depression on Latin American industry was generally more severe than its impact on industry elsewhere.

The correct answer is D.

RC00333-02
544. Which of the following conclusions about the Great Depression is best supported by the passage?

(A) It did not impede Latin American industrial growth as much as historians had previously thought.
(B) It had a more severe impact on the Brazilian and the Mexican textile industries than it had on Latin America as a region.
(C) It affected the Latin American textile industry more severely than it did any other industry in Latin America.
(D) The overall impact on Latin American industrial growth should be reevaluated by economic historians.
(E) Its impact on Latin America should not be compared with its impact on the United States.

Inference

This question asks which conclusion is most strongly supported by the passage. The passage presents the rationale of some historians for their conclusion that the Great Depression did not significantly interfere with economic growth in Latin America. It then critiques that rationale and conclusion. By questioning the historians' claims, the passage suggests that a reevaluation of the Great Depression's effect on Latin America is needed.

A The passage does not significantly support this. The passage indicates that, in fact, the Great Depression impeded Latin American economic development more than some historians had thought.
B The passage does not significantly support this. The passage does not compare the impact on the Brazilian and Mexican textile industries to the impact on the Latin American region.
C The passage does not significantly support this. The passage does not compare the effect of the Great Depression on the textile industry to its effect on other industries.
D **Correct.** As presented in the passage, the passage author's critique of the historians' rationale for their claims provides significant support for the conclusion that their claims should be reevaluated.

E The passage does not significantly support the claim that the comparison in question should not be made.

The correct answer is D.

RC00333-04
545. Which of the following, if true, would most strengthen the author's assertion regarding economic indicators in lines 25–27 ?

(A) During an economic depression, European textile manufacturers' profits rise while their industrial output remains steady.
(B) During a national economic recession, United States microchips manufacturers' profits rise sharply while United States steel manufacturers' profits plunge.
(C) During the years following a severe economic depression, textile manufacturers' output levels and profit levels increase in Brazil and Mexico but not in the rest of Latin America.
(D) Although Japanese industry as a whole recovers after an economic recession, it does not regain its previously high levels of production.
(E) While European industrial output increases in the years following an economic depression, total output remains below that of Japan or the United States.

Application

The question involves applying information from outside the passage to a claim made by the author. The text in lines 25–27 asserts that broad economic indicators pertaining to a nation or region can obscure differences between individual firms or industries within that nation or region. The question asks which evidence would most strengthen the support for that conclusion.

A This refers only to the relationship between a single industry's profits and its output, not to general economic indicators.
B **Correct.** The phrase *a national recession* refers to a general economic indicator. Suppose that in a situation described as a national recession, one industry (microchip manufacturing) prospers while another industry (steel manufacturing) does not.

This would provide some additional support, over and above that given in the passage, for the assertion that broad economic indicators may mask differences between industries.

C Economic differences between countries do not strengthen the support for the author's assertion regarding variations among different firms and industries in one country or region.

D This has no obvious bearing on how sweeping economic indicators can mask differences between industries or enterprises in a single country or region.

E A comparison of different countries does not pertain to the assertion regarding variation among firms and industries in the same country.

The correct answer is B.

Questions 546–549 refer to the passage on page 436.

RC00272-02

546. It can be inferred from the passage that a large plant might have to spend more than a similar but smaller plant on environmental compliance because the larger plant is

(A) more likely to attract attention from local regulators

(B) less likely to be exempt from permit and reporting requirements

(C) less likely to have regulatory costs passed on to it by companies that supply its raw materials

(D) more likely to employ older production technologies

(E) more likely to generate wastes that are more environmentally damaging than those generated by smaller plants

Inference

This item depends on understanding the implications of the passage's discussion of differences between large and small plants. It asks what might be true of a larger plant that would compel it to spend more than a smaller plant on environmental compliance. The passage addresses this issue by stating that smaller plants are often not subject to the same permit or reporting requirements that larger plants are.

A The likelihood of attracting regulatory attention is discussed only in the context of comparing plants that are *isolated* with small plants that are near large noncompliant ones. The passage does not suggest that size is generally the crucial determining factor in attracting regulatory attention.

B **Correct.** According to the passage, certain permit or reporting requirements may not apply to smaller plants; this suggests that larger plants are less likely than smaller plants to be exempt from these requirements, and thus that the larger plants would have to spend more to comply.

C The passage does not discuss the passing on of regulatory costs from suppliers to plants.

D The passage does not suggest that larger plants are any more likely than smaller plants to employ older production technologies.

E The passage does not distinguish between the types of wastes emitted by larger plants and those emitted by smaller plants.

The correct answer is B.

RC00272-04

547. According to the passage, which of the following statements about sulfur dioxide and nitrogen oxide outputs is true?

(A) Older production technologies cannot be adapted so as to reduce production of these outputs as waste products.

(B) Under the most recent environmental regulations, industrial plants are no longer permitted to produce these outputs.

(C) Although these outputs are environmentally hazardous, some plants still generate them as waste products despite the high compliance costs they impose.

(D) Many older plants have developed innovative technological processes that reduce the amounts of these outputs generated as waste products.

(E) Since the production processes that generate these outputs are less costly than alternative processes, these less expensive processes are sometimes adopted despite their acknowledged environmental hazards.

Supporting idea

This item depends on identifying what the passage states explicitly about outputs of sulfur dioxide and nitrogen oxide. The passage says that plants that produce these outputs are those that use older industrial coal-fired burners, and that such plants are subject to extensive compliance costs imposed by new regulations.

A   The passage does not address the question of whether older production technologies might be adapted to reduce outputs of sulfur dioxide and nitrogen oxide.
B   The passage states that new regulations have imposed high compliance costs on companies that produce sulfur dioxide and nitrogen oxide outputs, not that these outputs are prohibited.
C   **Correct.** The passage states that some companies are still using the older kinds of burners that generate sulfur dioxide and nitrogen oxide outputs, and that new regulations have imposed high compliance costs on these companies.
D   The passage does not address the question of whether older plants have developed new processes to reduce the amounts of sulfur dioxide and nitrogen oxide they produce.
E   Sulfur dioxide and nitrogen oxide outputs, the passage suggests, are produced only by older industrial coal-fired burners; newer facilities (using alternative processes) do not employ this technology, the expense of which is not mentioned in the passage.

The correct answer is C.

548. Which of the following best describes the relationship of the statement about large plants (lines 12–17) to the passage as a whole?

(A)   It presents a hypothesis that is disproved later in the passage.
(B)   It highlights an opposition between two ideas mentioned in the passage.
(C)   It provides examples to support a claim made earlier in the passage.
(D)   It exemplifies a misconception mentioned earlier in the passage.
(E)   It draws an analogy between two situations described in the passage.

Evaluation

This question asks about the role played in the passage by the following statement: *Additionally, large plants can spread compliance costs such as waste treatment across a larger revenue base; on the other hand, some smaller plants may not even be subject to certain provisions such as permit or reporting requirements by virtue of their size.* This statement describes situations in which compliance costs for plants of different sizes may differ, which serve as evidence in support of the passage's main claim: that environmental regulations do *not* affect all competitors in a given industry uniformly.

A   The statement in question is not a hypothesis; rather, it reports factors that are known to affect the varying impact of environmental regulations.
B   This is too vague to be a good description of the kind of relationship the question asks about. The statement in question does present a contrast—it suggests that larger plants' compliance costs are lower under some circumstances, while smaller plants' compliance costs are lower under other circumstances. But this purports to state two facts rather than mere *ideas*; they are contrasting facts but not in any meaningful sense *opposed*, since they can easily coexist.
C   **Correct.** The statement provides examples to support the initial claim made in the passage that regulatory costs fall unevenly on competitors in an industry: large plants can spread compliance costs around, and smaller plants may not even have to pay certain costs.
D   This statement helps to dispel, not exemplify, a misconception mentioned earlier in the passage—i.e., the myth that environmental regulations affect all companies in an industry the same way.
E   The statement does not suggest that the situation of larger and smaller plants is similar (or analogous) to any other situation mentioned in the passage.

The correct answer is C.

RC00272-07
549. The primary purpose of the passage is to

(A) address a widespread environmental management problem and suggest possible solutions
(B) illustrate varying levels of compliance with environmental regulation among different corporations
(C) describe the various alternatives to traditional methods of environmental management
(D) advocate increased corporate compliance with environmental regulation
(E) correct a common misconception about the impact of environmental regulations

Main idea

This question depends on understanding the passage as a whole. Its first sentence indicates its main purpose: to dispel a myth about environmental regulations that is often taken as fact.

A   The passage is not about the management of any environmental problem, which would be a problem about how to prevent or undo damage to the environment. The passage primarily aims to dispel a belief that the passage says is widely held by environmental managers.
B   The passage refers to variations in firms' levels of compliance with environmental regulations, but its primary purpose is not to illustrate those varying levels, nor does it do so.
C   The passage suggests that most environmental managers are mistaken about a key concept; its primary purpose is not to describe traditional methods of environmental management or alternatives to those traditional methods, nor does it do so.
D   The passage takes no position on whether companies should increase their compliance with environmental regulation.
E   **Correct.** The passage primarily aims to dispel the belief that environmental regulations affect all companies in an industry uniformly.

The correct answer is E.

Questions 550–555 refer to the passage on page 438.

RC00109-01
550. The primary purpose of the passage is to

(A) examine two sides of a historiographical debate
(B) call into question an author's approach to a historiographical debate
(C) examine one author's approach to a historiographical debate
(D) discuss two authors' works in relationship to a historiographical debate
(E) explain the prevalent perspective on a historiographical debate

Main idea

This question requires understanding what the passage as a whole is attempting to do. The passage opens by introducing two books published in 1984 that both concern the history of women in the United States. The passage then makes it clear that one book deals *directly* (line 15) with the issue of women's status, while the other does not. The passage then goes on to discuss the perspective that each book takes and what each book has to offer for an assessment of women's status in the eighteenth and nineteenth centuries.

A   The two books discussed in the passage do not take different sides on a particular debate but rather are described as being more or less useful to the debate itself.
B   The passage focuses on how two different books contain information useful to a particular historiographical debate but does not call into question the approach of either book.
C   The passage focuses on two authors' works, not one.
D   **Correct.** The passage discusses what two different books have to offer in relation to a particular historiographical debate.
E   The passage does not describe any perspective on a particular historiographical debate as being more prevalent than any other.

The correct answer is D.

RC00109-02
551. The author of the passage mentions the supervision of schools primarily in order to

   (A) remind readers of the role education played in the cultural changes of the nineteenth century in the United States
   (B) suggest an area in which nineteenth-century American women were relatively free to exercise power
   (C) provide an example of an occupation for which accurate data about women's participation are difficult to obtain
   (D) speculate about which occupations were considered suitable for United States women of the nineteenth century
   (E) illustrate how the answers to questions about women's status depend on particular contexts

Evaluation

Answering this question depends on understanding what role a particular piece of information plays in the passage as a whole. The author implicitly supports Lebsock's contention (beginning at line 20) that different frames of reference can produce different perspectives on the debate about women's status in the eighteenth and nineteenth centuries. The author then summarizes different contexts cited by Lebsock to support the contention about frames of reference. As part of this summary, the author refers to *supervising schools* (lines 24–25) as an example of a job that apparently showed women losing power.

   A   The passage does not discuss the role of education in the nineteenth century.
   B   The passage does mention some ways in which, according to Lebsock, *women ... gained power* (lines 25–26) in the nineteenth century, but *supervising schools* is not among them.
   C   The passage does not discuss the difficulty of obtaining data about particular occupations.
   D   The passage makes no judgments about the suitability for women of any jobs in the nineteenth century.
   E   **Correct.** The passage mentions supervising schools as part of an illustration of Lebsock's claim that the debate about women's status depends on the context being examined.

The correct answer is E.

RC00109-03
552. With which of the following characterizations of Lebsock's contribution to the controversy concerning women's status in the nineteenth-century United States would the author of the passage be most likely to agree?

   (A) Lebsock has studied women from a formerly neglected region and time period.
   (B) Lebsock has demonstrated the importance of frame of reference in answering questions about women's status.
   (C) Lebsock has addressed the controversy by using women's current status as a frame of reference.
   (D) Lebsock has analyzed statistics about occupations and property that were previously ignored.
   (E) Lebsock has applied recent historiographical methods to the biography of a nineteenth-century woman.

Supporting ideas

Answering this question requires recognizing information explicitly given in the passage. The passage introduces the work of Lebsock in line 6 and then goes on to describe several characteristics of Lebsock's book. In lines 20–22, the author introduces Lebsock's claim that the historiographical debate about women's status is dependent on frame of reference and calls that claim important; the passage then gives an example showing how frame of reference affects views of women's status. In so doing, the author displays an implicit agreement with Lebsock's discussion on this point.

   A   The author of the passage portrays neither the place nor time period that Lebsock focuses on as having been neglected by historians.
   B   **Correct.** The author describes as important Lebsock's idea that frame of reference informs the debate about women's status.
   C   According to the passage, Lebsock's book deals with women's status in the eighteenth and nineteenth centuries, not the present status of women.
   D   The passage does not mention or imply that Lebsock analyzed statistics in writing her book.
   E   Although the passage does describe Lebsock's book as pertaining to an ongoing historiographical debate, it identifies the book's topic as *women in one southern community* (lines 7–8), not the life of a single woman.

The correct answer is B.

RC00109-04

553. According to the passage, Lebsock's work differs from Buel and Buel's work in that Lebsock's work

(A) uses a large number of primary sources
(B) ignores issues of women's legal status
(C) refuses to take a position on women's status in the eighteenth century
(D) addresses larger historiographical issues
(E) fails to provide sufficient material to support its claims

Supporting ideas

This question asks for recognition of information contained in the passage. In the first sentence, the passage states that Buel and Buel's work and Lebsock's work have *contrasting approaches.* The passage then proceeds, using descriptions of each work's approach, to illustrate how the works differ. The passage notes that Buel and Buel's work *makes little effort* to place its biographical subject *in the context of recent historiography on women* (lines 5–6), whereas Lebsock's work attempts *to redirect two decades of historiographical debate* about women's status.

A   Primary sources are not mentioned in the passage in relation to either work discussed.
B   The legal status of women is not mentioned in the passage.
C   Lebsock's work is described in the passage as attempting to redirect the debate about women's status in the eighteenth and nineteenth centuries.
D   **Correct.** The passage suggests that by not placing its subject's story in the context of historiography, Buel and Buel's work does not therefore address larger historiographical issues, as Lebsock's does.
E   The passage tends to support Lebsock's views and does not refer to any lack of support for the claims made in Lebsock's work.

The correct answer is D.

RC00109-05

554. The passage suggests that Lebsock believes that compared to nineteenth-century American women, eighteenth-century American women were

(A) in many respects less powerful in relation to men
(B) more likely to own real estate
(C) generally more economically independent
(D) more independent in conducting their private lives
(E) less likely to work as school superintendents

Inference

This question requires making an inference based on information given in the passage. As part of the passage's description of Lebsock's contribution to the historiographical debate about women's status in the eighteenth and nineteenth centuries, Lebsock's conclusions about women's autonomy are described. As part of this description, the passage cites Lebsock's conclusion that nineteenth-century women lost economic autonomy when compared to eighteenth-century women (lines 17–20).

A   The passage states that in many ways women in the nineteenth century *lost power in relation to men* (line 23), which would imply that in those respects eighteenth-century women had more power in relation to men, not less. The only increase mentioned in nineteenth-century women's power is associated with owning more real estate.
B   The passage states that more nineteenth-century women owned real estate.
C   **Correct.** As the passage states, Lebsock concluded that nineteenth-century women lost economic autonomy compared to eighteenth-century women.
D   The passage states that nineteenth-century women gained more independence in their private lives.
E   The passage cites school superintendents as an example of an occupation more likely to be held by eighteenth-century women.

The correct answer is C.

555. The passage suggests that Buel and Buel's biography of Mary Fish provides evidence for which of the following views of women's history?

(A) Women have lost power in relation to men since the colonial era.
(B) Women of the colonial era were not as likely to be concerned with their status as were women in the nineteenth century.
(C) The colonial era was not as favorable for women as some historians have believed.
(D) Women had more economic autonomy in the colonial era than in the nineteenth century.
(E) Women's occupations were generally more respected in the colonial era than in the nineteenth century.

Inference

This question requires understanding what the passage implies. The approach that Buel and Buel's work takes is specifically described in lines 3–6 and again in lines 28–34. In lines 29–32, the passage states that Buel and Buel's work *provides ample raw material for questioning the myth ... of a colonial golden age in the eighteenth century*, referring to a myth about women's status. In describing this golden age as a myth fostered by some historians, the passage suggests that this era was not as favorable to women as these historians suggest.

A The passage describes Lebsock's work as providing such evidence, not Buel and Buel's work.
B The passage does not pertain to the level of concern women had for their status.
C **Correct.** The final paragraph of the passage describes Buel and Buel's work as providing material that calls into question claims that the eighteenth century was especially favorable to women.
D The passage refers to the economic autonomy of women in relation to Lebsock's work, not Buel and Buel's work.
E The passage does not refer to whether any particular occupations held by women were more respected at one time or another.

The correct answer is C.

Questions 556–558 refer to the passage on page 440.

556. The passage suggests that WIDC differed from WTUL in which of the following ways?

(A) WIDC believed that the existing safety regulations were adequate to protect women's health, whereas WTUL believed that such regulations needed to be strengthened.
(B) WIDC believed that unions could not succeed in pressuring employers to comply with such regulations, whereas WTUL believed that unions could succeed in doing so.
(C) WIDC believed that lead poisoning in white lead factories could be avoided by controlling conditions there, whereas WTUL believed that lead poisoning in such factories could not be avoided no matter how stringently safety regulations were enforced.
(D) At the time that the legislation concerning white lead factories was proposed, WIDC was primarily concerned with addressing health conditions in white lead factories, whereas WTUL was concerned with improving working conditions in all types of factories.
(E) At the time that WIDC was opposing legislative attempts to restrict women's labor, WTUL had already ceased to do so.

Inference

To answer this question you need to understand the differences between WIDC and WTUL as they are described in the passage. The only information about WTUL in the passage is that it had stopped opposing restrictions on women's labor in the late 1880s, and that, because existing safety regulations were not being enforced, it supported the proposal to prohibit women from working in white lead factories. WIDC, on the other hand, was formed in 1892 specifically to oppose restrictions on women's labor, and it opposed the proposal.

- A According to the passage, WIDC did believe that existing safety regulations, if enforced, could prevent lead poisoning. WTUL may or may not have believed that the safety regulations needed to be strengthened; all the passage states is that WTUL did not believe that the safety regulations were likely to be enforced.
- B The passage states that WTUL believed that because there were no unions to pressure employers, the employers would not comply with safety regulations. The passage does not present any information on which to base a conclusion about WIDC's beliefs regarding union pressure on employers.
- C Based on information in the passage, both WIDC and SPEW believed that enforcing safety regulations could protect women against lead poisoning. WIDC supported SPEW's position on the matter. WTUL believed that safety regulations were unlikely to be enforced because of the lack of unions.
- D The passage states that WIDC viewed the proposal to restrict women's employment in white lead factories as an instance of legislation designed to limit women's work opportunities—precisely the legislation that WIDC was formed to oppose. Thus, WIDC was not primarily concerned with the factories' health conditions.
- E **Correct.** WIDC began opposing legislative attempts to restrict women's labor in 1892 and continued to do so through at least 1895, when the Home Secretary proposed prohibiting women from working in white lead factories. WTUL stopped opposing restrictions on women's labor in the late 1880s, before WIDC was even founded. Thus, the passage suggests that WTUL had stopped opposing restrictions on women's labor well before WIDC worked to oppose such legislation.

The correct answer is E.

557. Which of the following, if true, would most clearly support the contention attributed to SPEW in lines 17–20 ?

    (A) Those white lead factories that most strongly enforced regulations concerning worker safety and hygiene had the lowest incidences of lead poisoning among employees.
    (B) The incidence of lead poisoning was much higher among women who worked in white lead factories than among women who worked in other types of factories.
    (C) There were many household sources of lead that could have contributed to the incidence of lead poisoning among women who also worked outside the home in the late nineteenth century.
    (D) White lead factories were more stringent than were certain other types of factories in their enforcement of workplace safety regulations.
    (E) Even brief exposure to the conditions typically found in white lead factories could cause lead poisoning among factory workers.

Evaluation

This question requires the reader to find a statement that would provide additional support for the contention made in the following statement: *SPEW contended, and WIDC concurred, that controllable conditions in such factories were responsible for the development of lead poisoning.* Information suggesting that when conditions were controlled, lead poisoning was less likely to develop would provide support for SPEW's contention.

A **Correct.** If incidences of lead poisoning were low in those factories that enforced hygiene and safety regulations, that would suggest that lead poisoning was not an inevitable result of working in a white lead factory—but rather that lead poisoning was the result of poor hygiene and safety practices.

B It would not be particularly surprising for the incidence of lead poisoning to be higher among women working in white lead factories than among women working in other kinds of factories—but such a finding would say nothing about whether controllable conditions had any effect on the development of lead poisoning.

C The existence of household sources of lead that might contribute to lead poisoning would weaken, not support, SPEW's contention that controllable factory conditions were responsible for the development of lead poisoning.

D If white lead factories enforced workplace safety regulations more stringently than did some other types of factories, it might be the case that SPEW's contention was incorrect: that even controlled conditions could not prevent a high incidence of lead poisoning.

E If the conditions typically found in white lead factories were particularly bad with regard to safety and hygiene, it could conceivably be the case that SPEW's contention was true—that is, that the conditions that caused lead poisoning were controllable. But it might also be the case that an uncontrollable aspect of those conditions caused lead poisoning. Thus, this neither supports nor undermines SPEW's contention clearly.

The correct answer is A.

RC00558-06
558. The passage is primarily concerned with

(A) presenting various groups' views of the motives of those proposing certain legislation

(B) contrasting the reasoning of various groups concerning their positions on certain proposed legislation

(C) tracing the process whereby certain proposed legislation was eventually enacted

(D) assessing the success of tactics adopted by various groups with respect to certain proposed legislation

(E) evaluating the arguments of various groups concerning certain proposed legislation

Main idea

Answering this question depends on identifying the overall point of the passage. The passage is mainly concerned with explaining the reasons behind the positions taken by WIDC and SPEW, which opposed the proposal to enact legislation prohibiting women from holding most white lead factory jobs, and the reasoning of WTUL, which supported the proposal.

A The passage explains how WIDC viewed the proposal, but it does not indicate what any of the groups believed about the motivations of the Home Secretary, who made the proposal.

B **Correct.** The passage contrasts the reasoning of the WIDC and SPEW, both of which believed that enforcing safety regulations would make the proposed legislation unnecessary, with the reasoning of WTUL, which thought that safety regulations were unlikely to be enforced and thus supported the proposal.

C The passage simply states that the proposal was eventually enacted; it does not trace the process by which this occurred.

D The passage implies that WIDC and SPEW were unsuccessful in their opposition to the proposed legislation, but it identifies only one tactic used in opposition to it: SPEW's attempt to challenge it by investigating the causes of lead poisoning.

E The passage does not evaluate the groups' arguments concerning the proposed legislation; rather, it presents those arguments without comment on their quality or value.

The correct answer is B.

Questions 559–564 refer to the passage on page 442.

RC00433-02

559. The author of the passage refers to Robert Filmer (see line 9) primarily in order to

(A) show that Royalist ideology was somewhat more radical than most historians appear to realize
(B) qualify the claim that patriarchalism formed the basis of Royalist ideology
(C) question the view that most early feminists were associated with the Royalist faction
(D) highlight an apparent tension between Royalist ideology and the ideas of early feminists
(E) argue that Royalists held conflicting opinions on issues of family organization and women's political rights

Evaluation

This question asks about the role of Filmer in the passage. The author states that Filmer's radical patriarchalism is associated with Royalist ideology and then goes on to define radical patriarchalism as an ideology that asserts the power of the king and the male head of the household. Early feminists, however, questioned the subordination of women in marriage. Thus, there seems to be a conflict between these two sets of ideas.

A Although the passage refers to Filmer's view as *radical patriarchalism*, it provides no evidence regarding any differences in the degrees to which historians consider that view, or Royalism in general, to be radical.
B Filmer's work supports the claim that patriarchalism was the basis of Royalist ideology; it does not qualify such a claim.
C That Filmer's approach was one of radical patriarchalism makes it surprising that early feminists were associated with the Royalist faction, but it does not provide any grounds for questioning whether they were so associated.

D **Correct.** There is apparent tension between Filmer's radical patriarchalism, if that is indeed essential to Royalist ideology, and the ideas of early feminists, who questioned such patriarchalism.
E The author refers to Filmer in order to suggest, initially, a uniformity among Royalists regarding family and women; it is only later in the passage that this view becomes more complicated.

The correct answer is D.

RC00433-11

560. The passage suggests which of the following about the seventeenth-century English women mentioned in line 2?

(A) Their status as forerunners of modern feminism is not entirely justified.
(B) They did not openly challenge the radical patriarchalism of Royalist Filmerian ideology.
(C) Cavendish was the first among these women to criticize women's subordination in marriage and assert women's equality with men.
(D) Their views on family organization and women's political rights were diametrically opposed to those of both Royalist and Parliamentarian ideology.
(E) Historians would be less puzzled if more of them were identified with the Parliamentarian side in the English Civil Wars.

Inference

The first sentence of the passage refers to women who are both regarded as forerunners of modern feminism and identified as Royalists. The passage goes on to suggest that, given Royalist ideology's association with Filmer's radical patriarchalism (equating absolute power of the king with absolute power of the male head of household), it is surprising that feminism would find any footing within such an ideology.

A Nothing in the passage disputes the idea that the seventeenth-century English women in question should be considered the forerunners of modern feminism.
B Gallagher provides the example of Margaret Cavendish as a writer who did openly challenge radical patriarchalism—albeit only in her writings.
C The passage states that Cavendish had successors among early feminists, but it does not indicate whether she herself was the first seventeenth-century English woman to assert women's equality.
D The passage does not indicate what the Parliamentarian view of family organization and women's political rights was, so there is no way to determine whether the Royalist forerunners of modern feminism were opposed to that view.
E **Correct.** The basic puzzle the passage sets out to solve is why the forerunners of modern feminism would have been associated with the Royalist side, which seems to have been based on radical patriarchalism. Historians would most likely have been less surprised if these women had been identified with the Parliamentarian side, which presumably did not embrace radical patriarchalism.

The correct answer is E.

561. The passage suggests that Margaret Cavendish's decision to become an author was motivated, at least in part, by a desire to

(A) justify her support for the Royalist cause
(B) encourage her readers to work toward eradicating Filmerian patriarchalism
(C) persuade other women to break free from their political and social isolation
(D) analyze the causes for women's exclusion from the pursuit of power
(E) create a world over which she could exercise total control

Inference

This question asks about Margaret Cavendish's reasons for becoming an author. The second paragraph describes her as someone who *insisted that she was a self-sufficient being*; she understood that, given the real-world strictures in place, she could achieve this self-sufficiency in her own mind and on paper as a writer. So her decision to become a writer can be inferred to be motivated by her desire to exercise power and control.

A The passage states that Cavendish justified her being the center of her own universe by invoking the Royalist figure of the absolute monarch; there is no suggestion in the passage that Cavendish felt the need to justify any support for the actual Royalist cause.
B The passage gives no direct indication that Cavendish was even aware of Filmerian patriarchalism.
C The second paragraph states that Cavendish's idea of absolute singularity carried with it the idea of social and political isolation; Cavendish was most likely not motivated by a desire to persuade other women to break free from such isolation.
D Cavendish took the exclusion of women from the pursuit of power for granted; the passage does not suggest that she was concerned with its causes.
E **Correct.** According to the passage, Cavendish considered herself a self-sufficient being who was at the center of her own universe; in her writing, she wanted to create a world in which this was also true.

The correct answer is E.

562. The phrase "a satellite orbiting a dominant male planet" (lines 41–42) refers most directly to

(A) Cavendish's concept that each woman is a sovereign self
(B) the complete political and social isolation of absolute singularity
(C) the immaterial world that a writer can create on paper
(D) the absolute subordination of women in a patriarchal society
(E) the metaphorical figure of the absolute monarch

Evaluation

The phrase in question is *a satellite orbiting a dominant male planet*. The passage states that this was the idea that Cavendish was reacting against; she preferred instead the idea that she was the center of her own universe, her own sovereign, subject to no one.

A   The idea of a satellite orbiting a dominant male planet refers not to Cavendish's idea that each woman is a sovereign self, but rather to the idea directly opposed to that: each woman must submit to a dominant male.
B   A *satellite orbiting a dominant male planet* is by definition not isolated, nor is it singular.
C   According to the passage, Cavendish wished to create her own world as a writer so that she did not have to be a *satellite*.
D   **Correct.** The phrase refers to the idea that in a patriarchal society, women are as satellites to men, who are the dominant planets.
E   While radical patriarchy does equate the monarch with the male head of the household, the in question phrase is most directly about the relationship, under patriarchy, between women and men.

The correct answer is D.

RC00433-06
563. The primary purpose of the passage is to

(A) trace the historical roots of a modern sociopolitical movement
(B) present one scholar's explanation for a puzzling historical phenomenon
(C) contrast two interpretations of the ideological origins of a political conflict
(D) establish a link between the ideology of an influential political theorist and that of a notoriously eccentric writer
(E) call attention to some points of agreement between opposing sides in an ideological debate

Main idea

This question asks about the passage as a whole. The passage is mainly concerned with outlining Catherine Gallagher's attempt to explain why, given Royalist ideology's apparent association with radical patriarchalism, Royalist women offered feminist critiques of women's subordination in marriage and asserted their equality with men.

A   The passage makes no connection between early feminism and its modern form.
B   **Correct.** The passage presents a puzzling historical phenomenon, that Royalist women critiqued patriarchalism, in the first paragraph, and then presents Catherine Gallagher's explanation for that phenomenon in the second paragraph.
C   While the passage discusses the political conflict between the Royalists and Parliamentarians in the English Civil Wars in the first paragraph, neither this conflict, nor its ideological origins are the focus of the passage. Furthermore, the passage does not offer any interpretations of the origins of the conflict.
D   The passage attempts to unlink the ideology of political theorist Robert Filmer and the eccentric author Margaret Cavendish by suggesting that Filmer's radical patriarchalism was not the only way of understanding Royalist ideology. Cavendish provided a different understanding entirely.
E   While both sides of the ideological debate did agree on the absolute monarchy, the passage as a whole does not focus on this agreement, but rather on the disagreement about where, theoretically, the idea of absolute monarchy leads.

The correct answer is B.

RC00433-09
564. Which of the following, if true, would most clearly undermine Gallagher's explanation of the link between Royalism and feminism?

(A) Because of their privileged backgrounds, Royalist women were generally better educated than were their Parliamentarian counterparts.
(B) Filmer himself had read some of Cavendish's early writings and was highly critical of her ideas.
(C) Cavendish's views were highly individual and were not shared by the other Royalist women who wrote early feminist works.
(D) The Royalist and Parliamentarian ideologies were largely in agreement on issues of family organization and women's political rights.
(E) The Royalist side included a sizable minority faction that was opposed to the more radical tendencies of Filmerian patriarchalism.

Inference

This question asks about how to undermine the way in which Gallagher connects Royalism and feminism. According to Gallagher, Cavendish's work exemplifies the connection between these ideas, because Cavendish took the idea of absolute monarchy and extended that to the idea of absolute self, an idea that should, Cavendish believed, apply to women as well as men.

A Gallagher's explanation of the link between Royalism and feminism does not depend on the education level of Royalist women relative to Parliamentarian women.
B Filmer most likely would have been critical of Cavendish's ideas, had he encountered them, but the passage does not indicate that Gallagher's argument had anything to do with whether Filmer read Cavendish's writings.
C **Correct.** Gallagher uses Cavendish's work to explain how Royalism gave rise to feminism, but if Cavendish's views were completely atypical of other Royalist women, then those views cannot explain the link as Gallagher suggests they do.
D The passage states in the first paragraph that if the Royalists and Parliamentarians were in agreement *on issues of family organization and women's political rights*, then feminists should have been divided between the two sides—but they were not. So this idea, if true, would undermine that statement, but not Gallagher's argument about the link between Royalists and feminists.
E If more Royalists were opposed to Filmer's radical patriarchalism, then Cavendish's writings would seem to be more representative of tendencies in Royalist ideology, thus making Gallagher's case stronger, not weaker.

The correct answer is C.

Questions 565–569 refer to the passage on page 444.

RC00312-01
565. The passage is primarily concerned with

(A) identifying two practices in medical research that may affect the accuracy of clinical trials
(B) describing aspects of medical research that tend to drive up costs
(C) evaluating an analysis of certain shortcomings of current medical research practices
(D) describing proposed changes to the ways in which clinical trials are conducted
(E) explaining how medical researchers have traditionally conducted clinical trials and how such trials are likely to change

Main idea

This question requires an understanding of what the passage as a whole is doing. The passage introduces Frazier and Mosteller as proposing changes to the ways clinical trials in medical research are currently conducted. The rest of the passage then describes these proposed changes together with the support Frazier and Mosteller provide for adopting these changes.

A The passage identifies practices in medical research to help illustrate the basis for Frazier and Mosteller's proposed changes.
B The passage mentions medical research costs as one example within the larger description of Frazier and Mosteller's proposed changes.
C The passage is not concerned with evaluating Frazier and Mosteller's proposed changes.

D   Correct. The passage describes the changes proposed by Frazier and Mosteller to the way clinical trials are conducted.
E   The passage is not concerned with establishing the likelihood of any changes to the way medical research is conducted.

The correct answer is D.

RC00312-03

566. Which of the following can be inferred from the passage about a study of the category of patients referred to in lines 20–22 ?

(A) Its findings might have limited applicability.
(B) It would be prohibitively expensive in its attempt to create ideal conditions.
(C) It would be the best way to sample the total population of potential patients.
(D) It would allow researchers to limit information collection without increasing the risk that important variables could be overlooked.
(E) Its findings would be more accurate if it concerned treatments for a progressive disease than if it concerned treatments for a nonprogressive disease.

Inference

This question requires drawing an inference from information given in the passage. In describing the proposals put forth by Frazier and Mosteller, the passage states in lines 15–20 that they propose using more patients in clinical trials than are currently being used, and that the trials would thereby obtain *a more representative sample of the total population with the disease under study*. The passage then states that researchers often *restrict* (lines 20–22) their trials to certain types of patients, therefore limiting the applicability of their findings.

A   Correct. The passage states that the researchers preferred to restrict the types of patients used in their studies, thereby using a less representative sample than if they used a more inclusive group of patients.
B   The passage mentions the added expense of clinical trials only in relation to data storage, collection, and analysis.
C   The passage describes the category of patients referred to as restricted and therefore unrepresentative of the total population.

D   While the passage does mention the amount of data collected about an individual patient, that topic is not connected to the category of patients referred to in lines 20–22.
E   The passage does not suggest that a study using the category of patients referred to would be more effective in investigating progressive diseases.

The correct answer is A.

RC00312-04

567. It can be inferred from the passage that a study limited to patients like those mentioned in lines 20–22 would have which of the following advantages over the kind of study proposed by Frazier and Mosteller?

(A) It would yield more data and its findings would be more accurate.
(B) It would cost less in the long term, though it would be more expensive in its initial stages.
(C) It would limit the number of variables researchers would need to consider when evaluating the treatment under study.
(D) It would help researchers to identify subgroups of patients with secondary conditions that might also be treatable.
(E) It would enable researchers to assess the value of an experimental treatment for the average patient.

Inference

This question requires understanding what the information in the passage implies. The passage explains that Frazier and Mosteller's proposal involves enrolling more patients in clinical trials (lines 18–19) than is the case with the category of patients referred to. The passage then explains that broadening the range of trial participants would allow an evaluation of particular treatments *under various conditions* and *for different patient subgroups* (line 29). This strongly suggests that limiting the patients used to those described in the referred text would limit the number of variables researchers would need to consider.

A   The passage suggests that not limiting the patients used in clinical trials will yield more data than restricting them will.

B   The passage refers to the costs of clinical trials only as they concern the collection, storage, and analysis of data collected from participants.
C   **Correct.** By limiting the patients used to those having the ailment under study, the passage suggests that researchers need to consider fewer variables in their assessment of a treatment.
D   The passage suggests that *not* limiting the types of patients used in clinical trials will better allow researchers to evaluate subgroups.
E   The passage suggests that limiting the types of patients available for clinical trials results in data for specific, rather than average, populations.

The correct answer is C.

568. The author mentions patients' ages (line 32) primarily in order to

(A) identify the most critical variable differentiating subgroups of patients

(B) cast doubt on the advisability of implementing Frazier and Mosteller's proposals about medical research

(C) indicate why progressive diseases may require different treatments at different stages

(D) illustrate a point about the value of enrolling a wide range of patients in clinical trials

(E) substantiate an argument about the problems inherent in enrolling large numbers of patients in clinical trials

Evaluation

Answering this question requires understanding how a particular piece of information functions in the passage as a whole. The passage is concerned with describing the proposals of Frazier and Mosteller. One of these proposals, described in the second paragraph, involves broadening the range of participants used in clinical trials. The passage states that in following this proposal, Frazier and Mosteller suggest that the effectiveness of treatments can be assessed for different patient subgroups. To affirm the value of broadening the range of participants, the passage then cites two examples of criteria by which relevant subgroups might be identified: disease stages and patients' ages.

A   The passage makes no judgment as to the value of the subgroups it refers to in relation to broadened participation in clinical trials.
B   The passage does not call into question the potential effectiveness of Frazier and Mosteller's proposals.
C   The passage's example of patients' ages is not intended to be causally connected to its previous example regarding progressive diseases.
D   **Correct.** Patients' ages are referred to in the passage to identify subgroups that could be evaluated if the range of participants in clinical trials were broadened.
E   The passage refers to patients' ages in support of Frazier and Mosteller's proposal that more patients be used in clinical trials.

The correct answer is D.

569. According to the passage, which of the following describes a result of the way in which researchers generally conduct clinical trials?

(A) They expend resources on the storage of information likely to be irrelevant to the study they are conducting.

(B) They sometimes compromise the accuracy of their findings by collecting and analyzing more information than is strictly required for their trials.

(C) They avoid the risk of overlooking variables that might affect their findings, even though doing so raises their research costs.

(D) Because they attempt to analyze too much information, they overlook facts that could emerge as relevant to their studies.

(E) In order to approximate the conditions typical of medical treatment, they base their methods of information collection on those used by hospitals.

Supporting ideas

This question asks for an identification of specific information given in the passage. The passage describes the proposals of Frazier and Mosteller as attempting to improve the way clinical trials have generally been conducted. In describing how current trials are generally conducted, the passage states that researchers *collect far more background information on patients than is strictly required for their trials* (lines 4–6) and that they therefore escalate the costs of the trials.

- A **Correct.** The passage states that researchers generally collect more information than they need to perform their clinical trials, which drives up the costs of the trials.
- B The passage makes no judgment about the accuracy of the information collected by researchers who currently hold clinical trials.
- C The passage states that the risk of overlooking relevant information in clinical trials is *never entirely eliminable* (line 11).
- D The passage states that researchers generally collect more information than is relevant, not that they overlook relevant information.
- E The passage states that, in general, researchers currently collect more information than hospitals do (line 6).

The correct answer is A.

Questions 570–575 refer to the passage on page 446.

RC00229-01
570. The primary purpose of the passage is to

   (A) assess the validity of a certain view
   (B) distinguish between two phenomena
   (C) identify the causes of a problem
   (D) describe a disturbing trend
   (E) allay concern about a particular phenomenon

Main idea

This question requires understanding, in general terms, the purpose of the passage as a whole. The first paragraph identifies an area of concern: declines in amphibian populations may constitute a crisis, one that indicates humans' catastrophic effects on the environment. The rest of the passage then goes on to evaluate, as the second paragraph states, whether claims of crisis-level extinctions as a result of human activity are valid. In making this evaluation, the passage discusses the possible causes of extinctions, biologists' prioritization of population declines over extinctions, and the fact that we lack extensive long-term data on amphibian populations.

- A **Correct.** The passage's main purpose is to assess whether the view that humans are causing crisis-level declines in amphibian populations is valid.
- B The passage takes care, particularly in the third paragraph, to distinguish between population declines and extinctions, but this is not its primary purpose.
- C The passage makes clear that it is difficult to identify the real extent of the problem facing amphibian populations, much less identify its causes.
- D The first paragraph notes what may seem to be a disturbing trend—the decline in amphibian populations—but the rest of the passage is concerned not with describing that trend in greater detail, but rather with determining whether it is in fact occurring.
- E While the passage provides possible grounds for concluding that concern about declining amphibian populations is overblown, it concludes by suggesting that we might, because we lack data, doom species and ecosystems to extinction. Thus, the overall purpose is not to allay concern.

The correct answer is A.

RC00229-02
571. It can be inferred from the passage that the author believes which of the following to be true of the environmentalists mentioned in lines 5–6 ?

   (A) They have wrongly chosen to focus on anecdotal reports rather than on the long-term data that are currently available concerning amphibians.
   (B) Their recommendations are flawed because their research focuses too narrowly on a single category of animal species.
   (C) Their certainty that population declines in general are caused by environmental degradation is not warranted.
   (D) They have drawn premature conclusions concerning a crisis in amphibian populations from recent reports of declines.
   (E) They have overestimated the effects of chance events on trends in amphibian populations.

Inference

This question asks about the author's view of the environmentalists mentioned in the first paragraph. These environmentalists have claimed, based on amphibian population declines, that the situation is a crisis and that immediate action must be taken. The author, however, states that the declines are only *apparently* drastic and questions whether they are real, thus suggesting that the environmentalists are drawing conclusions in the absence of a complete consideration of the situation.

A The passage indicates that anecdotal reports are insufficient, but so too are other resources. The fourth paragraph of the passage makes clear that there is not enough long-term data available on which to base conclusions about amphibian populations.
B The passage does not indicate that the environmentalists under discussion have conducted research on any animal species.
C The passage does not indicate that the environmentalists in question hold, with certainty, any particular view regarding population declines in general.
D Correct. The author argues that the recent declines may have several different causes, and that environmentalists have jumped to a conclusion about the cause of the declines as well as their significance.
E The environmentalists, in attributing population declines to intentional human activity, have more likely underestimated than overestimated the effects of chance events on amphibian populations.

The correct answer is D.

RC00229-03

572. It can be inferred from the passage that the author believes which of the following to be true of the amphibian extinctions that have recently been reported?

(A) They have resulted primarily from human activities causing environmental degradation.
(B) They could probably have been prevented if timely action had been taken to protect the habitats of amphibian species.
(C) They should not come as a surprise, because amphibian populations generally have been declining for a number of years.
(D) They have probably been caused by a combination of chance events.
(E) They do not clearly constitute evidence of general environmental degradation.

Inference

The author suggests throughout the passage that recently reported amphibian extinctions may have several different causes: they may be due to any number of chance events, for example, or may simply be the result of a small population that finds itself unable to continue under difficult conditions, whatever causes those conditions.

A The author states in the second paragraph that extinctions may occur without a proximate cause in human activities and does not make a commitment to any particular explanation of the amphibian extinctions.
B That chance events can cause extinctions suggests that even if habitats had been protected, extinctions still might have occurred.
C In the second paragraph, the author says that extinctions *should come as no great surprise*, but this option is imprecise. The amphibian populations have not generally *been declining for a number of years*. The author says in the third paragraph that amphibian populations show strong fluctuations; further, in the fourth paragraph, the author says that there is insufficient long-term data to conclude that amphibian populations have been, or are, in decline.
D The author suggests that the extinctions may have been caused by chance events, but there is not enough data to know whether or not this is probable.
E Correct. The reported extinctions could have resulted from several different causes; thus, they are not clear evidence of general environmental degradation.

The correct answer is E.

RC00229-04

573. According to the passage, each of the following is true of endangered amphibian species EXCEPT:

(A) They are among the rarest kinds of amphibians.
(B) They generally have populations that are small in size.

(C) They are in constant danger of extinction.
(D) Those with decreasing populations are the most likely candidates for immediate extinction.
(E) They are in danger of extinction due to events that sometimes have nothing to do with human activities.

Application

This question asks what the passage does not say is true of endangered amphibian species. The second paragraph discusses endangered species, stating that they are *always rare, almost always small, and, by definition, under constant threat of extinction*, which may be caused by chance events. The possibility of their extinction, the passage states, depends only on the population size, and not whether that population is increasing or decreasing.

A The second paragraph mentions rarity as a characteristic of endangered amphibian species.
B According to the second paragraph, endangered amphibian species are generally those of small populations.
C The second paragraph states that an endangered population is under constant threat of extinction.
D **Correct.** The last sentence of the second paragraph states that the probability of extinction due to chance events is independent of how a population changes in size. Immediate extinction would more likely come from such events, whereas population decline is gradual, even if fairly rapid.
E Endangered species, according to the second paragraph, may become extinct due to chance events—that is, events that have nothing to do with human activities.

The correct answer is D.

RC00229-05
574. Which of the following most accurately describes the organization of the passage?

(A) A question is raised, a distinction regarding it is made, and the question is answered.
(B) An interpretation is presented, its soundness is examined, and a warning is given.
(C) A situation is described, its consequences are analyzed, and a prediction is made.
(D) Two interpretations of a phenomenon are described, and one of them is rejected as invalid.
(E) Two methods for analyzing a phenomenon are compared, and further study of the phenomenon is recommended.

Evaluation

This question asks about the organization of the passage as a whole. In the first paragraph, the author tells about a situation that has been interpreted in a particular way by environmentalists. The passage then proceeds to consider whether that interpretation is valid, and while it does not come to a definitive conclusion on that point, the final paragraph warns about the possible consequences of not taking the action recommended by the environmentalists.

A The passage does initially raise a question regarding whether the environmentalists' interpretation of events is valid, but it does not answer that question, for the appropriate long-term data are not available.
B **Correct.** The passage presents environmentalists' interpretation of recent news regarding amphibians, then examines the soundness of that interpretation. Finally, the author warns that postponing environmental action may have disastrous consequences.
C The first paragraph describes a situation of possibly drastic declines in amphibian populations but does not follow this description with an analysis of its consequences.
D The passage suggests that apparent declines in amphibian populations may or may not constitute a crisis, but it does not reject either idea.
E While the passage does imply, in its final paragraph, that long-term data on amphibian populations should be collected, the passage does not compare two methods for analyzing amphibian populations or population declines in those populations.

The correct answer is B.

575. Which of the following best describes the function of the sentence in lines 35–38 ?

(A) To give an example of a particular kind of study
(B) To cast doubt on an assertion made in the previous sentence
(C) To raise an objection to a view presented in the first paragraph
(D) To provide support for a view presented in the first paragraph
(E) To introduce an idea that will be countered in the following paragraph

Evaluation

The sentence in question discusses the way in which anecdotal reports of population decreases cannot help biologists determine whether those decreases are normal fluctuations, take populations to lower levels that are not actually worrisome, or actually threaten extinctions. This indicates that the view mentioned in the first paragraph—reports of declines indicate a catastrophic crisis—may be mistaken.

A   The sentence does not address a particular kind of study; it objects to the use of anecdotal reports in place of actual study.
B   The previous sentence describes the possibilities referred to in the sentence in question. The sentence does not cast doubt on any of those possibilities.
C   **Correct.** The view that reports of amphibian population declines indicate a crisis, as presented in the first paragraph, is countered by the objection here that there are several possible causes for population declines, and anecdotal reports cannot distinguish among those possibilities.
D   The first paragraph is concerned with articulating the view that amphibian population declines constitute a crisis. This sentence does not support that view; instead, it offers reason to question it.
E   The sentence introduces the idea that amphibian populations have fluctuated in the past, and the following paragraph supports this idea by stating that several amphibian species that appeared almost extinct in the 1950s and 1960s have recovered. Thus, the paragraph does not counter the sentence.

The correct answer is C.

Questions 576–579 refer to the passage on page 448.

576. The passage mentions which of the following as a factor that affects the role of *P. ochraceus* as a keystone species within different habitats?

(A) The degree to which the habitat is sheltered from waves
(B) The degree to which other animals within a habitat prey on mussels
(C) The fact that mussel populations are often not dominant within some habitats occupied by *P. ochraceus*
(D) The size of the *P. ochraceus* population within the habitat
(E) The fact that there is great species diversity within some habitats occupied by *P. ochraceus*

Supporting idea

This question depends on recognizing what the passage states about the factors affecting *P. ochraceus*'s role as a keystone species, which is different in different habitats. According to the passage, *P. ochraceus* consumes and suppresses mussel populations in some habitats—specifically, those that are wave-exposed—making it a keystone predator in those habitats. But in wave-sheltered habitats, *P. ochraceus* does not play the same role in suppressing mussel populations.

A   **Correct.** The passage clearly states that *P. ochraceus*'s role in wave-exposed habitats differs from its role in wave-sheltered habitats.
B   The passage says that the impact of *P. ochraceus* predation on mussels is not strong in wave-sheltered habitats, but this is not—at least not at all sites—because other animals are preying on the mussels; rather, at least at some sites, it is because mussels are controlled by sand burial.
C   The passage does not suggest that mussel populations are dominant in any habitats occupied by *P. ochraceus*.

D   The size of the *P. ochraceus* population affects the size of the mussel population within wave-exposed habitats, but the passage does not suggest that *P. ochraceus*'s role as a keystone species depends on the size of its population within those habitats.

E   The only other species the passage mentions in conjunction with *P. ochraceus* habitats is the mussel; the passage does not address species diversity in these habitats.

The correct answer is A.

RC00556-04

577. Which of the following hypothetical experiments most clearly exemplifies the method of identifying species' roles that the author considers problematic?

(A) A population of seals in an Arctic habitat is counted in order to determine whether it is the dominant species in that ecosystem.

(B) A species of fish that is a keystone species in one marine ecosystem is introduced into another marine ecosystem to see whether the species will come to occupy a keystone role.

(C) In order to determine whether a species of monkey is a keystone species within a particular ecosystem, the monkeys are removed from that ecosystem and the ecosystem is then studied.

(D) Different mountain ecosystems are compared to determine how geography affects a particular species' ability to dominate its ecosystem.

(E) In a grassland experiencing a changing climate, patterns of species extinction are traced in order to evaluate the effect of climate changes on keystone species in that grassland.

Application

Answering this question depends on recognizing what the author says about identifying species' roles in habitats and then extending that to another situation. The author considers a particular method of studying keystone species problematic: removing a suspected keystone species from its habitat and observing what happens to the ecosystem. The author finds this problematic because interactions among species are complex.

A   The author does not discuss counting the members of a population as a problematic way of determining whether that population is a dominant species.

B   The method that the author finds problematic has to do with observing what happens to an ecosystem when a keystone species is removed from it, not with observing what happens to a different ecosystem when the species is introduced into it.

C   **Correct.** The author states explicitly that removing a species from a habitat in order to determine its keystone status is problematic. Removing the monkeys from their habitat is a clear example of this problematic practice.

D   Comparison of habitats in order to determine geography's effect on a particular species' dominance would most likely find favor with the author, for this is the approach the author seems to advocate in investigating *P. ochraceus*'s keystone status.

E   The author does not discuss tracing patterns of extinction or changing climates in the passage.

The correct answer is C.

RC00556-05

578. Which of the following, if true, would most clearly support the argument about keystone status advanced in the last sentence of the passage (lines 24–31)?

(A) A species of bat is primarily responsible for keeping insect populations within an ecosystem low, and the size of the insect population in turn affects bird species within that ecosystem.

(B) A species of iguana occupies a keystone role on certain tropical islands, but does not play that role on adjacent tropical islands that are inhabited by a greater number of animal species.

(C) Close observation of a savannah ecosystem reveals that more species occupy keystone roles within that ecosystem than biologists had previously believed.

(D) As a keystone species of bee becomes more abundant, it has a larger effect on the ecosystem it inhabits.

(E) A species of moth that occupies a keystone role in a prairie habitat develops coloration patterns that camouflage it from potential predators.

Evaluation

To answer this question, focus on the argument advanced in the last sentence of the passage and identify what information would support that argument. In the last sentence of the passage, the author claims that keystone status depends on context. The author then offers three contextual factors that may affect a species' keystone status: geography, community diversity (i.e., the number of species in a given habitat), and length of species interaction. Evidence supporting this argument would show that context is important to a species' keystone status.

A   This scenario does not indicate anything about keystone status; this is simply a description of how species populations in a single ecosystem affect one another.
B   **Correct.** That the iguana is a keystone species in a location that has limited species diversity but not a keystone species in a location that has greater species diversity suggests that keystone status does indeed depend on context. Thus, this example supports the author's argument in the last sentence of the passage.
C   That biologists were mistaken about keystone species in a particular ecosystem does not have a bearing on whether keystone status is context dependent.
D   It is not surprising that an increase in a species' population would lead to that species having a larger effect on its ecosystem—but this does not speak directly to the question of whether keystone status itself depends on context.
E   A keystone species enhancing its ability to survive in a single ecosystem does not lend any support to the idea that keystone status depends on context. The moth's keystone status would have to undergo some change for this to have a bearing on the question of context.

The correct answer is B.

579. The passage suggests which of the following about the identification of a species as a keystone species?

(A)   Such an identification depends primarily on the species' relationship to the dominant species.
(B)   Such an identification can best be made by removing the species from a particular ecosystem and observing changes that occur in the ecosystem.
(C)   Such an identification is likely to be less reliable as an ecosystem becomes less diverse.
(D)   Such an identification seems to depend on various factors within the ecosystem.
(E)   Such an identification can best be made by observing predation behavior.

Inference

Answering this question requires identifying how the passage suggests that keystone species should be identified. The passage identifies a particular way in which keystone status should *not* be determined: removing a species and observing what happens to the ecosystem. The passage also argues that keystone status depends strongly on context: that is, an ecosystem's characteristics, including its geography and inhabitants, determine its keystone species.

A   While the passage uses an example of a keystone species, *P. ochraceus*, which preys on a species that would, in the keystone species' absence, be dominant, there is nothing to suggest that a keystone species *must* have a particular relationship with the dominant, or potentially dominant, species in an ecosystem.
B   The passage explicitly states that this method of identification would be problematic.
C   A reduction in an ecosystem's diversity might alter which species occupy keystone roles in that ecosystem, the passage suggests, but there is no indication that identifying such species would become more difficult.
D   **Correct.** If, as the passage suggests, keystone status for any given species depends on the context of the ecosystem in which it lives, then it is likely that identifying keystone species depends strongly on understanding what factors of the ecosystem contribute to creating keystone status. The passage

lists such factors as geography, community diversity, and species interaction.

E While the passage uses a predator, *P. ochraceus*, as its example of a keystone species, there is no indication that predation is an essential component of the actual definition of keystone species (*one whose effects are much larger than would be predicted from its abundance*).

The correct answer is D.

Questions 580–582 refer to the passage on page 450.

RC00073-01

580. According to the passage, the anatomical evidence provided by the preserved soft bodies of conodonts led scientists to conclude that

- (A) conodonts had actually been invertebrate carnivores
- (B) conodonts' teeth were adapted from protective bony scales
- (C) conodonts were primitive vertebrate suspension feeders
- (D) primitive vertebrates with teeth appeared earlier than armored vertebrates
- (E) scientists' original observations concerning the phosphatic remains of conodonts were essentially correct

Supporting ideas

This question depends on understanding how a particular type of evidence—the preserved soft bodies of conodonts—supports a particular conclusion stated in the passage. The third paragraph makes this relationship explicit, explaining that certain features of conodonts show them to be more primitive than other vertebrates. Further, those features indicate that they came before ostracoderms and other armored jawless fishes. These remains support the conclusion stated in the second paragraph regarding teeth being more primitive than external armor.

A The passage states explicitly that conodonts were not invertebrates but rather vertebrates.

B This view is attributed to certain traditionalists but is contradicted by other paleontological evidence presented in the second and third paragraphs. According to the third paragraph, the evidence provided by the preserved soft bodies of conodonts undermines this traditional view.

C The final sentence of the passage indicates that the evidence in question supports the conclusion that conodonts were predators rather than suspension feeders.

D **Correct.** The third paragraph explains how conodonts' remains support the conclusion that teeth were more primitive than external armor.

E The second paragraph explains that originally, scientists thought that early vertebrates were not predators—but the remainder of the passage indicates that this idea is inconsistent with more recent evidence described in the passage.

The correct answer is D.

RC00073-03

581. The second paragraph in the passage serves primarily to

- (A) outline the significance of the 1981 discovery of conodont remains to the debate concerning the development of the vertebrate skeleton
- (B) contrast the traditional view of the development of the vertebrate skeleton with a view derived from the 1981 discovery of conodont remains
- (C) contrast the characteristics of the ostracoderms with the characteristics of earlier soft-bodied vertebrates
- (D) explain the importance of the development of teeth among the earliest vertebrate predators
- (E) present the two sides of the debate concerning the development of the vertebrate skeleton

531

Evaluation

This question depends on understanding the second paragraph in the context of the passage as a whole. The second paragraph begins by noting the traditional view of the vertebrate skeleton—that it was a defense against predators—and then goes on to explain that other paleontologists argued against this idea, claiming instead that vertebrates began as predators and that teeth were a more primary feature than external armor.

A The second paragraph focuses on describing the debate rather than on the distinctive contribution of the 1981 discovery to that debate.

B The second paragraph does not explicitly indicate whether the opposition to the traditional view originally rested on the 1981 discovery of conodont remains. In fact, the surrounding discussion, in the first and third paragraphs, suggests that the discovery in 1981 turned out to support the opposing view, which some paleontologists already held at that time.

C The mention of ostracoderms in the second paragraph merely serves to indicate how the traditionalists' arguments might have seemed plausible. The paragraph as a whole is not devoted to contrasting the ostracoderms with earlier soft-bodied vertebrates.

D The development of teeth figures in the second paragraph, but this development is mentioned first as a feature that some believed to have been adapted from protective scales; only the final sentence of the paragraph connects teeth to early vertebrate predators.

E **Correct.** According to the passage, the debate concerning the development of the vertebrate skeleton hinges on whether vertebrates began as predators, with teeth, or whether skeletal defenses such as external armor evolved first. The primary purpose of the second paragraph is to distinguish these two sides.

The correct answer is E.

582. It can be inferred that on the basis of the 1981 discovery of conodont remains, paleontologists could draw which of the following conclusions?

(A) The earliest vertebrates were sedentary suspension feeders.

(B) Ostracoderms were not the earliest vertebrates.

(C) Defensive armor preceded jaws among vertebrates.

(D) Paired eyes and adaptations for activity are definitive characteristics of vertebrates.

(E) Conodonts were unlikely to have been predators.

Inference

What could paleontologists conclude, based on the 1981 discovery of conodont remains? That discovery, according to the passage, supported the view of certain paleontologists that the earliest vertebrates were predators with teeth—unlike the ostracoderms, which had no jaws.

A According to the second paragraph, traditionalists believed that early vertebrates were sedentary suspension feeders. But the 1981 discovery supported instead the hypothesis that early vertebrates were predators instead.

B **Correct.** According to the third paragraph, the conodonts' body structures indicated that they were more primitive than the ostracoderms, so the ostracoderms must not have been the earliest vertebrates.

C Traditionalists argued that teeth were adapted from bony scales that provided defensive armor, but the 1981 discovery suggested that teeth preceded such scales.

D Paleontologists knew prior to the 1981 discovery that paired eyes and other adaptations are characteristics of vertebrates. They used this knowledge to help them interpret the 1981 discovery.

E The third paragraph indicates that conodonts, given their teeth, were most likely predators.

The correct answer is B.

7.6 Reading Comprehension Answer Explanations

Questions 583–590 refer to the passage on page 452.

RC00013-01

583. The primary purpose of the passage is to

(A) advocate a more positive attitude toward technological change
(B) discuss the implications for employees of the modernization of a telephone exchange
(C) consider a successful challenge to the constructivist view of technological change
(D) challenge the position of advocates of technological determinism
(E) suggest that the social causes of technological change should be studied in real situations

Main idea

This question asks for an assessment of what the passage as a whole is doing. The passage introduces Clark's study as a *solid contribution* (line 3) to the debate between technological determinists and social constructivists. In the second paragraph, Braverman is introduced as holding a position of social constructivism, a position that Clark takes issue with. In the final paragraph, the passage holds that *Clark refutes the extremes of the constructivists* (line 31), and Clark's arguments challenging social constructivism are then described.

A The passage takes no position on the merits of technological change but is concerned only with the role of such change in society.
B The passage mentions telephone exchange workers as an example that helps illustrate the more central debate between determinists and constructivists.
C **Correct.** The passage is mainly concerned with portraying Clark's view as a successful challenge to constructivism.
D The passage describes Clark's view as a successful challenge to social constructivism, not technological determinism.
E The passage is concerned with describing a challenge to social constructivism and not with suggesting the context in which technological change ought to be studied.

The correct answer is C.

RC00013-02

584. Which of the following statements about the modernization of the telephone exchange is supported by information in the passage?

(A) The new technology reduced the role of managers in labor negotiations.
(B) The modernization was implemented without the consent of the employees directly affected by it.
(C) The modernization had an impact that went significantly beyond maintenance routines.
(D) Some of the maintenance workers felt victimized by the new technology.
(E) The modernization gave credence to the view of advocates of social constructivism.

Supporting ideas

This question requires recognizing information contained in the passage. The passage states in the first paragraph that Clark's study focused on the modernization of a telephone exchange and the effect this had on maintenance work and workers. After describing Braverman's analysis in the second paragraph as being at odds with Clark's views, the passage discusses Clark's views in more detail in the final paragraph. As part of this discussion, the passage notes that Clark shows how a change from *maintenance-intensive electromechanical switches to semielectronic switching systems* at the telephone exchange *altered work tasks, skills, training opportunities, administration, and organization of workers* (lines 42–44). Thus, the passage shows that the modernization of the telephone exchange affected much more than maintenance routines.

A The passage does not discuss whether new technology reduces the role of managers in labor negotiations.
B The passage does not discuss the role of employee consent in the modernization of the telephone exchange.

533

C **Correct.** The passage states that the modernization of the telephone exchange affected tasks, skills, training, administration, and the organization of workers.
D The passage does not suggest that maintenance workers felt victimized by the modernization of the telephone exchange.
E The passage describes modernization as a fact viewable from a perspective of social constructivism or technological determinism, but that does not in itself support either view.

The correct answer is C.

RC00013-03

585. Which of the following most accurately describes Clark's opinion of Braverman's position?

(A) He respects its wide-ranging popularity.
(B) He disapproves of its misplaced emphasis on the influence of managers.
(C) He admires the consideration it gives to the attitudes of the workers affected.
(D) He is concerned about its potential to impede the implementation of new technologies.
(E) He is sympathetic to its concern about the impact of modern technology on workers.

Inference

Answering this question requires inferring what the passage's author likely believes. The passage describes Braverman's position as one of mainstream social constructivism (lines 23–24), a position that Clark takes issue with. Although it describes Braverman's position, the rest of the passage is devoted to showing how Clark's position takes issue with Braverman's. In the second paragraph, the passage describes Clark as holding that *technology can be a primary determinant of social and managerial organization* (lines 9–11), which suggests that managers are sometimes subordinate to technological change. In lines 15–17, however, Braverman is described as holding that *the shape of a technological system is subordinate to the manager's desire to wrest control of*

the labor process from the workers, which shows that Clark and Braverman are at odds on this point.

A Since the passage says that Clark believes an important insight *has been obscured by the recent sociological fashion* that Braverman's views exemplify (lines 11–14), one cannot infer that Clark respects the popularity of Braverman's views.
B **Correct.** The passage shows that Clark believes managers to have less influence over how technology affects an organization than Braverman claims that they have.
C The passage does not indicate that Clark admires any aspect of Braverman's position.
D The passage does not indicate that Clark considers impediments to modernization.
E The passage does not indicate that Clark is sympathetic to any concerns attributed to Braverman.

The correct answer is B.

RC00013-04

586. The information in the passage suggests that which of the following statements from hypothetical sociological studies of change in industry most clearly exemplifies the social constructivists' version of technological determinism?

(A) It is the available technology that determines workers' skills, rather than workers' skills influencing the application of technology.
(B) All progress in industrial technology grows out of a continuing negotiation between technological possibility and human need.
(C) Some organizational change is caused by people; some is caused by computer chips.
(D) Most major technological advances in industry have been generated through research and development.
(E) Some industrial technology eliminates jobs, but educated workers can create whole new skills areas by the adaptation of the technology.

Application

This question requires understanding different points of view discussed in the passage. In the first paragraph, the passage mentions the debate involving technological determinism and social constructivism. In the second and third paragraphs, the passage uses Braverman's analysis to illustrate the social constructivists' position and in the third paragraph suggests that the constructivists are *misrepresenting technological determinism* (line 24). In lines 29–30, the constructivists are reported to hold that technological determinism views technology as *existing outside society, capable of directly influencing skills and work organization.*

A   **Correct.** This statement is consistent with the constructivists' view that technological determinism sees technology as outside of society, influencing workers' skills.
B   The passage states that the constructivists hold that *technological determinists are supposed to believe . . . that machinery imposes appropriate forms of order on society* (lines 25–27), suggesting that no negotiation is present.
C   According to the description of them in the passage, constructivists portray technological determinists as believing that technology, not people, drives organizational change.
D   The passage does not portray either constructivists or determinists as being concerned with technological research and development.
E   The passage does not portray either constructivists or determinists as being concerned with technology-driven job elimination or creation.

The correct answer is A.

RC00013-05
587. The information in the passage suggests that Clark believes that which of the following would be true if social constructivism had not gained widespread acceptance?

(A) Businesses would be more likely to modernize without considering the social consequences of their actions.
(B) There would be greater understanding of the role played by technology in producing social change.
(C) Businesses would be less likely to understand the attitudes of employees affected by modernization.
(D) Modernization would have occurred at a slower rate.
(E) Technology would have played a greater part in determining the role of business in society.

Inference

Answering this question involves understanding a point of view as it is described in the passage. The passage aligns Clark's study closely with the technological determinists, summarizing his view in lines 9–11: *technology can be a primary determinant of social and managerial organization*. In the following sentence, the passage states that Clark believes that *this possibility is obscured by the recent sociological fashion, exemplified by Braverman's analysis* (lines 11–13). After illustrating Braverman's analysis, the passage then states that it represents *social constructivism*.

A   According to the passage, Clark holds that constructivists obscure how modernization might have social consequences.
B   **Correct.** According to the passage, Clark sees constructivism as obscuring the possibility that technology plays a primary role in social change.
C   The passage does not discuss how the attitudes of employees are perceived by their employers.
D   The passage describes a debate about the history and sociology of technology; it does not suggest that sociological analyses affect the pace of modernization.
E   The passage describes a debate about the history and sociology of technology; it does not suggest that sociological analyses affect the role that technology plays in business.

The correct answer is B.

588. According to the passage, constructivists employed which of the following to promote their argument?

(A) Empirical studies of business situations involving technological change
(B) Citation of managers supportive of their position
(C) Construction of hypothetical situations that support their view
(D) Contrasts of their view with a misstatement of an opposing view
(E) Descriptions of the breadth of impact of technological change

Supporting ideas

Answering this question involves recognizing information given in the passage. The passage indicates that a debate exists between technological determinists and social constructivists, suggesting that these views are in opposition. The passage goes on to state that *constructivists gain acceptance by misrepresenting technological determinism* (lines 23–24). This misrepresentation is presented as the *alternative to constructivism* (lines 27–28), suggesting that constructivists promoted their own view by contrasting it with a misrepresentation of determinists' views.

A   The passage mentions empirical studies in relation to Clark's study but not Braverman's analysis.
B   The passage does not mention that managers were supportive of any particular point of view within the sociology of technology.
C   The passage does not mention any hypothetical situations as being used by the constructivists in support of their view.
D   **Correct.** The passage indicates that the constructivists have come into fashion by contrasting their own views with a misrepresentation of the views of technological determinists.
E   The passage does not describe the constructivists as making determinations regarding the degree of impact that technological change has on social or managerial organization.

The correct answer is D.

589. The author of the passage uses the expression "are supposed to" in line 25 primarily in order to

(A) suggest that a contention made by constructivists regarding determinists is inaccurate
(B) define the generally accepted position of determinists regarding the implementation of technology
(C) engage in speculation about the motivation of determinists
(D) lend support to a comment critical of the position of determinists
(E) contrast the historical position of determinists with their position regarding the exchange modernization

Evaluation

This question requires understanding how a particular phrase functions in the passage as a whole. In the third paragraph the passage states that *constructivists gain acceptance by misrepresenting technological determinism* (lines 23–24) and follows this claim with an example of this misrepresentation, stating that *technological determinists are supposed to believe, for example* (lines 25–26). This line implies that the constructivist view of the determinists is inaccurate.

A   **Correct.** The passage uses the expression in part to provide an example of the constructivists' misrepresentation of the determinists.
B   The passage indicates that the view attributed to the determinists is a misrepresentation, not one that is generally accepted by determinists.
C   The expression in the passage is part of a discussion about the motivation of constructivists, not determinists.
D   The expression in the passage is part of a discussion that is critical of the constructivists, not the determinists.
E   The passage does not describe either the historical position of determinists or their position on the exchange modernization.

The correct answer is A.

7.6 Reading Comprehension Answer Explanations

RC00013-09

590. Which of the following statements about Clark's study of the telephone exchange can be inferred from information in the passage?

(A) Clark's reason for undertaking the study was to undermine Braverman's analysis of the function of technology.
(B) Clark's study suggests that the implementation of technology should be discussed in the context of conflict between labor and management.
(C) Clark examined the impact of changes in the technology of switching at the exchange in terms of overall operations and organization.
(D) Clark concluded that the implementation of new switching technology was equally beneficial to management and labor.
(E) Clark's analysis of the change in switching systems applies only narrowly to the situation at the particular exchange that he studied.

Inference

This question requires understanding what the passage implies in its discussion of a point of view. The details of Clark's views are discussed primarily in the final paragraph. The passage states that on an empirical level, Clark demonstrates that technological change regarding switches at the telephone exchange *altered work tasks, skills, training opportunities, administration, and organization of workers* (lines 42–44). The passage goes on to state Clark's contention that these changes even influenced negotiations between management and labor unions.

A The passage indicates that Clark's study addressed the extremes of both technological determinism and social constructivism. It cites Braverman as a proponent of social constructivism but provides no evidence that Clark's motivation in beginning his study was specifically to target an analysis offered by Braverman.
B The passage indicates that Clark attributed some organizational change to the way labor and management negotiated the introduction of technology but does not mention conflict between them.

C **Correct.** According to the passage, Clark concludes that changes to the technology of switches had an influence on several aspects of the overall operations and organization of the telephone exchange.
D The passage does not indicate that Clark assesses the benefits of technological change to either labor or management.
E The passage indicates that Clark believes the change in switching technology influenced many aspects of the overall operations of the telephone exchange.

The correct answer is C.

Questions 591–595 refer to the passage on page 454.

RC00650-02

591. The passage implies that which of the following was a reason that the proportion of verdicts in favor of patentees began to increase in the 1830s?

(A) Patent applications approved after 1836 were more likely to adhere closely to patent law.
(B) Patent laws enacted during the 1830s better defined patent rights.
(C) Judges became less prejudiced against patentees during the 1830s.
(D) After 1836, litigated cases became less representative of the population of patent disputes.
(E) The proportion of patent disputes brought to trial began to increase after 1836.

Inference

The question asks which statement can be reasonably inferred, from information provided in the passage, to be a reason for the increase in proportion of verdicts favoring patentees, starting in the 1830s. The second paragraph argues that what changed in that decade was not judges' attitudes toward patent law, but the types of patent cases that were litigated. It explains that a law passed in 1836 required that, for the first time in U.S. history, applications for patents had to be examined for their adherence to patent law before a patent would be issued. This information implies that patents granted after 1836 were more likely to adhere to patent law and were thus more likely to be upheld in court.

A **Correct.** The passage implies that patents granted after the 1836 law went into effect were more likely to adhere to patent law.
B The passage does not indicate that any law mentioned made changes to the definition of patent rights; rather, the passage indicates that the patent system was revised to require that patent applications be reviewed for adherence to existing law.
C The passage rejects the explanation that judges' attitudes toward patent rights became more favorable.
D The passage indicates that the population of disputes that were litigated changed after 1836, but it does not suggest that the population of litigated disputes differed from that of patent disputes as a whole.
E The passage does not indicate any change in the proportion of patent disputes brought to trial.

The correct answer is A.

RC00650-03

592. The passage implies that the scholars mentioned in line 8 would agree with which of the following criticisms of the American patent system before 1830?

(A) Its definition of property rights relating to inventions was too vague to be useful.
(B) Its criteria for the granting of patents were not clear.
(C) It made it excessively difficult for inventors to receive patents.
(D) It led to excessive numbers of patent-infringement suits.
(E) It failed to encourage national economic growth.

Inference

This question asks about a statement implied by the passage. The scholars mentioned in line 8 question whether U.S. patent law achieved its goal. That goal is described in the first sentence of the passage: to encourage America's economic growth. Thus, it is reasonable to conclude that the scholars would criticize the pre-1830 patent system for failing to encourage economic growth.

A The scholars contend that judges rejected patents for arbitrary reasons, not because the definition of property rights was vague.

B The passage does not indicate that the scholars were critical of the criteria for granting patents.
C The scholars are concerned with inventors' attempts to protect their patents, not the difficulty of acquiring a patent in the first place.
D The passage does not imply that the scholars in question believed that too many patent-infringement suits were brought to court, but rather that too few succeeded.
E **Correct.** The scholars doubt that patent law helped to achieve its goal, which was to encourage economic growth.

The correct answer is E.

RC00650-06

593. It can be inferred from the passage that the frequency with which pre-1830 cases have been cited in court decisions is an indication that

(A) judicial support for patent rights was strongest in the period before 1830
(B) judicial support for patent rights did not increase after 1830
(C) courts have returned to judicial standards that prevailed before 1830
(D) verdicts favoring patentees in patent-infringement suits did not increase after 1830
(E) judicial bias against patentees persisted after 1830

Inference

The question asks what is indicated by the frequency with which pre-1830 cases have been cited in court decisions. The second paragraph rejects some scholars' claims that judges prior to the 1830s were *antipatent*, while judges after that time were more accepting of patent rights. The passage supports its critique by pointing out that decisions made by judges before the 1830s have been cited as precedents by later judges just as frequently as post-1830s decisions have been. This implies that later judges' attitudes toward patent rights were similar to those of pre-1830s judges. Thus, there is no reason to believe judges' attitudes toward patent rights changed at that time.

A The passage argues that judicial support for patents did not change in the 1830s.
B **Correct.** Pre-1830s court decisions have been cited as frequently as later decisions, suggesting no change in judges' attitudes.
C The passage does not indicate that judicial standards changed from, and then returned to, those that prevailed before 1830.
D Although actual numbers of favorable verdicts are not mentioned, the passage indicates that the proportion of verdicts decided in favor of patentees did, in fact, increase beginning in the 1830s.
E The passage rejects the notion that judges were biased against patentees either before or after 1830.

The correct answer is B.

RC00650-07

594. It can be inferred from the passage that the author and the scholars referred to in line 21 disagree about which of the following aspects of the patents defended in patent-infringement suits before 1830?

(A) Whether the patents were granted for inventions that were genuinely useful
(B) Whether the patents were actually relevant to the growth of the United States economy
(C) Whether the patents were particularly likely to be annulled by judges
(D) Whether the patents were routinely invalidated for reasons that were arbitrary
(E) Whether the patents were vindicated at a significantly lower rate than patents in later suits

Inference

The question depends on recognizing differences between two explanations—one favored by the scholars mentioned in line 21, the other favored by the author—for the frequency with which patents were invalidated in U.S. courts prior to 1830. The first paragraph describes the scholars' view that judges before 1830 were *antipatent* and rejected patentees' claims for *arbitrary reasons*. The author of the passage rejects that view. As an alternate explanation, the author in the second paragraph implies that earlier patents often violated copyright law; this view is supported with reference to an 1836 revision to the patent system which instituted a procedure by which patent applications were inspected to ensure adherence to patent law.

A The author and the scholars are both focused on protecting inventors' property rights, not with their inventions' utility.
B Although the passage suggests that the scholars thought America's patent system did not help encourage economic growth, there is no suggestion that either the scholars or the author believes actual patents defended in court were irrelevant to economic growth.
C Both the scholars and the author believe that patents defended in court prior to 1830 were more likely to be invalidated than were patents in later legal disputes.
D **Correct.** The scholars claim that judges before 1830 decided against patentees for arbitrary reasons, but the passage suggests that the patents may have been invalidated because they failed to adhere to patent law.
E Both the scholars and the author accept that patents were upheld in court less often before 1830 than after.

The correct answer is D.

RC00650-08

595. The author of the passage cites which of the following as evidence challenging the argument referred to in lines 14–15 ?

(A) The proportion of cases that were decided against patentees in the 1820s
(B) The total number of patent disputes that were litigated from 1794 to 1830
(C) The fact that later courts drew upon the legal precedents set in pre-1830 patent cases
(D) The fact that the proportion of judicial decisions in favor of patentees began to increase during the 1830s
(E) The constitutional rationale for the 1836 revision of the patent system

Supporting idea

The question asks what evidence the author brings to bear against the argument referred to in lines 14–15. In the first paragraph, the author summarizes scholars' arguments to the conclusion that judges' attitudes toward patent rights shifted in the 1830s, based on the fact that judges earlier had routinely ruled against patentees in lawsuits whereas judges after that time provided more protection for patent rights. In the second paragraph the author challenges the claim that judges' attitudes shifted. The author provides evidence that judges after the 1830s cited legal precedents set in pre-1830s cases, suggesting that their views had not changed.

A The proportion of cases decided against patentees in the 1920s is cited as evidence that supports the scholars' argument in the first paragraph, not as evidence challenging their views.
B The total number of disputes litigated is not mentioned in the passage.
C **Correct.** The fact that judges after 1830 cited earlier cases as precedents is used as evidence to challenge scholars' claims that judges' attitudes shifted around 1830.
D The change in the proportion of decisions in favor of patentees is a fact that both the scholars and the author of the passage attempt to explain.
E No constitutional rationale for the 1836 law is mentioned in the passage.

The correct answer is C.

Questions 596–602 refer to the passage on page 456.

RC00313-01
596. The author of the passage discusses Krontiris primarily to provide an example of a writer who

(A) is highly critical of the writings of certain Renaissance women
(B) supports Kelly's view of women's status during the Renaissance
(C) has misinterpreted the works of certain Renaissance women
(D) has rejected the views of both Burckhardt and Kelly
(E) has studied Renaissance women in a wide variety of social and religious contexts

Evaluation

This question focuses on the author's reason for mentioning Krontiris's work. The passage states that Krontiris, in her discussion of six Renaissance women writers, is an example of scholars who are optimistic about women's achievements but also suggest that these women faced significant obstacles. She is a writer who, in other words, agrees with neither Kelly's negative views nor Burckhardt's positive approach.

A The passage indicates that Krontiris uses the Renaissance women writers' works as historical evidence, not that she offered any criticism of the works themselves.
B Krontiris's work, according to the author, is cautiously optimistic about women's achievements during the Renaissance. This contradicts Kelly's view that the status of women declined during this time.
C The author suggests that Krontiris may have erred in taking her six subjects as representative of all women during the Renaissance, not that she made any misinterpretations of their actual writing.
D **Correct.** The author uses Krontiris as an example of those feminist scholars who have rejected the overgeneralized approaches of both Kelly and Burckhardt.
E The author makes clear that Krontiris's study focuses on literate Renaissance women, who constituted a small minority.

The correct answer is D.

RC00313-02
597. According to the passage, Krontiris's work differs from that of the scholars mentioned in line 12 in which of the following ways?

(A) Krontiris's work stresses the achievements of Renaissance women rather than the obstacles to their success.
(B) Krontiris's work is based on a reinterpretation of the work of earlier scholars.
(C) Krontiris's views are at odds with those of both Kelly and Burkhardt.
(D) Krontiris's work focuses on the place of women in Renaissance society.
(E) Krontiris's views are based exclusively on the study of a privileged group of women.

Supporting idea

This question asks what the passage directly states about the difference between Krontiris's work and the feminist scholars mentioned in the first paragraph. The feminist scholars mentioned in the first paragraph explore differences among Renaissance women, particularly their social status and religion, and thus complicate Burckhardt's and Kelly's generalizations. Krontiris's work, on the other hand, focuses on Renaissance women writers, who are a distinctly privileged and small social group.

A The second paragraph makes clear that Krontiris addresses the obstacles faced by Renaissance women.
B The passage does not suggest that Krontiris is reinterpreting or drawing on reinterpretations of the work of earlier scholars.
C The second paragraph shows that Krontiris's work does complicate both Burckhardt's and Kelly's views, but in this, she is in agreement with the feminist scholars mentioned in the first paragraph.
D Both Krontiris and the feminist scholars mentioned in the first paragraph are concerned with the place of women in Renaissance society.
E **Correct.** The feminist scholars mentioned in the first paragraph are concerned with women of different social classes and religions, whereas Krontiris's work focuses on a limited social group.

The correct answer is E.

RC00313-03
598. According to the passage, feminist scholars cite Burckhardt's view of Renaissance women primarily for which of the following reasons?

(A) Burckhardt's view forms the basis for most arguments refuting Kelly's point of view.
(B) Burckhardt's view has been discredited by Kelly.
(C) Burckhardt's view is one that many feminist scholars wish to refute.
(D) Burckhardt's work provides rich historical evidence of inequality between Renaissance women and men.
(E) Burckhardt's work includes historical research supporting the arguments of the feminist scholars.

Supporting idea

This question asks what the passage says explicitly about why feminist scholars reference Burckhardt's view of Renaissance women. The first paragraph states that Burckhardt's view is that Renaissance women enjoyed *perfect equality* with men, and then follows that by noting how feminist scholars have *repeatedly cited* this view to contrast it with extensive evidence of women's inequality during the Renaissance.

A The passage does not indicate that any feminist scholars cite Burckhardt to refute Kelly's view. It uses Krontiris as an example of scholars who refute Kelly's point of view to a certain degree, but Krontiris does not use Burckhardt's view as her basis for doing so; Krontiris argues against Burckhardt as well.
B According to the first paragraph, Kelly's work was in certain ways inconsistent with Burckhardt's view, but that is not a reason why Burckhardt's view is cited by feminist scholars. Rather, according to the passage, they cite it in order to argue against it.
C **Correct.** Many feminist scholars wish to refute Burckhardt's view that Renaissance women and men were equal.
D As the first paragraph makes clear, Burckhardt's work emphasizes equality, not inequality, between Renaissance women and men.
E The passage does not discuss the historical research on which Burckhardt based his work.

The correct answer is C.

599. It can be inferred that both Burckhardt and Kelly have been criticized by the scholars mentioned in line 12 for which of the following?

(A) Assuming that women writers of the Renaissance are representative of Renaissance women in general
(B) Drawing conclusions that are based on the study of an atypical group of women
(C) Failing to describe clearly the relationship between social status and literacy among Renaissance women
(D) Failing to acknowledge the role played by Renaissance women in opposing cultural stereotypes
(E) Failing to acknowledge the ways in which social status affected the creative activities of Renaissance women

Inference

Line 12 refers to feminist scholars who have rejected both Kelly's and Burckhardt's views of the status of Renaissance women. The next sentence states that the feminist scholars use class and religious differences among Renaissance women to argue against Kelly's and Burckhardt's generalizations, which were based on upper-class Italian women.

A   The second paragraph suggests that Krontiris at times conflates Renaissance women writers and women in general, but the passage does not indicate that the feminist scholars believe this of Kelly or Burckhardt.
B   **Correct.** The feminist scholars mentioned study different types of Renaissance women and so reject Kelly's and Burckhardt's conclusions that were based on a group that was not in fact typical.
C   Krontiris, not Kelly and Burckhardt, is the scholar who, according to the passage, fails to address the relationship between literacy and social status.
D   The passage provides no grounds for determining whether Kelly, Burckhardt, or the feminist scholars mentioned in the first paragraph dealt with Renaissance women's opposition to cultural stereotypes; Krontiris's work is concerned with this question.

E   The first paragraph suggests that feminist scholars criticized Kelly and Burckhardt for failing to acknowledge the ways in which social status complicates any generalizations that can be made about Renaissance women's lives, not their creative activities specifically.

The correct answer is B.

600. The author of the passage suggests that Krontiris incorrectly assumes that

(A) social differences among Renaissance women are less important than the fact that they were women
(B) literacy among Renaissance women was more prevalent than most scholars today acknowledge
(C) during the Renaissance, women were able to successfully oppose cultural stereotypes relating to gender
(D) Renaissance women did not face many difficult social obstacles relating to their gender
(E) in order to attain power, Renaissance women attacked basic assumptions in the ideologies that oppressed them

Inference

The first statement the author makes about Krontiris, in the second paragraph, concerns what the author characterizes as a problem with Krontiris's work. Krontiris takes the Renaissance women writers she studies as representative of all Renaissance women; the author says that designating *women* as the most important grouping fails to consider whether other social differences might make for differences in experience.

A   **Correct.** The author indicates that Krontiris's error lies in assuming that women's identity as women trumps social and other differences.
B   The author does not suggest that Krontiris assumes inappropriate literacy levels among Renaissance women, but rather that Krontiris does not give sufficient consideration to the idea that women who could read and write most likely led lives very different from those of women who could not read and write.

C   The author says that Krontiris suggests that there were many cultural stereotypes that women were not able to oppose effectively.
D   Krontiris, according to the author, acknowledges the many social obstacles faced by women on the basis of their gender.
E   According to the author, Krontiris's concluding remarks suggest that Renaissance women *seldom attacked the basic assumptions in the ideologies that oppressed them.*

The correct answer is A.

RC00313-06

601. The last sentence in the passage serves primarily to

(A) suggest that Krontiris's work is not representative of recent trends among feminist scholars
(B) undermine the argument that literate women of the Renaissance sought to oppose social constraints imposed on them
(C) show a way in which Krontiris's work illustrates a "cautiously optimistic" assessment of Renaissance women's achievements
(D) summarize Krontiris's view of the effect of literacy on the lives of upper- and middle-class Renaissance women
(E) illustrate the way in which Krontiris's study differs from the studies done by Burckhardt and Kelly

Evaluation

The function of the final sentence of the passage is to indicate how Krontiris's work takes neither a completely positive nor completely negative view of Renaissance women's experiences—i.e., how her work is representative of those authors who are cautiously optimistic about the achievements of Renaissance women.

A   The passage discusses Krontiris's work as an example of the trend described in the latter part of the first paragraph and mentioned in the first line of the second paragraph. The last sentence in the passage shows that Krontiris's work is in fact representative of recent trends among feminist scholars.

B   The last sentence in the passage states that Renaissance women's opposition to cultural stereotypes was circumscribed, but it also suggests that these women did gain some power for themselves. Thus, the sentence does not serve primarily to undermine the argument that the women sought to oppose social constraints.

C   **Correct.** Krontiris's work illustrates the "cautiously optimistic" view by embracing both the idea that Renaissance women could gain a certain amount of power and the idea that the extent of their opposition was limited.

D   The last sentence in the passage summarizes Krontiris's view, but that view does not, according to the passage, take into account the effect of literacy on the members of a particular social class.

E   The main function of the final sentence of the passage is to take up the idea of the *cautiously optimistic* assessment offered in the penultimate sentence. This does mark a significant departure from both Burckhardt and Kelly, but the distinction between their work and that of other feminist scholars is marked more clearly earlier in the passage.

The correct answer is C.

RC00313-08

602. The author of the passage implies that the women studied by Krontiris are unusual in which of the following ways?

(A) They faced obstacles less formidable than those faced by other Renaissance women.
(B) They have been seen by historians as more interesting than other Renaissance women.
(C) They were more concerned about recording history accurately than were other Renaissance women.
(D) Their perceptions are more likely to be accessible to historians than are those of most other Renaissance women.
(E) Their concerns are likely to be of greater interest to feminist scholars than are the ideas of most other Renaissance women.

Inference

The women Krontiris studied are unusual, the author suggests, because they were literate, thus putting them among the minority of Renaissance women. That they could write, however, means that their written reflections are part of the historical record, whereas the direct impressions of experiences had by Renaissance women who could not write about their lives are lost to history.

A   The author implies that the obstacles faced by Krontiris's subjects may have been different from those faced by other women, not that they were less formidable.
B   The author does not imply that the women studied by Krontiris are seen as more interesting; rather, the author indicates that their work is that which is available for study.
C   The women Krontiris studies were able to record their own history because they, unlike most other Renaissance women, were literate. This does not imply that they were more concerned with recording history accurately.
D   **Correct.** Because Krontiris's subjects were literate, they were able to write down, and thus preserve for historians, their perceptions in a way that most other Renaissance women were not.
E   The author does not suggest that feminist scholars in general are more interested in the concerns of middle- and upper-class literate women than they are with women of other classes.

The correct answer is D.

Questions 603–606 refer to the passage on page 458.

RC00524-02
603. The passage implies which of the following about the five asteroids mentioned in line 12 ?

(A)   Their rotation rates are approximately the same.
(B)   They have undergone approximately the same number of collisions.
(C)   They are monoliths.
(D)   They are composed of fragments that have escaped the gravity of larger asteroids.
(E)   They were detected only recently.

Inference

In line 12, *five observed asteroids*, refers to the five asteroids whose rotation rates are exceptions to the strict limit on the rate of rotation found in all other observed asteroids. These five asteroids all have diameters smaller than 200 meters. The passage indicates that if asteroids were all monoliths—that is, single rocks—then their rotation rates would form a bell curve when graphed, but if asteroids were piles of rubble, the tail of the bell curve indicating very fast rotation rates would be missing. Among asteroids larger than 200 meters, this tail is missing, and only the five asteroids described as exceptions have rotation rates falling at the very high end of the bell curve.

A   All that the passage states about the rotation rates of these five asteroids is that they do not obey a strict limit. The passage does not rule out that their rates of rotation are significantly different from one another.
B   According to the passage, frequent collisions occur among asteroids. But the passage does not suggest that asteroids that are of similar sizes, or that have particularly high rotation rates, will be similar in terms of the number of collisions that they have undergone to reach those distinctive states.
C   **Correct.** The second paragraph states that *most small asteroids* should be monolithic, and the five observed asteroids are all smaller than 200 meters in diameter.
D   The five asteroids are most likely not composed of fragments because, as the passage states, small asteroids should be monoliths.
E   The passage notes that researchers have observed these five asteroids, along with others, but it does not indicate when these asteroids were originally detected.

The correct answer is C.

7.6 Reading Comprehension Answer Explanations

RC00524-04
604. The discovery of which of the following would call into question the conclusion mentioned in line 16?

(A) An asteroid 100 meters in diameter rotating at a rate of once per week
(B) An asteroid 150 meters in diameter rotating at a rate of 20 times per hour
(C) An asteroid 250 meters in diameter rotating at a rate of once per week
(D) An asteroid 500 meters in diameter rotating at a rate of once per hour
(E) An asteroid 1,000 meters in diameter rotating at a rate of once every 24 hours

Application

The conclusion that the text in line 16 points to is that asteroids with diameters greater than 200 meters are *multicomponent structures or rubble piles*. To call that conclusion into question, an observation would have to suggest that asteroids larger than 200 meters across are not such multicomponent structures. According to the first paragraph, rubble piles cannot be fast rotators: spinning faster than once every few hours would make them fly apart.

A   Nothing in the passage suggests that the behavior of an asteroid 100 meters in diameter is relevant to a conclusion about the behavior of asteroids greater than 200 meters in diameter.

B   Nothing in the passage suggests that the behavior of an asteroid 150 meters in diameter would have any effect on a conclusion about the constitution of asteroids with diameters greater than 200 meters.

C   An asteroid 250 meters in diameter rotating at a rate of once per week would be rotating at a slow enough rate to hold together a pile of rubble. Thus, this observation would be entirely consistent with the conclusion about asteroids larger than 200 meters in diameter.

D   **Correct.** Assuming that an asteroid composed of a pile of rubble is of a great enough density, a rotation rate greater than one revolution every few hours would make it fly apart. So a 500-meter asteroid rotating at a rate of once per hour—that is, faster than the crucial speed—would fly apart if it were not a monolith. The conclusion states that all asteroids larger than 200 meters are multicomponent structures (that is, are not monoliths), so the discovery of a 500-meter asteroid rotating at a rate of once an hour would call into question that conclusion.

E   An asteroid rotating at a rate of once every 24 hours would, regardless of size, be rotating much more slowly than the *once every few hours* that the passage claims would make a pile of rubble of a sufficient density fly apart. So an asteroid with a diameter of 1,000 meters that rotated once per day could be a pile of rubble and not conflict with the conclusion.

The correct answer is D.

RC00524-06
605. According to the passage, which of the following is a prediction that is based on the strength of the gravitational attraction of small asteroids?

(A) Small asteroids will be few in number.
(B) Small asteroids will be monoliths.
(C) Small asteroids will collide with other asteroids very rarely.
(D) Most small asteroids will have very fast rotation rates.
(E) Almost no small asteroids will have very slow rotation rates.

Supporting ideas

Regarding small asteroids, the second paragraph states that they have feeble gravity. Any fragments from impacts would escape that gravity, and thus, the passage states, the small asteroids *should be monolithic*.

545

A Small asteroids could be few in number, but the passage does not offer such a prediction.
B **Correct.** This prediction is offered in the second paragraph, based on the fact that small asteroids do not have strong gravitational attraction. Any impact fragments will easily escape the weak gravitational attraction of the small asteroids.
C The passage discusses large asteroids collisions in more detail than small-asteroid collisions, but it provides no basis for predicting how often large and small asteroids will, comparatively, be involved in such collisions.
D The first paragraph indicates that the rotation rates of small asteroids can exceed the upper limit on the rotation rates of large asteroids, but it does not indicate that most small asteroids have rotation rates that exceed this upper limit.
E The passage only indicates that there are few observed exceptions to the upper limit on rotation rates of large asteroids, and these exceptions are all smaller than 200 meters in diameter; the passage does not indicate that there are few small asteroids that have very slow rotation rates.

The correct answer is B.

RC00524-07
606. The author of the passage mentions "escape velocity" (see line 22) in order to help explain which of the following?

(A) The tendency for asteroids to become smaller rather than larger over time
(B) The speed with which impact fragments reassemble when they do not escape an asteroid's gravitational attraction after a collision
(C) The frequency with which collisions among asteroids occur
(D) The rotation rates of asteroids smaller than 200 meters in diameter
(E) The tendency for large asteroids to persist after collisions

Evaluation

This question asks about the purpose of the author's use of the phrase *escape velocity* in the second paragraph. The author is discussing what occurs after an asteroid collision, in which a large asteroid might be blasted to bits. The bits, according to the author, will move slower than their *mutual escape velocity*—that is, the speed at which they would have to move to get away from each other and not reassemble, under the influence of gravity, into a rubble pile.

A The author is emphasizing the asteroid bits that do not escape rather than those that do. Asteroids may become smaller over time, but the fact that most bits move slower than their escape velocity would not help to explain this shrinkage.
B That the bits of asteroid move slower than their escape velocity helps explain why the fragments reassemble, but it does not help explain the speed with which they reassemble.
C According to the author, asteroid collisions occur frequently, but the escape velocity of the resulting fragments does not help to explain that frequency.
D The concept of escape velocity may help explain why small asteroids are monoliths, but it has no relevance, at least as far as the passage indicates, to those asteroids' rotation rates.
E **Correct.** After a collision, it is the asteroid fragments' failure to reach escape velocity that allows the fragments' gravitational pull to reassemble them into a rubble pile.

The correct answer is E.

Questions 607–609 refer to the passage on page 460.

RC00301-04

607. The author of the passage mentions calculations about tunneling time and barrier thickness in order to

(A) suggest that tunneling time is unrelated to barrier thickness
(B) explain the evidence by which Wigner and Eisenbud discovered the phenomenon of tunneling
(C) describe data recently challenged by Raymond Chiao and colleagues
(D) question why particles engaged in quantum tunneling rarely achieve extremely high speeds
(E) explain the basis for Wigner and Eisenbud's hypothesis

Evaluation

This question asks why the author discusses calculations about tunneling time and barrier thickness. According to the passage, these calculations provided the grounds for Wigner and Eisenbud's hypothesis that tunneling particles may travel faster than light.

A The passage states that tunneling time is related to barrier thickness, up to the point at which tunneling time reaches a maximum.
B The passage indicates that the phenomenon of tunneling was noted at least as early as 1932. It provides no evidence that Wigner and Eisenbud discovered it.
C The passage uses Chiao's work to support the idea that tunneling particles may move faster than light, not challenge it.
D The author describes calculations about tunneling time and barrier thickness in order to explain that particles engaged in quantum tunneling may in fact achieve extremely high speeds, not to explain the rarity of the phenomenon.
E **Correct.** The calculations about tunneling time and barrier thickness supported Wigner and Eisenbud's hypothesis that quantum tunneling could occur at speeds faster than that of light.

The correct answer is E.

RC00301-03
608. The passage implies that if tunneling time reached no maximum in increasing with barrier thickness, then

(A) tunneling speed would increase with barrier thickness
(B) tunneling speed would decline with barrier thickness
(C) tunneling speed would vary with barrier thickness
(D) tunneling speed would not be expected to increase without limit
(E) successful tunneling would occur even less frequently than it does

Inference

The passage states that because tunneling time reaches a maximum, then tunneling speed must increase as barrier thickness increases. But if tunneling time did not reach such a maximum, then speed need not increase without limit; the particle could have as low a speed in thicker barriers as in thinner ones and take longer to tunnel through a barrier.

A If tunneling time could not reach a maximum, then speed might increase, decrease, or remain the same as barrier thickness increases.
B If tunneling time could not reach a maximum, then speed might increase, decrease, or remain the same as barrier thickness increases.
C Tunneling speed could vary with barrier thickness if tunneling time could not reach a maximum, but there is no basis in the passage on which to conclude that this is definitely so.
D **Correct.** The tunneling particle could have as low a speed in thicker barriers as in thinner ones and simply take longer to make its way through a thicker barrier.
E The passage states that the probability of successful tunneling declines as the thickness of the barrier increases. However, it does not address the issue of whether the differences in probability of successful tunneling are due to the greater time required to go through thicker barriers.

The correct answer is D.

609. Which of the following statements about the earliest scientific investigators of quantum tunneling can be inferred from the passage?

   (A) They found it difficult to increase barrier thickness continually.
   (B) They anticipated the later results of Chiao and his colleagues.
   (C) They did not suppose that tunneling particles could travel faster than light.
   (D) They were unable to observe instances of successful tunneling.
   (E) They made use of photons to study the phenomenon of tunneling.

Inference

This question asks about the earliest investigators of quantum tunneling. The passage notes that quantum tunneling's *extreme rapidity* was observed in 1932; thus, the earliest investigators of this phenomenon knew of its existence at that time. Not until 1955 did Wigner and Eisenbud hypothesize that the particles traveled faster than light. Thus, it is logical to infer that the earliest investigators did not imagine such a speed.

A   There is nothing in the passage to suggest that the earliest investigators of quantum tunneling had difficulty manipulating barrier thickness.

B   The passage states that Chiao and his colleagues measured photons moving at 1.7 times the speed of light—but the passage does not provide evidence that the earliest investigators anticipated such speeds.

C   **Correct.** The passage suggests that prior to 1955, investigators of quantum tunneling had not hypothesized that the particles could travel faster than the speed of light.

D   The passage indicates that by 1932, investigators had noted the rapidity of quantum tunneling; although this does not entail that they observed the phenomenon, it is consistent with their having been able to do so.

E   The passage indicates that Chiao's work involves photons, but it does not indicate the type of particles used or observed by the earliest investigators of the phenomenon.

The correct answer is C.

To register for the GMAT exam go to www.mba.com

8.0 Critical Reasoning

8.0 Critical Reasoning

Critical reasoning questions are designed to test the reasoning skills involved in:

1. constructing an argument
2. evaluating an argument, and
3. formulating or evaluating a plan of action.

The materials on which questions are based are drawn from a variety of sources. The GMAT exam does not expect any familiarity with the subject matter of those materials beyond what is generally known.

Critical reasoning questions are based on passages that are typically less than 100 words in length, and—unlike reading comprehension passages—each critical reasoning passage has just one question associated with it. On the exam, you will see only one passage and question at a time.

Answering critical reasoning questions requires no specialized knowledge. You do not need to know the terminology or conventions of formal logic, but you do need to be familiar with such generally known logical terms as "premise," "conclusion," and "assumption." The sample critical reasoning questions in this chapter illustrate the variety of topics the test may cover, the kinds of questions it may ask, and the level of analysis it requires.

8.1 What Is Measured

A set of critical reasoning questions provides one measure of your ability to deal with reasoning.

For the purposes of the GMAT, reasoning can be thought of as any series of statements of which at least one is given as logical support (evidence) for some other statement. Some examples include reasoning for the purpose of justifying belief in a statement, justifying some plan of action, or explaining why a certain phenomenon occurs.

Many of the passages in critical reasoning questions contain or report reasoning. Some passages display no reasoning and simply present information. Every critical reasoning question, however, will require you to engage in reasoning based on the passage. You may, for example, be asked to draw a conclusion from the given information, i.e., to identify among the answer choices the one statement that is logically supported by the information. Or you may be asked to identify the one statement that most plausibly explains why a phenomenon described in the passage occurred, or to evaluate whether a particular plan of action is likely to achieve the intended goal.

Many different skills are involved in the analysis and evaluation of reasoning. The following table lists the major skills that critical reasoning questions measure:

Question type	Skill	Examples
Analyzing reasoning structure	Ability to identify premises, conclusions, explanations, plan rationales, or background information in passages that contain reasoning	• [in a dialogue] "Ming uses which of the following techniques in responding to Wei?" • Which of the following most accurately describes the functions of each boldfaced part of the passage?
Drawing conclusions (inference)	Ability to infer a statement (draw a conclusion) from given information	• Which of the following is most strongly supported by the information provided? • Which of the following follows logically from the information provided?
Identifying sufficient or required assumptions	Ability to recognize an assumption that can help to complete a logical gap in a piece of reasoning associated with an explanation or the rationale for a policy or plan	• Which of the following is an assumption that Fang's reasoning requires? [or "on which Fang's reasoning depends"] • The conclusion follows logically if which of the following is assumed? • The plan will fail unless which of the following occurs?
Evaluating hypotheses	Ability to identify a hypothesis that most plausibly explains the occurrence of a phenomenon or event	• Which of the following, if true, most helps explain the failure to achieve the plan's objective? • Which of the following is most likely to contribute to the occurrence of the phenomenon observed? • In order to evaluate the force of the archaeologists' evidence, it would be most useful to determine which of the following?
Resolving apparent inconsistency	Ability to reconcile two apparently conflicting states of affairs	• Which of the following most helps to resolve the discrepancy between the reported level of rainfall and the occurrence of flooding in City X?
Identifying information that strengthens or weakens reasoning	Ability to identify information that either provides additional support or undermines reasoning	• Which of the following, if discovered, would cast the most doubt on the engineer's reasoning? • Which of the following, if true, would most strengthen the support for the physician's diagnosis?

Question type	Skill	Examples
Recognizing and describing logical flaws	Ability to identify errors in reasoning such as confusing correlation with causation or confusing a sufficient condition with a necessary one	• Which of the following, if true, most strongly indicates the existence of a flaw in the reasoning? • The reasoning attributed to the executive is most vulnerable to which of the following criticisms?
Identifying a point of disagreement	Ability to precisely identify the key issue on which two parties disagree, based on the statements they have made	• Which of the following is the main point of disagreement between Mandeep and Saumya?
Finding a solution to a practical problem	Ability to recognize a strategy for solving a practical problem	• Which of the following would most help the polling specialists overcome the difficulty they encountered in surveying a sample of likely voters?

8.2 Test-Taking Strategies

To answer critical reasoning questions, you must analyze and logically evaluate the passage on which each question is based, and then select the answer choice that most appropriately answers the question. Begin by carefully reading the passage and the question asked about the passage, then reading the five answer choices. If the correct answer is not immediately obvious to you, see whether you can eliminate some of the wrong answers. Reading the passage a second time may help illuminate subtleties not evident on first reading.

1. **Decide whether you benefit most from reading the passage or the question first.**

   Some test-takers may want to read the passage very carefully first and then read the question. But it can be advantageous to read the question first. Doing so can orient you toward noticing the content or structural features of the passage that are relevant to answering the question. Working through the practice questions in this guide should help you get a good feel for the approach that suits you best.

   Be careful to respond to the question asked. For example, here are two questions that, in a hurried reading, could easily be confused:

   (a) Which of the following is valued by most citizens of Nation X?

   (b) Which of the following is most valued by the citizens of Nation X?

   Something that is valued by most citizens of Nation X may not be the same as what is generally most valued by the citizens of Nation X. For example, the most justified answer to (a) could be "wealth" and the most justified answer to (b) could be "good community relations."

2. **Determine whether the passage contains reasoning or merely provides information.**

   To determine whether the passage contains reasoning, consider whether one or more of the statements are intended to support the truth of any other statement provided, or to justify a plan of action, or to explain some phenomenon. To help determine this, look for certain sorts of words or phrases, sometimes called "inference indicators," that authors may provide when they are presenting a piece of reasoning. For instance, the word *therefore* is frequently used to indicate a conclusion, and the word *because* is frequently used to indicate a premise or reason. Here are other examples (the list is not exhaustive):

- Conclusion indicators: *consequently, it follows that, so, hence*
- Premise indicators: *since, as, for, as is shown by, follows from*

Some of these words have other uses; for example, *since* can signify time or can signify causation. Also, keep in mind that a passage may contain reasoning even if no such indicators are present. Ask yourself whether any of the statements support the truth of another statement, help explain a phenomenon described in the passage, or help support a plan proposed in the passage.

3. **Identify the purpose and structure of any reasoning given in a passage.**

    A good first step in analyzing passages that contain reasoning is to determine the purpose of the reasoning. Does the reasoning aim to provide logical support for a conclusion? If so, then identifying that conclusion will help. Or perhaps the reasoning aims to explain a phenomenon, i.e., to indicate what has caused the phenomenon to occur. If so, identifying the statement that predicts or hypothesizes the occurrence of the phenomenon will help. A third possibility is that the reasoning provides a rationale for a plan or policy. If so, identifying a statement that indicates the goal of the plan or policy will help.

    Once you have identified the purpose of the reasoning, then you can look at the structure of the reasoning (i.e., *how* the author makes the argument). Pay attention to how sentences relate to one another. For example, the passage may begin with a conclusion followed by a premise that supports that conclusion—or the premise may come first. An intermediate conclusion may, in turn, be used as a premise to support a larger, final conclusion. Consider the following:

    > Among people currently employed, those who wish to retire early will probably not be able to afford to do so. Most people these days are spending almost all their income, and therefore few people are saving enough for early retirement.

    In this argument, "Few people are saving enough for early retirement" is an intermediate conclusion, because it is both a conclusion (for which "Most people these days are spending almost all of their income" is a premise) and a premise for the argument's main conclusion ("Among people currently employed, those who wish to retire early will probably not be able to afford to do so").

4. **To test reasoning, try to imagine scenarios where the premises are true and the conclusion false.**

    Many critical reasoning questions will require you to evaluate the soundness of the reasoning presented in a passage. To evaluate reasoning, you do not need to decide whether premises or conclusions are actually true. Determining actual truth is beyond the scope of the test: no test-taker could determine the truth or falsity of every assertion present in critical reasoning passages. Moreover, many critical reasoning passages refer to fictional scenarios. Normally, in evaluating a piece of reasoning, you should try to *imagine* a situation in which the premises would all be true with the conclusion false. If such a situation would be very unlikely to occur, then the reasoning is strong. On the other hand, if such a situation could likely occur, then the reasoning is poor.

This does not mean that considerations of what you know to be true about the real world will not at times be helpful in evaluating reasoning. Consider the following:

> Medical procedure A is as effective and cost-efficient as medical procedure B but has fewer unwanted side-effects than B. Therefore, medical procedure A should be preferred over medical procedure B.

In evaluating this reasoning, you can use the obvious fact that, all else being equal, the procedure with fewer unwanted side-effects is preferable.

There are degrees of logical support. A piece of reasoning can be very weak, moderately weak, moderately strong, or even absolutely certain. Even if you are not directly asked to do so, it is good practice to evaluate any reasoning in a passage, including the plausibility of an explanation or the persuasiveness of the rationale for a plan's success. Also, note that reasoning can be strengthened by adding new information that, along with the already given information, increases the likelihood that the conclusion inferred would be true provided that all the supporting information is true. Similarly, reasoning can be weakened by adding information that increases the likelihood of the conclusion being false provided that the supporting information is true.

8.3 Reasoning Concepts to Know for the GMAT Exam

The following is intended to provide some pointers to help you analyze the critical reasoning issues you may encounter on the GMAT exam.

1. **Be alert to any unstated assumption on which the reasoning may depend.**

    A statement that helps fill a "gap" in the information offered to support the conclusion is an unstated assumption. If the reasoning depends on such an assumption and the assumption is highly implausible, the reasoning would be subject to criticism on that basis. Note that assumptions can be of two kinds:

    - **Necessary assumptions:** unstated facts or opinions that must be assumed if the reasoning is to succeed logically. The GMAT question will often contain phrases like *an assumption that the argument (reasoning) requires, an assumption on which the argument depends (relies)*.

        > Mario has booked a flight scheduled to arrive at 5:00 pm—which should allow him to get here around 6:30 pm. So by 7:00 pm we will be going out to dinner with Mario.

        Assumption: The plane Mario is booked on will arrive not significantly later than the scheduled time. This assumption, though necessary, is not sufficient; for example, we also need to assume that Mario managed to catch his flight.

    - **Sufficient assumptions:** unstated facts or opinions that, if assumed, allow reasoning to succeed logically. One GMAT question form for sufficient assumptions is: *Which of the following, if assumed, would allow the conclusion to follow logically*.

        > The study of poetry is entirely without value, since poetry has no practical use.

        Assumption: The study of what has no practical use is entirely without value. This assumption, along with the premise given, provides sufficient support for the conclusion: if both the premise and the assumption are true, then the conclusion must also be true. But the following, more complex, assumption would also be sufficient:

        > Anything with no practical use is entirely without value, and the study of anything that is entirely without value is also entirely without value.

        This shows that two distinct assumptions can each be sufficient, neither of them being necessary.

2. **Understand the logic of *if-then* statements and associated inferences.**

   A conditional statement is a compound statement consisting of the part that expresses a condition (the "if" portion) and a part that expresses a supposed consequence: for example, "If it has rained today, then the ground is wet." (The order can be reversed, and the word *then* omitted: "The ground is wet if it has rained today.")

   There are certain errors that people often make in drawing inferences from conditional (*if-then*) statements. Consider the following:

   Attorney: If the jury finds the executive guilty of embezzlement, he will receive a prison sentence. But the jury will not find him guilty of embezzlement. So the executive is unlikely to receive a prison sentence. (Pattern: if A occurs, then B occurs. A does not occur. Therefore, B does not occur.)

   A little consideration will indicate that, in the absence of additional information (e.g., that the executive will not be found guilty of any other crime), the inference is faulty. Similarly, the following argument is in error:

   Attorney: If the jury finds the executive guilty of embezzlement, he will receive a prison sentence. He will, I believe, receive a prison sentence. Therefore, the jury will find him guilty of embezzlement. (Pattern: If A occurs, then B occurs. B occurs. Therefore, A occurs.)

   On the other hand, the following argument is logically correct (i.e., if both premises are true, then the conclusion must be true):

   Attorney: If the jury finds the executive guilty of embezzlement, he will receive a prison sentence. But he will not, I believe, receive a prison sentence. Therefore, the jury will not find him guilty of embezzlement. (Pattern: If A occurs, then B occurs. B does not occur. Therefore, A does not occur.)

   The following argument is also logically correct:

   Attorney: If the jury finds the executive guilty of embezzlement, he will receive a prison sentence. And the jury will find him guilty of embezzlement, I believe. So he will receive a prison sentence. (Pattern: If A occurs, then B occurs. A occurs. Therefore, B occurs.)

   In each of these cases, the second premise in the pattern is crucial: for correct reasoning, that premise should either affirm the *if*-clause, or deny the *then*-clause.

   To thoroughly understand the logic of *if-then* statements, it is useful to note the structural equivalence displayed in the following simple pair of examples:

   In daytime, if the sky is entirely clear, then there is sunshine.

   In daytime, if there is no sunshine, the sky is not entirely clear.

   The statements contain the same information, even if they can, in context, have differing rhetorical impacts. They are necessarily either both true or both false. Note, however, that we can easily imagine a situation where each of these statements is true but the following statement false:

   In daytime, if the sky is not entirely clear, then there is no sunshine.

Therefore, this third statement does not follow logically from either of the others.

Conditional Statements: Correct and Incorrect Inference Patterns

Premise(s)	Conclusion
If A occurs, B occurs. A does occur.	B occurs (correct)
If A occurs, B occurs. B does not occur.	A does not occur (correct)
If A occurs, B occurs. B does occur.	A occurs (incorrect)
If A occurs, B occurs. A does not occur	B does not occur (incorrect)

3. **Pay attention to statements that indicate a necessary condition or a sufficient condition.**

   There are many ways to indicate that something is necessary or sufficient for the occurrence of another event or phenomenon. Here is an example:

   Unless you sleep well tonight, you will not compete well in tomorrow's track events.

   This indicates that sleeping well tonight is a necessary condition of competing well in tomorrow's track events. This could be expressed by "Sleeping well tonight is necessary in order that you compete well in tomorrow's track events" or by "You will compete well in tomorrow's track events only if you sleep well tonight." *If-then* statements are sometimes used to indicate that something is a necessary condition or a sufficient condition, with the *if*-clause indicating a sufficient condition or the *then*-clause indicating a necessary condition. The statement "If you sleep well tonight, then you will compete well in tomorrow's track event" indicates that sleeping well tonight is a sufficient condition of competing well in tomorrow's track event—in the sense that, given the truth of the *if-then* statement, the situation where you sleep well tonight but do not compete well in tomorrow's track event will not occur.

   Fulfillment of an accurately expressed sufficient condition "guarantees" that something else will occur, but the fulfillment of a necessary condition is no guarantee that something else will occur. Suppose sleeping well tonight is a necessary (but not a sufficient) condition of competing well tomorrow in the track events. Then even if you do sleep well tonight (and therefore fulfill the condition said to be necessary), you may still not compete well tomorrow; there may be one or more other necessary conditions that have not been fulfilled (e.g., the condition that you will be in fine form with adequate energy).

4. **Be careful with negatives applied to AND statements and OR statements.**

   When someone denies an *and*-statement or denies an *or*-statement, it is quite easy to make an incorrect inference from a mistaken understanding of what the denial implies. Consider the following dialogue:

   John: Humidity is high today and the temperature is high today.

   Joanna: I believe that's not correct.

Is Joanna committed to the claim that humidity is not high today? Is she committed to the claim that the temperature is not high today? No. She is committed to the claim that humidity and temperature are *not both* high today—but not to the claim that neither is high today. Instead, her position can be paraphrased as: "At least one of the two, humidity and temperature, is not high today." To affirm the negation of an *and*-statement is, in effect, to affirm an *or*-statement—a principle that we could represent as follows:

"It is false that both statement 1 AND statement 2 are true" is equivalent to "Statement 1 is false OR statement 2 is false, OR both are false."

A related point—in reverse—can be made about *or*-statements. Consider the following dialogue:

Economist 1: Inflation will rise next year or equities will decline.

Economist 2: I believe that's incorrect.

Economist 2 denies the statement made by Economist 1. Economist 2 is committed to the view that there will *neither* be increased inflation *nor* a decline in equities—or equivalently, to the view that inflation will not rise and equities will not decline. If Economist 1 had said "Either inflation will rise next year or equities will decline," the meaning would be that one but not both effects will occur. Since the statement was not an *either-or* statement, just a simple *or*-statement, it asserts that at least one of the effects will occur, i.e., it leaves open the possibility that both effects could occur.

5. **Be aware of issues concerning general statements.**

    Statements about *all* or *some* members of a class are called "general statements." Some tempting inferences are incorrect—and sometimes obviously so, as in: "All primes are odd numbers. Therefore, all odd numbers are primes." The premise tells us that the subject class (primes) is entirely contained in the predicate class (odd numbers)—but there are odd numbers that are not primes, such as the number fifteen. So the premise is correct but the conclusion is false, and the following inference, which has an identical logical structure, is also incorrect: "All geniuses are exceptionally creative thinkers, so all exceptionally creative thinkers are geniuses."

    A similar point can be made regarding certain statements of the form *some As are not Bs*. From the premise "Some citizens of India are not residents of Mumbai," can it be correctly inferred that "Some residents of Mumbai are not citizens of India"? No—this inference is incorrect, since it has a true premise and a false conclusion, just as in "Some odd numbers are not primes, so some primes are not odd numbers." Compare with the following: "Some biologists are not researchers, so some researchers are not biologists." Based on common knowledge, both the premise and conclusion are true—but the structure of the argument is the same as in the preceding two examples, and the argument is therefore flawed.

    Even though "some" can sometimes be read, depending on the context, as meaning "some but not all," it should often be read as meaning "at least one"—even if a plural noun follows "some." If I say "Some voters are critical thinkers," that claim will be true whether all, or only one or two, voters are critical thinkers.

Some confusion can arise in cases where general statements are negated or denied. Consider the following dialogue:

Jana: Some voters in modern democracies are critical thinkers.

Julio: I wonder about that—in fact I think it's not true at all.

Julio's statement commits him to the claim that no voters in modern democracies are critical thinkers—not just to the weaker claim that some voters in modern democracies are not critical thinkers. And consider the following:

Jana: Every voter in modern democracies is a critical thinker.

Julio: I wonder about that—in fact I think that's not true at all.

Julio's statement commits him to the claim that some voters—one or more—in modern democracies are not critical thinkers—but not to the more sweeping claim that no such voters are (his claim will be true, of course, if no such voters are).

Not every general statement carries an implication that the subject class is not empty, i.e., contains at least one member. Consider the following:

Every *life-form native only to planets other than Earth is carbon-based.*

For all we know, the subject class—designated by the italicized phrase—may in reality be an "empty" class (equivalent to the null set), so we cannot correctly infer from this statement the following:

Some life-forms native only to planets other than Earth are carbon-based.

A *some*-statement always carries the implication that the subject class is non-empty, i.e., has at least one member.

Some general statements can easily be misread. Learn to distinguish carefully the following statements:

Some food is the favorite of every adult in Nation X.

Every adult in Nation X has some favorite food.

These statements are not equivalent. The first says something that is unlikely to be true: that there is a particular food that is a *universal* favorite among adults in Nation X. The second says only that each adult in Nation X has some food that is his or her favorite—which may well be true.

6. Note ways in which definitions can be defective.

Definitions serve various purposes, but all have the goal of making things adequately clear. A definition can simply give a conventional dictionary meaning—but many ordinary words have more than one meaning, and a definition may be needed if the meaning is not clear enough from context. Sometimes a new term needs to be introduced or an existing term needs to have a precise definition for a special (perhaps technical) purpose. Definitions are flawed if they are too vague for the intended purpose—when it is not sufficiently clear whether a given entity would fall inside or outside the class of things apparently targeted by the defined term. Also, a definition can be too broad or too narrow—when the definition incorrectly includes or excludes one or more items.

Consider the following: "An athlete is a fast runner or a high jumper." This is both too narrow and too imprecise—and perhaps too broad (depending on context): for example, does it include racehorses? A definition can be circular: "Atmospheric pressure is the air pressure in the earth's atmosphere." This is both circular and vague—and useless for scientific purposes.

7. Understand how hypotheses are confirmed.

A hypothesis is a proposed explanation that serves as a starting point for further investigation. On the GMAT exam, you may be asked to identify or evaluate a hypothesis that most plausibly explains a phenomenon or event. To do so, you should look for evidence that either supports or goes against the hypothesis.

Imagine the following research study designed to test the efficacy of a new teaching method for ten-year-old girls and boys. Sixty ten-year-old children are divided into two groups that are matched relative to gender distribution, measured performance in mathematics achievement, and all other factors presumed relevant. Method M, a new instructional method for teaching a set of designated mathematical skills, is applied to one of the groups, and an established method, Method E, for the same skills is applied to the other. Performance on the skills after ten weeks of instruction is measured for both groups, and a comparison made between the two data sets is appropriately processed. The goal is to discover whether the data confirms the following hypothesis (in the form of a prediction):

> If Method M is applied to groups of children like these, there will be a significantly larger gain in mathematical performance than if Method E is applied.

Suppose the data shows that the group subjected to Method M has a significantly larger gain in performance than the other group (the "control group"). This information provides some support for the hypothesis, provided that adequate scientific controls and statistical processing have been correctly executed (ensuring these two conditions are met is not always easy). The confirmatory evidence supports the superior efficacy of Method M, but it is not conclusive. What the evidence shows is that the experimental results for these children are *consistent with* the hypothesis that Method M generally has superior efficacy for such children. The *if*-clause is true of one of these groups of children—presumed typical of a larger population of ten-year-old children—and so is the *then*-clause. It is one piece of evidence that the hypothetical statement given above has not been falsified—and therefore is quite possibly correct. If the *then*-clause turned out false, this would be evidence against the hypothesis. Accumulation of confirmatory evidence through replicated experiments will greatly strengthen the confirmation of the hypothesis.

The finding of Method M's efficacy can be validly generalized only to groups of children that resemble in relevant respects the children featured in the study. In other words, the groups of children must be typical, i.e., *representative*, of the large population of ten-year-old children to whom Method M may be applied if it is scientifically validated. A similar principle of representativeness must govern sample selection in any study that aims to establish scientific results generalizable to a larger group or population.

8.4 Section Instructions

Go to www.mba.com/tutorial to view instructions for the section and get a feel for what the test center screens will look at on the actual GMAT exam.

8.5 Practice Questions

Each of the critical reasoning questions is based on a short argument, a set of statements, or a plan of action. For each question, select the best answer of the choices given.

610. Arts advocate: Few universities require that students who are specializing in science and technology take many art courses. However, real progress in science and technology requires an element of creativity, which the arts foster. Thus, to help science and technology students succeed in their careers, universities should increase the number of art courses required for them.

Which of the following would, if true, most strengthen the argument above?

(A) Universities required more art courses for science and technology students in the past.

(B) Participation in art courses increases students' creative thinking in their science and technology courses.

(C) More students who are interested in art would specialize in science and technology if the number of art courses required for those programs were increased.

(D) Some of the most prominent scientists began their careers as artists.

(E) Discussion of science and technology topics in art courses increases creative thinking among students in those courses.

611. A successful coffee stand that serves the workers in a large office building plans to increase its profits by adding oatmeal—a hot cereal popular among the workers—to its menu. The manager says that oatmeal is "the ultimate convenience food" because it can be served by the cup, as coffee is; further, offering oatmeal will enable the stand to get into the breakfast business without making a large investment, because it does not require elaborate cooking equipment.

Which of the following would, if true, most strengthen the likelihood that the manager's plan will achieve its goal?

(A) Some of the office building's businesses have recently begun providing free coffee to their employees.

(B) The ingredients needed to make oatmeal are inexpensive and do not spoil easily the way many fresh breakfast foods typically sold at coffee stands do.

(C) In order to offer more flexible schedules to their workers, several businesses in the office building will soon be expanding their hours.

(D) Supermarket sales of oatmeal and other cereals slowed this year following large gains last year.

(E) Oatmeal manufacturers have recently reduced their oatmeal offerings, which had included oatmeal in microwaveable cups and convenient cereal bars made with rolled oats.

612. Ramirez: The film industry claims that pirated DVDs, which are usually cheaper than legitimate DVDs and become available well before a film's official DVD release date, adversely affect its bottom line. But the industry should note what the spread of piracy indicates: consumers want lower prices and faster DVD releases. Lowering prices of DVDs and releasing them sooner would mitigate piracy's negative effect on film industry profits.

The argument above relies on which of the following assumptions?

(A) Releasing legitimate DVDs earlier would not cause any reduction in the revenue the film industry receives from the films' theatrical release.

(B) Some people who would otherwise purchase pirated DVDs would be willing to purchase legitimate DVDs if they were less expensive and released earlier than they are now.

(C) The film industry will in the future be able to produce DVDs more cheaply than is currently the case.

(D) Some current sellers of pirated DVDs would likely discontinue their businesses if legitimate DVDs were released faster and priced lower.

(E) Current purchasers of pirated DVDs are aware that those DVDs are not authorized by the film industry.

613. Harunia Province has a relatively dry climate and is attracting a fast-growing population that has put increasing demands on its water supply. The two companies that supply water to the region have struggled to keep up with demand and still remain profitable. Yet now they are asking Harunian authorities to write residential water-use regulations that could reduce their revenues and restrict their future flexibility in supplying water profitably.

Which of the following would, if true, most logically help explain why the water-supply companies are asking the authorities to regulate residential water use?

(A) The companies are planning large water-transportation and irrigation systems that require the approval of neighboring provinces.

(B) The companies believe regulation is inevitable and that having it in place now will allow better planning and thus future profitability.

(C) Few, if any, Harunian government officials have investments in the companies or serve on their boards of directors.

(D) The companies believe that the population is not likely to continue to grow.

(E) Long-term climate projections suggest that greater rainfall will eventually increase the amount of water available.

614. Loss of the Gocha mangrove forests has caused coastal erosion, reducing fish populations and requiring the Gocha Fishing Cooperative (GFC) to partially fund dredging and new shore facilities. However, as part of its subsidiary businesses, the GFC has now invested in a program to replant significant parts of the coast with mangrove trees. Given income from a controlled harvest of wood with continuing replanting, the mangrove regeneration effort makes it more likely that the cooperative will increase its net income.

Which of the following, if true, would most strengthen the argument that mangrove replanting will increase the Gocha cooperative's net income?

(A) The cost of dredging and shore facilities was shared with the local government.

(B) The GFC will be able to hire local workers to assist with the mangrove replanting.

(C) The GFC derives 10 percent of its revenue from salt-production facilities in an area previously cleared of mangroves.

(D) Mangrove forests tend to increase the commercial fish populations in coastal fishing grounds.

(E) A controlled harvesting of mangrove wood by the GFC would have little effect on coastal erosion.

615. Executives at the Fizzles Beverage Company plan to boost profits in Country X on their range of fruit-flavored drinks by introducing new flavors based on tropical fruits that are little known there. The executives reason that since the fruit drinks of other companies have none of these flavors, Fizzles will not have to compete for customers and thus will be able to sell the drinks at a higher price.

Which of the following, if true, presents the most serious potential weakness of the plan?

(A) The new fruit drinks would be priced significantly higher than other Fizzles fruit drinks with more conventional flavors.

(B) In a telephone survey, at least one of the consumers contacted said that they preferred many of the new flavors to all of the more familiar flavors.

(C) To build widespread demand for the new flavors, Fizzles would have to launch an advertising campaign to familiarize consumers with them.

(D) Consumers choosing among fruit-flavored drinks of different brands generally buy on the basis of name recognition and price rather than the specific fruit flavor.

(E) Few consumers who are loyal to a specific brand of fruit-flavored drinks would willingly switch to another brand that costs more.

616. Economist: In 2015, the average per-person amount paid for goods and services purchased by consumers in Country X was the equivalent of $17,570 in United States dollars, just 30 percent of the corresponding figure of $58,566 for Country Y. Yet in 2015, there was already a substantial middle class in Country X that had discretionary income for middle-class consumer goods such as new vehicles, computers, or major household appliances, while a significant portion of the middle class in Country Y did not have sufficient income to purchase such items.

Which of the following, if true, most helps explain the discrepancy in the relationships described by the economist?

(A) There are many consumer goods, such as household appliances, that are produced in Country X to be sold in the Country Y market.

(B) The volume of trade between Country X and Country Y is increasing rapidly in both directions.

(C) The economy of Country Y is recovering from a downturn that affected both Country Y and Country X.

(D) Country X residents pay much less than their Country Y counterparts for housing, transportation, and child care.

(E) In Country Y as well as in Country X, there are few assembly-line jobs in factories that pay a middle-class wage.

617. Neuroscientist: Memory evolved to help animals react appropriately to situations they encounter by drawing on the past experience of similar situations. But this does not require that animals perfectly recall every detail of all their experiences. Instead, to function well, memory should generalize from past experiences that are similar to the current one.

The neuroscientist's statements, if true, most strongly support which of the following conclusions?

(A) At least some animals perfectly recall every detail of at least some past experiences.

(B) Perfectly recalling every detail of all their past experiences could help at least some animals react more appropriately than they otherwise would to new situations they encounter.

(C) Generalizing from past experiences requires clear memories of most if not all the details of those experiences.

(D) Recalling every detail of all past experiences would be incompatible with any ability to generalize from those experiences.

(E) Animals can often react more appropriately than they otherwise would to situations they encounter if they draw on generalizations from past experiences of similar situations.

618. In Country X's last election, the Reform Party beat its main opponent, the Conservative Party, although pollsters, employing in-person interviews shortly before the vote, had projected a Conservative Party victory. Afterwards, the pollsters determined that, unlike Conservative Party supporters, Reform Party supporters were less likely to express their party preference during in-person interviews than they were during telephone interviews. Therefore, using only telephone interviews instead would likely result in more accurate projections for the next election.

Which of the following statements, if true, would most support the argument in the passage?

(A) The number of voters in Country X's next election will be significantly larger than the number of voters in the last election.

(B) The Conservative Party will win the next election.

(C) For each person interviewed in telephone polls before the next election, pollsters will be able to reasonably determine the likelihood of that person voting.

(D) People who expressed no party preference during the in-person interviews shortly before Country X's last election did not outnumber the people who expressed a preference for the Conservative Party.

(E) In the next election, pollsters will be able to conduct more in-person interviews than telephone interviews.

619. A company that manufactures plastic products from recyclable plastic is, surprisingly, unconcerned that economic conditions may worsen, despite analysts' belief that consumers would then consider ecofriendly plastic products an expensive luxury. But the company reasons that it will be able to lower its prices because, in a weakened economy, other ecofriendly plastic

manufacturers are likely to fail. Demand among manufacturers for recyclable plastics as raw materials would then plummet, creating an oversupply of such materials, making them less expensive for the manufacturer to purchase and thus lowering the company's costs.

Which of the following, if true, most weakens the company's reasoning?

(A) Smaller ecofriendly plastic manufacturers are more likely to fail in a weakened economy than larger ecofriendly manufacturers are.

(B) Some retailers whose sales include various companies' ecofriendly plastic products have struggled in recent years despite the overall good economy.

(C) Consumers would likely soon learn of the oversupply of recyclable plastics and cease recycling them, significantly raising manufacturers' raw-material costs.

(D) Retailers, including retailers that cater to consumers seeking certain types of ecofriendly products, may lose some business if economic conditions worsen.

(E) The plastics used by the company in its products were, after a recent investigation by a regulatory body, declared to be safe for consumers.

CR73241.01

620. Researchers asked volunteers to imagine they were running a five-kilometer race against 50 people and then against 500 people, races in each of which the top 10 percent would receive a $1,000 prize. Asked about the effort they would apply in the respective cases, the volunteers indicated, on average, that they would run slower in the race against the greater number of people. A likely explanation of this result is that those of the volunteers who were most *comparatively inclined*—those who most tended to compare themselves with others in the social environment—determined (perhaps unconsciously) that extreme effort would not be worthwhile in the 500-competitor race.

Which of the following would, if known to be true, most help justify the explanation offered above?

(A) The volunteers who were most comparatively inclined were also those that had the greatest desire to win a $1,000 prize.

(B) The volunteers who were the least comparatively inclined had no greater desire to win the $1,000 than those who were the most comparatively inclined.

(C) The volunteers who were most comparatively inclined were likely to indicate that they would run the two races at the same speed.

(D) The most comparatively inclined volunteers believed that they were significantly less likely to finish in the top 10 percent in the race against 500 than in the race against 50.

(E) Volunteers were chosen for participation in the study on the basis of answers to various questions designed to measure the degree to which the volunteers were comparatively inclined.

CR41141.01

621. According to a study, after a week of high-altitude living, twenty men had slimmed down. The men, middle-aged residents of low-altitude areas, had been taken to a research station at 2,650 meters (8,694 feet) above sea level. They had unrestricted access to food and were forbidden vigorous exercise, yet they lost an average of 1.5 kilograms (3.3 pounds) during their one-week stay. Clearly, the lower availability of oxygen at higher altitudes, or hypobaric hypoxia, can be said to have caused the weight loss, since _____.

Which of the following would, if true, most logically complete the argument?

(A) a decrease in oxygen intake has been shown to depress appetite

(B) the men all participated in the same kinds of exercise during their stay

(C) the foods available to the men had fewer calories than the foods they usually ate

(D) exercise at higher altitudes is more difficult than exercise at lower altitudes is

(E) several weeks after returning home, the men still weighed less than they had before the study

CR11741.01
622. Editorial: Our city's public transportation agency is facing a budget shortfall. The fastest growing part of the budget has been employee retirement benefits, which are exceptionally generous. Unless the budget shortfall is resolved, transportation service will be cut, and many transportation employees will lose their jobs. Thus, it would be in the employees' best interest for their union to accept cuts in retirement benefits.

Which of the following is an assumption the editorial's argument requires?

(A) The transportation employees' union should not accept cuts in retirement benefits if doing so would not be in the employees' best interest.

(B) The only feasible way for the agency to resolve the budget shortfall would involve cutting transportation service and eliminating jobs.

(C) Other things being equal, it is in the transportation employees' interest to have exceptionally generous retirement benefits.

(D) Cutting the retirement benefits would help resolve the agency's budget shortfall.

(E) The transportation employees' union will not accept cuts in retirement benefits if doing so will not allow more transportation employees to keep their jobs.

CR94231.01
623. Researchers hope to find clues about the A'mk peoples who lived in the Kaumpta region about one thousand years ago but who left few obvious traces. The researchers plan to hire the few remaining shamans of the modern-day indigenous people in Kaumpta, who are believed to be descended from the A'mk, to lead them to ancestral sites that may be the remains of A'mk buildings or ceremonial spaces. The shamans were taught the location of such sites as part of their traditional training as youths, and their knowledge of traditional Kaumpta customs may help determine the nature of any sites the researchers find.

Which of the following is an assumption on which the success of the plan depends?

(A) The researchers have reliable evidence that the A'mk of one thousand years ago built important ceremonial spaces.

(B) The shamans have a reasonably accurate memory of A'mk sites they learned about as youths.

(C) Kaumpta shamans are generally held in high esteem for their traditional knowledge.

(D) Modern technologies available to the researchers are likely to be able to find some A'mk sites easily.

(E) Most or all A'mk sites are likely to be found within the Kaumpta region.

CR09994
624. Astronomer: Most stars are born in groups of thousands, each star in a group forming from the same parent cloud of gas. Each cloud has a unique, homogeneous chemical composition. Therefore, whenever two stars have the same chemical composition as each other, they must have originated from the same cloud of gas.

Which of the following, if true, would most strengthen the astronomer's argument?

(A) In some groups of stars, not every star originated from the same parent cloud of gas.

(B) Clouds of gas of similar or identical chemical composition may be remote from each other.

(C) Whenever a star forms, it inherits the chemical composition of its parent cloud of gas.

(D) Many stars in vastly different parts of the universe are quite similar in their chemical compositions.

(E) Astronomers can at least sometimes precisely determine whether a star has the same chemical composition as its parent cloud of gas.

CR08017
625. With employer-paid training, workers have the potential to become more productive not only in their present employment but also in any number of jobs with different employers. To increase the productivity of their workforce, many firms are planning to maintain or even increase their investments in worker training. But some training experts object that if a trained worker is hired away by another firm, the employer that paid for the training has merely subsidized a competitor. They note that such hiring has been on the rise in recent years.

Which of the following would, if true, contribute most to defeating the training experts' objection to the firms' strategy?

(A) Firms that promise opportunities for advancement to their employees get, on average, somewhat larger numbers of job applications from untrained workers than do firms that make no such promise.

(B) In many industries, employees who take continuing-education courses are more competitive in the job market.

(C) More and more educational and training institutions are offering reduced tuition fees to firms that subsidize worker training.

(D) Research shows that workers whose training is wholly or partially subsidized by their employer tend to get at least as much training as do workers who pay for all their own training.

(E) For most firms that invest in training their employees, the value added by that investment in employees who stay exceeds the value lost through other employees' leaving to work for other companies.

CR93241.01

626. In emerging economies in Africa and other regions, large foreign banks that were set up during the colonial era have long played a major economic role. These institutions have tended to confine their business to the wealthier of banks' potential customers. But development of these countries' economies requires financing of the small businesses that dominate their manufacturing, farming, and services sectors. So economic growth will be likely to occur if local banks take on this portion of the financial services markets, since _____.

Which of the following completions would produce the strongest argument?

(A) local banks tend not to strive as much as large foreign banks to diversify their investments

(B) small farming and manufacturing businesses contribute to economic growth if they obtain adequate investment capital

(C) large foreign banks in emerging economies could, with local employees and appropriate local consultation, profitably expand their business to less wealthy clients

(D) some small businesses are among the wealthier customers of foreign banks in emerging economies

(E) local banks in emerging economies tend to be less risk-averse than foreign banks

CR49551.01

627. Exporters in Country X are facing lower revenues due to a shortage of the large metal shipping containers in which they send their goods by sea to other countries. Fewer containers arrive in Country X due to reductions in imports. This has meant lost orders, costly delays, and a scramble for alternatives, such as air freight, all of which are costlier. Moreover, the revenues of exporters in Country X will probably continue to decline in the near future. This is because other countries are likely to find it increasingly unprofitable to export their goods to Country X, and because _____.

Which of the following would most logically complete the passage?

(A) production of shipping containers in Country X is growing rapidly as a response to the shortage

(B) shipping companies are willing to move containers from country to country only when the containers are full

(C) the cost of shipping alternatives such as air freight is likely to stabilize in the near future

(D) consumers in Country X are purchasing more products than ever before

(E) the worldwide demand for goods made in Country X has only recently begun to rise after a long decline

CR01107

628. Candle Corporation's television stations are likely to have more income from advertisers than previously. This is because advertisers prefer to reach people in the 18- to 49-year-old age group and the number of people in that group watching Candle television is increasing. Furthermore, among Candle viewers, the percentage of viewers 18 to 49 years old is increasing.

Which of the following, if true, would most strengthen the argument that Candle Corporation will receive more income from advertisers?

(A) Advertisers carefully monitor the demographic characteristics of television audiences and purchase advertising time to reach the audiences they prefer to reach.

(B) Among people over 49 years old, fewer viewers of Candle stations buy products advertised on television than do viewers of other stations.

(C) There will be increasingly more advertisements on television that are directed at viewers who are over 49 years old.

(D) Candle stations plan to show reruns of television shows during hours when other stations run shows for the first time.

(E) People 18 to 49 years old generally have less disposable income to spend than do people over 49 years old.

629. A provincial government plans to raise the gasoline tax to give people an incentive to drive less, reducing traffic congestion in the long term. However, skeptics point out that most people in the province live in areas where cars are the only viable transportation to jobs and stores and therefore cannot greatly change their driving habits in response to higher gasoline prices.

In light of the skeptics' objection, which of the following, if true, would most logically support the prediction that the government's plan will achieve its goal of reducing traffic congestion?

(A) The revenue from the tax will be used to make public transportation a viable means of transportation to jobs and stores for far more people.

(B) The tax will encourage many residents to switch to more fuel-efficient cars, reducing air pollution and other problems.

(C) Because gasoline has been underpriced for decades, the province has many neighborhoods where cars are the only viable means of transportation.

(D) Most residents who cannot greatly change their driving habits could compensate for high gasoline prices by reducing other expenses.

(E) Traffic congestion is an especially serious problem for people for whom cars are the only viable means of transportation.

630. Editorial: The roof of Northtown's municipal equipment-storage building collapsed under the weight of last week's heavy snowfall. The building was constructed recently and met local building-safety codes in every particular, except that the nails used for attaching roof supports to the building's columns were of a smaller size than the codes specify for this purpose. Clearly, this collapse exemplifies how even a single, apparently insignificant departure from safety standards can have severe consequences.

Which of the following, if true, most seriously weakens the editorial's argument?

(A) The only other buildings to suffer roof collapses from the weight of the snowfall were older buildings constructed according to less exacting standards than those in the codes.

(B) The amount of snow that accumulated on the roof of the equipment-storage building was greater than the predicted maximum that was used in drawing up the safety codes.

(C) Because the equipment-storage building was not intended for human occupation, some safety-code provisions that would have applied to an office building did not apply to it.

(D) The municipality of Northtown itself has the responsibility for ensuring that buildings constructed within its boundaries meet the provisions of the building-safety codes.

(E) Because the equipment-storage building was used for storing snow-removal equipment, the building was almost completely empty when the roof collapsed.

631. Political theorist: Even with the best spies, area experts, and satellite surveillance, foreign policy assessments can still lack important information. In such circumstances intuitive judgment is vital. A national leader with such judgment can make good decisions about foreign policy even when current information is incomplete, since _____.

Which of the following, if true, most logically completes the argument?

(A) the central reason for failure in foreign policy decision making is the absence of critical information

(B) those leaders whose foreign policy decisions have been highly ranked have also been found to have good intuitive judgment

(C) both intuitive judgment and good information are required for sound decision making

(D) good foreign policy decisions often lead to improved methods of gathering information

(E) intuitive judgment can produce good decisions based on past experience, even when there are important gaps in current information

632. Supply shortages and signs of growing demand are driving cocoa prices upward. Unusually severe weather in cocoa-producing regions—too much rain in Brazil and too little in West Africa—has limited production. Further, Europe and North America recently reported stronger demand for cocoa. In the first quarter, grinding of cocoa beans—the first stage in processing cocoa for chocolate—rose 8.1 percent in Europe and 16 percent in North America. Analysts have concluded that cocoa's price will continue to rise at least into the near future.

Which of the following would, if true, most strengthen the reasoning above?

(A) Ground cocoa beans can be stored for long periods before they spoil.

(B) Several European and North American manufacturers that use cocoa have recently improved their processing capacity.

(C) It takes new cocoa trees five or six years before they start bearing fruit.

(D) Governments in Europe and North America are likely to change current restrictions on cocoa imports.

(E) Historically, cocoa production has varied widely from year to year.

633. During the earliest period of industrialization in Britain, steam engines were more expensive to build and operate than either windmills or water mills, the other practicable sources of power for factories. Yet despite their significant cost disadvantage, steam-powered factories were built in large numbers well before technical improvements brought their cost down. Furthermore, they were built even in regions where geographical conditions permitted the construction of wind- and water-powered factories close to major markets.

Which of the following, if true, most helps to explain the proliferation of steam-powered factories during the earliest period of industrialization in Britain?

(A) In many areas of Britain, there were fewer steam-powered factories than wind- or water-powered factories in the earliest period of industrialization.

(B) Unlike wind- or water-powered factories, steam-powered factories were fueled with coal, which sometimes had to be transported significant distances from the mine to the site of the factory.

(C) It was both difficult and expensive to convert a factory from wind power or water power to steam power.

(D) In the early period of industrialization, many goods sold in towns and cities could not be mass-produced in factories.

(E) In Britain, the number of sites where a wind- or water-powered factory could be built was insufficient to provide for all of the demand for factory-produced goods at the time.

634. Snowmaking machines work by spraying a mist that freezes immediately on contact with cold air. Because the sudden freezing kills bacteria, QuickFreeze is planning to market a wastewater purification system that works on the same principle. The process works only when temperatures are cold, however, so municipalities using it will still need to maintain a conventional system.

Which of the following, if true, provides the strongest grounds for a prediction that municipalities will buy QuickFreeze's purification system despite the need to maintain a conventional purification system as well?

(A) Bacteria are not the only impurities that must be removed from wastewater.

(B) Many municipalities have old wastewater purification systems that need to be replaced.

(C) Conventional wastewater purification systems have not been fully successful in killing bacteria at cold temperatures.

(D) During times of warm weather, when it is not in use, QuickFreeze's purification system requires relatively little maintenance.

(E) Places where the winters are cold rarely have a problem of water shortage.

635. **Plant scientists have used genetic engineering on seeds to produce crop plants that are highly resistant to insect damage**. Unfortunately, the seeds themselves are quite expensive, and the plants require more fertilizer and water to grow well than normal ones. Accordingly, **for most farmers the savings on pesticides would not compensate for the higher seed costs and the cost of additional fertilizer**. However, since consumer demand for grains, fruits, and vegetables grown without the use of pesticides continues to rise, the use of genetically engineered seeds of this kind is likely to become widespread.

In the argument given, the two portions in **boldface** play which of the following roles?

(A) The first supplies a context for the argument; the second is the argument's main conclusion.

(B) The first introduces a development that the argument predicts will have a certain outcome; the second is a state of affairs that, according to the argument, contributes to bringing about that outcome.

(C) The first presents a development that the argument predicts will have a certain outcome; the second acknowledges a consideration that tends to weigh against that prediction.

(D) The first provides evidence to support a prediction that the argument seeks to defend; the second is that prediction.

(E) The first and the second each provide evidence to support the argument's main conclusion.

636. Which of the following most logically completes the passage?

Leptin, a protein occurring naturally in the blood, appears to regulate how much fat the body carries by speeding up the metabolism and decreasing the appetite when the body has too much fat. Mice that do not naturally produce leptin have more fat than other mice, but lose fat rapidly when they are given leptin injections. Unfortunately, however, leptin cannot be used as a dietary supplement to control fat, since _____.

(A) the digestive system breaks down proteins before they can enter the bloodstream

(B) there are pharmaceuticals already available that can contribute to weight loss by speeding up the metabolism

(C) people with unusually low levels of leptin in their blood tend to have a high percentage of body fat

(D) the mice that do not naturally produce leptin were from a specially bred strain of mice

(E) mice whose bodies did produce leptin also lost some of their body fat when given leptin injections

637. Suncorp, a new corporation with limited funds, has been clearing large sections of the tropical Amazon forest for cattle ranching. This practice continues even though greater profits can be made from rubber tapping, which does not destroy the forest, than from cattle ranching, which does destroy the forest.

Which of the following, if true, most helps to explain why Suncorp has been pursuing the less profitable of the two economic activities mentioned above?

(A) The soil of the Amazon forest is very rich in nutrients that are important in the development of grazing lands.

(B) Cattle-ranching operations that are located in tropical climates are more profitable than cattle-ranching operations that are located in cold-weather climates.

(C) In certain districts, profits made from cattle ranching are more heavily taxed than profits made from any other industry.

(D) Some of the cattle that are raised on land cleared in the Amazon are killed by wildcats.

(E) The amount of money required to begin a rubber-tapping operation is twice as high as the amount needed to begin a cattle ranch.

638. Archaeologists use technology to analyze ancient sites. It is likely that this technology will advance considerably in the near future, allowing archaeologists to gather more information than is currently possible. If they study certain sites now, they risk contaminating or compromising them for future studies. Therefore, in order to maximize the potential for gathering knowledge in the long run, a team of archaeologists plans to delay the examination of a newly excavated site.

Which of the following would be most useful to investigate for the purpose of evaluating the plan's prospects for achieving its goal?

(A) Whether any of the contents of the site will significantly deteriorate before the anticipated technology is available

(B) Whether there will continue to be improvements on the relevant technology

(C) Whether the team can study a site other than the newly excavated site for the time being

(D) Whether the site was inhabited by a very ancient culture

(E) Whether the anticipated technology will damage objects under study

639. More and more law firms specializing in corporate taxes are paid on a contingency-fee basis. Under this arrangement, if a case is won, the firm usually receives more than it would have received if it had been paid on the alternate hourly rate basis. If the case is lost, the firm receives nothing. Most firms are likely to make more under the contingency-fee arrangement.

Which of the following, if true, would most strengthen the prediction above?

(A) Firms that work exclusively under the hourly rate arrangement spend, on average, fewer hours on cases that are won than on cases that are lost.

(B) Some litigation can last for years before any decision is reached, and, even then, the decision may be appealed.

(C) Firms under the contingency-fee arrangement still pay their employees on an hourly basis.

(D) Since the majority of firms specialize in certain kinds of cases, they are able to assess accurately their chances of winning each potential case.

(E) Firms working under the contingency-fee arrangement take in fewer cases per year than do firms working under the hourly rate arrangement.

640. Beginning in 1966 all new cars sold in Morodia were required to have safety belts and power steering. Previously, most cars in Morodia were without these features. Safety belts help to prevent injuries in collisions, and power steering helps to avoid collisions in the first place. But even though in 1966 one-seventh of the cars in Morodia were replaced with new cars, the number of car collisions and collision-related injuries did not decline.

Which of the following, if true about Morodia, most helps to explain why the number of collisions and collision-related injuries in Morodia failed to decline in 1966?

(A) Because of a driver-education campaign, most drivers and passengers in cars that did have safety belts used them in 1966.

(B) Most of the new cars bought in 1966 were bought in the months of January and February.

(C) In 1965, substantially more than one-seventh of the cars in Morodia were replaced with new cars.

(D) An excessive reliance on the new safety features led many owners of new cars to drive less cautiously in 1966 than before.

(E) The seat belts and power steering put into new cars sold in 1966 had to undergo strict quality-control inspections by manufacturers, whether the cars were manufactured in Morodia or not.

641. Enterprise Bank currently requires customers with checking accounts to maintain a minimum balance or pay a monthly fee. Enterprise plans to offer accounts with no monthly fee and no minimum-balance requirement; to cover their projected administrative costs of $3 per account per month they plan to charge $30 for overdrawing an account. Since each month on average slightly more than 10 percent of Enterprise's customers overdraw their accounts, bank officials predict the new accounts will generate a profit.

Which of the following, if true, most strongly supports the bank officials' prediction?

(A) Some of Enterprise Bank's current checking account customers are expected to switch to the new accounts once they are offered.

(B) One third of Enterprise Bank's revenues are currently derived from monthly fees tied to checking accounts.

(C) Many checking account customers who occasionally pay a fee for not maintaining a minimum balance in their account generally maintain a balance well above the minimum.

(D) Customers whose checking accounts do not have a minimum-balance requirement are more likely than others to overdraw their checking accounts.

(E) Customers whose checking accounts do not have a minimum-balance requirement are more likely than others to write checks for small amounts.

642. In virtually any industry, technological improvements increase labor productivity, which is the output of goods and services per person-hour worked. In Parland's industries, labor productivity is significantly higher than it is in Vergia's industries. Clearly, therefore, Parland's industries must, on the whole, be further advanced technologically than Vergia's are.

The argument is most vulnerable to which of the following criticisms?

(A) It offers a conclusion that is no more than a paraphrase of one of the pieces of information provided in its support.

(B) It presents as evidence in support of a claim information that is inconsistent with other evidence presented in support of the same claim.

(C) It takes one possible cause of a condition to be the actual cause of that condition without considering any other possible causes.

(D) It takes a condition to be the effect of something that happened only after the condition already existed.

(E) It makes a distinction that presupposes the truth of the conclusion that is to be established.

643. Chaco Canyon, a settlement of the ancient Anasazi culture in North America, had massive buildings. **It must have been a major Anasazi center**. Analysis of wood samples shows that some of the timber for the buildings came from the Chuska and San Mateo mountains, 50 miles from Chaco Canyon. **Only a major cultural center would have the organizational power to import timber from 50 miles away**.

In the argument given, the two portions in boldface play which of the following roles?

(A) The first is a premise used to support the argument's main conclusion; the second is the argument's main conclusion.

(B) The first is the argument's main conclusion; the second is a premise used to support that conclusion.

(C) The first is one of two premises used to support the argument's main conclusion; the second is the other of those two premises.

(D) The first is a premise used to support the argument's main conclusion; the second is a premise used to support another conclusion drawn in the argument.

(E) The first is inferred from another statement in the argument; the second is inferred from the first.

644. The Maxilux car company's design for its new luxury model, the Max 100, included a special design for the tires that was intended to complement the model's image. The winning bid for supplying these tires was submitted by Rubco. Analysts concluded that the bid would only just cover Rubco's costs on the tires, but Rubco executives claim that winning the bid will actually make a profit for the company.

Which of the following, if true, most strongly justifies the claim made by Rubco's executives?

(A) In any Maxilux model, the spare tire is exactly the same make and model as the tires that are mounted on the wheels.

(B) Rubco holds exclusive contracts to supply Maxilux with the tires for a number of other models made by Maxilux.

(C) The production facilities for the Max 100 and those for the tires to be supplied by Rubco are located very near each other.

(D) When people who have purchased a carefully designed luxury automobile need to replace a worn part of it, they almost invariably replace it with a part of exactly the same make and type.

(E) When Maxilux awarded the tire contract to Rubco, the only criterion on which Rubco's bid was clearly ahead of its competitors' bids was price.

645. Which of the following most logically completes the passage?

Most bicycle helmets provide good protection for the top and back of the head, but little or no protection for the temple regions on the sides of the head. A study of head injuries resulting from bicycle accidents showed that a large proportion were caused by blows to the temple area. Therefore, if bicycle helmets protected this area, the risk of serious head injury in bicycle accidents would be greatly reduced, especially since _____.

(A) among the bicyclists included in the study's sample of head injuries, only a very small proportion had been wearing a helmet at the time of their accident

(B) even those bicyclists who regularly wear helmets have a poor understanding of the degree and kind of protection that helmets afford

(C) a helmet that included protection for the temples would have to be somewhat larger and heavier than current helmets

(D) the bone in the temple area is relatively thin and impacts in that area are thus very likely to cause brain injury

(E) bicyclists generally land on their arm or shoulder when they fall to the side, which reduces the likelihood of severe impacts on the side of the head

646. Which of the following most logically completes the argument?

In a typical year, Innovair's airplanes are involved in 35 collisions while parked or being towed in airports, with a resulting yearly cost of $1,000,000 for repairs.

To reduce the frequency of ground collisions, Innovair will begin giving its ground crews additional training, at an annual cost of $500,000. Although this will cut the number of ground collisions by about half at best, the drop in repair costs can be expected to be much greater, since _____.

(A) most ground collisions happen when ground crews are rushing to minimize the time a delayed airplane spends on the ground

(B) a ground collision typically occurs when there are no passengers on the airplane

(C) the additional training will focus on helping ground crews avoid those kinds of ground collisions that cause the most costly damage

(D) the $500,000 cost figure for the additional training of ground crews includes the wages that those crews will earn during the time spent in actual training

(E) most ground collisions have been caused by the least experienced ground-crew members

647. Many agriculturally intensive areas of the world are beginning to encounter water scarcity problems. As a result, many farmers in these areas are likely to reduce their output as the water supply they need in order to maintain production shrinks. However, one group of farmers in such a region plans to increase their production by implementing techniques for water conservation.

Which of the following, if true, would most strongly support the prediction that the group's plan will succeed?

(A) Farmers that can gain a larger share of the food market in their regions will be better positioned to control more water resources.

(B) Most agricultural practices in areas with water shortages are water-intensive.

(C) Other regions of the world not facing water shortages are likely to make up for the reduction in agricultural output.

(D) Demand for agricultural products in the group's region is not expected to decline.

(E) More than half the water used for agriculture in the farmers' region is lost to evaporation or leakage from irrigation channels.

648. Hollywood restaurant is replacing some of its standard tables with tall tables and stools. The restaurant already fills every available seat during its operating hours, and the change in seating arrangements will not result in an increase in the restaurant's seating capacity. Nonetheless, the restaurant's management expects revenue to increase as a result of the seating change without any concurrent change in menu, prices, or operating hours.

Which of the following, if true, provides the best reason for the expectation?

(A) One of the taller tables takes up less floor space than one of the standard tables.

(B) Diners seated on stools typically do not linger over dinner as long as diners seated at standard tables.

(C) Since the restaurant will replace only some of its standard tables, it can continue to accommodate customers who do not care for the taller tables.

(D) Few diners are likely to avoid the restaurant because of the new seating arrangement.

(E) The standard tables being replaced by tall tables would otherwise have to be replaced with new standard tables at a greater expense.

649. A major network news organization experienced a drop in viewership in the week following the airing of a controversial report on the economy. The network also received a very large number of complaints regarding the report. The network, however, maintains that negative reactions to the report had nothing to do with its loss of viewers.

Which of the following, if true, most strongly supports the network's position?

(A) The other major network news organizations reported similar reductions in viewership during the same week.

(B) The viewers who registered complaints with the network were regular viewers of the news organization's programs.

(C) Major network news organizations publicly attribute drops in viewership to their own reports only when they receive complaints about those reports.

(D) This was not the first time that this network news organization has aired a controversial report on the economy that has inspired viewers to complain to the network.

(E) Most network news viewers rely on network news broadcasts as their primary source of information regarding the economy.

650. Only a reduction of 10 percent in the number of scheduled flights using Greentown's airport will allow the delays that are so common there to be avoided. Hevelia airstrip, 40 miles away, would, if upgraded and expanded, be an attractive alternative for fully 20 percent of the passengers using Greentown airport. Nevertheless, experts reject the claim that turning Hevelia into a full-service airport would end the chronic delays at Greentown.

    Which of the following, if true, most helps to justify the experts' position?

    (A) Turning Hevelia into a full-service airport would require not only substantial construction at the airport itself, but also the construction of new access highways.

    (B) A second largely undeveloped airstrip close to Greentown airport would be a more attractive alternative than Hevelia for many passengers who now use Greentown.

    (C) Hevelia airstrip lies in a relatively undeveloped area but would, if it became a full-service airport, be a magnet for commercial and residential development.

    (D) If an airplane has to wait to land, the extra jet fuel required adds significantly to the airline's costs.

    (E) Several airlines use Greentown as a regional hub, so that most flights landing at Greentown have many passengers who then take different flights to reach their final destinations.

651. Farmer: Worldwide, just three grain crops—rice, wheat, and corn—account for most human caloric intake. To maintain this level of caloric intake and also keep pace with global population growth, yields per acre from each of these crops will have to increase at least 1.5 percent every year, given that the supply of cultivated land is diminishing. Therefore, the government should increase funding for research into new ways to improve yields.

    Which of the following is an assumption on which the farmer's argument depends?

    (A) It is solely the government's responsibility to ensure that the amount of rice, wheat, and corn produced worldwide keeps pace with global population growth.

    (B) Increasing government funding for research into new ways to improve the yields per acre of rice, wheat, and corn crops would help to increase total worldwide annual production of food from these crops.

    (C) Increasing the yields per acre of rice, wheat, and corn is more important than increasing the yields per acre of other crops.

    (D) Current levels of funding for research into ways of improving grain crop yields per acre have enabled grain crop yields per acre to increase by more than 1.5 percent per year worldwide.

    (E) In coming decades, rice, wheat, and corn will become a minor part of human caloric intake, unless there is government-funded research to increase their yields per acre.

652. The air quality board recently informed Coffee Roast, a small coffee roasting firm, of a complaint regarding the smoke from its roaster. Recently enacted air quality regulations require machines roasting more than 10 pounds of coffee to be equipped with expensive smoke-dissipating afterburners. The firm, however, roasts only 8 pounds of coffee at a time. Nevertheless, the company has decided to purchase and install an afterburner.

    Which of the following, if true, most strongly supports the firm's decision?

    (A) Until settling on the new air quality regulations, the board had debated whether to require afterburners for machines roasting more than 5 pounds of coffee at a time.

    (B) Coffee roasted in a machine equipped with an afterburner has its flavor subtly altered.

    (C) The cost to the firm of an afterburner is less than the cost of replacing its roaster with a smaller one.

    (D) Fewer complaints are reported in areas that maintain strict rules regarding afterburners.

    (E) The firm has reason to fear that negative publicity regarding the complaints could result in lost sales.

653. People who do regular volunteer work tend to live longer, on average, than people who do not. It has been found that "doing good," a category that certainly includes volunteer work, releases endorphins, the brain's natural opiates, which induce in people a feeling of well-being. Clearly, there is a connection: Regular releases of endorphins must in some way help to extend people's lives.

    Which of the following, if true, most seriously undermines the force of the evidence given as support for the hypothesis that endorphins promote longevity?

    (A) People who do regular volunteer work are only somewhat more likely than others to characterize the work they do for a living as "doing good."

    (B) Although extremely high levels of endorphins could be harmful to health, such levels are never reached as a result of the natural release of endorphins.

    (C) There are many people who have done some volunteer work but who do not do such work regularly.

    (D) People tend not to become involved in regular volunteer work unless they are healthy and energetic to begin with.

    (E) Releases of endorphins are responsible for the sense of well-being experienced by many long-distance runners while running.

654. A study compared a sample of Swedish people older than 75 who needed in-home assistance with a similar sample of Israeli people. The people in the two samples received both informal assistance, provided by family and friends, and formal assistance, professionally provided. Although Sweden and Israel have equally well-funded and comprehensive systems for providing formal assistance, the study found that the people in the Swedish sample received more formal assistance, on average, than those in the Israeli sample.

    Which of the following, if true, does most to explain the difference that the study found?

    (A) A companion study found that among children needing special in-home care, the amount of formal assistance they received was roughly the same in Sweden as in Israel.

    (B) More Swedish than Israeli people older than 75 live in rural areas where formal assistance services are sparse or nonexistent.

    (C) Although in both Sweden and Israel much of the funding for formal assistance ultimately comes from the central government, the local structures through which assistance is delivered are different in the two countries.

    (D) In recent decades, the increase in life expectancy of someone who is 75 years old has been greater in Israel than in Sweden.

    (E) In Israel, people older than 75 tend to live with their children, whereas in Sweden people of that age tend to live alone.

655. Film Director: It is true that certain characters and plot twists in my newly released film *The Big Heist* are similar to characters and plot twists in *Thieves*, a movie that came out last year. Pointing to these similarities, the film studio that produced *Thieves* is now accusing me of taking ideas from that film. The accusation is clearly without merit. All production work on *The Big Heist* was actually completed months before *Thieves* was released.

    Which of the following, if true, provides the strongest support for the director's position?

    (A) Before *Thieves* began production, its script had been circulating for several years among various film studios, including the studio that produced *The Big Heist*.

    (B) The characters and plot twists that are most similar in the two films have close parallels in many earlier films of the same genre.

    (C) The film studio that produced *Thieves* seldom produces films in this genre.

    (D) The director of *Thieves* worked with the director of *The Big Heist* on several earlier projects.

    (E) Production work on *Thieves* began before production work on *The Big Heist* was started.

CR05412
656. In Mernia commercial fossil hunters often sell important fossils they have found, not to universities or museums, but to individual collectors, who pay much better but generally do not allow researchers access to their collections. To increase the number of fossils available for research, some legislators propose requiring all fossils that are found in Mernia to be sold only to universities or museums.

Which of the following, if true, most strongly indicates that the legislators' proposal will fail to achieve its goal?

(A) Some fossil hunters in Mernia are not commercial fossil hunters, but rather are amateurs who keep the fossils that they find.

(B) Most fossils found in Mernia are common types that have little scientific interest.

(C) Commercial fossil hunters in Mernia currently sell some of the fossils they find to universities and museums.

(D) Many universities in Mernia do not engage in fossil research.

(E) Most fossils are found by commercial fossil hunters, and they would give up looking for fossils if they were no longer allowed to sell to individual collectors.

CR02702
657. Economist: Tropicorp, which constantly seeks profitable investment opportunities, has been buying and clearing sections of tropical forest for cattle ranching, although pastures newly created there become useless for grazing after just a few years. The company has not gone into rubber tapping, even though greater profits can be made from rubber tapping, which leaves the forest intact. Thus, some environmentalists argue that **Tropicorp's actions do not serve even its own economic interest**. However, the initial investment required for a successful rubber-tapping operation is larger than that needed for a cattle ranch; there is a shortage of workers employable in rubber-tapping operations; and taxes are higher on profits from rubber tapping than on profits from cattle ranching. Consequently, **the environmentalists' conclusion is probably wrong**.

In the economist's argument, the two **boldface** portions play which of the following roles?

(A) The first supports the conclusion of the economist's argument; the second calls that conclusion into question.

(B) The first states the conclusion of the economist's argument; the second supports that conclusion.

(C) The first supports the conclusion of the environmentalists' argument; the second states that conclusion.

(D) The first states the conclusion of the environmentalists' argument; the second states the conclusion of the economist's argument.

(E) Each supports the conclusion of the economist's argument.

CR74231.01
658. Marketing executive for Magu Corporation: Whenever Magu opens a manufacturing facility in a new city, the company should sponsor, or make donations to, a number of nonprofit organizations in that city. Doing so would improve Magu's image in the community, and thus the money spent on such charitable ventures would lead to increased sales.

Which statement would, if true, point to the most serious weakness in the marketing executive's advice?

(A) Magu sells its products internationally, so sales in any one city represent only a small portion of total revenue.

(B) Spending on charitable ventures would require Magu to decrease direct advertisements, which are the most effective means of reaching its target customers.

(C) If market conditions change, Magu may have to close any such facility or relocate it.

(D) Some nonprofit organizations are poorly organized, so money donated to them would be of little benefit to the community.

(E) If workers at the manufacturing facility believed their wages or working conditions were poor, their complaints would outweigh any good impressions generated by Magu's donations or sponsorships.

659. Although the school would receive financial benefits if it had soft drink vending machines in the cafeteria, we should not allow them. Allowing soft drink machines there would not be in our students' interest. If our students start drinking more soft drinks, they will be less healthy.

The argument depends on which of the following?

(A) If the soft drink vending machines were placed in the cafeteria, students would consume more soft drinks as a result.

(B) The amount of soft drinks that most students at the school currently drink is not detrimental to their health.

(C) Students are apt to be healthier if they do not drink soft drinks at all than if they just drink small amounts occasionally.

(D) Students will not simply bring soft drinks from home if the soft drink vending machines are not placed in the cafeteria.

(E) The school's primary concern should be to promote good health among its students.

660. Many athletes inhale pure oxygen after exercise in an attempt to increase muscular reabsorption of oxygen. Measured continuously after exercise, however, the blood lactate levels of athletes who inhale pure oxygen are practically identical, on average, to those of athletes who breathe normal air. The lower the blood lactate level is, the higher the muscular reabsorption of oxygen is.

If the statements above are all true, they most strongly support which of the following conclusions?

(A) Athletes' muscular reabsorption of oxygen is not increased when they inhale pure oxygen instead of normal air.

(B) High blood lactate levels cannot be reduced.

(C) Blood lactate levels are a poor measure of oxygen reabsorption by muscles.

(D) The amount of oxygen reabsorbed by an athlete's muscles always remains constant.

(E) The inhaling of pure oxygen has no legitimate role in athletics.

661. Historian: Fifteenth-century advances in mapmaking contributed to the rise of modern nation-states. In medieval Europe (from the fifth to the fifteenth century), sovereignty centered in cities and towns and radiated outward, with boundaries often ambiguously defined. The conceptual shift toward the modern state began in the late fifteenth century, when mapmakers learned to reflect geography accurately by basing maps on latitude-longitude grids. By the mid-seventeenth century, nearly all maps showed boundary lines.

Which of the following would, if true, most strengthen the historian's reasoning?

(A) Borders did not become codified in Europe until certain treaties were signed in the early nineteenth century.

(B) During the medieval period, various authorities in Europe claimed power over collections of cities and towns, not contiguous territories.

(C) Many members of the political elite collected maps as a hobby during the late sixteenth and early seventeenth centuries.

(D) Seventeenth-century treatises and other sources of political authority describe areas of sovereignty rather than illustrate them using maps.

(E) During the fifteenth century in Europe, mapmakers simplified the borders of sovereignty by drawing clear lines of demarcation between political powers.

662. Sascha: The attempt to ban parliament's right to pass directed-spending bills—bills that contain provisions specifically funding the favorite projects of some powerful politicians—is antidemocratic. Our nation's constitution requires that money be drawn from our treasury only when so stipulated by laws passed by parliament, the branch of government most directly representative of the citizens. This requirement is based on the belief that exercising the power to spend public resources involves the ultimate exercise of state authority and that therefore _____.

Which of the following most logically completes Sascha's argument?

(A) designating funding specifically for the favorite projects of some powerful politicians should be considered antidemocratic

(B) the right to exercise such a power should belong exclusively to the branch of government most directly representative of the citizens

(C) exercising the power to spend public resources is in most cases—but not all—protected by the constitution

(D) modifications to any spending bills should be considered expenditures authorized by law

(E) only officials who are motivated by concerns for reelection should retain that power

663. Boreal owls range over a much larger area than do other owls of similar size. Scientists have hypothesized that **it is scarcity of prey that leads the owls to range so widely**. This hypothesis would be hard to confirm directly, since it is not possible to produce a sufficiently accurate count of the populations of small mammals inhabiting the forests where boreal owls live. Careful study of owl behavior has, however, shown that **boreal owls do range over larger areas when they live in regions where food of the sort eaten by small mammals is comparatively sparse**. This indicates that the scientists' hypothesis is not sheer speculation.

In the argument given, the two **boldfaced** portions play which of the following roles?

(A) The first presents an explanatory hypothesis; the second states the main conclusion of the argument.

(B) The first presents an explanatory hypothesis; the second presents evidence tending to support this hypothesis.

(C) The first presents an explanatory hypothesis; the second presents evidence to support an alternative explanation.

(D) The first describes a position that the argument opposes; the second presents evidence to undermine the support for the position being opposed.

(E) The first describes a position that the argument opposes; the second states the main conclusion of the argument.

664. Cognitive scientist: Using the pioneering work of comparative psychologist Gordon Gallup as a model, several studies have investigated animals' capacity for mirror self-recognition (MSR). Most animals exposed to a mirror respond only with social behavior, such as aggression. However, in the case of the great apes, repeated exposure to mirrors leads to self-directed behaviors, such as exploring the inside of the mouth, suggesting that these animals recognize the reflection as an image of self. The implication of these studies is that the great apes have a capacity for self-awareness unique among nonhuman species.

The cognitive scientist makes which of the following assumptions in the argument above?

(A) Gallup's work has established that the great apes have a capacity for MSR unique among nonhuman species.

(B) If an animal does not have the capacity for MSR, it does not have the capacity for self-awareness.

(C) If a researcher exposes an animal to a mirror and that animal exhibits social behavior, that animal is incapable of being self-aware.

(D) When exposed to a mirror, all animals display either social behavior or self-directed behavior.

(E) Animals that do not exhibit MSR may demonstrate a capacity for self-awareness in other ways.

665. Last year a record number of new manufacturing jobs were created. Will this year bring another record? Well, any new manufacturing job is created either within an existing company or by the start-up of a new company. **Within existing firms, new jobs have been created this year at well below last year's record pace.** At the same time, there is considerable evidence that the number of new companies starting up will be no higher this year than it was last year and **there is no reason to think that the new companies starting up this year will create more jobs per company than did last year's start-ups**. So clearly, the number of new jobs created this year will fall short of last year's record.

In the argument given, the two portions in **boldface** play which of the following roles?

(A) The first is a claim that the argument challenges; the second is an explicit assumption on which that challenge is based.

(B) The first is a claim that the argument challenges; the second is a judgment advanced in support of the main conclusion of the argument.

(C) The first provides evidence in support of the main conclusion of the argument; the second is an objection that has been raised against that main conclusion.

(D) The first provides evidence in support of the main conclusion of the argument; the second is a judgment advanced in support of that main conclusion.

(E) The first and the second are each claims that have been advanced in support of a position that the argument opposes.

666. A study of ticket sales at a summer theater festival found that people who bought tickets to individual plays had a no-show rate of less than 1 percent, while those who paid in advance for all ten plays being performed that summer had a no-show rate of nearly 30 percent. This may be at least in part because the greater the awareness customers retain about the cost of an item, the more likely they are to use it.

Which of the following would, if true, best serve as an alternative explanation of the results of the study?

(A) The price per ticket was slightly cheaper for those who bought all ten tickets in advance.

(B) Many people who attended the theater festival believed strongly that they should support it financially.

(C) Those who attended all ten plays became eligible for a partial refund.

(D) Usually, people who bought tickets to individual plays did so immediately prior to each performance that they attended.

(E) People who arrived just before the performance began could not be assured of obtaining seats in a preferred location.

667. Although there is no record of poet Edmund Spenser's parentage, we do know that as a youth Spenser attended the Merchant Tailors' School in London for a period between 1560 and 1570. Records from this time indicate that the Merchant Tailors' Guild then had only three members named Spenser: Robert Spenser, listed as a gentleman; Nicholas Spenser, elected the Guild's Warden in 1568; and John Spenser, listed as a "journeyman cloth-maker." Of these, the last was likely the least affluent of the three—and most likely Edmund's father, since school accounting records list Edmund as a scholar who attended the school at a reduced fee.

Which of the following is an assumption on which the argument depends?

(A) Anybody in sixteenth-century London who made clothing professionally would have had to be a member of the Merchant Tailors' Guild.

(B) The fact that Edmund Spenser attended the Merchant Tailors' School did not necessarily mean that he planned to become a tailor.

(C) No member of the Guild could become Guild warden in sixteenth-century London unless he was a gentleman.

(D) Most of those whose fathers were members of the Merchant Tailors' Guild were students at the Merchant Tailors' School.

(E) The Merchant Tailors' School did not reduce its fees for the children of the more affluent Guild members.

CR20831.01
668. Hea Sook: One should not readily believe urban legends. Most legends are propagated because the moral lesson underlying them supports a political agenda. People will repeat a tale if it fits their purpose. They may not deliberately spread untruths, but neither are they particularly motivated to investigate deeply to determine if the tale they are telling is true.

Kayla: But people would not repeat stories that they did not believe were true. Therefore, one can safely assume that if a story has been repeated by enough people then it is more likely to be true.

Kayla's reply is most vulnerable to the criticism that it

(A) does not specify how many people need to repeat a story before someone is justified believing it

(B) overstates the significance of political agendas in the retelling of stories

(C) fails to address the claim that people will not verify the truth of a story that fits their purpose

(D) implicitly supports the claim that the people repeating legends are not deliberately spreading untruths

(E) cannot distinguish people's motivations for repeating urban legends from their motivations for repeating other types of story

CR03749
669. Rainwater contains hydrogen of a heavy form called deuterium. The deuterium content of wood reflects the deuterium content of rainwater available to trees during their growth. Wood from trees that grew between 16,000 and 24,000 years ago in North America contains significantly more deuterium than wood from trees growing today. But water trapped in several North American caves that formed during that same early period contains significantly less deuterium than rainwater in North America contains today.

Which of the following, if true, most helps to reconcile the two findings?

(A) There is little deuterium in the North American caves other than the deuterium in the water trapped there.

(B) Exposure to water after a tree has died does not change the deuterium content of the wood.

(C) Industrialization in North America over the past 100 years has altered the deuterium content of rain.

(D) Trees draw on shallow groundwater from rain that falls during their growth, whereas water trapped in caves may have fallen as rainwater thousands of years before the caves formed.

(E) Wood with a high deuterium content is no more likely to remain preserved for long periods than is wood with a low deuterium content.

CR04925
670. Enforcement of local speed limits through police monitoring has proven unsuccessful in the town of Ardane. In many nearby towns, speed humps (raised areas of pavement placed across residential streets, about 300 feet apart) have reduced traffic speeds on residential streets by 20 to 25 percent. In order to reduce traffic speed and thereby enhance safety in residential neighborhoods, Ardane's transportation commission plans to install multiple speed humps in those neighborhoods.

Which of the following, if true, identifies a potentially serious drawback to the plan for installing speed humps in Ardane?

(A) On residential streets without speed humps, many vehicles travel at speeds more than 25 percent above the posted speed limit.

(B) Because of their high weight, emergency vehicles such as fire trucks and ambulances must slow almost to a stop at speed humps.

(C) The residential speed limit in Ardane is higher than that of the nearby towns where speed humps were installed.

(D) Motorists who are not familiar with the streets in Ardane's residential districts would be likely to encounter the speed humps unawares unless warned by signs and painted indicators.

(E) Bicyclists generally prefer that speed humps be constructed so as to leave a space on the side of the road where bicycles can travel without going over the humps.

CR00748

671. Which of the choices most logically completes the following argument?

NowNews, although still the most popular magazine covering cultural events in Kalopolis, has recently suffered a significant drop in advertising revenue because of falling circulation. Many readers have begun buying a competing magazine that, at 50 cents per copy, costs less than NowNews at $1.50 per copy. In order to boost circulation and thus increase advertising revenue, NowNews's publisher has proposed making it available at no charge. However, this proposal has a serious drawback, since _____.

(A) those Kalopolis residents with the greatest interest in cultural events are regular readers of both magazines.

(B) one reason NowNews's circulation fell was that its competitor's reporting on cultural events was superior.

(C) the newsstands and stores that currently sell NowNews will no longer carry it if it is being given away for free.

(D) at present, 10 percent of the total number of copies of each issue of NowNews are distributed free to students on college campuses in the Kalopolis area.

(E) NowNews's competitor would begin to lose large amounts of money if it were forced to lower its cover price.

CR07304

672. Archaeologist: Researchers excavating a burial site in Cyprus found a feline skeleton lying near a human skeleton. Both skeletons were in the same sediment at the same depth and equally well-preserved, suggesting that the feline and human were buried together about 9,500 years ago. This shows that felines were domesticated around the time farming began, when they would have been useful in protecting stores of grain from mice.

Which of the following, if true, would most seriously weaken the archaeologist's argument?

(A) Archaeologists have not found any remains of stores of grain in the immediate vicinity of the burial site.

(B) The burial site in Cyprus is substantially older than any other known burial site in which a feline skeleton and a human skeleton appear to have been buried together.

(C) Paintings found near the burial site seem to show people keeping felines as domestic companions, but do not show felines hunting mice.

(D) In Cyprus, there are many burial sites dating from around 9,500 years ago in which the remains of wild animals appear to have been buried alongside human remains.

(E) Before felines were domesticated, early farmers had no effective way to protect stores of grain from mice.

CR90061.01

673. Farmer: Several people in the past few years have claimed to have seen a mountain lion in the suburban outskirts—the latest just last month—and, while mountain lions were thought to have been driven from this entire region about twenty years ago, there is no reason for the people who reported seeing a mountain lion to have deliberately concocted a false report. Therefore, local wildlife managers should begin to urgently address the mountain lion's presence.

Which of the following would, if true, most seriously weaken the farmer's argument?

(A) Farmers in the suburban outskirts mostly raise cattle and hogs, which when fully grown are generally not attacked by mountain lions.

(B) Mountain lions are dissimilar in size and color to other wild animals found near the suburban outskirts.

(C) No person who claimed to have seen a mountain lion had anyone else with them at the purported sighting.

(D) There have been no regional reports in the past year of mountain lions migrating to the area.

(E) Recent surveys show that more than half of the people in the region report that they have never seen a mountain lion before.

674. The heavy traffic in Masana is a growing drain on the city's economy—the clogging of the streets of the central business district alone cost the economy more than $1.2 billion over the past year. In order to address this problem, officials plan to introduce congestion pricing, by which drivers would pay to enter the city's most heavily trafficked areas during the busiest times of the day.

Which of the following, if true, would most strongly indicate that the plan will be a success?

(A) Approximately one-fifth of the vehicles in the central business district are in transit from one side of the city to the other.

(B) Planners expect that, without congestion pricing, traffic in Masana is likely to grow by 6 percent in the next five years.

(C) In other urban areas, congestion pricing has strongly encouraged carpooling (sharing of rides by private commuters).

(D) Several studies have shown that a reduction in traffic of 15 percent in Masana could result in 5,500 or more new jobs.

(E) Over 30 percent of the vehicles in the city's center are occupied by more than one person.

675. Economist: The most economically efficient way to reduce emissions of air pollutants is to tax them in proportion to the damage they are likely to cause. But in Country Y, many serious pollutants are untaxed and unregulated, and policy makers strongly oppose new taxes. Therefore, the best way to achieve a reduction in air pollutant emissions in Country Y would be to institute fixed upper limits on them.

Which of the following is an assumption of the economist's argument?

(A) Policy makers in Country Y oppose all new taxes equally strongly, regardless of any benefits they may provide.

(B) Country Y's air pollutant emissions would not fall significantly if they were taxed in proportion to the damage they are likely to cause.

(C) Policy makers in Country Y strongly favor reductions in air pollutant emissions.

(D) Country Y's policy makers believe that air pollutant emissions should be reduced with maximum economic efficiency.

(E) Policy makers in Country Y do not oppose setting fixed upper limits on air pollutant emissions as strongly as they oppose new taxes.

676. Humans get Lyme disease from infected ticks. Ticks get infected by feeding on animals with Lyme disease, but the ease of transmission from host animal to tick varies. With most species of host animal, transmission of Lyme disease to ticks is extremely rare, but white-footed mice are an exception, readily passing Lyme disease to ticks. And white-footed mouse populations greatly expand, becoming the main food source for ticks, in areas where biodiversity is in decline.

The information in the passage most strongly supports which of the following?

(A) In areas where many humans are infected with Lyme disease, the proportion of ticks infected with Lyme disease is especially high.

(B) Very few animals that live in areas where there are no white-footed mice are infected with Lyme disease.

(C) Humans are less at risk of contracting Lyme disease in areas where biodiversity is high.

(D) Ticks feed on white-footed mice only when other host species are not available to them.

(E) The greater the biodiversity of an area, the more likely any given host animal in that area is to pass Lyme disease to ticks.

677. Many industrialized nations are trying to reduce atmospheric concentrations of carbon dioxide, a gas released by the burning of fossil fuels. One proposal is to replace conventional cement, which is made with calcium carbonate, by a new "eco-cement." This new cement, made with magnesium carbonate, absorbs large amounts of carbon dioxide when exposed to the atmosphere. Therefore, using eco-cement for new concrete building projects will significantly help reduce atmospheric concentrations of carbon dioxide.

Which of the following, if true, most strengthens the argument?

(A) The cost of magnesium carbonate, currently greater than the cost of calcium carbonate, probably will fall as more magnesium carbonate is used in cement manufacture.

(B) Eco-cement is strengthened when absorbed carbon dioxide reacts with the cement.

(C) Before the development of eco-cement, magnesium-based cement was considered too susceptible to water erosion to be of practical use.

(D) The manufacture of eco-cement uses considerably less fossil fuel per unit of cement than the manufacture of conventional cement does.

(E) Most building-industry groups are unaware of the development or availability of eco-cement.

CR00895

678. Advertisement: When your car's engine is running at its normal operating temperature, any major brand of motor oil will protect it about as well as Tuff does. When the engine is cold, it is a different story: Tuff motor oil flows better at lower temperatures than its major competitors do. So, if you want your car's engine to have maximum protection, you should use Tuff.

Which of the following, if true, most strengthens the argument in the advertisement?

(A) Tuff motor oil provides above-average protection for engines that happen to overheat.

(B) Tuff motor oil is periodically supplied free of charge to automobile manufacturers to use in factory-new cars.

(C) Tuff motor oil's share of the engine oil market peaked three years ago.

(D) Tuff motor oil, like any motor oil, is thicker and flows less freely at cold temperatures than at hot temperatures.

(E) Tuff motor oil is manufactured at only one refinery and shipped from there to all markets.

CR55541.01

679. Linguist: In English, the past is described as "behind" and the future "ahead," whereas in Aymara the past is "ahead" and the future "behind." Research indicates that English speakers sway backward when discussing the past and forward when discussing the future. Conversely, Aymara speakers gesture forward with their hands when discussing the past and backward when discussing the future. These bodily movements, therefore, suggest that the language one speaks affects how one mentally visualizes time.

The linguist's reasoning depends on assuming which of the following?

(A) At least some Aymara speakers sway forward when discussing the past and backward when discussing the future.

(B) Most people mentally visualize time as running either forward or backward.

(C) Not all English and Aymara speakers tend to sway or gesture forward or backward when discussing the present.

(D) How people move when discussing the future correlates to some extent with how they mentally visualize time.

(E) The researchers also examined the movements of at least some speakers of languages other than English and Aymara discussing the past and the future.

CR13108

680. *The Testament of William Thorpe* was published around 1530 as an appendix to Thorpe's longer *Examination*. Many scholars, however, doubt the attribution of the *Testament* to Thorpe because, whereas the *Examination* is dated 1406, the *Testament* is dated 1460. One scholar has recently argued that the 1460 date be amended to 1409, based on the observation that when these numbers are expressed as Roman numerals, MCCCCLX and MCCCCIX, it becomes easy to see how the dates might have become confused through scribal error.

Which of the following, if true, would most support the scholar's hypothesis concerning the date of the *Testament*?

(A) The sole evidence that historians have had that William Thorpe died no earlier than 1460 was the presumed date of publication of the *Testament*.

(B) In the preface to the 1530 publication, the editor attributes both works to William Thorpe.

(C) Few writers in fifteenth-century England marked dates in their works using only Roman numerals.

(D) The *Testament* alludes to a date, "Friday, September 20," as apparently contemporaneous with the writing of the *Testament*, and September 20 fell on a Friday in 1409 but not in 1460.

(E) The *Testament* contains few references to historical events that occurred later than 1406.

681. A prominent investor who holds a large stake in the Burton Tool Company has recently claimed that the company is mismanaged, citing as evidence the company's failure to slow down production in response to a recent rise in its inventory of finished products. It is doubtful whether an investor's sniping at management can ever be anything other than counterproductive, but in this case, it is clearly not justified. It is true that **an increased inventory of finished products often indicates that production is outstripping demand**, but in Burton's case it indicates no such thing. Rather, **the increase in inventory is entirely attributable to products that have already been assigned to orders received from customers**.

In the argument given, the two **boldfaced** portions play which of the following roles?

(A) The first states a generalization that underlies the position that the argument as a whole opposes; the second provides evidence to show that the generalization does not apply in the case at issue.

(B) The first states a generalization that underlies the position that the argument as a whole opposes; the second clarifies the meaning of a specific phrase as it is used in that generalization.

(C) The first provides evidence to support the conclusion of the argument as a whole; the second is evidence that has been used to support the position that the argument as a whole opposes.

(D) The first provides evidence to support the conclusion of the argument as a whole; the second states that conclusion.

(E) The first and the second each provide evidence against the position that the argument as a whole opposes.

682. To reduce productivity losses from employees calling in sick, Corporation X implemented a new policy requiring employees to come into work unless they were so sick that they had to go to a doctor. But a year after the policy was implemented, a study found that Corporation X's overall productivity losses due to reported employee illnesses had increased.

Which of the following, if true, would best explain why the policy produced the reverse of its intended effect?

(A) After the policy was implemented, employees more frequently went to the doctor when they felt sick.

(B) Before the policy was implemented, employees who were not sick at all often called in sick.

(C) Employees coming into work when sick often infect many of their coworkers.

(D) Unusually few employees became genuinely sick during the year after the policy was implemented.

(E) There are many other factors besides employee illness that can adversely affect productivity.

683. Advertising by mail has become much less effective, with fewer consumers responding. Because consumers are increasingly overwhelmed by the sheer amount of junk mail they receive, most discard almost all offers without considering them. Thus, an effective way for corporations to improve response rates would be to more carefully target the individuals to whom they mail advertising, thereby cutting down on the amount of junk mail each consumer receives.

Which of the following, if true, would most support the recommendation above?

(A) There are cost-effective means by which corporations that currently advertise by mail could improve response rates.

(B) Many successful corporations are already carefully targeting the individuals to whom they mail advertising.

(C) Any consumer who, immediately after receiving an advertisement by mail, merely glances at it, is very likely to discard it.

(D) Improvements in the quality of the advertising materials used in mail that is carefully targeted to individuals can improve the response rate for such mail.

(E) Response rates to carefully targeted advertisements by mail are considerably higher, on average, than response rates to most other forms of advertising.

684. Petrochemical industry officials have said that the extreme pressure exerted on plant managers during the last five years to improve profits by cutting costs has done nothing to impair the industry's ability to operate safely. However, environmentalists contend that the recent rash of serious oil spills and accidents at petrochemical plants is traceable to cost-cutting measures.

Which of the following, if true, would provide the strongest support for the position held by industry officials?

(A) The petrochemical industry benefits if accidents do not occur, since accidents involve risk of employee injury as well as loss of equipment and product.

(B) Petrochemical industry unions recently demanded that additional money be spent on safety and environmental protection measures, but the unions readily abandoned those demands in exchange for job security.

(C) Despite major cutbacks in most other areas of operation, the petrochemical industry has devoted more of its resources to environmental and safety measures in the last five years than in the preceding five years.

(D) There is evidence that the most damaging of the recent oil spills would have been prevented had cost-cutting measures not been instituted.

(E) Both the large fines and the adverse publicity generated by the most recent oil spill have prompted the petrochemical industry to increase the resources devoted to oil-spill prevention.

685. A company has developed a new sensing device that, according to the company's claims, detects weak, ultralow-frequency electromagnetic signals associated with a beating heart. These signals, which pass through almost any physical obstruction, are purportedly detected by the device even at significant distances. Therefore, if the company's claims are true, their device will radically improve emergency teams' ability to locate quickly people who are trapped within the wreckage of collapsed buildings.

Which of the following, if true, most strengthens the argument?

(A) People trapped within the wreckage of collapsed buildings usually have serious injuries that require prompt medical treatment.

(B) The device gives a distinctive reading when the signals it detects come from human beings rather than from any other living beings.

(C) Most people who have survived after being trapped in collapsed buildings were rescued within two hours of the building's collapse.

(D) Ultralow-frequency signals are not the only electromagnetic signals that can pass through almost any physical obstruction.

(E) Extensive training is required in order to operate the device effectively.

686. Economist: The price of tap water in our region should be raised drastically. **Supplies in local freshwater reservoirs have been declining for years** because water is being used faster than it can be replenished. Since the price of tap water has been low, **few users have bothered to adopt even easy conservation measures**.

The two sections in boldface play which of the following roles in the economist's argument?

(A) The first is a conclusion for which support is provided, and which in turn supports the main conclusion; the second is the main conclusion.

(B) The first is an observation for which the second provides an explanation; the second is the main conclusion but not the only conclusion.

(C) The first is a premise supporting the argument's main conclusion; so is the second.

(D) The first is the only conclusion; the second provides an explanation for the first.

(E) The first is the main conclusion; the second is a conclusion for which support is provided, and which in turn supports the first.

687. Politician: Hybrid cars use significantly less fuel per kilometer than nonhybrids. And fuel produces air pollution, which contributes to a number of environmental problems. Motorists can save money by driving cars that are more fuel efficient, and they will be encouraged to drive hybrid cars if we make them aware of that fact. Therefore, we can help reduce the total amount of pollution emitted by cars in this country by highlighting this advantage of hybrid cars.

Which of the following, if true, would most indicate a vulnerability of the politician's argument?

(A) People with more fuel-efficient cars typically drive more than do those with less fuel-efficient cars.

(B) Not all air pollution originates from automobiles.

(C) Hybrid cars have already begun to gain popularity.

(D) Fuel-efficient alternatives to hybrid cars will likely become available in the future.

(E) The future cost of gasoline and other fuel cannot be predicted with absolute precision or certainty.

CR99530.01
688. Mayor: False alarms from home security systems waste so much valuable police time that in many communities police have stopped responding to alarms from homes whose systems frequently produce false alarms. This policy reduces wastage of police time but results in a loss of protection for some residents. To achieve a comparable reduction in wastage without reducing protection for residents, the council has enacted a measure to fine residents for repeated false alarms.

Which of the following, if true, casts the most doubt on whether the measure enacted by the council will achieve its goal?

(A) A fine in the amount planned by the council will not cover the expenses police typically incur when they respond to a false alarm.
(B) Homes equipped with security systems are far less likely to be broken into than are homes without security systems.
(C) The threat of fines is likely to cause many residents to deactivate their security systems.
(D) The number of home security systems is likely to increase dramatically over the next five years.
(E) Many home security systems have never produced false alarms.

CR53341.01
689. Excavation of the house of a third-century Camarnian official revealed that he had served four magistrates—public officials who administer the law—over his thirty-year public career, in four provincial capital cities. However, given the Camarnian administrative system of that era, it is unclear whether he served them simultaneously, as a traveling administrator living for part of the year in each provincial capital, or else did so sequentially, leaving one magistrate after several years to join another.

Which of the following would, if found in the excavation, most likely help reveal the pattern of the official's administrative service?

(A) Maps and documents describing each of the four provincial capitals
(B) A cache of the official's documents related to work from early in his career
(C) A set of cups of a type made only in the city of the first magistrate whom the official is known to have served
(D) Several pieces of furniture in the styles of two of the provincial capital cities
(E) Heavy clothing appropriate only for the coldest of the four cities

CR80531.01
690. In 1563, in Florence's Palazzo Vecchio, Giorgio Vasari built in front of an existing wall a new wall on which he painted a mural. Investigators recently discovered a gap between Vasari's wall and the original, large enough to have preserved anything painted on the original. Historians believe that Leonardo da Vinci had painted, but left unfinished, a mural on the original wall; some historians had also believed that by 1563 the mural had been destroyed. However, it is known that in the late 1560s, when renovating another building, Santa Maria Novella, Vasari built a façade over its frescoes, and the frescoes were thereby preserved. Thus, Leonardo's Palazzo Vecchio mural probably still exists behind Vasari's wall.

Which of the following is an assumption on which the argument depends?

(A) Leonardo rarely if ever destroyed artworks that he left unfinished.
(B) Vasari was likely unaware that the mural in the Palazzo Vecchio had willingly been abandoned by Leonardo.
(C) Vasari probably would not have built the Palazzo Vecchio wall with a gap behind it except to preserve something behind the new wall.
(D) Leonardo would probably have completed the Palazzo Vecchio mural if he had had the opportunity to do so.
(E) When Vasari preserved the frescoes of Santa Maria Novella he did so secretly.

CR09534
691. Coffee shop owner: A large number of customers will pay at least the fair market value for a cup of coffee, even if there is no formal charge. Some will pay more than this out of appreciation of the trust that is placed in them. And our total number of customers is likely to increase. We could therefore improve our net cash flow by implementing an honor system in which customers pay what they wish for coffee by depositing money in a can.

Manager: We're likely to lose money on this plan. Many customers would cheat the system, paying a very small sum or nothing at all.

Which of the following, if true, would best support the owner's plan, in light of the manager's concern?

(A) The new system, if implemented, would increase the number of customers.

(B) By roasting its own coffee, the shop has managed to reduce the difficulties (and cost) of maintaining an inventory of freshly roasted coffee.

(C) Many customers stay in the cafe for long stretches of time.

(D) The shop makes a substantial profit from pastries and other food bought by the coffee drinkers.

(E) No other coffee shop in the area has such a system.

CR01900

692. The city of Workney, in raising bus fares from $1.00 to $1.25, proposed that 18 fare tokens be sold for $20.00 to alleviate the extra burden of the fare increase on the city's poor people. Critics suggested alternatively that 9 fare tokens be sold for $10.00, because a $20.00 outlay would be prohibitive for poor riders.

The alternative proposal depends on which of the following assumptions?

(A) Poor residents of Workney will continue to ride the buses in the same numbers despite the fare increase.

(B) Riders who are poor would be more likely to take advantage of the savings afforded by the 9-token offer than would riders who are not poor.

(C) The outlay of $10.00 for the purchase of 9 fare tokens would not be prohibitive for bus riders who are poor.

(D) The proposed fare increase is needed for the purchase of new buses for the city's bus system.

(E) Fewer riders would regularly purchase 18 fare tokens at once than would purchase only 9 fare tokens at once.

CR03272

693. Birds have been said to be descended from certain birdlike dinosaur species with which they share distinctive structural features. The fossil record, however, shows that this cannot be so, since there are bird fossils that are much older than the earliest birdlike dinosaur fossils that have been found.

Which of the following is an assumption on which the argument relies?

(A) The birdlike dinosaurs have no living descendants.

(B) There are no flightless dinosaur species that have the distinctive structural features shared by birds and birdlike dinosaurs.

(C) There are no birdlike dinosaur fossils that are older than the bird fossils but have not yet been unearthed.

(D) It could not have been the case that some birds were descended from one of the birdlike dinosaur species and other birds from another.

(E) Birds cannot have been descended from dinosaur species with which the birds do not share the distinctive structural features.

CR08239

694. City council member: Demand for electricity has been increasing by 1.5 percent a year, and there simply is no more space to build additional power plants to meet future demand increases. We must therefore begin to curtail usage, which is why I propose passing ordinances requiring energy-conservation measures in all city departments.

The city council member's proposal assumes which of the following?

(A) Existing power plants do not have the capacity to handle all of the projected increase in demand for electricity.

(B) No city departments have implemented energy-conservation measures voluntarily.

(C) Passing ordinances designed to curtail electricity usage will not have negative economic consequences for the city.

(D) Residential consumers are not responsible for the recent increases in demand for electricity.

(E) City departments that successfully conserve energy will set a good example for residential and industrial consumers of electricity.

695. Certain groups of Asian snails include both "left-handed" and "right-handed" species, with shells coiling to the left and right, respectively. Some left-handed species have evolved from right-handed ones. Also, researchers found that snail-eating snakes in the same habitat have asymmetrical jaws, allowing them to grasp right-handed snail shells more easily. If these snakes ate more right-handed snails over time, this would have given left-handed snails an evolutionary advantage over right-handed snails, with the left-handed snails eventually becoming a new species. Thus, the snakes' asymmetrical jaws probably helped drive the emergence of the left-handed snail species.

Which of the following would, if true, most strengthen the argument that asymmetrical snake jaws helped drive left-handed snail evolution?

(A) In one snake species, the snakes with asymmetrical jaws eat snails, while the snakes with symmetrical jaws do not eat snails.

(B) Some species of Asian snails contain either all right-handed snails, or all left-handed snails.

(C) Anatomical differences prevent left-handed snails from mating easily with right-handed snails.

(D) Some right-handed snails in this habitat have shells with a very narrow opening that helps prevent snakes from extracting the snails from inside their shells.

(E) Experiments show that the snail-eating snakes in this habitat fail more often in trying to eat left-handed snails than in trying to eat right-handed snails.

696. A moderately large city is redesigning its central downtown area and is considering a plan that would reduce the number of lanes for automobiles and trucks and increase those for bicycles and pedestrians. The intent is to attract more workers and shoppers to downtown businesses by making downtown easier to reach and more pleasant to move around in.

Which of the following would, if true, most strongly support the prediction that the plan would achieve its goal?

(A) People who make a habit of walking or bicycling whenever feasible derive significant health benefits from doing so.

(B) Most people who prefer to shop at suburban malls instead of downtown urban areas do so because parking is easier and cheaper at the former.

(C) In other moderately sized cities where measures were taken to make downtowns more accessible for walkers and cyclists, downtown businesses began to thrive.

(D) If the proposed lane restrictions on drivers are rigorously enforced, more people will likely be attracted to downtown businesses than would otherwise be.

(E) Most people who own and frequently ride bicycles for recreational purposes live at a significant distance from downtown urban areas.

697. Previously, Autoco designed all of its cars itself and then contracted with specialized parts suppliers to build parts according to its specifications. Now it plans to include its suppliers in designing the parts they are to build. Since many parts suppliers have more designers with specialized experience than Autoco has, Autoco expects this shift to reduce the overall time and cost of the design of its next new car.

Which of the following, if true, most strongly supports Autoco's expectation?

(A) When suppliers provide their own designs, Autoco often needs to modify its overall design.

(B) In order to provide designs for Autoco, several of the parts suppliers will have to add to their existing staffs of designers.

(C) Parts and services provided by outside suppliers account for more than 50 percent of Autoco's total costs.

(D) When suppliers built parts according to specifications provided by Autoco, the suppliers competed to win contracts.

(E) Most of Autoco's suppliers have on hand a wide range of previously prepared parts designs that can readily be modified for a new car.

698. In response to viral infection, the immune systems of mice typically produce antibodies that destroy the virus by binding to proteins on its surface. Mice infected with the herpesvirus generally develop keratitis, a degenerative disease affecting part of the eye. Since proteins on the surface of cells in this part of the eye

closely resemble those on the herpesvirus surface, scientists hypothesize that these cases of keratitis are caused by antibodies to the herpesvirus.

Which of the following, if true, most helps to support the scientists' reasoning?

(A) Other types of virus have surface proteins that closely resemble proteins found in various organs of mice.

(B) Mice that are infected with the herpesvirus but do not develop keratitis produce as many antibodies as infected mice that do develop keratitis.

(C) Mice infected with a new strain of the herpesvirus that has different surface proteins did not develop keratitis.

(D) Mice that have never been infected with the herpesvirus can sometimes develop keratitis.

(E) There are mice that are unable to form antibodies in response to herpes infections, and these mice contract herpes at roughly the same rate as other mice.

CR38931.01
699. One might expect that within a particular species, any individuals that managed to slow down the aging process would leave more offspring. Natural selection should therefore favor extreme longevity—but this does not seem to be the case. A possible explanation is that aging is a product of the inevitable wear and tear of living, similar to how household appliances generally accumulate faults that lead to their eventual demise. However, most researchers do not find this analogy satisfactory as an explanation.

Which of the following would, if true, provide the strongest explanation for the researchers' reaction?

(A) Some organisms are capable of living much longer than other organisms.

(B) Some organisms reproduce very quickly despite having short lifespans.

(C) There are several ways of defining "extreme longevity," and according to some definitions it occurs frequently.

(D) Organisms are capable of maintenance and self-repair and can remedy much of the damage that they accumulate.

(E) Some organisms generate much more wear and tear on their bodies than others.

CR02885
700. Last year a record number of new manufacturing jobs were created. Will this year bring another record? Well, **any new manufacturing job is created either within an existing company or by the start-up of a new company**. Within existing firms, new jobs have been created this year at well below last year's record pace. At the same time, there is considerable evidence that the number of new companies starting up this year will be no higher than it was last year and **there is no reason to think that the new companies starting up this year will create more jobs per company than did last year's start-ups**. So clearly, the number of new jobs created this year will fall short of last year's record.

In the argument given, the two portions in **boldface** play which of the following roles?

(A) The first provides evidence in support of the main conclusion of the argument; the second is a claim that the argument challenges.

(B) The first is a generalization that the argument seeks to establish; the second is a conclusion that the argument draws in order to support that generalization.

(C) The first is a generalization that the argument seeks to establish; the second is a judgment that has been advanced in order to challenge that generalization.

(D) The first is presented as an obvious truth on which the argument is based; the second is a claim that has been advanced in support of a position that the argument opposes.

(E) The first is presented as an obvious truth on which the argument is based; the second is a judgment advanced in support of the main conclusion of the argument.

701. Last year a record number of new manufacturing jobs were created. Will this year bring another record? Well, **any new manufacturing job is created either within an existing company or by the start-up of a new company**. Within existing firms, new jobs have been created this year at well below last year's record pace. At the same time, there is considerable evidence that the number of new companies starting up will be no higher this year than it was last year and there is no reason to think that the new companies starting up this year will create more jobs per company than did last year's start-ups. So clearly, **the number of new jobs created this year will fall short of last year's record**.

In the argument given, the two portions in **boldface** play which of the following roles?

(A) The first is presented as an obvious truth on which the argument is based; the second is the main conclusion of the argument.

(B) The first is presented as an obvious truth on which the argument is based; the second is a conclusion drawn in order to support the main conclusion of the argument.

(C) The first and the second each provide evidence in support of the main conclusion of the argument.

(D) The first is a generalization that the argument seeks to establish; the second is the main conclusion of the argument.

(E) The first is a generalization that the argument seeks to establish; the second is a conclusion that has been drawn in order to challenge that generalization.

702. In Stenland, many workers have been complaining that they cannot survive on minimum wage, the lowest wage an employer is permitted to pay. The government is proposing to raise the minimum wage. Many employers who pay their workers the current minimum wage argue that if it is raised, unemployment will increase because they will no longer be able to afford to employ as many workers.

Which of the following, if true in Stenland, most strongly supports the claim that raising the minimum wage there will not have the effects that the employers predict?

(A) For any position with wages below a living wage, the difficulty of finding and retaining employees adds as much to employment costs as would raising wages.

(B) Raising the minimum wage does not also increase the amount employers have to contribute in employee benefits.

(C) When inflation is taken into account, the proposed new minimum wage is not as high as the current one was when it was introduced.

(D) Many employees currently being paid wages at the level of the proposed new minimum wage will demand significant wage increases.

(E) Many employers who pay some workers only the minimum wage also pay other workers wages that are much higher than the minimum.

703. Biologists with a predilection for theory have tried—and largely failed—to define what it is that makes something a living thing. Organisms take in energy-providing materials and excrete waste products, but so do automobiles. Living things replicate and take part in evolution, but so do some computer programs. We must be open to the possibility that there are living things on other planets. Therefore, we will not be successful in defining what it is that makes something a living thing merely by examining living things on Earth—the only ones we know. Trying to do so is analogous to trying to specify _____.

Which of the following most logically completes the passage?

(A) the laws of physics by using pure mathematics
(B) what a fish is by listing its chemical components
(C) what an animal is by examining a plant
(D) what a machine is by examining a sketch of it
(E) what a mammal is by examining a zebra

704. For the period from the eighth century through the eleventh century, the shifting boundaries between Kingdom F and Kingdom G have not been well charted. Although a certain village in a border region between the two kingdoms usually belonged to Kingdom G, ninth-century artifacts found in the village were in the typical Kingdom F style of that time. It is unclear whether the village was actually a part of Kingdom F in the ninth century or whether it was a part of Kingdom G but had merely adopted Kingdom F's artistic styles under Kingdom F's cultural influence.

Which of the following would, if found in ninth-century sites in the village, best help in determining whether the village was a part of Kingdom F or Kingdom G in the ninth century?

(A) A trading contract written in the Kingdom G dialect

(B) A drawing of a dwelling complex known to have existed on the border of Kingdom F and Kingdom G in the ninth century

(C) Knives and other utensils made from metal typical of ninth-century mining sites in Kingdom F

(D) Some fragments of pottery made in the Kingdom G style from the seventh century out of materials only found in Kingdom F

(E) Numerous teeth from the ninth century with a chemical signature typical only of teeth from people who had grown up in the heart of Kingdom F

705. Sammy: For my arthritis, I am going to try my aunt's diet: large amounts of wheat germ and garlic. She was able to move more easily right after she started that diet.

Pat: When my brother began that diet, his arthritis got worse. But he has been doing much better since he stopped eating vegetables in the nightshade family, such as tomatoes and peppers.

Which of the following, if true, would provide a basis for explaining the fact that Sammy's aunt and Pat's brother had contrasting experiences with the same diet?

(A) A change in diet, regardless of the nature of the change, frequently brings temporary relief from arthritis symptoms.

(B) The compounds in garlic that can lessen the symptoms of arthritis are also present in tomatoes and peppers.

(C) Arthritis is a chronic condition whose symptoms improve and worsen from time to time without regard to diet.

(D) In general, men are more likely to have their arthritis symptoms alleviated by avoiding vegetables in the nightshade family than are women.

(E) People who are closely related are more likely to experience the same result from adopting a particular diet than are people who are unrelated.

706. Infotek, a computer manufacturer in Katrovia, has just introduced a new personal computer model that sells for significantly less than any other model. Market research shows, however, that very few Katrovian households without personal computers would buy a computer, regardless of its price. Therefore, introducing the new model is unlikely to increase the number of computers in Katrovian homes.

Which of the following is an assumption on which the argument depends?

(A) Infotek achieved the lower price of the new model by using components of lower quality than those used by other manufacturers.

(B) The main reason cited by consumers in Katrovia for replacing a personal computer is the desire to have an improved model.

(C) Katrovians in households that already have computers are unlikely to purchase the new Infotek model as an additional computer for home use.

(D) The price of other personal computers in Katrovia is unlikely to drop below the price of Infotek's new model in the near future.

(E) Most personal computers purchased in Katrovia are intended for home use.

707. Fast-food restaurants make up 45 percent of all restaurants in Canatria. Customers at these restaurants tend to be young; in fact, studies have shown that the older people get, the less likely they are to eat in fast-food restaurants. Since the average age of the Canatrian population is gradually rising and will continue to do so, the number of fast-food restaurants is likely to decrease.

Which of the following, if true, most seriously weakens the argument?

(A) Fast-food restaurants in Canatria are getting bigger, so each one can serve more customers.

(B) Some older people eat at fast-food restaurants more frequently than the average young person.

(C) Many people who rarely eat in fast-food restaurants nevertheless eat regularly in restaurants.

(D) The overall population of Canatria is growing steadily.

(E) As the population of Canatria gets older, more people are eating at home.

708. Last year a chain of fast-food restaurants, whose menu had always centered on hamburgers, added its first vegetarian sandwich, much lower in fat than the chain's other offerings. Despite heavy marketing, the new sandwich accounts for a very small proportion of the chain's sales. The sandwich's sales would have to quadruple to cover the costs associated with including it on the menu. Since such an increase is unlikely, the chain would be more profitable if it dropped the sandwich.

Which of the following, if true, most seriously weakens the argument?

(A) Although many of the chain's customers have never tried the vegetarian sandwich, in a market research survey most of those who had tried it reported that they were very satisfied with it.

(B) Many of the people who eat at the chain's restaurants also eat at the restaurants of competing chains and report no strong preference among the competitors.

(C) Among fast-food chains in general, there has been little or no growth in hamburger sales over the past several years as the range of competing offerings at other restaurants has grown.

(D) When even one member of a group of diners is a vegetarian or has a preference for low-fat food, the group tends to avoid restaurants that lack vegetarian or low-fat menu options.

(E) An attempt by the chain to introduce a lower-fat hamburger failed several years ago, since it attracted few new customers and most of the chain's regular customers greatly preferred the taste of the regular hamburgers.

709. Transportation expenses accounted for a large portion of the total dollar amount spent on trips for pleasure by residents of the United States in 1997, and about half of the total dollar amount spent on transportation was for airfare. However, the large majority of United States residents who took trips for pleasure in 1997 did not travel by airplane but used other means of transportation.

If the statements above are true, which of the following must also be true about United States residents who took trips for pleasure in 1997?

(A) Most of those who traveled by airplane did so because the airfare to their destination was lower than the cost of other available means of transportation.

(B) Most of those who traveled by airplane did so because other means of transportation to their destination were unavailable.

(C) Per mile traveled, those who traveled by airplane tended to spend more on transportation to their destination than did those who used other means of transportation.

(D) Overall, people who did not travel by airplane had lower average transportation expenses than people who did.

(E) Those who traveled by airplane spent about as much, on average, on other means of transportation as they did on airfare.

710. Voters commonly condemn politicians for being insincere, but politicians often must disguise their true feelings when they make public statements. If they expressed their honest views—about, say, their party's policies—then achieving politically necessary compromises would be much more difficult. Clearly, the very insincerity that people decry shows that our government is functioning well.

Which of the following, if true, most seriously undermines this reasoning?

(A) Achieving political compromises is not all that is necessary for the proper functioning of a government.

(B) Some political compromises are not in the best long-term interest of the government.

(C) Voters often judge politicians by criteria other than the sincerity with which they express their views.

(D) A political party's policies could turn out to be detrimental to the functioning of a government.

(E) Some of the public statements made by politicians about their party's policies could in fact be sincere.

711. To reduce waste of raw materials, the government of Sperland is considering requiring household appliances to be broken down for salvage when discarded. To cover the cost of salvage, the government is planning to charge a fee, which would be imposed when the appliance is first sold. Imposing the fee at the time of salvage would reduce waste more effectively, however, because consumers tend to keep old appliances longer if they are faced with a fee for discarding them.

Which of the following, if true, most seriously weakens the argument?

(A) Increasing the cost of disposing of an appliance properly increases the incentive to dispose of it improperly.

(B) The fee provides manufacturers with no incentive to produce appliances that are more durable.

(C) For people who have bought new appliances recently, the salvage fee would not need to be paid for a number of years.

(D) People who sell their used, working appliances to others would not need to pay the salvage fee.

(E) Many nonfunctioning appliances that are currently discarded could be repaired at relatively little expense.

712. When there is less rainfall than normal, the water level of Australian rivers falls and the rivers flow more slowly. Because algae whose habitat is river water grow best in slow-moving water, the amount of algae per unit of water generally increases when there has been little rain. By contrast, however, following a period of extreme drought, algae levels are low even in very slow-moving river water.

Which of the following, if true, does most to explain the contrast described above?

(A) During periods of extreme drought, the populations of some of the species that feed on algae tend to fall.

(B) The more slowly water moves, the more conducive its temperature is to the growth of algae.

(C) When algae populations reach very high levels, conditions within the river can become toxic for some of the other species that normally live there.

(D) Australian rivers dry up completely for short intervals in periods of extreme drought.

(E) Except during periods of extreme drought, algae levels tend to be higher in rivers in which the flow has been controlled by damming than in rivers that flow freely.

713. Increased use of incineration is sometimes advocated as a safe way to dispose of chemical waste. But opponents of incineration point to the 40 incidents involving unexpected releases of dangerous chemical agents that were reported just last year at two existing incinerators commissioned to destroy a quantity of chemical waste material. Since designs for proposed new incinerators include no additional means of preventing such releases, leaks will only become more prevalent if use of incineration increases.

Which of the following, if true, most seriously weakens the argument?

(A) At the two incinerators at which leaks were reported, staff had had only cursory training on the proper procedures for incinerating chemical waste.

(B) Other means of disposing of chemical waste, such as chemical neutralization processes, have not been proven safer than incineration.

(C) The capacity of existing incinerators is sufficient to allow for increased incineration of chemical waste without any need for new incinerators.

(D) The frequency of reports of unexpected releases of chemical agents at newly built incinerators is about the same as the frequency at older incinerators.

(E) In only three of the reported incidents of unexpected chemical leaks did the releases extend outside the property on which the incinerators were located.

714. Public health expert: **Increasing the urgency of a public health message may be counterproductive.** In addition to irritating the majority who already behave responsibly, **it may undermine all government pronouncements on health by convincing people that such messages are overly cautious.** And there is no reason to believe that those who ignore measured voices will listen to shouting.

The two sections in boldface play which of the following roles in the public health expert's argument?

(A) The first is a conclusion for which support is provided, but is not the argument's main conclusion; the second is an unsupported premise supporting the argument's main conclusion.

(B) The first is a premise supporting the only explicit conclusion; so is the second.

(C) The first is the argument's main conclusion; the second supports that conclusion and is itself a conclusion for which support is provided.

(D) The first is a premise supporting the argument's only conclusion; the second is that conclusion.

(E) The first is the argument's only explicit conclusion; the second is a premise supporting that conclusion.

715. Several industries have recently switched at least partly from older technologies powered by fossil fuels to new technologies powered by electricity. It is thus evident that less fossil fuel is being used as a result of the operations of these industries than would have been used if these industries had retained their older technologies.

Which of the following, if true, most strengthens the argument above?

(A) Many of the industries that have switched at least partly to the new technologies have increased their output.

(B) Less fossil fuel was used to manufacture the machinery employed in the new technologies than was originally used to manufacture the machinery employed in the older technologies.

(C) More electricity is used by those industries that have switched at least partly to the new technologies than by those industries that have not switched.

(D) Some of the industries that have switched at least partly to the new technologies still use primarily technologies that are powered by fossil fuels.

(E) The amount of fossil fuel used to generate the electricity needed to power the new technologies is less than the amount that would have been used to power the older technologies.

716. The difference in average annual income in favor of employees who have college degrees, compared with those who do not have such degrees, doubled between 1980 and 1990. Some analysts have hypothesized that increased competition between employers for employees with college degrees drove up income for such employees.

Which of the following, if true, most seriously undermines the explanation described above?

(A) During the 1980s a growing percentage of college graduates, unable to find jobs requiring a college degree, took unskilled jobs.

(B) The average age of all employees increased slightly during the 1980s.

(C) The unemployment rate changed very little throughout most of the 1980s.

(D) From 1980 to 1990 the difference in average income between employees with advanced degrees and those with bachelor's degrees also increased.

(E) During the 1980s there were some employees with no college degree who earned incomes comparable to the top incomes earned by employees with a college degree.

717. Which of the following most logically completes the passage?

According to the last pre-election poll in Whippleton, most voters believe that the three problems government needs to address, in order of importance, are pollution, crime, and unemployment. Yet in the election, candidates from parties perceived as strongly against pollution were defeated, while those elected were all from parties with a history of opposing legislation designed to reduce pollution. These results should not be taken to indicate that the poll was inaccurate, however, since _____.

(A) some voters in Whippleton do not believe that pollution needs to be reduced

(B) every candidate who was defeated had a strong antipollution record

(C) there were no issues other than crime, unemployment, and pollution on which the candidates had significant differences of opinion

(D) all the candidates who were elected were perceived as being stronger against both crime and unemployment than the candidates who were defeated

(E) many of the people who voted in the election refused to participate in the poll

718. Manufacturing plants in Arundia have recently been acquired in substantial numbers by investors from abroad. Arundian politicians are proposing legislative action to stop such investment, justifying the proposal by arguing that foreign investors, opportunistically exploiting a recent fall in the value of the Arundian currency, were able to buy Arundian assets at less than their true value.

Which of the following, if true, casts the most serious doubt on the adequacy of the Arundian politicians' justification for the proposed legislation?

(A) The Arundian government originally welcomed the fall in the value of the Arundian currency because the fall made Arundian exports more competitive on international markets.

(B) Foreign investors who acquired Arundian manufacturing plants generally did so with no intention of keeping and running those plants over the long term.

(C) Without the recent fall in the value of the Arundian currency, many of the Arundian assets bought by foreign investors would have been beyond the financial reach of those investors.

(D) In Concordia, a country broadly similar to Arundia, the share of manufacturing assets that is foreign-controlled is 60 percent higher than it is in Arundia.

(E) The true value of an investment is determined by the value of the profits from it, and the low value of the Arundian currency has depressed the value of any profits earned by foreign investors from Arundian assets.

719. Proposed new safety rules for Beach City airport would lengthen considerably the minimum time between takeoffs from the airport. In consequence, the airport would be able to accommodate 10 percent fewer flights than currently use the airport daily. The city's operating budget depends heavily on taxes generated by tourist spending, and most of the tourists come by plane. Therefore, the proposed new safety rules, if adopted, will reduce the revenue available for the operating budget.

The argument depends on assuming which of the following?

(A) There are no periods of the day during which the interval between flights taking off from the airport is significantly greater than the currently allowed minimum.

(B) Few, if any, of the tourists who use Beach City airport do so when their main destination is a neighboring community and not Beach City itself.

(C) If the proposed safety rules are adopted, the reduction in tourist numbers will not result mainly from a reduction in the number of tourists who spend relatively little in Beach City.

(D) Increasing the minimum time between takeoffs is the only way to achieve necessary safety improvements without a large expenditure by the city government on airport enhancements.

(E) The response to the adoption of the new safety rules would not include a large increase in the number of passengers per flight.

720. The introduction of new drugs into the market is frequently prevented by a shortage of human subjects for the clinical trials needed to show that the drugs are safe and effective. Since the lives and health of people in future generations may depend on treatments that are currently experimental, practicing physicians are morally in the wrong when, in the absence of any treatment proven to be effective, they fail to encourage suitable patients to volunteer for clinical trials.

Which of the following, if true, casts most doubt on the conclusion of the argument?

(A) Many drugs undergoing clinical trials are intended for the treatment of conditions for which there is currently no effective treatment.

(B) Patients do not share the physician's professional concern for public health, but everyone has a moral obligation to alleviate suffering when able to do so.

(C) Usually, half the patients in a clinical trial serve as a control group and receive a nonactive drug in place of the drug being tested.

(D) An experimental drug cannot legally be made available to patients unless those patients are subjects in clinical trials of the drug.

(E) Physicians have an overriding moral and legal duty to care for the health and safety of their current patients.

721. As a construction material, bamboo is as strong as steel and sturdier than concrete. Moreover, in tropical areas bamboo is a much less expensive construction material than either steel or concrete and is always readily available. In tropical areas, therefore, building with bamboo makes better economic sense than building with steel or concrete, except where land values are high.

Which of the following, if true, most helps to explain the exception noted above?

(A) Buildings constructed of bamboo are less likely to suffer earthquake damage than are steel and concrete buildings.

(B) Bamboo is unsuitable as a building material for multistory buildings.

(C) In order to protect it from being damaged by termites and beetles, bamboo must be soaked, at some expense, in a preservative.

(D) In some tropical areas, bamboo is used to make the scaffolding that is used during large construction projects.

(E) Bamboo growing in an area where land values are increasing is often cleared to make way for construction.

722. Newspaper editors should not allow reporters to write the headlines for their own stories. The reason for this is that, while the headlines that reporters themselves write are often clever, what typically makes them clever is that they allude to little-known information that is familiar to the reporter but that never appears explicitly in the story itself.

Which of the following, if true, most strengthens the argument?

(A) The reporter who writes a story is usually better placed than the reporter's editor is to judge what the story's most newsworthy features are.

(B) To write a headline that is clever, a person must have sufficient understanding of the story that the headline accompanies.

(C) Most reporters rarely bother to find out how other reporters have written stories and headlines about the same events that they themselves have covered.

(D) For virtually any story that a reporter writes, there are at least a few people who know more about the story's subject matter than does the reporter.

(E) The kind of headlines that newspaper editors want are those that anyone who has read a reporter's story in its entirety will recognize as clever.

CR03251

723. Scientists have modified feed corn genetically, increasing its resistance to insect pests. Farmers who tried out the genetically modified corn last season applied less insecticide to their corn fields and still got yields comparable to those they would have gotten with ordinary corn. Ordinary corn seed, however, costs less, and what these farmers saved on insecticide rarely exceeded their extra costs for seed. Therefore, for most feed-corn farmers, switching to genetically modified seed would be unlikely to increase profits.

Which of the following would it be most useful to know in order to evaluate the argument?

(A) Whether there are insect pests that sometimes reduce feed-corn yields, but against which commonly used insecticides and the genetic modification are equally ineffective

(B) Whether the price that farmers receive for feed corn has remained steady over the past few years

(C) Whether the insecticides typically used on feed corn tend to be more expensive than insecticides typically used on other crops

(D) Whether most of the farmers who tried the genetically modified corn last season applied more insecticide than was actually necessary

(E) Whether, for most farmers who plant feed corn, it is their most profitable crop

CR07318

724. Debater: The average amount of overtime per month worked by an employee in the manufacturing division of the Haglut Corporation is 14 hours. Most employees of the Haglut Corporation work in the manufacturing division. Furthermore, the average amount of overtime per month worked by any employee in the company generally does not fluctuate much from month to month. Therefore, each month, most employees of the Haglut Corporation almost certainly work at least some overtime.

The debater's argument is most vulnerable to criticism on which of these grounds?

(A) It takes for granted that the manufacturing division is a typical division of the corporation with regard to the average amount of overtime its employees work each month.

(B) It takes for granted that if a certain average amount of overtime is worked each month by each employee of the Haglut Corporation, then approximately the same amount of overtime must be worked each month by each employee of the manufacturing division.

(C) It confuses a claim from which the argument's conclusion about the Haglut Corporation would necessarily follow with a claim that would follow from the argument's conclusion only with a high degree of probability.

(D) It overlooks the possibility that even if, on average, a certain amount of overtime is worked by the members of some group, many members of that group may work no overtime at all.

(E) It overlooks the possibility that even if most employees of the corporation work some overtime each month, any one corporate employee may, in some months, work no overtime.

725. Proponents of the recently introduced tax on sales of new luxury boats had argued that a tax of this sort would be an equitable way to increase government revenue because the admittedly heavy tax burden would fall only on wealthy people and neither they nor anyone else would suffer any economic hardship. In fact, however, 20 percent of the workers employed by manufacturers of luxury boats have lost their jobs as a direct result of this tax.

The information given, if true, most strongly supports which of the following?

(A) The market for luxury boats would have collapsed even if the new tax on luxury boats had been lower.

(B) The new tax would produce a net gain in tax revenue for the government only if the yearly total revenue that it generates exceeds the total of any yearly tax-revenue decrease resulting from the workers' loss of jobs.

(C) Because many people never buy luxury items, imposing a sales tax on luxury items is the kind of legislative action that does not cost incumbent legislators much popular support.

(D) Before the tax was instituted, luxury boats were largely bought by people who were not wealthy.

(E) Taxes can be equitable only if their burden is evenly distributed over the entire population.

726. In Wareland last year, 16 percent of licensed drivers under 21 and 11 percent of drivers ages 21–24 were in serious accidents. By contrast, only 3 percent of licensed drivers 65 and older were involved in serious accidents. These figures clearly show that the greater experience and developed habits of caution possessed by drivers in the 65-and-older group make them far safer behind the wheel than the younger drivers are.

Which of the following is an assumption on which the argument depends?

(A) Drivers 65 and older do not, on average, drive very many fewer miles per year than drivers 24 and younger.

(B) Drivers 65 and older do not constitute a significantly larger percentage of licensed drivers in Wareland than drivers ages 18–24 do.

(C) Drivers 65 and older are less likely than are drivers 24 and younger to drive during weather conditions that greatly increase the risk of accidents.

(D) The difference between the accident rate of drivers under 21 and of those ages 21–24 is attributable to the greater driving experience of those in the older group.

(E) There is no age bracket for which the accident rate is lower than it is for licensed drivers 65 and older.

727. In the past the country of Malvernia has relied heavily on imported oil. Malvernia recently implemented a program to convert heating systems from oil to natural gas. Malvernia currently produces more natural gas each year than it uses, and oil production in Malvernian oil fields is increasing at a steady pace. If these trends in fuel production and usage continue, therefore, Malvernian reliance on foreign sources for fuel is likely to decline soon.

Which of the following would it be most useful to establish in evaluating the argument?

(A) When, if ever, will production of oil in Malvernia outstrip production of natural gas?

(B) Is Malvernia among the countries that rely most on imported oil?

(C) What proportion of Malvernia's total energy needs is met by hydroelectric, solar, and nuclear power?

(D) Is the amount of oil used each year in Malvernia for generating electricity and fuel for transportation increasing?

(E) Have any existing oil-burning heating systems in Malvernia already been converted to natural-gas-burning heating systems?

CR03618
728. Exposure to certain chemicals commonly used in elementary schools as cleaners or pesticides causes allergic reactions in some children. Elementary school nurses in Renston report that the proportion of schoolchildren sent to them for treatment of allergic reactions to those chemicals has increased significantly over the past ten years. Therefore, either Renston's schoolchildren have been exposed to greater quantities of the chemicals, or they are more sensitive to them than schoolchildren were ten years ago.

Which of the following is an assumption on which the argument depends?

(A) The number of school nurses employed by Renston's elementary schools has not decreased over the past ten years.

(B) Children who are allergic to the chemicals are no more likely than other children to have allergies to other substances.

(C) Children who have allergic reactions to the chemicals are not more likely to be sent to a school nurse now than they were ten years ago.

(D) The chemicals are not commonly used as cleaners or pesticides in houses and apartment buildings in Renston.

(E) Children attending elementary school do not make up a larger proportion of Renston's population now than they did ten years ago.

CR01854
729. Normally, the pineal gland governs a person's sleep-wake cycle by secreting melatonin in response to the daily cycle of light and darkness as detected by the eye. Nonetheless, many people who are totally blind due to lesions in the visual cortex of the brain easily maintain a 24-hour sleep-wake cycle. So the neural pathway by which the pineal gland receives information from the eye probably does not pass through the visual cortex.

For purposes of evaluating the argument it would be most useful to establish which of the following?

(A) Whether melatonin supplements help people who have difficulty maintaining a 24-hour sleep cycle to establish such a pattern

(B) Whether the melatonin levels of most totally blind people who successfully maintain a 24-hour sleep-wake cycle change in response to changes in exposure to light and darkness

(C) Whether melatonin is the only substance secreted by the pineal gland

(D) Whether most people who do not have a 24-hour sleep-wake cycle nevertheless have a cycle of consistent duration

(E) Whether there are any people with normal vision whose melatonin levels respond abnormally to periods of light and darkness

CR00942
730. **In countries where automobile insurance includes compensation for whiplash injuries sustained in automobile accidents, reports of having suffered such injuries are twice as frequent as they are in countries where whiplash is not covered.** Presently, no objective test for whiplash exists, so it is true that spurious reports of whiplash injuries cannot be readily identified. Nevertheless, these facts do not warrant the conclusion drawn by some commentators that in the countries with the higher rates of reported whiplash injuries, half of the reported cases are spurious. Clearly, **in countries where automobile insurance does not include compensation for whiplash, people often have little incentive to report whiplash injuries that they actually have suffered.**

In the argument given, the two boldfaced portions play which of the following roles?

(A) The first is a claim that the argument disputes; the second is a conclusion that has been based on that claim.

(B) The first is a claim that has been used to support a conclusion that the argument accepts; the second is that conclusion.

(C) The first is evidence that has been used to support a conclusion for which the argument provides further evidence; the second is the main conclusion of the argument.

(D) The first is a finding whose implications are at issue in the argument; the second is a claim presented in order to argue against deriving certain implications from that finding.

(E) The first is a finding whose accuracy is evaluated in the argument; the second is evidence presented to establish that the finding is accurate.

731. Last year Comfort Airlines had twice as many delayed flights as the year before, but the number of complaints from passengers about delayed flights went up three times. It is unlikely that this disproportionate increase in complaints was rooted in an increase in overall dissatisfaction with the service Comfort Airlines provides, since the airline made a special effort to improve other aspects of its service last year.

Which of the following, if true, most helps to explain the disproportionate increase in customer complaints?

(A) Comfort Airlines had more flights last year than the year before.
(B) Last year a single period of unusually bad weather caused a large number of flights to be delayed.
(C) Some of the improvements that Comfort Airlines made in its service were required by new government regulations.
(D) The average length of a flight delay was greater last year than it was the year before.
(E) The average number of passengers per flight was no higher last year than the year before.

732. Last year a global disturbance of weather patterns disrupted harvests in many of the world's important agricultural areas. Worldwide production of soybeans, an important source of protein for people and livestock alike, was not adversely affected, however. Indeed, last year's soybean crop was actually slightly larger than average. Nevertheless, the weather phenomenon is probably responsible for a recent increase in the world price of soybeans.

Which of the following, if true, provides the strongest justification for the attribution of the increase in soybean prices to the weather phenomenon?

(A) Last year's harvest of anchovies, which provide an important protein source for livestock, was disrupted by the effects of the weather phenomenon.
(B) Most countries that produce soybeans for export had above-average harvests of a number of food crops other than soybeans last year.
(C) The world price of soybeans also rose several years ago, immediately after an earlier occurrence of a similar global weather disturbance.
(D) Heavy rains attributable to the weather phenomenon improved grazing pastures last year, allowing farmers in many parts of the world to reduce their dependence on supplemental feed.
(E) Prior to last year, soybean prices had been falling for several years.

733. Most of the year, the hermit thrush, a North American songbird, eats a diet consisting mainly of insects, but in autumn, as the thrushes migrate to their Central and South American wintering grounds, they feed almost exclusively on wild berries. Wild berries, however, are not as rich in calories as insects, yet thrushes need to consume plenty of calories in order to complete their migration. One possible explanation is that berries contain other nutrients that thrushes need for migration and that insects lack.

Which of the following, if true, most seriously calls into question the explanation given for the thrush's diet during migration?

(A) Hermit thrushes, if undernourished, are unable to complete their autumn migration before the onset of winter.
(B) Insect species contain certain nutrients that are not found in wild berries.
(C) For songbirds, catching insects requires the expenditure of significantly more calories than eating wild berries does.
(D) Along the hermit thrushes' migration routes, insects are abundant throughout the migration season.
(E) There are some species of wild berries that hermit thrushes generally do not eat, even though these berry species are exceptionally rich in calories.

734. The kinds of hand and wrist injuries that result from extended use of a computer while maintaining an incorrect posture are common among schoolchildren in Harnville. Computers are important to the school curriculum there, so instead of reducing the amount their students use computers, teachers plan to bring about a sharp reduction in the number of these injuries by carefully monitoring their students' posture when using computers in the classroom.

Which of the following would it be most useful to know in order to assess the likelihood that the teachers' plan will be successful?

(A) Whether extended use of a computer while maintaining incorrect posture can cause injuries other than hand and wrist injuries

(B) Whether hand and wrist injuries not caused by computer use are common among schoolchildren in Harnville

(C) What proportion of schoolchildren in Harnville with hand and wrist injuries use computers extensively outside the classroom

(D) Whether changes in the curriculum could reduce the schools' dependence on computers

(E) What proportion of schoolchildren in Harnville already use correct posture while using a computer

CR04718
735. A certain cultivated herb is one of a group of closely related plants that thrive in soil with high concentrations of metals that are toxic to most other plants. Agronomists studying the growth of this herb have discovered that it produces large amounts of histidine, an amino acid that, in test-tube solutions, renders these metals chemically inert. Hence, the herb's high histidine production must be the key feature that allows it to grow in metal-rich soils.

In evaluating the argument, it would be most important to determine which of the following?

(A) Whether the herb can thrive in soil that does not have high concentrations of the toxic metals

(B) Whether others of the closely related group of plants also produce histidine in large quantities

(C) Whether the herb's high level of histidine production is associated with an unusually low level of production of some other amino acid

(D) Whether growing the herb in soil with high concentrations of the metals will, over time, reduce their concentrations in the soil

(E) Whether the concentration of histidine in the growing herb declines as the plant approaches maturity

CR01293
736. Many people suffer an allergic reaction to certain sulfites, including those that are commonly added to wine as preservatives. However, since there are several winemakers who add sulfites to none of the wines they produce, people who would like to drink wine but are allergic to sulfites can drink wines produced by these winemakers without risking an allergic reaction to sulfites.

Which of the following is an assumption on which the argument depends?

(A) These winemakers have been able to duplicate the preservative effect produced by adding sulfites by means that do not involve adding any potentially allergenic substances to their wine.

(B) Not all forms of sulfite are equally likely to produce the allergic reaction.

(C) Wine is the only beverage to which sulfites are commonly added.

(D) Apart from sulfites, there are no substances commonly present in wine that give rise to an allergic reaction.

(E) Sulfites are not naturally present in the wines produced by these winemakers in amounts large enough to produce an allergic reaction in someone who drinks these wines.

CR11447
737. A new law gives ownership of patents—documents providing exclusive right to make and sell an invention—to universities, not the government, when those patents result from government-sponsored university research. Administrators at Logos University plan to sell any patents they acquire to corporations in order to fund programs to improve undergraduate teaching.

Which of the following, if true, would cast the most doubt on the viability of the college administrators' plan described above?

(A) Profit-making corporations interested in developing products based on patents held by universities are likely to try to serve as exclusive sponsors of ongoing university research projects.

(B) Corporate sponsors of research in university facilities are entitled to tax credits under new federal tax-code guidelines.

(C) Research scientists at Logos University have few or no teaching responsibilities and participate little if at all in the undergraduate programs in their field.

(D) Government-sponsored research conducted at Logos University for the most part duplicates research already completed by several profitmaking corporations.

(E) Logos University is unlikely to attract corporate sponsorship of its scientific research.

738. Since it has become known that **several of a bank's top executives have been buying shares in their own bank,** the bank's depositors, who had been worried by rumors that the bank faced impending financial collapse, have been greatly relieved. They reason that, since top executives evidently have faith in the bank's financial soundness, those worrisome rumors must be false. Such reasoning might well be overoptimistic, however, since **corporate executives have been known to buy shares in their own company in a calculated attempt to dispel negative rumors about the company's health.**

In the argument given, the two boldfaced portions play which of the following roles?

(A) The first describes evidence that has been taken as supporting a conclusion; the second gives a reason for questioning that support.

(B) The first describes evidence that has been taken as supporting a conclusion; the second states a contrary conclusion that is the main conclusion of the argument.

(C) The first provides evidence in support of the main conclusion of the argument; the second states that conclusion.

(D) The first describes the circumstance that the argument as a whole seeks to explain; the second gives the explanation that the argument seeks to establish.

(E) The first describes the circumstance that the argument as a whole seeks to explain; the second provides evidence in support of the explanation that the argument seeks to establish.

739. Between 1980 and 2000 the sea otter population of the Aleutian Islands declined precipitously. There were no signs of disease or malnutrition, so there was probably an increase in the number of otters being eaten by predators. Orcas will eat otters when seals, their normal prey, are unavailable, and the Aleutian Islands seal population declined dramatically in the 1980s. Therefore, orcas were most likely the immediate cause of the otter population decline.

Which of the following, if true, most strengthens the argument?

(A) The population of sea urchins, the main food of sea otters, has increased since the sea otter population declined.

(B) Seals do not eat sea otters, nor do they compete with sea otters for food.

(C) Most of the surviving sea otters live in a bay that is inaccessible to orcas.

(D) The population of orcas in the Aleutian Islands has declined since the 1980s.

(E) An increase in commercial fishing near the Aleutian Islands in the 1980s caused a slight decline in the population of the fish that seals use for food.

740. Studies in restaurants show that the tips left by customers who pay their bill in cash tend to be larger when the bill is presented on a tray that bears a credit-card logo. Consumer psychologists hypothesize that simply seeing a credit-card logo makes many credit-card holders willing to spend more because it reminds them that their spending power exceeds the cash they have immediately available.

Which of the following, if true, most strongly supports the psychologists' interpretation of the studies?

(A) The effect noted in the studies is not limited to patrons who have credit cards.

(B) Patrons who are under financial pressure from their credit-card obligations tend to tip less when presented with a restaurant bill on a tray with a credit-card logo than when the tray has no logo.

(C) In virtually all of the cases in the studies, the patrons who paid bills in cash did not possess credit cards.

(D) In general, restaurant patrons who pay their bills in cash leave larger tips than do those who pay by credit card.

(E) The percentage of restaurant bills paid with a given brand of credit card increases when that credit card's logo is displayed on the tray with which the bill is presented.

741. In an experiment, each volunteer was allowed to choose between an easy task and a hard task and was told that another volunteer would do the other task. Each volunteer could also choose to have a computer assign the two tasks randomly. Most volunteers chose the easy task for themselves and under questioning later said they had acted fairly. But when the scenario was described to another group of volunteers, almost all said choosing the easy task would be unfair. This shows that most people apply weaker moral standards to themselves than to others.

Which of the following is an assumption required by this argument?

(A) At least some volunteers who said they had acted fairly in choosing the easy task would have said that it was unfair for someone else to do so.

(B) The most moral choice for the volunteers would have been to have the computer assign the two tasks randomly.

(C) There were at least some volunteers who were assigned to do the hard task and felt that the assignment was unfair.

(D) On average, the volunteers to whom the scenario was described were more accurate in their moral judgments than the other volunteers were.

(E) At least some volunteers given the choice between assigning the tasks themselves and having the computer assign them felt that they had made the only fair choice available to them.

742. Country X's recent stock-trading scandal should not diminish investors' confidence in the country's stock market. For one thing, **the discovery of the scandal confirms that Country X has a strong regulatory system**, as the following considerations show. In any stock market, some fraudulent activity is inevitable. If a stock market is well regulated, any significant stock-trading fraud in it will very likely be discovered. This deters potential perpetrators and facilitates improvement in regulatory processes.

In the argument, the portion in boldface plays which of the following roles?

(A) It is the argument's only conclusion.

(B) It is a conclusion for which the argument provides support and which itself is used to support the argument's main conclusion.

(C) It is the argument's main conclusion and is supported by another explicitly stated conclusion for which further support is provided.

(D) It is an assumption for which no explicit support is provided and is used to support the argument's only conclusion.

(E) It is a compound statement containing both the argument's main conclusion and an assumption used to support that conclusion.

743. **Delta Products Inc. has recently switched at least partly from older technologies using fossil fuels to new technologies powered by electricity.** The question has been raised whether it can be concluded that **for a given level of output Delta's operation now causes less fossil fuel to be consumed than it did formerly.** The answer, clearly, is yes, since the amount of fossil fuel used to generate the electricity needed to power the new technologies is less than the amount needed to power the older technologies, provided level of output is held constant.

In the argument given, the two boldfaced portions play which of the following roles?

(A) The first identifies the content of the conclusion of the argument; the second provides support for that conclusion.

(B) The first provides support for the conclusion of the argument; the second identifies the content of that conclusion.

(C) The first states the conclusion of the argument; the second calls that conclusion into question.

(D) The first provides support for the conclusion of the argument; the second calls that conclusion into question.

(E) Each provides support for the conclusion of the argument.

744. Theater Critic: The play *La Finestrina*, now at Central Theater, was written in Italy in the eighteenth century. The director claims that this production is as similar to the original production as is possible in a modern theater. Although the actor who plays Harlequin the clown gives a performance very reminiscent of the twentieth-century American comedian Groucho Marx, Marx's comic style was very much within the comic acting tradition that had begun in sixteenth-century Italy.

The considerations given best serve as part of an argument that

(A) modern audiences would find it hard to tolerate certain characteristics of a historically accurate performance of an eighteenth-century play

(B) Groucho Marx once performed the part of the character Harlequin in *La Finestrina*

(C) in the United States the training of actors in the twentieth century is based on principles that do not differ radically from those that underlay the training of actors in eighteenth-century Italy

(D) the performance of the actor who plays Harlequin in *La Finestrina* does not serve as evidence against the director's claim

(E) the director of *La Finestrina* must have advised the actor who plays Harlequin to model his performance on comic performances of Groucho Marx

745. Although the discount stores in Goreville's central shopping district are expected to close within five years as a result of competition from a SpendLess discount department store that just opened, those locations will not stay vacant for long. In the five years since the opening of Colson's, a nondiscount department store, a new store has opened at the location of every store in the shopping district that closed because it could not compete with Colson's.

Which of the following, if true, most seriously weakens the argument?

(A) Many customers of Colson's are expected to do less shopping there than they did before the SpendLess store opened.

(B) Increasingly, the stores that have opened in the central shopping district since Colson's opened have been discount stores.

(C) At present, the central shopping district has as many stores operating in it as it ever had.

(D) Over the course of the next five years, it is expected that Goreville's population will grow at a faster rate than it has for the past several decades.

(E) Many stores in the central shopping district sell types of merchandise that are not available at either SpendLess or Colson's.

746. Last year all refuse collected by Shelbyville city services was incinerated. This incineration generated a large quantity of residual ash. In order to reduce the amount of residual ash Shelbyville generates this year to half of last year's total, the city has revamped its collection program. This year city services will separate for recycling enough refuse to reduce the number of truckloads of refuse to be incinerated to half of last year's number.

Which of the following is required for the revamped collection program to achieve its aim?

(A) This year, no materials that city services could separate for recycling will be incinerated.

(B) Separating recyclable materials from materials to be incinerated will cost Shelbyville less than half what it cost last year to dispose of the residual ash.

(C) Refuse collected by city services will contain a larger proportion of recyclable materials this year than it did last year.

(D) The refuse incinerated this year will generate no more residual ash per truckload incinerated than did the refuse incinerated last year.

(E) The total quantity of refuse collected by Shelbyville city services this year will be no greater than that collected last year.

747. Veterinarians generally derive some of their income from selling several manufacturers' lines of pet-care products. Knowing that pet owners rarely throw away mail from their pet's veterinarian unread, one manufacturer of pet-care products offered free promotional materials on its products to veterinarians for mailing to their clients. Very few veterinarians accepted the offer, however, even though the manufacturer's products are of high quality.

Which of the following, if true, most helps to explain the veterinarians' reaction to the manufacturer's promotional scheme?

(A) Most of the veterinarians to whom the free promotional materials were offered were already selling the manufacturer's pet-care products to their clients.

(B) The special promotional materials were intended as a supplement to the manufacturer's usual promotional activities rather than as a replacement for them.

(C) The manufacturer's products, unlike most equally good competing products sold by veterinarians, are also available in pet stores and in supermarkets.

(D) Many pet owners have begun demanding quality in products they buy for their pets that is as high as that in products they buy for themselves.

(E) Veterinarians sometimes recommend that pet owners use products formulated for people when no suitable product specially formulated for animals is available.

CR00778

748. The average hourly wage of television assemblers in Vernland has long been significantly lower than that in neighboring Borodia. Since Borodia dropped all tariffs on Vernlandian televisions three years ago, the number of televisions sold annually in Borodia has not changed. However, recent statistics show a drop in the number of television assemblers in Borodia. Therefore, updated trade statistics will probably indicate that the number of televisions Borodia imports annually from Vernland has increased.

Which of the following is an assumption on which the argument depends?

(A) The number of television assemblers in Vernland has increased by at least as much as the number of television assemblers in Borodia has decreased.

(B) Televisions assembled in Vernland have features that televisions assembled in Borodia do not have.

(C) The average number of hours it takes a Borodian television assembler to assemble a television has not decreased significantly during the past three years.

(D) The number of televisions assembled annually in Vernland has increased significantly during the past three years.

(E) The difference between the hourly wage of television assemblers in Vernland and the hourly wage of television assemblers in Borodia is likely to decrease in the next few years.

CR05725

749. Guidebook writer: I have visited hotels throughout the country and have noticed that in those built before 1930 the quality of the original carpentry work is generally superior to that in hotels built afterward. Clearly carpenters working on hotels before 1930 typically worked with more skill, care, and effort than carpenters who have worked on hotels built subsequently.

Which of the following, if true, most seriously weakens the guidebook writer's argument?

(A) The quality of original carpentry in hotels is generally far superior to the quality of original carpentry in other structures, such as houses and stores.

(B) Hotels built since 1930 can generally accommodate more guests than those built before 1930.

(C) The materials available to carpenters working before 1930 were not significantly different in quality from the materials available to carpenters working after 1930.

(D) The better the quality of original carpentry in a building, the less likely that building is to fall into disuse and be demolished.

(E) The average length of apprenticeship for carpenters has declined significantly since 1930.

750. Scientists typically do their most creative work before the age of forty. It is commonly thought that this happens because aging by itself brings about a loss of creative capacity. However, studies show that **of scientists who produce highly creative work beyond the age of forty, a disproportionately large number entered their field at an older age than is usual**. Since by the age of forty the large majority of scientists have been working in their field for at least fifteen years, the studies' finding strongly suggests that the real reason why scientists over forty rarely produce highly creative work is not that they have aged but rather that **scientists over forty have generally spent too long in their field**.

In the argument given, the two portions in boldface play which of the following roles?

(A) The first is a claim, the accuracy of which is at issue in the argument; the second is a conclusion drawn on the basis of that claim.

(B) The first is an objection that has been raised against a position defended in the argument; the second is that position.

(C) The first is evidence that has been used to support an explanation that the argument challenges; the second is that explanation.

(D) The first is evidence that has been used to support an explanation that the argument challenges; the second is a competing explanation that the argument favors.

(E) The first provides evidence to support an explanation that the argument favors; the second is that explanation.

751. NorthAir charges low fares for its economy-class seats, but it provides very cramped seating and few amenities. Market research shows that economy passengers would willingly pay more for wider seating and better service, and additional revenue provided by these higher ticket prices would more than cover the additional cost of providing these amenities. Even though NorthAir is searching for ways to improve its profitability, it has decided not to make these improvements.

Which of the following, if true, would most help to explain NorthAir's decision in light of its objectives?

(A) None of NorthAir's competitors offers significantly better seating and service to economy-class passengers than NorthAir does.

(B) On many of the routes that NorthAir flies, it is the only airline to offer direct flights.

(C) A few of NorthAir's economy-class passengers are satisfied with the service they receive, given the low price they pay.

(D) Very few people avoid flying on NorthAir because of the cramped seating and poor service offered in economy class.

(E) The number of people who would be willing to pay the high fares NorthAir charges for its business-class seats would decrease if its economy-class seating were more acceptable.

752. Which of the following most logically completes the argument given?

Asthma, a chronic breathing disorder, is significantly more common today among adult competitive swimmers than it is among competitive athletes who specialize in other sports. Although chlorine is now known to be a lung irritant and swimming pool water is generally chlorinated, it would be rash to assume that frequent exposure to chlorine is the explanation of the high incidence of asthma among these swimmers, since _____.

(A) young people who have asthma are no more likely to become competitive athletes than are young people who do not have asthma

(B) competitive athletes who specialize in sports other than swimming are rarely exposed to chlorine

(C) competitive athletes as a group have a significantly lower incidence of asthma than do people who do not participate in competitive athletics

(D) until a few years ago, physicians routinely recommended competitive swimming to children with asthma, in the belief that this form of exercise could alleviate asthma symptoms

(E) many people have asthma without knowing they have it and thus are not diagnosed with the condition until they begin engaging in very strenuous activities, such as competitive athletics

753. In the country of Marut, the Foreign Trade Agency's records were reviewed in 1994 in light of information then newly available about neighboring Goro. The review revealed that in every year since 1963, the agency's projection of what Goro's gross national product (GNP) would be five years later was a serious underestimate. The review also revealed that in every year since 1963, the agency estimated Goro's GNP for the previous year—a Goro state secret—very accurately.

Of the following claims, which is most strongly supported by the statements given?

(A) Goro's GNP fluctuated greatly between 1963 and 1994.

(B) Prior to 1995, Goro had not released data intended to mislead the agency in making its five-year projections.

(C) The amount by which the agency underestimated the GNP it projected for Goro tended to increase over time.

(D) Even before the new information came to light, the agency had reason to think that at least some of the five-year projections it had made were inaccurate.

(E) The agency's five-year projections of Goro's GNP had no impact on economic planning in Marut.

754. Vargonia has just introduced a legal requirement that student-teacher ratios in government-funded schools not exceed a certain limit. All Vargonian children are entitled to education, free of charge, in these schools. When a recession occurs and average incomes fall, the number of children enrolled in government-funded schools tends to increase. Therefore, though most employment opportunities contract in economic recessions, getting a teaching job in Vargonia's government-funded schools will not be made more difficult by a recession.

Which of the following would be most important to determine in order to evaluate the argument?

(A) Whether in Vargonia there are any schools not funded by the government that offer children an education free of charge

(B) Whether the number of qualified applicants for teaching positions in government-funded schools increases significantly during economic recessions

(C) What the current student-teacher ratio in Vargonia's government-funded schools is

(D) What proportion of Vargonia's workers currently hold jobs as teachers in government-funded schools

(E) Whether in the past a number of government-funded schools in Vargonia have had student-teacher ratios well in excess of the new limit

755. In Colorado subalpine meadows, nonnative dandelions co-occur with a native flower, the larkspur. Bumblebees visit both species, creating the potential for interactions between the two species with respect to pollination. In a recent study, researchers selected 16 plots containing both species; all dandelions were removed from eight plots; the remaining eight control plots were left undisturbed. The control plots yielded significantly more larkspur seeds than the dandelion-free plots, leading the researchers to conclude that the presence of dandelions facilitates pollination (and hence seed production) in the native species by attracting more pollinators to the mixed plots.

Which of the following, if true, most seriously undermines the researchers' reasoning?

(A) Bumblebees preferentially visit dandelions over larkspurs in mixed plots.

(B) In mixed plots, pollinators can transfer pollen from one species to another to augment seed production.

(C) If left unchecked, nonnative species like dandelions quickly crowd out native species.

(D) Seed germination is a more reliable measure of a species' fitness than seed production.

(E) Soil disturbances can result in fewer blooms, and hence lower seed production.

756. An experiment was done in which human subjects recognize a pattern within a matrix of abstract designs and then select another design that completes that pattern. The results of the experiment were surprising. The lowest expenditure of energy in neurons in the brain was found in those subjects who performed most successfully in the experiments.

Which of the following hypotheses best accounts for the findings of the experiment?

(A) The neurons of the brain react less when a subject is trying to recognize patterns than when the subject is doing other kinds of reasoning.

(B) Those who performed best in the experiment experienced more satisfaction when working with abstract patterns than did those who performed less well.

(C) People who are better at abstract pattern recognition have more energy-efficient neural connections.

(D) The energy expenditure of the subjects' brains increases when a design that completes the initially recognized pattern is determined.

(E) The task of completing a given design is more capably performed by athletes, whose energy expenditure is lower when they are at rest.

757. With seventeen casinos, Moneyland operates the most casinos in a certain state. Although intent on expanding, it was outmaneuvered by Apex Casinos in negotiations to acquire the Eldorado chain. To complete its acquisition of Eldorado, Apex must sell five casinos to comply with a state law forbidding any owner to operate more than one casino per county. Since Apex will still be left operating twenty casinos in the state, it will then have the most casinos in the state.

Which of the following, if true, most seriously undermines the prediction?

(A) Apex, Eldorado, and Moneyland are the only organizations licensed to operate casinos in the state.

(B) The majority of Eldorado's casinos in the state will need extensive renovations if they are to continue to operate profitably.

(C) Some of the state's counties do not permit casinos.

(D) Moneyland already operates casinos in the majority of the state's counties.

(E) Apex will use funds it obtains from the sale of the five casinos to help fund its acquisition of the Eldorado chain.

758. It is widely assumed that people need to engage in intellectual activities such as solving crossword puzzles or mathematics problems in order to maintain mental sharpness as they age. In fact, however, simply talking to other people—that is, participating in social interaction, which engages many mental and perceptual skills—suffices. Evidence to this effect comes from a study showing that the more social contact people report, the better their mental skills.

Which of the following, if true, most seriously weakens the force of the evidence cited?

(A) As people grow older, they are often advised to keep exercising their physical and mental capacities in order to maintain or improve them.

(B) Many medical conditions and treatments that adversely affect a person's mental sharpness also tend to increase that person's social isolation.

(C) Many people are proficient both in social interactions and in solving mathematical problems.

(D) The study did not itself collect data but analyzed data bearing on the issue from prior studies.

(E) The tasks evaluating mental sharpness for which data were compiled by the study were more akin to mathematics problems than to conversation.

8.6 Answer Key

610. B	648. B	686. C	724. D
611. B	649. A	687. A	725. B
612. B	650. E	688. C	726. A
613. B	651. B	689. B	727. D
614. D	652. E	690. C	728. C
615. D	653. D	691. D	729. B
616. D	654. E	692. C	730. D
617. E	655. B	693. C	731. D
618. C	656. E	694. A	732. A
619. C	657. D	695. E	733. C
620. D	658. B	696. C	734. C
621. A	659. A	697. E	735. B
622. D	660. A	698. C	736. E
623. B	661. E	699. D	737. D
624. C	662. B	700. E	738. A
625. E	663. B	701. A	739. C
626. B	664. B	702. A	740. B
627. B	665. D	703. E	741. A
628. A	666. D	704. E	742. B
629. A	667. E	705. C	743. B
630. B	668. C	706. C	744. D
631. E	669. D	707. D	745. B
632. C	670. B	708. D	746. D
633. E	671. C	709. D	747. C
634. C	672. D	710. A	748. C
635. C	673. C	711. A	749. D
636. A	674. C	712. D	750. E
637. E	675. E	713. A	751. E
638. A	676. C	714. E	752. D
639. D	677. D	715. E	753. D
640. D	678. A	716. A	754. B
641. D	679. D	717. D	755. E
642. C	680. D	718. E	756. C
643. B	681. A	719. E	757. A
644. D	682. C	720. E	758. B
645. D	683. E	721. B	
646. C	684. C	722. E	
647. E	685. B	723. D	

8.7 Answer Explanations

The following discussion is intended to familiarize you with the most efficient and effective approaches to critical reasoning questions. The particular questions in this chapter are generally representative of the kinds of critical reasoning questions you will encounter on the GMAT exam. Remember that it is the problem solving strategy that is important, not the specific details of a particular question.

*CR70041.01
610. Arts advocate: Few universities require that students who are specializing in science and technology take many art courses. However, real progress in science and technology requires an element of creativity, which the arts foster. Thus, to help science and technology students succeed in their careers, universities should increase the number of art courses required for them.

Which of the following would, if true, most strengthen the argument above?

(A) Universities required more art courses for science and technology students in the past.
(B) Participation in art courses increases students' creative thinking in their science and technology courses.
(C) More students who are interested in art would specialize in science and technology if the number of art courses required for those programs were increased.
(D) Some of the most prominent scientists began their careers as artists.
(E) Discussion of science and technology topics in art courses increases creative thinking among students in those courses.

Argument Evaluation

Situation The arts advocate argues that universities should increase the number of art courses required for students specializing in science and technology, with the goal of helping these students succeed in their careers. Few universities require students in these fields to take many art courses.

Reasoning *What piece of information, if true and added to the argument, would most strengthen it?* One of the arts advocate's premises is that progress in science and technology requires creativity. Another premise is that courses in the arts foster creativity. The conclusion is that universities should, for the sake of promoting career success, require students specializing in science and technology to take more courses in art. Suppose that participation in art courses enriches students' participation in the science and technology courses: that would be a further reason for universities to require that the students take more art courses.

A This does not indicate that increasing art offerings now for science and technology students is the most prudent course of action. Universities' past decision to offer fewer art courses for science and technology students may have resulted from review of data, careful analysis, and prudent policy assumptions. For example, the decision may have been required in order to finance provision of more science and technology courses.

B **Correct.** This suggests that participation in art courses increases the value of science and technology courses, an additional piece of information that strengthens the argument.

C The argument does not suggest that the goal of requiring science and technology students to take more art courses is to persuade more students interested in art to specialize in science and technology. This information is therefore largely irrelevant to the arts advocate's Reasoning.

D This information does not address the role art may have played in the scientists' achievements in science and technology. Several of these scientists may well have been aspiring artists who failed or became disenchanted and discovered that they could better exploit their talents in science and technology.

E The arts advocate does not advocate that science and technology topics be addressed in art courses. The arts advocate's Reasoning focuses on the value of art courses in fostering creativity.

The correct answer is B.

---
*These numbers correlate with the online test bank question number. See the GMAT Official Guide Online Index in the back of this book.

8.7 Critical Reasoning Answer Explanations

CR48541.01
611. A successful coffee stand that serves the workers in a large office building plans to increase its profits by adding oatmeal—a hot cereal popular among the workers—to its menu. The manager says that oatmeal is "the ultimate convenience food" because it can be served by the cup, as coffee is; further, offering oatmeal will enable the stand to get into the breakfast business without making a large investment, because it does not require elaborate cooking equipment.

Which of the following would, if true, most strengthen the likelihood that the manager's plan will achieve its goal?

(A) Some of the office building's businesses have recently begun providing free coffee to their employees.
(B) The ingredients needed to make oatmeal are inexpensive and do not spoil easily the way many fresh breakfast foods typically sold at coffee stands do.
(C) In order to offer more flexible schedules to their workers, several businesses in the office building will soon be expanding their hours.
(D) Supermarket sales of oatmeal and other cereals slowed this year following large gains last year.
(E) Oatmeal manufacturers have recently reduced their oatmeal offerings, which had included oatmeal in microwaveable cups and convenient cereal bars made with rolled oats.

Evaluation of a Plan

Situation   Hoping to increase profits, a successful coffee stand plans to add hot cereal, specifically oatmeal, to its menu. Oatmeal can be added without making a large investment, and it is convenient because it can be served by the cup.

Reasoning   *What statement would most support the claim that the coffee stand's plan will achieve its goal?* We are told that the initial investment involved in offering oatmeal would not be large, but it would be helpful to know whether the regular costs of offering oatmeal are low. If the ingredients are not expensive, and they are unlikely to spoil before they can be sold to a customer, then there is a greater chance that the coffee stand can sell oatmeal profitably.

A   If the businesses at the office building have started providing free coffee to their workers, and those workers are the coffee stand's primary customers, it is quite possible that the coffee stand's profits will decline even if its offering of hot cereal proves popular. Any profits made from the sale of hot cereal may be outweighed by decreases in profits from coffee sales.

B   **Correct.** Although the information given provides some reason to think that the cost of offering hot cereal will not be prohibitive to profitability, the fact that the ingredients needed to make oatmeal are inexpensive and do not spoil easily lends even more support to the belief that offering hot cereal could increase profits.

C   Because we are not told what the current work hours are for the workers in the building, it is unclear whether giving workers more flexible schedules would increase or decrease the number of workers in the building at breakfast time.

D   A decline in the sales of oatmeal and other cereals at supermarkets might indicate an overall decrease in demand for such cereals, which would suggest that the coffee stand's plan may not be useful in achieving the goal of increased profitability.

E   Oatmeal manufacturers may have reduced their oatmeal offerings because of a decline in demand for oatmeal, which would suggest that the coffee stand's plan may not be useful in achieving the goal of increased profitability.

The correct answer is B.

CR53631.01
612. Ramirez: The film industry claims that pirated DVDs, which are usually cheaper than legitimate DVDs and become available well before a film's official DVD release date, adversely affect its bottom line. But the industry should note what the spread of piracy indicates: consumers want lower prices and faster DVD releases. Lowering prices of DVDs and releasing them sooner would mitigate piracy's negative effect on film industry profits.

The argument above relies on which of the following assumptions?

(A) Releasing legitimate DVDs earlier would not cause any reduction in the revenue the film industry receives from the films' theatrical release.

(B) Some people who would otherwise purchase pirated DVDs would be willing to purchase legitimate DVDs if they were less expensive and released earlier than they are now.

(C) The film industry will in the future be able to produce DVDs more cheaply than is currently the case.

(D) Some current sellers of pirated DVDs would likely discontinue their businesses if legitimate DVDs were released faster and priced lower.

(E) Current purchasers of pirated DVDs are aware that those DVDs are not authorized by the film industry.

Argument Construction

Situation Pirated DVDs of films are released earlier than the film's official DVD release day. They are also sold more cheaply. These practices cut into the revenue expected from a film's official DVD sales. According to Ramirez, the prevalence of piracy indicates that consumers want lower prices and earlier release. He concludes that if the official DVDs were sold more cheaply and released earlier, the impact of piracy on film industry profits might be reduced.

Reasoning *What must Ramirez assume for his argument to be logically correct?* Suppose none of the current purchasers of pirated film DVDs were to purchase the official DVDs even if these were released earlier and at a significantly lower price. If that were to occur, then the measures Ramirez suggests would not mitigate piracy.

A This does not have to be assumed for Ramirez's reasoning to be logically good. Earlier release of the official DVDs at a lower price could somewhat reduce revenue from movie theater showings of the films. But if the revenue from official DVDs released earlier and priced lower were greatly boosted through greatly increased official DVD sales, overall revenue for each film could be higher than would be the case with widespread piracy.

B **Correct.** If all existing purchasers of pirated film DVDs continued to purchase such DVDs even after implementation of the changes Ramirez advocates, then the changes would not mitigate the destructive consequences of piracy. Thus, Ramirez's reasoning must assume that the changes he recommends would cause at least some former purchasers of pirated DVDs to begin purchasing the official DVDs.

C This might improve profits provided revenue did not also decline. Ramirez's argument does not depend on the assumption that the cost of producing DVDs will decline. His reasoning assumes that total sales volume for official DVDs would increase if piracy were reduced.

D Ideally this would occur with the change Ramirez recommends, but it does not have to be assumed for his reasoning to be logically good. For example, the result Ramirez predicts could occur if all existing sellers of pirated DVDs continued to sell them but sold fewer.

E This is likely true but is not an assumption that Ramirez needs to make for his reasoning to be logically good. Even if some DVDs sold by DVD sellers were pirated without the sellers being aware of it, e.g., if they purchased them from a fraudulent wholesaler, the fact that the pirated DVDs are sold more cheaply and before the release of the official DVD would reduce the filmmakers' total revenue.

The correct answer is B.

8.7 Critical Reasoning Answer Explanations

CR79041.01

613. Harunia Province has a relatively dry climate and is attracting a fast-growing population that has put increasing demands on its water supply. The two companies that supply water to the region have struggled to keep up with demand and still remain profitable. Yet now they are asking Harunian authorities to write residential water-use regulations that could reduce their revenues and restrict their future flexibility in supplying water profitably.

Which of the following would, if true, most logically help explain why the water-supply companies are asking the authorities to regulate residential water use?

(A) The companies are planning large water-transportation and irrigation systems that require the approval of neighboring provinces.
(B) The companies believe regulation is inevitable and that having it in place now will allow better planning and thus future profitability.
(C) Few, if any, Harunian government officials have investments in the companies or serve on their boards of directors.
(D) The companies believe that the population is not likely to continue to grow.
(E) Long-term climate projections suggest that greater rainfall will eventually increase the amount of water available.

Argument Construction

Situation   Two water-supply companies are asking the authorities in Harunia Province to regulate residential water use, even though regulation could reduce their revenues and restrict their flexibility in supplying water profitably in the future.

Reasoning   *Which piece of information would most help explain why the companies are advocating water-use regulations that would restrict their operations?* The companies are already struggling to keep up with demand from a fast-growing population in the region. So why would they advocate regulations that could, at least in the immediate term, reduce their profits and restrict them? Is there any advantage that the companies perceive—an advantage that would outweigh any disadvantages—in getting regulations instituted soon?

A   It is unclear how this information bears on the companies' request for regulations in Harunia Province, since neighboring provinces seem primarily involved.

B   **Correct.** The companies presumably must strategically plan their capital investments to cope with increasing water demand in Harunia Province and to receive adequate return on that investment. In that context it seems critically important for the companies to have certainty at the planning stage about future regulatory requirements. Moreover, given possible shortfalls in water supply, the companies would reasonably expect government regulation even if they did not request it.

C   This suggests that, in framing water regulations, Harunian government officials will not be influenced by financial interests, so the companies cannot expect to obtain special favors from the regulatory authorities in the framing of water regulations.

D   If anything, this suggests that the companies could continue to operate without any regulatory regime that might restrict their operations.

E   This would presumably result in a weakening of the case for residential water-use regulation and would also make it easier for the water-supply companies to meet demand.

The correct answer is B.

CR31551.01
614. Loss of the Gocha mangrove forests has caused coastal erosion, reducing fish populations and requiring the Gocha Fishing Cooperative (GFC) to partially fund dredging and new shore facilities. However, as part of its subsidiary businesses, the GFC has now invested in a program to replant significant parts of the coast with mangrove trees. Given income from a controlled harvest of wood with continuing replanting, the mangrove regeneration effort makes it more likely that the cooperative will increase its net income.

Which of the following, if true, would most strengthen the argument that mangrove replanting will increase the Gocha cooperative's net income?

(A) The cost of dredging and shore facilities was shared with the local government.
(B) The GFC will be able to hire local workers to assist with the mangrove replanting.
(C) The GFC derives 10 percent of its revenue from salt-production facilities in an area previously cleared of mangroves.
(D) Mangrove forests tend to increase the commercial fish populations in coastal fishing grounds.
(E) A controlled harvesting of mangrove wood by the GFC would have little effect on coastal erosion.

Argument Evaluation

Situation A subsidiary business of the Gocha Fishing Cooperative (GFC) has invested in a program to replant significant parts of the coast with mangrove trees.

Reasoning *What additional information, if true, would most strengthen the argument's support for the conclusion that the mangrove regeneration effort will increase the GFC's net income?* If the regeneration effort helped the GFC's fishing operations, this could lead to an increase in GFC's income.

A If the local government helped with the cost of dredging and shore facilities, that would help reduce the GFC's costs, but that is not directly related to the impact of the GFC's mangrove regeneration effort on GFC's net income.

B It is unclear whether hiring local workers to assist with mangrove replanting would be less costly than hiring workers from elsewhere, so it is unclear whether this would help the GFC increase its net income.

C The information provided does not indicate whether the mangrove regeneration effort will have any effect on its salt-production facilities, or any revenue or profit that it derives from these facilities, so this does not strengthen the argument.

D **Correct.** If the mangrove restoration effort helps increase the commercial fish population in coastal fishing grounds, then there is a good chance that the GFC's income from its fishing operations will increase as a result.

E The information provided does not indicate what, if any, effect coastal erosion has on GFC's net income, so the fact that controlled harvesting of mangrove wood would have little effect on coastal erosion does not strengthen the argument.

The correct answer is D.

8.7 Critical Reasoning Answer Explanations

CR07651.01
615. Executives at the Fizzles Beverage Company plan to boost profits in Country X on their range of fruit-flavored drinks by introducing new flavors based on tropical fruits that are little known there. The executives reason that since the fruit drinks of other companies have none of these flavors, Fizzles will not have to compete for customers and thus will be able to sell the drinks at a higher price.

Which of the following, if true, presents the most serious potential weakness of the plan?

(A) The new fruit drinks would be priced significantly higher than other Fizzles fruit drinks with more conventional flavors.

(B) In a telephone survey, at least one of the consumers contacted said that they preferred many of the new flavors to all of the more familiar flavors.

(C) To build widespread demand for the new flavors, Fizzles would have to launch an advertising campaign to familiarize consumers with them.

(D) Consumers choosing among fruit-flavored drinks of different brands generally buy on the basis of name recognition and price rather than the specific fruit flavor.

(E) Few consumers who are loyal to a specific brand of fruit-flavored drinks would willingly switch to another brand that costs more.

Evaluation of a Plan

Situation Fizzle Beverage Company's executives plan to offer drinks with tropical fruit flavors that are little known in Country X in the hope that doing so will boost profits in that country. They reason that because their competitors in that country do not offer drinks with these flavors, Fizzle will be able to sell the drinks at a premium price.

Reasoning *What casts the most doubt on the claim that the executive's plan will effectively allow them to sell fruit-flavored drinks at a higher price?* The executives believe that the lack of a direct competitor to these drinks will allow the company to sell the drinks for a higher price. But any information indicating that something other than the specific fruit flavor of the drink drives sales of fruit-flavored drinks would cast doubt on the plan.

A We have already been told that the prices will be higher. The question is whether they will be able to sell the drink successfully at these higher prices as a result of the plan.

B This provides at least some very slight support for the belief that the plan would succeed (if no one at all preferred the new drinks, then the plan would almost certainly fail); however, the question asks for something that would cast doubt on the effectiveness of the plan.

C When introducing a new product, companies usually have to launch advertising campaigns, and quite frequently such campaigns effectively create demand for the product, so the fact that Fizzles will have to launch an advertising campaign does not cast doubt on the plan.

D **Correct.** The plan depends on consumers wanting the drinks because of their unique, unfamiliar flavors, and being willing to pay a higher price for them because of their uniqueness in the market. If price (presumably a lower one) and name recognition, rather than the specific fruit flavor, are what generally drive sales, then it seems unlikely that the executives' plan will succeed.

E Nothing in the information provided indicates how many consumers are loyal to any specific brand of fruit-flavored drinks. Perhaps the vast majority of consumers are willing to switch brands. If that is so, then the fact that the very few who are loyal to a specific brand would not be willing to switch would not cast much doubt on the effectiveness of the plan.

The correct answer is D.

CR33061.01
616. Economist: In 2015, the average per-person amount paid for goods and services purchased by consumers in Country X was the equivalent of $17,570 in United States dollars, just 30 percent of the corresponding figure of $58,566 for Country Y. Yet in 2015, there was already a substantial middle class in Country X that had discretionary income for middle-class consumer goods such as new vehicles, computers, or major household appliances, while a significant portion of the middle class in Country Y did not have sufficient income to purchase such items.

Which of the following, if true, most helps explain the discrepancy in the relationships described by the economist?

(A) There are many consumer goods, such as household appliances, that are produced in Country X to be sold in the Country Y market.
(B) The volume of trade between Country X and Country Y is increasing rapidly in both directions.
(C) The economy of Country Y is recovering from a downturn that affected both Country Y and Country X.
(D) Country X residents pay much less than their Country Y counterparts for housing, transportation, and child care.
(E) In Country Y as well as in Country X, there are few assembly-line jobs in factories that pay a middle-class wage.

Argument Construction

Situation An economist points out that even though in 2015 the average per-person amount paid for goods and services in Country X was only 30 percent of the corresponding figure in Country Y, a substantial middle class in Country X had discretionary income for consumer goods whereas a substantial portion of the middle class in Country Y did not.

Reasoning *What, if true, would most help explain the discrepancies described by the economist?* Information indicating that residents in Country X pay much less for nondiscretionary items than do residents of Country Y would help explain why, even though people in Country Y pay on average three times more for goods and services than people in Country X, Country X has a more substantial middle class capable of buying discretionary goods than does Country Y.

A That many consumer goods produced in Country X are intended to be sold in Country Y does not help explain why many people in Country Y are not able to afford such goods.

B An increasing volume of trade between Country X and Country Y—which, for all we know, is perfectly balanced—would not help explain any discrepancies between the two countries.

C That the economies of both Country X and Country Y both suffered a downturn, and Country Y is recovering, could not plausibly explain why many people in Country Y have trouble paying for discretionary goods unless we had the information that Country Y's recovery was significantly slower than Country X's; but we do not have that information.

D **Correct.** That people in one nation pay far less for nondiscretionary goods than people in another nation would potentially be helpful in explaining how the people in the former nation would more easily be able to afford discretionary goods.

E If a claim is true of both Country X and Country Y, it would not help explain a discrepancy between the two countries.

The correct answer is D.

617. Neuroscientist: Memory evolved to help animals react appropriately to situations they encounter by drawing on the past experience of similar situations. But this does not require that animals perfectly recall every detail of all their experiences. Instead, to function well, memory should generalize from past experiences that are similar to the current one.

The neuroscientist's statements, if true, most strongly support which of the following conclusions?

(A) At least some animals perfectly recall every detail of at least some past experiences.
(B) Perfectly recalling every detail of all their past experiences could help at least some animals react more appropriately than they otherwise would to new situations they encounter.
(C) Generalizing from past experiences requires clear memories of most if not all the details of those experiences.
(D) Recalling every detail of all past experiences would be incompatible with any ability to generalize from those experiences.
(E) Animals can often react more appropriately than they otherwise would to situations they encounter if they draw on generalizations from past experiences of similar situations.

Argument Construction

Situation   A neuroscientist claims that memory evolved to help animals learn how to react appropriately by generalizing from past experiences but that this does not require animals to remember all details of those experiences.

Reasoning   *What conclusion would the neuroscientist's theory about memory most strongly support?* The neuroscientist asserts that the evolutionary function of memory is to help animals learn to react appropriately by drawing on generalizations from similar experiences they have had. If memory is to serve this function, drawing on generalizations must actually help animals learn to react more appropriately than they otherwise would, even when they do not remember all the details of past experiences.

A   Even if no animal ever recalls all the details of any past experience, animals could still learn through generalizations, as the neuroscientist claims.

B   This statement could be false even if all of what the neuroscientist says is true. Even if it were never helpful for any animal to recall every detail of all its past experiences, animals could still benefit by learning through generalizations.

C   Generalizations from experiences might be made while the experiences are occurring, so that only the generalizations and not the details need to be remembered.

D   The neuroscientist only claims that remembering perfect details is not required for memory to serve its function, not that such perfect recall is incompatible with memory serving its function.

E   **Correct.** If the evolutionary function of memory is to help animals react more appropriately by drawing on generalizations from past experiences, it follows that animal memories can often successfully serve this function in this manner.

The correct answer is E.

CR52061.01
618. In Country X's last election, the Reform Party beat its main opponent, the Conservative Party, although pollsters, employing in-person interviews shortly before the vote, had projected a Conservative Party victory. Afterwards, the pollsters determined that, unlike Conservative Party supporters, Reform Party supporters were less likely to express their party preference during in-person interviews than they were during telephone interviews. Therefore, using only telephone interviews instead would likely result in more accurate projections for the next election.

Which of the following statements, if true, would most support the argument in the passage?

(A) The number of voters in Country X's next election will be significantly larger than the number of voters in the last election.
(B) The Conservative Party will win the next election.
(C) For each person interviewed in telephone polls before the next election, pollsters will be able to reasonably determine the likelihood of that person voting.
(D) People who expressed no party preference during the in-person interviews shortly before Country X's last election did not outnumber the people who expressed a preference for the Conservative Party.
(E) In the next election, pollsters will be able to conduct more in-person interviews than telephone interviews.

Argument Evaluation

Situation — Pollsters, using in-person interviews shortly before the last election in Country X, incorrectly predicted that the Conservative Party would win that election, whereas the Reform Party won instead. The pollsters determined that Reform Party supporters, unlike Conservative Party supporters, are less likely to give their party preference in person than in telephone interviews.

Reasoning — *What additional information, if true, would most strengthen the support, in light of the given information, for the prediction that using only telephone interviews would result in more accurate projections in the next election in Country X?* Even if in telephone interviews pollsters are more likely to get accurate information about which party a person interviewed supports, the pollsters' projections may not be accurate if the pollsters are unable to determine whether that person is actually likely to vote. So, information indicating that pollsters will be able to determine the likelihood that a person will vote would strengthen support for the conclusion.

A If this larger number of voters in the next election is not anticipated by pollsters, then it may affect the accuracy of their predictions. However, the effect would likely be a decrease, rather than an increase, in accuracy. If the pollsters are able to accurately predict voter turnout, then their predictions for the next election could be more accurate. But we have no indication as to whether their turnout predictions will be accurate.

B If the Conservative Party will win the next election, an underestimate of Reform Party support will be less important for the accuracy of the projection of which party will win.

C **Correct.** It would certainly be helpful if the pollsters were able to determine how likely the person they were interviewing would be to vote.

D This is irrelevant to the argument. The conclusion concerns the relative accuracy of telephone interviews in predicting voting numbers in the next election.

E If pollsters are able to do more in-person interviews than telephone interviews for the next election, that at least weakly suggests that they might not be able to conduct a sufficient number of telephone interviews to get a representative sample—which would weaken support for the conclusion, not strengthen it.

The correct answer is C.

619. A company that manufactures plastic products from recyclable plastic is, surprisingly, unconcerned that economic conditions may worsen, despite analysts' belief that consumers would then consider ecofriendly plastic products an expensive luxury. But the company reasons that it will be able to lower its prices because, in a weakened economy, other ecofriendly plastic manufacturers are likely to fail. Demand among manufacturers for recyclable plastics as raw materials would then plummet, creating an oversupply of such materials, making them less expensive for the manufacturer to purchase and thus lowering the company's costs.

Which of the following, if true, most weakens the company's reasoning?

(A) Smaller ecofriendly plastic manufacturers are more likely to fail in a weakened economy than larger ecofriendly manufacturers are.
(B) Some retailers whose sales include various companies' ecofriendly plastic products have struggled in recent years despite the overall good economy.
(C) Consumers would likely soon learn of the oversupply of recyclable plastics and cease recycling them, significantly raising manufacturers' raw-material costs.
(D) Retailers, including retailers that cater to consumers seeking certain types of ecofriendly products, may lose some business if economic conditions worsen.
(E) The plastics used by the company in its products were, after a recent investigation by a regulatory body, declared to be safe for consumers.

Argument Evaluation

Situation   A company that manufactures products from recyclable plastics believes that if economic conditions worsen it will be able to lower its prices. It believes its costs will decline because other ecofriendly plastic manufacturers will fail, thereby reducing the demand for recyclable plastics as raw materials.

Reasoning   *What would most weaken the reasoning?* Suppose the company's costs did not decline and the company consequently could not reduce its prices. Even if demand for recyclable plastics as raw materials weakens in an economic downturn, the company's costs may nonetheless not decline if for some reason the supply of recyclable plastics also declines. If so, then the company may well not be able to lower its prices and stay profitable.

A   We are not told whether the company in question is a smaller ecofriendly plastic manufacturer or a larger one. Given that, the fact that smaller such companies are more likely to fail than larger ones may strengthen the argument rather than weaken it (assuming the company in question is a larger such company).

B   If some retailers whose sales include various companies' ecofriendly plastic products have struggled in a healthy economy, they may well struggle even more in a weak economy. This could help drive the company's competitors out of business, which is what the company argues is likely to happen in an economic downturn; so rather than weakening the argument, this arguably strengthens it.

C   **Correct.** Suppose consumers learn of the oversupply of recyclable plastics and stop recycling them as a result; the oversupply may therefore not last long, and indeed a shortage might arise. This would lead not to lower raw-material costs, as the company argues, but to higher raw-material costs.

D   The information that retailers' lost business might result in a decrease in sales of the competing products does not weaken the argument. A loss of business due to worsening economic conditions is a presupposition of the argument.

E   The fact that the plastics used by the company have been declared safe has probably helped boost demand for the company's products, and perhaps for the competing products as well, yet an economic downturn could still hurt the company's competitors. So, this does little to weaken the company's argument.

The correct answer is C.

CR73241.01
620. Researchers asked volunteers to imagine they were running a five-kilometer race against 50 people and then against 500 people, races in each of which the top 10 percent would receive a $1,000 prize. Asked about the effort they would apply in the respective cases, the volunteers indicated, on average, that they would run slower in the race against the greater number of people. A likely explanation of this result is that those of the volunteers who were most *comparatively inclined*—those who most tended to compare themselves with others in the social environment—determined (perhaps unconsciously) that extreme effort would not be worthwhile in the 500-competitor race.

Which of the following would, if known to be true, most help justify the explanation offered above?

(A) The volunteers who were most comparatively inclined were also those that had the greatest desire to win a $1,000 prize.

(B) The volunteers who were the least comparatively inclined had no greater desire to win the $1,000 than those who were the most comparatively inclined.

(C) The volunteers who were most comparatively inclined were likely to indicate that they would run the two races at the same speed.

(D) The most comparatively inclined volunteers believed that they were significantly less likely to finish in the top 10 percent in the race against 500 than in the race against 50.

(E) Volunteers were chosen for participation in the study on the basis of answers to various questions designed to measure the degree to which the volunteers were comparatively inclined.

Argument Construction

Situation Volunteers were asked how much effort they would expend when running a five-kilometer race against 50 people and how much they would expend in such a race against 500 people, when the prize for each race is $1,000 for finishing in the top 10 percent. The volunteers indicated, on average, that they would run more slowly in the race against 500 people than in the race against 50 people. This result is likely because comparatively inclined volunteers believed that extreme effort would not have been worthwhile in the race against 500 competitors.

Reasoning *What would most help to justify the explanation proposed above?* If comparatively inclined volunteers thought it was at least as likely that they would finish in the top 10 percent in the race against 500 as in the race against 50, the proposed explanation would fail. Thus, it would help justify the explanation if we knew that the comparatively inclined volunteers believed they were less likely to win in the race against 500 than in the race against 50.

A If one knew that the volunteers who were most comparatively inclined had the greatest desire to win the $1,000, one might actually be more puzzled about why these volunteers said they would expend less effort against the 500 competitors. If they expended less effort, they would probably be less likely to finish in the top 10 percent.

B If one knew that the volunteers who were more comparatively inclined had no less desire to win a $1,000 prize than those who were least comparatively inclined, one would have at least some reason to think the comparatively inclined volunteers wanted to win the $1,000; this clearly cannot explain why they would not expend as much effort in the 500-competitor race as in the 50-competitor race.

C If the most comparatively inclined volunteers were likely to indicate that they would run the two races at the same speed, then the proposed explanation cannot be correct.

D **Correct.** If the most comparatively inclined volunteers believed they would be far less likely to finish in the top 10 percent in the race against 500 than in the race against 50, then they would likely believe that extreme effort would not be worthwhile in the race with more people. This therefore is likely to be at least part of the explanation.

E Even if volunteers were chosen on the basis of answers to questions designed to measure how comparatively inclined they were, we are not told whether the volunteers were chosen because of the degree to which they were comparatively inclined.

The correct answer is D.

8.7 Critical Reasoning Answer Explanations

CR41141.01
621. According to a study, after a week of high-altitude living, twenty men had slimmed down. The men, middle-aged residents of low-altitude areas, had been taken to a research station at 2,650 meters (8,694 feet) above sea level. They had unrestricted access to food and were forbidden vigorous exercise, yet they lost an average of 1.5 kilograms (3.3 pounds) during their one-week stay. Clearly, the lower availability of oxygen at higher altitudes, or hypobaric hypoxia, can be said to have caused the weight loss, since _____.

Which of the following would, if true, most logically complete the argument?

(A) a decrease in oxygen intake has been shown to depress appetite
(B) the men all participated in the same kinds of exercise during their stay
(C) the foods available to the men had fewer calories than the foods they usually ate
(D) exercise at higher altitudes is more difficult than exercise at lower altitudes is
(E) several weeks after returning home, the men still weighed less than they had before the study

Argument Construction

Situation   Twenty middle-aged men lived at a high-altitude research station for one week. They had unrestricted access to food but did no vigorous exercise. By the end of their stay they had lost an average 1.5 kilograms (3.3 pounds) of weight.

Reasoning   *Which additional information, if true, would most help support the claim that lower availability of oxygen at higher altitudes caused the weight loss?* The puzzlement arises from the fact that the twenty men had free access to food and did no vigorous exercise. And consuming less of the types of food they would normally eat would have caused weight loss. But suppose one or both of these behaviors had not occurred?

A   **Correct.** This information helps support the explanatory hypothesis that lower oxygen levels accounted for the weight loss. The men's intake of oxygen certainly decreased at an altitude of 2,650 meters (8694 feet), since they normally lived in low-altitude areas. Moreover, reduced appetite would provide a mechanism by which weight loss could have occurred.

B   The men were forbidden vigorous exercise and we can assume that, in a research context, they followed this restriction. Mild exercise would be unlikely to explain the weight loss.

C   This does not support the explanatory hypothesis concerning the role of oxygen reduction in the weight loss.

D   Even if this is generally true, it does not support the hypothesis that lower oxygen levels accounted for the weight loss.

E   This provides no support for the explanatory hypothesis that lower oxygen levels accounted for the weight loss. It might even cast some doubt on the hypothesis, since over a period of several weeks following the study, the men's weight did not increase with their return to their normal oxygen levels.

The correct answer is A.

CR11741.01

622. Editorial: Our city's public transportation agency is facing a budget shortfall. The fastest growing part of the budget has been employee retirement benefits, which are exceptionally generous. Unless the budget shortfall is resolved, transportation service will be cut, and many transportation employees will lose their jobs. Thus, it would be in the employees' best interest for their union to accept cuts in retirement benefits.

Which of the following is an assumption the editorial's argument requires?

(A) The transportation employees' union should not accept cuts in retirement benefits if doing so would not be in the employees' best interest.
(B) The only feasible way for the agency to resolve the budget shortfall would involve cutting transportation service and eliminating jobs.
(C) Other things being equal, it is in the transportation employees' interest to have exceptionally generous retirement benefits.
(D) Cutting the retirement benefits would help resolve the agency's budget shortfall.
(E) The transportation employees' union will not accept cuts in retirement benefits if doing so will not allow more transportation employees to keep their jobs.

Argument Construction

Situation An editorial indicates that the fastest growing part of a particular city's public transportation agency's budget is employee retirement benefits. The agency's budget has a shortfall. If the shortfall is not resolved, transportation service will be cut and many of the employees will lose their jobs.

Reasoning *What must be true if we are to accept the editorial's conclusion, that it is in the employee's best interest to accept cuts in retirement benefits?* If cutting the employees' retirement benefits would not be sufficient to resolve the budget shortfall, then it may well not be in employees' best interest to accept such cuts. The reasons given for accepting the cuts are related to the undesirable consequences of a continued shortfall.

A The argument is about whether the union's accepting the cuts is in fact in the employees' best interest, and does not require any assumption about whether employees should accept what is in their best interest.
B This is incompatible with an assumption made by the argument. The argument assumes that cutting the retirement benefits of the employees would help resolve the budget shortfall.
C The argument would actually be stronger if it were NOT the case that it is in the employees' interest to have exceptionally generous retirement benefits.
D **Correct.** If cutting retirement benefits would not help resolve the agency's budget shortfall, then cutting those benefits would not help the employees avoid job cuts.
E The argument does not depend on assuming anything regarding what factors would motivate the union's acceptance.

The correct answer is D.

623. Researchers hope to find clues about the A'mk peoples who lived in the Kaumpta region about one thousand years ago but who left few obvious traces. The researchers plan to hire the few remaining shamans of the modern-day indigenous people in Kaumpta, who are believed to be descended from the A'mk, to lead them to ancestral sites that may be the remains of A'mk buildings or ceremonial spaces. The shamans were taught the location of such sites as part of their traditional training as youths, and their knowledge of traditional Kaumpta customs may help determine the nature of any sites the researchers find.

Which of the following is an assumption on which the success of the plan depends?

(A) The researchers have reliable evidence that the A'mk of one thousand years ago built important ceremonial spaces.
(B) The shamans have a reasonably accurate memory of A'mk sites they learned about as youths.
(C) Kaumpta shamans are generally held in high esteem for their traditional knowledge.
(D) Modern technologies available to the researchers are likely to be able to find some A'mk sites easily.
(E) Most or all A'mk sites are likely to be found within the Kaumpta region.

Evaluation of a Plan

Situation Researchers wish to find sites of an ancient people, the A'mk, who lived in the Kaumpta region one thousand years ago. Indigenous people believed to be descended from the A'mk live in that region today. Their shamans, as youths, were taught about such sites. To discover some of these sites, the researchers plan to hire the shamans.

Reasoning *What must be true for the success of the researchers' plan to find the sites by relying on the shamans' assistance?* The plan would fail, for example, if there were no such sites in the Kaumpta region. Therefore, the researchers' plan depends on assuming that Kaumpta have some such sites—but not that most of the sites are there. The plan also requires that the shamans collectively have reasonably accurate recall of what they learned about the sites as youths.

A The researchers hope to find buildings or ceremonial spaces or both. However, the plan does not require ceremonial spaces to be found or that the researchers have evidence of them.

B **Correct.** If the shamans collectively have no "reasonably accurate memory" of what they learned of the location of such sites, then the researchers' plan is not a useful one and can have no reasonable expectation of success.

C This is likely to be so if the indigenous group from which they come is still committed to maintaining their traditional knowledge. But the plan does not rely on the shamans being honored among their own people. It must be assumed, of course, that the shamans currently possess "traditional knowledge" and are willing to share it.

D The researchers' reliance on the shamans' assistance suggests that it is not so easy for the researchers to rely entirely on "modern technologies" in this case.

E The plan can succeed even if this is not correct. What must be assumed is that at least some of the A'mk sites are within the Kaumpta region; it need not be assumed that most or all are.

The correct answer is B.

CR09994

624. Astronomer: Most stars are born in groups of thousands, each star in a group forming from the same parent cloud of gas. Each cloud has a unique, homogeneous chemical composition. Therefore, whenever two stars have the same chemical composition as each other, they must have originated from the same cloud of gas.

Which of the following, if true, would most strengthen the astronomer's argument?

(A) In some groups of stars, not every star originated from the same parent cloud of gas.
(B) Clouds of gas of similar or identical chemical composition may be remote from each other.
(C) Whenever a star forms, it inherits the chemical composition of its parent cloud of gas.
(D) Many stars in vastly different parts of the universe are quite similar in their chemical compositions.
(E) Astronomers can at least sometimes precisely determine whether a star has the same chemical composition as its parent cloud of gas.

Argument Evaluation

Situation   Most stars are born in groups, any one of which forms from a parent gas cloud with a unique, homogenous chemical composition.

Reasoning   What would be additional evidence that any two stars with the same chemical composition originated from the same gas cloud? The implicit reasoning is that since the chemical composition of each gas cloud is unique and homogenous, any two stars that formed from gas with the same chemical composition must have originated from the same cloud. The astronomer then infers that if two stars have the same composition now, they must have originated from the same cloud. This inference requires the assumption that the composition each star has now depends only on the composition of the cloud in which it originated. Any evidence that supports this assumption will strengthen the argument.

A   Whether or not stars born in different clouds of gas are ever in the same "group" is not clearly relevant to whether or not they ever have the same chemical composition.

B   How remote clouds of similar compositions are from each other is not clearly relevant to whether stars that have the same chemical composition may have formed from different clouds of gas. Also, the suggestion that different gas clouds may have identical compositions conflicts with the astronomer's premise that the composition of each cloud from which stars form is unique.

C   **Correct.** If each star's composition is identical to that of its parent cloud, and each cloud's composition is unique, then any two stars identical in composition must have formed from the same parent cloud.

D   If anything, this would suggest that stars with the same composition might have formed from different clouds, so it would weaken rather than strengthen the argument.

E   If astronomers could do this, they might be able to obtain additional evidence for or against the position taken in the argument, but this, in itself, provides no reason to suppose that the evidence would support, rather than weaken, that position. They might find that the stars' compositions do not precisely correlate with the compositions of the stars' parent gas clouds.

The correct answer is C.

8.7 Critical Reasoning Answer Explanations

CR08017

625. With employer-paid training, workers have the potential to become more productive not only in their present employment but also in any number of jobs with different employers. To increase the productivity of their workforce, many firms are planning to maintain or even increase their investments in worker training. But some training experts object that if a trained worker is hired away by another firm, the employer that paid for the training has merely subsidized a competitor. They note that such hiring has been on the rise in recent years.

Which of the following would, if true, contribute most to defeating the training experts' objection to the firms' strategy?

(A) Firms that promise opportunities for advancement to their employees get, on average, somewhat larger numbers of job applications from untrained workers than do firms that make no such promise.
(B) In many industries, employees that take continuing-education courses are more competitive in the job market.
(C) More and more educational and training institutions are offering reduced tuition fees to firms that subsidize worker training.
(D) Research shows that workers whose training is wholly or partially subsidized by their employer tend to get at least as much training as do workers who pay for all their own training.
(E) For most firms that invest in training their employees, the value added by that investment in employees who stay exceeds the value lost through other employees' leaving to work for other companies.

Evaluation of a Plan

Situation Many firms pay to train their workers in order to increase their workforces' productivity. But in recent years firms have been increasingly hiring away from each other workers who have had such training.

Reasoning *What would most help address the concern that firms that pay to train workers are thereby subsidizing competitors that hire away those workers?* In order for the employer-paid training to be worthwhile for a given firm despite the risk of subsidizing competitors that may hire away the trained workers, that firm has to gain more benefits from the training than it loses by subsidizing such competitors. Any evidence that this is true for most firms would help to address the experts' concern.

A A typical firm does not necessarily want larger numbers of applications from unqualified workers. And if hired, those workers can still be hired away by competitors after the firm has paid to train them, just as the experts warned.

B This suggests that in many industries, companies, rather than investing in employee training, prefer to hire employees who already have specifically relevant training (perhaps funded by other companies). If anything, this slightly supports, rather than defeats, the training experts' view. No firm has an interest in making its own employees more competitive in the job market unless the firm is likely to benefit from their being so.

C Even firms that pay reduced tuition fees for worker training may lose the money they pay for those fees and effectively subsidize competitors that hire the trained employees away. So this does not defeat the training experts' objection.

D The more highly trained workers—regardless of whether their training was company subsidized or not—would presumably be prime targets for recruitment by competing firms, just as the experts warned. The research finding in question does not help defeat the experts' objection.

E **Correct.** This explicitly indicates that most firms gain more than they lose from the general practice of firms paying to train their workers.

The correct answer is E.

CR93241.01
626. In emerging economies in Africa and other regions, large foreign banks that were set up during the colonial era have long played a major economic role. These institutions have tended to confine their business to the wealthier of banks' potential customers. But development of these countries' economies requires financing of the small businesses that dominate their manufacturing, farming, and services sectors. So economic growth will be likely to occur if local banks take on this portion of the financial services markets, since _____.

Which of the following completions would produce the strongest argument?

(A) local banks tend not to strive as much as large foreign banks to diversify their investments
(B) small farming and manufacturing businesses contribute to economic growth if they obtain adequate investment capital
(C) large foreign banks in emerging economies could, with local employees and appropriate local consultation, profitably expand their business to less wealthy clients
(D) some small businesses are among the wealthier customers of foreign banks in emerging economies
(E) local banks in emerging economies tend to be less risk-averse than foreign banks

Argument Construction

Situation: Large foreign banks have long played an economic role in emerging economies, but they have typically confined their business to wealthier customers. Economic development in these countries requires the financing of small businesses that dominate their manufacturing, farming, and services sectors.

Reasoning: *What would most help support the claim that growth in emerging economies will likely occur if local banks help finance small businesses in the relevant sectors of these emerging markets?* If it were the case that these small businesses would actually be likely to contribute to economic growth, given adequate investment capital, then economic growth would indeed be likely to occur if local banks provided the investment capital.

A It could be the case that whatever sorts of investments local banks make—diversified or not—economic growth will not tend to occur; for instance, it could be that the businesses they invest in do not use the capital wisely. So, this claim does not help support the conclusion.

B **Correct.** If small farming and manufacturing businesses will contribute to economic growth if they obtain adequate investment capital, then we have fairly good reason to think that economic growth is likely to occur if local banks take on the financing of such small businesses (we merely need to also assume that they will provide adequate investment capital when they take on this financing).

C Even if large foreign banks could profitably expand their businesses to less-wealthy clients, we have been given no reason to think they will. Furthermore, the claim in need of support is that economic growth will occur if local, rather than foreign, banks financially support these small businesses.

D The claim that economic growth will occur if local banks finance small business in certain sectors is not supported by the claim that there are some small businesses supported by foreign banks. If these businesses are already financially supported and yet there is not the sort of economic growth discussed, then that might even suggest that economic growth is unlikely to occur.

E It could be that, if local banks are less risk-averse than foreign banks, they will invest in risky businesses that fail, which would not tend to support the claim that economic growth will likely result if local banks in emerging counties provide financial support for the relevant sectors.

The correct answer is B.

8.7 Critical Reasoning Answer Explanations

CR49551.01

627. Exporters in Country X are facing lower revenues due to a shortage of the large metal shipping containers in which they send their goods by sea to other countries. Fewer containers arrive in Country X due to reductions in imports. This has meant lost orders, costly delays, and a scramble for alternatives, such as air freight, all of which are costlier. Moreover, the revenues of exporters in Country X will probably continue to decline in the near future. This is because other countries are likely to find it increasingly unprofitable to export their goods to Country X, and because _____.

Which of the following would most logically complete the passage?

(A) production of shipping containers in Country X is growing rapidly as a response to the shortage
(B) shipping companies are willing to move containers from country to country only when the containers are full
(C) the cost of shipping alternatives such as air freight is likely to stabilize in the near future
(D) consumers in Country X are purchasing more products than ever before
(E) the worldwide demand for goods made in Country X has only recently begun to rise after a long decline

Argument Construction

Situation   Exporters in Country X are finding that there is an insufficient number of shipping containers for them to use for their exports, because the number of such containers arriving in Country X has declined because of reduced imports. Also, alternative methods of shipping are relatively costly. Furthermore, other countries will likely find shipping goods to Country X to be less and less profitable.

Reasoning   *What would most support the prediction that Country X's exporters' revenues will likely see further declines in revenue in the near future?* If the number of shipping containers available to exporters is likely to decrease, then the prediction would have further support. We know that other countries exporting to Country X will find it increasingly unprofitable, so there is reason to believe their exports will decline further—meaning there will be fewer imports into Country X, which means fewer shipping containers arriving in Country X carrying imported goods, unless the shipping containers shipped in the future are less full than when they are shipped now. If shipping companies are willing to move such containers to another country only when the containers are full, then that will not occur.

A   If production of shipping containers in Country X were rapidly increasing, then the reason given for the decline in revenue for exporters in Country X—that there is an insufficient number of shipping containers—would be undermined, and so therefore would be the conclusion.

B   **Correct.** If shipping companies are unwilling to move containers from country to country unless the containers are full, then, given Country X's decline in imports, there will likely be fewer shipping containers available to Country X's exporters, which provides support for the claim that their revenues will likely decline.

C   If the cost of shipping alternatives such as air freight is likely to stabilize, then those alternative methods of shipping might become economically viable, which would undermine rather than support the conclusion.

D   The fact that consumers in Country X are purchasing more goods than ever before does not affect how much revenue is generated by exporting goods from Country X.

E   If there is increased demand for goods from Country X, then the price of such goods might increase sufficiently to make alternative methods of shipping economically viable, which would undermine rather than support the conclusion.

The correct answer is B.

628. Candle Corporation's television stations are likely to have more income from advertisers than previously. This is because advertisers prefer to reach people in the 18- to 49-year-old age group and the number of people in that group watching Candle television is increasing. Furthermore, among Candle viewers, the percentage of viewers 18 to 49 years old is increasing.

Which of the following, if true, would most strengthen the argument that Candle Corporation will receive more income from advertisers?

(A) Advertisers carefully monitor the demographic characteristics of television audiences and purchase advertising time to reach the audiences they prefer to reach.

(B) Among people over 49 years old, fewer viewers of Candle stations buy products advertised on television than do viewers of other stations.

(C) There will be increasingly more advertisements on television that are directed at viewers who are over 49 years old.

(D) Candle stations plan to show reruns of television shows during hours when other stations run shows for the first time.

(E) People 18 to 49 years old generally have less disposable income to spend than do people over 49 years old.

Argument Evaluation

Situation   Both the number and the percentage of Candle television viewers who are 18 to 49 years old are increasing. Advertisers prefer to reach people in this age group.

Reasoning   *What evidence, when combined with the cited facts, would most support the prediction that Candle will receive more income from advertisers?* The argument assumes that the increasing number and percentage of Candle viewers in the age group that advertisers prefer to reach will probably encourage advertisers to spend more on advertising with Candle. This assumption could be supported by evidence that the advertisers realize that Candle is getting more viewers in that preferred age range or by evidence that this awareness will influence the advertisers' purchase of advertising time.

A   **Correct.** Advertisers monitoring demographics will probably realize that Candle has increasing numbers of viewers in their preferred age range. If they purchase advertising to reach viewers in that age range, then they will probably purchase more advertising time with Candle.

B   This gives advertisers less reason to advertise on Candle to reach viewers over 49 years old. Other things being equal, that makes Candle likely to receive less income from advertisers, not more income.

C   Since the percentage of Candle viewers 18 to 49 years old is growing, the percentage over 49 years old is probably shrinking. This could make advertisers seeking to reach older viewers less inclined to advertise on Candle even as they increase their overall television advertising.

D   Advertisers are not necessarily inclined to purchase more advertising during showings of reruns than during original airings of television shows and may even be inclined to purchase less advertising during such showings.

E   This gives advertisers less incentive to try to reach audiences between 18 and 49 years old and hence less reason to purchase advertising on Candle.

The correct answer is A.

CR12584
629. A provincial government plans to raise the gasoline tax to give people an incentive to drive less, reducing traffic congestion in the long term. However, skeptics point out that most people in the province live in areas where cars are the only viable transportation to jobs and stores and therefore cannot greatly change their driving habits in response to higher gasoline prices.

In light of the skeptics' objection, which of the following, if true, would most logically support the prediction that the government's plan will achieve its goal of reducing traffic congestion?

(A) The revenue from the tax will be used to make public transportation a viable means of transportation to jobs and stores for far more people.
(B) The tax will encourage many residents to switch to more fuel-efficient cars, reducing air pollution and other problems.
(C) Because gasoline has been underpriced for decades, the province has many neighborhoods where cars are the only viable means of transportation.
(D) Most residents who cannot greatly change their driving habits could compensate for high gasoline prices by reducing other expenses.
(E) Traffic congestion is an especially serious problem for people for whom cars are the only viable means of transportation.

Evaluation of a Plan

Situation A provincial government plans to raise the gasoline tax in order to reduce traffic congestion by discouraging people from driving. But skeptics point out that most people in the province have no viable form of transportation other than driving.

Reasoning *What would suggest that raising the gasoline tax will reduce traffic congestion even though most people in the province have no viable form of transportation other than driving?* The skeptics point out that since most people in the province have no way to reach jobs or stores except by car, they will not be able to reduce their driving much even if the gasoline tax increases. Any evidence that raising the gasoline tax would reduce traffic congestion despite this obstacle would help to support the plan in light of the skeptics' objection.

A **Correct.** If the tax will fund these public transit improvements, then far more people will have a viable means of transportation other than driving, undermining the basis of the skeptics' objection.
B People switching to fuel-efficient cars would not reduce traffic congestion.
C This essentially only tends to support the skeptics' objection. Unless the plan somehow helps to alleviate the necessity of driving (by, for example, making alternative transportation available), the information provided gives no reason to suppose that the higher costs would significantly reduce traffic congestion.
D If residents cannot greatly change their driving habits, then the tax will not reduce traffic congestion.
E This suggests that many residents in the province could benefit if the plan did reduce traffic congestion, but it does not provide a reason to believe the plan will have that effect.

The correct answer is A.

CR03940

630. Editorial: The roof of Northtown's municipal equipment-storage building collapsed under the weight of last week's heavy snowfall. The building was constructed recently and met local building-safety codes in every particular, except that the nails used for attaching roof supports to the building's columns were of a smaller size than the codes specify for this purpose. Clearly, this collapse exemplifies how even a single, apparently insignificant departure from safety standards can have severe consequences.

Which of the following, if true, most seriously weakens the editorial's argument?

(A) The only other buildings to suffer roof collapses from the weight of the snowfall were older buildings constructed according to less exacting standards than those in the codes.

(B) The amount of snow that accumulated on the roof of the equipment-storage building was greater than the predicted maximum that was used in drawing up the safety codes.

(C) Because the equipment-storage building was not intended for human occupation, some safety-code provisions that would have applied to an office building did not apply to it.

(D) The municipality of Northtown itself has the responsibility for ensuring that buildings constructed within its boundaries meet the provisions of the building-safety codes.

(E) Because the equipment-storage building was used for storing snow-removal equipment, the building was almost completely empty when the roof collapsed.

Argument Evaluation

Situation   The roof of a recently constructed building collapsed under heavy snowfall. The only way the building did not meet safety standards was that some nails for the roof supports were smaller than prescribed by the building codes.

Reasoning   *What would make it less likely that the building's collapse resulted from a single, apparently minor departure from safety standards?* The building met safety standards except for the size of the nails. So if the collapse exemplifies how a departure from safety standards can have severe consequences, as the conclusion claims, then the size of the nails had to be responsible for the collapse. Thus, evidence that a factor other than the size of the nails could fully account for the collapse would weaken the argument.

A   This suggests that the snow would not have been heavy enough to collapse the roof if the construction had completely met the safety standards, so it strengthens, rather than weakens, the argument.

B   **Correct.** This suggests that the snow could have collapsed the roof even if the nails had met the safety standards, thus casting doubt on the assumption that the nails' inadequacy was responsible for the collapse.

C   The claim that the safety requirements for this building were weaker than some others tends slightly to strengthen, rather than weaken, the hypothesis that the bad consequences resulted partly from a failure to comply. Even if safety-code provisions for an equipment-storage building differ from those for an office building, they may still be adequate to ensure the roof's stability.

D   The question of who was responsible for ensuring compliance with the safety codes is irrelevant to whether a failure to comply was responsible for the roof's collapse.

E   This suggests that the alleged consequences of failing to meet safety standards were less severe than they could have been, but it is irrelevant to determining the cause of the collapse.

The correct answer is B.

CR12078
631. Political theorist: Even with the best spies, area experts, and satellite surveillance, foreign policy assessments can still lack important information. In such circumstances intuitive judgment is vital. A national leader with such judgment can make good decisions about foreign policy even when current information is incomplete, since _____.

Which of the following, if true, most logically completes the argument?

(A) the central reason for failure in foreign policy decision making is the absence of critical information
(B) those leaders whose foreign policy decisions have been highly ranked have also been found to have good intuitive judgment
(C) both intuitive judgment and good information are required for sound decision making
(D) good foreign policy decisions often lead to improved methods of gathering information
(E) intuitive judgment can produce good decisions based on past experience, even when there are important gaps in current information

Argument Construction

Situation   National leaders sometimes must make foreign policy decisions while lacking important information.

Reasoning   *What would most help support the claim that a national leader with intuitive judgment can make good foreign policy decisions without complete information?* The word *since* preceding the blank indicates that the blank should be filled with a premise supporting the statement immediately before the blank. So an observation that supports the claim that a national leader with intuitive judgment can make good foreign policy decisions without complete information would logically complete the argument.

A   This gives us no reason to suppose that intuitive judgment helps national leaders avoid such failures.

B   This does not specify who ranked the foreign policy decisions, nor how they determined the rankings, so it gives us no reason to accept those rankings. For all we know, the anonymous rankers may have used the dubious rankings they created as the sole evidence for their so-called findings about which leaders have good intuitive judgment.

C   This implies that intuitive judgment alone is inadequate without good information, so it undermines rather than supports the claim that national leaders can make good foreign policy decisions with intuitive judgment while lacking complete information.

D   This gives us no reason to suppose that good foreign policy decisions can be made in the first place by leaders lacking important information.

E   **Correct.** This suggests that national leaders can make good foreign policy decisions using intuitive judgment based on their past foreign policy experience, even without complete information about the current situations they're facing.

The correct answer is E.

CR51141.01
632. Supply shortages and signs of growing demand are driving cocoa prices upward. Unusually severe weather in cocoa-producing regions—too much rain in Brazil and too little in West Africa—has limited production. Further, Europe and North America recently reported stronger demand for cocoa. In the first quarter, grinding of cocoa beans—the first stage in processing cocoa for chocolate—rose 8.1 percent in Europe and 16 percent in North America. Analysts have concluded that cocoa's price will continue to rise at least into the near future.

Which of the following would, if true, most strengthen the reasoning above?

(A) Ground cocoa beans can be stored for long periods before they spoil.
(B) Several European and North American manufacturers that use cocoa have recently improved their processing capacity.
(C) It takes new cocoa trees five or six years before they start bearing fruit.
(D) Governments in Europe and North America are likely to change current restrictions on cocoa imports.
(E) Historically, cocoa production has varied widely from year to year.

Argument Evaluation

Situation There has been limited production of cocoa beans due to severe weather and also increased demand for cocoa; as a result, cocoa prices have risen.

Reasoning *What would help support the analysts' inference that cocoa prices will continue to rise at least into the near future?* If the price of cocoa is to continue to rise, then the conditions that have led to the recent increase in price must not be ameliorated. They would be ameliorated if demand for cocoa beans declined, e.g., because price increases made people less likely to want ground cocoa; they would also be ameliorated if supply increased, e.g., because many new cocoa trees were planted and very quickly started bearing fruit. If we had reason to believe that one or more of these ameliorating factors is unlikely to happen, then we have more reason to think that prices might stay high, and possibly even rise further.

A That ground cocoa beans can be stored for long periods without spoiling does not tell us whether supply and demand conditions will stay stable, improve, or get worse.

B The fact that these manufacturers have recently improved their processing capacity might help explain why the grinding of cocoa beans has increased recently; but it does not indicate that this increased capacity will be fully utilized. Often, if end-product demand decreases, industrial capacity will become underutilized.

C **Correct.** If it takes new cocoa trees several years to start bearing fruit, then it is less likely that supply can quickly be increased, which in turn makes it less likely that supply can quickly meet any increased demand and thereby relieve pricing pressures.

D These governments may change current restrictions on cocoa imports, but for all we know they may make them more restrictive rather than less restrictive. If they made them more restrictive, demand might decrease, in which case prices might actually fall.

E If cocoa production varies from year to year, it could be that next year cocoa production increases, in which case, as long as demand does not increase as well, prices might fall.

The correct answer is C.

CR01295

633. During the earliest period of industrialization in Britain, steam engines were more expensive to build and operate than either windmills or water mills, the other practicable sources of power for factories. Yet despite their significant cost disadvantage, steam-powered factories were built in large numbers well before technical improvements brought their cost down. Furthermore, they were built even in regions where geographical conditions permitted the construction of wind- and water-powered factories close to major markets.

Which of the following, if true, most helps to explain the proliferation of steam-powered factories during the earliest period of industrialization in Britain?

(A) In many areas of Britain, there were fewer steam-powered factories than wind- or water-powered factories in the earliest period of industrialization.
(B) Unlike wind- or water-powered factories, steam-powered factories were fueled with coal, which sometimes had to be transported significant distances from the mine to the site of the factory.
(C) It was both difficult and expensive to convert a factory from wind power or water power to steam power.
(D) In the early period of industrialization, many goods sold in towns and cities could not be mass-produced in factories.
(E) In Britain, the number of sites where a wind- or water-powered factory could be built was insufficient to provide for all of the demand for factory-produced goods at the time.

Argument Construction

Situation Although steam engines were more expensive than windmills and water mills in early industrial Britain, many steam-powered factories were built even in regions where the construction of wind- and water-powered factories was geographically feasible.

Reasoning *Why might steam-powered factories have proliferated despite their cost disadvantage?* Early industrialists would have needed some positive reason to choose steam over less expensive power sources for their factories. For example, steam engines might have operated faster or more effectively than windmills or water mills. Or steam engines might have received government subsidies. Or conditions restricting the number or locations of windmills and water mills might have forced industrialists to use steam power instead.

A This suggests that the steam-powered factories did not initially proliferate as widely as they might have, but it does not explain why they proliferated to the extent that they did.

B The inconvenience of transporting coal for steam-powered factories would have made those factories less likely to proliferate, not more likely.

C The difficulty of converting factories to steam power would have made steam-powered factories less likely to proliferate, not more likely.

D The technological inability to mass-produce popular products in factories would have made factories in general less likely to proliferate, including steam-powered factories.

E **Correct.** The inadequate number of sites for wind- and water-powered factories might have encouraged early industrialists to build steam-powered factories instead, since the high demand for factory-produced goods could have made these factories profitable despite their cost disadvantage.

The correct answer is E.

CR03938
634. Snowmaking machines work by spraying a mist that freezes immediately on contact with cold air. Because the sudden freezing kills bacteria, QuickFreeze is planning to market a wastewater purification system that works on the same principle. The process works only when temperatures are cold, however, so municipalities using it will still need to maintain a conventional system.

Which of the following, if true, provides the strongest grounds for a prediction that municipalities will buy QuickFreeze's purification system despite the need to maintain a conventional purification system as well?

- (A) Bacteria are not the only impurities that must be removed from wastewater.
- (B) Many municipalities have old wastewater purification systems that need to be replaced.
- (C) Conventional wastewater purification systems have not been fully successful in killing bacteria at cold temperatures.
- (D) During times of warm weather, when it is not in use, QuickFreeze's purification system requires relatively little maintenance.
- (E) Places where the winters are cold rarely have a problem of water shortage.

Evaluation of a Plan

Situation QuickFreeze is planning to market wastewater purification systems that work by spraying a mist that freezes on contact with cold air. The sudden freezing kills bacteria. Because the system works only at cold temperatures, municipalities using it will still need to maintain a conventional system.

Reasoning *Which statement provides the strongest grounds for thinking that at least some municipalities will buy the purification system despite the need to maintain a conventional purification system as well?* The passage tells us why a municipality using a QuickFreeze wastewater purification system would still need a conventional system. But why would a municipality want the QuickFreeze system *in addition* to a conventional system? If conventional systems are not fully effective at cold temperatures, the QuickFreeze system would allow municipalities that sometimes experience cold temperatures to purify their wastewater more effectively.

A There is no basis in the passage for determining whether the QuickFreeze system will help remove impurities other than bacteria from wastewater. If it does not, this answer choice implies that the QuickFreeze system would not be sufficient for purifying wastewater. This would actually undermine the prediction.

B The passage states that municipalities using the QuickFreeze system would still need a conventional system. Thus, the old conventional wastewater systems would still need to be replaced with new conventional systems. This answer choice provides no reason to think municipalities would buy the QuickFreeze system.

C **Correct.** This statement, if true, would strengthen the prediction, because it provides a valid reason why the QuickFreeze system could be needed alongside conventional ones: it is more effective in cold weather.

D Although this claim does undercut one reason for thinking municipalities might *not* be likely to purchase the QuickFreeze system, it provides little reason to think that they will purchase such a system. Perhaps in times of cold weather, the QuickFreeze system is very expensive to maintain.

E The issue of whether or not there are water shortages in places where winters are cold is not directly relevant. If conventional wastewater systems are sufficient to purify water in such places, municipalities would not need the QuickFreeze system (as they would still need to maintain a conventional purification system).

The correct answer is C.

CR05080

635. **Plant scientists have used genetic engineering on seeds to produce crop plants that are highly resistant to insect damage**. Unfortunately, the seeds themselves are quite expensive, and the plants require more fertilizer and water to grow well than normal ones. Accordingly, **for most farmers the savings on pesticides would not compensate for the higher seed costs and the cost of additional fertilizer**. However, since consumer demand for grains, fruits, and vegetables grown without the use of pesticides continues to rise, the use of genetically engineered seeds of this kind is likely to become widespread.

In the argument given, the two portions in **boldface** play which of the following roles?

(A) The first supplies a context for the argument; the second is the argument's main conclusion.
(B) The first introduces a development that the argument predicts will have a certain outcome; the second is a state of affairs that, according to the argument, contributes to bringing about that outcome.
(C) The first presents a development that the argument predicts will have a certain outcome; the second acknowledges a consideration that tends to weigh against that prediction.
(D) The first provides evidence to support a prediction that the argument seeks to defend; the second is that prediction.
(E) The first and the second each provide evidence to support the argument's main conclusion.

Argument Construction

Situation Seeds genetically engineered by plant scientists produce crops highly resistant to insect damage and require less use of pesticides. The seeds would be costly to use and would not help most farmers increase their profitability. Nonetheless, consumer demand for pesticide-free food materials is increasing, so genetically engineered seeds are likely to become widely used.

Reasoning *What function is served by the statement that plant scientists have used genetic engineering on seeds to produce insect-resistant crop plants? What function is served by the statement that for most farmers the savings on pesticides would not outweigh other associated costs?* The first describes an innovation—genetically engineered seeds—that allows crops to be grown with little or no use of pesticides. The second notes that despite savings on pesticide use, most farmers would not increase their profits by using the new seeds. The argument's main conclusion, however, is the prediction that use of such genetically engineered seeds will become widespread.

A The second statement is a conclusion—but not the main conclusion—that has the first statement as partial support.
B This correctly characterizes the first statement but not the second. The second statement is not meant to indicate a factor that contributes to the predicted outcome; it indicates, rather, a factor that somewhat counts against the argument's prediction.
C **Correct.** This correctly characterizes both statements.
D The first statement provides partial support for the prediction stated in the argument's main conclusion; the second statement does not state that prediction.
E The second cannot accurately be described as giving evidence to support the prediction stated in the argument's main conclusion.

The correct answer is C.

CR04159
636. Which of the following most logically completes the passage?

Leptin, a protein occurring naturally in the blood, appears to regulate how much fat the body carries by speeding up the metabolism and decreasing the appetite when the body has too much fat. Mice that do not naturally produce leptin have more fat than other mice, but lose fat rapidly when they are given leptin injections. Unfortunately, however, leptin cannot be used as a dietary supplement to control fat, since _____.

(A) the digestive system breaks down proteins before they can enter the bloodstream
(B) there are pharmaceuticals already available that can contribute to weight loss by speeding up the metabolism
(C) people with unusually low levels of leptin in their blood tend to have a high percentage of body fat
(D) the mice that do not naturally produce leptin were from a specially bred strain of mice
(E) mice whose bodies did produce leptin also lost some of their body fat when given leptin injections

Argument Construction

Situation   Leptin, a protein naturally occurring in the bloodstream, speeds up metabolism to induce loss of excessive fat. Mice that lack leptin have more fat than other mice, but lose fat when given leptin injections. However, leptin cannot be used as a dietary supplement to control fat.

Reasoning   *What would explain the fact that a dietary supplement of leptin will not help to control fat?* Leptin injected into the bloodstream—but not leptin taken as a dietary supplement—helps control fat. So leptin taken as a dietary supplement is either inactivated in the gastrointestinal system or for some other reason fails to enter the bloodstream.

A   **Correct.** The digestive system breaks down proteins and would therefore break down leptin, which is a protein. This means that leptin given as a dietary supplement would never reach the bloodstream.

B   The question concerns leptin alone, and this new information fails to explain why leptin cannot help control fat if administered as a dietary supplement.

C   It is unsurprising that this would be so, but this information does nothing to explain why leptin consumed as a supplement would fail to control fat.

D   Presumably leptin administered as a dietary supplement was first tested on mice bred to lack leptin. However, the question about leptin does not concern only mice, but presumably humans and other mammals.

E   This suggests that boosting existing normal leptin levels with injections can induce further fat loss. However, this has no obvious relevance to the question raised about why dietary supplements of leptin fail to produce fat loss.

The correct answer is A.

CR05452
637. Suncorp, a new corporation with limited funds, has been clearing large sections of the tropical Amazon forest for cattle ranching. This practice continues even though greater profits can be made from rubber tapping, which does not destroy the forest, than from cattle ranching, which does destroy the forest.

Which of the following, if true, most helps to explain why Suncorp has been pursuing the less profitable of the two economic activities mentioned above?

(A) The soil of the Amazon forest is very rich in nutrients that are important in the development of grazing lands.
(B) Cattle-ranching operations that are located in tropical climates are more profitable than cattle-ranching operations that are located in cold-weather climates.
(C) In certain districts, profits made from cattle ranching are more heavily taxed than profits made from any other industry.
(D) Some of the cattle that are raised on land cleared in the Amazon are killed by wildcats.
(E) The amount of money required to begin a rubber-tapping operation is twice as high as the amount needed to begin a cattle ranch.

Argument Construction

Situation Suncorp is a new corporation with limited funds. It has been clearing large sections of the tropical Amazon forest for ranching, even though rubber-tapping would be more profitable.

Reasoning *What would explain why Suncorp is clearing sections of the rain forest for ranching, even though rubber tapping would be more profitable?* Because Suncorp has limited funds, if rubber tapping has much higher start-up costs, Suncorp might not have enough money to start rubber-tapping operations. If cattle ranching has much lower start-up costs than rubber tapping, Suncorp might be able to afford such an operation.

A This statement gives a reason why cattle ranching in the Amazon might be more profitable than one might otherwise think it would be. However, we already know from the passage that rubber tapping would be more profitable than cattle ranching. So, this answer choice does not help explain why cattle ranching might be preferable to rubber tapping.

B The comparison between the profitableness of cattle ranching in tropical climates and in cold-weather climates is irrelevant. The passage only covers cattle ranching in the tropical Amazon forest. This answer choice would at most explain why Suncorp is undertaking cattle ranching in the Amazon rather than in some cold-weather location.

C This statement makes what needs to be explained harder to understand, for it indicates that cattle ranching in the Amazon might be less profitable than one would otherwise think.

D Like answer choice (C), this statement indicates a disadvantage of cattle ranching in the Amazon. So, it does not explain why cattle ranching would be preferred to some other economic activity.

E **Correct.** Because it costs less to begin cattle ranching than it does to begin rubber tapping, Suncorp—which has limited funds—would have a reason to pursue cattle ranching over a potentially more profitable activity.

The correct answer is E.

CR09963
638. Archaeologists use technology to analyze ancient sites. It is likely that this technology will advance considerably in the near future, allowing archaeologists to gather more information than is currently possible. If they study certain sites now, they risk contaminating or compromising them for future studies. Therefore, in order to maximize the potential for gathering knowledge in the long run, a team of archaeologists plans to delay the examination of a newly excavated site.

Which of the following would be most useful to investigate for the purpose of evaluating the plan's prospects for achieving its goal?

(A) Whether any of the contents of the site will significantly deteriorate before the anticipated technology is available
(B) Whether there will continue to be improvements on the relevant technology
(C) Whether the team can study a site other than the newly excavated site for the time being
(D) Whether the site was inhabited by a very ancient culture
(E) Whether the anticipated technology will damage objects under study

Evaluation of a Plan

Situation   To avoid prematurely compromising a newly excavated site, an archaeological team plans to postpone examining it until more advanced technology is developed that will let them gather more information from it. Their goal is to maximize the potential for gathering knowledge.

Reasoning   *What would be most helpful to investigate in order to assess how likely it is that delaying examination of the site will maximize the potential for gathering knowledge from it?* In order to maximize (or even increase) the potential for gathering knowledge from the site by delaying its examination, the risk of compromising the site by examining it now has to be greater than the risk that the site will be compromised as much or more by delaying the examination. The delay might also increase the risk that the site will never be examined at all—for example, the team might lose its funding while it delays, or changes in local political conditions might prevent the site's future examination. Investigating any of these risks could be helpful in assessing the likelihood that the team's plan will achieve its goal.

A   **Correct.** If any of the site's contents will significantly deteriorate before the technology becomes available, that could reduce the ability to gather future information from the site even more than examining and compromising the site now would.

B   The passage already tells us that it is likely the technology *will advance considerably in the near future*. Given this information, further inquiry into whether there will be any ongoing (perhaps minor) improvements is somewhat redundant and probably of minimal value with respect to evaluating the plan's likelihood of success.

C   Even if the team can study a second site in the meanwhile, they might maximize the overall potential for gathering knowledge by delaying the examination of either site, both sites, or neither site until more advanced technology is available.

D   The age of the culture that inhabited the site is irrelevant to assessing the risks of delaying the site's examination until more advanced technology is available.

E   Even if the anticipated technology will damage or destroy the objects under study, it might still maximize the amount of knowledge that can be gathered from those objects. Without any comparison between the damage risk that would be incurred by proceeding with the current technology and the damage risk that would be incurred by waiting, the mere fact that some damage would occur is irrelevant.

The correct answer is A.

CR01102

639. More and more law firms specializing in corporate taxes are paid on a contingency-fee basis. Under this arrangement, if a case is won, the firm usually receives more than it would have received if it had been paid on the alternate hourly rate basis. If the case is lost, the firm receives nothing. Most firms are likely to make more under the contingency-fee arrangement.

Which of the following, if true, would most strengthen the prediction above?

(A) Firms that work exclusively under the hourly rate arrangement spend, on average, fewer hours on cases that are won than on cases that are lost.

(B) Some litigation can last for years before any decision is reached, and, even then, the decision may be appealed.

(C) Firms under the contingency-fee arrangement still pay their employees on an hourly basis.

(D) Since the majority of firms specialize in certain kinds of cases, they are able to assess accurately their chances of winning each potential case.

(E) Firms working under the contingency-fee arrangement take in fewer cases per year than do firms working under the hourly rate arrangement.

Argument Evaluation

Situation Law firms of a certain type are increasingly working on a contingency-fee basis, whereby the firm is only paid if the case won. For the individual cases that are thus taken and won, the payments are generally greater than the total payments would have been if the firms had been paid on an hourly basis. Furthermore, although cases taken on a contingency-fee basis present a significant risk of working for many hours on a case and not being paid, the passage claims that most firms are likely to make more money, on average, than they would if they took their cases on an hourly basis.

Reasoning *What would most strongly indicate that, despite the risks, the law firms working on a contingency fee basis are likely to make more money, on average, than they would have otherwise?* Our task is to find the statement that would most strongly support this prediction.

A Supposing that the firms mentioned in this option changed from working on an hourly-rate basis to working on a contingency-fee basis, we would not have enough information to predict what the results would be. For example, we may have no reason to expect that the firm would accept the same cases that they would have accepted if they were working on an hourly-rate basis. As such, patterns of work on cases taken on an hourly basis may be irrelevant for determining how much the firms would make if they were to take their cases on a contingency-fee basis.

B This option indicates that firms taking cases on a contingency-fee basis can work on the cases for years without payment. Rather than supporting the point that firms would make more money if they worked on a contingency-fee basis, the option illustrates an aspect of the risks associated with this payment arrangement.

C This option also helps to illustrate the risk associated with taking cases on a contingency-fee basis. Even though firms working on such cases will only be paid if they win and not until then, they will still incur significant costs when working on their cases.

D **Correct.** This option suggests that firms working on a contingency-fee basis would be able to select cases that they would be likely to win and therefore be paid for. This makes it more likely that the firms would make more money working on a contingency-fee basis than they would if working on an hourly basis.

E Although the difference in numbers of cases described in this option could, given certain possible facts, be relevant to the prediction made by the argument, we have not been given any such facts.

The correct answer is D.

CR00766
640. Beginning in 1966 all new cars sold in Morodia were required to have safety belts and power steering. Previously, most cars in Morodia were without these features. Safety belts help to prevent injuries in collisions, and power steering helps to avoid collisions in the first place. But even though in 1966 one-seventh of the cars in Morodia were replaced with new cars, the number of car collisions and collision-related injuries did not decline.

Which of the following, if true about Morodia, most helps to explain why the number of collisions and collision-related injuries in Morodia failed to decline in 1966?

(A) Because of a driver-education campaign, most drivers and passengers in cars that did have safety belts used them in 1966.

(B) Most of the new cars bought in 1966 were bought in the months of January and February.

(C) In 1965, substantially more than one-seventh of the cars in Morodia were replaced with new cars.

(D) An excessive reliance on the new safety features led many owners of new cars to drive less cautiously in 1966 than before.

(E) The seat belts and power steering put into new cars sold in 1966 had to undergo strict quality-control inspections by manufacturers, whether the cars were manufactured in Morodia or not.

Argument Construction

Situation Starting in 1966, new cars sold in Morodia were required to have safety belts and power steering. But the numbers of car collisions and collision-related injuries did not decline that year.

Reasoning *What could explain why the newly required safety features did not reduce the numbers of collisions and collision-related injuries in 1966?* The passage says that power steering helps to prevent collisions and that safety belts help to prevent collision-related injuries. Since most Morodian cars previously lacked these features, and one-seventh of them were replaced with new cars in 1966, the proportion of cars with these features must have increased that year. This should have reduced the numbers of collisions and collision-related injuries unless some other factor counteracted the reductions. Evidence of any such countervailing factor would help to explain why the numbers did not decrease.

A Increased usage of safety belts should have reduced the number of collision-related injuries, so it would not help explain why this number did not decrease.

B If the new cars bought in 1966 were mostly purchased early in the year, the increased proportion of cars with the newly required safety features should have started more significantly reducing the numbers of collisions and collision-related injuries early in the year, producing greater reductions for the year as a whole.

C However, many cars were replaced in the year before the safety features were required, in 1966 the replacement of one-seventh of all Morodian cars should still have increased the overall proportion of Morodian cars with the safety features and thus reduced the numbers of collisions and collision-related injuries.

D **Correct.** If many owners of the cars with the new safety features drove less cautiously, their recklessness could have increased the overall numbers of collisions and collision-related injuries despite any benefits from the safety features.

E Strict quality-control inspections should have made the safety features more reliable, further reducing the numbers of collisions and collision-related injuries.

The correct answer is D.

CR04882
641. Enterprise Bank currently requires customers with checking accounts to maintain a minimum balance or pay a monthly fee. Enterprise plans to offer accounts with no monthly fee and no minimum-balance requirement; to cover their projected administrative costs of $3 per account per month they plan to charge $30 for overdrawing an account. Since each month on average slightly more than 10 percent of Enterprise's customers overdraw their accounts, bank officials predict the new accounts will generate a profit.

Which of the following, if true, most strongly supports the bank officials' prediction?

(A) Some of Enterprise Bank's current checking account customers are expected to switch to the new accounts once they are offered.

(B) One third of Enterprise Bank's revenues are currently derived from monthly fees tied to checking accounts.

(C) Many checking account customers who occasionally pay a fee for not maintaining a minimum balance in their account generally maintain a balance well above the minimum.

(D) Customers whose checking accounts do not have a minimum-balance requirement are more likely than others to overdraw their checking accounts.

(E) Customers whose checking accounts do not have a minimum-balance requirement are more likely than others to write checks for small amounts.

Evaluation of a Plan

Situation Enterprise Bank gives customers checking accounts with no monthly fee provided they maintain a certain minimum balance. However, the bank plans to offer accounts with no minimum-balance requirement and no monthly fee. It plans to cover the bank's $3 per account per month administrative cost by charging a $30 penalty for overdrafts. Only slightly more than 10 percent of customers, on average, overdraw their accounts in a month. The bank officials predict the new accounts will generate a profit.

Reasoning *What new information, if accurate, would most strongly support the prediction?* If about only one customer in ten, on average, currently has an overdraft in a month, and if this trend continues among customers who sign up for the new account, then the proposed $30 penalty per overdraft will cover the $30 cost of maintaining checking accounts for 10 customers per month. Would removing the minimum-balance requirement significantly increase the 10 percent overdraft rate? If so, then significantly more than one in ten customers, on average, would pay a $30 penalty. If this were so, then the new plan would yield a profit, as predicted.

A "Some" might mean only a few, and this would probably not be sufficient to make the new plan significantly profitable.

B This suggests that many customers with the current minimum-balance no-monthly-fee account do not maintain the minimum-balance requirement and pay fees instead. However, this information by itself seems to have little bearing on the new plan.

C Such customers would be likely to overdraw their accounts less frequently. This suggests that if a preponderance of the customers for the proposed new account were such customers, the overdraft rate would decrease, and the proposed new account would be less profitable, or even unprofitable.

D **Correct.** This information provides strong support for the bank officials' prediction. It indicates that the currently roughly 10 percent overdraft rate might increase drastically with the no-minimum-balance account and, on average, cause the imposition of a $30 penalty on significantly more than 10 percent of customers per month. This would make the new account significantly profitable.

E This suggests that a check written by one of these customers is more likely to be for a small amount and is therefore somewhat less likely to cause an overdraft (unless such customers typically have small checking balances, which we are not told). If there were many such customers for the proposed new account, the overdraft rate might be less than 10 percent; this would indicate that the new account might not turn out to be profitable.

The correct answer is D.

CR05667
642. In virtually any industry, technological improvements increase labor productivity, which is the output of goods and services per person-hour worked. In Parland's industries, labor productivity is significantly higher than it is in Vergia's industries. Clearly, therefore, Parland's industries must, on the whole, be further advanced technologically than Vergia's are.

The argument is most vulnerable to which of the following criticisms?

(A) It offers a conclusion that is no more than a paraphrase of one of the pieces of information provided in its support.
(B) It presents as evidence in support of a claim information that is inconsistent with other evidence presented in support of the same claim.
(C) It takes one possible cause of a condition to be the actual cause of that condition without considering any other possible causes.
(D) It takes a condition to be the effect of something that happened only after the condition already existed.
(E) It makes a distinction that presupposes the truth of the conclusion that is to be established.

Argument Evaluation

Situation | Technological improvements in nearly every industry increase labor productivity, which is the output of goods and services per person-hour worked. Because labor productivity is significantly higher in Parland than Vergia, Parland's industries are, in general, more technologically advanced than Vergia's.

Reasoning | *To which criticism is the argument most vulnerable?* Though one factor, such as technological advancements, may lead to greater labor productivity, it may not be the only such factor, or even a necessary factor, leading to great labor productivity. Therefore, the mere fact that one region's labor is more productive than another's is not sufficient to establish that the former region is more technologically advanced than the latter region is.

A   The conclusion is not merely a paraphrase of the pieces of information provided in its support. Indeed, the problem with the argument is that the conclusion goes too far beyond what the premises merit.
B   The premises of the argument are not inconsistent with one another.
C   **Correct.** This accurately describes the flaw in the argument because the reasons given in the argument for its conclusion would be good reasons only if there were no other plausible explanations for Parland's greater labor productivity.
D   The argument does not mention how long Parland has had more productive labor, or when technological improvements would have occurred.
E   Neither of the premises contains anything that presupposes the conclusion to be true.

The correct answer is C.

CR08471
643. Chaco Canyon, a settlement of the ancient Anasazi culture in North America, had massive buildings. **It must have been a major Anasazi center**. Analysis of wood samples shows that some of the timber for the buildings came from the Chuska and San Mateo mountains, 50 miles from Chaco Canyon. **Only a major cultural center would have the organizational power to import timber from 50 miles away**.

In the argument given, the two portions in boldface play which of the following roles?

(A) The first is a premise used to support the argument's main conclusion; the second is the argument's main conclusion.

(B) The first is the argument's main conclusion; the second is a premise used to support that conclusion.

(C) The first is one of two premises used to support the argument's main conclusion; the second is the other of those two premises.

(D) The first is a premise used to support the argument's main conclusion; the second is a premise used to support another conclusion drawn in the argument.

(E) The first is inferred from another statement in the argument; the second is inferred from the first.

Argument Construction

Situation　The ancient Anasazi settlement at Chaco Canyon had massive buildings, for which some of the timber came from mountains 50 miles away.

Reasoning　*What roles do the statement that Chaco Canyon must have been a major Anasazi center and the statement that only a major center would have the organizational power to import timber from 50 miles away play in the argument?* The first and third sentences in the passage are both factual observations. Since no further support is provided for either of them, neither can be a conclusion in the argument. The fourth sentence is a speculative generalization about major cultural centers. None of the other statements gives us any reason to think this generalization is true, so it cannot be a conclusion in the argument, either. However, the third and fourth sentences together imply that Chaco Canyon was a major cultural center, and the first sentence indicates that it was Anasazi. So together, the first, third, and fourth sentences all support the claim that Chaco Canyon was a major Anasazi cultural center and thus more generally a major Anasazi center, as the second sentence asserts. Therefore, the first, third, and fourth sentences are all premises that jointly support the second sentence as a conclusion.

A　As explained above, the first boldface sentence is a conclusion supported by the latter, not the other way around.

B　**Correct.** As explained above, the first boldface sentence is the argument's only stated conclusion, and in that sense its main conclusion, while all the other sentences are premises used to support it.

C　As explained above, the first boldface sentence is the argument's conclusion, not a premise used to support the conclusion.

D　As explained above, the first boldface sentence is the argument's only stated conclusion, and there is no reason to suppose that the argument is intended to lead to any other tacit conclusion that the second boldface sentence is intended to support.

E　As explained above, the first boldface sentence is inferred from the three other statements in the argument together, not from any one of them alone. The second boldface sentence is a speculative generalization that cannot be, and is not meant to be, inferred from the former or from any other statement in the argument.

The correct answer is B.

CR04364
644. The Maxilux car company's design for its new luxury model, the Max 100, included a special design for the tires that was intended to complement the model's image. The winning bid for supplying these tires was submitted by Rubco. Analysts concluded that the bid would only just cover Rubco's costs on the tires, but Rubco executives claim that winning the bid will actually make a profit for the company.

Which of the following, if true, most strongly justifies the claim made by Rubco's executives?

(A) In any Maxilux model, the spare tire is exactly the same make and model as the tires that are mounted on the wheels.
(B) Rubco holds exclusive contracts to supply Maxilux with the tires for a number of other models made by Maxilux.
(C) The production facilities for the Max 100 and those for the tires to be supplied by Rubco are located very near each other.
(D) When people who have purchased a carefully designed luxury automobile need to replace a worn part of it, they almost invariably replace it with a part of exactly the same make and type.
(E) When Maxilux awarded the tire contract to Rubco, the only criterion on which Rubco's bid was clearly ahead of its competitors' bids was price.

Argument Construction

Situation   Rubco won a bid for supplying tires for the Max 100, a new luxury model by Maxilux. The bid would barely cover the cost of the tires, but Rubco executives claim that winning the bid will be profitable.

Reasoning   *What would support the executives' claim?* Rubco is not expected to make a profit from supplying the tires for the new cars, so we must look for some other way that Rubco could derive a profit as a result of winning the bid. If by winning the bid Rubco created an inevitable market for itself in replacement tires—on which Rubco could earn a profit—then the executives' claim may be justified.

A   We have already been told that the bid is expected to barely cover the costs of supplying the tires on the new cars, so the analysts mentioned in the passage have presumably already taken into account that there is a spare tire supplied for the Max 100.

B   If winning the bid led Rubco to win more exclusive contracts with the Maxilux, that might help support the executives' claim. But this statement indicates only that Rubco already has several exclusive contracts to supply Maxilux with tires, not that winning the bid has led to, or will lead to, more such contracts, which is what would be needed.

C   As in answer choice (A), this is relevant to the costs of supplying the tires for the Max 100, but presumably this was taken into account by the analysts when they concluded that the bid would barely cover Rubco's costs on the tires.

D   **Correct.** This indicates that by winning the bid Rubco has created a way to profit from the contract with Maxilux, specifically, by creating a market for replacement tires.

E   This is likely one of the reasons that Rubco's bid only just covers Rubco's costs on the tires; it does nothing to justify the executives' claims that the bid will lead to a profit for Rubco.

The correct answer is D.

8.7 Critical Reasoning Answer Explanations

CR05186

645. Which of the following most logically completes the passage?

Most bicycle helmets provide good protection for the top and back of the head, but little or no protection for the temple regions on the sides of the head. A study of head injuries resulting from bicycle accidents showed that a large proportion were caused by blows to the temple area. Therefore, if bicycle helmets protected this area, the risk of serious head injury in bicycle accidents would be greatly reduced, especially since _____.

(A) among the bicyclists included in the study's sample of head injuries, only a very small proportion had been wearing a helmet at the time of their accident

(B) even those bicyclists who regularly wear helmets have a poor understanding of the degree and kind of protection that helmets afford

(C) a helmet that included protection for the temples would have to be somewhat larger and heavier than current helmets

(D) the bone in the temple area is relatively thin and impacts in that area are thus very likely to cause brain injury

(E) bicyclists generally land on their arm or shoulder when they fall to the side, which reduces the likelihood of severe impacts on the side of the head

Argument Construction

Situation Bicycle helmets protect the top and back of the head, but not the sides or temples. A study found that a large proportion of head injuries caused by biking accidents were caused by blows to the temple area.

Reasoning *Why would the risk of serious head injury in bicycle accidents be greatly reduced if bicycle helmets protected the temple regions?* If for some reason a serious head injury is particularly likely when there is impact to the temple area, then bicycle helmets that protect that area would be apt to reduce the number of serious head injuries from bicycle accidents. One such reason is that the bone in the temple area is relatively thin.

A   This point is irrelevant because it gives us no information about the seriousness or the likelihood of injuries due to impact to the temple area.

B   Whether bicyclists who regularly wear helmets have a good understanding of what protection their helmets afford is not relevant as to whether serious head injuries are particularly likely to occur from impact to the temple area.

C   This point is relevant only to what a helmet that protected the temple area would be like, not to the seriousness of injuries resulting from impact to that area. If anything, this point counts as a reason *against* the conclusion, not *for* it. If such helmets are heavier and larger, they may be used less than they otherwise would be. If fewer helmets are used, then improvements to helmet design will have less of an effect in reducing serious head injuries.

D   **Correct.** This statement provides a reason why the temple area of the rider's head needs protection: impacts to this area are very likely to cause brain injuries.

E   This is largely irrelevant. Even if it suggests that head injuries do not generally result from bicyclists falling to the side, it does not indicate that such injuries are rare or that there is not great risk of serious injury in those cases in which there is impact to the temple area.

The correct answer is D.

CR01867
646. Which of the following most logically completes the argument?

In a typical year, Innovair's airplanes are involved in 35 collisions while parked or being towed in airports, with a resulting yearly cost of $1,000,000 for repairs.

To reduce the frequency of ground collisions, Innovair will begin giving its ground crews additional training, at an annual cost of $500,000. Although this will cut the number of ground collisions by about half at best, the drop in repair costs can be expected to be much greater, since _____.

(A) most ground collisions happen when ground crews are rushing to minimize the time a delayed airplane spends on the ground
(B) a ground collision typically occurs when there are no passengers on the airplane
(C) the additional training will focus on helping ground crews avoid those kinds of ground collisions that cause the most costly damage
(D) the $500,000 cost figure for the additional training of ground crews includes the wages that those crews will earn during the time spent in actual training
(E) most ground collisions have been caused by the least experienced ground-crew members

Evaluation of a Plan

Situation   An airline will give its ground crews additional training to reduce the frequency of the collisions its airplanes are involved in while parked or being towed in airports.

Reasoning   *What premise would most logically support the conclusion that the additional training will reduce repair costs from ground collisions much more than it reduces the number of such collisions?* The key word *since* before the blank shows that the argument should be completed with a premise that supports the preceding claim that the *drop in repair costs can be expected to be much greater*. A suitable premise might provide evidence that the training will disproportionately help to prevent the ground collisions that result in the higher repair costs as opposed to the less serious collisions that result in lower repair costs.

A   We are given no reason to believe that the additional training would affect how much ground crews rush to minimize delays.
B   The number of passengers is not clearly relevant to the repair costs resulting from a ground collision and in any case would not be affected by additional ground crew training.
C   **Correct.** If the training especially helps the ground crews avoid those kinds of collisions that cause the most costly damage, then it will probably reduce repair costs even more than it reduces the number of collisions.
D   Whether the cited expense for training includes wages is irrelevant to whether the training will reduce repair costs more than it reduces the number of collisions.
E   This suggests that the additional training may help reduce the number of collisions, not that it will reduce repair costs more than it reduces the number of collisions.

The correct answer is C.

CR12558
647. Many agriculturally intensive areas of the world are beginning to encounter water scarcity problems. As a result, many farmers in these areas are likely to reduce their output as the water supply they need in order to maintain production shrinks. However, one group of farmers in such a region plans to increase their production by implementing techniques for water conservation.

Which of the following, if true, would most strongly support the prediction that the group's plan will succeed?

(A) Farmers who can gain a larger share of the food market in their regions will be better positioned to control more water resources.
(B) Most agricultural practices in areas with water shortages are water-intensive.
(C) Other regions of the world not facing water shortages are likely to make up for the reduction in agricultural output.
(D) Demand for agricultural products in the group's region is not expected to decline.
(E) More than half the water used for agriculture in the farmers' region is lost to evaporation or leakage from irrigation channels.

Evaluation of a Plan

Situation   Farmers in many agriculturally intensive regions will probably reduce their output because the regions' water supplies are dwindling, but one group of farmers in such a region plans to use water conservation techniques to increase their output.

Reasoning   *What would provide evidence that water conservation techniques will help the farmers increase production despite their region's dwindling water supplies?* In order for the water conservation techniques to be effective, they must result in significantly more water becoming available for the farmers to use. Because overall supplies are shrinking, rather than growing, that can only happen if the farmers are currently losing or wasting a great deal of water in ways that could be prevented with water conservation techniques.

A   This suggests an advantage the farmers will gain if their water conservation plan enables them to increase production, but it provides no evidence that the plan actually will enable them to increase production.

B   This suggests that the plan would have to yield quite a lot of conserved water in order for the farmers to increase production, but it offers no evidence that the plan will do so. Thus, it provides some reason to question whether the plan will succeed.

C   Whether regions without water shortages will increase production is not directly relevant to the question of whether a particular measure would lead to increased production in one region that does have a water shortage.

D   This has some slight, indirect relevance to the question of whether the farmers' plan will succeed: it suggests that if the farmers do manage to increase production, they will continue to have a market for what they produce. However, it does not address the issue of whether they will be able to increase production. Furthermore, even if demand for agricultural products in the group's region were expected to decline, it could still remain high enough to support the farmers' increased output from their water conservation plan.

E   **Correct.** This suggests that the farmers are losing a lot of water in ways that the water conservation techniques might prevent, so it provides evidence that employing some such techniques could enable the farmers to save enough water to increase their output.

The correct answer is E.

CR03367
648. Hollywood restaurant is replacing some of its standard tables with tall tables and stools. The restaurant already fills every available seat during its operating hours, and the change in seating arrangements will not result in an increase in the restaurant's seating capacity. Nonetheless, the restaurant's management expects revenue to increase as a result of the seating change without any concurrent change in menu, prices, or operating hours.

Which of the following, if true, provides the best reason for the expectation?

(A) One of the taller tables takes up less floor space than one of the standard tables.

(B) Diners seated on stools typically do not linger over dinner as long as diners seated at standard tables.

(C) Since the restaurant will replace only some of its standard tables, it can continue to accommodate customers who do not care for the taller tables.

(D) Few diners are likely to avoid the restaurant because of the new seating arrangement.

(E) The standard tables being replaced by tall tables would otherwise have to be replaced with new standard tables at a greater expense.

Argument Construction

Situation Hollywood restaurant is replacing some of its tables with taller tables and stools, and the management expects this will increase revenue, despite the fact that the restaurant already fills all of its available seats and that this change will not increase seating capacity. Furthermore, there will not be any change in menu, prices, or operating hours.

Reasoning *What would strongly support the management's expectation?* Since the new seating will not increase the restaurant's seating capacity, the management's expectations must be based on a belief that the change to taller tables and stools will somehow change diners' behavior, perhaps by leading them to order more food, or to stay at their tables for a shorter time, thereby allowing the restaurant to serve more diners during its operating hours without increasing seating capacity. If diners seated at tall tables and on tall stools spend less time lingering over their dinners, then they will leave sooner, opening up the tables for more diners. Because the restaurant, before the change, already fills every available seat during its operating hours, it is reasonable to think that it will be able to serve more diners than it currently does, thereby selling more food and thus increasing revenue.

A This would be relevant if we could infer from it that seating capacity will increase. However, the passage indicates that the new seating arrangement will not result in greater capacity.

B **Correct.** Because the restaurant will be able to serve more meals during its operating hours, the restaurant's revenue can be expected to increase.

C This may indicate that the restaurant is less likely to alienate customers who do not care for tall tables and stools, but that only supports the claim that the restaurant will not lose customers and therefore lose revenue; it does not indicate that the restaurant will see revenue increase.

D Again, this merely indicates that there will not be a loss—or much loss—of revenue, not that there will be an increase in revenue.

E Less expensive tables will decrease the restaurant's costs, but it will not increase the restaurant's revenue.

The correct answer is B.

CR07660
649. A major network news organization experienced a drop in viewership in the week following the airing of a controversial report on the economy. The network also received a very large number of complaints regarding the report. The network, however, maintains that negative reactions to the report had nothing to do with its loss of viewers.

Which of the following, if true, most strongly supports the network's position?

(A) The other major network news organizations reported similar reductions in viewership during the same week.
(B) The viewers who registered complaints with the network were regular viewers of the news organization's programs.
(C) Major network news organizations publicly attribute drops in viewership to their own reports only when they receive complaints about those reports.
(D) This was not the first time that this network news organization has aired a controversial report on the economy that has inspired viewers to complain to the network.
(E) Most network news viewers rely on network news broadcasts as their primary source of information regarding the economy.

Argument Construction

Situation   A major network news organization aired a controversial report on the economy, and the following week the network's viewership declined. The network claims that the loss of viewers was not connected with negative reactions to the report.

Reasoning   *Which statement most strongly supports the network's position?* If other major news network organizations had similar drops in viewership, it is implausible to think that the controversial report accounted for the other organizations' drops in viewership. On the other hand, it is not implausible to suppose that whatever did cause the drop in the viewership experienced by other network news organizations—e.g., holidays, weather, popular non-news programming—also had that effect on the organization that ran the controversial report. This would give some reason to believe that it was not the report that accounts for the organization's drop in viewership.

A **Correct.** This statement indicates that something other than the airing of the report could account for the subsequent drop in the organization's viewership.
B If anything, this statement tends to undermine the network's claim, because it suggests that the report offended people who otherwise might have continued to watch the organization's programming.
C Since the network did in fact receive complaints about the report, this statement is irrelevant.
D The fact that the network has received complaints before about controversial reports on the economy that the network's news organization has aired tells us nothing about whether this recent report caused a subsequent drop in viewership.
E The fact that viewers turn to network news broadcasts as their primary source of information about the economy tells us nothing about whether viewers might stop watching a particular network news organization's programs as a result of its airing a controversial report on the economy.

The correct answer is A.

CR04366
650. Only a reduction of 10 percent in the number of scheduled flights using Greentown's airport will allow the delays that are so common there to be avoided. Hevelia airstrip, 40 miles away, would, if upgraded and expanded, be an attractive alternative for fully 20 percent of the passengers using Greentown airport. Nevertheless, experts reject the claim that turning Hevelia into a full-service airport would end the chronic delays at Greentown.

Which of the following, if true, most helps to justify the experts' position?

(A) Turning Hevelia into a full-service airport would require not only substantial construction at the airport itself, but also the construction of new access highways.

(B) A second largely undeveloped airstrip close to Greentown airport would be a more attractive alternative than Hevelia for many passengers who now use Greentown.

(C) Hevelia airstrip lies in a relatively undeveloped area but would, if it became a full-service airport, be a magnet for commercial and residential development.

(D) If an airplane has to wait to land, the extra jet fuel required adds significantly to the airline's costs.

(E) Several airlines use Greentown as a regional hub, so that most flights landing at Greentown have many passengers who then take different flights to reach their final destinations.

Evaluation of a Plan

Situation   To avoid the delays now common at Greentown's airport, the number of scheduled flights there would need to be reduced by 10 percent. If the nearby Hevelia airstrip were expanded and upgraded, it would be an attractive alternative for 20 percent of Greentown airport's passengers. Still, experts do not believe that the delays at Greentown would end even if Hevelia were turned into a full-service airport.

Reasoning   *Which statement most supports the experts' position?* If the number of flights at Greentown's airport did not drop by at least 10 percent, despite the fact that 20 percent of the passengers who currently use Greentown's airport would find nearby Hevelia airstrip an attractive alternative, then the delays would not be avoided. Airlines generally use certain airports as regional hubs—an airport through which an airline routes most of its traffic—so, even if many passengers would be willing to use Hevelia airstrip, the number of flights at Greentown may not decline significantly, or at all.

A   The experts' position concerns what would happen to the flight delays at Greentown airport if the Hevelia airstrip were converted into a full-service airport. So the fact that there are great costs involved in making such a conversion—possibly making such a conversion unlikely—has no bearing on the effects such a conversion would have on flight delays at Greentown if the conversion were to be carried out.

B   This statement indicates that the undeveloped airstrip near Greentown might be a better way to alleviate flight delays at Greentown, but it tells us nothing about the effects that converting the Hevelia airstrip to a full-service airport would have were it to be carried out.

C   This in no way explains why converting the Hevelia airstrip into a full-service airport would not alleviate the problem with flight delays at Greentown.

D   This provides a reason to think that reducing the number of flights at Greentown might make the airport more efficient. But that has no bearing on the effect that converting the Hevelia airstrip to a full-service airport might have on flight delays at Greentown.

E   **Correct.** This statement provides support for the experts' position because it gives a reason for thinking that the number of scheduled flights at Greentown would not be reduced, even if Hevelia airstrip became an attractive alternative for some 20 percent of Greentown's passengers.

The correct answer is E.

651. Farmer: Worldwide, just three grain crops—rice, wheat, and corn—account for most human caloric intake. To maintain this level of caloric intake and also keep pace with global population growth, yields per acre from each of these crops will have to increase at least 1.5 percent every year, given that the supply of cultivated land is diminishing. Therefore, the government should increase funding for research into new ways to improve yields.

Which of the following is an assumption on which the farmer's argument depends?

(A) It is solely the government's responsibility to ensure that the amount of rice, wheat, and corn produced worldwide keeps pace with global population growth.

(B) Increasing government funding for research into new ways to improve the yields per acre of rice, wheat, and corn crops would help to increase total worldwide annual production of food from these crops.

(C) Increasing the yields per acre of rice, wheat, and corn is more important than increasing the yields per acre of other crops.

(D) Current levels of funding for research into ways of improving grain crop yields per acre have enabled grain crop yields per acre to increase by more than 1.5 percent per year worldwide.

(E) In coming decades, rice, wheat, and corn will become a minor part of human caloric intake, unless there is government-funded research to increase their yields per acre.

Argument Construction

Situation The farmer states that although the worldwide human population is increasing, the supply of cultivated land is decreasing. We thus need to increase yields for the food crops that account for most of human caloric intake—rice, wheat, and corn—if we are to maintain our existing caloric intake. The increase in yields, according to the farmer, would need to be at least 1.5 percent every year.

Reasoning *What must be true if we are to accept the farmer's conclusion, that the government should increase funding for research into new ways to improve crop yields, on the basis of the above statements?* The farmer uses the above statements as premises of an argument for an increase in government funding for research on crop yields. Supposing that the farmer's statements are true, we need to find in the available options the statement that, if added to the argument, may allow us to accept the farmer's conclusion, based on the argument.

A Whether or not nongovernmental entities such as NGOs (nongovernmental organizations) are responsible for helping to ensure that humans have an adequate amount of food, governments may or may not also have this responsibility.

B **Correct.** If government funding of this research does not increase crop yields, then the premises of the argument provide no support for the conclusion that the government should provide such funding. The cogency of the argument thus depends on this statement.

C Crops in addition to rice, wheat, and corn could also be very important, and perhaps essential for human existence. However, this would not diminish the importance of food crops such as rice, wheat, and corn.

D This option may suggest that current levels of funding of research into crop yields are sufficient for purposes of our obtaining the necessary crop yields.

E This option suggests that rice, wheat, and corn may be replaced by other crops, because the other crops have better yields. Because we might thus have a means for increasing crop yields that does not involve an increase in government research funding, this option may actually decrease the support for the conclusion.

The correct answer is B.

CR08770
652. The air quality board recently informed Coffee Roast, a small coffee roasting firm, of a complaint regarding the smoke from its roaster. Recently enacted air quality regulations require machines roasting more than 10 pounds of coffee to be equipped with expensive smoke-dissipating afterburners. The firm, however, roasts only 8 pounds of coffee at a time. Nevertheless, the company has decided to purchase and install an afterburner.

Which of the following, if true, most strongly supports the firm's decision?

(A) Until settling on the new air quality regulations, the board had debated whether to require afterburners for machines roasting more than 5 pounds of coffee at a time.
(B) Coffee roasted in a machine equipped with an afterburner has its flavor subtly altered.
(C) The cost to the firm of an afterburner is less than the cost of replacing its roaster with a smaller one.
(D) Fewer complaints are reported in areas that maintain strict rules regarding afterburners.
(E) The firm has reason to fear that negative publicity regarding the complaints could result in lost sales.

Evaluation of a Plan

Situation   After being informed of a complaint about smoke from its coffee roaster, a firm decided to purchase and install an afterburner to reduce or eliminate emissions of smoke, even though the roaster roasts too little coffee at a time for an afterburner to be legally required.

Reasoning   *What would have been a good reason for the firm to buy and install the afterburner?* The only factors mentioned that might give the firm reason to buy an afterburner are the complaint about smoke and the regulations requiring an afterburner. Since the regulations do not apply in this case, the complaint is more likely to have motivated the firm's decision. Any serious potential consequences the firm might have faced from failure to address the complaint could have provided a good reason to buy and install the afterburner.

A   If this debate had still been ongoing when the firm made its decision, uncertainty about the pending regulations might have justified the decision. But the debate had already been settled before the firm decided to purchase the afterburner, and the regulations clearly did not require one.

B   An unspecified alteration in flavor is not clearly a good reason to use an afterburner—the afterburner might worsen the flavor.

C   The firm's roaster was already small enough that the regulations did not require it to be replaced, even without an afterburner.

D   This reason relates only to rules regarding afterburners, not to Coffee Roast's purchase of an afterburner, which was not mandated by regulations. Furthermore, it could be that the air quality regulations recently enacted are among the strictest in any region, which could result in fewer complaints regardless of whether Coffee Roast installs an afterburner.

E   **Correct.** Since installing an afterburner is a plausible way to address the complaint and prevent future complaints, the firm has plausible reasons to believe this strategy will help it avoid the negative publicity and lost sales it fears. These considerations could have reasonably justified its decision.

The correct answer is E.

CR03695
653. People who do regular volunteer work tend to live longer, on average, than people who do not. It has been found that "doing good," a category that certainly includes volunteer work, releases endorphins, the brain's natural opiates, which induce in people a feeling of well-being. Clearly, there is a connection: Regular releases of endorphins must in some way help to extend people's lives.

Which of the following, if true, most seriously undermines the force of the evidence given as support for the hypothesis that endorphins promote longevity?

(A) People who do regular volunteer work are only somewhat more likely than others to characterize the work they do for a living as "doing good."
(B) Although extremely high levels of endorphins could be harmful to health, such levels are never reached as a result of the natural release of endorphins.
(C) There are many people who have done some volunteer work but who do not do such work regularly.
(D) People tend not to become involved in regular volunteer work unless they are healthy and energetic to begin with.
(E) Releases of endorphins are responsible for the sense of well-being experienced by many long-distance runners while running.

Argument Evaluation

Situation: People who volunteer regularly live longer on average than people who do not. Doing good work, including volunteer work, releases endorphins, which induce a feeling of well-being.

Reasoning: *What additional findings would suggest that the cited evidence does not indicate that endorphins increase longevity?* The argument implicitly assumes that the reason regular volunteers tend to live longer is that volunteering lengthens their lives. It further assumes that no factor that is correlated with volunteering, other than the endorphin release, would plausibly explain how volunteering could have this effect. Findings that cast doubt on either of these assumptions would undermine the connection between the cited evidence and the conclusion that endorphins promote longevity.

A Volunteering might greatly boost volunteers' endorphin levels even if the work the volunteers do for a living is no different from other people's work.
B Even if unnaturally high endorphin levels could harm health, the levels attainable through volunteer work may promote health.
C The argument is about an observed correlation in a certain group of people (those who regularly do volunteer work). How many people are outside that group (i.e., do not regularly do volunteer work) is independent of the question of what causes the observed correlation. Even if some people volunteer only occasionally, volunteering regularly may promote longevity by causing regular releases of endorphins.
D **Correct.** This suggests that the initially better health of people who choose to volunteer could fully explain the cited correlation between volunteering and longevity.
E Unless we are also given evidence that long-distance runners tend not to live longer than other people, this does not undermine the purported evidence in the argument. Endorphins might promote longevity in both regular volunteers and long-distance runners.

The correct answer is D.

CR04140
654. A study compared a sample of Swedish people older than 75 who needed in-home assistance with a similar sample of Israeli people. The people in the two samples received both informal assistance, provided by family and friends, and formal assistance, professionally provided. Although Sweden and Israel have equally well-funded and comprehensive systems for providing formal assistance, the study found that the people in the Swedish sample received more formal assistance, on average, than those in the Israeli sample.

Which of the following, if true, does most to explain the difference that the study found?

(A) A companion study found that among children needing special in-home care, the amount of formal assistance they received was roughly the same in Sweden as in Israel.

(B) More Swedish than Israeli people older than 75 live in rural areas where formal assistance services are sparse or nonexistent.

(C) Although in both Sweden and Israel much of the funding for formal assistance ultimately comes from the central government, the local structures through which assistance is delivered are different in the two countries.

(D) In recent decades, the increase in life expectancy of someone who is 75 years old has been greater in Israel than in Sweden.

(E) In Israel, people older than 75 tend to live with their children, whereas in Sweden people of that age tend to live alone.

Argument Construction

Situation   A study of elder care in Israel and Sweden found that in Sweden, of the total amount of care that people older than 75 and needing in-home assistance received, the proportion of care that was formal, i.e., provided by professional care personnel, was greater than in Israel. Both Sweden and Israel had equally good systems for providing formal care, and in both countries, the elderly also received informal care, i.e., care provided by friends and family.

Reasoning   *Among the factors given, which would most contribute to explaining the difference the study found between Sweden and Israel with respect to elder care?* A good guess would be that there is a difference in some societal factor that affects the difference the study found. For example, perhaps elders in one of the countries regard maintaining independence as a higher priority than elders in the other and consequently try to rely less on friends and family? Perhaps patterns of decline in ability to remain independent are different in the two countries? Or perhaps a greater proportion of elders live alone in one of the countries than in the other?

A   The difference to be explained concerns only elder care, not care of children.

B   The fact that formal elder care is less available in Swedish rural areas than in Israeli rural areas might suggest that there would be a greater reliance on informal care in such areas in Sweden. But this new information throws little light on how the overall proportions of formal and informal care in each country would be affected.

C   This information is not specific enough to help explain the precise difference found in the study. It is reasonable to assume that the study was conducted with sufficient rigor to take account of any relevant structural differences in the delivery of formal elder care.

D   This could suggest either that the greater proportion of informal elder care in Israel contributes to greater life expectancy or that greater life expectancy signals greater fitness during old age that would make it more practical for friends and family to provide informal elder care.

E   **Correct.** The prevalence in Israel of elders living in family settings—in contrast to Sweden, where elders tend to live alone—offers a plausible explanation of the difference that the study found in the patterns of elder care in Israel and Sweden. It seems reasonable to think that, all things being equal, elders living alone would use formal elder care services more often than elders living with friends or family.

The correct answer is E.

CR05077
655. Film Director: It is true that certain characters and plot twists in my newly released film *The Big Heist* are similar to characters and plot twists in *Thieves*, a movie that came out last year. Pointing to these similarities, the film studio that produced *Thieves* is now accusing me of taking ideas from that film. The accusation is clearly without merit. All production work on *The Big Heist* was actually completed months before *Thieves* was released.

Which of the following, if true, provides the strongest support for the director's position?

(A) Before *Thieves* began production, its script had been circulating for several years among various film studios, including the studio that produced *The Big Heist*.

(B) The characters and plot twists that are most similar in the two films have close parallels in many earlier films of the same genre.

(C) The film studio that produced *Thieves* seldom produces films in this genre.

(D) The director of *Thieves* worked with the director of *The Big Heist* on several earlier projects.

(E) Production work on *Thieves* began before production work on *The Big Heist* was started.

Argument Evaluation

Situation The director of the film *The Big Heist* has been accused, by the studio that produced the film *Thieves*, of taking ideas from the film. The director responds that the accusation lacks merit, since all production work on *The Big Heist* was completed before *Thieves* appeared last year in theaters.

Reasoning *Which of the five statements most strongly supports the director's position?* Crime thrillers, as a film genre, are likely to have stock characters and plot lines that reflect a long tradition. So it would be no surprise if some of the characters or plot twists in one such film would resemble, to a greater or lesser extent, the characters and plot twists in another. The studio might be correct in identifying such resemblances between *The Big Heist* and *Thieves*. But it would not necessarily be correct that characters or plot lines in *The Big Heist* were derived from *Thieves*.

A This undercuts the director's position, since it provides information that indicates an opportunity for the director to copy ideas from the script for *Thieves*.

B **Correct.** This information strengthens the support for the director's claim that the studio's accusation lacks merit. Since both *Thieves* and *The Big Heist* fall within a long tradition of crime thriller films, the characters and plot lines in both films reflect that tradition, and so any resemblances do not imply deliberate copying of the ideas in *Thieves* by the director of *The Big Heist*.

C This information seems largely irrelevant to the issue raised and does not strengthen support for the director's conclusion.

D This does little to indicate that the director's conclusion is correct. For example, the then-future director of *Thieves* might have discussed with the future director of *The Big Heist* specific ideas about character and plot for a planned crime thriller film.

E This does not support the director's claim. For example, it raises the possibility that information about *Thieves* leaked during the early stages of production—information that could have been exploited in the production of *The Big Heist*.

The correct answer is B.

CR05412
656. In Mernia commercial fossil hunters often sell important fossils they have found, not to universities or museums, but to individual collectors, who pay much better but generally do not allow researchers access to their collections. To increase the number of fossils available for research, some legislators propose requiring all fossils that are found in Mernia to be sold only to universities or museums.

Which of the following, if true, most strongly indicates that the legislators' proposal will fail to achieve its goal?

(A) Some fossil hunters in Mernia are not commercial fossil hunters, but rather are amateurs who keep the fossils that they find.
(B) Most fossils found in Mernia are common types that have little scientific interest.
(C) Commercial fossil hunters in Mernia currently sell some of the fossils they find to universities and museums.
(D) Many universities in Mernia do not engage in fossil research.
(E) Most fossils are found by commercial fossil hunters, and they would give up looking for fossils if they were no longer allowed to sell to individual collectors.

Evaluation of a Plan

Situation Fossil hunters in Mernia often sell important fossils to collectors who do not make them accessible to researchers. To increase the number of fossils available for research, some legislators propose requiring all fossils found in Mernia to be sold only to universities or museums.

Reasoning *What would most strongly suggest that requiring all fossils found in Mernia to be sold only to universities or museums would not increase the number of fossils available for research?* To increase the number of fossils available for research, the proposed requirement will have to be implemented and effectively enforced. It will presumably have to increase the total number of fossils sold to universities and museums. And those institutions will have to make more of the fossils in their collections available to researchers than the private collectors do. Evidence that any of those conditions will not be fulfilled would suggest that the legislators' proposal will fail to achieve its goal.

A Even if the legislation does not affect fossils kept by amateurs, it might still result in many more fossils being sold to universities or museums rather than to private collectors, and thus might still increase the number of fossils available for research.

B Even if few Mernian fossils are interesting to researchers, the legislation could still achieve its goal of making more fossils available for research.

C Even if commercial fossil hunters already sell a few fossils to universities and museums, the legislation could encourage them to sell many more fossils.

D The universities that do not engage in fossil research presumably will not be interested in buying fossils even if the legislation passes. But the fossil hunters can just sell their fossils to other universities and museums that do engage in fossil research.

E **Correct.** This suggests that if the legislation passes, fossils will simply be left in the ground rather than sold to private collectors. That would not increase the total number of fossils available for research.

The correct answer is E.

CR02702

657. Economist: Tropicorp, which constantly seeks profitable investment opportunities, has been buying and clearing sections of tropical forest for cattle ranching, although pastures newly created there become useless for grazing after just a few years. The company has not gone into rubber tapping, even though greater profits can be made from rubber tapping, which leaves the forest intact. Thus, some environmentalists argue that **Tropicorp's actions do not serve even its own economic interest**. However, the initial investment required for a successful rubber-tapping operation is larger than that needed for a cattle ranch; there is a shortage of workers employable in rubber-tapping operations; and taxes are higher on profits from rubber tapping than on profits from cattle ranching. Consequently, **the environmentalists' conclusion is probably wrong**.

In the economist's argument, the two **boldface** portions play which of the following roles?

(A) The first supports the conclusion of the economist's argument; the second calls that conclusion into question.
(B) The first states the conclusion of the economist's argument; the second supports that conclusion.
(C) The first supports the conclusion of the environmentalists' argument; the second states that conclusion.
(D) The first states the conclusion of the environmentalists' argument; the second states the conclusion of the economist's argument.
(E) Each supports the conclusion of the economist's argument.

Argument Construction

Situation — According to an economist, the firm Tropicorp has been investing in tropical forest that it has cleared for cattle ranching. But its new pastures are useless for grazing after a few years. In contrast, rubber tapping—which would avoid cutting trees—could be more profitable. According to the economist, environmentalists consequently argue that Tropicorp's investment does not serve the firm's economic interest. However, the economist argues, investing in rubber tapping involves some potential costs and risks greater than those that investing in cattle ranching involves. Consequently, the economist argues, the environmentalists' conclusion is probably wrong.

Reasoning — *What function is served by the statement that Tropicorp's actions do not serve even its own economic interest? What function is served by the statement that the environmentalists' conclusion is probably wrong?* The first statement is a conclusion that the economist attributes to environmentalists. The second statement is the conclusion of an argument presented by the economist.

A   The first states the conclusion of the argument that is attributed to environmentalists; it does not support—nor is it meant to—the conclusion of the economist.
B   The second statement, not the first, is the conclusion of the economist's argument.
C   The first is the conclusion attributed to environmentalists and is not meant merely as support for that conclusion.
D   **Correct.** The first states the conclusion of the environmentalists' argument as the economist presents it; the second is the conclusion of the economist's argument.
E   Neither statement is meant as support for the economist's conclusion, nor does it offer such support.

The correct answer is D.

CR74231.01
658. Marketing executive for Magu Corporation: Whenever Magu opens a manufacturing facility in a new city, the company should sponsor, or make donations to, a number of nonprofit organizations in that city. Doing so would improve Magu's image in the community, and thus the money spent on such charitable ventures would lead to increased sales.

Which statement would, if true, point to the most serious weakness in the marketing executive's advice?

(A) Magu sells its products internationally, so sales in any one city represent only a small portion of total revenue.
(B) Spending on charitable ventures would require Magu to decrease direct advertisements, which are the most effective means of reaching its target customers.
(C) If market conditions change, Magu may have to close any such facility or relocate it.
(D) Some nonprofit organizations are poorly organized, so money donated to them would be of little benefit to the community.
(E) If workers at the manufacturing facility believed their wages or working conditions were poor, their complaints would outweigh any good impressions generated by Magu's donations or sponsorships.

Evaluation of a Plan

Situation A marketing executive for Magu Corporation argues that Magu can increase its sales if it sponsors or donates to nonprofit organizations in any city in which it opens a new manufacturing facility, because doing so would improve its image in that city and increase sales.

Reasoning *What would most strongly suggest that Magu would not increase sales even if it followed the plan proposed by the marketing executive?* Sponsoring or donating to nonprofit organizations would require the use of financial assets that therefore cannot be spent elsewhere. If as a result Magu had to cut other expenditures that drive sales more effectively than funding nonprofit organizations drives sales, the plan may not succeed.

A Because Magu sells its products internationally and no one city represents more than a small portion of revenue, any increase in sales in any given city will have only a slight effect on total sales; nonetheless, sales could still rise.

B **Correct.** If sponsoring or donating to a nonprofit would require Magu to reduce advertising, and advertising is the most effective means of reaching its target customers, then any positive influence on sales resulting from the charitable venture might be overwhelmed by a decrease in sales because of the advertising cuts.

C The fact that Magu might have to close or relocate one of these new facilities does not suggest that the marketing executive's plan would not work; Magu's image could, nonetheless, improve and sales could increase as a result.

D Even if some nonprofit organizations are poorly organized, others may not be, and Magu could limit its support to those.

E Even if such complaints from workers would outweigh any benefit arising from Magu's support of nonprofit organizations, this does not indicate that the marketing executive's plan will not work, because we have no reason to think that the workers will in fact be dissatisfied with their wages or working conditions.

The correct answer is B.

CR08831
659. Although the school would receive financial benefits if it had soft drink vending machines in the cafeteria, we should not allow them. Allowing soft drink machines there would not be in our students' interest. If our students start drinking more soft drinks, they will be less healthy.

The argument depends on which of the following?

(A) If the soft drink vending machines were placed in the cafeteria, students would consume more soft drinks as a result.
(B) The amount of soft drinks that most students at the school currently drink is not detrimental to their health.
(C) Students are apt to be healthier if they do not drink soft drinks at all than if they just drink small amounts occasionally.
(D) Students will not simply bring soft drinks from home if the soft drink vending machines are not placed in the cafeteria.
(E) The school's primary concern should be to promote good health among its students.

Argument Construction

Situation   Allowing soft drink vending machines in a school cafeteria would financially benefit the school, but students who drink more soft drinks would become less healthy.

Reasoning   *What must be true in order for the claim that students drinking more soft drinks would cause them to become less healthy to justify the conclusion that soft drink vending machines should not be allowed in the cafeteria?* The argument is that because drinking more soft drinks would be unhealthy for the students, allowing the vending machines would not be in the students' interest, so the vending machines should not be allowed. This reasoning depends on the implicit factual assumption that allowing the vending machines would result in the students drinking more soft drinks. It also depends on the implicit value judgment that receiving financial benefits should be less important to the school than preventing a situation that would make the students less healthy.

A   **Correct.** If the cafeteria vending machines would not result in students consuming more soft drinks, then allowing the machines would not harm the students' health in the way the argument assumes.
B   Even if the amount of soft drinks the students currently drink were unhealthy, enabling the students to drink more could make them even less healthy.
C   Even if drinking small amounts of soft drinks occasionally would not harm the students, vending machines in the cafeteria could lead the students to drink excessive amounts.
D   Even if students who cannot buy soft drinks in the cafeteria sometimes bring them from home instead, adding vending machines in the cafeteria could increase the students' overall soft drink consumption.
E   A concern does not have to be the primary one in order to be valid and important. It could be held that promoting students' good health should not be the schools' primary concern but should still be a more important concern than the financial benefits from the vending machines.

The correct answer is A.

CR01112
660. Many athletes inhale pure oxygen after exercise in an attempt to increase muscular reabsorption of oxygen. Measured continuously after exercise, however, the blood lactate levels of athletes who inhale pure oxygen are practically identical, on average, to those of athletes who breathe normal air. The lower the blood lactate level is, the higher the muscular reabsorption of oxygen is.

If the statements above are all true, they most strongly support which of the following conclusions?

(A) Athletes' muscular reabsorption of oxygen is not increased when they inhale pure oxygen instead of normal air.
(B) High blood lactate levels cannot be reduced.
(C) Blood lactate levels are a poor measure of oxygen reabsorption by muscles.
(D) The amount of oxygen reabsorbed by an athlete's muscles always remains constant.
(E) The inhaling of pure oxygen has no legitimate role in athletics.

Argument Construction

Situation: Blood lactate levels after exercise are practically identical in athletes who breathe normal air and in those who inhale pure oxygen after exercise. The lower the blood lactate level, the higher the muscular reabsorption of oxygen.

Reasoning: *What conclusion do the stated facts most strongly support?* We are told that lower blood lactate levels correspond consistently to higher muscular reabsorption of oxygen. Since athletes who breathe pure oxygen after exercise have blood lactate levels practically identical to those in athletes who breathe normal air, probably muscular reabsorption of oxygen does not differ significantly between athletes who breathe pure oxygen and those who breathe pure air.

A **Correct.** As explained above, the stated facts suggest that muscular reabsorption of oxygen does not differ significantly between athletes who breathe pure oxygen and those who breathe pure air. So breathing pure oxygen instead of normal air after exercise probably does not increase athletes' muscular reabsorption of oxygen.

B None of the statements indicates that blood lactate levels cannot be reduced by means other than inhaling pure oxygen.

C We are told that blood lactate levels are negatively correlated with muscular reabsorption of oxygen. This negative correlation might allow muscular reabsorption of oxygen to be precisely determined by measuring blood lactate levels.

D Muscular reabsorption of oxygen might vary for reasons unrelated to whether an athlete has been inhaling pure oxygen.

E Inhaling pure oxygen might have some legitimate role unrelated to muscular reabsorption of oxygen.

The correct answer is A.

CR79751.01

661. Historian: Fifteenth-century advances in mapmaking contributed to the rise of modern nation-states. In medieval Europe (from the fifth to the fifteenth century), sovereignty centered in cities and towns and radiated outward, with boundaries often ambiguously defined. The conceptual shift toward the modern state began in the late fifteenth century, when mapmakers learned to reflect geography accurately by basing maps on latitude-longitude grids. By the mid-seventeenth century, nearly all maps showed boundary lines.

Which of the following would, if true, most strengthen the historian's reasoning?

(A) Borders did not become codified in Europe until certain treaties were signed in the early nineteenth century.
(B) During the medieval period, various authorities in Europe claimed power over collections of cities and towns, not contiguous territories.
(C) Many members of the political elite collected maps as a hobby during the late sixteenth and early seventeenth centuries.
(D) Seventeenth-century treatises and other sources of political authority describe areas of sovereignty rather than illustrate them using maps.
(E) During the fifteenth century in Europe, mapmakers simplified the borders of sovereignty by drawing clear lines of demarcation between political powers.

Argument Evaluation

Situation — A historian claims that fifteenth-century advances in mapmaking contributed to the rise of modern nation states. In earlier centuries boundaries of sovereignty in Europe were poorly defined but in the fifteenth century maps were made based on grids showing latitude and longitude.

Reasoning — *What additional piece of information, if true and added to the argument, would most improve the support offered for the conclusion that improved mapping contributed to the rise of nation states?* The historian claims that there was a cause–effect relationship between progress in mapmaking and the rise of the nation state. This claim is supported by information that territories of sovereignty were vague and ill-defined before the fifteenth century, when latitude-longitude grids began to allow progressively greater accuracy in the delineation of territories on maps. The argument assumes that the rise of nation states would have required a high degree of clarity about each state's non-overlapping area of sovereignty.

A   This indicates the role of treaties in the evolution of nation states but provides no additional support for the historian's causal claim.
B   This information is consistent with the historian's belief that nothing resembling the modern state existed before the fifteenth century, but it provides no additional support for the historian's causal claim.
C   The relevance of this information to the argument is tenuous at best. There could be many non-political explanations for the interest of political elites in collecting maps. Many people other than political elites may also have collected maps during the period mentioned.
D   This information tends to minimize the role of maps in defining areas of sovereignty and to cast some doubt on the historian's causal claim.
E   **Correct.** This information makes explicit the role of mapmakers in providing clarity about the geographical boundaries of each political entity's sovereignty. It thus provides additional evidence for the historian's causal claim and strengthens the historian's reasoning.

The correct answer is E.

CR11751.01
662. Sascha: The attempt to ban parliament's right to pass directed-spending bills—bills that contain provisions specifically funding the favorite projects of some powerful politicians—is antidemocratic. Our nation's constitution requires that money be drawn from our treasury only when so stipulated by laws passed by parliament, the branch of government most directly representative of the citizens. This requirement is based on the belief that exercising the power to spend public resources involves the ultimate exercise of state authority and that therefore _____.

Which of the following most logically completes Sascha's argument?

(A) designating funding specifically for the favorite projects of some powerful politicians should be considered antidemocratic

(B) the right to exercise such a power should belong exclusively to the branch of government most directly representative of the citizens

(C) exercising the power to spend public resources is in most cases—but not all—protected by the constitution

(D) modifications to any spending bills should be considered expenditures authorized by law

(E) only officials who are motivated by concerns for reelection should retain that power

Argument Construction

Situation According to Sascha, restricting parliament's ability to direct public money to the projects favored by powerful politicians would be undemocratic. Sascha argues that such a restriction on directed spending would be inconsistent with constitutional requirements.

Reasoning *What piece of information would most logically complete Sascha's argument?* What piece of information would most strongly associate parliament's spending authority with the concept of democracy? A good guess would be: some information that connects parliament's public representation role with its spending authority.

A Sascha believes that democratic constitutional principles require that parliament remain free to do what is described in this sentence.

B **Correct.** This statement makes explicit the connection, implicitly relied on by Sascha's argument, between parliament's spending authority and its role in representing the public.

C This statement may be true but fails to associate parliament's spending authority under the constitution with the notion of democracy.

D Bills are merely works-in-progress, texts of proposed laws. Modifications of bills do not in themselves provide legal authority for any public spending item.

E Sascha opposes restrictions on parliament's spending power, and this would seem to imply that Sascha believes every parliamentary representative should be free to vote on such measures regardless of their levels of concern for reelection.

The correct answer is B.

8.7 Critical Reasoning Answer Explanations

CR02143

663. Boreal owls range over a much larger area than do other owls of similar size. Scientists have hypothesized that **it is scarcity of prey that leads the owls to range so widely**. This hypothesis would be hard to confirm directly, since it is not possible to produce a sufficiently accurate count of the populations of small mammals inhabiting the forests where boreal owls live. Careful study of owl behavior has, however, shown that **boreal owls do range over larger areas when they live in regions where food of the sort eaten by small mammals is comparatively sparse**. This indicates that the scientists' hypothesis is not sheer speculation.

In the argument given, the two **boldfaced** portions play which of the following roles?

(A) The first presents an explanatory hypothesis; the second states the main conclusion of the argument.
(B) The first presents an explanatory hypothesis; the second presents evidence tending to support this hypothesis.
(C) The first presents an explanatory hypothesis; the second presents evidence to support an alternative explanation.
(D) The first describes a position that the argument opposes; the second presents evidence to undermine the support for the position being opposed.
(E) The first describes a position that the argument opposes; the second states the main conclusion of the argument.

Argument Construction

Situation The boreal owl range over a much larger area than owls of similar size. Scientists hypothesize they do so because of prey scarcity. Counting the owls' prey—small mammals—in the boreal owls' habitat is inherently difficult. This makes the scientists' hypothesis hard to confirm directly. However, it has been found that boreal owls range widely when they inhabit regions with relatively little food for the small mammals they prey on.

Reasoning *What function is served by the statement that it is scarcity of prey that leads the owls to range so widely? What function is served by the statement that boreal owls range widely if food for their small-mammal prey is relatively sparse in the region they inhabit?* The first statement expresses a hypothesis that seeks to explain the comparatively wide range of boreal owls. The second statement serves to provide some indirect evidence for the scientists' hypothesis.

A The main conclusion of the argument is that the scientists' hypothesis is not sheer speculation, i.e., that the scientists have based their hypothesis on some evidence that they have discovered. The first statement presents the scientists' hypothesis. The second statement cites some evidence for the hypothesis and is not the main conclusion of the argument.

B **Correct.** As stated, the first presents an explanatory hypothesis, while the second cites some indirect evidence for the hypothesis.

C The second statement cites some indirect evidence for the scientists' hypothesis, not for some other hypothesis.

D The argument does not oppose the scientists' hypothesis, presented in the first statement; the second statement cites evidence for the hypothesis, and does not cite evidence for a position the argument opposes.

E The second statement does not present the argument's main conclusion. The main conclusion is that the scientists' hypothesis is not mere speculation.

The correct answer is B.

CR18731.01
664. Cognitive scientist: Using the pioneering work of comparative psychologist Gordon Gallup as a model, several studies have investigated animals' capacity for mirror self-recognition (MSR). Most animals exposed to a mirror respond only with social behavior, such as aggression. However, in the case of the great apes, repeated exposure to mirrors leads to self-directed behaviors, such as exploring the inside of the mouth, suggesting that these animals recognize the reflection as an image of self. The implication of these studies is that the great apes have a capacity for self-awareness unique among nonhuman species.

The cognitive scientist makes which of the following assumptions in the argument above?

(A) Gallup's work has established that the great apes have a capacity for MSR unique among nonhuman species.
(B) If an animal does not have the capacity for MSR, it does not have the capacity for self-awareness.
(C) If a researcher exposes an animal to a mirror and that animal exhibits social behavior, that animal is incapable of being self-aware.
(D) When exposed to a mirror, all animals display either social behavior or self-directed behavior.
(E) Animals that do not exhibit MSR may demonstrate a capacity for self-awareness in other ways.

Argument Construction

Situation   A cognitive scientist claims that several studies, modeled on Gordon Gallup's work, have investigated animals' capacity for mirror self-recognition (MSR), and found that, whereas most animals exposed to a mirror exhibit only social behavior in response, great apes can come to respond with self-directed behavior. The cognitive scientist infers from this that the great apes, unique among nonhumans, have a capacity for self-awareness.

Reasoning   *What must be true for the studies to support the cognitive scientist's conclusion?* The implicit reasoning is that an animal has self-awareness only if the animal has the capacity for MSR; if the latter is lacking, so is the capacity for self-awareness.

A   The studies the cognitive scientist's inference is based on were not necessarily conducted by Gallup himself. We are told only that they are modeled on his work.

B   **Correct.** If it were possible for an animal to have the capacity for self-awareness even if the animal lacks the capacity for MSR, then the studies would not imply that the great apes have a capacity for self-awareness that other nonhuman animal species lack.

C   The cognitive scientist's reasoning does not require that an animal with the capacity for self-awareness never exhibits social behavior when exposed to a mirror; it merely requires that it does not exhibit only such behavior.

D   The cognitive scientist's reasoning is compatible with an animal's displaying no behavior in response to exposure to a mirror.

E   The cognitive scientist's reasoning is compatible with the claim that an animal that does not exhibit MSR has no capacity at all for self-awareness.

The correct answer is B.

8.7 Critical Reasoning Answer Explanations

665. Last year a record number of new manufacturing jobs were created. Will this year bring another record? Well, any new manufacturing job is created either within an existing company or by the start-up of a new company. **Within existing firms, new jobs have been created this year at well below last year's record pace**. At the same time, there is considerable evidence that the number of new companies starting up will be no higher this year than it was last year and **there is no reason to think that the new companies starting up this year will create more jobs per company than did last year's start-ups**. So clearly, the number of new jobs created this year will fall short of last year's record.

In the argument given, the two portions in **boldface** play which of the following roles?

(A) The first is a claim that the argument challenges; the second is an explicit assumption on which that challenge is based.

(B) The first is a claim that the argument challenges; the second is a judgment advanced in support of the main conclusion of the argument.

(C) The first provides evidence in support of the main conclusion of the argument; the second is an objection that has been raised against that main conclusion.

(D) The first provides evidence in support of the main conclusion of the argument; the second is a judgment advanced in support of that main conclusion.

(E) The first and the second are each claims that have been advanced in support of a position that the argument opposes.

Argument Construction

Situation　Manufacturing jobs are created either within existing companies or in start-ups. Manufacturing jobs are being created at a much slower rate this year than last year. It seems likely that the number of new start-ups will not exceed last year's number and that the average number of manufacturing jobs per start-up will not exceed last year's number. So fewer manufacturing jobs are likely to be created this year than last year.

Reasoning　*What function is served by the statement that within existing firms, new jobs have been created this year at well below last year's record pace? What function is served by the statement that there is no reason to think that the new companies starting up this year will create more jobs per company than did last year's start-ups?* The first statement is one of the statements used as support for the argument's main conclusion (the prediction about this year's job creation). The second statement gives another premise used as support for that prediction.

A　The argument does not challenge the claim made by the first statement; it uses the first and the second statement as support for the argument's main conclusion, the prediction about this year's job creation.

B　The argument does not challenge the claim made by the first statement, but uses the first and second statements as support for the argument's main conclusion.

C　The first provides evidence in support of the main conclusion of the argument; the second is not an objection that has been raised against the main conclusion.

D　**Correct.** The first provides evidence in support of the main conclusion of the argument; the second also provides support for the main conclusion.

E　Neither the first nor the second is meant to support a position that the argument opposes; rather, they are both meant to support the argument's main conclusion.

The correct answer is D.

CR07809
666. A study of ticket sales at a summer theater festival found that people who bought tickets to individual plays had a no-show rate of less than 1 percent, while those who paid in advance for all ten plays being performed that summer had a no-show rate of nearly 30 percent. This may be at least in part because the greater the awareness customers retain about the cost of an item, the more likely they are to use it.

Which of the following would, if true, best serve as an alternative explanation of the results of the study?

(A) The price per ticket was slightly cheaper for those who bought all ten tickets in advance.
(B) Many people who attended the theater festival believed strongly that they should support it financially.
(C) Those who attended all ten plays became eligible for a partial refund.
(D) Usually, people who bought tickets to individual plays did so immediately prior to each performance that they attended.
(E) People who arrived just before the performance began could not be assured of obtaining seats in a preferred location.

Argument Construction

Situation People who bought tickets to individual plays at a theater festival had a much lower no-show rate than did people who paid in advance for all ten plays.

Reasoning *What factor other than greater awareness of the ticket costs could explain why people who bought tickets individually were more likely to attend the plays?* The passage suggests that people who bought tickets individually were more likely to attend the plays because they were more vividly aware of what they had paid for each ticket. But there are other possible explanations—perhaps the people who bought the tickets individually were more eager to attend each play for its own sake, or had other characteristics or incentives that made them more likely to attend the plays.

A A slight price difference would not plausibly explain why the no-show rate was thirty times greater among those who bought all the tickets in advance than among those who bought them individually.

B This could be true of many people who bought their tickets individually as well as many who bought them in advance.

C This would provide an added incentive for those who bought tickets in advance to attend all the plays.

D **Correct.** If people who bought individual tickets usually did so right before each performance, they would have much less time after buying the tickets to change their minds about whether to attend than would people who bought all the tickets in advance.

E If anything, this might present an additional difficulty for those who bought individual tickets without advance planning, so it would not help to explain the lower no-show rate among buyers of individual tickets.

The correct answer is D.

8.7 Critical Reasoning Answer Explanations

CR12019

667. Although there is no record of poet Edmund Spenser's parentage, we do know that as a youth Spenser attended the Merchant Tailors' School in London for a period between 1560 and 1570. Records from this time indicate that the Merchant Tailors' Guild then had only three members named Spenser: Robert Spenser, listed as a gentleman; Nicholas Spenser, elected the Guild's Warden in 1568; and John Spenser, listed as a "journeyman cloth-maker." Of these, the last was likely the least affluent of the three—and most likely Edmund's father, since school accounting records list Edmund as a scholar who attended the school at a reduced fee.

Which of the following is an assumption on which the argument depends?

(A) Anybody in sixteenth century London who made clothing professionally would have had to be a member of the Merchant Tailors' Guild.
(B) The fact that Edmund Spenser attended the Merchant Tailors' School did not necessarily mean that he planned to become a tailor.
(C) No member of the Guild could become Guild warden in sixteenth century London unless he was a gentleman.
(D) Most of those whose fathers were members of the Merchant Tailors' Guild were students at the Merchant Tailors' School.
(E) The Merchant Tailors' School did not reduce its fees for the children of the more affluent Guild members.

Argument Construction

Situation   Records indicate that the poet Edmund Spenser attended the Merchant Tailors' School for a reduced fee as a youth. There is no record of his parentage, but at the time the Merchant Tailors' Guild had only three members named Spenser, of whom the least affluent was probably John Spenser.

Reasoning   *What must be true in order for the cited facts to support the conclusion that John Spenser was probably Edmund Spenser's father?* The implicit reasoning is that since Edmund Spenser attended the Merchant Tailors' School at a reduced fee, his father must have been poor. And since John Spenser was probably the poorest of the three men named Spenser in the Merchant Tailors' Guild, he was probably Edmund Spenser's father. This reasoning assumes that only the children of poor parents had reduced fees at the Merchant Tailors' School, that the children at the school generally had fathers in the Merchant Tailors' Guild, that children in that time and place generally shared their fathers' surnames, and that the two other Spensers in the Merchant Tailors' Guild were not poor enough for their children to qualify for reduced fees.

A   John Spenser, as a tailor and member of the guild, could have been Edmund Spenser's father even if some other professional tailors did not belong to the guild and did not have children at the school.
B   Although Edmund Spenser became a poet as an adult, he and all his classmates might have attended the school as children because they planned to become tailors.
C   The argument assumes that a Guild's Warden probably would have been wealthier than a journeyman cloth-maker, but that might have been probable even if the Guild's Warden were not a "gentleman."
D   Even if most children of fathers in the guild did not attend the school, all the children who did attend the school might have had fathers in the guild.
E   **Correct.** If the school reduced its fees for children of wealthier guild members, then the fact that Edmund Spenser's fees were reduced would not provide evidence that his father was the poorest of the three Spensers in the guild, as the argument requires.

The correct answer is E.

CR20831.01
668. Hea Sook: One should not readily believe urban legends. Most legends are propagated because the moral lesson underlying them supports a political agenda. People will repeat a tale if it fits their purpose. They may not deliberately spread untruths, but neither are they particularly motivated to investigate deeply to determine if the tale they are telling is true.

Kayla: But people would not repeat stories that they did not believe were true. Therefore, one can safely assume that if a story has been repeated by enough people then it is more likely to be true.

Kayla's reply is most vulnerable to the criticism that it

(A) does not specify how many people need to repeat a story before someone is justified believing it
(B) overstates the significance of political agendas in the retelling of stories
(C) fails to address the claim that people will not verify the truth of a story that fits their purpose
(D) implicitly supports the claim that the people repeating legends are not deliberately spreading untruths
(E) cannot distinguish people's motivations for repeating urban legends from their motivations for repeating other types of story

Argument Evaluation

Situation Hea Sook and Kayla have a difference of opinion on how likely urban legends are to be true.

Reasoning *What criticism is Kayla's reply most vulnerable to?* Hea Sook argues that because urban legends generally are propagated for political purposes, people are not particularly motivated to carefully investigate whether the story they are telling is true. These people may not be deliberately telling an untruth, but they have not taken care to establish whether the story is true. Kayla responds that people would not repeat a story that they did not believe to be true, but Hea Sook not only does not attempt to deny that, but she suggests that it may be true. Kayla ignores the fact that sometimes people believe that something is true without carefully determining whether it actually is true, and that they are less likely to verify whether it is true when the story fits their purposes.

A Kayla does not specify how many people need to repeat a story before one is justified in believing it, but she does not need to. Her claim—that there is some number sufficient for such belief to be justified—could be true even if she does not specify what that number is.

B It is Hea Sook, not Kayla, who asserts that political agendas are a significant factor in whether one retells a story.

C **Correct.** Kayla does not address whether people are unlikely to verify whether a story is true if the story fits their purpose.

D Kayla does not merely implicitly claim that people who repeat legends are not deliberately spreading untruths; she explicitly states this, but in this she and Hea Sook agree.

E We have no reason to think that Kayla cannot distinguish people's motivations for repeating urban legends from their motivations for repeating other types of stories. She may well be able to do this.

The correct answer is C.

8.7 Critical Reasoning Answer Explanations

CR03749
669. Rainwater contains hydrogen of a heavy form called deuterium. The deuterium content of wood reflects the deuterium content of rainwater available to trees during their growth. Wood from trees that grew between 16,000 and 24,000 years ago in North America contains significantly more deuterium than wood from trees growing today. But water trapped in several North American caves that formed during that same early period contains significantly less deuterium than rainwater in North America contains today.

Which of the following, if true, most helps to reconcile the two findings?

(A) There is little deuterium in the North American caves other than the deuterium in the water trapped there.
(B) Exposure to water after a tree has died does not change the deuterium content of the wood.
(C) Industrialization in North America over the past 100 years has altered the deuterium content of rain.
(D) Trees draw on shallow groundwater from rain that falls during their growth, whereas water trapped in caves may have fallen as rainwater thousands of years before the caves formed.
(E) Wood with a high deuterium content is no more likely to remain preserved for long periods than is wood with a low deuterium content.

Argument Construction

Situation In North America, wood from trees that grew 16,000 to 24,000 years ago contains more deuterium than wood from trees growing today. But water in caves that formed during that same period contains less deuterium than rainwater contains today.

Reasoning *What could explain the puzzling discrepancy between the observed deuterium levels in wood and in caves?* Since the deuterium content of wood from trees reflects the deuterium content of rainwater available to the trees while they grew, the deuterium levels observed in wood suggests that North American rainwater contained more deuterium 16,000 to 24,000 years ago than it contains today. But this conclusion seems at odds with the low deuterium levels in water in caves that formed 16,000 to 24,000 years ago. Several factors might explain the discrepancy: the water in those caves might not be rainwater from the period when the caves formed; or some natural process might have altered the deuterium levels in the cave water or the wood; or the wood or caves in which deuterium levels were measured might be statistically abnormal somehow.

A If the caves had absorbed deuterium out of the rainwater trapped in them, there would probably be deuterium in the cave walls. So the observation that there is little deuterium in the caves apart from that in the water eliminates one possible explanation for the oddly low deuterium levels in the cave water.

B This suggests that the deuterium levels in the wood accurately reflect higher deuterium levels in rainwater that fell 16,000 to 24,000 years ago, but it does not explain why the deuterium levels are so low in water in the caves that formed then.

C This could explain why deuterium levels in rainwater have changed, but it does not help explain the discrepancy between the high deuterium levels in the wood and the low deuterium levels in the cave water.

D **Correct.** If the water in the caves fell as rainwater thousands of years before the caves formed, it may date from a period when rainwater contained much less deuterium than during the period 16,000 to 24,000 years ago, and much less than today.

E If wood with high deuterium content were more likely to be preserved, then wood from 16,000 to 24,000 years ago might have a high deuterium content even if the rainwater then had a low deuterium content. So the observation that wood with more deuterium is not more likely to be preserved eliminates one possible explanation for the discrepancy.

The correct answer is D.

CR04925
670. Enforcement of local speed limits through police monitoring has proven unsuccessful in the town of Ardane. In many nearby towns, speed humps (raised areas of pavement placed across residential streets, about 300 feet apart) have reduced traffic speeds on residential streets by 20 to 25 percent. In order to reduce traffic speed and thereby enhance safety in residential neighborhoods, Ardane's transportation commission plans to install multiple speed humps in those neighborhoods.

Which of the following, if true, identifies a potentially serious drawback to the plan for installing speed humps in Ardane?

(A) On residential streets without speed humps, many vehicles travel at speeds more than 25 percent above the posted speed limit.

(B) Because of their high weight, emergency vehicles such as fire trucks and ambulances must slow almost to a stop at speed humps.

(C) The residential speed limit in Ardane is higher than that of the nearby towns where speed humps were installed.

(D) Motorists who are not familiar with the streets in Ardane's residential districts would be likely to encounter the speed humps unawares unless warned by signs and painted indicators.

(E) Bicyclists generally prefer that speed humps be constructed so as to leave a space on the side of the road where bicycles can travel without going over the humps.

Evaluation of a Plan

Situation Ardane's difficulty in getting compliance with speed limits has led it to propose the installation of speed humps to slow traffic. In nearby towns, speed humps have reduced speeds in residential areas by up to 25 percent.

Reasoning *Which one of the statements presented identifies a major disadvantage of the proposed installation of speed humps?* Is it possible that they might slow traffic too much? Clearly, there is a general need for traffic to flow smoothly. Would speed humps affect all types of traffic equally? Perhaps not. For example, certain emergency vehicles must sometimes need to travel quickly through residential neighborhoods. A problem with speed humps is that some heavier vehicles must go very slowly over speed humps.

A This indicates a drawback of not installing speed humps.

B **Correct.** This information indicates a significant drawback—possibly leading to loss of life and property—of the plan to install the speed humps.

C This suggests that installing speed humps might lower speeds significantly below the current speed limits. If speeds became very low, the result could be traffic gridlock that would have unforeseen consequences. However, we have insufficient information to evaluate such possibilities.

D This is unlikely to be a drawback, since such warning signs are typically put in place whenever speed humps are installed.

E This information provides no evidence of a drawback in Ardane's plan for speed humps, since the design of Ardane's planned speed humps is not indicated.

The correct answer is B.

8.7 Critical Reasoning Answer Explanations

CR00748
671. Which of the following most logically completes the argument below?

NowNews, although still the most popular magazine covering cultural events in Kalopolis, has recently suffered a significant drop in advertising revenue because of falling circulation. Many readers have begun buying a competing magazine that, at 50 cents per copy, costs less than *NowNews* at $1.50 per copy. In order to boost circulation and thus increase advertising revenue, *NowNews*'s publisher has proposed making it available at no charge, but this proposal has a serious drawback, since _____.

(A) Those Kalopolis residents with the greatest interest in cultural events are regular readers of both magazines.
(B) One reason *NowNews*'s circulation fell was that its competitor's reporting on cultural events was superior.
(C) The newsstands and stores that currently sell *NowNews* will no longer carry it if it is being given away for free.
(D) At present, 10 percent of the total number of copies of each issue of *NowNews* are distributed free to students on college campuses in the Kalopolis area.
(E) *NowNews*'s competitor would begin to lose large amounts of money if it were forced to lower its cover price.

Argument Construction

Situation *NowNews* is suffering declines in circulation and advertising revenue due to competition from a lower-priced magazine. The publisher proposes offering *NowNews* for free to reverse these declines.

Reasoning *What would suggest that the publisher's proposal will fail to increase circulation and advertising revenue?* The proposal's intended effect is simply to increase advertising revenue by increasing circulation. Any evidence that offering the magazine for free will not result in more copies being circulated or will not attract advertisers would therefore be evidence of a drawback in the proposal. So a statement offering such evidence would logically complete the argument.

A The fact that certain highly motivated Kalopolis residents still read *NowNews* even at a cost of $1.50 per issue leaves open the possibility that providing the magazine free might still boost readership.

B This suggests that improving its cultural reporting might help *NowNews* increase its circulation, not that the publisher's proposal will fail to do so.

C **Correct.** If the proposal leads newsstands and stores to stop carrying *NowNews*, circulation and advertising revenue would probably decline as a result.

D Even if 10 percent of the copies of *NowNews* are already distributed for free, distributing the remaining 90 percent for free could still increase circulation and advertising revenue as the publisher intends.

E Forcing a competing magazine to lower its cover price and lose lots of money would be an advantage rather than a drawback of the proposal, as far as the publisher of *NowNews* was concerned.

The correct answer is C.

672. Archaeologist: Researchers excavating a burial site in Cyprus found a feline skeleton lying near a human skeleton. Both skeletons were in the same sediment at the same depth and equally well-preserved, suggesting that the feline and human were buried together about 9,500 years ago. This shows that felines were domesticated around the time farming began, when they would have been useful in protecting stores of grain from mice.

Which of the following, if true, would most seriously weaken the archaeologist's argument?

(A) Archaeologists have not found any remains of stores of grain in the immediate vicinity of the burial site.

(B) The burial site in Cyprus is substantially older than any other known burial site in which a feline skeleton and a human skeleton appear to have been buried together.

(C) Paintings found near the burial site seem to show people keeping felines as domestic companions, but do not show felines hunting mice.

(D) In Cyprus, there are many burial sites dating from around 9,500 years ago in which the remains of wild animals appear to have been buried alongside human remains.

(E) Before felines were domesticated, early farmers had no effective way to protect stores of grain from mice.

Argument Evaluation

Situation: A human skeleton and a feline skeleton were apparently buried together in Cyprus about 9,500 years ago.

Reasoning: *What would most strongly suggest that the skeletons do not show that felines were domesticated around the time farming began?* The argument implicitly assumes that farming in Cyprus began around 9,500 years ago, so evidence against that assumption would weaken the argument. The argument could also be weakened by evidence that felines were domesticated much earlier, that the feline skeleton was not from a domesticated cat, or that the two skeletons were not actually buried together around 9,500 years ago.

A Even if archaeologists searched for evidence of a grain store, the fact that no such evidence was found near the burial site is at best only weak evidence that no grain store existed there or slightly farther away.

B The lack of corroborating evidence from other burial sites would weaken the argument slightly but would still be compatible with the hypothesis that this site revealed one of the very first burials of a domesticated cat.

C This would cast doubt on the hypothesis that cats were domesticated mainly to protect stores of grain, but not on the argument's conclusion that cats were domesticated around the time farming began.

D **Correct.** If many wild animals were buried alongside humans in Cyprus around 9,500 years ago, then the feline skeleton is just as likely to be that of a wild animal than that of a domesticated cat.

E Since this would provide an additional reason why early farmers might have domesticated the local cats, it would strengthen rather than weaken the argument.

The correct answer is D.

673. Farmer: Several people in the past few years have claimed to have seen a mountain lion in the suburban outskirts—the latest just last month—and, while mountain lions were thought to have been driven from this entire region about twenty years ago, there is no reason for the people who reported seeing a mountain lion to have deliberately concocted a false report. Therefore, local wildlife managers should begin to urgently address the mountain lion's presence.

Which of the following would, if true, most seriously weaken the farmer's argument?

(A) Farmers in the suburban outskirts mostly raise cattle and hogs, which when fully grown are generally not attacked by mountain lions.

(B) Mountain lions are dissimilar in size and color to other wild animals found near the suburban outskirts.

(C) No person who claimed to have seen a mountain lion had anyone else with them at the purported sighting.

(D) There have been no regional reports in the past year of mountain lions migrating to the area.

(E) Recent surveys show that more than half of the people in the region report that they have never seen a mountain lion before.

Argument Evaluation

Situation   A farmer argues that, because several people in recent years, including someone just last month, have claimed to have seen a mountain lion in the suburban outskirts, local wildlife managers need to address the mountain lion's presence. The farmer claims that people would not intentionally create a false story about seeing a mountain lion.

Reasoning   *What would most seriously call into question the farmer's argument that because there have been reports of mountain lion sightings, wildlife managers should address the issue?* Even if it is true that people would not intentionally create a false report of having seen a mountain lion, it is possible that people have mistakenly believed they have seen a mountain lion when in fact what they saw was something else. If some fact called into question the accuracy of the reports of mountain lion sightings, then the farmer's conclusion would have weaker support.

A   Even if most fully grown animals raised by farmers would not be attacked by mountain lions, there could still be good reason to be concerned about the presence of mountain lions in the suburban outskirts. The mountain lion might attack animals before they are fully grown.

B   A dissimilarity in size and color between mountain lions and other wild animals in the area where the mountain lions were purportedly sighted would make it less likely that people mistakenly believed that an animal they spotted was a mountain lion. So, this would strengthen the farmer's argument, not weaken it.

C   **Correct.** If there actually were at least one mountain lion in the area, and several people over a period of a few years accurately claim to have seen one, then it seems likely that on at least some occasions a person would have been in the presence of someone else at the time, given the frequency with which people are in the company of others. So, if there have been no instances of a person reporting seeing a mountain lion when in the company of another, perhaps that is because when someone has mistakenly believed that an animal is a mountain lion, the other person helps correct the mistaken belief. With no one else present, an illusory sighting would be less likely to be corrected.

D   There have been purported sightings of a mountain lion in the area for several years, so presumably, if the sightings are accurate, there has been at least one mountain lion for several years, so the sightings could be accurate even if no mountain lion has migrated to the area in the past year.

E   It might be likely that most people living in the area would not have seen a mountain lion even if one lived in the area. For instance, the mountain lion might intentionally try to avoid people.

The correct answer is C.

CR09117
674. The heavy traffic in Masana is a growing drain on the city's economy—the clogging of the streets of the central business district alone cost the economy more than $1.2 billion over the past year. In order to address this problem, officials plan to introduce congestion pricing, by which drivers would pay to enter the city's most heavily trafficked areas during the busiest times of the day.

Which of the following, if true, would most strongly indicate that the plan will be a success?

(A) Approximately one-fifth of the vehicles in the central business district are in transit from one side of the city to the other.
(B) Planners expect that, without congestion pricing, traffic in Masana is likely to grow by 6 percent in the next five years.
(C) In other urban areas, congestion pricing has strongly encouraged carpooling (sharing of rides by private commuters).
(D) Several studies have shown that a reduction in traffic of 15 percent in Masana could result in 5,500 or more new jobs.
(E) Over 30 percent of the vehicles in the city's center are occupied by more than one person.

Evaluation of a Plan

Situation Traffic congestion in Masana has been harming the city's economy. To address the problem, officials plan to make drivers pay to enter the city's most heavily trafficked areas during the busiest times of day.

Reasoning *What would most strongly suggest that the plan will reduce the harm to Masana's economy from traffic congestion?* In order to succeed, the plan will have to be implemented and effectively enforced. Furthermore, the prices drivers pay will have to be high enough to significantly change their behavior in ways that reduce the amount of traffic congestion in the city. Finally, the economic benefits from the reduced traffic congestion will have to substantially outweigh any economically damaging side effects of the congestion pricing. Any evidence that any of these conditions will hold would provide at least some support for the prediction that the plan will succeed.

A   This provides no evidence that the congestion pricing would affect the behavior of either the one-fifth of drivers whose vehicles traverse the city or of the other four-fifths of drivers, nor does it give any evidence that the plan would produce overriding economic benefits.

B   This indicates that the traffic problem will grow worse if the plan is not implemented, but it does not provide any evidence that the plan will help address the problem.

C   **Correct.** This indicates that similar plans have successfully changed drivers' behavior in other cities in a way likely to reduce the number of cars on the road in heavily trafficked areas at busy times of day without producing harmful economic side effects. Thus, it provides evidence that the strategy could also be successful in Masana.

D   Although this suggests that reducing traffic congestion would be economically beneficial, it doesn't provide any evidence that the plan will succeed in reducing traffic congestion.

E   This suggests that many drivers in the city center are already carpooling, which, if anything, indicates that the plan will be less able to further affect those drivers' behavior and thus could be less effective than it might otherwise be.

The correct answer is C.

675. **Economist:** The most economically efficient way to reduce emissions of air pollutants is to tax them in proportion to the damage they are likely to cause. But in Country Y, many serious pollutants are untaxed and unregulated, and policy makers strongly oppose new taxes. Therefore, the best way to achieve a reduction in air pollutant emissions in Country Y would be to institute fixed upper limits on them.

Which of the following is an assumption of the economist's argument?

(A) Policy makers in Country Y oppose all new taxes equally strongly, regardless of any benefits they may provide.
(B) Country Y's air pollutant emissions would not fall significantly if they were taxed in proportion to the damage they are likely to cause.
(C) Policy makers in Country Y strongly favor reductions in air pollutant emissions.
(D) Country Y's policy makers believe that air pollutant emissions should be reduced with maximum economic efficiency.
(E) Policy makers in Country Y do not oppose setting fixed upper limits on air pollutant emissions as strongly as they oppose new taxes.

Argument Construction

Situation   Although taxing air pollution emissions in proportion to the damage they cause is the most economically efficient way to reduce those emissions, many serious pollutants in Nation Y are untaxed and unregulated, and the nation's policy makers strongly oppose new taxes. Therefore, fixed upper limits on such emissions would more effectively reach this goal.

Reasoning   *What must be true in order for the factors the economist cites to support the claim that fixing upper limits on air pollutant emissions in Nation Y would be the best way to reduce those emissions?* Political opposition to taxation in Nation Y is the only factor the economist cites to support the argument's conclusion that it would be best to institute fixed upper limits on air pollutants. In order for the premise to support the conclusion, there must be less political opposition in Nation Y to instituting such limits than there would be to the proportional taxation approach the economist prefers.

A   Even if the policy makers oppose some new taxes less than others, they could still oppose the proportional taxation approach strongly enough for it to be utterly infeasible.

B   Even if the proportional taxation scheme would significantly reduce emissions, it still might not be the best approach for Nation Y if it would generate too much political opposition to be viable there.

C   Even if policy makers in Nation Y do not strongly favor reducing emissions, fixing upper limits on emissions might still be a better and more politically feasible way to reduce emissions than any alternative is.

D   Since fixing upper emissions limits would be no more economically efficient than the proportional taxation scheme, the policy makers' support for economic efficiency would not make the former approach any more politically feasible than the latter.

E   **Correct.** If the policy makers opposed fixing upper emissions limits as strongly as they oppose new taxes, then their opposition to new taxes would no longer support the conclusion that fixing the emissions limits is a better way to reduce emissions.

The correct answer is E.

CR04986
676. Humans get Lyme disease from infected ticks. Ticks get infected by feeding on animals with Lyme disease, but the ease of transmission from host animal to tick varies. With most species of host animal, transmission of Lyme disease to ticks is extremely rare, but white-footed mice are an exception, readily passing Lyme disease to ticks. And white-footed mouse populations greatly expand, becoming the main food source for ticks, in areas where biodiversity is in decline.

The information in the passage most strongly supports which of the following?

(A) In areas where many humans are infected with Lyme disease, the proportion of ticks infected with Lyme disease is especially high.

(B) Very few animals that live in areas where there are no white-footed mice are infected with Lyme disease.

(C) Humans are less at risk of contracting Lyme disease in areas where biodiversity is high.

(D) Ticks feed on white-footed mice only when other host species are not available to them.

(E) The greater the biodiversity of an area, the more likely any given host animal in that area is to pass Lyme disease to ticks.

Argument Construction

Situation White-footed mice readily pass Lyme disease to ticks, which pass it to humans. White-footed mouse populations expand where biodiversity is declining.

Reasoning *What conclusion do the stated facts support?* Since declining biodiversity causes white-footed mouse populations to increase, and white-footed mice are especially likely to pass Lyme disease to ticks, and ticks pass it to humans, declining biodiversity could reasonably be expected to increase the incidence of Lyme disease in both ticks and humans.

A In areas where many humans are infected with Lyme disease, the total number of ticks may be unusually high, so even if the number of infected ticks is unusually high, the proportion of infected ticks may not be unusually high

B Most animals with Lyme disease may get it from sources other than ticks that have fed on infected mice.

C **Correct.** If biodiversity is high, then any biodiversity decline that has already begun has likely not yet reached a point where white-footed mouse populations have greatly expanded, so the risk of people contracting Lyme disease is still relatively less than in areas where biodiversity is low and where significant decline in biodiversity has likely already occurred.

D Even if ticks feed on white-footed mice when few other species are available for them to feed on, they may also sometimes feed on white-footed mice when there are many other species for them to feed on.

E The passage suggests that the overall incidence of Lyme disease is probably lower in more biodiverse areas, so any given host animal in those areas would probably be less likely to pass Lyme disease to a tick.

The correct answer is C.

677. Many industrialized nations are trying to reduce atmospheric concentrations of carbon dioxide, a gas released by the burning of fossil fuels. One proposal is to replace conventional cement, which is made with calcium carbonate, by a new "eco-cement." This new cement, made with magnesium carbonate, absorbs large amounts of carbon dioxide when exposed to the atmosphere. Therefore, using eco-cement for new concrete building projects will significantly help reduce atmospheric concentrations of carbon dioxide.

Which of the following, if true, most strengthens the argument?

(A) The cost of magnesium carbonate, currently greater than the cost of calcium carbonate, probably will fall as more magnesium carbonate is used in cement manufacture.
(B) Eco-cement is strengthened when absorbed carbon dioxide reacts with the cement.
(C) Before the development of eco-cement, magnesium-based cement was considered too susceptible to water erosion to be of practical use.
(D) The manufacture of eco-cement uses considerably less fossil fuel per unit of cement than the manufacture of conventional cement does.
(E) Most building-industry groups are unaware of the development or availability of eco-cement.

Argument Evaluation

Situation: Many nations are trying to reduce atmospheric concentrations of carbon dioxide. One proposed method is to use a new type of "eco-cement" that absorbs carbon dioxide from air.

Reasoning: *What evidence, combined with the cited facts, would most support the prediction that using eco-cement will significantly help reduce atmospheric concentrations of carbon dioxide?* The prediction assumes that the use of eco-cement would be an effective way to reduce carbon dioxide levels. Any evidence supporting this assumption will support the prediction.

A Since eco-cement uses magnesium carbonate, the prediction that magnesium carbonate prices will fall suggests that a potential financial barrier to widespread eco-cement use will diminish. However, those prices may not fall enough to make eco-cement cost-competitive with regular cement.

B Even if absorbed carbon dioxide strengthens eco-cement, the strengthened eco-cement might still be much weaker than regular cement and thus might never become widely used, in which case it will not significantly help reduce atmospheric concentrations of carbon dioxide.

C Even if eco-cement is less susceptible to water erosion than earlier forms of magnesium-based cement were, it might still be much more susceptible to water erosion than regular cement is, and thus might never become widely used.

D **Correct.** This suggests that manufacturing eco-cement produces much less carbon dioxide than manufacturing regular cement does, so it supports the claim that widespread use of eco-cement would be an effective way to reduce carbon dioxide levels.

E If anything, this lack of awareness makes it less likely that eco-cement will become widely used, which in turn makes it less likely that eco-cement will significantly help reduce atmospheric concentrations of carbon dioxide.

The correct answer is D.

CR00895
678. Advertisement: When your car's engine is running at its normal operating temperature, any major brand of motor oil will protect it about as well as Tuff does. When the engine is cold, it is a different story: Tuff motor oil flows better at lower temperatures than its major competitors do. So, if you want your car's engine to have maximum protection, you should use Tuff.

Which of the following, if true, most strengthens the argument in the advertisement?

(A) Tuff motor oil provides above-average protection for engines that happen to overheat.
(B) Tuff motor oil is periodically supplied free of charge to automobile manufacturers to use in factory-new cars.
(C) Tuff motor oil's share of the engine oil market peaked three years ago.
(D) Tuff motor oil, like any motor oil, is thicker and flows less freely at cold temperatures than at hot temperatures.
(E) Tuff motor oil is manufactured at only one refinery and shipped from there to all markets.

Argument Evaluation

Situation   An advertisement argues that since Tuff motor oil flows better than its major competitors at low temperatures and works about as well as they do at normal temperatures, it provides *maximum protection* for car engines.

Reasoning   *What additional evidence would suggest that Tuff motor oil provides the best available protection for car engines?* The argument requires the assumptions that no type of motor oil other than the "major brands" provides superior protection, that flowing better at lower temperatures ensures superior protection at those temperatures, and that Tuff protects car engines at least as well as its competitors do at above-normal temperatures. Any evidence supporting any of these assumptions would strengthen the argument.

A   **Correct.** If Tuff provides above-average protection when engines overheat, in addition to the solid protection it provides at normal and low temperatures, it may well provide the best available protection overall.
B   The company that makes Tuff might give automobile manufacturers free motor oil as a promotional gimmick even if Tuff is an inferior product.
C   Tuff's sales might have declined over the past three years because consumers have realized that Tuff is an inferior product.
D   The similar responses of Tuff and other motor oils to temperature changes do not suggest that Tuff provides better protection overall than those other motor oils do.
E   Even if Tuff is manufactured at only one refinery, it may still be an inferior product.

The correct answer is A.

679. Linguist: In English, the past is described as "behind" and the future "ahead," whereas in Aymara the past is "ahead" and the future "behind." Research indicates that English speakers sway backward when discussing the past and forward when discussing the future. Conversely, Aymara speakers gesture forward with their hands when discussing the past and backward when discussing the future. These bodily movements, therefore, suggest that the language one speaks affects how one mentally visualizes time.

The linguist's reasoning depends on assuming which of the following?

(A) At least some Aymara speakers sway forward when discussing the past and backward when discussing the future.
(B) Most people mentally visualize time as running either forward or backward.
(C) Not all English and Aymara speakers tend to sway or gesture forward or backward when discussing the present.
(D) How people move when discussing the future correlates to some extent with how they mentally visualize time.
(E) The researchers also examined the movements of at least some speakers of languages other than English and Aymara discussing the past and the future.

Argument Construction

Situation A linguist argues that the language one speaks affects how one mentally visualizes time. The linguist's argument is based on the fact that English speakers, who refer to the past as "behind" and the future as "ahead," display backward and forward bodily movements when speaking of the past and the future, while speakers of Aymara, who refer to the past as "ahead" and the future as "behind" display correspondingly different body movements.

Reasoning *What must be true if we are to accept the linguist's conclusion from the given information that the language one speaks affects how one mentally visualizes time?* The linguist's evidence will support the conclusion only if there is some correlation between people's bodily movements and how they mentally visualize time. So, the linguist's reasoning requires an assumption to that effect.

A The linguist's reasoning is based on the differences in bodily movements discussed in the argument—that is, that Aymara speakers gesture in certain ways and that English speakers sway in certain ways; thus, the linguist's reasoning does not require that Aymara speakers sway in any way whatsoever when they discuss the past or future.

B The linguist's reasoning is based only on speakers of English and Aymara, so no claim related to speakers of other languages—who make up a majority of people—is required.

C The linguist's argument would actually be stronger if all English and Aymara speakers sway or gesture in the ways discussed, so the argument certainly does not depend on assuming that not all such speakers sway or gesture in these ways.

D **Correct.** The fact that English and Aymara speakers sway or gesture in the ways described would be irrelevant to the linguist's conclusion if how people move when discussing the future does not correlate at least to some extent with how they visualize time.

E It might be helpful to the linguist's argument to examine the movements of speakers of other languages when they discuss the past and the future, but the linguist's argument does not require this.

The correct answer is D.

680. *The Testament of William Thorpe* was published around 1530 as an appendix to Thorpe's longer *Examination*. Many scholars, however, doubt the attribution of the *Testament* to Thorpe because, whereas the *Examination* is dated 1406, the *Testament* is dated 1460. One scholar has recently argued that the 1460 date be amended to 1409, based on the observation that when these numbers are expressed as Roman numerals, MCCCCLX and MCCCCIX, it becomes easy to see how the dates might have become confused through scribal error.

Which of the following, if true, would most support the scholar's hypothesis concerning the date of the *Testament*?

(A) The sole evidence that historians have had that William Thorpe died no earlier than 1460 was the presumed date of publication of the *Testament*.

(B) In the preface to the 1530 publication, the editor attributes both works to William Thorpe.

(C) Few writers in fifteenth-century England marked dates in their works using only Roman numerals.

(D) The *Testament* alludes to a date, "Friday, September 20," as apparently contemporaneous with the writing of the *Testament*, and September 20 fell on a Friday in 1409 but not in 1460.

(E) The *Testament* contains few references to historical events that occurred later than 1406.

Argument Construction

Situation *The Testament of William Thorpe*, dated 1460, was published around 1530 as an appendix to Thorpe's *Examination*, dated 1406. But when expressed in Roman numerals, 1460 could easily be confused with 1409.

Reasoning *Given the facts cited, what would provide additional evidence that Thorpe's* Testament *dates from 1409 rather than 1460?* The scholar's hypothesis that the work dates from 1409 is based on the observation that in Roman numerals, 1409 might easily have been improperly transcribed as 1460. This hypothesis could be supported by evidence that the manuscripts were dated in Roman numerals, or by any independent evidence that 1409 is a more likely date for the *Testament* than 1460.

A This suggests that scholars have no biographical evidence that the *Testament* was published in 1460, but they could still have abundant evidence of other types to support that date, such as the text's cultural allusions or references to other works.

B The editor of the 1530 publication could easily have been mistaken about the authorship of one or both works. And even if the editor were correct, Thorpe might have lived long enough to write one work in 1406 and the other in 1460.

C This would cast doubt on the scholar's argument by providing evidence that the original manuscripts were not dated only in Roman numerals.

D Correct. This provides strong evidence directly supporting the hypothesis that the *Testament* dates from 1409 specifically.

E Even if the *Testament* contained only one reference to a historical event that occurred later than 1406 (for example, one event in 1459), that reference alone could provide strong evidence that the work dates from 1460 rather than 1409.

The correct answer is D.

8.7 Critical Reasoning Answer Explanations

CR00777

681. A prominent investor who holds a large stake in the Burton Tool Company has recently claimed that the company is mismanaged, citing as evidence the company's failure to slow down production in response to a recent rise in its inventory of finished products. It is doubtful whether an investor's sniping at management can ever be anything other than counterproductive, but in this case, it is clearly not justified. It is true that **an increased inventory of finished products often indicates that production is outstripping demand**, but in Burton's case it indicates no such thing. Rather, **the increase in inventory is entirely attributable to products that have already been assigned to orders received from customers**.

In the argument given, the two **boldfaced** portions play which of the following roles?

(A) The first states a generalization that underlies the position that the argument as a whole opposes; the second provides evidence to show that the generalization does not apply in the case at issue.

(B) The first states a generalization that underlies the position that the argument as a whole opposes; the second clarifies the meaning of a specific phrase as it is used in that generalization.

(C) The first provides evidence to support the conclusion of the argument as a whole; the second is evidence that has been used to support the position that the argument as a whole opposes.

(D) The first provides evidence to support the conclusion of the argument as a whole; the second states that conclusion.

(E) The first and the second each provide evidence against the position that the argument as a whole opposes.

Argument Construction

Situation An investor has criticized a company, based on the company's recent increase in inventory and on its not decreasing production as a result of this increase.

Reasoning *What roles do the two boldfaced statements play in the argument?* The argument suggests that the investor's criticism is based on a principle that increased inventory of finished products often indicates that production is faster than it should be, given the existing demand for a company's products. However, the argument then states that the increase in inventory at the company in question is "entirely attributable" to existing orders of products. The argument thus suggests that the investor's criticism is misplaced, based on a suggestion as to (1) a principle that the investor could be using to support her argument and (2) an explanation as to why the principle does not apply to the company. The two boldfaced portions state these respective elements.

A **Correct.** The first boldfaced portion states the principle that may provide the basis of the investor's criticism, which the argument as a whole opposes. The second boldfaced portion is a statement that, if true, the generalization would not apply to the company in question.

B This option correctly describes the first of the boldfaced portions. However, rather than clarifying an aspect of the meaning of the first generalization, the second boldfaced portion indicates why the first generalization may not apply to the company.

C This option incorrectly describes both of the boldfaced portions. The first boldfaced portion states a general principle that could support the position that the argument *opposes*. The second boldfaced portion then criticizes the application of the principle.

D Because the second boldfaced portion describes a fundamental premise rather than the conclusion, the description in this option of the second boldfaced portion is incorrect.

E If we think of an argument as a set of statements that are meant to support, or provide evidence for, a conclusion, then, because the boldfaced statements are indeed part of the argument, they may be seen as providing evidence for the position the argument opposes. However, a description of the roles of the boldfaced statements in this argument would need to provide more detail, such as what option A provides.

The correct answer is A.

CR10028

682. To reduce productivity losses from employees calling in sick, Corporation X implemented a new policy requiring employees to come into work unless they were so sick that they had to go to a doctor. But a year after the policy was implemented, a study found that Corporation X's overall productivity losses due to reported employee illnesses had increased.

Which of the following, if true, would best explain why the policy produced the reverse of its intended effect?

(A) After the policy was implemented, employees more frequently went to the doctor when they felt sick.
(B) Before the policy was implemented, employees who were not sick at all often called in sick.
(C) Employees coming into work when sick often infect many of their coworkers.
(D) Unusually few employees became genuinely sick during the year after the policy was implemented.
(E) There are many other factors besides employee illness that can adversely affect productivity.

Evaluation of a Plan

Situation After a company started requiring employees to come to work unless they were sick enough to have to go to a doctor, the company's productivity losses from reported employee illness increased.

Reasoning *What would explain why the policy increased productivity losses from reported employee illness?* Any factors that could have plausibly caused the policy to increase employee absenteeism from reported illness or to reduce the employees' productivity at work as a result of reported illness could explain why the policy increased productivity losses from reported illness.

A Even though the policy required sick employees to consult a doctor, there is no reason to think that employees' doing so would have made them less productive than they would otherwise have been when absent from work.

B This suggests that the policy made it more difficult for employees to falsely claim illness as an excuse for a work absence. Reduction in absences should result in productivity gains rather than losses.

C **Correct.** This could have been a result of the policy and would have led to productivity losses possibly greater than those seen before the policy was introduced.

D This would help to explain lower productivity losses from reported illness after the policy was implemented, not higher productivity losses.

E The question is what could explain how the policy increased productivity losses from reported employee illness specifically, not productivity losses from any other factors.

The correct answer is C.

CR08443
683. Advertising by mail has become much less effective, with fewer consumers responding. Because consumers are increasingly overwhelmed by the sheer amount of junk mail they receive, most discard almost all offers without considering them. Thus, an effective way for corporations to improve response rates would be to more carefully target the individuals to whom they mail advertising, thereby cutting down on the amount of junk mail each consumer receives.

Which of the following, if true, would most support the recommendation above?

(A) There are cost-effective means by which corporations that currently advertise by mail could improve response rates.

(B) Many successful corporations are already carefully targeting the individuals to whom they mail advertising.

(C) Any consumer who, immediately after receiving an advertisement by mail, merely glances at it is very likely to discard it.

(D) Improvements in the quality of the advertising materials used in mail that is carefully targeted to individuals can improve the response rate for such mail.

(E) Response rates to carefully targeted advertisements by mail are considerably higher, on average, than response rates to most other forms of advertising.

Evaluation of a Plan

Situation	Advertising by mail has become less effective because consumers overwhelmed with the amount of junk mail they receive discard almost all of it without considering it.

Reasoning	*What would most help to support the claim that making mail advertising more carefully targeted would improve response rates?* The passage recommends targeted advertising, reasoning that since targeted advertising would reduce the total amount of junk mail consumers receive, it would generate higher response rates. Any additional evidence for the claim that carefully targeted advertising would improve response rates would support this recommendation.

A	Even if targeted advertising and every other means of improving response rates were too expensive to be cost-effective, targeted advertising could still be effective for any corporation willing to pay the expense.

B	If many corporations already mail targeted advertising, and mail advertising is nonetheless yielding declining response rates, that suggests that targeted mail is an ineffective way to increase response rates.

C	This could be equally true for targeted and untargeted mail advertising, so it does not suggest that the former is more effective.

D	The question under consideration is whether more carefully targeted mail advertising would in itself increase response rates, not whether higher quality advertising would do so.

E	**Correct.** This provides some evidence that carefully targeted mail advertising is associated with higher response rates than untargeted mail advertising is, and therefore that targeting mail advertising more carefully would improve response rates.

The correct answer is E.

CR01905
684. Petrochemical industry officials have said that the extreme pressure exerted on plant managers during the last five years to improve profits by cutting costs has done nothing to impair the industry's ability to operate safely. However, environmentalists contend that the recent rash of serious oil spills and accidents at petrochemical plants is traceable to cost-cutting measures.

Which of the following, if true, would provide the strongest support for the position held by industry officials?

(A) The petrochemical industry benefits if accidents do not occur, since accidents involve risk of employee injury as well as loss of equipment and product.
(B) Petrochemical industry unions recently demanded that additional money be spent on safety and environmental protection measures, but the unions readily abandoned those demands in exchange for job security.
(C) Despite major cutbacks in most other areas of operation, the petrochemical industry has devoted more of its resources to environmental and safety measures in the last five years than in the preceding five years.
(D) There is evidence that the most damaging of the recent oil spills would have been prevented had cost-cutting measures not been instituted.
(E) Both the large fines and the adverse publicity generated by the most recent oil spill have prompted the petrochemical industry to increase the resources devoted to oil-spill prevention.

Argument Evaluation

Situation Petrochemical industry officials claim that pressure on plant managers to cut costs over the past five years has not made the industry's operations any less safe. Environmentalists claim that recent oil spills and accidents show otherwise.

Reasoning *What evidence would most strongly suggest that the cost-cutting pressure was not responsible for the recent rash of oil spills and accidents?* Evidence that the plant managers did not cut costs in any specific ways likely to have increased the likelihood of oil spills and accidents would support the industry officials' position that the cost-cutting pressure has not made petrochemical operations any less safe.

A   Even if the petrochemical industry has good reasons to try to prevent accidents, the recent rash of serious accidents suggests that it is failing to do so and that the cost-cutting pressure might be responsible.

B   This suggests that the unions, whose members could directly observe the cost-cutting pressure's effects, share the environmentalists' belief that this pressure contributed to the oil spills and accidents. Because the unions abandoned their demands, their concerns probably have not been addressed.

C   **Correct.** This suggests that, as the industry officials claim, the cost-cutting pressure has not in itself reduced the industry's effectiveness at preventing oil spills and accidents. Thus, it suggests that other factors are probably responsible for the recent problems.

D   This clearly suggests that the cost-cutting measures have indeed caused the industry to operate less safely, as the environmentalists claim.

E   Although this suggests that the industry is now trying to address the recent problems, the cost-cutting measures might nonetheless have caused all those problems.

The correct answer is C.

8.7 Critical Reasoning Answer Explanations

CR01368

685. A company has developed a new sensing device that, according to the company's claims, detects weak, ultralow-frequency electromagnetic signals associated with a beating heart. These signals, which pass through almost any physical obstruction, are purportedly detected by the device even at significant distances. Therefore, if the company's claims are true, their device will radically improve emergency teams' ability to locate quickly people who are trapped within the wreckage of collapsed buildings.

Which of the following, if true, most strengthens the argument?

(A) People trapped within the wreckage of collapsed buildings usually have serious injuries that require prompt medical treatment.

(B) The device gives a distinctive reading when the signals it detects come from human beings rather than from any other living beings.

(C) Most people who have survived after being trapped in collapsed buildings were rescued within two hours of the building's collapse.

(D) Ultralow-frequency signals are not the only electromagnetic signals that can pass through almost any physical obstruction.

(E) Extensive training is required in order to operate the device effectively.

Argument Evaluation

Situation   A new sensing device can detect—at significant distances and even behind obstructions such as walls—weak, ultralow-frequency electromagnetic signals that are characteristic of heartbeats. It is predicted, based on this information, that the new device will shorten the time it currently takes to locate people buried under collapsed buildings but still alive.

Reasoning   *What new information, if accurate, would provide further evidence that would support the prediction?* The existing evidence fails to tell us whether the new device can distinguish between human heartbeats and heartbeats from other species. If the device does not quickly provide signals characteristic of human heartbeats, then the prediction might not be correct; even if the prediction eventually turns out to be correct, the evidence given for it is insufficient. Any new information that implies the signals provided by the device can discern a human heartbeat from those of nonhuman species will strengthen support for the prediction.

A   This implies that prompt rescue of people trapped under collapsed buildings is vitally important. The prediction is that the new device will speed rescue of such people, but the new information here does nothing to indicate that the prediction is accurate.

B   **Correct.** This information fills an important gap (already discussed) in the evidence for the prediction.

C   Even if this is true, shortening the time for locating and rescuing people from collapsed buildings would clearly be beneficial. However, the new information given here does not make it more likely that the prediction is correct.

D   If this is correct, then if anything, it somewhat undermines the evidence given for the prediction, since it raises the possibility that the detection ability of the device might be impeded by "noise" from irrelevant electromagnetic signals near the collapsed building.

E   This could lead to practical obstacles when using the device even in emergency situations, with the result that the device might never actually be used by competent personnel to "improve emergency teams' ability" because the "extensive training" would cost too much.

The correct answer is B.

CR11639
686. Economist: The price of tap water in our region should be raised drastically. **Supplies in local freshwater reservoirs have been declining for years** because water is being used faster than it can be replenished. Since the price of tap water has been low, **few users have bothered to adopt even easy conservation measures**.

The two sections in boldface play which of the following roles in the economist's argument?

(A) The first is a conclusion for which support is provided, and which in turn supports the main conclusion; the second is the main conclusion.
(B) The first is an observation for which the second provides an explanation; the second is the main conclusion but not the only conclusion.
(C) The first is a premise supporting the argument's main conclusion; so is the second.
(D) The first is the only conclusion; the second provides an explanation for the first.
(E) The first is the main conclusion; the second is a conclusion for which support is provided, and which in turn supports the first.

Argument Construction

Situation: Local water supplies have been declining for years because of excessive water use and low prices. Few users have adopted even easy conservation measures.

Reasoning: *What roles do the two boldface statements play in the argument?* Both are factual observations. Since no further evidence or support is provided for either, neither can be a conclusion in the argument. However, interconnected causal explanations, signaled by *because* and *since,* are provided for both. The observation in the first boldface statement is causally explained by the further observation that water is being used faster than it can be replenished, which in turn is causally explained by the entire final sentence. The observation in the second boldface statement is causally explained by the observation that the price of tap water has been low. The only remaining portion of the argument is the initial sentence, a recommendation supported by these four observations together, and by the causal claims in which they are embedded. Thus, the four observations (including the two boldface statements) and the causal claims containing them are all premises, and the initial statement is the argument's only conclusion.

A As explained above, the two boldface statements are premises of the argument. Although causal explanations are provided for both, no support or evidence is provided for either.

B As explained above, the second boldface statement does provide part of the causal explanation for the observation in the first boldface statement. But no support is provided for either statement, so neither is a conclusion.

C **Correct.** As explained above, each of the statements is a premise that serves along with other claims to support the recommendation in the initial sentence, which is the argument's only conclusion, and in that sense its main conclusion.

D As explained above, the second boldface statement does provide part of the causal explanation for the observation in the first boldface statement. But no support is provided for either statement, so neither is a conclusion in the argument.

E As explained above, the two boldface statements are premises of the argument. Although causal explanations are provided for both, no support or evidence is provided for either.

The correct answer is C.

687. Politician: Hybrid cars use significantly less fuel per kilometer than nonhybrids. And fuel produces air pollution, which contributes to a number of environmental problems. Motorists can save money by driving cars that are more fuel efficient, and they will be encouraged to drive hybrid cars if we make them aware of that fact. Therefore, we can help reduce the total amount of pollution emitted by cars in this country by highlighting this advantage of hybrid cars.

Which of the following, if true, would most indicate a vulnerability of the politician's argument?

(A) People with more fuel-efficient cars typically drive more than do those with less fuel-efficient cars.
(B) Not all air pollution originates from automobiles.
(C) Hybrid cars have already begun to gain popularity.
(D) Fuel-efficient alternatives to hybrid cars will likely become available in the future.
(E) The future cost of gasoline and other fuel cannot be predicted with absolute precision or certainty.

Argument Evaluation

Situation According to a politician, hybrid cars use less fuel per kilometer than nonhybrids, and fuel produces air pollution. Motorists can save money by driving fuel-efficient cars, and will be encouraged to do so if made aware of the fact. The politician concludes that highlighting this fact will result in a reduction in air pollution.

Reasoning *What would suggest that telling motorists they can save money by driving fuel-efficient cars would not reduce automotive air pollution, despite the facts cited by the politician?* The politician's implicit reasoning is that since hybrid cars use less fuel per kilometer, and fuel produces air pollution, motorists who drive hybrid cars must produce less air pollution than those who drive nonhybrids. The politician concludes that encouraging motorists to drive hybrid cars by telling them they would save money on fuel will therefore reduce automotive air pollution. Evidence that motorists who drive hybrid cars produce just as much automotive air pollution as those who drive nonhybrids would undermine this argument.

A **Correct.** If drivers of hybrid cars tend to drive more kilometers than drivers of nonhybrids, then they may consume just as much fuel and produce just as much air pollution as the nonhybrid car drivers do, despite their lower fuel use per kilometer.
B The politician's argument is only about air pollution from cars specifically, not air pollution from all sources.
C Even if hybrid cars are beginning to gain popularity, informing motorists of the cost savings from fuel efficiency could help these cars become more popular than they would otherwise be.
D Encouraging motorists to switch to hybrid cars now could reduce fuel use and automotive air pollution in the near future even if other, more fuel-efficient vehicles will become available further in the future.
E Even if the future cost of fuel cannot be predicted accurately, encouraging motorists to switch to hybrid cars could reduce air pollution as the politician argues.

The correct answer is A.

CR99530.01
688. Mayor: False alarms from home security systems waste so much valuable police time that in many communities police have stopped responding to alarms from homes whose systems frequently produce false alarms. This policy reduces wastage of police time but results in a loss of protection for some residents. To achieve a comparable reduction in wastage without reducing protection for residents, the council has enacted a measure to fine residents for repeated false alarms.

Which of the following, if true, casts the most doubt on whether the measure enacted by the council will achieve its goal?

(A) A fine in the amount planned by the council will not cover the expenses police typically incur when they respond to a false alarm.
(B) Homes equipped with security systems are far less likely to be broken into than are homes without security systems.
(C) The threat of fines is likely to cause many residents to deactivate their security systems.
(D) The number of home security systems is likely to increase dramatically over the next five years.
(E) Many home security systems have never produced false alarms.

Evaluation of a Plan

Situation   In many communities, police have been responding to false home-security alarms but have ceased to respond to alarms from homes that often have such false alarms. To reduce wastage of police time without compromising residents' home protection, one town council has enacted a new measure that will fine home residents for repeated false alarms.

Reasoning   *What fact or occurrence would most reduce the likelihood that the town council's newly enacted measure would achieve its goal, which is to reduce wastage of police time without compromising home protection? Note that the goal is not to eliminate all wastage of police time or to pay all the costs of it; some random wastage is to be expected. But if many residents deactivated their security alarms (even well-functioning systems) because they wish to avoid being fined, this could reduce the level of home protection for those residents.*

A The goal is to reduce wastage of police time resulting from false security-system alarms, not necessarily to cover all the costs in police time for such alarms.

B This seems obviously true, but it is also irrelevant to the frequency of false home-security alarms. It is therefore irrelevant, also, to whether the council's measure will effectively address wastage of police time stemming from such alarms.

C **Correct.** If this occurred, it would result in a lower level of home protection for some residents and would mean that the town council's measure would have failed to achieve its goal.

D This scenario does not make the council's measure more likely to fail to achieve its goal. If the increase in alarm systems occurs, it will likely result in more protection for the homes of more residents. Assuming vigorous enforcement of the new measure, we have no reason to believe that the number of false alarms would increase.

E This has little bearing on the likelihood of the council's measure succeeding. Any home-security system that has never produced a false alarm could do so tomorrow, for all kinds of reasons.

The correct answer is C.

CR53341.01

689. Excavation of the house of a third-century Camarnian official revealed that he had served four magistrates—public officials who administer the law—over his thirty-year public career, in four provincial capital cities. However, given the Camarnian administrative system of that era, it is unclear whether he served them simultaneously, as a traveling administrator living for part of the year in each provincial capital, or else did so sequentially, leaving one magistrate after several years to join another.

Which of the following would, if found in the excavation, most likely help reveal the pattern of the official's administrative service?

(A) Maps and documents describing each of the four provincial capitals
(B) A cache of the official's documents related to work from early in his career
(C) A set of cups of a type made only in the city of the first magistrate whom the official is known to have served
(D) Several pieces of furniture in the styles of two of the provincial capital cities
(E) Heavy clothing appropriate only for the coldest of the four cities

Argument Construction

Situation   Evidence from an excavation makes clear that a particular third-century Camarnian official served four magistrates in four provincial capitals over his thirty-year career, but it is unclear whether he served the magistrates simultaneously or sequentially.

Reasoning   *What evidence, if it were also found in the excavation, would be most helpful in determining whether the official served the magistrates simultaneously or sequentially?* It would be helpful to find documents from throughout the magistrate's career indicating at what times he worked for each magistrate, or even documents from just one period, as long as there were a large number, because this would likely show whether he was working for just one magistrate or for all four.

A   We already know that the official worked in each of the four capitals. The fact that maps and documents describing the capitals were at his house tells us nothing about whether he worked for magistrates in these capitals simultaneously or not.

B   **Correct.** Presumably the work-related documents would show whom he was working for at the time, and for how long—and would provide evidence as to whether he was working for multiple magistrates or for just one.

C   Merely finding a set of cups made only in one of the cities tells us little. Even if we knew when he acquired the set, he need not have been working for the magistrate of that city at the time he acquired it; perhaps he had simply traveled to that city.

D   One frequently moves furniture when moving from one city to another, so the fact that the official had pieces of furniture that may have come from different cities does not give us any indication of whether the official worked for all four magistrates simultaneously or not.

E   The fact that heavy clothing appropriate only for the coldest of the four cities was found in the excavation of the official's house does not imply that other clothing, appropriate for one or more of the other cities, was not found. Consistent with the finding of the heavy clothing, the official may have worked exclusively in the city for which that clothing was appropriate, or worked intermittently in this city.

The correct answer is B.

CR80531.01
690. In 1563, in Florence's Palazzo Vecchio, Giorgio Vasari built in front of an existing wall a new wall on which he painted a mural. Investigators recently discovered a gap between Vasari's wall and the original, large enough to have preserved anything painted on the original. Historians believe that Leonardo da Vinci had painted, but left unfinished, a mural on the original wall; some historians had also believed that by 1563 the mural had been destroyed. However, it is known that in the late 1560s, when renovating another building, Santa Maria Novella, Vasari built a façade over its frescoes, and the frescoes were thereby preserved. Thus, Leonardo's Palazzo Vecchio mural probably still exists behind Vasari's wall.

Which of the following is an assumption on which the argument depends?

(A) Leonardo rarely if ever destroyed artworks that he left unfinished.
(B) Vasari was likely unaware that the mural in the Palazzo Vecchio had willingly been abandoned by Leonardo.
(C) Vasari probably would not have built the Palazzo Vecchio wall with a gap behind it except to preserve something behind the new wall.
(D) Leonardo would probably have completed the Palazzo Vecchio mural if he had had the opportunity to do so.
(E) When Vasari preserved the frescoes of Santa Maria Novella he did so secretly.

Argument Construction

Situation   Georgio Vasari built a new wall in front of an existing wall in the Palazzo Vecchio that historians believe had had an unfinished mural by Leonardo da Vinci painted on it. Some historians, however, believe the mural had been destroyed by the time Vasari built the new wall. There is a gap between the old and new wall, large enough to have preserved anything painted on it, as there is in Santa Maria Novella, where Vasari also constructed a new wall in front of an old wall; on that wall, the building's frescoes were preserved.

Reasoning   *What claim needs to be true for the cited facts to support the conclusion that Leonardo's Palazzo Vecchio mural likely still exists behind Vasari's wall?* If there are other equally likely reasons that Vasari would have left a gap between the old wall and a new wall, besides preserving any painting on the old wall, the stated facts would not support the conclusion. After all, it may be only fortuitous that the frescoes in the Santa Maria Novella were preserved when Vasari built the new wall with a gap between it and the old wall. Therefore, the argument depends on assuming that it is unlikely that Vasari would have created a gap between the old and new walls unless he had been trying to preserve something painted on the old wall.

A   The argument does not depend on the claim that Leonardo rarely if ever destroyed his unfinished artworks. Obviously, it does depend on the claim that he did not always do so, but even if he fairly regularly destroyed unfinished artworks, this mural could be one of the ones he did not—perhaps the reason the mural was left unfinished was that he died before completing it.

B   The argument does not depend on Vasari knowing that Leonardo had willingly abandoned the mural. Even if Leonardo did willingly leave it unfinished, Vasari could nonetheless have thought the mural was of value and wanted to preserve it.

C   **Correct.** If there had been other likely reasons for Vasari to have built a gap behind the new wall other than to preserve something painted on the old wall, the cited facts would not be a good reason to believe that Vasari built the gap for the purpose of preserving anything painted on it.

D   Leonardo may have had no interest in finishing the mural. Vasari could nevertheless have thought that there was value in preserving it.

E   There is no need to assume that Vasari preserved the frescoes at Santa Maria Novella secretly. Even if he did not do so in this instance, he could have preserved other paintings secretly by the same means, or he may have let others know that he was preserving Leonardo's mural, although there is no historical record that he did let them know.

The correct answer is C.

691. Coffee shop owner: A large number of customers will pay at least the fair market value for a cup of coffee, even if there is no formal charge. Some will pay more than this out of appreciation of the trust that is placed in them. And our total number of customers is likely to increase. We could therefore improve our net cash flow by implementing an honor system in which customers pay what they wish for coffee by depositing money in a can.

Manager: We're likely to lose money on this plan. Many customers would cheat the system, paying a very small sum or nothing at all.

Which of the following, if true, would best support the owner's plan, in light of the manager's concern?

(A) The new system, if implemented, would increase the number of customers.
(B) By roasting its own coffee, the shop has managed to reduce the difficulties (and cost) of maintaining an inventory of freshly roasted coffee.
(C) Many customers stay in the cafe for long stretches of time.
(D) The shop makes a substantial profit from pastries and other food bought by the coffee drinkers.
(E) No other coffee shop in the area has such a system.

Evaluation of a Plan

Situation   The owner and the manager of a coffee shop disagree about whether allowing customers to pay for coffee on an honor system would increase or decrease profits.

Reasoning   *What would be the best evidence that the honor-system plan would increase profits even if many customers cheated the system?* The owner argues that profits would increase because many customers will choose to pay as much or more than before and the total number of customers will likely increase. But the manager points out that many customers would also choose to pay little or nothing. Assuming that the manager is correct about that, what further support could the owner present for the claim that the plan would still be profitable?

A   Since the owner has already basically asserted this, asserting it again would not provide any significant additional support for the plan.
B   This suggests that the shop is already profitable, not that the honor-system plan would make it more profitable.
C   Customers who stay in the cafe for long stretches would not necessarily pay any more per cup on the honor-system plan than other customers would.
D   **Correct.** If the customer base increases (as both the owner and the manager seem to agree), more customers will likely purchase highly profitable pastries and other foods, thus boosting profits.
E   The reason no other coffee shop in the area has an honor system may be that their owners and managers have determined that it would not be profitable.

The correct answer is D.

CR01900
692. The city of Workney, in raising bus fares from $1.00 to $1.25, proposed that 18 fare tokens be sold for $20.00 to alleviate the extra burden of the fare increase on the city's poor people. Critics suggested alternatively that 9 fare tokens be sold for $10.00, because a $20.00 outlay would be prohibitive for poor riders.

The alternative proposal depends on which of the following assumptions?

(A) Poor residents of Workney will continue to ride the buses in the same numbers despite the fare increase.
(B) Riders who are poor would be more likely to take advantage of the savings afforded by the 9-token offer than would riders who are not poor.
(C) The outlay of $10.00 for the purchase of 9 fare tokens would not be prohibitive for bus riders who are poor.
(D) The proposed fare increase is needed for the purchase of new buses for the city's bus system.
(E) Fewer riders would regularly purchase 18 fare tokens at once than would purchase only 9 fare tokens at once.

Evaluation of a Plan

Situation The city of Workney raised bus fares from $1.00 to $1.25. To help poor people, the city proposed allowing people to block-purchase 18 tickets for $20.00. But critics argued that poor people could ill-afford to pay $20.00 at one time. Their alternative proposal was: allow block-purchase of 9 tickets for $10.00.

Reasoning *What did the critics assume in making their alternative proposal?* The city's block-purchase proposal would result in a saving of $4.50 over the cost of purchasing 18 tickets separately, and the critics' alternative block-purchase proposal would result in a saving of $2.25 over the cost of purchasing 9 tickets separately. The savings per ticket on either proposal would be identical. But the critics' proposal assumes that people who would not be able to block-purchase 18 tickets for $20.00 would be able to block-purchase 9 tickets for $10.00.

A The critics assume something incompatible with this. Their alternative was proposed because they believed that some poor residents would otherwise, at least sometimes, be unable to purchase bus tickets.

B Nothing in the critics' proposal allows only poor people to benefit from the proposal. No information is given about the relative likelihoods of poor or nonpoor riders availing of the block-purchase option perhaps for convenience rather than for savings.

C **Correct.** The critics' proposal depends on the assumption that poor bus riders would generally be able to block-purchase 9 tickets for $10.00.

D The alternative proposal does not depend on assuming this. The proposal could still make sense even if the additional revenue from the fare increases was needed to pay higher wages to bus drivers.

E The critics' proposal does not depend on assuming this. How many riders would block-purchase 18 tickets? How many would block-purchase 9 tickets? These are open questions, as far as the critics' proposal is concerned. The 9-ticket option might or might not turn out to be more frequently purchased than the 18-ticket option. The critics' concern is to make the 9-ticket option available to poor riders, not to prevent nonpoor riders from availing of it.

The correct answer is C.

CR03272
693. Birds have been said to be descended from certain birdlike dinosaur species with which they share distinctive structural features. The fossil record, however, shows that this cannot be so, since there are bird fossils that are much older than the earliest birdlike dinosaur fossils that have been found.

Which of the following is an assumption on which the argument relies?

(A) The birdlike dinosaurs have no living descendants.
(B) There are no flightless dinosaur species that have the distinctive structural features shared by birds and birdlike dinosaurs.
(C) There are no birdlike dinosaur fossils that are older than the bird fossils but have not yet been unearthed.
(D) It could not have been the case that some birds were descended from one of the birdlike dinosaur species and other birds from another.
(E) Birds cannot have been descended from dinosaur species with which the birds do not share the distinctive structural features.

Argument Construction

Situation   Although birds have been said to be descended from birdlike dinosaurs, some bird fossils predate the earliest known birdlike dinosaur fossils.

Reasoning   *What must be true in order for the premise that some bird fossils predate the earliest known birdlike dinosaur fossils to support the conclusion that birds are not descended from birdlike dinosaurs?* The argument implicitly reasons that since the cited bird fossils predate the earliest known birdlike dinosaur fossils, they must be from birds that lived before the earliest birdlike dinosaurs, and which therefore could not have been descended from birdlike dinosaurs. This reasoning assumes that any birdlike dinosaurs that lived before the first birds would have left fossils that still exist. It also assumes that no undiscovered birdlike dinosaur fossils predate the cited bird fossils.

A   The argument is only about whether birds are descended from birdlike dinosaurs. Whether birdlike dinosaurs have any living descendants other than birds is irrelevant.

B   The argument is only about birds and birdlike dinosaurs. It is not about other types of dinosaurs that were not birdlike.

C   **Correct.** If any undiscovered birdlike dinosaur fossils predate the cited bird fossils, then the latter fossils' age does not support the conclusion that birds are not descended from birdlike dinosaurs.

D   The argument purports to establish that the relative ages of bird fossils and birdlike dinosaur fossils show that birds cannot be descended from any of the known birdlike dinosaur species. In doing this, it acknowledges multiple birdlike dinosaur species and leaves open the question of whether some birds may be descended from one such species and other birds from another such species.

E   The argument does not claim that the known fossil record shows that birds cannot be descended from dinosaurs. It only claims that the record shows that they cannot be descended from the birdlike dinosaurs that shared their distinctive structural features.

The correct answer is C.

694. City council member: Demand for electricity has been increasing by 1.5 percent a year, and there simply is no more space to build additional power plants to meet future demand increases. We must therefore begin to curtail usage, which is why I propose passing ordinances requiring energy-conservation measures in all city departments.

The city council member's proposal assumes which of the following?

(A) Existing power plants do not have the capacity to handle all of the projected increase in demand for electricity.
(B) No city departments have implemented energy-conservation measures voluntarily.
(C) Passing ordinances designed to curtail electricity usage will not have negative economic consequences for the city.
(D) Residential consumers are not responsible for the recent increases in demand for electricity.
(E) City departments that successfully conserve energy will set a good example for residential and industrial consumers of electricity.

Argument Construction

Situation: A city council member proposes energy-conservation measures for all city government departments because there is no room to build new power plants to meet future increases in the demand for electricity.

Reasoning: *What must be true in order for the factors the city council member cites to help justify the proposal?* The city council member says electricity usage must be curtailed on account of an increasing demand for electricity and a lack of space for new power plants that could meet future demand increases. In order for this reasoning to help justify the proposal, the cited factors must actually establish a need to curtail electricity usage.

A **Correct.** If current power plants could satisfy the projected increased demand for electricity, then the increasing demand and the lack of room to build new plants would not establish a need to curtail electricity usage.

B The proposed ordinances could still be necessary even if one city department had voluntarily implemented energy-conservation measures.

C Passing the ordinances could still be necessary even if they would have some negative economic effects.

D No matter who is responsible for the recent increases in demand, curtailing the city government's electricity usage could still help to reduce demand.

E Ordinances to curtail the city government's energy usage could be economically necessary regardless of whether or not departments that obey the ordinances set a good example.

The correct answer is A.

CR32441.01
695. Certain groups of Asian snails include both "left-handed" and "right-handed" species, with shells coiling to the left and right, respectively. Some left-handed species have evolved from right-handed ones. Also, researchers found that snail-eating snakes in the same habitat have asymmetrical jaws, allowing them to grasp right-handed snail shells more easily. If these snakes ate more right-handed snails over time, this would have given left-handed snails an evolutionary advantage over right-handed snails, with the left-handed snails eventually becoming a new species. Thus, the snakes' asymmetrical jaws probably helped drive the emergence of the left-handed snail species.

Which of the following would, if true, most strengthen the argument that asymmetrical snake jaws helped drive left-handed snail evolution?

(A) In one snake species, the snakes with asymmetrical jaws eat snails, while the snakes with symmetrical jaws do not eat snails.

(B) Some species of Asian snails contain either all right-handed snails, or all left-handed snails.

(C) Anatomical differences prevent left-handed snails from mating easily with right-handed snails.

(D) Some right-handed snails in this habitat have shells with a very narrow opening that helps prevent snakes from extracting the snails from inside their shells.

(E) Experiments show that the snail-eating snakes in this habitat fail more often in trying to eat left-handed snails than in trying to eat right-handed snails.

Argument Evaluation

Situation   There are both Asian snails with shells that coil to the right and Asian snails with shells that coil to the left, and the latter have evolved from the former; furthermore, there are snakes that have asymmetrical jaws that allow the snakes to grasp the snails with right-coiled shells more easily.

Reasoning   *What fact would help support the claim that the snakes' asymmetrical jaws helped drive the emergence of species of snails with left-coiled shells?* We are told that if over time the snakes with asymmetrical jaws ate more snails with right-coiled shells than snails with left-coiled shells, then this would give snails with left-coiled shells an evolutionary survival advantage. So, if some evidence showed that the snakes with such jaws in fact were more likely to have successfully eaten the snails with the right-coiled shells, then we would have good reason to think the snakes' asymmetrical jaws helped drive the emergence of snails with left-coiled shells.

A   The fact that snakes with asymmetrical jaws eat snails and other snakes do not does not give any indication as to whether snails with left-coiled shells have any evolutionary advantages over snails with right-coiled shells. At best it only tells us that if snakes drove the evolution of snails with left-coiled shells, it would likely have been the snakes with asymmetrical jaws.

B   The fact that some species of Asian snails have no variation in the direction in which their shells coil tells us nothing about what, if any, evolutionary advantages they have relative to other snails, or whether the snakes' asymmetrical jaws had any effect on any such evolutionary advantages.

C   The inability of snails with left-coiled shells to mate easily with snails with right-coiled shells in and of itself tells us nothing about whether the snakes' asymmetrical jaws had any effect on the emergence of snails with left-coiled shells. Although it does suggest a different factor that could have contributed to the emergence of the snail species with left-coiled shells, it does not exclude the possibility that the snakes were also a factor.

D   The fact that snakes cannot extract some snails with right-coiled shells from their shells would suggest that these snails might have an evolutionary advantage; but the argument's conclusion is about an evolutionary advantage that snails with left-coiled shells presumably have, not an advantage that snails with right-coiled shells would have.

E   **Correct.** The fact that experiments show that the snakes are more successful at eating snails with right-coiled shells than they are at eating snails with left-coiled shells would support the claim that these snakes did in fact eat more snails with right-coiled shells, and hence the snails with left-coiled shells would as a result have an evolutionary advantage.

The correct answer is E.

CR95631.01
696. A moderately large city is redesigning its central downtown area and is considering a plan that would reduce the number of lanes for automobiles and trucks and increase those for bicycles and pedestrians. The intent is to attract more workers and shoppers to downtown businesses by making downtown easier to reach and more pleasant to move around in.

Which of the following would, if true, most strongly support the prediction that the plan would achieve its goal?

(A) People who make a habit of walking or bicycling whenever feasible derive significant health benefits from doing so.
(B) Most people who prefer to shop at suburban malls instead of downtown urban areas do so because parking is easier and cheaper at the former.
(C) In other moderately sized cities where measures were taken to make downtowns more accessible for walkers and cyclists, downtown businesses began to thrive.
(D) If the proposed lane restrictions on drivers are rigorously enforced, more people will likely be attracted to downtown businesses than would otherwise be.
(E) Most people who own and frequently ride bicycles for recreational purposes live at a significant distance from downtown urban areas.

Evaluation of a Plan

Situation A moderately large city desires to attract more workers and shoppers to downtown businesses by making the downtown area more pleasant and easier to travel to. In light of this goal, the city is considering a plan that would reduce the number of lanes for automobiles and trucks and increase those for bicycles and pedestrians.

Reasoning *What would most strongly support the prediction that reducing the number of lanes for automobiles and trucks and increasing those for bicycles and pedestrians would achieve the goal of attracting more people to downtown businesses?* If other moderately sized cities that have improved the accessibility of their downtown areas to pedestrians and cyclists have seen increased downtown business, then it is reasonable to think that the city in question will have improved downtown business as well.

A If people who make a habit of walking or bicycling derive significant health benefits, that would provide further motivation for trying to encourage people to walk or ride a bicycle, but it does not provide much support for the claim that adding lanes for pedestrians and cyclists will successfully bring people to shop or work more in the city's downtown. Perhaps people will merely use the new lanes for exercise, but not to get to the downtown area to do business.

B Because the plan as described does not provide for additional parking, the fact that parking is a major concern motivating people to shop at suburban malls does not give us good reason to think that the city's plan will help achieve the city's goal.

C **Correct.** If other moderately sized cities that have made their downtown areas more accessible to pedestrians and cyclists have seen their downtown businesses begin to thrive soon afterwards, this is evidence—even if not conclusive—that the changes produced the thriving. Consequently, it is reasonable to think that the same will result for the city in question.

D It might be the case that rigorously enforcing lane restrictions will attract more people to downtown businesses than would otherwise be the case, but the information provided does not indicate how strictly lane restrictions will be enforced.

E The city's plan is aimed at increasing the use of bicycles for the purposes of shopping or getting to work, not only for recreational purposes. And even if people who use their bicycles for recreational purposes would also be likely to use them for shopping or getting to work, the fact that most recreational cyclists live at a significant distance from the city's downtown area may suggest that the city's plan will not be successful, because the cyclists may live too far away to use their bicycles for these purposes, even if it would be somewhat easier for them to do so once the plan has been implemented.

The correct answer is C.

697. Previously, Autoco designed all of its cars itself and then contracted with specialized parts suppliers to build parts according to its specifications. Now it plans to include its suppliers in designing the parts they are to build. Since many parts suppliers have more designers with specialized experience than Autoco has, Autoco expects this shift to reduce the overall time and cost of the design of its next new car.

Which of the following, if true, most strongly supports Autoco's expectation?

(A) When suppliers provide their own designs, Autoco often needs to modify its overall design.

(B) In order to provide designs for Autoco, several of the parts suppliers will have to add to their existing staffs of designers.

(C) Parts and services provided by outside suppliers account for more than 50 percent of Autoco's total costs.

(D) When suppliers built parts according to specifications provided by Autoco, the suppliers competed to win contracts.

(E) Most of Autoco's suppliers have on hand a wide range of previously prepared parts designs that can readily be modified for a new car.

Evaluation of a Plan

Situation A car manufacturer plans to have its parts suppliers start helping to design the parts they build for the manufacturer. Many parts suppliers have more designers with specialized experience than the manufacturer has.

Reasoning *What would make it more likely that having the parts suppliers help design the parts will reduce the time and cost of designing the manufacturer's next new car?* In order for the change to reduce the time and cost, the parts suppliers involved in designing the next car will probably have to do their portion of the design process faster and cheaper than the manufacturer would have, and the design collaboration process will have to avoid producing substantial new inefficiencies.

A The additional need to modify the overall design would probably make the design process slower and more expensive, not faster and cheaper.

B The additional need to hire more designers would probably increase design costs, not reduce them.

C Although this suggests that the change is likely to substantially affect the design's expense, it does not indicate whether the expense will increase or decrease.

D If anything, this competition probably made Autoco's previous design process cheaper. It does not suggest that the new design process, which may involve less competition, will be faster or cheaper than the previous one.

E **Correct.** Modifying the previously prepared parts designs will probably be faster and cheaper than creating new designs from scratch.

The correct answer is E.

698. In response to viral infection, the immune systems of mice typically produce antibodies that destroy the virus by binding to proteins on its surface. Mice infected with the herpesvirus generally develop keratitis, a degenerative disease affecting part of the eye. Since proteins on the surface of cells in this part of the eye closely resemble those on the herpesvirus surface, scientists hypothesize that these cases of keratitis are caused by antibodies to the herpesvirus.

Which of the following, if true, most helps to support the scientists' reasoning?

(A) Other types of virus have surface proteins that closely resemble proteins found in various organs of mice.

(B) Mice that are infected with the herpesvirus but do not develop keratitis produce as many antibodies as infected mice that do develop keratitis.

(C) Mice infected with a new strain of the herpesvirus that has different surface proteins did not develop keratitis.

(D) Mice that have never been infected with the herpesvirus can sometimes develop keratitis.

(E) There are mice that are unable to form antibodies in response to herpes infections, and these mice contract herpes at roughly the same rate as other mice.

Argument Evaluation

Situation Mice infected with the herpesvirus tend to develop keratitis, an eye disease. The surface of the eye cells have proteins that resemble those on the herpesvirus surface. Based on this finding, scientists have hypothesized that keratitis develops in mice because antibodies that attack herpesvirus surface proteins can also attack eyes.

Reasoning *What other information, if correct, would provide the strongest support for the scientists' hypothesis?* The clue that led the scientists to form their hypothesis was the close resemblance of the proteins on the mouse eye surface to those on the herpesvirus surface. The resemblance could cause antibodies to bind to both types of proteins, in one case eliminating the herpesvirus and in the other case causing keratitis.

A   Even if this is correct, we lack information as to whether the antibodies to those other types of virus can damage the organs that display the closely resembling proteins. If such a damage process were confirmed, it could count as evidence—even if not sufficient—to confirm the scientists' hypothesis.

B   If anything, this would, absent further information, raise doubts about the correctness of the scientists' proposed explanation.

C   **Correct.** This provides strong confirmation of the scientists' hypothesis. The proteins on the new strain of the herpesvirus no longer sufficiently resemble the proteins on the eye surface to cause the antibodies to attack those proteins and cause keratitis.

D   For all we know, keratitis may have multiple independent causes and may sometimes be caused by processes other than the protein misidentification hypothesized by the scientists. This information neither confirms nor refutes the scientists' hypothesis.

E   The rates at which mice contract herpes is not discussed. We lack any information as to whether mice that lack antibodies to the herpesvirus sometimes contract keratitis along with herpes infection.

The correct answer is C.

CR38931.01
699. One might expect that within a particular species, any individuals that managed to slow down the aging process would leave more offspring. Natural selection should therefore favor extreme longevity—but this does not seem to be the case. A possible explanation is that aging is a product of the inevitable wear and tear of living, similar to how household appliances generally accumulate faults that lead to their eventual demise. However, most researchers do not find this analogy satisfactory as an explanation.

Which of the following would, if true, provide the strongest explanation for the researchers' reaction?

(A) Some organisms are capable of living much longer than other organisms.
(B) Some organisms reproduce very quickly despite having short lifespans.
(C) There are several ways of defining "extreme longevity," and according to some definitions it occurs frequently.
(D) Organisms are capable of maintenance and self-repair and can remedy much of the damage that they accumulate.
(E) Some organisms generate much more wear and tear on their bodies than others.

Argument Construction

Situation   One possible explanation for the fact that natural selection does not favor extreme longevity, despite the fact that a slowed-down aging process would leave more offspring, is that aging is the product of wear and tear, much like household appliances eventually no longer function because of wear and tear; most researchers, however, reject this analogy as an explanation.

Reasoning   *What would explain the researchers' rejection of the explanation?* The explanation is based on analogy between organisms and household appliances. If there were a crucial difference between appliances and organisms, such as the fact that organisms are capable of self-repair in a way that household appliances are not, then it would be reasonable for the researchers to reject the explanation.

A   The fact that some organisms can live much longer than other organisms is not a good reason to reject the analogy; after all, some household appliances may last much longer than others, perhaps because they receive a different amount of wear and tear.

B   Even if some organisms reproduce very quickly despite having short lifespans, that does not mean that they would not have even more offspring if they lived longer; also, this is irrelevant as to whether the analogy between the aging process and the wear and tear on household appliances is any good.

C   It is unclear what these different ways of defining "extreme longevity" are—perhaps the definition is merely a relative one; some organisms live much longer than others, and those that do have "extreme longevity." But presumably some household appliances last much longer than others, so this would not indicate a difference, and thus would not explain why most researchers reject the analogy.

D   **Correct.** Household appliances cannot repair themselves as organisms can, so the wear and tear of living is quite different from the wear and tear in household appliances.

E   Presumably some household appliances receive much more wear and tear than other household appliances, so the fact that some organisms generate more wear and tear on their bodies than others does not indicate a difference between appliances and organisms, and thus does not explain why the researchers reject the analogy.

The correct answer is D.

CR02885

700. Last year a record number of new manufacturing jobs were created. Will this year bring another record? Well, **any new manufacturing job is created either within an existing company or by the start-up of a new company**. Within existing firms, new jobs have been created this year at well below last year's record pace. At the same time, there is considerable evidence that the number of new companies starting up this year will be no higher than it was last year and **there is no reason to think that the new companies starting up this year will create more jobs per company than did last year's start-ups**. So clearly, the number of new jobs created this year will fall short of last year's record.

In the argument given, the two portions in **boldface** play which of the following roles?

(A) The first provides evidence in support of the main conclusion of the argument; the second is a claim that the argument challenges.

(B) The first is a generalization that the argument seeks to establish; the second is a conclusion that the argument draws in order to support that generalization.

(C) The first is a generalization that the argument seeks to establish; the second is a judgment that has been advanced in order to challenge that generalization.

(D) The first is presented as an obvious truth on which the argument is based; the second is a claim that has been advanced in support of a position that the argument opposes.

(E) The first is presented as an obvious truth on which the argument is based; the second is a judgment advanced in support of the main conclusion of the argument.

Argument Construction

Situation Manufacturing jobs are created either within existing companies or in start-ups. Manufacturing jobs are being created at a much slower rate this year than last year. It seems likely that the number of new start-ups will not exceed last year's number and that the average number of manufacturing jobs per start-up will not exceed last year's number. So fewer manufacturing jobs are likely to be created this year than last year.

Reasoning *What function is served by the statement that any new manufacturing job is created either within an existing company or by the start-up of a new company? What function is served by the statement that there is no reason to think that the new companies starting up this year will create more jobs per company than did last year's start-ups?* The first statement makes explicit a general background assumption that there are just two ways in which manufacturing jobs are created. This assumption is used, along with other information, to support the argument's main conclusion, i.e., the prediction about job creation this year. The second statement gives a premise meant to help support the prediction about this year's manufacturing-job creation.

A The first is a general statement making explicit an assumption on which the argument's reasoning depends, but the second is a statement affirmed as part of the argument and does not express a claim that the argument challenges.

B The first is a generalization that is simply stated, without any support being offered. The second is not a conclusion and is not offered in support of the first.

C The second is not presented as a challenge to the generalization that is given in the first statement. The argument does not seek to establish the first statement, but merely asserts it.

D The second is information offered in support of the argument's main conclusion rather than a statement offered in support of a position opposed by the argument.

E **Correct.** The first, stating a truism, is merely asserted and requires no support in the argument, for which it provides a foundation; the second is a piece of information meant to support the prediction that is the argument's main conclusion.

The correct answer is E.

701. Last year a record number of new manufacturing jobs were created. Will this year bring another record? Well, **any new manufacturing job is created either within an existing company or by the start-up of a new company**. Within existing firms, new jobs have been created this year at well below last year's record pace. At the same time, there is considerable evidence that the number of new companies starting up will be no higher this year than it was last year and there is no reason to think that the new companies starting up this year will create more jobs per company than did last year's start-ups. So clearly, **the number of new jobs created this year will fall short of last year's record**.

In the argument given, the two portions in boldface play which of the following roles?

(A) The first is presented as an obvious truth on which the argument is based; the second is the main conclusion of the argument.

(B) The first is presented as an obvious truth on which the argument is based; the second is a conclusion drawn in order to support the main conclusion of the argument.

(C) The first and the second each provide evidence in support of the main conclusion of the argument.

(D) The first is a generalization that the argument seeks to establish; the second is the main conclusion of the argument.

(E) The first is a generalization that the argument seeks to establish; the second is a conclusion that has been drawn in order to challenge that generalization.

Argument Construction

Situation   Manufacturing jobs are created either within existing companies or in start-ups. Manufacturing jobs are being created at a much slower rate this year than last year. It seems likely that the number of new start-ups will not exceed last year's number and that the average number of new manufacturing jobs per start-up will not exceed last year's number. So fewer manufacturing jobs are likely to be created this year than last year.

Reasoning   *What function is served by the statement that any new manufacturing job is created either within an existing company or by the start-up of a new company? What function is served by the statement that the number of new jobs created this year will fall short of last year's record number?* The first statement makes explicit a general background assumption that manufacturing jobs are created in just two ways. This assumption is used, along with other information, to support the argument's main conclusion. The second statement gives the argument's main conclusion, a prediction about how this year's manufacturing-job creation will compare with last year's.

A   **Correct.** The first statement states a truism that is meant to provide support for the second statement; the second statement is the argument's main conclusion.

B   The second statement is the argument's main conclusion, not an intermediate conclusion used to support the argument's main conclusion.

C   The second statement is the main conclusion of the argument, not a statement used as support for the main conclusion.

D   The argument merely asserts, and does not "seek to establish," the first statement. The first statement is a truism that does not need to be supported with evidence.

E   The second statement is the argument's main conclusion and is not meant to present a challenge to the first statement. The first statement serves to provide partial support for the argument's main conclusion.

The correct answer is A.

CR00827
702. In Stenland, many workers have been complaining that they cannot survive on minimum wage, the lowest wage an employer is permitted to pay. The government is proposing to raise the minimum wage. Many employers who pay their workers the current minimum wage argue that if it is raised, unemployment will increase because they will no longer be able to afford to employ as many workers.

Which of the following, if true in Stenland, most strongly supports the claim that raising the minimum wage there will not have the effects that the employers predict?

(A) For any position with wages below a living wage, the difficulty of finding and retaining employees adds as much to employment costs as would raising wages.

(B) Raising the minimum wage does not also increase the amount employers have to contribute in employee benefits.

(C) When inflation is taken into account, the proposed new minimum wage is not as high as the current one was when it was introduced.

(D) Many employees currently being paid wages at the level of the proposed new minimum wage will demand significant wage increases.

(E) Many employers who pay some workers only the minimum wage also pay other workers wages that are much higher than the minimum.

Argument Evaluation

Situation Stenland's government proposes to raise the minimum wage because many workers have complained they cannot survive on it. But many employers claim that raising the minimum wage will increase unemployment.

Reasoning *What evidence would most strongly suggest that raising the minimum wage will not increase unemployment?* The employers with minimum-wage workers implicitly reason that because raising the minimum wage will increase the wages they have to pay each worker, it will reduce the number of workers they can afford to employ, and thus will increase unemployment. Evidence that the increased wage would not actually increase the employers' expenses per employee would cast doubt on their prediction, as would evidence that reducing the number of minimum-wage workers would not increase the nation's overall unemployment rate.

A **Correct.** This suggests that raising the minimum wage would make it easier for employers to find and retain minimum-wage employees, and that the savings would fully offset the cost of paying the higher wages. If there were such offsetting savings, the employers should still be able to afford to employ as many workers as they currently do.

B Even if raising the minimum wage does not increase employers' costs for employee benefits, paying the higher wage might still in itself substantially increase employers' overall costs per employee.

C For all we know, the current minimum wage might have substantially increased unemployment when it was introduced.

D These additional demands would probably raise employers' overall costs per employee, making it more likely that increasing the minimum wage would increase overall unemployment.

E Even if some workers receive more than the minimum wage, raising that wage could still raise employers' expenses for employing low-wage workers, making it too expensive for the employers to employ as many workers overall.

The correct answer is A.

8.7 Critical Reasoning Answer Explanations

CR07810

703. Biologists with a predilection for theory have tried—and largely failed—to define what it is that makes something a living thing. Organisms take in energy-providing materials and excrete waste products, but so do automobiles. Living things replicate and take part in evolution, but so do some computer programs. We must be open to the possibility that there are living things on other planets. Therefore, we will not be successful in defining what it is that makes something a living thing merely by examining living things on Earth—the only ones we know. Trying to do so is analogous to trying to specify _____.

Which of the following most logically completes the passage?

(A) the laws of physics by using pure mathematics
(B) what a fish is by listing its chemical components
(C) what an animal is by examining a plant
(D) what a machine is by examining a sketch of it
(E) what a mammal is by examining a zebra

Argument Construction

Situation   Some biologists have tried, unsuccessfully, to find a theoretically defensible account of what it means for something to be a living thing. Some of the suggested definitions are too broad, because they include things that we would not regard as living. To find life on other planets, we must not narrow our conception of life by basing it simply on the kinds of life encountered on Earth.

Reasoning   *Which of the five choices would be the logically most appropriate completion of the argument?* The argument points out that life-forms elsewhere in the universe may be very different from any of the life-forms on Earth. Both life-forms on Earth and life-forms discovered elsewhere would all qualify as members of a very large class, the class of all life-forms. Taking life-forms on Earth, a mere subset of the class of all life-forms, as representative of all life-forms would be a logical mistake and would not lead to success in defining what it means for something to be a living thing.

A   This would not involve a logical mistake like the one already identified.
B   This would not involve a logical mistake closely resembling the one already identified.
C   Plants are not a subclass of the class of animals, so this does not involve the logical mistake of taking a subclass as representative of a larger class.
D   This does not involve a logical mistake closely resembling the one already discussed.
E   **Correct.** This involves the logical mistake of taking the class of zebras, a subclass of the class of mammals, as representative of the class of mammals. Logically, it resembles taking the class of life-forms on Earth as representative of the class of all life-forms.

The correct answer is E.

CR74541.01
704. For the period from the eighth century through the eleventh century, the shifting boundaries between Kingdom F and Kingdom G have not been well charted. Although a certain village in a border region between the two kingdoms usually belonged to Kingdom G, ninth-century artifacts found in the village were in the typical Kingdom F style of that time. It is unclear whether the village was actually a part of Kingdom F in the ninth century or whether it was a part of Kingdom G but had merely adopted Kingdom F's artistic styles under Kingdom F's cultural influence.

Which of the following would, if found in ninth-century sites in the village, best help in determining whether the village was a part of Kingdom F or Kingdom G in the ninth century?

(A) A trading contract written in the Kingdom G dialect
(B) A drawing of a dwelling complex known to have existed on the border of Kingdom F and Kingdom G in the ninth century
(C) Knives and other utensils made from metal typical of ninth-century mining sites in Kingdom F
(D) Some fragments of pottery made in the Kingdom G style from the seventh century out of materials only found in Kingdom F
(E) Numerous teeth from the ninth century with a chemical signature typical only of teeth from people who had grown up in the heart of Kingdom F

Argument Construction

Situation   From the eighth century to the eleventh century, the boundaries between two kingdoms, F and G, shifted, but these shifts are not well documented. A certain village in a border region was usually part of Kingdom G, but ninth-century artifacts in the village are typical of the style of ninth-century artifacts from Kingdom F.

Reasoning   *What evidence, if it were found in the ninth-century sites in the village, would be most helpful in determining which of the two kingdoms the village was a part of during that century?* Information strongly indicating that during the ninth century the village was primarily settled by people clearly from Kingdom F would lend support to the claim that the village was part of Kingdom F in the ninth century.

A   A trading contract found at a ninth-century site in the village written in Kingdom G dialect would not settle whether the village was part of Kingdom G, because it could be the case that such a document would be written in that dialect even if the village were part of Kingdom F but regularly traded with Kingdom G.

B   Finding at a ninth-century site in the village a drawing of a dwelling complex known to have been on the border of Kingdom F and Kingdom G would not be useful in determining to which kingdom the village belonged at the time. We are not told in which kingdom that dwelling complex existed, and even if we were told, it could be that a villager in the other kingdom had a drawing of that complex for some reason (e.g., the villager could have had it because that complex was going to be attacked in a skirmish between the kingdoms).

C   Because there could have been trade between Kingdom F and Kingdom G, the fact that utensils made from metal typical of ninth-century mining sites in Kingdom F would not be very helpful in determining to which of the two kingdoms the village belonged in that century.

D   If fragments of pottery from the seventh century made in the Kingdom G style but from materials found only in Kingdom F were discovered, it would be unclear in which kingdom the pottery had been made. Given that the fragments may be from two centuries earlier than the period in question, and that we do not even know what kingdom the pottery was created in, these fragments would be of no use in determining to which kingdom the village belonged in the ninth century.

E **Correct.** Although the mere presence of people from Kingdom F in the village would not provide strong support for the claim that the village was part of Kingdom F during the ninth century—the village could have shifted from Kingdom F to Kingdom G while maintaining much of its Kingdom F population—the presence of significant numbers of people from the heart of Kingdom F would support the claim that there was widespread migration of people from Kingdom F to the village. This is what one might reasonably expect if the village was part of Kingdom F during the ninth century. The discovery of numerous teeth that clearly belonged to people who grew up in the heart of Kingdom F in the ninth century would support the claim that many such people lived in the village during that century.

The correct answer is E.

CR02829
705. Sammy: For my arthritis, I am going to try my aunt's diet: large amounts of wheat germ and garlic. She was able to move more easily right after she started that diet.

Pat: When my brother began that diet, his arthritis got worse. But he has been doing much better since he stopped eating vegetables in the nightshade family, such as tomatoes and peppers.

Which of the following, if true, would provide a basis for explaining the fact that Sammy's aunt and Pat's brother had contrasting experiences with the same diet?

(A) A change in diet, regardless of the nature of the change, frequently brings temporary relief from arthritis symptoms.
(B) The compounds in garlic that can lessen the symptoms of arthritis are also present in tomatoes and peppers.
(C) Arthritis is a chronic condition whose symptoms improve and worsen from time to time without regard to diet.
(D) In general, men are more likely to have their arthritis symptoms alleviated by avoiding vegetables in the nightshade family than are women.
(E) People who are closely related are more likely to experience the same result from adopting a particular diet than are people who are unrelated.

Argument Construction

Situation   Sammy's aunt's arthritis apparently improved after she consumed large amounts of wheat germ and garlic. Pat's brother's arthritis deteriorated after he followed the same diet. Since he stopped eating vegetables in the nightshade family, such as tomatoes and peppers, his arthritis has improved.

Reasoning   *What could account for the fact that Sammy's aunt's arthritis improved and Pat's brother's arthritis got worse after they both followed the wheat germ and garlic diet?* The fact that a person has a health improvement following a diet is, by itself, very weak evidence for the claim that the diet caused the improvement. More generally, the fact that one event follows another is seldom, by itself, evidence that the earlier event caused the later. This applies to both the experience of Sammy's aunt and that of Pat's brother with the wheat germ and garlic diet.

A   In theory, this could be somewhat relevant to Sammy's aunt's experience but not to Pat's brother's experience. It is, however, insufficient to explain either.

B   Even if this is true, it might be the case that a large quantity of the compounds in question must be consumed in concentrated form to benefit arthritis. No evidence is given to indicate whether this is so. Regardless, the puzzle as to why the wheat germ and garlic diet was followed by arthritis improvement in one case and not in the other remains.

C   **Correct.** If we know there are typically fluctuations in the severity of arthritis symptoms and these can occur independent of diet, then the divergent experiences of the two people can be attributed to such fluctuations—even if it is conceded that some diets can affect arthritis symptoms in some manner. The wheat germ and garlic diet may, or may not, be such a diet.

D   This could throw light on Pat's brother's experience but not on Sammy's aunt's experience.

E   If this is correct, it is still far too general to provide a basis for explaining why the experiences of the two people were different. Does it apply to arthritis? We're not told. Nor are we told that it applies to the wheat germ and garlic diet. Is Pat's brother closely related to Sammy's aunt? We don't know.

The correct answer is C.

8.7 Critical Reasoning Answer Explanations

CR05756

706. Infotek, a computer manufacturer in Katrovia, has just introduced a new personal computer model that sells for significantly less than any other model. Market research shows, however, that very few Katrovian households without personal computers would buy a computer, regardless of its price. Therefore, introducing the new model is unlikely to increase the number of computers in Katrovian homes.

Which of the following is an assumption on which the argument depends?

(A) Infotek achieved the lower price of the new model by using components of lower quality than those used by other manufacturers.

(B) The main reason cited by consumers in Katrovia for replacing a personal computer is the desire to have an improved model.

(C) Katrovians in households that already have computers are unlikely to purchase the new Infotek model as an additional computer for home use.

(D) The price of other personal computers in Katrovia is unlikely to drop below the price of Infotek's new model in the near future.

(E) Most personal computers purchased in Katrovia are intended for home use.

Argument Construction

Situation   In Katrovia, a new personal computer model costs less than any other model. But market research shows that very few Katrovian households without personal computers would buy even cheap ones.

Reasoning   *What must be true in order for the stated facts to support the conclusion that introducing the new computer model is unlikely to increase the overall number of computers in Katrovian homes?* The market research supports the conclusion that no new computer model is likely to significantly increase the number of computers in Katrovian homes that currently lack computers. But the overall number of computers in Katrovian homes will still increase if Katrovian homes that already have computers buy additional computers while keeping their existing ones. So the argument has to assume that the new computer model will not increase the number of additional computers purchased for Katrovian homes that already have computers.

A   Even if Infotek used high-quality components in the new computer model, Katrovians might still refuse to buy it.

B   Replacing a personal computer does not change the overall number of personal computers in homes, so Katrovians' motives for replacing their computers are irrelevant to the argument.

C   **Correct.** As explained above, unless computers of the new model are purchased as additional computers for Katrovian homes that already have computers, the new model's introduction is unlikely to increase the overall number of computers in Katrovian homes.

D   The assumption that other personal computer prices would stay relatively high does not help establish the link between its premises and its conclusion. If answer choice D were false, the argument would be no weaker than it is without any consideration of other computers' potential prices.

E   If most personal computers purchased in Katrovia were not intended for home use, then the new model's introduction would be even less likely to increase the number of personal computers in Katrovian homes. So the argument does not depend on assuming that most of the computers purchased are for home use.

The correct answer is C.

CR05501
707. Fast-food restaurants make up 45 percent of all restaurants in Canatria. Customers at these restaurants tend to be young; in fact, studies have shown that the older people get, the less likely they are to eat in fast-food restaurants. Since the average age of the Canatrian population is gradually rising and will continue to do so, the number of fast-food restaurants is likely to decrease.

Which of the following, if true, most seriously weakens the argument?

(A) Fast-food restaurants in Canatria are getting bigger, so each one can serve more customers.
(B) Some older people eat at fast-food restaurants more frequently than the average young person.
(C) Many people who rarely eat in fast-food restaurants nevertheless eat regularly in restaurants.
(D) The overall population of Canatria is growing steadily.
(E) As the population of Canatria gets older, more people are eating at home.

Argument Evaluation

Situation   In Canatria, the older people get, the less likely they are to eat in fast-food restaurants. The average age of Canatrians is increasing.

Reasoning   *What evidence would most weaken the support provided by the cited facts for the prediction that the number of fast-food restaurants in Canatria is likely to decrease?* The argument implicitly reasons that since studies have shown that Canatrians tend to eat in fast-food restaurants less as they get older, and since Canatrians are getting older on average, the proportion of Canatrians eating in fast-food restaurants will decline. The argument assumes that this means the overall number of fast-food restaurant customers will decline and that demand will decrease enough to reduce the number of fast-food restaurants that can sustain profitability. Consequently, fewer new fast-food restaurants will open or more old ones will close, or both. Thus, the number of fast-food restaurants in Canatria will fall. Any evidence casting doubt on any inference in this chain of implicit reasoning will weaken the argument.

A   This strengthens the argument by providing additional evidence that the total number of fast-food restaurants will decrease. If the average number of customers per fast-food restaurant is increasing, then fewer fast-food restaurants will be needed to serve the same—or a lesser—number of customers.

B   Even if a few individuals do not follow the general trends described, those trends could still reduce the overall demand for and number of fast-food restaurants.

C   The argument is only about fast-food restaurants, not restaurants of other types.

D   **Correct.** This suggests that even if the proportion of Canatrians eating at fast-food restaurants declines, the total number doing so may not decline. Thus, the total demand for and profitability of fast-food restaurants may not decline either, so the total number of fast-food restaurants in Canatria may not decrease.

E   If anything, this strengthens the argument by pointing out an additional trend likely to reduce the demand for, and thus the number of, fast-food restaurants in Canatria.

The correct answer is D.

708. Last year a chain of fast-food restaurants, whose menu had always centered on hamburgers, added its first vegetarian sandwich, much lower in fat than the chain's other offerings. Despite heavy marketing, the new sandwich accounts for a very small proportion of the chain's sales. The sandwich's sales would have to quadruple to cover the costs associated with including it on the menu. Since such an increase is unlikely, the chain would be more profitable if it dropped the sandwich.

Which of the following, if true, most seriously weakens the argument?

(A) Although many of the chain's customers have never tried the vegetarian sandwich, in a market research survey most of those who had tried it reported that they were very satisfied with it.

(B) Many of the people who eat at the chain's restaurants also eat at the restaurants of competing chains and report no strong preference among the competitors.

(C) Among fast-food chains in general, there has been little or no growth in hamburger sales over the past several years as the range of competing offerings at other restaurants has grown.

(D) When even one member of a group of diners is a vegetarian or has a preference for low-fat food, the group tends to avoid restaurants that lack vegetarian or low-fat menu options.

(E) An attempt by the chain to introduce a lower-fat hamburger failed several years ago, since it attracted few new customers and most of the chain's regular customers greatly preferred the taste of the regular hamburgers.

Argument Evaluation

Situation Last year a fast-food restaurant chain specializing in hamburgers started offering a low-fat vegetarian sandwich and marketed it heavily. The new sandwich's sales are far too low to cover the costs associated with including it on the menu.

Reasoning *What evidence would most weaken the support provided by the cited facts for the prediction that it would be more profitable for the chain to drop the sandwich?* The implicit argument is that since the new sandwich's sales are too low to cover the costs associated with including it on the menu, offering the sandwich diminishes the chain's profitability and will continue to do so if the sandwich continues to be offered. This reasoning assumes that the sandwich provides the chain no substantial indirect financial benefits except through its direct sales. It also assumes that the sandwich's sales will not increase sufficiently to make the sandwich a viable product. Any evidence casting doubt on either of these assumptions will weaken the argument.

A This gives information only about the respondents to the survey who had tried the sandwich (possibly very few), who were probably already more open to liking a vegetarian sandwich than any of the chain's other customers. So their responses are probably unrepresentative of the chain's customers in general and do not suggest that the sandwich has enough market potential.

B Although the issue of competition with other restaurants is not raised in the information provided, this new information, if anything, strengthens the argument, by suggesting that the introduction of the new sandwich has not significantly enhanced customer preference for eating at the restaurants that offer the new sandwich.

C This suggests that the cause of stagnation in fast-food restaurants' hamburger sales has been competition from non-fast-food restaurants, but not that the non-fast-food restaurants competed by offering vegetarian options.

D **Correct.** This suggests that even if the sandwich's sales are low, it may indirectly increase the chain's overall profits by encouraging large groups to eat at the chain.

E This strengthens the argument by suggesting that the chain's customers are generally not interested in low-fat menu options such as the new sandwich.

The correct answer is D.

CR03727
709. Transportation expenses accounted for a large portion of the total dollar amount spent on trips for pleasure by residents of the United States in 1997, and about half of the total dollar amount spent on transportation was for airfare. However, the large majority of United States residents who took trips for pleasure in 1997 did not travel by airplane but used other means of transportation.

If the statements above are true, which of the following must also be true about United States residents who took trips for pleasure in 1997?

(A) Most of those who traveled by airplane did so because the airfare to their destination was lower than the cost of other available means of transportation.

(B) Most of those who traveled by airplane did so because other means of transportation to their destination were unavailable.

(C) Per mile traveled, those who traveled by airplane tended to spend more on transportation to their destination than did those who used other means of transportation.

(D) Overall, people who did not travel by airplane had lower average transportation expenses than people who did.

(E) Those who traveled by airplane spent about as much, on average, on other means of transportation as they did on airfare.

Argument Construction

Situation In 1997, about half of total transportation spending by U.S. residents taking trips for pleasure was for airfare. But the large majority of U.S. residents who took trips for pleasure in 1997 did not travel by airplane.

Reasoning *What can be deduced from the stated facts?* The information provided indicates that among U.S. residents who took trips for pleasure in 1997, those who traveled by airplane were a small minority. Yet this small minority's spending for airfare accounted for half of all transportation spending among residents taking trips for pleasure. It follows that on average, those who traveled by airplane must have spent far more per person on transportation than those who did not travel by airplane.

A This does not follow logically from the information given. Most of those who traveled by airplane may have done so even if flying was more expensive than other modes of transportation—for example, because flying was faster or more comfortable.

B This does not follow from the information given. Most of those who traveled by airplane may have done so even if many other modes of transportation were available—the other modes may all have been less desirable.

C This does not follow from the information given. Those who traveled by airplane may have traveled much farther on average than those who used other means of transportation, so their transportation spending per mile traveled need not have been greater.

D **Correct.** As explained above, those who traveled by airplane must have spent more per person on transportation than those who did not travel by airplane, on average. In other words, those who did not travel by airplane must have had lower average transportation expenses than those who did.

E This does not follow from the information given. Although half the total dollar spending on transportation was for airfare, much of the transportation spending that was not for airfare was by the large majority of U.S. residents who did not travel by airplane.

The correct answer is D.

8.7 Critical Reasoning Answer Explanations

CR12051
710. Voters commonly condemn politicians for being insincere, but politicians often must disguise their true feelings when they make public statements. If they expressed their honest views—about, say, their party's policies—then achieving politically necessary compromises would be much more difficult. Clearly, the very insincerity that people decry shows that our government is functioning well.

Which of the following, if true, most seriously undermines this reasoning?

(A) Achieving political compromises is not all that is necessary for the proper functioning of a government.
(B) Some political compromises are not in the best long-term interest of the government.
(C) Voters often judge politicians by criteria other than the sincerity with which they express their views.
(D) A political party's policies could turn out to be detrimental to the functioning of a government.
(E) Some of the public statements made by politicians about their party's policies could in fact be sincere.

Argument Evaluation

Situation Politicians must often make insincere public statements because expressing their true feelings would make it harder for them to achieve politically necessary compromises.

Reasoning *What would suggest that the argument's premises do not establish that politicians' insincerity shows our government is functioning well?* The implicit reasoning is that insincerity helps politicians achieve politically necessary compromises, and these compromises help our government to function well, so insincerity must show that our government is functioning well. Evidence that these necessary compromises do not ensure that our government functions well would undermine the argument's reasoning, as would evidence that politicians' insincerity has other substantial effects that hinder the government's functioning.

A **Correct.** If governments may function poorly even when insincerity allows necessary political compromises to be made, then the argument's premises do not establish that politicians' insincerity shows our government is functioning well.

B The argument does not require that all political compromises help government to function well, only that politically necessary compromises do.

C Even if voters often judge politicians by criteria other than their sincerity, they may also often decry politicians' insincerity, not realizing or caring that such insincerity helps the government function well.

D Even if a political party's policies impair the government's functioning, politically necessary compromises by politicians in that party could improve the government's functioning.

E Even if politicians sometimes speak sincerely about their party's policies, their general willingness to be insincere as needed to achieve politically necessary compromises could be a sign that the government is functioning well.

The correct answer is A.

CR06728
711. To reduce waste of raw materials, the government of Sperland is considering requiring household appliances to be broken down for salvage when discarded. To cover the cost of salvage, the government is planning to charge a fee, which would be imposed when the appliance is first sold. Imposing the fee at the time of salvage would reduce waste more effectively, however, because consumers tend to keep old appliances longer if they are faced with a fee for discarding them.

Which of the following, if true, most seriously weakens the argument?

(A) Increasing the cost of disposing of an appliance properly increases the incentive to dispose of it improperly.
(B) The fee provides manufacturers with no incentive to produce appliances that are more durable.
(C) For people who have bought new appliances recently, the salvage fee would not need to be paid for a number of years.
(D) People who sell their used, working appliances to others would not need to pay the salvage fee.
(E) Many nonfunctioning appliances that are currently discarded could be repaired at relatively little expense.

Evaluation of a Plan

Situation A government is considering requiring household appliances to be broken down for salvage when discarded. To cover the salvage costs, the government plans to charge a fee on appliance sales.

Reasoning *What would suggest that charging the fee at the time of salvage would less effectively reduce waste than charging the fee at the time of sale would?* The argument is that charging the fee at the time of salvage would reduce waste of raw materials because it would encourage consumers to keep their appliances longer before salvaging them. This argument could be weakened by pointing out other factors that might increase waste if the fee is charged at the time of salvage or reduce waste if the fee is charged at the time of sale.

A **Correct.** This suggests that charging the fee at the time of salvage rather than the time of sale would encourage consumers to discard their appliances illegally, thereby increasing waste of raw materials by reducing the proportion of discarded appliances that are salvaged.

B This factor would remain the same regardless of whether the fee was charged at the time of sale or the time of salvage.

C This might be a reason for consumers to prefer the fee be charged at the time of salvage rather than the time of sale, but it does not suggest that charging the fee at the time of salvage would reduce waste less effectively.

D This provides an additional reason to expect that charging the fee at the time of salvage would help reduce waste, so it strengthens rather than weakens the argument.

E This would give consumers an additional reason to keep using their old appliances and postpone paying a fee at the time of salvage, so it strengthens rather than weakens the argument.

The correct answer is A.

8.7 Critical Reasoning Answer Explanations

CR02866
712. When there is less rainfall than normal, the water level of Australian rivers falls and the rivers flow more slowly. Because algae whose habitat is river water grow best in slow-moving water, the amount of algae per unit of water generally increases when there has been little rain. By contrast, however, following a period of extreme drought, algae levels are low even in very slow-moving river water.

Which of the following, if true, does most to explain the contrast described above?

(A) During periods of extreme drought, the populations of some of the species that feed on algae tend to fall.
(B) The more slowly water moves, the more conducive its temperature is to the growth of algae.
(C) When algae populations reach very high levels, conditions within the river can become toxic for some of the other species that normally live there.
(D) Australian rivers dry up completely for short intervals in periods of extreme drought.
(E) Except during periods of extreme drought, algae levels tend to be higher in rivers in which the flow has been controlled by damming than in rivers that flow freely.

Argument Construction

Situation When Australian rivers flow slowly due to little rain, algae populations in those rivers increase. But after periods of extreme drought, algae levels are low even in water moving at speeds that would normally show population increases.

Reasoning *What would explain the contrast between algae levels in slow-moving water resulting from little rain and slow-moving water after a drought?* There must be some difference between what happens during periods in which there is simply less rainfall than normal and periods in which there is extreme drought, a difference that affects the algae population.

A This indicates one of the consequences of drought, and slightly suggests that this might be due to a lower algae level. But it does nothing to explain why algae levels might be lower after a drought.

B This could explain why some rivers that are slow-moving and have little water might have a high algae level—but not why the algae level is low in such rivers after a period of drought.

C This explains why levels of other species might be low when algae populations are high, not why algae populations are high when there is little rain, but low following a period of extreme drought.

D **Correct.** This statement properly identifies something that helps explain the contrast. According to the information given, the habitat of the algae under discussion is river water. If the river dries up, the algae will probably not survive. Then after the drought, algae population levels would likely take a while to rise again.

E This emphasizes that there is a contrast between what happens to algae during periods of extreme drought and what happens to them at other times, but it does not help explain that contrast.

The correct answer is D.

CR04924
713. Increased use of incineration is sometimes advocated as a safe way to dispose of chemical waste. But opponents of incineration point to the 40 incidents involving unexpected releases of dangerous chemical agents that were reported just last year at two existing incinerators commissioned to destroy a quantity of chemical waste material. Since designs for proposed new incinerators include no additional means of preventing such releases, leaks will only become more prevalent if use of incineration increases.

Which of the following, if true, most seriously weakens the argument?

(A) At the two incinerators at which leaks were reported, staff had had only cursory training on the proper procedures for incinerating chemical waste.

(B) Other means of disposing of chemical waste, such as chemical neutralization processes, have not been proven safer than incineration.

(C) The capacity of existing incinerators is sufficient to allow for increased incineration of chemical waste without any need for new incinerators.

(D) The frequency of reports of unexpected releases of chemical agents at newly built incinerators is about the same as the frequency at older incinerators.

(E) In only three of the reported incidents of unexpected chemical leaks did the releases extend outside the property on which the incinerators were located.

Argument Evaluation

Situation   Last year, at two chemical waste incinerators, there were forty reported incidents involving unexpected releases of dangerous chemicals. Designs for proposed new incinerators include no additional safeguards against such releases. Therefore, increased use of incineration will likely make such releases more prevalent.

Reasoning   *What would undermine the support provided for the conclusion that leaks will become more prevalent if more chemical waste is disposed of through incineration?* The argument draws a general conclusion about chemical waste incineration from evidence about only two particular incinerators. This reasoning would be undermined by any evidence that the leaks at those two incinerators were the result of something other than insufficient safeguards against such releases.

A   **Correct.** If the staff training at the two incinerators was cursory, then the leaks may have been the results of staff not knowing how to use safeguards with which the incinerators are equipped that, if properly used, would have prevented the release of dangerous chemicals. Therefore, if staff at newer incinerators will be better trained, leaks might not become more prevalent even if chemical waste incineration becomes more common.

B   Other chemical waste disposal methods may be safer than incineration even if no one has proven so; and even if they're not safer overall, they may involve fewer leaks.

C   Continuing to use existing incinerators might well produce just as many leaks as switching to new incinerators would.

D   This suggests that new incinerators produce as many leaks as older incinerators do, a finding that provides additional evidence that increased incineration even with proposed new incinerators would lead to more leaks.

E   The argument is not about how far the releases from leaks extend, only about how many of them are likely to occur.

The correct answer is A.

CR10049
714. Public health expert: **Increasing the urgency of a public health message may be counterproductive**. In addition to irritating the majority who already behave responsibly, **it may undermine all government pronouncements on health by convincing people that such messages are overly cautious**. And there is no reason to believe that those who ignore measured voices will listen to shouting.

The two sections in boldface play which of the following roles in the public health expert's argument?

(A) The first is a conclusion for which support is provided, but is not the argument's main conclusion; the second is an unsupported premise supporting the argument's main conclusion.

(B) The first is a premise supporting the only explicit conclusion; so is the second.

(C) The first is the argument's main conclusion; the second supports that conclusion and is itself a conclusion for which support is provided.

(D) The first is a premise supporting the argument's only conclusion; the second is that conclusion.

(E) The first is the argument's only explicit conclusion; the second is a premise supporting that conclusion.

Argument Construction

Situation   A public health expert argues against increasing the urgency of public health messages by pointing out negative effects that may arise from such an increase, as well as by questioning its efficacy.

Reasoning   *What roles are played in the argument by the two claims in boldface?* The first claim in boldface states that increasing the urgency of public health messages may be counterproductive. After making this claim, the public health expert mentions two specific reasons this could be so: it could irritate people who already behave responsibly, and it could convince people that all public health messages are too cautious. (The latter reason in the second claim in boldface). The phrase [i]n *addition to* indicates that neither claim in the second sentence is intended to support or explain the other. However, since each claim in the second sentence gives a reason to believe the claim in the first sentence, each independently supports the first sentence as a conclusion. The word [a]nd beginning the third sentence reveals that its intended role in the argument is the same as that of the two claims in the second sentence.

A   Everything stated after the first sentence is intended to help support it, so the first sentence is the argument's main conclusion.

B   Everything stated after the first sentence is intended to help support it, so the first sentence is a conclusion, not a premise.

C   Each of the three claims in the second and third sentences is presented as an independent reason to accept the general claim in the first sentence. Therefore, nothing in the passage is intended to support the second statement in boldface as a conclusion.

D   Everything stated after the first sentence is intended to help support it, so the first sentence is a conclusion, not a premise.

E   **Correct.** Each of the three claims in the second and third sentences is presented as an independent reason to accept the general claim in the first sentence. Thus, each of those claims is a premise supporting the claim in the first sentence as the argument's only conclusion.

The correct answer is E.

715. Several industries have recently switched at least partly from older technologies powered by fossil fuels to new technologies powered by electricity. It is thus evident that less fossil fuel is being used as a result of the operations of these industries than would have been used if these industries had retained their older technologies.

Which of the following, if true, most strengthens the argument above?

(A) Many of the industries that have switched at least partly to the new technologies have increased their output.
(B) Less fossil fuel was used to manufacture the machinery employed in the new technologies than was originally used to manufacture the machinery employed in the older technologies.
(C) More electricity is used by those industries that have switched at least partly to the new technologies than by those industries that have not switched.
(D) Some of the industries that have switched at least partly to the new technologies still use primarily technologies that are powered by fossil fuels.
(E) The amount of fossil fuel used to generate the electricity needed to power the new technologies is less than the amount that would have been used to power the older technologies.

Argument Evaluation

Situation Several industries have now switched, at least partly, to technologies using electricity rather than fossil fuels. Thus, less fossil fuel will be consumed as a result of the operation of these industries than otherwise would have been.

Reasoning *Which option most strengthens the argument?* One way to strengthen an argument is to eliminate or minimize one of its flaws or weaknesses. Because the conclusion is stated in terms of "fossil fuel consumed *as a result* of the operation of these industries," the claim would encompass even any fossil fuel that might be used to generate the electricity that the newer technologies use. Yet the premise of the argument does not address this issue. So the argument is strengthened if it turns out that less fossil fuel was used to produce the electricity than would have been used to power the older technologies.

A In an indirect way, this option slightly weakens rather than strengthens the argument. For *if* fossil fuels are used to produce the electricity now used by the industries and *if* it is because of these newer technologies that output has increased, the argument's conclusion is *less* likely.

B It does not matter how much fossil fuel was used to manufacture the older technologies *originally*. That has no bearing on whether more fossil fuel would have been expended as a result of the *continued operation* of the industries if the partial switch to newer technologies had not occurred.

C This is what we would expect, but it in no way strengthens the argument.

D This may seem to weaken the argument by indicating that the switch from older technologies will have less of an impact on fossil fuel consumption by these industries than we might have assumed. But since the conclusion makes no claim about how much consumption has been reduced, it is not clear that this option has any bearing on the strength of the argument one way or the other.

E **Correct.** This is the option that most strengthens the argument.

The correct answer is E.

CR00792
716. The difference in average annual income in favor of employees who have college degrees, compared with those who do not have such degrees, doubled between 1980 and 1990. Some analysts have hypothesized that increased competition between employers for employees with college degrees drove up income for such employees.

Which of the following, if true, most seriously undermines the explanation described above?

(A) During the 1980s a growing percentage of college graduates, unable to find jobs requiring a college degree, took unskilled jobs.
(B) The average age of all employees increased slightly during the 1980s.
(C) The unemployment rate changed very little throughout most of the 1980s.
(D) From 1980 to 1990 the difference in average income between employees with advanced degrees and those with bachelor's degrees also increased.
(E) During the 1980s there were some employees with no college degree who earned incomes comparable to the top incomes earned by employees with a college degree.

Argument Evaluation

Situation   The amount by which average annual income for employees with college degrees exceeds that for employees without such degrees doubled between 1980 and 1990.

Reasoning   *What evidence would most strongly suggest that increased competition among employers for employees with college degrees does not explain the relative increase in those employees' incomes?* Such increased competition could not explain the relative increase in income for employees with college degrees if the competition did not actually increase, or if such competition occurred but did not result in employers paying higher wages or salaries, or if the increase in competition to hire employees without college degrees was even greater. So evidence that any of those conditions existed would undermine the analysts' explanation.

A **Correct.** This suggests that the supply of college graduates grew relative to employers' demand for them, and hence that employers' competition for college-educated employees did not actually increase.
B The average age might have increased equally for employees with college degrees and for those without them, so the increase is not clearly relevant to explaining why the difference between these two groups' average incomes grew.
C Even if the overall unemployment rate did not change, competition for college-educated employees could have increased while competition for other employees decreased.
D This statement gives information comparing income trends among two groups of those with college degrees, and is irrelevant to the comparison of income trends for those with college degrees and those without college degrees.
E Even if there was strong competition and high pay for certain unusual types of employees without college degrees, increasing competition for employees with college degrees might have explained the overall growing difference in average pay between employees with college degrees and those without.

The correct answer is A.

CR01239
717. Which of the following most logically completes the passage?

According to the last pre-election poll in Whippleton, most voters believe that the three problems government needs to address, in order of importance, are pollution, crime, and unemployment. Yet in the election, candidates from parties perceived as strongly against pollution were defeated, while those elected were all from parties with a history of opposing legislation designed to reduce pollution. These results should not be taken to indicate that the poll was inaccurate, however, since _____.

(A) some voters in Whippleton do not believe that pollution needs to be reduced
(B) every candidate who was defeated had a strong antipollution record
(C) there were no issues other than crime, unemployment, and pollution on which the candidates had significant differences of opinion
(D) all the candidates who were elected were perceived as being stronger against both crime and unemployment than the candidates who were defeated
(E) many of the people who voted in the election refused to participate in the poll

Argument Construction

Situation   A pre-election poll indicated that most voters believed the three problems government needs to address, in order of importance, are pollution, crime, and unemployment. But in the election, candidates from parties with a history of opposing anti-pollution legislation beat candidates from parties perceived as more strongly against pollution.

Reasoning   *What would most help explain how the poll might have been accurate despite the election results?* Since the poll indicated that voters were most concerned about pollution, it suggested that candidates from anti-pollution parties would be more likely to be elected, other things being equal—and yet those candidates were not elected. There are many possible explanations for this outcome that are compatible with the poll having been accurate. For example, voters might have been swayed by the candidates' personalities, qualifications, or advertising more than by their positions on the issues. Or some candidates might have convinced voters that their personal positions on the issues were different from those of their parties. Or voters might have chosen candidates based on their positions on crime and unemployment, considering those issues together more important than pollution alone. Any statement suggesting that any such factors explained the election results would logically complete the passage by providing a reason to believe that the poll could have been accurate despite those results.

A   If the number of voters who did not believe that pollution needed to be reduced was large enough to explain the election results, then the poll was probably inaccurate. So this does not explain how the poll might have been accurate despite those results.

B   This eliminates the possibility that candidates were defeated for having weak antipollution records conflicting with their parties' antipollution stances, so it eliminates one explanation of how the poll might have been accurate despite the election results. Thus, it slightly weakens the conclusion of the argument instead of providing a premise to support it.

C   This eliminates the possibility that differences of opinion among the candidates on these other issues might explain the election results, but it does not explain how the poll could have been accurate despite the election results.

D   **Correct.** The poll indicated that voters believed that the government needs to address crime and unemployment as well as pollution. So if the poll was accurate, the election outcome might have resulted from voters considering candidates' positions on crime and unemployment to be jointly more important than their positions on pollution.

E   If anything, this provides a reason to doubt that the poll accurately reflected voters' opinions. It does not explain how the poll might have accurately reflected those opinions despite the election results.

The correct answer is D.

CR01153

718. Manufacturing plants in Arundia have recently been acquired in substantial numbers by investors from abroad. Arundian politicians are proposing legislative action to stop such investment, justifying the proposal by arguing that foreign investors, opportunistically exploiting a recent fall in the value of the Arundian currency, were able to buy Arundian assets at less than their true value.

Which of the following, if true, casts the most serious doubt on the adequacy of the Arundian politicians' justification for the proposed legislation?

(A) The Arundian government originally welcomed the fall in the value of the Arundian currency because the fall made Arundian exports more competitive on international markets.

(B) Foreign investors who acquired Arundian manufacturing plants generally did so with no intention of keeping and running those plants over the long term.

(C) Without the recent fall in the value of the Arundian currency, many of the Arundian assets bought by foreign investors would have been beyond the financial reach of those investors.

(D) In Concordia, a country broadly similar to Arundia, the share of manufacturing assets that is foreign-controlled is 60 percent higher than it is in Arundia.

(E) The true value of an investment is determined by the value of the profits from it, and the low value of the Arundian currency has depressed the value of any profits earned by foreign investors from Arundian assets.

Argument Evaluation

Situation   After a recent fall in the value of Arundian currency, foreign investors have been acquiring many Arundian manufacturing plants. Arundian politicians are proposing legislation to stop such investment.

Reasoning   *What would most undermine the Arundian politicians' justification for the proposed legislation?* The politicians are justifying their proposal by claiming that foreign investors have been exploiting the fall in the currency's value by buying Arundian assets at less than their *true value* (whatever that means). Any evidence that their claim is false or meaningless would undermine their justification for the proposal, as would any evidence that the claim, even if true, does not provide a good reason to stop the foreign investments.

A   This suggests that the foreign investors got a good deal on the manufacturing plants, since it provides evidence that those plants will now be more competitive and profitable. So, if anything, it supports the politicians' justification for their proposal rather than undermining it.

B   This suggests that the foreign investors generally believe the manufacturing plants are undervalued, and intend to sell them at a profit as soon as the currency rises enough. So it supports the politicians' justification for their proposal rather than undermining it.

C   This suggests that the recent fall in the currency's value made Arundian assets cost less than usual for foreign investors, thus arguably allowing the investors to buy the assets at less than their *true value*. So, if anything, it supports the politicians' justification for their proposal rather than undermining it.

D   The Arundian politicians might consider the example of Concordia to be a warning of the disaster that could befall Arundia unless the legislation is enacted. So the situation in Concordia might be cited as support for the politicians' justification of their proposal.

E   **Correct.** This implies that the fall in the Arundian currency's value has reduced the *true value* of Arundian manufacturing plants and any profits they may make, so it undermines the politicians' claim that the foreign investors exploited the fall in the currency's value to acquire the plants for less than their *true value*.

The correct answer is E.

CR04964
719. Proposed new safety rules for the Beach City airport would lengthen considerably the minimum time between takeoffs from the airport. In consequence, the airport would be able to accommodate 10 percent fewer flights than currently use the airport daily. The city's operating budget depends heavily on taxes generated by tourist spending, and most of the tourists come by plane. Therefore, the proposed new safety rules, if adopted, will reduce the revenue available for the operating budget.

The argument depends on assuming which of the following?

(A) There are no periods of the day during which the interval between flights taking off from the airport is significantly greater than the currently allowed minimum.

(B) Few, if any, of the tourists who use the Beach City airport do so when their main destination is a neighboring community and not Beach City itself.

(C) If the proposed safety rules are adopted, the reduction in tourist numbers will not result mainly from a reduction in the number of tourists who spend relatively little in Beach City.

(D) Increasing the minimum time between takeoffs is the only way to achieve necessary safety improvements without a large expenditure by the city government on airport enhancements.

(E) The response to the adoption of the new safety rules would not include an increase in the number of passengers per flight.

Argument Construction

Situation   Proposed safety rules for a city airport would reduce the number of daily flights the airport can accommodate. The city's operating budget depends heavily on taxes generated by tourists, who mostly come by plane. Therefore, adopting the safety rules will result in lower revenue available for the operating budget.

Reasoning   *What must be true in order for the cited facts to support the conclusion that the proposed rules would reduce the revenue for the operating budget?* The implicit reasoning is that since the rules would reduce the number of flights that can be accommodated, they would thereby reduce the number of tourists arriving by plane, which in turn would reduce the tax revenue that tourist spending generates for the operating budget. This assumes that the actual number of daily flights would fall along with the number that the airport can accommodate; that fewer daily flights would mean fewer people flying into the airport; that fewer people flying into the airport would mean fewer tourists flying into the airport; that fewer tourists flying into the airport would mean fewer tourists visiting the city; that fewer tourists visiting the city would mean less taxable spending by tourists; and that less taxable spending by tourists would mean less revenue overall for the operating budget.

A   Even if flights depart the airport less frequently during some periods of the day, increasing the minimum time between flights at busy times of day could reduce the total number of daily flights from the airport.

B   Even if half the tourists flying into the airport were bound for other nearby towns, the other half could still spend enough in town to generate lots of revenue for the operating budget.

C   It is possible that most tourists spend relatively little in the city, but a few spend a lot. In that case, even if a reduction in tourist numbers resulted mainly from a declining number of tourists who spend relatively little, it could also greatly reduce the already small number of tourists who spend a lot.

D   This suggests that the proposed rules might be financially better for the city than any alternative way to improve safety, whereas the argument's conclusion is that the proposed rules are financially disadvantageous.

E   **Correct.** If adopting the proposed rules would result in a large increase in the number of passengers per flight, fewer daily flights would not necessarily mean fewer passengers or fewer tourists overall.

The correct answer is E.

720. The introduction of new drugs into the market is frequently prevented by a shortage of human subjects for the clinical trials needed to show that the drugs are safe and effective. Since the lives and health of people in future generations may depend on treatments that are currently experimental, practicing physicians are morally in the wrong when, in the absence of any treatment proven to be effective, they fail to encourage suitable patients to volunteer for clinical trials.

Which of the following, if true, casts most doubt on the conclusion of the argument?

(A) Many drugs undergoing clinical trials are intended for the treatment of conditions for which there is currently no effective treatment.
(B) Patients do not share the physician's professional concern for public health, but everyone has a moral obligation to alleviate suffering when able to do so.
(C) Usually, half the patients in a clinical trial serve as a control group and receive a nonactive drug in place of the drug being tested.
(D) An experimental drug cannot legally be made available to patients unless those patients are subjects in clinical trials of the drug.
(E) Physicians have an overriding moral and legal duty to care for the health and safety of their current patients.

Argument Evaluation

Situation: A shortage of human subjects for clinical trials needed to show that new drugs are safe and effective often prevents those drugs from being introduced into the market. The lives and health of future generations may depend on treatments that are now experimental.

Reasoning: *What would cast doubt on the judgment that doctors are morally obligated to encourage their patients to volunteer for clinical trials?* Note that the argument's conclusion, unlike its premises, is a moral judgment. This judgment could be cast into doubt by a moral principle that would be likely to conflict with it under the conditions described. For example, a principle suggesting that it is sometimes morally unacceptable for doctors to encourage their patients to volunteer for clinical trials would also suggest that they are not morally obligated to encourage their patients to volunteer for clinical trials, since anything morally obligatory must also be morally acceptable.

A If anything, this highlights how important it is to ensure that these drugs undergo clinical trials to benefit future generations, so it supports rather than casts doubt on the argument's conclusion.

B This suggests that patients are morally obligated to volunteer for clinical trials to help prevent suffering in future generations. If anything, this supports the claim that doctors are morally obligated to encourage their patients to volunteer.

C The clinical trial will probably not harm any patients in the control group, yet their participation will benefit future generations. So, if anything, this supports the claim that doctors should encourage their patients to volunteer.

D This legal barrier makes it even more essential for the drugs to undergo clinical trials in order to benefit patients, so it supports rather than casts doubt on the argument's conclusion.

E **Correct.** Since the experimental drugs' safety is being tested during the trials, the drugs may prove unsafe for subjects in the trials. If doctors have an overriding moral duty to keep their current patients safe, then it may be morally unacceptable for them to encourage those patients to volunteer for the trials.

The correct answer is E.

CR01285
721. As a construction material, bamboo is as strong as steel and sturdier than concrete. Moreover, in tropical areas bamboo is a much less expensive construction material than either steel or concrete and is always readily available. In tropical areas, therefore, building with bamboo makes better economic sense than building with steel or concrete, except where land values are high.

Which of the following, if true, most helps to explain the exception noted above?

(A) Buildings constructed of bamboo are less likely to suffer earthquake damage than are steel and concrete buildings.
(B) Bamboo is unsuitable as a building material for multistory buildings.
(C) In order to protect it from being damaged by termites and beetles, bamboo must be soaked, at some expense, in a preservative.
(D) In some tropical areas, bamboo is used to make the scaffolding that is used during large construction projects.
(E) Bamboo growing in an area where land values are increasing is often cleared to make way for construction.

Argument Construction

Situation Bamboo is as strong as steel and sturdier than concrete when used as a construction material. In tropical areas, bamboo is much less expensive and is always readily available.

Reasoning *What explains the exception specified in the conclusion?* The argument's conclusion is that in tropical areas bamboo is a more economical building material than steel or concrete, *except where land values are high*. The information in the passage makes clear why bamboo is a more economical building material in tropical areas than are concrete or steel. So the question is: Why must an exception be made for areas where land values are high? Multistory buildings are particularly desirable in areas where land values are high, but bamboo may not be suitable for such buildings.

A   This explains why bamboo would be preferable to steel or concrete in tropical areas especially prone to earthquakes. However, there is no clear connection to be made between areas where land values are high and areas especially prone to earthquakes.

B   **Correct.** Multistory buildings provide a greater area of floor space for a given site area, and in that sense are more economical. A single-story building with the same floor space will occupy a much bigger site, so the higher the land values, the more likely it is that a multistory building will be built on that land. Thus, given this information, bamboo is less suitable for areas where land values are high.

C   This undermines, to some extent, the claim that bamboo is an economical building material. But it does nothing to explain why it would be less economical specifically in areas where land values are high.

D   This is irrelevant. Bamboo is used to build scaffolding for construction projects and as a building material for permanent structures. There is no way to infer from this that bamboo is less economical specifically in areas where land values are high.

E   The fact that bamboo is cleared from an area to make room for construction in no way implies that bamboo would not be a suitable and economical building material for the area once it has been cleared.

The correct answer is B.

8.7 Critical Reasoning Answer Explanations

CR00788

722. Newspaper editors should not allow reporters to write the headlines for their own stories. The reason for this is that, while the headlines that reporters themselves write are often clever, what typically makes them clever is that they allude to little-known information that is familiar to the reporter but that never appears explicitly in the story itself.

Which of the following, if true, most strengthens the argument?

(A) The reporter who writes a story is usually better placed than the reporter's editor is to judge what the story's most newsworthy features are.

(B) To write a headline that is clever, a person must have sufficient understanding of the story that the headline accompanies.

(C) Most reporters rarely bother to find out how other reporters have written stories and headlines about the same events that they themselves have covered.

(D) For virtually any story that a reporter writes, there are at least a few people who know more about the story's subject matter than does the reporter.

(E) The kind of headlines that newspaper editors want are those that anyone who has read a reporter's story in its entirety will recognize as clever.

Argument Evaluation

Situation   The headlines newspaper reporters write for their own stories are often clever only because they allude to little-known information that never appears explicitly in the stories themselves.

Reasoning   *What would most help the argument support the conclusion that newspaper editors should not allow reporters to write headlines for their own stories?* The argument's only explicit premise is that the headlines newspaper reporters write for their own stories are often clever only because they allude to little-known information that never appears explicitly in the stories themselves. In order for this premise to support the conclusion that newspaper editors should not allow reporters to write their own headlines, it would be helpful to be given a reason why editors should avoid headlines alluding to such little-known information.

A   This suggests that reporters are likely to write better headlines for their stories than editors are, so it weakens the argument that editors should not allow reporters to write their own headlines.

B   Since a reporter who wrote a story is likely to understand that story well, this does not provide a reason why editors should not allow reporters to write their own headlines.

C   If most reporters did what is suggested, they could perhaps hone their headline-writing skills—unless almost all reporters are weak in such skills, as suggested in the given information. The fact that they do not bother to do so may help explain why reporters' headline-writing skills are weak. An explanation of why this is so does not provide additional support for the argument's conclusion.

D   The people who know more about a story's subject matter than the reporter writing the story might be just as likely to see the cleverness of allusions to little-known information as the reporters are. So, to the extent that this is relevant at all, it slightly weakens the argument by suggesting that obscurely clever headlines sometimes function as intended.

E   **Correct.** The argument's explicit premise suggests that typically a reporter's headline for his or her own story cannot be recognized as clever by a reader who has read the whole story. So if editors want headlines that anyone who has read the accompanying stories would recognize as clever, they have a reason not to let reporters write the headlines.

The correct answer is E.

CR03251
723. Scientists have modified feed corn genetically, increasing its resistance to insect pests. Farmers who tried out the genetically modified corn last season applied less insecticide to their corn fields and still got yields comparable to those they would have gotten with ordinary corn. Ordinary corn seed, however, costs less, and what these farmers saved on insecticide rarely exceeded their extra costs for seed. Therefore, for most feed-corn farmers, switching to genetically modified seed would be unlikely to increase profits.

Which of the following would it be most useful to know in order to evaluate the argument?

(A) Whether there are insect pests that sometimes reduce feed-corn yields, but against which commonly used insecticides and the genetic modification are equally ineffective
(B) Whether the price that farmers receive for feed corn has remained steady over the past few years
(C) Whether the insecticides typically used on feed corn tend to be more expensive than insecticides typically used on other crops
(D) Whether most of the farmers who tried the genetically modified corn last season applied more insecticide than was actually necessary
(E) Whether, for most farmers who plant feed corn, it is their most profitable crop

Argument Evaluation

Situation Farmers who grew feed corn genetically engineered to be pest resistant got yields comparable to those of farmers growing ordinary feed corn, but did so while using less pesticide. Since the amount saved on pesticide was rarely in excess of the extra costs for the genetically modified corn, most farmers will probably not increase profits by choosing the genetically engineered variety.

Reasoning *Which would be most useful to know in evaluating the argument?* To answer a question such as this, one should look for information that would strengthen or weaken the argument. If one had information that the farmers growing the genetically modified corn could have increased their yields last year at lower cost, this would be helpful in evaluating the argument, because this would show that the argument is weak.

A It does not matter to the argument whether there are pests against which pesticides and genetic resistance are equally ineffective, because that is compatible with there being pests against which they are not equally effective.
B Whether prices of feed corn go up or down affects the comparison groups equally.
C The relative cost of insecticides for other crops has no bearing on the argument because the argument is concerned with only feed corn.
D **Correct.** This option provides the information that it would be most useful to know in evaluating the argument. It shows that farmers growing genetically modified corn last year could have attained higher profits than they in fact did.
E The argument concerns only the relative profitability of growing one variety of feed corn versus another.

The correct answer is D.

CR07318
724. Debater: The average amount of overtime per month worked by an employee in the manufacturing division of the Haglut Corporation is 14 hours. Most employees of the Haglut Corporation work in the manufacturing division. Furthermore, the average amount of overtime per month worked by any employee in the company generally does not fluctuate much from month to month. Therefore, each month, most employees of the Haglut Corporation almost certainly work at least some overtime.

The debater's argument is most vulnerable to criticism on which of these grounds?

(A) It takes for granted that the manufacturing division is a typical division of the corporation with regard to the average amount of overtime its employees work each month.

(B) It takes for granted that if a certain average amount of overtime is worked each month by each employee of the Haglut Corporation, then approximately the same amount of overtime must be worked each month by each employee of the manufacturing division.

(C) It confuses a claim from which the argument's conclusion about the Haglut Corporation would necessarily follow with a claim that would follow from the argument's conclusion only with a high degree of probability.

(D) It overlooks the possibility that even if, on average, a certain amount of overtime is worked by the members of some group, many members of that group may work no overtime at all.

(E) It overlooks the possibility that even if most employees of the corporation work some overtime each month, any one corporate employee may, in some months, work no overtime.

Argument Evaluation

Situation   Most of the employees of the Haglut Corporation work in the manufacturing division, where employees average 14 hours per month in overtime. The average amount of overtime per month for employees at Haglut does not fluctuate much from month to month.

Reasoning   *What is the argument's greatest weakness?* The argument's conclusion is that almost certainly each month most of the employees of Haglut work at least some overtime. Answer choice (D) identifies the argument's greatest weakness because it points out how the conclusion of the argument could be false even if all of the supporting information were true. For example, it could be that less than half of the employees work any overtime at all, but those that do work overtime work much more than 14 hours per month.

A   The argument leaves open the possibility that in some divisions of the corporation, the average monthly overtime of its employees is quite different from 14 hours, even if (as the argument states) that average does not change much from month to month.

B   The argument does not assume that there is a monthly amount of overtime worked by each employee of the manufacturing division equivalent to the company-wide average monthly overtime per employee.

C   This does not identify a weakness that can be detected in the argument. Since the claims mentioned here are not specified, the passage provides no evidence that clearly indicates that this type of confusion is playing a role in the argument.

D   **Correct.** The argument ignores the possibility that most of the employees of Haglut work no overtime at all in a particular month—which is quite consistent with the argument's assertion that the average number of monthly overtime hours per employee within the manufacturing division is 14.

E   The possibility described by this is not overlooked by the argument, because this possibility is consistent with the conclusion. It could easily be that most employees of the corporation work some overtime each month—as the conclusion envisions—but that there are always some employees who do not work any overtime.

The correct answer is D.

725. Proponents of the recently introduced tax on sales of new luxury boats had argued that a tax of this sort would be an equitable way to increase government revenue because the admittedly heavy tax burden would fall only on wealthy people and neither they nor anyone else would suffer any economic hardship. In fact, however, 20 percent of the workers employed by manufacturers of luxury boats have lost their jobs as a direct result of this tax.

The information given, if true, most strongly supports which of the following?

(A) The market for luxury boats would have collapsed even if the new tax on luxury boats had been lower.

(B) The new tax would produce a net gain in tax revenue for the government only if the yearly total revenue that it generates exceeds the total of any yearly tax-revenue decrease resulting from the workers' loss of jobs.

(C) Because many people never buy luxury items, imposing a sales tax on luxury items is the kind of legislative action that does not cost incumbent legislators much popular support.

(D) Before the tax was instituted, luxury boats were largely bought by people who were not wealthy.

(E) Taxes can be equitable only if their burden is evenly distributed over the entire population.

Argument Construction

Situation Proponents of a recently introduced tax on sales of new luxury boats argued that it would be an equitable way to increase government revenue because the tax would fall only on the wealthy and cause no economic hardship. But because of the tax, 20 percent of luxury-boat manufacturing workers have lost their jobs.

Reasoning *What conclusion do the statements about the proponents' argument and the tax's effects support?* Since the tax caused many workers to lose their jobs, apparently the proponents were incorrect in asserting that it would cause no one to suffer any economic hardship. Thus, their justification for concluding that the tax is an equitable way to increase government revenue is factually inaccurate, casting doubt on that conclusion.

A The passage indicates that the tax directly caused a significant decrease (though not necessarily a collapse) in the market for luxury boats. But the passage contains no evidence about whether such a decrease might not have occurred if the new tax had been somewhat lower.

B **Correct.** Since the tax caused the workers to lose their jobs, it might have made the government lose revenue from payroll taxes that the laid-off workers would have paid if they had kept their jobs. So if the yearly total revenue generated directly and indirectly by the tax were less than those total yearly payroll taxes and any other tax revenue that was lost as a result of the tax, the tax would have caused a net loss in tax revenue.

C The passage contains no information about what types of legislative actions cost, or do not cost, incumbent legislators popular support.

D Although the passage suggests that some of the tax proponents' assumptions were wrong, it contains no information suggesting that those proponents were wrong in thinking that luxury boats are purchased mainly by wealthy people.

E The passage does not provide any basis for determining what makes a tax equitable or about whether the luxury boat tax is equitable. The tax's proponents evidently felt that a tax whose burden falls only on the wealthy rather than evenly on the entire population can be equitable.

The correct answer is B.

CR05191
726. In Wareland last year, 16 percent of licensed drivers under 21 and 11 percent of drivers ages 21–24 were in serious accidents. By contrast, only 3 percent of licensed drivers 65 and older were involved in serious accidents. These figures clearly show that the greater experience and developed habits of caution possessed by drivers in the 65-and-older group make them far safer behind the wheel than the younger drivers are.

Which of the following is an assumption on which the argument depends?

(A) Drivers 65 and older do not, on average, drive very many fewer miles per year than drivers 24 and younger.
(B) Drivers 65 and older do not constitute a significantly larger percentage of licensed drivers in Wareland than drivers ages 18–24 do.
(C) Drivers 65 and older are less likely than are drivers 24 and younger to drive during weather conditions that greatly increase the risk of accidents.
(D) The difference between the accident rate of drivers under 21 and of those ages 21–24 is attributable to the greater driving experience of those in the older group.
(E) There is no age bracket for which the accident rate is lower than it is for licensed drivers 65 and older.

Argument Evaluation

Situation   Last year in Wareland, a much higher percentage of drivers 24 and under than of drivers 65 and older were in serious accidents.

Reasoning   *What must be true for the observation about the accident rates to support the conclusion that the greater experience and caution of drivers 65 and older make them safer behind the wheel than the younger drivers?* Several factors other than greater experience and caution could explain the lower accident rate among the older drivers. For example, the older drivers might simply drive much less than the younger ones, but still get in just as many accidents per mile driven. Or perhaps because the older drivers are more often retired, their schedules less often lead them to drive at times of day when accident rates are greater for everyone. Or they might be more likely to live in rural areas with less traffic and lower accident rates. The argument depends on assuming that none of these factors fully explains the difference in accident rates.

A **Correct.** Although we are given no information about the possible extent of any difference in average miles driven, the (somewhat vague) information that drivers 65 and older drive *very many fewer miles per year*, on average, than drivers 24 and younger would cast serious doubt on the statistical argument given. The argument assumes that the difference in miles driven is not sufficiently substantial to undermine the argument.

B The argument is only about the discrepancy between the percentages of the drivers in two specific age groups who were in serious accidents last year. The percentages of licensed drivers who fall in these age groups are irrelevant.

C Even if drivers 65 and older are just as likely as younger drivers to drive in inclement weather, they may do so far more carefully than the younger drivers, so the older drivers' greater experience and caution could still explain their lower accident rates.

D Even if greater experience does not explain the difference between the accident rates of the two younger groups of drivers, it might still explain the differences between the accident rate of those two younger groups taken together and that of drivers aged 65 and older.

E The accident rate could be lower for drivers in late middle age than for those 65 and older because drivers in late middle age are also cautious and experienced, but their reflexes and vision tend to be less impaired. Even if that were true, the experience and caution of the drivers 65 and older might still make them safer than drivers 24 and under.

The correct answer is A.

CR05614
727. In the past the country of Malvernia has relied heavily on imported oil. Malvernia recently implemented a program to convert heating systems from oil to natural gas. Malvernia currently produces more natural gas each year than it uses, and oil production in Malvernian oil fields is increasing at a steady pace. If these trends in fuel production and usage continue, therefore, Malvernian reliance on foreign sources for fuel is likely to decline soon.

Which of the following would it be most useful to establish in evaluating the argument?

(A) When, if ever, will production of oil in Malvernia outstrip production of natural gas?
(B) Is Malvernia among the countries that rely most on imported oil?
(C) What proportion of Malvernia's total energy needs is met by hydroelectric, solar, and nuclear power?
(D) Is the amount of oil used each year in Malvernia for generating electricity and fuel for transportation increasing?
(E) Have any existing oil-burning heating systems in Malvernia already been converted to natural-gas-burning heating systems?

Argument Evaluation

Situation Malvernia has relied heavily on imported oil, but recently began a program to convert heating systems from oil to natural gas. Malvernia produces more natural gas than it uses, so it will probably reduce its reliance on imported oils if these trends continue.

Reasoning *Which option provides the information that it would be most useful to know in evaluating the argument?* In other words, we are looking for the option which—depending on whether it was answered yes or no—would either most weaken or most strengthen the argument. The argument indicates that Malvernia will be using less oil for heating and will be producing more oil domestically. But the conclusion that Malvernia's reliance on foreign oil will decline, assuming the current trends mentioned continue, would be seriously undermined if there was something in the works that was bound to offset these trends, for instance, if it turned out that the country's need for oil was going to rise drastically in the coming years.

A Since both counteract the need for imported oil, it makes little difference to the argument whether domestic oil production exceeds domestic natural gas.
B Whether there are many countries that rely more on foreign oil than Malvernia would have little impact on whether Malvernia's need for foreign oil can be expected to decline.
C Since there is no information in the argument about whether Malvernia can expect an increase or decrease from these other energy sources, it does not matter how much they now provide.
D **Correct.** This option provides the information that it would be most useful to know in evaluating the argument.
E The argument tells us that a program has begun *recently* to convert heating systems from oil to gas. So, even if no such conversions have been completed, the argument still indicates that they can be expected to occur.

The correct answer is D.

8.7 Critical Reasoning Answer Explanations

728. Exposure to certain chemicals commonly used in elementary schools as cleaners or pesticides causes allergic reactions in some children. Elementary school nurses in Renston report that the proportion of schoolchildren sent to them for treatment of allergic reactions to those chemicals has increased significantly over the past ten years. Therefore, either Renston's schoolchildren have been exposed to greater quantities of the chemicals, or they are more sensitive to them than schoolchildren were ten years ago.

Which of the following is an assumption on which the argument depends?

(A) The number of school nurses employed by Renston's elementary schools has not decreased over the past ten years.
(B) Children who are allergic to the chemicals are no more likely than other children to have allergies to other substances.
(C) Children who have allergic reactions to the chemicals are not more likely to be sent to a school nurse now than they were ten years ago.
(D) The chemicals are not commonly used as cleaners or pesticides in houses and apartment buildings in Renston.
(E) Children attending elementary school do not make up a larger proportion of Renston's population now than they did ten years ago.

Argument Construction

Situation   Some children have allergic reactions to some of the chemicals commonly used in elementary schools as cleaners and pesticides. The number of children sent to elementary school nurses in Renston for allergic reactions to such chemicals has risen significantly over the past ten years.

Reasoning   *What must the argument assume?* The argument's conclusion presents just two alternatives: either the children are exposed to more of the chemicals than children in earlier years *or* they are more sensitive. But there is a third possible explanation for the significant increase in school-nurse visits that the school nurses have reported: that children are just more inclined to go to the school nurse when they experience an allergic reaction than were children several years ago. For the conclusion to follow from its premises, the argument must assume that this is not the correct explanation.

A   If the number of elementary school nurses in Renston elementary schools had decreased over the past ten years, that would in no way explain the rise in the proportion of children reporting to school nurses for allergic reactions.

B   Only school-nurse visits for allergic reactions to the cleaners and pesticides used in elementary schools are in question in the argument. Of course there could be school-nurse visits for allergic reactions to other things, but that issue does not arise in the argument.

C   **Correct.** This can be seen by considering whether the argument would work if we assume that this were false, i.e., that a school-nurse visit *is* more likely in such cases. As noted above, this provides an alternative to the two explanations that the conclusion claims are the sole possibilities.

D   This does not need to be assumed by the argument. The argument's conclusion suggests that children may in recent years have had greater exposure to the chemicals, not that this exposure has occurred exclusively in the schools. The argument does not rely on this latter assumption.

E   The argument does not need to make this assumption. The argument is framed in terms of proportions of children having school-nurse visits for certain allergic reactions. *How many* children there are or what proportion such children are of Renston's total population is not directly relevant to the argument.

The correct answer is C.

CR01854

729. Normally, the pineal gland governs a person's sleep-wake cycle by secreting melatonin in response to the daily cycle of light and darkness as detected by the eye. Nonetheless, many people who are totally blind due to lesions in the visual cortex of the brain easily maintain a 24-hour sleep-wake cycle. So the neural pathway by which the pineal gland receives information from the eye probably does not pass through the visual cortex.

For purposes of evaluating the argument it would be most useful to establish which of the following?

(A) Whether melatonin supplements help people who have difficulty maintaining a 24-hour sleep cycle to establish such a pattern

(B) Whether the melatonin levels of most totally blind people who successfully maintain a 24-hour sleep-wake cycle change in response to changes in exposure to light and darkness

(C) Whether melatonin is the only substance secreted by the pineal gland

(D) Whether most people who do not have a 24-hour sleep-wake cycle nevertheless have a cycle of consistent duration

(E) Whether there are any people with normal vision whose melatonin levels respond abnormally to periods of light and darkness

Argument Evaluation

Situation   Normally, a person's sleep-wake cycle is governed by the pineal gland secreting melatonin in response to the daily cycle of light and darkness as detected by the eye. Yet many people who are totally blind due to lesions of the visual cortex easily maintain a 24-hour sleep-wake cycle.

Reasoning   *What additional information would be most helpful in evaluating the argument?* The argument's conclusion is that the neural pathway by which the pineal gland receives information probably does not pass through the visual cortex. This is suggested by the fact that people without a well-functioning visual cortex (e.g., people with a certain type of blindness) can nonetheless maintain a 24-hour sleep-wake cycle. Is it by the pineal gland's secretion of melatonin that they do so? The argument tells us that *normally* (i.e., in sighted people), this is the mechanism for sleep regulation. But the argument depends on assuming that a similar mechanism is operating in people who are blind but have well-regulated sleep cycles. The best choice will be the one that helps us decide whether that assumption is correct.

A   This question would not give us an answer that would help in evaluating the argument. A "no" answer would not clarify whether the pineal gland-melatonin mechanism operates in people who are blind. A "yes" answer would do no better. The question refers only to people who have sleep dysfunctions (which the argument does not address).

B   **Correct.** Answering this question would provide the most useful information for evaluating the argument. A "yes" answer would help confirm a key assumption of the argument: that blind people rely on the pineal gland-melatonin mechanism for sleep regulation. A "no" answer would help disconfirm that assumption.

C   Whether or not there are other substances secreted by the pineal gland makes no difference to the reasoning. The argument relies on the premise that the pineal gland governs the sleep cycle *by secreting melatonin*. For example, if the pineal gland sometimes secreted adrenaline, that would still have no bearing on the argument.

D   The consistency or inconsistency of the duration of some people's sleep patterns has no relevance to the reasoning. Their sleep patterns could be due to any of a number of factors.

E   This does not help, for there could be sighted people whose melatonin levels respond abnormally simply because of a pineal-gland abnormality.

The correct answer is B.

730. **In countries where automobile insurance includes compensation for whiplash injuries sustained in automobile accidents, reports of having suffered such injuries are twice as frequent as they are in countries where whiplash is not covered.** Presently, no objective test for whiplash exists, so it is true that spurious reports of whiplash injuries cannot be readily identified. Nevertheless, these facts do not warrant the conclusion drawn by some commentators that in the countries with the higher rates of reported whiplash injuries, half of the reported cases are spurious. Clearly, **in countries where automobile insurance does not include compensation for whiplash, people often have little incentive to report whiplash injuries that they actually have suffered.**

In the argument given, the two boldfaced portions play which of the following roles?

(A) The first is a claim that the argument disputes; the second is a conclusion that has been based on that claim.
(B) The first is a claim that has been used to support a conclusion that the argument accepts; the second is that conclusion.
(C) The first is evidence that has been used to support a conclusion for which the argument provides further evidence; the second is the main conclusion of the argument.
(D) The first is a finding whose implications are at issue in the argument; the second is a claim presented in order to argue against deriving certain implications from that finding.
(E) The first is a finding whose accuracy is evaluated in the argument; the second is evidence presented to establish that the finding is accurate.

Argument Evaluation

Situation   Reported whiplash injuries are twice as common in countries where car insurance companies pay compensation for such injuries as they are in countries where insurance companies do not. Although there is no objective test for whiplash, this does not mean, as some suggest, that half of the reports of such injuries are fake. It could simply be that where insurance will not pay for such injuries, people are less inclined to report them.

Reasoning   *What roles do the two boldfaced portions play in the argument?* The first portion tells us about the correlation between reported cases of whiplash in countries and the willingness of insurance companies in those countries to compensate for whiplash injuries. The argument next states that whiplash is difficult to objectively verify. The argument then asserts that *although* this last fact, taken together with the first boldfaced portion, has led some to infer that over half of the reported cases in countries with the highest whiplash rates are spurious, such an inference is unwarranted. The second boldfaced portion then helps to explain why such an inference is not necessarily warranted by offering an alternative explanation.

A   The claim made in the first boldfaced portion is never disputed in the argument; at dispute is how to account for the fact that this claim is true. The second is not the argument's conclusion.
B   In a manner of speaking, perhaps, the argument uses the first portion to support its conclusion; but there is no indication that it has been used elsewhere to do so. In any case, the second boldfaced portion is not the argument's conclusion.
C   The first has been used to support a conclusion that the argument *rejects*; the second boldfaced portion is not the argument's conclusion.
D   **Correct.** This option correctly identifies the roles played in the argument by the boldfaced portions.
E   The accuracy of the first boldfaced portion is never questioned in the argument; nor is the second intended to somehow help show that the first is accurate. Rather, the argument assumes that the first portion is accurate.

The correct answer is D.

CR03859
731. Last year Comfort Airlines had twice as many delayed flights as the year before, but the number of complaints from passengers about delayed flights went up three times. It is unlikely that this disproportionate increase in complaints was rooted in an increase in overall dissatisfaction with the service Comfort Airlines provides, since the airline made a special effort to improve other aspects of its service last year.

Which of the following, if true, most helps to explain the disproportionate increase in customer complaints?

(A) Comfort Airlines had more flights last year than the year before.
(B) Last year a single period of unusually bad weather caused a large number of flights to be delayed.
(C) Some of the improvements that Comfort Airlines made in its service were required by new government regulations.
(D) The average length of a flight delay was greater last year than it was the year before.
(E) The average number of passengers per flight was no higher last year than the year before.

Argument Construction

Situation Last year Comfort Airlines had twice as many delayed flights as it did the year before, but three times as many passenger complaints about delayed flights. The airline made a special effort to improve other aspects of its service last year.

Reasoning *What could explain why the number of complaints about delayed flights increased disproportionately to the number of delayed flights last year?* In other words, why did the average number of passenger complaints per delayed flight go up last year? One obvious possibility is that the average number of passengers per delayed flight was greater last year than it had been the year before. Another is that the flight delays tended to cause worse problems for passengers last year than they had the year before, so that on average each delay was more upsetting for the passengers.

A This helps explain why the airline had more delayed flights last year, but not why the increase in complaints about delayed flights was disproportionate to the increase in delayed flights.

B This helps explain why the airline had more delayed flights last year. But, if anything, the situation should have reduced the number of passenger complaints per delayed flight, since many passengers should have realized that the unusually bad weather was not the airline's fault.

C If any of the improvements concerned handling of flight delays, for example, and passengers were aware that government regulations addressed this, then passengers might have complained more than previously. But the information we are given here is too general and too vague to explain the disproportionate increase in complaints.

D **Correct.** Longer flight delays would have more severely inconvenienced passengers and thus would probably have generated more passenger complaints per delay.

E This rules out the possibility that an increased number of passengers per delayed flight could have caused the disproportionate increase in the number of complaints about delayed flights. But no alternative explanation is offered.

The correct answer is D

8.7 Critical Reasoning Answer Explanations

CR01337

732. Last year a global disturbance of weather patterns disrupted harvests in many of the world's important agricultural areas. Worldwide production of soybeans, an important source of protein for people and livestock alike, was not adversely affected, however. Indeed, last year's soybean crop was actually slightly larger than average. Nevertheless, the weather phenomenon is probably responsible for a recent increase in the world price of soybeans.

Which of the following, if true, provides the strongest justification for the attribution of the increase in soybean prices to the weather phenomenon?

(A) Last year's harvest of anchovies, which provide an important protein source for livestock, was disrupted by the effects of the weather phenomenon.

(B) Most countries that produce soybeans for export had above-average harvests of a number of food crops other than soybeans last year.

(C) The world price of soybeans also rose several years ago, immediately after an earlier occurrence of a similar global weather disturbance.

(D) Heavy rains attributable to the weather phenomenon improved grazing pastures last year, allowing farmers in many parts of the world to reduce their dependence on supplemental feed.

(E) Prior to last year, soybean prices had been falling for several years.

Argument Construction

Situation | A weather disturbance last year disrupted harvests worldwide but did not reduce production of soybeans, a protein source for both people and livestock. Soybean prices increased nonetheless, likely a result of the weather.

Reasoning | *What evidence would suggest that the weather disturbance caused the increase in soybean prices even though it did not reduce soybean production?* Prices tend to increase when the supply of a product falls relative to the demand for the product. But the production of soybeans did not fall. Evidence that the weather disturbance either hindered the global distribution of soybeans or increased global demand for soybeans could support the claim that the weather disturbance caused the increase in soybean prices.

A **Correct.** If the weather disturbance reduced the anchovy harvest, and anchovies provide protein for livestock just as soybeans do, then more soybeans for livestock feed would be needed to compensate for the lack of anchovies. The resulting increase in demand for soybeans could thus have increased global soybean prices.

B This is not surprising, given that the weather disturbance did not severely affect the soybean-producing countries, but it does not explain how the weather disturbance could have caused soybean prices to increase.

C The rise in soybean prices after the earlier weather disturbance could easily have been a coincidence. Or, unlike last year's disturbance, the earlier disturbance could have reduced soybean production.

D This suggests that demand for soybeans should have fallen as a result of the weather disturbance, so it does not explain why soybean prices rose.

E If soybean prices were unusually low for some temporary reason when the weather disturbance occurred, they might have been likely to rise back to normal levels even without the weather disturbance.

The correct answer is A.

CR03541
733. Most of the year, the hermit thrush, a North American songbird, eats a diet consisting mainly of insects, but in autumn, as the thrushes migrate to their Central and South American wintering grounds, they feed almost exclusively on wild berries. Wild berries, however, are not as rich in calories as insects, yet thrushes need to consume plenty of calories in order to complete their migration. One possible explanation is that berries contain other nutrients that thrushes need for migration and that insects lack.

Which of the following, if true, most seriously calls into question the explanation given for the thrush's diet during migration?

(A) Hermit thrushes, if undernourished, are unable to complete their autumn migration before the onset of winter.
(B) Insect species contain certain nutrients that are not found in wild berries.
(C) For songbirds, catching insects requires the expenditure of significantly more calories than eating wild berries does.
(D) Along the hermit thrushes' migration routes, insects are abundant throughout the migration season.
(E) There are some species of wild berries that hermit thrushes generally do not eat, even though these berry species are exceptionally rich in calories.

Argument Evaluation

Situation   Hermit thrushes are songbirds that usually eat insects but switch to eating berries when migrating. The thrushes need lots of calories to migrate, but berries contain fewer calories than insects do. Perhaps the berries contain nutrients that insects do not provide.

Reasoning   *What would cast doubt on the claim that the thrushes switch to berries because berries contain nutrients that insects lack and that the thrushes need for their migration?* Evidence that berries do not contain such nutrients or that thrushes do not decrease their net calorie consumption by eating berries would cast doubt on the proposed explanation. So would any evidence that supported an alternative explanation for the diet change during migration—for example, seasonal or regional differences in the amount or quality of berries or insects available for the thrushes to consume.

A   Even if thrushes need to be well-nourished to finish migrating before winter, extra nutrients found in berries but not insects might help provide the nourishment they need.

B   Even if insects contain *certain nutrients* not found in wild berries, those specific nutrients may not be the ones the thrushes need for their migration.

C   **Correct.** This suggests that the thrushes might gain more net calories from eating berries than from eating insects, which could explain why they switch to eating berries even if the berries contain no extra nutrients.

D   By ruling out a lack of insects to eat while migrating as an alternative explanation for why the thrushes switch to eating berries, this would support the proposed explanation.

E   The calorie-rich species of berries the thrushes do not eat might be poisonous or indigestible for them, even if the species of berries the thrushes do eat contain nutrients they need to migrate.

The correct answer is C.

734. The kinds of hand and wrist injuries that result from extended use of a computer while maintaining an incorrect posture are common among schoolchildren in Harnville. Computers are important to the school curriculum there, so instead of reducing the amount their students use computers, teachers plan to bring about a sharp reduction in the number of these injuries by carefully monitoring their students' posture when using computers in the classroom.

Which of the following would it be most useful to know in order to assess the likelihood that the teachers' plan will be successful?

(A) Whether extended use of a computer while maintaining incorrect posture can cause injuries other than hand and wrist injuries

(B) Whether hand and wrist injuries not caused by computer use are common among schoolchildren in Harnville

(C) What proportion of schoolchildren in Harnville with hand and wrist injuries use computers extensively outside the classroom

(D) Whether changes in the curriculum could reduce the schools' dependence on computers

(E) What proportion of schoolchildren in Harnville already use correct posture while using a computer

Evaluation of a Plan

Situation   Hand and wrist injuries from using computers while maintaining poor posture are common among schoolchildren in Harnville. Teachers plan to greatly reduce the number of such injuries by monitoring their students' posture while the students use computers in the classroom.

Reasoning   *What would be most helpful to know to determine the likelihood that the teachers' plan will succeed?* The primary concern is the *posture* students adopt while using computers. To succeed, the teachers' plan must reduce the time students spend with poor posture while using computers and reduce it enough to greatly reduce the number of injuries. To know how likely this is, it would help to know how effectively the teachers will be able to monitor and improve their students' posture inside the classroom. But how many of the students use computers *outside of school* while maintaining poor posture and how often do they do so? If many students do so quite often, they may develop hand and wrist injuries regardless of what happens in school.

A   The teachers do not plan to reduce any injuries other than hand and wrist injuries, so whether computer use with poor posture causes any such other injuries is irrelevant to the likelihood that their plan will produce its intended effect.

B   The plan being discussed concerns only the reduction of hand and wrist injuries caused specifically by computer use with poor posture, so the frequency of hand and wrist injuries from other causes is irrelevant to the likelihood that the plan will produce its intended effect.

C   **Correct.** If the students' school use of computers is a large part of their overall computer use, any retraining that accompanies the monitoring might have some effect on their posture and related injury rates overall. However, the greater the proportion of children with hand and wrist injuries who use computers extensively outside the classroom, the more children are likely to keep developing the injuries regardless of any monitoring at school, so the less effective the teachers' plan involving only computer use at school is likely to be.

D   Knowing whether this is the case might help in developing a potential alternative to the teachers' plan, but if it did, this would not help significantly toward assessing the likelihood that the actual plan will succeed. The teachers' actual plan involves monitoring computer use in school without reducing such use. Other possible means of achieving the plan's goal are not part of the plan and are therefore irrelevant to the likelihood that the teachers' actual plan will succeed.

E   The passage indicates that the proportion of the schoolchildren maintaining poor posture while using computers is high enough for many to develop hand and wrist injuries as a result. Whatever the exact proportion is, the teachers' plan may or may not succeed in reducing it.

The correct answer is C.

CR04718
735. A certain cultivated herb is one of a group of closely related plants that thrive in soil with high concentrations of metals that are toxic to most other plants. Agronomists studying the growth of this herb have discovered that it produces large amounts of histidine, an amino acid that, in test-tube solutions, renders these metals chemically inert. Hence, the herb's high histidine production must be the key feature that allows it to grow in metal-rich soils.

In evaluating the argument, it would be most important to determine which of the following?

(A) Whether the herb can thrive in soil that does not have high concentrations of the toxic metals
(B) Whether others of the closely related group of plants also produce histidine in large quantities
(C) Whether the herb's high level of histidine production is associated with an unusually low level of production of some other amino acid
(D) Whether growing the herb in soil with high concentrations of the metals will, over time, reduce their concentrations in the soil
(E) Whether the concentration of histidine in the growing herb declines as the plant approaches maturity

Argument Evaluation

Situation   A certain herb and closely related species thrive in soil full of metals toxic to most plants. The herb produces much histidine, which makes those metals chemically inert. Histidine production, therefore, is largely what accounts for the herb's thriving in metal-rich soils.

Reasoning   *What evidence would help determine whether the herb's histidine production is what enables it to thrive in metal-rich soils?* The argument is that since the herb's histidine chemically neutralizes the metals that are toxic to most plants, it must explain why the herb can thrive in metal-rich soils. To evaluate this argument, it would be helpful to know about the relationship between other closely related plant species' histidine production and the ability to thrive in metal-rich soils. It would also be helpful to know about any other factors that might plausibly explain why the herb can thrive in those soils.

A   Whether or not the herb thrives in metal-free soils, histidine production could enable it to thrive in soils that contain toxic metals.
B   **Correct.** If the closely related plants do not produce much histidine, whatever other factor allows them to thrive in metal-rich soils would likely account for why the herb thrives in those soils as well.
C   The given information suggests no particular reason to suppose that a low level of some unspecified amino acid would enable a plant to thrive in metal-rich soils.
D   The herb might absorb metals from any metal-rich soil it grows in, regardless of why it thrives in that soil.
E   Whether or not histidine concentrations in the herb decline as it approaches maturity, there could still be enough histidine in the growing herb to neutralize the metals and explain why it can grow in metal-rich soil.

The correct answer is B.

CR01293

736. Many people suffer an allergic reaction to certain sulfites, including those that are commonly added to wine as preservatives. However, since there are several winemakers who add sulfites to none of the wines they produce, people who would like to drink wine but are allergic to sulfites can drink wines produced by these winemakers without risking an allergic reaction to sulfites.

Which of the following is an assumption on which the argument depends?

(A) These winemakers have been able to duplicate the preservative effect produced by adding sulfites by means that do not involve adding any potentially allergenic substances to their wine.
(B) Not all forms of sulfite are equally likely to produce the allergic reaction.
(C) Wine is the only beverage to which sulfites are commonly added.
(D) Apart from sulfites, there are no substances commonly present in wine that give rise to an allergic reaction.
(E) Sulfites are not naturally present in the wines produced by these winemakers in amounts large enough to produce an allergic reaction in someone who drinks these wines.

Argument Construction

Situation   People who are allergic to certain sulfites can avoid risking an allergic reaction by drinking wine from one of the several producers that does not add sulfites.

Reasoning   *On what assumption does the argument depend?* Drinking wine to which no sulfites have been *added* will not prevent exposure to sulfites if, for instance, sulfites occur naturally in wines. In particular, if the wines that do not have sulfites added have sulfites present naturally in quantities sufficient to produce an allergic reaction, drinking these wines will not prevent an allergic reaction. The argument therefore depends on assuming that this is not the case.

A   The argument does not require this because the conclusion does not address allergic reactions to substances other than sulfites.

B   The argument specifically refers to "certain sulfites" producing allergic reactions. It is entirely compatible with certain other forms of sulfites not producing allergic reactions in anyone.

C   This is irrelevant. The argument does not claim that one can avoid having an allergic reaction to sulfites *from any source* just by restricting one's wine consumption to those varieties to which no sulfites have been added.

D   Once again, the argument's conclusion does not address allergic reactions to substances other than sulfites in wine.

E   **Correct.** The argument relies on this assumption.

The correct answer is E.

CR11447
737. A new law gives ownership of patents—documents providing exclusive right to make and sell an invention—to universities, not the government, when those patents result from government-sponsored university research. Administrators at Logos University plan to sell any patents they acquire to corporations in order to fund programs to improve undergraduate teaching.

Which of the following, if true, would cast the most doubt on the viability of the college administrators' plan described above?

(A) Profit-making corporations interested in developing products based on patents held by universities are likely to try to serve as exclusive sponsors of ongoing university research projects.
(B) Corporate sponsors of research in university facilities are entitled to tax credits under new federal tax-code guidelines.
(C) Research scientists at Logos University have few or no teaching responsibilities and participate little if at all in the undergraduate programs in their field.
(D) Government-sponsored research conducted at Logos University for the most part duplicates research already completed by several profit-making corporations.
(E) Logos University is unlikely to attract corporate sponsorship of its scientific research.

Evaluation of a Plan

Situation   Universities own the patents resulting from government-sponsored research at their institutions. One university plans to sell its patents to corporations to fund a program to improve teaching.

Reasoning   *Which point casts doubt on the university's plan?* The university's plan assumes there will be a market for its patents, and that the corporations will want to buy them. What might make this untrue? If some of the corporations have already done the same or similar research, they will not be prospective buyers of the university's patents.

A   This point is irrelevant to the plan to sell patents in order to fund a program.
B   The university plans to sell the patents to the corporations, not to invite the corporations to sponsor research.
C   This point is irrelevant to the university's plan to sell off patents since the plan does not specify that the research scientists will be involved in the programs to improve undergraduate teaching.
D   **Correct.** This statement properly identifies a factor that casts doubt on the university's plan to sell its patents to corporations.
E   The plan concerns selling patents resulting from government-sponsored research, not attracting corporate sponsorship for research.

The correct answer is D.

8.7 Critical Reasoning Answer Explanations

CR01848

738. Since it has become known that **several of a bank's top executives have been buying shares in their own bank**, the bank's depositors, who had been worried by rumors that the bank faced impending financial collapse, have been greatly relieved. They reason that, since top executives evidently have faith in the bank's financial soundness, those worrisome rumors must be false. Such reasoning might well be overoptimistic, however, since **corporate executives have been known to buy shares in their own company in a calculated attempt to dispel negative rumors about the company's health.**

In the argument given, the two boldfaced portions play which of the following roles?

(A) The first describes evidence that has been taken as supporting a conclusion; the second gives a reason for questioning that support.

(B) The first describes evidence that has been taken as supporting a conclusion; the second states a contrary conclusion that is the main conclusion of the argument.

(C) The first provides evidence in support of the main conclusion of the argument; the second states that conclusion.

(D) The first describes the circumstance that the argument as a whole seeks to explain; the second gives the explanation that the argument seeks to establish.

(E) The first describes the circumstance that the argument as a whole seeks to explain; the second provides evidence in support of the explanation that the argument seeks to establish.

Argument Evaluation

Situation Top executives at a bank that has been rumored to be in financial trouble have been buying shares in the bank. Bank depositors see this as a good sign, because they believe that it indicates that the executives have faith in the bank. However, corporate executives sometimes do this just to dispel rumors about a company's health.

Reasoning *What is the role that the two boldfaced portions play in the argument?* The first boldfaced portion states that bank executives are buying bank shares, which the passage indicates is taken by bank depositors to be evidence of the executives' faith in the bank. The passage then tells us what some have inferred from this, and finally offers in the second boldfaced statement evidence that undermines this inference.

A **Correct.** This option correctly identifies the roles played by the boldfaced portions.

B This correctly describes the first statement's role, but the second statement is not offered as a conclusion—no evidence is given for it; rather it is evidence for something else.

C The second statement is not offered as a conclusion; no evidence is given for it.

D The second statement is not itself offered as an explanation of why these bank executives are investing in the bank; if it were, that would mean that the bank executives are doing so *because* corporate executives are known to do such things in a calculated effort to dispel worries. Furthermore the argument does not conclude that this other explanation (which the boldfaced portion points to) is correct, only that the one inferred by depositors may not be.

E The argument is not so much seeking to establish an explanation of its own as it is trying to undermine that inferred by the depositors.

The correct answer is A.

CR03814
739. Between 1980 and 2000 the sea otter population of the Aleutian Islands declined precipitously. There were no signs of disease or malnutrition, so there was probably an increase in the number of otters being eaten by predators. Orcas will eat otters when seals, their normal prey, are unavailable, and the Aleutian Islands seal population declined dramatically in the 1980s. Therefore, orcas were most likely the immediate cause of the otter population decline.

Which of the following, if true, most strengthens the argument?

(A) The population of sea urchins, the main food of sea otters, has increased since the sea otter population declined.
(B) Seals do not eat sea otters, nor do they compete with sea otters for food.
(C) Most of the surviving sea otters live in a bay that is inaccessible to orcas.
(D) The population of orcas in the Aleutian Islands has declined since the 1980s.
(E) An increase in commercial fishing near the Aleutian Islands in the 1980s caused a slight decline in the population of the fish that seals use for food.

Argument Evaluation

Situation: A sea otter population declined even though there were no signs of disease or malnutrition. The local seal population also declined. Orcas eat otters when seals are unavailable, and thus are probably the cause of the decline in the otter population.

Reasoning: *What would be evidence that predation by orcas reduced the sea otter population?* Disease and malnutrition are ruled out as alternative explanations of the decline in the sea otter population. The argument could be further strengthened by casting doubt on other possible explanations, such as predation by other animals, or by presenting observations that predation of otters by orcas would help to explain.

A Regardless of whether or not orcas ate the sea otters, the sea urchin population would most likely have increased when the population of sea otters preying on them decreased.

B Because the seal population declined during the initial years of the otter population decline, predation by and competition with seals were already implausible explanations of the otter population decline.

C **Correct.** Orcas eating most of the accessible otters could plausibly explain this observation, which therefore provides additional evidence that orca predation reduced the sea otter population.

D If the orca population declined at the same time as the sea otter population, it would be less likely that increasing predation by orcas reduced the otter population.

E Since the sea otters showed no signs of malnutrition, they were probably getting enough fish. But if they were not, commercial fishing rather than orcas might have caused the otter population decline.

The correct answer is C.

8.7 Critical Reasoning Answer Explanations

CR05960

740. Studies in restaurants show that the tips left by customers who pay their bill in cash tend to be larger when the bill is presented on a tray that bears a credit-card logo. Consumer psychologists hypothesize that simply seeing a credit-card logo makes many credit-card holders willing to spend more because it reminds them that their spending power exceeds the cash they have immediately available.

Which of the following, if true, most strongly supports the psychologists' interpretation of the studies?

(A) The effect noted in the studies is not limited to patrons who have credit cards.

(B) Patrons who are under financial pressure from their credit-card obligations tend to tip less when presented with a restaurant bill on a tray with a credit-card logo than when the tray has no logo.

(C) In virtually all of the cases in the studies, the patrons who paid bills in cash did not possess credit cards.

(D) In general, restaurant patrons who pay their bills in cash leave larger tips than do those who pay by credit card.

(E) The percentage of restaurant bills paid with a given brand of credit card increases when that credit card's logo is displayed on the tray with which the bill is presented.

Argument Evaluation

Situation Studies have found that restaurant customers give more generous tips when their bills are brought on trays bearing a credit-card logo. Psychologists speculate that this is because the logo reminds customers of their ability to spend more money than they have.

Reasoning *Which of the options most helps to support the psychologists' explanation of the studies?* The psychologists' hypothesis is that the credit-card logos on the trays bring to the minds of those who tip more the fact that they have more purchasing power than merely the cash that they have at hand. This explanation would not be valid even if those people who are *not* reminded of their own excess purchasing power—if in fact they have any such power—when they see such a logo nonetheless tip more in such trays. Thus, if restaurant patrons who are under financial pressure from their credit-card obligations do not tip more when their bills are presented on trays bearing credit-card logos, then the psychologists' interpretation of the studies is supported.

A This undermines the psychologists' interpretation, for it shows that the same phenomenon occurs even when the alleged cause has been removed.

B **Correct.** This option identifies the result that would most strengthen the psychologists' interpretation.

C This undermines the psychologists' interpretation by showing that the same phenomenon occurs even when the alleged cause has been removed; patrons cannot be reminded of something that is not there.

D To the extent that this bears on the interpretation of the study, it weakens it. Patrons *using* credit cards are surely aware that they have credit, and yet they spend *less* generously.

E This does not support the idea that being reminded that one has a credit card induces one to be *more generous*, only that it induces one to *use* that credit card.

The correct answer is B.

CR11633
741. In an experiment, each volunteer was allowed to choose between an easy task and a hard task and was told that another volunteer would do the other task. Each volunteer could also choose to have a computer assign the two tasks randomly. Most volunteers chose the easy task for themselves and under questioning later said they had acted fairly. But when the scenario was described to another group of volunteers, almost all said choosing the easy task would be unfair. This shows that most people apply weaker moral standards to themselves than to others.

Which of the following is an assumption required by this argument?

(A) At least some volunteers who said they had acted fairly in choosing the easy task would have said that it was unfair for someone else to do so.
(B) The most moral choice for the volunteers would have been to have the computer assign the two tasks randomly.
(C) There were at least some volunteers who were assigned to do the hard task and felt that the assignment was unfair.
(D) On average, the volunteers to whom the scenario was described were more accurate in their moral judgments than the other volunteers were.
(E) At least some volunteers given the choice between assigning the tasks themselves and having the computer assign them felt that they had made the only fair choice available to them.

Argument Construction

Situation   In an experiment, most volunteers chose to do an easy task themselves and leave a hard task for someone else. They later said they had acted fairly, but almost all volunteers in another group to which the scenario was described said choosing the easy task would be unfair, indicating that most people apply weaker moral standards to themselves.

Reasoning   *What must be true in order for the facts presented to support the conclusion that most people apply weaker moral standards to themselves than to others?* One set of volunteers said they had acted fairly in taking the easy task, whereas different volunteers said that doing so would be unfair. In neither case did any of the volunteers actually judge their own behavior differently from how they judged anyone else's. So the argument implicitly infers from the experimental results that most of the volunteers would judge their own behavior differently from someone else's if given the chance. This inference assumes that the volunteers in the second group would have applied the same moral standards that those in the first group did if they had been in the first group's position, and vice versa.

A   **Correct.** If none of the volunteers who said their own behavior was fair would have judged someone else's similar behavior as unfair, then their relaxed moral judgment of themselves would not suggest that they applied weaker moral standards to themselves than to others.
B   Even if this is so, the experimental results could still suggest that the volunteers would apply weaker moral standards to themselves than to others.
C   The argument would be equally strong even if volunteers who were assigned the hard task did not know that someone else had gotten an easier task—or even if no volunteers were actually assigned the hard task at all.
D   Even if the moral standards applied by the volunteers who judged themselves were as accurate as those applied by the volunteers to whom the scenario was described, the former standards were still weaker.
E   Even if all the volunteers in the first group had felt that all the choices available to them would have been fair for them to make personally, they might have applied stricter moral standards to someone else in the same position.

The correct answer is A.

8.7 Critical Reasoning Answer Explanations

CR08527
742. Country X's recent stock-trading scandal should not diminish investors' confidence in the country's stock market. For one thing, **the discovery of the scandal confirms that Country X has a strong regulatory system**, as the following considerations show. In any stock market, some fraudulent activity is inevitable. If a stock market is well regulated, any significant stock-trading fraud in it will very likely be discovered. This deters potential perpetrators and facilitates improvement in regulatory processes.

In the argument, the portion in boldface plays which of the following roles?

(A) It is the argument's only conclusion.
(B) It is a conclusion for which the argument provides support and which itself is used to support the argument's main conclusion.
(C) It is the argument's main conclusion and is supported by another explicitly stated conclusion for which further support is provided.
(D) It is an assumption for which no explicit support is provided and is used to support the argument's only conclusion.
(E) It is a compound statement containing both the argument's main conclusion and an assumption used to support that conclusion.

Argument Construction

Situation Country X recently had a stock-trading scandal.

Reasoning *What role does the statement that the scandal's discovery confirms that Country X has a strong regulatory system play in the argument?* In the sentence containing the boldface statement, the phrase *For one thing* indicates that the statement is being used to justify the claim in the preceding sentence. Thus, the boldface statement must support that preceding sentence as a conclusion. Directly after the boldface statement, the phrase as *the following considerations show* indicates that the subsequent sentences are being used to support the boldface statement. Thus, the boldface statement is a conclusion supported by the sentences following it, and this statement itself supports the sentence preceding it, which must be the argument's main conclusion.

A   As explained above, the boldface statement supports the claim in the preceding sentence, so it cannot be the argument's only conclusion.
B   **Correct.** As explained above, the boldface statement is supported by the statements following it and in turn is used to support the argument's main conclusion in the statement preceding it.
C   As explained above, the boldface statement cannot be the argument's main conclusion, because it supports a further conclusion presented in the sentence preceding it.
D   As explained above, the sentences following the boldface statement are the explicit support provided for it.
E   As explained above, the argument's main conclusion is stated only in the first sentence, which precedes the boldface statement. It is not repeated anywhere in the boldface statement.

The correct answer is B.

CR05644
743. **Delta Products Inc. has recently switched at least partly from older technologies using fossil fuels to new technologies powered by electricity.** The question has been raised whether it can be concluded that **for a given level of output Delta's operation now causes less fossil fuel to be consumed than it did formerly.** The answer, clearly, is yes, since the amount of fossil fuel used to generate the electricity needed to power the new technologies is less than the amount needed to power the older technologies, provided level of output is held constant.

In the argument given, the two boldfaced portions play which of the following roles?

(A) The first identifies the content of the conclusion of the argument; the second provides support for that conclusion.
(B) The first provides support for the conclusion of the argument; the second identifies the content of that conclusion.
(C) The first states the conclusion of the argument; the second calls that conclusion into question.
(D) The first provides support for the conclusion of the argument; the second calls that conclusion into question.
(E) Each provides support for the conclusion of the argument.

Argument Evaluation

Situation   Delta switched from technologies using fossil fuels to ones using electricity. It has been asked whether this results in less fossil fuel used per level of output. The answer is that it does.

Reasoning   *What roles do the two boldfaced portions play in the argument?* The first boldfaced statement is simply asserted by the passage. But the second boldfaced statement, when it is first introduced, is not asserted to be true, but rather is identified as something that might be inferred from the first statement. By the end of the passage the argument concludes that the second statement is true.

A   This option simply reverses the roles that the statements play in the argument.
B   **Correct.** This option identifies the roles the boldfaced portions play.
C   Nothing in the passage is intended to support the first statement; and the second statement is not supposed to call the first into question.
D   This correctly identifies the role of the first statement, but the second boldfaced portion does not call the argument's conclusion into question—it is part of a sentence that refers to the question whether that conclusion can be drawn from the first statement.
E   Again, this is only half right. The second boldfaced portion is not offered as support for the conclusion; if it were offered as such support, the argument would be guilty of circular reasoning, since the second boldfaced portion states exactly what the argument concludes.

The correct answer is B.

CR00907
744. Theater Critic: The play *La Finestrina*, now at Central Theater, was written in Italy in the eighteenth century. The director claims that this production is as similar to the original production as is possible in a modern theater. Although the actor who plays Harlequin the clown gives a performance very reminiscent of the twentieth-century American comedian Groucho Marx, Marx's comic style was very much within the comic acting tradition that had begun in sixteenth-century Italy.

The considerations given best serve as part of an argument that

(A) modern audiences would find it hard to tolerate certain characteristics of a historically accurate performance of an eighteenth-century play

(B) Groucho Marx once performed the part of the character Harlequin in *La Finestrina*

(C) in the United States the training of actors in the twentieth century is based on principles that do not differ radically from those that underlay the training of actors in eighteenth-century Italy

(D) the performance of the actor who plays Harlequin in *La Finestrina* does not serve as evidence against the director's claim

(E) the director of *La Finestrina* must have advised the actor who plays Harlequin to model his performance on comic performances of Groucho Marx

Argument Construction

Situation The director of the local production of *La Finestrina* says it is as similar to the original production as is possible in a modern theater. The actor playing Harlequin gives a performance reminiscent of Groucho Marx, whose comic style falls within an acting tradition which began in sixteenth-century Italy.

Reasoning *For which of the options would the consideration given best serve as an argument?* The actor's performance was reminiscent of someone who fell within a tradition going back to sixteenth-century Italy. The play was written, and therefore was likely first performed, in eighteenth-century Italy. All of this suggests that there could be a similarity between the performances of Harlequin in the local production and in the original production. While the two performances *might* have been quite dissimilar, there is nothing *here* that supports that.

A Regardless of how plausible this option might be on its own merits, the passage provides no support for it because the passage provides no information about the characteristics of a historically accurate performance of an eighteenth-century play.

B The passage neither says this nor implies it.

C The passage says nothing about the training of actors, so this option would be supported by the passage only in a very roundabout, indirect way.

D **Correct.** This is the option that the considerations most support.

E That the performance reminded the theater critic of Groucho Marx hardly shows that the similarity was intentional, let alone that it was at the director's instruction.

The correct answer is D.

CR07257

745. Although the discount stores in Goreville's central shopping district are expected to close within five years as a result of competition from a SpendLess discount department store that just opened, those locations will not stay vacant for long. In the five years since the opening of Colson's, a nondiscount department store, a new store has opened at the location of every store in the shopping district that closed because it could not compete with Colson's.

Which of the following, if true, most seriously weakens the argument?

(A) Many customers of Colson's are expected to do less shopping there than they did before the SpendLess store opened.

(B) Increasingly, the stores that have opened in the central shopping district since Colson's opened have been discount stores.

(C) At present, the central shopping district has as many stores operating in it as it ever had.

(D) Over the course of the next five years, it is expected that Goreville's population will grow at a faster rate than it has for the past several decades.

(E) Many stores in the central shopping district sell types of merchandise that are not available at either SpendLess or Colson's.

Argument Evaluation

Situation   Due to competition from a recently opened SpendLess discount department store, discount stores in Goreville's central shopping district are expected to close within five years. But those locations will not be vacant long, for new stores have replaced all those that closed because of the opening five years ago of a Colson's nondiscount department store.

Reasoning   *The question is which option would most weaken the argument?* The arguer infers that stores that leave because of the SpendLess will be replaced in their locations by other stores because that is what happened after the Colson's department store came in. Since the reasoning relies on a presumed similarity between the two cases, any information that brings to light a relevant dissimilarity would weaken the argument. If the stores that were driven out by Colson's were replaced mostly by discount stores, that suggests that the stores were replaced because of a need that no longer exists after the opening of SpendLess.

A   The fact that Colson's may be seeing fewer customers does not mean that the discount stores that close will not be replaced; they might be replaced by stores that in no way compete with Colson's or SpendLess.

B   **Correct.** This option most seriously weakens the argument.

C   If anything, this strengthens the argument by indicating that Goreville's central shopping district is thriving.

D   This, too, strengthens the argument because one is more likely to open a new store in an area with a growing population.

E   Because this statement does not indicate whether any of these stores that offer goods not sold at SpendLess or Colson's will be among those that are closing, it is not possible to determine what effect it has on the strength of the argument.

The correct answer is B.

CR05685
746. Last year all refuse collected by Shelbyville city services was incinerated. This incineration generated a large quantity of residual ash. In order to reduce the amount of residual ash Shelbyville generates this year to half of last year's total, the city has revamped its collection program. This year city services will separate for recycling enough refuse to reduce the number of truckloads of refuse to be incinerated to half of last year's number.

Which of the following is required for the revamped collection program to achieve its aim?

(A) This year, no materials that city services could separate for recycling will be incinerated.
(B) Separating recyclable materials from materials to be incinerated will cost Shelbyville less than half what it cost last year to dispose of the residual ash.
(C) Refuse collected by city services will contain a larger proportion of recyclable materials this year than it did last year.
(D) The refuse incinerated this year will generate no more residual ash per truckload incinerated than did the refuse incinerated last year.
(E) The total quantity of refuse collected by Shelbyville city services this year will be no greater than that collected last year.

Argument Construction

Situation: To cut in half the residual ash produced at its incinerator, the city will separate for recycling enough refuse to cut in half the number of truckloads of refuse going to the incinerator.

Reasoning: *Which option is required if the city's revamped collection program is to achieve its aim?* Cutting the number of truckloads of refuse in half must reduce the amount of residual ash to half last year's level. But if removal of the recycled refuse does not proportionately reduce the amount of ash, this will not happen. So if the amount of residual ash produced per truckload increases after recycling, then the amount of ash produced will not be cut in half by cutting in half the number of truckloads.

A This merely indicates that no further reduction of ash through recycling could be achieved this year; it indicates nothing about how much the ash will be reduced.
B This suggests a further benefit from recycling, but does not bear on the amount of ash that will be produced.
C Since no information is provided about how much, if any, recyclable materials were removed from the refuse last year, this does not affect the reasoning.
D **Correct.** This states a requirement for the collection program to achieve its aim.
E This is not a requirement because even if the city collects more refuse this year, it could still cut in half the amount of residual ash by cutting in half the number of truckloads going to the incinerator.

The correct answer is D.

CR01801
747. Veterinarians generally derive some of their income from selling several manufacturers' lines of pet-care products. Knowing that pet owners rarely throw away mail from their pet's veterinarian unread, one manufacturer of pet-care products offered free promotional materials on its products to veterinarians for mailing to their clients. Very few veterinarians accepted the offer, however, even though the manufacturer's products are of high quality.

Which of the following, if true, most helps to explain the veterinarians' reaction to the manufacturer's promotional scheme?

(A) Most of the veterinarians to whom the free promotional materials were offered were already selling the manufacturer's pet-care products to their clients.

(B) The special promotional materials were intended as a supplement to the manufacturer's usual promotional activities rather than as a replacement for them.

(C) The manufacturer's products, unlike most equally good competing products sold by veterinarians, are also available in pet stores and in supermarkets.

(D) Many pet owners have begun demanding quality in products they buy for their pets that is as high as that in products they buy for themselves.

(E) Veterinarians sometimes recommend that pet owners use products formulated for people when no suitable product specially formulated for animals is available.

Evaluation of a Plan

Situation Veterinarians generally derive some income from selling various manufacturers' pet-care products, but very few veterinarians accepted free promotional materials from one such manufacturer to mail to their clients.

Reasoning *What would most help explain why so few veterinarians accepted the free promotional materials to mail to their clients?* The passage says that veterinarians generally derive income from selling pet-care products, which suggests that it should have been in many veterinarians' financial interest to accept and mail out the free promotional materials to increase sales. Any evidence that mailing out these specific promotional materials from this manufacturer would not actually have been in many veterinarians' financial interest could help explain why so few veterinarians accepted the materials.

A This suggests that most of the veterinarians should have had a financial interest in accepting and mailing out the promotional materials in order to increase their sales of the manufacturer's products.

B Even if the promotional materials supplemented the manufacturer's usual promotional activities, they could still have increased the veterinarians' sales of the manufacturer's products and thus generated more income for the veterinarians.

C **Correct.** If this manufacturer's products are available in pet stores and supermarkets but most other products sold by veterinarians are not, then distributing the manufacturer's promotional materials could have encouraged customers to buy this manufacturer's products from pet stores and supermarkets rather than to buy competing products from the veterinarians. Thus, the veterinarians may have been concerned that the promotions would reduce their profits.

D The passage says the manufacturer's products are of high quality, so we have no reason to suppose that clients' demand for quality products would discourage veterinarians from accepting the manufacturer's promotional materials.

E Presumably the manufacturer's products are specially formulated for pets, so any products veterinarians recommend only when no specially formulated pet-care products are available would not reduce the veterinarians' interest in promoting the manufacturer's products.

The correct answer is C.

CR00778

748. The average hourly wage of television assemblers in Vernland has long been significantly lower than that in neighboring Borodia. Since Borodia dropped all tariffs on Vernlandian televisions three years ago, the number of televisions sold annually in Borodia has not changed. However, recent statistics show a drop in the number of television assemblers in Borodia. Therefore, updated trade statistics will probably indicate that the number of televisions Borodia imports annually from Vernland has increased.

Which of the following is an assumption on which the argument depends?

(A) The number of television assemblers in Vernland has increased by at least as much as the number of television assemblers in Borodia has decreased.
(B) Televisions assembled in Vernland have features that televisions assembled in Borodia do not have.
(C) The average number of hours it takes a Borodian television assembler to assemble a television has not decreased significantly during the past three years.
(D) The number of televisions assembled annually in Vernland has increased significantly during the past three years.
(E) The difference between the hourly wage of television assemblers in Vernland and the hourly wage of television assemblers in Borodia is likely to decrease in the next few years.

Argument Construction

Situation Television assemblers in Vernland are paid less than those in neighboring Borodia. The number of televisions sold in Borodia has not dropped since its tariffs on Vernlandian TVs were lowered three years ago, but the number of TV assemblers in Borodia has. So TV imports from Vernland have likely increased.

Reasoning *What assumption does the argument depend on?* The fact that fewer individuals in Borodia are working as TV assemblers is offered as evidence that TV imports from Vernland into Borodia have likely increased. That piece of evidence is relevant *only* as an indication that the number of TVs being produced within Borodia has decreased. But a drop in the number of TV assemblers does not indicate a drop in the number of TVs being assembled *if* the number of TVs an average assembler puts together has increased. Thus, the argument must be assuming that the average time it takes an assembler to put together a TV has not significantly decreased.

A The argument does not rely on any information about the number of television assemblers in Vernland nor for that matter on the number of TVs assembled in Vernland.

B The argument need not assume there is any difference in the features of the TVs produced in the two countries. Increased sales of Vernlandian TVs in Borodia could be due to any number of other reasons, such as price or quality.

C **Correct.** This option states an assumption on which the argument depends.

D The argument does not depend upon this being so: Vernland's domestic TV sales (or perhaps its exports to countries other than Borodia) may have decreased by more than its imports into Borodia have increased.

E The argument's conclusion addresses what *has* happened; the argument in no way relies on any assumptions about what may or may not happen in the coming years.

The correct answer is C.

CR05725
749. Guidebook writer: I have visited hotels throughout the country and have noticed that in those built before 1930 the quality of the original carpentry work is generally superior to that in hotels built afterward. Clearly carpenters working on hotels before 1930 typically worked with more skill, care, and effort than carpenters who have worked on hotels built subsequently.

Which of the following, if true, most seriously weakens the guidebook writer's argument?

(A) The quality of original carpentry in hotels is generally far superior to the quality of original carpentry in other structures, such as houses and stores.
(B) Hotels built since 1930 can generally accommodate more guests than those built before 1930.
(C) The materials available to carpenters working before 1930 were not significantly different in quality from the materials available to carpenters working after 1930.
(D) The better the quality of original carpentry in a building, the less likely that building is to fall into disuse and be demolished.
(E) The average length of apprenticeship for carpenters has declined significantly since 1930.

Argument Evaluation

Situation   The original carpentry in hotels built before 1930 shows superior care, skill, and effort to that in hotels built after 1930. This leads to the conclusion that carpenters working on hotels before 1930 were superior in skill, care, and effort to those that came after.

Reasoning   *Which option most seriously weakens the argument?* The argument draws an inference from a comparison between carpentry in hotels of different eras to a judgment about the carpenters working on hotels in those eras. One way to weaken this inference is by finding some way in which the carpentry in the hotels may be unrepresentative of the skill, care, and effort of the carpenters working in the eras. The comparison is between the carpentry evident in hotels of the two eras *that still exist*. Thus, if there is some reason to think that hotels with good carpentry survive longer than those with bad carpentry, then still-existing hotels from the older era will have disproportionately more good carpentry, even assuming no difference between the skill, care, and effort of the carpenters from the two eras.

A   This option applies equally to both eras, so it has no bearing on the argument.
B   It is not clear whether carpenters working on larger hotels would exercise more, less, or the same skill and care as those working on smaller hotels; thus this option does not weaken the argument.
C   The argument does not rely, even implicitly, on there being any difference in the quality of materials used in the two eras, so it does not weaken the argument to point out that no such difference exists.
D   **Correct.** This weakens the reasoning in the argument by showing a respect in which the comparison between *existing* hotels is unrepresentative.
E   The longer a carpenter works as an apprentice, the more skill he or she is apt to have upon becoming a full-fledged carpenter. So this option would tend to slightly strengthen rather than weaken the argument.

The correct answer is D.

8.7 Critical Reasoning Answer Explanations

CR02997

750. Scientists typically do their most creative work before the age of forty. It is commonly thought that this happens because aging by itself brings about a loss of creative capacity. However, studies show that **of scientists who produce highly creative work beyond the age of forty, a disproportionately large number entered their field at an older age than is usual.** Since by the age of forty the large majority of scientists have been working in their field for at least fifteen years, the studies' finding strongly suggests that the real reason why scientists over forty rarely produce highly creative work is not that they have aged but rather that **scientists over forty have generally spent too long in their field.**

In the argument given, the two portions in boldface play which of the following roles?

(A) The first is a claim, the accuracy of which is at issue in the argument; the second is a conclusion drawn on the basis of that claim.

(B) The first is an objection that has been raised against a position defended in the argument; the second is that position.

(C) The first is evidence that has been used to support an explanation that the argument challenges; the second is that explanation.

(D) The first is evidence that has been used to support an explanation that the argument challenges; the second is a competing explanation that the argument favors.

(E) The first provides evidence to support an explanation that the argument favors; the second is that explanation.

Argument Evaluation

Situation   It is generally thought that the reason scientists tend to do their most creative work before age forty is that creative capacity declines with age. Yet those scientists who do creative work after forty tend, disproportionately, to have started their careers in science later in life. So a better explanation is that many scientists over forty have just been at it too long.

Reasoning   *What roles do the two portions of the argument that are in boldface play?* The argument describes a phenomenon and what is commonly thought to explain it. Then, the first boldfaced statement introduces evidence that suggests that there may be another explanation. After this evidence is further developed, the argument then concludes that there is indeed a better explanation for the phenomenon; that explanation is stated in the second boldfaced portion.

A   The accuracy of the first statement is never called into question by the argument; rather, it is relied upon as the basis for the argument's conclusion.

B   The first statement is not an objection against the position the argument defends; instead, it is a basis for that position.

C   The first statement is not used to support a position the argument challenges, and the second statement is the explanation the argument supports, not the one it challenges.

D   The second statement is indeed an explanation that the argument favors; but the first statement is not used to support a competing explanation that the argument challenges.

E   **Correct.** This option correctly identifies the roles played by the boldfaced portions of the argument.

The correct answer is E.

751. NorthAir charges low fares for its economy-class seats, but it provides very cramped seating and few amenities. Market research shows that economy passengers would willingly pay more for wider seating and better service, and additional revenue provided by these higher ticket prices would more than cover the additional cost of providing these amenities. Even though NorthAir is searching for ways to improve its profitability, it has decided not to make these improvements.

Which of the following, if true, would most help to explain NorthAir's decision in light of its objectives?

(A) None of NorthAir's competitors offers significantly better seating and service to economy-class passengers than NorthAir does.
(B) On many of the routes that NorthAir flies, it is the only airline to offer direct flights.
(C) A few of NorthAir's economy-class passengers are satisfied with the service they receive, given the low price they pay.
(D) Very few people avoid flying on NorthAir because of the cramped seating and poor service offered in economy class.
(E) The number of people who would be willing to pay the high fares NorthAir charges for its business-class seats would decrease if its economy-class seating were more acceptable.

Evaluation of a Plan

Situation   Market research shows that improving some amenities for economy-class passengers would allow NorthAir to raise its economy ticket prices more than enough to cover the additional cost of providing those amenities. But NorthAir has decided not to improve those amenities, even though it is looking for ways to improve its profitability.

Reasoning   *What would most help explain why NorthAir decided not to improve the seating and other amenities, even though the resulting increase in economy-class ticket prices would more than cover the expense?* NorthAir is looking for ways to improve its profitability. Making improvements that would increase ticket prices enough to generate more revenue than they cost should improve profitability, other things being equal. But if improving the amenities would generate side effects that reduced profitability, those side effects would provide a good reason for NorthAir's decision not to improve the amenities and hence would help explain why NorthAir made that decision.

A   The passage says that for NorthAir, the cost of providing better economy seating and other amenities would be more than met by the increased revenue from the higher ticket prices that passengers would be willing to pay. This could give NorthAir a competitive edge, with improved profitability.

B   Even if NorthAir faces little or no competition on certain routes, offering extra amenities might increase passengers' interest in flying those routes. It might also lead passengers to choose NorthAir on other routes that competing airlines also serve. Both of these effects could improve NorthAir's profitability.

C   Even if a few NorthAir economy passengers would not pay more for extra amenities, the market research indicates that most of them would, so offering the amenities could still improve NorthAir's profits attributable to economy-class seating.

D   This suggests that improving the amenities would not increase the total number of NorthAir passengers. But improving the amenities might still enable the airline to increase its ticket prices per passenger enough to improve its profitability.

E   **Correct.** This suggests that improving the economy-class amenities would reduce NorthAir's revenue from sales of business-class tickets, which are likely much more expensive than economy-class tickets. This reduction in revenue could be enough to reduce NorthAir's total profitability despite the increased revenue from economy-class ticket sales.

The correct answer is E.

8.7 Critical Reasoning Answer Explanations

CR00774

752. Which of the following most logically completes the argument given?

Asthma, a chronic breathing disorder, is significantly more common today among adult competitive swimmers than it is among competitive athletes who specialize in other sports. Although chlorine is now known to be a lung irritant and swimming pool water is generally chlorinated, it would be rash to assume that frequent exposure to chlorine is the explanation of the high incidence of asthma among these swimmers, since _____.

(A) young people who have asthma are no more likely to become competitive athletes than are young people who do not have asthma

(B) competitive athletes who specialize in sports other than swimming are rarely exposed to chlorine

(C) competitive athletes as a group have a significantly lower incidence of asthma than do people who do not participate in competitive athletics

(D) until a few years ago, physicians routinely recommended competitive swimming to children with asthma, in the belief that this form of exercise could alleviate asthma symptoms

(E) many people have asthma without knowing they have it and thus are not diagnosed with the condition until they begin engaging in very strenuous activities, such as competitive athletics

Argument Construction

Situation Asthma is more common among competitive swimmers than among other competitive athletes. Chlorine is a lung irritant generally present in swimming pool water.

Reasoning *What would cast doubt on the hypothesis that exposure to chlorine in swimming pools accounts for the high incidence of asthma among adult competitive swimmers?* Evidence of any other factor that would provide an alternative explanation of why asthma is more common among adult competitive swimmers than among other competitive athletes would make it rash to assume that frequent exposure to chlorine explains the high incidence of asthma among these swimmers, so a statement providing such evidence would logically fill in the blank at the end of the passage to complete the argument.

A This might help explain why competitive athletes in general are not especially likely to have asthma, but it does not explain why adult competitive swimmers are more likely to have asthma than other competitive athletes are.

B This provides additional evidence that exposure to chlorine explains why adult competitive swimmers are more likely to have asthma than other competitive athletes are, so it does not cast doubt on that hypothesis.

C A lower incidence of asthma among competitive athletes than among nonathletes does not help explain the higher incidence of asthma among adult competitive swimmers than among other competitive athletes.

D **Correct.** Routinely encouraging children with asthma to take up competitive swimming would likely have made the proportion of adult competitive swimmers with asthma exceed the proportion of other competitive athletes with asthma, even if chlorine in swimming pool water never causes asthma in swimmers.

E This might help explain why people with asthma are just as likely as other people to become competitive athletes, but it does not help explain why adult competitive swimmers are more likely to have asthma than other competitive athletes are.

The correct answer is D.

CR01289

753. In the country of Marut, the Foreign Trade Agency's records were reviewed in 1994 in light of information then newly available about neighboring Goro. The review revealed that in every year since 1963, the agency's projection of what Goro's gross national product (GNP) would be five years later was a serious underestimate. The review also revealed that in every year since 1963, the agency estimated Goro's GNP for the previous year—a Goro state secret—very accurately.

Of the following claims, which is most strongly supported by the statements given?

(A) Goro's GNP fluctuated greatly between 1963 and 1994.
(B) Prior to 1995, Goro had not released data intended to mislead the agency in making its five-year projections.
(C) The amount by which the agency underestimated the GNP it projected for Goro tended to increase over time.
(D) Even before the new information came to light, the agency had reason to think that at least some of the five-year projections it had made were inaccurate.
(E) The agency's five-year projections of Goro's GNP had no impact on economic planning in Marut.

Argument Construction

Situation   A review in 1994 revealed that every year since 1963, Marut's Foreign Trade Agency had seriously underestimated what Goro's GNP would be five years later, but accurately estimated what Goro's GNP had been the previous year.

Reasoning   *What conclusion do the stated facts most strongly support?* Goro's GNP in each year at least from 1969 through 1993 had been seriously underestimated by the agency five years in advance, yet was then accurately estimated by the agency one year after the fact. It follows that for each of these years, the agency's earlier projection of Goro's GNP must have been much lower than its later estimate.

A   This is not supported by the information given. The fact that the agency consistently underestimated each year's GNP in its five-year projections and then correctly estimated it after the fact does not indicate that Goro's GNP fluctuated greatly.

B   This is not supported by the information given. The reason the agency's five-year projections were inaccurate might well have been that Goro deliberately released data intended to mislead the agency in making those projections.

C   This is not supported by the information given. The fact that the underestimates remained large throughout the years in question does not indicate that the underestimates increased over time.

D   **Correct.** As explained above, for many years there were serious discrepancies between the agency's five-year projections of Goro's GNP and its retrospective estimates of each previous year's trade. In any year at least from 1970 through 1993, these discrepancies, if noticed, would have given the agency reason to doubt some of the five-year projections.

E   This is not supported by the information given. Even though at least some of the five-year projections were eventually known to be serious underestimates, they could still have affected Marut's economic planning. The economic planners might have retained an unreasonable faith in the accuracy of the most recent projections.

The correct answer is D.

8.7 Critical Reasoning Answer Explanations

CR05082
754. Vargonia has just introduced a legal requirement that student-teacher ratios in government-funded schools not exceed a certain limit. All Vargonian children are entitled to education, free of charge, in these schools. When a recession occurs and average incomes fall, the number of children enrolled in government-funded schools tends to increase. Therefore, though most employment opportunities contract in economic recessions, getting a teaching job in Vargonia's government-funded schools will not be made more difficult by a recession.

Which of the following would be most important to determine in order to evaluate the argument?

(A) Whether in Vargonia there are any schools not funded by the government that offer children an education free of charge
(B) Whether the number of qualified applicants for teaching positions in government-funded schools increases significantly during economic recessions
(C) What the current student-teacher ratio in Vargonia's government-funded schools is
(D) What proportion of Vargonia's workers currently hold jobs as teachers in government-funded schools
(E) Whether in the past a number of government-funded schools in Vargonia have had student-teacher ratios well in excess of the new limit

Argument Evaluation

Situation   During a recession, the number of children in government-funded schools in Vargonia tends to increase. Vargonian children are entitled to a free education in these schools. A new law requires student-teacher ratios in these schools to remain below a certain limit.

Reasoning   *Which of the five questions would provide us with the best information for evaluating the argument?* The argument's conclusion is that recessions do not make teaching jobs in Vargonia's government-funded schools harder to get. During recessions, the reasoning goes, more students will enroll in Vargonia's government-funded schools than in nonrecession times. Implicit in the argument is the thought that, because the new law sets an upper limit on the average number of students per teacher, schools that get an influx of new students would have to hire more teachers. During a recession, however, there might be much more competition in the labor market for teachers because many more qualified people are applying for teaching jobs.

A   This information is not significant in the context of the argument, which does not need to assume that only government-funded schools provide free education.

B   **Correct.** Getting an answer to this question would provide us with specific information useful in evaluating the argument. A "yes" answer to this question would suggest that competition for teaching jobs in Vargonian government-funded schools would be keener during recessions. A "no" answer would suggest that the level of competition would decrease during recessions.

C   Discovering the current student-teacher ratio in Vargonia's schools would be of no value, by itself, in evaluating the argument. We do not know what the new upper limit on the student-teacher ratio is, and we do not know whether Vargonia is currently in a recession.

D   Finding out whether the proportion this refers to is 1 percent, for example, or 4 percent, would tell us nothing about whether getting teaching jobs at government-funded schools in Vargonia becomes more difficult during a recession. Among other things, we do not know whether Vargonia is currently in a recession, and we do not know what proportion of Vargonia's workers would be qualified candidates for teaching jobs.

E   This is of no relevance in evaluating the argument because, presumably, the new limit on student-teacher ratios will be complied with. Thus, even if student-teacher ratios in the past would have exceeded the new limit, the argument concerns whether, *in the future*, getting a teaching job in Vargonia's government-funded schools will be made more difficult by a recession.

The correct answer is B.

CR09951
755. In Colorado subalpine meadows, nonnative dandelions co-occur with a native flower, the larkspur. Bumblebees visit both species, creating the potential for interactions between the two species with respect to pollination. In a recent study, researchers selected 16 plots containing both species; all dandelions were removed from eight plots; the remaining eight control plots were left undisturbed. The control plots yielded significantly more larkspur seeds than the dandelion-free plots, leading the researchers to conclude that the presence of dandelions facilitates pollination (and hence seed production) in the native species by attracting more pollinators to the mixed plots.

Which of the following, if true, most seriously undermines the researchers' reasoning?

(A) Bumblebees preferentially visit dandelions over larkspurs in mixed plots.
(B) In mixed plots, pollinators can transfer pollen from one species to another to augment seed production.
(C) If left unchecked, nonnative species like dandelions quickly crowd out native species.
(D) Seed germination is a more reliable measure of a species' fitness than seed production.
(E) Soil disturbances can result in fewer blooms, and hence lower seed production.

Argument Evaluation

Situation   Bumblebees visit both larkspur and dandelions in certain meadows. A study found that more larkspur seeds were produced in meadow plots in which both larkspur and dandelions grew than in similar plots from which all dandelions had been removed. The researchers inferred that dandelions facilitate larkspur pollination.

Reasoning   *What evidence would cast the most doubt on the inference from the study's findings to the conclusion that dandelions facilitate larkspur pollination by attracting more pollinators?* The argument assumes that the only relevant difference between the two types of plots was whether dandelions were present. Evidence that the plots differed in some other way that could provide a plausible alternative explanation of why more larkspur seeds were produced in the plots with dandelions would weaken the argument.

A   This would suggest that the larkspur pollination should have been lower in the plots with dandelions, so it does not provide a plausible alternative explanation for the study's findings.

B   This is fully compatible with the claim that the dandelions attracted more pollinators to the mixed plots, and it would also help to support the argument's conclusion that dandelions facilitated larkspur pollination in those plots.

C   Although this suggests that the mixed plots won't remain mixed for long, it does not provide a plausible alternative explanation for the study's finding that larkspur seed production was higher in the mixed plots.

D   The argument is not about how fit larkspurs are as a species, but about why they produced different numbers of seeds in the different plots.

E   **Correct.** This provides a plausible alternative explanation for why larkspur seed production was lower in the plots from which dandelions had been removed, since digging them out would have disturbed the soil.

The correct answer is E.

CR11453
756. An experiment was done in which human subjects recognize a pattern within a matrix of abstract designs and then select another design that completes that pattern. The results of the experiment were surprising. The lowest expenditure of energy in neurons in the brain was found in those subjects who performed most successfully in the experiments.

Which of the following hypotheses best accounts for the findings of the experiment?

(A) The neurons of the brain react less when a subject is trying to recognize patterns than when the subject is doing other kinds of reasoning.
(B) Those who performed best in the experiment experienced more satisfaction when working with abstract patterns than did those who performed less well.
(C) People who are better at abstract pattern recognition have more energy-efficient neural connections.
(D) The energy expenditure of the subjects' brains increases when a design that completes the initially recognized pattern is determined.
(E) The task of completing a given design is more capably performed by athletes, whose energy expenditure is lower when they are at rest.

Argument Construction

Situation   Experimental subjects worked with pattern recognition and completion. The subjects who performed best showed the lowest expenditure of energy in neurons in the brain.

Reasoning   *Which hypothesis best accounts for the findings?* In order to account for the findings, the hypothesis must suggest a plausible link between successful performance and the energy expenditure of neurons in the brain. Consider each answer choice, and evaluate its plausibility and logic. Where is there a reasonably direct relationship between the given factors and the conclusion that is drawn? Understand that hypotheses based on factors not included in the experiment cannot be used to account for the findings.

A   The experiment did not compare types of reasoning so this hypothesis does not account for the results.
B   No information is provided about subjects' satisfaction, so this hypothesis is not warranted.
C   **Correct.** This statement properly identifies a hypothesis that connects subjects' performance with their energy expenditure and so could account for the experiment's results.
D   The most successful subjects would presumably not have completed fewer patterns than average, so the posited increase in energy would likely lead to higher energy expenditures for them, not lower.
E   No information is offered on the subjects, so no hypothesis about athletes is warranted.

The correct answer is C.

CR01202
757. With seventeen casinos, Moneyland operates the most casinos in a certain state. Although intent on expanding, it was outmaneuvered by Apex Casinos in negotiations to acquire the Eldorado chain. To complete its acquisition of Eldorado, Apex must sell five casinos to comply with a state law forbidding any owner to operate more than one casino per county. Since Apex will still be left operating twenty casinos in the state, it will then have the most casinos in the state.

Which of the following, if true, most seriously undermines the prediction?

(A) Apex, Eldorado, and Moneyland are the only organizations licensed to operate casinos in the state.
(B) The majority of Eldorado's casinos in the state will need extensive renovations if they are to continue to operate profitably.
(C) Some of the state's counties do not permit casinos.
(D) Moneyland already operates casinos in the majority of the state's counties.
(E) Apex will use funds it obtains from the sale of the five casinos to help fund its acquisition of the Eldorado chain.

Argument Evaluation

Situation Moneyland operates seventeen casinos, the most in a certain state, and is intent on expanding. Another operator, Apex Casinos, is acquiring the Eldorado casino chain, but must sell five casinos to comply with a state law forbidding any owner to operate more than one casino per county. After these transactions, Apex will operate twenty casinos in the state.

Reasoning *What observation would cast the most doubt on the prediction that Apex will have the most casinos in the state after the transactions?* Apex will operate twenty casinos, whereas Moneyland now operates just seventeen, and no one else operates even that many. It follows that Apex will operate more casinos after its transactions than Moneyland or any other one owner now operates. However, if Moneyland also acquires three or more casinos during the transactions, then Apex will not have the most casinos in the state afterward. Thus, any observation suggesting that Moneyland is about to acquire several casinos would undermine the prediction.

A **Correct.** Since Apex is acquiring Eldorado, Moneyland and Apex will be the only remaining licensed casino operators in the state. Therefore, Moneyland is the only likely buyer for the five casinos Apex needs to sell. So Moneyland is likely to acquire the five casinos during the sale and end up with twenty-two casinos—more than Apex.

B This does not undermine the prediction. Even if the Eldorado casinos cannot operate profitably for long without extensive renovations, Apex will still have twenty casinos immediately after its transactions.

C This supports rather than undermines the prediction. If fewer counties permit casinos, there will be fewer opportunities for Moneyland or any other operator to acquire more casinos to surpass the twenty Apex will own.

D This supports rather than undermines the prediction. If Moneyland's seventeen casinos are in most of the state's counties already, then there are fewer counties in which Moneyland could acquire additional casinos to surpass the twenty Apex will own.

E This supports rather than undermines the prediction. Apex's use of the funds from selling the five casinos to acquire the Eldorado chain will not help anyone else to acquire more casinos to surpass the twenty Apex will own.

The correct answer is A.

CR05093
758. It is widely assumed that people need to engage in intellectual activities such as solving crossword puzzles or mathematics problems in order to maintain mental sharpness as they age. In fact, however, simply talking to other people—that is, participating in social interaction, which engages many mental and perceptual skills—suffices. Evidence to this effect comes from a study showing that the more social contact people report, the better their mental skills.

Which of the following, if true, most seriously weakens the force of the evidence cited?

(A) As people grow older, they are often advised to keep exercising their physical and mental capacities in order to maintain or improve them.

(B) Many medical conditions and treatments that adversely affect a person's mental sharpness also tend to increase that person's social isolation.

(C) Many people are proficient both in social interactions and in solving mathematical problems.

(D) The study did not itself collect data but analyzed data bearing on the issue from prior studies.

(E) The tasks evaluating mental sharpness for which data were compiled by the study were more akin to mathematics problems than to conversation.

Argument Evaluation

Situation A study shows that the more social contact people report, the better their mental skills are, so engaging in social interaction is sufficient for maintaining mental sharpness.

Reasoning *What would suggest that the study does not establish the truth of the conclusion?* The study shows a correlation between mental sharpness and social interaction but does not indicate why this correlation exists. Evidence that mental sharpness contributes to social interaction or that some third factor affects both mental sharpness and social interaction, could provide an alternative explanation for the correlation and thus cast doubt on the explanation that social interaction contributes to mental sharpness.

A People are often wrongly advised to do things that are not actually beneficial. And even if exercising mental capacities does help to maintain them, the passage says that social interaction provides such exercise.

B **Correct.** This provides evidence that the correlation observed in the study results from mental sharpness facilitating social interaction, in which case the study results do not indicate that social interaction facilitates mental sharpness.

C This would be expected, given the argument's conclusion that social interaction helps to maintain better mental skills overall.

D A study that analyzes data from prior studies can provide evidence just as well as a study that collects its own data can.

E The argument's conclusion would be compatible with this observation, and would then suggest that social interaction contributes to the mental sharpness needed for tasks similar to math problems.

The correct answer is B.

9.0 Sentence Correction

9.0 Sentence Correction

Sentence correction questions appear in the Verbal Reasoning section of the GMAT™ exam. The Verbal Reasoning section uses multiple-choice questions to measure your ability to read and comprehend written material, to reason and evaluate arguments, and to correct written material to express ideas effectively in standard written English. Because the Verbal Reasoning section includes passages from several different content areas, you may be generally familiar with some of the material; however, neither the passages nor the questions assume detailed knowledge of the topics discussed. Sentence correction questions are intermingled with critical reasoning and reading comprehension questions throughout the Verbal Reasoning section of the test. You will have 65 minutes to complete the Verbal Reasoning section or about 1¾ minutes to answer each question.

Sentence correction questions present a statement in which words are underlined. The questions ask you to select the best expression of the idea or relationship described in the underlined section from the answer options. The first answer choice always repeats the original phrasing, whereas the other four provide alternatives. In some cases, the original phrasing is the best choice. In other cases, the underlined section has obvious or subtle errors that require correction. These questions require you to be familiar with the stylistic conventions and grammatical rules of standard written English and to demonstrate your ability to improve incorrect or ineffective expressions. Sentence correction questions may include English-language idioms, which are standard constructions not derived from the most basic rules of grammar and vocabulary, but idioms are not intended to measure any specialized knowledge of colloquialisms or regionalisms.

You should begin these questions by reading the sentence carefully. Note whether there are any obvious grammatical errors as you read the underlined section. Then read the five answer choices carefully. If there was a subtle error you did not recognize the first time you read the sentence, it may become apparent after you have read the answer choices. If the error is still unclear, see whether you can eliminate some of the answers as being incorrect. Remember that in some cases, the original selection may be the best answer.

9.1 Some Comments About How It Works

Sentence Correction questions require a good understanding of how the conventions of standard written English can be used for effective communication. However, that understanding does not have to come from extensive explicit training in grammar and usage or from knowledge of specialized linguistic terminology. Many people may have the needed insights without being able to explain them in technical terms. Analogously, without knowing the scientific name of baker's yeast or the chemistry of the Maillard reaction, a talented baker or food critic may be able to tell whether a loaf of bread was properly prepared. This is not to say that explicit training in grammar and usage is unhelpful. As an adjunct to critical reading and writing experience, it can be a useful approach to developing insights into good written communication. It is good to be cautious, though; books and websites offering advice about how to write may occasionally stipulate outmoded or idiosyncratic rules that are not generally followed in effective professional writing.

The problems posed in Sentence Correction take a different approach and fall within a different domain from those in the other Verbal Reasoning section types. But like those other types, they test skills of critical reasoning, problem solving, and reading comprehension. Sentence Correction tasks can be aptly thought of as requiring detective work. A key part of this work consists in understanding the differences among formulations offered in the answer choices and in seeing that some do not make sense when they are plugged into the larger sentence. In this way, the Sentence Correction questions pose some of the most refined and closely targeted reading comprehension tasks in the GMAT exam. To see why certain wordings do not work, you will need to use critical analysis, forming hypotheses about what the writer is trying to express and being ready to revise the hypotheses as you read through the answer choices.

The more difficult questions are not essentially designed to test for knowledge of rules or facts that are harder to learn or that require more technical training. Difficulty often stems from complexity and subtlety among the interconnected parts of the sentence and involves critical application of principles that all astute users of English should understand. Sentence Correction tasks are puzzles of a sort, but they are not merely arbitrarily contrived. Typically, the incorrect answer choices represent flaws that even an experienced writer might introduce by temporarily losing track of the structure of a sentence or by accidentally moving a piece of text to an unintended position.

Sometimes you may be able to think of a wording that works better than any of the options presented, but the task is to find the most effective of the available choices within the parameters of the problem posed. In writing, there are almost always tradeoffs. For example, conciseness is sometimes the enemy of precision and adequate specificity. Certain types of redundancy can be annoying and can make the writer seem inept, but other types of repetition and paraphrasing can improve readability and comprehension. Language serves many purposes, not all of which are cooperative or directly informative. In sincere straightforwardly informative writing—although not in all advertising, entertainment, and poetry—one should minimize ambiguity, yet in the end every sentence is at least somewhat open to multiple interpretations. Because one can never absolutely eliminate the risk of unintended interpretations, Sentence Correction answers should minimize that risk relative to the context, setting, and ordinary assumptions about the intent of the writer. It is safe to assume that any GMAT Sentence Correction sentence you encounter will be intended to sincerely inform, instruct, or inquire, rather than to parody bad writing, confuse the reader, or provoke laughter, outrage, or derision.

You will not be expected to take sides in contentious controversies about grammar, usage, or style or to apply rules that are widely regarded as highly pedantic or outdated. A few of these are mentioned in the discussions of the specific categories that follow.

9.2 The Eight Sentence Correction Categories

The problems to be solved in Sentence Correction questions are classified into eight grammar and usage categories. Each incorrect answer choice contains a flaw in at least one of these categories, and some span two or more categories. Each test contains questions representing a wide range of different types of problems. In the answer explanations in section 9.9, the categories shown in the heading for each question are the most salient, but many of the questions contain problems in other categories as well. Although these eight categories represent the full range of Sentence Correction problems, the discussions within each category below are not exhaustive and are not intended as a comprehensive guide to English grammar and usage. For each category, the discussion aims to provide a general understanding of the kinds of reasoning that may be involved in solving Sentence Correction problems of that type.

Agreement

Effective verbal communication requires clarity about how the elements of a sentence relate to one another. The conventions of agreement help maintain such clarity; constructions that violate these conventions can be confusing or even nonsensical. There are two types of agreement: subject-verb agreement and agreement of terms that have the same referent.

Subject-verb agreement: Singular subjects take singular verbs, whereas plural subjects take plural verbs. Standard contemporary English makes few distinctions in verb form among persons and numbers, but most English verbs do have a distinct present-tense form for third person singular, and *to be* has distinctive forms for first person singular (*am*, *was*).

Examples:
Correct: "I **walk** to the store."
Incorrect: "I **walks** to the store."

Correct: "Each of the circuits **has** its own switch."
Incorrect: "Each of the circuits **have** its own switch."

Correct: "The masses **have** spoken."
Incorrect: "The masses **has** spoken."

Agreement between terms that have the same referent: A pronoun that stands for another element in the discourse—a noun, a noun phrase, or another pronoun—must agree with its antecedent in person, number, and gender. Where a noun or noun phrase has the same referent as another noun or noun phrase, the two terms should agree in number.

Examples:
Correct: "When **you** dream, **you** are usually asleep."
Incorrect: "When **one** dreams, **you** are usually asleep."

The incorrect version is by no means ungrammatical, but it is puzzling and appears not to be intended to mean what it literally says. Thus, it is also a matter of logical predication and rhetorical construction, categories that are discussed under those headings below.

Correct: "I threw away the banana and the mango because **they were** both spoiled."
Incorrect: "I threw away the banana and the mango because **it was** both spoiled."

Correct: "The engineers are **friends** of mine."
Incorrect: "The engineers are **a friend** of mine."

Almost all educated users of English have internalized the conventions of agreement, yet we all occasionally make mistakes of this sort by accident or because we lose track of the structure of our wording. Keep in mind that as you evaluate different wording choices, context is vitally important. We can see immediately that an entire clause consisting of the words "You is working" would be incorrect. On the other hand, that same sequence of words is correct in the following sentence: "The team member who used to assist you is working on a different project now." This is easy to see, but doing so depends on recognizing that the subject of *is* is not *you* but rather the entire noun phrase preceding the verb. This recognition may be either intuitive or based on explicit analysis.

Similarly, no one would seriously claim that the plural *they* should stand for the singular noun *proposal*, but one might more easily overlook the failure of agreement in the following sentence: "From among the six submitted proposals, they chose number four, believing that they could be more easily implemented than the other five." Many readers may see the problem quickly, but in doing so they are noting some complex features of the sentence structure. In principle, *they* could refer to the six proposals or to those who chose from among them, but neither of those tentative interpretations makes sense. Here the reasoning overlaps with that involved in the category of logical predication. The choosers are not the sorts of things that could be implemented, and the comparative phrase *than the other five* rules out the hypothesis that the antecedent of *they* is the plural *six submitted proposals*. Changing *they* to *it* resolves the discrepancy by using a pronoun that clearly has the singular noun phrase *number four* as its antecedent.

Some complicating factors to consider:

When analyzing potential agreement issues in Sentence Correction, keep in mind that not all cases conform obviously and straightforwardly to the most basic rules of agreement. Here are a few special considerations. These are not intended to be exhaustive.

Quantities and quantifying phrases: In some cases, formally plural quantities may take plural verbs, and in other cases they are construed as singular. For example, "Six dollars were withdrawn from the box, one at a time" is correct, but so is "Six dollars is a high price for that."

Quantifying phrases (such as *a number of* and *a percentage of*) often function as subject modifiers in what could appear to be a subject position. In such cases, they are treated similarly to numbers. "A large proportion of the trees are flowering" is essentially like "Three of the trees are flowering." In other cases, similar phrases function as subjects. Consider, for example, the following correct phrases: "a small percentage of our profits is reinvested" and "a small percentage of our employees oppose the new plan."

As a pronoun, *each* is singular, distributing individually to the members of the set or collection referred to, as illustrated in "Each of the circuits has its own switch." When *each* is used as an adjective before a noun, the noun is singular ("Each machine has been inspected"), but in the predicate position *each* modifies the entire plural collection ("The machines have each been inspected").

Plurals that appear singular: All English users are aware that for some words the plural is the same as the singular (*sheep* and *deer*, for example), but there are subtle cases, as when a formally singular noun referring to a group or culture is construed as plural. No simple rule governs the use of such terms; one can say, for example, "the British are" or "the Inuit are" but not "the German are" or "the Cuban are." *Police* is plural, but many similar group words, such as *navy*, are typically construed as singular.

Collective nouns construed as singular or plural: Many nouns referring to groups of people or collections of things have a singular form (team, choir, platoon, crew, assembly, for example). In some editorial styles—and especially in British usage—these can sometimes be construed as plural. This occurs where the writer's intention is to distribute the predicate to the individual members of the group rather than to refer to the group as a single abstract entity. Thus, one may say "the staff are working in small groups" but also "the staff is larger than it used to be."

Plurals construed as singular: Some formally plural nouns, such as *news*, are construed as singular in normal usage. A title that has a plural form (such as *The Grapes of Wrath*) takes a singular verb if it refers to a single work, and some names of organizations or political entities may be construed as singular even though they have a plural form. For example, the phrase *the Cayman Islands* may be singular when referring to the country as a political entity and plural when referring to the islands as multiple pieces of land.

Singular verbs that could appear plural: For most English verbs (with the notable exception of *to be*), the infinitive is the same as the present plural, and the present subjunctive for all persons is the same as the infinitive. Furthermore, the singular past subjunctive is the same as the plural. Thus, there is a risk that at first glance a correct verb form used with a singular subject may appear plural. "The researcher suspend further testing" and "I were you" would be incorrect as complete sentences, but in the following sentences they are in the subjunctive mood and are correct: "We considered it imperative that the researcher suspend further testing." "I wouldn't do that if I were you." As a complete sentence, "The mayor attend the hearings" would be incorrect, but in the sentence, "In none of these cases will either the councilor or the mayor attend the hearings," the verb form is correct; it is an infinitive preceded by the auxiliary verb *will*.

Some issues that are not tested:

The following are a few examples of issues that are outside the scope of the agreement-related Sentence Correction questions.

Especially in informal discourse, the plural pronoun *they* and related forms *them*, *their*, and *theirs* are sometimes used as nonspecific, genderless ways of referring to a singular person. Consider, for example, "Somebody left their notebook on the conference room table." The reasoning surrounding such usage and the alternatives (*he*, *she*, *she or he*, *she/he*) is complex and evolving. You should not expect to see questions that require you to judge which usage is preferable.

Although you should be able to recognize commonly used irregular plurals or special classes of plurals (such as *phenomena*, *cacti*, *genera*), you will not be asked to correct an improper plural spelling. For example, you will not be asked to correct "the genuses are" to "the genera are."

You will also not be expected to know whether certain highly technical terms or local organization names take singular or plural verbs and pronouns unless the context makes it clear whether they are singular or plural. For example, those who are very familiar with the Centers for Disease Control (a U.S. government organization) will know that it is normally referred to in the singular, but others would not be able to determine this merely from seeing the name.

Diction

Sentences that are structurally well formed can still be confusing, or can make the writer seem inept, if the words are not chosen appropriately and effectively. Effective diction involves using the right part of speech and observing other conventions regarding which words to use in which contexts. Word choices involving agreement and verb form may also be thought of partly as matters of diction, but they are treated separately under the Agreement and Verb Form headings. The diction issues you may encounter in Sentence Correction are too many and varied to list here, but here are a few salient categories into which risks of ineffective diction may fall:

Parts of speech: Even accomplished writers sometimes accidentally use an inappropriate part of speech, such as an adjective where an adverb is needed or a preposition where a conjunction is needed.

Examples:
Correct: "I could **easily** tell that the cat was friendly."
Incorrect: "I could **easy** tell that the cat was friendly."

Correct: "The concerto was **beautiful**."
Incorrect: "The concerto was **beautifully**."

Pronoun cases: Pronouns should be in the right case. A writer might compromise clarity by using a subject form of a pronoun as an object or vice versa or a reflexive pronoun in a nonreflexive context.

Examples:
Correct: "**She** and her friend were walking in the park."
Incorrect: "**Her** and her friend were walking in the park."

Correct: "We sent an email to **them**."
Incorrect: "We sent an email to **they**."

Correct: "I gave **him** a good performance rating."
Incorrect: "I gave **himself** a good performance rating."

Counting and quantifying: Although the conventions for quantification of mass nouns and count nouns have some subtle complexities, keep in mind the general rule that mass nouns are quantified by an amount, whereas count nouns are quantified by numbers or by words (such as *many*) that indicate multiple units. Except in certain technical mathematical contexts, *less* and *least* are typically reserved for comparisons of amount or degree, whereas *fewer* and *fewest* express comparisons of number. However, *more* and *most* are used for both comparisons of number and comparisons of degree. *Both* is appropriate only in referring to two entities or qualities.

Examples:
Correct: "We bought only a **small amount of** rice." "She wished me **much happiness**."
Incorrect: "We bought only **a few** rice." "She wished me **many happinesses**."

Correct: "**Fewer** deliveries arrived today than yesterday."
Incorrect: "**Less** deliveries arrived today than yesterday."

Correct: "**All five of the** trees in the garden need pruning."
Incorrect: "**Both of the five** trees in the garden need pruning."

Prepositions: Subtle differences of relationship are often expressed by different prepositions that function similarly to one another. Consider, for example, in/into/within, to/toward, on/onto/above, through/throughout, beside/besides, beside/along/against, and on/over/above.

Examples:
Correct: "We were standing **beside** the river."
Incorrect: "We were standing **besides** the river."

The incorrect version can also be thought of as displaying a problem of logical predication in that it appears to say illogically that the river was also standing.

Correct: "The editor was sitting **in** his office all afternoon."
Incorrect: "The editor was sitting **into** his office all afternoon."

Word choices that are inherently very simple and obvious can become a little more difficult in complex settings, and a Sentence Correction answer choice that appears appropriate on its own may not work when plugged into the larger sentence. In isolation, "distributed throughout" is recognizable as a standard phrase, but in the following sentence it does not make sense: "The computers were distributed throughout the generosity of a group of donors." Replacing *throughout* with *through* solves the problem. The issue here is a matter not only of diction but also of logical predication: the wording causes the sentence to make an illogical claim about the computers.

"We were confident" is fine as a freestanding sentence, but it is nonsense in the following context: "The lawyer who consulted with we were confident that we could negotiate a settlement." This displays combined problems of diction (*with we*), agreement (the plural *were* with the singular subject *lawyer*), and grammatical construction. "Us was confident" is strange out of context, but substituting *us was* for the offending part of the sentence solves the problem: "The lawyer who consulted with us was confident that we could negotiate a settlement."

Some complicating factors to consider:

The following are only a few examples of the types of subtleties and complexities that may be involved in deciding what words are appropriate.

Potentially misleading grammatical constructions: In some contexts, a verb might superficially appear to require an adverb in the predicate position when in fact a predicate adjective is appropriate. For example, it is correct to say "The surface feels rough" rather than "The surface feels roughly." "The animal does not smell well" means something very different from "The animal does not smell good." Both can be correct depending on what the writer wants to convey.

Words ending in *ing* that are derived from verbs (such as *going, assessing,* and *hurting*) can often be either gerunds or participles. Generally, in carefully crafted formal writing, a pronoun or noun that modifies a gerund will be possessive ("The schedule depends on our receiving the materials on time," not "depends on us receiving"). However, in similar constructions the *ing* word is intended as a participle with the noun or pronoun as its subject. This can be seen in the following two examples: (1) "I was concerned about my friend's lying on the ground." Here the focus of the concern is on the situation the friend was in. (2) "I was concerned about my friend lying on the ground." In this case, the writer may intend the focus to be explicitly on the friend who was in that situation.

Words with multiple functions: In English, almost any noun can function as an adjective. Nouns that function also as verbs are well known (as in "she chaired the meeting" or "he tabled the motion"), but words that are not normally used as verbs can also be pressed into special service as verbs on an ad hoc basis. One could say, for example, "She plans to greenhouse her tender plants when the weather turns cold." Some words regularly function as both adjectives and adverbs. One can say, for example, both "This is a hard job" and "We are working hard." Likewise, *fast* is used correctly as both adjective and adverb in the following sentence: "This is not usually a fast train, but it is moving fast at this moment."

Considerations in applying between and among: Among is generally not appropriate for relationships that involve only two entities. It is standard to say "the distance between my house and yours," not "the distance among my house and yours." *Among* is usually needed instead of *between* for relationships involving more than two entities, but there are exceptions. *Between* is sometimes the more accurate preposition to use where the relationship holds, independently, between each member of the group and some other member. Thus, for example, it would be appropriate to say, "In planning your trip to the five destinations, consider the distances between cities and the driving conditions you may encounter."

Some issues that are not tested:

The following are a few examples of issues that are outside the scope of the diction-related Sentence Correction questions.

Which/that: Some American publishers have adopted the convention that *which*, used as a relative pronoun, should always be nonrestrictive and should be replaced with *that* in restrictive contexts (as in "Laws which have been repealed are no longer enforced" versus "laws that have been repealed are no longer enforced"). You should not expect to see questions for which the deciding factor is merely whether the writer adheres to this convention.

Object words with to be: Some usage advisors prescribe the use of nominative (subject) pronouns in both the subject position and the object position with the verb *to be*. According to this convention, "If I were her, I would be happy to accept the job" is incorrect; it should be "If I were she, I would be happy to accept the job." In some contexts, this latter form of expression could seem annoyingly stilted and pedantic and thus could violate other standards of effective expression. You should not expect to see questions for which the deciding factor is merely whether the writer adheres to this convention.

Slang, archaic diction, and words that are distinctively regional or limited to certain subsets of English: You will not be expected, for example, to correct *thou* or *you-all* to *you*, to understand that *skint* could be paraphrased as *lacking resources*, to judge whether *mickle* is a synonym of *muckle* or whether either of these should be paraphrased with *large*, or to understand that *give* (a test) in some usages is synonymous with *take* (a test) in others.

Variant forms and spellings: You will not be asked to choose between variant forms that have the same function and meaning. Some examples of such variant pairs are: *whilst/while, toward/towards, until/till,* and *outward/outwards.*

Grammatical Construction

Many issues of agreement, verb form, parallelism, diction, and idiom can be described as matters of grammar, but those categories by no means cover the full range of grammar-related tasks in Sentence Correction. The Grammatical Construction category concerns issues of grammar that are not treated elsewhere in this classification scheme. For the most part, these are matters of syntax—the ways in which the elements of a sentence are arranged. Effective communication depends on shared understandings between the writer and reader about how the relative positions of words and phrases help convey meaning. A series of words and punctuation marks that does not follow predictable conventions of syntax can be puzzling, annoying, or even incomprehensible. Here are a few major principles guiding effective grammatical construction:

Complete structure: In English, a well-formed sentence or independent clause needs both a subject and a predicate containing a main verb.

Examples:
Correct: "The shipping **company promised that** the package would be delivered on time."
Incorrect: "The shipping **company that** the package would be delivered on time."

Here the main subject, *the shipping company*, has no verb; the only verb phrase, *would be delivered*, has *the package* as its subject and is embedded in the clause beginning with *that*.

Correct: "**In any case, the contract is** acceptable."
Incorrect: "**In any case is** acceptable." In this incorrect example, there is no discernible subject.

Correct: "**Rushing to defend its nest, the swan** pecked at the intruder."
Incorrect: "**Rushing to defend its nest. The swan** pecked at the intruder."

The first part of this incorrect example represents a stereotypical variety of incompletely formed sentence known as a sentence fragment. Sentence fragments are punctuated as sentences but are grammatically incomplete and often seem to be left stranded from a preceding or following sentence.

Clear and correct linkages and punctuation: For clarity of meaning, the elements of a sentence need to be linked to, and separated from, one another with standard punctuation and with appropriate links such as conjunctions and relative pronouns.

Examples:
Correct: "The cupboard **contained two boxes of tea, a bag of rice, and a jar of pickles**."
Incorrect: "The cupboard **contained two boxes of tea a bag of rice, and contained a jar of pickles**."

In this case, the structure is both ungrammatical and confusingly nonparallel. Issues of the latter type are discussed under the Parallelism heading below.

Correct: "The weather yesterday was **hot, and there were** thunderstorms in the evening."
Incorrect: "The weather yesterday was **hot there were** thunderstorms in the evening."

Correct: "We should cancel the **cricket match; the rain will continue** all afternoon."
Incorrect: "We should cancel the **cricket match the rain will continue,** all afternoon."

Proper ordering of words and phrases: A sentence whose components do not follow standard conventions for English governing the sequence of parts can be confusing and can make the writer appear unfamiliar with the language.

Examples:
Correct: "The director's name is Juan."
Incorrect: "Is Juan, the director's name."

Correct: "The geranium has outgrown its pot and will need to be transplanted to a larger container."
Incorrect: "Outgrown its pot to a larger container and the geranium will need to be transplanted."

Correct: "Please call me tomorrow to discuss the contract."
Incorrect: "To discuss me please the contract tomorrow call."

This is an extreme case of obviously ungrammatical word arrangement. Incoherent word sequences such as this are sometimes described as "word salad." To the extent that this example makes any sense, it also appears illogically to be asking someone to telephone a contract and thus displays a problem of logical predication (discussed later under that heading).

To see how an answer choice affects a sentence's grammatical construction, you may need to analyze the relationship between widely separated parts. Consider the sentence, "If you clean the filter before it becomes so clogged that it impedes the flow can prevent costly repairs in the long run." It is important to see that the main verb phrase is *can prevent*; the intervening verbs are embedded in the clause modifying *clean the filter*. The opening phrase, *if you clean . . .* is not grammatically structured to function as a subject, but if that phrase is replaced with *cleaning*, the sentence becomes well-formed and makes sense: "Cleaning the filter before it becomes so clogged that it impedes the flow can prevent costly repairs in the long run." The problem with *if you clean* involves both grammatical construction and verb form (discussed later under that heading).

Consider also the following ungrammatical sentence: "The headphones provided with the audio player that **although she bought them last year, they never worked**." The phrase "she bought last year never worked" would be ungrammatical in isolation, but if substituted for the boldface phrase, it makes the sentence grammatically correct: "The headphones provided with the audio player that **she bought last year never worked**." The crucial relationship here is between the opening words (*the headphones*) and the final phrase of the sentence.

Some complicating factors to consider:

Idiomatic constructions: Some idiomatic wording formats, especially those that use parallel structure to express comparisons, are widely treated as well-formed sentences even though they do not follow the basic conventions of grammatical construction. Some examples are: "The greater the thread count, the higher the price." "Better a small nutritious meal than a large unwholesome one." "Here today, gone tomorrow."

Inverted structures: In contemporary English, standard sentence structure puts subjects ahead of their verbs, but there are many exceptions for special purposes, including some quotations, negative constructions, and questions. Each of the following is readily recognizable as a well-formed sentence: "'Tell me about it,' said his uncle." "Were you at the meeting?" "In neither case could I find the needed information."

Elliptical constructions: In informal contexts and in many formal contexts where economy of words and smoothness of flow are key considerations, certain sentence elements may be omitted when the writer's intent is entirely clear without them. For example, *that* is often omitted at the start of a relative clause, as in "The film I saw last night was boring" or "I was afraid they might be angry." It is also often considered acceptable to omit infinitive verbs in some cases to avoid awkward repetition, with the preposition *to* left dangling, as in "I reviewed the report even though I didn't want to."

Some issues that are not tested:

The following are a few examples of issues that are outside the scope of the grammatical-construction-related Sentence Correction questions.

Fragments that function as complete sentences in special contexts: A group of words that has no subject or no verb can sometimes stand as a well-formed sentence. "No" can be a complete sentence in answer to a stated or hypothetical question, as can "The one on the left." Similarly, a clause beginning with a conjunction and not followed by any other clause can sometimes be an acceptable sentence, as, for example, "Because the delivery was late." Exclamations such as "Not again!" are also complete and well formed in special contexts. You should not expect to see a Sentence Correction question that appears likely to be drawn from a context in which it is intended to function in any of these ways or as a headline, title, or line of poetry.

Punctuation as editorial style: You will need to judge issues of punctuation only insofar as they involve standard conventions that make a difference for the meaning and coherence of the sentence. Beyond the basic grammatical principles, some punctuation conventions vary by region or academic discipline, are matters of pure style, or are determined by publishers or editors for their own purposes. You will not need to judge, for example, whether a comma should be inside or outside a closing quotation mark, whether emphasis should be indicated by italics, or whether an apostrophe should be inserted before the *s* in a plural non-word such as *IOUs/IOU's* or *1980s/1980's*.

Idiom

Idioms are standard forms of expression that consist of ordinary words but whose uses cannot be inferred from the meanings of their component parts or the basic conventions of grammar and usage. There is ultimately no logical reason why English speakers say "on average" rather than "at average" or "depending on" rather than "depending from." This is simply how we do things. Thus, knowing idiomatic constructions is rather like knowing vocabulary words. Accidentally using the wrong combination of words in an idiomatic construction or structuring a phrase in an unidiomatic way can make it difficult for readers to discern the writer's intended meaning. Here are a few major categories of idiomatic wording issues that you may encounter in Sentence Correction:

Prepositions with abstract concepts: For abstract concepts, there is no top, bottom, inside, or outside, yet with these we often use the same prepositions that denote spatial relationships between concrete objects. There are some patterns, but for the most part knowing which preposition to use with which abstract noun or verb depends on familiarity. The idiomatic pairings of prepositions with abstract concepts are far too many and varied to list here. A few illustrations are: *in* love, different *from* (also different *to* in British usage), *in* a while, *on* guard, *at* work.

Examples:
Correct: "**With regard to** your party invitation, I may not be able to go, because I will be **on call** at the clinic that evening."
Incorrect: "**On regard with** your party invitation, I may not be able to go, because I will be **in call** at the clinic that evening."

Correct: "The cost of the repairs will **depend on** what clever solutions the contractors **come up with**."
Incorrect: "The cost of the repairs will **depend from** what clever solutions the contractors **come out through**."

Correlatives: Certain standard correlative structures provide economical ways of expressing relationships between concepts. For example, it can be more efficient to say "Neither she nor he is going" than to say "He is not going, and she is also not going." However, if such structures are not skillfully handled in accordance with standard conventions, they can be puzzling and misleading. Other examples of such idiomatic correlative structures are *as . . . as, more/less/greater/smaller/etc. . . . than*, and *not only . . . but also*.

Examples:
Correct: "**Neither** the pomegranates **nor** the melons have arrived yet from the vendor."
Incorrect: "**Neither** the pomegranates have arrived yet **neither** the melons from the vendor."

Correct: "She was almost **as** sure that if we installed this system it would fail **as** that we would need some such system."
Incorrect: "She was almost **as** sure that if we installed this system it would fail **than** that we would need some such system."

Correct: "The prolonged drought is stressing **not only** the rabbits **but also** the wallabies."
Incorrect: "The prolonged drought is stressing the rabbits, **not** the wallabies **just only**."

Verb phrases: Many combinations of verbs with adverbs or prepositions, or with both adverbs and prepositions, have conventional meanings that do not follow directly from the meanings of their component parts. These include such phrases as *give up, give up on, come through with, come up, come up with, come down with, do without, have at, get over, get on with, go through, go through with*, and *get through with*. Similarly, there are many idiomatic combinations of verb and object, such as *have had it, make waves, make one's mark*, and *put one's finger on*.

Examples:
Correct: "The investigator has **given up on** determining what **happened to** the missing funds."
Incorrect: "The investigator has **given through over** determining what **happened on** the missing funds."

Correct: "When they checked the patient's temperature, it **turned out** that he was **running a fever**."
Incorrect: "When they checked the patient's temperature, it **veered off** that he was **doing a fever**."

Pronouns with no reference: English requires stated subjects in most sentences with active verb forms. Where there is no real subject, one uses specific referentless placeholder pronouns: *it* and *there*.

Examples:
Correct: "**It was raining** yesterday."
Incorrect: "**They were raining** yesterday."

Correct: "**There are** several reasons to prefer this theory over the proposed alternative."
Incorrect: "**Several reasons are** to prefer this theory over the proposed alternative."

Compound modifiers: Some adverbs and adjectives are idiomatically built out of multiple words. A few examples are: *all in all, by and by, by and large, on the whole, through and through, on the up and up,* and *on the other hand* (sometimes, but not always, correlated with *on the one hand*).

Examples:
Correct: "She listened to the radio **off and on** throughout the day."
Incorrect: "She listened to the radio **off but again on** throughout the day."

Correct: "You wondered whether anyone would mention you at the meeting; **in fact**, two people **did so**."
Incorrect: "You wondered whether anyone would mention you at the meeting; **in the fact**, two people **did thus and so**."

Idiom-related problems do not always involve identifying malformed idioms. Sometimes the crucial insight may involve determining which of multiple idiomatic meanings is intended or whether a phrase should be treated as an idiom or a non-idiom. The meaning of the sentence "She asked for information **on** purpose of the order I had submitted" is unclear. However, a plausible hypothesis is that the writer meant to say "information on the purpose," with *on* serving as an informal equivalent of *regarding*. On that reading, the apparent use of the idiom *on purpose* results from an accidental juxtaposition of the two words. Substituting a phrase such as *regarding the* for the boldface word *on* can turn this into a meaningful, well-formed sentence: "She asked for information **regarding the** purpose of the order I had submitted."

In the following sentence, *as long as* could appear at first glance to refer to a length of time: "We should be able to restart our assembly line tomorrow **as long as receiving** the replacement parts today." However, on that interpretation the temporal relationship does not make sense. The sentence can be made coherent by replacing *receiving* with *we receive*, but doing so requires reinterpreting the phrase *as long as* so that it functions as an idiom equivalent to *provided that*. The sentence then becomes "We should be able to restart our assembly line tomorrow **as long as we receive** the replacement parts today."

Some complicating factors to consider:

Here are just a few of the many subtleties that one may encounter in judging whether idiomatic usages are correct and effective:

Similar phrases often have very different idiomatic uses and meanings; consider, for example, *come through with*, *come down with*, and *come up with*. Some idiomatic preposition-plus-noun phrases have alternate forms. For example, it is correct to say either "with regard to" or "in regard to." Many idiomatic phrases have multiple meanings, which are not always similar. For example, *come out with* in some contexts means *express* and in others *publish* or *begin marketing*.

For many idiomatic expressions, there are special exceptions to the standard forms. For example, *not only . . . but* phrases are standardly completed with *also*, but there are special cases in which *also* is unnecessary or misleading. This can be seen in the following sentence: "Surprisingly, the endangered species was found not only at the lowest elevations but throughout the entire valley." If the lowest elevations referred to are in the valley, *but also* would misleadingly seem to indicate that the entire valley was a separate category rather than a more general category encompassing the lower elevations.

Words that form standard pairs, such as *neither* and *nor,* often have other meanings and uses as well. In some contexts, *neither* or *nor* might appear at first glance to need the other term. However, *neither* often occurs as an adjective (as in "neither book has been opened"), a pronoun (as in "neither of them has been opened"), or a freestanding clause negator (as in "My supervisor is not fond of filing reports, but neither am I"). Similarly, *nor* can occur without *neither* (as in "None of the strata in the escarpment were fractured in the earthquake, nor were any of the exposed formations displaced").

Some issues that are not tested:

GMAT Sentence Correction questions neither assess nor presuppose knowledge of obsolete forms of idiomatic expression, highly specialized technical jargon, distinctive dialect constructions, or slang idioms that have not become standard forms of expression.

Logical Predication

Correct grammar is by no means the only type of structural relationship that matters for effective communication. Logical relationships among sentence elements are also crucial. A writer may accidentally structure a completely grammatical sentence in a way that has unintended meanings or implications. Issues of logical predication intersect with all the other categories discussed here and are involved in many of the Sentence Correction questions. Here are a few ways in which they may occur:

Position and scope of modifiers: Modifiers should be positioned so it is clear what word or words they are meant to modify. If modifiers are not positioned clearly, they can cause illogical references or comparisons or otherwise distort the meaning of the sentence.

Examples:
Correct: "I put **the cake that I baked** by the door."
Incorrect: "I put the cake by **the door that I baked**."

Although the better-worded version contains the potentially ambiguous phrase *I baked by the door*, the meaning is made clear by the fact that *put the cake* requires completion by an indication of where or how the cake was put. Therefore, *by the door* binds to the verb *put*.

Correct: "**Concerned that the snake might be venomous, the workers** left it in the crate untouched."
Incorrect: "**Concerned that it might be venomous, the snake** was left untouched by **the workers in the crate**."

Pronoun-antecedent relationships: A misplaced pronoun can bind to the wrong noun, pronoun, or noun phrase and thus create an unintended meaning.

Examples:
Correct: "The baker informed the customers **that the cakes were moldy** and would have to be discarded."
Incorrect: "The baker informed **the customers that they were moldy** and the cakes would have to be discarded."

Correct: "**After reviewing** the report from the consultants, **the company** may consider changing the logo."
Incorrect: "**After it has reviewed** the report from the consultants, **the logo** may be considered for changing by the company."

Compatibility of concepts: Careless wording can cause a predicate to say something inconsistent with the nature of the subject and vice versa.

Examples:
Correct: "The **three types** of wildlife most often seen in the park are sparrows, mallards, and squirrels, **in that order**."
Incorrect: "The **single** most often **type** of wildlife seen in the park is the sparrow, the mallard, and the squirrel, **in that order**."

Correct: "Stock prices **rose** abruptly today **to an all-time high**."
Incorrect: "Stock prices **dropped** abruptly today **to an all-time high**."

Ellipses and extraneous elements: Omission of a crucial word or phrase or inclusion of an extraneous element can shift the subject to an unintended element while leaving the sentence grammatically well formed. Accidents of this sort can also make an unintended noun or pronoun the subject or object of a verb.

Examples:
Correct: "Work on the stadium renovations **is temporarily at** a standstill."
Incorrect: "Work on the stadium renovations **is temporarily** a standstill."

Here the omission of *at* causes the sentence to make an illogical claim about the work (that it is a standstill).

Correct: "**The car was traveling** slowly along the highway."
Incorrect: "**The car's speed was traveling** slowly along the highway."

The redundant reference to speed causes this sentence to say, absurdly, that the speed was traveling along the highway.

Reversed relationships: An unintended meaning can result from accidentally or misguidedly reversing a relationship between sentence elements.

Examples:
Correct: "Last week's unusually high sales of electric fans can almost certainly be **blamed on** the unseasonably hot weather."
Incorrect: "Last week's unusually high sales of electric fans can almost certainly be **blamed for** the unseasonably hot weather."

This also involves an issue of idiomatic usage of prepositions (discussed under the Idiom category above).

Correct: "**Forecasters said the cold front** will move through the region tomorrow."
Incorrect: "**Forecasters, said the cold front,** will move through the region tomorrow."

Ambiguous words and phrases: Writers should be cautious in using words or phrases that have multiple standard meanings. Often the context makes it clear which meaning is intended, but sometimes it does not. Paraphrasing to rule out unwanted meanings can sometimes require adding words or increasing the structural complexity of a sentence.

Examples:
Correct: "She has studied Greek and **speaks** that language **in addition to** Gujarati."
Incorrect: "She has studied Greek and **speaks** it **as well as** Gujarati."

As well as is an entirely acceptable equivalent of *and also* or *in addition to*, but it can be an unfortunate choice of words for a context in which *well* makes perfect sense as an evaluative judgment. Since there is no firm basis for deciding which way the latter version is intended, an alternate correct version could be "She has studied Greek and speaks it as well as she speaks Gujarati."

Correct: "Although visitors **are not permitted to** enter the loading docks, they **might** occasionally wander into the area."
Incorrect: "Although visitors **may not** enter the loading docks, they **may** occasionally wander into the area."

Here again, there is no firm basis for deciding which way the latter version is intended. In the incorrect version, both occurrences of *may* could mean either *are permitted to* or *might*.

Few incorrect answers in actual Sentence Correction questions will be as easy to dismiss as the most obvious of these illustrative examples. Most logical predication decisions will require careful analysis of the relationships between the answer choice and the nonunderlined portions of the sentence. Be alert for all types of problematic relationships among sentence parts, not just for stereotypical dangling modifiers.

Some complicating factors to consider:

Given that all Sentence Correction questions are presented out of context, there may be no basis for certainty about which of several possible interpretations the writer intended to convey. You will not be given multiple equally good versions of a sentence and asked to guess which one accurately represents the writer's true intention. In principle, almost any illogically constructed sentence could be intended to convey a bizarre meaning. One could hypothesize that the writer of the first example under *Position and scope of modifiers* really did intend to say that she or he had baked the door. Even on that hypothesis, the most reasonable judgment for Sentence Correction purposes would be that the sentence is poorly constructed. A careful writer who wants to convey a straightforward message should make it clear that the unusual meaning is the intended one instead of leading the reader to believe that she or he is ineptly trying to convey the more plausible meaning.

Some issues that are not tested:

Occasionally, you may find a poorly worded version of a sentence amusing. However, you should not expect to see Sentence Correction sentences that can be most charitably interpreted as jokes. Among the answer choices, there will always be a serious way of resolving ambiguities and illogical meanings.

Parallelism

Words or phrases that have similar roles in a sentence should be treated in ways that make the similarity clear. This often requires ensuring that parallel clauses have parallel structure, that verbs having the same function are in the same form, and that elements within the scope of a modifier all relate to the modifier in the same way. Here are some major categories in which parallelism can be an issue:

Elements of a series: Where the elements of a series all have the same role or function, they should be in parallel form.

Examples:
Correct: "I **ate** supper, **went** for a walk, and then **visited** some friends."
Incorrect: "I **ate** supper, then **walking**, and then **visitation** of some friends."

Correct: "She tackled the problem **calmly**, **efficiently**, and **analytically**."
Incorrect: "She tackled the problem **calmly, by being efficient in tackling it**, and **was analytic**."

In both these examples, the nonparallel version is also awkward and wordy. Problems of these types are further discussed under the category of rhetorical construction.

Correlations and comparisons: The sides of a correlative structure often need parallel treatment to make the relationship clear and accurate.

Examples:
Correct: "We are neither **planning to** hire any new developers nor **trying to** find ways to reduce the workloads of the current staff."
Incorrect: "We are planning neither **to hire** any new developers nor **attempts at finding ways to** reduce workloads of the current staff."

Correct: "We were impressed not only **by the** beauty of the inlets and beaches but also **by the** diversity of the plant life."
Incorrect: "We were impressed not only **by the** beauty of the inlets and beaches but also **the diversity** of the plant life **impressed us**."

Issues of scope and repetition of elements: To determine what elements of a sentence should be made parallel to each other, it is sometimes necessary to determine how much of the wording should fall within the scope of a verb, preposition, or modifier. The scope may determine which elements need to be in parallel form and whether certain elements need to be repeated. Issues of this type overlap with those illustrated above.

Examples:
Correct: "He mended the torn fabric with **a needle and thread**."
Incorrect: "He **mended** the torn fabric **with a needle** and **mended** it **with thread**."

Assuming that the needle and thread were used together as a unit, the repetition of *with* misrepresents the relationship. In the correct version, the parallelism is between the two nouns, which are both within the scope of *mended with*. In the incorrect version, the parallelism is between the two verb phrases *mended with* . . . and *mended with* . . .

Correct: "He **punched holes** in the decoration **with a needle** and **tied** it to the lamp **with thread**."
Incorrect: "He **punched holes** in and **tied** the decoration to the lamp with **a needle and thread**."

Correct: "The house that was **on fire** was **on the list** of historically significant buildings."
Incorrect: "The house was **on fire and the list** of historically significant buildings."

On functions so differently in the two phrases that it makes no sense to subsume both the fire and the list under a single occurrence of the preposition. Therefore, we need the repetition of *on*.

Correct: "The mixture contains **dates, raisins, and figs**."
Incorrect: "The mixture **contains** dates, **contains** raisins, and **contains** figs."

The correct version has a parallelism among the three objects of the verb *contains*. In the incorrect version, the verb is awkwardly repeated, creating an unnecessary parallelism among three verb phrases. This also displays a problem of rhetorical construction.

Corresponding series: Where the elements of one series are supposed to correspond to those of another series, the order of elements in each series should parallel the order of elements in the other. This parallelism can help prevent confusion about how the two series relate to each other without using cumbersome repetition.

Example:
Correct: "Last week we had four meetings, of which the **first, second, and third** were on **Tuesday, Wednesday, and Thursday** and the last on Friday."
Incorrect: "Last week we had four meetings, of which the last was on Friday, with the **first, second, and third** being on **Thursday, Tuesday, and Wednesday**."

Grammatical considerations: Some requirements of parallelism, including some of those illustrated above, are also requirements of grammatical construction.

Examples:
Correct: "If **the warranty has expired, we will have to pay** for the repairs."
Incorrect: "If **the warranty has expired, our paying** for the repairs."

In the correct version, the two sides of the conditional are parallel in that each is a complete clause with a subject and predicate.

Correct: "**The shipping delays** and **the** two-day **closure** have caused a backlog of orders."
Incorrect: "**The shipping delays** and **we were closed** for two days have caused a backlog of orders."

To function properly as subjects of *have caused*, both of the stated causes need to be in the form of noun phrases.

Some complicating factors to consider:

Problems of idiomatic structure and of logical predication sometimes involve parallelism as well. The following sentence displays all three: "Not only the CEO, and also the executive vice president's proposed policies, have been distributed to the relevant people in middle management." In presenting a faulty parallelism between the *not only* term and the *and also* term, it appears illogically to claim that the CEO has been distributed. It also falls short of the clarity that could be achieved with a more standardly idiomatic *not only . . . but also* structure.

Agreement, as discussed under that heading above, represents a special kind of parallelism. For example, where a singular noun and a pronoun refer to the same thing, the two terms should be parallel in both being singular, and when a verb has a plural subject, the two should be parallel in both being plural. However, in the Sentence Correction classification scheme, agreement is treated as a distinct category. Thus, agreement-related answer explanations in section 9.9 of this book will not automatically carry the parallelism label as well.

Some issues that are not tested:

Sentence Correction questions do not require decisions about purely aesthetic or decorative types of parallelism. For example, you will not be asked to decide whether a rhymed pair such as *highways and byways* would be preferable to another phrase that is equivalent in meaning and function.

Rhetorical Construction

A sentence that is grammatically and idiomatically correct and conforms to good standards of parallelism and logical predication may still be unclear or annoying or may appear ineptly written. Rhetorical construction problems arise in many ways, including the following.

Economy of wording: Superfluous words or unneeded punctuation, pointless redundancies, or convoluted structures that do not enhance precision and adequacy of detail can make a sentence confusing or simply annoying.

Examples:
Correct: "Bananas are almost always harvested green and allowed to ripen in transit or on supermarket shelves."
Incorrect: "With regard to the ways in which people harvest bananas, people almost always harvest such fruits—fruits of the banana variety—in a green condition, and since the thus-harvested bananas have a low ripeness level, people allow these unripe future-delectable-golden morsels to do their ripening while traveling ensconced in cargo devices after harvest, or even when, after transit, they have landed serenely on supermarket shelves."

Correct: "We will carefully review your memo and let you know whether we are interested in the solutions you propose."
Incorrect: "We will 'review'—i.e., carefully scrutinize—your memo submitted, letting you know, vis-à-vis the memo's contained proposal details, whether there is interest, on our part, or not, in those."

Precision and adequacy of detail: Wording that is too vague, sparse, indeterminate, or incomplete can fail to effectively communicate the intended message. Precision often requires the inclusion of details and qualifying phrases. How much specificity and qualification are required depends on the purpose of the communication. Scientific and legal contexts, for example, often require far more precision than do casual communications between friends.

Examples:
Correct: "In medical diagnosis, influenza can be understood as an acute respiratory infection caused by any of the influenza viruses."
Incorrect: "In medical diagnosis, influenza can be understood as when a virus affects you."

Correct: "The contractor shall deliver the completed materials, as defined in Section 5 of this agreement, no later than the thirtieth calendar day after the date on which the signed and ratified contract is distributed to the contracting parties."
Incorrect: "The contractor shall finish taking the actions for relevant agreement sections in a month of distribution and related events."

The latter version of this sentence is indisputably badly constructed and very vague. The judgment that the former version is acceptable is based on the adequacy of the wording for the apparently intended purpose, but there is no way to tell, without background information, whether it refers to the right agreement section or delivery deadline.

Active and passive voice: The better-worded version of the "banana" sentence above uses passive verbs (*are harvested and [are] allowed*). Passive voice is a means of bringing the object of a verb into the subject position. It can sometimes be more straightforward and economical than active voice where the cause of an effect is unknown or irrelevant. However, passive-voice constructions are often objectionably vague, awkward, or indirect.

Examples:
Correct: "We **had** lunch in the hotel and then **spent** the afternoon **looking** at paintings and sculptures in the museum."
Incorrect: "Lunch **was had** in the hotel **by** us before the afternoon **was spent** in the museum where there were paintings and sculptures **being looked at**."

Correct: "The fruits **are left** to dry for two weeks and then **collected**, **sorted**, and **packaged** for shipment."
Incorrect: "**Relevant people leave** the fruits to dry for two weeks, and then **people, devices, and systems collect** and sort them and package them before **someone or something ships** them."

Other types of awkwardness and inelegance: Problems of rhetorical construction take many different forms, some of which do not fall neatly into standard categories.

Examples:
Correct: "As expected, she did the job very well."
Incorrect: "Expectedly, the goodness of her doing the job was considerable."

Correct: "She hoped that humans would be able to explore some of the planets in other solar systems."
Incorrect: "Her hope was for other solar systems' planets' possible human exploration."

Some complicating factors to consider:

Because rhetorical construction is one of the points tested in Sentence Correction, some people might be tempted to guess that shorter answer choices are a safer bet than longer ones. Wordiness is a stereotypical feature of some inelegant writing, and teachers and writing coaches often emphasize conciseness as a goal. Conversely, some might guess that a longer version or one with more qualifiers and caveats is more likely correct. No such guessing strategy is justified. Sentence Correction questions are designed to represent a wide range of issues. Highly professional expert question writers and test assemblers would be extremely unlikely to create predictable patterns that could be exploited in guessing. There is simply no substitute for careful analysis and understanding of the content of each question and answer choice.

Some issues that are not tested:

Sentence Correction questions do not require judgments about rhetorical appropriateness that depend on knowledge of highly technical or specialized vocabulary or syntax. Similarly, you should not expect to see questions for which the deciding factor is merely whether the writer uses jargon or buzzwords. For example, you would not be asked to determine whether *contact* might be preferable to *reach out to*—or whether *sunsetting* might be an effective substitute for *phasing out*—in a sentence such as: "I will reach out to various stakeholders to leverage decisions about the timeframe for phasing out the product."

Verb Form

Verbs should be in the right tenses and moods and should have the right relationships to other verbs. Uses of infinitives and participles should follow standard conventions so that the intended meanings are clear. Some of the problems posed in Sentence Correction questions involve choices among verb tenses, but many are concerned with other verb-form issues. Here are some categories in which verb-form problems may occur:

Temporal relationships: Because Sentence Correction questions are presented without any context, it is sometimes impossible to tell when they were written or whether the events they refer to were in the past, present, or future from the writer's point of view. Therefore, to the extent that verb tenses are at issue, they are often a matter of internal coherence of the parts of the sentence.

Examples:
Correct: "Chili peppers **belong** to the Solanaceae family of flowering plants."
Incorrect: "Chili peppers **are belonging** to the Solanaceae family of flowering plants."

The present progressive form is used unidiomatically in the incorrect version. That form indicates that the event or condition referred to is ongoing at the time of writing and may not continue. The simple present form *belong* is coherent with the permanence and timelessness of the stated fact.

Correct: "I am looking forward to my stay in Tianjin, a city that I **have never visited** before."
Incorrect: "I am looking forward to my stay in Tianjin, a city that I **will never visited** before."

In the correct version, the present perfect form *have never visited* effectively describes the writer's relationship to unspecified times in the past. In the incorrect version, the future form *will* is incompatible with the past-looking perspective indicated by *before* and *visited*.

Correct: "When the researcher **begins** the next phase of the experiment, she **will have been working** on the experiment for six weeks."
Incorrect: "When the researcher **will begin** the next phase of the experiment, she **had been working** on the experiment for six weeks."

The simple present, as used in the correct version, is the appropriate way in English to express a future event on which another future event is predicated. One could similarly use the present perfect *has begun*, which would have a slightly different nuance of meaning. In the incorrect version, *when . . . will begin* is unidiomatic, and the past perfect *had been working* makes no sense in this future context.

Correct: "When I **arrived** at the office, my colleagues **had** already **left**."
Incorrect: "When I **arrived** at the office, my colleagues **will** already **have been leaving**."

In the correct version, the past perfect form *had left* clearly indicates that the action of leaving was already completed at the past time referred to by the simple past form *arrived*. In the incorrect version, the future perfect progressive form makes no sense in relation to the overall past setting established by the verb *arrived*.

Conditionals and subjunctives: Conditional verb forms referring to conjectural or counterfactual events are typically created with the auxiliary *would*. *Would* constructions often require the antecedent (the "if" clause) to be in subjunctive form, but subjunctives have other purposes as well. Although English uses subjunctives less commonly than do some other languages, such forms are sometimes needed to clarify the meaning of a sentence. They appear in prescriptive and conjectural contexts and make no commitment to whether an action will occur. Consider the difference between the following two sentences: "It is important that he eats high-calorie meals." "It is important that he eat high-calorie meals." The former presupposes that the person actually does eat such meals, and it says that the fact that he does so is important. Using the subjunctive form, the latter prescribes his eating high-calorie meals but makes no commitment to whether he actually does so. For some persons and tenses, the subjunctive is indistinguishable from the past or some other indicative forms.

Examples:
Correct: "If the piano **needed** tuning, I would pay to have that done, but I don't believe it needs tuning."
Incorrect: "When the piano **will need** tuning, I would pay to have that done, but I don't believe it needs tuning."

Correct: "**Were the piano** out of tune, **I would pay** to have it tuned."
Incorrect: "**The piano be** out of tune, **I pay** to have it tuned."

Correct: "If the piano **is** out of tune, I **will pay** to have it tuned."
Incorrect: "If the piano **were** out of tune, I **am going to pay** to have it tuned."

Auxiliary verbs: English uses auxiliary verbs for many purposes, some of which are mentioned in the discussions of temporal relationships and conditionals above. For effective communication, the use of auxiliary verbs should conform to standard conventions.

Examples:
Correct: "**Does the professor teach** that course often?"
Incorrect: "**Teaches** the professor that course often?"

In contemporary English, interrogative forms of most verbs are created using appropriate forms of the auxiliary verb *to do*. The simple inversion of subject and verb seen in the incorrect version is an obsolete form.

Correct: "We **cannot** find the website you recommended."
Incorrect: "We **do not can** find the website you recommended."

Can is a modal verb whose negative and interrogative forms are not created with *do*. Furthermore, *can* is one of a few verbs that have no infinitive form; its infinitive is expressed by a phrase such as *to be able*.

Correct: "The new book **might** turn out **to be** a best seller."
Incorrect: "The new book **might will** turn out **being** a best seller."

Treatment of participles, gerunds, and infinitives: Present participles (such as *finding* and *taking*) are used with the verb *to be* to express progressive verb forms (*is finding, had been taking*). They also function as modifiers in phrases such as "he bought the book, hoping he would like it" and as nouns in phrases such as "his buying the book was unexpected." When used as nouns, they are known as gerunds. Past participles (such as *found* and *taken*) are used with the verb *to have* to express perfect verb forms (*has found, will have taken*). They also function as adjectives in phrases such as "the book published last year" and "The plant is withered." The infinitive form is used for verbs that are modified by other verbs. With some modifying verbs, the infinitive must be preceded by *to*. With other verbs (certain modal and auxiliary verbs) it must not. With yet others (such as *help, go,* and *need*) it can be used either with or without *to*. Infinitives can be treated as nouns, serving as subjects or objects of verbs, as in "to laugh at one's own mistakes can be therapeutic."

Examples:
Correct: "**Having** nowhere else to go, **I wandered** through the airport all day."
Incorrect: "**My having** nowhere else to go **wandered** through the airport all day."

In that the incorrect version makes *having* the subject of *wandered*, it also exemplifies a problem of logical predication (discussed under that heading above).

Correct: "**Widely disliked**, the software went unused."
Incorrect: "**To have widely disliked it**, the software went unused."

Like the one above, this example contains a problem of both verb form and logical predication.

Correct: "You **must make** the reservation at least two days in advance."
Incorrect: "You **must to make** the reservation at least two days in advance."

Correct: "My colleague **went to find** another microphone."
Incorrect: "My colleague **went find** another microphone."

Although such expressions as *go find* and *go get* are standard, they are unidiomatic in affirmative past tenses, which require the preposition *to* with the infinitive ("went to find").

Some complicating factors to consider:

English verb forms and surrounding idiomatic wording conventions have many peculiarities and nuances. The following are reminders of just a few such complications.

It is important to keep in mind that the subtleties of how English tenses are used cannot always be inferred from the names of the tenses. For example, in some other European languages, actions that are currently occurring are indicated by the simple present tense. English typically uses the present progressive form for that purpose, as in "The dog is barking" or "The car is running." The simple present tense in English is typically reserved instead for events and conditions that occur at indefinite or unspecified times or that recur, as in "Dogs bark for various reasons" or "The car runs on unleaded fuel."

"Going to (do or happen)" is a standard way of expressing the future tense, but unlike in French, there is no parallel form "coming from (doing or happening)." To indicate that an action was recently completed, English uses the idiom *has/have/had just*, as in "I had just finished composing the email."

The preposition *to* has many different uses in combination with verbs. These differences can sometimes lead to ambiguous constructions and potential confusion. Stereotypically, *to* before a verb is thought of as an infinitive marker, but it can also indicate purpose or intention. Thus, for example, "I need your truck to haul the boxes" is indeterminate between two meanings. More precise expressions of these could be "I need your truck so that I can haul the boxes" and "It is essential for me that your truck haul the boxes." The latter may seem very formal but could be appropriate where precision is needed. *To* with a verb can also be prescriptive, as in "The borrower is to pay a fine if the materials are not returned by the due date," or simply predictive, as in "The visitors are to arrive soon." It can even express a past tense in a construction such as "but I was never to see him again" or "she was the last one to leave the building."

Shall also has multiple meanings. As a simple future-tense indicator, it is an alternative to *will* for first person verbs ("I shall tell you about it tomorrow"). However, it can also be used prescriptively, similarly to *must*, as in "The borrower shall pay a fine if the materials are not returned by the due date."

Some issues that are not tested:

You may hear that some usage advisors object to placing anything between *to* and an infinitive verb, as in "To finally reach the destination." You should not expect to see Sentence Correction questions for which the deciding factor is merely whether the writer follows this advice. However, you might encounter a sentence that is awkward and unclear because too many words—or words that would go better elsewhere—are crammed in between the preposition and the verb. This occurs in the following sentence: "I try to remember to scrupulously every day before I leave work log off my computer." This is an issue of general unclarity and inelegance falling under the heading of rhetorical construction, and not a mere case of "split infinitive."

9.3 Study Suggestions

There are two basic ways you can study for sentence correction questions:

- **Read material that reflects standard usage.**
  One way to gain familiarity with the basic conventions of standard written English is simply to read. Suitable material will usually be found in good magazines and nonfiction books, editorials in outstanding newspapers, and the collections of essays used by many college and university writing courses.

- **Review basic rules of grammar and practice with writing exercises.**
  Begin by reviewing the grammar rules laid out in this chapter. Then, if you have school assignments (such as essays and research papers) that have been carefully evaluated for grammatical errors, it may be helpful to review the comments and corrections.

9.4 What Is Measured

Sentence correction questions test three broad aspects of language proficiency:

- **Correct expression**
  A correct sentence is grammatically and structurally sound. It conforms to all the rules of standard written English, including noun-verb agreement, noun-pronoun agreement, pronoun consistency, pronoun case, and verb tense sequence. A correct sentence will not have dangling, misplaced, or improperly formed modifiers; unidiomatic or inconsistent expressions; or faults in parallel construction.

- **Effective expression**
  An effective sentence expresses an idea or relationship clearly and concisely as well as grammatically. This does not mean that the choice with the fewest and simplest words is necessarily the best answer. It means that there are no superfluous words or needlessly complicated expressions in the best choice.

- **Proper diction**
  An effective sentence also uses proper diction. (Diction refers to the standard dictionary meanings of words and the appropriateness of words in context.) In evaluating the diction of a sentence, you must be able to recognize whether the words are well chosen, accurate, and suitable for the context.

9.5 Test-Taking Strategies

1. **Read the entire sentence carefully.**
   Try to understand the specific idea or relationship that the sentence should express.

2. **Evaluate the underlined passage for errors and possible corrections before reading the answer choices.**
   This strategy will help you discriminate among the answer choices. Remember, in some cases the underlined passage is correct.

3. **Read each answer choice carefully.**
   The first answer choice always repeats the underlined portion of the original sentence. Choose this answer if you think that the sentence is best as originally written, but do so *only after* examining all the other choices.

4. **Try to determine how to correct what you consider to be wrong with the original sentence.**
   Some of the answer choices may change things that are not wrong, whereas others may not change everything that is wrong.

5. **Make sure that you evaluate the sentence and the choices thoroughly.**
   Pay attention to general clarity, grammatical and idiomatic usage, economy and precision of language, and appropriateness of diction.

6. **Read the whole sentence, substituting the choice that you prefer for the underlined passage.**
   A choice may be wrong because it does not fit grammatically or structurally with the rest of the sentence. Remember that some sentences will require no correction. When the given sentence requires no correction, choose the first answer.

9.6 Section Instructions

Go to www.mba.com/tutorial to view instructions for the section and get a feel for what the test center screens will look at on the actual GMAT exam.

9.7 Practice Questions

Each of the sentence correction questions presents a sentence, part or all of which is underlined. Beneath the sentence you will find five ways of phrasing the underlined part. The first of these repeats the original; the other four are different. Follow the requirements of standard written English to choose your answer, paying attention to grammar, word choice, and sentence construction. Select the answer that produces the most effective sentence; your answer should make the sentence clear, exact, and free of grammatical error. It should also minimize awkwardness, ambiguity, and redundancy.

*SC01527

759. According to some critics, watching television <u>not only undermines one's ability to think critically but also impairs one's</u> overall ability to perceive.

(A) not only undermines one's ability to think critically but also impairs one's
(B) not only undermines one's ability of critical thinking but also impairs the
(C) undermines not only one's ability to think critically but also impairs one's
(D) undermines not only one's ability of critical thinking but also impairs the
(E) undermines one's ability not only to think critically but also impairs one's

SC12999

760. In her presentation, the head of the Better Business Bureau emphasized that companies should think of the cost of conventions and other similar gatherings <u>as not an expense, but as</u> an investment in networking that will pay dividends.

(A) as not an expense, but as
(B) as not expense but
(C) not an expense, rather
(D) not as an expense, but as
(E) not in terms of expense, but

SC15382

761. Recent interdisciplinary studies advance the argument that emotions, including those deemed personal or <u>private is a social phenomenon, though one inseparable</u> from bodily response.

(A) private is a social phenomenon, though one inseparable
(B) private, are social phenomena that are inseparable
(C) private are a social phenomenon but are not those separable
(D) private—are social phenomena but not separable
(E) also as private emotions, are social phenomena not inseparable

SC01455

762. In a speech before the Senate Banking Committee, the chairman of the Federal Reserve painted an optimistic picture of the economy, <u>suggesting to investors the central bank in the near future is not lowering interest rates</u>.

(A) suggesting to investors the central bank in the near future is not lowering interest rates
(B) suggesting to investors that the central bank would not lower interest rates in the near future
(C) which suggests that to investors in the near future interest rates will not be lowered by the central bank
(D) with the suggestion to investors in the near future that interest rates would not be lowered by the central bank
(E) with the suggestion to investors of interest rates not being lowered in the near future by the central bank

763. As with ants, the elaborate social structure of termites includes a few individuals reproducing and the rest serve the colony by tending juveniles, gathering food, building the nest, or battling intruders.

(A) As with ants, the elaborate social structure of termites includes a few individuals reproducing

(B) As do ants, termites have an elaborate social structure, which includes a few individuals to reproduce

(C) Just as with ants, termite social structure is elaborate, including a few individuals for reproducing

(D) Like ants, termites have an elaborate social structure in which a few individuals reproduce

(E) Like that of ants, the termite social structure is elaborate, including a few individuals that reproduce

764. While Noble Sissle may be best known for his collaboration with Eubie Blake, as both a vaudeville performer and as a lyricist for songs and Broadway musicals, also enjoying an independent career as a singer with such groups as Hahn's Jubilee Singers.

(A) and as a lyricist for songs and Broadway musicals, also enjoying

(B) and writing lyrics for songs and Broadway musicals, also enjoying

(C) and a lyricist for songs and Broadway musicals, he also enjoyed

(D) as well as writing lyrics for songs and Broadway musicals, he also enjoyed

(E) as well as a lyricist for songs and Broadway musicals, he had also enjoyed

765. Air traffic routes over the North Pole are currently used by only two or three planes a day, but it was found by a joint Canadian–Russian study to be both feasible as well as desirable if those routes are opened to thousands more commercial planes a year.

(A) Air traffic routes over the North Pole are currently used by only two or three planes a day, but it was found by a joint Canadian–Russian study to be both feasible as well as desirable if those routes are opened to thousands more commercial planes a year.

(B) Currently used by only two or three planes a day, a joint Canadian–Russian study has found that if air traffic routes over the North Pole are opened to thousands more commercial planes a year, it would be both feasible and desirable.

(C) A joint Canadian–Russian study, finding it to be both feasible as well as desirable to open air traffic routes over the North Pole, which are currently used by only two or three planes a day, to thousands more commercial planes a year.

(D) Although air traffic routes over the North Pole are currently used by only two or three planes a day, a joint Canadian–Russian study has found that opening those routes to thousands more commercial planes a year is both feasible and desirable.

(E) With air traffic routes over the North Pole currently used by only two or three planes a day, opening those routes to thousands more commercial planes a year has been found by a joint Canadian—Russian study as both feasible and desirable.

766. From an experiment using special extrasensory perception cards, each bearing one of a set of symbols, parapsychologist Joseph Banks Rhine claimed statistical proof for subjects who could use thought transference to identify a card in the dealer's hand.

(A) for subjects who could use thought transference to identify a card in the dealer's hand

(B) for a card in the dealer's hand to be identified by subjects with thought transference

(C) of subjects able to identify with thought transference a card in the dealer's hand

(D) that subjects could identify a card in the dealer's hand by using thought transference

(E) that subjects are capable to use thought transference for identifying a card in the dealer's hand

767. A long-term study of some 1,000 physicians indicates that the more coffee these doctors drank, the more they had a likelihood of coronary disease.

(A) more they had a likelihood of coronary disease
(B) more was their likelihood of having coronary disease
(C) more they would have a likelihood to have coronary disease
(D) greater was their likelihood of having coronary disease
(E) greater was coronary disease likely

768. Hurricanes at first begin traveling from east to west, because that direction is the way the prevailing winds in the tropics blow, but they then veer off toward higher latitudes, in many cases changing direction toward the east before dissipating over the colder, more northerly waters or over land.

(A) Hurricanes at first begin traveling from east to west, because that direction is the way the prevailing winds in the tropics blow, but
(B) At first, hurricanes travel from east to west, because that is the direction of the prevailing winds in the tropics, but
(C) While hurricanes travel from east to west at first, the direction of the prevailing winds blowing in the tropics, and
(D) Because hurricanes at first travel from east to west, since it is the direction of the prevailing winds in the tropics,
(E) Hurricanes, beginning by traveling from east to west, because this is the direction of the prevailing winds in the tropics,

769. Travelers from Earth to Mars would have to endure low levels of gravity for long periods of time, avoiding large doses of radiation, plus contending with the chemically reactive Martian soil, and perhaps even ward off contamination by Martian life-forms.

(A) Mars would have to endure low levels of gravity for long periods of time, avoiding large doses of radiation, plus contending
(B) Mars would have to endure low levels of gravity for long periods of time, avoid large doses of radiation, contend

(C) Mars, having to endure low levels of gravity for long periods of time, would also have to avoid large doses of radiation, plus contending
(D) Mars, having to endure low levels of gravity for long periods of time, avoid large doses of radiation, plus contend
(E) Mars, who would have to endure low levels of gravity for long periods of time, avoid large doses of radiation, contend with

770. Unlike the virginal, whose single set of strings runs parallel to the front edge of the instrument, the harpsichord's several sets of strings are placed at right angles to its front edge.

(A) whose single set of strings runs parallel to the front edge of the instrument, the harpsichord's several sets of strings are
(B) with a single set of strings running parallel to the front edge of the instrument, the several sets of strings of the harpsichord are
(C) which has a single set of strings that runs parallel to the front edge of the instrument, in the case of the harpsichord, several sets of strings are
(D) which has a single set of strings that run parallel to the front edge of the instrument, the harpsichord has several sets of strings
(E) in which a single set of strings run parallel to the front edge of the instrument, the harpsichord's several sets of strings are

771. Although Alice Walker published a number of essays, poetry collections, and stories during the 1970s, her third novel, *The Color Purple*, which was published in 1982, brought her the widest acclaim in that it won both the National Book Award as well as the Pulitzer Prize.

(A) which was published in 1982, brought her the widest acclaim in that it won both the National Book Award as well as the Pulitzer Prize
(B) published in 1982, bringing her the widest acclaim by winning both the National Book Award and the Pulitzer Prize
(C) published in 1982, brought her the widest acclaim, winning both the National Book Award and the Pulitzer Prize

(D) was published in 1982 and which, winning both the National Book Award and the Pulitzer Prize, brought her the widest acclaim

(E) was published in 1982, winning both the National Book Award as well as the Pulitzer Prize, and bringing her the widest acclaim

772. Heating oil and natural gas futures rose sharply yesterday, as long-term forecasts for much colder temperatures in key heating regions raised fears <u>of insufficient supplies capable of meeting</u> the demand this winter.

(A) of insufficient supplies capable of meeting
(B) of supplies that would be insufficient for meeting
(C) of insufficient supplies that are unable to meet
(D) that there would be supplies insufficient for meeting
(E) that supplies would be insufficient to meet

773. Because it regarded the environmentalists as members of an out-of-state organization, the city council voted <u>that they are denied permission for participating</u> in the parade.

(A) that they are denied permission for participating
(B) that they be denied permission for participating
(C) denying them permission for participation
(D) the denial of permission that they participate
(E) to deny them permission to participate

774. In 1913, the largely self-taught Indian mathematician Srinivasa Ramanujan mailed 120 of his theorems to three different British mathematicians; <u>only one, G. H. Hardy, recognized the brilliance of these theorems, but</u> thanks to Hardy's recognition, Ramanujan was eventually elected to the Royal Society of London.

(A) only one, G. H. Hardy, recognized the brilliance of these theorems, but
(B) they were brilliant, G. H. Hardy alone recognized, but
(C) these theorems were brilliant, but only one, G. H. Hardy recognized;
(D) but, only one, G. H. Hardy, recognizing their brilliance,
(E) only one G. H. Hardy recognized, but these theorems were brilliant

775. Cost cutting and restructuring <u>has allowed the manufacturing company to lower its projected losses for the second quarter, and they are forecasting</u> a profit before the end of the year.

(A) has allowed the manufacturing company to lower its projected losses for the second quarter, and they are forecasting
(B) has allowed for the manufacturing company to lower its projected losses in the second quarter and to forecast
(C) have allowed that the manufacturing company can lower the projected losses for the second quarter, and to forecast
(D) have allowed the manufacturing company to lower its projected second-quarter losses and to forecast
(E) have allowed for the manufacturing company to lower the projected losses in the second quarter, as well as forecasting

776. The Life and Casualty Company hopes that by increasing its environmental fund reserves to $1.2 billion, <u>that it has set aside enough to pay for environmental claims and no longer has</u> to use its profits and capital to pay those claims bit by bit, year by year.

(A) that it has set aside enough to pay for environmental claims and no longer has
(B) enough has been set aside with which environmental claims can be paid and it will have no longer
(C) it has set aside enough for payment of environmental claims and thus no longer having
(D) enough has been set aside to pay for environmental claims, thus no longer having
(E) it has set aside enough to pay for environmental claims and will no longer have

777. <u>Like ancient Egyptian architectural materials that were recycled in the construction of</u> ancient Greek Alexandria, so ancient Greek materials from the construction of that city were reused in subsequent centuries by Roman, Muslim, and modern builders.

(A) Like ancient Egyptian architectural materials that were recycled in the construction of
(B) Like recycling ancient Egyptian architectural materials to construct

(C) Just as ancient Egyptian architectural materials were recycled in the construction of

(D) Just as they recycled ancient Egyptian architectural materials in constructing

(E) Just like ancient Egyptian architectural materials that were recycled in constructing

SC09877
778. Especially in the early years, new entrepreneurs may need to find resourceful ways, like renting temporary office space or using answering services, that make their company seem large and more firmly established than they may actually be.

(A) that make their company seem large
(B) to make their companies seem larger
(C) thus making their companies seem larger
(D) so that the companies seem larger
(E) of making their company seem large

SC01975
779. Unlike the nests of leaf cutters and most other ants, situated underground or in pieces of wood, raider ants make a portable nest by entwining their long legs to form "curtains" of ants that hang from logs or boulders, providing protection for the queen and the colony larvae and pupae.

(A) the nests of leaf cutters and most other ants,
(B) the nests of leaf cutters and most other ants, which are
(C) leaf cutters and most other ants, whose nests are
(D) leaf cutters and most other ants in having nests
(E) those of leaf cutters and most other ants with nests

SC04452
780. Turtles, like other reptiles, can endure long fasts, in their ability to survive on weekly or even monthly feedings; however, when food is readily available, they may eat frequently and grow very fat.

(A) fasts, in their ability to survive
(B) fasts, having their ability to survive
(C) fasts, due to having the ability of surviving
(D) fasts because they are able to survive
(E) fasts because of having the ability of surviving

SC02025
781. Thai village crafts, as with other cultures, have developed through the principle that form follows function and incorporate readily available materials fashioned using traditional skills.

(A) as with
(B) as did those of
(C) as they have in
(D) like in
(E) like those of

SC01554
782. To estimate the expansion rate of the universe is a notoriously difficult problem because there is a lack of a single yardstick that all distances can be measured by.

(A) To estimate the expansion rate of the universe is a notoriously difficult problem because there is a lack of a single yardstick that all distances can be measured by.

(B) Estimating the expansion rate of the universe is a notoriously difficult problem because there is no single yardstick by which all distances can be measured.

(C) Because there is a lack of a single yardstick to measure all distances by, estimating the expansion rate of the universe is a notoriously difficult problem.

(D) A notoriously difficult problem is to estimate the expansion rate of the universe because a single yardstick is lacking by which all distances can be measured.

(E) It is a notoriously difficult problem to estimate the expansion rate of the universe because by no single yardstick can all distances be measured.

SC01059
783. The Commerce Department reported that the nation's economy grew at a brisk annual pace of 3.7 percent in the second quarter, but that while businesses were expanding their production, unsold goods piled up on store shelves as consumer spending is slowed sharply.

(A) unsold goods piled up on store shelves as consumer spending is slowed sharply
(B) unsold goods were piling up on store shelves as consumer spending slowed sharply
(C) unsold goods had piled up on store shelves with a sharp slowing of consumer spending
(D) consumer spending was slowing sharply, with the piling up of unsold goods on store shelves
(E) consumer spending has slowed sharply, with unsold goods piling up on store shelves

SC01470
784. Thomas Mann's novel Doctor Faustus offers an examination not only of how difficult it is to reconcile reason, will, and passion together in any art form, but also a skillfully navigated exploration of the major concerns of modernism.

(A) an examination not only of how difficult it is to reconcile reason, will, and passion together in any art form, but
(B) an examination not only about the difficulty of reconciling reason, will, and passion in any art form, and
(C) not only an examination of how difficult it is to reconcile reason, will, and passion in any art form, and
(D) not only an examination about the difficulty with reconciling reason, will, and passion together in any art form, but
(E) not only an examination of the difficulty of reconciling reason, will, and passion in any art form, but

SC00981
785. According to a recent study, retirees in the United States are four times more likely to give regular financial aid to their children as to receive it from them.

(A) retirees in the United States are four times more likely to give regular financial aid to their children as
(B) retirees in the United States are four times as likely to give regular financial aid to their children as it is for them

(C) retirees in the United States are four times more likely to give regular financial aid to their children than
(D) it is four times more likely for retirees in the United States to give regular financial aid to their children than they are
(E) it is four times as likely that retirees in the United States will give their children regular financial aid as they are

SC04093
786. Discussion of greenhouse effects have usually had as a focus the possibility of Earth growing warmer and to what extent it might, but climatologists have indicated all along that precipitation, storminess, and temperature extremes are likely to have the greatest impact on people.

(A) Discussion of greenhouse effects have usually had as a focus the possibility of Earth growing warmer and to what extent it might,
(B) Discussion of greenhouse effects has usually had as its focus whether Earth would get warmer and what the extent would be,
(C) Discussion of greenhouse effects has usually focused on whether Earth would grow warmer and to what extent,
(D) The discussion of greenhouse effects have usually focused on the possibility of Earth getting warmer and to what extent it might,
(E) The discussion of greenhouse effects has usually focused on whether Earth would grow warmer and the extent that is,

SC02102
787. In the seventh century B.C., the Roman alphabet was adapted from the Etruscan alphabet, which in turn had been adapted in the previous century from a western Greek alphabet, which itself had been adapted earlier in the same century from the Phoenician alphabet.

(A) which itself had been adapted earlier
(B) adapting itself earlier
(C) itself being adapted earlier
(D) having been earlier adapted itself
(E) earlier itself having been adapted

788. The foundation works to strengthen local and regional agricultural markets and cooperating with governments, improving access for farmers for productive resources such as land and credit.

   (A) cooperating with governments, improving access for farmers for
   (B) cooperates with governments to improve access for farmers to
   (C) cooperate with governments for improvements of access for farmers to
   (D) cooperate with governments and improve accessibility for farmers for their
   (E) in cooperation with governments to improve access for farmers for

789. A professor at the university has taken a sabbatical to research on James Baldwin's books that Baldwin wrote in France while he was living there.

   (A) on James Baldwin's books that Baldwin wrote in France while he was living there
   (B) about the books James Baldwin wrote in France
   (C) into James Baldwin's books written while in France
   (D) on the books of James Baldwin, written while he lived in France
   (E) the books James Baldwin wrote while he lived in France

790. When working with overseas clients, an understanding of cultural norms is at least as important as grasping the pivotal business issues for the global manager.

   (A) When working with overseas clients, an understanding of cultural norms is at least as important as grasping the pivotal business issues for the global manager.
   (B) When they work with overseas clients, understanding cultural norms is at least of equivalent importance to grasping the pivotal business issues for the global manager.
   (C) For global managers working with overseas clients, understanding cultural norms is at least as important as grasping the pivotal business issues.
   (D) For global managers working with overseas clients, an understanding of cultural norms is at least as important to them as grasping the pivotal business issues.
   (E) Global managers working with overseas clients find an understanding of cultural norms to be equally important to grasping the pivotal business issues.

791. Often major economic shifts are so gradual as to be indistinguishable at first from ordinary fluctuations in the financial markets.

   (A) so gradual as to be indistinguishable
   (B) so gradual they can be indistinguishable
   (C) so gradual that they are unable to be distinguished
   (D) gradual enough not to be distinguishable
   (E) gradual enough so that one cannot distinguish them

792. Researchers now regard interferon as not a single substance, but it is rather a biological family of complex molecules that play an important, though not entirely defined, role in the immune system.

   (A) as not a single substance, but it is rather a biological family of complex molecules that play
   (B) as not a single substance but as a biological family of complex molecules playing
   (C) not as a single substance but as a biological family of complex molecules that play
   (D) not to be a single substance but rather a biological family of complex molecules playing
   (E) not as a single substance but instead as being a biological family of complex molecules that play

793. The remarkable similarity of Thule artifacts throughout a vast region can, in part, be explained as a very rapid movement of people from one end of North America to the other.

   (A) The remarkable similarity of Thule artifacts throughout a vast region can, in part, be explained as
   (B) Thule artifacts being remarkably similar throughout a vast region, one explanation is
   (C) That Thule artifacts are remarkably similar throughout a vast region is, in part, explainable as
   (D) One explanation for the remarkable similarity of Thule artifacts throughout a vast region is that there was
   (E) Throughout a vast region Thule artifacts are remarkably similar, with one explanation for this being

SC12841.01
794. Regulators are likely to end what are, in effect, long-standing exemptions permitting pilots of small turboprop aircraft at small carriers to fly <u>as much as 20 percent more hours per month than pilots at larger airlines fly, with the consequence that</u> some carriers could be forced to hire additional pilots.

(A) as much as 20 percent more hours per month than pilots at larger airlines fly, with the consequence that

(B) as many as 20 percent more hours per month as pilots at larger airlines, and

(C) more hours per month, as much as 20 percent, than pilots at larger airlines; consequently

(D) as much as 20 percent more hours per month as larger airlines' pilots, so

(E) as many as 20 percent more hours per month than pilots at larger airlines do, and consequently

SC24751.01
795. Self-compassion is made up of mindfulness, the ability to manage thoughts and emotions without being carried <u>away or repressing them, common humanity, or empathy with the suffering of others,</u> and self-kindness, a recognition of your own suffering and a commitment to solving the problem.

(A) away or repressing them, common humanity, or empathy with the suffering of others,

(B) away, or repression of them, and common humanity, or empathy with the suffering of others,

(C) away, or repressing them, common humanity, empathy with the suffering of others;

(D) away or repressing them; common humanity, an empathy with the suffering of others;

(E) away or repress them; common humanity, to empathize with the suffering of others

SC83751.01
796. According to the laws of this nation, individuals are minors until they reach the age of eighteen, <u>although this is less in some countries and more in others</u>.

(A) although this is less in some countries and more in others

(B) but this age is lower in some countries; higher in others

(C) although in some countries, it is lower and in others it is higher

(D) although it is less than that in some countries and more than that in others

(E) but the relevant age is lower in some countries and higher in others

SC32261.01
797. <u>Rather than ignore a company that seems about to fail,</u> investment analysts should recognize that its reorganization and recent uptick in revenue, combined with its dynamic new leadership, indicate that the firm's prospects must be taken seriously.

(A) Rather than ignore a company that seems about to fail,

(B) Rather than ignoring a company that is about to seemingly fail,

(C) Instead of a company that is seemingly about to fail being ignored,

(D) Instead of ignore a company that seems about to fail,

(E) In place of ignoring a company's imminent failure seemingly about to occur,

SC01490
798. Between 14,000 and 8,000 B.C. the ice cap that covered northern Asia, Europe, and America <u>began to melt, uncovering vast new areas that were to be occupied</u> by migrating peoples moving northward.

(A) began to melt, uncovering vast new areas that were to be occupied

(B) began melting, to uncover vast new areas to be occupied

(C) began, by melting, to uncover vast new areas for occupation

(D) began, after melting, uncovering vast new areas which are to be occupied

(E) would begin to uncover, through melting, vast new areas for occupation

SC01472
799. Bengal-born writer, philosopher, and educator Rabindranath Tagore had the greatest admiration <u>for Mohandas K. Gandhi the person and also as a politician, but Tagore had been</u> skeptical of Gandhi's form of nationalism and his conservative opinions about India's cultural traditions.

(A) for Mohandas K. Gandhi the person and also as a politician, but Tagore had been

(B) for Mohandas K. Gandhi as a person and as a politician, but Tagore was also

(C) for Mohandas K. Gandhi not only as a person and as a politician, but Tagore was also

(D) of Mohandas K. Gandhi as a person and as also a politician, but Tagore was

(E) of Mohandas K. Gandhi not only as a person and as a politician, but Tagore had also been

SC04704
800. Traffic safety officials predict that drivers will be equally likely to exceed the proposed speed limit as the current one.

(A) equally likely to exceed the proposed speed limit as

(B) equally likely to exceed the proposed speed limit as they are

(C) equally likely that they will exceed the proposed speed limit as

(D) as likely that they will exceed the proposed speed limit as

(E) as likely to exceed the proposed speed limit as they are

SC04562
801. Written early in the French Revolution, Mary Wollstonecraft's *A Vindication of the Rights of Man* (1790) and *A Vindication of the Rights of Woman* (1792) attributed Europe's social and political ills to be the result of the dominance of aristocratic values and patriarchal hereditary privilege.

(A) Mary Wollstonecraft's *A Vindication of the Rights of Man* (1790) and *A Vindication of the Rights of Woman* (1792) attributed Europe's social and political ills to be the result of

(B) Mary Wollstonecraft's *A Vindication of the Rights of Man* (1790) and *A Vindication of the Rights of Woman* (1792) attributed Europe's social and political ills to result from

(C) Mary Wollstonecraft's *A Vindication of the Rights of Man* (1790) and *A Vindication of the Rights of Woman* (1792) attributed Europe's social and political ills to

(D) in *A Vindication of the Rights of Man* (1790) and *A Vindication of the Rights of Woman* (1792), Mary Wollstonecraft attributed Europe's social and political ills to have been the result of

(E) Mary Wollstonecraft, in *A Vindication of the Rights of Man* (1790) and *A Vindication of the Rights of Woman* (1792), attributed Europe's social and political ills to

SC01498
802. Using study groups managed by the principal popular organizations and political parties, the Swedish public was informed by the government about energy and nuclear power.

(A) the Swedish public was informed by the government about energy and nuclear power

(B) the government informed the Swedish public about energy and nuclear power

(C) energy and nuclear power information was given to the Swedish public by the government

(D) information about energy and nuclear power was given to the Swedish public by the government

(E) the public of Sweden was given energy and nuclear power information by the government

SC07446
803. The use of the bar code, or Universal Product Code, which was created in part to enable supermarkets to process customers at a faster rate, has expanded beyond supermarkets to other retail outlets and have become readily accepted despite some initial opposition when it was first introduced in 1974.

(A) have become readily accepted despite some initial opposition when it was first introduced in 1974

(B) has become readily accepted despite some initial opposition when they were first introduced in 1974

(C) have become readily accepted despite some initial opposition when first introduced in 1974

(D) has become readily accepted despite some initial opposition when the bar code was first introduced in 1974

(E) bar codes have become readily accepted despite some initial opposition when it was first introduced in 1974

SC01595
804. Normally a bone becomes fossilized through the action of groundwater, which permeates the bone, washes away its organic components, and replaces them with minerals.

(A) which permeates the bone, washes away its organic components, and replaces them

(B) which permeates the bone, washes away its organic components, and those are replaced

(C) which permeates the bone, washing away its organic components, to be replaced

(D) permeating the bone, washing away its organic components, to be replaced

(E) permeating the bone, washing away its organic components and replacing them

805. The Organization of Petroleum Exporting Countries (OPEC) had long been expected to announce a reduction in output to bolster sagging oil prices, but officials of the organization just recently announced that the group will pare daily production by 1.5 million barrels by the beginning of next year, but only if non-OPEC nations, including Norway, Mexico, and Russia, were to trim output by a total of 500,000 barrels a day.

(A) year, but only if non-OPEC nations, including Norway, Mexico, and Russia, were to trim output

(B) year, but only if the output of non-OPEC nations, which includes Norway, Mexico, and Russia, is trimmed

(C) year only if the output of non-OPEC nations, including Norway, Mexico, and Russia, would be trimmed

(D) year only if non-OPEC nations, which includes Norway, Mexico, and Russia, were trimming output

(E) year only if non-OPEC nations, including Norway, Mexico, and Russia, trim output

806. Over the past ten years cultivated sunflowers have become a major commercial crop, second only to soybeans as a source of vegetable oil.

(A) second only to soybeans as a source of vegetable oil

(B) second in importance to soybeans only as a source of vegetable oil

(C) being second in importance only to soybeans as a source of vegetable oil

(D) which, as a source of vegetable oil, is only second to soybeans

(E) as a source of vegetable oil only second to soybeans

807. Not trusting themselves to choose wisely among the wide array of investment opportunities on the market, stockbrokers are helping many people who turn to them to buy stocks that could be easily bought directly.

(A) stockbrokers are helping many people who turn to them to buy stocks that could be easily

(B) stockbrokers are helping many people who are turning to them for help in buying stocks that they could easily have

(C) many people are turning to stockbrokers for help from them to buy stocks that could be easily

(D) many people are turning to stockbrokers for help to buy stocks that easily could have been

(E) many people are turning to stockbrokers for help in buying stocks that could easily be

808. In the 1940s popular magazines in the United States began to report on the private lives of persons from the entertainment industry, in despite of the fact that they previously had featured individuals in business and politics.

(A) in despite of the fact that they previously had featured individuals

(B) in spite of the fact previously that these publications featured articles on those

(C) whereas previously there were those individuals featured in articles

(D) whereas previously those individuals they featured were

(E) whereas previously these publications had featured articles on individuals

809. In the early part of the twentieth century, many vacationers found that driving automobiles and sleeping in tents allowed them to enjoy nature close at hand and tour at their own pace, with none of the restrictions of passenger trains and railroad timetables or with the formalities, expenses, and impersonality of hotels.

(A) with none of the restrictions of passenger trains and railroad timetables or with the

(B) with none of the restrictions of passenger trains, railroad timetables, nor

(C) without the restrictions of passenger trains and railroad timetables nor

(D) without the restrictions of passenger trains and railroad timetables or with the

(E) without the restrictions of passenger trains and railroad timetables or the

9.7 Sentence Correction Practice Questions

810. Over the next few years, increasing demands on the Chattahoochee River, which flows into the Apalachicola River, could alter the saline content of Apalachicola Bay, which would rob the oysters there of their flavor, and to make them decrease in size, less distinctive, and less in demand.

    (A) which would rob the oysters there of their flavor, and to make them decrease in size,
    (B) and it would rob the oysters there of their flavor, make them smaller,
    (C) and rob the oysters there of their flavor, making them decrease in size,
    (D) robbing the oysters there of their flavor and making them smaller,
    (E) robbing the oysters there of their flavor, and making them decrease in size,

811. Elizabeth Barber, the author of both *Prehistoric Textiles*, a comprehensive work on cloth in the early cultures of the Mediterranean, and also of *Women's Work*, a more general account of early cloth manufacture, is an expert authority on textiles in ancient societies.

    (A) also of *Women's Work*, a more general account of early cloth manufacture, is an expert authority on
    (B) also *Women's Work*, a more general account of cloth manufacture, is an expert authority about
    (C) of *Women's Work*, a more general account about early cloth manufacture, is an authority on
    (D) of *Women's Work*, a more general account about early cloth manufacture, is an expert authority about
    (E) *Women's Work*, a more general account of early cloth manufacture, is an authority on

812. Digging in sediments in northern China, evidence has been gathered by scientists suggesting that complex life-forms emerged much earlier than they had previously thought.

    (A) evidence has been gathered by scientists suggesting that complex life-forms emerged much earlier than they had
    (B) evidence gathered by scientists suggests a much earlier emergence of complex life-forms than had been
    (C) scientists have gathered evidence suggesting that complex life-forms emerged much earlier than
    (D) scientists have gathered evidence that suggests a much earlier emergence of complex life-forms than that which was
    (E) scientists have gathered evidence which suggests a much earlier emergence of complex life-forms than that

813. Employing many different techniques throughout his career, Michelangelo produced a great variety of art works, including paintings, for example, in the Sistine Chapel, to sculpture, for example, the statue of David.

    (A) including paintings, for example, in the Sistine Chapel, to sculpture, for example,
    (B) including paintings, for example, in the Sistine Chapel, to sculpture, like
    (C) including paintings, such as those in the Sistine Chapel, and sculpture, as
    (D) ranging from paintings, such as those in the Sistine Chapel, to sculpture, such as
    (E) ranging from paintings, such as in the Sistine Chapel, and sculpture, such as

814. According to a recent study of consumer spending on prescription medications, increases in the sales of the 50 drugs that were advertised most heavily accounts for almost half of the $20.8 billion increase in drug spending last year, the remainder of which came from sales of the 9,850 prescription medicines that companies did not advertise or advertised very little.

    (A) heavily accounts for almost half of the $20.8 billion increase in drug spending last year, the remainder of which came
    (B) heavily were what accounted for almost half of the $20.8 billion increase in drug spending last year; the remainder of the increase coming
    (C) heavily accounted for almost half of the $20.8 billion increase in drug spending last year, the remainder of the increase coming
    (D) heavily, accounting for almost half of the $20.8 billion increase in drug spending last year, while the remainder of the increase came
    (E) heavily, which accounted for almost half of the $20.8 billion increase in drug spending last year, with the remainder of it coming

795

815. Technically, "quicksand" is the term for sand that is so saturated with water as to acquire a liquid's character.

(A) that is so saturated with water as to acquire a liquid's character
(B) that is so saturated with water that it acquires the character of a liquid
(C) that is saturated with water enough to acquire liquid characteristics
(D) saturated enough with water so as to acquire the character of a liquid
(E) saturated with water so much as to acquire a liquid character

816. At the end of 2001, motion picture industry representatives said that there were about a million copies of Hollywood movies available online and expected piracy to increase with high-speed Internet connections that become more widely available.

(A) online and expected piracy to increase with high-speed Internet connections that become more widely available
(B) online and expect the increase of piracy with the wider availability of high-speed Internet connections
(C) online, and they expect more piracy to increase with the wider availability of high-speed Internet connections
(D) online, and that they expected the increase of piracy as high-speed Internet connections would become more widely available
(E) online, and that they expected piracy to increase as high-speed Internet connections became more widely available

817. Making things even more difficult has been general market inactivity lately, if not paralysis, which has provided little in the way of pricing guidance.

(A) has been general market inactivity lately, if not paralysis, which has provided
(B) there is general market inactivity, if not paralysis, lately it has provided
(C) general market inactivity, if not paralysis, has lately provided
(D) lately, general market inactivity, if not paralysis, has provided
(E) is that lately general market inactivity, if not paralysis, which provides

818. Ryūnosuke Akutagawa's knowledge of the literatures of Europe, China, and that of Japan were instrumental in his development as a writer, informing his literary style as much as the content of his fiction.

(A) that of Japan were instrumental in his development as a writer, informing his literary style as much as
(B) that of Japan was instrumental in his development as a writer, and it informed both his literary style as well as
(C) Japan was instrumental in his development as a writer, informing both his literary style and
(D) Japan was instrumental in his development as a writer, as it informed his literary style as much as
(E) Japan were instrumental in his development as a writer, informing both his literary style in addition to

819. Many stock traders in the United States have set out to become global investors, convinced that limiting their investments to the U.S. stock market, even though it is certainly home to the stocks of some of the world's great corporations, restricted their gains.

(A) even though it is certainly
(B) which, while it is certainly
(C) despite that that market is certainly
(D) which, though certainly
(E) although, certainly as

820. According to scientists who monitored its path, an expanding cloud of energized particles ejected from the Sun recently triggered a large storm in the magnetic field that surrounds Earth, which brightened the Northern Lights and also possibly knocking out a communications satellite.

(A) an expanding cloud of energized particles ejected from the Sun recently triggered a large storm in the magnetic field that surrounds Earth, which brightened the Northern Lights and also possibly knocking
(B) an expanding cloud of energized particles ejected from the Sun was what recently triggered a large storm in the magnetic field that surrounds Earth, and it brightened the Northern Lights and also possibly knocked

(C) an expanding cloud of energized particles ejected from the Sun recently triggered a large storm in the magnetic field that surrounds Earth, brightening the Northern Lights and possibly knocking

(D) a large storm in the magnetic field that surrounds Earth, recently triggered by an expanding cloud of energized particles, brightened the Northern Lights and it possibly knocked

(E) a large storm in the magnetic field surrounding Earth was recently triggered by an expanding cloud of energized particles, brightening the Northern Lights and it possibly knocked

SC01033

821. Because many of Australia's marsupials, such as the koala, are cute and cuddly, as well as being biologically different than North American marsupials, they have attracted a lot of attention after their discovery in the 1700s.

(A) being biologically different than North American marsupials, they have attracted a lot of attention after

(B) being biologically different from North American marsupials, they attracted a lot of attention since

(C) biologically different than North American marsupials, they attracted a lot of attention since

(D) biologically different than North American marsupials, they have attracted a lot of attention after

(E) biologically different from North American marsupials, they have attracted a lot of attention since

SC02448

822. Having been named for a mythological nymph who cared for the infant Jupiter, the asteroid named Ida, in the middle of the belt of asteroids that orbit the Sun between Mars and Jupiter, was discovered in 1884.

(A) Having been named for a mythological nymph who cared for the infant Jupiter, the asteroid named Ida, in the middle of the belt of asteroids that orbit the Sun between Mars and Jupiter, was discovered in 1884.

(B) Discovered in 1884, the asteroid Ida, named for a mythological nymph who cared for the infant Jupiter, is in the middle of the belt of asteroids that orbit the Sun between Mars and Jupiter.

(C) In the middle of the belt of asteroids that orbit the Sun between Mars and Jupiter, the asteroid Ida, discovered in 1884 and named for a mythological nymph who cared for the infant Jupiter.

(D) The asteroid Ida, named for a mythological nymph who cared for the infant Jupiter and discovered in 1884, is in the middle of the belt of asteroids to orbit the Sun between Mars and Jupiter.

(E) Ida, an asteroid discovered in 1884 and which was named for a mythological nymph who cared for the infant Jupiter, is in the middle of the belt of asteroids to orbit the Sun between Mars and Jupiter.

SC20121.01

823. Custodian fees and expenses, as described in the statement of operations, include interest expense incurred by the fund on any cash overdrafts of its custodian account during the period.

(A) include interest expense incurred by the fund on any cash overdrafts of its custodian account during the period

(B) are to include interest expenses on any cash overdrafts of its custodian account the fund incurred during the period

(C) includes interest expense the fund incurred during the period on any cash overdrafts of its custodian account

(D) may include interest expense during the period that the fund was to incur on any cash overdrafts of its custodian account

(E) including interest expense on any cash overdrafts of its custodian account incurred by the fund during the period

SC36241.01

824. Although some had accused Smith, the firm's network manager, of negligence when the crucial data went missing, the CEO defused a situation that was quite tense with her public statement that the debacle was not Smith's fault.

(A) a situation that was quite tense with her public statement that the debacle was not Smith's fault

(B) a situation that was quite tense, by publicly stating that the debacle was not Smith's fault

(C) a situation, which was quite tense, by stating publicly that Smith was not responsible for the debacle

(D) a quite tense situation with a public statement about the debacle not being Smith's fault

(E) a quite tense situation by publicly stating the debacle not to have been Smith's fault

SC01077

825. Many utilities obtain most of their electric power from large coal and nuclear operations at costs that are sometimes two to three times higher as that of power from smaller, more efficient plants that can both make use of waste heat and take advantage of the current abundance of natural gas.

(A) two to three times higher as that of power from smaller, more efficient plants that can both

(B) higher by two to three times as that from smaller, more efficient plants that both can

(C) two to three times higher than those for power from smaller, more efficient plants that can both

(D) between two to three times higher as those for power from smaller, more efficient plants that both can

(E) between two to three times higher than from smaller, more efficient plants that they can both

SC01523

826. When viewed from the window of a speeding train, the speed with which nearby objects move seems faster than that of more distant objects.

(A) the speed with which nearby objects move seems faster than that of

(B) the speed that nearby objects move seems faster than for

(C) the speed of nearby objects seems faster than

(D) nearby objects' speeds seem to be faster than those of

(E) nearby objects seem to move at a faster speed than do

SC41451.01

827. Ramón pointed out that food high in whole-grain fiber creates the energy we need to fight illnesses—as do vegetables and lean proteins.

(A) fiber creates the energy we need to fight illnesses—as do vegetables and lean proteins

(B) fiber in addition to vegetables and lean proteins, create the energy we need to fight illnesses

(C) fiber creates the energy we need to fight illnesses, along with vegetables and lean proteins

(D) fiber, vegetables, and lean proteins creates the energy we need to fight illnesses

(E) fiber, as vegetables and lean proteins, create the energy we need to fight illnesses

SC01487

828. The English physician Edward Jenner found that if experimental subjects were deliberately infected with cowpox, which caused only a mild illness, they are immune from smallpox.

(A) which caused only a mild illness, they are immune from

(B) causing only a mild illness, they become immune from

(C) which causes only a mild illness, they are immune to

(D) causing only a mild illness, they became immune from

(E) which caused only a mild illness, they would become immune to

SC00989

829. The final decades of the twentieth century not only saw an explosion of the literary production among women, but there was also an intense interest in the lives and works of women writers.

(A) not only saw an explosion of the literary production among women, but there was also

(B) not only saw an explosion of literary production in women, but there was also

(C) saw not only an explosion of literary production among women, but also

(D) saw not only an explosion of the literary production by women, but it also saw

(E) saw not only an explosion of literary production by women, but also saw

SC01070

830. Covering 71 percent of Earth's surface, the oceans play an essential role in maintaining the conditions for human existence on land, moderating temperature by the absorption of heat and carbon dioxide, and giving pure water back to the atmosphere through evaporation.

(A) Covering 71 percent of Earth's surface, the oceans play an essential role in maintaining the conditions for human existence on land, moderating

9.7 Sentence Correction Practice Questions

(B) Covering 71 percent of Earth's surface and playing an essential role in maintaining the conditions for human existence on land, the oceans moderate

(C) The oceans cover 71 percent of Earth's surface and play an essential role in maintaining conditions for human existence on land, and by moderating

(D) The oceans cover 71 percent of Earth's surface, play an essential role in maintaining the conditions for human existence on land, and moderate

(E) The oceans cover 71 percent of Earth's surface, playing an essential role in maintaining the conditions for human existence on land, and they moderate

SC11850.01

831. Although the rise in the Producer Price Index was greater than expected, most analysts agreed that the index was unlikely to continue going up and that inflation remained essentially under control.

(A) that the index was unlikely to continue going up and that inflation remained

(B) that it was unlikely for the index continuing to go up and for inflation to remain

(C) that the index was unlikely to continue to go up, with inflation to remain

(D) on the unlikelihood that the index would continue going up and that inflation remained

(E) on the unlikelihood that the index would continue to go up and for inflation to remain

SC17041.01

832. Severely hindered by problems with local suppliers, the fact that the AQ division also had a new management team to adapt to was not seen by the board of directors as a legitimate excuse for such low productivity.

(A) Severely hindered by problems with local suppliers, the fact that the AQ division also had a new management team to adapt to

(B) Though severely hindered by local supply problems, the fact that the AQ division also had a new management team to which to adapt

(C) Severely hindered by problems with local suppliers, the AQ division also had to adapt to a new management team, but this

(D) Severely hindered by local supply problems, that the AQ division also had to adapt to a new management team

(E) Though severely hindered by problems with local suppliers, the AQ division's also having a new management team to which it had to adapt

SC01037

833. The Eastern State Penitentiary was established in 1822 by reformers advocating that prisoners be held in solitary confinement and hard labor so as to reform them.

(A) advocating that prisoners be held in solitary confinement and hard labor so as to reform them

(B) who were advocating prisoners to be held in solitary confinement and hard labor for their reform

(C) advocating solitary confinement and hard labor as the means to reform prisoners

(D) who advocated solitary confinement and hard labor for the means of prisoner reform

(E) advocating as the means for prisoner reform solitary confinement and hard labor

SC03288

834. Some anthropologists believe that the genetic homogeneity evident in the world's people is the result of a "population bottleneck"—at some time in the past our ancestors suffered an event, greatly reducing their numbers and thus our genetic variation.

(A) at some time in the past our ancestors suffered an event, greatly reducing their numbers

(B) that at some time in the past our ancestors suffered an event that greatly reduced their numbers

(C) that some time in the past our ancestors suffered an event so that their numbers were greatly reduced,

(D) some time in the past our ancestors suffered an event from which their numbers were greatly reduced

(E) some time in the past, that our ancestors suffered an event so as to reduce their numbers greatly,

799

835. Through experimenting designed to provide information that will ultimately prove useful in the treatment of hereditary diseases, mice have received bone marrow transplants that give them a new gene.

(A) Through experimenting designed to provide information that will ultimately prove
(B) Through experiments designed to provide information ultimately proving
(C) In experimentation designed to provide information that ultimately proves
(D) In experimenting designed to provide information ultimately proving
(E) In experiments designed to provide information that will ultimately prove

836. Linking arrangements among secondary schools and the workplace never evolved in the United States as they have in most other developed countries.

(A) among secondary schools and the workplace never evolved in the United States as they have
(B) in the United States among secondary schools and the workplace never evolved as they did
(C) between secondary schools and the workplace never evolved in the United States as
(D) in the United States between secondary schools and the workplace never evolved as they have
(E) between secondary schools and the workplace never evolved in the United States as they did

837. The United Parcel Service plans to convert its more than 2,000 gasoline-powered trucks in the Los Angeles area to run on cleaner-burning natural gas.

(A) to convert its more than 2,000 gasoline-powered trucks in the Los Angeles area to
(B) to convert its more than 2,000 trucks in the Los Angeles area that are powered by gasoline to
(C) on converting its more than 2,000 gasoline-powered trucks in the Los Angeles area that will
(D) for its more than 2,000 gasoline-powered trucks in the Los Angeles area to convert to
(E) that its more than 2,000 trucks in the Los Angeles area that are powered by gasoline will convert to

838. Foraging at all times of the day and night, but interspersing their feeding with periods of rest that last between one and eight hours, a sperm whale could eat so much as a ton of squid a day.

(A) between one and eight hours, a sperm whale could eat so
(B) between one and eight hours, sperm whales can eat as
(C) between one to eight hours, sperm whales could eat as
(D) from one to eight hours, sperm whales could eat so
(E) from one to eight hours, a sperm whale can eat so

839. In some types of pine tree, a thick layer of needles protects the buds from which new growth proceeds; consequently they are able to withstand forest fires relatively well.

(A) a thick layer of needles protects the buds from which new growth proceeds; consequently they are able to withstand forest fires relatively well
(B) a thick needle layer protects buds from where new growth proceeds, so that they can withstand forest fires relatively well
(C) a thick layer of needles protect the buds from which new growth proceeds; thus, they are able to withstand relatively well any forest fires
(D) since the buds from which new growth proceeds are protected by a thick needle layer, consequently they can therefore withstand forest fires relatively well
(E) because the buds where new growth happens are protected by a thick layer of needles, they are able to withstand forest fires relatively easily as a result

840. The tourism commission has conducted surveys of hotels in the most popular resorts, with the ultimate goal of reducing the guests who end up expressing overall dissatisfaction with the service in the hotels.

(A) with the ultimate goal of reducing the guests who end up expressing overall dissatisfaction with the service in the hotels
(B) with the goal to ultimately reduce the number of guests who end up expressing overall dissatisfaction with the hotels' service

(C) ultimately with the goal to reduce expressions of overall dissatisfaction by the guests with the hotel service

(D) in an ultimate attempt to reduce the number of guests that ends up expressing overall dissatisfaction with the hotels' service

(E) with the ultimate goal of reducing the number of guests who express overall dissatisfaction with the hotels' service

SC01607
841. A new study suggests that the conversational pace of everyday life may be so brisk <u>it hampers the ability of some children for distinguishing discrete sounds and words and, the result is, to make</u> sense of speech.

(A) it hampers the ability of some children for distinguishing discrete sounds and words and, the result is, to make

(B) that it hampers the ability of some children to distinguish discrete sounds and words and, as a result, to make

(C) that it hampers the ability of some children to distinguish discrete sounds and words and, the result of this, they are unable to make

(D) that it hampers the ability of some children to distinguish discrete sounds and words, and results in not making

(E) as to hamper the ability of some children for distinguishing discrete sounds and words, resulting in being unable to make

SC07035
842. The nineteenth-century chemist Humphry Davy presented the results of his early experiments in his "Essay on Heat and Light," <u>a critique of all chemistry since Robert Boyle as well as a vision of a</u> new chemistry that Davy hoped to found.

(A) a critique of all chemistry since Robert Boyle as well as a vision of a

(B) a critique of all chemistry following Robert Boyle and also his envisioning of a

(C) a critique of all chemistry after Robert Boyle and envisioning as well

(D) critiquing all chemistry from Robert Boyle forward and also a vision of

(E) critiquing all the chemistry done since Robert Boyle as well as his own envisioning of

SC02280
843. To attract the most talented workers, some companies are offering a wider range of <u>benefits, letting employees pick those most important to them</u>.

(A) benefits, letting employees pick those most important to them

(B) benefits, letting employees pick the most important of them to themselves

(C) benefits and letting employees pick the most important to themselves

(D) benefits and let employees pick the most important to them

(E) benefits and let employees pick those that are most important to themselves

SC01583
844. Many of the earliest known images of Hindu deities in India date from the time of the Kushan <u>Empire, fashioned either from the spotted sandstone of Mathura or</u> Gandharan grey schist.

(A) Empire, fashioned either from the spotted sandstone of Mathura or

(B) Empire, fashioned from either the spotted sandstone of Mathura or from

(C) Empire, either fashioned from the spotted sandstone of Mathura or

(D) Empire and either fashioned from the spotted sandstone of Mathura or from

(E) Empire and were fashioned either from the spotted sandstone of Mathura or from

SC01051
845. Tides typically range from three to six feet, but while some places show no tides at all, <u>some others, such as the Bay of Fundy, have tides of at least thirty feet and more</u>.

(A) some others, such as the Bay of Fundy, have tides of at least thirty feet and more

(B) the others, such as the Bay of Fundy, that have tides of more than thirty feet

(C) others, such as the Bay of Fundy, have tides of more than thirty feet

(D) those at the Bay of Fundy, which has tides of more than thirty feet

(E) the ones at the Bay of Fundy have tides of at least thirty feet and more

SC01028
846. A leading figure in the Scottish Enlightenment, Adam Smith's two major books are to democratic capitalism what Marx's *Das Kapital* is to socialism.

(A) Adam Smith's two major books are to democratic capitalism what

(B) Adam Smith's two major books are to democratic capitalism like

(C) Adam Smith's two major books are to democratic capitalism just as

(D) Adam Smith wrote two major books that are to democratic capitalism similar to

(E) Adam Smith wrote two major books that are to democratic capitalism what

SC04331
847. Researchers studying the brain scans of volunteers who pondered ethical dilemmas have found that the basis for making tough moral judgments is emotion, not logic or analytical reasoning.

(A) the brain scans of volunteers who pondered ethical dilemmas have found that the basis for making tough moral judgments is

(B) the brain scans of volunteers who pondered ethical dilemmas and found the basis to make tough moral decisions to be

(C) the brain scans of volunteers pondering ethical dilemmas and found that the basis for making tough moral decisions is

(D) volunteers' brain scans while pondering ethical dilemmas have found the basis to make tough moral judgments to be

(E) volunteers' brain scans while they pondered ethical dilemmas have found that the basis for making tough moral judgments is

SC02060
848. Rivaling the pyramids of Egypt or even the ancient cities of the Maya as an achievement, the army of terra-cotta warriors created to protect Qin Shi Huang, China's first emperor, in his afterlife is more than 2,000 years old and took 700,000 artisans more than 36 years to complete.

(A) the army of terra-cotta warriors created to protect Qin Shi Huang, China's first emperor, in his afterlife is more than 2,000 years old and took 700,000 artisans more than 36 years to complete

(B) Qin Shi Huang, China's first emperor, was protected in his afterlife by an army of terra-cotta warriors that was created more than 2,000 years ago by 700,000 artisans who took more than 36 years to complete it

(C) it took 700,000 artisans more than 36 years to create an army of terra-cotta warriors more than 2,000 years ago that would protect Qin Shi Huang, China's first emperor, in his afterlife

(D) more than 2,000 years ago, 700,000 artisans worked more than 36 years to create an army of terra-cotta warriors to protect Qin Shi Huang, China's first emperor, in his afterlife

(E) more than 36 years were needed to complete the army of terra-cotta warriors that 700,000 artisans created 2,000 years ago to protect Qin Shi Huang, China's first emperor, in his afterlife

SC03675
849. In California, a lack of genetic variation in the Argentine ant has allowed the species to spread widely; due to their being so genetically similar to one another, the ants consider all their fellows to be a close relative and thus do not engage in the kind of fierce intercolony struggles that limits the spread of this species in its native Argentina.

(A) due to their being so genetically similar to one another, the ants consider all their fellows to be a close relative and thus do not engage in the kind of fierce intercolony struggles that limits

(B) due to its being so genetically similar, the ant considers all its fellows to be a close relative and thus does not engage in the kind of fierce intercolony struggles that limit

(C) because it is so genetically similar, the ant considers all its fellows to be close relatives and thus does not engage in the kind of fierce intercolony struggles that limits

(D) because they are so genetically similar to one another, the ants consider all their fellows to be close relatives and thus do not engage in the kind of fierce intercolony struggles that limit

(E) because of being so genetically similar to one another, the ants consider all their fellows to be a close relative and thus do not engage in the kind of fierce intercolony struggles that limits

850. Next month, state wildlife officials are scheduled to take over the job of increasing the wolf population in the federally designated recovery area, the number of which will however ultimately be dictated by the number of prey in the area.

(A) area, the number of which will however
(B) area; the size of the population, however, will
(C) area, however the number of wolves will
(D) area; the number of which will, however,
(E) area, when the size of the population will, however,

851. About 5 million acres in the United States have been invaded by leafy spurge, a herbaceous plant from Eurasia with milky sap that gives mouth sores to cattle, displacing grasses and other cattle food and rendering rangeland worthless.

(A) States have been invaded by leafy spurge, a herbaceous plant from Eurasia with milky sap that gives mouth sores to cattle, displacing grasses and other cattle food and rendering
(B) States have been invaded by leafy spurge, a herbaceous plant from Eurasia, with milky sap, that gives mouth sores to cattle and displaces grasses and other cattle food, rendering
(C) States have been invaded by leafy spurge, a herbaceous plant from Eurasia having milky sap that gives mouth sores to cattle and displacing grasses and other cattle food, rendering
(D) States, having been invaded by leafy spurge, a herbaceous plant from Eurasia with milky sap that gives mouth sores to cattle, displaces grasses and other cattle food, and renders
(E) States, having been invaded by leafy spurge, a herbaceous plant from Eurasia that has milky sap giving mouth sores to cattle and displacing grasses and other cattle food, rendering

852. While it costs about the same to run nuclear plants as other types of power plants, it is the fixed costs that stem from building nuclear plants that makes it more expensive for them to generate electricity.

(A) While it costs about the same to run nuclear plants as other types of power plants, it is the fixed costs that stem from building nuclear plants that makes it more expensive for them to generate electricity.

(B) While the cost of running nuclear plants is about the same as for other types of power plants, the fixed costs that stem from building nuclear plants make the electricity they generate more expensive.
(C) Even though it costs about the same to run nuclear plants as for other types of power plants, it is the fixed costs that stem from building nuclear plants that makes the electricity they generate more expensive.
(D) It costs about the same to run nuclear plants as for other types of power plants, whereas the electricity they generate is more expensive, stemming from the fixed costs of building nuclear plants.
(E) The cost of running nuclear plants is about the same as other types of power plants, but the electricity they generate is made more expensive because of the fixed costs stemming from building nuclear plants.

853. The 32 species that make up the dolphin family are closely related to whales and in fact include the animal known as the killer whale, which can grow to be 30 feet long and is famous for its aggressive hunting pods.

(A) include the animal known as the killer whale, which can grow to be 30 feet long and is
(B) include the animal known as the killer whale, growing as big as 30 feet long and
(C) include the animal known as the killer whale, growing up to 30 feet long and being
(D) includes the animal known as the killer whale, which can grow as big as 30 feet long and is
(E) includes the animal known as the killer whale, which can grow to be 30 feet long and it is

854. The first trenches that were cut into a 500-acre site at Tell Hamoukar, Syria, have yielded strong evidence for centrally administered complex societies in northern regions of the Middle East that were arising simultaneously with but independently of the more celebrated city-states of southern Mesopotamia, in what is now southern Iraq.

(A) that were cut into a 500-acre site at Tell Hamoukar, Syria, have yielded strong evidence for centrally administered complex societies in northern regions of the Middle East that were arising simultaneously with but

- (B) that were cut into a 500-acre site at Tell Hamoukar, Syria, yields strong evidence that centrally administered complex societies in northern regions of the Middle East were arising simultaneously with but also
- (C) having been cut into a 500-acre site at Tell Hamoukar, Syria, have yielded strong evidence that centrally administered complex societies in northern regions of the Middle East were arising simultaneously but
- (D) cut into a 500-acre site at Tell Hamoukar, Syria, yields strong evidence of centrally administered complex societies in northern regions of the Middle East arising simultaneously but also
- (E) cut into a 500-acre site at Tell Hamoukar, Syria, have yielded strong evidence that centrally administered complex societies in northern regions of the Middle East arose simultaneously with but

SC02317

855. Companies are relying more and more on networked computers for such critical tasks as inventory management, electronic funds transfer, and electronic data interchange, <u>in which standard business transactions are handled via computer rather than on paper</u>.

- (A) in which standard business transactions are handled via computer rather than on paper
- (B) where computers handle standard business transactions rather than on paper
- (C) in which computers handle standard business transactions instead of on paper
- (D) where standard business transactions are handled, not with paper, but instead via computer
- (E) in which standard business transactions are being handled via computer, in place of on paper

SC07231

856. Combining enormous physical strength with higher intelligence, the Neanderthals <u>appear as equipped for facing any obstacle the environment could put in their path,</u> but their relatively sudden disappearance during the Paleolithic era indicates that an inability to adapt to some environmental change led to their extinction.

- (A) appear as equipped for facing any obstacle the environment could put in their path,
- (B) appear to have been equipped to face any obstacle the environment could put in their path,
- (C) appear as equipped to face any obstacle the environment could put in their paths,
- (D) appeared as equipped to face any obstacle the environment could put in their paths,
- (E) appeared to have been equipped for facing any obstacle the environment could put in their path,

SC02135

857. To map Earth's interior, geologists use a network of seismometers to chart seismic waves that originate in the earth's crust and ricochet around its <u>interior, most rapidly traveling through cold, dense regions and slower</u> through hotter rocks.

- (A) interior, most rapidly traveling through cold, dense regions and slower
- (B) interior, which travel most rapidly through cold, dense regions, and more slowly
- (C) interior, traveling most rapidly through cold, dense regions and more slowly
- (D) interior and most rapidly travel through cold, dense regions, and slower
- (E) interior and that travel most rapidly through cold, dense regions and slower

SC02470

858. Prices at the producer level are only 1.3 percent higher now <u>than a year ago and are going down, even though floods in the Midwest and drought in the South are hurting crops and therefore raised</u> corn and soybean prices.

- (A) than a year ago and are going down, even though floods in the Midwest and drought in the South are hurting crops and therefore raised
- (B) than those of a year ago and are going down, even though floods in the Midwest and drought in the South are hurting crops and therefore raising
- (C) than a year ago and are going down, despite floods in the Midwest and drought in the South, and are hurting crops and therefore raising
- (D) as those of a year ago and are going down, even though floods in the Midwest and drought in the South hurt crops and therefore raise
- (E) as they were a year ago and are going down, despite floods in the Midwest and drought in the South, and are hurting crops and therefore raising

859. Fossils of the arm of a sloth found in Puerto Rico in 1991, and dated at 34 million years old, made it the earliest known mammal of the Greater Antilles Islands.

    (A) sloth found in Puerto Rico in 1991, and dated at 34 million years old, made it the earliest known mammal of
    (B) sloth, that they found in Puerto Rico in 1991, has been dated at 34 million years old, thus making it the earliest mammal known on
    (C) sloth that was found in Puerto Rico in 1991, was dated at 34 million years old, making this the earliest known mammal of
    (D) sloth, found in Puerto Rico in 1991, have been dated at 34 million years old, making the sloth the earliest known mammal on
    (E) sloth which, found in Puerto Rico in 1991, was dated at 34 million years old, made the sloth the earliest known mammal of

860. Recently physicians have determined that stomach ulcers are not caused by stress, alcohol, or rich foods, but a bacterium that dwells in the mucous lining of the stomach.

    (A) not caused by stress, alcohol, or rich foods, but
    (B) not caused by stress, alcohol, or rich foods, but are by
    (C) caused not by stress, alcohol, or rich foods, but by
    (D) caused not by stress, alcohol, and rich foods, but
    (E) caused not by stress, alcohol, and rich foods, but are by

861. The eyes of the elephant seal adapt to darkness more quickly than any other animal yet tested, thus allowing it to hunt efficiently under the gloomy conditions at its feeding depth of between 300 and 700 meters.

    (A) The eyes of the elephant seal adapt to darkness more quickly than any other animal yet tested, thus allowing it
    (B) The eyes of the elephant seal adapt to darkness more quickly than does any other animal yet tested, allowing them
    (C) The eyes of the elephant seal adapt to darkness more quickly than do those of any other animal yet tested, allowing it
    (D) Because they adapt to darkness more quickly than any other animal yet tested, the eyes of the elephant seal allow it
    (E) Because the eyes of the elephant seal adapt to darkness more quickly than do those of any other animal yet tested, it allows them

862. A mutual fund having billions of dollars in assets will typically invest that money in hundreds of companies, rarely holding more than one percent of the shares of any particular corporation.

    (A) companies, rarely holding more than one percent
    (B) companies, and it is rare to hold at least one percent or more
    (C) companies and rarely do they hold more than one percent
    (D) companies, so that they rarely hold more than one percent
    (E) companies; rarely do they hold one percent or more

863. Positing an enormous volcanic explosion at the end of the Permian period would explain the presence of a buried crater, account for the presence of the element iridium (originating deep within the earth), and the presence of quartz having been shattered by high-impact shock waves.

    (A) account for the presence of the element iridium (originating deep within the earth), and the presence of quartz having been
    (B) of the element iridium (originating deep within the earth), and of quartz
    (C) the element iridium (originating deep within the earth), and explain the presence of quartz having been
    (D) the presence of the element iridium (originating deep within the earth), and explain the presence of quartz
    (E) explain the element iridium (originating deep within the earth), and the presence of quartz

864. The 19-year-old pianist and composer performed his most recent work all over Europe, Asia, and North America last year, winning prestigious awards in both London as well as Tokyo for his achievement at so young an age, and he is hoping to continue composing now that he has returned to Chicago.

(A) winning prestigious awards in both London as well as Tokyo for his achievement at so young an age, and he is hoping

(B) winning prestigious awards both in London and Tokyo for his achievement at such a young age, and hoping

(C) having won prestigious awards both in London and Tokyo for his achievement at so young an age, hoping

(D) winning prestigious awards in both London and Tokyo for his achievement at such a young age, and he hopes

(E) having won prestigious awards both in London as well as Tokyo for his achievement at so young an age, and he hopes

865. Starfish, with anywhere from five to eight arms, have a strong regenerative ability, and if one arm is lost it quickly replaces it, sometimes by the animal overcompensating and growing an extra one or two.

(A) one arm is lost it quickly replaces it, sometimes by the animal overcompensating and

(B) one arm is lost it is quickly replaced, with the animal sometimes overcompensating and

(C) they lose one arm they quickly replace it, sometimes by the animal overcompensating,

(D) they lose one arm they are quickly replaced, with the animal sometimes overcompensating,

(E) they lose one arm it is quickly replaced, sometimes with the animal overcompensating,

866. In 2000, a mere two dozen products accounted for half the increase in spending on prescription drugs, a phenomenon that is explained not just because of more expensive drugs but by the fact that doctors are writing many more prescriptions for higher-cost drugs.

(A) a phenomenon that is explained not just because of more expensive drugs but by the fact that doctors are writing

(B) a phenomenon that is explained not just by the fact that drugs are becoming more expensive but also by the fact that doctors are writing

(C) a phenomenon occurring not just because of drugs that are becoming more expensive but because of doctors having also written

(D) which occurred not just because drugs are becoming more expensive but doctors are also writing

(E) which occurred not just because of more expensive drugs but because doctors have also written

867. Similar to other early Mississippi Delta blues singers, the music of Robert Johnson arose from an oral tradition beginning with a mixture of chants, fiddle tunes, and religious music and only gradually evolved into the blues.

(A) Similar to other early Mississippi Delta blues singers, the music of Robert Johnson arose from an oral tradition beginning with

(B) Similar to that of other early Mississippi Delta blues singers, Robert Johnson made music that arose from an oral tradition that began with

(C) As with other early Mississippi Delta blues singers, Robert Johnson made music that arose from an oral tradition beginning as

(D) Like other early Mississippi Delta blues singers, Robert Johnson's music arose from an oral tradition beginning with

(E) Like the music of other early Mississippi Delta blues singers, the music of Robert Johnson arose from an oral tradition that began as

868. Thelonious Monk, who was a jazz pianist and composer, produced a body of work both rooted in the stride-piano tradition of Willie (The Lion) Smith and Duke Ellington, yet in many ways he stood apart from the mainstream jazz repertory.

(A) Thelonious Monk, who was a jazz pianist and composer, produced a body of work both rooted

(B) Thelonious Monk, the jazz pianist and composer, produced a body of work that was rooted both

(C) Jazz pianist and composer Thelonious Monk, who produced a body of work rooted

(D) Jazz pianist and composer Thelonious Monk produced a body of work that was rooted

(E) Jazz pianist and composer Thelonious Monk produced a body of work rooted both

SC06898

869. Nobody knows exactly how many languages there are in the world, partly because of the difficulty of distinguishing between a language <u>and the sublanguages or dialects within it, but those who have tried to count typically have found</u> about five thousand.

(A) and the sublanguages or dialects within it, but those who have tried to count typically have found

(B) and the sublanguages or dialects within them, with those who have tried counting typically finding

(C) and the sublanguages or dialects within it, but those who have tried counting it typically find

(D) or the sublanguages or dialects within them, but those who tried to count them typically found

(E) or the sublanguages or dialects within them, with those who have tried to count typically finding

SC08719

870. Although a number of excellent studies narrate the development of domestic technology and its impact on housewifery, these works do not discuss the contributions of the women employed <u>by manufacturers and utility companies as product demonstrators and publicists,</u> who initially promoted new and unfamiliar technology to female consumers.

(A) by manufacturers and utility companies as product demonstrators and publicists,

(B) to be product demonstrators and publicists by manufacturers and utility companies,

(C) to demonstrate and publicize their products by manufacturers and utility companies

(D) by manufacturers and utility companies to be demonstrators and publicists of their products

(E) by manufacturers and utility companies to demonstrate and publicize their products

SC01577

871. The absence <u>from business and financial records of the nineteenth century of statistics about women leave us with no record of the jobs that were performed by women and</u> how they survived economically.

(A) from business and financial records of the nineteenth century of statistics about women

leave us with no record of the jobs that were performed by women and

(B) from business and financial records of statistics about women from the nineteenth century leave us with no record of what jobs women performed or

(C) of statistics for women from business and financial records in the nineteenth century leaves us with no record of either the jobs that women were performing and of

(D) of statistics on women from business and financial records in the nineteenth century leave us with no record of the jobs that women performed or of

(E) of statistics about women from business and financial records of the nineteenth century leaves us with no record of either what jobs women performed or

SC02138

872. <u>Heating-oil prices are expected to be higher this year than last because refiners are paying about $5 a barrel more for crude oil than they were</u> last year.

(A) Heating-oil prices are expected to be higher this year than last because refiners are paying about $5 a barrel more for crude oil than they were

(B) Heating-oil prices are expected to rise higher this year over last because refiners pay about $5 a barrel for crude oil more than they did

(C) Expectations are for heating-oil prices to be higher this year than last year's because refiners are paying about $5 a barrel for crude oil more than they did

(D) It is the expectation that heating-oil prices will be higher for this year over last because refiners are paying about $5 a barrel more for crude oil now than what they were

(E) It is expected that heating-oil prices will rise higher this year than last year's because refiners pay about $5 a barrel for crude oil more than they did

SC01443

873. <u>Even though Clovis points, spear points with longitudinal grooves chipped onto their faces, have been found all over North America, they are named for the New Mexico site where they were first discovered in 1932.</u>

(A) Even though Clovis points, spear points with longitudinal grooves chipped onto their faces, have been found all over North America, they are named for the New Mexico site where they were first discovered in 1932.

(B) Although named for the New Mexico site where first discovered in 1932, Clovis points are spear points of longitudinal grooves chipped onto their faces and have been found all over North America.

(C) Named for the New Mexico site where they have been first discovered in 1932, Clovis points, spear points of longitudinal grooves chipped onto the faces, have been found all over North America.

(D) Spear points with longitudinal grooves that are chipped onto the faces, Clovis points, even though named for the New Mexico site where first discovered in 1932, but were found all over North America.

(E) While Clovis points are spear points whose faces have longitudinal grooves chipped into them, they have been found all over North America, and named for the New Mexico site where they have been first discovered in 1932.

874. Heavy commitment by an executive to a course of action, especially if it has worked well in the past, makes it likely to miss signs of incipient trouble or misinterpret them when they do appear.

(A) Heavy commitment by an executive to a course of action, especially if it has worked well in the past, makes it likely to miss signs of incipient trouble or misinterpret them when they do appear.

(B) An executive who is heavily committed to a course of action, especially one that worked well in the past, makes missing signs of incipient trouble or misinterpreting ones likely when they do appear.

(C) An executive who is heavily committed to a course of action is likely to miss or misinterpret signs of incipient trouble when they do appear, especially if it has worked well in the past.

(D) Executives' being heavily committed to a course of action, especially if it has worked well in the past, makes them likely to miss signs of incipient trouble or misinterpreting them when they do appear.

(E) Being heavily committed to a course of action, especially one that has worked well in the past, is likely to make an executive miss signs of incipient trouble or misinterpret them when they do appear.

875. According to recent studies comparing the nutritional value of meat from wild animals and meat from domesticated animals, wild animals have less total fat than do livestock fed on grain and more of a kind of fat they think is good for cardiac health.

(A) wild animals have less total fat than do livestock fed on grain and more of a kind of fat they think is

(B) wild animals have less total fat than livestock fed on grain and more of a kind of fat thought to be

(C) wild animals have less total fat than that of livestock fed on grain and have more fat of a kind thought to be

(D) total fat of wild animals is less than livestock fed on grain and they have more fat of a kind thought to be

(E) total fat is less in wild animals than that of livestock fed on grain and more of their fat is of a kind they think is

876. Yellow jackets number among the 900 or so species of the world's social wasps, wasps living in a highly cooperative and organized society where they consist almost entirely of females—the queen and her sterile female workers.

(A) wasps living in a highly cooperative and organized society where they consist almost entirely of

(B) wasps that live in a highly cooperative and organized society consisting almost entirely of

(C) which means they live in a highly cooperative and organized society, almost all

(D) which means that their society is highly cooperative, organized, and it is almost entirely

(E) living in a society that is highly cooperative, organized, and it consists of almost all

877. Before 1988, insurance companies in California were free to charge whatever rates the market would bear, needing no approval from regulators before raising rates.

(A) needing no approval from regulators before raising

(B) and it needed no approval by regulators before raising

(C) and needing no approval from regulators before they raised

(D) with approval not needed by regulators before they raised

(E) with no approval needed from regulators before the raising of

SC01022
878. Marconi's conception of the radio was as a substitute for the telephone, a tool for private conversation; instead, it is precisely the opposite, a tool for communicating with a large, public audience.

(A) Marconi's conception of the radio was as a substitute for the telephone, a tool for private conversation; instead, it is

(B) Marconi conceived of the radio as a substitute for the telephone, a tool for private conversation, but which is

(C) Marconi conceived of the radio as a tool for private conversation that could substitute for the telephone; instead, it has become

(D) Marconi conceived of the radio to be a tool for private conversation, a substitute for the telephone, which has become

(E) Marconi conceived of the radio to be a substitute for the telephone, a tool for private conversation, other than what it is,

SC02611
879. Because there are provisions of the new maritime code that provide that even tiny islets can be the basis for claims to the fisheries and oil fields of large sea areas, they have already stimulated international disputes over uninhabited islands.

(A) Because there are provisions of the new maritime code that provide that even tiny islets can be the basis for claims to the fisheries and oil fields of large sea areas, they have already stimulated

(B) Because the new maritime code provides that even tiny islets can be the basis for claims to the fisheries and oil fields of large sea areas, it has already stimulated

(C) Even tiny islets can be the basis for claims to the fisheries and oil fields of large sea areas under provisions of the new maritime code, already stimulating

(D) Because even tiny islets can be the basis for claims to the fisheries and oil fields of large sea areas under provisions of the new maritime code, this has already stimulated

(E) Because even tiny islets can be the basis for claims to the fisheries and oil fields of large sea areas under provisions of the new maritime code, which is already stimulating

SC02576
880. Unlike the automobile company, whose research was based on crashes involving sport utility vehicles, the research conducted by the insurance company took into account such factors as a driver's age, sex, and previous driving record.

(A) company, whose research was based on
(B) company, which researched
(C) company, in its research of
(D) company's research, having been based on
(E) company's research on

SC12131
881. Gusty westerly winds will continue to usher in a seasonally cool air mass into the region, as a broad area of high pressure will build and bring fair and dry weather for several days.

(A) to usher in a seasonally cool air mass into the region, as a broad area of high pressure will build and

(B) ushering in a seasonally cool air mass into the region and a broad area of high pressure will build that

(C) to usher in a seasonally cool air mass to the region, a broad area of high pressure building, and

(D) ushering a seasonally cool air mass in the region, with a broad area of high pressure building and

(E) to usher a seasonally cool air mass into the region while a broad area of high pressure builds, which will

SC02008
882. With the patience of its customers and with its network strained to the breaking point, the on-line service company announced a series of new initiatives trying to relieve the congestion that has led to at least four class-action lawsuits and thousands of complaints from frustrated customers.

(A) the patience of its customers and with its network strained to the breaking point, the on-line service company announced a series of new initiatives trying to relieve

(B) the patience of its customers and its network strained to the breaking point, the on-line service company announced a series of new initiatives that try to relieve

(C) its network and the patience of its customers strained to the breaking point, the on-line service company announced a series of new initiatives to try to relieve

(D) its network and with the patience of its customers strained to the breaking point, the on-line service company announced a series of initiatives to try relieving

(E) its network and its customers' patience strained to the breaking point, the on-line service company announced a series of new initiatives to try relieving

883. November is traditionally the strongest month for sales of light trucks, but sales this past November, even when compared with sales in previous Novembers, accounted for a remarkably large share of total vehicle sales.

(A) but sales this past November, even when compared with sales in previous Novembers,

(B) but even when it is compared with previous Novembers, this past November's sales

(C) but even when they are compared with previous Novembers, sales of light trucks this past November

(D) so that compared with previous Novembers, sales of light trucks this past November

(E) so that this past November's sales, even compared with previous Novembers' sales,

884. Most of the country's biggest daily newspapers had lower circulation in the six months from October 1995 through March 1996 than a similar period a year earlier.

(A) a similar period
(B) a similar period's
(C) in a similar period
(D) that in a similar period
(E) that of a similar period

885. Mauritius was a British colony for almost 200 years, excepting for the domains of administration and teaching, the English language was never really spoken on the island.

(A) excepting for
(B) except in
(C) but except in
(D) but excepting for
(E) with the exception of

886. Although appearing less appetizing than most of their round and red supermarket cousins, heirloom tomatoes, grown from seeds saved during the previous year—they are often green and striped, or have plenty of bumps and bruises—heirlooms are more flavorful and thus in increasing demand.

(A) Although appearing less appetizing than most of their round and red supermarket cousins, heirloom tomatoes, grown from seeds saved during the previous year

(B) Although heirloom tomatoes, grown from seeds saved during the previous year, appear less appetizing than most of their round and red supermarket cousins

(C) Although they appear less appetizing than most of their round and red supermarket cousins, heirloom tomatoes, grown from seeds saved during the previous year

(D) Grown from seeds saved during the previous year, heirloom tomatoes appear less appetizing than most of their round and red supermarket cousins

(E) Heirloom tomatoes, grown from seeds saved during the previous year, although they appear less appetizing than most of their round and red supermarket cousins

887. The World Wildlife Fund has declared that global warming, a phenomenon most scientists agree to be caused by human beings in burning fossil fuels, will create havoc among migratory birds by altering the environment in ways harmful to their habitats.

(A) a phenomenon most scientists agree to be caused by human beings in burning fossil fuels,

(B) a phenomenon most scientists agree that is caused by fossil fuels burned by human beings,

(C) a phenomenon that most scientists agree is caused by human beings' burning of fossil fuels,

(D) which most scientists agree on as a phenomenon caused by human beings who burn fossil fuels,

(E) which most scientists agree to be a phenomenon caused by fossil fuels burned by human beings,

SC02216
888. The largest of all the planets, <u>not only is Jupiter three times so massive as Saturn, the next larger</u> planet, but also possesses four of the largest satellites, or moons, in our solar system.

(A) not only is Jupiter three times so massive as Saturn, the next larger

(B) not only is Jupiter three times as massive as Saturn, the next largest

(C) Jupiter, not only three times as massive as Saturn, the next largest

(D) Jupiter not only is three times as massive as Saturn, the next largest

(E) Jupiter is not only three times so massive as Saturn, the next larger

SC01587
889. While many of the dinosaur fossils found recently in northeast China seem to provide evidence of the kinship between dinosaurs and birds, the wealth of enigmatic fossils <u>seem more likely at this stage that they will inflame debates over the origin of birds rather than</u> settle them.

(A) seem more likely at this stage that they will inflame debates over the origin of birds rather than

(B) seem more likely that it will inflame debates over the origin of birds at this stage than

(C) seems more likely to inflame debates on the origin of birds at this stage rather than

(D) seems more likely at this stage to inflame debates over the origin of birds than to

(E) seems more likely that it will inflame debates on the origin of birds at this stage than to

SC01622
890. <u>Found only in the Western Hemisphere and surviving through extremes of climate, hummingbirds' range extends</u> from Alaska to Tierra del Fuego, from sea-level rain forests to the edges of Andean snowfields and ice fields at altitudes of 15,000 feet.

(A) Found only in the Western Hemisphere and surviving through extremes of climate, hummingbirds' range extends

(B) Found only in the Western Hemisphere, hummingbirds survive through extremes of climate, their range extending

(C) Hummingbirds, found only in the Western Hemisphere and surviving through extremes of climate, with their range extending

(D) Hummingbirds, found only in the Western Hemisphere and surviving through extremes of climate, their range extends

(E) Hummingbirds are found only in the Western Hemisphere, survive through extremes of climate, and their range extends

SC01761
891. <u>She was less successful after she had emigrated to New York compared to</u> her native Germany, photographer Lotte Jacobi nevertheless earned a small group of discerning admirers, and her photographs were eventually exhibited in prestigious galleries across the United States.

(A) She was less successful after she had emigrated to New York compared to

(B) Being less successful after she had emigrated to New York as compared to

(C) Less successful after she emigrated to New York than she had been in

(D) Although she was less successful after emigrating to New York when compared to

(E) She had been less successful after emigrating to New York than in

SC02259
892. Scientists have recently found evidence that black holes—regions of space in which matter is so concentrated and the pull of gravity so powerful that nothing, not even light, can emerge from them—probably <u>exist at the core of nearly all galaxies and the mass of each black hole is proportional to</u> its host galaxy.

(A) exist at the core of nearly all galaxies and the mass of each black hole is proportional to

(B) exist at the core of nearly all galaxies and that the mass of each black hole is proportional to that of

(C) exist at the core of nearly all galaxies, and that the mass of each black hole is proportional to

(D) exists at the core of nearly all galaxies, and that the mass of each black hole is proportional to that of

(E) exists at the core of nearly all galaxies and the mass of each black hole is proportional to that of

893. The use of lie detectors is based on the assumption that lying produces emotional reactions in an individual <u>that, in turn, create unconscious physiological responses</u>.

(A) that, in turn, create unconscious physiological responses

(B) that creates unconscious physiological responses in turn

(C) creating, in turn, unconscious physiological responses

(D) to create, in turn, physiological responses that are unconscious

(E) who creates unconscious physiological responses in turn

894. Australian embryologists have found evidence <u>that suggests that the elephant is descended from an aquatic animal, and its trunk originally evolving</u> as a kind of snorkel.

(A) that suggests that the elephant is descended from an aquatic animal, and its trunk originally evolving

(B) that has suggested the elephant descended from an aquatic animal, its trunk originally evolving

(C) suggesting that the elephant had descended from an aquatic animal with its trunk originally evolved

(D) to suggest that the elephant had descended from an aquatic animal and its trunk originally evolved

(E) to suggest that the elephant is descended from an aquatic animal and that its trunk originally evolved

895. Most efforts to combat such mosquito-borne diseases <u>like malaria and dengue have focused either on the vaccination of humans or on exterminating</u> mosquitoes with pesticides.

(A) like malaria and dengue have focused either on the vaccination of humans or on exterminating

(B) like malaria and dengue have focused either on vaccinating of humans or on the extermination of

(C) as malaria and dengue have focused on either vaccinating humans or on exterminating

(D) as malaria and dengue have focused on either vaccinating of humans or on extermination of

(E) as malaria and dengue have focused on either vaccinating humans or exterminating

896. Among the Tsonga, a Bantu-speaking group of tribes in southeastern Africa, dance teams represent their own chief at <u>the court of each other, providing entertainment in return for</u> food, drink, and lodging.

(A) the court of each other, providing entertainment in return for

(B) the court of another and provide entertainment in return for

(C) the court of the other, so as to provide entertainment as a return on

(D) each other's court, entertainment being provided in return for

(E) another's court and provide entertainment as a return on

897. Almost like clones in their similarity to one another, <u>the cheetah species' homogeneity makes them especially vulnerable to disease</u>.

(A) the cheetah species' homogeneity makes them especially vulnerable to disease

(B) the cheetah species is especially vulnerable to disease because of its homogeneity

(C) the homogeneity of the cheetah species makes it especially vulnerable to disease

(D) homogeneity makes members of the cheetah species especially vulnerable to disease

(E) members of the cheetah species are especially vulnerable to disease because of their homogeneity

898. As sources of electrical power, windmills now account for only about 2,500 megawatts nationwide, but production is <u>almost expected to double by the end of the year, which would provide</u> enough electricity for 1.3 million households.

(A) almost expected to double by the end of the year, which would provide

(B) almost expected that it will double by the end of the year, thus providing

(C) expected that it will almost double by the end of the year to provide

(D) expected almost to double by the end of the year and thus to provide

(E) expected almost to double by the end of the year, which would thus be providing

SC03154
899. While most of the earliest known ball courts in Mesoamerica date to 900–400 B.C., <u>waterlogged latex balls found at El Manati and representations of ballplayers painted on ceramics found at San Lorenzo attest</u> to the fact that the Mesoamerican ballgame was well established by the mid-thirteenth century B.C.

(A) waterlogged latex balls found at El Manati and representations of ballplayers painted on ceramics found at San Lorenzo attest

(B) waterlogged latex balls found at El Manati and the painting of representations of ballplayers on ceramics found at San Lorenzo attests

(C) waterlogged latex balls found at El Manati and ceramics painted with representations of ballplayers found at San Lorenzo attests

(D) the finding of waterlogged latex balls at El Manati and the painting of representations of ballplayers on ceramics found at San Lorenzo attests

(E) the finding of waterlogged latex balls at El Manati and of representations of ballplayers painted on ceramics at San Lorenzo attest

SC04899
900. As criminal activity on the Internet becomes more and more sophisticated, not only are thieves able to divert cash from company bank accounts, <u>they can also pilfer valuable information such as business development strategies, new product specifications, and contract bidding plans, and sell</u> the data to competitors.

(A) they can also pilfer valuable information such as business development strategies, new product specifications, and contract bidding plans, and sell

(B) they can also pilfer valuable information that includes business development strategies, new product specifications, and contract bidding plans, and selling

(C) also pilfering valuable information including business development strategies, new product specifications, and contract bidding plans, selling

(D) but also pilfer valuable information such as business development strategies, new product specifications, and contract bidding plans to sell

(E) but also pilfering valuable information such as business development strategies, new product specifications, and contract bidding plans and selling

SC05785
901. Last week local shrimpers held a news conference to take some credit for the resurgence of the rare Kemp's ridley turtle, saying that their compliance with laws <u>requiring that turtle-excluder devices be on shrimp nets protect</u> adult sea turtles.

(A) requiring that turtle-excluder devices be on shrimp nets protect

(B) requiring turtle-excluder devices on shrimp nets is protecting

(C) that require turtle-excluder devices on shrimp nets protect

(D) to require turtle-excluder devices on shrimp nets are protecting

(E) to require turtle-excluder devices on shrimp nets is protecting

SC03752
902. <u>A ruined structure found at Aqaba, Jordan, was probably a church, as indicated in its eastward orientation and by its overall plan, as well as</u> artifacts, such as glass oil-lamp fragments, found at the site.

(A) A ruined structure found at Aqaba, Jordan, was probably a church, as indicated in its eastward orientation and by its overall plan, as well as

(B) A ruined structure found at Aqaba, Jordan, once probably being a church, was indicated by its eastward orientation, overall plan, and

(C) Indicating that a ruined structure found at Aqaba, Jordan, was probably a church were its eastward orientation and overall plan, but also the

(D) A ruined structure found at Aqaba, Jordan, was probably a church, as indicates its eastward orientation and overall plan, as well as the

(E) That a ruined structure found at Aqaba, Jordan, was probably a church is indicated by its eastward orientation and overall plan, as well as by the

903. In the major cities of industrialized countries at the end of the nineteenth century, important public places such as theaters, restaurants, shops, and banks had installed electric lighting, but electricity was in less than 1 percent of homes, where lighting was still provided mainly by candles or gas.

(A) electricity was in less than 1 percent of homes, where lighting was still

(B) electricity was in less than 1 percent of homes and lighting still

(C) there had been less than 1 percent of homes with electricity, where lighting was still being

(D) there was less than 1 percent of homes that had electricity, having lighting that was still

(E) less than 1 percent of homes had electricity, where lighting had still been

904. By 1999, astronomers had discovered 17 nearby stars that are orbited by planets about the size of Jupiter.

(A) had discovered 17 nearby stars that are orbited by planets

(B) had discovered 17 nearby stars with planets orbiting them that were

(C) had discovered that there were 17 nearby stars that were orbited by planets

(D) have discovered 17 nearby stars with planets orbiting them that are

(E) have discovered that 17 nearby stars are orbited by planets

905. Although she was considered among her contemporaries to be the better poet than her husband, later Elizabeth Barrett Browning was overshadowed by his success.

(A) Although she was considered among her contemporaries to be the better poet than her husband, later Elizabeth Barrett Browning was overshadowed by his success.

(B) Although Elizabeth Barrett Browning was considered among her contemporaries as a better poet than her husband, she was later overshadowed by his success.

(C) Later overshadowed by the success of her husband, Elizabeth Barrett Browning's poetry had been considered among her contemporaries to be better than that of her husband.

(D) Although Elizabeth Barrett Browning's success was later overshadowed by that of her husband, among her contemporaries she was considered the better poet.

(E) Elizabeth Barrett Browning's poetry was considered among her contemporaries as better than her husband, but her success was later overshadowed by his.

906. In no other historical sighting did Halley's Comet cause such a worldwide sensation as did its return in 1910–1911.

(A) did its return in 1910–1911

(B) had its 1910–1911 return

(C) in its return of 1910–1911

(D) its return of 1910–1911 did

(E) its return in 1910–1911

907. Rock samples taken from the remains of an asteroid about twice the size of the 6-mile-wide asteroid that eradicated the dinosaurs has been dated to be 3.47 billion years old and thus is evidence of the earliest known asteroid impact on Earth.

(A) has been dated to be 3.47 billion years old and thus is

(B) has been dated at 3.47 billion years old and thus

(C) have been dated to be 3.47 billion years old and thus are

(D) have been dated as being 3.47 billion years old and thus

(E) have been dated at 3.47 billion years old and thus are

9.8 Answer Key

759. A	797. A	835. E	873. A
760. D	798. A	836. E	874. E
761. B	799. B	837. A	875. B
762. B	800. E	838. B	876. B
763. D	801. C	839. A	877. A
764. C	802. B	840. E	878. C
765. D	803. D	841. B	879. B
766. D	804. A	842. A	880. E
767. D	805. E	843. A	881. E
768. B	806. A	844. E	882. C
769. B	807. E	845. C	883. A
770. D	808. E	846. E	884. C
771. C	809. E	847. A	885. C
772. E	810. D	848. A	886. B
773. E	811. E	849. D	887. C
774. A	812. C	850. B	888. D
775. D	813. D	851. B	889. D
776. E	814. C	852. B	890. B
777. C	815. B	853. A	891. C
778. B	816. E	854. E	892. B
779. C	817. D	855. A	893. A
780. D	818. C	856. B	894. E
781. E	819. A	857. C	895. E
782. B	820. C	858. B	896. B
783. B	821. E	859. D	897. E
784. E	822. B	860. C	898. D
785. C	823. A	861. C	899. A
786. C	824. B	862. A	900. A
787. A	825. C	863. B	901. B
788. B	826. E	864. D	902. E
789. E	827. A	865. B	903. A
790. C	828. E	866. B	904. A
791. A	829. C	867. E	905. D
792. C	830. A	868. D	906. C
793. D	831. A	869. A	907. E
794. E	832. C	870. A	
795. D	833. C	871. E	
796. E	834. B	872. A	

9.9 Answer Explanations

The following discussion of sentence correction is intended to familiarize you with the most efficient and effective approaches to these kinds of questions. The particular questions in this chapter are generally representative of the kinds of sentence correction questions you will encounter on the GMAT exam.

*SC01527

759. According to some critics, watching television <u>not only undermines one's ability to think critically but also impairs one's</u> overall ability to perceive.

(A) not only undermines one's ability to think critically but also impairs one's
(B) not only undermines one's ability of critical thinking but also impairs the
(C) undermines not only one's ability to think critically but also impairs one's
(D) undermines not only one's ability of critical thinking but also impairs the
(E) undermines one's ability not only to think critically but also impairs one's

Grammatical Construction; Parallelism

The sentence correctly uses the structure *not only … but also …* to convey two points about the effects that critics believe result from watching television. The phrases placed in the blanks must be in parallel form.

A **Correct.** Two verbal phrases *undermines … and impairs …* are coordinated and placed in the correct positions, in parallel form. Also, *ability to think* (where *to think* is the infinitive form of the verb) is the idiomatically correct usage, parallel with *ability to perceive*.

B The phrase *ability of thinking* is unidiomatic. The use of *the* instead of *one's* impairs the parallelism.

C The phrase *not only* should precede the verb *undermines*. This obliterates the parallelism and makes the sentence incoherent.

D This makes the sentence incoherent because it obliterates the parallelism: the phrase *not only* should precede the verb *undermines*. A further deficiency is the use of *the* instead of *one's*.

E This obliterates the parallelism and makes the sentence incoherent. The phrase *not only* should precede the verb *undermines*.

The correct answer is A.

SC12999

760. In her presentation, the head of the Better Business Bureau emphasized that companies should think of the cost of conventions and other similar gatherings <u>as not an expense, but as</u> an investment in networking that will pay dividends.

(A) as not an expense, but as
(B) as not expense but
(C) not an expense, rather
(D) not as an expense, but as
(E) not in terms of expense, but

Parallelism; Idiom

This sentence is constructed around *not as X, but as Y*, which must start with the word *not* in accordance with this idiomatic pattern, and express both parts in a parallel way.

A This sentence improperly places *as* before *not*.
B This sentence improperly places *as* before *not*.
C This version lacks the required words *as* and *but*.
D **Correct.** The idiom has all of its parts and expresses the two opposed concepts in parallel terms.
E Although *in terms of* is an acceptable substitute for *as*, the construction is no longer parallel due to the lack of a second *in terms of* (or *as*) after *but*.

The correct answer is D.

---
*These numbers correlate with the online test bank question number. See the GMAT Official Guide Online Index in the back of this book.

9.9 Sentence Correction Answer Explanations

SC15382

761. Recent interdisciplinary studies advance the argument that emotions, including those deemed personal or <u>private is a social phenomenon, though one inseparable</u> from bodily response.

   (A) private is a social phenomenon, though one inseparable
   (B) private, are social phenomena that are inseparable
   (C) private are a social phenomenon but are not those separable
   (D) private—are social phenomena but not separable
   (E) also as private emotions, are social phenomena not inseparable

Agreement; Rhetorical Construction

The main problem is one of agreement: in the subordinate clause starting with *that*, the subject is the plural *emotions*, which demands the verb *are*, not *is*. Also, the phrase starting with *including* is a parenthetical expression that needs to be set off from the rest of the clause, with some punctuation to indicate a pause at its end (after *private*).

A   The verb form *is* is incorrect, and should instead be *are*; the parenthetical expression is not separated at its end from the rest of the clause.

B   **Correct.** *Are* is the correct agreeing verb form, and the comma after *private* correctly sets off the parenthetical expression.

C   *Are* is correct, but nothing after *private* sets off the parenthetical expression from the subsequent material. In addition, *not those separable* is awkwardly phrased; it would be better as *not separable* or *inseparable* as in the correct answer choice B.

D   The dash would be correct to set off the parenthetical expression only if *including* had been immediately preceded by a dash; otherwise a comma is needed. The phrase *not separable* is awkward; it would be better as *are not separable* or *are inseparable*.

E   The phrase *also as private emotions* is wordy and unidiomatic. The phrase *social phenomena not inseparable* not only does not express the intended meaning, but is also awkward without a verb and a relative pronoun such as *that*: a better phrasing is *social phenomena that are not separable*.

The correct answer is B.

SC01455

762. In a speech before the Senate Banking Committee, the chairman of the Federal Reserve painted an optimistic picture of the economy, <u>suggesting to investors the central bank in the near future is not lowering interest rates</u>.

   (A) suggesting to investors the central bank in the near future is not lowering interest rates
   (B) suggesting to investors that the central bank would not lower interest rates in the near future
   (C) which suggests that to investors in the near future interest rates will not be lowered by the central bank
   (D) with the suggestion to investors in the near future that interest rates would not be lowered by the central bank
   (E) with the suggestion to investors of interest rates not being lowered in the near future by the central bank

Grammatical Construction; Verb Form

The sentence seeks to report, in indirect-speech form (i.e., using a *that*-clause), a thought expressed by the chairman of the United States Federal Reserve (the central bank) concerning the central bank's intentions. For example, the chairman might have said: "The central bank will not lower interest rates in the near future." In simplified form, the report of that past speech would have been correct as follows: "The chairman said that the central bank would not lower interest rates in the near future." Notice how *will not lower* has to morph into *would not lower* in the indirect-speech transformation of the past direct speech. However, in the indirect-speech report that is given, the sequence of the verb forms is incorrect.

A   The present-continuous form *is not lowering* is incorrect because the report refers to a past speech of the chairman that referred to what the central bank then intended.

B   **Correct.** This clearly and correctly reports the chairman's past speech about what the central bank intended at that time.

C   The antecedent of the relative pronoun *which* is unclear: is it *the economy*, *an optimistic picture of the economy*, or *the* chairman ... the economy? The sequence suggests that *to investors* is unnecessarily awkward and implausibly puts *to investors* within the scope of the reported speech, i.e., within the *that*-clause.

D The placement of the adverbial phrase *in the near future* incorrectly removes it outside the scope of the reported speech, and leaves it unclear what verb or adjective it is meant to modify.

E Indirect speech is normally best expressed in a *that*-clause; the attempt to express it by the prepositional phrase *of interest rates not being lowered ...* is unnecessarily awkward.

The correct answer is B.

SC03014

763. As with ants, the elaborate social structure of termites includes a few individuals reproducing and the rest serve the colony by tending juveniles, gathering food, building the nest, or battling intruders.

(A) As with ants, the elaborate social structure of termites includes a few individuals reproducing

(B) As do ants, termites have an elaborate social structure, which includes a few individuals to reproduce

(C) Just as with ants, termite social structure is elaborate, including a few individuals for reproducing

(D) Like ants, termites have an elaborate social structure in which a few individuals reproduce

(E) Like that of ants, the termite social structure is elaborate, including a few individuals that reproduce

Grammatical Construction; Parallelism

The sentence describes the organization of reproduction and labor among termites. As written, the sentence seems, illogically, to compare a social structure with ants, not with another social structure. Overall, the sentence structure is unnecessarily awkward.

A The phrases *a few individuals reproducing* and *the rest serve ...* are nonparallel, contrary to what would be expected given the coordinating conjunction *and*.

B The *and* seems as if it should coordinate two parallel elements in a complex relative clause; yet *a few individuals reproducing* is not parallel with *the rest serve ... intruders*.

C This illogically compares a social structure with ants. The structure *including ... and ...* raises an expectation that there would be a phrase following *and* that would be parallel with the phrase *a few individuals for reproducing*. However, *the rest serve ... intruders* is not parallel. The participle *including* is often used to introduce instances of a class; its use here is confusing since a social structure is not a class that has termites as its members.

D **Correct.** The sentence concisely notes that termites resemble ants in having an elaborate social structure. The complex relative clause *in which ... and ...* has two coordinated elements correctly parallel in structure: *a few individuals reproduce* and *the rest serve ... intruders*.

E The phrase *that of ants* is not parallel with *the termite social structure*; also, the forward reference of *that* is unnecessarily awkward and impairs readability. As already noted, the use of the participle *including* is confusing. The conjunction *and* indicates coordination of two parallel elements, but *a few individuals that reproduce* cannot be correctly coordinated with anything that follows it.

The correct answer is D.

SC02078

764. While Noble Sissle may be best known for his collaboration with Eubie Blake, as both a vaudeville performer and as a lyricist for songs and Broadway musicals, also enjoying an independent career as a singer with such groups as Hahn's Jubilee Singers.

(A) and as a lyricist for songs and Broadway musicals, also enjoying

(B) and writing lyrics for songs and Broadway musicals, also enjoying

(C) and a lyricist for songs and Broadway musicals, he also enjoyed

(D) as well as writing lyrics for songs and Broadway musicals, he also enjoyed

(E) as well as a lyricist for songs and Broadway musicals, he had also enjoyed

Grammatical Construction; Idiom; Parallelism

As worded, this sentence opens with a dependent clause (a clause that cannot stand on its own), which requires a main clause (also known as an independent clause) to complete the sentence; however, there is no main clause. Also, given the placement of *as* before *both*, the *as* before *a lyricist* is incorrect. It would be acceptable to write *as both a vaudeville performer and a lyricist* or to write *both as a vaudeville performer and as a lyricist*; it is not acceptable to mix the two forms, as is done here.

A The dependent clause, *While . . . Broadway musicals*, is followed by a participial phrase rather than a main clause and is therefore ungrammatical. Furthermore, the word *as* before *a lyricist* violates the parallel structure required by the phrase *both . . . and*.

B The construction *as both a performer and writing lyrics* is incorrect. Also, like (A), this version of the sentence does not supply a main clause.

C **Correct.** Unlike (A) and (B), this version has a main clause. Also, unlike the other version, it correctly uses the *both x and y* form.

D Although this version does supply the main clause anticipated by *While . . .*, its use as *both a vaudeville performer as well as writing lyrics* is incorrect.

E This version's use of *both x as well as y* instead of *both x and y* is incorrect. It also introduces an inexplicable past perfect verb, *had . . . enjoyed*, in the main clause.

The correct answer is C.

SC03881

765. Air traffic routes over the North Pole are currently used by only two or three planes a day, but it was found by a joint Canadian–Russian study to be both feasible as well as desirable if those routes are opened to thousands more commercial planes a year.

(A) Air traffic routes over the North Pole are currently used by only two or three planes a day, but it was found by a joint Canadian–Russian study to be both feasible as well as desirable if those routes are opened to thousands more commercial planes a year.

(B) Currently used by only two or three planes a day, a joint Canadian–Russian study has found that if air traffic routes over the North Pole are opened to thousands more commercial planes a year, it would be both feasible and desirable.

(C) A joint Canadian–Russian study, finding it to be both feasible as well as desirable to open air traffic routes over the North Pole, which are currently used by only two or three planes a day, to thousands more commercial planes a year.

(D) Although air traffic routes over the North Pole are currently used by only two or three planes a day, a joint Canadian–Russian study has found that opening those routes to thousands more commercial planes a year is both feasible and desirable.

(E) With air traffic routes over the North Pole currently used by only two or three planes a day, opening those routes to thousands more commercial planes a year has been found by a joint Canadian–Russian study as both feasible and desirable.

Rhetorical Construction; Verb Form; Logical Predication

The point of the sentence is to share the results of a study about air routes over the North Pole, but the wording is confusing and verbose. The passive construction *it was found by a joint Canadian–Russian study to be* could be expressed more directly and clearly in active voice: *a joint Canadian–Russian study has found*.

A The passive construction *it was found by a joint Canadian–Russian study to be*, especially followed by the conditional *if*, is wordy, awkward, and unclear.

B *Used by only two or three planes* illogically modifies *a joint Canadian–Russian study*; the pronoun *it* has no clear antecedent.

C The subject *A joint Canadian–Russian study* has no verb; *to thousands more commercial planes* is located too far away from *to open*, which it is intended to modify.

D **Correct.** The sentence uses correctly placed modifiers and the active voice to explain clearly what *a joint Canadian–Russian study has found*.

E   The passive construction *opening those routes . . . has been found by a joint Canadian–Russian study as both* is wordy and unidiomatic.

The correct answer is D.

SC01680

766. From an experiment using special extrasensory perception cards, each bearing one of a set of symbols, parapsychologist Joseph Banks Rhine claimed statistical proof <u>for subjects who could use thought transference to identify a card in the dealer's hand</u>.

(A) for subjects who could use thought transference to identify a card in the dealer's hand

(B) for a card in the dealer's hand to be identified by subjects with thought transference

(C) of subjects able to identify with thought transference a card in the dealer's hand

(D) that subjects could identify a card in the dealer's hand by using thought transference

(E) that subjects are capable to use thought transference for identifying a card in the dealer's hand

Idiom; Rhetorical Construction

This sentence is meant to indicate that Joseph Banks Rhine claimed that a certain experiment statistically proved that subjects could identify what symbol was on a card in a dealer's hand by using thought transference. The present version of the sentence does not convey the intended meaning well, however. What should follow *proof* is a statement of the assertion that Rhine claims the experiment has statistically proved, linked to the word *proof* by the word *that*. Instead *proof* is followed by a prepositional phrase *for subjects who*. . . .

A   This version of the sentence inappropriately attempts to describe the claim by using a prepositional phrase, *for subjects who*. . . .

B   Like (A), this version of the sentence inappropriately attempts to describe the claim by using a prepositional phrase, *for a card in*. . . .

C   Like (A) and (B), this version of the sentence inappropriately attempts to describe the claim by using a prepositional phrase. While

proof might reasonably be followed by *of*, the phrase that follows the preposition is ungrammatical, requiring a participle to modify *subjects*, such as *being able to*. . . .

D   **Correct.** This version correctly uses the idiom *proof that* followed by an assertion.

E   While this version of the sentence correctly follows *proof* with *that* followed by an assertion, it fails to use the appropriate idiom with *capable*; instead of *capable to use*, it should have *capable of using*.

The correct answer is D.

SC02272

767. A long-term study of some 1,000 physicians indicates that the more coffee these doctors drank, the <u>more they had a likelihood of coronary disease</u>.

(A) more they had a likelihood of coronary disease

(B) more was their likelihood of having coronary disease

(C) more they would have a likelihood to have coronary disease

(D) greater was their likelihood of having coronary disease

(E) greater was coronary disease likely

Idiom; Rhetorical Construction

This sentence describes the results of a study in which researchers found a correlation between the amounts of coffee that people drank and their likelihood of coronary disease. It most eloquently expresses this correlation as a comparison of parallel forms, using the idiom *the + comparative adjective phrase . . . the + comparative adjective phrase*. The two adjective phrases should have the same grammatical form.

A   This version obscures the intended correlation between *coffee* and *likelihood*. The phrase *the more they had a likelihood* somewhat illogically indicates that the research subjects had likelihood to a greater degree rather than that their likelihood was greater.

B   Although the adverb *more* is used to indicate a greater degree or extent in phrases such as *more likely*, the adjective *more* normally indicates greater quantity. Thus, the use of *more* as an adjective modifying *their likelihood* is nonstandard. Differences in a particular type of likelihood are normally thought of as matters of degree, not of quantity. *Greater* is the preferred adjective for indicating such differences.

C The conditional verb phrase *would have a likelihood to have* is redundant, wordy, and not comparable to the simple past tense *drank*.

D **Correct.** This version uses proper wording and is clear and concise.

E This completion of the comparison is not idiomatic; moreover, it is ungrammatical, attempting to use an adjective *greater* to describe an adverb, *likely*.

The correct answer is D.

SC02096

768. Hurricanes at first begin traveling from east to west, because that direction is the way the prevailing winds in the tropics blow, but they then veer off toward higher latitudes, in many cases changing direction toward the east before dissipating over the colder, more northerly waters or over land.

(A) Hurricanes at first begin traveling from east to west, because that direction is the way the prevailing winds in the tropics blow, but

(B) At first, hurricanes travel from east to west, because that is the direction of the prevailing winds in the tropics, but

(C) While hurricanes travel from east to west at first, the direction of the prevailing winds blowing in the tropics, and

(D) Because hurricanes at first travel from east to west, since it is the direction of the prevailing winds in the tropics,

(E) Hurricanes, beginning by traveling from east to west, because this is the direction of the prevailing winds in the tropics,

Rhetorical Construction; Grammatical Construction

Hurricanes at first begin traveling is redundant. The sentence could start with *At first, hurricanes travel* or with *Hurricanes begin traveling*; there is no need to have both *at first* and *begin*. A concise version of the sentence would also avoid *that direction is the way the prevailing winds in the tropics blow*. The meaning of *way* here is already conveyed by *direction*.

A *At first* and *begin* are redundant. Also, *that direction is the way the prevailing winds blow* is unnecessarily wordy.

B **Correct.** This version of the sentence is grammatically correct and lacks redundancy.

C This sentence begins with a dependent clause (that is, a clause that cannot stand on its own), anticipating a main clause (also known as an independent clause) to complete the sentence; a main clause does follow, but it is connected to the initial dependent clause by the coordinating conjunction *and*, which would be appropriate here only if the initial clause was of the same grammatical type (that is, was also a main clause).

D The causal conjunction *Because* suggests that the direction in which hurricanes initially travel causes them later to veer off to the north, but this make little logical sense.

E This sentence opens with a main subject, *Hurricanes*, but this subject has no verb. The sentence's main verb, *veer*, has as a subject *they*.

The correct answer is B.

SC03083

769. Travelers from Earth to Mars would have to endure low levels of gravity for long periods of time, avoiding large doses of radiation, plus contending with the chemically reactive Martian soil, and perhaps even ward off contamination by Martian life-forms.

(A) Mars would have to endure low levels of gravity for long periods of time, avoiding large doses of radiation, plus contending

(B) Mars would have to endure low levels of gravity for long periods of time, avoid large doses of radiation, contend

(C) Mars, having to endure low levels of gravity for long periods of time, would also have to avoid large doses of radiation, plus contending

(D) Mars, having to endure low levels of gravity for long periods of time, avoid large doses of radiation, plus contend

(E) Mars, who would have to endure low levels of gravity for long periods of time, avoid large doses of radiation, contend with

Grammatical Construction; Parallelism

The sentence lists a series of things that travelers from Earth to Mars would have to do in order to successfully handle challenging conditions. Listing elements in a series requires parallelism in wording for each element, together with the use of a conjunction immediately preceding the final element.

A The parallelism requirement is not fulfilled; for example, *endure ... time* is not parallel with *avoiding ... radiation* or *contending ... soil*. The word *plus* is not a coordinating conjunction and its inclusion impairs the structure of the series.

B **Correct.** The parallelism requirement is fulfilled, with the following elements: *endure ...*, *avoid ...*, *contend ...*, *and perhaps even ward off*.

C The parallelism requirement is not fulfilled; for example, *would have to avoid* is not parallel with *contending*. The word *plus* is not a coordinating conjunction.

D This is not a valid sentence since it lacks an independent clause.

E This is not a valid sentence since it lacks an independent clause.

The correct answer is B.

SC01739

770. Unlike the virginal, <u>whose single set of strings runs parallel to the front edge of the instrument, the harpsichord's several sets of strings are</u> placed at right angles to its front edge.

(A) whose single set of strings runs parallel to the front edge of the instrument, the harpsichord's several sets of strings are

(B) with a single set of strings running parallel to the front edge of the instrument, the several sets of strings of the harpsichord are

(C) which has a single set of strings that runs parallel to the front edge of the instrument, in the case of the harpsichord, several sets of strings are

(D) which has a single set of strings that run parallel to the front edge of the instrument, the harpsichord has several sets of strings

(E) in which a single set of strings run parallel to the front edge of the instrument, the harpsichord's several sets of strings are

Parallelism; Agreement

The point of the sentence is to contrast two instruments, but the sentence has been written to contrast the *virginal* with the *sets of strings* on the harpsichord. The proper contrast is between the *virginal* and the *harpsichord*.

A The *virginal* is illogically contrasted with the *sets of strings* on the harpsichord. Note the possessive form *harpsichord's* in contrast to virginal.

B The *virginal* is illogically contrasted with the *sets of strings* on the harpsichord.

C *In the case of the harpsichord* is not parallel to the *virginal*.

D **Correct.** The contrast is properly drawn between *the virginal* and *the harpsichord*.

E The *virginal* is illogically contrasted with the *sets of strings* on the harpsichord; the verb *run* does not agree with the singular subject *set*.

The correct answer is D.

SC02000

771. Although Alice Walker published a number of essays, poetry collections, and stories during the 1970s, her third novel, The Color Purple, <u>which was published in 1982, brought her the widest acclaim in that it won both the National Book Award as well as the Pulitzer Prize</u>.

(A) which was published in 1982, brought her the widest acclaim in that it won both the National Book Award as well as the Pulitzer Prize

(B) published in 1982, bringing her the widest acclaim by winning both the National Book Award and the Pulitzer Prize

(C) published in 1982, brought her the widest acclaim, winning both the National Book Award and the Pulitzer Prize

(D) was published in 1982 and which, winning both the National Book Award and the Pulitzer Prize, brought her the widest acclaim

(E) was published in 1982, winning both the National Book Award as well as the Pulitzer Prize, and bringing her the widest acclaim

Idiom; Grammatical Construction

This sentence claims that the 1982 novel *The Color Purple* brought Alice Walker more acclaim than her many publications in the 1970s.

A The construction *both the American Book Award as well as the Pulitzer Prize* is unidiomatic; the correct idiomatic form is *both x and y*.

B Because this sentence uses only participial phrases in the clause following the initial, dependent clause, the sentence lacks a main verb and is therefore ungrammatical.

C **Correct.** This version correctly uses the form *both x and y* and is grammatically correct.

D The use of *which* is inappropriate here; although it would still be rhetorically inferior to the correct answer (C), this version would be acceptable if the word *which* were deleted.

E Like (A), this version of the sentence uses the unidiomatic form *both x as well as y*.

The correct answer is C.

SC01436

772. Heating oil and natural gas futures rose sharply yesterday, as long-term forecasts for much colder temperatures in key heating regions raised fears <u>of insufficient supplies capable of meeting</u> the demand this winter.

(A) of insufficient supplies capable of meeting

(B) of supplies that would be insufficient for meeting

(C) of insufficient supplies that are unable to meet

(D) that there would be supplies insufficient for meeting

(E) that supplies would be insufficient to meet

Rhetorical Construction; Verb Form

The wording of the underlined portion of this sentence is incoherent because it suggests that supplies that are "insufficient" are "capable of meeting the demand." The phrase *fears of insufficient supplies* is awkward and unclear: it suggests that the object of the fears already exists, i.e., that supplies are already insufficient. How can the intended meaning—regarding a fear that something might occur—be best expressed in the context of the sentence as a whole?

A This produces an incoherent sentence that forces us to guess at what might have been intended.

B This is wordy and unnecessarily awkward. The phrase *insufficient to meet* would be more idiomatic than *insufficient for meeting*.

C The present tense *are* fails to express the future-oriented nature of the fears: that future supplies might turn out to be insufficient relative to demand.

D The awkward expression here is misleading. What the fears were about was not that there would be supplies but that the supplies would be insufficient.

E **Correct.** What was feared was the following: future supplies will be insufficient to meet the demand. Because we are told that the fears were raised in the past, the futurity of the feared occurrence must be expressed by *would be* (rather than by *will be*) in the context of the *that*-clause, which clearly conveys what was feared (the object of the "fears").

The correct answer is E.

SC00970

773. Because it regarded the environmentalists as members of an out-of-state organization, the city council voted <u>that they are denied permission for participating</u> in the parade.

(A) that they are denied permission for participating

(B) that they be denied permission for participating

(C) denying them permission for participation

(D) the denial of permission that they participate

(E) to deny them permission to participate

Verb Form; Logical Predication

The sentence describes a vote that has been taken by a city council and suggests an explanation as to why the city council voted the particular way it did. The underlined portion, together with the three words that follow it, serves to describe the particular way the council voted and begins immediately after the verb *voted*. The word *that* at the beginning of the underlined portion introduces a subordinate clause that introduces the particular way the city council voted.

A When we vote for something, what we vote for is something that perhaps should happen, rather than a fact or a description of an actual state of affairs. The statement *they are denied permission* would, if used properly, simply describe an actual state of affairs. It is therefore something that would not be voted for. The wording of the sentence thus needs to be changed, so that what is described as being voted for is not described as if it were an existing state of affairs. Furthermore, as discussed in connection with option B, the use of "for participating" may also be incorrect.

B   The use of "for participating" in this option may be incorrect. The noun *permission* as used in this statement describes an official act of allowing someone or something *to* do something. In this statement, it would be better if *permission* were followed by an infinitive form of a verb (beginning with the word "to"). For example, *permission to participate* would be correct.

C   In addition to the flaw described in connection with option B, this option has a flaw associated with the use of the word *denying*. Between *voted* and whatever form of the verb "deny" we may choose, we need a term, such as an infinitive (e.g., *to*) or a preposition (e.g., *for* or *on*) to introduce the statement describing the vote. In this way, *to deny*, *for denying*, and *on denying* could be correct. This option lacks such an introducing term.

D   One flaw in this option is somewhat like the flaw in option C. For option D, the option is a noun phrase, which, when preceded by the verb "voted," needs a preposition such as *for* or *on* to precede it. For example, *voted for the denial of permission* might be correct. The use of *that they participate* is also incorrect. This flaw could be fixed if, as discussed in connection with option B, we used *to participate* instead.

E   **Correct.** This option has none of the flaws discussed in connection with options A through D.

The correct answer is E.

SC07348

774. In 1913, the largely self-taught Indian mathematician Srinivasa Ramanujan mailed 120 of his theorems to three different British mathematicians; <u>only one, G. H. Hardy, recognized the brilliance of these theorems, but</u> thanks to Hardy's recognition, Ramanujan was eventually elected to the Royal Society of London.

(A) only one, G. H. Hardy, recognized the brilliance of these theorems, but

(B) they were brilliant, G. H. Hardy alone recognized, but

(C) these theorems were brilliant, but only one, G. H. Hardy recognized;

(D) but, only one, G. H. Hardy, recognizing their brilliance,

(E) only one G. H. Hardy recognized, but these theorems were brilliant

Logical Predication; Grammatical Construction

The point of the sentence is that only one of the British mathematicians with whom Srinivasa Ramanujan initially shared his theorems recognized their brilliance, but that recognition was sufficient to earn Ramanujan acclaim. The sentence has been correctly constructed, with the phrase *only one* referring clearly to *British mathematicians* and the noun *theorems* repeated to avoid confusion.

A   **Correct.** The phrase *only one* refers clearly to *British mathematicians*, and the noun *theorems* is repeated to avoid confusion.

B   *They* is intended to refer to *theorems* but instead refers to *mathematicians*, causing confusion.

C   Structured in this way, the sentence does not make sense. *Only one* is intended to refer to *G. H. Hardy* but instead seems to refer to *theorems*, causing confusion. If *only one* is taken to refer to *G. H. Hardy*, the absence of a comma after the name and the absence of an object for *recognized* make the sentence ungrammatical.

D   The sentence is ungrammatical because *G. H. Hardy* serves as the subject of a clause but is not paired with a verb.

E   *Only one G. H. Hardy recognized* incorrectly implies (in an awkwardly inverted wording structure) that Hardy recognized only one theorem; *these theorems were brilliant thanks to Hardy's recognition* illogically suggests that Hardy's recognition is what made the theorems brilliant.

The correct answer is A.

9.9 Sentence Correction Answer Explanations

SC05201

775. Cost cutting and restructuring <u>has allowed the manufacturing company to lower its projected losses for the second quarter, and they are forecasting</u> a profit before the end of the year.

   (A) has allowed the manufacturing company to lower its projected losses for the second quarter, and they are forecasting
   (B) has allowed for the manufacturing company to lower its projected losses in the second quarter and to forecast
   (C) have allowed that the manufacturing company can lower the projected losses for the second quarter, and to forecast
   (D) have allowed the manufacturing company to lower its projected second-quarter losses and to forecast
   (E) have allowed for the manufacturing company to lower the projected losses in the second quarter, as well as forecasting

Agreement; Idiom; Verb Form

The point of the sentence is to explain the two main effects of the changes made by the company. However, the singular verb *has allowed* does not agree with the compound subject *cost cutting and restructuring*, which are far more plausibly understood as two actions rather than as two facets of a single action. In principle, *the manufacturing company* could be construed as plural (referring collectively to the decision makers and spokespeople who are projecting losses and forecasting a profit), but the plural pronoun *they* does not agree with the earlier *its*, which treats the antecedent as singular.

A The singular verb *has allowed* does not agree with the compound subject *cost cutting and restructuring*; the plural pronoun *they* does not agree with the intended singular antecedent *company*.

B The singular verb *has allowed* does not agree with the compound subject *cost cutting and restructuring*; *allowed for* is not the correct idiom.

C *Allowed that* is not the correct idiom; *can lower* and *to forecast* are not grammatically parallel.

D **Correct.** The sentence uses the correct subject–verb combination *cost cutting and restructuring have allowed*; the two occurrences of the pronoun *its* agree with each other in treating their antecedent *company* as singular; and the two effects *to lower* and *to forecast* are parallel and idiomatic.

E *Allowed for* is not the correct idiom; *to lower* and *as well as forecasting* are not parallel.

The correct answer is D.

SC13010

776. The Life and Casualty Company hopes that by increasing its environmental fund reserves to $1.2 billion, <u>that it has set aside enough to pay for environmental claims and no longer has</u> to use its profits and capital to pay those claims bit by bit, year by year.

   (A) that it has set aside enough to pay for environmental claims and no longer has
   (B) enough has been set aside with which environmental claims can be paid and it will have no longer
   (C) it has set aside enough for payment of environmental claims and thus no longer having
   (D) enough has been set aside to pay for environmental claims, thus no longer having
   (E) it has set aside enough to pay for environmental claims and will no longer have

Grammatical Construction; Logical Predication

All predicates need a proper logical subject. Here, the relevant predicates are the verbs *increase*, *set aside*, and *have*. With *it* as the subject for *set aside*—referring back to the Life and Casualty Company—all three verbs should have this as their understood subject. With a different subject for *set aside*, at least one of the other verbs lacks a proper logical subject. Also, this sentence uses the word *that* after *hope* to start the subordinate clause, but then incorrectly repeats the *that* after the initial adverbial phrase (*by increasing . . . billion*). Only the first *that* is grammatically correct.

A The additional *that* makes the sentence ungrammatical. Also, because in this context the hope is forward-looking (*bit by bit, year by year*), it would be preferable to use the future tense, *will no longer have to*, instead of the present *no longer has to*.

B   With *enough* as the subject of *set aside*, the next subject (*it*) is naturally interpreted as *enough*, but this is not a logical choice for the subject of *use*.

C   The phrase *no longer having* is ungrammatical when connected to the rest of the sentence by *and*, which should connect two regular clauses; *no longer having . . .* is a mere phrase, not a clause, and *no longer has* would be correct.

D   For *no longer having*, illogically, the implied subject is *enough*; the implied subject, instead, should be the company referred to at the beginning of the sentence.

E   **Correct.** There is only one *that*, and *will no longer have to use* has its proper logical subject (*it*) from the clause preceding it.

The correct answer is E.

SC03079

777. Like ancient Egyptian architectural materials that were recycled in the construction of ancient Greek Alexandria, so ancient Greek materials from the construction of that city were reused in subsequent centuries by Roman, Muslim, and modern builders.

   (A)   Like ancient Egyptian architectural materials that were recycled in the construction of
   (B)   Like recycling ancient Egyptian architectural materials to construct
   (C)   Just as ancient Egyptian architectural materials were recycled in the construction of
   (D)   Just as they recycled ancient Egyptian architectural materials in constructing
   (E)   Just like ancient Egyptian architectural materials that were recycled in constructing

Diction; Parallelism

When two situations are asserted to be similar, the proper way to express this is with the paired expressions *just as . . . so . . .*, not *like . . . so*. Moreover, the two compared situations should be expressed as clauses, not as noun phrases. Thus the clause *ancient Egyptian architectural materials were recycled . . .* is correct, as opposed to a noun phrase like *ancient Egyptian architectural materials that were recycled . . .*

A   *Just as* and a following clause with a passive verb are preferred, but instead this option has *like* and a following noun phrase (*ancient Egyptian materials . . .*). It appears, somewhat implausibly, to say that the ancient Greek materials were similar to the earlier ancient Egyptian ones in that both were used by Roman, Muslim, and modern builders.

B   *Just as* and a following clause with a passive verb are preferred, but instead this option has *like* and a following noun phrase (*recycling ancient Egyptian materials . . .*). It appears illogically to say that the action of recycling was similar to the ancient Greek materials in that both were reused in subsequent centuries.

C   **Correct.** The expressions *just as* and *so* are paired to link the two clauses in parallel, and both clauses use the passive construction.

D   *Just as* is used to connect two clauses, which is good, but the first clause employs the active construction rather than the preferred passive, so there is a failure of parallelism. Also, it is unclear what *they* refers to. The sentence appears to say illogically that some unidentified group's action of recycling was similar to the ancient Greek materials' being reused.

E   *Just as* introducing a clause with a passive verb is preferable, but this sentence uses *like* and a following noun phrase (*ancient Egyptian materials . . .*). It appears, somewhat implausibly, to say that the ancient Greek materials were similar to the earlier ancient Egyptian ones in that both were used by Roman, Muslim, and modern builders.

The correct answer is C.

SC09877

778. Especially in the early years, new entrepreneurs may need to find resourceful ways, like renting temporary office space or using answering services, that make their company seem large and more firmly established than they may actually be.

   (A)   that make their company seem large
   (B)   to make their companies seem larger
   (C)   thus making their companies seem larger
   (D)   so that the companies seem larger
   (E)   of making their company seem large

Grammatical Construction; Diction

The clause beginning with *that* suggests that a company can be made to seem better than it actually is. The comparison signaled by *than* appears to be intended to apply to both the size of the company and the degree to which the company is firmly established. In that case, it is a mistake to use *large* instead of *larger*. If, on the other hand, *large* is not intended to be part of the comparison, it would be better to clarify this by separating the two topics in a construction such as *make their company seem large and also make it seem more firmly established*.... The phrase *resourceful ways* suggests purpose, so *ways* should connect with *to* or *of*, rather than a *that* clause to capture the intended meaning.

A   *Large* is the incorrect form to express comparison; it should be *larger*; the *that* clause does not adequately capture the idea of purpose implicit in *ways*. The singular *company* does not agree with the plural pronoun *they*. Thus, the sentence either commits an agreement mistake or illogically says that entrepreneurs need to find ways to make themselves seem large and more firmly established.

B   **Correct.** *Larger* is the correct form to express the comparative meaning, and *to* correctly follows *way*. *Companies* agrees with the plural *they*.

C   The phrase beginning *thus making* does not capture the idea of purpose implicit in *ways*.

D   Clauses beginning *so that* can express purpose, but do not fit with *ways* in the manner required here: *to* or *of* is needed after *ways*.

E   *Large* is the incorrect form to express comparison; it should be *larger*. The singular *company* does not agree with the plural pronoun *they*. Thus, the sentence either commits an agreement mistake or illogically says that entrepreneurs need to find ways to make themselves seem large and more firmly established.

The correct answer is B.

SC01975

779. Unlike <u>the nests of leaf cutters and most other ants,</u> situated underground or in pieces of wood, raider ants make a portable nest by entwining their long legs to form "curtains" of ants that hang from logs or boulders, providing protection for the queen and the colony larvae and pupae.

(A) the nests of leaf cutters and most other ants,
(B) the nests of leaf cutters and most other ants, which are
(C) leaf cutters and most other ants, whose nests are
(D) leaf cutters and most other ants in having nests
(E) those of leaf cutters and most other ants with nests

Logical Predication

As worded, this sentence draws a contrast between raider ants and the nests of leaf cutters and most other ants. The appropriate contrast would be with leaf cutters and most other ants themselves, not their nests.

A   As indicated above, the appropriate contrast is between raider ants and other kinds of ants (namely leaf cutters and most ants). As worded, this version of the sentence says something obviously true: of course the nests of leaf cutters and most other ants do not make portable nests.

B   Like (A), this sentence compares nests with raider ants. Also, the referent of the relative pronoun *which* is ambiguous, possibly modifying *ants*, and possibly modifying *nests*.

C   **Correct.** This version correctly draws the contrast between raider ants and other kinds of ants. Furthermore, unlike in (B) and (D), it is clear here that *situated underground or in pieces of wood* applies to the nests of leaf cutters and most other ants.

D   This sentence correctly compares leaf cutters and other ants with raider ants, but the prepositional phrase *in having nests* suggests that it is raider ants, not leaf cutters and most other ants, that have nests situated underground or in pieces of wood; however, the rest of the sentence indicates that in fact raider ants' nests are not situated in such locations.

E   The referent of *those* is unclear; presumably it refers to *nests*, but grammatically it has no clear antecedent. If it is taken to refer to nests, *those* creates an illogical comparison with *raider ants*.

The correct answer is C.

SC04452

780. Turtles, like other reptiles, can endure long fasts, in their ability to survive on weekly or even monthly feedings; however, when food is readily available, they may eat frequently and grow very fat.

- (A) fasts, in their ability to survive
- (B) fasts, having their ability to survive
- (C) fasts, due to having the ability of surviving
- (D) fasts because they are able to survive
- (E) fasts because of having the ability of surviving

Idiom; Diction

To express why turtles can endure long fasts—their ability to survive on only occasional feedings—it is clearer and more idiomatic to use *because* than to use *in* or *having*. Also, the noun *ability* here requires *to* introducing a noun phrase denoting the nature of the ability.

A *In* does not express the causal relationship clearly, whereas *because* does.

B *Having* does not express the causal relationship clearly.

C *Ability of* is incorrect; *ability* must be followed by *to* in order to express the intended meaning. *Due to having the ability* is awkward, nonstandard, and unnecessarily wordy.

D **Correct.** This option uses *because* to express the causal relation and uses *to* after *ability*.

E *Ability of* is incorrect; *ability* must be followed by *to* in order to express the intended meaning. *Because of having the ability* is awkward, nonstandard, and unnecessarily wordy.

The correct answer is D.

SC02025

781. Thai village crafts, as with other cultures, have developed through the principle that form follows function and incorporate readily available materials fashioned using traditional skills.

- (A) as with
- (B) as did those of
- (C) as they have in
- (D) like in
- (E) like those of

Logical Predication; Diction; Verb Form

The phrase *as with other cultures* is initially confusing given that no culture has been specifically mentioned; Thai village culture is indirectly referenced by the mention of *Thai village crafts*, so perhaps that is what is meant. But then, looking at the phrase in context, it becomes clear that the sentence is intended to indicate that the *crafts* of other cultures are similar in certain ways to Thai village crafts. Thus, the sentence should say *those of other cultures*. Furthermore, the use here of *as with* is questionable. To do the job it is supposed to do here (to indicate that the crafts of Thai villages are like the crafts of other cultures in a particular way), *as with* should be at the beginning of the sentence: *As with the crafts of other cultures, Thai village crafts have developed. . . .* Alternatively, *like* could be used here instead of *as with*.

A The appropriate comparison is between Thai village crafts and those (i.e., crafts) of other cultures, not the other cultures themselves. Additionally, *like* would be more appropriate here than *as with*.

B The verb form here is incorrect. [*D*]*id* is not parallel to *have* later in the sentence. The phrase *as have those of other cultures* would be parallel, but it is in the wrong position. To be correct, it would need to occur after the main verb is introduced: *Thai village crafts have developed, as have those of other cultures, . . .*

C The use of the pronoun *they* is inaccurate; the reader is likely to take its antecedent to be *Thai village crafts*, not *crafts*. Furthermore, even if the pronoun here were not problematic, if the construction *as they have in other cultures* is used, it should occur after the main verb (*have developed*) is introduced.

D The comparative term *like* compares two nouns or noun phrases, but in this version of the sentence, *like* compares a noun (*crafts*) with a prepositional phrase (*in other cultures*).

E **Correct.** [*T*]*hose of other cultures* clearly refers to the crafts of other cultures; *like* is appropriate for making a comparison between two sorts of things (*crafts*).

The correct answer is E.

782. To estimate the expansion rate of the universe is a notoriously difficult problem because there is a lack of a single yardstick that all distances can be measured by.

(A) To estimate the expansion rate of the universe is a notoriously difficult problem because there is a lack of a single yardstick that all distances can be measured by.

(B) Estimating the expansion rate of the universe is a notoriously difficult problem because there is no single yardstick by which all distances can be measured.

(C) Because there is a lack of a single yardstick to measure all distances by, estimating the expansion rate of the universe is a notoriously difficult problem.

(D) A notoriously difficult problem is to estimate the expansion rate of the universe because a single yardstick is lacking by which all distances can be measured.

(E) It is a notoriously difficult problem to estimate the expansion rate of the universe because by no single yardstick can all distances be measured.

Rhetorical Construction; Logical Predication

The sentence seeks to explain the difficulty of estimating the expansion rate of the universe and uses a *because*-clause to present the explanation. Issues in the given sentence include the following: is the infinitive verb form *to estimate* best here? And is there a more straightforward and more readable way to express the explanation?

A The wording with the infinitive verb form *to estimate* is less than ideal here (as opposed to *how to estimate*, for example). The phrase *there is a lack of a single yardstick* is wordy. The placement of the preposition *by* so far from the relative pronoun it governs (*that*) is unnecessarily awkward.

B **Correct.** Use of the verbal noun *estimating* is acceptable here. The phrase *there is no single yardstick* is much more direct and readable than *there is a lack of a single yardstick*. The preposition *by* is adjacent to *which*, the relative pronoun that it governs.

C The phrase *there is a lack of a single yardstick* is wordy. The placement of the preposition *by* at the end of the phrase *a single yardstick to measure all distances by* is unnecessarily

awkward, in that it separates *by* from the noun that it is meant to govern.

D Compared with the given sentence, this sentence involves a reordering of the ideas and a shifting of emphases in a way that is confusing. For example, is this sentence to be understood as citing one instance of "a notoriously difficult problem"? This was not the purpose of the given sentence. In addition, the phrase *to estimate* is less clear than would be *how to estimate*. Finally, the wide separation of the *because*-clause from the reference to difficulty produces a sentence that is unnecessarily awkward, if not incoherent (for example, structurally it seems to make the adverbial *because*-clause modify the verb *estimate*). Contrast this with the given sentence, where the *because*-clause is placed adjacent to the phrase *difficult problem*.

E The phrase *to estimate* is less clear than would be *how to estimate*. The *because*-clause, which is meant to explain why estimating the expansion rate of the universe is difficult, is too widely separated from the reference to difficulty. In the *because*-clause, the inversion of the normal subject-verb order is unnecessarily awkward.

The correct answer is B.

783. The Commerce Department reported that the nation's economy grew at a brisk annual pace of 3.7 percent in the second quarter, but that while businesses were expanding their production, unsold goods piled up on store shelves as consumer spending is slowed sharply.

(A) unsold goods piled up on store shelves as consumer spending is slowed sharply

(B) unsold goods were piling up on store shelves as consumer spending slowed sharply

(C) unsold goods had piled up on store shelves with a sharp slowing of consumer spending

(D) consumer spending was slowing sharply, with the piling up of unsold goods on store shelves

(E) consumer spending has slowed sharply, with unsold goods piling up on store shelves

Verb Form; Rhetorical Construction

The sentence summarizes a government report about four business and economic processes occurring over a single quarter: economic growth, increasing production, unsold goods accumulating in retail stores, and a sharp slowing in consumer spending. A problem in the verb *is slowed* is use of the passive form, which in this context is awkward and unidiomatic. It is also present tense, whereas *piled up* is simple-past tense—a breach of proper tense sequence.

A This fails because of the inappropriate and in context unidiomatic use of the passive voice. Also, *piled up* does not clearly indicate a process.

B **Correct.** The verb *were piling up* correctly indicates a process as opposed to a single event; with the *as*-clause, the verb *slowed* indicates a process simultaneous with another process (and, implicitly, contributing to it).

C The verb *had piled up* suggests an event that occurred before businesses were expanding their production, even though the *while*-clause indicates that the piling-up occurred simultaneously with that expansion.

D The import of the *with*-phrase is insufficiently clear. It could be read as indicating that the piling-up was also slowing. But this reading fails to capture the idea of a causal relationship implicitly conveyed in the given sentence.

E The verb *has slowed* suggests a process that occurred in the recent past and impinges on the present (not necessarily in "the second quarter"). The verb tense does not match the verb tense *were expanding* in the *while*-clause, and does not convey simultaneity with the expansion referred to.

The correct answer is B.

SC01470

784. Thomas Mann's novel Doctor Faustus offers <u>an examination not only of how difficult it is to reconcile reason, will, and passion together in any art form, but</u> also a skillfully navigated exploration of the major concerns of modernism.

(A) an examination not only of how difficult it is to reconcile reason, will, and passion together in any art form, but

(B) an examination not only about the difficulty of reconciling reason, will, and passion in any art form, and

(C) not only an examination of how difficult it is to reconcile reason, will, and passion in any art form, and

(D) not only an examination about the difficulty with reconciling reason, will, and passion together in any art form, but

(E) not only an examination of the difficulty of reconciling reason, will, and passion in any art form, but

Grammatical Construction; Idiom

The sentence, in its most correct form, would use the structure *not only ... but also ...* to coordinate parallel references to an "examination" and to an "exploration." However, the given sentence errs in placing the phrase *not only* after the first of the items meant to be coordinated. This impairs the required parallelism and the grammatical structure of the sentence as a whole—as if the "examination" referred to was not only an examination of the difficulty of a certain reconciliation but was also an examination of a skillfully navigated exploration. This does not seem to be the intended meaning, and if it were, the latter *of*, not included, would be required.

A In addition to the structural problem already noted, the word *together* is superfluous because its meaning is already included in *reconcile*.

B The word *examination* should be followed in this context by the preposition *of* rather than by *about*. The coordinate conjunction *and* is unidiomatic, given the earlier occurrence of *not only*.

C The coordinate conjunction *and* is unidiomatic in this context, given the earlier occurrence of *not only*.

D The prepositions *about* and *with* are unidiomatic here (as opposed to *of* in both cases). As noted earlier, *together* is superfluous with *reconcile*.

E **Correct.** The coordination of the parallel reference to an examination and an exploration is successfully executed here using the structure *not only ... but also*.

The correct answer is E.

9.9 Sentence Correction Answer Explanations

SC00981

785. According to a recent study, <u>retirees in the United States are four times more likely to give regular financial aid to their children as</u> to receive it from them.

(A) retirees in the United States are four times more likely to give regular financial aid to their children as

(B) retirees in the United States are four times as likely to give regular financial aid to their children as it is for them

(C) retirees in the United States are four times more likely to give regular financial aid to their children than

(D) it is four times more likely for retirees in the United States to give regular financial aid to their children than they are

(E) it is four times as likely that retirees in the United States will give their children regular financial aid as they are

Diction; Parallelism

The sentence notes a difference, for retirees in the United States, between the likelihood that they will give regular financial aid to their children and the likelihood that they will receive regular financial aid from their children. The elements of the comparison need to be expressed in parallel and in a proper construction.

A This sentence improperly implements the construction *four times more likely to X than to Y*, with *X* corresponding to *give regular financial aid to their children* and *Y* corresponding to *receive it from them*. Instead of the word *than* that would be used in this construction, the sentence improperly uses *as*.

B This sentence, like sentence A, improperly uses *as*. It also lacks parallelism, because *to give regular financial aid to their children* is not parallel to *it is for them to receive it from them*.

C **Correct.** This sentence resolves both of the issues discussed in connection with sentences A and B. In addition to properly using *than* in the construction *four times more likely to X than to Y*, the sentence properly lists in parallel the two elements being compared—*to give regular financial aid to their children* and *to receive it from them*.

D This sentence, in addition to being somewhat more wordy than necessary, lacks parallelism. The phrase *to give regular financial aid to their children* is not parallel to *they are to receive it from them*. The words *they are* in the second phrase are superfluous and make the sentence more difficult to read than necessary, and can simply be removed.

E This sentence is hard to parse and lacks parallelism. It is difficult to see what two phrases represent the elements to be compared and thus what needs to be parallel with what. This makes the sentence difficult to read.

The correct answer is C.

SC04093

786. <u>Discussion of greenhouse effects have usually had as a focus the possibility of Earth growing warmer and to what extent it might,</u> but climatologists have indicated all along that precipitation, storminess, and temperature extremes are likely to have the greatest impact on people.

(A) Discussion of greenhouse effects have usually had as a focus the possibility of Earth growing warmer and to what extent it might,

(B) Discussion of greenhouse effects has usually had as its focus whether Earth would get warmer and what the extent would be,

(C) Discussion of greenhouse effects has usually focused on whether Earth would grow warmer and to what extent,

(D) The discussion of greenhouse effects have usually focused on the possibility of Earth getting warmer and to what extent it might,

(E) The discussion of greenhouse effects has usually focused on whether Earth would grow warmer and the extent that is,

Agreement; Parallelism

The sentence contrasts climatologists' views concerning greenhouse effects with other views that emphasize global warming. The main subject of the sentence is *discussion . . .*, which is singular, so the main verb should be singular. The two things that are said to be the focus of discussion should be in parallel form.

A The plural verb *have . . . had* does not agree with the singular subject *discussion*. The phrases *the possibility . . . warmer* and *to what . . . might* are not parallel.

831

B   The verb form *has had as its focus* is unnecessarily wordy; the noun clauses are parallel in form, but it is not clear what *the extent* refers to.

C   **Correct.** This has correct subject-verb agreement, eliminates the wordiness of the original sentence, and the phrases *whether . . . warmer* and *to what extent* are parallel.

D   The singular subject *discussion* does not agree with the plural verb *have focused*. *The possibility of . . .* is not parallel with *to what extent. . . .*

E   The two phrases following *on* are not in parallel form. What *that* refers to in *the extent that is* is unclear.

The correct answer is C.

787. In the seventh century B.C., the Roman alphabet was adapted from the Etruscan alphabet, which in turn had been adapted in the previous century from a western Greek alphabet, <u>which itself had been adapted earlier</u> in the same century from the Phoenician alphabet.

(A) which itself had been adapted earlier
(B) adapting itself earlier
(C) itself being adapted earlier
(D) having been earlier adapted itself
(E) earlier itself having been adapted

Rhetorical Construction; Verb Form; Logical Predication

This sentence describes a string of adaptations of the alphabet, tracing back from the seventh century BC through two points in the eighth century BC. Because the latest of the three adaptations is temporally located in past tense, earlier adaptations should be located in the past perfect tense.

A   **Correct.** This sentence is properly constructed and uses the appropriate verb forms for the relationships among the events that it describes.

B   It is unclear what the participial phrase *adapting itself earlier . . .* refers to. The present participle could be used for an event that was simultaneous with, or part of, the event mentioned before the underlined portion. However, it is inappropriate for describing an event that took place even earlier than the seventh century BC, which has already been designated in the sentence as past tense. The reflexive form *adapting itself* is nonsensical in this sentence.

C   The present tense of the reflexive participial phrase is inappropriate for describing an event prior to the seventh century BC, given that the seventh century BC has already been designated in the sentence as past tense.

D   Without commas around *itself*, the pronoun appears to be reflexive. The combination of passive and reflexive then makes no sense. If *itself* is intended simply for emphasis, rather than as a reflexive pronoun, it would be preferable, in this context, to set it off with commas. But if it were intended in that way, it would seem to refer to the Roman alphabet, and the claim made in the sentence would be confusing and nearly nonsensical. This modifier is confusingly placed before the designation of time (*in the same century*) and source (*from the Phoenician alphabet*).

E   The adverb *earlier* is misplaced before the pronoun *itself*; it should be immediately before the phrase *in the same century*.

The correct answer is A.

788. The foundation works to strengthen local and regional agricultural markets and <u>cooperating with governments, improving access for farmers for</u> productive resources such as land and credit.

(A) cooperating with governments, improving access for farmers for
(B) cooperates with governments to improve access for farmers to
(C) cooperate with governments for improvements of access for farmers to
(D) cooperate with governments and improve accessibility for farmers for their
(E) in cooperation with governments to improve access for farmers for

Parallelism; Rhetorical Construction

As written, this sentence does not clearly indicate whether *and* is intended to conjoin two things that the foundation does (working to strengthen markets and cooperating with governments) or two things that the foundation works to accomplish (strengthening markets and cooperating with governments). The latter is less plausible because of the redundancy of *works to cooperate*. In the former, the proper verb form, parallel with the present-tense *works*, would be *cooperates*. In the latter, the proper verb form, parallel with the infinitive *to strengthen*, would be *to cooperate* or simply *cooperate*. Only one of the answer choices resolves the uncertainty of meaning in a coherent and well-formed way.

A *Cooperating* is incorrect, since it is not in the same form as either *works* or *to strengthen*.

B **Correct.** This version correctly represents the foundation's two actions by putting the verbs *works* and *cooperates* in parallel form. *Cooperates . . . to improve* is the most concise phrasing to express the purpose of improving access.

C *Cooperate . . . for improvements of access for farmers* is awkwardly phrased and unnecessarily wordy.

D *Cooperate . . . and improve accessibility for farmers* is awkwardly phrased and unnecessarily wordy.

E *In cooperation* destroys the parallelism required by *works to*: there should be a verb following *works to*, not this prepositional phrase.

The correct answer is B.

SC07338

789. A professor at the university has taken a sabbatical to research <u>on James Baldwin's books that Baldwin wrote in France while he was living there</u>.

(A) on James Baldwin's books that Baldwin wrote in France while he was living there

(B) about the books James Baldwin wrote in France

(C) into James Baldwin's books written while in France

(D) on the books of James Baldwin, written while he lived in France

(E) the books James Baldwin wrote while he lived in France

Diction; Rhetorical Construction

The phrasing of this sentence is wordy and redundant: *books that Baldwin wrote in France while he was living there* could more concisely be expressed with *books James Baldwin wrote while he lived in France*. The verb *research* requires a direct object, not a preposition followed by its object.

A *On* incorrectly follows *to research*, and *books that Baldwin wrote in France while he was living there* includes redundant information.

B *About* incorrectly follows *to research*.

C *Into* incorrectly follows *to research*. Given this sentence structure, *while in France* seems to say, illogically, that the books were written while they were in France.

D *On* incorrectly follows *to research*; also, there is no need to make *written while he lived in France* into an independent phrase instead of a relative clause.

E **Correct.** *Research* takes a direct object, which describes the books directly without redundancy.

The correct answer is E.

SC12710.01

790. When working with overseas clients, an understanding of cultural norms is at least as important as grasping the pivotal business issues for the global manager.

(A) When working with overseas clients, an understanding of cultural norms is at least as important as grasping the pivotal business issues for the global manager.

(B) When they work with overseas clients, understanding cultural norms is at least of equivalent importance to grasping the pivotal business issues for the global manager.

(C) For global managers working with overseas clients, understanding cultural norms is at least as important as grasping the pivotal business issues.

(D) For global managers working with overseas clients, an understanding of cultural norms is at least as important to them as grasping the pivotal business issues.

(E) Global managers working with overseas clients find an understanding of cultural norms to be equally important to grasping the pivotal business issues.

Idiom; Rhetorical Construction; Logical Predication

The sentence compares the relative importance of two kinds of understanding that are important for global managers working with overseas clients: understanding of cultural norms and grasping the pivotal business issues. The sentence and its variants seem intended to assert that the first is at least as important as the second. The idiomatic usage *as important as* is the most effective way to make the comparison, but some of the variants do not make it in this way. In the given sentence, the initial phrase *when ... clients*, by virtue of its position, should modify the main subject of the sentence, *an understanding of cultural norms*, but that reading is untenable and results in a logical-predication error. The adverbial modifier *for the global manager* is not well placed to make clear that it modifies the adjective *important*.

A   This version fails for the reasons already explained: misleading placement of the initial phrase, and misleading placement of an adverbial modifier.

B   The pronoun *they* should refer forward to a plural noun or pronoun but does not do so here. To make a comparison, the awkward phrase *of equivalent importance to* is used instead of the more idiomatic *as important as*. The modifying phrase *for the global manager* fails to show clearly what it is intended to modify.

C   **Correct.** The initial adverbial phrase *for global ... clients* signals clearly that it modifies the adjective *important*. The comparison is made clearly and idiomatically.

D   The phrase *to them* is redundant with *for global managers*. The phrase *an understanding of cultural norms* is not parallel with the verbal-noun construction *grasping the pivotal business issues*.

E   The wording used to express the comparison is awkward and unidiomatic. The phrase *an understanding of cultural norms* is not parallel with the verbal-noun construction *grasping the pivotal business issues*. Also, preferable to *equally important to* would be *as important as*.

The correct answer is C.

---

791. Often major economic shifts are <u>so gradual as to be indistinguishable</u> at first from ordinary fluctuations in the financial markets.

(A) so gradual as to be indistinguishable
(B) so gradual they can be indistinguishable
(C) so gradual that they are unable to be distinguished
(D) gradual enough not to be distinguishable
(E) gradual enough so that one cannot distinguish them

Idiom; Rhetorical Construction

The idiom *so ... as to ...* is correctly used as a predicate of the subject in the given sentence. None of the variants offered uses the idiom correctly, and some of them have rhetorical issues such as redundancy or awkwardness.

A   **Correct.** The underlined portion is an example of correct use of the idiom mentioned above. The sentence contains no other errors.

B   Based on the given sentence, which is correct, the word *can* is redundant here, given the ending *-able* of *indistinguishable*. The intended sense could be conveyed by *so gradual that they are indistinguishable*—even though this would not be a use of the idiom mentioned above.

C   This contains awkward verbiage in the phrase *are unable to*. The intended sense would be better conveyed by *cannot*—even though this would not be a use of the idiom mentioned above.

D   This is unnecessarily awkward, and the use of *enough* often carries the nuance that the sufficiency is of something desirable—which seems not to be so in this context. The idiomatic use above would be better.

E   This is wordy and unnecessarily awkward. As explained, the use of *enough* is inappropriate in the context, and use of the idiom explained above would be much better.

The correct answer is A.

792. Researchers now regard interferon <u>as not a single substance, but it is rather a biological family of complex molecules that play</u> an important, though not entirely defined, role in the immune system.

(A) as not a single substance, but it is rather a biological family of complex molecules that play

(B) as not a single substance but as a biological family of complex molecules playing

(C) not as a single substance but as a biological family of complex molecules that play

(D) not to be a single substance but rather a biological family of complex molecules playing

(E) not as a single substance but instead as being a biological family of complex molecules that play

Parallelism; Rhetorical Construction

This sentence draws a contrast between how interferon is and is not regarded by researchers. However, the two parts of the contrast are not expressed in parallel form since the first is a prepositional phrase (*as not a single substance*), and the second is a clause (*it is rather a biological family*). Furthermore, the wording *regard interferon as not* is awkward and confusing. For clarity and proper parallelism, the contrast should be constructed using the expression *not as X but as Y*, where *X* and *Y* are both noun phrases.

A The contrast is not expressed using parallel grammatical structure, and *regard interferon as not* is awkward and confusing.

B The wording *regard interferon as not* is awkward and confusing and violates proper parallelism.

C **Correct.** The contrast is expressed using the parallel structure *not as a single substance but as a biological family*.

D The main defect here is that *regard interferon not to be a single substance* is unidiomatic; *regard . . . as . . .* is the correct form; and completing the parallelism correctly would require the repetition of *as*, in the phrase *but rather as . . .*

E The contrast is not expressed using parallel grammatical structure since *a single substance* is a noun phrase, while *being a biological family* is a participial phrase; omitting the unnecessary words *being* and *instead* would improve the sentence.

The correct answer is C.

793. <u>The remarkable similarity of Thule artifacts throughout a vast region can, in part, be explained as</u> a very rapid movement of people from one end of North America to the other.

(A) The remarkable similarity of Thule artifacts throughout a vast region can, in part, be explained as

(B) Thule artifacts being remarkably similar throughout a vast region, one explanation is

(C) That Thule artifacts are remarkably similar throughout a vast region is, in part, explainable as

(D) One explanation for the remarkable similarity of Thule artifacts throughout a vast region is that there was

(E) Throughout a vast region Thule artifacts are remarkably similar, with one explanation for this being

Logical Predication; Grammatical Construction; Rhetorical Construction

The intended meaning of the sentence is that the rapid movement of people across North America is one explanation of the *similarity of Thule artifacts throughout a vast region*. As worded, however, the sentence is illogical: The sentence indicates that the similarity in artifacts was a rapid movement of people, which makes no sense. Instead of equating similarity with movement, the sentence needs to identify this movement of people as a cause of similarity among artifacts.

A As worded, this version of the sentence makes the illogical statement that the similarity among artifacts is explainable *as a very rapid movement*. It should specify that the similarity of artifacts may be a consequence of the rapid population movement.

B This version of the sentence is syntactically awkward, and leaves unclear what the main subject, *one explanation*, is supposed to be an explanation of.

C Like (A), this version of the sentence equates the similarity of artifacts with the movement of people, when a causal connection is what is intended.

D **Correct.** This version adequately expresses the intended causal connection.

E   This version is awkward, introducing the causal connection with the unnecessarily wordy and indirect string of prepositional phrases, *with one explanation for this....*

The correct answer is D.

SC12841.01

794. Regulators are likely to end what are, in effect, long-standing exemptions permitting pilots of small turboprop aircraft at small carriers to fly <u>as much as 20 percent more hours per month than pilots at larger airlines fly, with the consequence that</u> some carriers could be forced to hire additional pilots.

(A) as much as 20 percent more hours per month than pilots at larger airlines fly, with the consequence that

(B) as many as 20 percent more hours per month as pilots at larger airlines, and

(C) more hours per month, as much as 20 percent, than pilots at larger airlines; consequently

(D) as much as 20 percent more hours per month as larger airlines' pilots, so

(E) as many as 20 percent more hours per month than pilots at larger airlines do, and consequently

Grammatical Construction; Diction

The sentence is meant to convey that an exemption to maximum flying-time regulations for pilots at smaller airlines may soon be ended and that this will entail that such airlines will have to hire more pilots. The most significant error in the given sentence is in the final clause, which seems to indicate that pilots' flying as many as 20 percent more hours per month could result in carriers having to hire additional pilots. This "consequence" is wrongly assigned to the extra flying time rather than to the (probable) ending of the exemption—a logical predication error. A second significant error, a diction error, in some of the variants is the use of *as* in a context where *than* is required to express a comparison. A usage that is preferable to *as much as*, given that the noun it modifies is plural, is *as many as*.

A   This version fails because of the errors identified above.

B   The comparison of flying times here is erroneously expressed by the third occurrence of *as* where *than* is required. The verb *do* should be inserted immediately following *airlines* to complete the clause. Also, the idea of consequence present in the given sentence is not conveyed by using *and* without some such word as *consequently*.

C   Inserting the percentage as a parenthesis fails to indicate clearly that what is intended is 20 percent more hours than the flying time of pilots at larger airlines.

D   The comparison of flying times here is erroneously expressed by the third occurrence of *as*, where *than* is required. The verb *do* should be inserted immediately following *airlines* to complete the clause.

E   **Correct.** None of the errors identified in the given sentence is present here. The consequence referred to is correctly assigned to the possible ending of the exemption. The comparison between the maximum flying times for the two classes of pilots is correctly expressed using *than*.

The correct answer is E.

SC24751.01

795. Self-compassion is made up of mindfulness, the ability to manage thoughts and emotions without being carried <u>away or repressing them, common humanity, or empathy with the suffering of others,</u> and self-kindness, a recognition of your own suffering and a commitment to solving the problem.

(A) away or repressing them, common humanity, or empathy with the suffering of others,

(B) away, or repression of them, and common humanity, or empathy with the suffering of others,

(C) away or repressing them, common humanity, empathy with the suffering of others;

(D) away or repressing them; common humanity, an empathy with the suffering of others;

(E) away or repress them; common humanity, to empathize with the suffering of others

Parallelism; Grammatical Construction

This sentence seems meant to present a list of three elements that make up self-compassion: mindfulness, common humanity, and self-kindness. However, the sentence is not well formed, especially with respect to punctuation. Also, the use of the conjunction *or* is haphazard and its function unclear. The description of each of the three elements is complex, comprising a noun that names the element, followed by a noun phrase that gives a definition of that noun. For clarity, the sentence should be structured in a way that highlights the parallelism among the three elements. Because of the complexity and length of the description of each element, the sentence would be made clearest by separating the descriptions of the elements with semicolons.

A   The second occurrence of *or* could function to introduce a definition of a term but its use here is confusing and nonparallel with its first occurrence. The lack of appropriate punctuation creates a reading difficulty.

B   The first occurrence of *or* is meant to coordinate two items, but the naming of the items impairs the formal parallelism that should be present; *being carried away*, a verbal noun, is nonparallel with *repression*, which is a noun but not a verbal noun. As indicated above, the function of the second occurrence of *or* is not clear: for example, does it introduce a definition of *common humanity*? If so, the description of the second element in the series is nonparallel with the descriptions of the other two elements.

C   The effect of the final semicolon here is to coalesce, in a very confusing way, the descriptions of the first two elements; to avoid this, a semicolon should also immediately precede *common humanity*.

D   **Correct.** This version produces a sentence in which each of the descriptions of the three elements of self-compassion is set off with a semicolon and clearly distinguished from the others in a way that makes salient the parallelism among the three descriptions and facilitates the reader in understanding the sentence.

E   The punctuation here is confusing: the first semicolon is not matched by a semicolon immediately after *others*. The verb *repress* is nonparallel with the verbal noun *being carried away*.

The correct answer is D.

SC83751.01

796. According to the laws of this nation, individuals are minors until they reach the age of eighteen, <u>although this is less in some countries and more in others</u>.

(A) although this is less in some countries and more in others

(B) but this age is lower in some countries; higher in others

(C) although in some countries, it is lower and in others it is higher

(D) although it is less than that in some countries and more than that in others

(E) but the relevant age is lower in some countries and higher in others

Logical Predication; Diction

What the pronoun *this* refers to in the underlined clause is unclear. Could it be the age of majority? No, because this is not mentioned in the preceding context. Could it be *the age of eighteen*? No, because it makes no sense to say the age of eighteen is *less in some countries* (this would be a logical predication error). If *lower* were substituted for *less,* but no other change was made, the sentence would not be any better—even if, in general, the adjective *lower* is a more appropriate modifier with *age* than is *less*.

A   As explained, this version fails because of a logical predication error and a diction error.

B   This version also contains a logical predication error. The semicolon, rather than a comma or a coordinating conjunction *and*, is inappropriate: it turns *higher in others* into a mere sentence fragment.

C   The context fails to provide an antecedent that makes sense for the pronoun *it*; if *the age of eighteen* were the antecedent, there would be a logical predication error. The comma after *countries* is unnecessary and confusing.

D   Again, as explained, the reference of the pronoun *it* is unclear. The predicates *less than that* and *more than that* create a logical predication error if they are predicates of *the age of eighteen*.

E **Correct.** The phrase *the relevant age* clearly refers to the age at which minors reach the age of majority. The sentence indicates that in some countries that age is lower than eighteen and in some others higher.

The correct answer is E.

SC32261.01

797. Rather than ignore a company that seems about to fail, investment analysts should recognize that its reorganization and recent uptick in revenue, combined with its dynamic new leadership, indicate that the firm's prospects must be taken seriously.

    (A) Rather than ignore a company that seems about to fail,
    (B) Rather than ignoring a company that is about to seemingly fail,
    (C) Instead of a company that is seemingly about to fail being ignored,
    (D) Instead of ignore a company that seems about to fail,
    (E) In place of ignoring a company's imminent failure seemingly about to occur,

Diction; Verb Form; Parallelism

The underlined phrase raises two main issues: Is *rather than* the appropriate way of introducing the modifying underlined phrase? Is the verb form *ignore* correct? The phrases *instead of* and *in place of* both function as prepositions and must therefore be followed, even if not immediately, by a word or phrase that functions as a noun or pronoun (this could include verbal nouns, ending in *-ing*). The phrase *rather than* indicates a comparison or contrast. (However, *rather than* can function as a preposition in some contexts.)

A **Correct.** *Rather than* does not function as a preposition here. Its function is to coordinate two verbs, in parallel form, that indicate actions compared in the sentence (some have called *rather than* in this function a "quasi-conjunction").

B The phrase *rather than ignoring* is correct and accepted in some usages, where *rather than* functions prepositionally, as here. But B is incorrect because the phrase *about to seemingly fail* does not coherently capture the intended idea. To see this, notice that the idea to be conveyed is that actual failure seems about to occur, not that the appearance of failure is about to occur.

C The passive verb form is quite unnecessary and produces an unnecessarily awkward phrase that is also incorrect in another way: the complex noun phrase *instead of ... being ignored* is mistakenly placed in parallel with *investment analysts*.

D *Instead of* normally functions as a preposition and can govern only a word or phrase that functions as a noun or pronoun, not a finite verb form (a verb form that is neither a verbal noun nor an infinitive) such as *ignore*.

E *In place of* is a preposition that can do the same work as *instead of* in some contexts but is somewhat awkward here. In the noun phrase *a company's imminent failure seemingly about to occur*, the adjectival phrase *seemingly about to occur* is redundant with the adjective *imminent*.

The correct answer is A.

SC01490

798. Between 14,000 and 8,000 B.C. the ice cap that covered northern Asia, Europe, and America began to melt, uncovering vast new areas that were to be occupied by migrating peoples moving northward.

    (A) began to melt, uncovering vast new areas that were to be occupied
    (B) began melting, to uncover vast new areas to be occupied
    (C) began, by melting, to uncover vast new areas for occupation
    (D) began, after melting, uncovering vast new areas which are to be occupied
    (E) would begin to uncover, through melting, vast new areas for occupation

Verb Form; Logical Predication

The sentence explains what happened when an ice cap *began to melt*. The participial phrase *uncovering vast new areas* succinctly describes the immediate effects of the melting. The verb form *were to be occupied* is used to indicate that occupation would take place at a time in the future from the time of the melting.

A **Correct.** The sentence succinctly expresses immediate and future effects of the melting of an ice cap.

B The infinitive *to uncover* incorrectly implies that the ice cap melted for the purpose of uncovering new areas.

C Since *melting* is what caused new areas to be uncovered, that word should be part of the main verb, not placed in the nonrestrictive prepositional phrase *by melting*.

D It does not make sense to say that the ice cap *began . . . uncovering* new areas *after* it had melted—since the ice cap no longer existed in the areas where it had melted.

E Since *melting* is what caused new areas to be uncovered, that word should be part of the main verb, not placed in the nonrestrictive prepositional phrase *through melting*.

The correct answer is A.

SC01472

799. Bengal-born writer, philosopher, and educator Rabindranath Tagore had the greatest admiration <u>for Mohandas K. Gandhi the person and also as a politician, but Tagore had been</u> skeptical of Gandhi's form of nationalism and his conservative opinions about India's cultural traditions.

(A) for Mohandas K. Gandhi the person and also as a politician, but Tagore had been

(B) for Mohandas K. Gandhi as a person and as a politician, but Tagore was also

(C) for Mohandas K. Gandhi not only as a person and as a politician, but Tagore was also

(D) of Mohandas K. Gandhi as a person and as also a politician, but Tagore was

(E) of Mohandas K. Gandhi not only as a person and as a politician, but Tagore had also been

Rhetorical Construction; Parallelism

This sentence describes the writer and philosopher Tagore's two types of feelings for Gandhi. The underlined part of the sentence has to express correctly the time line of these two feelings (they happened simultaneously). The underlined part also has to express the correct relationship between the complements of admiration and skepticism.

A To maintain parallelism, it is important for two conjoined phrases to be of the same grammatical type. Thus, it is appropriate to conjoin *Gandhi the person and the politician,* or *Gandhi as a person and as a politician,* but it is nonstandard in English to mix and match. In addition, the use of the past perfect tense *had been* places the skepticism earlier on the time line than the admiration, which is misleading.

B **Correct.** This version correctly conjoins two parallel phrases, *Gandhi as a person and as a politician,* and, in using two simple past tenses to introduce the two emotions, marks them as holding at the same time.

C The phrase *not only X but also Y* matches the meaning of this sentence: Tagore had not only admiration but also skepticism. However *not only* has to precede *admiration* for this rhetorical construction to be parallel.

D The noun *admiration* as it is positioned in this sentence should take the preposition *for,* not *of,* since it refers to a person. The adverb *also* is redundant because it expresses the same meaning as the conjunction *and.*

E As in (D), the noun *admiration* should take the preposition *for.* As in (C), the rhetorical structure of *not only X but also Y* is violated. Finally, the use of the past perfect tense *had been* is misleading with respect to the time line.

The correct answer is B.

SC04704

800. Traffic safety officials predict that drivers will be <u>equally likely to exceed the proposed speed limit as</u> the current one.

(A) equally likely to exceed the proposed speed limit as

(B) equally likely to exceed the proposed speed limit as they are

(C) equally likely that they will exceed the proposed speed limit as.

(D) as likely that they will exceed the proposed speed limit as

(E) as likely to exceed the proposed speed limit as they are

839

Idiom; Parallelism

This sentence reports on a prediction that compares the likelihood of drivers exceeding a proposed new speed limit with the likelihood of drivers exceeding the current speed limit. The idiom *as x as y*, rather than the incorrect form *equally . . . as*, should be used to express the comparison.

A   *Equally likely . . . as* is not an idiomatic form of comparison.

B   This also offers a nonidiomatic form of comparison.

C   The comparison is expressed nonidiomatically. Also, *the drivers will be equally likely* should be followed by *to exceed* rather than by *that they will exceed*. The resulting sentence is wordy and structurally flawed.

D   The resulting sentence is wordy and structurally flawed. The idiomatic phrase *as x as y* is somewhat in use, but *as likely that they* is awkward, and the comparison is unclear and not parallel.

E   **Correct.** The idiomatic phrase *as x as y* is properly used, and the comparison is clear and parallel.

The correct answer is E.

SC04562

801. Written early in the French Revolution, Mary Wollstonecraft's *A Vindication of the Rights of Man* (1790) and *A Vindication of the Rights of Woman* (1792) attributed Europe's social and political ills to be the result of the dominance of aristocratic values and patriarchal hereditary privilege.

   (A)   Mary Wollstonecraft's *A Vindication of the Rights of Man* (1790) and *A Vindication of the Rights of Woman* (1792) attributed Europe's social and political ills to be the result of

   (B)   Mary Wollstonecraft's *A Vindication of the Rights of Man* (1790) and *A Vindication of the Rights of Woman* (1792) attributed Europe's social and political ills to result from

   (C)   Mary Wollstonecraft's *A Vindication of the Rights of Man* (1790) and *A Vindication of the Rights of Woman* (1792) attributed Europe's social and political ills to

   (D)   in *A Vindication of the Rights of Man* (1790) and *A Vindication of the Rights of Woman* (1792), Mary Wollstonecraft attributed Europe's social and political ills to have been the result of

   (E)   Mary Wollstonecraft, in *A Vindication of the Rights of Man* (1790) and *A Vindication of the Rights of Woman* (1792), attributed Europe's social and political ills to

Logical Predication; Idiom

The phrase at the beginning needs a subject for *written*; most logically here it would be the books mentioned written by Mary Wollstonecraft; any other main-clause subject is therefore incorrect. The verb *attribute* idiomatically requires the preposition *to* followed by a noun phrase, not the infinitive marker *to* followed by a verb.

A   The main subject is correctly predicated of *written*, but *attribute* is incorrectly followed by the infinitive *to* plus a verb (*be*).

B   The main subject is correctly predicated of *written*, but *attribute* is incorrectly followed by the infinitive *to* plus a verb (*result*).

C   **Correct.** The main subject is correctly predicated of *written*, and *attribute* is correctly followed by the preposition *to*.

D   The subject of the main clause is *Mary Wollstonecraft*, and so this phrase is illogically forced to be taken as the subject of *written*. Also, *attribute* is incorrectly followed by *to* plus a verb (*have been*).

E   The subject of the main clause is *Mary Wollstonecraft*, and so this phrase is illogically forced to be taken as the subject of *written*.

The correct answer is C.

SC01498

802. Using study groups managed by the principal popular organizations and political parties, the Swedish public was informed by the government about energy and nuclear power.

   (A)   the Swedish public was informed by the government about energy and nuclear power

   (B)   the government informed the Swedish public about energy and nuclear power

   (C)   energy and nuclear power information was given to the Swedish public by the government

(D) information about energy and nuclear power was given to the Swedish public by the government

(E) the public of Sweden was given energy and nuclear power information by the government

Logical Predication; Rhetorical Construction

This sentence tries to describe a situation in which the government used study groups to inform the Swedish public. Therefore, it is incorrect to use *the Swedish public* as the subject of *inform* in this sentence, because doing so in this case illogically makes *the Swedish public* the subject of *using* as well. Additionally, *inform* is a more concise and direct way to express the idea in *give information*.

A   Using *the Swedish public* as the subject of the main clause incorrectly makes it the subject of *using* as well.

B   Correct. Using *the government* as the main subject correctly allows it to count as the subject of using; *inform* is a concise phrasing for the main action of the sentence.

C   Energy and nuclear power information does not work as the subject of the main clause, since this also, illogically, makes it the subject of *using*. Also, this phrase delays the reader's understanding of the important noun *information* (a clearer phrasing is *information about energy and nuclear power*) and employs *give information* rather than the more concise *inform*.

D   *Energy and nuclear power information* does not work as the main clause subject, since this also, illogically, makes it the subject of *using*. In addition, this version awkwardly uses *give information to* instead of the more concise *inform*.

E   *The public of Sweden* is awkward compared to *the Swedish public*, and in any case is illogically taken as the subject of using; *given . . . information* could be phrased more concisely with *inform*.

The correct answer is B.

803. The use of the bar code, or Universal Product Code, which was created in part to enable supermarkets to process customers at a faster rate, has expanded beyond supermarkets to other retail outlets and <u>have become readily accepted despite some initial opposition when it was first introduced in 1974</u>.

(A) have become readily accepted despite some initial opposition when it was first introduced in 1974

(B) has become readily accepted despite some initial opposition when they were first introduced in 1974

(C) have become readily accepted despite some initial opposition when first introduced in 1974

(D) has become readily accepted despite some initial opposition when the bar code was first introduced in 1974

(E) bar codes have become readily accepted despite some initial opposition when it was first introduced in 1974

Agreement; Rhetorical Construction

The subject of this sentence is *the use of the bar code*, the main noun of which is the singular *use*; thus, the corresponding main verb should be in the singular form *has*, not the plural *have*. The actual subject for this verb is merely understood, but when it is present, any pronoun that refers back to it must agree with it in number.

A   The verb form *have* does not agree with the sentence's subject. The referent of *it* is potentially unclear.

B   *Has* is correct; however, the rest of its clause is badly worded, because its subject *they* does not clearly refer back to the singular *Universal Product Code* (or *bar code*); a better choice is *it*.

C   The plural *have* does not agree with the singular subject *use*.

D   Correct. The verb is in the correct form *has*, and using *bar code* as the last clause's subject avoids an agreement problem.

E   Restating the subject as the plural *bar codes* allows the following verb to be *have*, but it is then incorrect to use *it* later in the sentence, since *it* does not agree in number with *bar codes*.

The correct answer is D.

804. Normally a bone becomes fossilized through the action of groundwater, which permeates the bone, washes away its organic components, and replaces them with minerals.

(A) which permeates the bone, washes away its organic components, and replaces them
(B) which permeates the bone, washes away its organic components, and those are replaced
(C) which permeates the bone, washing away its organic components, to be replaced
(D) permeating the bone, washing away its organic components, to be replaced
(E) permeating the bone, washing away its organic components and replacing them

Logical Predication; Grammatical Construction

The sentence explains the process by which groundwater produces fossilization of bones. The grammatically correct sentence describes a series of three stages in the process.

A **Correct.** Three parallel verbal phrases—*permeates ..., washes ..., and replaces ...*—are correctly coordinated within a relative clause that has *which* as its subject referring to *groundwater*.

B The third component of the series, *and those are replaced*, is nonparallel, and therefore incorrect. This renders the sentence ungrammatical.

C This lacks the appropriate parallelism; based on structure, the phrase *to be replaced ...* should modify *which*, a relative pronoun referring to *groundwater*. But this would not express the thought intended in the given sentence, which indicates that organic components are replaced.

D The participles *permeating* and *washing away* should, based on structure, have the subject of the sentence, *a bone*, as their implicit subject. But this produces nonsense. It is unclear what the phrase *to be replaced* modifies: based on the intended meaning, it should be *its organic components*, but the structure does not indicate this, given that the subject of the sentence is *a bone*.

E The three participles *permeating, washing away*, and *replacing* have the subject of the sentence (*a bone*) as their implicit subject. This produces nonsense. Also, any three-element series must have a comma immediately following each of its first two elements.

The correct answer is A.

805. The Organization of Petroleum Exporting Countries (OPEC) had long been expected to announce a reduction in output to bolster sagging oil prices, but officials of the organization just recently announced that the group will pare daily production by 1.5 million barrels by the beginning of next year, but only if non-OPEC nations, including Norway, Mexico, and Russia, were to trim output by a total of 500,000 barrels a day.

(A) year, but only if non-OPEC nations, including Norway, Mexico, and Russia, were to trim output
(B) year, but only if the output of non-OPEC nations, which includes Norway, Mexico, and Russia, is trimmed
(C) year only if the output of non-OPEC nations, including Norway, Mexico, and Russia, would be trimmed
(D) year only if non-OPEC nations, which includes Norway, Mexico, and Russia, were trimming output
(E) year only if non-OPEC nations, including Norway, Mexico, and Russia, trim output

Rhetorical Construction; Logical Predication

The underlined part of this sentence deals with the conditions under which OPEC members will lower their own oil production by 1.5 million barrels by the beginning of next year. The important thing to notice here is the following logical relation: *X will do something only if Y does something else.*

A This version has redundant words, *were to* in front of *trim*, that do not add anything more in meaning. Furthermore, *were to trim* is not the proper verb form to accompany *will pare*. The addition of *but* before *only* is also redundant.

B This version uses the passive construction in the conditional clause *only if the output ... is trimmed*. This use of the passive voice makes this sentence vague; it is now unclear who needs to trim the output of non-OPEC nations. Finally, the addition of *but* before *only* is redundant.

C   As in (B), this version also introduces vagueness by using the passive construction. In addition, *would* in front of the passive verb *be trimmed* is redundant.

D   This version uses an active verb, but in the past progressive form, *were trimming*. The progressive tense denotes actions in progress, so its use is not normally warranted in conditional sentences such as this one.

E   **Correct.** This version uses the correct and most concise conditional structure, without redundancies.

The correct answer is E.

SC01507

806. Over the past ten years cultivated sunflowers have become a major commercial crop, second only to soybeans as a source of vegetable oil.

(A) second only to soybeans as a source of vegetable oil

(B) second in importance to soybeans only as a source of vegetable oil

(C) being second in importance only to soybeans as a source of vegetable oil

(D) which, as a source of vegetable oil, is only second to soybeans

(E) as a source of vegetable oil only second to soybeans

Rhetorical Construction; Idiom

The sentence makes the point that cultivated sunflowers are the second largest source of vegetable oil, soybeans alone being larger. Where *only* is placed in the sentence greatly affects the sense.

A   **Correct.** The placement of *only* allows the sentence to correctly express the thought that cultivated sunflowers rank second as a source of vegetable oil, with soybeans alone ranking first.

B   The placement of *only* creates an ambiguity: does it modify *soybeans* or the phrase *as a source of vegetable oil*? In the latter case, the sense would be that being a source of vegetable oil is the only respect in which soybeans are more important than sunflower seeds. However, this does not seem to be the intended sense of the given sentence. The phrase *in importance* is unnecessary and would make the sentence wordy.

C   The word *being* and the phrase *in importance* are unnecessary and make the sentence wordy.

D   The phrase *only second to soybeans* appears to minimize the importance, initially suggested, of sunflowers' being second to soybeans as a source of vegetable oil.

E   The word *only* is misplaced, given the intended sense, and it is unclear whether it modifies the phrase *as a source of vegetable oil*, or the phrase *second to soybeans*. In either case it fails to capture the sense of the given sentence.

The correct answer is A.

SC00985

807. Not trusting themselves to choose wisely among the wide array of investment opportunities on the market, stockbrokers are helping many people who turn to them to buy stocks that could be easily bought directly.

(A) stockbrokers are helping many people who turn to them to buy stocks that could be easily

(B) stockbrokers are helping many people who are turning to them for help in buying stocks that they could easily have

(C) many people are turning to stockbrokers for help from them to buy stocks that could be easily

(D) many people are turning to stockbrokers for help to buy stocks that easily could have been

(E) many people are turning to stockbrokers for help in buying stocks that could easily be

Logical Predication; Grammatical Construction; Verb Form

This sentence is intended to be about people who, because they do not trust themselves to make wise investment decisions, turn to stockbrokers for advice. As the sentence is worded, however, it is stockbrokers who do not trust themselves to choose wisely. The sentence is made even more incomprehensible by the peculiar placement of the adverbs in the phrase, *could be easily bought directly*.

A This version of the sentence incorrectly identifies the subject described by the opening modifier as *stockbrokers*; the adverb *easily* is misplaced in the phrase *could be easily bought*.

B As in (A), the opening clause illogically modifies *stockbrokers* rather than *many people*. The tense of the verb phrase *could easily have bought* does not match the tense of *are helping* earlier in the main clause.

C Although the opening modifier is correctly attached to *people* rather than *stockbrokers*, the sentence is unnecessarily wordy (*for help from them*).

D *To buy* is not idiomatic in this context—*in buying* would be correct—and the tense of the verb *could have been* does not match the tense of the verb earlier in the clause; the point is not that people are turning to stockbrokers for help in buying stocks that at some earlier time could have been bought directly, but rather that the stocks could be bought by the people directly at the very time they are seeking help from the stockbrokers.

E **Correct.** The opening clause correctly modifies *many people*, and the adverb is correctly placed.

The correct answer is E.

SC01007

808. In the 1940s popular magazines in the United States began to report on the private lives of persons from the entertainment industry, <u>in despite of the fact that they previously had featured individuals</u> in business and politics.

(A) in despite of the fact that they previously had featured individuals

(B) in spite of the fact previously that these publications featured articles on those

(C) whereas previously there were those individuals featured in articles

(D) whereas previously those individuals they featured were

(E) whereas previously these publications had featured articles on individuals

Idiom; Parallelism; Logical Predication

The sentence compares the reporting by popular magazines in the 1940s to the reporting by these magazines before the 1940s. Whereas previously the publications featured articles on people in business and politics, in the 1940s the magazines began to report on the private lives of persons in the entertainment industry. The two elements being compared should be described clearly and in a parallel fashion.

A This sentence appears to misuse the *in spite of* idiom by using *despite* instead of *spite*. The use of *despite* is incorrect. Furthermore, although we can discern what the pronoun *they* is meant to refer to, the sentence would be easier to read if *these publications* were used in place of *they*.

B The word *previously*, which is misplaced in this sentence, should be between *publications* and *featured*, and perhaps preceded with *had*. The wording of the relevant portion of the sentence would thus be *fact that these publications had previously featured*. Furthermore, although we can discern what (or who) *those in business and politics* is meant to refer to, more specific wording would have made this phrase in the sentence easier to read. For example, we could substitute *individuals* for *those*.

C In this sentence, the phrase, *there were those individuals featured in articles in business and politics* is an assertion that individuals thus featured existed. Although we can guess that the writer would have meant to indicate that it was the magazines that were doing the featuring, the sentence fails to make this point clear. The sentence thus lacks clarity.

D This sentence may present an improvement over sentences A, B, and C. However, the sentence would be more readable if the phrase *those individuals they featured* was made parallel with the corresponding portion of the other element of the comparison. For example, *they featured those individuals* would be parallel with *popular magazines ... began to report on the private lives of persons ...* It would also help if *they* were replaced with a more specific term such as *the magazines*.

E **Correct.** This sentence is clear and relatively easy to read.

The correct answer is E.

809. In the early part of the twentieth century, many vacationers found that driving automobiles and sleeping in tents allowed them to enjoy nature close at hand and tour at their own pace, with none of the restrictions of passenger trains and railroad timetables or with the formalities, expenses, and impersonality of hotels.

(A) with none of the restrictions of passenger trains and railroad timetables or with the

(B) with none of the restrictions of passenger trains, railroad timetables, nor

(C) without the restrictions of passenger trains and railroad timetables nor

(D) without the restrictions of passenger trains and railroad timetables or with the

(E) without the restrictions of passenger trains and railroad timetables or the

Rhetorical Construction; Diction

The sentence lays out some advantages that car travel and tent camping were perceived to offer over rail travel. The sentence attempts to describe these advantages in terms of the absence of any of a series of annoyances accompanying rail travel. But the sentence fails because of the mismatch between *with none of...* and *or with....* One way to successfully convey the intended meaning is to use the preposition *without* governing all the items in the series, expressed as nouns or noun phrases.

A By using *none of...* to introduce the first drawback of rail travel, and *or* to introduce the rest of them, this sentence suggests that the presence of drawbacks on the final list is an alternative to the absence of *restrictions*.

B *With none...nor...* is nonidiomatic (as opposed to *neither...nor...*).

C The structure *without...nor...* in the way used here is nonidiomatic. The negative *without* governs the whole list of drawbacks at the end of the sentence.

D The coupling of *without* and *or with* is confusing, suggesting, as in (A), that the drawbacks on the final list are an alternative to the absence of *restrictions*.

E **Correct.** The sentence is unambiguous and constructed in a way that *without* clearly distributes over all the items in the series.

The correct answer is E.

810. Over the next few years, increasing demands on the Chattahoochee River, which flows into the Apalachicola River, could alter the saline content of Apalachicola Bay, which would rob the oysters there of their flavor, and to make them decrease in size, less distinctive, and less in demand.

(A) which would rob the oysters there of their flavor, and to make them decrease in size,

(B) and it would rob the oysters there of their flavor, make them smaller,

(C) and rob the oysters there of their flavor, making them decrease in size,

(D) robbing the oysters there of their flavor and making them smaller,

(E) robbing the oysters there of their flavor, and making them decrease in size,

Category

The sentence claims that demands for river water may change the saline content of the bay, possibly altering the flavor and size of oysters there and diminishing the oysters' marketability. The sentence is not parallel. It should read *which would rob the oysters...and make them decrease* to be parallel and grammatical. The series of three phrases after *make them* that describes what will happen to the oysters also needs to be parallel.

A The referent of the relative pronoun, *which*, is ambiguous; the two effects of altered saline content are not expressed in parallel form, with a relative clause expressing the first effect, and an infinitive phrase expressing the second.

B The referent of the pronoun *it* is ambiguous. Also, the effects of the bay's altered saline content are not expressed in parallel form—the first being an independent clause and the second a verb phrase.

C The comma before the conjunction *and* signals that an independent clause will follow *and*, but a verb phrase follows instead. The series of phrases following *making them* lacks appropriate parallelism.

D **Correct.** The potential effects on the oysters are expressed by two parallel participial phrases, the second of which lists three adjectives correctly in a series.

E The series of phrases following *making them* lacks appropriate parallelism.

The correct answer is D.

811. Elizabeth Barber, the author of both *Prehistoric Textiles*, a comprehensive work on cloth in the early cultures of the Mediterranean, and <u>also of *Women's Work*, a more general account of early cloth manufacture, is an expert authority on</u> textiles in ancient societies.

    (A) also of *Women's Work*, a more general account of early cloth manufacture, is an expert authority on

    (B) also *Women's Work*, a more general account of cloth manufacture, is an expert authority about

    (C) of *Women's Work*, a more general account about early cloth manufacture, is an authority on

    (D) of *Women's Work*, a more general account about early cloth manufacture, is an expert authority about

    (E) *Women's Work*, a more general account of early cloth manufacture, is an authority on

Rhetorical Construction; Idiom; Parallelism

Using a lot of parenthetical elements, this sentence communicates the main idea that Elizabeth Barber is an authority on textiles in ancient societies. It is the main rhetorical goal of the sentence to position the parenthetical elements so that they do not obscure the main idea. The parenthetical descriptions need to be streamlined enough to be informative, but not too long. In addition, several versions repeat *of* before the title *Women's Work* and doing so makes the sentence unparallel; the first *of* comes before *both* and so should distribute over both clauses.

A The use of *also of* before *Women's Work* is redundant and unparallel. It is sufficient to connect the two book titles like this: *both X and Y*. The meanings of the two nouns *expert* and *authority* largely overlap, so there is no need to modify one with the other.

B The use of *also* before *Women's Work* is redundant. It is sufficient to connect the two book titles like this: *both X and Y*. The meanings of the two nouns *expert* and *authority* largely overlap, so there is no need to modify one with the other. Finally, the noun *authority* takes the preposition *on*, not *about*.

C As in (A), repeating the preposition *of* before *Women's Work* makes the sentence unparallel. The noun *account* takes the preposition *of*, not *about*.

D As in (A) and (C), repeating the preposition *of* before *Women's Work* makes the sentence unparallel. The noun *account* takes the preposition *of*, not *about*. It is redundant to modify *authority* with *expert* because they express the same idea. Finally, the noun *authority* takes the preposition *on*, not *about*.

E **Correct.** This version is parallel, uses the most concise structure of the parenthetical descriptions, eschews the redundant modification of *authority*, and employs the correct prepositions.

The correct answer is E.

812. Digging in sediments in northern China, <u>evidence has been gathered by scientists suggesting that complex life-forms emerged much earlier than they had</u> previously thought.

    (A) evidence has been gathered by scientists suggesting that complex life-forms emerged much earlier than they had

    (B) evidence gathered by scientists suggests a much earlier emergence of complex life-forms than had been

    (C) scientists have gathered evidence suggesting that complex life-forms emerged much earlier than

    (D) scientists have gathered evidence that suggests a much earlier emergence of complex life-forms than that which was

    (E) scientists have gathered evidence which suggests a much earlier emergence of complex life-forms than that

Logical Predication; Modification

In principle, the relationship described in the first part of the underlined portion could be expressed with *scientists* as the subject (*scientists gathered evidence*) or with *evidence* as the subject (*evidence was gathered by scientists*). The latter construction could be effective in some contexts, but here its relationship to the rest of the sentence appears to commit the writer to the claim that the evidence was digging in China.

A   This version has a dangling participle, *digging*. ... *Digging in sediments in northern China* must modify *scientists*, not *evidence*. The passive structure of the main clause also creates an inadvisable distance between the words *evidence* and *suggesting*. Furthermore, the dependent clause starting with *suggesting* may be construed with either the evidence or the scientists, which makes this version unnecessarily ambiguous.

B   This version has a dangling participle, *digging*. ... *Digging in sediments in northern China* must modify *scientists*, not *evidence*.

C   **Correct.** Choosing *scientists* as the subject of *gathered*, this version corrects the dangling participle. It also uses a parallel active form of the verb *emerge*, and does not use redundant material.

D   In this context it would be preferable to use a verb (*emerged*). The phrasing used here (*suggests a much earlier emergence of*) sounds more stilted and is less clear and direct. In addition, inserting *that which* before *previously thought* is not only redundant but incorrect English.

E   The problems described in (D) above are also in evidence here.

The correct answer is C.

SC01521

813. Employing many different techniques throughout his career, Michelangelo produced a great variety of art works, including paintings, for example, in the Sistine Chapel, to sculpture, for example, the statue of David.

(A) including paintings, for example, in the Sistine Chapel, to sculpture, for example,

(B) including paintings, for example, in the Sistine Chapel, to sculpture, like

(C) including paintings, such as those in the Sistine Chapel, and sculpture, as

(D) ranging from paintings, such as those in the Sistine Chapel, to sculpture, such as

(E) ranging from paintings, such as in the Sistine Chapel, and sculpture, such as

Parallelism; Rhetorical Construction

This sentence names painting and sculpture as two of the many kinds of art created by Michelangelo and provides examples of his work in those two art forms. Although the two sets of examples are expressed in parallel form, the position of the phrase *for example* that introduces them creates a choppy and awkward sentence since it must be surrounded by commas. A more concise way to construct parallel sets of examples is to express each using a phrase introduced by *such as*.

A   The sentence is choppy and awkward due to the twofold use of the phrase *for example*, which must be surrounded by commas. The preposition *to*, in context, suggests a range, but it would then be needed to be preceded by *from*.

B   The examples of art are not in parallel form since the first is introduced by *for example* followed by the prepositional phrase *in the Sistine Chapel*, and the second is introduced by the prepositional phrase *like*... The preposition *to* is unidiomatic and awkwardly used here.

C   The examples of art are not in parallel form since the first is introduced by *such as*, and the second is introduced by *as*.

D   **Correct.** The examples of art are in parallel form, each introduced with the words *such as*.

E   Although the examples of art are both introduced by *such as*, the form is not parallel since the first is a prepositional phrase (*in the Sistine Chapel*) and the second is a noun phrase (*the statue of David*).

The correct answer is D.

SC04422

814. According to a recent study of consumer spending on prescription medications, increases in the sales of the 50 drugs that were advertised most heavily accounts for almost half of the $20.8 billion increase in drug spending last year, the remainder of which came from sales of the 9,850 prescription medicines that companies did not advertise or advertised very little.

(A) heavily accounts for almost half of the $20.8 billion increase in drug spending last year, the remainder of which came

(B) heavily were what accounted for almost half of the $20.8 billion increase in drug spending last year; the remainder of the increase coming

(C) heavily accounted for almost half of the $20.8 billion increase in drug spending last year, the remainder of the increase coming

(D) heavily, accounting for almost half of the $20.8 billion increase in drug spending last year, while the remainder of the increase came

(E) heavily, which accounted for almost half of the $20.8 billion increase in drug spending last year, with the remainder of it coming

Grammatical Construction; Verb Form

The sentence indicates that according to research, increases in sales of the relatively small number of the most heavily advertised drugs accounted for nearly half of last year's total increase in drug spending. The sentence is flawed because of subject-verb disagreement, and an ambiguity in the referent of *which*.

A   The singular verb form *accounts* fails to agree in number with the plural subject *increases*. What the relative pronoun *which* refers to is unclear; to make clear sense, it should refer to *the ... increase*.

B   The phrase *were what accounted* is unnecessarily wordy; the semicolon before *the remainder* signals that a complete clause will follow, but what follows is not a complete clause.

C   **Correct.** The sentence is clear and grammatically correct. The subject and verb agree.

D   In the resulting sentence, no main verb follows the main subject *increases*.

E   The resulting sentence lacks a main verb for the main subject *increases*.

The correct answer is C.

SC00971

815. Technically, "quicksand" is the term for sand <u>that is so saturated with water as to acquire a liquid's character</u>.

(A) that is so saturated with water as to acquire a liquid's character

(B) that is so saturated with water that it acquires the character of a liquid

(C) that is saturated with water enough to acquire liquid characteristics

(D) saturated enough with water so as to acquire the character of a liquid

(E) saturated with water so much as to acquire a liquid character

Rhetorical Construction; Logical Predication

The statement provides a definition of the term *quicksand* as sand that has been saturated with water to a certain degree. Many of the flaws in the incorrect options have to do with how this degree of saturation is described.

A   The matter of degree in this option is introduced with the word *so*, which is used to indicate that the relevant degree of saturation will be specified with a clause that states a condition—a statement that includes both a subject and a verb—that implies a certain degree of saturation. Lacking a subject, this sentence fails to state a clear condition.

B   **Correct.** In this option, the clause introduced with *that* contains a proper statement—with both a subject and verb—which implies a degree of saturation with water. This option thus has none of the flaws discussed in connection with option A.

C   In this option, we might immediately note that the word (adjective) *enough*, which qualifies the word *water* is misplaced. In English (with, as almost always, exceptions), qualifiers of nouns are generally placed before the noun. In this case, it should be *enough water*.

D   The words *so as* make this option a poor choice. In the case of option D, if we cut out "so as" and write, *"quicksand" is the term for sand saturated enough to acquire the character of a liquid*, then our statement would be much improved. However, as it stands, option D is at best awkward.

E   We might immediately note that this option is awkward—*so much* qualifies *saturated*, yet it is placed after the word *water*, well after *saturated*. This makes the statement unnecessarily difficult to read. A modification of this part of the sentence so as to read *saturated so much with water* would be an improvement. Furthermore, as discussed in connection with options A and B, option E would be better if *as to acquire a liquid character* were replaced with *that it acquires a liquid character* (or, as in B, *that it acquires the character of a liquid*).

The correct answer is B.

9.9 Sentence Correction Answer Explanations

SC07232

816. At the end of 2001, motion picture industry representatives said that there were about a million copies of Hollywood movies available <u>online and expected piracy to increase with high-speed Internet connections that become more widely available</u>.

(A) online and expected piracy to increase with high-speed Internet connections that become more widely available

(B) online and expect the increase of piracy with the wider availability of high-speed Internet connections

(C) online, and they expect more piracy to increase with the wider availability of high-speed Internet connections

(D) online, and that they expected the increase of piracy as high-speed Internet connections would become more widely available

(E) online, and that they expected piracy to increase as high-speed Internet connections became more widely available

Rhetorical Construction; Grammatical Construction

Every clause needs a subject, either an overt subject or an understood subject (whose interpretation can come from a coordinated clause or some other nearby clause). In this sentence, the clause containing *expected* lacks a clear subject. The intended subject is *motion picture industry representatives*, but to clearly indicate that, the subject should either be repeated or be replaced with the pronoun *they*. Furthermore, *piracy to increase with high-speed Internet connections that become more widely available* is awkward, and it fails to clearly communicate the idea that piracy will increase as a result of high-speed Internet connections becoming available.

A The second clause is awkward and unclear; there is no clear subject for *expected*.

B There is no clear subject for *expect*.

C It is redundant to use both *more* and *increase*.

D This wording makes the meaning very unclear. *They expected the increase in piracy* appears to refer to a particular (past) increase, but this does not clearly make sense with the ensuing use of the conditional verb form *would become*, which is inappropriate here.

E **Correct.** In this version the verb *expect* has an overt subject, and the following phrasing clearly indicates that the expected increase in piracy is the result of high-speed Internet connections becoming more widely available.

The correct answer is E.

SC14066

817. Making things even more difficult <u>has been general market inactivity lately, if not paralysis, which has provided</u> little in the way of pricing guidance.

(A) has been general market inactivity lately, if not paralysis, which has provided

(B) there is general market inactivity, if not paralysis, lately it has provided

(C) general market inactivity, if not paralysis, has lately provided

(D) lately, general market inactivity, if not paralysis, has provided

(E) is that lately general market inactivity, if not paralysis, which provides

Grammatical Construction; Rhetorical Construction

This sentence uses a special inverted structure, putting the predicate (*Making things even more difficult*) before the verb (*has been*) and the subject. In this construction, the subject (*general market inactivity*) can be directly compared with *paralysis*. Such contrasts are best made using phrases that are adjacent, not separated by other material (here, the adverb *lately*). If a more normal clause structure is used, *making things even more difficult* becomes a modifier, not the main predicate, so it should be clearly set off from the rest of the clause with a comma.

A This inverted structure makes *general market activity* the subject of *Making things even more difficult*. This would be legitimate by itself, but it requires *general market inactivity* to be next to both *if not paralysis* (for contrast) and *which* (marking a relative clause modifying *inactivity*). It cannot be next to both of these simultaneously.

B This is a run-on sentence, with two independent clauses (*Making things even more difficult there is general market inactivity, if not paralysis, and lately it has*

849

provided little in the way of pricing guidance) conjoined merely by a comma, rather than by a coordinating conjunction, such as and. Also, the initial topic phrase (*Making things even more difficult*) is awkward without a following comma.

C   The initial topic phrase (*Making things even more difficult*) should be followed by a comma.

D   **Correct.** The topic phrase (*Making things even more difficult*) is properly separated from the subject by a comma, and *inactivity* and *if not paralysis* are adjacent for the clearest connection between them.

E   This is a sentence fragment.

The correct answer is D.

SC01946

818. Ryūnosuke Akutagawa's knowledge of the literatures of Europe, China, and that of Japan were instrumental in his development as a writer, informing his literary style as much as the content of his fiction.

(A) that of Japan were instrumental in his development as a writer, informing his literary style as much as

(B) that of Japan was instrumental in his development as a writer, and it informed both his literary style as well as

(C) Japan was instrumental in his development as a writer, informing both his literary style and

(D) Japan was instrumental in his development as a writer, as it informed his literary style as much as

(E) Japan were instrumental in his development as a writer, informing both his literary style in addition to

Logical Predication; Agreement

When a verb follows a complex noun phrase made up of several parts, it agrees with the first noun in the phrase. In this case, *knowledge of the literatures of Europe, China, and Japan* is a singular noun and the correct verb form is *was*, not *were*. The various parts of an enumeration have to be alike: *the literatures of Europe, China, and Japan*. The logical relationship between the predicates is important.

A   This version of the sentence violates the correct subject-verb agreement, and the correct structure of enumeration is disrupted by the addition of *that of* in front of *Japan*.

B   The correct structure of enumeration is disrupted by the addition of *that of* in front of *Japan*. Both … as well as … is incorrect usage.

C   **Correct.** The structure of the enumeration (*Europe, China, and Japan*) as well as the conjunction structure (*both X and Y*) are correct. The logical relationships among the parts of the sentence are clearly expressed.

D   This phrasing makes it unclear what the writer is claiming. It appears to indicate that the effect of Akutagawa's knowledge on his development as a writer was due to the fact that both of the aspects of his writing were influenced to the same extent. However, it is implausible to suppose that this is what the writer intends. Furthermore, the comparison is ambiguous: did his knowledge inform his style as much as it informed the content, or did it inform his style as much as the content informed his style?

E   The subject-verb agreement in this version is incorrect. *Both X in addition to Y* is incorrect usage.

The correct answer is C.

SC24321.01

819. Many stock traders in the United States have set out to become global investors, convinced that limiting their investments to the U.S. stock market, even though it is certainly home to the stocks of some of the world's great corporations, restricted their gains.

(A) even though it is certainly

(B) which, while it is certainly

(C) despite that that market is certainly

(D) which, though certainly

(E) although, certainly as

Grammatical Construction; Diction

This sentence contains no errors. A major error in three of the variants of the underlined portion is to create a mere sentence fragment through failure to complete, with a verb, the noun clause that would normally be introduced by the phrase *convinced that*.

A   **Correct.** The phrase *convinced that* introduces a noun clause: *limiting their investments to the U.S. stock market restricted* *their gains.* The clause introduced by *even though* is a parenthesis inserted in the noun clause.

B   This creates a sentence fragment by leaving the noun clause introduced by *convinced that* with no verb to complete it. The relative pronoun *which* introduces a relative clause; this clause takes *restricted* as its verb and *the U.S. stock market* as the antecedent of *which*.

C   There is a diction error here. The phrase *despite that* is not a subordinating conjunction; the word *despite* is normally used as a preposition. A preposition must be followed by a noun, noun phrase, or pronoun that it governs (as in "despite that fact, …") but is not so followed in this case. The conjunction *although* would better serve the function intended for *despite that*.

D   This creates a sentence fragment by leaving the noun clause introduced by *convinced that* without a verb to complete it.

E   This creates a sentence fragment and deprives the verb *restricted* of a subject. The word *although* is a subordinating conjunction used only to introduce a subordinate clause, which is required to have its own verb. But these requirements are not fulfilled here, so we have a diction error.

The correct answer is A.

SC01973

820. According to scientists who monitored its path, <u>an expanding cloud of energized particles ejected from the Sun recently triggered a large storm in the magnetic field that surrounds Earth, which brightened the Northern Lights and also possibly knocking</u> out a communications satellite.

(A)   an expanding cloud of energized particles ejected from the Sun recently triggered a large storm in the magnetic field that surrounds Earth, which brightened the Northern Lights and also possibly knocking

(B)   an expanding cloud of energized particles ejected from the Sun was what recently triggered a large storm in the magnetic field that surrounds Earth, and it brightened the Northern Lights and also possibly knocked

(C)   an expanding cloud of energized particles ejected from the Sun recently triggered a large storm in the magnetic field that surrounds Earth, brightening the Northern Lights and possibly knocking

(D)   a large storm in the magnetic field that surrounds Earth, recently triggered by an expanding cloud of energized particles, brightened the Northern Lights and it possibly knocked

(E)   a large storm in the magnetic field surrounding Earth was recently triggered by an expanding cloud of energized particles, brightening the Northern Lights and it possibly knocked

Logical Predication; Rhetorical Construction; Verb Form

The timing and logical relationships among the events described in this sentence are of utmost importance. The scientists monitored a cloud ejected from the Sun. The cloud triggered a large storm, whose consequences were the brightening of the Northern Lights and the possible knocking out of a satellite. The latter two events are in a conjunction, so they should be represented by similar verb forms.

A   In this context, the shift in verb form from *which brightened* to *and also possibly knocking* is ungrammatical. The two verbs should be in the same verb form for parallel construction.

B   *X was what triggered Y* is wordy and awkward, and its meaning is unclear in this context. Given the most plausible intended meaning of the sentence, the two conjunctions *and … and …* in the last clause are redundant. The comma after *Earth* turns the final part of the sentence into an independent clause, and it is unclear whether this is part of what the scientists claimed or a separate claim made by the writer.

C   **Correct.** The conjoined elements are of parallel forms, and the logical relations between the events are clear and concisely communicated.

D   The wording in this answer choice makes the intended meaning unclear. The information that the cloud particles were ejected from the Sun is lost. The sentence is ungrammatical; the second conjoined main verb, *knocked*, needs no pronoun subject *it* because its subject is *a large storm*.

E   The wording in this answer choice makes the intended meaning unclear. The information that the cloud particles were ejected from the Sun is lost. The two conjoined verbs are of different form; the second conjoined verb includes an unnecessary pronoun subject.

The correct answer is C.

SC01033

821. Because many of Australia's marsupials, such as the koala, are cute and cuddly, as well as <u>being biologically different than North American marsupials, they have attracted a lot of attention after</u> their discovery in the 1700s.

(A) being biologically different than North American marsupials, they have attracted a lot of attention after

(B) being biologically different from North American marsupials, they attracted a lot of attention since

(C) biologically different than North American marsupials, they attracted a lot of attention since

(D) biologically different than North American marsupials, they have attracted a lot of attention after

(E) biologically different from North American marsupials, they have attracted a lot of attention since

Verb Form; Parallelism

In seeking to explain why Australian marsupials have attracted much attention in North America, the sentence ascribes two attributes to them: they differ biologically from North American marsupials and seem friendly and appealing. The structure *are ... as well as ...* is used to coordinate the description of the two properties—but incorrectly, because the insertion of *being* impairs the required parallelism: *are cute and cuddly* is not parallel to *[are] being biologically different*. Also, there is a lack of fit between the verb form *have attracted* and the preposition *after*.

A   The phrase *cute and cuddly* is adjectival, as is *biologically different ...*; adding the word *being* is not useful and impairs parallelism. The verb form *have attracted* suggests a process continuing from some point in the past, but the word *after* is most naturally read as indicating the time of a single event relative to an earlier point in time.

B   The word *being* is superfluous here. The word *since* indicates continuation over a past period, whereas the verb *attracted* indicates a single event occurring within a period.

C   The word *being* is superfluous here and impairs parallelism. The verb *attracted*, indicating a single event, does not match the use of the word *since*, which indicates a continuing duration relative to the time of an earlier event.

D   The verb *have attracted*, indicating continuation, does not match the use of the word *after*, which is appropriate in order to give the time of a single event relative to an earlier point in time.

E   **Correct.** The superfluous word *being* is omitted, preserving the parallelism between the two adjectival phrases in the description of the attribute following *as well as*. The preposition *since* is the appropriate usage with the verb form *have attracted*.

The correct answer is E.

SC02448

822. <u>Having been named for a mythological nymph who cared for the infant Jupiter, the asteroid named Ida, in the middle of the belt of asteroids that orbit the Sun between Mars and Jupiter, was discovered in 1884.</u>

(A) Having been named for a mythological nymph who cared for the infant Jupiter, the asteroid named Ida, in the middle of the belt of asteroids that orbit the Sun between Mars and Jupiter, was discovered in 1884.

(B) Discovered in 1884, the asteroid Ida, named for a mythological nymph who cared for the infant Jupiter, is in the middle of the belt of asteroids that orbit the Sun between Mars and Jupiter.

(C) In the middle of the belt of asteroids that orbit the Sun between Mars and Jupiter, the asteroid Ida, discovered in 1884 and named for a mythological nymph who cared for the infant Jupiter.

(D) The asteroid Ida, named for a mythological nymph who cared for the infant Jupiter and discovered in 1884, is in the middle of the belt of asteroids to orbit the Sun between Mars and Jupiter.

(E) Ida, an asteroid discovered in 1884 and which was named for a mythological nymph who cared for the infant Jupiter, is in the middle of the belt of asteroids to orbit the Sun between Mars and Jupiter

Rhetorical Construction; Logical Predication; Grammatical Construction

This sentence describes a discovery that occurred in 1884 and provides some additional information about the object that was discovered. The most effectively worded answer choice opens with a past-participial phrase (*discovered* . . .) describing the subject of the sentence, *the asteroid Ida*. Ida's discovery is logically prior to its naming, described in a second past, following the subject (*named* . . .). The sentence is then completed with a present tense linking verb *is* + prepositional phrase to explain Ida's location.

A   Opening with a past perfect passive verb, *Having been named*, this version of the sentence illogically suggests that being named for a mythological nymph preceded the discovery of Ida.

B   **Correct.** This version is clear, logically coherent, and grammatically correct.

C   This version of the sentence is ungrammatical; it has no main verb for the subject *the asteroid Ida*.

D   The sequence of events is obscured by the placement of *named* before *discovered* in the compound participial phrases. The infinitive form *to orbit* is ungrammatical in place of the relative clause.

E   This sentence awkwardly attempts to use a compound conjunction *and* to join the past participial phrase *discovered in 1884* with the relative clause *which was named*. . . . The infinitive form *to orbit* is ungrammatical in place of the relative clause.

The correct answer is B.

SC20121.01
823. Custodian fees and expenses, as described in the statement of operations, <u>include interest expense incurred by the fund on any cash overdrafts of its custodian account during the period</u>.

(A) include interest expense incurred by the fund on any cash overdrafts of its custodian account during the period

(B) are to include interest expenses on any cash overdrafts of its custodian account the fund incurred during the period

(C) includes interest expense the fund incurred during the period on any cash overdrafts of its custodian account

(D) may include interest expense during the period that the fund was to incur on any cash overdrafts of its custodian account

(E) including interest expense on any cash overdrafts of its custodian account incurred by the fund during the period

Logical Predication; Agreement; Grammatical Construction; Verb Form

The given sentence is correct. The subject of the main verb is plural; the word *custodian* functions as an adjective modifying *fees and expenses*. The complex adjectival phrase *incurred . . . period* (which includes embedded adverbial modifiers such as *by the fund*) modifies the noun phrase *interest expense*. The adverbial phrase *during the period* modifies the verb *incurred*. Errors occurring in the other versions include misplaced modifiers, errors in subject-verb agreement, and a grammatical construction error.

A   **Correct.** This has none of the errors listed above. The use of the singular *expense*, an abstract noun with no plural, is legitimate—as is also the use of the plural concrete noun *expenses* (a "count noun") elsewhere in the sentence.

B   The phrase *are to include* can convey either a future sense or an imperative sense, but nothing in the given sentence indicates that either of these senses is appropriate. The relative clause [*that*] *the fund incurred . . .* is misleadingly attached to *account* rather than to *expenses*—a logical predication error.

C   The verb *includes* is singular but its subject is plural.

D   The introduction of *may* and *was to* do not improve on the given sentence and introduce superfluous words. The force of *was to* is unclear. The relative clause *that . . . incur* is misleadingly attached to *period* rather than to *expense*.

E   This version is no longer a sentence—as opposed to an extended noun phrase—because the present participle *including* has replaced the finite verb *include*. The adjectival modifier *incurred by ... period* is misleadingly attached to *account* rather than *expense*.

The correct answer is A.

SC36241.01

824. Although some had accused Smith, the firm's network manager, of negligence when the crucial data went missing, the CEO defused <u>a situation that was quite tense with her public statement that the debacle was not Smith's fault.</u>

(A) a situation that was quite tense with her public statement that the debacle was not Smith's fault

(B) a situation that was quite tense, by publicly stating that the debacle was not Smith's fault

(C) a situation, which was quite tense, by stating publicly that Smith was not responsible for the debacle

(D) a quite tense situation with a public statement about the debacle not being Smith's fault

(E) a quite tense situation by publicly stating the debacle not to have been Smith's fault

Logical Predication; Rhetorical Construction

The sentence is awkwardly and ambiguously worded. The phrase *with her public statement that the debacle was not Smith's fault* could be read as modifying *tense* or as expressing the means by which the CEO defused the situation, which is surely what is intended.

A   The sentence is flawed for the reasons discussed above.

B   **Correct.** This clearly conveys the intended meaning that the CEO defused the situation *by publicly stating that the debacle was not Smith's fault*.

C   By setting *which was quite tense* apart with commas, the tenseness of the situation appears to be inessential, but surely the fact that the situation was quite tense is an important part of the intended meaning. Thus, this version of the sentence fails rhetorically.

D   *With a public statement about the debacle not being Smith's fault* could be taken to be modifying *situation* or to be indicating the means by which the CEO defused the situation. Therefore, this version is ambiguous.

E   *By publicly stating the debacle not to have been Smith's fault* is awkward and lacks rhetorical force.

The correct answer is B.

SC01077

825. Many utilities obtain most of their electric power from large coal and nuclear operations at costs that are sometimes <u>two to three times higher as that of power from smaller, more efficient plants that can both</u> make use of waste heat and take advantage of the current abundance of natural gas.

(A) two to three times higher as that of power from smaller, more efficient plants that can both

(B) higher by two to three times as that from smaller, more efficient plants that both can

(C) two to three times higher than those for power from smaller, more efficient plants that can both

(D) between two to three times higher as those for power from smaller, more efficient plants that both can

(E) between two to three times higher than from smaller, more efficient plants that they can both

Grammatical Construction; Diction

The sentence compares utilities' high costs of power obtained from large producers with the costs of power obtained from smaller, more economic producers. The comparative form *higher* must be followed by the preposition *than*, not by *as*. The sentence uses the plural *costs*; therefore, the singular pronoun *that* in the phrase *as that of power from ...* incorrectly refers to a plural antecedent *costs*. An issue that arises in some of the five choices concerns the placing of *both* in a *both ... and ...* construction that is meant to indicate parallelism between the clauses *that make use of ...* and *[that] take advantage of ...*.

A   As indicated, the use of *as* with *higher* in the comparison between costs is incorrect. Use of the singular pronoun *that* to refer to the plural *costs* is incorrect.

B   The phrase *higher by two to three times* is unclear, and the use of *as* is unidiomatic here. Also, *higher as* is incorrect.

C **Correct.** The comparative *higher* is correctly followed by *than*. The plural pronoun *those* is correctly used to refer back to *costs*. The placement of *both* indicates correctly the parallel clauses.

D The phrase *higher as* is unidiomatic. The placement of *both* is ambiguous: either suggesting that the number of "more efficient plants" is just two, or that the verb *can* is not to be read as going along with *take* (this reading would create a grammatical-construction flaw, and render *take advantage … gas* into a sentence fragment).

E This omits a pronoun that would refer back to costs and so fails to capture the comparison intended in the given sentence. It compares the costs of power from large plants with power from smaller plants, i.e., it nonsensically compares costs with power.

The correct answer is C.

SC01523

826. When viewed from the window of a speeding train, the speed with which nearby objects move seems faster than that of more distant objects.

(A) the speed with which nearby objects move seems faster than that of

(B) the speed that nearby objects move seems faster than for

(C) the speed of nearby objects seems faster than

(D) nearby objects' speeds seem to be faster than those of

(E) nearby objects seem to move at a faster speed than do

Logical Predication; Parallelism

The intended meaning of the sentence is easily discerned: objects viewed from a speeding train seem to move faster than more distant objects. However, the sentence is defective in structure. One problem is that the participle *viewed* seems to apply to the subject of the main clause, the noun phrase *the speed with which nearby objects move*. Since this produces nonsense, the sentence needs to be reshaped. Comparing the speed of nearby objects with the speed of more distant objects would ideally be done with parallelism in phrasing, but that is lacking in the given sentence.

A The subject of the main clause should be *nearby objects* and not *the speed with which nearby objects move*, given the participle in the *when*-clause.

B The phrase *the speed … move* is erroneously made the subject of the main clause, but the phrase contains an additional problem: structurally it makes the relative pronoun *that* the object of the verb *move*.

C The phrase *the speed … objects* is erroneously made the subject of the main clause.

D The phrase *nearby objects' speeds* is erroneously made the subject of the main clause.

E **Correct.** The phrase *nearby objects* is correctly made the subject of the verb *seem*, and this fits with the participle in the *when*-clause. Additionally, there is a strict parallelism between *nearby objects* and *more distant objects*, which are being compared with respect to their apparent speed.

The correct answer is E.

SC41451.01

827. Ramón pointed out that food high in whole-grain fiber creates the energy we need to fight illnesses—as do vegetables and lean proteins.

(A) fiber creates the energy we need to fight illnesses—as do vegetables and lean proteins

(B) fiber in addition to vegetables and lean proteins, create the energy we need to fight illnesses

(C) fiber creates the energy we need to fight illnesses, along with vegetables and lean proteins

(D) fiber, vegetables, and lean proteins creates the energy we need to fight illnesses

(E) fiber, as vegetables and lean proteins, create the energy we need to fight illnesses

Logical Predication; Grammatical Construction; Agreement

The sentence is clear and correctly constructed. Its variants go wrong in three different ways. One error is to make the verb number plural where the subject of the verb is singular. Another error consists of the misapplication of a predicate. In the given sentence, the predicate *creates the energy we need to fight illnesses* is correctly applied, and the verb is singular because the subject of the verb is given by the noun phrase *food high in whole grain fiber*. A third error concerns the use of *as*. In the given sentence, it functions correctly as a conjunction introducing a clause that compares foods high in whole-grain fiber with vegetables and lean proteins.

A **Correct.** As explained above, this avoids errors that appear in the variant versions of the sentence.

B This fails in two ways. First, the comma immediately following *proteins* in effect creates two sentence fragments which do not comprise a sentence and neither of which can stand on its own as an independent clause. This is a grammatical construction error. Even if the comma were removed, a plural verb is paired with the singular subject designated by *food high in whole-grain fiber*. The phrase *in addition to … proteins* is an adjectival modifier of the subject and does not generate a plural subject.

C The main error here arises from the placement of the final phrase *along with … proteins*. Inserting it instead immediately after *fiber* would make the meaning clearer for the reader. It would then be an adjectival modifier of the noun phrase *food high in whole-grain fiber*. But as it stands, it can be read as an adverbial modifier, though it is unclear which verb it would modify.

D It would make sense to describe a meal plan as rich in vegetables. But vegetables are not parallel to fiber as components of a food, and this indicates that the series *fiber, vegetables, and lean proteins* has logical predication and parallelism issues.

E The verb *create* is incorrect in being plural, given that its subject *food high in whole-grain fiber* is singular. The role of *as* here is ambiguous: is it meant to function as a preposition—which must govern a noun, noun phrase, or pronoun—or as a conjunction that would introduce a subordinate clause? In the given sentence, it functions, correctly, as a conjunction. Here, though, it is unclear, and looks more like a preposition, since the phrase *as vegetables and lean proteins* contains no verb. However, if taken as a propositional phrase, the phrase could imply that vegetables and lean proteins are high in whole-grain fiber (obviously false). This would be a logical predication error.

The correct answer is A.

SC01487

828. The English physician Edward Jenner found that if experimental subjects were deliberately infected with cowpox, <u>which caused only a mild illness, they are immune from</u> smallpox.

(A) which caused only a mild illness, they are immune from

(B) causing only a mild illness, they become immune from

(C) which causes only a mild illness, they are immune to

(D) causing only a mild illness, they became immune from

(E) which caused only a mild illness, they would become immune to

Verb Form

This sentence describes the result of infecting volunteers with cowpox. A conditional verb form is used to describe the cowpox infection: *if experimental subjects were deliberately infected*. The sentence then incorrectly uses simple present tense for the effects of that infection: *they are immune*. However, since the effects are dependent on an action that may or may not occur, the correct way to express those effects is by using another conditional verb form: *they would become immune*.

A The effects of a conditional situation are incorrectly expressed using the simple present tense verb *are*.

B The participle *causing* suggests that infecting the subjects with cowpox caused a mild illness only in some of the cases—but this does not seem to be the intended meaning. The effects of a conditional situation are incorrectly expressed using the simple present tense verb *become*. The preposition *from* is incorrect with *immune*; it should be *to*.

C The effects of a conditional situation are incorrectly expressed using the simple present tense verb *are*.

D   See above the comment on *causing* in (B). The effects of a conditional situation are incorrectly expressed using the simple past tense verb *became*. The preposition with *immune* should be *to*.

E   **Correct.** The effects of a conditional situation are correctly expressed using the conditional verb *would become*. The preposition *to* (rather than *from*) is correct with *immune*.

The correct answer is E.

SC00989

829. The final decades of the twentieth century not only saw an explosion of the literary production among women, but there was also an intense interest in the lives and works of women writers.

(A) not only saw an explosion of the literary production among women, but there was also

(B) not only saw an explosion of literary production in women, but there was also

(C) saw not only an explosion of literary production among women, but also

(D) saw not only an explosion of the literary production by women, but it also saw

(E) saw not only an explosion of literary production by women, but also saw

Parallelism; Diction

The sentence, about twentieth century literary production by women and the interest in women writers, contains a common type of construction that requires parallelism.

A   The predicate of this sentence begins with what would be the first part of the construction *not only saw ... but also saw*. In this construction, *not also saw* would be parallel with *but also saw*, thus allowing for a statement that is easy for a human to process. However, instead of *but also saw*, the sentence uses *but there was also*. The sentence thus lacks parallelism and is unnecessarily difficult to read.

B   This sentence has the same flaw as does sentence A with respect to *but there was also*. Furthermore, the use of *in* in *production in women* is incorrect and should be replaced with *among*.

C   **Correct.** This sentence correctly uses, after the main verb *saw*, the construction *not only ... but also*. It also uses *among* as suggested for sentence B.

D   The portion of this sentence that follows the main verb *saw* starts with what would be the construction *not only ... but also*. However, instead of *but also*, the sentence uses *but it also saw*. This is incorrect on various grounds. First, the portion is in the predicate and it is clear what the subject is. The pronoun *it*, which refers to the subject, is thus unnecessary. Second, because it fails to correctly follow the construction *not only ... but also*, the sentence lacks parallelism.

E   The main flaw in this sentence is the inclusion of *saw* after *also*. This use of *saw* is redundant and lacks parallelism.

The correct answer is C.

SC01070

830. Covering 71 percent of Earth's surface, the oceans play an essential role in maintaining the conditions for human existence on land, moderating temperature by the absorption of heat and carbon dioxide, and giving pure water back to the atmosphere through evaporation.

(A) Covering 71 percent of Earth's surface, the oceans play an essential role in maintaining the conditions for human existence on land, moderating

(B) Covering 71 percent of Earth's surface and playing an essential role in maintaining the conditions for human existence on land, the oceans moderate

(C) The oceans cover 71 percent of Earth's surface and play an essential role in maintaining conditions for human existence on land, and by moderating

(D) The oceans cover 71 percent of Earth's surface, play an essential role in maintaining the conditions for human existence on land, and moderate

(E) The oceans cover 71 percent of Earth's surface, playing an essential role in maintaining the conditions for human existence on land, and they moderate

Parallelism; Rhetorical Construction; Grammatical Construction

This sentence about the essential role oceans play in maintaining conditions for human existence on

857

land begins with a participial phrase describing the vastness of the oceans, followed by the main clause (*oceans play an essential role* . . .). The object, *role*, is modified by a prepositional phrase that indicates what kind of role the oceans play (it plays a role *in maintaining the conditions for human existence on land*). This statement about the ocean's role in maintaining terrestrial conditions is elucidated by two parallel participial phrases that describe the oceans, explaining how they maintain conditions essential for human existence on land (*moderating* . . . *and giving* . . .).

A **Correct.** This version of the sentence effectively conveys the means by which the ocean plays an essential role in maintaining the conditions for human existence on land, using parallel verb forms.

B This version of the sentence is ungrammatical; *and giving* . . . suggests that this is part of a series of participial phrases, but it is not.

C The conjunction followed by a prepositional phrase *and by moderating* . . . anticipates a new subject—an agent that does something by moderating—but this subject never appears.

D This version of the sentence is structured as a series of verbs—*cover*, *play*, and *moderate*—all describing things the oceans do; the final participial phrase *giving* . . . *water* . . . violates the parallel structure set up in the sentence.

E This version of the sentence correctly makes *playing an essential role* . . . a function of the oceans' coverage of Earth's surface, but the introduction of a new main verb *moderate* fails to indicate that what follows (moderating temperature and returning pure water) identifies the role oceans play in maintaining conditions for human existence on land. Furthermore, the participial phrase *and giving pure water* . . . violates the parallel structure set up by the series of main verbs that appear earlier in this version of the sentence.

The correct answer is A.

SC11850.01

831. Although the rise in the Producer Price Index was greater than expected, most analysts agreed <u>that the index was unlikely to continue going up and that inflation remained</u> essentially under control.

(A) that the index was unlikely to continue going up and that inflation remained

(B) that it was unlikely for the index continuing to go up and for inflation to remain

(C) that the index was unlikely to continue to go up, with inflation to remain

(D) on the unlikelihood that the index would continue going up and that inflation remained

(E) on the unlikelihood that the index would continue to go up and for inflation to remain

Rhetorical Construction; Verb Form

The given sentence is a better version than any of its variants. The analysts agreed on two points, each expressed in a noun clause, with each clause introduced by *that*. The first point of agreement is on a prediction, the second on a determination of fact. Each of these noun clauses is an object of the verb *agreed*. There is a rhetorically valuable parallelism between the two clauses, a parallelism not preserved, however, in three of the four variants. Note also that when a past-tense verb takes a *that*-clause as its object, the tense of that clause should be past (e.g., *was*, *remained*).

A **Correct.** As noted above, this preserves an important parallelism and correctly uses a past-tense verb in each of the noun clauses.

B This variant loses the rhetorically valuable parallelism noted above. It substitutes another, badly functioning, parallelism between two phrases each introduced by *for*. The verb forms in the phrases *for the index continuing* and *for inflation to remain* are not parallel, and both constructions are awkward and nonidiomatic.

C Although *continue to go* is not in itself wrong, avoiding the repetition of *to* by using the equally correct *continue going* would be rhetorically better. The phrase *with inflation to remain* conveys no clear information and leaves us guessing: for example, is it meant to indicate in context that it was agreed that inflation's remaining under control would impede the continuation of the increase in the index? If this is the intended meaning—not a meaning conveyed in the best version of the sentence above—it would be better expressed by, e.g., the clause *if inflation remained* . . ., plus dropping the comma immediately preceding it.

D   This is awkward and contains avoidable verbiage. Compare *agreed on the unlikelihood that the index would* with *agreed that the index was unlikely to*. The second is more direct and shorter. The parallelism between two *that*-clauses here is introduced, not by *agreed* but by *unlikelihood*. The sentence formed in this way indicates (contrary to the given sentence above, which is error-free) that it was agreed that inflation was unlikely to remain under control.

E   There is an undesirable lack of parallelism between *unlikelihood that* and [*unlikelihood*] *for*. The first is idiomatic and the second not so. Moreover, the sentence formed in this way indicates—contrary to the given sentence above, which is error-free—that it was agreed that inflation was unlikely to remain under control.

The correct answer is A.

SC17041.01

832. Severely hindered by problems with local suppliers, the fact that the AQ division also had a new management team to adapt to was not seen by the board of directors as a legitimate excuse for such low productivity.

(A) Severely hindered by problems with local suppliers, the fact that the AQ division also had a new management team to adapt to

(B) Though severely hindered by local supply problems, the fact that the AQ division also had a new management team to which to adapt

(C) Severely hindered by problems with local suppliers, the AQ division also had to adapt to a new management team, but this

(D) Severely hindered by local supply problems, that the AQ division also had to adapt to a new management team

(E) Though severely hindered by problems with local suppliers, the AQ division's also having a new management team to which it had to adapt

Logical Predication; Rhetorical Construction

The adjectival phrase *severely ... suppliers* should, because of its position, modify the subject of the main clause, the noun phrase *the fact ... to*. On this interpretation, the sentence lacks a coherent interpretation and has a logical predication error. The noun phrase that was meant to be modified is probably *the AQ division*. A second flaw concerns the phrase *had a new management team to adapt to*, which is unnecessarily awkward, especially with *to adapt to*.

A   As explained above, this sentence fails because of two flaws.

B   A logical predication flaw similar to the one noted above is present in this variant. The relative clause *to which to adapt* is unnecessarily awkward.

C   **Correct.** This makes clear that the adjectival phrase *severely ... suppliers* modifies the noun phrase *the AQ division*. This version is a rhetorical improvement on the given sentence in that unnecessary verbiage such as *the fact that* is dropped and the terminal preposition *to* is eliminated.

D   This has a logical predication problem like that noted in the given sentence: the initial adjectival phrase, rather than modifying *the AQ division*, appears to modify a noun clause *that ... team* but this would yield an incoherent interpretation of the sentence.

E   This also has a logical predication flaw; because of its position, the phrase *though severely ... suppliers* seems to modify a complex noun phrase, i.e., the phrase *the AQ division's also having a new management team to which it had to adapt*.

The correct answer is C.

SC01037

833. The Eastern State Penitentiary was established in 1822 by reformers advocating that prisoners be held in solitary confinement and hard labor so as to reform them.

(A) advocating that prisoners be held in solitary confinement and hard labor so as to reform them

(B) who were advocating prisoners to be held in solitary confinement and hard labor for their reform

(C) advocating solitary confinement and hard labor as the means to reform prisoners

(D) who advocated solitary confinement and hard labor for the means of prisoner reform

(E) advocating as the means for prisoner reform solitary confinement and hard labor

Idiom; Rhetorical Construction

The sentence describes an effect—reform of prisoners—that those who founded a prison in 1822 hoped would result from two types of punishment they advocated. The phrase *held in solitary confinement and hard labor* is problematic because *held in hard labor* is nonidiomatic. The adverbial phrase *so as to reform them* is wordy; it is also grammatically problematic because the subject of the passive-voice verb is *prisoners*, whereas the implicit subject of the verb *to reform* is presumably the punishments or the prison staff.

A   This is wordy, unidiomatic, and grammatically flawed, as explained.

B   An alternative wording *that prisoners be held ...* would be much clearer and less awkward; the phrase *advocating prisoners ...* makes it misleadingly appear that *prisoners* is the object of *advocating*. As indicated, the phrase *held in solitary confinement and hard labor* is unidiomatic.

C   **Correct.** The wording here conveys the intended meaning correctly and idiomatically, as well as with clarity and brevity. It indicates that reform of prisoners is the hoped-for result of the advocated punishments.

D   The phrase *for the means of prisoner reform* is wordy and unidiomatic and conveys no clear meaning. For example, is it intended to suggest that prisoner reform is a means to something else? Probably not. Is it intended to suggest that the two punishment types are means to reform? If so, then *as* would work much better than *for*.

E   The insertion of *as the means for prisoner reform* placed before (rather than after) *confinement and hard labor*—the object of the verb *advocating*—renders the resulting sentence unnecessarily awkward.

The correct answer is C.

SC03288

834. Some anthropologists believe that the genetic homogeneity evident in the world's people is the result of a "population bottleneck"—<u>at some time in the past our ancestors suffered an event, greatly reducing their numbers</u> and thus our genetic variation.

(A) at some time in the past our ancestors suffered an event, greatly reducing their numbers

(B) that at some time in the past our ancestors suffered an event that greatly reduced their numbers

(C) that some time in the past our ancestors suffered an event so that their numbers were greatly reduced,

(D) some time in the past our ancestors suffered an event from which their numbers were greatly reduced

(E) some time in the past, that our ancestors suffered an event so as to reduce their numbers greatly,

Grammatical Construction; Parallelism

The underlined part of this sentence is an explanatory rewording of the clause that follows *believe*. Scientists believe that X—[in other words,] that Y. In this construction, X and Y are parallel clauses.

A   The omission of *that* after the dash makes the function of the final clause unclear. The structure makes that clause appear to be an awkward and rhetorically puzzling separate assertion that the writer has appended to the prior claim about what the anthropologists believe. The agent or cause of *reducing* is unclear.

B   **Correct.** Repetition of *that* effectively signals the paraphrasing of the belief.

C   The preposition *at* before *some time* is missing; without *at* the adverb *sometime* would be needed instead of this two-word noun phrase. The modifier of *event* is expressed with a wordy passive construction, which destroys the parallelism between it and what follows.

D   Repetition of *that* signals the paraphrasing of the belief and is therefore needed. The preposition *at* before *some time* is missing. The modifier of *event* is expressed with a wordy passive construction, which destroys the parallelism between it and what follows.

E *That* is repeated in the paraphrase, but in the wrong place. A possible, and absurd, reading of this version is that our ancestors suffered an event in order to willfully reduce their own numbers and thus our genetic variation.

The correct answer is B.

SC01493

835. Through experimenting designed to provide information that will ultimately prove useful in the treatment of hereditary diseases, mice have received bone marrow transplants that give them a new gene.

(A) Through experimenting designed to provide information that will ultimately prove

(B) Through experiments designed to provide information ultimately proving

(C) In experimentation designed to provide information that ultimately proves

(D) In experimenting designed to provide information ultimately proving

(E) In experiments designed to provide information that will ultimately prove

Rhetorical Construction; Diction

The sentence reports that mice received a new gene by means of a bone marrow transplant, in the context of experiments aimed at improving treatment of hereditary disease. Issues arise concerning use of the preposition *through*, use of the verb form *experimenting*, and use of certain forms of the verb *prove*. The hoped-for result is more clearly expressed by the future tense *will ... prove* than by other forms of the verb.

A The verb form *experimenting* is inappropriate here because it seems to have *mice* as its implicit subject, which would be nonsensical, presuming scientists ran the experiment. The preposition *through* awkwardly signals that the experiments were the means by which—rather than the context in which—the bone marrow transplants were administered.

B The use of *through* is awkward for the reason already indicated. Compared with *will ... prove*, the present participle *proving* less clearly signals the prospective nature of the experimenters' goal.

C The word *experimentation*, because it can simply mean "trying out new things or ideas," is unnecessarily imprecise compared with *experiments*. The present tense *prove* does not clearly signal the prospective nature of the experimenters' goal.

D The use of the verbal noun *experimenting* is less idiomatic than *experiments*. Compared with *will ... prove*, the present participle *proving* less clearly signals the prospective nature of the experimenters' goal.

E **Correct.** The use of the preposition *in*, the word *experiments*, and the future *will ... prove* create a sentence that avoids some of the potential problems identified.

The correct answer is E.

SC48420.01

836. Linking arrangements among secondary schools and the workplace never evolved in the United States as they have in most other developed countries.

(A) among secondary schools and the workplace never evolved in the United States as they have

(B) in the United States among secondary schools and the workplace never evolved as they did

(C) between secondary schools and the workplace never evolved in the United States as

(D) in the United States between secondary schools and the workplace never evolved as they have

(E) between secondary schools and the workplace never evolved in the United States as they did

Diction; Verb Form

The sentence presents a contrast between the United States and other countries with respect to the relationship (or lack thereof) between school and workplace. The sentence has two flaws. The first flaw is the use of *among*, which should be used to indicate only a relationship of more than two entities. Here, the use of *among* suggests a relationship among secondary schools. But the intended relationship is between two entities: secondary schools on the one hand and the workplace on the other. The preposition *between* is a better usage. The second flaw relates to the use of *have*. It would be appropriate as a proxy for a preceding occurrence of the past-perfect verb *have evolved*, rather than the simple-past verb from, *evolved*, used in the first part of the sentence. The simple-past verb form *did* is a better proxy for *evolved*.

A   The sentence is flawed in the ways explained.

B   The default reading of the phrase *in the United States* would treat it as a modifier of *arrangements*, but this reading is nonsensical in the context of the sentence as a whole; it makes no sense to say that linking arrangements in the United States have evolved in other countries. The parallelism that would help to highlight the intended comparison is lost. Also, the preposition *among* is not correct, for the reason explained above.

C   This can convey what is likely an unintended meaning: that the linking arrangements never evolved in the United States and never evolved in most other developed countries.

D   The default reading of the phrase *in the United States* would treat it as a modifier of *arrangements*, but this reading is nonsensical in the context of the sentence as a whole; it makes no sense to say that linking arrangements in the United States have evolved in other countries. The phrase would be better treated as an adverbial modifier of the verb *evolved*. The parallelism that would help to highlight the comparison is lost.

E   **Correct.** None of the flaws identified above, nor any other flaw, is present here.

The correct answer is E.

SC01603

837. The United Parcel Service plans <u>to convert its more than 2,000 gasoline-powered trucks in the Los Angeles area to</u> run on cleaner-burning natural gas.

(A) to convert its more than 2,000 gasoline-powered trucks in the Los Angeles area to

(B) to convert its more than 2,000 trucks in the Los Angeles area that are powered by gasoline to

(C) on converting its more than 2,000 gasoline-powered trucks in the Los Angeles area that will

(D) for its more than 2,000 gasoline-powered trucks in the Los Angeles area to convert to

(E) that its more than 2,000 trucks in the Los Angeles area that are powered by gasoline will convert to

Verb Form; Logical Predication

The sentence reports a company's plan to convert certain of its trucks to run on natural gas. Issues to note include: what construction should follow the verb *plan* and how the class of trucks that are to be converted is described.

A   **Correct.** The planned action is described by the infinitive form *to convert*. Of the company's trucks, those in question are specified by the adjective *gasoline-powered* and by the adjectival phrase *in the Los Angeles area*. The goal of the conversion is given by the infinitive verbal phrase *to run ... gas*.

B   The introduction of the relative clause *that are powered by gasoline* is unnecessarily awkward, especially because the relative pronoun *that* is not adjacent to its antecedent *trucks*.

C   The construction *plans on converting ...* is not a standard form, even if sometimes used informally. The future tense in the relative clause *that will run ...* does not clearly specify that the trucks' running on natural gas is the goal of the planned conversion.

D   This fails to capture the thought in the given sentence, which indicates that the company plans to convert the trucks, rather than (as here) the trucks converting. In this version, *to convert* is being used intransitively (without an object), with its implicit subject being the noun phrase *its more than ... area*, which refers to the trucks.

E   This refers to a plan that the trucks will convert (where *convert* is used intransitively), rather than to a plan to convert the trucks. This intransitive use makes no sense in the context. The introduction of the relative clause *that are powered by gasoline* is unnecessarily awkward.

The correct answer is A.

9.9 Sentence Correction Answer Explanations

SC02443

838. Foraging at all times of the day and night, but interspersing their feeding with periods of rest that last <u>between one and eight hours, a sperm whale could eat so</u> much as a ton of squid a day.

- (A) between one and eight hours, a sperm whale could eat so
- (B) between one and eight hours, sperm whales can eat as
- (C) between one to eight hours, sperm whales could eat as
- (D) from one to eight hours, sperm whales could eat so
- (E) from one to eight hours, a sperm whale can eat so

Agreement; Diction

Although this sentence, as presented, uses the conditional or past verb form *could*, it is more plausibly intended to make a general statement about the actual behavior of a species, a statement that holds in the present day. For that purpose, the present indicative *can* is preferable. *So much as* is not the correct wording to express the upper level of a variable amount; *as much as* should be used instead. Also, although the singular *a sperm whale* can be used to refer to sperm whales generally, the plural *their* needs to refer to the plural *sperm whales*.

- A This sentence incorrectly uses *so*. Also, the plural *their* does not agree with the singular *sperm whale*.
- **B Correct.** Both *can* and *as* are used; also, *sperm whales* agrees with the plural *their*.
- C *To* is the wrong word to use with *between*. The proper construction would be *between . . . and* or *from . . . to*.
- D This sentence incorrectly uses *so*.
- E *So* is not the correct form; also the use of the singular *a sperm whale* does not agree with the plural *their*.

The correct answer is B.

SC14796

839. In some types of pine tree, <u>a thick layer of needles protects the buds from which new growth proceeds; consequently they are able to withstand forest fires relatively well</u>.

- (A) a thick layer of needles protects the buds from which new growth proceeds; consequently they are able to withstand forest fires relatively well
- (B) a thick needle layer protects buds from where new growth proceeds, so that they can withstand forest fires relatively well
- (C) a thick layer of needles protect the buds from which new growth proceeds; thus, they are able to withstand relatively well any forest fires
- (D) since the buds from which new growth proceeds are protected by a thick needle layer, consequently they can therefore withstand forest fires relatively well
- (E) because the buds where new growth happens are protected by a thick layer of needles, they are able to withstand forest fires relatively easily as a result

Grammatical Construction; Rhetorical Construction

This sentence is fine as written. It uses the correct *from which* to introduce the relative clause modifying *buds* and avoids redundant expressions of causation, such as *consequently . . . therefore*, or *because . . . as a result*.

- **A Correct.** The relative clause starting with *from which* is in the correct form, and the causality is expressed efficiently and clearly with one word, *consequently*.
- B In this context, *needle layer* is less precise than the more standard *layer of needles*, which makes it clear that the layer is composed of needles rather than being, for example, a layer of a needle. *From where* is not the correct form, because it is redundant in using two words that express the idea of location (*from* and *where*) instead of one.
- C The short direct object *any forest fires* is separated from its verb *withstand* by an adverb phrase; this word order is awkward, and is acceptable only with very long direct objects and in some cases where there is no other reasonable way to eliminate ambiguity.
- D This version is unnecessarily redundant in expressing causation, using all of *since*, *consequently*, and *therefore*. As in answer choice B, *layer of needles* would be more precise than *needle layer*.
- E This version is unnecessarily redundant in expressing causation, using both *because* and *as a result*.

The correct answer is A.

SC08577

840. The tourism commission has conducted surveys of hotels in the most popular resorts, <u>with the ultimate goal of reducing the guests who end up expressing overall dissatisfaction with the service in the hotels.</u>

(A) with the ultimate goal of reducing the guests who end up expressing overall dissatisfaction with the service in the hotels

(B) with the goal to ultimately reduce the number of guests who end up expressing overall dissatisfaction with the hotels' service

(C) ultimately with the goal to reduce expressions of overall dissatisfaction by the guests with the hotel service

(D) in an ultimate attempt to reduce the number of guests that ends up expressing overall dissatisfaction with the hotels' service

(E) with the ultimate goal of reducing the number of guests who express overall dissatisfaction with the hotels' service

Verb Form; Rhetorical Construction

This sentence seems to be saying something absurd: that the goal is to reduce the guests themselves, instead of to reduce the **number** of guests or the expressions of dissatisfaction. It is also awkward in introducing the superfluous *end up*; but at least, if it does so, the correct form to agree with the subject *guests* is *end up*, not *ends up*, which is used in answer choice D. In general, direct modifiers (such as *with the (hotel) service*) should not be separated from the word they modify (such as *dissatisfaction*) if possible.

A *Reducing the guests* is clearly not the intent of the sentence; it should be phrased as reducing the number of guests or the expressions of dissatisfaction.

B *With the goal to ultimately reduce* is awkward and unidiomatic.

C *With the hotel service* should be placed next to *dissatisfaction*; also, *ultimately with the goal* is awkward, better phrased as *with the ultimate goal*.

D The relative clause *that ends up . . .* modifies the plural *guests* (not, in this context, *number*), so the correct verb form is *end up*.

E **Correct.** The *with* phrase is concise, and it is the number of guests, not the guests themselves, that is to be reduced. *With the hotel's service* is adjacent to *dissatisfaction*. Also, in the relative clause starting with *who*, the implicit subject of *express* is *guests*, so this verb correctly agrees with its subject.

The correct answer is E.

SC01607

841. A new study suggests that the conversational pace of everyday life may be so brisk <u>it hampers the ability of some children for distinguishing discrete sounds and words and, the result is, to make</u> sense of speech.

(A) it hampers the ability of some children for distinguishing discrete sounds and words and, the result is, to make

(B) that it hampers the ability of some children to distinguish discrete sounds and words and, as a result, to make

(C) that it hampers the ability of some children to distinguish discrete sounds and words and, the result of this, they are unable to make

(D) that it hampers the ability of some children to distinguish discrete sounds and words, and results in not making

(E) as to hamper the ability of some children for distinguishing discrete sounds and words, resulting in being unable to make

Rhetorical Construction; Parallelism; Diction

The sentence describes a hypothesized causal series: The fast conversational pace impairs children's ability to distinguish individual sounds and words, and this, in turn, impairs their ability to make sense of speech. These two consequences, both impaired abilities, are most clearly and efficiently expressed in parallel infinitive phrases (*to distinguish* and *to make*). The explanatory phrase *as a result* before the second infinitive clarifies the sequence. The term *ability* should be followed by the preposition *to*, not *for*.

A *For* is the wrong preposition to follow *ability*; the phrase *and, the result is*, introduces a new clause which indicates that children's inability to distinguish sounds enables them to make sense of speech.

B **Correct.** The two abilities hampered by the fast pace of conversation are described with the parallel infinitive phrases *to distinguish* and *to make*.

C *The result of this* is a new subject that grammatically requires a new verb; the phrase is wordy and unclear.

D This version of the sentence nonsensically suggests that the pace of speech results in not making sense of speech, removing the children from the picture as the ones who are affected.

E The phrase is awkward, wordy, and unclear; *for* is the incorrect preposition to follow ability.

The correct answer is B.

SC07035

842. The nineteenth-century chemist Humphry Davy presented the results of his early experiments in his "Essay on Heat and Light," a critique of all chemistry since Robert Boyle as well as a vision of a new chemistry that Davy hoped to found.

    (A) a critique of all chemistry since Robert Boyle as well as a vision of a
    (B) a critique of all chemistry following Robert Boyle and also his envisioning of a
    (C) a critique of all chemistry after Robert Boyle and envisioning as well
    (D) critiquing all chemistry from Robert Boyle forward and also a vision of
    (E) critiquing all the chemistry done since Robert Boyle as well as his own envisioning of

Parallelism; Rhetorical Construction

The main objective of the sentence is to describe "Essay on Heat and Light" as Davy's presentation of his own experiments and to further explain that the essay served as both a critique of previous chemistry and a vision of a new kind of chemistry. The clearest, most effective form for providing this explanation of the essay's function is to make *critique* and *vision* both appositives of "Essay on Heat and Light," and to present them in a parallel structure.

A **Correct.** The phrases describing the essay's function are presented in parallel form.

B *Critique* and *his envisioning* are not parallel; the phrase *and also his envisioning* is unnecessarily wordy; it is also unclear to whom *his* refers.

C The two descriptors are not parallel.
D The two descriptors are not parallel.
E The meaning is confused in the assertion that Davy critiqued his own vision of chemistry.

The correct answer is A.

SC02280

843. To attract the most talented workers, some companies are offering a wider range of benefits, letting employees pick those most important to them.

    (A) benefits, letting employees pick those most important to them
    (B) benefits, letting employees pick the most important of them to themselves
    (C) benefits and letting employees pick the most important to themselves
    (D) benefits and let employees pick the most important to them
    (E) benefits and let employees pick those that are most important to themselves

Diction; Parallelism; Verb Form

The sentence describes the benefit options offered by some companies, which allow employees to *pick those most important to them*. *Letting* maintains the progressive sense of *are offering*; *those* refers clearly and concisely to *benefits*; and *them* is the correct pronoun to serve as the object of the preposition *to*.

A **Correct.** The sentence clearly and concisely explains benefit options that allow employees to *pick those most important to them*.

B *The most important of them to themselves* is wordy, and the function of *themselves* is unclear. Normally, *themselves* would be either reflexive or emphatic, but in this case it cannot reasonably be taken in either of those ways. This nonstandard use of the pronoun makes it unclear whether *to themselves* is supposed to modify *pick* or *most important of them*.

C The pronoun *themselves* is used incorrectly, and its intended function is unclear. Normally, *themselves* would be either reflexive or emphatic, but in this case it cannot reasonably be taken in either of those ways. This nonstandard use of the pronoun makes it unclear whether *to themselves* is supposed to modify *pick* or *most important of them*.

D The present tense verb *let* incorrectly shifts tense from the present progressive *are offering*.

E The present tense verb *let* incorrectly shifts tense from the present progressive *are offering*; the function of *themselves* is unclear. Normally, *themselves* would be either reflexive or emphatic, but in this case it cannot reasonably be taken in either of those ways. This nonstandard use of the pronoun makes it unclear whether *to themselves* is supposed to modify *pick* or *most important of them*.

The correct answer is A.

SC01583

844. Many of the earliest known images of Hindu deities in India date from the time of the Kushan Empire, fashioned either from the spotted sandstone of Mathura or Gandharan grey schist.

(A) Empire, fashioned either from the spotted sandstone of Mathura or

(B) Empire, fashioned from either the spotted sandstone of Mathura or from

(C) Empire, either fashioned from the spotted sandstone of Mathura or

(D) Empire and either fashioned from the spotted sandstone of Mathura or from

(E) Empire and were fashioned either from the spotted sandstone of Mathura or from

Logical Predication; Parallelism

The sentence makes two claims about the earliest known images of Hindu deities in India: They date from the Kushan Empire, and they are made from sandstone or schist. The clearest, most effective way to incorporate these two claims into a single sentence is to provide two parallel predicates for the single subject, *the earliest known images of Hindu deities in India*. The two options of media, presented as either/or choices, must also be given in parallel structure: *either from ... or from ... or from either ... or ...*.

A Placement of the modifier *fashioned ...* suggests that the *Empire* (the closest noun), not the images of the deities, was fashioned out of these materials; to parallel *either from*, the preposition *from* should also follow *or*.

B Parallelism requires that *either* precede the first appearance of *from* or that the second appearance of *from* be eliminated.

C As in (A) and (B), the placement of the modifier after *Empire* is misleading; parallelism requires that the phrase *fashioned from*, or another comparable verb and preposition, follow *or*.

D Parallelism requires that a verb follow *or*, since a verb follows *either*.

E **Correct.** Two verbs, *date* and *were fashioned*, introduce parallel predicates for the subject, *earliest known images*; the choices of media are correctly presented with the structure *either from ... or from*.

The correct answer is E.

SC01051

845. Tides typically range from three to six feet, but while some places show no tides at all, some others, such as the Bay of Fundy, have tides of at least thirty feet and more.

(A) some others, such as the Bay of Fundy, have tides of at least thirty feet and more

(B) the others, such as the Bay of Fundy, that have tides of more than thirty feet

(C) others, such as the Bay of Fundy, have tides of more than thirty feet

(D) those at the Bay of Fundy, which has tides of more than thirty feet

(E) the ones at the Bay of Fundy have tides of at least thirty feet and more

Idiom; Grammatical Construction

This sentence defines typical tides and then draws a contrast between locations with tides lower than that norm and locations with tides higher than the norm. The proper idiom for drawing this contrast is *some places* and *others*—not *some places* and *some others* as written. The height of tides in places such as the Bay of Fundy is expressed in a confusing manner since *at least thirty feet* sets a lower limit on the height. This wording is pointlessly redundant with the phrase *and more*, which follows it. *At least* would normally be used to indicate that the writer does not know, or prefers not to say, whether the tides are sometimes higher. *And more* rhetorically conflicts with this by signaling a definite commitment to the claim that they are (at least sometimes) higher. A charitable reading suggests that *tides of more than thirty feet* is the intended meaning.

A The sentence contains repetitive and redundant wording—*some places* and *some others*, and *at least thirty feet and more*.

B The final clause is incomplete because *that* introduces a subordinate clause, leaving the subject *others* with no main verb.

C **Correct.** A contrast is drawn between places with low tides and places with high tides using the expression *some places* and *others*, and the height of the high tides is expressed clearly and without redundancy.

D The pronoun *those*, which refers to *places*, does not make sense along with *at the Bay of Fundy*, which names a single place; the final clause is incomplete because *which* introduces a subordinate clause, leaving the subject *those* with no verb.

E The word *ones*, which refers to *places*, does not make sense along with *at the Bay of Fundy*, which names a single place; *at least thirty feet and more* is redundant and confusing.

The correct answer is C.

SC01028

846. A leading figure in the Scottish Enlightenment, Adam Smith's two major books are to democratic capitalism what Marx's *Das Kapital* is to socialism.

(A) Adam Smith's two major books are to democratic capitalism what

(B) Adam Smith's two major books are to democratic capitalism like

(C) Adam Smith's two major books are to democratic capitalism just as

(D) Adam Smith wrote two major books that are to democratic capitalism similar to

(E) Adam Smith wrote two major books that are to democratic capitalism what

Idiom; Logical Predication

A leading figure in the Scottish Enlightenment describes Adam Smith, not his two books, so the name of Adam Smith must immediately follow the opening phrase. The comparison between Smith's books and Marx's book is expressed as a ratio, so the correct idiomatic expression is *x is to y what a is to b*.

A The opening phrase is a dangling modifier because it describes Smith, not his books.

B The opening phrase is a dangling modifier; *like* is an incorrect word for making the comparison.

C The opening phrase is a dangling modifier; *just as* is an incorrect term for the comparison.

D *Similar to* is an incorrect conclusion to the comparison introduced by *are to*.

E **Correct.** The opening phrase is followed by the subject that it modifies, Adam Smith, and the comparison of the two men's work is presented idiomatically.

The correct answer is E.

SC04331

847. Researchers studying the brain scans of volunteers who pondered ethical dilemmas have found that the basis for making tough moral judgments is emotion, not logic or analytical reasoning.

(A) the brain scans of volunteers who pondered ethical dilemmas have found that the basis for making tough moral judgments is

(B) the brain scans of volunteers who pondered ethical dilemmas and found the basis to make tough moral decisions to be

(C) the brain scans of volunteers pondering ethical dilemmas and found that the basis for making tough moral decisions is

(D) volunteers' brain scans while pondering ethical dilemmas have found the basis to make tough moral judgments to be

(E) volunteers' brain scans while they pondered ethical dilemmas have found the basis for making tough moral judgments is

Logical Predication; Grammatical Construction

The sentence reports that researchers got volunteers to ponder ethical dilemmas and make moral judgments. Brain scans revealed that the volunteers' judgments were based on emotion rather than logical analysis. The main clause of this sentence is *Researchers . . . have found that . . .*; embedded within this sentence, the present participial phrase *studying . . .* describes the researchers, the relative clause *who pondered . . .* describes the volunteers, and the object of the main verb appears as a noun clause *that the basis . . . is. . . .*

A **Correct.** The sentence is coherent and grammatically correct.

B The use of the conjunction *and* immediately before *found* indicates that the past tense verbs *pondered* and *found* both have *volunteers* as subject, but this changes the original sentence, making it a long noun phrase rather than a complete sentence.

C The conjunction *and* leaves the verb *found* without a subject, and this changes the original sentence into a sequence of incoherently connected phrases rather than a complete sentence.

D The phrase *the basis to make* is unidiomatic, a sufficient reason for rejecting this option. The placement of the modifier *while pondering* appears in a form parallel to *studying* and means that the researchers, not the volunteers, were pondering ethical dilemmas. This does not make the sentence incoherent, but creates a sentence that fails to capture the meaning clearly intended in the original sentence.

E Because the word *volunteers'* is a possessive form, and functions adjectivally as a modifier of *brain scans*, *they* must refer back to *researchers* rather than to *volunteers'*. This is not incorrect in itself, but, as with (D), the resulting sentence fails to capture the intended meaning of the original sentence.

The correct answer is A.

SC02060

848. Rivaling the pyramids of Egypt or even the ancient cities of the Maya as an achievement, <u>the army of terra-cotta warriors created to protect Qin Shi Huang, China's first emperor, in his afterlife is more than 2,000 years old and took 700,000 artisans more than 36 years to complete</u>.

(A) the army of terra-cotta warriors created to protect Qin Shi Huang, China's first emperor, in his afterlife is more than 2,000 years old and took 700,000 artisans more than 36 years to complete

(B) Qin Shi Huang, China's first emperor, was protected in his afterlife by an army of terra-cotta warriors that was created more than 2,000 years ago by 700,000 artisans who took more than 36 years to complete it

(C) it took 700,000 artisans more than 36 years to create an army of terra-cotta warriors more than 2,000 years ago that would protect Qin Shi Huang, China's first emperor, in his afterlife

(D) more than 2,000 years ago, 700,000 artisans worked more than 36 years to create an army of terra-cotta warriors to protect Qin Shi Huang, China's first emperor, in his afterlife

(E) more than 36 years were needed to complete the army of terra-cotta warriors that 700,000 artisans created 2,000 years ago to protect Qin Shi Huang, China's first emperor, in his afterlife

Logical Predication; Rhetorical Construction

The opening modifier, *Rivaling the pyramids … describes the army of terra-cotta warriors*, which must immediately follow the modifier. The placement of the predicates that follow is important; they must clarify two things about the army of terra-cotta warriors: how old it is and how long it took to complete. The clearest and most effective way to express these two assertions is as parallel verb phrases, *is more than 2,000 years old* and *took … more than 36 years to complete*.

A **Correct.** The opening phrase correctly modifies the subject, *the army of terra-cotta warriors*; the placement of modifiers and predicates in the main clause makes the meaning of the sentence clear.

B Opening phrase is a dangling modifier because it does not describe the subject *Qin Shi Huang*; in addition, the sentence is awkward and unclear.

C Opening phrase is a dangling modifier because it does not describe the subject *it*; the sequence of information presented is confusing and unclear.

D Opening phrase is a dangling modifier because it does not describe the subject *700,000 artisans*.

E Opening phrase is a dangling modifier because it does not describe the subject *more than 36 years*.

The correct answer is A.

849. In California, a lack of genetic variation in the Argentine ant has allowed the species to spread widely; <u>due to their being so genetically similar to one another, the ants consider all their fellows to be a close relative and thus do not engage in the kind of fierce intercolony struggles that limits</u> the spread of this species in its native Argentina.

(A) due to their being so genetically similar to one another, the ants consider all their fellows to be a close relative and thus do not engage in the kind of fierce intercolony struggles that limits

(B) due to its being so genetically similar, the ant considers all its fellows to be a close relative and thus does not engage in the kind of fierce intercolony struggles that limit

(C) because it is so genetically similar, the ant considers all its fellows to be close relatives and thus does not engage in the kind of fierce intercolony struggles that limits

(D) because they are so genetically similar to one another, the ants consider all their fellows to be close relatives and thus do not engage in the kind of fierce intercolony struggles that limit

(E) because of being so genetically similar to one another, the ants consider all their fellows to be a close relative and thus do not engage in the kind of fierce intercolony struggles that limits

Diction; Agreement

Words that express comparisons, such as *similar*, require either a plural object, with an optional expression of the entities being compared, or a singular object, in which case this explicit comparison is required. Thus *its being so genetically similar*, without this explicit comparison, is incorrect. Also, the two sides of the construction *consider . . . to be* must agree in number (*fellows . . . close relatives*, not *fellows . . . a close relative*).

A *Consider all their fellows to be a close relative* shows incorrect agreement, with plural *fellows* and singular *a close relative*.

B *Its being so genetically similar* is incorrect because there is no explicit statement of what the ant is similar to; also, the plural *fellows* and *singular a close relative* do not agree.

C *It is so genetically similar* is incorrect because there is no explicit statement of what the ant is similar to.

D **Correct.** The clause with *similar* uses the plural *they* and an explicit *to one another*, and agreement is respected between *ants* and *fellows*.

E The plural *fellows* and singular *a close relative* do not agree.

The correct answer is D.

850. Next month, state wildlife officials are scheduled to take over the job of increasing the wolf population in the federally designated recovery <u>area, the number of which will however</u> ultimately be dictated by the number of prey in the area.

(A) area, the number of which will however

(B) area; the size of the population, however, will

(C) area, however the number of wolves will

(D) area; the number of which will, however,

(E) area, when the size of the population will, however,

Grammatical Construction; Diction

The point of the sentence is that the ultimate size of the wolf population will be determined according to the number of prey in the area. However, the phrase *the number of which* has no referent since it cannot logically refer to the noncount noun *population* or to the singular *wolf*, which is used adjectivally here to modify *population*. The idea can be expressed clearly by making *the size of the population* the subject of a new independent clause: *the size of the population will be dictated by the number of prey.*

A *The number of which* cannot logically refer to the noncount noun *population* or to the singular *wolf*, which is used adjectivally here to modify *population*.

B **Correct.** The idea is expressed clearly with an independent clause: *the size of the population will be dictated by the number of prey.*

C *However* is intended to serve as a conjunctive adverb between the two independent clauses, but the punctuation of the sentence creates confusion by suggesting that *however* is modifying *are scheduled*. A semicolon after *area* and a comma after *however* would make the intended function of *however* clear.

D *The number of which* cannot logically refer to the noncount noun *population*; the semicolon creates confusion since it is not followed by an independent clause.

E *When* illogically suggests that the size of the population will be determined at the moment wildlife officials take over the task. This conflicts with the ensuing claim that the determination will *ultimately* depend on a long-term condition (*the number of prey in the area*).

The correct answer is B.

851. About 5 million acres in the United <u>States have been invaded by leafy spurge, a herbaceous plant from Eurasia with milky sap that gives mouth sores to cattle, displacing grasses and other cattle food and rendering</u> rangeland worthless.

(A) States have been invaded by leafy spurge, a herbaceous plant from Eurasia with milky sap that gives mouth sores to cattle, displacing grasses and other cattle food and rendering

(B) States have been invaded by leafy spurge, *a herbaceous plant from Eurasia*, with milky sap, that gives mouth sores to cattle and displaces grasses and other cattle food, rendering

(C) States have been invaded by leafy spurge, a herbaceous plant from Eurasia having milky sap that gives mouth sores to cattle and displacing grasses and other cattle food, rendering

(D) States, having been invaded by leafy spurge, a herbaceous plant from Eurasia with milky sap that gives mouth sores to cattle, displaces grasses and other cattle food, and renders

(E) States, having been invaded by leafy spurge, a herbaceous plant from Eurasia that has milky sap giving mouth sores to cattle and displacing grasses and other cattle food, rendering

Logical Predication; Grammatical Construction

The sentence explains that leafy spurge causes mouth sores in cattle and also displaces other plants eaten by cattle. However, the structure of the sentence seems, illogically, to indicate that *displacing grasses* modifies either the immediately preceding phrase (*that gives mouth sores to cattle*) or the main subject of the sentence (*about 5 million acres in the United States*). A clearer way to express the effects of the leafy spurge invasion is with a compound predicate in the subordinate clause: *that gives mouth sores ... and displaces grasses*.

A *Displacing grasses* appears illogically to modify either *about 5 million acres in the United States* or *that gives mouth sores to cattle*.

B **Correct.** The effects of the leafy spurge invasion are expressed clearly with a compound predicate in the subordinate clause: *that gives mouth sores ... and displaces grasses*. The parenthetical commas around *with milky sap* make it clear that the entire phrase *that gives ... and displaces ... rendering ...* is intended to modify *a herbaceous plant from Eurasia*. Although the sap may well be the means by which the plant gives mouth sores to cattle, the sentence can be well formed and meaningful without making a definite commitment to whether that is the case.

C *Having* and *displacing* should not be expressed in parallel form since the first is a permanent characteristic of leafy spurge and the second refers to an effect of the plant's invasion.

D The subject of the sentence, *5 million acres* is not clearly paired with a verb. The structure of the sentence suggests that *5 million acres* may be the intended subject of both *displaces* and *renders* but it is illogical to say that 5 million acres displaces grasses and renders rangeland worthless.

E The subject of the sentence, *5 million acres* is not clearly paired with a verb. The structure of the sentence suggests that *5 million acres* may be the intended subject of both *displaces* and *renders* but it is illogical to say that 5 million acres displaces grasses and renders rangeland worthless.

The correct answer is B.

852. <u>While it costs about the same to run nuclear plants as other types of power plants, it is the fixed costs that stem from building nuclear plants that makes it more expensive for them to generate electricity.</u>

(A) While it costs about the same to run nuclear plants as other types of power plants, it is the fixed costs that stem from building nuclear plants that makes it more expensive for them to generate electricity.

(B) While the cost of running nuclear plants is about the same as for other types of power plants, the fixed costs that stem from building nuclear plants make the electricity they generate more expensive.

(C) Even though it costs about the same to run nuclear plants as for other types of power plants, it is the fixed costs that stem from building nuclear plants that makes the electricity they generate more expensive.

(D) It costs about the same to run nuclear plants as for other types of power plants, whereas the electricity they generate is more expensive, stemming from the fixed costs of building nuclear plants.

(E) The cost of running nuclear plants is about the same as other types of power plants, but the electricity they generate is made more expensive because of the fixed costs stemming from building nuclear plants.

Agreement; Logical Predication

The emphatic construction *it is X that does Y* (as in the phrase *it is Jane who knows the answer*) should be used only when there is a compelling reason to emphasize the doer of the action. In this sentence, the emphatic construction is used without good reason.

A   This sentence uses the emphatic structure *it is ... that* without justification. The singular verb *makes* violates the agreement within the structure. The verb *makes* should agree with the notional subject (*the fixed costs*), not with the pronoun *it*.

B   **Correct.** This answer choice clearly and succinctly compares the two types of costs.

C   In addition to using the more cumbersome emphatic structure, this version violates the agreement within the structure. The verb should agree with the notional subject (*the fixed costs*), not with the pronoun *it*.

D   The preposition *for* is redundant in comparing the two objects of *run*. Since it is not clear what *stemming ... refers to*, this is a dangling modifier.

E   The passive construction *electricity ... is made more expensive because of ...* is wordy and cumbersome. The preposition *for* is necessary in the comparison of the costs.

The correct answer is B.

SC03207

853. The 32 species that make up the dolphin family are closely related to whales and in fact <u>include the animal known as the killer whale, which can grow to be 30 feet long and is</u> famous for its aggressive hunting pods.

(A) include the animal known as the killer whale, which can grow to be 30 feet long and is

(B) include the animal known as the killer whale, growing as big as 30 feet long and

(C) include the animal known as the killer whale, growing up to 30 feet long and being

(D) includes the animal known as the killer whale, which can grow as big as 30 feet long and is

(E) includes the animal known as the killer whale, which can grow to be 30 feet long and it is

Rhetorical Construction; Agreement

The subject of the sentence is *the 32 species that make up the dolphin family*, and the sentence makes two claims about them: They are closely related, and they include the killer whale. The relative pronoun *which* restates the object of the second verb, reintroducing *the animal known as the killer whale* as the subject of a relative clause followed by two parallel verbs: *can grow* and *is famous*.

A   **Correct.** In this concise sentence, verbs agree in number with their subjects and the relative pronoun *which* indicates clearly that *the animal known as the killer whale* is the subject of the verbs in the dependent clause.

B   Changing the verb to the participial *growing* introduces ambiguity, because it could refer back to the subject of the sentence (*32 species*).

C   The participial *growing* might refer to *the 32 species*; the introduction of *being* is unnecessarily wordy and adds nothing in terms of meaning.

D   *as big as* is an idiomatically incorrect expression of the comparison; the plural verb form *include* is needed to match the plural subject *the 32 species*.

E   *It* simply restates the subject of the previous phrase, introducing more words but no additional meaning; the singular verb form *includes* should be the plural form *include*.

The correct answer is A.

SC06611

854. The first trenches <u>that were cut into a 500-acre site at Tell Hamoukar, Syria, have yielded strong evidence for centrally administered complex societies in northern regions of the Middle East that were arising simultaneously with but</u> independently of the more celebrated city-states of southern Mesopotamia, in what is now southern Iraq.

(A) that were cut into a 500-acre site at Tell Hamoukar, Syria, have yielded strong evidence for centrally administered complex societies in northern regions of the Middle East that were arising simultaneously with but

(B) that were cut into a 500-acre site at Tell Hamoukar, Syria, yields strong evidence that centrally administered complex societies in northern regions of the Middle East were arising simultaneously with but also

(C) having been cut into a 500-acre site at Tell Hamoukar, Syria, have yielded strong evidence that centrally administered complex societies in northern regions of the Middle East were arising simultaneously but

(D) cut into a 500-acre site at Tell Hamoukar, Syria, yields strong evidence of centrally administered complex societies in northern regions of the Middle East arising simultaneously but also

(E) cut into a 500-acre site at Tell Hamoukar, Syria, have yielded strong evidence that centrally administered complex societies in northern regions of the Middle East arose simultaneously with but

Rhetorical Construction; Agreement; Grammatical Construction

This sentence, explaining interconnections among a number of events, needs to be streamlined as much as possible in order to become understandable. To this end, unnecessary words and structures should be eliminated. Prominent among these are the relative clauses beginning with *that*. Additionally, the subject of this sentence is the plural *trenches*, which requires a plural verb.

A   *That were cut …* and *that were arising …* are unnecessarily wordy and create an unnecessarily complicated and confusing sentence structure.

B   In addition to the unnecessarily wordy relative clauses, the singular verb *yields* does not agree with the plural subject *trenches*.

C   *Having been cut …* is unnecessarily wordy; *arising simultaneously* must be followed by the preposition *with* in order to make sense.

D   The singular verb *yields* does not agree with the plural subject *trenches*; *also* adds no meaning to the sentence.

E   **Correct.** Unnecessary clauses and phrases are avoided, and the subject and verb of the main clause agree in number.

The correct answer is E.

SC02317

855. Companies are relying more and more on networked computers for such critical tasks as inventory management, electronic funds transfer, and electronic data interchange, <u>in which standard business transactions are handled via computer rather than on paper</u>.

(A) in which standard business transactions are handled via computer rather than on paper

(B) where computers handle standard business transactions rather than on paper

(C) in which computers handle standard business transactions instead of on paper

(D) where standard business transactions are handled, not with paper, but instead via computer

(E) in which standard business transactions are being handled via computer, in place of on paper

Idiom; Logical Predication; Rhetorical Construction

The concluding comparison in this sentence uses the idiom *rather than*, which requires parallel structures. In this sentence the prepositional phrase *via computer* parallels *on paper*. Substituting *where* for *in which* creates a nonstandard idiom.

A   **Correct.** This sentence uses standard idiomatic constructions and avoids the problems that are found in the other versions.

B *Where* is a nonstandard way to refer to a noun that does not name a location. If electronic data interchange were a location, this version would entail the odd claim that *on paper* is an alternative location at which computers would be expected to process information.

C The comparison of the clause *computers handle...* with the prepositional phrase *on paper* illogically treats a location (*on paper*) as an alternative to an activity (*computers handle*).

D As in (B), *where* is a nonstandard idiom. The commas around *not with paper* appear to make this phrase parenthetical; thus, it is somewhat unclear what *instead via computer* is contrasted with.

E The pile of prepositions in the phrase *in place of on paper* is unnecessarily confusing and wordy.

The correct answer is A.

SC07231

856. Combining enormous physical strength with higher intelligence, the Neanderthals <u>appear as equipped for facing any obstacle the environment could put in their path,</u> but their relatively sudden disappearance during the Paleolithic era indicates that an inability to adapt to some environmental change led to their extinction.

(A) appear as equipped for facing any obstacle the environment could put in their path,

(B) appear to have been equipped to face any obstacle the environment could put in their path,

(C) appear as equipped to face any obstacle the environment could put in their paths,

(D) appeared as equipped to face any obstacle the environment could put in their paths,

(E) appeared to have been equipped for facing any obstacle the environment could put in their path,

Verb Form; Diction

Because Neanderthals "disappeared," the verb describing their apparent abilities cannot be present tense, so *as equipped* must be changed to *to have been equipped*. The expression *equipped to face* is clearer and more direct than *equipped for facing*.

A *As equipped* indicates that Neanderthals still appear this way; *equipped* should be followed by an infinitive form instead of a prepositional phrase.

B **Correct.** The verb tense clearly indicates that the current evidence is about Neanderthals in the past.

C *As equipped* does not indicate that Neanderthals appeared this way in the past; while individual Neanderthals may well have followed different paths, this sentence is about the single evolutionary path taken by Neanderthals as a species.

D Present-tense *appear* is needed to parallel present-tense *indicates* and to reinforce that this is current evidence about Neanderthals in the past; as in (C), *paths* should be singular.

E *For facing* is an incorrect substitution of a prepositional phrase for an infinitive.

The correct answer is B.

SC02135

857. To map Earth's interior, geologists use a network of seismometers to chart seismic waves that originate in the earth's crust and ricochet around its <u>interior, most rapidly traveling through cold, dense regions and slower</u> through hotter rocks.

(A) interior, most rapidly traveling through cold, dense regions and slower

(B) interior, which travel most rapidly through cold, dense regions, and more slowly

(C) interior, traveling most rapidly through cold, dense regions and more slowly

(D) interior and most rapidly travel through cold, dense regions, and slower

(E) interior and that travel most rapidly through cold, dense regions and slower

Grammatical Construction; Parallelism

This sentence explains in detail an activity of geologists (using seismometers to chart waves), focusing primarily on the object, seismic waves. A description of these waves is developed in a relative clause (*that originate... hotter rocks*) that contains a compound verb phrase (*originate... ricochet...*). The action, *ricochet*, is further described in a participial phrase in which *traveling...* is then further described in a comparison of travel speeds in cold and hot regions of Earth's crust.

A The two expressions of comparison should be parallel. Because *most rapidly* is placed before the verb, it appears to modify the entire ensuing phrase, including *slower*. This and the contrast between the forms of *rapidly* and *slower* make the comparisons nonparallel. Some usage advisers consider *slower* to be only an adjective. Although *slower* is sometimes used as an adverb, that usage would be more appropriate with the parallel *faster*. The stark contrast between this typically adjectival form and the clearly adverbial *ly* form is somewhat jarring.

B   The referent of the relative pronoun *which* is unclear.

C   **Correct.** The modifiers are parallel and correctly positioned in relation to the verb.

D   This version of the sentence offers *travel* as a compound verb parallel with *originate* and *ricochet* rather than as a description of how the waves ricochet. It has the same problems with parallelism as (A).

E   Adding a relative clause *and that . . .* makes this sentence wordy and awkward.

The correct answer is C.

SC02470

858. Prices at the producer level are only 1.3 percent higher now <u>than a year ago and are going down, even though floods in the Midwest and drought in the South are hurting crops and therefore raised</u> corn and soybean prices.

(A) than a year ago and are going down, even though floods in the Midwest and drought in the South are hurting crops and therefore raised

(B) than those of a year ago and are going down, even though floods in the Midwest and drought in the South are hurting crops and therefore raising

(C) than a year ago and are going down, despite floods in the Midwest and drought in the South, and are hurting crops and therefore raising

(D) as those of a year ago and are going down, even though floods in the Midwest and drought in the South hurt crops and therefore raise

(E) as they were a year ago and are going down, despite floods in the Midwest and drought in the South, and are hurting crops and therefore raising

Logical Predication; Verb Form

The sentence as written makes an illogical comparison between *prices at the producer level* and a time period (*a year ago*); surely the intended comparison is between such prices now and those of a year ago. The clause at the end of the sentence states that flooding and a drought *are hurting* crops, and as a result of this, they have *raised* prices of certain crops. *Are hurting* is in the present progressive tense, indicating an ongoing process; *raised* is in the simple past tense, indicating a completed action. It would be more appropriate to use the present progressive tense here as well, *[are] raising*.

A   The first part of this version of the sentence illogically compares prices to a time; the second part of the sentence indicates that a completed action (*raised . . . prices*) results from an ongoing present condition (*floods . . . and drought . . . are hurting crop*s).

B   **Correct.** This version of the sentence makes an appropriate comparison (between prices now and those of a year ago), and uses tenses in an appropriate way.

C   Like (A), this version of the sentence illogically compares prices to time past. Furthermore, in this version, *Prices* is the subject not only for the verb *are* but also for the verbs *are hurting* and *[are] raising*, which makes no sense.

D   The comparative adjective *higher* requires the comparative term *than* instead of *as*; the tenses of the verbs in the latter half of the sentence, *hurt* (simple past) and *raise* (simple present), do not work together logically.

E   Like (D), this version inappropriately uses *as* instead of *than* with *higher*. Furthermore, like (C), in this version [*p*]*rices* is the subject not only for the verb *are* but also for the verbs *are hurting* and *[are] raising*.

The correct answer is B.

SC07117

859. Fossils of the arm of a <u>sloth found in Puerto Rico in 1991, and dated at 34 million years old, made it the earliest known mammal of</u> the Greater Antilles Islands.

(A) sloth found in Puerto Rico in 1991, and dated at 34 million years old, made it the earliest known mammal of

(B) sloth, that they found in Puerto Rico in 1991, has been dated at 34 million years old, thus making it the earliest mammal known on

(C) sloth that was found in Puerto Rico in 1991, was dated at 34 million years old, making this the earliest known mammal of

(D) sloth, found in Puerto Rico in 1991, have been dated at 34 million years old, making the sloth the earliest known mammal on

(E) sloth which, found in Puerto Rico in 1991, was dated at 34 million years old, made the sloth the earliest known mammal of

Agreement; Logical Predication

The subject of the sentence is the plural *fossils*, not *sloth*, and therefore requires a plural verb. *It* therefore does not have a singular antecedent. To clarify the identification of the oldest known mammal, the noun *the sloth* must be explicitly identified.

A   Because *sloth* is the object of a preposition and not the subject of the sentence, there is no reasonable antecedent for the pronoun *it*; in this construction, the subject of *made* is *fossils*, but it makes no sense to say that the *fossils* made it the earliest known mammal.

B   The introduction of the mysterious *they*, a pronoun without a reference, adds confusion to this sentence; the singular verb does not agree with the plural subject.

C   The relative clause *that was ...* is wordy and awkward; the singular verb does not agree with the plural subject.

D   **Correct.** The plural verb agrees with its plural subject, and *the sloth* is explicitly identified as *the earliest known mammal*.

E   The singular verb does not agree with the plural subject.

The correct answer is D.

SC01550

860. Recently physicians have determined that stomach ulcers are not caused by stress, alcohol, or rich foods, but a bacterium that dwells in the mucous lining of the stomach.

(A) not caused by stress, alcohol, or rich foods, but

(B) not caused by stress, alcohol, or rich foods, but are by

(C) caused not by stress, alcohol, or rich foods, but by

(D) caused not by stress, alcohol, and rich foods, but

(E) caused not by stress, alcohol, and rich foods, but are by

Parallelism; Diction

The formula used in this sentence *not this but that* requires parallel elements following *not* and *but*. This means that *not by stress, alcohol, or rich foods* must be balanced by *but by a bacterium*. ... There is no need to repeat the verb *are caused*, or even the auxiliary verb *are*, because the verb precedes the *not by ... but by ...* formula. The substitution of the conjunction *and* for the conjunction *or* changes the meaning of the sentence: *Stress, alcohol and rich foods* identifies the combination of these three factors as a suggested cause of stomach ulcers, whereas *stress, alcohol, or rich foods* offers three individual possibilities. There is no way to tell which one of these is the intended meaning of the sentence.

A   To preserve parallelism, *but* should be followed by *by*.

B   There is no reason to repeat the auxiliary verb *are*.

C   **Correct.** This sentence correctly uses the *not by ... but by ...* formula.

D   To preserve parallelism, *but* should be followed by *by*.

E   To preserve parallelism, *but* should be followed by *by*.

The correct answer is C.

SC05848

861. The eyes of the elephant seal adapt to darkness more quickly than any other animal yet tested, thus allowing it to hunt efficiently under the gloomy conditions at its feeding depth of between 300 and 700 meters.

(A) The eyes of the elephant seal adapt to darkness more quickly than any other animal yet tested, thus allowing it

(B) The eyes of the elephant seal adapt to darkness more quickly than does any other animal yet tested, allowing them

(C) The eyes of the elephant seal adapt to darkness more quickly than do those of any other animal yet tested, allowing it

(D) Because they adapt to darkness more quickly than any other animal yet tested, the eyes of the elephant seal allow it

(E) Because the eyes of the elephant seal adapt to darkness more quickly than do those of any other animal yet tested, it allows them

Logical Predication; Agreement

Logically, the eyes of the elephant seal should be contrasted with the eyes of other animals, not with the animals themselves. The sentence must make this comparison directly and precisely, with each subject interpretable as the subject of *adapt*. Given the correct subject (*those of any other animal yet tested*), which is plural, any reference to it must also be plural.

A *Any other animal yet tested* is incorrectly set up as the subject of *adapt*.

B *Any other animal yet tested* is incorrectly set up as the subject of *adapt*. The plural pronoun *them* seems to refer to eyes. Although there is a sense in which eyes can hunt, it is more reasonable to suppose that, in this context, the writer's intention is to mention how the eyes' quick adaptation allows the seal to hunt efficiently.

C **Correct.** The subject of the comparative phrase is correctly *those of any other animal yet tested*, the plural verb *do* correctly agrees with this subject (*those*), and the singular pronoun *it* correctly agrees with its antecedent (*elephant seal*).

D *Any other animal yet tested* is incorrectly set up as the subject of *adapt*.

E The subject is correct, but in the following clause *it* has no clear referent.

The correct answer is C.

SC01068

862. A mutual fund having billions of dollars in assets will typically invest that money in hundreds of <u>companies, rarely holding more than one percent</u> of the shares of any particular corporation.

(A) companies, rarely holding more than one percent

(B) companies, and it is rare to hold at least one percent or more

(C) companies and rarely do they hold more than one percent

(D) companies, so that they rarely hold more than one percent

(E) companies; rarely do they hold one percent or more

Agreement; Logical Predication

The participial phrase starting with *rarely holding* is predicated of the main subject *a mutual fund*. It elaborates on the effect of the main clause verb: since a mutual fund invests in hundreds of companies, it rarely holds more than one percent in any particular corporation.

A **Correct.** The participle *holding* in the embedded clause correctly refers to *a mutual fund*. It also correctly expresses the cause-and-effect relationship between investing in many companies and holding little in each company.

B The antecedent of *it is rare to hold* is not clear. The use of *it is rare* instead of *rarely* could be misleading.

C The use of *and* between the clauses makes them both main clauses. Thus, the cause-and-effect relationship between investing and holding is lost. The referent of *they* is unclear. It makes no sense to suppose that it refers to the hundreds of companies. Since it presumably refers to *a mutual fund*, it should be singular.

D The pronoun *they* refers to *a mutual fund* and thus should be singular.

E The pronoun *they* refers to *a mutual fund* and thus should be singular.

The correct answer is A.

SC08083

863. Positing an enormous volcanic explosion at the end of the Permian period would explain the presence of a buried crater, <u>account for the presence of the element iridium (originating deep within the earth), and the presence of quartz having been</u> shattered by high-impact shock waves.

(A) account for the presence of the element iridium (originating deep within the earth), and the presence of quartz having been

(B) of the element iridium (originating deep within the earth), and of quartz

(C) the element iridium (originating deep within the earth), and explain the presence of quartz having been

(D) the presence of the element iridium (originating deep within the earth), and explain the presence of quartz

(E) explain the element iridium (originating deep within the earth), and the presence of quartz

Parallelism; Rhetorical Construction

The sentence indicates that a volcanic explosion would explain the presence of three features, but those features are not expressed using parallel grammatical structures. The first two items in the list are verb phrases that involve needless repetition—*explain the presence of* and *account for the presence of*—while the third is an awkwardly worded noun phrase—*the presence of quartz having been shattered*. The three features can be identified more concisely with a list of prepositional phrases following *explain the presence*: *of a buried crater*, *of the element iridium*, and *of quartz*.

A The three features are not listed in parallel form; the sentence is wordy and awkward.

B **Correct.** The three features are identified with parallel prepositional phrases.

C The three features are not listed in parallel form since the first and third are verb phrases, while the second is a noun phrase; the wording is awkward and needlessly repetitive.

D The three features are not listed in parallel form since the first and third are verb phrases, while the second is a noun phrase; the wording is needlessly repetitive.

E The three features are not listed in parallel form since the first and second are verb phrases, while the third is a noun phrase; the sentence illogically states that an explosion would *explain the element iridium*, rather than explain the *presence* of the element.

The correct answer is B.

SC01561

864. The 19-year-old pianist and composer performed his most recent work all over Europe, Asia, and North America last year, winning prestigious awards in both London as well as Tokyo for his achievement at so young an age, and he is hoping to continue composing now that he has returned to Chicago.

(A) winning prestigious awards in both London as well as Tokyo for his achievement at so young an age, and he is hoping

(B) winning prestigious awards both in London and Tokyo for his achievement at such a young age, and hoping

(C) having won prestigious awards both in London and Tokyo for his achievement at so young an age, hoping

(D) winning prestigious awards in both London and Tokyo for his achievement at such a young age, and he hopes

(E) having won prestigious awards both in London as well as Tokyo for his achievement at so young an age, and he hopes

Idiom; Grammatical Construction

This sentence is about the past accomplishments and the future ambitions of a musician who recently won awards on a world tour. In some of the versions of the sentence, the phrase *as well as* is redundant with the word *both* before *London* and *Tokyo*. Idiomatically, the simple conjunction *and* completes the phrase beginning with *both*.

A The phrase *as well as* between *London* and *Tokyo* is not idiomatic (the idiomatic formula is *both X and Y*). The present progressive verb *is hoping* is unnecessarily wordy.

B Because *hoping* is parallel with *winning*, it suggests that the *hoping* and *winning* are contemporaneous, whereas in fact the musician won his awards last year but is now, in the present, upon his return, hoping to continue composing.

C The present-perfect participial phrase *having won* suggests that his winning took place before his performance tour. Furthermore, the use of *hoping* in this version of the sentence suggests that hoping is something the pianist did while on his performance tour *last year*, but the final phrase, *now that he has returned to Chicago*, indicates this is not so.

D **Correct.** This version of the sentence uses the correct idiomatic formula (*both X and Y*).

E The participial phrase *having won*... inaccurately states that the musician won his awards prior to his performance tour. Furthermore, *both in London as well as Tokyo* is unidiomatic, as indicated in the discussion of (A) above, and unparallel (*in* should either precede *both*, or else *in* should be added before *Tokyo*).

The correct answer is D.

SC01474
865. Starfish, with anywhere from five to eight arms, have a strong regenerative ability, and if <u>one arm is</u> <u>lost it quickly replaces it, sometimes by the animal overcompensating and</u> growing an extra one or two.

(A) one arm is lost it quickly replaces it, sometimes by the animal overcompensating and

(B) one arm is lost it is quickly replaced, with the animal sometimes overcompensating and

(C) they lose one arm they quickly replace it, sometimes by the animal overcompensating,

(D) they lose one arm they are quickly replaced, with the animal sometimes overcompensating,

(E) they lose one arm it is quickly replaced, sometimes with the animal overcompensating,

Agreement; Idiom

In a conditional sentence *if X, (then) Y*, rhetorical flow is enhanced by the two clauses sharing the same structure. If one clause is passive, the other should be passive; if one clause is active, the other should be active, too.

A The conditional clause has a passive verb, while the result clause has an active verb. The pronoun *it* should be plural since it refers to *starfish*. We know that *starfish* is plural in this sentence because it agrees with *have* in the main clause.

B **Correct.** The conditional structure is clear and correct.

C This answer choice allows the unintended reading that the animal replaces the missing arm by overcompensating. The logical connection between *overcompensating* and *growing* is unclear.

D The conditional clause has an active verb, while the result clause has a passive verb. The second *they* should refer to *arm*, so the agreement is not correct. The logical connection between *overcompensating* and *growing* is unclear.

E The conditional clause has an active verb, while the result clause has a passive verb. The logical connection between *overcompensating* and *growing* is unclear.

The correct answer is B.

SC04249
866. In 2000, a mere two dozen products accounted for half the increase in spending on prescription drugs, <u>a phenomenon that is explained not just because of more expensive drugs but by the fact that doctors are writing</u> many more prescriptions for higher-cost drugs.

(A) a phenomenon that is explained not just because of more expensive drugs but by the fact that doctors are writing

(B) a phenomenon that is explained not just by the fact that drugs are becoming more expensive but also by the fact that doctors are writing

(C) a phenomenon occurring not just because of drugs that are becoming more expensive but because of doctors having also written

(D) which occurred not just because drugs are becoming more expensive but doctors are also writing

(E) which occurred not just because of more expensive drugs but because doctors have also written

Rhetorical Construction; Idiom

This sentence explains that a few high-cost products account for increased spending for two reasons—rising drug prices and more prescriptions for high-priced drugs. To present these two causes, the sentence employs a formula that requires parallel elements: *not just because of x, but because of y*, with *x* and *y* assuming the same grammatical form. One way to create this parallelism is to phrase both contributing causes as noun clauses beginning with *the fact that*. To streamline the sentence, unnecessary words and redundancies should be eliminated. One such redundancy is the repetition of meaning in *explained* and *because of*.

A It is redundant and confusing to say that the phenomenon in question is *explained … because of*; the sentence structure is not parallel.

B **Correct.** This sentence correctly uses parallel structure.

C The phrasing *drugs that are becoming* and *doctors having also written* are awkward and confusing; the placement of *also* is incorrect.

D The structure of this sentence is not parallel.

E The placement of *also* is incorrect; the structure of the sentence is not parallel.

The correct answer is B.

867. Similar to other early Mississippi Delta blues singers, the music of Robert Johnson arose from an oral tradition beginning with a mixture of chants, fiddle tunes, and religious music and only gradually evolved into the blues.

(A) Similar to other early Mississippi Delta blues singers, the music of Robert Johnson arose from an oral tradition beginning with

(B) Similar to that of other early Mississippi Delta blues singers, Robert Johnson made music that arose from an oral tradition that began with

(C) As with other early Mississippi Delta blues singers, Robert Johnson made music that arose from an oral tradition beginning as

(D) Like other early Mississippi Delta blues singers, Robert Johnson's music arose from an oral tradition beginning with

(E) Like the music of other early Mississippi Delta blues singers, the music of Robert Johnson arose from an oral tradition that began as

Logical Predication; Verb Form

The sentence aims to compare the music of early Mississippi Delta Blues singers with the music of Robert Johnson. But what it does is illogically compare singers themselves with the music of Johnson. The second half of the sentence describes two stages of the oral tradition from which blues developed.

A *Similar to* is a wordy and imprecise form of comparison here. The second half of the sentence attempts to describe the stages of the oral tradition, but in a nonparallel form, presenting the first stage as a participial phrase and the second as a verb phrase.

B *Similar to* is wordy and imprecise. The pronoun *that* lacks a grammatical referent.

C The comparative phrase *as with* is an inappropriate form for comparing nouns and noun phrases. The second half of the sentence violates parallelism, attempting to express the first stage of the oral tradition as a present-participle phrase and the second as a past-tense verb phrase.

D This makes a sentence that illogically compares *singers* with *music*. It violates parallelism by coupling a participial phrase *beginning with*... with a verb phrase *evolved into*....

E **Correct.** The resulting sentence compares like with like. It uses a relative clause to describe the oral tradition from which blues developed, indicating the two stages of development with two verbs in parallel.

The correct answer is E.

868. Thelonious Monk, who was a jazz pianist and composer, produced a body of work both rooted in the stride-piano tradition of Willie (The Lion) Smith and Duke Ellington, yet in many ways he stood apart from the mainstream jazz repertory.

(A) Thelonious Monk, who was a jazz pianist and composer, produced a body of work both rooted

(B) Thelonious Monk, the jazz pianist and composer, produced a body of work that was rooted both

(C) Jazz pianist and composer Thelonious Monk, who produced a body of work rooted

(D) Jazz pianist and composer Thelonious Monk produced a body of work that was rooted

(E) Jazz pianist and composer Thelonious Monk produced a body of work rooted both

Grammatical Construction; Rhetorical Construction

The subject of the sentence is *Thelonious Monk*, and the sentence tells about two things that he did: *produced* and *stood apart*. The work he produced was rooted in the mainstream (*stride piano*) jazz tradition, yet at the same time, he deviated from this tradition. The use of a relative clause (*who was a jazz pianist*...) or an appositive (*the jazz pianist*...) introduces unnecessary wordiness and grammatical complexity. Since only one point is being made about Monk's body of work, the appearance of the word *both* in the clause presenting the claim about Monk's work is deceptive as well as grammatically incorrect.

A The relative clause introduces wordiness and confusion.

B The appositive introduces wordiness and unnecessary grammatical complexity.

C The sentence is a fragment because the main subject, *Thelonious Monk*, has no verb.

D **Correct.** The sentence concisely identifies Thelonious Monk and expresses the single point about his work without unnecessary or misleading words.

E   The appearance of *both* is misleading, since only one point is being made about where Monk's musical roots are located.

The correct answer is D.

SC06898

869. Nobody knows exactly how many languages there are in the world, partly because of the difficulty of distinguishing between a language <u>and the sublanguages or dialects within it, but those who have tried to count typically have found</u> about five thousand.

(A)   and the sublanguages or dialects within it, but those who have tried to count typically have found

(B)   and the sublanguages or dialects within them, with those who have tried counting typically finding

(C)   and the sublanguages or dialects within it, but those who have tried counting it typically find

(D)   or the sublanguages or dialects within them, but those who tried to count them typically found

(E)   or the sublanguages or dialects within them, with those who have tried to count typically finding

Agreement; Idiom

This sentence first introduces a condition that makes it difficult to count languages and then, with the conjunction *but*, introduces the topic of those who defy these difficulties and try to count the world's languages anyway. Connecting these two parts of the sentence with *but* indicates that the second clause of the sentence is counter to expectation. The challenges of the task are explained using the example of a single language and its many sublanguages or dialects. When this example is referred to with a pronoun, the pronoun should be singular; when the languages being counted are referred to with a pronoun, this pronoun must be plural.

A   **Correct.** The pronoun *it* agrees in number to its singular antecedent, and *but* indicates that the idea expressed in the final clause defies expectations.

B   The plural pronoun *them* incorrectly refers to the singular antecedent *language*; connecting the two clauses with the preposition *with* loses the sense that counting languages despite the difficulties defies expectations.

C   The second appearance of *it*, referring to world languages, is incorrect because it does not agree in number with *languages*.

D   The conjunction *or* is incorrect—the idiomatic expression is *distinguishing between x and y*; the plural pronoun *them* does not agree with the singular antecedent *language*.

E   The plural pronoun *them* incorrectly refers to the singular antecedent, *language; with* is an imprecise connector for the two clauses, losing the *counter-to-expectation* relationship between them.

The correct answer is A.

SC08719

870. Although a number of excellent studies narrate the development of domestic technology and its impact on housewifery, these works do not discuss the contributions of the women employed <u>by manufacturers and utility companies as product demonstrators and publicists</u>, who initially promoted new and unfamiliar technology to female consumers.

(A)   by manufacturers and utility companies as product demonstrators and publicists,

(B)   to be product demonstrators and publicists by manufacturers and utility companies,

(C)   to demonstrate and publicize their products by manufacturers and utility companies

(D)   by manufacturers and utility companies to be demonstrators and publicists of their products

(E)   by manufacturers and utility companies to demonstrate and publicize their products

Logical Predication; Rhetorical Construction

The point of the sentence is that studies do not include the contributions of women who promoted new domestic technology. The sentence indicates clearly that the women were *employed by manufacturers and utility companies*, worked as *product demonstrators and publicists*, and promoted new technology *to female consumers*.

A   **Correct.** The sentence clearly describes the women's employment and contributions.

B   This sentence structure appears to make *who initially promoted* refer to *manufacturers and utility companies* rather than to *the women*. This conflicts with the use of the word *who*, which would normally be expected to refer to persons rather than to abstract entities such as companies.

C   *Their* refers to *the women*, incorrectly suggesting that the *products* belong to them. This sentence structure appears to make *who initially promoted* refer to *manufacturers and utility companies* rather than to *the women*. This conflicts with the word *who*, which would normally be expected to refer to persons rather than to abstract entities such as companies.

D   *Who initially promoted* follows, and appears to refer to, *products*, which cannot logically be the referent.

E   *Who initially promoted* follows, and appears to refer to, *products*, which cannot logically be the referent.

The correct answer is A.

SC01577

871. The absence <u>from business and financial records of the nineteenth century of statistics about women leave us with no record of the jobs that were performed by women and</u> how they survived economically.

(A) from business and financial records of the nineteenth century of statistics about women leave us with no record of the jobs that were performed by women and

(B) from business and financial records of statistics about women from the nineteenth century leave us with no record of what jobs women performed or

(C) of statistics for women from business and financial records in the nineteenth century leaves us with no record of either the jobs that women were performing and of

(D) of statistics on women from business and financial records in the nineteenth century leave us with no record of the jobs that women performed or of

(E) of statistics about women from business and financial records of the nineteenth century leaves us with no record of either what jobs women performed or

Rhetorical Construction; Agreement

This sentence is phrased awkwardly in two ways. The first relates to *absence of statistics*: it is best to place a noun modifier right next to the noun that it modifies, with no intervening material. Second, *jobs that were performed by women* is more complicated than necessary—*jobs women performed* is better, for example. Also, the singular noun *absence* requires the correct agreeing verb form *leaves*.

A   *Absence* and *of statistics* are widely separated, and *leave* does not properly agree with its subject, *absence*.

B   *Absence* and *of statistics* are widely separated, and *leave* does not properly agree with its subject, *absence*.

C   *Jobs that women were performing* is unnecessarily long and complex. The *either* construction should be completed with *or*, not *and*.

D   *Leave* does not properly agree with its subject, *absence*.

E   **Correct.** *Leaves* agrees with *absence*. The phrase *of statistics* is next to the noun it modifies (*absence*), and *jobs women performed* is a nicely simple phrasing.

The correct answer is E.

SC02138

872. <u>Heating-oil prices are expected to be higher this year than last because refiners are paying about $5 a barrel more for crude oil than they were</u> last year.

(A) Heating-oil prices are expected to be higher this year than last because refiners are paying about $5 a barrel more for crude oil than they were

(B) Heating-oil prices are expected to rise higher this year over last because refiners pay about $5 a barrel for crude oil more than they did

(C) Expectations are for heating-oil prices to be higher this year than last year's because refiners are paying about $5 a barrel for crude oil more than they did

(D) It is the expectation that heating-oil prices will be higher for this year over last because refiners are paying about $5 a barrel more for crude oil now than what they were

(E) It is expected that heating-oil prices will rise higher this year than last year's because refiners pay about $5 a barrel for crude oil more than they did

Rhetorical Construction; Idiom

The sentence connects a comparison between this year's and last year's heating-oil prices with a comparison between this year's and last year's crude-oil prices. The most efficient, parallel expression of those comparisons is to use two comparative expressions, *higher than* and *more than*.

881

A **Correct.** This sentence expresses the comparison in succinct, parallel phrases.

B The comparative form, *higher*, anticipates the comparative term *than*, not *over*; in the second clause, the comparative terms *more than* should immediately follow *$5 a barrel*.

C *Expectations are for …* is an unnecessarily wordy and indirect expression; the possessive *year's* is not parallel with the adverbial phrase *this year*.

D *It is the expectation that …* is wordy and awkward; *for* and *what* are unnecessary.

E *It is expected that …* is wordy and awkward; the possessive *last year's* does not parallel the adverbial phrase *this year*.

The correct answer is A.

SC01443

873. Even though Clovis points, spear points with longitudinal grooves chipped onto their faces, have been found all over North America, they are named for the New Mexico site where they were first discovered in 1932.

(A) Even though Clovis points, spear points with longitudinal grooves chipped onto their faces, have been found all over North America, they are named for the New Mexico site where they were first discovered in 1932.

(B) Although named for the New Mexico site where first discovered in 1932, Clovis points are spear points of longitudinal grooves chipped onto their faces and have been found all over North America.

(C) Named for the New Mexico site where they have been first discovered in 1932, Clovis points, spear points of longitudinal grooves chipped onto the faces, have been found all over North America.

(D) Spear points with longitudinal grooves that are chipped onto the faces, Clovis points, even though named for the New Mexico site where first discovered in 1932, but were found all over North America.

(E) While Clovis points are spear points whose faces have longitudinal grooves chipped into them, they have been found all over North America, and named for the New Mexico site where they have been first discovered in 1932.

Verb Form; Rhetorical Construction; Logical Predication

Even though, *although*, and *while* introduce clauses that appear to be logically incompatible but in fact are not. In this sentence, the apparent incompatibility that must be clearly expressed is that although the spear points are named for a particular place in New Mexico, they are in fact found throughout North America. Because their discovery took place in 1932 and is not ongoing, the correct verb tense is simple past, not present perfect.

A **Correct.** The *even though* clause expresses clearly that the seeming incompatibility is between where the spear points have been found (*all over North America*) and the naming of the spear points for a single site in New Mexico.

B The sentence structure indicates that the expected incompatibility is between the geographically based name of the points and their physical properties, which makes no sense; *where discovered* is missing a subject—the correct form is *where they were first discovered*.

C *Have been first discovered* is the wrong tense, since the discovery is a discrete event completed in the past.

D The sequence of information in this sentence is confusing; *even though* and *but* both introduce information that is contrary to expectation, so to use them both to describe a single apparent contradiction is redundant and nonsensical.

E *While* introduces a description of Clovis points and suggests that this appears incompatible with their appearance all over North America, which makes no sense; *have been first discovered* is the wrong tense.

The correct answer is A.

SC04408

874. Heavy commitment by an executive to a course of action, especially if it has worked well in the past, makes it likely to miss signs of incipient trouble or misinterpret them when they do appear.

(A) Heavy commitment by an executive to a course of action, especially if it has worked well in the past, makes it likely to miss signs of incipient trouble or misinterpret them when they do appear.

(B) An executive who is heavily committed to a course of action, especially one that worked well in the past, makes missing signs of incipient trouble or misinterpreting ones likely when they do appear.

(C) An executive who is heavily committed to a course of action is likely to miss or misinterpret signs of incipient trouble when they do appear, especially if it has worked well in the past.

(D) Executives' being heavily committed to a course of action, especially if it has worked well in the past, makes them likely to miss signs of incipient trouble or misinterpreting them when they do appear.

(E) Being heavily committed to a course of action, especially one that has worked well in the past, is likely to make an executive miss signs of incipient trouble or misinterpret them when they do appear.

Rhetorical Construction; Logical Predication

This sentence explains that an executive who is blindly committed to a proven course of action is likely to overlook or misinterpret indicators that the plan may no longer be working. The sentence needs to make clear *who* may misinterpret these indicators.

A The passive construction causes the sentence to be wordy and confusing; the reference for *it* is ambiguous, leaving the reader with questions about who or what is likely to miss these signs.

B The sentence structure indicates that the *executive*, not his or her strategy, causes signs to be overlooked; the modifier *when they do appear* is misplaced.

C The reference for the pronoun *it* is unclear because many nouns have intervened between the appearance of the logical referent (*course of action*) and *it*.

D *Misinterpreting* should be an infinitive verb form to parallel *miss*; the phrasing throughout the sentence is wordy and awkward.

E **Correct.** The grammatical structure of this sentence and the appropriate placement of modifiers expresses the meaning clearly and concisely.

The correct answer is E.

SC06740
875. According to recent studies comparing the nutritional value of meat from wild animals and meat from domesticated animals, <u>wild animals have less total fat than do livestock fed on grain and more of a kind of fat they think is</u> good for cardiac health.

(A) wild animals have less total fat than do livestock fed on grain and more of a kind of fat they think is

(B) wild animals have less total fat than livestock fed on grain and more of a kind of fat thought to be

(C) wild animals have less total fat than that of livestock fed on grain and have more fat of a kind thought to be

(D) total fat of wild animals is less than livestock fed on grain and they have more fat of a kind thought to be

(E) total fat is less in wild animals than that of livestock fed on grain and more of their fat is of a kind they think is

Logical Predication; Rhetorical Construction

The sentence reports research findings on the comparison between the fat content of wild animals and that of domestic livestock. The most significant error in the sentence is in the phrase *they think*: the pronoun *they* either lacks a referent or is meant to refer back to *wild animals*, which would be nonsensical.

A The pronoun *they* fails to refer correctly.

B **Correct.** The phrase *thought to be* eliminates the most significant error in the original sentence. Note that while the phrase *less total fat than livestock* differs from the phrase *less total fat than do livestock* in the original, either would be correct here.

C The resulting sentence is unnecessarily wordy and confusing. The pronoun *that* is not only superfluous, but it fails to refer back to anything.

D The resulting sentence makes a nonsensical comparison between *total fat* and *livestock*.

E The resulting sentence is wordy and confusing. It lacks the required parallelism *in wild animals . . . in livestock*. The referent of the possessive pronoun *their* is ambiguous, as is the referent of the pronoun *they*.

The correct answer is B.

876. Yellow jackets number among the 900 or so species of the world's social wasps, <u>wasps living in a highly cooperative and organized society where they consist almost entirely of</u> females—the queen and her sterile female workers.

(A) wasps living in a highly cooperative and organized society where they consist almost entirely of

(B) wasps that live in a highly cooperative and organized society consisting almost entirely of

(C) which means they live in a highly cooperative and organized society, almost all

(D) which means that their society is highly cooperative, organized, and it is almost entirely

(E) living in a society that is highly cooperative, organized, and it consists of almost all

Idiom; Logical Predication; Rhetorical Construction

This sentence identifies yellow jackets as one of 900 types of social wasps and provides an explanation of the term *social wasps*. In this explanation, the society or population—not the individual wasps themselves—consists almost entirely of females. The three descriptors of social wasps (*cooperative, organized,* and *consisting almost entirely of females*) are most effectively expressed in parallel structures.

A *They*, referring to wasps, is an incorrect subject for *consist*.

B **Correct.** The three descriptors of the wasp society are in parallel form, and *consisting* properly modifies *society*.

C The sentence structure makes it unclear what *almost all females* describes.

D *And it is …* violates the parallelism of the three descriptors of social wasps.

E *And it consists …* violates the parallelism of the three descriptors.

The correct answer is B.

877. Before 1988, insurance companies in California were free to charge whatever rates the market would bear, <u>needing no approval from regulators before raising</u> rates.

(A) needing no approval from regulators before raising

(B) and it needed no approval by regulators before raising

(C) and needing no approval from regulators before they raised

(D) with approval not needed by regulators before they raised

(E) with no approval needed from regulators before the raising of

Logical Predication; Rhetorical Construction

The sentence explains that, prior to 1988, insurance companies in California could raise rates without regulators' approval. This idea is expressed concisely using a participial phrase and two prepositional phrases: *needing no approval from regulators before raising rates.* Unlike some of the answer choices that contain errors involving antecedents, this construction uses no pronouns and contains no such errors.

A **Correct.** The combination of a participial phrase and two prepositional phrases expresses the idea clearly with no errors involving pronouns or antecedents.

B The singular pronoun *it* has no clear antecedent. If *it* is taken to refer to the market (the only grammatically plausible antecedent), the sentence is illogical. *Whatever rates the market would bear* clearly indicates that *market* is being used in the sense of an abstract set of forces affecting prices. To say that the market, in that sense, raised taxes and that it needed no approval to do so is nonsensical.

C The construction *were … and needing* is ungrammatical. The pronoun *they* is intended to refer to *companies* but could also seem, illogically, to refer to *regulators*.

D *By regulators* illogically indicates that regulators are the ones who did not need approval; the pronoun *they* is intended to refer to *companies* but could also seem, illogically, to refer to *regulators*.

E *Before the raising of* is wordy and awkward. Both that phrase and *with no approval needed* are strangely uninformative and rhetorically ineffective in that they appear to pointedly avoid telling who did not need the approval or who might have raised the rates.

The correct answer is A.

878. Marconi's conception of the radio was as a substitute for the telephone, a tool for private conversation; instead, it is precisely the opposite, a tool for communicating with a large, public audience.

- (A) Marconi's conception of the radio was as a substitute for the telephone, a tool for private conversation; instead, it is
- (B) Marconi conceived of the radio as a substitute for the telephone, a tool for private conversation, but which is
- (C) Marconi conceived of the radio as a tool for private conversation that could substitute for the telephone; instead, it has become
- (D) Marconi conceived of the radio to be a tool for private conversation, a substitute for the telephone, which has become
- (E) Marconi conceived of the radio to be a substitute for the telephone, a tool for private conversation, other than what it is,

Rhetorical Construction; Logical Predication

The main point of this sentence is to explain that while Marconi felt the radio would substitute for the phone as an instrument of private communication, in fact it has become an instrument of mass communication. It is less wordy to use *Marconi* as the subject of the active verb *conceived* than to use the subject *conception* with the static verb *was*. The pronoun *it* positioned as the subject of the final verb *has become* refers back to *radio*. Versions of the sentence that use the relative pronoun *which* indicate that the telephone has become a mass medium.

- A The nominalized subject, *conception*, leads to a wordy and awkward sentence.
- B The reference for the relative pronoun *which* is ambiguous; the sentence as a whole is awkward.
- C **Correct.** An active verb makes the first clause more concise; *it* in the second clause clearly refers to *the radio*.
- D *Conceived of* … should be followed by *as* rather than *to be*.
- E *Conceived of* … should be followed by *as* rather than *to be*; *other than what it is* is awkward, wordy, and redundant, overlapping the meaning of *precisely the opposite* … .

The correct answer is C.

879. Because there are provisions of the new maritime code that provide that even tiny islets can be the basis for claims to the fisheries and oil fields of large sea areas, they have already stimulated international disputes over uninhabited islands.

- (A) Because there are provisions of the new maritime code that provide that even tiny islets can be the basis for claims to the fisheries and oil fields of large sea areas, they have already stimulated
- (B) Because the new maritime code provides that even tiny islets can be the basis for claims to the fisheries and oil fields of large sea areas, it has already stimulated
- (C) Even tiny islets can be the basis for claims to the fisheries and oil fields of large sea areas under provisions of the new maritime code, already stimulating
- (D) Because even tiny islets can be the basis for claims to the fisheries and oil fields of large sea areas under provisions of the new maritime code, this has already stimulated
- (E) Because even tiny islets can be the basis for claims to the fisheries and oil fields of large sea areas under provisions of the new maritime code, which is already stimulating

Logical Predication; Grammatical Construction

In this sentence, the *there are … that …* construction contributes nothing more than unnecessary words. The sentence needs to make clear whether *provisions* or *code* is the subject of the main verb *stimulated*.

- A The *there are … that …* construction is unnecessarily wordy; in the predicate nominative instead of the subject position, *provisions* is not an obvious referent for the pronoun *they*.
- B **Correct.** In this sentence, *the new maritime code* is clearly the antecedent of *it* in the main clause and thus the subject of *has already stimulated*.
- C *Under provisions of the new maritime code* is a misplaced modifier, seeming to describe *sea areas*; the sentence does not make clear what is *stimulating … disputes*.
- D The referent of *this* is unclear.

E   The sentence is a fragment, opening with a dependent clause (*Because ... code*) and concluding with a relative clause, but lacking a main, independent clause.

The correct answer is B.

880. Unlike the automobile company, whose research was based on crashes involving sport utility vehicles, the research conducted by the insurance company took into account such factors as a driver's age, sex, and previous driving record.

    (A) company, whose research was based on
    (B) company, which researched
    (C) company, in its research of
    (D) company's research, having been based on
    (E) company's research on

Logical Predication; Rhetorical Construction

The point of the sentence is to contrast the research conducted by the automobile company and that conducted by the insurance company, but the sentence has been written in a way that contrasts *the automobile company* with *research*. The correct contrast is between *automobile company's research* and *research conducted by the insurance company*.

A   *Automobile company* is incorrectly contrasted with *research*.

B   *Automobile company* is incorrectly contrasted with *research*.

C   *Automobile company* is incorrectly contrasted with *research*.

D   *Having been based on* is wordy. This construction makes it unclear whether *having been based on crashes involving sport utility vehicles* is intended to modify *the automobile company's research* or *the research conducted by the insurance company*. The sentence structure slightly favors the latter interpretation, but it is somewhat implausible to suppose that this is the intended meaning.

E   **Correct.** The sentence concisely contrasts the *automobile company's research* and *research conducted by the insurance company*.

The correct answer is E.

881. Gusty westerly winds will continue to usher in a seasonally cool air mass into the region, as a broad area of high pressure will build and bring fair and dry weather for several days.

    (A) to usher in a seasonably cool air mass into the region, as a broad area of high pressure will build and
    (B) ushering in a seasonably cool air mass into the region and a broad area of high pressure will build that
    (C) to usher in a seasonably cool air mass to the region, a broad area of high pressure building, and
    (D) ushering a seasonably cool air mass in the region, with a broad area of high pressure building and
    (E) to usher a seasonably cool air mass into the region while a broad area of high pressure builds, which will

Verb Form; Grammatical Construction; Diction

The sentence offers a prediction that two concurrent weather events will bring a certain type of weather, but its use of the phrase *as ... will build* causes confusion. The wording makes the sequence of events and the causal relationships among them unclear. Future tense is used to indicate that winds *will continue*. The relation of *as* to the rest of the sentence makes it unclear whether *as* is intended as a logical indicator (similar to *because*) or as a temporal indicator (equivalent to *while*). If *as* is intended in the former way, it would be preferable to resolve the ambiguity by using a word or phrase such as *because* or *given that*. If it is intended in the latter way, a present tense verb would be needed following *as* or *while* to show that the second event is concurrent with, or part of, the future situation: *while high pressure builds*. In addition, *usher in ... into* is redundant and unidiomatic. A clear, concise way to express this idea is *will continue to usher a seasonably cool air mass into the region while a broad area of high pressure builds*.

A   *Usher in ... into* is redundant and unidiomatic. *As ... will build* causes confusion.

B   The absence of a comma after *region* makes this ungrammatical. *Ushering in ... into* is redundant; *will build* is the wrong verb tense; the plural verb *bring* does not agree with *area*, the singular antecedent of *that*.

C The grammatical function of *a broad area of high pressure building* is unclear.

D *Ushering ... in the region* is incorrect since *into* is needed to indicate movement from outside in; the subject of the verb *bring* is unclear.

E **Correct.** The idea is expressed with clear, correct combinations of verbs and subjects.

The correct answer is E.

SC02008

882. With the patience of its customers and with its network strained to the breaking point, the on-line service company announced a series of new initiatives trying to relieve the congestion that has led to at least four class-action lawsuits and thousands of complaints from frustrated customers.

(A) the patience of its customers and with its network strained to the breaking point, the on-line service company announced a series of new initiatives trying to relieve

(B) the patience of its customers and its network strained to the breaking point, the on-line service company announced a series of new initiatives that try to relieve

(C) its network and the patience of its customers strained to the breaking point, the on-line service company announced a series of new initiatives to try to relieve

(D) its network and with the patience of its customers strained to the breaking point, the on-line service company announced a series of initiatives to try relieving

(E) its network and its customers' patience strained to the breaking point, the on-line service company announced a series of new initiatives to try relieving

Logical Predication; Rhetorical Construction

The sentence explains the online service provider's efforts to relieve congestion, but it has been written with confusing ambiguities. Because *the patience of its customers* is in a separate prepositional phrase from *its network*, it is not clear whether both or only the latter is *strained to the breaking point*. The phrase *trying to relieve* is probably meant to explain the purpose of the initiatives, but does not do so unambiguously (for example, *trying* could modify either *the company* or *initiatives*, and it is not clear which is intended). An unambiguous wording of the sentence would clarify that both *the patience of its customers* and *its network* are *strained to the breaking point* and that the purpose of the initiatives is *to try to relieve* the congestion.

A *The patience of its customers* is not clearly linked to *strained to the breaking point*; *trying to relieve* is an ambiguous and unidiomatic way of expressing the purpose of the initiatives.

B *That try to relieve* fails to express the purpose of the initiatives in a rhetorically acceptable way; moreover the present tense *try* is illogical here. The phrase *the patience of its customers and its network* is rhetorically flawed in that its structure makes it seem to be attributing *patience* to the *network*.

C **Correct.** The sentence indicates clearly that both *the patience of its customers* and *its network* are *strained to the breaking point* and that the company introduced initiatives aimed at relieving the congestion.

D *Its network* is not clearly linked to *strained to the breaking point*; with *to try*, the infinitive form *to relieve* is more rhetorically appropriate here than the verbal noun form *relieving*, in order to indicate the goal of the intervention.

E With *to try*, the infinitive form *to relieve* is more rhetorically appropriate here than the verbal noun form *relieving*, in order to indicate the goal of the intervention.

The correct answer is C.

SC02094

883. November is traditionally the strongest month for sales of light trucks, but sales this past November, even when compared with sales in previous Novembers, accounted for a remarkably large share of total vehicle sales.

(A) but sales this past November, even when compared with sales in previous Novembers,

(B) but even when it is compared with previous Novembers, this past November's sales

(C) but even when they are compared with previous Novembers, sales of light trucks this past November

(D) so that compared with previous Novembers, sales of light trucks this past November

(E) so that this past November's sales, even compared with previous Novembers' sales,

Logical Predication; Agreement

This sentence identifies November as traditionally being the month with the strongest sales of light trucks, and then goes on to indicate that even when compared to previous Novembers, this past November's sales accounted for a notably large portion of overall sales. It makes sense to make a comparison between sales in one November with sales in other Novembers. It does not make sense to compare sales to months, as in (C) and (D).

A **Correct.** This version makes the correct comparison between sales in one particular November and sales in previous Novembers.

B The antecedent of the word *it* is unclear. The sentence begins with the word *November*, which is used to refer not to a specific November, but to the month generally. If the antecedent of *it* is taken to be *November*, then the sentence compares November, taken generally, to previous Novembers. But previous to what? Since taking *November* to be the antecedent renders the sentence nonsensical, we may be inclined to look for the antecedent elsewhere; the only other possible candidate, however, is *this past November's sales*, which is ruled out because *it* is singular and *sales* is plural.

C The antecedent of the pronoun *they* is *sales*, making the comparison between *they* and *previous Novembers* illogical.

D The sentence illogically compares sales of light trucks with previous Novembers. The conjunction *so that* nonsensically introduces a causal relationship between November's typically strong sales and the aforementioned comparison.

E Like (D), this sentence introduces a nonsensical causal relationship, in this case between the fact that November typically has the strongest sales and the fact that this past November's sales accounted for a remarkably large share of total vehicle sales.

The correct answer is A.

SC05760
884. Most of the country's biggest daily newspapers had lower circulation in the six months from October 1995 through March 1996 than <u>a similar period</u> a year earlier.

(A) a similar period
(B) a similar period's
(C) in a similar period
(D) that in a similar period
(E) that of a similar period

Logical Predication; Parallelism

The sentence compares newspaper circulation during two separate periods, but the comparison is not parallel because it has been drawn using a prepositional phrase, *in the six months*, and a noun phrase, *a similar period*. Both phrases compared by *than* should be prepositional phrases: *lower in the six months . . . than in a similar period.*

A *In the six months* and *a similar period* are not grammatically parallel. The sentence appears illogically to compare a period of time with an amount of circulation.

B *In the six months* and *a similar period's* are not grammatically parallel.

C **Correct.** *In the six months* and *in a similar period* are both prepositional phrases, making the comparison clear and properly idiomatic.

D *In the six months* and *that in a similar period* are not grammatically parallel; it is unclear what the antecedent of *that* is supposed to be.

E *In the six months* and *that of a similar period* are not grammatically parallel; it is unclear what the antecedent of *that* is supposed to be.

The correct answer is C.

SC01714
885. Mauritius was a British colony for almost 200 years, <u>excepting for</u> the domains of administration and teaching, the English language was never really spoken on the island.

(A) excepting for
(B) except in
(C) but except in
(D) but excepting for
(E) with the exception of

Idiom; Grammatical Construction

This two-clause sentence describes an apparent incompatibility: as a British colony, Mauritius might be expected to be English-speaking, but in fact it was not. To describe this apparent contradiction and to avoid a comma splice, the clauses should be joined by the conjunction *but*. *Domains* describes places *in* which English is spoken; *for* is the incorrect preposition. *Excepting* is not idiomatic English in this case.

A The lack of a conjunction causes a comma splice; *excepting for* is non-idiomatic.

B The lack of a conjunction causes a comma splice.

C **Correct.** The two independent clauses are separated by *but*, and *except in* is an appropriate idiom.

D *Excepting for* is non-idiomatic.

E The lack of a conjunction causes a comma splice.

The correct answer is C.

SC04853

886. Although appearing less appetizing than most of their round and red supermarket cousins, heirloom tomatoes, grown from seeds saved during the previous year—they are often green and striped, or have plenty of bumps and bruises—heirlooms are more flavorful and thus in increasing demand.

(A) Although appearing less appetizing than most of their round and red supermarket cousins, heirloom tomatoes, grown from seeds saved during the previous year

(B) Although heirloom tomatoes, grown from seeds saved during the previous year, appear less appetizing than most of their round and red supermarket cousins

(C) Although they appear less appetizing than most of their round and red supermarket cousins, heirloom tomatoes, grown from seeds saved during the previous year

(D) Grown from seeds saved during the previous year, heirloom tomatoes appear less appetizing than most of their round and red supermarket cousins

(E) Heirloom tomatoes, grown from seeds saved during the previous year, although they appear less appetizing than most of their round and red supermarket cousins

Rhetorical Construction; Grammatical Construction

The intended meaning could be communicated more effectively by mentioning heirloom tomatoes as early as possible in the sentence, so that we know that the writer is comparing heirloom tomatoes with supermarket tomatoes. The placement of *heirloom tomatoes* and *heirlooms* makes the sentence ungrammatical.

A This is ungrammatical. If *heirloom tomatoes* is the subject of *are more flavorful* ... then *heirlooms* has no predicate and is nonsensically superfluous. If *heirlooms* is the subject, *heirloom tomatoes* has no predicate.

B **Correct.** The noun *heirloom tomatoes* is mentioned early in the sentence, followed by a parenthetical definition, and is the subject of the verb *appear*, and *heirlooms* is the subject of *are*.

C The noun *heirloom tomatoes* appears too late in the sentence. Parsing is made harder by introducing the pronoun *they* and revealing its antecedent later in the sentence. The sentence is also ungrammatical. If *heirloom tomatoes* is the subject of *are more flavorful* ... then *heirlooms* has no predicate and is nonsensically superfluous. If *heirlooms* is the subject, *heirloom tomatoes* has no predicate.

D Beginning the sentence with the explanatory clause *grown from seeds ...* gives it too much importance. It could be construed as the reason why heirloom tomatoes appear less appetizing, which is contrary to the truth. The sentence is also ungrammatical.

E Rhetorical structure requires that *although* appear in the beginning of the clause to which it pertains. Placing it later necessitates the pronoun *they* with antecedent *heirloom tomatoes*, which is redundant. The sentence is also ungrammatical.

The correct answer is B.

SC01987

887. The World Wildlife Fund has declared that global warming, a phenomenon most scientists agree to be caused by human beings in burning fossil fuels, will create havoc among migratory birds by altering the environment in ways harmful to their habitats.

(A) a phenomenon most scientists agree to be caused by human beings in burning fossil fuels,

(B) a phenomenon most scientists agree that is caused by fossil fuels burned by human beings,

(C) a phenomenon that most scientists agree is caused by human beings' burning of fossil fuels,

(D) which most scientists agree on as a phenomenon caused by human beings who burn fossil fuels,

(E) which most scientists agree to be a phenomenon caused by fossil fuels burned by human beings,

Logical Predication; Rhetorical Construction

The underlined portion of the sentence is an appositive defining *global warming* as a phenomenon caused by the burning of fossil fuels by humans. Because this appositive intervenes between the subject (*global warming*) and verb (*will create*) of a clause, it should be expressed as clearly and economically as possible so as not to confuse the meaning of the sentence as a whole.

A *To be caused* and *in burning* are wordy, awkward, and indirect.

B *That is* should immediately follow *phenomenon*, not *agree*.

C **Correct.** The phrase *human beings' burning* is more economical than constructions with prepositional phrases or relative clauses.

D The phrasing is wordy and indirect.

E The phrasing is wordy and the meaning is imprecise; it is not fossil fuels that cause global warming—it is the burning of fossil fuels by humans.

The correct answer is C.

SC02216

888. The largest of all the planets, <u>not only is Jupiter three times so massive as Saturn, the next larger</u> planet, but also possesses four of the largest satellites, or moons, in our solar system.

(A) not only is Jupiter three times so massive as Saturn, the next larger

(B) not only is Jupiter three times as massive as Saturn, the next largest

(C) Jupiter, not only three times as massive as Saturn, the next largest

(D) Jupiter not only is three times as massive as Saturn, the next largest

(E) Jupiter is not only three times so massive as Saturn, the next larger

Diction; Idiom

This sentence begins with a phrase, [*t*]*he largest . . .*, describing the main subject *Jupiter*. The remainder of the sentence describes Jupiter's size and possession of moons, using the idiom *not only x but y* to introduce parallel adjective phrases.

A In this version of the sentence, *so massive as Saturn* violates the parallelism established by the idiom *as + adjective + as + noun*. For the sake of clarity, the noun described by the opening adjectival phrase should immediately follow that phrase. The phrase *next larger* is unidiomatic and unclear. The superlative (*largest*) is appropriate in this consideration of all the planets.

B As in (A), *Jupiter* should immediately follow the opening phrase.

C This version of the sentence violates the parallelism of the idiom *not only x but y*, following the first half of the template with an adjective phrase and the second half with a verb phrase.

D **Correct.** The placement of the subject in relation to the opening modifier, the properly constructed phrasing, and the proper use of comparison words make the meaning of the sentence clear.

E The phrase *so massive as* violates the idiom *as x as y*. Consideration of Jupiter's size among all the planets, including Saturn, requires the superlative form, *largest*.

The correct answer is D.

SC01587

889. While many of the dinosaur fossils found recently in northeast China seem to provide evidence of the kinship between dinosaurs and birds, the wealth of enigmatic fossils <u>seem more likely at this stage that they will inflame debates over the origin of birds rather than</u> settle them.

(A) seem more likely at this stage that they will inflame debates over the origin of birds rather than

(B) seem more likely that it will inflame debates over the origin of birds at this stage than

(C) seems more likely to inflame debates on the origin of birds at this stage rather than

(D) seems more likely at this stage to inflame debates over the origin of birds than to

(E) seems more likely that it will inflame debates on the origin of birds at this stage than to

Agreement; Parallelism

This sentence states that whereas many dinosaur fossils from China suggest that there is a kinship between dinosaurs and birds, the *wealth* of fossils are more ambiguous about what they suggest about the ancestry of birds. The word *wealth* is a mass noun followed by a prepositional phrase; because *wealth* follows the article *the*, the emphasis is on it rather than on the noun in the prepositional phrase, *fossils*. The singular *wealth* requires a singular main verb (*seems*). The comparative expression *more likely*... must be followed by an infinitive verb (*to inflame*) so it will be parallel to the verb with which it is compared (*to settle*).

A The singular subject *wealth* does not agree with the plural verb *seem*; both items being compared should be in parallel form (*inflame* and *settle*); the relative clause *that they will inflame* violates the parallelism.

B Again, the relative clause violates the desired parallelism; the singular subject, *wealth*, requires a singular verb, *seems*.

C The subject and the verb agree with one another, but the placement of the modifier *at this stage* makes the modifier appear to describe *origin of the birds* rather than the verb *seems*.

D **Correct.** The verb *seems* agrees in number with the noun *wealth*; the infinitive *to inflame* is parallel with the verb to which it is compared, *to settle*.

E The clause *wealth... seems more likely that it will inflame* is not idiomatic, and *that it will inflame* is not parallel with the infinitive verb *to settle*.

The correct answer is D.

SC01622
890. Found only in the Western Hemisphere and surviving through extremes of climate, hummingbirds' range extends from Alaska to Tierra del Fuego, from sea-level rain forests to the edges of Andean snowfields and ice fields at altitudes of 15,000 feet.

(A) Found only in the Western Hemisphere and surviving through extremes of climate, hummingbirds' range extends

(B) Found only in the Western Hemisphere, hummingbirds survive through extremes of climate, their range extending

(C) Hummingbirds, found only in the Western Hemisphere and surviving through extremes of climate, with their range extending

(D) Hummingbirds, found only in the Western Hemisphere and surviving through extremes of climate, their range extends

(E) Hummingbirds are found only in the Western Hemisphere, survive through extremes of climate, and their range extends

Logical Predication; Grammatical Construction

This sentence makes three points about hummingbirds: they live in the Western Hemisphere, they survive extreme climates, and their range is wide and varied. *Hummingbirds*, not *hummingbirds' range*, should be the subject of the sentence.

A The opening modifier, *found... and surviving...* should modify *hummingbirds*, not, as it does, *hummingbirds' range*.

B **Correct.** *Hummingbirds* is the subject of the sentence, and the use of the absolute phrase *their range extending* appropriately connects the final clause to the rest of the sentence.

C This version of the sentence has no main verb for the subject *Hummingbirds* and as a result is ungrammatical.

D Like (C), this version of the sentence has no main verb for the subject *Hummingbirds*.

E This version of the sentence begins with the subject *Hummingbirds* attached to a pair of verb phrases (*are found...* and *survive...*) followed by the conjunction *and*, which suggests that what follows should also be a verb phrase; instead, a new subject is introduced, *their range*. Replacing the comma before *survive* with *and* would render the sentence acceptable.

The correct answer is B.

SC01761

891. <u>She was less successful after she had emigrated to New York compared to</u> her native Germany, photographer Lotte Jacobi nevertheless earned a small group of discerning admirers, and her photographs were eventually exhibited in prestigious galleries across the United States.

(A) She was less successful after she had emigrated to New York compared to

(B) Being less successful after she had emigrated to New York as compared to

(C) Less successful after she emigrated to New York than she had been in

(D) Although she was less successful after emigrating to New York when compared to

(E) She had been less successful after emigrating to New York than in

Idiom; Grammatical Construction; Logical Predication

This sentence compares the success Jacobi experienced after moving to New York to the success she had previously experienced in Germany. The phrase *less successful* anticipates the conclusion of the comparison with the phrase *than*. ... The main subject of the sentence is *photographer Lotte Jacobi*, and the main verb is *earned*. The opening clause *She was less successful ...* therefore creates a comma splice if the comma is not followed by a conjunction. The most efficient way to incorporate the information about Jacobi's comparative successes in Germany and in New York is to turn this clause into an adjectival phrase describing Jacobi.

A *Less successful* ... anticipates *than* rather than *compared to* ...; a comma is insufficient to join two independent clauses into a single sentence.

B *As compared to* is an incorrect way to complete the comparison introduced by *less*; *Being* ... is unnecessarily wordy and awkward.

C **Correct.** The idiomatic construction *less successful ... than* is incorporated into an introductory adjectival phrase modifying *Lotte Jacobi*.

D *When compared to* is an incorrect phrase to complete the comparison introduced by *less*.

E A comma is insufficient to join two independent clauses into a single sentence; past-perfect tense is misleading, since it refers to Jacobi's experience in New York, which in fact followed her experience in Germany.

The correct answer is C.

SC02259

892. Scientists have recently found evidence that black holes—regions of space in which matter is so concentrated and the pull of gravity so powerful that nothing, not even light, can emerge from them—probably <u>exist at the core of nearly all galaxies and</u> <u>the mass of each black hole is proportional to</u> its host galaxy.

(A) exist at the core of nearly all galaxies and the mass of each black hole is proportional to

(B) exist at the core of nearly all galaxies and that the mass of each black hole is proportional to that of

(C) exist at the core of nearly all galaxies, and that the mass of each black hole is proportional to

(D) exists at the core of nearly all galaxies, and that the mass of each black hole is proportional to that of

(E) exists at the core of nearly all galaxies and the mass of each black hole is proportional to that of

Logical Predication; Agreement

This sentence focuses attention on two hypotheses about black holes—one about their location and the other about their mass. These hypotheses appear as parallel relative clauses *that black holes ... exist at ...* and *that the mass ... is proportional*. The subject of the first relative clause (*black holes*) is plural, so the clause must be completed with the plural form of *exist*.

A This version of the sentence does not provide the relative pronoun *that* to provide parallel structure for presenting the two things scientific evidence reveals about black holes. This leaves it somewhat unclear whether the final clause is intended to convey part of what the scientists discovered or to express a claim that the writer is making independently of the scientists' discovery. The sentence illogically compares *mass* to *galaxy*.

B **Correct.** The structure of the sentence makes the meaning clear, and the plural verb form agrees with the plural subject.

C The comma appears to signal that the final part of the sentence is intended as an independent clause expressing a separate claim rather than describing part of the scientists' discovery. But if it were intended in that way, it should be set off as a separate sentence, not conjoined with the preceding clause. Like (A), this version makes an illogical comparison between *mass* and *galaxy*.

D The singular verb *exists* does not agree with the plural subject *black holes*. As in (C), the comma is inappropriate because it does not introduce a new independent clause.

E The singular verb *exists* does not agree with the plural subject *black holes*. Like (A), this version lacks the relative pronoun *that*, which would clarify the relationship between the two clauses.

The correct answer is B.

SC02346

893. The use of lie detectors is based on the assumption that lying produces emotional reactions in an individual <u>that, in turn, create unconscious physiological responses</u>.

(A) that, in turn, create unconscious physiological responses

(B) that creates unconscious physiological responses in turn

(C) creating, in turn, unconscious physiological responses

(D) to create, in turn, physiological responses that are unconscious

(E) who creates unconscious physiological responses in turn

Agreement; Rhetorical Construction; Logical Predication

This sentence describes a cause-and-effect sequence; in the underlined portion of the sentence, the relative pronoun *that* refers to the plural noun *reactions*. The verb in the relative clause must therefore be a plural verb. The causal sequence is most clearly expressed by a relative clause that turns the object *emotional reactions* (from the clause *lying causes emotional reactions in an individual*) into the subject (*that*) of a new clause (*that in turn create unconscious physiological responses*). *In turn* is best placed before the verb of the second relative clause, *create*, to clarify that a chain of events is being described.

A **Correct.** This construction clearly indicates the causal sequence.

B The singular verb *creates* does not agree with the subject referenced by the relative pronoun *that* (*reactions*).

C This construction is less successful at clarifying the chain of events because *creating* seems to refer back to *lying*; if used as a participial, *creating* would have to be preceded by a comma.

D This construction does not make clear the causal chain of events, because it is unclear which noun *to create* should attach to; the infinitive construction implies intent, which does not really make sense.

E Because *reactions* is not a person, *who* is the wrong relative pronoun to use.

The correct answer is A.

SC04213

894. Australian embryologists have found evidence <u>that suggests that the elephant is descended from an aquatic animal, and its trunk originally evolving</u> as a kind of snorkel.

(A) that suggests that the elephant is descended from an aquatic animal, and its trunk originally evolving

(B) that has suggested the elephant descended from an aquatic animal, its trunk originally evolving

(C) suggesting that the elephant had descended from an aquatic animal with its trunk originally evolved

(D) to suggest that the elephant had descended from an aquatic animal and its trunk originally evolved

(E) to suggest that the elephant is descended from an aquatic animal and that its trunk originally evolved

Parallelism; Verb Form

The clearest, most economical way of expressing the two things suggested by Australian embryologists' evidence is to format them as relative clauses serving as parallel direct objects of the verb *suggest*. It is awkward and confusing to string together relative clauses: *evidence that suggests that the elephant. ... A* clearer way of making this connection is to turn the verb *suggests* into a participle modifying *evidence*. The word *descended* is a predicate adjective following the present-tense verb *is* and describing the present-day elephant. The verb *evolved* should be past tense because it describes how the trunk of the elephant *originally* evolved, not how it is evolving today.

A The string of relative phrases is awkward and confusing; the phrase following the conjunction *and* is not parallel with the relative clause *that the elephant is descended. ...*

B The evidence *still* suggests these things about the evolution of the elephant and its trunk, so the present-perfect verb tense is inaccurate.

C *Had descended* is the wrong verb tense; *with* cannot be followed by an independent clause.

D *Had descended* is the wrong tense; the phrase following the conjunction *and* does not parallel the relative clause that precedes the conjunction.

E **Correct.** The two dependent clauses beginning with *that* are in parallel form and contain verbs in the correct tenses.

The correct answer is E.

SC01957

895. Most efforts to combat such mosquito-borne diseases like malaria and dengue have focused either on the vaccination of humans or on exterminating mosquitoes with pesticides.

(A) like malaria and dengue have focused either on the vaccination of humans or on exterminating

(B) like malaria and dengue have focused either on vaccinating of humans or on the extermination of

(C) as malaria and dengue have focused either on vaccinating humans or on exterminating

(D) as malaria and dengue have focused on either vaccinating of humans or on extermination of

(E) as malaria and dengue have focused on either vaccinating humans or exterminating

Diction; Parallelism

The phrase *such ... diseases like malaria and dengue* is not a correct way in English to indicate that the two diseases mentioned are examples of a larger category; the correct expression is *such ... as. ...*

A This use of *such ... like ...* is incorrect English; the correct expression is *such ... as. ...* It is better to keep the preposition *on* close to the verb it goes with, *focus*, so as not to repeat it.

B The correct expression is *such ... as. ...* It is better to keep the preposition *on* close to the verb it goes with, *focus*, so as not to repeat it. This use of the gerund *vaccinating* (followed by *of*) would normally be preceded by *the*, but this would make the phrase awkward. It would be preferable to use *vaccination*, which is parallel to *extermination*.

C This answer choice incorrectly repeats the preposition *on* before *exterminating*.

D This answer choice incorrectly repeats the preposition *on* before *extermination*. This use of the gerund *vaccinating* (followed by *of*) would normally be preceded by *the*, but this would make the phrase awkward. It would be preferable to use *vaccination*, which is parallel to *extermination*.

E **Correct.** This version uses *either ... or ...* correctly and appropriately uses the parallel forms *vaccinating* and *exterminating*.

The correct answer is E.

SC02344

896. Among the Tsonga, a Bantu-speaking group of tribes in southeastern Africa, dance teams represent their own chief at the court of each other, providing entertainment in return for food, drink, and lodging.

(A) the court of each other, providing entertainment in return for

(B) the court of another and provide entertainment in return for

(C) the court of the other, so as to provide entertainment as a return on

(D) each other's court, entertainment being provided in return for

(E) another's court and provide entertainment as a return on

Diction; Idiom

The point of the sentence is that dancers representing one chief perform at the court of another chief *in return for* gifts. *The court of each other* is unidiomatic and unclear. It could be intended to indicate, somewhat implausibly, that each team has a court that the other teams visit, but *represent their own chief* strongly suggests that the court referred to is the court of another chief. The correct pronoun to refer to a different chief is *another*.

A *The court of each other* is unidiomatic and unclear. *Each other* seems to refer, somewhat illogically, to the dancers.

B **Correct.** The sentence clearly explains the idea, using the correct pronoun *another* and the correct idiom *in return for*.

C This could be confusing in that *the other* indicates that there is only one other chief, whereas *group of tribes* suggests that there may be a number of chiefs. *As a return on* is the incorrect idiom; *a return on* normally refers to a gain from an investment, not a direct exchange of one good for another.

D *Each other's court* somewhat illogically indicates that the dancers each have a court. *Entertainment being provided in return for* is awkward and indirect.

E *As a return on* is the incorrect idiom; *a return on* normally refers to a gain from an investment, not a direct exchange of one good for another.

The correct answer is B.

SC06633

897. Almost like clones in their similarity to one another, the cheetah species' homogeneity makes them especially vulnerable to disease.

(A) the cheetah species' homogeneity makes them especially vulnerable to disease

(B) the cheetah species is especially vulnerable to disease because of its homogeneity

(C) the homogeneity of the cheetah species makes it especially vulnerable to disease

(D) homogeneity makes members of the cheetah species especially vulnerable to disease

(E) members of the cheetah species are especially vulnerable to disease because of their homogeneity

Agreement; Logical Predication

Genetic homogeneity is presented as a cause of cheetahs' vulnerability to disease. The opening adjectival phrase refers to the fact that individual cheetahs are almost like clones of one another because of how genetically similar they are. This adjectival phrase should be followed by what it describes, individual cheetahs. But the structure of the sentence makes it seem that this adjectival phrase is meant—illogically—to describe *the cheetah species' homogeneity*. The sentence structure also fails to make clear that the intended reference is to just one (the only) cheetah species.

A The sentence nonsensically presents the opening phrase as describing *homogeneity*.

B The resulting sentence opens with a reference to a plurality of individuals (*to one another*), but confusingly identifies this with a single (collective) entity, a species.

C The resulting sentence nonsensically presents the opening phrase as describing *homogeneity*.

D The resulting sentence nonsensically presents the opening phrase as describing *homogeneity*.

E **Correct.** The sentence is clear and the opening phrase correctly modifies *members of the cheetah species*.

The correct answer is E.

SC04330

898. As sources of electrical power, windmills now account for only about 2,500 megawatts nationwide, but production is almost expected to double by the end of the year, which would provide enough electricity for 1.3 million households.

(A) almost expected to double by the end of the year, which would provide

(B) almost expected that it will double by the end of the year, thus providing

(C) expected that it will almost double by the end of the year to provide

(D) expected almost to double by the end of the year and thus to provide

(E) expected almost to double by the end of the year, which would thus be providing

Rhetorical Construction; Idiom

The intended meaning of the sentence seems to be that the electricity production of windmills is expected to approximately double by year's end. But instead of saying *almost double*, we have *almost expected*, which is an unclear idea. Also unclear is what the relative pronoun *which* refers to.

A   The placement of *almost* makes it nonsensically modify *is expected*. What the relative pronoun *which* refers to is ambiguous: for example, does it refer to the expectation, the possible doubling, or the year?

B   The resulting sentence misplaces the adverb *almost*.

C   The phrase *production is expected that it will . . .* makes no sense—as opposed to, for example, *it is expected that production will. . . .*

D   **Correct.** This sentence clearly conveys the expectations of production: *almost to double* and *thus to provide*. There is no ambiguity as to what will be providing *enough electricity*.

E   The referent of the relative pronoun *which* is ambiguous, and the conditional verb form *would thus be providing* is unnecessarily wordy.

The correct answer is D.

SC03154

899. While most of the earliest known ball courts in Mesoamerica date to 900–400 B.C., <u>waterlogged latex balls found at El Manati and representations of ballplayers painted on ceramics found at San Lorenzo attest</u> to the fact that the Mesoamerican ballgame was well established by the mid-thirteenth century B.C.

(A) waterlogged latex balls found at El Manati and representations of ballplayers painted on ceramics found at San Lorenzo attest

(B) waterlogged latex balls found at El Manati and the painting of representations of ballplayers on ceramics found at San Lorenzo attests

(C) waterlogged latex balls found at El Manati and ceramics painted with representations of ballplayers found at San Lorenzo attests

(D) the finding of waterlogged latex balls at El Manati and the painting of representations of ballplayers on ceramics found at San Lorenzo attests

(E) the finding of waterlogged latex balls at El Manati and of representations of ballplayers painted on ceramics at San Lorenzo attest

Logical Predication; Agreement

The sentence points out two pieces of evidence that prove the early existence of ballgames in Mesoamerica: *waterlogged latex balls* and *representations of ballplayers*. The two noun phrases together serve as subjects for the verb *attest*, creating a sentence that logically and correctly expresses its main idea.

A   **Correct.** *Waterlogged latex balls* and *representations of ballplayers* together serve as subjects for the verb *attest*.

B   *Painting* could refer to something that has been painted, but on that interpretation the sentence does not make sense, because the painting is itself the representation and a single painting would not plausibly be on multiple ceramics. Alternatively, it could refer to an ongoing act of painting, which could not plausibly constitute the kind of evidence referred to. The singular verb *attests* does not agree with the compound subject *balls* and *painting*.

C   The singular verb *attests* does not agree with the compound subject *balls* and *ceramics*.

D   *Balls*, not *finding*, should be the subject of the verb since the balls are the evidence. *Painting* could refer to something that has been painted, but on that interpretation the sentence does not make sense, because the painting is itself the representation and a single painting would not plausibly be on multiple ceramics. Alternatively, it could refer to an ongoing act of painting, which could not plausibly constitute the kind of evidence referred to. The singular verb *attests* does not agree with the compound subject *finding* and *painting*.

E   *Balls* and *representations* should be the subject of the verb *attest* since they are the evidence—not *finding*; the plural verb *attest* does not agree with the singular subject *finding*.

The correct answer is A.

9.9 Sentence Correction Answer Explanations

SC04899

900. As criminal activity on the Internet becomes more and more sophisticated, not only are thieves able to divert cash from company bank accounts, <u>they can also pilfer valuable information such as business development strategies, new product specifications, and contract bidding plans, and sell</u> the data to competitors.

   (A) they can also pilfer valuable information such as business development strategies, new product specifications, and contract bidding plans, and sell
   (B) they can also pilfer valuable information that includes business development strategies, new product specifications, and contract bidding plans, and selling
   (C) also pilfering valuable information including business development strategies, new product specifications, and contract bidding plans, selling
   (D) but also pilfer valuable information such as business development strategies, new product specifications, and contract bidding plans to sell
   (E) but also pilfering valuable information such as business development strategies, new product specifications, and contract bidding plans and selling

Grammatical Construction; Verb Form

The two clauses in this *not only . . .* construction normally require subjects, which this sentence has. The second clause (beginning with *they can*) further divides into two clauses about pilfering and selling; here, the two verbs must have the same form, since each one is the main verb of its clause.

   A **Correct.** *They* supplies the needed subject, and *pilfer* and *sell* are both in the bare verb form.
   B *Selling* is the wrong form for the main verb of a finite clause; it should be *sell*.
   C There is no subject for the *pilfer* clause, and *pilfering* would be the wrong form even if a subject were added.
   D There is no subject for the *pilfer* clause.
   E There is no subject for the *pilfer* clause, and both *selling* and *pilfering* have the wrong verb for the main verb of a finite clause; they should be *sell* and *pilfer*, respectively.

The correct answer is A.

SC05785

901. Last week local shrimpers held a news conference to take some credit for the resurgence of the rare Kemp's ridley turtle, saying that their compliance with laws <u>requiring that turtle-excluder devices be on shrimp nets protect</u> adult sea turtles.

   (A) requiring that turtle-excluder devices be on shrimp nets protect
   (B) requiring turtle-excluder devices on shrimp nets is protecting
   (C) that require turtle-excluder devices on shrimp nets protect
   (D) to require turtle-excluder devices on shrimp nets are protecting
   (E) to require turtle-excluder devices on shrimp nets is protecting

Rhetorical Construction; Agreement

The subject of the clause introduced by *saying that* is the singular noun *compliance*. This subject requires the singular form of the verb *protect*. The clearest, most economical way to describe the laws in question is to follow the word *laws* with a present participle *requiring*. To use an infinitive, *to require*, seems to indicate that requiring these devices is the objective of the laws, when in fact the objective is to protect the sea turtles.

   A The plural verb *protect* does not agree with the singular subject *compliance*.
   B **Correct.** The singular verb *is protecting* agrees with the singular subject *compliance*, and the participial phrase beginning with *requiring* concisely and accurately describes the laws.
   C The relative clause *that require* introduces unnecessary wordiness; the plural verb *protect* does not agree with the singular subject *compliance*.
   D *To require* obscures the purpose of the laws; the plural verb phrase *are protecting* does not agree with the singular subject *compliance*.
   E *To require* obscures the purpose of the laws.

The correct answer is B.

SC03752

902. <u>A ruined structure found at Aqaba, Jordan, was probably a church, as indicated in its eastward orientation and by its overall plan, as well as</u> artifacts, such as glass oil-lamp fragments, found at the site.

(A) A ruined structure found at Aqaba, Jordan, was probably a church, as indicated in its eastward orientation and by its overall plan, as well as

(B) A ruined structure found at Aqaba, Jordan, once probably being a church, was indicated by its eastward orientation, overall plan, and

(C) Indicating that a ruined structure found at Aqaba, Jordan, was probably a church were its eastward orientation and overall plan, but also the

(D) A ruined structure found at Aqaba, Jordan, was probably a church, as indicates its eastward orientation and overall plan, as well as the

(E) That a ruined structure found at Aqaba, Jordan, was probably a church is indicated by its eastward orientation and overall plan, as well as by the

Logical Predication; Parallelism

This sentence explains why a currently ruined structure probably used to be a church. In the best-worded answer choice, the abstract subject (the probability that a certain hypothesis is true) is explained abstractly in a relative clause (*That a ruined structure was probably . . .*) followed by a passive verb (*is indicated*), followed by the prepositional phrase (*by . . .*), which is completed by a parallel listing of forms of evidence, all presented as noun phrases in the expression, (*by*) (*its*) A + B, as well as (*by*) C.

A This version makes the relationship between *as well as . . .* and the rest of the sentence unclear. The most plausible hypothesis is that the artifacts are another of the types of evidence, parallel with the structure's orientation and its plan. The sentence violates the parallelism required in the list by failing to supply the preposition in the final item following *as well as*.

B The subject of this version of the sentence, *structure*, is completed by the verb *was indicated*, creating the illogical assertion that the structure itself, rather than its probable identity, was indicated by its orientation, plan, and attendant artifacts.

C Opening the sentence with the predicate adjective *indicating* leads to a confusing and awkward withholding of the subjects *orientation . . . plan . . . artifacts*.

D The only plausible subject for the singular verb *indicates* is the plural *orientation . . . plan, as well as the artifacts*. Very little about this sentence makes sense.

E **Correct.** The relationships among the parts of the sentence are clear and logical.

The correct answer is E.

SC04343

903. In the major cities of industrialized countries at the end of the nineteenth century, important public places such as theaters, restaurants, shops, and banks had installed electric lighting, but <u>electricity was in less than 1 percent of homes, where lighting was still</u> provided mainly by candles or gas.

(A) electricity was in less than 1 percent of homes, where lighting was still

(B) electricity was in less than 1 percent of homes and lighting still

(C) there had been less than 1 percent of homes with electricity, where lighting was still being

(D) there was less than 1 percent of homes that had electricity, having lighting that was still

(E) less than 1 percent of homes had electricity, where lighting had still been

Rhetorical Construction; Verb Form

In this type of usage, a participle such as *provided* normally must be preceded by some form of the verb *be*. The best choice for this is the past tense *was*, since the main part of the clause describes the situation in the past tense (*electricity was . . .*). To link the ideas of lighting and electricity in homes, *where* is the most efficient and direct expression, superior to alternatives such as *and* or *having*.

A **Correct.** The participle is preceded by the appropriate form *was*, and the clauses are linked efficiently by *where*.

B There is no form of *be* in the second clause, and *and* does not clearly indicate the connection between the two clauses.

C *Had been* and *was being* represent inappropriate tenses, and the *there had been* construction is longer than necessary.

D Both *having lighting* and the *there was* construction are longer and more complicated than necessary. This sentence structure makes *there*, instead of *homes*, the subject of *having*.

E   *Had been* is not the appropriate tense for this situation.

The correct answer is A.

SC02965
904. By 1999, astronomers <u>had discovered 17 nearby stars that are orbited by planets</u> about the size of Jupiter.

(A) had discovered 17 nearby stars that are orbited by planets
(B) had discovered 17 nearby stars with planets orbiting them that were
(C) had discovered that there were 17 nearby stars that were orbited by planets
(D) have discovered 17 nearby stars with planets orbiting them that are
(E) have discovered that 17 nearby stars are orbited by planets

Verb Form; Rhetorical Construction

Opening with a past date (*1999*) describing the end point of a period of discovery, this sentence calls for a past perfect main verb to follow the subject *astronomers*. In order to economize on words and maximize clarity, the object of the main clause, *stars*, is modified by a passive relative clause *that are orbited by planets* followed by the adjective phrase *about the size of Jupiter*. This structure avoids an awkward and confusing string of relative clauses and prepositional phrases.

A   Correct. This version is clear and uses the correct verb form *had discovered*.

B   The use of a prepositional phrase *with planets* necessitates the introduction of a relative clause *that were . . .*, in which the referent of the relative pronoun *that* is somewhat uncertain (stars? or planets?). The past tense verb *were* suggests, improbably, that the size of the planets may have changed significantly since 1999.

C   The string of relative clauses is awkward and wordy.

D   If the sentence was written after 1999, the present perfect tense is illogical, because 1999 is in the past. If it was written in 1999, this way of referring to the then-present time is odd and misleading. The prepositional phrase is wordy and indirect.

E   As in (D), the present perfect tense is illogical.

The correct answer is A.

SC01647
905. <u>Although she was considered among her contemporaries to be the better poet than her husband, later Elizabeth Barrett Browning was overshadowed by his success.</u>

(A) Although she was considered among her contemporaries to be the better poet than her husband, later Elizabeth Barrett Browning was overshadowed by his success.
(B) Although Elizabeth Barrett Browning was considered among her contemporaries as a better poet than her husband, she was later overshadowed by his success.
(C) Later overshadowed by the success of her husband, Elizabeth Barrett Browning's poetry had been considered among her contemporaries to be better than that of her husband.
(D) Although Elizabeth Barrett Browning's success was later overshadowed by that of her husband, among her contemporaries she was considered the better poet.
(E) Elizabeth Barrett Browning's poetry was considered among her contemporaries as better than her husband, but her success was later overshadowed by his.

Idiom; Verb Form; Logical Predication

The sentence misuses the locution *the better poet*. It is acceptable to say *a better poet than* but not *the better poet than*. If you have already mentioned two poets *X* and *Y*, and you want to say that *X* is better than *Y*, you can either say *X is a better poet than Y*, or simply, *X is the better poet*.

A   This version of the sentence misuses the idiom *the better poet*, most likely confusing it with the idiom *a better poet than*.

B   [W]*as considered among her contemporaries as* is awkward and unnecessarily creates a potential misreading (she was considered to be among her contemporaries).

C   The subject here is *Elizabeth Barrett Browning's poetry*, not *Elizabeth Barrett Browning*, so the antecedent of *her* in *her husband* could comically be taken to be *Elizabeth Barrett Browning's poetry*. Furthermore, the tense of *had been considered* pairs oddly with *Later overshadowed*. Each seems to be in reaction to some particular time *T*—later than *T* and earlier than *T*, but when *T* was or its significance is never indicated.

D   **Correct.** This version avoids the problems of the other versions.

   E   This sentence comically compares Elizabeth Barrett Browning's poetry to her husband.

The correct answer is D.

906. In no other historical sighting did Halley's Comet cause such a worldwide sensation as did its return in 1910–1911.

   (A)   did its return in 1910–1911
   (B)   had its 1910–1911 return
   (C)   in its return of 1910–1911
   (D)   its return of 1910–1911 did
   (E)   its return in 1910–1911

Parallelism; Verb Form; Logical Predication

The single subject of this sentence is *Halley's Comet*, and its single verb phrase is *did cause*. The comparison presented by the sentence is between adverbial phrases describing times when the comet was seen. Grammatically, the items being compared are parallel prepositional phrases beginning with the preposition *in*: *in no other sighting* and *in its return in 1910–1911*. This is the clearest, most economical way of presenting the information. The options that introduce a second verb (*did* or *had*) violate the parallelism and introduce a comparison between the comet itself (subject of the verb *did cause*) and the comet's return (subject of the verb *did* or *had*).

   A   This sentence implies a comparison between the comet and its return.

   B   This sentence implies a comparison between the comet and its return; *had* is the wrong auxiliary verb form because it must be followed by *caused* instead of *cause*.

   C   **Correct.** The parallel prepositional phrases in this sentence correctly compare times when the comet was sighted.

   D   This sentence implies a comparison between the comet and its return.

   E   This sentence violates parallelism, implying a comparison between a prepositional phrase and a noun phrase.

The correct answer is C.

907. Rock samples taken from the remains of an asteroid about twice the size of the 6-mile-wide asteroid that eradicated the dinosaurs has been dated to be 3.47 billion years old and thus is evidence of the earliest known asteroid impact on Earth.

   (A)   has been dated to be 3.47 billion years old and thus is
   (B)   has been dated at 3.47 billion years old and thus
   (C)   have been dated to be 3.47 billion years old and thus are
   (D)   have been dated as being 3.47 billion years old and thus
   (E)   have been dated at 3.47 billion years old and thus are

Agreement; Idiom

The plural subject of this sentence, *Rock samples*, requires plural verb phrases—*have been dated* and *are* rather than *has been dated* and *is*. The idiomatic way of expressing estimation of age is with the phrase *dated at*.

   A   The subject and verbs do not agree; *dated to be …* is not idiomatic.

   B   The subject and verb do not agree; the conjunction *and thus* should be followed by a verb.

   C   *Dated to be* is not idiomatic.

   D   *As being* is not idiomatic; the conjunction *and thus* should be followed by a verb.

   E   **Correct.** The plural verbs match the plural subject, and the wording of the sentence is idiomatic.

The correct answer is E.

To register for the GMAT exam go to www.mba.com

10.0 Integrated Reasoning

> Please visit gmat.wiley.com and use the unique access code found on the inside front cover of this book to access Integrated Reasoning questions and answer explanations.

10.0 Integrated Reasoning

This chapter contains an overview of integrated reasoning question types, explains what they measure, and offers some tips and strategies for answering them. Because of the way integrated reasoning questions are presented on a computer screen, this book does *not* contain any integrated reasoning practice questions. **For Integrated Reasoning practice questions, you can go to gmat.wiley.com and log into your account using the access code located on the inside front cover of this book.**

Overview of the Integrated Reasoning Section:

The Integrated Reasoning section of the GMAT™ exam measures your ability to understand and evaluate multiple sources and types of information—numeric, graphic, and verbal—as they relate to one another.

In this section, you will:

- Use quantitative and verbal reasoning skills to solve complex problems,
- Solve multiple problems in relation to one another, and
- Provide answers in different response formats, rather than only traditional multiple choice.

The Integrated Reasoning section consists of 12 questions to be completed over 30 minutes. Four types of questions are used throughout the section, and some require multiple responses. The questions involve both quantitative and verbal reasoning, either separately or in combination. Questions with a **quantitative component** require a basic knowledge of arithmetic, elementary algebra, and commonly known concepts of geometry and statistics. Questions with a **verbal component** require the ability to understand written material and to reason and evaluate arguments.

Special Features:

- The Integrated Reasoning section is unique from the Quantitative Reasoning and Verbal Reasoning sections of the GMAT™ exam in that it is not computer-adaptive. This means that your performance on earlier questions does not determine the selection of later questions.

- Unlike the other sections of the GMAT™ exam, integrated reasoning questions may have multiple questions on a single screen. For these questions, you can change answers while on the current screen before clicking "Next" to advance to the next question. However, once you move to a new screen, you cannot return to the previous screen.

- The Integrated Reasoning section may contain quantitative elements but is not a test of quantitative skills. An online calculator with basic functions will be available for this section only, whereas it is not available for the Quantitative Reasoning section.

10.1 What Is Measured

The Integrated Reasoning section of the GMAT™ exam measures how well you integrate data to solve complex problems. Specifically, the Integrated Reasoning section tests you in the following skill categories:

Skill Category	Details	Examples
Apply	Ability to understand principles, rules, or other concepts and apply them to a new context or predict consequences that would follow if new information were incorporated	• Decide whether new examples would comply with or violate established rules • Determine how a trend would be affected by new scenarios • Use established principles to draw conclusions about new data
Evaluate	Ability to make judgments about the quality of information	• Decide whether a claim made in one source is supported or weakened by information provided in another source • Determine whether information provided is sufficient to justify a course of action • Judge the strength of evidence in support of an argument or plan • Identify errors or gaps in the information provided
Infer	Ability to draw conclusions based on information or ideas that are not explicitly stated in the materials provided, but can be derived from them	• Calculate the probability of an outcome based on given data • Indicate whether statements follow logically from the information provided • Determine the meaning of a term within a given context • Identify the rate of change in data gathered over time
Recognize	Ability to identify information that is directly presented in the materials provided, including specific facts, details, or relationships between pieces of information	• Identify areas of agreement and disagreement between sources of information • Determine the strength of correlation between two variables • Indicate rank within a table within a combination of categories (e.g., which product maximizes revenue and minimizes costs) • Identify facts provided as evidence in an argument
Strategize	Ability to work toward a goal within the context of particular needs or constraints	• Choose a plan of action that minimizes risks and maximizes value • Identify trade-offs required to reach a goal • Specify the mathematical formula that will yield a desired result • Determine which means of completing a task are consistent within given constraints

10.2 Question Types and Test-Taking Strategies

There are four types of questions in the Integrated Reasoning section:

| Multi-Source Reasoning | Table Analysis | Graphics Interpretation | Two-Part Analysis |

Multi-Source Reasoning

What will be displayed:

- Two or three sources of information presented on multiple tabs on the left side of your screen
- A question prompt with answer choices on the right side of your screen
- Multiple tabs for you to click on to view information and determine what is needed to answer the question. At least one tab will contain a written passage (e.g., an email or report)
- Other sources may be tables, graphs, diagrams, or other visual information

Example of information sources presented on multiple tabs:

For outside laboratory tests, the museum's first-year budget for the Kaxna collection allows unlimited IRMS testing, and a total of $7,000—equal to the cost of 4 TL tests plus 15 radiocarbon tests, or the cost of 40 ICP-MS tests—for all other tests. For each technique applied by an outside lab, the museum is charged a fixed price per artifact.

The response type:

- For some questions, you will receive a traditional multiple-choice question with five answer choices
- For some questions, you will receive a set of three conditional statements for you to indicate true/false or yes/no
  - Select one answer choice PER ROW (i.e., conditional statement)
  - All three conditional statements must be answered correctly to receive credit for the question

Example of a conditional statement question:

For each of the following artifacts in the museum's Kaxna collection, select *Yes* if, based on the museum's assumptions, a range of dates for the object's creation can be obtained using one of the techniques in the manner described. Otherwise, select *No*.

Yes No
○   ○   Bronze statue of a deer
○   ○   Fired-clay pot
○   ○   Wooden statue of a warrior

Strategies for Answering Multi-Source Reasoning Questions

- **Do not expect to be completely familiar with the material presented in multi-source reasoning sets.**

  All the information you will need to answer the questions correctly will be provided. Even so, you may find some graphs, charts, tables, or verbal passages easier to understand than others; all the material is designed to be challenging.

- **Analyze each source of information carefully, as the questions require detailed understanding of the information presented.**

  Text passages often build ideas sequentially, so note as you read how each statement adds to the main idea of the passage as a whole. Some of the passages used with multi-source reasoning questions will be entirely descriptive; others may contain strong opinions.

  The graphic elements in the multi-source reasoning questions come in various forms, such as tables, graphs, diagrams, or charts. Briefly familiarize yourself with the information presented. If scales are provided, note the marked values and labels. Also note the major graphical elements of the information presented.

- **Read the questions carefully, making sure you understand what is being asked.**

  Some questions may require you to recognize discrepancies among different sources of information or to draw inferences using information from different sources. Other questions may require you to determine which one of the information sources is relevant.

  You can refer back to any of the information at any time while you are answering the multi-source reasoning questions by clicking on the tabs in the graphics.

- **Select the answer choices that have the most support based on the information provided.**

  If you happen to be familiar with the subject matter, do not let this knowledge influence your answer. Consider only the information provided in the question when selecting an answer.

Table Analysis

What will be displayed:

- A data table similar to a spreadsheet, which you will be able to sort by each data column

Example of data table with sorting drop-down menu:

The table displays data on *Brazilian agricultural* products in 2009.

Sort By: Production, world share (%) ▼

Commodity	Production, world share (%)	Production, world rank	Exports, world share (%)	Exports, world rank
Pork	4	4	12	4
Cotton	5	5	10	4
Corn	8	4	10	2
Chickens	15	3	38	1
Beef	16	2	22	1
Sugar	21	1	44	1
Soybeans	27	2	40	2
Coffee	40	1	32	1
Orange juice	56	1	82	1

The response type:

- A set of three conditional statements for you to indicate true/false or yes/no
  - Select one answer choice PER ROW (i.e., conditional statement)
  - All three conditional statements must be answered correctly to receive credit for the question

Example of a conditional statement question:

For each of the following statements, select *Yes* if the statement can be shown to be true based on the information in the table. Otherwise select *No*.

Yes	No	
○	○	No individual country produces more than one-fourth of the world's sugar.
○	○	If Brazil produces less than 20% of the world's supply of any commodity listed in the table, Brazil is not the world's top exporter of that commodity.
○	○	Of the commodities in th table for which Brazil ranks first in world exports, Brazil produces more than 20% of the world's supply.

Strategies for Answering Table Analysis Questions

- **Examine the table and accompanying text to determine the type of information provided.**

  Orienting yourself to the data at the start will make it easier to locate the information you need.

- **Read the question carefully.**

  The question will contain the condition that each phrase, statement, numerical value, or algebraic expression does or does not meet. If you clearly understand the condition (e.g., "*is consistent with the information provided*" or "*can be inferred from the information provided*"), you will find it easier to understand what choice you need to make. Some questions involve quantitative skills, but others involve subsets, conditions, or consistency of data, which are not necessarily mathematical.

- **Read each phrase, statement, numerical value, or algebraic expression carefully to determine the data analysis required.**

  Often, the phrase, statement, numerical value, or algebraic expression indicates a relationship that you can clarify by sorting the table by one or more of its columns. Understanding how the data is organized and sorted can help you work more efficiently.

- **Judge each phrase, statement, numerical value, or algebraic expression carefully based on the condition specified.**

  For each, the two answer choices (such as *yes* or *no*, *true* or *false*, *consistent* or *inconsistent*) are mutually exclusive and only one answer selection for each phrase, statement, numerical value, or algebraic expression is correct. Focus your attention on whether the given condition has been met.

Graphics Interpretation

What will be displayed:

- A graph, diagram, or other visual representation
  - Graphics may include (but are not limited to) bar graphs, line graphs, scatterplots, bubble charts, pie charts, flow charts, or organizational charts

- One or more statements with blank/missing information

Example of graphics:

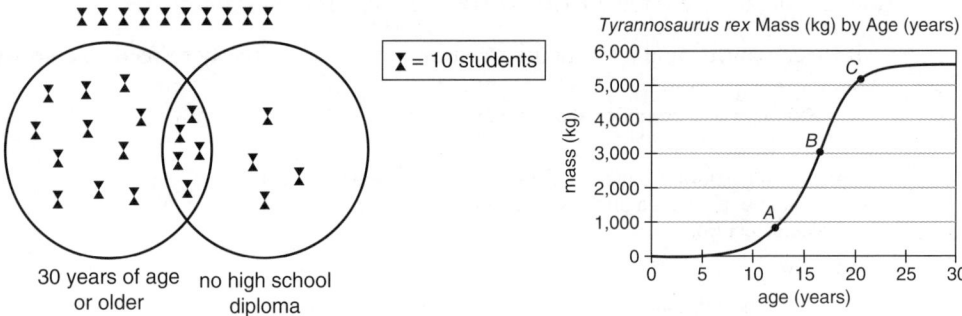

Example of statement with blank/missing information and drop-down menus:

Use the drop-down menus to complete each statement according to the information presented in the diagram.

If one student is selected at random from the 300 surveyed, the chance that the student will be under 30 or a high school graduate or both is [Select... ▼]

If one student is selected at random from the 300 surveyed, the chance that the student will be both under 30 and high school graduate is [1 out of 3 ▼]

Select...
1 out of 6
1 out of 3
2 out of 3
5 out of 6

The response type:

- Drop-down menus containing a word, number, or phrase
  - If there is more than one blank, all drop-down menus must be answered correctly in order to receive credit for the question
- Interpret the graphic and complete each statement with the most accurate word, number, or phrase from an embedded drop-down menu

Strategies for Answering Graphics Interpretation Questions

- **Make sure you understand what the problem is asking you to do.**

  Graphics interpretation problems involve interpreting and integrating data, discerning relationships, and making inferences from a set of data. You may have to do some quantitative analysis, such as calculating change in a given value over time or comparing different rates of growth.

- **Read the graphic carefully.**

  Familiarize yourself with the information presented in the graphic. If there are scales on the axes, make note of the marked values. If there are labels, be sure to note any discrepancy between the units in the graph and the units discussed in the text.

- **Read any accompanying text carefully.**

  If there is accompanying text, it may clarify the meaning of the graphic. The text might also present information that is not contained in the graphic but is necessary to answer the question.

- **Read all the choices in the drop-down menu.**

  By checking the menu options, you may find additional information about the task involved.

- **Choose the option that best completes the statement.**

  More than one option in the drop-down menu may seem plausible; choose the one that makes the statement most accurate or logical. If the drop-down menu is preceded by a phrase, such as *nearest to* or *closest to*, choose the option that is closest to your calculated answer. You might find it helpful to read the statement again with your answer choice in place.

Two-Part Analysis

Two-part analysis questions, which measure your ability to solve complex problems, cover a wide range of content and could be quantitative, verbal, or some combination of both. The versatility of the format lends itself to a wide range of content and skills measured, including the ability to evaluate trade-offs, solve simultaneous equations, and discern relationships between two entities.

What is displayed:

- A brief written scenario or problem
- A table with two related choices relevant to the information provided
  - The two related choices are represented by the first two columns
  - Your answer options are listed in the third column of the table

Example of a written scenario:

A literature department at a small university in an English-speaking country is organizing a two-day festival in which it will highlight the works of ten writers who have been the subjects of recent scholarly work by the faculty. Five writers will be featured each day. To reflect the department's strengths, the majority of writers scheduled for one of the days will be writers whose primary writing language is not English. On the other day of the festival, at least four of the writers will be women. Neither day should have more than two writers from the same country. Departmental members have already agreed on a schedule for eight of the writers. That schedule showing names, along with each writer's primary writing language and country of origin, is shown.

- Day 1:

  Achebe (male, English, Nigeria)

  Weil (female, French, France)

  Gavalda (female, French, France)

  Barrett Browning (female, English, UK)

- Day 2:

  Rowling (female, English, UK)

  Austen (female, English, UK)

  Ocantos (male, Spanish, Argentina)

  Lu Xun (male, Chinese, China)

Example of a response based on passage information:

Select a writer who could be added to the schedule for either day. Then select a writer who could be added to the schedule for neither day. Make only two selections, one in each column.

Either day	Neither day	Writer
○	○	LeGuin (female, English, USA)
○	○	Longfellow (make, English, USA)
○	○	Murasaki (female, Japanese, Japan)
○	○	Colette (female, French, France)
○	○	Vargas Llosa (male, Spanish, Peru)
○	○	Zola (male, French, France)

The response type:

- Select one response PER COLUMN (not per row)
  - A single correct answer must be selected for each column to receive credit for the question
  - The same answer choice can be selected for both response columns (i.e., the two answer choices are not mutually exclusive)

Strategies for Answering Two-Part Analysis Questions

- **Read the information carefully.**

  All the material presented is designed to be challenging. If you happen to be familiar with the subject matter, do not let this knowledge influence your choice. Answer the question only on the basis of what is given.

- **Determine exactly what the question is asking.**

  Do not assume that the headings in the two response columns are complete descriptions of the tasks to be performed. Pay close attention to how the question describes the tasks. Often the headings in the two response columns are shorthand references to the tasks.

- **Remember that you are only supposed to make two choices.**

  Select one answer in each of the first two columns of the response table. You do not need to make a choice for each *row* of the table. The third column contains possible answers to the two questions.

- **Review all available answers before making a final choice.**

  Do not assume you have chosen the best answers in the two columns without reading all the options.

- **Determine whether tasks are dependent or independent.**

  Some two-part analysis questions pose two tasks that can be carried out individually. Others pose one task with two dependent parts, each of which you must carry out correctly to create a single correct response. With dependent questions, you cannot answer the question logically without making both choices. Be sure to examine your answers in relation to one another.

- **Keep in mind that the same answer choice might be the correct response for both columns.**

  If the tasks associated with the two response columns are *not* mutually exclusive, it is possible that one answer option satisfies the conditions of both response columns.

Additional Tips for the Integrated Reasoning Section

Examine and analyze all given data

- Do not expect to be completely familiar with all the material presented. You may find some graphs, charts, tables, or verbal passages to be easier to understand than others. All the material is designed to be challenging, but if you have familiarity with the subject matter, do not let this knowledge influence your answer choices. Answer all questions based on the information that is provided.

- For graphs and charts, make sure you take note of the scales on the axes and read all accompanying text carefully, as it may help clarify the meaning of the graphic or provide additional valuable information.

Read each question carefully

- Make sure you are clear about exactly what the question is asking. Fully read each question problem, including the accompanying text, which usually comes before the answer tables.

Scan the answer choices

- It may be helpful to scan the answer choices prior to doing any work; sometimes the answer choices will give you additional information about the task involved.

Manage your time wisely

- You have 30 minutes to complete 12 questions in the Integrated Reasoning section, which is 2½ minutes per question.

- Remember that many questions have a considerable amount of information to comprehend and consist of multiple parts.

Additional Integrated Reasoning Samples

For additional sample questions in each question format, visit mba.com:

https://www.mba.com/us/the-gmat-exam/gmat-exam-format-timing/integrated-reasoning/ir-sample-question-types.aspx

Additional Integrated Reasoning Practice

Use your unique access code found in the inside front cover of this book to access 74 Integrated Reasoning practice questions with answer explanations at gmat.wiley.com. Additional Integrated Reasoning practice questions are available for purchase on mba.com.

10.3 Section Instructions

Go to www.mba.com/tutorial to view instructions for the section and get a feel for what the test center screens will look at on the actual GMAT exam.

11.0 Analytical Writing Assessment

11.0 Analytical Writing Assessment

The Analytical Writing Assessment (AWA) consists of one 30-minute writing task called the Analysis of an Argument. In this section, you must read a brief argument, analyze the reasoning behind it, and then write a critique of the argument. You are not asked to state your opinion but rather to analyze the one given. For example, you may, consider what questionable assumptions underlie the author's thinking, what alternative explanations or counterexamples might weaken the conclusion, or what sort of evidence could help strengthen or refute the argument.

For this task, you will use the computer keyboard to type your response. You will be able to use typical word-processing functions—that is, you can cut, copy, paste, undo, and redo. These functions can be accessed either by using the keyboard or by using the mouse to click on icons on the screen. You will be able to take notes when planning your response.

It is important that you plan carefully before you begin writing. Read the specific analytical writing task several times to make sure you understand exactly what is expected. Think about how you might present your analysis. You may want to sketch an outline to help you plan and organize. Keep in mind the 30-minute time limit as you plan your response—keep your analysis brief enough to allow for plenty of time to write a first draft, read it over carefully, and make any necessary corrections or revisions before you run out of time. As you write, try to keep your language clear, your sentences concise, and the flow of your ideas logical. State your premise clearly at the beginning, and make sure you present a strong conclusion at the end.

11.1 What Is Measured

The Analytical Writing Assessment is designed as a direct measure of your ability to think critically and communicate your ideas. More specifically, the Analysis of an Argument task tests your ability to formulate an appropriate and constructive critique of a prescribed conclusion based upon a specific line of thinking.

The argument that you will analyze may concern a topic of general interest, possibly related to business, or to a variety of other subjects. It is important to note, however, that no Analysis of an Argument question presupposes any specific knowledge of business or other specific content areas. Only your capacity to write analytically is assessed.

Professional essay raters, including college and university faculty members from various subject-matter areas, including but not limited to management education, will evaluate your essay. For information on how readers are qualified, visit mba.com. Readers are trained to be sensitive and fair in evaluating the responses of nonnative speakers of English. A computer scoring program will also evaluate your essays. Your responses will be scored on the basis of:

- the overall quality of your ideas
- your ability to organize, develop, and express those ideas
- how well you provide relevant supporting reasons and examples
- your ability to control the elements of standard written English

11.2 Test-Taking Strategies

1. **Read the question carefully.**
   Make sure you have taken all parts of a question into account before you begin to respond to it.

2. **Do not start to write immediately.**
   Take a few minutes to think about the question and plan a response before you begin writing. You may find it helpful to write a brief outline or jot down some ideas on the erasable notepad provided. Take care to organize your ideas and develop them fully, but leave time to reread your response and make any revisions that you think would improve it.

3. **Focus on the task of analyzing and critiquing a line of thinking or reasoning.**
   Get used to asking yourself questions such as the following: *What questionable assumptions might underlie the thinking? What alternative explanations might be given? What counterexamples might be raised? What additional evidence might prove useful in fully and fairly evaluating the reasoning?*

4. **Develop fully any examples you use.**
   Do not simply list your examples—explain how they illustrate your point.

5. **Discuss alternative explanations or counterexamples.**
   These techniques allow you to introduce illustrations and examples drawn from your observations, experiences, and reading.

6. **Make sure your response reads like a narrative.**
   Your response should not read like an outline. It should use full sentences, a coherent organizational scheme, logical transitions between points, and appropriately introduced and developed examples.

11.3 The Directions

These are the directions that you will see for the Analysis of an Argument essay. If you read them carefully and understand them clearly before going to sit for the test, you will not need to spend too much time reviewing them when you take the GMAT™ exam. They read as follows:

ANALYSIS OF AN ARGUMENT

In this section, you will be asked to write a critique of the argument presented. *You are not asked to present your own views on the subject.*

Writing Your Response: Take a few minutes to evaluate the argument and plan a response before you begin writing. Be sure to leave enough time to reread your response and make any revisions that you think are necessary.

Evaluation of Your Response: Scores will reflect how well you:

- organize, develop, and express your ideas about the argument presented
- provide relevant supporting reasons and examples
- control the elements of standard written English

11.4 GMAT™ Scoring Guide: Analysis of an Argument

6 Outstanding

A 6 paper presents a cogent, well-articulated critique of the argument and demonstrates mastery of the elements of effective writing.

A typical paper in this category exhibits the following characteristics:

- clearly identifies important features of the argument and analyzes them insightfully
- develops ideas cogently, organizes them logically, and connects them with clear transitions
- effectively supports the main points of the critique
- demonstrates control of language, including diction and syntactic variety
- demonstrates facility with the conventions of standard written English but may have minor flaws

5 Strong

A 5 paper presents a well-developed critique of the argument and demonstrates good control of the elements of effective writing.

A typical paper in this category exhibits the following characteristics:

- clearly identifies important features of the argument and analyzes them in a generally thoughtful way
- develops ideas clearly, organizes them logically, and connects them with appropriate transitions
- sensibly supports the main points of the critique
- demonstrates control of language, including diction and syntactic variety
- demonstrates facility with the conventions of standard written English but may have occasional flaws

4 Adequate

A 4 paper presents a competent critique of the argument and demonstrates adequate control of the elements of writing.

A typical paper in this category exhibits the following characteristics:

- identifies and analyzes important features of the argument
- develops and organizes ideas satisfactorily but may not connect them with transitions
- supports the main points of the critique
- demonstrates sufficient control of language to convey ideas with reasonable clarity
- generally follows the conventions of standard written English but may have some flaws

3 Limited

A 3 paper demonstrates some competence in analytical writing skills and in its control of the elements of writing but is plainly flawed.

A typical paper in this category exhibits one or more of the following characteristics:

- does not identify or analyze most of the important features of the argument, although some analysis of the argument is present
- mainly analyzes tangential or irrelevant matters, or reasons poorly
- is limited in the logical development and organization of ideas
- offers support of little relevance and value for points of the critique
- does not convey meaning clearly
- contains occasional major errors or frequent minor errors in grammar, usage, and mechanics

2 Seriously Flawed

A 2 paper demonstrates serious weaknesses in analytical writing skills.

A typical paper in this category exhibits one or more of the following characteristics:

- does not present a critique based on logical analysis, but may instead present the writer's own views on the subject
- does not develop ideas, or is disorganized and illogical
- provides little, if any, relevant or reasonable support
- has serious and frequent problems in the use of language and in sentence structure
- contains numerous errors in grammar, usage, and mechanics that interfere with meaning

1 Fundamentally Deficient

A 1 paper demonstrates fundamental deficiencies in analytical writing skills.

A typical paper in this category exhibits more than one of the following characteristics:

- provides little evidence of the ability to understand and analyze the argument
- provides little evidence of the ability to develop an organized response
- has severe and persistent errors in language and sentence structure
- contains a pervasive pattern of errors in grammar, usage, and mechanics that results in incoherence

0 No Score

A paper in this category is off topic, not written in English, is merely attempting to copy the topic, or consists only of keystroke characters.

NR Blank

11.5 Sample: Analysis of an Argument

Read the statement and the instructions that follow it, and then make any notes that will help you plan your response.

The following appeared as part of an article in a daily newspaper:

"The computerized on-board warning system that will be installed in commercial airliners will virtually solve the problem of midair plane collisions. One plane's warning system can receive signals from another's transponder—a radio set that signals a plane's course—in order to determine the likelihood of a collision and recommend evasive action."

Discuss how well reasoned you find this argument. In your discussion, be sure to analyze the line of reasoning and the use of evidence in the argument. For example, you may need to consider what questionable assumptions underlie the thinking and what alternative explanations or counterexamples might weaken the conclusion. You can also discuss what sort of evidence would strengthen or refute the argument, what changes in the argument would make it more logically sound, and what, if anything, would help you better evaluate its conclusion.

Sample Paper 6

The argument that this warning system will virtually solve the problem of midair plane collisions omits some important concerns that must be addressed to substantiate the argument. The statement that follows the description of what this warning system will do simply describes the system and how it operates. This alone does not constitute a logical argument in favor of the warning system, and it certainly does not provide support or proof of the main argument.

Most conspicuously, the argument does not address the cause of the problem of midair plane collisions, the use of the system by pilots and flight specialists, or who is involved in the midair plane collisions. First, the argument assumes that the cause of the problem is that the planes' courses, the likelihood of collisions, and actions to avoid collisions are unknown or inaccurate. In a weak attempt to support its claim, the argument describes a system that makes all of these things accurately known. But if the cause of the problem of midair plane collisions is that pilots are not paying attention to their computer systems or flight operations, the warning system will not solve the collision problem. Second, the argument never addresses the interface between individuals and the system and how this will affect the warning system's objective of obliterating the problem of collisions. If the pilot or flight specialist does not conform to what the warning system suggests, midair collisions will not be avoided. Finally, if planes other than commercial airliners are involved in the collisions, the problem of these collisions cannot be solved by a warning system that will not be installed on non-commercial airliners. The argument also does not address what would happen in the event that the warning system collapses, fails, or does not work properly.

Because the argument leaves out several key issues, it is not sound or persuasive. If it included the items discussed above instead of solely explaining what the system supposedly does, the argument would have been more thorough and convincing.

Explanation of Score 6

This response is, as the scoring guide requires of a 6, "cogent" and "well articulated": all the points made not only bear directly on the argument to be analyzed, but also contribute to a single, integrated development of the writer's critique. The writer begins by making the controlling point that a mere description of the warning system's mode of operation cannot serve as a true argument proving the system's effectiveness, since the description overlooks several major considerations. The writer then identifies these considerations—what causes midair collisions, how pilots will actually use the commercial airline warning system, what kinds of airplanes are typically involved in midair collisions—and, citing appropriate counterexamples (e.g., what if pilots do not pay attention to their instruments?), explains fully how each oversight undermines the conclusion that the warning system will virtually eliminate midair plane collisions.

Throughout, the writer complements the logically organized development of this critique with good, clear prose that demonstrates the ability not only to control language and vary sentence structure but also to express ideas forcibly (e.g., "the argument never addresses the interface between individuals and the system"). Of course, as in any response written under time constraints, occasional minor flaws can be found. For example, "the argument assumes that the cause of the problem is that the planes' courses, the likelihood of collisions, and actions to avoid collisions are unknown or inaccurate" is wordy and imprecise: how can a course, a likelihood, or actions be inaccurate? But flaws such as these, minor and infrequent, do not interfere with the overall clarity and forcefulness of this outstanding response.

Sample Paper 4

The argument is not logically convincing. It does not state whether all planes can receive signals from each other. It does not state whether planes constantly receive signals. If they only receive signals once every certain time interval, collisions will not definitely be prevented. Further if they receive a signal right before they are about to crash, they cannot avoid each other.

The main flaw in the argument is that it assumes that the two planes, upon receiving each other's signals, will know which evasive action to take. For example, the two planes could be going towards each other and then receive the signals. If one turns at an angle to the left and the other turns at an angle to the right, the two planes will still crash. Even if they receive an updated signal, they will not have time to avoid each other.

The following argument would be more sound and persuasive. The new warning system will solve the problem of midair plane collisions. Each plane will receive constant, continual signals from each other. If the two planes are headed in a direction where they will crash, the system will coordinate the signals, and tell one plane to go one way, and the other plane to go another way. The new system will ensure that the two planes will turn in different directions so they don't crash by trying to prevent the original crash. In addition, the two planes will be able to see themselves and the other on a computer screen, to aid in the evasive action.

Explanation of Score 4

This response competently cites a number of deficiencies in the argument presented: the information given about the nature of the signals sent and received and the evasive action recommended does not warrant the conclusion that the onboard warning system "will virtually solve the problem of midair plane collisions." However, in discussing these insufficiencies in the argument, the response reveals an unevenness in the quality of its reasoning. For example, while it is perfectly legitimate to point out that the argument assumes too much and says too little about the evasive action that will be recommended by the warning system, it is farfetched to suggest that the system might be so poorly designed as to route two approaching airplanes to the same spot. Likewise, while it is fair to question the effectiveness of a warning signal about which the argument says so little, it is not reasonable to assume that the system would be designed to space signals so far apart that they would prove useless. Rather than invent implausibly bad versions of the warning system to prove that it might be ineffective, a stronger response would analyze unexplored possibilities inherent in the information that is given—for example, the possibility that pilots might not be able to respond quickly and effectively to the radio signals the argument says they will receive when the new system is installed. The "more sound and persuasive argument" in the last paragraph, while an improvement on the original, continues to overlook this possibility and also assumes that other types of aircraft without transponders will pose no problems.

The organization of ideas, while generally sound, is sometimes weakened by needless repetition of the same points, as in sentences 4 and 5 of the last paragraph. The writing contains minor instances of awkwardness (e.g., "Each plane will receive constant, continual signals from each other" in paragraph 3), but is free of flaws that make understanding difficult. However, though the writing is generally clean and clear, the syntax does not show much variety. A few sentences begin with "if" clauses, but almost all the rest, even those that begin with a transitional phrase such as "for example" or "in addition," conform to a "subject, verb, complement" pattern. The first paragraph, in which the second and third sentences begin the same way ("It does not state"), is particularly repetitious.

Sample Paper 2

This argument has no information about air collisions. I think most cases happen in new airports because the air traffic I heavy. In this case sound airport control could solve the problem.

I think this argument is logically reasonable. Its assumption is that plane collisions are caused by planes that don't know each others positions. So pilots can do nothing, if they know each others position through the system it will solve the problem.

If it can provide evidence the problem is lack of knowledge of each others positions, it will be more sound and persuasive.

More information about air collisions is helpful, (the reason for air collisions).

Explanation of Score 2

This response is seriously flawed in several ways. First of all, it has very little substance. The writer appears to make only one point—that while it seems reasonable to assume that midair collisions would be less likely if pilots were sure of each other's positions, readers cannot adequately judge this assumption without more information about where, why, and how such collisions occur. This point, furthermore, is neither explained by a single reason beyond what is given in the topic nor supported by a single example. Legitimate though it is, it cannot, alone and undeveloped, serve as an adequate response to the argument.

Aside from being undeveloped, the response is confusing. At the outset, it seems to be critical of the argument. The writer begins by pointing to the inadequacy of the information given; then speculates, without evidence, that "most cases happen in new airports"; and then suggests that the problem should be addressed by improving "airport control," not (it is implied) by installing onboard warning systems. After criticizing the argument in the first paragraph, the writer confusingly seems to endorse it in the second. Then, in the remainder of the response, the writer returns to a critical stance.

The general lack of coherence is reflected in the serious and frequent writing problems that make meaning hard to determine—for example, the elliptical and ungrammatical "So pilots can do nothing, if they know each others position through the system it will solve the problem" (paragraph 2) or "If it can provide evidence the problem is lack of knowledge of each others positions, it will be more sound and persuasive" (paragraph 3). The prose suffers from a variety of basic errors in grammar, usage, and mechanics.

11.6 Analysis of an Argument Sample Topics

The following appeared as part of an annual report sent to stockholders by Olympic Foods, a processor of frozen foods:

"Over time, the costs of processing go down because as organizations learn how to do things better, they become more efficient. In color film processing, for example, the cost of a 3-by-5-inch print fell from 50 cents for five-day service in 1970 to 20 cents for one-day service in 1984. The same principle applies to the processing of food. And since Olympic Foods will soon celebrate its 25th birthday, we can expect that our long experience will enable us to minimize costs and thus maximize profits."

Discuss how well reasoned you find this argument. In your discussion be sure to analyze the line of reasoning and the use of evidence in the argument. For example, you may need to consider what questionable assumptions underlie the thinking and what alternative explanations or counterexamples might weaken the conclusion. You can also discuss what sort of evidence would strengthen or refute the argument, what changes in the argument would make it more logically sound, and what, if anything, would help you better evaluate its conclusion.

The following appeared in a memorandum from the business department of the Apogee Company:

"When the Apogee Company had all its operations in one location, it was more profitable than it is today. Therefore, the Apogee Company should close down its field offices and conduct all its operations from a single location. Such centralization would improve profitability by cutting costs and helping the company maintain better supervision of all employees."

Discuss how well reasoned … etc.

The following appeared in a memorandum issued by a large city's council on the arts:

"In a recent citywide poll, 15 percent more residents said that they watch television programs about the visual arts than was the case in a poll conducted five years ago. During these past five years, the number of people visiting our city's art museums has increased by a similar percentage. Since the corporate funding that supports public television, where most of the visual arts programs appear, is now being threatened with severe cuts, we can expect that attendance at our city's art museums will also start to decrease. Thus some of the city's funds for supporting the arts should be reallocated to public television."

Discuss how well reasoned … etc.

The following appeared in a report presented for discussion at a meeting of the directors of a company that manufactures parts for heavy machinery:

"The falling revenues that the company is experiencing coincide with delays in manufacturing. These delays, in turn, are due in large part to poor planning in purchasing metals. Consider further that the manager of the department that handles purchasing of raw materials has an excellent background in general business, psychology, and sociology, but knows little about the properties of metals. The company should, therefore, move the purchasing manager to the sales department and bring in a scientist from the research division to be manager of the purchasing department."

Discuss how well reasoned … etc.

The following appeared in an announcement issued by the publisher of *The Mercury*, a weekly newspaper:

"Since a competing lower-priced newspaper, *The Bugle*, was started five years ago, *The Mercury*'s circulation has declined by 10,000 readers. The best way to get more people to read *The Mercury* is to reduce its price below that of *The Bugle*, at least until circulation increases to former levels. The increased circulation of *The Mercury* will attract more businesses to buy advertising space in the paper."

Discuss how well reasoned ... etc.

The following appeared as part of an article in a magazine devoted to regional life:

"Corporations should look to the city of Helios when seeking new business opportunities or a new location. Even in the recent recession, Helios's unemployment rate was lower than the regional average. It is the industrial center of the region, and historically it has provided more than its share of the region's manufacturing jobs. In addition, Helios is attempting to expand its economic base by attracting companies that focus on research and development of innovative technologies."

Discuss how well reasoned ... etc.

The following appeared in the health section of a magazine on trends and lifestyles:

"People who use the artificial sweetener aspartame are better off consuming sugar, since aspartame can actually contribute to weight gain rather than weight loss. For example, high levels of aspartame have been shown to trigger a craving for food by depleting the brain of a chemical that registers satiety, or the sense of being full. Furthermore, studies suggest that sugars, if consumed after at least 45 minutes of continuous exercise, actually enhance the body's ability to burn fat. Consequently, those who drink aspartame-sweetened juices after exercise will also lose this calorie-burning benefit. Thus it appears that people consuming aspartame rather than sugar are unlikely to achieve their dietary goals."

Discuss how well reasoned ... etc.

The following appeared in the editorial section of a corporate newsletter:

"The common notion that workers are generally apathetic about management issues is false, or at least outdated: a recently published survey indicates that 79 percent of the nearly 1,200 workers who responded to survey questionnaires expressed a high level of interest in the topics of corporate restructuring and redesign of benefits programs."

Discuss how well reasoned ... etc.

The following appeared in the opinion column of a financial magazine:

"On average, middle-aged consumers devote 39 percent of their retail expenditure to department store products and services, while for younger consumers the average is only 25 percent. Since the number of middle-aged people will increase dramatically within the next decade, department stores can expect retail sales to increase significantly during that period. Furthermore, to take advantage of the trend, these stores should begin to replace some of those products intended to attract the younger consumer with products intended to attract the middle-aged consumer."

Discuss how well reasoned ... etc.

The following appeared in the editorial section of a local newspaper:

"This past winter, 200 students from Waymarsh State College traveled to the state capitol building to protest against proposed cuts in funding for various state college programs. The other 12,000 Waymarsh students evidently weren't so concerned about their education: they either stayed on campus or left for winter break. Since the group who did not protest is far more numerous, it is more representative of the state's college students than are the protesters. Therefore the state legislature need not heed the appeals of the protesting students."

Discuss how well reasoned ... etc.

The following appeared in the editorial section of a local newspaper:

"In the first four years that Montoya has served as mayor of the city of San Perdito, the population has decreased and the unemployment rate has increased. Two businesses have closed for each new business that has opened. Under Varro, who served as mayor for four years before Montoya, the unemployment rate decreased and the population increased. Clearly, the residents of San Perdito would be best served if they voted Montoya out of office and reelected Varro."

Discuss how well reasoned ... etc.

The following appeared as part of a promotional campaign to sell advertising space in the *Daily Gazette* to grocery stores in the Marston area:

"Advertising the reduced price of selected grocery items in the *Daily Gazette* will help you increase your sales. Consider the results of a study conducted last month. Thirty sale items from a store in downtown Marston were advertised in *The Gazette* for four days. Each time one or more of the 30 items was purchased, clerks asked whether the shopper had read the ad. Two-thirds of the 200 shoppers asked answered in the affirmative. Furthermore, more than half the customers who answered in the affirmative spent over $100 at the store."

Discuss how well reasoned ... etc.

The following appeared as part of a campaign to sell advertising time on a local radio station to local businesses:

"The Cumquat Café began advertising on our local radio station this year and was delighted to see its business increase by 10 percent over last year's totals. Their success shows you how you can use radio advertising to make your business more profitable."

Discuss how well reasoned ... etc.

The following appeared as part of a newspaper editorial:

"Two years ago Nova High School began to use interactive computer instruction in three academic subjects. The school dropout rate declined immediately, and last year's graduates have reported some impressive achievements in college. In future budgets the school board should use a greater portion of the available funds to buy more computers, and all schools in the district should adopt interactive computer instruction throughout the curriculum."

Discuss how well reasoned ... etc.

The following appeared as a part of an advertisement for Adams, who is seeking re-election as governor:

"Re-elect Adams, and you will be voting for proven leadership in improving the state's economy. Over the past year alone, 70 percent of the state's workers have had increases in their wages, 5,000 new jobs have been created, and six corporations have located their headquarters here. Most of the respondents in a recent poll said they believed that the economy is likely to continue to improve if Adams is re-elected. Adams's opponent, Zebulon, would lead our state in the wrong direction, because Zebulon disagrees with many of Adams's economic policies."

Discuss how well reasoned ... etc.

The following appeared as part of an article in the education section of a Waymarsh city newspaper:

"Throughout the last two decades, those who earned graduate degrees found it very difficult to get jobs teaching their academic specialties at the college level. Those with graduate degrees from Waymarsh University had an especially hard time finding such jobs. But better times are coming in the next decade for all academic job seekers, including those from Waymarsh. Demographic trends indicate that an increasing number of people will be reaching college age over the next 10 years; consequently, we can expect that the job market will improve dramatically for people seeking college-level teaching positions in their fields."

Discuss how well reasoned ... etc.

The following appeared in an article in a consumer-products magazine:

"Two of today's best-selling brands of full-strength prescription medication for the relief of excess stomach acid, Acid-Ease and Pepticaid, are now available in milder nonprescription forms. Doctors have written 76 million more prescriptions for full-strength Acid-Ease than for full-strength Pepticaid. So people who need an effective but milder nonprescription medication for the relief of excess stomach acid should choose Acid-Ease."

Discuss how well reasoned ... etc.

The following is an excerpt from a memo written by the head of a governmental department:

"Neither stronger ethics regulations nor stronger enforcement mechanisms are necessary to ensure ethical behavior by companies doing business with this department. We already have a code of ethics that companies doing business with this department are urged to abide by, and virtually all of these companies have agreed to follow it. We also know that the code is relevant to the current business environment because it was approved within the last year, and in direct response to specific violations committed by companies with which we were then working—not in abstract anticipation of potential violations, as so many such codes are."

Discuss how well reasoned ... etc.

The following appeared as part of an article in the travel section of a newspaper:

"Over the past decade, the restaurant industry in the country of Spiessa has experienced unprecedented growth. This surge can be expected to continue in the coming years, fueled by recent social changes: personal incomes are rising, more leisure time is available, single-person households are more common, and people have a greater interest in gourmet food, as evidenced by a proliferation of publications on the subject."

Discuss how well reasoned ... etc.

The following appeared in an article in a health and fitness magazine:

"Laboratory studies show that Saluda Natural Spring Water contains several of the minerals necessary for good health and that it is completely free of bacteria. Residents of Saluda, the small town where the water is bottled, are hospitalized less frequently than the national average. Even though Saluda Natural Spring Water may seem expensive, drinking it instead of tap water is a wise investment in good health."

Discuss how well reasoned ... etc.

The following appeared as part of an editorial in an industry newsletter:

"While trucking companies that deliver goods pay only a portion of highway maintenance costs and no property tax on the highways they use, railways spend billions per year maintaining and upgrading their facilities. The government should lower the railroad companies' property taxes, since sending goods by rail is clearly a more appropriate mode of ground transportation than highway shipping. For one thing, trains consume only a third of the fuel a truck would use to carry the same load, making them a more cost-effective and environmentally sound mode of transport. Furthermore, since rail lines already exist, increases in rail traffic would not require building new lines at the expense of taxpaying citizens."

Discuss how well reasoned … etc.

The following appeared in the editorial section of a newspaper:

"As public concern over drug abuse has increased, authorities have become more vigilant in their efforts to prevent illegal drugs from entering the country. Many drug traffickers have consequently switched from marijuana, which is bulky, or heroin, which has a market too small to justify the risk of severe punishment, to cocaine. Thus enforcement efforts have ironically resulted in an observed increase in the illegal use of cocaine."

Discuss how well reasoned … etc.

The following appeared in a speech delivered by a member of the city council:

"Twenty years ago, only half of the students who graduated from Einstein High School went on to attend a college or university. Today, two-thirds of the students who graduate from Einstein do so. Clearly, Einstein has improved its educational effectiveness over the past two decades. This improvement has occurred despite the fact that the school's funding, when adjusted for inflation, is about the same as it was 20 years ago. Therefore, we do not need to make any substantial increase in the school's funding at this time."

Discuss how well reasoned … etc.

The following appeared in a memo from the customer service division to the manager of Mammon Savings and Loan:

"We believe that improved customer service is the best way for us to differentiate ourselves from competitors and attract new customers. We can offer our customers better service by reducing waiting time in teller lines from an average of six minutes to an average of three. By opening for business at 8:30 instead of 9:00, and by remaining open for an additional hour beyond our current closing time, we will be better able to accommodate the busy schedules of our customers. These changes will enhance our bank's image as the most customer-friendly bank in town and give us the edge over our competition."

Discuss how well reasoned … etc.

The following appeared as part of an article in a magazine on lifestyles:

"Two years ago, City L was listed fourteenth in an annual survey that ranks cities according to the quality of life that can be enjoyed by those living in them. This information will enable people who are moving to the state in which City L is located to confidently identify one place, at least, where schools are good, housing is affordable, people are friendly, the environment is safe, and the arts flourish."

Discuss how well reasoned … etc.

The following appeared in a memorandum from a member of a financial management and consulting firm:

"We have learned from an employee of Windfall, Ltd., that its accounting department, by checking about 10 percent of the last month's purchasing invoices for errors and inconsistencies, saved the company some $10,000 in overpayments. In order to help our clients increase their net gains, we should advise each of them to institute a policy of checking all purchasing invoices for errors. Such a recommendation could also help us get the Windfall account by demonstrating to Windfall the rigorousness of our methods."

Discuss how well reasoned … etc.

The following appeared in a newspaper editorial:

"As violence in movies increases, so do crime rates in our cities. To combat this problem we must establish a board to censor certain movies, or we must limit admission to persons over 21 years of age. Apparently our legislators are not concerned about this issue since a bill calling for such actions recently failed to receive a majority vote."

Discuss how well reasoned … etc.

The following appeared in the editorial section of a local newspaper:

"Commuter use of the new subway train is exceeding the transit company's projections. However, commuter use of the shuttle buses that transport people to the subway stations is below the projected volume. If the transit company expects commuters to ride the shuttle buses to the subway rather than drive there, it must either reduce the shuttle bus fares or increase the price of parking at the subway stations."

Discuss how well reasoned … etc.

The following was excerpted from the speech of a spokesperson for Synthetic Farm Products, Inc.:

"Many farmers who invested in the equipment needed to make the switch from synthetic to organic fertilizers and pesticides feel that it would be too expensive to resume synthetic farming at this point. But studies of farmers who switched to organic farming last year indicate that their current crop yields are lower. Hence their purchase of organic farming equipment, a relatively minor investment compared to the losses that would result from continued lower crop yields, cannot justify persisting on an unwise course. And the choice to farm organically is financially unwise, given that it was motivated by environmental rather than economic concerns."

Discuss how well reasoned … etc.

The following appeared in a newspaper story giving advice about investments:

"As overall life expectancy continues to rise, the population of our country is growing increasingly older. For example, more than 20 percent of the residents of one of our more populated regions are now at least 65 years old, and occupancy rates at resort hotels in that region declined significantly during the past six months. Because of these two related trends, a prudent investor would be well advised to sell interest in hotels and invest in hospitals and nursing homes instead."

Discuss how well reasoned … etc.

The following appeared as part of the business plan of an investment and financial consulting firm:

"Studies suggest that an average coffee drinker's consumption of coffee increases with age, from age 10 through age 60. Even after age 60, coffee consumption remains high. The average cola drinker's consumption of cola, however, declines with increasing age. Both of these trends have remained stable for the past 40 years. Given that the number of older adults will significantly increase as the population ages over the next 20 years, it follows that the demand for coffee will increase and the demand for cola will decrease during this period. We should, therefore, consider transferring our investments from Cola Loca to Early Bird Coffee."

Discuss how well reasoned … etc.

The following appeared in the editorial section of a West Cambria newspaper:

"A recent review of the West Cambria volunteer ambulance service revealed a longer average response time to accidents than was reported by a commercial ambulance squad located in East Cambria. In order to provide better patient care for accident victims and to raise revenue for our town by collecting service fees for ambulance use, we should disband our volunteer service and hire a commercial ambulance service."

Discuss how well reasoned … etc.

The following is part of a business plan being discussed at a board meeting of the Perks Company:

"It is no longer cost-effective for the Perks Company to continue offering its employees a generous package of benefits and incentives year after year. In periods when national unemployment rates are low, Perks may need to offer such a package in order to attract and keep good employees, but since national unemployment rates are now high, Perks does not need to offer the same benefits and incentives. The money thus saved could be better used to replace the existing plant machinery with more technologically sophisticated equipment, or even to build an additional plant."

Discuss how well reasoned … etc.

The following appeared as part of a plan proposed by an executive of the Easy Credit Company to the president:

"The Easy Credit Company would gain an advantage over competing credit card services if we were to donate a portion of the proceeds from the use of our cards to a well-known environmental organization in exchange for the use of its symbol or logo on our card. Since a recent poll shows that a large percentage of the public is concerned about environmental issues, this policy would attract new customers, increase use among existing customers, and enable us to charge interest rates that are higher than the lowest ones available."

Discuss how well reasoned ... etc.

The following appeared as part of a recommendation from the financial planning office to the administration of Fern Valley University:

"In the past few years, Fern Valley University has suffered from a decline in both enrollments and admissions applications. The reason can be discovered from our students, who most often cite poor teaching and inadequate library resources as their chief sources of dissatisfaction with Fern Valley. Therefore, in order to increase the number of students attending our university, and hence to regain our position as the most prestigious university in the greater Fern Valley metropolitan area, it is necessary to initiate a fund-raising campaign among the alumni that will enable us to expand the range of subjects we teach and to increase the size of our library facilities."

Discuss how well reasoned ... etc.

The following appeared in an article in a college departmental newsletter:

"Professor Taylor of Jones University is promoting a model of foreign language instruction in which students receive 10 weeks of intensive training, then go abroad to live with families for 10 weeks. The superiority of the model, Professor Taylor contends, is proved by the results of a study in which foreign language tests given to students at 25 other colleges show that first-year foreign language students at Jones speak more fluently after only 10 to 20 weeks in the program than do 9 out of 10 foreign language majors elsewhere at the time of their graduation."

Discuss how well reasoned ... etc.

The following appeared as part of an article in the business section of a local newspaper:

"Motorcycle X has been manufactured in the United States for more than 70 years. Although one foreign company has copied the motorcycle and is selling it for less, the company has failed to attract motorcycle X customers—some say because its product lacks the exceptionally loud noise made by motorcycle X. But there must be some other explanation. After all, foreign cars tend to be quieter than similar American-made cars, but they sell at least as well. Also, television advertisements for motorcycle X highlight its durability and sleek lines, not its noisiness, and the ads typically have voice-overs or rock music rather than engine-roar on the sound track."

Discuss how well reasoned ... etc.

The following appeared in the editorial section of a campus newspaper:

"Because occupancy rates for campus housing fell during the last academic year, so did housing revenues. To solve the problem, campus housing officials should reduce the number of available housing units, thereby increasing the occupancy rates. Also, to keep students from choosing to live off-campus, housing officials should lower the rents, thereby increasing demand."

Discuss how well reasoned ... etc.

The following appeared in an Avia Airlines departmental memorandum:

"On average, 9 out of every 1,000 passengers who traveled on Avia Airlines last year filed a complaint about our baggage-handling procedures. This means that although some 1 percent of our passengers were unhappy with those procedures, the overwhelming majority were quite satisfied with them; thus it would appear that a review of the procedures is not important to our goal of maintaining or increasing the number of Avia's passengers."

Discuss how well reasoned ... etc.

The following appeared as part of an article in a weekly newsmagazine:

"The country of Sacchar can best solve its current trade deficit problem by lowering the price of sugar, its primary export. Such an action would make Sacchar better able to compete for markets with other sugar-exporting countries. The sale of Sacchar's sugar abroad would increase, and this increase would substantially reduce Sacchar's trade deficit."

Discuss how well reasoned ... etc.

The following appeared as part of an article in a trade publication:

"Stronger laws are needed to protect new kinds of home-security systems from being copied and sold by imitators. With such protection, manufacturers will naturally invest in the development of new home-security products and production technologies. Without stronger laws, therefore, manufacturers will cut back on investment. From this will follow a corresponding decline not only in product quality and marketability, but also in production efficiency, and thus ultimately a loss of manufacturing jobs in the industry."

Discuss how well reasoned ... etc.

The following appeared in the opinion section of a national newsmagazine:

"To reverse the deterioration of the postal service, the government should raise the price of postage stamps. This solution will no doubt prove effective, since the price increase will generate larger revenues and will also reduce the volume of mail, thereby eliminating the strain on the existing system and contributing to improved morale."

Discuss how well reasoned ... etc.

The following appeared in an article in the health section of a newspaper:

"There is a common misconception that university hospitals are better than community or private hospitals. This notion is unfounded, however: the university hospitals in our region employ 15 percent fewer doctors, have a 20 percent lower success rate in treating patients, make far less overall profit, and pay their medical staff considerably less than do private hospitals. Furthermore, many doctors at university hospitals typically divide their time among teaching, conducting research, and treating patients. From this it seems clear that the quality of care at university hospitals is lower than that at other kinds of hospitals."

Discuss how well reasoned ... etc.

The following is part of a business plan created by the management of the Megamart grocery store:

"Our total sales have increased this year by 20 percent since we added a pharmacy section to our grocery store. Clearly, the customer's main concern is the convenience afforded by one-stop shopping. The surest way to increase our profits over the next couple of years, therefore, is to add a clothing department along with an automotive supplies and repair shop. We should also plan to continue adding new departments and services, such as a restaurant and a garden shop, in subsequent years. Being the only store in the area that offers such a range of services will give us a competitive advantage over other local stores."

Discuss how well reasoned ... etc.

The following appeared as part of a column in a popular entertainment magazine:

"The producers of the forthcoming movie *3003* will be most likely to maximize their profits if they are willing to pay Robin Good several million dollars to star in it—even though that amount is far more than any other person involved with the movie will make. After all, Robin has in the past been paid a similar amount to work in several films that were very financially successful."

Discuss how well reasoned ... etc.

The following appeared in a memorandum from the directors of a security and safety consulting service:

"Our research indicates that over the past six years no incidents of employee theft have been reported within ten of the companies that have been our clients. In analyzing the security practices of these ten companies, we have further learned that each of them requires its employees to wear photo identification badges while at work. In the future, therefore, we should recommend the use of such identification badges to all of our clients."

Discuss how well reasoned ... etc.

The following appeared as part of an article in the business section of a local newspaper:

"The owners of the Cumquat Cafe evidently made a good business decision in moving to a new location, as can be seen from the fact that the Cafe will soon celebrate its second anniversary there. Moreover, it appears that businesses are not likely to succeed at the old location: since the Cafe's move, three different businesses—a tanning salon, an antique emporium, and a pet-grooming shop—have occupied its former spot."

Discuss how well reasoned ... etc.

The following appeared in the editorial section of a local newspaper:

"The profitability of Croesus Company, recently restored to private ownership, is a clear indication that businesses fare better under private ownership than under public ownership."

Discuss how well reasoned ... etc.

The following appeared in the editorial section of a local newspaper:

"If the paper from every morning edition of the nation's largest newspaper were collected and rendered into paper pulp that the newspaper could reuse, about 5 million trees would be saved each year. This kind of recycling is unnecessary, however, since the newspaper maintains its own forests to ensure an uninterrupted supply of paper."

Discuss how well reasoned ... etc.

The following appeared as part of a business plan recommended by the new manager of a musical rock group called Zapped:

"To succeed financially, Zapped needs greater name recognition. It should therefore diversify its commercial enterprises. The rock group Zonked plays the same type of music that Zapped plays, but it is much better known than Zapped because, in addition to its concert tours and four albums, Zonked has a series of posters, a line of clothing and accessories, and a contract with a major advertising agency to endorse a number of different products."

Discuss how well reasoned ... etc.

The following appeared in a magazine article on trends and lifestyles:

"In general, people are not as concerned as they were a decade ago about regulating their intake of red meat and fatty cheeses. Walk into the Heart's Delight, a store that started selling organic fruits and vegetables and whole-grain flours in the 1960s, and you will also find a wide selection of cheeses made with high butterfat content. Next door, the owners of the Good Earth Cafe, an old vegetarian restaurant, are still making a modest living, but the owners of the new House of Beef across the street are millionaires."

Discuss how well reasoned ... etc.

The following editorial appeared in the Elm City paper:

"The construction last year of a shopping mall in downtown Oak City was a mistake. Since the mall has opened, a number of local businesses have closed, and the downtown area suffers from an acute parking shortage, and arrests for crime and vagrancy have increased in the nearby Oak City Park. Elm City should pay attention to the example of the Oak City mall and deny the application to build a shopping mall in Elm City."

Discuss how well reasoned ... etc.

The following appeared as part of an editorial in a weekly newsmagazine:

"Historically, most of this country's engineers have come from our universities; recently, however, our university-age population has begun to shrink, and decreasing enrollments in our high schools clearly show that this drop in numbers will continue throughout the remainder of the decade. Consequently, our nation will soon be facing a shortage of trained engineers. If we are to remain economically competitive in the world marketplace, then we must increase funding for education—and quickly."

Discuss how well reasoned ... etc.

The following appeared in an Excelsior Company memorandum:

"The Excelsior Company plans to introduce its own brand of coffee. Since coffee is an expensive food item, and since there are already many established brands of coffee, the best way to gain customers for the Excelsior brand is to do what Superior, the leading coffee company, did when it introduced the newest brand in its line of coffees: conduct a temporary sales promotion that offers free samples, price reductions, and discount coupons for the new brand."

Discuss how well reasoned ... etc.

The following appeared as part of an article in a health club trade publication:

"After experiencing a decline in usage by its members, Healthy Heart fitness center built an indoor pool. Since usage did not increase significantly, it appears that health club managers should adopt another approach—lowering membership fees rather than installing expensive new features."

Discuss how well reasoned ... etc.

The following appeared as part of an article in a popular arts-and-leisure magazine:

"The safety codes governing the construction of public buildings are becoming far too strict. The surest way for architects and builders to prove that they have met the minimum requirements established by these codes is to construct buildings by using the same materials and methods that are currently allowed. But doing so means that there will be very little significant technological innovation within the industry, and hence little evolution of architectural styles and design—merely because of the strictness of these safety codes."

Discuss how well reasoned ... etc.

The following is from a campaign by Big Boards Inc. to convince companies in River City that their sales will increase if they use Big Boards billboards for advertising their locally manufactured products:

"The potential of Big Boards to increase sales of your products can be seen from an experiment we conducted last year. We increased public awareness of the name of the current national women's marathon champion by publishing her picture and her name on billboards in River City for a period of three months. Before this time, although the champion had just won her title and was receiving extensive national publicity, only 5 percent of 15,000 randomly surveyed residents of River City could correctly name the champion when shown her picture; after the three-month advertising experiment, 35 percent of respondents from a second survey could supply her name."

Discuss how well reasoned ... etc.

The following appeared as part of an article on government funding of environmental regulatory agencies:

"When scientists finally learn how to create large amounts of copper from other chemical elements, the regulation of copper mining will become unnecessary. For one thing, since the amount of potentially available copper will no longer be limited by the quantity of actual copper deposits, the problem of over-mining will quickly be eliminated altogether. For another, manufacturers will not need to use synthetic copper substitutes, the production of which creates pollutants. Thus, since two problems will be settled—over-mining and pollution—it makes good sense to reduce funding for mining regulation and either save the money or reallocate it where it is needed more."

Discuss how well reasoned ... etc.

The following appeared as part of an article in a popular science magazine:

"Scientists must typically work 60 to 80 hours a week if they hope to further their careers; consequently, good and affordable all-day child care must be made available to both male and female scientists if they are to advance in their fields. Moreover, requirements for career advancement must be made more flexible so that preschool-age children can spend a significant portion of each day with a parent."

Discuss how well reasoned ... etc.

The following appeared as part of a recommendation by one of the directors of the Beta Company:

"The Alpha Company has just reduced its workforce by laying off 15 percent of its employees in all divisions and at all levels, and it is encouraging early retirement for other employees. As you know, the Beta Company manufactures some products similar to Alpha's, but our profits have fallen over the last few years. To improve Beta's competitive position, we should try to hire a significant number of Alpha's former workers, since these experienced workers can provide valuable information about Alpha's successful methods, will require little training, and will be particularly motivated to compete against Alpha."

Discuss how well reasoned ... etc.

The following appeared in the letters-to-the-editor section of a local newspaper:

"*Muscle Monthly*, a fitness magazine that regularly features pictures of bodybuilders using state-of-the-art exercise machines, frequently sells out, according to the owner of Skyview Newsstand. To help maximize fitness levels in our town's residents, we should, therefore, equip our new community fitness center with such machines."

Discuss how well reasoned ... etc.

The following appeared as part of an article in the business section of a local newspaper:

"The Cumquat Cafe made a mistake in moving to a new location. After one year at the new spot, it is doing about the same volume of business as before, but the owners of the RoboWrench plumbing supply wholesale outlet that took over its old location are apparently doing better: RoboWrench is planning to open a store in a neighboring city."

Discuss how well reasoned ... etc.

The following appeared in a memorandum from the director of human resources to the executive officers of Company X:

"Last year, we surveyed our employees on improvements needed at Company X by having them rank, in order of importance, the issues presented in a list of possible improvements. Improved communications between employees and management was consistently ranked as the issue of highest importance by the employees who responded to the survey. As you know, we have since instituted regular communications sessions conducted by high-level management, which the employees can attend on a voluntary basis. Therefore, it is likely that most employees at Company X now feel that the improvement most needed at the company has been made."

Discuss how well reasoned ... etc.

The following appeared in a memorandum from the vice president of Road Food, an international chain of fast-food restaurants:

"This past year, we spent almost as much on advertising as did our main competitor, Street Eats, which has fewer restaurants than we do. Although it appeared at first that our advertising agency had created a campaign along the lines we suggested, in fact our total profits were lower than those of Street Eats. In order to motivate our advertising agency to perform better, we should start basing the amount that we pay it on how much total profit we make each year."

Discuss how well reasoned ... etc.

The following appeared in the promotional literature for Cerberus dog food:

"Obesity is a great problem among pet dogs, just as it is among their human owners. Obesity in humans is typically caused by consuming more calories than the body needs. For humans, a proper diet for losing weight is a reduced-calorie diet that is high in fiber and carbohydrates but low in fat. Therefore, the best way for dog owners to help their dogs lose weight in a healthy way is to restrict the dog's diet to Cerberus reduced-calorie dog food, which is high in fiber and carbohydrates but low in fat."

Discuss how well reasoned ... etc.

The following appeared in an article in a travel magazine:

"After the airline industry began requiring airlines to report their on-time rates, Speedee Airlines achieved the number one on-time rate, with more than 89 percent of its flights arriving on time each month. And now Speedee is offering more flights to more destinations than ever before. Clearly, Speedee is the best choice for today's business traveler."

Discuss how well reasoned ... etc.

The following appeared in a memorandum to the planning department of an investment firm:

"Costs have begun dropping for several types of equipment currently used to convert solar energy into electricity. Moreover, some exciting new technologies for converting solar energy are now being researched and developed. Hence we can expect that solar energy will soon become more cost efficient and attractive than coal or oil as a source of electrical power. We should, therefore, encourage investment in Solario, a new manufacturer of solar-powered products. After all, Solario's chief executive was once on the financial planning team for Ready-to-Ware, a software engineering firm that has shown remarkable growth since its recent incorporation."

Discuss how well reasoned ... etc.

The following appeared in a memorandum from a company's marketing department:

"Since our company started manufacturing and marketing a deluxe air filter six months ago, sales of our economy filter—and company profits—have decreased significantly. The deluxe air filter sells for 50 percent more than the economy filter, but the economy filter lasts for only one month while the deluxe filter can be used for two months before it must be replaced. To increase repeat sales of our economy filter and maximize profits, we should discontinue the deluxe air filter and concentrate all our advertising efforts on the economy filter."

Discuss how well reasoned ... etc.

The following appeared in a memorandum from the president of a company that makes shampoo:

"A widely publicized study claims that HR2, a chemical compound in our shampoo, can contribute to hair loss after prolonged use. This study, however, involved only 500 subjects. Furthermore, we have received no complaints from our customers during the past year, and some of our competitors actually use more HR2 per bottle of shampoo than we do. Therefore, we do not need to consider replacing the HR2 in our shampoo with a more expensive alternative."

Discuss how well reasoned ... etc.

The following appeared in the editorial section of a local newspaper:

"The tragic crash of a medical helicopter last week points out a situation that needs to be addressed. The medical-helicopter industry supposedly has more stringent guidelines for training pilots and maintaining equipment than do most other airline industries, but these guidelines do not appear to be working: statistics reveal that the rate of medical-helicopter accidents is much higher than the rate of accidents for nonmedical helicopters or commercial airliners."

Discuss how well reasoned ... etc.

The following appeared as part of a recommendation from the business manager of a department store:

"Local clothing stores reported that their profits decreased, on average, for the three-month period between August 1 and October 31. Stores that sell products for the home reported that, on average, their profits increased during this same period. Clearly, consumers are choosing to buy products for their homes instead of clothing. To take advantage of this trend, we should reduce the size of our clothing departments and enlarge our home furnishings and household products departments."

Discuss how well reasoned ... etc.

The following appeared in a letter to the editor of a regional newspaper:

"In response to petitions from the many farmers and rural landowners throughout our region, the legislature has spent valuable time and effort enacting severe laws to deter motorists from picking fruit off the trees, trampling through the fields, and stealing samples of foliage. But how can our local lawmakers occupy themselves with such petty vandalism when crime and violence plague the nation's cities? The fate of apples and leaves is simply too trivial to merit their attention."

Discuss how well reasoned ... etc.

The following appeared as part of an editorial in a campus newspaper:

"With an increasing demand for highly skilled workers, this nation will soon face a serious labor shortage. New positions in technical and professional occupations are increasing rapidly, while at the same time the total labor force is growing slowly. Moreover, the government is proposing to cut funds for aid to education in the near future."

Discuss how well reasoned ... etc.

The following appeared as part of a memorandum from a government agency:

"Given the limited funding available for the building and repair of roads and bridges, the government should not spend any money this year on fixing the bridge that crosses the Styx River. This bridge is located near a city with a weakening economy, so it is not as important as other bridges; moreover, the city population is small and thus unlikely to contribute a significant enough tax revenue to justify the effort of fixing the bridge."

Discuss how well reasoned ... etc.

The following appeared as part of an article in an entertainment magazine:

"A series of books based on the characters from a popular movie are consistently best sellers in local bookstores. Seeking to capitalize on the books' success, Vista Studios is planning to produce a movie sequel based on the books. Due to the success of the books and the original movie, the sequel will undoubtedly be profitable."

Discuss how well reasoned … etc.

The following appeared in a letter to the editor of a popular science and technology magazine:

"It is a popular myth that consumers are really benefiting from advances in agricultural technology. Granted, consumers are, on the average, spending a decreasing proportion of their income on food. But consider that the demand for food does not rise in proportion with real income. As real income rises, therefore, consumers can be expected to spend a decreasing proportion of their income on food. Yet agricultural technology is credited with having made our lives better."

Discuss how well reasoned … etc.

The following appeared in the editorial section of a local newspaper:

"This city should be able to improve existing services and provide new ones without periodically raising the taxes of the residents. Instead, the city should require that the costs of services be paid for by developers who seek approval for their large new building projects. After all, these projects can be highly profitable to the developers, but they can also raise a city's expenses and increase the demand for its services."

Discuss how well reasoned … etc.

The following appeared in the editorial section of a local newspaper:

"In order to avoid the serious health threats associated with many landfills, our municipality should build a plant for burning trash. An incinerator could offer economic as well as ecological advantages over the typical old-fashioned type of landfill: incinerators can be adapted to generate moderate amounts of electricity, and ash residue from some types of trash can be used to condition garden soil."

Discuss how well reasoned … etc.

The following appeared in the editorial section of a monthly business newsmagazine:

"Most companies would agree that as the risk of physical injury occurring on the job increases, the wages paid to employees should also increase. Hence it makes financial sense for employers to make the workplace safer; they could thus reduce their payroll expenses and save money."

Discuss how well reasoned … etc.

The following appeared as part of a company memorandum:

"Adopting an official code of ethics regarding business practices may in the long run do our company more harm than good in the public eye. When one of our competitors received unfavorable publicity for violating its own code of ethics, it got more attention from the media than it would have if it had had no such code. Rather than adopt an official code of ethics, therefore, we should instead conduct a publicity campaign that stresses the importance of protecting the environment and assisting charitable organizations."

Discuss how well reasoned ... etc.

The following appeared in the editorial section of a daily newspaper:

"Although forecasts of presidential elections based on opinion polls measure current voter preference, many voters keep changing their minds about whom they prefer until the last few days before the balloting. Some do not even make a final decision until they enter the voting booth. Forecasts based on opinion polls are therefore little better at predicting election outcomes than a random guess would be."

Discuss how well reasoned ... etc.

The following appeared in the editorial section of a newspaper in the country of West Cambria:

"The practice of officially changing speed limits on the highways—whether by increasing or decreasing them—is a dangerous one. Consider what happened over the past decade whenever neighboring East Cambria changed its speed limits: an average of 3 percent more automobile accidents occurred during the week following the change than had occurred during the week preceding it—even when the speed limit was lowered. This statistic shows that the change in speed limit adversely affected the alertness of drivers."

Discuss how well reasoned ... etc.

The following appeared as part of a memorandum from the vice president of Nostrum, a large pharmaceutical corporation:

"The proposal to increase the health and retirement benefits that our employees receive should not be implemented at this time. An increase in these benefits is not only financially unjustified, since our last year's profits were lower than those of the preceding year, but also unnecessary, since our chief competitor, Panacea, offers its employees lower health and retirement benefits than we currently offer. We can assume that our employees are reasonably satisfied with the health and retirement benefits that they now have since a recent survey indicated that two-thirds of the respondents viewed them favorably."

Discuss how well reasoned ... etc.

The following appeared as part of an article on trends in television:

"A recent study of viewers' attitudes toward prime-time television programs shows that many of the programs that were judged by their viewers to be of high quality appeared on (noncommercial) television networks, and that, on commercial television, the most popular shows are typically sponsored by the bestselling products. Thus, it follows that businesses who use commercial television to promote their products will achieve the greatest advertising success by sponsoring only highly rated programs—and, ideally, programs resembling the highly rated noncommercial programs on public channels as much as possible."

Discuss how well reasoned ... etc.

The following appeared as part of an article in the business section of a daily newspaper:

"Company A has a large share of the international market in video-game hardware and software. Company B, the pioneer in these products, was once a $12 billion-a-year giant but collapsed when children became bored with its line of products. Thus Company A can also be expected to fail, especially given the fact that its games are now in so many American homes that the demand for them is nearly exhausted."

Discuss how well reasoned ... etc.

The following appeared as part of an article in a photography magazine:

"When choosing whether to work in color or in black-and-white, the photographer who wishes to be successful should keep in mind that because color photographs are more true to life, magazines use more color photographs than black-and-white ones, and many newspapers are also starting to use color photographs. The realism of color also accounts for the fact that most portrait studios use more color film than black-and-white film. Furthermore, there are more types of color film than black-and-white film available today. Clearly, photographers who work in color have an advantage over those who work in black-and-white."

Discuss how well reasoned ... etc.

The following appeared as part of a letter to the editor of a local newspaper:

"It makes no sense that in most places 15-year-olds are not eligible for their driver's license while people who are far older can retain all of their driving privileges by simply renewing their license. If older drivers can get these renewals, often without having to pass another driving test, then 15-year-olds should be eligible to get a license. Fifteen-year-olds typically have much better eyesight, especially at night; much better hand-eye coordination; and much quicker reflexes. They are also less likely to feel confused by unexpected developments or disoriented in unfamiliar surroundings, and they recover from injuries more quickly."

Discuss how well reasoned ... etc.

The following appeared in an ad for a book titled *How to Write a Screenplay for a Movie*:

"Writers who want to succeed should try to write film screenplays rather than books, since the average film tends to make greater profits than does even a best-selling book. It is true that some books are also made into films. However, our nation's film producers are more likely to produce movies based on original screenplays than to produce films based on books, because in recent years the films that have sold the most tickets have usually been based on original screenplays."

Discuss how well reasoned ... etc.

The following appeared as part of an article in a daily newspaper:

"The computerized onboard warning system that will be installed in commercial airliners will virtually solve the problem of midair plane collisions. One plane's warning system can receive signals from another's transponder—a radio set that signals a plane's course—in order to determine the likelihood of a collision and recommend evasive action."

Discuss how well reasoned ... etc.

The following appeared in a memorandum from the ElectroWares company's marketing department:

"Since our company started manufacturing and marketing a deluxe light bulb six months ago, sales of our economy light bulb—and company profits—have decreased significantly. Although the deluxe light bulb sells for 50 percent more than the economy bulb, it lasts twice as long. Therefore, to increase repeat sales and maximize profits, we should discontinue the deluxe light bulb."

Discuss how well reasoned ... etc.

The following is taken from an editorial in a local newspaper:

"Over the past decade, the price per pound of citrus fruit has increased substantially. Eleven years ago, Megamart charged 15 cents a pound for lemons, but today it commonly charges over a dollar a pound. In only one of these last 11 years was the weather unfavorable for growing citrus crops. Evidently, then, citrus growers have been responsible for the excessive increase in the price of citrus fruit, and strict pricing regulations are needed to prevent them from continuing to inflate prices."

Discuss how well reasoned ... etc.

The following appeared as part of an article in a local newspaper:

"Over the past three years the tartfish industry has changed markedly: fishing technology has improved significantly, and the demand for tartfish has grown in both domestic and foreign markets. As this trend continues, the tartfish industry on Shrimp Island can expect to experience the same overfishing problems that are already occurring with mainland fishing industries: without restrictions on fishing, fishers see no reason to limit their individual catches. As the catches get bigger, the tartfish population will be dangerously depleted while the surplus of tartfish will devalue the catch for fishers. Government regulation is the only answer: tartfish-fishing should be allowed only during the three-month summer season, when tartfish reproduce and thus are most numerous, rather than throughout the year."

Discuss how well reasoned ... etc.

The following appeared in a proposal from the development office at Platonic University:

"Because Platonic University has had difficulty in meeting its expenses over the past three years, we need to find new ways to increase revenues. We should consider following the example of Greene University, which recently renamed itself after a donor who gave it $100 million. If Platonic University were to advertise to its alumni and other wealthy people that it will rename either individual buildings or the entire university itself after the donors who give the most money, the amount of donations would undoubtedly increase."

Discuss how well reasoned ... etc.

The following appeared as part of an article in the business section of a local newspaper:

"Hippocrene Plumbing Supply recently opened a wholesale outlet in the location once occupied by the Cumquat Café. Hippocrene has apparently been quite successful there because it is planning to open a large outlet in a nearby city. But the Cumquat Café, one year after moving to its new location, has seen its volume of business drop somewhat from the previous year's. Clearly, the former site was the better business location, and the Cumquat Café has made a mistake in moving to its new address."

Discuss how well reasoned ... etc.

The following appeared in the editorial section of a local paper:

"Applications for advertising spots on KMTV, our local cable television channel, decreased last year. Meanwhile a neighboring town's local channel, KOOP, changed its focus to farming issues and reported an increase in advertising applications for the year. To increase applications for its advertisement spots, KMTV should focus its programming on farming issues as well."

Discuss how well reasoned ... etc.

The following appeared as part of an article in a computer magazine:

"A year ago Apex Manufacturing bought its managers computers for their homes and paid for telephone connections so that they could access Apex computers and data files from home after normal business hours. Since last year, productivity at Apex has increased by 15 percent. Other companies can learn from the success at Apex: given home computers and access to company resources, employees will work additional hours at home and thereby increase company profits."

Discuss how well reasoned ... etc.

The following was excerpted from an article in a farming trade publication:

"Farmers who switched from synthetic to organic farming last year have seen their crop yields decline. Many of these farmers feel that it would be too expensive to resume synthetic farming at this point, given the money that they invested in organic farming supplies and equipment. But their investments will be relatively minor compared to the losses from continued lower crop yields. Organic farmers should switch to synthetic farming rather than persist in an unwise course. And the choice to farm organically is financially unwise, given that it was motivated by environmental rather than economic concerns."

Discuss how well reasoned ... etc.

The following appeared in a letter to prospective students from the admissions office at Plateau College:

"Every person who earned an advanced degree in science or engineering from Olympus University last year received numerous offers of excellent jobs. Typically, many graduates of Plateau College have gone on to pursue advanced degrees at Olympus. Therefore, enrolling as an undergraduate at Plateau College is a wise choice for students who wish to ensure success in their careers."

Discuss how well reasoned ... etc.

The following appeared in a memorandum sent by a vice-president of the Nadir Company to the company's human resources department:

"Nadir does not need to adopt the costly 'family-friendly' programs that have been proposed, such as part-time work, work at home, and jobsharing. When these programs were made available at the Summit Company, the leader in its industry, only a small percentage of employees participated in them. Rather than adversely affecting our profitability by offering these programs, we should concentrate on offering extensive training that will enable employees to increase their productivity."

Discuss how well reasoned ... etc.

The following appeared as part of an article in a trade magazine for breweries:

"Magic Hat Brewery recently released the results of a survey of visitors to its tasting room last year. Magic Hat reports that the majority of visitors asked to taste its low-calorie beers. To boost sales, other small breweries should brew low-calorie beers as well."

Discuss how well reasoned ... etc.

The following appeared in an editorial from a newspaper serving the town of Saluda:

"The Saluda Consolidated High School offers more than 200 different courses from which its students can choose. A much smaller private school down the street offers a basic curriculum of only 80 different courses, but it consistently sends a higher proportion of its graduating seniors on to college than Consolidated does. By eliminating at least half of the courses offered there and focusing on a basic curriculum, we could improve student performance at Consolidated and also save many tax dollars."

Discuss how well reasoned ... etc.

The following appeared as part of an article in the book section of a newspaper:

"Currently more and more books are becoming available in electronic form—either free-of-charge on the Internet or for a very low price-per-book on compact disc. Thus literary classics are likely to be read more widely than ever before. People who couldn't have purchased these works at bookstore prices will now be able to read them for little or no money; similarly, people who find it inconvenient to visit libraries and wait for books to be returned by other patrons will now have access to whatever classic they choose from their home or work computers. This increase in access to literary classics will radically affect the public taste in reading, creating a far more sophisticated and learned reading audience than has ever existed before."

Discuss how well reasoned ... etc.

The following appeared as an editorial in a magazine concerned with educational issues:

"In our country, the real earnings of men who have only a high-school degree have decreased significantly over the past 15 years, but those of male college graduates have remained about the same. Therefore, the key to improving the earnings of the next generation of workers is to send all students to college. Our country's most important educational goal, then, should be to establish enough colleges and universities to accommodate all high school graduates."

Discuss how well reasoned ... etc.

The following appeared as part of a business plan created by the management of the Take Heart Fitness Center:

"After opening the new swimming pool early last summer, Take Heart saw a 12 percent increase in the use of the center by its members. Therefore, in order to increase membership in Take Heart, we should continue to add new recreational facilities in subsequent years: for example, a multipurpose game room, a tennis court, and a miniature golf course. Being the only center in the area offering this range of activities would give us a competitive advantage in the health and recreation market."

Discuss how well reasoned ... etc.

The following appeared in a letter from a staff member in the office of admissions at Argent University:

"The most recent nationwide surveys show that undergraduates choose their major field primarily based on their perception of job prospects in that field. At our university, economics is now the most popular major, so students must perceive this field as having the best job prospects. Therefore, we can increase our enrollment if we focus our advertising and recruiting on publicizing the accomplishments of our best-known economics professors and the success of our economics graduates in finding employment."

Discuss how well reasoned ... etc.

The following appeared as part of a memorandum from the loan department of the Frostbite National Bank:

"We should not approve the business loan application of the local group that wants to open a franchise outlet for the Kool Kone chain of ice cream parlors. Frostbite is known for its cold winters, and cold weather can mean slow ice cream sales. For example, even though Frostbite is a town of 10,000 people, it has only one ice cream spot—the Frigid Cow. Despite the lack of competition, the Frigid Cow's net revenues fell by 10 percent last winter."

Discuss how well reasoned ... etc.

The following appeared as part of a letter to the editor of a local newspaper:

"Bayview High School is considering whether to require all of its students to wear uniforms while at school. Students attending Acorn Valley Academy, a private school in town, earn higher grades on average and are more likely to go on to college. Moreover, Acorn Valley reports few instances of tardiness, absenteeism, or discipline problems. Since Acorn Valley requires its students to wear uniforms, Bayview High School would do well to follow suit and require its students to wear uniforms as well."

Discuss how well reasoned ... etc.

The following appeared in a memo to the Saluda town council from the town's business manager:

"Research indicates that those who exercise regularly are hospitalized less than half as often as those who don't exercise. By providing a well-equipped gym for Saluda's municipal employees, we should be able to reduce the cost of our group health insurance coverage by approximately 50 percent and thereby achieve a balanced town budget."

Discuss how well reasoned ... etc.

The following appeared in a memorandum written by the assistant manager of a store that sells gourmet food items from various countries:

"A local wine store made an interesting discovery last month: it sold more French than Italian wine on days when it played recordings of French accordion music, but it sold more Italian than French wine on days when Italian songs were played. Therefore, I recommend that we put food specialties from one particular country on sale for a week at a time and play only music from that country while the sale is going on. By this means we will increase our profits in the same way that the wine store did, and we will be able to predict more precisely what items we should stock at any given time."

Discuss how well reasoned ... etc.

The following appeared in a memorandum from the director of research and development at Ready-to-Ware, a software engineering firm:

"The package of benefits and incentives that Ready-to-Ware offers to professional staff is too costly. Our quarterly profits have declined since the package was introduced two years ago, at the time of our incorporation. Moreover, the package had little positive effect, as we have had only marginal success in recruiting and training high-quality professional staff. To become more profitable again, Ready-to-Ware should, therefore, offer the reduced benefits package that was in place two years ago and use the savings to fund our current research and development initiatives."

Discuss how well reasoned ... etc.

The following appeared as a memorandum from the vice-president of the Dolci candy company:

"Given the success of our premium and most expensive line of chocolate candies in a recent taste test and the consequent increase in sales, we should shift our business focus to producing additional lines of premium candy rather than our lower-priced, ordinary candies. When the current economic boom ends and consumers can no longer buy major luxury items, such as cars, they will still want to indulge in small luxuries, such as expensive candies."

Discuss how well reasoned ... etc.

The following appeared in a memorandum from the business office of the Lovin' Cupful, a national restaurant chain:

"The Lovin' Cupful franchises in our northeast region have begun serving customers Almost, a brand new powdered instant tea, in place of brewed tea. Waiters report that only about 2 percent of the customers have complained, and that customers who want refills typically ask for 'more tea.' It appears, then, that 98 percent of the customers are perfectly happy with the switch, or else they cannot tell powdered instant from brewed tea. Therefore, in order to take advantage of the lower price per pound of Almost, all of our restaurants should begin substituting it for brewed tea."

Discuss how well reasoned ... etc.

The following appeared in a memorandum from the director of marketing for a pharmaceutical company:

"According to a survey of 5,000 urban residents, the prevalence of stress headaches increases with educational level, so that stress headaches occur most often among people with graduate-school degrees. It is well established that, nationally, higher educational levels usually correspond with higher levels of income. Therefore, in marketing our new pain remedy, Omnilixir, we should send free samples primarily to graduate students and to people with graduate degrees, and we should concentrate on advertising in professional journals rather than in general interest magazines."

Discuss how well reasoned ... etc.

The following appeared as part of an editorial in the Waymarsh city newspaper:

"Last year the parents of first graders in our school district expressed satisfaction with the reading skills their children developed but complained strongly about their children's math skills. To remedy this serious problem and improve our district's elementary education, everyone in the teacher-training program at Waymarsh University should be required to take more courses in mathematics."

Discuss how well reasoned ... etc.

The following appeared in a letter to the editor of a River City newspaper:

"The Clio Development Group should not be permitted to build a multilevel parking garage on Dock Street since most of the buildings on the block would have to be demolished. Because these buildings were erected decades ago, they have historic significance and must therefore be preserved as economic assets in the effort to revitalize a restored riverfront area. Recall how Lakesburg has benefited from business increases in its historic downtown center. Moreover, there is plenty of vacant land for a parking lot elsewhere in River City."

Discuss how well reasoned ... etc.

The following appeared in a corporate planning memorandum for a company that develops amusement parks:

"Because travel from our country to foreign countries has increased dramatically in recent years, our next project should be a 'World Tour' theme park with replicas of famous foreign buildings, rides that have international themes, and refreshment stands serving only foods from the country represented by the nearest ride. The best location would be near our capital city, which has large percentages of international residents and of children under the age of 16. Given the advantages of this site and the growing interest in foreign countries, the 'World Tour' theme park should be as successful as our space-travel theme park, where attendance has increased tenfold over the past decade."

Discuss how well reasoned ... etc.

The following appeared in a memorandum from the publisher to the staff of *The Clarion*, a large metropolitan newspaper:

"During the recent campaign for mayor, a clear majority of city readers who responded to our survey indicated a desire for more news about city government. To increase circulation, and thus our profits, we should therefore consistently devote a greater proportion of space in all editions of *The Clarion* to coverage of local news."

Discuss how well reasoned ... etc.

The following appeared in a memorandum from the assistant manager of Pageturner Books:

"Over the past two years, Pageturner's profits have decreased by 5 percent, even though we have added a popular café as well as a music section selling CDs and tapes. At the same time, we have experienced an increase in the theft of merchandise. We should therefore follow the example of Thoreau Books, which increased its profits after putting copies of its most frequently stolen books on a high shelf behind the payment counter. By doing likewise with copies of the titles that our staff reported stolen last year, we too can increase profitability."

Discuss how well reasoned ... etc.

The following appeared in a letter to the editor of a River City newspaper:

"The Clio Development Group's plan for a multilevel parking garage on Dock Street should be approved in order to strengthen the economy of the surrounding area. Although most of the buildings on the block would have to be demolished, they are among the oldest in the city and thus of little current economic value. Those who oppose the project should realize that historic preservation cannot be the only consideration: even Athens or Jerusalem will knock down old buildings to put up new ones that improve the local economy."

Discuss how well reasoned ... etc.

The following appeared in a memorandum from the owner of Carlo's Clothing to the staff:

"Since Disc Depot, the music store on the next block, began a new radio advertising campaign last year, its business has grown dramatically, as evidenced by the large increase in foot traffic into the store. While the Disc Depot's owners have apparently become wealthy enough to retire, profits at Carlo's Clothing have remained stagnant for the past three years. In order to boost our sales and profits, we should therefore switch from newspaper advertising to frequent radio advertisements like those for Disc Depot."

Discuss how well reasoned ... etc.

The following appeared as part of the business plan of the Capital Idea investment firm:

"Across town in the Park Hill district, the Thespian Theater, Pizzazz Pizza, and the Niblick Golf Club have all had business increases over the past two years. Capital Idea should therefore invest in the Roxy Playhouse, the Slice-o'-Pizza, and the Divot Golf Club, three new businesses in the Irongate district. As a condition, we should require them to participate in a special program: Any customer who patronizes two of the businesses will receive a substantial discount at the third. By motivating customers to patronize all three, we will thus contribute to the profitability of each and maximize our return."

Discuss how well reasoned ... etc.

The following appeared as part of an article in a newsletter for farmers:

"Users of Solacium, a medicinal herb now grown mainly in Asia, report that it relieves tension and promotes deep sleep. A recent study indicates that a large number of college students who took pills containing one of the ingredients in Solacium suffered less anxiety. To satisfy the anticipated demands for this very promising therapeutic herb and to reap the financial benefits, farmers in this country should begin growing it."

Discuss how well reasoned ... etc.

The following appeared in a memorandum from the president of Aurora, a company that sells organic milk (milk produced without the use of chemical additives):

"Sales of organic food products in this country have tripled over the past five years. If Aurora is to profit from this continuing trend, we must diversify and start selling products such as organic orange juice and organic eggs in addition to our regular product line. With the recent increase of articles in health magazines questioning the safety of milk and other food products, customers are even more likely to buy our line of organic products. And to help ensure our successful expansion, we should hire the founder of a chain of health-food stores to serve as our vice president of marketing."

Discuss how well reasoned ... etc.

The following appeared in a memorandum from the human resources department of Diversified Manufacturing:

"Managers at our central office report that their employees tend to be most productive in the days immediately preceding a vacation. To help counteract our declining market share, we could increase the productivity of our professional staff members, who currently receive four weeks paid vacation a year, by limiting them to a maximum of one week's continuous vacation time. They will thus take more vacation breaks during a year and give us more days of maximum productivity."

Discuss how well reasoned ... etc.

The following appeared in a memorandum from a regional supervisor of post office operations:

"During a two-week study of postal operations, the Presto City post office handled about twice as many items as the Lento City post office, even though the cities are about the same size. Moreover, customer satisfaction appears to be higher in Presto City, since the study found fewer complaints regarding the Presto City post office. Therefore, the postmasters at these two offices should exchange assignments: the Presto City postmaster will solve the problems of inefficiency and customer dissatisfaction at the Lento City office while the Lento City postmaster learns firsthand the superior methods of Presto City."

Discuss how well reasoned ... etc.

The following appeared in a memorandum written by the managing director of the Exeunt Theater Company:

"Now that we have moved to a larger theater, we can expect to increase our revenues from ticket sales. To further increase profits, we should start producing the plays that have been most successful when they were performed in our nation's largest cities. In addition, we should hire the Adlib Theater Company's director of fund-raising, since corporate contributions to Adlib have increased significantly over the three years that she has worked for Adlib."

Discuss how well reasoned ... etc.

The following appeared in a memorandum from the human resources department of HomeStyle, a house remodeling business:

"This year, despite HomeStyle's move to new office space, we have seen a decline in both company morale and productivity, and a corresponding increase in administrative costs. To rectify these problems, we should begin using a newly developed software package for performance appraisal and feedback. Managers will save time by simply choosing comments from a preexisting list; then the software will automatically generate feedback for the employee. The human resources department at CounterBalance, the manufacturer of the countertops we install, reports satisfaction with the package."

Discuss how well reasoned ... etc.

The following appeared as part of an article in a weekly newsmagazine:

"The country of Oleum can best solve the problem of its balance-of-trade deficit by further increasing the tax on its major import, crude oil. After Oleum increased the tax on imported crude oil four months ago, consumption of gasoline declined by 20 percent. Therefore, by imposing a second and significantly higher tax increase next year, Oleum will dramatically decrease its balance-of-trade deficit."

Discuss how well reasoned ... etc.

The following appeared as part of a business plan by the Capital Idea investment firm:

"In recent years the worldwide demand for fish has grown, and improvements in fishing technology have made larger catches, and thus increased supply, possible: for example, last year's tuna catch was 9 percent greater than the previous year's. To capitalize on these trends, we should therefore invest in the new tartfish processing plant on Tartfish Island, where increasing revenues from tourism indicate a strong local economy."

Discuss how well reasoned ... etc.

The following appeared in a speech by a stockholder of Consolidated Industries at the company's annual stockholders' meeting:

"In the computer hardware division last year, profits fell significantly below projections, the product line decreased from 20 to only 5 items, and expenditures for employee benefits increased by 15 percent. Nevertheless, Consolidated's board of directors has approved an annual salary of more than $1 million for our company's chief executive officer. The present board members should be replaced because they are unconcerned about the increasing costs of employee benefits and salaries, in spite of the company's problems generating income."

Discuss how well reasoned ... etc.

The following appeared in a memorandum from the business planning department of Avia Airlines:

"Of all the cities in their region, Beaumont and Fletcher are showing the fastest growth in the number of new businesses. Therefore, Avia should establish a commuter route between them as a means of countering recent losses on its main passenger routes. And to make the commuter route more profitable from the outset, Avia should offer a 1/3 discount on tickets purchased within two days of the flight. Unlike tickets bought earlier, discount tickets will be nonrefundable, and so gain from their sale will be greater."

Discuss how well reasoned ... etc.

The following appeared in a memorandum from the vice president of Gigantis, a development company that builds and leases retail store facilities:

"Nationwide over the past five years, sales have increased significantly at outlet stores that deal exclusively in reduced-price merchandise. Therefore, we should publicize the new mall that we are building at Pleasantville as a central location for outlet shopping and rent store space only to outlet companies. By taking advantage of the success of outlet stores, this plan should help ensure full occupancy of the mall and enable us to recover quickly the costs of building the mall."

Discuss how well reasoned ... etc.

The following appeared in a memorandum written by the chair of the music department to the president of Omega University:

"Mental health experts have observed that symptoms of mental illness are less pronounced in many patients after group music-therapy sessions, and job openings in the music-therapy field have increased during the past year. Consequently, graduates from our degree program for music therapists should have no trouble finding good positions. To help improve the financial status of Omega University, we should therefore expand our music-therapy degree program by increasing its enrollment targets."

Discuss how well reasoned ... etc.

The following appeared in a memorandum to the work-group supervisors of the GBS Company:

"The CoffeeCart beverage and food service located in the lobby of our main office building is not earning enough in sales to cover its costs, and so the cart may discontinue operating at GBS. Given the low staff morale, as evidenced by the increase in the number of employees leaving the company, the loss of this service could present a problem, especially since the staff morale questionnaire showed widespread dissatisfaction with the snack machines. Therefore, supervisors should remind the employees in their group to patronize the cart—after all, it was leased for their convenience so that they would not have to walk over to the cafeteria on breaks."

Discuss how well reasoned … etc.

The following appeared as part of an article in a trade magazine:

"During a recent trial period in which government inspections at selected meat-processing plants were more frequent, the amount of bacteria in samples of processed chicken decreased by 50 percent on average from the previous year's level. If the government were to institute more frequent inspections, the incidence of stomach and intestinal infections throughout the country could thus be cut in half. In the meantime, consumers of Excel Meats should be safe from infection because Excel's main processing plant has shown more improvement in eliminating bacterial contamination than any other plant cited in the government report."

Discuss how well reasoned … etc.

To register for the GMAT exam go to www.mba.com

12.0 Official Guide Question Index

12.0 Official Guide Question Index

The Official Guide Question index is organized by difficulty level, GMAT section, and then by math or verbal concept. All numbers below are associated with the problem numbers in the guide and not the page numbers.

There are different ways to classify and categorize each of the different types of problems. Below are the GMAC classification and categorization of the practice problems in this section of the guide.

Difficulty: Easy

Critical Reasoning:

Argument Construction: 612, 613, 616, 617, 620, 621, 622, 626, 627, 631, 633, 635, 636, 637, 640, 643, 644, 645, 648, 649, 651, 654, 657

Argument Evaluation: 610, 614, 618, 619, 624, 628, 630, 632, 639, 642, 653, 655

Evaluation of a Plan: 611, 615, 623, 625, 629, 634, 638, 641, 646, 647, 650, 652, 656, 658

Data Sufficiency: Algebra

Applied problems: 251, 276, 287

Equations: 257, 262

Exponents: 252, 259

Exponents and radicals: 302

Inequalities: 256, 278, 281

Measurement conversion: 309

Operations with radicals: 286

Probability: 277

Ratios: 297

Sets: 258, 283

Simplifying algebraic equations: 296, 305

Simultaneous equations: 232, 233, 236, 248, 254, 255, 294, 295, 303

Statistics: 304

Data Sufficiency: Arithmetic

Applied problems: 231, 244, 249, 264, 280

Applied problems; Percents: 260, 263, 267

Inequalities: 282

Operations with integers: 266, 290

Order: 270

Order; Ratio: 240

Percents: 247, 279

Probability: 245

Properties of integers: 288, 291, 293, 299, 301

Properties of numbers: 265, 284, 285, 300, 308

Ratio and proportion: 235, 238, 243

Ratios: 239

Sequences: 250

Series and sequences: 292, 298

Sets: 274, 275

Statistics: 234, 241, 242, 253

Data Sufficiency: Geometry

Angles: 237

Circles: 261

Circles; Area: 271

Circles; Pythagorean theorem: 273

Coordinate geometry: 272

Lines and segments: 269, 307

Triangles: 289, 306

Triangles; Area: 268

Triangles; Pythagorean theorem: 246

Problem Solving: Algebra

Algebraic expressions: 60, 73

Applied problems: 34, 55, 64, 69, 77

Coordinate geometry: 62, 68, 84

First-degree equations: 10, 13, 20, 22, 74, 92

Functions: 95

Inequalities: 26, 61, 85

Properties of numbers: 88

Simplifying algebraic expressions: 38, 90

Simultaneous equations: 47

Simultaneous first-degree equations: 29

Statistics: 21

Problem Solving: Arithmetic

Applied problems: 4, 5, 9, 23, 33, 35, 45, 51, 71, 75, 83

Applied problems; Percents: 54, 78

Applied problems; Properties of numbers: 14

Applied problems; Sequences: 79

Estimation: 28, 50, 53, 57

Exponents: 41

Fractions: 89

Interpretation of graphs and tables: 49

Interpretation of tables: 2, 46

Operations on radical expressions: 76

Operations on rational numbers: 8

Operations with integers: 27, 86

Operations with radical expressions: 82

Operations with rational numbers: 11, 18, 42, 43, 80

Percents: 7, 16, 19, 67, 87, 93, 94

Probability: 24

Profit and loss: 36

Properties of numbers: 58, 66, 81

Rate: 65

Ratio and proportion: 12, 39, 48

Sequences: 59

Statistics: 3, 15, 17, 30, 63, 91

Problem Solving: Geometry

Angles: 56

Angles and their measure: 32

Applied problems: 31

Area: 52, 70

Circles; Circumference; Perimeter: 25

Circles; Pythagorean theorem: 72

Perimeter: 1

Pythagorean theorem: 40

Simple coordinate geometry; Triangles: 6

Triangles: 37

Volume: 44

Reading Comprehension:

Application: 470

Evaluation: 467, 476, 481, 484, 487, 494, 498

Inference: 465, 469, 472, 478, 479, 480, 488, 491, 492, 495, 501

Main idea: 461, 463, 464, 475, 477, 482, 500

Supporting idea: 462, 483, 485, 486, 489, 490, 493

Supporting ideas: 466, 468, 471, 473, 474, 496, 497, 499

Sentence Correction:

Agreement; Idiom; Verb form: 775

Agreement; Parallelism: 786

Agreement; Rhetorical construction: 761

Diction; Parallelism: 777, 785

Diction; Rhetorical construction: 789

Grammatical construction; Diction: 778

Grammatical construction; Idiom: 784

Grammatical construction; Idiom; Parallelism: 764

Grammatical construction; Logical predication: 776

Grammatical construction; Parallelism: 759, 763, 769

Grammatical construction; Verb form: 762

Idiom; Diction: 780

Idiom; Grammatical construction: 771

Idiom; Rhetorical construction: 766, 767, 791

Idiom; Rhetorical construction; Logical predication: 790

Logical predication: 779

Logical predication; Diction; Verb form: 781

Logical predication; Grammatical construction: 774

Parallelism; Agreement: 770

Parallelism; Idiom: 760

Parallelism; Rhetorical construction: 788

Rhetorical construction; Grammatical construction: 768

Rhetorical construction; Logical predication: 782

Rhetorical construction; Verb form: 772

Rhetorical construction; Verb form; Logical predication: 765, 787

Verb form; Logical predication: 773

Verb form; Rhetorical construction: 783

Difficulty: Medium

Critical Reasoning:

Argument Construction: 659, 660, 662, 663, 664, 665, 666, 667, 669, 671, 675, 676, 679, 680, 681, 686, 689, 690, 693, 694, 699, 700, 701, 703, 704, 705, 706, 709

Argument Evaluation: 661, 668, 672, 673, 677, 678, 684, 685, 687, 695, 698, 702, 707, 708, 710

Evaluation of a Plan: 670, 674, 682, 683, 688, 691, 692, 696, 697

Data Sufficiency: Algebra

Inequalities: 362

Applied problems: 366, 381

Applied problems; Percents: 378

Applied problems; Proportions: 336

Exponents: 316

First-degree equations: 346, 363, 373

Functions: 353

Inequalities: 320, 367

Properties of numbers: 347

Ratios: 323

Ratios; Simultaneous equations: 319

Series and sequences: 326

Sets: 361

Simplifying algebraic expressions: 337, 359

Simultaneous equations: 313, 314, 315, 327, 349

Data Sufficiency: Arithmetic

Applied problems: 340, 342, 354, 356, 383

Applied problems; Percents: 368, 379

Arithmetic operations: 311

Computation with integers: 365, 380

Exponents: 348

Inequalities: 375

Number line: 386

Operations with integers: 370

Operations with integers; Order: 350

Percents: 344

Probability: 355

Properties of integers: 310, 318, 241, 385

Properties of numbers: 343, 351, 352, 364, 372, 374

Series and sequences: 312

Statistics: 338, 339, 377, 382, 384

Statistics; Simplifying algebraic expressions: 357

Data Sufficiency: Geometry

Angles: 360

Applied problems; Circles: 345

Circles: 321

Circles; Area: 322

Polygons: 369

Quadrilaterals: 324, 335

Quadrilaterals; Area: 317

Quadrilaterals; Perimeter: 331

Rectangles; Perimeter: 358

Surface area: 376

Triangles: 328, 330

Triangles; Area: 325, 329, 332

Triangles; Area; Pythagorean theorem: 334

Volume: 333

Volume; Surface area: 371

Problem Solving: Algebra

Applied problems: 110, 118, 130, 131, 133

Functions: 129

Inequalities: 122

Percents: 105, 135

Percents; First-degree equations: 112

Ratio and proportion: 102

Second-degree equations: 104, 116, 128

Sets: 123

Simplifying algebraic expressions; Operations on rational numbers: 115

Simultaneous equations; Inequalities: 138

Problem Solving: Arithmetic

Absolute value; Number line: 121

Estimation: 132

Operations on integers: 120

Operations on radical expressions: 117

Operations with decimals; Place value: 139

Operations with integers: 101, 111, 137

Percents: 113, 125, 126

Percents; Ratio and proportion: 114

Properties of numbers: 103, 127

Remainders: 108

Sets: 124

Statistics: 107, 134, 136

Problem Solving: Geometry

Area: 109

Circles; Triangles: 106

Circles; Rectangles: 96

Quadrilaterals; Area: 100

Quadrilaterals; Pythagorean theorem: 97

Rectangles: 98

Triangles; Area: 99

Volume: 119

Reading Comprehension:

Application: 517, 522, 531, 540, 545

Evaluation: 504, 505, 507, 511, 513, 523, 530, 535, 541, 542, 548

Inference: 503, 506, 509, 510, 512, 516, 518, 519, 528, 529, 534, 538, 544, 546

Main idea: 508, 525, 532, 533, 543, 549

Supporting idea: 502, 526, 527, 536, 537, 547

Supporting ideas: 514, 515, 520, 521, 524, 539

Sentence Correction:

Agreement; Diction: 838

Agreement; Rhetorical construction: 803

Category: 810

Diction; Verb form: 836

Diction; Verb form; Parallelism: 797

Grammatical construction; Diction: 794, 819, 825

Grammatical construction; Parallelism: 834

Grammatical construction; Rhetorical construction: 817, 839

Grammatical construction; Verb form: 814

Idiom; Parallelism: 800

Idiom; Parallelism; Logical predication: 808

Idiom; Rhetorical construction: 833

Logical predication; Agreement: 818

Logical predication; Agreement; Grammatical construction; Verb form: 823

Logical predication; Diction: 796

Logical predication; Grammatical construction: 804

Logical predication; Grammatical construction; Agreement: 827

Logical predication; Grammatical construction; Rhetorical construction: 793

Logical predication; Grammatical construction; Verb form: 807

Logical predication; Idiom: 801

Logical predication; Modification: 812

Logical Predication; Parallelism: 826

Logical predication; Rhetorical construction: 802, 824, 832

Logical predication; Rhetorical construction; Verb form: 820

Parallelism, Diction: 829

Parallelism; Grammatical construction: 795

Parallelism; Rhetorical construction: 792, 813

Parallelism; Rhetorical construction; Grammatical construction: 830

Rhetorical construction; Diction: 809, 835

Rhetorical construction; Grammatical construction: 816

Rhetorical construction; Idiom: 806

Rhetorical construction; Idiom; Parallelism: 811

Rhetorical construction; Logical predication: 805, 815

Rhetorical construction; Logical predication; Grammatical construction: 822

Rhetorical construction; Parallelism: 799

Rhetorical construction; Verb form: 831

Verb form: 828

Verb form; Logical predication: 798, 837

Verb form; Parallelism: 821

Verb form; Rhetorical construction: 840

Difficulty: Hard

Critical Reasoning:

Argument Construction: 712, 714, 717, 719, 721, 725, 728, 731, 732, 736, 741, 742, 744, 746, 748, 752, 753, 756

Argument Evaluation: 713, 715, 716, 718, 720, 722, 723, 724, 726, 727, 729, 730, 733, 735, 738, 739, 740, 743, 745, 749, 750, 754, 755, 757, 758

Evaluation of a Plan: 711, 734, 737, 747, 751

Data Sufficiency: Algebra

Absolute value: 447

Applied problems: 394, 395, 407, 449

Computation with integers: 415

Coordinate geometry: 403, 439

Exponents: 406

Functions: 420

Inequalities: 417, 429, 432, 457

Order: 400

Properties of numbers: 426

Rate problems: 397

Ratios: 411

Second-degree equations: 422

Simplifying algebraic expressions: 460

Simultaneous equations: 401, 408

Data Sufficiency: Arithmetic

Applied problems: 392, 416, 430, 453

Applied problems; Estimating: 436

Computation with integers: 393

Elementary combinations: 387

Operations on rational numbers: 443

Operations with radicals: 398

Percents: 388, 396

Place value: 405, 444

Properties of integers: 412, 421

Properties of numbers: 390, 410, 413, 419, 428, 433, 446, 451, 455, 459

Proportions: 458

Ratio and proportion: 424

Rounding; Estimating: 389

Sets: 418, 445

Statistics: 404, 414, 431, 434, 437. 441, 448, 450, 452

Data Sufficiency: Geometry

Angles: 456

Area: 454

Circles: 425, 435

Coordinate geometry: 438

Cylinders; Volume: 399

Polygons: 423

Rectangular solids and cylinder: 427

Simple coordinate geometry: 218

Triangles: 442

Triangles; Area: 402, 409

Triangles; Perimeter: 440

Problem Solving: Algebra

Algebra equations: 180

Applied numbers: 190

Applied problems: 160, 167, 179, 184, 190, 191, 199, 219, 220, 227

Applied problems; Simultaneous equations: 186

Coordinate geometry: 183

Inequalities: 185, 193, 228

Order: 391

Percents: 207

Second-degree equations: 168, 188, 202, 222, 226

Second-degree equations; Simultaneous equations: 155

Sequences: 206

Simplifying algebraic expressions: 198, 212

Simultaneous equations: 149, 216

Simultaneous equations; Inequalities: 157

Statistics: 171, 211

Statistics; Applied problems; Simultaneous equations: 217

Systems of equations: 150

Problem Solving: Arithmetic

Applied problems: 143, 152, 208

Elementary combinations: 140, 148,182, 201, 214

Estimation: 192

Interpretation of graphs and tables; Statistics: 164

Negative exponents: 209, 230

Operations on rational numbers: 161, 163, 187, 197, 203, 215, 223, 225

Operations with integers: 173

Percents: 153, 169, 172, 210

Probability: 142, 162, 170, 221

Profit and loss: 196

Properties of numbers: 141, 154, 175, 176, 178, 181, 189, 195, 200, 213

Properties of numbers; Decimals: 147

Property of numbers: 165

Rate: 205

Sets: 229

Simplifying expressions; Computation with integers: 204

Statistics: 144, 151, 158, 166

Algebra Statistics; Applied problems: 194

Problem Solving: Geometry

Area: 146

Circles: 177

Perimeter: 156

Polygons: 224

Quadrilaterals; Triangles: 174

Triangles: 145

Arithmetic Volume; Ratio and proportion: 159

Reading Comprehension:

Application: 573, 577, 586, 604

Evaluation: 551, 557, 559, 562, 568, 574, 575, 578, 581, 589, 596, 601, 606, 607

Inference: 554, 555, 556, 560, 561, 564, 566, 567, 571, 572, 579, 582, 585, 587, 590, 591, 592, 593, 594, 599, 600, 602, 603, 608, 609

Main idea: 550, 558, 563, 565, 570, 583

Supporting idea: 595, 597, 598

Supporting ideas: 552, 553, 569, 576, 580, 584, 588, 605

Sentence Correction:

Agreement; Idiom: 865, 869, 907

Agreement; Logical predication: 852, 859, 862, 897

Agreement; Parallelism: 889

Agreement; Rhetorical construction; Logical predication: 893

Diction; Agreement: 849

Diction; Idiom: 888, 896

Diction; Parallelism: 895

Diction; Parallelism; Verb form: 843

Grammatical construction; Diction: 850

Grammatical construction; Parallelism: 857

Grammatical construction; Rhetorical construction: 868

Grammatical construction; Verb form: 900

Idiom; Grammatical construction: 845, 864, 885

Idiom; Grammatical construction; Logical predication: 891

Idiom; Logical predication: 846

Idiom; Logical predication; Rhetorical construction: 855, 876

Idiom; Verb form; Logical predication: 905

Logical predication; Agreement: 861, 883, 892, 899

Logical predication; Grammatical construction: 847, 851, 879, 890

Logical predication; Parallelism: 844, 884, 902

Logical predication; Rhetorical construction: 848, 870, 875, 877, 880, 882, 887

Logical predication; Verb form: 858, 867

Parallelism; Diction: 860

Parallelism; Rhetorical construction: 842, 863

Parallelism; Verb form: 894

Parallelism; Verb form; Logical predication: 906

Rhetorical construction; Agreement: 853, 871, 901

Rhetorical construction; Agreement; Grammatical construction: 854

Rhetorical construction; Grammatical construction: 886

Rhetorical construction; Idiom: 866, 872, 898

Rhetorical construction; Logical predication: 874, 878

Rhetorical construction; Parallelism; Diction: 841

Rhetorical construction; Verb form: 903

Verb form; Diction: 856

Verb form; Grammatical construction; Diction: 881

Verb form; Rhetorical construction: 904

Verb form; Rhetorical construction; Logical predication: 873

13.0 GMAT Official Guide Online Index

GMAT Official Guide Online Index

ARE YOU USING BOTH THE BOOK AND THE ONLINE QUESTION BANK TO STUDY? If so, use the following index to locate a question from the online question bank in the book.

To locate a question from the online question bank in the book – Every question in the online question bank has a unique ID, called the Practice Question Identifier or PQID, which appears below the question number. Look up the PQID in the table to find its problem number and page number in the book.

PQID	Question #	Page
CR00766	640	571
CR01102	639	570
CR01107	628	567
CR01112	660	577
CR01295	633	569
CR01867	646	572
CR02143	663	578
CR02702	657	576
CR02888	665	579
CR03367	648	573
CR03695	653	575
CR03938	634	569
CR03940	630	568
CR04140	654	575
CR04159	636	570
CR04364	644	572
CR04366	650	574
CR04882	641	571
CR05077	655	575
CR05080	635	569
CR05186	645	572
CR05412	656	576
CR05452	637	570
CR05667	642	571
CR07651.01	615	563
CR07660	649	573
CR07712	651	574
CR07809	666	579
CR08017	625	566
CR08471	643	572
CR08770	652	574
CR08831	659	577
CR09616	617	564
CR09963	638	570
CR09994	624	566
CR11741.01	622	566
CR11751.01	662	578
CR12019	667	579

PQID	Question #	Page
CR12078	631	568
CR12558	647	573
CR12584	629	568
CR18731.01	664	578
CR31551.01	614	563
CR33061.01	616	564
CR40751.01	619	564
CR41141.01	621	565
CR48541.01	611	562
CR49551.01	627	567
CR51141.01	632	568
CR52061.01	618	564
CR53631.01	612	562
CR70041.01	610	562
CR73241.01	620	565
CR74231.01	658	576
CR79041.01	613	563
CR79751.01	661	577
CR93241.01	626	567
CR94231.01	623	566
DS00172	414	289
DS00254	242	274
DS00328	429	291
DS00340	446	293
DS00602.01	319	280
DS00660	253	275
DS00764	416	289
DS00858	251	274
DS01049	424	290
DS01168	380	286
DS01216	279	277
DS01257	356	284
DS01324	386	287
DS01341	339	282
DS01383	408	289
DS01425	284	277
DS01427	443	292
DS01473	434	291

PQID	Question #	Page	PQID	Question #	Page
DS01544	275	276	DS06318	406	289
DS01602.01	291	278	DS06397	261	275
DS01619	282	277	DS06475	259	275
DS01641	450	293	DS06537	359	284
DS02441	276	276	DS06633	257	275
DS02450	267	276	DS06657	420	290
DS02541	244	274	DS06659	387	287
DS02562	231	273	DS06662	250	274
DS02585	281	277	DS06789	412	289
DS02706	357	284	DS06802	249	274
DS02888	423	290	DS06861	440	292
DS02939	338	282	DS06869	409	289
DS03045	355	284	DS06875	456	294
DS03046	422	290	DS06901	268	276
DS03057	393	287	DS06905	264	275
DS03138	241	274	DS07262	391	287
DS03422	235	273	DS07441	447	293
DS03628	280	277	DS07502.01	310	279
DS03680	407	289	DS07508	415	289
DS03802	233	273	DS07713	439	292
DS03999	277	277	DS07813	262	275
DS04057	337	282	DS07822	238	273
DS04157	365	285	DS07839	260	275
DS04366	269	276	DS07949	258	275
DS04409	449	293	DS07953	395	288
DS04428	358	284	DS08054	245	274
DS04536	283	277	DS08091.01	377	286
DS04540	378	286	DS08105	410	289
DS04594	246	274	DS08197	374	286
DS04602.01	307	279	DS08231	390	287
DS04605	255	275	DS08301	428	291
DS04630	247	274	DS08308	286	277
DS04631	405	289	DS08365	379	286
DS04852	360	284	DS08420	336	282
DS04897	427	291	DS08451	433	291
DS05049	345	283	DS08502.01	315	280
DS05162	445	293	DS08723	254	275
DS05265	403	288	DS08730	271	276
DS05269	382	286	DS08995	436	292
DS05312	287	277	DS09315	278	277
DS05330	354	284	DS09379	348	283
DS05338	240	273	DS09603	404	288
DS05377	341	283	DS09973	441	292
DS05631	366	285	DS10471	232	273
DS05639	392	287	DS10602.01	290	278
DS05668	394	287	DS10687	243	274
DS05772	347	283	DS11109	263	275
DS05863	234	273	DS11254	256	275
DS06027	372	285	DS11257	364	285
DS06038	417	290	DS11287	342	283
DS06065	252	275	DS11538	448	293
DS06096	361	284	DS11602.01	292	278
DS06315	397	288	DS11723	444	293

13.0 GMAT Official Guide Online Index

PQID	Question #	Page
DS11805	270	276
DS12008	418	290
DS12031	265	275
DS12047	431	291
DS12062	248	274
DS12070	435	291
DS12239	437	292
DS12265	236	273
DS12533	272	276
DS12602.01	298	278
DS12718	421	290
DS12730	398	288
DS12806	438	292
DS12943	351	283
DS13122	274	276
DS13130	375	286
DS13408	344	283
DS13541	368	285
DS13588	362	284
DS13602.01	327	281
DS13641	426	290
DS13841.01	370	285
DS13857	442	292
DS13949	350	283
DS13958	432	291
DS13965	413	289
DS13982	399	288
DS14406	396	288
DS14502	285	277
DS14527	383	286
DS14569	340	282
DS14788	352	284
DS15045	385	287
DS15377	266	276
DS15561	367	285
DS15940	239	273
DS16078	388	287
DS16085	459	294
DS16164	430	291
DS16168	455	294
DS16188	453	294
DS16197	400	288
DS16204	460	294
DS16361	419	290
DS16368	451	293
DS16370	457	294
DS16384	411	289
DS16529	389	287
DS16536	402	288
DS16542	425	290
DS16565	452	293
DS16572	454	294
DS16589	458	294

PQID	Question #	Page
DS17615	343	283
DS17639	237	273
DS18414	401	288
DS19199	349	283
DS19520	273	276
DS21602.01	293	278
DS22602.01	302	279
DS24571.01	353	284
DS24602.01	329	281
DS24751.01	346	283
DS27502.01	289	278
DS28502.01	317	280
DS30602.01	321	280
DS32602.01	299	278
DS34602.01	330	281
DS37502.01	311	279
DS38502.01	316	280
DS41602.01	296	278
DS42602.01	303	279
DS43602.01	304	279
DS45530.01	373	285
DS45602.01	309	279
DS47502.01	314	280
DS47651.01	376	286
DS49502.01	318	280
DS50351.01	371	285
DS51602.01	324	280
DS52602.01	300	278
DS53602.01	305	279
DS57502.01	312	279
DS59502.01	322	280
DS61602.01	323	280
DS63602.01	306	279
DS64602.01	331	281
DS65602.01	308	279
DS69502.01	320	280
DS70602.01	294	278
DS71521.01	381	286
DS71602.01	325	281
DS72602.01	301	279
DS72951.01	363	285
DS74602.01	332	282
DS75271.01	369	285
DS75602.01	335	282
DS76502.01	288	277
DS81602.01	297	278
DS83602.01	328	281
DS84602.01	333	282
DS86502.01	313	279
DS89950.01	384	287
DS90602.01	295	278
DS92602.01	326	281
DS94602.01	334	282

971

PQID	Question #	Page	PQID	Question #	Page
PS00015	59	154	PS03371	61	155
PS00041	175	173	PS03513	204	177
PS00087	27	150	PS03635	80	158
PS00096	62	155	PS03686	209	178
PS00307	79	158	PS03768	151	169
PS00419	76	157	PS03823	135	167
PS00422	164	171	PS03972	26	149
PS00428	133	167	PS04089	123	165
PS00526	69	156	PS04305	211	178
PS00534	32	150	PS04448	112	163
PS00562	147	169	PS04482	102	162
PS00564	200	177	PS04571	30	150
PS00574	215	179	PS04617	130	166
PS00633	117	164	PS04651	176	173
PS00907	74	157	PS04677	208	178
PS00947	224	180	PS04688	172	172
PS00984	21	149	PS04711	157	170
PS01233	35	151	PS04734	92	160
PS01248	14	148	PS04797	41	152
PS01315	73	157	PS05001	9	147
PS01622	111	163	PS05100	49	153
PS01648	225	181	PS05140	214	179
PS01761	101	161	PS05239	28	150
PS01987	152	169	PS05308	51	153
PS02007	36	151	PS05410	8	147
PS02017	139	168	PS05544	52	153
PS02102	75	157	PS05560	105	162
PS02111	142	168	PS05680	40	152
PS02127	24	149	PS05682	66	155
PS02209	71	156	PS05747	42	152
PS02286	18	148	PS05882	195	176
PS02295	11	147	PS05888	168	172
PS02325	120	164	PS05957	72	157
PS02338	47	153	PS05962	122	165
PS02382	13	148	PS05973	132	166
PS02405	213	178	PS06133	124	165
PS02534	46	152	PS06215	170	172
PS02555	113	163	PS06243	50	153
PS02599	6	147	PS06497	173	173
PS02600	128	166	PS06498	205	177
PS02649	145	168	PS06558	197	176
PS02695	68	156	PS06562	184	174
PS02704	127	166	PS06570	163	171
PS02749	137	167	PS06592	44	152
PS02764	17	148	PS06601	70	156
PS02777	138	167	PS06674	166	171
PS02820	109	163	PS06946	88	159
PS02903	149	169	PS06948	183	174
PS02947	84	158	PS07081	179	174
PS02991	1	146	PS07112	119	164
PS02996	78	158	PS07197	65	155
PS03144	216	179	PS07308	4	146
PS03214	81	158	PS07325	104	162

13.0 GMAT Official Guide Online Index

PQID	Question #	Page
PS07357	144	168
PS07369	15	148
PS07408	56	154
PS07459	167	172
PS07465	87	159
PS07491	188	175
PS07536	174	173
PS07547	182	174
PS07555	210	178
PS07672	94	160
PS07712	229	181
PS07730	169	172
PS07799	5	146
PS08025	58	154
PS08173	55	154
PS08209	165	171
PS08219	156	170
PS08280	148	169
PS08313	159	170
PS08385	60	154
PS08399	121	164
PS08441	125	165
PS08461	12	148
PS08480	202	177
PS08552	207	178
PS08570	199	177
PS08732	206	177
PS08768	57	154
PS08865	118	164
PS08877	7	147
PS08886	230	181
PS08966	134	167
PS09403	203	177
PS09707	23	149
PS09708	115	164
PS09737	110	163
PS09868	2	146
PS09899	95	160
PS10002	3	146
PS10307	114	163
PS10391	103	162
PS10470	53	153
PS10546	129	166
PS10568	63	155
PS10628	37	151
PS10982	141	168
PS11065	154	170
PS11091	85	159
PS11121	116	164
PS11308	106	162
PS11396	93	160
PS11600	136	167
PS11756	108	162

PQID	Question #	Page
PS11906	19	148
PS12078	177	173
PS12114	54	154
PS12177	178	174
PS12287	67	156
PS12536	181	174
PS12542	25	149
PS12577	131	166
PS12760	91	160
PS12764	82	158
PS12786	38	151
PS12949	90	160
PS13101	83	158
PS13159	45	152
PS13244	171	172
PS13691	201	177
PS13707	34	151
PS13724	140	168
PS13801	31	150
PS13827	146	169
PS13831	39	151
PS13996	180	174
PS14203	228	181
PS14236	77	157
PS14250	48	153
PS14467	86	159
PS14861	16	148
PS14972	43	152
PS14989	89	159
PS15111	126	165
PS15358	22	149
PS15402	29	150
PS15517	107	162
PS15523	64	155
PS15957	20	149
PS16088	153	170
PS16100	198	176
PS16107	185	175
PS16115	226	181
PS16116	196	176
PS16122	162	171
PS16146	212	178
PS16214	158	170
PS16259	150	169
PS16410	143	168
PS16802	155	170
PS16810	160	171
PS16811	161	171
PS16823	186	175
PS16824	187	175
PS16828	189	175
PS16830	190	175
PS16831	191	175

973

PQID	Question #	Page		PQID	Question #	Page
PS16832	192	176		RC00223-07	542	433
PS16833	193	176		RC00229-01	570	446
PS16835	194	176		RC00229-02	571	446
PS16890	217	179		RC00229-03	572	446
PS16893	218	179		RC00229-04	573	447
PS16894	219	179		RC00229-05	574	447
PS16896	220	180		RC00229-06	575	447
PS16897	221	180		RC00272-02	546	436
PS16898	222	180		RC00272-04	547	436
PS16899	223	180		RC00272-06	548	437
PS16904	227	181		RC00272-07	549	437
PS17479	33	150		RC00301-02	609	460
PS17812	10	147		RC00301-03	608	460
PS19502.01	99	161		RC00301-04	607	460
PS40602.01	100	161		RC00312-01	565	444
PS58502.01	97	161		RC00312-03	566	444
PS77502.01	96	160		RC00312-04	567	445
PS98502.01	98	161		RC00312-05	568	445
RC00013-01	583	452		RC00312-06	569	445
RC00013-02	584	452		RC00313-01	596	456
RC00013-03	585	452		RC00313-02	597	456
RC00013-04	586	453		RC00313-03	598	457
RC00013-05	587	453		RC00313-04	599	457
RC00013-07	588	453		RC00313-05	600	457
RC00013-08	589	453		RC00313-06	601	457
RC00013-09	590	453		RC00313-08	602	457
RC00017-02	490	414		RC00333-01	543	434
RC00017-03	491	414		RC00333-02	544	434
RC00017-04	492	415		RC00333-04	545	435
RC00017-05	493	415		RC00344-02	469	404
RC00073-01	580	450		RC00344-04	470	404
RC00073-03	581	450		RC00344-05	471	405
RC00073-08	582	451		RC00344-06	472	405
RC00109-01	550	438		RC00349-02	520	424
RC00109-02	551	438		RC00349-03	521	424
RC00109-03	552	439		RC00349-04	522	425
RC00109-04	553	439		RC00349-05	523	425
RC00109-05	554	439		RC00349-06	524	425
RC00109-06	555	439		RC00359-01	473	406
RC00120-01	535	431		RC00359-03	474	406
RC00120-02	536	431		RC00359-05	475	407
RC00120-03	537	431		RC00359-06	476	407
RC00120-04	538	431		RC00394-02	510	420
RC00120-05	533	430		RC00394-03	511	420
RC00120-06	534	430		RC00394-04	512	421
RC00121-01	528	428		RC00394-05	513	421
RC00121-02	529	428		RC00394-06	514	421
RC00121-03	530	428		RC00419-01	477	408
RC00121-05	531	429		RC00419-02	478	408
RC00121-07	532	429		RC00419-04	479	409
RC00223-03	539	432		RC00419-05	480	409
RC00223-04	540	432		RC00419-06	481	409
RC00223-05	541	433		RC00423-01	515	422

PQID	Question #	Page
RC00423-02	516	422
RC00423-03	517	422
RC00423-04	518	422
RC00423-05	519	423
RC00433-02	559	442
RC00433-04	561	443
RC00433-06	563	443
RC00433-08	562	443
RC00433-09	564	443
RC00433-11	560	443
RC00455-03	467	402
RC00455-05	468	403
RC00458-01	482	410
RC00458-02	483	410
RC00458-03	484	411
RC00458-05	485	411
RC00497-02	486	412
RC00497-03	487	412
RC00497-04	488	413
RC00497-05	489	413
RC00504-01	461	398
RC00504-04	463	399
RC00504-05	462	398
RC00524-02	603	458
RC00524-04	604	458
RC00524-06	605	459
RC00524-07	606	459
RC00525-01	464	400
RC00525-02	465	400
RC00525-07	466	401
RC00556-03	576	448
RC00556-04	577	448
RC00556-05	578	449
RC00556-06	579	449
RC00558-01	556	440
RC00558-02	557	441
RC00558-06	558	441
RC00633-01	525	426
RC00633-02	526	426
RC00633-06	527	427
RC00650-02	591	454
RC00650-03	592	454
RC00650-06	593	454
RC00650-07	594	455
RC00650-08	595	455
RC38200-01.01	494	416
RC38200-02.01	495	416
RC38200-03.01	496	417
RC38200-04.01	497	417
RC38200-05.01	498	417
RC38200-06.01	499	417
RC38200-07.01	500	417
RC38200-08.01	501	417

PQID	Question #	Page
RC74000-01.01	502	418
RC74000-02.01	503	418
RC74000-03.01	504	418
RC74000-04.01	505	419
RC74000-05.01	506	419
RC74000-06.01	507	419
RC74000-07.01	508	419
RC74000-08.01	509	419
SC00970	773	788
SC00971	815	796
SC00981	785	790
SC00985	807	794
SC00989	829	798
SC00994	812	795
SC01007	808	794
SC01018	793	791
SC01022	878	809
SC01028	846	802
SC01033	821	797
SC01037	833	799
SC01051	845	801
SC01059	783	790
SC01068	862	805
SC01070	830	798
SC01077	825	798
SC01436	772	788
SC01443	873	807
SC01445	852	803
SC01455	762	785
SC01469	811	795
SC01470	784	790
SC01472	799	792
SC01474	865	806
SC01487	828	798
SC01490	798	792
SC01493	835	800
SC01498	802	793
SC01506	792	791
SC01507	806	794
SC01521	813	795
SC01523	826	798
SC01527	759	785
SC01550	860	805
SC01554	782	789
SC01561	864	806
SC01577	871	807
SC01583	844	801
SC01587	889	811
SC01595	804	793
SC01603	837	800
SC01607	841	801
SC01618	906	814
SC01622	890	811

PQID	Question #	Page		PQID	Question #	Page
SC01647	905	814		SC04408	874	808
SC01680	766	786		SC04416	805	794
SC01714	885	810		SC04422	814	795
SC01739	770	787		SC04452	780	789
SC01761	891	811		SC04562	801	793
SC01946	818	796		SC04704	800	793
SC01957	895	812		SC04760	810	795
SC01973	820	796		SC04770	809	794
SC01975	779	789		SC04836	907	814
SC01987	887	810		SC04853	886	810
SC02000	771	787		SC04899	900	813
SC02008	882	809		SC05201	775	788
SC02025	781	789		SC05393	867	806
SC02060	848	802		SC05760	884	810
SC02078	764	786		SC05785	901	813
SC02094	883	810		SC05848	861	805
SC02096	768	787		SC06611	854	803
SC02102	787	790		SC06633	897	812
SC02135	857	804		SC06740	875	808
SC02138	872	807		SC06898	869	807
SC02216	888	811		SC07035	842	801
SC02259	892	811		SC07117	859	805
SC02272	767	787		SC07231	856	804
SC02280	843	801		SC07232	816	796
SC02317	855	804		SC07338	789	791
SC02344	896	812		SC07348	774	788
SC02346	893	812		SC07446	803	793
SC02443	838	800		SC07758	850	803
SC02448	822	797		SC08083	863	805
SC02470	858	804		SC08577	840	800
SC02539	877	808		SC08719	870	807
SC02576	880	809		SC09185	788	791
SC02611	879	809		SC09877	778	789
SC02710	851	803		SC11850.01	831	799
SC02965	904	814		SC12131	881	809
SC03014	763	786		SC12710.01	790	791
SC03079	777	788		SC12841.01	794	792
SC03083	769	787		SC12999	760	785
SC03154	899	813		SC13010	776	788
SC03207	853	803		SC14066	817	796
SC03288	834	799		SC14796	839	800
SC03292	876	808		SC15382	761	785
SC03675	849	802		SC17041.01	832	799
SC03752	902	813		SC20121.01	823	797
SC03805	868	806		SC24321.01	819	796
SC03881	765	786		SC24751.01	795	792
SC04093	786	790		SC32261.01	797	792
SC04213	894	812		SC36241.01	824	797
SC04249	866	806		SC41451.01	827	798
SC04330	898	812		SC48420.01	836	800
SC04331	847	802		SC83751.01	796	792
SC04343	903	814		SC87460.01	791	791

Appendix A Answer Sheets

Diagnostic Answer Sheet—Quantitative

1.
2.
3.
4.
5.
6.
7.
8.
9.
10.
11.
12.
13.
14.
15.
16.
17.
18.
19.
20.
21.
22.
23.
24.
25.
26.
27.
28.
29.
30.
31.
32.
33.
34.
35.
36.
37.
38.
39.
40.
41.
42.
43.
44.
45.
46.
47.
48.

Diagnostic Answer Sheet—Verbal

49.
50.
51.
52.
53.
54.
55.
56.
57.
58.
59.
60.
61.
62.
63.
64.
65.
66.
67.
68.
69.
70.
71.
72.
73.
74.
75.
76.
77.
78.
79.
80.
81.
82.
83.
84.
85.
86.
87.
88.
89.
90.
91.
92.
93.
94.
95.
96.
97.
98.
99.
100.

Problem Solving Answer Sheet

1.	32.	63.	94.	125.	156.	187.	218.
2.	33.	64.	95.	126.	157.	188.	219.
3.	34.	65.	96.	127.	158.	189.	220.
4.	35.	66.	97.	128.	159.	190.	221.
5.	36.	67.	98.	129.	160.	191.	222.
6.	37.	68.	99.	130.	161.	192.	223.
7.	38.	69.	100.	131.	162.	193.	224.
8.	39.	70.	101.	132.	163.	194.	225.
9.	40.	71.	102.	133.	164.	195.	226.
10.	41.	72.	103.	134.	165.	196.	227.
11.	42.	73.	104.	135.	166.	197.	228.
12.	43.	74.	105.	136.	167.	198.	229.
13.	44.	75.	106.	137.	168.	199.	230.
14.	45.	76.	107.	138.	169.	200.	
15.	46.	77.	108.	139.	170.	201.	
16.	47.	78.	109.	140.	171.	202.	
17.	48.	79.	110.	141.	172.	203.	
18.	49.	80.	111.	142.	173.	204.	
19.	50.	81.	112.	143.	174.	205.	
20.	51.	82.	113.	144.	175.	206.	
21.	52.	83.	114.	145.	176.	207.	
22.	53.	84.	115.	146.	177.	208.	
23.	54.	85.	116.	147.	178.	209.	
24.	55.	86.	117.	148.	179.	210.	
25.	56.	87.	118.	149.	180.	211.	
26.	57.	88.	119.	150.	181.	212.	
27.	58.	89.	120.	151.	182.	213.	
28.	59.	90.	121.	152.	183.	214.	
29.	60.	91.	122.	153.	184.	215.	
30.	61.	92.	123.	154.	185.	216.	
31.	62.	93.	124.	155.	186.	217.	

Data Sufficiency Answer Sheet

231.	266.	301.	336.	371.	406.	441.
232.	267.	302.	337.	372.	407.	442.
233.	268.	303.	338.	373.	408.	443.
234.	269.	304.	339.	374.	409.	444.
235.	270.	305.	340.	375.	410.	445.
236.	271.	306.	341.	376.	411.	446.
237.	272.	307.	342.	377.	412.	447.
238.	273.	308.	343.	378.	413.	448.
239.	274.	309.	344.	379.	414.	449.
240.	275.	310.	345.	380.	415.	450.
241.	276.	311.	346.	381.	416.	451.
242.	277.	312.	347.	382.	417.	452.
243.	278.	313.	348.	383.	418.	453.
244.	279.	314.	349.	384.	419.	454.
245.	280.	315.	350.	385.	420.	455.
246.	281.	316.	351.	386.	421.	456.
247.	282.	317.	352.	387.	422.	457.
248.	283.	318.	353.	388.	423.	458.
249.	284.	319.	354.	389.	424.	459.
250.	285.	320.	355.	390.	425.	460.
251.	286.	321.	356.	391.	426.	
252.	287.	322.	357.	392.	427.	
253.	288.	323.	358.	393.	428.	
254.	289.	324.	359.	394.	429.	
255.	290.	325.	360.	395.	430.	
256.	291.	326.	361.	396.	431.	
257.	292.	327.	362.	397.	432.	
258.	293.	328.	363.	398.	433.	
259.	294.	329.	364.	399.	434.	
260.	295.	330.	365.	400.	435.	
261.	296.	331.	366.	401.	436.	
262.	297.	332.	367.	402.	437.	
263.	298.	333.	368.	403.	438.	
264.	299.	334.	369.	404.	439.	
265.	300.	335.	370.	405.	440.	

Reading Comprehension Answer Sheet

461.	491.	521.	551.	581.
462.	492.	522.	552.	582.
463.	493.	523.	553.	583.
464.	494.	524.	554.	584.
465.	495.	525.	555.	585.
466.	496.	526.	556.	586.
467.	497.	527.	557.	587.
468.	498.	528.	558.	588.
469.	499.	529.	559.	589.
470.	500.	530.	560.	590.
471.	501.	531.	561.	591.
472.	502.	532.	562.	592.
473.	503.	533.	563.	593.
474.	504.	534.	564.	594.
475.	505.	535.	565.	595.
476.	506.	536.	566.	596.
477.	507.	537.	567.	597.
478.	508.	538.	568.	598.
479.	509.	539.	569.	599.
480.	510.	540.	570.	600.
481.	511.	541.	571.	601.
482.	512.	542.	572.	602.
483.	513.	543.	573.	603.
484.	514.	544.	574.	604.
485.	515.	545.	575.	605.
486.	516.	546.	576.	606.
487.	517.	547.	577.	607.
488.	518.	548.	578.	608.
489.	519.	549.	579.	609.
490.	520.	550.	580.	

Critical Reasoning Answer Sheet

610.	640.	670.	700.	730.
611.	641.	671.	701.	731.
612.	642.	672.	702.	732.
613.	643.	673.	703.	733.
614.	644.	674.	704.	734.
615.	645.	675.	705.	735.
616.	646.	676.	706.	736.
617.	647.	677.	707.	737.
618.	648.	678.	708.	738.
619.	649.	679.	709.	739.
620.	650.	680.	710.	740.
621.	651.	681.	711.	741.
622.	652.	682.	712.	742.
623.	653.	683.	713.	743.
624.	654.	684.	714.	744.
625.	655.	685.	715.	745.
626.	656.	686.	716.	746.
627.	657.	687.	717.	747.
628.	658.	688.	718.	748.
629.	659.	689.	719.	749.
630.	660.	690.	720.	750.
631.	661.	691.	721.	751.
632.	662.	692.	722.	752.
633.	663.	693.	723.	753.
634.	664.	694.	724.	754.
635.	665.	695.	725.	755.
636.	666.	696.	726.	756.
637.	667.	697.	727.	757.
638.	668.	698.	728.	758.
639.	669.	699.	729.	

Sentence Correction Answer Sheet

759.	789.	819.	849.	879.
760.	790.	820.	850.	880.
761.	791.	821.	851.	881.
762.	792.	822.	852.	882.
763.	793.	823.	853.	883.
764.	794.	824.	854.	884.
765.	795.	825.	855.	885.
766.	796.	826.	856.	886.
767.	797.	827.	857.	887.
768.	798.	828.	858.	888.
769.	799.	829.	859.	889.
770.	800.	830.	860.	890.
771.	801.	831.	861.	891.
772.	802.	832.	862.	892.
773.	803.	833.	863.	893.
774.	804.	834.	864.	894.
775.	805.	835.	865.	895.
776.	806.	836.	866.	896.
777.	807.	837.	867.	897.
778.	808.	838.	868.	898.
779.	809.	839.	869.	899.
780.	810.	840.	870.	900.
781.	811.	841.	871.	901.
782.	812.	842.	872.	902.
783.	813.	843.	873.	903.
784.	814.	844.	874.	904.
785.	815.	845.	875.	905.
786.	816.	846.	876.	906.
787.	817.	847.	877.	907.
788.	818.	848.	878.	

Graduate Management Admission Council™

Caution!

The penalties for cheating on the GMAT™ Exam are severe.

The following is considered cheating:

- Hiring someone to take the test
- Taking the test for someone else
- Memorizing test questions
- Sharing answers with others

The penalties for cheating are:

- Cancellation of your scores
- Ban on future testing
- School notification
- Possible legal prosecution

Has someone been trying to get you to cheat?
File a report via email: pvtestsecurity@pearson.com

Pearson VUE

© 2019 Graduate Management Admission Council (GMAC). All rights reserved. GMAT™ and Graduate Management Admission Council™ are trademarks of GMAC in the United States and other countries. Pearson VUE is a trademark in the US and other countries of Pearson Education, Inc., or its affiliates.

Notes

Notes

Notes